INTRODUCTION TO JAVA PROGRAMMING
Seventh Edition

W9-AGG-378

Thank you for purchasing a new copy of *Introduction to Java Programming,* Seventh Edition, by Y. Daniel Liang. The information below provides instruction on how to access VideoNotes, Pearson's new visual tool for teaching and reinforcing key programming concepts and techniques.

VideoNotes are step-by-step videos that demonstrate how to solve problems from design through coding. VideoNotes allow for self-paced instruction with easy navigation including the ability to play, rewind, fast-forward, and stop within each VideoNote exercise.

 – Margin icons in your textbook let you know that a VideoNotes tutorial is available for a particular concept or representative homework problem.

To access VideoNotes for Liang, 7e:

1. Go to www.prenhall.com/liang
2. Click on the title *Introduction to Java Programming,* Seventh Edition.
3. Click on the link to VideoNotes. There you can register as a First-Time User and Returning User.
4. Use a coin to scratch off the coating below and reveal your student access code.
   **Do not use a knife or other sharp object as it may damage the code.

L ، C	

5. On the registration page, enter your student access code. Do not type the dashes. You can use lower or uppercase letters.
6. Follow the on-screen instructions. If you need help during the online registration process, simply click on Need Help?
7. Once your personal Login Name and Password are confirmed, you can begin viewing your VideoNotes.

To login to VideoNotes for the first time after you've registered:

Follow steps 1 and 2 to return to the VideoNotes link. Then, follow the prompts for "Returning Users" to enter your Login Name and Password.

Note to Instructors: For access to the Instructor Resource Center, contact your Pearson Representative.

IMPORTANT: The access code on this page can only be used once to establish a subscription to the Liang, *Introduction to Java Programming,* Seventh Edition VideoNotes. If this access code has already been scratched off, it may no longer be valid. If this is the case, you can purchase a subscription by going to the *www.prenhall.com/liang* website and selecting "Get Access."

PEARSON
Prentice Hall

Upper Saddle River, NJ 07458
www.prenhall.com

To get help with registration, visit *http://247.prenhall.com*

INTRODUCTION TO

JAVA™

PROGRAMMING

COMPREHENSIVE VERSION

Seventh Edition

Y. Daniel Liang

Armstrong Atlantic State University

PEARSON

Prentice
Hall

Upper Saddle River, New Jersey 07458

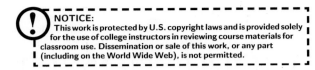
Editorial Director, Computer Science and Engineering: Marcia J. Horton
Executive Editor: Tracy Dunkelberger
Editorial Assistant: Melinda Haggerty
Director of Marketing: Margaret Waples
Marketing Manager: Christopher Kelly
Associate Editor: ReeAnne Davies
Senior Managing Editor: Scott Disanno
Production Editor: Irwin Zucker
Art Director: Kenny Beck
Media Editor: David Dulles
Media Editor: David Alick
Manufacturing Manager: Alan Fischer
Manufacturing Buyer: Lisa McDowell

The author and publisher of this book have used their best efforts in preparing this book. These efforts include the development, research, and testing of the theories and programs to determine their effectiveness. The author and publisher make no warranty of any kind, expressed or implied, with regard to these programs or the documentation contained in this book. The author and published shall not be liable in any event for incidental or consequential damages in connection with, or arising out of, the furnishing, performance, or use of these programs.

Pearson Education Ltd., London
Pearson Education Singapore, Pte, Ltd.
Pearson Education Canada, Inc.
Pearson Education-Japan
Pearson Education Australia PTY, Limited
Pearson Education North Asia, Ltd., Hong Kong
Pearson Education de Mexico, S. A. de C. V.
Pearson Education Malaysia, Pte. Ltd.
Pearson Education, Upper Saddle River, New Jersey

PEARSON
Prentice
Hall

10 9 8 7 6 5 4 3 2 1

ISBN 10: 0-13-208494-5
ISBN 13: 978-0-13-208494-9

To Samantha, Michael, and Michelle

PREFACE

Since 1997, six editions of *Introduction to Java Programming* have been published. Each new edition has substantially improved the previous one. This seventh edition is another great leap forward. We added the new Chapter 9, "Thinking in Objects," to bridge the differences between the procedural programming and object-oriented programming and show students when and how to apply OOP effectively. We expanded the coverage on data structures in Chapters 20–28 to serve a full course on data structures. We moved all advanced and nonessential language features to the Companion Web site, so that students can focus on problem solving and fundamental programming techniques in the early chapters. We refined the teaching method using the problem-driven approach. We enhanced the presentation to make the book more accessible to new programmers. We modified the contents to keep up with new Java technologies. We created a wide variety of new interesting examples and exercises to better motivate students. We renovated the Companion Web site to provide more useful supporting materials including a brand new *LiveLab*. We invite you to take a close look and be the judge.

This comprehensive book covers fundamentals of programming, object-oriented programming, GUI programming, data structures, concurrency, networking, internationalization, advanced GUI, database, and Web programming. It is designed to prepare students to become proficient Java programmers. A brief version (*Introduction to Java Programming, Brief Version, 7E*) is available for a first course on programming, commonly known as CS1. The brief version contains the first twenty chapters in the comprehensive version.

The book uses the *fundamentals-first* and *problem-driven* pedagogy to teach problem solving and programming.

Fundamentals First

imperative and OOP

Both imperative and OOP are important programming paradigms with distinct advantages for certain applications. Some programs should be developed using the imperative approach, and others are better developed using the object-oriented approach. Today's students need to know both paradigms and use them effectively in harmony. This book introduces both imperative and OOP paradigms. Students will learn when and how to apply these two paradigms effectively.

fundamentals-first

The imperative paradigm is fundamental in programming. There are several strategies in teaching Java. This book adopts the fundamentals-first strategy. It begins with all the necessary and important basic concepts, then moves to object-oriented programming, and then to the use of the object-oriented approach to build interesting GUI applications and applets with exception handling and advanced features.

fundamental programming techniques

My own experience, confirmed by the experiences of many colleagues, demonstrates that new programmers in order to succeed must learn basic logic and fundamental programming techniques like loops and stepwise refinement. The fundamental concepts and techniques on loops, methods, and arrays are the foundation for programming. Building the foundation prepares students to learn object-oriented programming, GUI, and database and Web programming.

using OOP effectively

The fundamentals-first approach reinforces object-oriented programming by first presenting the procedural solutions and demonstrating how they can be improved using the object-oriented approach. Students can learn when and how to apply OOP effectively.

Problem-Driven

problem solving

Programming isn't just syntax, classes, or objects. It is really *problem solving*. Variables, data types, operators and expressions, sequential statements, selection statements, loops, functions, and arrays are fundamental techniques for problem solving. From fundamental programming techniques to object-oriented programming, there are many layers of abstraction.

Classes are simply a layer of abstraction. Applying the concept of abstraction in the design and implementation of software projects is the key to developing software. The overriding objective of the book, therefore, is to teach students to use many layers of abstraction in solving problems and to see problems in small and in large. The examples and exercises throughout the book center on problem solving and foster the concept of developing reusable components and using them to create practical projects.

This book uses the problem-driven approach to teach problem solving. Interesting and practical examples are used not only to illustrate syntax but also to teach problem solving and programming. Interesting and practical problems introduce each chapter and are solved within the chapter. The book uses a wide variety of problems with various levels of difficulty to motivate students. The problems cover many application areas in gaming, math, business, science, animation, and multimedia. Here are some representative problems in the book:

problem-driven

Example 1: We start Chapter 2 with a simple problem of computing a circle's area given its radius (§2.2, "Writing Simple Programs"). To solve this problem, we introduce variables for storing data and data types for declaring variables. We also introduce expressions for computing area. Initially, the input value for radius is coded in the program. This is not convenient. Later we introduce how to prompt the user to enter data at runtime using the `Scanner` class (§2.11) and the input dialog box (§2.16).

Example 2: The comparison operators and `boolean` type are introduced with the `AdditionQuiz` game (Listing 3.3) that automatically generates an addition question and grades the user's answers. Later we introduce the need for a selection statement in the `SubtractionQuiz` game (Listing 3.4) that automatically generates a subtraction question (i.e., `firstNumber – secondNumber`) and grades the user's answers. Since we require that the first number be greater than the second, a selection statement must be used to write this program.

Example 3: The `SubtractionQuiz` game generates just one question. To repeatedly generate random questions, you have to use loops. In Chapter 4, we revise `SubtractionQuiz` to generate ten questions in `SubtractionQuizLoop` (Listing 4.3).

Example 4: The `GreatestCommonDivisor` program (Listing 4.8) computes the greatest common divisor (gcd) of two numbers. This program is not reusable because all the code is in the main method. To make the code modular and reusable, we revise the program to create a method for computing gcd in Listing 5.5.

Example 5: Listing 3.6, ComputeBMI.java, gives a program for computing Body Mass Index. Suppose you want to store the user's information. The program is difficult to expand in the procedural paradigm. We redesign the program using classes in §9.6, "Object-Oriented Thinking," and use this problem to demonstrate the advantages of using the object-oriented paradigm over the procedural paradigm.

Learning Strategies

A programming course is quite different from other courses. In a programming course, you learn from examples, from practice, and *from mistakes*. You need to devote a lot of time to writing programs, testing them, and fixing errors.

learn from mistakes

For first-time programmers, learning Java is like learning any high-level programming language. The fundamental point in learning programming is to develop the critical skills of formulating programmatic solutions for real problems and translating them into programs using selection statements, loops, methods, and arrays.

programmatic solution

Once you acquire the basic skills of writing programs using loops, methods, and arrays, you can begin to learn how to develop object-oriented software using class encapsulation and inheritance.

object-oriented programming

When you know how to program and understand the concept of object-oriented programming, learning Java becomes a matter of learning the Java API. The Java API establishes a framework for programmers to develop applications using Java. You have to use the classes and interfaces in the API and follow their conventions and rules to create applications. The best way to learn the Java API is to imitate examples and do exercises.

Java API

What's New in This Edition?

This edition substantially improves *Introduction to Java Programming, Sixth Edition*. The major improvements are as follows:

complete revision

■ The book is completely revised in every detail to enhance clarity, presentation, content, examples, and exercises. Every section has been reworked.

focus on problem solving

■ Nonessential language topics are moved to the Companion Web site so that students can focus on learning problem solving and programming techniques. These topics include the **&** and **|** operators, the discussion of how expressions are evaluated internally in Java, regular expressions, initialization blocks, how to package Java projects into archive files, etc.

new examples

■ The book provides many new examples to stimulate student interest in programming in early chapters. For example, new guess number, body mass index, guess birth date, and Sudoku problems are provided in Chapters 3–6.

new exercises

■ A wide variety of new exercises (in many application areas such as gaming, math business, science, animation, and multimedia) are provided throughout the book.

separate GUI sections

■ The text introduces both console input using the **Scanner** class and GUI input using the **JOptionPane** class in Chapters 1–6. For consistency and ordering flexibility, the GUI examples are placed in separate sections and may be omitted.

design patterns

■ Design patterns are introduced throughout the book.

new Chapter 9

■ Chapter 7 in the preceding edition has been broken into two chapters. The new Chapter 9 focuses on class design and explores the differences between the procedural paradigm and object-oriented paradigm.

new data structures chapters

■ Chapter 21, "Generics," presents an in-depth coverage of generics. Generics is now covered before Java Collections Framework so it can be incorporated with the data structures. Brand-new Chapter 23, "Algorithm Efficiency," uses many concrete examples to introduce algorithm analysis and design. New Chapters 27–28 introduce graph algorithms and applications.

using **StringBuilder**

■ The code using **StringBuffer** is now replaced by **StringBuilder** to improve efficiency, starting from Chapter 8.

Java 6 splash screen

■ Java 6 splash screen is introduced in §13.10, "Image Icons."

new concurrency features

■ Thread pooling, locks, conditions, semaphores, and blocking queues are introduced in Chapter 29.

SwingWorker

■ **SwingWorker** is introduced in Chapter 29 to perform time-consuming tasks on a thread separately from the event dispatch thread.

autosort and filtering

■ Java 6 autosort and filtering for **JTable** are introduced in Chapter 36.

new JDBC features

■ New features such as automatic driver discovery, scrollable and updatable result sets, **RowSet**, and callable statements are covered in Chapters 37 and 38.

JavaServer Faces

■ JavaServer Faces is introduced in Chapter 41.

Web services

■ Web services are introduced in Chapter 42.

Pedagogical Features

The philosophy of the Liang Java Series is *teaching by example and learning by doing*. Basic features are explained by example so that you can learn by doing. The book uses the following elements to get the most from the material:

- **Objectives** list what students should have learned from the chapter. This will help them to determine whether they have met the objectives after completing the chapter.

- **Introduction** opens the discussion with the type of problems that will be solved in the chapter. The book is written using the problem-driven approach.

- **Examples**, carefully chosen and presented in an easy-to-follow style, teach programming concepts. The book uses many small, simple, and stimulating examples to demonstrate important ideas.

- **Chapter Summary** reviews the important subjects that students should understand and remember. It helps them to reinforce the key concepts they have learned in the chapter.

- **Review Questions** are grouped by sections to help students track their progress and evaluate their learning.

- **Programming Exercises** are grouped by sections to provide students with opportunities to apply on their own the new skills they have learned. The level of difficulty is rated as easy (no asterisk), moderate (*), hard (**), or challenging (***). The trick of learning programming is practice, practice, and practice. To that end, the book provides a great many exercises.

- **Notes, Tips,** and **Cautions** are inserted throughout the text to offer valuable advice and insight on important aspects of program development.

Note
Provides additional information on the subject and reinforces important concepts.

Tip
Teaches good programming style and practice.

Caution
Helps students steer away from the pitfalls of programming errors.

Design Guide
Provides the guidelines for designing programs.

Flexible Chapter Orderings

The book provides flexible chapter orderings to enable earlier coverage of GUI, exception handling, recursion, generics, and the Java Collections Framework. Four common alternative orderings are shown as follows:

GUI Early Ordering

Chapter 10
Chapter 13
Chapter 14
Chapter 11
Chapter 15
Chapter 16
Chapter 17

Exception and Binary I/O
Early Ordering

Chapter 10
Chapter 18
Chapter 19

Recursion Early Ordering

Chapter 6
Chapter 20

Generics and Collections
Early Ordering

Chapter 10
Chapter 21
Chapter 22

Many of the chapters after Chapter 17 can be covered in any order. The accompanying diagram shows the chapter dependencies.

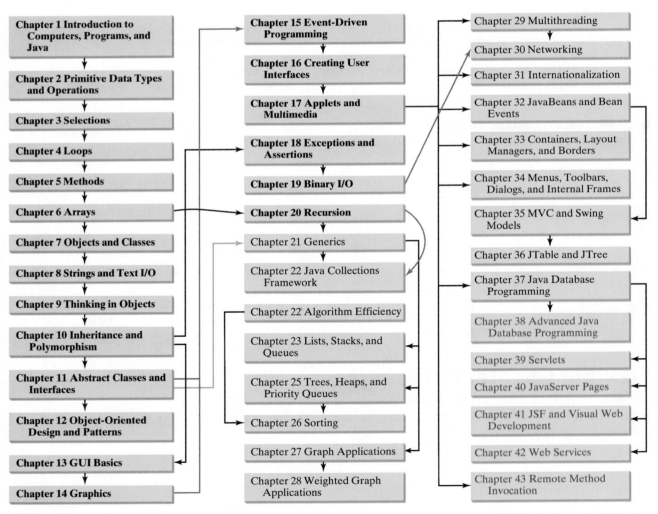

Chapters 1-20 are in the Brief Version

Bonus Chapters 38-43 in the Companion Web site

Organization of the Book

The chapters can be grouped into eight parts that, taken together, form a comprehensive introduction to Java programming. Because knowledge is cumulative, the early chapters provide the conceptual basis for understanding Java and guide students through simple examples and exercises; subsequent chapters progressively present Java programming in detail, culminating with the development of comprehensive Java applications.

Part I: Fundamentals of Programming (Chapters 1–6)

The first part of the book is a stepping stone, preparing you to embark on the journey of learning Java. You will begin to know Java (Chapter 1), and will learn fundamental programming techniques with primitive data types (Chapter 2), control statements (Chapters 3–4), methods (Chapter 5), and arrays (Chapter 6).

Part II: Object-Oriented Programming (Chapters 7–12)

This part introduces object-oriented programming. Java is an object-oriented programming language that uses abstraction, encapsulation, inheritance, and polymorphism to provide great flexibility, modularity, and reusability in developing software. You will learn programming with objects and classes (Chapters 7–9), class inheritance (Chapter 10), polymorphism (Chapter 10), abstract classes (Chapter 11), interfaces (Chapter 11), and object-oriented design and patterns (Chapter 12). Processing strings will be introduced in Chapter 8.

Part III: GUI Programming (Chapters 13–17)

This part introduces Java GUI programming. Major topics include GUI basics (Chapter 13), drawing shapes (Chapter 14), event-driven programming (Chapter 15), creating graphical user interfaces (Chapter 16), and writing applets (Chapter 17). You will learn the architecture of Java GUI programming API and use the GUI components to develop applications and applets.

Part IV: Exception Handling and Binary IO (Chapters 18–19)

This part introduces the use of exception handling (Chapter 18) to make your programs robust and correct and the use of input and output to manage and process a large quantity of binary data stored in files (Chapter 19).

Part V: Algorithms and Data Structures (Chapters 20–28)

This part introduces the main subjects in a typical data structures course. Chapter 20 introduces recursion to write methods for solving inherently recursive problems. Chapter 21 introduces how to measure algorithm efficiency in order to choose an appropriate algorithm for applications. Chapter 22 introduces JDK 1.5 generics to improve software reliability. Chapter 23 introduces Java Collection Framework, which defines a set of useful API for data structures. You will learn how to implement several popular data structures in Chapter 24 and Chapter 25. Chapter 26 introduces classic sorting algorithms. Chapters 27–28 introduce graph applications.

Part VI: Currency, Networking, and Internationalization (Chapters 29–31)

This part of the book is devoted to three unique and useful features of Java. Chapter 29 treats the use of multithreading to make programs more responsive and interactive. Chapter 30 introduces how to write programs that talk with each other from different hosts over the Internet. Chapter 31 covers the use of internationalization support to develop projects for international audiences.

Part VII: Advanced GUI (Chapters 32–36)

Part III, "GUI Programming,"covers how to develop GUI programs, event-driven programming, creating user interfaces, and applets. This part introduces Java GUI programming in more depth and breadth. You will delve into JavaBeans and will learn how to develop custom events and source components in Chapter 32, review and explore new containers, layout managers, and borders in Chapter 33, learn how to create GUI with menus, popup menus, toolbars, dialogs, and internal frames in Chapter 34, develop components using the MVC approach and explore the advanced Swing components `JSpinner`, `JList`, `JComboBox`, `JSpinner`, and `JTable`, and `JTree` in Chapters 35 and 36.

Part VIII: Database and Web Programming (Chapters 37–43)

This part is devoted to the development of database and Web applications using Java. Chapter 37 introduces the use of Java to develop database projects, Chapter 38 introduces advanced Java database programming, and Chapters 39 and 40 introduce how to use Java servlets and JSP to generate dynamic contents from Web servers. Chapter 41 introduces rapid Web application development using JavaServer Faces. Chapter 42 introduces Web services. Chapter 43 introduces remote method invocation.

Java Development Tools

You can use a text editor, such as the Windows Notepad or WordPad, to create Java programs, and to compile and run the programs from the command window. You can also use a Java development tool, such as TextPad, NetBeans, Eclipse, or JBuilder. These tools support an integrated development environment (IDE) for rapidly developing Java programs. Editing, compiling, building, executing, and debugging programs are integrated in one graphical user interface. Using these tools effectively can greatly increase your programming productivity. TextPad is a primitive IDE tool. NetBeans, Eclipse, and JBuilder are more sophisticated, but they are easy to use if you follow the tutorials. Tutorials on TextPad, NetBeans, Eclipse, and JBuilder can be found in the supplements on the Companion Web site.

IDE Tutorials

Instructor Resource Materials

Instructor Resources associated with this book can be accessed via www.prenhall.com/liang or directly at www.cs.armstrong.edu/liang/intro7e . Access to some instructor material may require a password to the Pearson Instructor Resource Center (IRC). Contact your local Pearson Sales Representative for access to the IRC material.

The Instructor Resource site contains the following resources:

- **Interactive PowerPoint slides** with interactive buttons to view full-color, syntax-highlighted source code and to run programs without leaving the slides.

- **Solutions** to all the review questions and exercises. (Students will have access to the solutions of even-numbered programming exercises.)

- **Web-based quiz generator.** Instructors can choose chapters to generate quizzes from a large database of more than 2000 questions.

- **Sample Exams.** In general, each exam has four parts:

  - Multiple-choice questions or short-answer questions

  - Correct programming errors

- Trace programs

- Write programs

- **MyTest.** Testbank of exam questions

Web-Based Course Assessment and Management System (LiveLab)

This system provides three conveniences:

- **Automatic Grading System (AGS):** It can automatically grade programs

- **Quiz Creation/Submission/Grading System:** It enables instructors to create/modify quizzes and let students take them, and be graded automatically.

- **Tracking grades, attendance, etc.:** The system enables the students to track their own grades and instructors to view the grades of all students and track attendance.

The hallmark features of the **Automatic Grading System (AGS)** are as follows:

- Allows students to compile, run and submit exercises online (letting them know if their program runs correctly with student test cases–students can continue to run and submit the program before the due date)

- Allows instructors to review submissions; run programs with instructor test cases; correct them online; and provide feedback to students online.

- Allows instructors to create/modify their own exercises, create public and secret test cases, assign exercises, and set due dates.

- Provides more than 200 exercises that can be assigned to students.

- Allows instructors to sort and filter all exercises and check grades (by time frame, student, date, and/or exercise).

- Allows instructors to delete students from the system.

- Allows students and instructors to track grades on exercises.

Advantages and conveniences of **the Online Quiz System** are as follows:

- Allows instructors to create/modify quizzes from a test bank, from a text file, or create a completely new test online.

- Allows instructors to assign the quizzes to students, set a due date, and test time limit.

- Allows students and instructors to review submitted quizzes.

- Allows students and instructors to track grades on quizzes.

VideoNotes

VideoNotes are Pearson's new visual tool designed for teaching students key programming concepts and techniques and are available at www.prenhall.com/liang. These short step-by-step videos demonstrate how to solve problems from design through coding. VideoNotes allow for self-paced instruction with easy navigation including the ability to select, play, rewind, fast-forward, and stop within each VideoNote exercise.

VideoNote margin icons in your textbook let you know when a VideoNotes video is available for a particular concept or homework problem.

VideoNotes are free with the purchase of a new book. To *purchase* access to VideoNotes, go to www.prenhall.com/liang and click on VideoNotes under *Student Resources*.

GOAL

Gradiance Online Accelerated Learning (GOAL) is Pearson's premier online homework and assessment system and available at www.prenhall.com/liang. GOAL is designed to minimize student frustration while providing an interactive teaching experience outside the classroom.

With GOAL's immediate feedback and book-specific hints and pointers, students will have a more efficient and effective learning experience. GOAL delivers immediate assessment and feedback via two kinds of assignments: multiple choice homework exercises and interactive lab projects.

The homework consists of a set of multiple choice questions designed to test student knowledge of a solved problem. When answers are graded as incorrect, students are given a hint and directed back to a specific section in the course textbook for helpful information. The interactive Lab Projects, unlike syntax checkers and compilers, GOAL checks for both syntactic and semantic errors. GOAL determines if the student's program runs but more importantly, when checked against a hidden data set, verifies that it returns the correct result. By testing the code and providing immediate feedback, GOAL lets you know exactly which concepts the students have grasped and which ones need to be revisited.

Instructors should contact their local Pearson Sales Representative for sales and ordering information for the GOAL Student Access Code and Liang Introduction to Java Programming, 7eValue Pack.

Student Resources

Resources associated with this book can be accessed via www.prenhall.com/liang or directly at www.cs.armstrong.edu/liang/intro7e.

The Student Resource Web site contains the following resources:

- Answers to review questions
- Solutions to even-numbered programming exercises
- Source code for the examples in the book
- Interactive Self-Test (organized by sections for each chapter)
- LiveLabs
- Supplemental material
- Resource links
- Errata

Additional Supplemental Material

The text covers the essential subjects. The supplements extend the text to introduce additional topics that might be of interest to readers. The supplements listed in this table are available from the Companion Web site.

Supplements on the Companion Website

Part I General Supplements
A Glossary
B Installing and Configuring JDK
C Compiling and Running Java from the Command Window
D Java Coding Style Guidelines
E Creating Desktop Shortcuts for Java Applications on Windows
F Using Packages to Organize the Classes in the Text

Part II IDE Supplements
A TextPad Tutorial
B JBuilder Tutorial
C Learning Java Effectively with JBuilder
D NetBeans Tutorial
E Learning Java Effectively with NetBeans
F Eclipse Tutorial
G Learning Java Effectively with Eclipse
H JBuilder 2007 Tutorial
I Visual GUI Development Using NetBeans

Part III Java Supplements
A Discussion on Operator and Operand Evaluations
B The & and | Operators
C Bitwise Operations
D Statement Labels with break and continue
E Enumerated Types
F Packages
G Regular Expressions
H Formatted Strings
I The Methods in the Object Class
J Hiding Data Fields and Static Methods
K Initialization Blocks
L Extended Discussions on Overriding Methods

M Design Patterns
N Text I/O Prior to JDK 1.5 (Reader and Writer Classes)
O Assertions
P Generics
Q Java Archiving
R Java 2D
S GridBagLayout | OverlayLayout | SpringLayout
T Networking Using Datagram Protocol
U Creating Internal Frames
V Pluggable Look and Feel
W UML Graphical Notations
X Testing Classes Using JUnit
Y JNI

Part IV Database Supplements
A SQL Statements for Creating and Initializing Tables Used in the Book
B MySQL Tutorial
C Oracle Tutorial
D Microsoft Access Tutorial
E Introduction to Database Systems
F Relational Database Concept
G Database Design
H SQL Basics
I Advanced SQL

Part V Web Programming Supplements
A HTML and XHTML Tutorial
B CSS Tutorial
C XML
D Java and XML
E Tomcat Tutorial
F More Examples on JSF and Visual Web Development

Part VI Data Structures Supplements
A AVL Trees
B 2-3 Trees
C Red-Black Trees
D Hashing

Acknowledgments

I would like to thank Armstrong Atlantic State University for enabling me to teach what I write and for supporting me in writing what I teach. Teaching is the source of inspiration for continuing to improve the book. I am grateful to the instructors and students who have offered comments, suggestions, bug reports, and praise.

This book was greatly enhanced thanks to outstanding reviews for this and previous editions. The reviewers are: Elizabeth Adams (James Madison University), Yang Ang

(University of Wollongong, Australia), Kevin Bierre (Rochester Institute of Technology), David Champion (DeVry Institute), James Chegwidden (Tarrant County College), Anup Dargar (University of North Dakota), Charles Dierbach (Towson University), Erica Eddy (University of Wisconsin at Parkside), Deena Engel (New York University), Henry A Etlinger (Rochester Institute of Technology), James Ten Eyck (Marist College), Olac Fuentes (University of Texas at El Paso), Harold Grossman (Clemson University), Ron Hofman (Red River College, Canada), Stephen Hughes (Roanoke College), Vladan Jovanovic (Georgia Southern University), Edwin Kay (Lehigh University), Larry King (University of Texas at Dallas), Nana Kofi (Langara College, Canada), Roger Kraft (Purdue University at Calumet), Hong Lin (DeVry Institute), Dan Lipsa (Armstrong Atlantic State University), James Madison (Rensselaer Polytechnic Institute), Frank Malinowski (Aelera Corporation), Tim Margush (University of Akron), Debbie Masada (Sun Microsystems), Blayne Mayfield (Oklahoma State University), John McGrath (J.P. McGrath Consulting), Shyamal Mitra (University of Texas at Austin), Michel Mitri (James Madison University), Kenrick Mock (University of Alaska Anchorage), Jun Ni (University of Iowa), Benjamin Nystuen (University of Colorado at Colorado Spring), Gavin Osborne (University of Saskatchewan), Kevin Parker (Idaho State University), Mark Pendergast (Florida Gulf Coast University), Richard Povinelli (Marquette University), Roger Priebe (University of Texas at Austin), Mary Ann Pumphrey (De Anza Junior College), Ronald F. Taylor (Wright State University), Carolyn Schauble (Colorado State University), David Scuse (University of Manitoba), Ashraf Shirani (San Jose State University), Daniel Spiegel (Kutztown University), Lixin Tao (Pace University), Russ Tront (Simon Fraser University), Deborah Trytten (University of Oklahoma), Kent Vidrine (George Washington University), and Bahram Zartoshty (California State University at Northridge).

It is a great pleasure, honor, and privilege to work with Prentice Hall. I would like to thank Marcia Horton, Tracy Dunkelberger, Margaret Waples, Chris Kelly, Erin Davis, Jake Warde, Melinda Haggerty, ReeAnne Davies, Vince O'Brien, Scott Disanno, Irwin Zucker, and their colleagues for organizing, producing, and promoting this project, and Robert Lentz for copy editing.

As always, I am indebted to my wife, Samantha, for her love, support, and encouragement.

Y. Daniel Liang
y.daniel.liang@gmail.com
www.cs.armstrong.edu/liang

BRIEF CONTENTS

1 Introduction to Computers, Programs, and Java 1
2 Elementary Programming 25
3 Selections 67
4 Loops 103
5 Methods 141
6 Arrays 179
7 Objects and Classes 229
8 Strings and Text I/O 263
9 Thinking in Objects 303
10 Inheritance and Polymorphism 329
11 Abstract Classes and Interfaces 361
12 Object-Oriented Design and Patterns 393
13 GUI Basics 419
14 Graphics 445
15 Event-Driven Programming 483
16 Creating User Interfaces 513
17 Applets and Multimedia 557
18 Exception Handling 597
19 Binary I/O 623
20 Recursion 655
21 Generics 685
22 Java Collections Framework 705
23 Algorithm Efficiency 741
24 Lists, Stacks, and Queues 767
25 Trees, Iterators, Heaps, and Priority Queues 799
26 Sorting 835
27 Graph Applications 857
28 Weighted Graphs Applications 901

29 Multithreading 929
30 Networking 975
31 Internationalization 1015
32 JavaBeans and Bean Events 1049
33 Containers, Layout Managers, and Borders 1069
34 Menus, Toolbars, and Dialogs 1107
35 MVC and Swing Models 1145
36 JTable and JTree 1183
37 Java Database Programming 1231

Chapters are available from the companion Web site:

38 Advanced Java Database Programming 38-1
39 Servlents 39-1
40 JavaServer Pages 40-1
41 JSF and Visual Web Development 41-1
42 Web Services 42-1
43 Remote Method Invocation 43-1

APPENDIXES

A Java Keywords 1267
B The ASCII Character Set 1268
C Operator Precedence Chart 1270
D Java Modifiers 1272
E Special Floating-Point Values 1274

INDEX 1275

CONTENTS

Chapter 1 Introduction to Computers, Programs, and Java   1

  1.1   Introduction   2
  1.2   What Is a Computer?   2
  1.3   Programs   5
  1.4   Operating Systems   7
  1.5   Number Systems   8
  1.6   Java, World Wide Web, and Beyond   12
  1.7   The Java Language Specification, API, JDK, and IDE   14
  1.8   A Simple Java Program   15
  1.9   Creating, Compiling, and Executing a Java Program   16
  1.10 (GUI) Displaying Text in a Message Dialog Box   19

Chapter 2 Elementary Programming   25

  2.1   Introduction   26
  2.2   Writing Simple Programs   26
  2.3   Identifiers   28
  2.4   Variables   29
  2.5   Assignment Statements and Assignment Expressions   30
  2.6   Constants   31
  2.7   Numeric Data Types and Operations   32
  2.8   Numeric Type Conversions   39
  2.9   Character Data Type and Operations   40
  2.10 The String Type   43
  2.11 Console Input Using the Scanner Class   44
  2.12 Case Studies   46
  2.13 Programming Style and Documentation   51
  2.14 Programming Errors   53
  2.15 Debugging   54
  2.16 (GUI) Getting Input from Input Dialogs   55

Chapter 3 Selections   67

  3.1   Introduction   68
  3.2   boolean Data Type and Operations   68
  3.3   if Statements   72
  3.4   switch Statements   86

3.5	Conditional Expressions	88
3.6	Formatting Console Output	89
3.7	Operator Precedence and Associativity	91
3.8	(GUI) Confirmation Dialogs	92

Chapter 4   Loops   103

4.1	Introduction	104
4.2	The while Loop	104
4.3	The do-while Loop	110
4.4	The for Loop	111
4.5	Which Loop to Use?	113
4.6	Nested Loops	115
4.7	Minimizing Numeric Errors	116
4.8	Case Studies	117
4.9	Keywords break and continue	122
4.10	(GUI) Controlling a Loop with a Confirmation Dialog	127

Chapter 5   Methods   141

5.1	Introduction	142
5.2	Defining a Method	142
5.3	Calling a Method	143
5.4	void Method Example	145
5.5	Passing Parameters by Values	147
5.6	Modularizing Code	149
5.7	Overloading Methods	151
5.8	The Scope of Variables	153
5.9	The Math Class	154
5.10	Case Study: Generating Random Characters	157
5.11	Method Abstraction and Stepwise Refinement	159

Chapter 6   Arrays   179

6.1	Introduction	180
6.2	Array Basics	180
6.3	Copying Arrays	188
6.4	Passing Arrays to Methods	189
6.5	Returning an Array from a Method	192
6.6	Variable-Length Argument Lists	195
6.7	Searching Arrays	196
6.8	Sorting Arrays	199
6.9	The Arrays Class	202
6.10	Two-Dimensional Arrays	203
6.11	Multidimensional Arrays	215

Chapter 7	Objects and Classes	229
7.1	Introduction	230
7.2	Defining Classes for Objects	230
7.3	Constructing Objects Using Constructors	232
7.4	Accessing Objects via Reference Variables	232
7.5	Using Classes from the Java Library	238
7.6	Static Variables, Constants, and Methods	241
7.7	Visibility Modifiers	245
7.8	Data Field Encapsulation	247
7.9	Passing Objects to Methods	249
7.10	Array of Objects	251

Chapter 8	Strings and Text I/O	263
8.1	Introduction	264
8.2	The String Class	264
8.3	The Character Class	273
8.4	The StringBuilder/StringBuffer Class	276
8.5	Command-Line Arguments	280
8.6	The File Class	283
8.7	File Input and Output	285
8.8	(GUI) File Dialogs	290

Chapter 9	Thinking in Objects	303
9.1	Introduction	304
9.2	Immutable Objects and Classes	304
9.3	The Scope of Variables	305
9.4	The this Reference	306
9.5	Class Abstraction and Encapsulation	307
9.6	Object-Oriented Thinking	311
9.7	Designing the Course Class	313
9.8	Designing a Class for Stacks	316
9.9	Designing the GuessDate Class	318

Chapter 10	Inheritance and Polymorphism	329
10.1	Introduction	330
10.2	Superclasses and Subclasses	330
10.3	Extending the JFrame Class	335
10.4	Using the super Keyword	336
10.5	Overriding Methods	338
10.6	Overriding vs. Overloading	339
10.7	The Object Class and Its Methods	340

10.8	Polymorphism, Dynamic Binding, and Generic Programming	341
10.9	Casting Objects and the instanceof Operator	343
10.10	The ArrayList Class	345
10.11	A Custom Stack Class	349
10.12	The protected Data and Methods	350
10.13	Preventing Extending and Overriding	351

Chapter 11 · Abstract Classes and Interfaces   361

11.1	Introduction	362
11.2	Abstract Classes	362
11.3	Example: Calendar and GregorianCalendar	366
11.4	Interfaces	369
11.5	Example: The Comparable Interface	370
11.6	Example: The ActionListener Interface	373
11.7	Example: The Cloneable Interface	374
11.8	Interfaces vs. Abstract Classes	377
11.9	Processing Primitive Data Type Values as Objects	380
11.10	Sorting an Array of Objects	382
11.11	Automatic Conversion between Primitive Types and Wrapper Class Types	384
11.12	The BigInteger and BigDecimal Classes	385

Chapter 12 · Object-Oriented Design and Patterns   393

12.1	Introduction	394
12.2	Software Life Cycle	394
12.3	Discovering Classes	395
12.4	Discovering Class Relationships	396
12.5	Case Study: Object-Oriented Design	400
12.6	Case Study: The Rational Class	405
12.7	Class Design Guidelines	410
12.8	Framework-Based Programming Using Java API	413
12.9	Design Patterns	414

Chapter 13 · GUI Basics   419

13.1	Introduction	420
13.2	Swing vs. AWT	420
13.3	The Java GUI API	420
13.4	Frames	423
13.5	Layout Managers	425
13.6	The Color Class	432
13.7	The Font Class	432
13.8	Using Panels as Subcontainers	433

13.9	Common Features of Swing GUI Components	435
13.10	Image Icons	437

Chapter 14 Graphics 445

14.1	Introduction	446
14.2	Graphical Coordinate Systems	446
14.3	The Graphics Class	446
14.4	The paintComponent Method	449
14.5	Drawing Graphics on Panels	450
14.6	Drawing Strings, Lines, Rectangles, and Ovals	451
14.7	Case Study: The FigurePanel Class	452
14.8	Drawing Arcs	456
14.9	Drawing Polygons and Polylines	458
14.10	Centering a String Using the FontMetrics Class	460
14.11	Case Study: The MessagePanel Class	462
14.12	Case Study: The StillClock Class	467
14.13	Displaying Images	471
14.14	Case Study: The ImageViewer Class	473

Chapter 15 Event-Driven Programming 483

15.1	Introduction	484
15.2	Event and Event Source	484
15.3	Listeners, Registrations, and Handling Events	485
15.4	Mouse Events	498
15.5	Key Events	501
15.6	Animation Using the Timer Class	503

Chapter 16 Creating User Interfaces 513

16.1	Introduction	514
16.2	Buttons	514
16.3	Check Boxes	520
16.4	Radio Buttons	523
16.5	Labels	525
16.6	Text Fields	526
16.7	Text Areas	528
16.8	Combo Boxes	531
16.9	Lists	534
16.10	Scroll Bars	538
16.11	Sliders	541
16.12	Creating Multiple Windows	543

Chapter 17   Applets and Multimedia   557

17.1   Introduction   558
17.2   The Applet Class   558
17.3   The JApplet Class   560
17.4   The HTML File and the <applet> Tag   561
17.5   Enabling Applets to Run as Applications   567
17.6   Passing Strings to Applets   568
17.7   Case Study: TicTacToe   572
17.8   Case Study: Bouncing Ball   577
17.9   Locating Resources Using the URL Class   580
17.10 Playing Audio in Any Java Program   581
17.11 Case Study: Multimedia Animations   582

Chapter 18   Exception Handling   597

18.1   Introduction   598
18.2   Exception-Handling Overview   598
18.3   Exception-Handling Advantages   600
18.4   Exception Types   601
18.5   Understanding Exception Handling   604
18.6   The finally Clause   611
18.7   When to Use Exceptions   612
18.8   Rethrowing Exceptions   612
18.9   Chained Exceptions   613
18.10 Creating Custom Exception Classes   614

Chapter 19   Binary I/O   623

19.1   Introduction   624
19.2   How is I/O Handled in Java?   624
19.3   Text I/O vs. Binary I/O   624
19.4   Binary I/O Classes   626
19.5   Problem: Copying Files   633
19.6   Object I/O   635
19.7   Random Access Files   639
19.8   Problem: Creating an Address Book   642

Chapter 20   Recursion   655

20.1   Introduction   656
20.2   Problem: Computing Factorials   656
20.3   Problem: Computing Fibonacci Numbers   659
20.4   Problem Solving Using Recursion   661

20.5	Recursive Helper Methods	662
20.6	Problem: Finding the Directory Size	665
20.7	Problem: Tower of Hanoi	666
20.8	Problem: Fractals	670
20.9	Problem: Eight Queens	673
20.10	Recursion versus Iteration	675

Chapter 21 Generics 685

21.1	Introduction	686
21.2	Motivations and Benefits	686
21.3	Declaring Generic Classes and Interfaces	688
21.4	Generic Methods	690
21.5	Raw Type and Backward Compatibility	691
21.6	Wildcard Generic Types	692
21.7	Erasure and Restrictions on Generics	694
21.8	Case Study: Generic Matrix Class	697

Chapter 22 Java Collections Framework 705

22.1	Introduction	706
22.2	The `Collection` Interface and the `AbstractCollection` Class	707
22.3	Sets	708
22.4	The Comparator Interface	714
22.5	Lists	716
22.6	Static Methods for Lists and Collections	720
22.7	Performance of Sets and Lists	723
22.8	The Vector and Stack Classes	724
22.9	Queues and Priority Queues	726
22.10	Maps	728
22.11	Singleton and Unmodifiable Collections and Maps	733

Chapter 23 Algorithm Efficiency 741

23.1	Introduction	742
23.2	Big O Notation	742
23.3	Examples: Determining Big O	743
23.4	Analyzing Binary Search	745
23.5	Analyzing Selection Sort	745
23.6	Analyzing Insertion Sort	746
23.7	Analyzing the Towers of Hanoi Problem	746
23.8	Comparing Common Growth Functions	747
23.9	Case Studies: Finding Fibonacci Numbers	747

23.10	Case Studies: Finding Greatest Common Divisors	749
23.11	Case Studies: Finding Prime Numbers	752
23.12	Case Studies: Closest Pair of Points	758
23.13	Preview of Other Algorithms	760

Chapter 24 Lists, Stacks, and Queues — 767

24.1	Introduction	768
24.2	Common Features for Lists	768
24.3	Array Lists	771
24.4	Linked Lists	776
24.5	Variations of Linked Lists	787
24.6	Stacks and Queues	788
24.7	Case Study: Evaluating Expressions	790

Chapter 25 Trees, Iterators, Heaps, and Priority Queues — 799

25.1	Introduction	800
25.2	Binary Search Trees	800
25.3	Deleting Elements in a BST	812
25.4	Tree Visualization	816
25.5	Iterators	820
25.6	Heaps	822
25.7	Priority Queues	828

Chapter 26 Sorting — 835

26.1	Introduction	836
26.2	Bubble Sort	836
26.3	Merge Sort	838
26.4	Quick Sort	841
26.5	Heap Sort	845
26.6	Bucket Sort and Radix Sort	846
26.7	External Sort	848

Chapter 27 Graph Applications — 857

27.1	Introduction	858
27.2	Basic Graph Terminologies	859
27.3	Representing Graphs	860
27.4	Modeling Graphs	864
27.5	Graph Traversals	874
27.6	Depth-First Search	875

27.7   Breadth-First Search   879
27.8   Case Study: The Nine Tail Problem   882
27.9   Case Study: The Knight's Tour Problem   888

Chapter 28   **Weighted Graphs Applications**   901

28.1   Introduction   902
28.2   Representing Weighted Graphs   902
28.3   The WeightedGraph Class   904
28.4   Minimum Spanning Trees   910
28.5   Finding Shortest Paths   915
28.6   Case Study: The Weighted Nine Tail Problem   922

Chapter 29   **Multithreading**   929

29.1   Introduction   930
29.2   Thread Concepts   930
29.3   Creating Tasks and Threads   930
29.4   The Thread Class   933
29.5   Example: Flashing Text   936
29.6   GUI Event Dispatch Thread   937
29.7   Case Study: Clock with Audio   938
29.8   Thread Pools   941
29.9   Thread Synchronization   943
29.10   Synchronization Using Locks   947
29.11   Cooperation among Threads   949
29.12   Case Study: Producer/Consumer   953
29.13   Blocking Queues   956
29.14   Semaphores   958
29.15   Avoiding Deadlocks   959
29.16   Thread States   960
29.17   Synchronized Collections   960
29.18   SwingWorker   962
29.19   Displaying Progress Using JProgressBar   965

Chapter 30   **Networking**   975

30.1   Introduction   976
30.2   Client/Server Computing   976
30.3   The InetAddress Class   983
30.4   Serving Multiple Clients   984
30.5   Applet Clients   987
30.6   Sending and Receiving Objects   989
30.7   Retrieving Files from Web Servers   994

30.8	JEditorPane	997
30.9	Case Studies: Distributed TicTacToe Games	999

Chapter 31　Internationalization　1015

31.1	Introduction	1016
31.2	The Locale Class	1016
31.3	Displaying Date and Time	1018
31.4	Formatting Numbers	1029
31.5	Resource Bundles	1035
31.6	Character Encoding	1042

Chapter 32　JavaBeans and Bean Events　1049

32.1	Introduction	1050
32.2	JavaBeans	1050
32.3	Bean Properties	1051
32.4	Java Event Model Review	1052
32.5	Creating Custom Source Components	1055
32.6	Creating Custom Event Sets	1059

Chapter 33　Containers, Layout Managers, and Borders　1069

33.1	Introduction	1070
33.2	Swing Container Structures	1070
33.3	Layout Managers	1072
33.4	Creating Custom Layout Managers	1081
33.5	JScrollPane	1086
33.6	JTabbedPane	1090
33.7	JSplitPane	1091
33.8	Swing Borders	1094

Chapter 34　Menus, Toolbars, and Dialogs　1107

34.1	Introduction	1108
34.2	Menus	1108
34.3	Popup Menus	1114
34.4	JToolBar	1116
34.5	Processing Actions Using the Action Interface	1118
34.6	JOptionPane Dialogs	1122
34.7	Creating Custom Dialogs	1129
34.8	JColorChooser	1132
34.9	JFileChooser	1134

Chapter 35   MVC and Swing Models   1145

35.1   Introduction   1146
35.2   MVC   1146
35.3   MVC Variations   1152
35.4   Swing Model-View-Controller Architecture   1153
35.5   JSpinner   1154
35.6   Spinner Models and Editors   1156
35.7   JList   1163
35.8   List Models   1167
35.9   List Cell Renderer   1170
35.10   JComboBox   1174

Chapter 36   JTable and JTree   1183

36.1   Introduction   1184
36.2   JTable   1184
36.3   Table Models and Table Column Models   1189
36.4   Auto Sort and Filtering   1193
36.5   Case Study: Modifying Rows and Columns   1195
36.6   Table Renderers and Editors   1200
36.7   Custom Table Renderers and Editors   1203
36.8   Table Model Events   1205
36.9   JTree   1208
36.10   TreeModel and DefaultTreeModel   1212
36.11   TreeNode, MutableTreeNode, and DefaultMutableTreeNode   1214
36.12   TreePath and TreeSelectionModel   1217
36.13   Case Study: Modifying Trees   1220
36.14   Tree Node Rendering and Editing   1223
36.15   Tree Events   1225

Chapter 37   Java Database Programming   1231

37.1   Introduction   1232
37.2   Relational Database Systems   1232
37.3   SQL   1236
37.4   JDBC   1244
37.5   PreparedStatement   1253
37.6   CallableStatement   1255
37.7   Retrieving Metadata   1258

Chapters are available from the companion Web site:

Chapter 38 Advanced Java Database Programming   38–1

38.1	Introduction	38–2
38.2	A Universal SQL Client	38–2
38.3	Batch Processing	38–6
38.4	Scrollable and Updatable Result Set	38–11
38.5	RowSet, JdbcRowSet, and CachedRowSet	38–14
38.6	RowSetTableModel	38–19
38.7	Storing and Retrieving Images in JDBC	38–26

Chapter 39 Servlets   39–1

39.1	Introduction	39–2
39.2	HTML and Common Gateway Interface	39–2
39.3	Creating and Running Servlets	39–4
39.4	The Servlet API	39–8
39.5	Creating Servlets	39–11
39.6	HTML Forms	39–14
39.7	Database Programming in Servlets	39–20
39.8	Session Tracking	39–24
39.9	Sending Images from Servlets	39–39

Chapter 40 JavaServer Pages   40–1

40.1	Introduction	40–2
40.2	Creating a Simple JSP Page	40–2
40.3	How Is a JSP Page Processed?	40–3
40.4	JSP Scripting Constructs	40–4
40.5	Predefined Variables	40–6
40.6	JSP Directives	40–8
40.7	Using JavaBeans in JSP	40–10
40.8	Getting and Setting Properties	40–13
40.9	Associating Properties with Input Parameters	40–13
40.10	Forwarding Requests from JavaServer Pages	40–22
40.11	Case Study: Browsing Database Tables	40–22

Chapter 41 JSF and Visual Web Development   41–1

| 41.1 | Introduction | 41–2 |
| 41.2 | Getting Started with JSF | 41–2 |

41.3   JSF UI Components   41–6
41.4   JSF UI Containers   41–11
41.5   Binding Data with UI Components   41–14
41.6   Session Tracking   41–20
41.7   Validating Input   41–23
41.8   Virtual Forms   41–26

Chapter 42   **Web Services**   42–1

42.1   Introduction   42–2
42.2   Creating Web Services   42–2
42.3   Deploying and Testing Web Services   42–4
42.4   Consuming Web Services   42–5
42.5   Passing and Returning Arguments   42–9
42.6   Web Service Session Tracking   42–16

Chapter 43   **Remote Method Invocation**   43–1

43.1   Introduction   43–2
43.2   RMI Basics   43–2
43.3   Developing RMI Applications   43–5
43.4   RMI vs. Socket-Level Programming   43–10
43.5   Developing Three-Tier Applications Using RMI   43–11
43.6   RMI Callbacks   43–14

Appendixes

Appendix A   Java Keywords   1267
Appendix B   The ASCII Character Set   1268
Appendix C   Operator Precedence Chart   1270
Appendix D   Java Modifiers   1272
Appendix E   Special Floating-Point Values   1274

Index   1275

CHAPTER 1

INTRODUCTION TO COMPUTERS, PROGRAMS, AND JAVA

Objectives

- To review computer basics, programs, and operating systems (§§1.2–1.4).

- To represent numbers in binary, decimal, and hexadecimal (§1.5).

- To explore the relationship between Java and the World Wide Web (§1.6).

- To distinguish the terms API, IDE, and JDK (§1.7).

- To write a simple Java program (§1.8).

- To display output on the console (§1.8).

- To create, compile, and run Java programs (§1.9).

- To explain the basic syntax of a Java program (§1.9).

- (GUI) To display output using the `JOptionPane` output dialog boxes (§1.10).

1.1 Introduction

why Java?

You use word processors to write documents, Web browsers to explore the Internet, and email programs to send email over the Internet. These are all examples of software that runs on computers. Software is developed using programming languages. There are many programming languages—so *why Java*? The answer is that Java enables users to develop and deploy applications on the Internet for servers, desktop computers, and small hand-held devices. The future of computing is being profoundly influenced by the Internet, and Java promises to remain a big part of that future. Java is *the* Internet programming language.

You are about to begin an exciting journey, learning a powerful programming language. At the outset, it is helpful to review computer basics, programs, and operating systems and to become familiar with number systems. If you are already familiar with such terms as CPU, memory, disks, operating systems, and programming languages, you may skip the review in §§1.2–1.4. You may also skip §1.5 and use it as reference when you have questions regarding binary and hexadecimal numbers.

1.2 What Is a Computer?

hardware
software

A computer is an electronic device that stores and processes data. It includes both *hardware* and *software*. In general, hardware comprises the visible, physical elements of the computer, and software provides the invisible instructions that control the hardware and make it perform specific tasks. Writing instructions for computers to perform is called computer programming. Knowing computer hardware isn't essential to your learning a programming language, but it does help you understand better the effect of the program instructions. This section introduces computer hardware components and their functions.

A computer consists of the following major hardware components (Figure 1.1):

- Central processing unit (CPU)

- Memory (main memory)

- Storage devices (disks, CDs, tapes)

- Input and output devices (monitors, keyboards, mice, printers)

- Communication devices [modems and network interface cards (NICs)]

FIGURE 1.1 A computer consists of CPU, memory, storage devices, input devices, output devices, and communication devices.

The components are connected through a subsystem called a *bus* that transfers data or power between them.

1.2.1 Central Processing Unit

CPU

The *central processing unit* (CPU) is the computer's brain. It retrieves instructions from memory and executes them. The CPU usually has two components: a *control unit* and an *arithmetic/logic unit*. The control unit controls and coordinates the actions of the other components. The arithmetic and logic unit performs numeric operations (addition, subtraction, multiplication, division) and logical operations (comparisons).

Today's CPU is built on a small silicon semiconductor chip with millions of transistors. Every computer has an internal clock, which emits electronic pulses at a constant rate. These pulses are used to control and synchronize the pace of operations. The higher the clock speed, the more instructions are executed in a given period of time. The unit of measurement of clock speed is the *hertz* (Hz), with 1 hertz equaling 1 pulse per second. The clock speed of computers is usually stated in megahertz (MHz) (1 MHz is 1 million Hz). CPU speed has been improved continuously. Intel's Pentium 3 Processor runs at about 500 megahertz and its Intel Pentium 4 Processor at about 3 gigahertz (GHz) (1 GHz is 1000 MHz).

speed

hertz
megahertz

gigahertz

1.2.2 Memory

To store and process information, computers use *off* or *on* electrical states, referred to by convention as *0* and *1*. These 0s and 1s are interpreted as digits in the binary number system and called *bits* (*b*inary dig*its*). Data of various kinds, such as numbers, characters, and strings, are encoded as series of bits. Data and program instructions for the CPU to execute are stored as groups of bits, or bytes, each byte composed of eight bits, in a computer's *memory*. A memory unit is an ordered sequence of *bytes*, as shown in Figure 1.2.

bit

byte

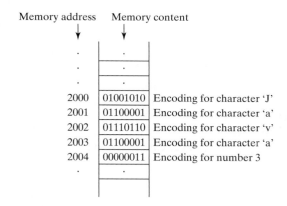

FIGURE 1.2 Memory stores data and program instructions.

The programmer need not be concerned about the encoding and decoding of data, which the system performs automatically, based on the encoding scheme. In the popular ASCII encoding scheme, for example, character '`J`' is represented by `01001010` in one byte.

A byte is the minimum storage unit. A small number such as `3` can be stored in a single byte. To store a number that cannot fit into a single byte, the computer uses several adjacent bytes. No two data items can share or split the same byte.

A memory byte is never empty, but its initial content may be meaningless to your program. The current content of a memory byte is lost whenever new information is placed in it.

A program and its data must be brought to memory before they can be executed.

Every byte has a unique address. The address is used to locate the byte for storing and retrieving data. Since the bytes can be accessed in any order, the memory is also referred to as *RAM* (random-access memory). Today's personal computers usually have at least 512 megabytes of RAM. A *megabyte* (abbreviated MB) is about 1 million bytes. For a precise definition of megabyte, please see http://en.wikipedia.org/wiki/Megabyte. Like the CPU, memory is built on silicon semiconductor chips containing thousands of transistors embedded on their surface. Compared to CPU chips, memory chips are less complicated, slower, and less expensive.

RAM

megabyte
megabyte URL

1.2.3 Storage Devices

Memory is volatile, because information is lost when the power is turned off. Programs and data are permanently stored on storage devices and, when the computer actually uses them are moved to memory, which is much faster than storage devices.

There are four main types of storage devices:

- Disk drives (hard disks and floppy disks)
- CD drives (CD-R, CD-RW, and DVD)
- Tape drives
- USB flash drives

drive

Drives are devices for operating a medium, such as disks, CDs, and tapes.

Disks

hard disk
floppy disk

There are two kinds of disks: *hard disks* and *floppy disks*. Personal computers have a hard drive with an optional 3.5-inch floppy disk drive. Hard disks provide much faster performance and larger capacity than floppy disks. A floppy disk has a fixed capacity of about 1.44 MB. The hard disks of the latest PCs store from 30 to 160 gigabytes. Often both disk drives are encased inside the computer, with the floppy disk being removable and the hard disk not. Removable hard disks are also available. Floppy disks are being replaced by CD-RW and flash drives.

CDs and DVDs

CD-R
CD-RW

CD stands for compact disk. There are two types of CD drives: *CD-R* and *CD-RW*. A CD-R is for read-only permanent storage; the user cannot modify its contents once they are recorded. A CD-RW can be used like a floppy disk, and thus can be both read and rewritten. A single CD can hold up to 700 MB. Most software is distributed through CD-ROMs. Most new PCs are equipped with a CD-RW drive that can work with both CD-R and CD-RW.

DVD stands for digital versatile disc or digital video disk. DVDs and CDs look alike, and you can use either to store data. A DVD can hold more information than a CD. A standard DVD storage capacity is 4.7 GB.

Tapes

Tapes are mainly used for backup of data and programs. Unlike disks and CDs, tapes store information sequentially. The computer must retrieve information in the order it was stored. Tapes are very slow. It would take one to two hours to back up a 1-gigabyte hard disk. The new trend is to back up data using flash drives or external hard disks.

USB Flash Drives

USB flash drives are devices for storing and transporting data. A flash drive is small—about the size of a pack of gum. It acts like a portable hard drive that can be plugged into the USB port of your computer. USB flash drives are currently available with up to 20 GB storage capacity.

1.2.4 Input and Output Devices

Input and output devices let the user communicate with the computer. The common input devices are *keyboards* and *mice*. The common output devices are *monitors* and *printers*.

The Keyboard

A computer *keyboard* resembles a typewriter keyboard except that it has extra keys for certain special functions.

function key

Function keys are located at the top of the keyboard and are numbered with prefix F. Their use depends on the software.

A *modifier key* is a special key (e.g., *Shift*, *Alt*, *Ctrl*) that modifies the normal action of another key when the two are pressed in combination.

The *numeric keypad,* located on the right-hand corner of the keyboard, is a separate set of keys for quick input of numbers.

Arrow keys, located between the main keypad and the numeric keypad, are used to move the cursor up, down, left, and right.

The *Insert, Delete, Page Up,* and *Page Dn keys*, located above the arrow keys, are used in word processing for performing insert, delete, page up, and page down.

The Mouse

A *mouse* is a pointing device. It is used to move an electronic pointer called a cursor around the screen or to click on an object on the screen to trigger it to respond.

The Monitor

The *monitor* displays information (text and graphics). The screen resolution and dot pitch determine the quality of the display.

The *screen resolution* specifies the number of pixels per square inch. Pixels (short for "picture elements") are tiny dots that form an image on the screen. A common resolution for a 17-inch screen, for example, is 1024 pixels wide and 768 pixels high. The resolution can be set manually. The higher the resolution, the sharper and clearer the image is.

The *dot pitch* is the amount of space between pixels. Typically, it has ranges from 0.21 to 0.81 millimeters. The smaller the dot pitch, the better the display.

1.2.5 Communication Devices

Computers can be networked through communication devices, such as the dialup modem (*mo*dulator/*dem*odulator), DSL, cable modem, and network interface card. A dialup modem uses a phone line and can transfer data at a speed up to 56,000 bps (bits per second). A DSL (digital subscriber line) also uses a phone line and can transfer data at a speed twenty times faster. A cable modem uses the TV cable line maintained by the cable company and is as fast as a DSL. A network interface card (NIC) is a device that connects a computer to a local area network (LAN). The LAN is commonly used in business, universities, and government organizations. A typical NIC called *10BaseT* can transfer data at 10 mbps (million bits per second).

1.3 Programs

Computer *programs*, known as *software*, are instructions to the computer, telling it what to do. Computers do not understand human languages, so you need to use computer languages in computer programs.

The computer's native language, which differs among different types of computers, is its *machine language*—a set of built-in primitive instructions. These instructions are in the form of binary code, so in telling the machine what to do, you have to enter binary code. Programming in machine language is a tedious process. Moreover, the programs are highly difficult to read and modify. For example, to add two numbers, you might have to write an instruction in binary like this:

```
1101101010011010
```

Assembly language is a low-level programming language in which a mnemonic is used to represent each of the machine-language instructions. For example, to add two numbers, you might write an instruction in assembly code like this:

```
ADDF3 R1, R2, R3
```

Margin terms: modifier key · numeric keypad · screen resolution · dot pitch · modem · DSL · NIC · LAN · mbps · software · machine language · assembly language assembler

Assembly languages were developed to make programming easy. However, since the computer cannot understand assembly language, a program called an *assembler* is used to convert assembly-language programs into machine code, as shown in Figure 1.3.

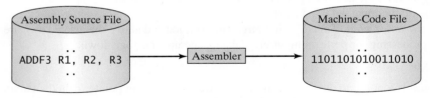

FIGURE 1.3 Assembler translates assembly-language instructions to machine code.

Assembly programs are written in terms of machine instructions with easy-to-remember mnemonic names. Since assembly language is machine dependent, an assembly program can be executed only on a particular kind of machine. The high-level languages were developed in order to overcome the platform-specific problem and make programming easier.

high-level language

The *high-level languages* are English-like and easy to learn and program. Here, for example, is a high-level language statement that computes the area of a circle with radius 5:

```
area = 5 * 5 * 3.1415;
```

There are over one hundred high-level languages. The well-known ones are:

- COBOL (COmmon Business Oriented Language)
- FORTRAN (FORmula TRANslation)
- BASIC (Beginner's All-purpose Symbolic Instruction Code)
- Pascal (named for Blaise Pascal)
- Ada (named for Ada Lovelace)
- C (whose developer designed B first)
- Visual Basic (Basic-like visual language developed by Microsoft)
- Delphi (Pascal-like visual language developed by Borland)
- C++ (an object-oriented language, based on C)
- C# (a Java-like language developed by Microsoft)
- Java

Each of these languages was designed for a specific purpose. COBOL was designed for business applications and now is used primarily for business data processing. FORTRAN was designed for mathematical computations and is used mainly for numeric computations. BASIC was designed to be learned and used easily. Ada was developed for the Department of Defense and is mainly used in defense projects. C combines the power of an assembly language with the ease of use and portability of a high-level language. Visual Basic and Delphi are used in developing graphical user interfaces and in rapid application development. C++ is popular for system software projects such as writing compilers and operating systems. The Microsoft Windows operating system was coded using C++.

source program
compiler

A program written in a high-level language is called a *source program or source code*. Since a computer cannot understand a source program, a program called a *compiler* is used to translate the source program into a machine-language program. The machine-language program is often then linked with other supporting library code to form an executable file. The executable file can be run on the machine, as shown in Figure 1.4. On Windows, executable files have extension .exe.

FIGURE 1.4 A source program is compiled into a machine-language file, which is then linked with the system library to form an executable file.

You can port (i.e., move) a source program to any machine with appropriate compilers. The source program must be recompiled, however, because the machine-language program can run only on a specific kind of machine. Nowadays computers are networked to work together. Java was designed to run on any platform. With Java, you write the program once and compile the source program into a special type of machine-language code known as *bytecode*. The bytecode can then run on any computer with a Java Virtual Machine (JVM), as shown in Figure 1.5. Java Virtual Machine is software that interprets Java bytecode.

bytecode
JVM

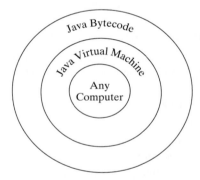

FIGURE 1.5 Java bytecode can be executed on any computer with a Java Virtual Machine.

Note

Java bytecode is interpreted. The difference between compiling and interpreting is as follows. Compiling translates the high-level code into a target-language code as a single unit. Interpreting translates the individual steps in a high-level program one at a time rather than the whole program as a single unit. Each step is executed immediately after it is translated.

compiling vs. interpreting

1.4 Operating Systems

The *operating system* (OS), the most important program that runs on a computer, enables it to manage and control its activities. Application programs, such as a Web browser or a word processor, cannot run without an operating system. You are probably using Microsoft Windows (currently the most popular PC operating system), Mac OS, or Linux. The interrelationship of hardware, operating system, application software, and the user is shown in Figure 1.6.

OS

```
┌──────────────────────┐
│        User          │──────┐
└──────────────────────┘      │
           │                  │
           ▼                  │
┌──────────────────────┐      │
│ Application Programs  │      │
└──────────────────────┘      │
           │                  │
           ▼                  │
┌──────────────────────┐      │
│  Operating System     │◄─────┘
└──────────────────────┘
           │
           ▼
┌──────────────────────┐
│      Hardware         │
└──────────────────────┘
```

FIGURE 1.6   The operating system is the software that controls and manages the system.

The major tasks of the operating system are:

- Controlling and monitoring system activities
- Allocating and assigning system resources
- Scheduling operations

1.4.1   Controlling and Monitoring System Activities

Operating systems perform basic tasks, such as recognizing input from the keyboard, sending output to the monitor, keeping track of files and directories on the disk, and controlling peripheral devices, such as disk drives and printers. Operating systems also make sure that different programs and users running at the same time do not interfere with each other, and they are responsible for security, ensuring that unauthorized users do not access the system.

1.4.2   Allocating and Assigning System Resources

The OS is responsible for determining what computer resources a program needs (e.g., CPU, memory, disks, input and output devices) and for allocating and assigning them to run the program.

1.4.3   Scheduling Operations

The OS is responsible for scheduling programs to use the system resources efficiently. Many of today's operating systems support such techniques as *multiprogramming*, *multithreading*, or *multiprocessing* to increase system performance.

multiprogramming

   Multiprogramming allows multiple programs to run simultaneously by sharing the CPU. The CPU is much faster than the other components. As a result, it is idle most of the time—for example, while waiting for data to be transferred from the disk or from other sources. A multiprogramming OS takes advantage of this by allowing multiple programs to use the CPU when it would otherwise be idle. For example, you may use a word processor to edit a file at the same time as the Web browser is downloading a file.

multithreading

   Multithreading allows concurrency within a program, so that its subunits can run at the same time. For example, a word-processing program allows users to simultaneously edit text and save it to a file. In this example, editing and saving are two tasks within the same application. These two tasks may run on separate threads concurrently.

multiprocessing

   Multiprocessing, or parallel processing, uses two or more processors together to perform a task. It is like a surgical operation where several doctors work together on one patient.

1.5 Number Systems

 Pedagogical NOTE

You can skip this section and use it as reference when you have questions regarding binary and hexadecimal numbers.

Computers use binary numbers internally, because storage devices like memory and disks are made to store 0s and 1s. The binary number system has two digits, 0 and 1. A number or a character inside a computer is stored as a sequence of 0s and 1s. Each 0 or 1 is called a *bit*.

binary number

Since we use decimal numbers in our daily life, binary numbers are not intuitive. When you write a number like 20 in a program, it is assumed to be a decimal number. Internally, computer software is used to convert decimal numbers into binary numbers, and vice versa.

decimal number

You write programs using decimal number systems. However, if you write programs to deal with a system like an operating system, you need to use binary numbers to reach down to the "machine level." Binary numbers tend to be very long and cumbersome. Hexadecimal numbers are often used to abbreviate binary numbers, with each hexadecimal digit representing exactly four binary digits. The hexadecimal number system has sixteen digits: 0–9, A–F. The letters A, B, C, D, E, and F correspond to the decimal numbers 10, 11, 12, 13, 14, and 15.

hexadecimal number

The digits in the decimal number system are 0, 1, 2, 3, 4, 5, 6, 7, 8, and 9. A decimal number is represented using a sequence of one or more of these digits. The value that each digit in the sequence represents depends on its position, which has a value that is an integral power of 10. For example, the digits 7, 4, 2, and 3 in decimal number 7423 represent 7000, 400, 20, and 3, respectively, as shown below:

$$\boxed{7 \mid 4 \mid 2 \mid 3} = 7 \times 10^3 + 4 \times 10^2 + 2 \times 10^1 + 3 \times 10^0$$
$$10^3 \ 10^2 \ 10^1 \ 10^0 \ = 7000 + 400 + 20 + 3 = 7423$$

The decimal number system has ten digits, and the position values are integral powers of 10. We say that 10 is the *base* or *radix* of the decimal number system. Similarly, the base of the binary number system is 2, since the binary number system has two digits, and the base of the hex number system is 16, since the hex number system has sixteen digits.

base
radix

If 1101 is a binary number, the digits 1, 1, 0, and 1 represent 1×2^3, 1×2^2, 0×2^1, and 1×2^0, respectively, as shown below:

$$\boxed{1 \mid 1 \mid 0 \mid 1} = 1 \times 2^3 + 1 \times 2^2 + 0 \times 2^1 + 1 \times 2^0$$
$$2^3 \ \ 2^2 \ \ 2^1 \ \ 2^0 \ = 8 + 4 + 0 + 1 = 13$$

If 7423 is a hex number, the digits 7, 4, 2, and 3 represent 7×16^3, 4×16^2, 2×16^1, and 3×16^0, respectively, as shown below:

$$\boxed{7 \mid 4 \mid 2 \mid 3} = 7 \times 16^3 + 4 \times 16^2 + 2 \times 16^1 + 3 \times 16^0$$
$$16^3 \ 16^2 \ 16^1 \ 16^0 \ = 28672 + 1024 + 32 + 3 = 29731$$

1.5.1 Conversions Between Binary Numbers and Decimal Numbers

Given a binary number $b_n b_{n-1} b_{n-2} \ldots b_2 b_1 b_0$, the equivalent decimal value is

$$b_n \times 2^n + b_{n-1} \times 2^{n-1} + b_{n-2} \times 2^{n-2} + \ldots + b_2 \times 2^2 + b_1 \times 2^1 + b_0 \times 2^0$$

The following are examples of converting binary numbers to decimals:

binary to decimal

Binary	Conversion Formula	Decimal
10	$1 \times 2^1 + 0 \times 2^0$	2
1000	$1 \times 2^3 + 0 \times 2^2 + 0 \times 2^1 + 0 \times 2^0$	8
10101011	$1 \times 2^7 + 0 \times 2^6 + 1 \times 2^5 + 0 \times 2^4 + 1 \times 2^3 + 0 \times 2^2 +$ $1 \times 2^1 + 1 \times 2^0$	171

decimal to binary

To convert a decimal number d to a binary number is to find the bits $b_n, b_{n-1}, b_{n-2}, \ldots, b_2, b_1$, and b_0 such that

$$d = b_n \times 2^n + b_{n-1} \times 2^{n-1} + b_{n-2} \times 2^{n-2} + \ldots + b_2 \times 2^2 + b_1 \times 2^1 + b_0 \times 2^0$$

These bits can be found by successively dividing d by 2 until the quotient is 0. The remainders are $b_0, b_1, b_2, \ldots, b_{n-2}, b_{n-1}$, and b_n.

For example, the decimal number 123 is 1111011 in binary. The conversion is done as follows:

 Tip
The Windows Calculator, as shown in Figure 1.7, is a useful tool for performing number conversions. To run it, choose *Programs*, *Accessories*, and *Calculator* from the Start button.

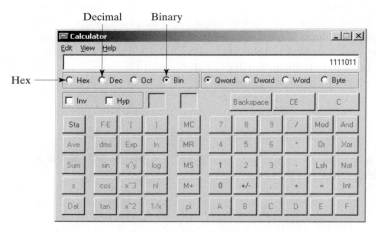

FIGURE 1.7 You can perform number conversions using the Windows Calculator.

1.5.2 Conversions Between Hexadecimal Numbers and Decimal Numbers

Given a hexadecimal number $h_n h_{n-1} h_{n-2} \ldots h_2 h_1 h_0$, the equivalent decimal value is

$$h_n \times 16^n + h_{n-1} \times 16^{n-1} + h_{n-2} \times 16^{n-2} + \ldots + h_2 \times 16^2 + h_1 \times 16^1 + h_0 \times 16^0$$

hex to decimal

The following are examples of converting hexadecimal numbers to decimals:

Hexadecimal	Conversion Formula	Decimal
7F	$7 \times 16^1 + 15 \times 16^0$	127
FFFF	$15 \times 16^3 + 15 \times 16^2 + 15 \times 16^1 + 15 \times 16^0$	65535
431	$4 \times 16^2 + 3 \times 16^1 + 1 \times 16^0$	1073

To convert a decimal number d to a hexadecimal number is to find the hexadecimal digits $h_n, h_{n-1}, h_{n-2}, \ldots, h_2, h_1$, and h_0 such that

$$d = h_n \times 16^n + h_{n-1} \times 16^{n-1} + h_{n-2} \times 16^{n-2} + \ldots + h_2 \times 16^2$$
$$+ h_1 \times 16^1 + h_0 \times 16^0$$

These numbers can be found by successively dividing d by 16 until the quotient is 0. The remainders are $h_0, h_1, h_2, \ldots, h_{n-2}, h_{n-1}$, and h_n.

For example, the decimal number 123 is 7B in hexadecimal. The conversion is done as follows:

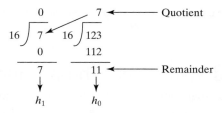

1.5.3 Conversions Between Binary Numbers and Hexadecimal Numbers

To convert a hexadecimal number to a binary number, simply convert each digit in the hexadecimal number into a four-digit binary number using Table 1.1.

TABLE 1.1 Converting Hexadecimal to Binary

Hexadecimal	Binary	Decimal
0	0000	0
1	0001	1
2	0010	2
3	0011	3
4	0100	4
5	0101	5
6	0110	6
7	0111	7
8	1000	8
9	1001	9
A	1010	10
B	1011	11
C	1100	12
D	1101	13
E	1110	14
F	1111	15

For example, the hexadecimal number 7B is 1111011, where 7 is 111 in binary, and B is 1011 in binary.

binary to hex

To convert a binary number to a hexadecimal, convert every four binary digits from right to left in the binary number into a hexadecimal number.

For example, the binary number 1110001101 is 38D, since 1101 is D, 1000 is 8, and 11 is 3, as shown below.

 Note

Octal numbers are also useful. The octal number system has eight digits, 0 to 7. A decimal number 8 is represented as 10 in the octal system.

1.6 Java, World Wide Web, and Beyond

This book introduces Java programming. Java was developed by a team led by James Gosling at Sun Microsystems. Originally called *Oak*, it was designed in 1991 for use in embedded chips in consumer electronic appliances. In 1995, renamed *Java*, it was redesigned for developing Internet applications. For the history of Java, see java.sun.com/features/1998/05/birthday.html.

Java has become enormously popular. Its rapid rise and wide acceptance can be traced to its design characteristics, particularly its promise that you can write a program once and run it anywhere. As stated by Sun, Java is *simple, object-oriented, distributed, interpreted, robust, secure, architecture-neutral, portable, high-performance, multithreaded,* and *dynamic*. For the anatomy of Java characteristics, see www.cs.armstrong.edu/liang/intro7e/JavaCharacteristics.pdf.

Java is a full-featured, general-purpose programming language that is capable of developing robust mission-critical applications. Today, it is used not only for Web programming, but also for developing standalone applications across platforms on servers, desktops, and mobile devices. It was used to develop the code to communicate with and control the robotic rover that rolled on Mars. Many companies that once considered Java to be more hype than substance are now using it to create distributed applications accessed by customers and partners across the Internet. For every new project being developed today, companies are asking how they can use Java to make their work easier.

The World Wide Web is an electronic information repository that can be accessed on the Internet from anywhere in the world. The Internet is the infrastructure of the Web. The Internet has been around for more than thirty years. The colorful World Wide Web and sophisticated Web browsers are the major reason for its popularity.

The primary authoring language for the Web is the Hypertext Markup Language (HTML). HTML is a simple language for laying out documents, linking documents on the Internet, and bringing images, sound, and video alive on the Web. However, it cannot interact with the user except through simple forms. Web pages in HTML are essentially static and flat.

applet

Java initially became attractive because Java programs can be run from a Web browser. Such programs are called *applets*. Applets use a modern graphical user interface with buttons, text fields, text areas, radio buttons, and so on, to interact with users on the Web and process their requests. Applets make the Web responsive, interactive, and fun to use. Figure 1.8 shows an applet running from a Web browser.

 Tip

For a demonstration of Java applets, visit java.sun.com/applets. This site provides a rich Java resource as well as links to other cool applet demo sites. java.sun.com is the official Sun Java Website.

Enter this URL from a
Web browser

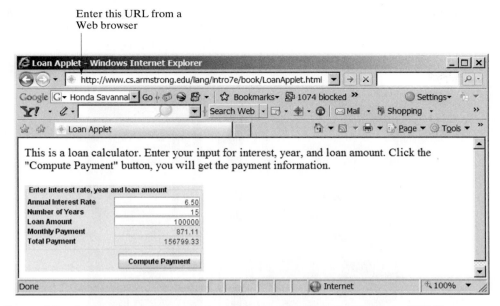

FIGURE 1.8 A Java applet for computing loan payments is embedded in an HTML page. The user can use the applet to compute the loan payments.

Java can also be used to develop applications on the server side. These applications can be run from a Web server to generate dynamic Web pages. The LiveLab accompanying this book, as shown in Figure 1.9, was developed using Java.

Enter this URL from a
Web browser

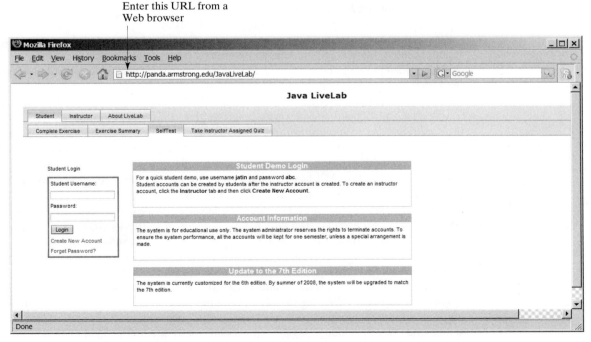

FIGURE 1.9 Java was used to develop the LiveLab for this book.

Java is a versatile programming language. You can use it to develop applications on your desktop and on the server. You can also use it to develop applications for small hand-held devices, such as personal digital assistants and cell phones. Figure 1.10 shows a Java program that displays the calendar on a BlackBerry© and on a cell phone.

Figure 1.10 Java can be used to develop applications for hand-held and wireless devices, such as a BlackBerry© (left) and a cell phone (right).

1.7 The Java Language Specification, API, JDK, and IDE

Computer languages have strict rules of usage. If you do not follow the rules when writing a program, the computer will be unable to understand it. The Java language specification and Java API define the Java standard.

Java language specification

The *Java language specification* is a technical definition of the language that includes the syntax and semantics of the Java programming language. The complete Java language specification can be found at java.sun.com/docs/books/jls.

API

The *application program interface* (*API*) contains predefined classes and interfaces for developing Java programs. The Java language specification is stable, but the API is still expanding. At the Sun Java Website (java.sun.com), you can view and download the latest version of the Java API.

Java SE, EE, and ME

Java is a full-fledged and powerful language that can be used in many ways. It comes in three editions: *Java Standard Edition* (*Java SE*), *Java Enterprise Edition* (*Java EE*), and *Java Micro Edition* (*Java ME*). Java SE can be used to develop client-side standalone applications or applets. Java EE can be used to develop server-side applications, such as Java servlets and JavaServer Pages. Java ME can be used to develop applications for mobile devices, such as cell phones. This book uses Java SE to introduce Java programming.

JDK 1.6 = JDK 6

There are many versions of Java SE. The latest is Java SE 6, which will be used in this book. Sun releases each version with a *Java Development Toolkit* (JDK). For Java SE 6, the Java Development Toolkit is called *JDK 1.6* (also known as *Java 6* or *JDK 6*).

Java IDE

JDK consists of a set of separate programs for developing and testing Java programs, each of which is invoked from a command line. Besides JDK, you can use a Java development tool (e.g., NetBeans, Eclipse, JBuilder, and TextPad)—software that provides an *integrated development environment* (*IDE*) for rapidly developing Java programs. Editing, compiling, building, debugging, and online help are integrated in one graphical user interface. Just enter source code in one window or open an existing file in a window, then click a button, menu item, or function key to compile and run the program.

Pedagogical NOTE

If you wish to use NetBeans, Eclipse, JBuilder, or TextPad for developing Java programs, please see Supplement II for tutorials.

Supplement II

1.8 A Simple Java Program

A Java program can be written in many ways. This book introduces Java applications, applets, and servlets. *Applications* are standalone programs that can be executed from any computer with a JVM. *Applets* are special kinds of Java programs that run from a Web browser. Servlets are special kinds of Java programs that run from a Web server to generate dynamic Web contents. Applets will be introduced in Chapter 17 and servlets in Chapter 39.

application
applet

Let us begin with a simple Java program that displays the message "Welcome to Java!" on the console. The program is shown in Listing 1.1.

Video Note
Your first Java program

LISTING 1.1   Welcome.java

```java
1 public class Welcome {
2   public static void main(String[] args) {
3     // Display message Welcome to Java! to the console
4     System.out.println("Welcome to Java!");
5   }
6 }
```

class
main method
comment
display message

```
Welcome to Java!
```

The line numbers are not part of the program, but are displayed for reference purposes. So, don't type line numbers in your program.

line numbers

Line 1 defines a class. Every Java program must have at least one class. Each class has a name. By convention, class names start with an uppercase letter. In this example, the class name is Welcome.

class name

Line 2 defines the main method. In order to run a class, the class must contain a method named main. The JVM executes the program by invoking the main method.

main method

A method is a construct that contains statements. The main method in this program contains the System.out.println statement. This statement prints a message "Welcome to Java!" to the console (line 4). Every statement in Java ends with a semicolon (;), known as the *statement terminator*.

statement terminator
reserved word

Reserved words, or *keywords,* have a specific meaning to the compiler and cannot be used for other purposes in the program. For example, when the compiler sees the word class, it understands that the word after class is the name for the class. Other reserved words in this program are public, static, and void.

Line 3 is a *comment* that documents what the program is and how it is constructed. Comments help programmers to communicate and understand the program. They are not programming statements and thus are ignored by the compiler. In Java, comments are preceded by two slashes (//) on a line, called a *line comment*, or enclosed between /* and */ on one or several lines, called a *block comment*. When the compiler sees //, it ignores all text after // on the same line. When it sees /*, it scans for the next */ and ignores any text between /* and */. Here are examples of comments:

comment

```
// This application program prints Welcome to Java!
/* This application program prints Welcome to Java! */
/* This application program
   prints Welcome to Java! */
```

block

The braces in the program form a *block* that groups the components of the program. In Java, each block begins with an opening brace ({) and ends with a closing brace (}). Every class has a *class block* that groups the data and methods of the class. Every method has a *method block* that groups the statements in the method. Blocks can be *nested*, meaning that one block can be placed within another, as shown in the following code.

```
public class Welcome {
  public static void main(String[] args) {                Class block
    System.out.println("Welcome to Java!");  Method block
  }
}
```

Tip

matching braces

An opening brace must be matched by a closing brace. Whenever you type an opening brace, immediately type a closing brace to prevent the missing-brace error. Most Java IDEs automatically insert the closing brace for each opening brace.

Note

You are probably wondering why the `main` method is declared this way and why `System.out.println(...)` is used to display a message to the console. For the time being, simply accept that this is how things are done. Your questions will be fully answered in subsequent chapters.

Note

syntax rules

Like any programming language, Java has its own syntax, and you need to write code that obeys the syntax rules. If your program violates the rules—for example if the semicolon is missing, a brace is missing, a quotation mark is missing, or `String` is misspelled—the Java compiler will report syntax errors. Try to compile the program with these errors and see what the compiler reports.

The program in Listing 1.1 displays one message. Once you understand the program, it is easy to extend it to display more messages. For example, you can rewrite the program to display three messages, as shown in Listing 1.2.

LISTING 1.2 Welcome1.java

class
main method
display message

```
1 public class Welcome1 {
2   public static void main(String[] args) {
3     System.out.println("Programming is fun!");
4     System.out.println("Fundamentals First");
5     System.out.println("Problem Driven");
6   }
7 }
```

```
Programming is fun!
Fundamentals First
Problem Driven
```

1.9 Creating, Compiling, and Executing a Java Program

You have to create your program and compile it before it can be executed. This process is repetitive, as shown in Figure 1.11. If your program has compilation errors, you have to fix them by modifying the program, then recompile it. If your program has runtime errors or does not produce the correct result, you have to modify the program, recompile it, and execute it again.

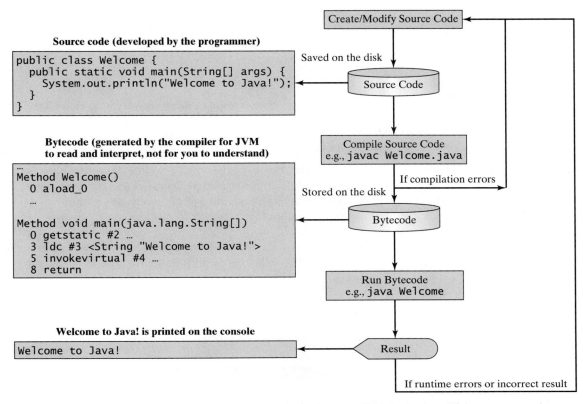

FIGURE 1.11 The Java program-development process consists of repeatedly creating/modifying source code, compiling, and executing programs.

You can use any text editor or IDE to create and edit a Java source-code file. Figure 1.12 shows how to use NotePad to create and edit the source-code file.

editor

FIGURE 1.12 You can create the Java source file using Windows NotePad.

Note

The source file must end with the extension .java and must have the exact same name as the public class name. For example, the file for the source code in Listing 1.1 should be named Welcome.java, since the public class name is `Welcome`.

.java file

A Java compiler translates a Java source file into a Java bytecode file. The following command compiles Welcome.java:

compile

```
javac Welcome.java
```

Note

You must first install and configure JDK before compiling and running programs. See Supplement I.B, "Installing and Configuring JDK 6," on how to install JDK and set up the environment to compile and run Java programs. If you have trouble compiling and running programs,

Supplement I.B

Supplement I.C

please see Supplement I.C, "Compiling and Running Java from the Command Window." This supplement also explains how to use basic DOS commands and how to use Windows NotePad and WordPad to create and edit files. All the supplements are accessible from the Companion Website.

Caution

case sensitive

Java source programs are case sensitive. It would be wrong, for example, to replace **main** in the program with **Main**. Program filenames are case sensitive on UNIX but generally not on Windows; JDK treats filenames as case sensitive on any platform. If you try to compile the program using **javac welcome.java**, you will get a file-not-found error.

.class bytecode file

If there are no syntax errors, the *compiler* generates a bytecode file with a .class extension. So the preceding command generates a file named **Welcome.class**. The bytecode is similar to machine instructions but is architecture neutral and can run on any platform that has a JVM. This is one of Java's primary advantages: *Java bytecode can run on a variety of hardware platforms and operating systems.*

run

To execute a Java program is to run the program's bytecode. You can execute the bytecode on any platform with a JVM. The following command runs the bytecode:

```
java Welcome
```

Figure 1.13 shows the **javac** command for compiling Welcome.java. The compiler generated the Welcome.class file. This file is executed using the **java** command.

Video Note

Compile and run a Java program

FIGURE 1.13 The output of Listing 1.1 displays the message Welcome to Java!

Note

c:\book

For simplicity and consistency, all source code and class files are placed under **c:\book** unless specified otherwise.

Caution

java ClassName

Do not use the extension .class in the command line when executing the program. Use **java ClassName** to run the program. If you use **java ClassName.class** in the command line, the system will attempt to fetch **ClassName.class.class**.

Tip

NoClassDefFoundError

If you execute a class file that does not exist, a **NoClassDefFoundError** will occur. If you execute a class file that does not have a **main** method or you mistype the **main** method (e.g., by typing **Main** instead of **main**), a **NoSuchMethodError** will occur.

NoSuchMethodError

Note

When executing a Java program, the JVM first loads the bytecode of the class to memory using a program called the *class loader*. If your program uses other classes, the class loader dynamically loads them just before they are needed. After a class is loaded, the JVM uses a program called *bytecode verifier* to check the validity of the bytecode and ensure that the bytecode does not violate Java's security restrictions. Java enforces strict security to make sure that Java programs arriving from the network do not harm your computer.

class loader

bytecode verifier

Pedagogical NOTE

Instructors may require students to use packages. For example, you may place all programs in this chapter in a package named *chapter1*. For instructions on how to use packages, please see Supplement I.F, "Using Packages to Organize the Classes in the Text."

using package

1.10 (GUI) Displaying Text in a Message Dialog Box

The program in Listing 1.1 displays the text on the console, as shown in Figure 1.13. You can rewrite the program to display the text in a message dialog box. To do so, you need to use the showMessageDialog method in the JOptionPane class. JOptionPane is one of the many predefined classes in the Java system that can be reused rather than "reinventing the wheel." You can use the showMessageDialog method to display any text in a message dialog box, as shown in Figure 1.14. The new program is given in Listing 1.3.

JOptionPane

showMessageDialog

Video Note

Display an output message dialog box

FIGURE 1.14 "Welcome to Java!" is displayed in a message box.

LISTING 1.3 WelcomeInMessageDialogBox.java

```
 1  /*  This application program displays Welcome to Java!
 2   *  in a message dialog box.
 3   */
 4  import javax.swing.JOptionPane;
 5
 6  public class WelcomeInMessageDialogBox {
 7    public static void main(String[] args) {
 8      // Display Welcome to Java! in a message dialog box
 9      JOptionPane.showMessageDialog(null, "Welcome to Java!");
10    }
11  }
```

block comment

import

main method

display message

This program uses a Java class JOptionPane (line 9). Java's predefined classes are grouped into packages. JOptionPane is in the javax.swing package. JOptionPane is imported to the program using the import statement in line 4 so that the compiler can locate the class without the full name javax.swing.JOptionPane.

package

Note

If you replace JOptionPane on line 9 with javax.swing.JOptionPane, you don't need to import it in line 4. javax.swing.JOptionPane is the full name for the JOptionPane class.

The `showMessageDialog` method is a *static* method. Such a method should be invoked by using the class name followed by a dot operator (`.`) and the method name with arguments. Methods will be introduced in Chapter 5, "Methods." The `showMessageDialog` method can be invoked with two arguments, as in line 9.

The first argument can always be `null`. `null` is a Java keyword that will be fully introduced in Chapter 7, "Objects and Classes." The second argument is a string for text to be displayed.

two versions of
showMessageDialog

There are several ways to use the `showMessageDialog` method. For the time being, all you need to know are two ways to invoke it. One is to use a statement, as shown in the example:

```
JOptionPane.showMessageDialog(null, x);
```

where `x` is a string for the text to be displayed.

The other is to use a statement like this one:

```
JOptionPane.showMessageDialog(null, x,
    y, JOptionPane.INFORMATION_MESSAGE));
```

where `x` is a string for the text to be displayed, and `y` is a string for the title of the message box. The fourth argument can be `JOptionPane.INFORMATION_MESSAGE`, which causes the icon ( ) to be displayed in the message box, as shown in the following example.

 Note

specific import

There are two types of `import` statements: *specific import* and *wildcard import*. The *specific import* specifies a single class in the import statement. For example, the following statement imports `JOptionPane` from package `javax.swing`.

```
import javax.swing.JOptionPane;
```

wildcard import

The *wildcard import* imports all the classes in a package. For example, the following statement imports all classes from package `javax.swing`.

```
import javax.swing.*;
```

no performance difference

The information for the classes in an imported package is not read in at compile time or runtime unless the class is used in the program. The import statement simply tells the compiler where to locate the classes. There is no performance difference between a specific import and a wildcard import declaration.

Note

java.lang
implicitly imported

Recall that you have used the `System` class in the statement *System.out.println("Welcome to Java");* in Listing 1.1. The `System` class is not imported because it is in the `java.lang` package. All the classes in the `java.lang` package are *implicitly* imported in every Java program.

KEY TERMS

.class file   18
.java file   17
assembly language   6
binary numbers   3, 9
bit   3
block   16
block comment   15
byte   3
bytecode   7
bytecode verifier   19
cable modem   5
central processing unit (CPU)   2
class loader   19
comment   15
compiler   6
dot pitch   5
DSL (digital subscriber line)   5
hardware   2
hexadecimal numbers   9
high-level language   6
Integrated Development Environment
    (IDE)   14

java command   18
javac command   17
Java Development Toolkit (JDK)   14
Java Virtual Machine (JVM)   7
keyword (or reserved word)   15
line comment   15
machine language   5
main method   15
modem   5
memory   3
network interface card (NIC)   5
operating system (OS)   7
pixel   5
resolution   5
software   2
source code   6, 15
source file   6, 15
specific import   20
storage devices   4
statement   15
wildcard import   20

Note

The above terms are defined in the present chapter. Supplement I.A, "Glossary," on the Companion Web site lists all the key terms and descriptions in the book, organized by chapters.

CHAPTER SUMMARY

■ A computer is an electronic device that stores and processes data. A computer includes both *hardware* and *software*. In general, hardware is the visible, physical aspect of the computer, and software is the invisible instructions that control the hardware and make it perform tasks.

■ Computer *programs*, known as *software*, are instructions to the computer. You tell a computer what to do through programs. Computer programming consists of writing instructions for computers to perform.

■ The *machine language* is a set of primitive instructions built into every computer. *Assembly language* is a low-level programming language in which a mnemonic is used to represent each of the machine-language instructions.

■ *High-level languages* are English-like and much easier to learn and program. There are over one hundred high-level languages. A program written in a high-level language is called a *source program*. Since a computer cannot understand a source program, a program called a *compiler* is used to translate it into a machine-language program, which is then linked with other supporting library code to form an executable file.

- The *operating system* (OS) is a program that manages and controls a computer's activities. Application programs, such as Web browsers and word processors, cannot run without an operating system.

- Java was developed by a team led by James Gosling at Sun Microsystems. It is an Internet programming language. Since its inception in 1995, it has quickly become a premier language for building software.

- Java is platform independent, meaning that you can write a program once and run it anywhere.

- Java programs can be embedded in HTML pages and downloaded by Web browsers to bring live animation and interaction to Web clients.

- Java source files end with the .java extension. Every class is compiled into a separate bytecode file that has the same name as the class and ends with the .class extension.

- To compile a Java source-code file from the command line, use the **javac** command. To run a Java class, use the **java** command.

- Every Java program is a set of class definitions. The keyword `class` introduces a class definition. The contents of the class are included in a block. A block begins with an opening brace ({) and ends with a closing brace (}). Methods are contained in a class.

- A Java application must have a `main` method. The `main` method is the entry point where the application program starts when it is executed.

REVIEW QUESTIONS

 Note
Answers to review questions are on the Companion Website.

Sections 1.2–1.4

1.1   Define hardware and software.

1.2   List the main components of the computer.

1.3   Define machine language, assembly language, and high-level programming language.

1.4   What is a source program? What is a compiler?

1.5   What is the JVM?

1.6   What is an operating system?

Section 1.5

1.7   Convert the following decimal numbers into hexadecimal and binary numbers.

100; 4340; 2000

1.8   Convert the following binary numbers into hexadecimal numbers and decimal numbers.

1000011001; 100000000; 100111

1.9   Convert the following hexadecimal numbers into binary and decimal numbers.

FEFA9; 93; 2000

Sections 1.6–1.7

1.10   Describe the history of Java. Can Java run on any machine? What is needed to run Java on a computer?

1.11   What are the input and output of a Java compiler?

1.12   List some Java development tools. Are tools like NetBeans, Eclipse, and JBuilder different languages from Java, or are they dialects or extensions of Java?

1.13   What is the relationship between Java and HTML?

Sections 1.8–1.10

1.14   Explain the Java keywords. List some Java keywords you learned in this chapter.

1.15   Is Java case sensitive? What is the case for Java keywords?

1.16   What is the Java source filename extension, and what is the Java bytecode filename extension?

1.17   What is a comment? Is the comment ignored by the compiler? How do you denote a comment line and a comment paragraph?

1.18   What is the statement to display a string on the console? What is the statement to display the message "Hello world" in a message dialog box?

1.19   The following program is wrong. Reorder the lines so that the program displays morning followed by afternoon.

```java
    public static void main(String[] args) {
    }
public class Welcome {
    System.out.println("afternoon");
    System.out.println("morning");
}
```

1.20   Identify and fix the errors in the following code:

```java
1 public class Welcome {
2   public void Main(String[] args) {
3     System.out.println('Welcome to Java!);
4   }
5 }
```

1.21   What is the command to compile a Java program? What is the command to run a Java application?

1.22   If a NoClassDefFoundError occurs when you run a program, what is the cause of the error?

1.23   If a NoSuchMethodError occurs when you run a program, what is the cause of the error?

1.24   Why does the System class not need to be imported?

1.25   Are there any performance differences between the following two import statements?

```java
import javax.swing.JOptionPane;
import javax.swing.*;
```

PROGRAMMING EXERCISES

level of difficulty

Note

NOTE: Solutions to even-numbered exercises are on the Companion Website. Solutions to all exercises are on the Instructor Resource Website. The level of difficulty is rated easy (no star), moderate (*), hard (**), or challenging (***).

1.1 (*Creating, compiling, and running a Java program*) Create a source file containing a Java program. Perform the following steps to compile the program and run it (see §1.9, "Creating, Compiling, and Executing a Java Program" earlier in this chapter):

1. Create a file named **Welcome.java** for Listing 1.1. You can use any editor that will save your file in text format.
2. Compile the source file.
3. Run the bytecode.
4. Replace `"Welcome to Java"` with `"My first program"` in the program; save, compile, and run the program. You will see the message `"My first program"` displayed.
5. Replace `class` with `Class`, and recompile the source code. The compiler returns an error message because the Java program is case sensitive.
6. Change it back, and compile the program again.
7. Instead of using the command `java Welcome` to run the program, use `java Welcome.class`. What happens?

1.2 (*Displaying five messages*) Write a Java program that displays `Welcome to Java` five times.

1.3* (*Displaying a pattern*) Write a Java program that displays the following pattern:

Video Note
Display five messages

```
J   A   V   V   A
J   A A   V V   A A
J J AAAAA   V V   AAAAA
J J A   A   V   A   A
```

CHAPTER 2

ELEMENTARY PROGRAMMING

Objectives

- To write Java programs to perform simple calculations (§2.2).

- To use identifiers to name variables, constants, methods, and classes (§2.3).

- To use variables to store data (§§2.4–2.5).

- To program with assignment statements and assignment expressions (§2.5).

- To use constants to store permanent data (§2.6).

- To declare Java primitive data types: `byte`, `short`, `int`, `long`, `float`, `double`, and `char` (§§2.7–2.9).

- To use Java operators to write numeric expressions (§§2.7–2.8).

- To represent characters using the `char` type (§2.9).

- To represent a string using the `String` type (§2.10).

- To obtain input from the console using the `Scanner` class (§§2.11–2.12).

- To become familiar with Java documentation, programming style, and naming conventions (§2.13).

- To distinguish syntax errors, runtime errors, and logic errors (§2.14).

- To debug logic errors (§2.15).

- (GUI) To obtain input using the `JOptionPane` input dialog boxes (§2.16).

2.1 Introduction

In Chapter 1 you learned how to create, compile, and run a Java program. Now you will learn how to solve practical problems programmatically. You will learn Java primitive data types and related subjects, such as variables, constants, data types, operators, expressions, and input and output.

2.2 Writing Simple Programs

problem

To begin, let's look at a simple problem for computing the area of a circle. How do we write a program for solving this problem?

algorithm

Writing a program involves designing algorithms and data structures, as well as translating algorithms into programming code. An *algorithm* describes how a problem is solved in terms of the actions to be executed and the order of their execution. Algorithms can help the programmer plan a program before writing it in a programming language. The algorithm for this program can be described as follows:

1. Read in the radius.

2. Compute the area using the following formula:

$$\text{area} = \text{radius} \times \text{radius} \times \pi$$

3. Display the area.

floating-point number
primitive data types

Data structures involve data representation and manipulation. Java provides data types for representing integers, floating-point numbers (i.e., numbers with a decimal point), characters, and Boolean types. These types are known as *primitive data types*. Java also supports array and string types as objects. Some advanced data structures, such as stacks, sets, and lists, have built-in implementation in Java.

To novice programmers, coding is a daunting task. When you *code*, you translate an algorithm into a programming language the computer understands. You already know that every Java program begins with a class declaration in which the keyword `class` is followed by the class name. Assume that you have chosen `ComputeArea` as the class name. The outline of the program would look like this:

```java
public class ComputeArea {
  // Data and methods to be given later
}
```

As you know, every application must have a `main` method where program execution begins. So the program is expanded as follows:

```java
public class ComputeArea {
  public static void main(String[] args) {
    // Step 1: Read in radius

    // Step 2: Compute area

    // Step 3: Display the area
  }
}
```

The program needs to read the radius entered by the user from the keyboard. This raises two important issues:

- Reading the radius.

- Storing the radius in the program.

Let's address the second issue first. In order to store the radius, the program needs to declare a symbol called a *variable* that will represent the radius. Variables are used to store data and computational results in the program.

Rather than using x and y as variable names, choose descriptive names: in this case, radius for radius, and area for area. To let the compiler know what radius and area are, specify their data types—integer, float, or something else. Declare radius and area as double-precision floating-point numbers. The program can be expanded as follows:

```java
public class ComputeArea {
  public static void main(String[] args) {
    double radius;
    double area;
    // Step 1: Read in radius

    // Step 2: Compute area

    // Step 3: Display the area
  }
}
```

The program declares radius and area as variables. The reserved word double indicates that radius and area are double-precision floating-point values stored in the computer.

The first step is to read in radius. Reading a number from the keyboard is not a simple matter. For the time being, let us assign a fixed number to radius in the program. In §2.11, "Console Input Using the Scanner Class," and §2.16, "Getting Input from Input Dialogs," you will learn how to obtain a numeric value from the console and from an input dialog.

The second step is to compute area by assigning the expression radius * radius * 3.14159 to area.

In the final step, print area on the console by using the System.out.println method.

The complete program is shown in Listing 2.1. A sample run of the program is shown in Figure 2.1.

Compile →
Run →

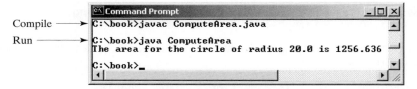

FIGURE 2.1 The program displays the area of a circle.

LISTING 2.1 ComputeArea.java

```java
1  public class ComputeArea {
2    /** Main method */                            Memory
3    public static void main(String[] args) {
4      double radius; // Declare radius        radius   no value
5      double area; // Declare area            area     no value
6
7      // Assign a radius
8      radius = 20; // New value is radius     radius   20
9
10     // Compute area
11     area = radius * radius * 3.14159;       area     1256.636
12
13     // Display results
```

```
14      System.out.println("The area for the circle of radius " +
15        radius + " is " + area);
16   }
17 }
```

declaring variable

assign value

Variables such as `radius` and `area` correspond to memory locations. Every variable has a name, a type, a size, and a value. Line 4 declares that `radius` can store a `double` value. The value is not defined until you assign a value. Line 8 assigns `20` into `radius`. Similarly, line 5 declares variable `area`, and line 11 assigns a value into `area`. Figure 2.2 shows the value in the memory for `area` and `radius` as the program is executed.

line#	radius	area
4	no value	
5		no value
8	20	
11		1256.636

FIGURE 2.2 The variable values stored in the memory are changed during execution.

concatenating strings

concatenating strings with numbers

The plus sign (+) has two meanings: one for addition and the other for concatenating strings. The plus sign (+) in lines 14–15 is called a *string concatenation operator*. It combines two strings if two operands are strings. If one of the operands is a nonstring (e.g., a number), the nonstring value is converted into a string and concatenated with the other string. So the plus signs (+) in lines 14–15 concatenate strings into a longer string, which is then displayed in the output. Strings and string concatenation will be discussed further in §2.10, "The `String` Type."

Caution

breaking a long string

A string constant cannot cross lines in the source code. Thus the following statement would result in a compilation error:

```
System.out.println("Introduction to Java Programming,
  by Y. Daniel Liang");
```

To fix the error, break the string into separate substrings, and use the concatenation operator (+) to combine them:

```
System.out.println("Introduction to Java Programming, " +
  "by Y. Daniel Liang");
```

Tip

incremental development and testing

This example consists of three steps. It is a good approach to develop and test these steps incrementally by adding them one at a time.

2.3 Identifiers

Just as every entity in the real world has a name, so you need to choose names for the things you will refer to in your programs. Programming languages use special names called *identifiers* for such programming entities as variables, constants, methods, classes, and packages. Here are the rules for naming identifiers:

naming identifiers

- An identifier is a sequence of characters that consists of letters, digits, underscores (_), and dollar signs ($).

- An identifier must start with a letter, an underscore (_), or a dollar sign ($). It cannot start with a digit.

- An identifier cannot be a reserved word. (See Appendix A, "Java Keywords," for a list of reserved words.)

- An identifier cannot be `true`, `false`, or `null`.

- An identifier can be of any length.

For example, `$2`, `ComputeArea`, `area`, `radius`, and `showMessageDialog` are legal identifiers, whereas `2A` and `d+4` are not because they do not follow the rules. The Java compiler detects illegal identifiers and reports syntax errors.

Note

Since Java is case sensitive, `X` and `x` are different identifiers.

case-sensitive

Tip

Identifiers are used for naming variables, constants, methods, classes, and packages. Descriptive identifiers make programs easy to read. Besides choosing descriptive names for identifiers, you should follow naming conventions for different kinds of identifiers. Naming conventions are summarized in §2.15, "Programming Style and Documentation."

descriptive names

Tip

Do not name identifiers with the `$` character. By convention, the `$` character should be used only in mechanically generated source code.

the `$` character

2.4 Variables

Variables are used to store data in a program. In the program in Listing 2.1, `radius` and `area` are variables of double-precision, floating-point type. You can assign any numerical value to `radius` and `area`, and the values of `radius` and `area` can be reassigned. For example, you can write the code shown below to compute the area for different radii:

```
// Compute the first area
radius = 1.0;
area = radius * radius * 3.14159;
System.out.println("The area is " + area + " for radius " + radius);

// Compute the second area
radius = 2.0;
area = radius * radius * 3.14159;
System.out.println("The area is " + area + " for radius " + radius);
```

2.4.1 Declaring Variables

Variables are for representing data of a certain type. To use a variable, you declare it by telling the compiler its name as well as what type of data it represents. This *variable declaration* tells the compiler to allocate appropriate memory space for the variable based on its data type. The syntax for declaring a variable is

```
datatype variableName;
```

Here are some examples of variable declarations:

declaring variable

```
int x;              // Declare x to be an integer variable;
double radius;      // Declare radius to be a double variable;
double interestRate; // Declare interestRate to be a double variable;
char a;             // Declare a to be a character variable;
```

The examples use the data types `int`, `double`, and `char`. Later you will be introduced to additional data types, such as `byte`, `short`, `long`, `float`, `char`, and `boolean`.

If variables are of the same type, they can be declared together, as follows:

```
datatype variable1, variable2, ..., variablen;
```

The variables are separated by commas. For example,

```
int i, j, k; // Declare i, j, and k as int variables
```

Note

naming variables

By convention, variable names are in lowercase. If a name consists of several words, concatenate all of them and capitalize the first letter of each word except the first. Examples of variables are `radius` and `interestRate`.

2.5 Assignment Statements and Assignment Expressions

assignment statement
assignment operator

After a variable is declared, you can assign a value to it by using an *assignment statement*. In Java, the equal sign (=) is used as the *assignment operator*. The syntax for assignment statements is as follows:

```
variable = expression;
```

expression

An *expression* represents a computation involving values, variables, and operators that, taking them together, evaluates to a value. For example, consider the following code:

```
int x = 1;                 // Assign 1 to variable x;
double radius = 1.0;       // Assign 1.0 to variable radius;
x = 5 * (3 / 2) + 3 * 2;   // Assign the value of the expression to x;
x = y + 1;                 // Assign the addition of y and 1 to x;
area = radius * radius * 3.14159; // Compute area
```

A variable can also be used in an expression. For example,

```
x = x + 1;
```

In this assignment statement, the result of x + 1 is assigned to x. If x is 1 before the statement is executed, then it becomes 2 after the statement is executed.

To assign a value to a variable, the variable name must be on the left of the assignment operator. Thus, 1 = x would be wrong.

Note:

In mathematics, x = x + 1 denotes an equation. However, in Java, x = x + 1 is an assignment statement that assigns a new value to x.

assignment expression

In Java, an assignment statement can also be treated as an expression that evaluates to the value being assigned to the variable on the left-hand side of the assignment operator. For this reason, an assignment statement is also known as an *assignment expression*. For example, the following statement is correct:

```
System.out.println(x = 1);
```

which is equivalent to

```
x = 1;
System.out.println(x);
```

The following statement is also correct:

```
i = j = k = 1;
```

which is equivalent to

```
k = 1;
j = k;
i = j;
```

Note

In an assignment statement, the data type of the variable on the left must be compatible with the data type of the value on the right. For example, `int x = 1.0` would be illegal because the data type of `x` is `int`. You cannot assign a `double` value (`1.0`) to an `int` variable without using type casting. Type casting is introduced in §2.8, "Numeric Type Conversions."

2.5.1 Declaring and Initializing Variables in One Step

Variables often have initial values. You can declare a variable and initialize it in one step. Consider, for instance, the following code:

```
int x = 1;
```

This is equivalent to the next two statements:

```
int x;
x = 1;
```

You can also use a shorthand form to declare and initialize variables of the same type together. For example,

```
int i = 1, j = 2;
```

Tip

A variable must be declared before it can be assigned a value. A variable declared in a method must be assigned a value before it can be used. Whenever possible, declare a variable and assign its initial value in one step. This will make the program easy to read and avoid programming errors.

2.6 Constants

The value of a variable may change during the execution of the program, but a *constant* represents permanent data that never changes. In our `ComputeArea` program, π is a constant. If you use it frequently, you don't want to keep typing `3.14159`; instead, you can define a constant for π. Here is the syntax for declaring a constant:

constant

```
final datatype CONSTANTNAME = VALUE;
```

A constant must be declared and initialized in the same statement. The word `final` is a Java keyword which means that the constant cannot be changed. For example, in the `ComputeArea` program, you could define π as a constant and rewrite the program as follows:

```
// ComputeArea.java: Compute the area of a circle
public class ComputeArea {
  public static void main(String[] args) {
    final double PI = 3.14159; // Declare a constant

    // Assign a radius
    double radius = 20;

    // Compute area
    double area = radius * radius * PI ;
```

```
    // Display results
    System.out.println("The area for the circle of radius " +
      radius + " is " + area);
  }
}
```

naming constants

Caution

By convention, constants are named in uppercase: `PI`, not `pi` or `Pi`.

benefits of constants

Note

There are three benefits of using constants: (1) you don't have to repeatedly type the same value; (2) the value can be changed in a single location, if necessary; (3) a descriptive name for a constant makes the program easy to read.

2.7 Numeric Data Types and Operations

Every data type has a range of values. The compiler allocates memory space to store each variable or constant according to its data type. Java provides eight primitive data types for numeric values, characters, and Boolean values. This section introduces numeric data types.

Table 2.1 lists the six numeric data types, their ranges, and their storage sizes.

TABLE 2.1 Numeric Data Types

Name	Range	Storage Size
`byte`	-2^7 (-128) to $2^7 - 1$ (127)	8-bit signed
`short`	-2^{15} (-32768) to $2^{15} - 1$ (32767)	16-bit signed
`int`	-2^{31} (-2147483648) to $2^{31} - 1$ (2147483647)	32-bit signed
`long`	-2^{63} to $2^{63} - 1$ (i.e., -9223372036854775808 to 9223372036854775807)	64-bit signed
`float`	Negative range: $-3.4028235E + 38$ to $-1.4E - 45$ Positive range: $1.4E{-}45$ to $3.4028235E + 38$	32-bit IEEE 754
`double`	Negative range: $-1.7976931348623157E + 308$ to $-4.9E - 324$ Positive range: $4.9E - 324$ to $1.7976931348623157E + 308$	64-bit IEEE 754

Note

IEEE 754 is a standard approved by the Institute of Electrical and Electronics Engineers for representing floating-point numbers on computers. The standard has been widely adopted. Java has adopted the 32-bit **IEEE 754** for the `float` type and the 64-bit **IEEE 754** for the `double` type. The **IEEE 754** standard also defines special values in Appendix E, "Special Floating-Point Values."

integer types

Java uses four types for integers: `byte`, `short`, `int`, and `long`. Choose the type that is most appropriate for your variable. For example, if you know an integer stored in a variable is within a range of byte, declare the variable as a `byte`.

Java uses two types for floating-point numbers: `float` and `double`. The `double` type is twice as big as `float`. So, the `double` is known as *double precision*, while `float` is known as *single precision*. Normally, you should use the `double` type because it is more accurate than the `float` type.

floating-point

Caution

When a variable is assigned a value that is too large to be stored, it causes *overflow*. For example, executing the following statement causes *overflow*, because the largest value that can be stored in a variable of the `int` type is `2147483647`. `2147483648` is too large.

what is overflow?

```
int value = 2147483647 + 1;
```

When a variable is assigned a value that is too small to be stored, it causes *underflow*. For example, executing the following statement causes *underflow*, because the smallest value that can be stored in a variable of the `int` type is `-2147483648`. `-2147483649` is too small.

what is underflow?

```
int value = -2147483648 - 1;
```

Java does not report warnings or errors on overflow and underflow. So be careful when working with numbers close to the maximum or minimum range of a given type.

2.7.1 Numeric Operators

The operators for numeric data types include the standard arithmetic operators: addition (+), subtraction (−), multiplication (*), division (/), and remainder (%), as shown in Table 2.2.

operators +, −, *, /, %

TABLE 2.2 Numeric Operators

Name	Meaning	Example	Result
+	Addition	34 + 1	35
−	Subtraction	34.0 − 0.1	33.9
*	Multiplication	300 * 30	9000
/	Division	1.0 / 2.0	0.5
%	Remainder	20 % 3	2

The result of integer division is an integer. The fractional part is truncated. For example, `5 / 2` yields `2`, not `2.5`, and `-5 / 2` yields `-2`, not `-2.5`.

integer division

The `%` operator yields the remainder after division. The left-hand operand is the dividend and the right-hand operand is the divisor. Therefore, `7 % 3` yields `1`, `12 % 4` yields `0`, `26 % 8` yields `2`, and `20 % 13` yields `7`.

```
   2            3            3                          1  ←──── Quotient
3) 7         4) 12        8) 26          Divisor ──→ 13) 20  ←──── Dividend
   6            12           24                         13
  ───          ───          ───                        ───
   1            0            2                           7  ←──── Remainder
```

The % operator is often used for positive integers but can be used also with negative integers and floating-point values. The remainder is negative only if the dividend is negative. For example, `-7 % 3` yields `-1`, `-12 % 4` yields `0`, `-26 % -8` yields `-2`, and `20 % -13` yields `7`.

Remainder is very useful in programming. For example, an even number `% 2` is always `0` and an odd number `% 2` is always `1`. So you can use this property to determine whether a number is even or odd. Suppose today is Saturday, you and your friend are going to meet in `10` days. What day is in `10` days? You can find that the day is Tuesday using the following expression:

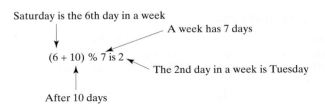

Saturday is the 6th day in a week

A week has 7 days

(6 + 10) % 7 is 2

The 2nd day in a week is Tuesday

After 10 days

Listing 2.2 gives a program that obtains minutes and remaining seconds from an amount of time in seconds. For example, `500` seconds contains `8` minutes and `20` seconds.

LISTING 2.2 DisplayTime.java

```
1 public class DisplayTime {
2   public static void main(String[] args) {
3     int seconds = 500;
4     int minutes = seconds / 60;
5     int remainingSeconds = seconds % 60;
6     System.out.println(seconds + " seconds is " + minutes +
7       " minutes and " + remainingSeconds + " seconds");
8   }
9 }
```

divide

remainder

```
500 seconds is 8 minutes and 20 seconds
```

Line 4 obtains the minutes using `seconds / 60`. Line 5 (`seconds % 60`) obtains the remaining seconds after taking away the minutes.

unary operator

binary operator

The + and - operators can be both unary and binary. A *unary* operator has only one operand; a *binary* operator has two operands. For example, the - operator in `-5` can be considered a unary operator to negate number `5`, whereas the - operator in `4 - 5` is a binary operator for subtracting `5` from `4`.

Note

floating-point approximation

Calculations involving floating-point numbers are approximated because these numbers are not stored with complete accuracy. For example,

```
System.out.println(1.0 - 0.1 - 0.1 - 0.1 - 0.1 - 0.1);
```

displays `0.5000000000000001`, not `0.5`, and

```
System.out.println(1.0 - 0.9);
```

displays `0.09999999999999998`, not `0.1`. Integers are stored precisely. Therefore, calculations with integers yield a precise integer result.

2.7.2 Numeric Literals

A *literal* is a constant value that appears directly in a program. For example, `34`, `1000000`, and `5.0` are literals in the following statements:

literal

```
int i = 34;
long k = 1000000;
double d = 5.0;
```

Integer Literals

An integer literal can be assigned to an integer variable as long as it can fit into the variable. A compilation error would occur if the literal were too large for the variable to hold. The statement `byte b = 128`, for example, would cause a compilation error, because 128 cannot be stored in a variable of the `byte` type. (Note that the range for a byte value is from -128 to 127.)

An integer literal is assumed to be of the `int` type, whose value is between -2^{31} (-2147483648) and $2^{31} - 1$ (2147483647). To denote an integer literal of the `long` type, append the letter `L` or `l` to it (e.g., `2147483648L`). `L` is preferred because `l` (lowercase L) can easily be confused with 1 (the digit one). To write integer `2147483648` in a Java program, you have to write it as denote `2147483648L`, because `2147483648` exceeds the range for the `int` value.

long literal

> **Note**
>
> By default, an integer literal is a decimal number. To denote an octal integer literal, use a leading 0 (zero), and to denote a hexadecimal integer literal, use a leading 0x or 0X (zero x). For example, the following code displays the decimal value 65535 for hexadecimal number FFFF.
>
> octal and hex literals
>
> ```
> System.out.println( 0x FFFF);
> ```
>
> Hexadecimal numbers, binary numbers, and octal numbers were introduced in §1.5, "Number Systems."

Floating-Point Literals

Floating-point literals are written with a decimal point. By default, a floating-point literal is treated as a `double` type value. For example, `5.0` is considered a `double` value, not a `float` value. You can make a number a `float` by appending the letter `f` or `F`, and you can make a number a `double` by appending the letter `d` or `D`. For example, you can use `100.2f` or `100.2F` for a `float` number, and `100.2d` or `100.2D` for a `double` number.

suffix f or F
suffix d or D

> **Note**
>
> The `double` type values are more accurate than the `float` type values. For example,
>
> **double** vs. **float**
>
> ```
> System.out.println("1.0 / 3.0 is " + 1.0 / 3.0);
> ```
>
> displays `1.0 / 3.0 is 0.3333333333333333`.
>
> ```
> System.out.println("1.0F / 3.0F is " + 1.0F / 3.0F);
> ```
>
> displays `1.0F / 3.0F is 0.33333334`.

Scientific Notation

Floating-point literals can also be specified in scientific notation; for example, `1.23456e+2`, the same as `1.23456e2`, is equivalent to $1.23456 \times 10^2 = 123.456$, and `1.23456e-2` is equivalent to $1.23456 \times 10^{-2} = 0.0123456$. `E` (or `e`) represents an exponent and can be in either lowercase or uppercase.

why called floating-point?

Note
The **float** and **double** types are used to represent numbers with a decimal point. Why are they called *floating-point numbers*? These numbers are stored in scientific notation. When a number such as **50.534** is converted into scientific notation, such as **5.0534e+1**, its decimal point is moved (i.e., floated) to a new position.

2.7.3 Evaluating Java Expressions

Writing a numeric expression in Java involves a straightforward translation of an arithmetic expression using Java operators. For example, the arithmetic expression

$$\frac{3 + 4x}{5} - \frac{10(y - 5)(a + b + c)}{x} + 9\left(\frac{4}{x} + \frac{9 + x}{y}\right)$$

can be translated into a Java expression as:

```
(3 + 4 * x) / 5 - 10 * (y - 5) * (a + b + c) / x +
9 * (4 / x + (9 + x) / y)
```

evaluating an expression

Though Java has its own way to evaluate an expression behind the scene, the result of a Java expression and its corresponding arithmetic expression are the same. Therefore, you can safely apply the arithmetic rule for evaluating a Java expression. Operators contained within pairs of parentheses are evaluated first. Parentheses can be nested, in which case the expression in the inner parentheses is evaluated first. Multiplication, division, and remainder operators are applied next. If an expression contains several multiplication, division, and remainder operators, they are applied from left to right. Addition and subtraction operators are applied last. If an expression contains several addition and subtraction operators, they are applied from left to right. Here is an example of how an expression is evaluated:

```
3 + 4 * 4 + 5 * (4 + 3) - 1                    (1) inside parentheses first
3 + 4 * 4 + 5 * 7 - 1                          (2) multiplication
3 + 16 + 5 * 7 - 1                             (3) multiplication
3 + 16 + 35 - 1                                (4) addition
19 + 35 - 1                                    (5) addition
54 - 1                                         (6) subtraction
53
```

Listing 2.3 gives a program that converts a Fahrenheit degree to Celsius using the formula $celsius = \left(\frac{5}{9}\right)(fahrenheit - 32)$.

LISTING 2.3 FahrenheitToCelsius.java

divide

```
1 public class FahrenheitToCelsius {
2   public static void main(String[] args) {
3     double fahrenheit = 100; // Say 100;
4     double celsius = (5.0 / 9) * (fahrenheit - 32);
5     System.out.println("Fahrenheit " + fahrenheit + " is " +
```

```
6        celsius + " in Celsius");
7    }
8 }
```

```
Fahrenheit 100.0 is 37.77777777777778 in Celsius
```

Be careful when applying division. Division of two integers yields an integer in Java. $\frac{5}{9}$ is translated to **5.0 / 9** instead of **5 / 9** in line 4, because **5 / 9** yields **0** in Java.

integer vs. decimal division

2.7.4 Shorthand Operators

Very often the current value of a variable is used, modified, and then reassigned back to the same variable. For example, the following statement adds the current value of **i** with **8** and assigns the result back to **i**:

```
i = i + 8;
```

Java allows you to combine assignment and addition operators using a shorthand operator. For example, the preceding statement can be written as:

shorthand operator

```
i += 8;
```

The **+=** is called the *addition assignment operator*. Other shorthand operators are shown in Table 2.3.

shorthand operator

TABLE 2.3 Shorthand Operators

Operator	Name	Example	Equivalent
+=	Addition assignment	i += 8	i = i + 8
-=	Subtraction assignment	f -= 8.0	f = f - 8.0
*=	Multiplication assignment	i *= 8	i = i * 8
/=	Division assignment	i /= 8	i = i / 8
%=	Remainder assignment	i %= 8	i = i % 8

Caution

There are no spaces in the shorthand operators. For example, + = should be +=.

There are two more shorthand operators for incrementing and decrementing a variable by **1**. This is handy because that's often how much the value needs to be changed. These two operators are **++** and **--**. They can be used in prefix or suffix notation, as shown in Table 2.4.

++ and --

TABLE 2.4 Increment and Decrement Operators

Operator	Name	Description
++var	preincrement	The expression (++var) increments var by 1 and evaluates to the *new* value in var *after* the increment.
var++	postincrement	The expression (var++) evaluates to the *original* value in var and increments var by 1.
--var	predecrement	The expression (--var) decrements var by 1 and evaluates to the *new* value in var *after* the decrement.
var--	postdecrement	The expression (var--) evaluates to the *original* value in var and decrements var by 1.

If the operator is *before* (prefixed to) the variable, the variable is incremented or decremented by 1, then the *new* value of the variable is returned. If the operator is *after* (suffixed to) the variable, the original *old* value of the variable is returned, then the variable is incremented or decremented by 1. Therefore, the prefixes ++x and −−x are referred to, respectively, as the

preincrement, predecrement
postincrement, postdecrement

preincrement operator and the *predecrement operator*; and the suffixes x++ and x−− are referred to, respectively, as the *postincrement operator* and the *postdecrement operator*. The prefix form of ++ (or −−) and the suffix form of ++ (or −−) are the same if they are used in isolation, but they cause different effects when used in an expression. The following code illustrates this:

```
int i = 10;                    Same effect as      int newNum = 10 * i;
int newNum = 10 * i++;       ───────────────►      i = i + 1;
```

In this case, i is incremented by 1, then the *old* value of i is returned and used in the multiplication. So newNum becomes 100. If i++ is replaced by ++i as follows,

```
int i = 10;                     Same effect as      i = i + 1;
int newNum = 10 * (++i);      ───────────────►      int newNum = 10 * i;
```

i is incremented by 1, and the new value of i is returned and used in the multiplication. Thus newNum becomes 110.

Here is another example:

```
double x = 1.0;
double y = 5.0;
double z = x-- + (++y);
```

After all three lines are executed, y becomes 6.0, z becomes 7.0, and x becomes 0.0.

The increment operator ++ and the decrement operator −− can be applied to all integer and floating-point types. These operators are often used in loop statements. A *loop statement* is a structure that controls how many times an operation or a sequence of operations is performed in succession. This structure, and the subject of loop statements, are introduced in Chapter 4, "Loops."

Tip

Using increment and decrement operators makes expressions short, but it also makes them complex and difficult to read. Avoid using these operators in expressions that modify multiple variables or the same variable multiple times, such as this one: int k = ++i + i.

Note

Like the assignment operator (=), the operators (+=, −=, *=, /=, %=, ++, and −−) can be used to form an assignment statement as well as an expression. For example, in the following code, x = 2 is a statement in the first line and an expression in the second line.

```
x = 2; // Statement
System.out.println( x = 2); // Expression
```

expression statement

If a statement is used as an expression, it is called an *expression statement*.

2.8 Numeric Type Conversions

Often it is necessary to mix numeric values of different types in a computation. Consider the following statements:

```
byte i = 100;
long k = i * 3 + 4;
double d = i * 3.1 + k / 2;
```

Are these statements correct? Java allows binary operations on values of different types. When performing a binary operation involving two operands of different types, Java automatically converts the operand based on the following rules:

converting operands

1. If one of the operands is `double`, the other is converted into `double`.

2. Otherwise, if one of the operands is `float`, the other is converted into `float`.

3. Otherwise, if one of the operands is `long`, the other is converted into `long`.

4. Otherwise, both operands are converted into `int`.

For example, the result of `1 / 2` is `0`, because both operands are `int` values. The result of `1.0 / 2` is `0.5`, since `1.0` is `double` and `2` is converted to `2.0`.

The range of numeric types increases in this order:

range increases
———————————————————————————————————→
byte, short, int, long, float, double

You can always assign a value to a numeric variable whose type supports a larger range of values; thus, for instance, you can assign a `long` value to a `float` variable. You cannot, however, assign a value to a variable of a type with smaller range unless you use *type casting*. Casting is an operation that converts a value of one data type into a value of another data type. Casting a variable of a type with a small range to a variable of a type with a larger range is known as *widening a type*. Casting a variable of a type with a large range to a variable of a type with a smaller range is known as *narrowing a type*. Widening a type can be performed automatically without explicit casting. Narrowing a type must be performed explicitly.

type casting

widening a type
narrowing a type

The syntax for casting gives the target type in parentheses, followed by the variable's name or the value to be cast. For example,

```
float f = (float)10.7;
int i = (int)f;
```

In the first line, the `double` value `10.7` is cast into `float`. In the second line, `i` has a value of `10`; the fractional part in `f` is *truncated*. Note that the fractional part is truncated, not rounded.

truncated

Caution

Casting is necessary if you are assigning a value to a variable of a smaller type range, such as assigning a `double` value to an `int` variable. A compilation error will occur if casting is not used in situations of this kind. Be careful when using casting. Lost information might lead to inaccurate results.

possible loss of precision

Note

Casting does not change the variable being cast. For example, `d` is not changed after casting in the following code:

```
double d = 4.5;
int i = (int)d;  // i becomes 4, but d is not changed
```

Note

To assign a variable of the `int` type to a variable of the `short` or `byte` type, explicit casting must be used. For example, the following statements have a compilation error:

```
int i = 1;
byte b = i; // Error because explicit casting is required
```

However, so long as the integer literal is within the permissible range of the target variable, explicit casting is not needed to assign an integer literal to a variable of the `short` or `byte` type. Please refer to §2.7.2, "Numeric Literals."

Listing 2.4 gives a program that displays the sales tax with two digits after the decimal point.

LISTING 2.4 SalesTax.java

```
1 public class SalesTax {
2   public static void main(String[] args) {
3     double purchaseAmount = 197.55;
4     double tax = purchaseAmount * 0.06;
5     System.out.println("Sales tax is " + (int)(tax * 100) / 100.0);
6   }
7 }
```

```
Sales tax is 11.85
```

formatting numbers

Variable `purchaseAmount` is `197.55` (line 3). The sales tax is `6%` of the purchase, so the `tax` is evaluated as `11.853` (line 4). The statement in line 5 displays the tax `11.85` with two digits after the decimal point. Note that `(int)(tax * 100)` is `1185`, so `(int)(tax * 100) / 100.0` is `11.85`.

2.9 Character Data Type and Operations

char type

The character data type, `char`, is used to represent a single character. A character literal is enclosed in single quotation marks. Consider the following code:

```
char letter = 'A';
char numChar = '4';
```

The first statement assigns character `A` to the `char` variable `letter`. The second statement assigns the digit character `4` to the `char` variable `numChar`.

Caution

char literal

A string literal must be enclosed in quotation marks. A character literal is a single character enclosed in single quotation marks. So `"A"` is a string, and `'A'` is a character.

2.9.1 Unicode and ASCII code

Computers use binary numbers internally. A character is stored as a sequence of 0s and 1s in a computer. The process of converting a character to its binary representation is called *encoding*. There are different ways to encode a character. How characters are encoded is defined by an *encoding scheme*.

character encoding

Unicode

original Unicode

Java supports *Unicode*, an encoding scheme established by the Unicode Consortium to support the interchange, processing, and display of written texts in the world's diverse languages. Unicode was originally designed as a 16-bit character encoding. The primitive data type `char` was intended to take advantage of this design by providing a simple data type that could hold any character. However, it turned out that the **65,536** characters possible in a 16-bit encoding are not sufficient to represent all the characters in the world. The Unicode standard therefore has been extended to allow up to **1,112,064** characters. Those characters that go beyond the original 16-bit limit are called *supplementary characters*. JDK 1.5 supports supplementary characters. The processing and representing of supplementary characters are beyond the scope of this book. For simplicity, this book considers only the original 16-bit Unicode characters. These characters can be stored in a **char** type variable.

supplementary Unicode

A 16-bit Unicode takes two bytes, preceded by **\u**, expressed in four hexadecimal digits that run from **'\u0000'** to **'\uFFFF'**. For example, the word "welcome" is translated into Chinese using two characters, 欢迎 . The Unicodes of these two characters are "**\u6B22\u8FCE**".

Listing 2.5 gives a program that displays two Chinese characters and three Greek letters.

LISTING 2.5 DisplayUnicode.java

```
 1  import javax.swing.JOptionPane;
 2
 3  public class DisplayUnicode {
 4    public static void main(String[] args) {
 5      JOptionPane.showMessageDialog(null,
 6        "\u6B22\u8FCE \u03b1 \u03b2 \u03b3",
 7        "\u6B22\u8FCE Welcome",
 8        JOptionPane.INFORMATION_MESSAGE);
 9    }
10  }
```

If no Chinese font is installed on your system, you will not be able to see the Chinese characters. The Unicodes for the Greek letters α β γ are **\u03b1 \u03b2 \u03b3**.

Most computers use *ASCII (American Standard Code for Information Interchange)*, a 7-bit encoding scheme for representing all uppercase and lowercase letters, digits, punctuation marks, and control characters. Unicode includes ASCII code, with **'\u0000'** to **'\u007F'** corresponding to the 128 ASCII characters. (See Appendix B, "The ASCII Character Set," for a list of ASCII characters and their decimal and hexadecimal codes.) You can use ASCII characters such as **'X'**, **'1'**, and **'$'** in a Java program as well as Unicodes. Thus, for example, the following statements are equivalent:

ASCII

```
char letter = 'A';
char letter = '\u0041'; // Character A's Unicode is 0041
```

Both statements assign character **A** to **char** variable **letter**.

Note
The increment and decrement operators can also be used on **char** variables to get the next or preceding Unicode character. For example, the following statements display character **b**.

char increment and decrement

```
char ch = 'a';
System.out.println(++ch);
```

2.9.2 Escape Sequences for Special Characters

Suppose you want to print a message with quotation marks in the output. Can you write a statement like this?

```
System.out.println("He said "Java is fun"");
```

No, this statement has a syntax error. The compiler thinks the second quotation character is the end of the string and does not know what to do with the rest of characters.

To overcome this problem, Java defines escape sequences to represent special characters, as shown in Table 2.5. An escape sequence begins with the backslash character (\) followed by a character that has a special meaning to the compiler.

TABLE 2.5 Java Escape Sequences

Character Escape Sequence	Name	Unicode Code
\b	Backspace	\u0008
\t	Tab	\u0009
\n	Linefeed	\u000A
\f	Formfeed	\u000C
\r	Carriage Return	\u000D
\\	Backslash	\u005C
\'	Single Quote	\u0027
\"	Double Quote	\u0022

So, now you can print the quoted message using the following statement:

```
System.out.println("He said \"Java is fun\"");
```

The output is

```
He said "Java is fun"
```

2.9.3 Casting between char and Numeric Types

A char value can be cast into any numeric type, and vice versa. When an integer is cast into a char, only its lower sixteen bits of data are used; the other part is ignored. For example, see the following code:

```
char ch = (char)0XAB0041; // The lower 16 bits hex code 0041 is
                          // assigned to ch
System.out.println(ch);   // ch is character A
```

When a floating-point value is cast into a char, the floating-point value is first cast into an int, which is then cast into a char.

```
char ch = (char)65.25;    // Decimal 65 is assigned to ch
System.out.println(ch);   // ch is character A
```

When a char is cast into a numeric type, the character's Unicode is cast into the specified numeric type.

```
int i = (int)'A'; // The Unicode of character A is assigned to i
System.out.println(i);  // i is 65
```

Implicit casting can be used if the result of a casting fits into the target variable. Otherwise, explicit casting must be used. For example, since the Unicode of 'a' is 97, which is within the range of a byte, these implicit castings are fine:

```
byte b = 'a';
int i = 'a';
```

But the following casting is incorrect, because the Unicode \uFFF4 cannot fit into a byte:

```
byte b = '\uFFF4';
```

To force assignment, use explicit casting, as follows:

```
byte b = (byte)'\uFFF4';
```

Any positive integer between 0 and FFFF in hexadecimal can be cast into a character implicitly. Any number not in this range must be cast into a char explicitly.

Note

All numeric operators can be applied to char operands. A char operand is automatically cast into a number if the other operand is a number or a character. If the other operand is a string, the character is concatenated with the string. For example, the following statements

numeric operators on characters

```
int i = '2' + '3'; // (int)'2' is 50 and (int)'3' is 51
System.out.println("i is " + i);

int j = 2 + 'a'; // (int)'a' is 97
System.out.println("j is " + j);
System.out.println(j + " is the Unicode for character " + (char)j);

System.out.println("Chapter " + '2');
```

display

```
i is 101
j is 99
99 is the Unicode for character c
Chapter 2
```

Note

The Unicodes for lowercase letters are consecutive integers starting from the Unicode for 'a', then for 'b', 'c', ..., and 'z'. The same is true for the uppercase letters. Furthermore, the Unicode for 'a' is greater than the Unicode for 'A'. So 'a' - 'A' is the same as 'b' - 'B'. For a lowercase letter *ch*, its corresponding uppercase letter is (char)('A' + (ch - 'a')).

2.10 The **String** Type

The char type represents only one character. To represent a string of characters, use the data type called String. For example, the following code declares the message to be a string with value "Welcome to Java".

```
String message = "Welcome to Java";
```

String is actually a predefined class in the Java library just like the System class and JOptionPane class. The String type is not a primitive type. It is known as a *reference type*. Any Java class can be used as a reference type for a variable. Reference data types will be thoroughly discussed in Chapter 7, "Classes and Objects." For the time being, you need to know only how to declare a String variable, how to assign a string to the variable, and how to concatenate strings.

As first shown in Listing 2.1, two strings can be concatenated. The plus sign (+) is the concatenation operator if one of the operands is a string. If one of the operands is a nonstring (e.g., a number), the nonstring value is converted into a string and concatenated with the other string. Here are some examples:

concatenating strings and numbers

```
// Three strings are concatenated
String message = "Welcome " + "to " + "Java";
```

```
// String Chapter is concatenated with number 2
String s = "Chapter" + 2; // s becomes Chapter2

// String Supplement is concatenated with character B
String s1 = "Supplement" + 'B'; // s becomes SupplementB
```

If neither of the operands is a string, the plus sign (+) is the addition operator that adds two numbers.

The shorthand += operator can also be used for string concatenation. For example, the following code appends the string " and Java is fun" with the string "Welcome to Java" in **message**.

```
message += " and Java is fun";
```

So the new **message** is "Welcome to Java and Java is fun".

Suppose that i = 1 and j = 2, what is the output of the following statement?

```
System.out.println("i + j is " + i + j);
```

The output is "i + j is 12" because "i + j is " is concatenated with the value of i first. To force i + j to be executed first, enclose i + j in the parentheses, as follows:

```
System.out.println("i + j is " + (i + j));
```

2.11 Console Input Using the **Scanner** Class

In Listing 2.1, the radius is fixed in the source code. To use a different radius, you have to modify the source code and recompile it. Obviously, this is not convenient. You can use the **Scanner** class for console input.

Java uses **System.out** to refer to the standard output device and **System.in** to the standard input device. By default the output device is the console, and the input device is the keyboard. To perform console output, you simply use the **println** method to display a primitive value or a string to the console. Console input is not directly supported in Java, but you can use the **Scanner** class to create an object to read input from **System.in**, as follows:

```
Scanner input = new Scanner(System.in);
```

Scanner is a new class in JDK 1.5. The syntax *new Scanner(System.in)* creates an object of the **Scanner** type. The syntax *Scanner input* declares that **input** is a variable whose type is **Scanner**. The whole line *Scanner input = new Scanner(System.in)* creates a **Scanner** object and assigns its reference to the variable **input**. An object may contain methods. Invoking a method on an object is to ask the object to perform a task. A **Scanner** object contains the methods for reading input, as shown in Table 2.6:

TABLE 2.6 Methods for Scanner Objects

Method	Description
nextByte()	reads an integer of the byte type.
nextShort()	reads an integer of the short type.
nextInt()	reads an integer of the int type.
nextLong()	reads an integer of the long type.
nextFloat()	reads a number of the float type.
nextDouble()	reads a number of the double type.
next()	reads a string that ends before a whitespace.
nextLine()	reads a line of character (i.e., a string ending with a line separator).

A **Scanner** object reads an item separated by whitespaces. A whitespace character is ' ',
'\t', '\f', '\r', or '\n'. For example, the following statements prompt the user to enter a
double value from the console.

whitespace

```
System.out. print("Enter a double value: ");
Scanner input = new Scanner(System.in);
double d = input.nextDouble();
```

The **print** method is identical to the **println** method except that **println** moves the
cursor to the next line after displaying the string, but **print** does not advance the cursor to the
next line when completed.

print vs. **println**

More details on objects will be introduced in Chapter 7, "Objects and Classes." For the
time being, simply accept that this is how to obtain input from the console.

Listing 2.6 gives an example that reads various types of data from the console using the
Scanner class.

Video Note
Obtain console input

LISTING 2.6 TestScanner.java

```
1  import java.util.Scanner; // Scanner is in java.util
2
3  public class TestScanner {
4    public static void main(String args[]) {
5      // Create a Scanner
6      Scanner input = new Scanner(System.in);
7
8      // Prompt the user to enter an integer
9      System.out.print("Enter an integer: ");
10     int intValue = input.nextInt();
11     System.out.println("You entered the integer " + intValue);
12
13     // Prompt the user to enter a double value
14     System.out.print("Enter a double value: ");
15     double doubleValue = input.nextDouble();
16     System.out.println("You entered the double value "
17       + doubleValue);
18
19     // Prompt the user to enter a string
20     System.out.print("Enter a string without space: ");
21     String string = input.next();
22     System.out.println("You entered the string " + string);
23   }
24 }
```

import class

create a **Scanner**

read an **int**

read a **double**

read a **string**

```
Enter an integer: 4 ↵Enter
You entered the integer 4


Enter a double value: 23.55 ↵Enter
You entered the double value 23.55


Enter a string without space: Java ↵Enter
You entered the string Java
```

The **Scanner** class is in the **java.util** package. It is imported in line 1. Line 6 creates a **Scanner**
object. Line 10 reads an **int** value. Line 15 reads a **double** value. Line 21 reads a string.

avoiding input errors

Important Caution

To *avoid input errors*, do not use `nextLine()` after `nextByte()`, `nextShort()`, `nextInt()`, `nextLong()`, `nextFloat()`, `nextDouble()`, and `next()`. The reasons will be explained in §8.7.3, "How Does `Scanner` Work?"

2.12 Case Studies

In the preceding sections, you learned about variables, constants, primitive data types, operators, expressions, and console input. You are now ready to use them to write interesting programs. This section presents three problems: computing loan payments, breaking a sum of money down into smaller units, and displaying the current time.

2.12.1 Problem: Computing Loan Payments

The problem is to write a program that computes loan payments. The loan can be a car loan, a student loan, or a home mortgage loan. The program lets the user enter the interest rate, number of years, and loan amount, and displays the monthly and total payments.

The formula to compute the monthly payment is as follows:

$$\frac{loanAmount \times monthlyInterestRate}{1 - \dfrac{1}{(1 + monthlyInterestRate)^{numberOfYears \times 12}}}$$

You don't have to know how this formula is derived. Nonetheless, given the monthly interest rate, number of years, and loan amount, you can use it to compute the monthly payment.

In the formula, you have to compute $(1 + monthlyInterestRate)^{numberOfYears \times 12}$. The `pow(a, b)` method in the `Math` class can be used to compute a^b. The `Math` class, which comes with the Java API, is available to all Java programs. The `Math` class is introduced in Chapter 5, "Methods."

pow(a, b) method

Here are the steps in developing the program:

1. Prompt the user to enter the annual interest rate, number of years, and loan amount.

2. Obtain the monthly interest rate from the annual interest rate.

3. Compute the monthly payment using the preceding formula.

4. Compute the total payment, which is the monthly payment multiplied by 12 and multiplied by the number of years.

5. Display the monthly payment and total payment.

Listing 2.7 gives the complete program.

Video Note
Program Mathematical computations

import class

LISTING 2.7 **ComputeLoan.java**

```
1 import java.util.Scanner;
2
3 public class ComputeLoan {
4   public static void main(String[] args) {
5     // Create a Scanner
6     Scanner input = new Scanner(System.in);
7
```

create a **Scanner**

```
8      // Enter yearly interest rate
9      System.out.print("Enter yearly interest rate, for example 8.25: ");
10     double annualInterestRate = input.nextDouble();                        enter interest rate
11
12     // Obtain monthly interest rate
13     double monthlyInterestRate = annualInterestRate / 1200;
14
15     // Enter number of years
16     System.out.print(
17       "Enter number of years as an integer, for example 5: ");
18     int numberOfYears = input.nextInt();                                   enter years
19
20     // Enter loan amount
21     System.out.print("Enter loan amount, for example 120000.95: ");
22     double loanAmount = input.nextDouble();                               enter loan amount
23
24     // Calculate payment
25     double monthlyPayment = loanAmount * monthlyInterestRate / (1         monthlyPayment
26       - 1 / Math.pow(1 + monthlyInterestRate, numberOfYears * 12));
27     double totalPayment = monthlyPayment * numberOfYears * 12;            totalPayment
28
29     // Format to keep two digits after the decimal point
30     monthlyPayment = (int)(monthlyPayment * 100) / 100.0;
31     totalPayment = (int)(totalPayment * 100) / 100.0;
32
33     // Display results
34     System.out.println("The monthly payment is " + monthlyPayment);      display result
35     System.out.println("The total payment is " + totalPayment);
36   }
37 }
```

```
Enter yearly interest rate, for example 8.25: 5.75  ↵Enter
Enter number of years as an integer, for example 5: 15  ↵Enter
Enter loan amount, for example 120000.95: 250000  ↵Enter
The monthly payment is 2076.02
The total payment is 373684.53
```

Line 10 reads the yearly interest rate, which is converted into monthly interest rate in line 13. If you entered an input other than a numeric value, a runtime error would occur. In Chapter 18, "Exception Handling," you will learn how to handle the exception so that the program can continue to run.

Each variable in a method such as `main` must be declared once and only once. Choose the most appropriate data type for the variable. For example, `numberOfYears` is best declared as an `int` (line 18), although it could be declared as a `long`, `float`, or `double`. Note that `byte` might be the most appropriate for `numberOfYears`. For simplicity, however, the examples in this book will use `int` for integer and `double` for floating-point values.

The formula for computing the monthly payment is translated into Java code in lines 25–27.

The statements in lines 30–31 are for formatting the number to keep two digits after the decimal point. For example, if `monthlyPayment` is `2076.0252175`, `(int)(monthlyPayment * 100)` is `207602`. Therefore, `(int)(monthlyPayment * 100) / 100.0` yields `2076.02`.   formatting numbers java.lang package

The program uses the Scanner class, imported in line 1. The program also uses the Math class; why isn't it imported? The Math class is in the java.lang package. All classes in the java.lang package are implicitly imported. So, there is no need to explicitly import the Math class.

2.12.2 Problem: Counting Monetary Units

Suppose you want to develop a program that classifies a given amount of money into smaller monetary units. The program lets the user enter an amount as a double value representing a total in dollars and cents, and outputs a report listing the monetary equivalent in dollars, quarters, dimes, nickels, and pennies, as shown in the sample output.

Your program should report the maximum number of dollars, then the maximum number of quarters, and so on, in this order.

Here are the steps in developing the program:

1. Prompt the user to enter the amount as a decimal number, such as 11.56.

2. Convert the amount (e.g., 11.56) into cents (1156).

3. Divide the cents by 100 to find the number of dollars. Obtain the remaining cents using the cents remainder 100.

4. Divide the remaining cents by 25 to find the number of quarters. Obtain the remaining cents using the remaining cents remainder 25.

5. Divide the remaining cents by 10 to find the number of dimes. Obtain the remaining cents using the remaining cents remainder 10.

6. Divide the remaining cents by 5 to find the number of nickels. Obtain the remaining cents using the remaining cents remainder 5.

7. The remaining cents are the pennies.

8. Display the result.

The complete program is given in Listing 2.8.

LISTING 2.8 ComputeChange.java

import class

```
 1 import java.util.Scanner;
 2
 3 public class ComputeChange {
 4   public static void main(String[] args) {
 5     // Create a Scanner
 6     Scanner input = new Scanner(System.in);
 7
 8     // Receive the amount
 9     System.out.print(
10       "Enter an amount in double, for example 11.56: ");
11     double amount = input.nextDouble();
12
13     int remainingAmount = (int)(amount * 100);
14
15     // Find the number of one dollars
16     int numberOfOneDollars = remainingAmount / 100;
17     remainingAmount = remainingAmount % 100;
18
```

enter input (at line 11)

dollars (at line 16)

```
19        // Find the number of quarters in the remaining amount
20        int numberOfQuarters = remainingAmount / 25;
21        remainingAmount = remainingAmount % 25;
22
23        // Find the number of dimes in the remaining amount
24        int numberOfDimes = remainingAmount / 10;
25        remainingAmount = remainingAmount % 10;
26
27        // Find the number of nickels in the remaining amount
28        int numberOfNickels = remainingAmount / 5;
29        remainingAmount = remainingAmount % 5;
30
31        // Find the number of pennies in the remaining amount
32        int numberOfPennies = remainingAmount;
33
34        // Display results
35        String output = "Your amount " + amount + " consists of \n" +
36          "\t" + numberOfOneDollars + " dollars\n" +
37          "\t" + numberOfQuarters + " quarters\n" +
38          "\t" + numberOfDimes + " dimes\n" +
39          "\t" + numberOfNickels + " nickels\n" +
40          "\t" + numberOfPennies + " pennies";
41        System.out.println(output);
42      }
43 }
```

quarters

dimes

nickels

pennies

prepare output

```
Enter an amount in double, for example 11.56: 11.56 ⏎Enter
Your amount 11.56 consists of
11 dollars
2 quarters
0 dimes
1 nickels
1 pennies
```

The variable `amount` stores the amount entered from the console (line 11). This variable is not changed because the amount has to be used at the end of the program to display the results. The program introduces the variable `remainingAmount` (line 13) to store the changing `remainingAmount`.

The variable `amount` is a `double` decimal representing dollars and cents. It is converted to an `int` variable `remainingAmount`, which represents all the cents. For instance, if `amount` is `11.56`, then the initial `remainingAmount` is `1156`. The division operator yields the integer part of the division. So `1156 / 100` is `11`. The remainder operator obtains the remainder of the division. So `1156 % 100` is `56`.

The program extracts the maximum number of singles from the total amount and obtains the remaining amount in the variable `remainingAmount` (lines 16–17). It then extracts the maximum number of quarters from `remainingAmount` and obtains a new `remainingAmount` (lines 20–21). Continuing the same process, the program finds the maximum number of dimes, nickels, and pennies in the remaining amount.

One serious problem with this example is the possible loss of precision when casting a `double` amount to an `int remainingAmount`. This could lead to an inaccurate result. If you try to enter the amount `10.03`, `10.03 * 100` becomes `1002.9999999999999`. You will find that the program displays `10` dollars and `2` pennies. To fix the problem, enter the amount as an integer value representing cents (see Exercise 2.9).

loss of precision

As shown in the sample output, **0** dimes, **1** nickels, and **1** pennies are displayed in the result. It would be better not to display **0** dimes, and to display **1** nickel and **1** penny using the singular forms of the words. You will learn how to use selection statements to modify this program in the next chapter (see Exercise 3.7).

2.12.3 Problem: Displaying the Current Time

The problem is to develop a program that displays the current time in GMT (Greenwich Mean Time) in the format hour:minute:second, such as 13:19:8.

currentTimeMillis

The `currentTimeMillis` method in the `System` class returns the current time in milliseconds elapsed since the time **00:00:00** on January 1, 1970 GMT, as shown in Figure 2.3. This time is known as the *Unix epoch*, because **1970** was the year when the Unix operating system was formally introduced.

Unix epoch

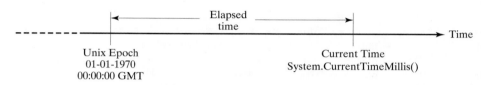

FIGURE 2.3 The `System.currentTimeMillis()` returns the number of milliseconds since the Unix epoch.

You can use this method to obtain the current time, and then compute the current second, minute, and hour as follows.

1. Obtain the total milliseconds since midnight, Jan 1, 1970, in `totalMilliseconds` by invoking `System.currentTimeMillis()` (e.g., 1103203148368 milliseconds).

2. Obtain the total seconds `totalSeconds` by dividing `totalMilliseconds` by 1000 (e.g., 1103203148368 milliseconds / 1000 = 1103203148 seconds).

3. Compute the current second from `totalSeconds % 60` (e.g., 1103203148 seconds % 60 = 8,which is the current second).

4. Obtain the total minutes `totalMinutes` by dividing `totalSeconds` by 60 (e.g., 1103203148 seconds / 60 = 18386719 minutes).

5. Compute the current minute from `totalMinutes % 60` (e.g., 18386719 minutes % 60 = 19, which is the current minute).

6. Obtain the total hours `totalHours` by dividing `totalMinutes` by 60 (e.g.,18386719 minutes / 60 = 306445 hours).

7. Compute the current hour from `totalHours % 24` (e.g., 306445 hours % 24 = 19, which is the current hour).

Listing 2.9 gives the complete program.

Video Note
Use operators / and %

totalMilliseconds

LISTING 2.9 ShowCurrentTime.java

```java
1 public class ShowCurrentTime {
2   public static void main(String[] args) {
3     // Obtain the total milliseconds since the midnight, Jan 1, 1970
4     long totalMilliseconds = System.currentTimeMillis();
5
6     // Obtain the total seconds since the midnight, Jan 1, 1970
```

```
 7      long totalSeconds = totalMilliseconds / 1000;                    totalSeconds
 8
 9      // Compute the current second in the minute in the hour
10      int currentSecond = (int)(totalSeconds % 60);                    currentSecond
11
12      // Obtain the total minutes
13      long totalMinutes = totalSeconds / 60;                           totalMinutes
14
15      // Compute the current minute in the hour
16      int currentMinute = (int)(totalMinutes % 60);                    currentMinute
17
18      // Obtain the total hours
19      long totalHours = totalMinutes / 60;                             totalHours
20
21      // Compute the current hour
22      int currentHour = (int)(totalHours % 24);                        currentHour
23
24      // Display results
25      System.out.println("Current time is " + currentHour + ":"        preparing output
26        + currentMinute + ":" + currentSecond + " GMT");
27    }
28 }
```

```
Current time is 13:19:8 GMT
```

When `System.currentTimeMillis()` (line 4) is invoked, it returns the difference, measured in milliseconds, between the current GMT and midnight, January 1, 1970 GMT. This method returns the milliseconds as a `long` value.

2.13 Programming Style and Documentation

Programming style deals with what programs look like. A program can compile and run properly even if written on only one line, but writing it all on one line would be bad programming style because it would be hard to read. *Documentation* is the body of explanatory remarks and comments pertaining to a program. Programming style and documentation are as important as coding. Good programming style and appropriate documentation reduce the chance of errors and make programs easy to read. So far you have learned some good programming styles. This section summarizes them and gives several guidelines. More detailed guidelines can be found in Supplement I.D, "Java Coding Style Guidelines," on the Companion Website.

programming style

documentation

2.13.1 Appropriate Comments and Comment Styles

Include a summary at the beginning of the program to explain what the program does, its key features, its supporting data structures, and any unique techniques it uses. In a long program, you should also include comments that introduce each major step and explain anything that is difficult to read. It is important to make comments concise so that they do not crowd the program or make it difficult to read.

In addition to line comment // and block comment /*, Java supports comments of a special type, referred to as *javadoc comments*. javadoc comments begin with /** and end with */. They can be extracted into an HTML file using JDK's `javadoc` command. For more information, see java.sun.com/j2se/javadoc.

javadoc comment

Use javadoc comments (/** ... */) for commenting on an entire class or an entire method. These comments must precede the class or the method header in order to be extracted in a javadoc HTML file. For commenting on steps inside a method, use line comments (//).

2.13.2 Naming Conventions

Make sure that you choose descriptive names with straightforward meanings for the variables, constants, classes, and methods in your program. Names are case sensitive. Listed below are the conventions for naming variables, methods, and classes.

naming variables and methods

- Use lowercase for variables and methods. If a name consists of several words, concatenate them into one, making the first word lowercase and capitalizing the first letter of each subsequent word—for example, the variables `radius` and `area` and the method `showInputDialog`.

naming classes

- Capitalize the first letter of each word in a class name—for example, the class names `ComputeArea`, `Math`, and `JOptionPane`.

naming constants

- Capitalize every letter in a constant, and use underscores between words—for example, the constants `PI` and `MAX_VALUE`.

It is important to become familiar with the naming conventions. Understanding them will help you to understand Java programs. If you stick with the naming conventions, other programmers will better understand your program.

 Caution

naming classes

Do not choose class names that are already used in the Java library. For example, since the `Math` class is defined in Java, you should not name your class `Math`.

 Tip

using full descriptive names

Avoid using abbreviations for identifiers. Using complete words is more descriptive. For example, `numberOfStudents` is better than `numStuds`, `numOfStuds`, or `numOfStudents`.

2.13.3 Proper Indentation and Spacing

indent code

A consistent indentation style makes programs clear and easy to read. *Indentation* is used to illustrate the structural relationships between a program's components or statements. Java can read the program even if all of the statements are in a straight line, but it is easier to read and maintain code that is aligned properly. Indent each subcomponent or statement at least *two* spaces more than the structure within which it is nested.

A single space should be added on both sides of a binary operator, as shown in the following statement:

A single space line should be used to separate segments of the code to make the program easier to read.

2.13.4 Block Styles

A block is a group of statements surrounded by braces. There are two popular styles, *next-line* style and *end-of-line* style, as shown below.

The next-line style aligns braces vertically and makes programs easy to read, whereas the end-of-line style saves space and may help avoid some subtle programming errors. Both are acceptable block styles. The choice depends on personal or organizational preference. You should use a style consistently. Mixing styles is not recommended. This book uses the *end-of-line* style to be consistent with the Java API source code.

```
public class Test
{
  public static void main(String[] args)
  {
    System.out.println("Block Styles");
  }
}
```
Next-line style

```
public class Test {
  public static void main(String[] args) {
    System.out.println("Block Styles");
  }
}
```
End-of-line style

2.14 Programming Errors

Programming errors are unavoidable, even for experienced programmers. Errors can be categorized into three types: syntax errors, runtime errors, and logic errors.

2.14.1   Syntax Errors

Errors that occur during compilation are called *syntax errors* or *compilation errors*. Syntax errors result from errors in code construction, such as mistyping a keyword, omitting some necessary punctuation, or using an opening brace without a corresponding closing brace. These errors are usually easy to detect, because the compiler tells you where they are and what caused them. For example, compiling the following program results in a syntax error, as shown in Figure 2.4.

syntax errors

```
// ShowSyntaxErrors.java: The program contains syntax errors
public class ShowSyntaxErrors {
  public static void main(String[] args) {
    i = 30;
    System.out.println(i + 4);
  }
}
```
syntax error

Compile

```
C:\book>javac ShowSyntaxErrors.java
ShowSyntaxErrors.java:4: cannot resolve symbol
symbol  : variable i
location: class ShowSyntaxErrors
    i = 30;
    ^
ShowSyntaxErrors.java:5: cannot resolve symbol
symbol  : variable i
location: class ShowSyntaxErrors
    System.out.println(i + 4);
                       ^
2 errors

C:\book>
```

FIGURE 2.4   The compiler reports syntax errors.

Two errors are detected. Both are the result of not declaring variable i. Since a single error will often display many lines of compilation errors, it is a good practice to start debugging from the top line and work downward. Fixing errors that occur earlier in the program may also fix additional errors that occur later.

2.14.2 Runtime Errors

runtime errors

Runtime errors are errors that cause a program to terminate abnormally. Runtime errors occur while an application is running if the environment detects an operation that is impossible to carry out. Input errors typically cause runtime errors.

An *input error* occurs when the user enters an unexpected input value that the program cannot handle. For instance, if the program expects to read in a number, but instead the user enters a string, this causes data-type errors to occur in the program. To prevent input errors, the program should prompt the user to enter the correct type of values. It may display a message like "Please enter an integer" before reading an integer from the keyboard.

Another common source of runtime errors is division by zero. This happens when the divisor is zero for integer divisions. For instance, the following program would cause a runtime error, as shown in Figure 2.5.

```java
// ShowRuntimeErrors.java: Program contains runtime errors
public class ShowRuntimeErrors {
  public static void main(String[] args) {
    int i = 1 / 0;
  }
}
```

Run ⟶

FIGURE 2.5 The runtime error causes the program to terminate abnormally.

2.14.3 Logic Errors

logic errors

Logic errors occur when a program does not perform the way it was intended to. Errors of this kind occur for many different reasons. For example, suppose you wrote the following program to add **number1** to **number2**.

```java
// ShowLogicErrors.java: The program contains a logic error
public class ShowLogicErrors {
  public static void main(String[] args) {
    // Add number1 to number2
    int number1 = 3;
    int number2 = 3;
    number2 += number1 + number2;
    System.out.println("number2 is " + number2);
  }
}
```

The program does not have syntax errors or runtime errors, but it does not print the correct result for **number2**. See if you can find the error.

2.15 Debugging

In general, syntax errors are easy to find and easy to correct because the compiler gives indications as to where the errors came from and why they are there. Runtime errors are not difficult to find either, since the Java interpreter displays them on the console when the program aborts. Finding logic errors, on the other hand, can be very challenging.

Logic errors are called *bugs*. The process of finding and correcting errors is called *debugging*. A common approach to debugging is to use a combination of methods to narrow down to the part of the program where the bug is located. You can *hand-trace* the program (i.e., catch errors by reading the program), or you can insert print statements in order to show the values of the variables or the execution flow of the program. This approach might work for a short, simple program. But for a large, complex program, the most effective approach for debugging is to use a debugger utility.

JDK includes a command-line debugger (jdb), which is invoked with a class name. jdb is itself a Java program, running its own copy of Java interpreter. All the Java IDE tools, such as NetBeans, Eclipse, and JBuilder, include integrated debuggers. The debugger utilities let you follow the execution of a program. They vary from one system to another, but they all support most of the following helpful features:

- **Executing a single statement at a time:** The debugger allows you to execute one statement at a time so that you can see the effect of each.

- **Tracing into or stepping over a method:** If a method is being executed, you can ask the debugger to enter the method and execute one statement at a time in the method, or you can ask it to step over the entire method. You should step over the entire method if you know that the method works. For example, always step over system-supplied methods, such as `System.out.println`.

- **Setting breakpoints:** You can also set a breakpoint at a specific statement. Your program pauses when it reaches a breakpoint and displays the line with the breakpoint. You can set as many breakpoints as you want. Breakpoints are particularly useful when you know where your programming error starts. You can set a breakpoint at that line and have the program execute until it reaches the breakpoint.

- **Displaying variables:** The debugger lets you select several variables and display their values. As you trace through a program, the content of a variable is continuously updated.

- **Displaying call stacks:** The debugger lets you trace all of the method calls and lists all pending methods. This feature is helpful when you need to see a large picture of the program-execution flow.

- **Modifying variables:** Some debuggers enable you to modify the value of a variable when debugging. This is convenient when you want to test a program with different samples but do not want to leave the debugger.

 Pedagogical Note
An IDE not only helps debug errors but also is an effective pedagogical tool. Supplement II shows you how to use a debugger to trace programs and how debugging can help in learning Java effectively.

(margin notes: bugs; debugging; hand-traces; debugging in IDE; learning tool)

2.16 (GUI) Getting Input from Input Dialogs

You can obtain input from the console. Alternatively, you may obtain input from an input dialog box by invoking the `JOptionPane.showInputDialog` method, as shown in Figure 2.6.

*(margin note: **JOptionPane** class)*

FIGURE 2.6 The input dialog box enables the user to enter a string.

When this method is executed, a dialog is displayed to enable you to enter an input value. After entering a string, click OK to accept the input and dismiss the dialog box. The input is returned from the method as a string.

Note

showInputDialog method

There are several ways to use the **showInputDialog** method. For the time being, you need to know only two ways to invoke it.

One is to use a statement like this one:

```
JOptionPane.showInputDialog(x);
```

where x is a string for the prompting message.

The other is to use a statement as shown in the example:

```
String string = JOptionPane.showInputDialog(null, x,
    y, JOptionPane.QUESTION_MESSAGE);
```

where x is a string for the prompting message, and y is a string for the title of the input dialog box, as shown in the following example.

2.16.1 Converting Strings to Numbers

The input returned from the input dialog box is a string. If you enter a numeric value such as `123`, it returns `"123"`. You have to convert a string into a number to obtain the input as a number.

Integer.parseInt method

To convert a string into an `int` value, use the **parseInt** method in the **Integer** class, as follows:

```
int intValue = Integer.parseInt(intString);
```

where `intString` is a numeric string such as `"123"`.

Double.parseDouble method

To convert a string into a `double` value, use the **parseDouble** method in the **Double** class, as follows:

```
double doubleValue = Double.parseDouble(doubleString);
```

where `doubleString` is a numeric string such as `"123.45"`.

The **Integer** and **Double** classes are both included in the `java.lang` package, and thus are automatically imported.

2.16.2 Using Input Dialog Boxes

Listing 2.7 reads input from the console. Alternatively, you can use input dialog boxes. A sample run of the new program is shown in Figure 2.7.

Listing 2.10 gives the complete program. Figure 2.7 shows a sample run of the program.

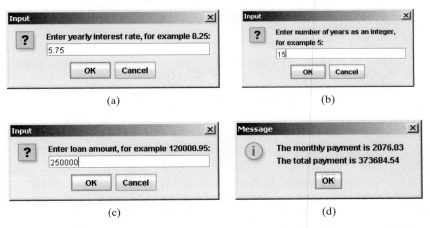

FIGURE 2.7 The program accepts the annual interest rate (a), number of years (b), and loan amount (c), then displays the monthly payment and total payment (d).

LISTING 2.10 ComputeLoanUsingInputDialog.java

```
1  import javax.swing.JOptionPane;
2
3  public class ComputeLoanUsingInputDialog {
4    public static void main(String[] args) {
5      // Enter yearly interest rate
6      String annualInterestRateString = JOptionPane.showInputDialog(
7        "Enter yearly interest rate, for example 8.25:");
8
9      // Convert string to double
10     double annualInterestRate =
11       Double.parseDouble(annualInterestRateString);
12
13     // Obtain monthly interest rate
14     double monthlyInterestRate = annualInterestRate / 1200;
15
16     // Enter number of years
17     String numberOfYearsString = JOptionPane.showInputDialog(
18       "Enter number of years as an integer, \nfor example 5:");
19
20     // Convert string to int
21     int numberOfYears = Integer.parseInt(numberOfYearsString);
22
23     // Enter loan amount
24     String loanString = JOptionPane.showInputDialog(
25       "Enter loan amount, for example 120000.95:");
26
27     // Convert string to double
28     double loanAmount = Double.parseDouble(loanString);
29
30     // Calculate payment
31     double monthlyPayment = loanAmount * monthlyInterestRate / (1
32       - 1 / Math.pow(1 + monthlyInterestRate, numberOfYears * 12));
33     double totalPayment = monthlyPayment * numberOfYears * 12;
34
35     // Format to keep two digits after the decimal point
36     monthlyPayment = (int)(monthlyPayment * 100) / 100.0;
```

enter interest rate

convert string to double

monthlyPayment

totalPayment

preparing output

```
37      totalPayment = (int)(totalPayment * 100) / 100.0;
38
39      // Display results
40      String output = "The monthly payment is " + monthlyPayment +
41        "\nThe total payment is " + totalPayment;
42      JOptionPane.showMessageDialog(null, output);
43    }
44 }
```

The `showInputDialog` method in lines 6–7 displays an input dialog. Enter the interest rate as a double value and click OK to accept the input. The value is returned as a string that is assigned to the `String` variable `annualInterestRateString`. The `Double.parseDouble(annualInterestRateString)` (line 11) is used to convert the string into a `double` value. If you entered an input other than a numeric value or clicked *Cancel* in the input dialog box, a runtime error would occur. In Chapter 18, "Exception Handling," you will learn how to handle the exception so that the program can continue to run.

 Pedagogical Note

JOptionPane or Scanner?

For obtaining input you can use `JOptionPane` or `Scanner`, whichever is convenient. For consistency most examples in the book use `Scanner` for getting input. You can easily revise the examples using `JOptionPane` for getting input.

KEY TERMS

algorithm 26
assignment operator (=) 30
assignment statement 30
backslash (\) 42
`byte` type 33
casting 39
`char` type 40
constant 31
data type 32
debugger 55
debugging 55
declaration 29
decrement operator (−−) 37
`double` type 32
`encoding` 40
`final` 31
`float` type 32
floating-point number 26
expression 30
expression statement 38

identifier 28
increment operator (++) 37
incremental development and testing 28
indentation 52
`int` type 32
literal 35
logic error 54
`long` type 32
narrowing (of types) 39
operator 33
primitive data type 26
runtime error 54
`short` type 32
syntax error 53
supplementary Unicode 41
Unicode 40
Unix epoch 50
variable 27
widening (of types) 39
whitespace 45

CHAPTER SUMMARY

■ Java provides four integer types (`byte`, `short`, `int`, `long`) that represent integers of four different sizes, and two floating-point types (`float`, `double`) that represent floating-point numbers of two different precisions. Character type (`char`) represents a single character. These are called primitive data types. Java's primitive types are portable across all computer platforms. They have exactly the same values on all platforms. When they are declared, the variables of these types are created and assigned memory space.

■ Java provides operators that perform numeric operations: + (addition), – (subtraction), * (multiplication), / (division), and % (remainder). Integer division (/) yields an integer result. The remainder operator (%) yields the remainder of the division.

■ The increment operator (++) and the decrement operator (−−) increment or decrement a variable by 1. If the operator is prefixed to the variable, the variable is first incremented or decremented by 1, then used in the expression. If the operator is a suffix to the variable, the variable is incremented or decremented by 1, but then the original old value is used in the expression.

■ All the numeric operators can be applied to characters. When an operand is a character, the character's Unicode value is used in the operation.

■ You can use casting to convert a value of one type into another type. Casting a variable of a type with a small range to a variable of a type with a larger range is known as *widening a type*. Casting a variable of a type with a large range to a variable of a type with a smaller range is known as *narrowing a type*. Widening a type can be performed automatically without explicit casting. Narrowing a type must be performed explicitly.

■ Programming errors can be categorized into three types: syntax errors, runtime errors, and logic errors. Errors that occur during compilation are called *syntax errors* or *compilation errors*. *Runtime errors* are errors that cause a program to terminate abnormally. *Logic errors* occur when a program does not perform the way it was intended to.

REVIEW QUESTIONS

Sections 2.2–2.6

2.1 Which of the following identifiers are valid?

```
applet, Applet, a++, --a, 4#R, $4, #44, apps
```

2.2 Which of the following are Java keywords?

```
class, public, int, x, y, radius
```

2.3 Translate the following algorithm into Java code:
   ■ Step 1: Declare a `double` variable named `miles` with initial value `100`;
   ■ Step 2: Declare a `double` constant named `MILE_TO_KILOMETER` with value `1.609`;
   ■ Step 3: Declare a `double` variable named `kilometer`, multiply miles and `MILE_TO_KILOMETER`, and assign the result to `kilometer`.
   ■ Step 4: Display `kilometer` to the console.
   What is `kilometer` after Step 4?

2.4 What are the benefits of using constants? Declare an `int` constant `SIZE` with value `20`.

Section 2.7 Numeric Data Types and Operations

2.5 Assume that `int a = 1` and `double d = 1.0`, and that each expression is independent. What are the results of the following expressions?

```
a = 46 / 9;
a = 46 % 9 + 4 * 4 - 2;
a = 45 + 43 % 5 * (23 * 3 % 2);
a %= 3 / a + 3;
d = 4 + d * d + 4;
d += 1.5 * 3 + (++a);
d -= 1.5 * 3 + a++;
```

2.6 Show the result of the following remainders.

```
56 % 6
78 % -4
-34 % 5
-34 % -5
5 % 1
1 % 5
```

2.7 Find the largest and smallest **byte**, **short**, **int**, **long**, **float**, and **double**. Which of these data types requires the least amount of memory?

2.8 What is the result of `25 / 4`? How would you rewrite the expression if you wished the result to be a floating-point number?

2.9 Are the following statements correct? If so, show the output.

```
System.out.println("the output for 25 / 4 is " + 25 / 4);
System.out.println("the output for 25 / 4.0 is " + 25 / 4.0);
```

2.10 How would you write the following arithmetic expression in Java?

$$\frac{4}{3(r + 34)} - 9(a + bc) + \frac{3 + d(2 + a)}{(a + bd)}$$

2.11 Suppose `m` and `r` are integers. Write a Java expression for mr^2 to obtain a floating-point result?

2.12 Which of these statements are true?
(a) Any expression can be used as a statement.
(b) The expression `x++` can be used as a statement.
(c) The statement `x = x + 5` is also an expression.
(d) The statement `x = y = x = 0` is illegal.

2.13 Which of the following are correct literals for floating-point numbers?

```
12.3, 12.3e+2, 23.4e-2, -334.4, 20, 39F, 40D
```

2.14 Identify and fix the errors in the following code:

```
 1 public class Test {
 2   public void main(string[] args) {
 3     int i;
 4     int k = 100.0;
 5     int j = i + 1;
 6
 7     System.out.println("j is " + j + " and
 8       k is " + k);
 9   }
10 }
```

Section 2.8 Numeric Type Conversions

2.15 Can different types of numeric values be used together in a computation?

2.16 What does an explicit conversion from a **double** to an **int** do with the fractional part of the *double* value? Does casting change the variable being cast?

2.17 Show the following output.

```
float f = 12.5F;
int i = (int)f;
System.out.println("f is " + f);
System.out.println("i is " + i);
```

Section 2.9 Character Data Type and Operations

2.18 Use print statements to find out the ASCII code for `'1'`, `'A'`, `'B'`, `'a'`, `'b'`. Use print statements to find out the character for the decimal code 40, 59, 79, 85, 90. Use print statements to find out the character for the hexadecimal code 40, 5A, 71, 72, 7A.

2.19 Which of the following are correct literals for characters?

```
'1', '\u345dE', '\u3fFa','\b', \t
```

2.20 How do you display characters \ and "?

2.21 Evaluate the following:

```
int i = '1';
int j = '1' + '2';
int k = 'a';
char c = 90;
```

2.22 Can the following conversions involving casting be allowed? If so, find the converted result.

```
char c = 'A';
i = (int)c;

float f = 1000.34f;
int i = (int)f;

double d = 1000.34;
int i = (int)d;

int i = 97;
char c = (char)i;
```

Section 2.10 The String Type

2.23 Show the output of the following statements (write a program to verify your result):

```
System.out.println("1" + 1);
System.out.println('1' + 1);
System.out.println("1" + 1 + 1);
System.out.println("1" + (1 + 1));
System.out.println('1' + 1 + 1);
```

2.24 Evaluate the following expressions (write a program to verify your result):

```
1 + "Welcome " + 1 + 1
1 + "Welcome " + (1 + 1)
```

```
1 + "Welcome " + ('\u0001'  + 1)
1 + "Welcome " + 'a'  + 1
```

Sections 2.11–2.12

2.25 How do you convert a decimal string into a `double` value? How do you convert an integer string into an `int` value?

2.26 How do you obtain the current minute using the `System.currentTimeMillis()` method?

Sections 2.14–2.15

2.27 What are the naming conventions for class names, method names, constants, and variables? Which of the following items can be a constant, a method, a variable, or a class according to the Java naming conventions?

`MAX_VALUE, Test, read, readInt`

2.28 Reformat the following program according to the programming style and documentation guidelines. Use the next-line brace style.

```java
public class Test
{
  // Main method
  public static void main(String[] args) {
  /** Print a line */
  System.out.println("2 % 3 = "+2%3);
  }
}
```

2.29 Describe syntax errors, runtime errors, and logic errors.

Section 2.16 (GUI) Getting Input from Input Dialogs

2.30 Why do you have to import `JOptionPane` but not the `Math` class?

2.31 How do you prompt the user to enter an input using a dialog box?

2.32 How do you convert a string to an integer? How do you convert a string to a double?

PROGRAMMING EXERCISES

Pedagogical Note

fixed input

Students may first write a program with a fixed input value and later modify it using the console input or an input dialog box. The solutions are provided for both console and dialog boxes.

Debugging Tip

learn from examples

The compiler usually gives a reason for a syntax error. If you don't know how to correct it, compare your program closely with similar examples in the text character by character.

Sections 2.2–2.8

2.1 (*Converting Celsius to Fahrenheit*) Write a program that reads a Celsius degree in double from the console, then converts it to Fahrenheit and displays the result. The formula for the conversion is as follows:

`fahrenheit = (9 / 5) * celsius + 32`

Hint: In Java, $9 / 5$ is 1, so you need to write $9.0 / 5$ in the program to obtain the correct result.

2.2 (*Computing the volume of a cylinder*) Write a program that reads in the radius and length of a cylinder and computes volume using the following formulas:

```
area = radius * radius * π
volume = area * length
```

2.3 (*Converting feet into meters*) Write a program that reads a number in feet, converts it to meters, and displays the result. One foot is 0.305 meters.

2.4 (*Converting pounds into kilograms*) Write a program that converts pounds into kilograms. The program prompts the user to enter a number in pounds, converts it to kilograms, and displays the result. One pound is 0.454 kilograms.

2.5* (*Financial application: calculating tips*) Write a program that reads the subtotal and the gratuity rate, and computes the gratuity and total. For example, if the user enters 10 for subtotal and 15% for gratuity rate, the program displays $\$1.5$ as gratuity and $\$11.5$ as total.

2.6** (*Summing the digits in an integer*) Write a program that reads an integer between 0 and 1000 and adds all the digits in the integer. For example, if an integer is 932, the sum of all its digits is 14.

Hint: Use the % operator to extract digits, and use the / operator to remove the extracted digit. For instance, $932 \% 10 = 2$ and $932 / 10 = 93$.

Section 2.9 Character Data Type and Operations

2.7* (*Converting an uppercase letter to lowercase*) Write a program that converts an uppercase letter to a lowercase letter. The character is typed in the source code as a literal value. In Chapter 9, "Strings and Text I/O," you will learn how to enter a character input.

Hint: In the ASCII table (see Appendix B), uppercase letters appear before lowercase letters. The offset between any uppercase letter and its corresponding lowercase letter is the same. So you can find a lowercase letter from its corresponding uppercase letter, as follows:

```
int offset = (int)'a' - (int)'A';
int unicodeForUppercase = (int)uppercase;
int unicodeForLowercase = unicodeForUppercase + offset;
char lowercase = (char)unicodeForLowercase;
```

2.8* (*Finding the character of an ASCII code*) Write a program that receives an ASCII code (an integer between 0 and 128) and displays its character. For example, if the user enters 97, the program displays character a.

Sections 2.10–2.12

2.9* (*Financial application: monetary units*) Rewrite Listing 2.8, ComputeChange.java, to fix the possible loss of accuracy when converting a `double` value to an `int` value. Enter the input as an integer whose last two digits represent the cents. For example, the input 1156 represents 11 dollars and 56 cents.

Section 2.16 (GUI) Getting Input from Input Dialogs

2.10* (*Using the GUI input*) Rewrite Listing 2.8, ComputeChange.java, using the GUI input and output.

Comprehensive

2.11* (*Financial application: payroll*) Write a program that reads the following information and prints a payroll statement:

Employee's name (e.g., Smith)

Number of hours worked in a week (e.g., 10)

Hourly pay rate (e.g., 6.75)

Federal tax withholding rate (e.g., 20%)

State tax withholding rate (e.g., 9%)

Write this program in two versions: (a) Use dialog boxes to obtain input and display output; (b) Use console input and output. A sample run of the console input and output is shown below:

```
Enter employee's name: Smith ↵Enter
Enter number of hours worked in a week: 10 ↵Enter
Enter hourly pay rate: 6.75 ↵Enter
Enter federal tax withholding rate: 0.20 ↵Enter
Enter state tax withholding rate: 0.09 ↵Enter
Employee Name: Smith
Hours Worked:  10.0
Pay Rate:  $6.75
Gross Pay:  $67.5
Deductions:
   Federal Withholding (20.0%):  $13.5
   State Withholding (9.0%):  $6.07
   Total Deduction:  $19.57
Net Pay:  $47.92
```

2.12* (*Financial application: calculating interest*) If you know the balance and the annual percentage interest rate, you can compute the interest on the next monthly payment using the following formula:

$$\text{interest} = \text{balance} \times (\text{annualInterestRate} / 1200)$$

Write a program that reads the balance and the annual percentage interest rate and displays the interest for the next month in two versions: (a) Use dialog boxes to obtain input and display output; (b) Use console input and output. A sample run of the console input and output is shown below:

```
Enter balance: 100000 ↵Enter
Enter annual interest rate: 4.625 ↵Enter
The interest is 385.41
```

2.13* (*Financial application: calculating the future investment value*) Write a program that reads in investment amount, annual interest rate, and number of years, and displays the future investment value using the following formula:

```
futureInvestmentValue =
  investmentAmount x (1 + monthlyInterestRate)numberOfYears*12
```

For example, if you enter amount `1000`, annual interest rate `3.25%`, and number of years `1`, the future investment value is `1032.98`.

Hint: Use the `Math.pow(a, b)` method to compute `a` raised to the power of `b`.

2.14 (*Health application: computing BMI*) Body Mass Index (BMI) is a measure of health on weight. It can be calculated by taking your weight in kilograms and dividing by the square of your height in meters. Write a program that prompts the user to enter a weight in pounds and height in inches and display the BMI. Note that one pound is `0.45359237` kilograms and one inch is `0.0254` meters.

Video Note
Compute BMI

2.15**(*Financial application: compound value*) Suppose you save `$100` *each* month into a savings account with the annual interest rate 5%. So, the monthly interest rate is 0.05 / 12 = 0.00417. After the first month, the value in the account becomes

$$100 * (1 + 0.00417) = 100.417$$

After the second month, the value in the account becomes,

$$(100 + 100.417) * (1 + 0.00417) = 201.252$$

After the third month, the value in the account becomes,

$$(100 + 201.252) * (1 + 0.00417) = 302.507$$

and so on.

Write a program to display the account value after the sixth month. (In Exercise 4.30, you will use a loop to simplify the code and display the account value for any month.)

2.16 (*Science: calculating energy*) Write a program that calculates the energy needed to heat water from an initial temperature to a final temperature. Your program should prompt the user to enter the amount of water in kilograms and the initial and final temperatures of the water. The formula to compute the energy is

```
Q = M * (final temperature - initial temperature) * 4184
```

where `M` is the weight of water in kilograms, temperatures are in degrees Celsius, and energy `Q` is measured in joules.

2.17* (*Science: wind-chill temperature*) How cold is it outside? The temperature alone is not enough to provide the answer. Other factors including wind speed, relative humidity, and sunshine play important roles in determining coldness outside. In 2001, the National Weather Service (NWS) implemented the new wind-chill temperature to measure the coldness using temperature and wind speed. The formula is given as follows:

$$t_{wc} = 35.74 + 0.6215t_a - 35.75v^{0.16} + 0.4275t_a v^{0.16}$$

where t_a is the outside temperature measured in degrees Fahrenheit and v is the speed measured in miles per hour. t_{wc} is the wind-chill temperature. The formula cannot be used for wind speeds below 2 mph or temperatures below -58°F or above 41°F.

Write a program that prompts the user to enter a temperature between $-58°F$ and $41°F$ and a wind speed greater than or equal to 2 and displays the wind-chill temperature. Use `Math.pow(a, b)` to compute $v^{0.16}$ (see §2.12.1).

2.18 (*Printing a table*) Write a program that displays the following table:

```
a       b       pow(a, b)
1       2       1
2       3       8
3       4       81
4       5       1024
5       6       15625
```

SELECTIONS

Objectives

- To declare `boolean` type and use Boolean values `true` and `false` (§3.2).

- To apply relational operators (<, <=, ==, !=, >, >=) and logic operators (!, &&, ||, ^) to write Boolean expressions (§3.2).

- To use Boolean expressions to control selection statements (§§3.3–3.5).

- To implement selection control using `if` and nested `if` statements (3.3).

- To implement selection control using `switch` statements (§3.4).

- To write expressions using the conditional operator (§3.5).

- To display formatted output using the `System.out.printf` method and to format strings using the `String.format` method (§3.6).

- To examine the rules governing operator precedence and associativity (§3.7).

- (GUI) To get user confirmation using confirmation dialogs (§3.8).

3.1 Introduction

problem

If you assign a negative value for `radius` in Listing 2.1, ComputeArea.java, the program prints an invalid result. If the radius is negative, you don't want the program to compute the area. How can you deal with this situation?

pseudocode

Like all high-level programming languages, Java provides selection statements that let you choose actions with two or more alternative courses. You can use selection statements in the following *pseudocode* (i.e., natural language mixed with programming code) to rewrite Listing 2.1:

```
if the radius is negative
    the program displays a message indicating a wrong input;
else
    the program computes the area and displays the result;
```

Selection statements use conditions. Conditions are Boolean expressions. This chapter first introduces Boolean types, values, operators, and expressions.

3.2 **boolean** Data Type and Operations

comparison operators

How do you compare two values, such as whether a radius is greater than 0, equal to 0, or less than 0? Java provides six *comparison operators* (also known as *relational operators*), shown in Table 3.1, which can be used to compare two values. The result of the comparison is a Boolean value: `true` or `false`. For example, the following statement displays `true`:

```
double radius = 1;
System.out.println(radius > 0);
```

TABLE 3.1 Comparison Operators

Operator	Name	Example	Result
<	less than	1 < 2	true
<=	less than or equal to	1 <= 2	true
>	greater than	1 > 2	false
>=	greater than or equal to	1 >= 2	false
==	equal to	1 == 2	false
!=	not equal to	1 != 2	true

Note

compare characters

You can also compare characters. Comparing characters is the same as comparing their Unicodes. For example, `'a'` is larger than `'A'` because the Unicode of `'a'` is larger than the Unicode of `'A'`.

Caution

== vs. =

The equality comparison operator is two equal signs (`==`), not a single equal sign (`=`). The latter symbol is for assignment.

Boolean variable

A variable that holds a Boolean value is known as a *Boolean variable*. The `boolean` data type is used to declare Boolean variables. A `boolean` variable can hold one of the two values: `true` and `false`. For example, the following statement assigns `true` to the variable `lightsOn`:

```
boolean lightsOn = true;
```

`true` and `false` are literals, just like a number such as `10`. They are reserved words and can- **Boolean literals**
not be used as identifiers in your program.

Boolean operators
Boolean operators, also known as logical operators, operate on Boolean values to create a new Boolean value. Table 3.2 gives a list of Boolean operators. Table 3.3 defines the not (`!`) operator. The not (`!`) operator negates `true` to `false` and `false` to `true`. Table 3.4 defines the and (`&&`) operator. The and (`&&`) of two Boolean operands is `true` if and only if both operands are `true`. Table 3.5 defines the or (`||`) operator. The or (`||`) of two Boolean operands is `true` if at least one of the operands is `true`. Table 3.6 defines the exclusive or (`^`) operator. The exclusive or (`^`) of two Boolean operands is `true` if and only if the two operands have different Boolean values.

TABLE 3.2   Boolean Operators

Operator	Name	Description
`!`	not	logical negation
`&&`	and	logical conjunction
`||`	or	logical disjunction
`^`	exclusive or	logical exclusion

TABLE 3.3   Truth Table for Operator `!`

p	!p	Example
true	false	`!(1 > 2)` is `true`, because `(1 > 2)` is `false`.
false	true	`!(1 > 0)` is `false`, because `(1 > 0)` is `true`.

TABLE 3.4   Truth Table for Operator `&&`

p1	p2	p1 && p2	Example
false	false	false	`(2 > 3) && (5 > 5)` is `false`, because
false	true	false	either `(2 > 3)` or `(5 > 5)` is `false`.
true	false	false	`(3 > 2) && (5 > 5)` is `false`, because `(5 > 5)` is `false`.
true	true	true	`(3 > 2) && (5 >= 5)` is `true`, because `(3 > 2)` and `(5 >= 5)` are both `true`.

TABLE 3.5   Truth Table for Operator `||`

p1	p2	p1 || p2	Example
false	false	false	`(2 > 3) || (5 > 5)` is `false`, because `(2 > 3)` and `(5 > 5)` are both `false`.
false	true	true	
true	false	true	`(3 > 2) || (5 > 5)` is `true`, because `(3 > 2)` is `true`.
true	true	true	

TABLE 3.6   Truth Table for Operator `^`

p1	p2	p1 ^ p2	Example
false	false	false	`(2 > 3) ^ (5 > 1)` is `true`, because `(2 > 3)` is false and `(5 > 1)` is `true`.
false	true	true	
true	false	true	`(3 > 2) ^ (5 > 1)` is `false`, because both `(3 > 2)` and `(5 > 1)` are `true`.
true	true	false	

Listing 3.1 gives a program that checks whether a number is divisible by 2 and 3, whether a number is divisible by 2 or 3, and whether a number is divisible by 2 or 3 but not both:

LISTING 3.1 TestBoolean.java

import class

```java
 1  import java.util.Scanner;
 2
 3  public class TestBoolean {
 4    public static void main(String[] args) {
 5      // Create a Scanner
 6      Scanner input = new Scanner(System.in);
 7
 8      // Receive an input
 9      System.out.print("Enter an integer: ");
10      int number = input.nextInt();
11
12      System.out.println("Is " + number +
13        "\n\tdivisible by 2 and 3? " +
14        (number % 2 == 0 && number % 3 == 0)
15        + "\n\tdivisible by 2 or 3? " +
16        (number % 2 == 0 || number % 3 == 0) +
17        "\n\tdivisible by 2 or 3, but not both? "
18        + (number % 2 == 0 ^ number % 3 == 0));
19    }
20  }
```

input

and

or

exclusive or

```
Enter an integer: 18  ↵Enter
Is 18
   divisible by 2 and 3? true
   divisible by 2 or 3? true
   divisible by 2 or 3, but not both? false
```

A long string is formed by concatenating the substrings in lines 12–18. The three \n characters display the string in four lines. (number % 2 == 0 && number % 3 == 0) (line 14) checks whether the number is divisible by 2 and 3. (number % 2 == 0 || number % 3 == 0) (line 16) checks whether the number is divisible by 2 or 3. (number % 2 == 0 ^ number % 3 == 0) (line 18) checks whether the number is divisible by 2 or 3, but not both.

Caution

In mathematics, the expression

```
1 <= numberOfDaysInAMonth <= 31
```

is correct. However, it does not make sense in Java, because `1 <= numberOfDaysInAMonth` is evaluated to a **boolean** value, which cannot be compared with `31`. Here, two operands (a **boolean** value and a numeric value) are *incompatible*. The correct expression in Java is

incompatible operands

```
(1 <= numberOfDaysInAMonth) && (numberOfDaysInAMonth <= 31)
```

Note

As shown in the preceding chapter, a **char** value can be cast into an **int** value, and vice versa. A **boolean** value, however, cannot be cast into a value of other types, nor can a value of other types be cast into a **boolean** value.

cannot cast **boolean**

Note

De Morgan's law, named after Indian-born British mathematician and logician Augustus De Morgan (1806-1871), can be used to simplify Boolean expressions. The law states

De Morgan's law

> !(condition1 && condition2) is same as !condition1 || !condition2
> !(condition1 || condition2) is same as !condition1 && !condition2

For example,

> !(n == 2 || n == 3) is same as n != 2 && n != 3
> !(n % 2 == 0 && n % 3 == 0) is same as n % 2 != 0 || n % 3 != 0

Note

When evaluating p1 && p2, Java first evaluates p1 and then, if p1 is true, evaluates p2; if p1 is false, it does not evaluate p2. When evaluating p1 || p2, Java first evaluates p1 and then, if p1 is false, evaluates p2; if p1 is true, it does not evaluate p2. Therefore, && is referred to as the *conditional* or *short-circuit AND* operator, and || is referred to as the *conditional* or *short-circuit OR* operator.

conditional operator
short-circuit operator

3.2.1 Problem: Determining Leap Year

A year is a *leap year* if it is divisible by 4 but not by 100 or if it is divisible by 400. So you can use the following Boolean expression to check whether a year is a leap year:

leap year

$$(year \% 4 == 0 \text{ \&\& } year \% 100 \mathrel{!=} 0) \mathrel{||} (year \% 400 == 0)$$

Listing 3.2 gives the program that lets the user enter a year and checks whether it is a leap year.

LISTING 3.2 LeapYear.java

```
1  import java.util.Scanner;
2
3  public class LeapYear {
4    public static void main(String args[]) {
5      // Create a Scanner
6      Scanner input = new Scanner(System.in);
7      System.out.print("Enter a year: ");
8      int year = input.nextInt();
9
10     // Check if the year is a leap year
11     boolean isLeapYear =
12       (year % 4 == 0 && year % 100 != 0) || (year % 400 == 0);
13
14     // Display the result
15     System.out.println(year + " is a leap year? " + isLeapYear);
16   }
17 }
```

input

leap year?

display result

```
Enter a year: 2008 ↵Enter
2008 is a leap year? true
```

```
Enter a year: 2002 ↵Enter
2002 is a leap year? false
```

3.2.2 Problem: A Simple Math Learning Tool

Suppose you want to develop a program to let a first-grader practice addition. The program randomly generates two single-digit integers, `number1` and `number2`, and displays to the student a question such as "What is 7 + 9?", as shown in the sample output. After the student types the answer, the program displays a message to indicate whether the answer is true or false.

There are several ways to generate random numbers. For now, generate the first integer using `System.currentTimeMillis() % 10` and the second using `System.currentTimeMillis() * 7 % 10`. Listing 3.3 gives the program. Lines 5–6 generate two numbers, `number1` and `number2`. Line 14 obtains an answer from the user. The answer is graded in line 18 using a Boolean expression `number1 + number2 == answer`.

Video Note
Program addition quiz

generate number1

generate number2

show question

display result

LISTING 3.3 AdditionQuiz.java

```java
1  import java.util.Scanner;
2
3  public class AdditionQuiz {
4    public static void main(String[] args) {
5      int number1 = (int)(System.currentTimeMillis() % 10);
6      int number2 = (int)(System.currentTimeMillis() * 7 % 10);
7
8      // Create a Scanner
9      Scanner input = new Scanner(System.in);
10
11      System.out.print(
12        "What is " + number1 + " + " + number2 + "? ");
13
14      int answer = input.nextInt();
15
16      System.out.println(
17        number1 + " + " + number2 + " = " + answer + " is " +
18        (number1 + number2 == answer));
19    }
20  }
```

```
What is 1 + 7? 8  ↵Enter
1 + 7 = 8 is true
```

```
What is 4 + 8? 9  ↵Enter
4 + 8 = 9 is false
```

3.3 if Statements

why **if** statement?

The preceding program displays a message such as "6 + 2 = 7 is false." If you wish the message to be "6 + 2 = 7 is incorrect," you have to use a selection statement to carry out this minor change.

This section introduces selection statements. Java has several types of selection statements: simple `if` statements, `if . . . else` statements, nested `if` statements, `switch` statements, and conditional expressions.

3.3.1 Simple **if** Statements

A simple **if** statement executes an action if and only if the condition is **true**. The syntax for a simple **if** statement is shown below:

```
if (booleanExpression) {
  statement(s);
}
```

if statement

The execution flow chart is shown in Figure 3.1(a).

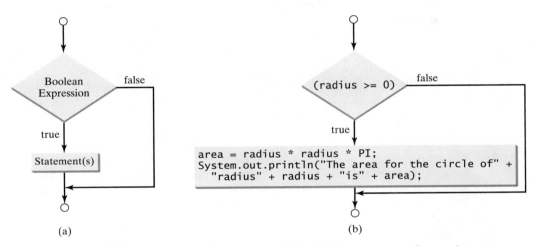

(a)   (b)

FIGURE 3.1 An **if** statement executes statements if the **booleanExpression** evaluates to **true**.

If the **booleanExpression** evaluates to **true**, the statements in the block are executed. As an example, see the following code:

```
if (radius >= 0) {
  area = radius * radius * PI;
  System.out.println("The area for the circle of radius " +
    radius + " is " + area);
}
```

The flow chart of the preceding statement is shown in Figure 3.1(b). If the value of **radius** is greater than or equal to **0**, then the **area** is computed and the result is displayed; otherwise, the two statements in the block will not be executed.

As another example, the following statement determines whether a number is even or odd:

```
if (number % 2 == 0)
  System.out.println(number + " is even.");

if (number % 2 != 0)
  System.out.println(number + " is odd.");
```

The `booleanExpression` is enclosed in parentheses. For example, the code in (a) below is wrong. It should be corrected, as shown in (b).

```
if (i > 0) && (i < 10) {
   System.out.println("i is an " +
      + "integer between 0 and 10");
}
```

```
if ((i > 0) && (i < 10))
   System.out.println("i is an " +
      + "integer between 0 and 10");
```

(a) Wrong   (b) Correct

The braces can be omitted if they enclose a single statement. For example, the following statements are equivalent.

```
if ((i > 0) && (i < 10)) {
   System.out.println("i is an " +
      + "integer between 0 and 10");
}
```

Equivalent

```
if ((i > 0) && (i < 10))
   System.out.println("i is an " +
      + "integer between 0 and 10");
```

(a)   (b)

Caution

Forgetting the braces when they are needed for grouping multiple statements is a common programming error. If you modify the code by adding new statements in an `if` statement without braces, you will have to insert the braces if they are not already in place.

Caution

Adding a semicolon at the end of an `if` clause, as shown in (a) below, is a common mistake.

Logic Error

```
if (radius >= 0);
{
   area = radius * radius * PI;
   System.out.println("The area "
      + " is " + area);
}
```

Equivalent

Empty Body

```
if (radius >= 0) { };
{
   area = radius * radius * PI;
   System.out.println("The area "
      + " is " + area);
}
```

(a)   (b)

This mistake is hard to find, because it is neither a compilation error nor a runtime error; it is a logic error. The code in (a) is equivalent to that in (b) with an empty block.

This error often occurs when you use the next-line block style. Using the end-of-line block style will prevent this error.

3.3.2 `if . . . else` Statements

A simple `if` statement takes an action if the specified condition is `true`. If the condition is `false`, nothing is done. But what if you want to take alternative actions when the condition is `false`? You can use an `if . . . else` statement. The actions that an `if . . . else` statement specifies differ based on whether the condition is `true` or `false`.

Here is the syntax for this type of statement:

if-else statement

```
if (booleanExpression) {
   statement(s)-for-the-true-case;
}
```

```
else {
    statement(s)-for-the-false-case;
}
```

The flow chart of the statement is shown in Figure 3.2.

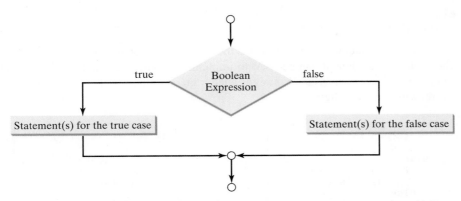

FIGURE 3.2   An **if . . . else** statement executes statements for the **true** case if the **boolean** expression evaluates to **true**; otherwise, statements for the **false** case are executed.

If the **booleanExpression** evaluates to **true**, the **statement(s)** for the true case are executed; otherwise, the **statement(s)** for the false case are executed. For example, consider the following code:

```
if (radius >= 0) {
    area = radius * radius * PI;
    System.out.println("The area for the circle of radius " +
        radius + " is " + area);
}
else {
    System.out.println("Negative input");
}
```

If **radius >= 0** is **true**, **area** is computed and displayed; if it is **false**, the message **"Negative input"** is printed.

As usual, the braces can be omitted if there is only one statement within them. The braces enclosing the **System.out.println("Negative input")** statement can therefore be omitted in the preceding example.

Using the **if ... else** statement, you can rewrite the code for determining whether a number is even or odd in the preceding section, as follows:

```
if (number % 2 == 0)
    System.out.println(number + " is even.");
else
    System.out.println(number + " is odd.");
```

This is more efficient because whether **number % 2** is **0** is tested only once.

3.3.3   Nested **if** Statements

The statement in an **if** or **if . . . else** statement can be any legal Java statement, including another **if** or **if . . . else** statement. The inner **if** statement is said to be *nested* inside the outer **if** statement. The inner **if** statement can contain another **if** statement; in fact, there is no limit to the depth of the nesting. For example, the following is a nested `if` statement:

nested **if** statement

```
if (i > k) {
  if (j > k)
    System.out.println("i and j are greater than k");
}
else
  System.out.println("i is less than or equal to k");
```

The `if (j > k)` statement is nested inside the `if (i > k)` statement.

The nested `if` statement can be used to implement multiple alternatives. The statement given in Figure 3.3(a), for instance, assigns a letter grade to the variable `grade` according to the score, with multiple alternatives.

```
if (score >= 90.0)
  grade = 'A';
else
  if (score >= 80.0)
    grade = 'B';
  else
    if (score >= 70.0)
      grade = 'C';
    else
      if (score >= 60.0)
        grade = 'D';
      else
        grade = 'F';
```

Equivalent ——————

This is better

```
if (score >= 90.0)
  grade = 'A';
else if (score >= 80.0)
  grade = 'B';
else if (score >= 70.0)
  grade = 'C';
else if (score >= 60.0)
  grade = 'D';
else
  grade = 'F';
```

            (a)   (b)

FIGURE 3.3 A preferred format for multiple alternative `if` statements is shown in (b).

The execution of this `if` statement proceeds as follows. The first condition (`score >= 90.0`) is tested. If it is `true`, the grade becomes `'A'`. If it is `false`, the second condition (`score >= 80.0`) is tested. If the second condition is `true`, the grade becomes `'B'`. If that condition is `false`, the third condition and the rest of the conditions (if necessary) continue to be tested until a condition is met or all of the conditions prove to be `false`. If all of the conditions are `false`, the grade becomes `'F'`. Note that a condition is tested only when all of the conditions that come before it are `false`.

The `if` statement in Figure 3.3(a) is equivalent to the `if` statement in Figure 3.3(b). In fact, Figure 3.3(b) is the preferred writing style for multiple alternative `if` statements. This style avoids deep indentation and makes the program easy to read.

 Note

matching **else** with **if**

The `else` clause matches the most recent unmatched `if` clause in the same block. For example, the statement in (a) below is equivalent to the statement in (b).

```
int i = 1;
int j = 2;
int k = 3;

if (i > j)
  if (i > k)
    System.out.println("A");
else
  System.out.println("B");
```

Equivalent ——————

This is better with correct indentation

```
int i = 1;
int j = 2;
int k = 3;

if (i > j)
  if (i > k)
    System.out.println("A");
  else
    System.out.println("B");
```

            (a)   (b)

The compiler ignores indentation. Nothing is printed from the statement in (a) and (b). To force the `else` clause to match the first `if` clause, you must add a pair of braces:

```java
int i = 1; int j = 2; int k = 3;

if(i > j) {
  if (i > k)
    System.out.println("A");
}
else
  System.out.println("B");
```

This statement prints B.

Tip

assign **boolean** variable

Often new programmers write the code that assigns a test condition to a `boolean` variable like the code in (a):

(a)   (b)

The code can be simplified by assigning the test value directly to the variable, as shown in (b).

Caution

test **boolean** value

To test whether a `boolean` variable is `true` or `false` in a test condition, it is redundant to use the equality comparison operator like the code in (a):

```java
if (even == true)              Equivalent       if (even)
  System.out.println(                             System.out.println(
    "It is even.");                                 "It is even.");
```

(a)   (b)

This is better

Instead, it is better to use the `boolean` variable directly, as shown in (b). Another good reason to use the `boolean` variable directly is to avoid errors that are difficult to detect. Using the `=` operator instead of the `==` operator to compare equality of two items in a test condition is a common error. It could lead to the following erroneous statement:

```java
if (even = true)
  System.out.println("It is even.");
```

This statement does not have syntax errors. It assigns `true` to `even` so that `even` is always `true`.

3.3.4 Problem: An Improved Math Learning Tool

Suppose you want to develop a program for a first-grader to practice subtraction. The program randomly generates two single-digit integers, `number1` and `number2`, with `number1 > number2` and displays to the student a question such as "What is 9 − 2?" After the student enters the answer, the program displays a message to indicate whether the answer is correct.

The previous programs generate random numbers using `System.currentTimeMillis()`. A better way to generate a random number is to use the `random()` method in the `Math` class.   **random()** method

Invoking this method returns a random double value **d** such that $0.0 \leq d < 1.0$. So, `(int)(Math.random() * 10)` returns a random single-digit integer (i.e., a number between 0 and 9).

The program may work as follows:

- Generate two single-digit integers into **number1** and **number2**.

- If **number1 < number2**, swap **number1** with **number2**.

- Prompt the student to answer "What is number1 – number2?"

- Check the student's answer and display whether the answer is correct.

The complete program is shown in Listing 3.4.

Video Note
Program subtraction quiz

LISTING 3.4 SubtractionQuiz.java

random numbers

get answer

check the answer

```
 1 import java.util.Scanner;
 2
 3 public class SubtractionQuiz {
 4   public static void main(String[] args) {
 5     // 1. Generate two random single-digit integers
 6     int number1 = (int)(Math.random() * 10);
 7     int number2 = (int)(Math.random() * 10);
 8
 9     // 2. If number1 < number2, swap number1 with number2
10     if (number1 < number2) {
11       int temp = number1;
12       number1 = number2;
13       number2 = temp;
14     }
15
16     // 3. Prompt the student to answer "What is number1 - number2?"
17     System.out.print
18       ("What is " + number1 + " - " + number2 + "? ");
19     Scanner input = new Scanner(System.in);
20     int answer = input.nextInt();
21
22     // 4. Grade the answer and display the result
23     if (number1 - number2 == answer)
24       System.out.println("You are correct!");
25     else
26       System.out.println("Your answer is wrong.\n" + number1 + " - "
27         + number2 + " should be " + (number1 - number2));
28   }
29 }
```

```
What is 6 - 6? 0 ↵Enter
You are correct!
```

```
What is 9 - 2? 5 ↵Enter
Your answer is wrong.
9 - 2 should be 7
```

To swap two variables **number1** and **number2**, a temporary variable **temp** (line 11) is used to first hold the value in **number1**. The value in **number2** is assigned to **number1** (line 12), and the value in **temp** is assigned to **number2**.

3.3.5 Problem: Lottery

Suppose you want to develop a program to play lottery. The program randomly generates a lottery of a two-digit number, prompts the user to enter a two-digit number, and determines whether the user wins according to the following rule:

1. If the user input matches the lottery in exact order, the award is $10,000.

2. If the user input matches the lottery, the award is $3,000.

3. If one digit in the user input matches a digit in the lottery, the award is $1,000.

The complete program is shown in Listing 3.5.

LISTING 3.5 Lottery.java

```java
 1 import java.util.Scanner;
 2
 3 public class Lottery {
 4   public static void main(String[] args) {
 5     // Generate a lottery
 6     int lottery = (int)(Math.random() * 100);          generate a lottery
 7
 8     // Prompt the user to enter a guess
 9     Scanner input = new Scanner(System.in);
10     System.out.print("Enter your lottery pick (two digits): ");
11     int guess = input.nextInt();                       enter a guess
12
13     // Check the guess
14     if (guess == lottery)                              exact match?
15       System.out.println("Exact match: you win $10,000");
16     else if (guess % 10 == lottery / 10                match all digits?
17         && guess / 10 == lottery % 10)
18       System.out.println("Match all digits: you win $3,000");
19     else if (guess % 10 == lottery / 10 || guess % 10 == lottery % 10    match one digit?
20         || guess / 10 == lottery / 10 || guess / 10 == lottery % 10)
21       System.out.println("Match one digit: you win $1,000");
22     else
23       System.out.println("Sorry, no match");
24   }
25 }
```

```
Enter your lottery pick (two digits):  45  ↵Enter
Sorry, no match
```

```
Enter your lottery pick:  23  ↵Enter
Exact match: you win $10,000
```

The program generates a lottery using the `Math.random()` method (line 6) and prompts the user to enter a guess (line 11). The program then checks the guess against the lottery number in this order:

1. First check whether the guess matches the lottery exactly (line 14).

2. If not, check whether the reversal of the guess matches the lottery (lines 16–17).

3. If not, check whether one digit is in the lottery (lines 19-20).

4. If not, nothing matches.

Note that `guess % 10` obtains the last digit from `guess` and `guess / 10` obtains the first digit from `guess`, since `guess` is a two-digit number.

3.3.6 Problem: Computing Body Mass Index

Body Mass Index (BMI) is a measure of health on weight. It can be calculated by taking your weight in kilograms and dividing by the square of your height in meters. The interpretation of BMI for people 16 years or older is as follows:

BMI	Interpretation
below 16	serious underweight
16-18	underweight
18-24	normal weight
24-29	overweight
29-35	seriously overweight
above 35	gravely overweight

Write a program that prompts the user to enter a weight in pounds and height in inches and display the BMI. Note that one pound is `0.45359237` kilograms and one inch is `0.0254` meters. Listing 3.6 gives the program.

Video Note
Use multiple alternative if statements

LISTING 3.6 ComputeBMI.java

```java
1 import java.util.Scanner;
2
3 public class ComputeBMI {
4   public static void main(String[] args) {
5     Scanner input = new Scanner(System.in);
6
7     // Prompt the user to enter weight in pounds
8     System.out.print("Enter weight in pounds: ");
9     double weight = input.nextDouble();
10
11    // Prompt the user to enter height in inches
12    System.out.print("Enter height in inches: ");
13    double height = input.nextDouble();
14
15    final double KILOGRAMS_PER_POUND = 0.45359237; // Constant
16    final double METERS_PER_INCH = 0.0254; // Constant
17
18    // Compute BMI
19    double bmi = weight * KILOGRAMS_PER_POUND /
20      ((height * METERS_PER_INCH) * (height * METERS_PER_INCH));
21
22    // Display result
23    System.out.println("Your BMI is " + bmi);
24    if (bmi < 16)
25      System.out.println("You are seriously underweight");
26    else if (bmi < 18)
27      System.out.println("You are underweight");
28    else if (bmi < 24)
29      System.out.println("You are normal weight");
30    else if (bmi < 29)
31      System.out.println("You are overweight");
32    else if (bmi < 35)
33      System.out.println("You are seriously overweight");
```

input weight

input height

compute bmi

display output

```
34      else
35        System.out.println("You are gravely overweight");
36   }
37 }
```

```
Enter weight in pounds:  146  ↵Enter
Enter height in inches:  70   ↵Enter
Your BMI is 20.948603801493316
You are normal weight
```

Two constants KILOGRAMS_PER_POUND and METERS_PER_INCH are defined in lines 15–16. Using constants here makes programs easy to read.

3.3.7 Problem: Computing Taxes

The United States federal personal income tax is calculated based on filing status and taxable income. There are four filing statuses: single filers, married filing jointly, married filing separately, and head of household. The tax rates vary every year. Table 3.7 shows the rates for 2002. If you are, say, single with a taxable income of $10,000, the first $6,000 is taxed at 10% and the other $4,000 is taxed at 15%. So your tax is $1,200.

TABLE 3.7   2002 U.S. Federal Personal Tax Rates

Tax rate	Single filers	Married filing jointly or qualifying widow/widower	Married filing separately	Head of household
10%	Up to $6,000	Up to $12,000	Up to $6,000	Up to $10,000
15%	$6,001 – $27,950	$12,001 – $46,700	$6,001 – $23,350	$10,001 – $37,450
27%	$27,951 – $67,700	$46,701 – $112,850	$23,351 – $56,425	$37,451 – $96,700
30%	$67,701 – $141,250	$112,851 – $171,950	$56,426 – $85,975	$96,701 – $156,600
35%	$141,251 – $307,050	$171,951 – $307,050	$85,976 – $153,525	$156,601 – $307,050
38.6%	$307,051 or more	$307,051 or more	$153,526 or more	$307,051 or more

You are to write a program to compute personal income tax. Your program should prompt the user to enter the filing status and taxable income and compute the tax. Enter 0 for single filers, 1 for married filing jointly, 2 for married filing separately, and 3 for head of household.

Your program computes the tax for the taxable income based on the filing status. The filing status can be determined using if statements outlined as follows:

```
if (status == 0) {
  // Compute tax for single filers
}
else if (status == 1) {
  // Compute tax for married filing jointly
}
else if (status == 2) {
  // Compute tax for married filing separately
}
else if (status == 3) {
  // Compute tax for head of household
}
else {
  // Display wrong status
}
```

For each filing status there are six tax rates. Each rate is applied to a certain amount of taxable income. For example, of a taxable income of $400,000 for single filers, $6,000 is taxed at 10%, (27,950 − 6,000) at 15%, (67,700 − 27,950) at 27%, (141,250 − 67,700) at 35%, and (400,000 − 307,050) at 38.6%.

Listing 3.7 gives the solution to compute taxes for single filers. The complete solution is left as an exercise.

LISTING 3.7 ComputeTax.java

```java
1  import java.util.Scanner;
2
3  public class ComputeTax {
4    public static void main(String[] args) {
5      // Create a Scanner
6      Scanner input = new Scanner(System.in);
7
8      // Prompt the user to enter filing status
9      System.out.print(
10        "(0-single filer, 1-married jointly,\n" +
11        "2-married separately, 3-head of household)\n" +
12        "Enter the filing status: ");
13      int status = input.nextInt();
14
15      // Prompt the user to enter taxable income
16      System.out.print("Enter the taxable income: ");
17      double income = input.nextDouble();
18
19      // Compute tax
20      double tax = 0;
21
22      if (status == 0) { // Compute tax for single filers
23        if (income <= 6000)
24          tax = income * 0.10;
25        else if (income <= 27950)
26          tax = 6000 * 0.10 + (income - 6000) * 0.15;
27        else if (income <= 67700)
28          tax = 6000 * 0.10 + (27950 - 6000) * 0.15 +
29            (income - 27950) * 0.27;
30        else if (income <= 141250)
31          tax = 6000 * 0.10 + (27950 - 6000) * 0.15 +
32            (67700 - 27950) * 0.27 + (income - 67700) * 0.30;
33        else if (income <= 307050)
34          tax = 6000 * 0.10 + (27950 - 6000) * 0.15 +
35            (67700 - 27950) * 0.27 + (141250 - 67700) * 0.30 +
36            (income - 141250) * 0.35;
37        else
38          tax = 6000 * 0.10 + (27950 - 6000) * 0.15 +
39            (67700 - 27950) * 0.27 + (141250 - 67700) * 0.30 +
40            (307050 - 141250) * 0.35 + (income - 307050) * 0.386;
41      }
42      else if (status == 1) { // Compute tax for married filing jointly
43        // Left as exercise
44      }
45      else if (status == 2) { // Compute tax for married filing separately
46        // Left as exercise
47      }
48      else if (status == 3) { // Compute tax for head of household
49        // Left as exercise
50      }
```

input status

input income

compute tax

```
51      else {
52        System.out.println("Error: invalid status");
53        System.exit(0);
54      }
55
56      // Display the result
57      System.out.println("Tax is " + (int)(tax * 100) / 100.0);
58  }
59 }
```

exit program

display output

```
(0-single filer, 1-married jointly,
2-married separately, 3-head of household)
Enter the filing status: 0  ↵Enter
Enter the taxable income: 400000  ↵Enter
Tax is 130598.7
```

The program receives the filing status and taxable income. The multiple alternative `if` statements (lines 22, 42, 45, 48, 51) check the filing status and compute the tax based on the filing status.

`System.exit(0)` (line 53) is defined in the `System` class. Invoking this method terminates the program. The argument `0` indicates that the program is terminated normally.

`System.exit(0)`

An initial value of `0` is assigned to `tax` (line 20). A syntax error would occur if it had no initial value, because all of the other statements that assign values to `tax` are within the `if` statement. The compiler thinks that these statements may not be executed and therefore reports a syntax error.

To test a program, you should provide the input that covers all cases. For this program, your input should cover all statuses (`0`, `1`, `2`, `3`). For each status, test the tax for each of the six brackets. So, there are a total of 24 cases.

test all cases

Tip

For all programs, you should write a small amount of code and test it before moving on to add more code. This is called *incremental development and testing*. This approach makes debugging easier, because the errors are likely in the new code you just added.

incremental development and testing

3.3.8 Problem: Guessing Birth Dates

You can find out your friend's birth date by asking five questions. Each question asks whether the date is in one of five sets of numbers, as shown in Figure 3.4:

The birth date is the sum of the first numbers in the sets where the date appears. For example, if the birth date is `19`, it appears in Set1, Set3, and Set5. The first numbers in these three sets are `1`, `2`, and `16`. Their sum is `19`.

The way the numbers are placed in the five sets is intrigue. The numbers are not put together by accident. The starting numbers in each set are 1, 2, 4, 8, and 16, which correspond to 1, 10, 100, 1000, and 10000 in binary. If a date's binary number has a digit 1 in position k, the number should appear in Setk. For example, number 19 is 10011, so it appears in Set1, Set2, and Set5. It is binary 1 + 10 + 10000 = 10011 or decimal 1 + 2 + 16 = 19. Number 31 is 11111, so it appears in Set1, Set2, Set3, Set4, and Set5. It is binary 1 + 10 + 100 + 1000 + 10000 = 11111 and it is decimal 1 + 2 + 4 + 8 + 16 = 31.

Listing 3.8 gives a program that prompts the user to answer whether the date is in Set1 (lines 41–47), in Set2 (lines 50–56), in Set3 (lines 59–65), in Set4 (lines 68–74), and in Set5 (lines 77–83). If the number is in the set, the program adds the first number in the set to `date` (lines 47, 56, 65, 74, 83).

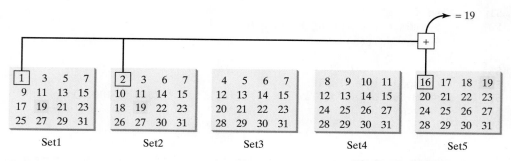

FIGURE 3.4 The birth date is the sum of the first numbers in the sets where the date appears.

LISTING 3.8 GuessBirthDate.java

```
1  import java.util.Scanner;
2
3  public class GuessBirthDate {
4    public static void main(String[] args) {
5      String set1 =
6        "  1   3   5   7\n" +
7        "  9  11  13  15\n" +
8        " 17  19  21  23\n" +
9        " 25  27  29  31";
10
11     String set2 =
12       "  2   3   6   7\n" +
13       " 10  11  14  15\n" +
14       " 18  19  22  23\n" +
15       " 26  27  30  31";
16
17     String set3 =
18       "  4   5   6   7\n" +
19       " 12  13  14  15\n" +
20       " 20  21  22  23\n" +
21       " 28  29  30  31";
22
23     String set4 =
24       "  8   9  10  11\n" +
25       " 12  13  14  15\n" +
26       " 24  25  26  27\n" +
27       " 28  29  30  31";
28
29     String set5 =
30       " 16  17  18  19\n" +
31       " 20  21  22  23\n" +
32       " 24  25  26  27\n" +
33       " 28  29  30  31";
34
35     int date = 0;
36
37     // Create a Scanner
38     Scanner input = new Scanner(System.in);
39
40     // Prompt the user to answer questions
41     System.out.print("Is your birthdate in Set1?\n");
42     System.out.print(set1);
43     System.out.print("\nEnter 0 for No and 1 for Yes: ");
44     int answer = input.nextInt();
```

date to be determined

```
45
46      if (answer == 1)                                                    in Set1?
47        date += 1;
48
49      // Prompt the user to answer questions
50      System.out.print("\nIs your birthdate in Set2?\n");
51      System.out.print(set2);
52      System.out.print("\nEnter 0 for No and 1 for Yes: ");
53      answer = input.nextInt();
54
55      if (answer == 1)                                                    in Set2?
56        date += 2;
57
58      // Prompt the user to answer questions
59      System.out.print("Is your birthdate in Set3?\n");
60      System.out.print(set3);
61      System.out.print("\nEnter 0 for No and 1 for Yes: ");
62      answer = input.nextInt();
63
64      if (answer == 1)                                                    in Set3?
65        date += 4;
66
67      // Prompt the user to answer questions
68      System.out.print("\nIs your birthdate in Set4?\n");
69      System.out.print(set4);
70      System.out.print("\nEnter 0 for No and 1 for Yes: ");
71      answer = input.nextInt();
72
73      if (answer == 1)                                                    in Set4?
74        date += 8;
75
76      // Prompt the user to answer questions
77      System.out.print("\nIs your birthdate in Set5?\n");
78      System.out.print(set5);
79      System.out.print("\nEnter 0 for No and 1 for Yes: ");
80      answer = input.nextInt();
81
82      if (answer == 1)                                                    in Set5?
83        date += 16;
84
85      System.out.println("\nYour birthdate is " + date + "!");
86   }
87 }
```

```
Is your birth date in Set1?
 1  3  5  7
 9 11 13 15
17 19 21 23
25 27 29 31
Enter 0 for No and 1 for Yes:  1  [↵Enter]

Is your birth date in Set2?
 2  3  6  7
10 11 14 15
18 19 22 23
26 27 30 31
Enter 0 for No and 1 for Yes:  1  [↵Enter]
```

```
Is your birth date in Set3?
 4  5  6  7
12 13 14 15
20 21 22 23
28 29 30 31
Enter 0 for No and 1 for Yes:  0  ⏎Enter

Is your birth date in Set4?
 8  9 10 11
12 13 14 15
24 25 26 27
28 29 30 31
Enter 0 for No and 1 for Yes:  0  ⏎Enter

Is your birth date in Set5?
16 17 18 19
20 21 22 23
24 25 26 27
28 29 30 31
Enter 0 for No and 1 for Yes:  1  ⏎Enter
Your birth date is 19
```

3.4 **switch** Statements

The **if** statement in Listing 3.5 makes selections based on a single **true** or **false** condition. There are four cases for computing taxes, which depend on the value of **status**. To fully account for all the cases, nested **if** statements were used. Overuse of nested **if** statements makes a program difficult to read. Java provides a **switch** statement to handle multiple conditions efficiently. You could write the following **switch** statement to replace the nested **if** statement in Listing 3.5:

```
switch (status) {
  case 0:  compute taxes for single filers;
           break;
  case 1:  compute taxes for married filing jointly;
           break;
  case 2:  compute taxes for married filing separately;
           break;
  case 3:  compute taxes for head of household;
           break;
  default: System.out.println("Errors: invalid status");
           System.exit(0);
}
```

The flow chart of the preceding **switch** statement is shown in Figure 3.5.

This statement checks to see whether the status matches the value **0**, **1**, **2**, or **3**, in that order. If matched, the corresponding tax is computed; if not matched, a message is displayed. Here is the full syntax for the **switch** statement:

switch statement

```
switch (switch-expression) {
  case value1: statement(s)1;
               break;
  case value2: statement(s)2;
               break;
```

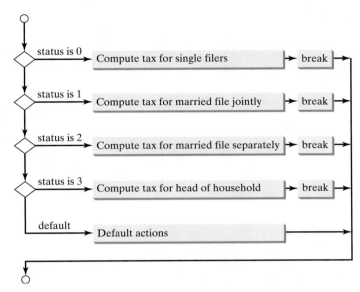

FIGURE 3.5 The `switch` statement checks all cases and executes the statements in the matched case.

```
    ...
    case valueN: statement(s)N;
                 break;
    default:     statement(s)-for-default;
  }
```

The `switch` statement observes the following rules:

- The `switch-expression` must yield a value of `char`, `byte`, `short`, or `int` type and must always be enclosed in parentheses.

- The `value1`, ..., and `valueN` must have the same data type as the value of the `switch-expression`. Note that `value1`, ..., and `valueN` are constant expressions, meaning that they cannot contain variables, such as `1 + x`.

- When the value in a `case` statement matches the value of the `switch-expression`, the statements *starting from this case* are executed until either a `break` statement or the end of the switch statement is reached.

- The keyword `break` is optional. The `break` statement immediately ends the `switch` statement.

- The `default` case, which is optional, can be used to perform actions when none of the specified cases matches the `switch-expression`.

- The `case` statements are checked in sequential order, but the order of the cases (including the default case) does not matter. However, it is good programming style to follow the logical sequence of the cases and place the default case at the end.

Caution

Do not forget to use a `break` statement when one is needed. Once a case is matched, the statements starting from the matched case are executed until a `break` statement or the end of the `switch` statement is reached. This is referred to as *fall-through behavior*. For example, the following code prints character a three times if `ch` is 'a':

without **break**

fall-through behavior

```
switch (ch) {
  case 'a': System.out.println(ch);
  case 'b': System.out.println(ch);
  case 'c': System.out.println(ch);
}
```

Tip

To avoid programming errors and improve code maintainability, it is a good idea to put a comment in a case clause if **break** is purposely omitted.

3.5 Conditional Expressions

You might want to assign a value to a variable that is restricted by certain conditions. For example, the following statement assigns 1 to y if x is greater than 0, and -1 to y if x is less than or equal to 0.

```
if (x > 0)
  y = 1;
else
  y = -1;
```

Alternatively, as in this example, you can use a conditional expression to achieve the same result.

```
y = (x > 0) ? 1 : -1;
```

Conditional expressions are in a completely different style, with no explicit **if** in the statement. The syntax is shown below:

conditional expression

```
booleanExpression ? expression1 : expression2;
```

The result of this conditional expression is **expression1** if **booleanExpression** is true; otherwise the result is **expression2**.

Suppose you want to assign the larger number between variable **num1** and **num2** to **max**. You can simply write a statement using the conditional expression:

```
max = (num1 > num2) ? num1 : num2;
```

For another example, the following statement displays the message "num is even" if **num** is even, and otherwise displays "num is odd."

```
System.out.println((num % 2 == 0) ? "num is even" : "num is odd");
```

Note

The symbols **?** and **:** appear together in a conditional expression. They form a conditional operator. It is called a *ternary operator* because it uses three operands. It is the only ternary operator in Java.

3.6 Formatting Console Output

If you wish to display only two digits after the decimal point in a floating-point value, you may write the code like this:

```
double x = 2.0 / 3;
System.out.println("x is " + (int)(x * 100) / 100.0);
```

```
x is 0.66
```

However, a better way to accomplish this task is to format the output using the `printf` method. The syntax to invoke this method is

printf

```
System.out.printf(format, item1, item2, ..., itemk)
```

where `format` is a string that may consist of substrings and format specifiers.

A format specifier specifies how an item should be displayed. An item may be a numeric value, a character, a Boolean value, or a string. A simple specifier consists of a percent sign (%) and a conversion code. Table 3.8 lists some frequently used simple specifiers:

specifier

TABLE 3.8 Frequently Used Specifiers

Specifier	Output	Example
%b	a Boolean value	true or false
%c	a character	'a'
%d	a decimal integer	200
%f	a floating-point number	45.460000
%e	a number in standard scientific notation	4.556000e+01
%s	a string	"Java is cool"

Here is an example:

Items must match the specifiers in order, in number, and in exact type. For example, the specifier for `count` is `%d` and for `amount` is `%f`. By default, a floating-point value is displayed with six digits after the decimal point. You can specify the width and precision in a specifier, as shown in the examples in Table 3.9.

The code presented in the beginning of this section for displaying only two digits after the decimal point in a floating-point value can be revised using the `printf` method as follows:

TABLE 3.9 Examples of Specifying Width and Precision

Example	Output
`%5c`	Output the character and add four spaces before the character item.
`%6b`	Output the Boolean value and add one space before the false value and two spaces before the true value.
`%5d`	Output the integer item with width at least 5. If the number of digits in the item is < 5, add spaces before the number. If the number of digits in the item is > 5, the width is automatically increased.
`%10.2f`	Output the floating-point item with width at least 10 including a decimal point and two digits after the point. Thus there are 7 digits allocated before the decimal point. If the number of digits before the decimal point in the item is < 7, add spaces before the number. If the number of digits before the decimal point in the item is > 7, the width is automatically increased.
`%10.2e`	Output the floating-point item with width at least 10 including a decimal point, two digits after the point and the exponent part. If the displayed number in scientific notation has width less than 10, add spaces before the number.
`%12s`	Output the string with width at least 12 characters. If the string item has less than 12 characters, add spaces before the string. If the string item has more than 12 characters, the width is automatically increased.

left justify

By default, the output is right justified. You can put the minus sign (–) in the specifier to specify that the item is left justified in the output within the specified field. For example, the following statements

```
System.out.printf("%8d%8s%8.1f\n", 1234, "Java", 5.6);
System.out.printf("%-8d%-8s%-8.1f \n", 1234, "Java", 5.6);
```

display

8 characters		8 characters		8 characters	
1 2 3 4		J a v a		5 . 6	
1 2 3 4		J a v a		5 . 6	

Caution
The items must match the specifiers in exact type. The item for the specifier `%f` or `%e` must be a floating-point type value such as 40.0, not 40. Thus an `int` variable cannot match `%f` or `%e`.

Tip
The `%` sign denotes a specifier. To output a literal `%` in the format string, use `%%`.

3.7 Operator Precedence and Associativity

Operator precedence and associativity determine the order in which operators are evaluated. Suppose that you have this expression:

```
3 + 4 * 4 > 5 * (4 + 3) - 1
```

What is its value? What is the execution order of the operators?

Arithmetically, the expression in the parentheses is evaluated first. (Parentheses can be nested, in which case the expression in the inner parentheses is executed first.) When evaluating an expression without parentheses, the operators are applied according to the precedence rule and the associativity rule.

The precedence rule defines precedence for operators, as shown in Table 3.10, which contains the operators you have learned so far. Operators are listed in decreasing order of precedence from top to bottom. Operators with the same precedence appear in the same group. (See Appendix C, "Operator Precedence Chart," for a complete list of Java operators and their precedence.)

precedence

TABLE 3.10 Operator Precedence Chart

Precedence	Operator
	var++ and var– (Postfix)
	+, – (Unary plus and minus), ++var and --var (Prefix)
	(type) (Casting)
	! (Not)
	*, /, % (Multiplication, division, and remainder)
	+, – (Binary addition and subtraction)
	<, <=, >, >= (Comparison)
	==, != (Equality)
	∧ (Exclusive OR)
	&& (AND)
	|| (OR)
	=, +=, –=, *=, /=, %= (Assignment operator)

If operators with the same precedence are next to each other, their *associativity* determines the order of evaluation. All binary operators except assignment operators are *left associative*. For example, since + and – are of the same precedence and are left associative, the expression

associativity

$$a - b + c - d \quad \underline{\quad equivalent \quad} \quad ((a - b) + c) - d$$

Assignment operators are *right associative*. Therefore, the expression

$$a = b += c = 5 \quad \underline{\quad equivalent \quad} \quad a = (b += (c = 5))$$

Suppose a, b, and c are 1 before the assignment; after the whole expression is evaluated, a becomes 6, b becomes 6, and c becomes 5. Note that left associativity for the assignment operator would not make sense.

Note

Java has its own way to evaluate an expression internally. The result of a Java evaluation is the same as its corresponding arithmetic evaluation. Interested readers may refer to Supplement IV.M for more discussions on how an expression is evaluated in Java *behind the scenes*.

behind scenes

3.8 (GUI) Confirmation Dialogs

You have used `showMessageDialog` to display a message dialog box and `showInputDialog` to display an input dialog box. Occasionally it is useful to answer a question with a confirmation dialog box. A confirmation dialog can be created using the following statement:

```
int option =
    JOptionPane.showConfirmDialog
        (null, "Continue");
```

When a button is clicked, the method returns an option value. The value is `JOptionPane.YES_OPTION` (0) for the *Yes* button, `JOptionPane.NO_OPTION` (1) for the *No* button, and `JOptionPane.CANCEL_OPTION` (2) for the *Cancel* button.

You may rewrite the guess-birth-date program in Listing 3.8 using confirmation dialog boxes, as shown in Listing 3.9. Figure 3.6 shows a sample run of the program for the date 19.

LISTING 3.9 GuessBirthDateUsingConfirmationDialog.java

import class

set1

set2

set3

set4

set5

```
 1  import javax.swing.JOptionPane;
 2
 3  public class GuessBirthDateUsingConfirmationDialog {
 4    public static void main(String[] args) {
 5      String set1 =
 6        "  1  3  5  7\n" +
 7        "  9 11 13 15\n" +
 8        "17 19 21 23\n" +
 9        "25 27 29 31";
10
11      String set2 =
12        "  2  3  6  7\n" +
13        "10 11 14 15\n" +
14        "18 19 22 23\n" +
15        "26 27 30 31";
16
17      String set3 =
18        "  4  5  6  7\n" +
19        "12 13 14 15\n" +
20        "20 21 22 23\n" +
21        "28 29 30 31";
22
23      String set4 =
24        "  8  9 10 11\n" +
25        "12 13 14 15\n" +
26        "24 25 26 27\n" +
27        "28 29 30 31";
28
29      String set5 =
30        "16 17 18 19\n" +
31        "20 21 22 23\n" +
32        "24 25 26 27\n" +
33        "28 29 30 31";
34
```

```
35      int date = 0;
36
37      // Prompt the user to answer questions
38      int answer = JOptionPane.showConfirmDialog(null,                    confirmation dialog
39        "Is your birthdate in these numbers?\n" + set1);
40
41      if (answer == JOptionPane.YES_OPTION)                               in set1?
42        date += 1;
43
44      answer = JOptionPane.showConfirmDialog(null,
45        "Is your birthdate in these numbers?\n" + set2);
46
47      if (answer == JOptionPane.YES_OPTION)                               in set2?
48        date += 2;
49
50      answer = JOptionPane.showConfirmDialog(null,
51        "Is your birthdate in these numbers?\n" + set3);
52
53      if (answer == JOptionPane.YES_OPTION)                               in set3?
54        date += 4;
55
56      answer = JOptionPane.showConfirmDialog(null,
57        "Is your birthdate in these numbers?\n" + set4);
58
59      if (answer == JOptionPane.YES_OPTION)                               in set4?
60        date += 8;
61
62      answer = JOptionPane.showConfirmDialog(null,
63        "Is your birthdate in these numbers?\n" + set5);
64
65      if (answer == JOptionPane.YES_OPTION)                               in set5?
66        date += 16;
67
68      JOptionPane.showMessageDialog(null, "Your birthdate is " +
69        date + "!");
70    }
71 }
```

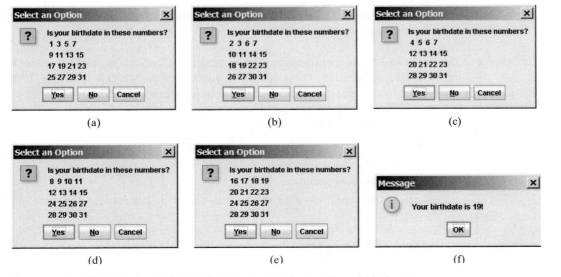

FIGURE 3.6 Click Yes in (a), No in (b), Yes in (c), Yes in (d), and No in (e).

The program displays confirmation boxes to prompt the user to answer whether a number is in Set1 (line 38), Set2 (line 44), Set3 (line 50), Set4 (line 56), and Set5 (line 62). If the answer is Yes, the first number in the set is added to `date` (lines 42, 48, 54, 60, and 66).

KEY TERMS

boolean expression 68	fall-through behavior 87
boolean value 68	operator associativity 91
`boolean` type 68	operator precedence 91
`break` statement 86	selection statement 72
conditional operator 88	short-circuit evaluation 71

CHAPTER SUMMARY

- The `boolean` type represents a `true` or `false` value.

- The relational operators (`<`, `<=`, `==`, `!=`, `>`, `>=`) work with numbers and characters, and yield a Boolean value.

- The Boolean operators `&&`, `||`, `!`, and `^` operate with Boolean values and variables.

- When evaluating `p1 && p2`, Java first evaluates `p1` and then evaluates `p2` if `p1` is `true`; if `p1` is `false`, it does not evaluate `p2`. When evaluating `p1 || p2`, Java first evaluates `p1` and then evaluates `p2` if `p1` is `false`; if `p1` is `true`, it does not evaluate `p2`. Therefore, `&&` is referred to as the *conditional* or *short-circuit AND* operator, and `||` is referred to as the *conditional* or *short-circuit OR* operator.

- Selection statements are used for programming with alternative courses. There are several types of selection statements: `if` statements, `if . . . else` statements, nested `if` statements, `switch` statements, and conditional expressions.

- The various `if` statements all make control decisions based on a Boolean expression. Based on the `true` or `false` evaluation of the expression, these statements take one of two possible courses.

- The `switch` statement makes control decisions based on a switch expression of type `char`, `byte`, `short`, or `int`.

- The keyword `break` is optional in a switch statement, but it is normally used at the end of each case in order to terminate the remainder of the `switch` statement. If the `break` statement is not present, the next `case` statement will be executed.

REVIEW QUESTIONS

Section 3.2 `boolean` Data Type and Operations

3.1   List six comparison operators.

3.2   Assuming that `x` is `1`, show the result of the following Boolean expressions.

```
(true) && (3 > 4)
!(x > 0) && (x > 0)
(x > 0) || (x < 0)
```

```
(x != 0) || (x == 0)
(x >= 0) || (x < 0)
(x != 1) == !(x == 1)
```

3.3 Write a Boolean expression that evaluates to `true` if a number stored in variable `num` is between `1` and `100`.

3.4 Write a Boolean expression that evaluates to `true` if a number stored in variable `num` is between `1` and `100` or the number is negative.

3.5 Assume that `x` and `y` are `int` type. Which of the following are legal Java expressions?

```
x > y > 0
x = y && y
x /= y
x or y
x and y
(x != 0) || (x = 0)
```

3.6 Can the following conversions involving casting be allowed? If so, find the converted result.

```
boolean b = true;
i = (int)b;

int i = 1;
boolean b = (boolean)i;
```

3.7 Suppose that `x` is `1`. What is `x` after the evaluation of the following expression?

```
(x >= 1) && (x++ > 1)
```

3.8 Suppose that `x` is `1`. What is `x` after the evaluation of the following expression?

```
(x > 1) && (x++ > 1)
```

3.9 Show the output of the following program:

```
public class Test {
  public static void main(String[] args) {
    char x = 'a';
    char y = 'c';

    System.out.println(++y);
    System.out.println(y++);
    System.out.println(x > y);
    System.out.println(x - y);
  }
}
```

3.10 Write a Boolean expression that evaluates true if `age` is greater than `13` and less than `18`.

3.11 Write a Boolean expression that evaluates true if `weight` is greater than `50` or height is greater than `160`.

3.12 Write a Boolean expression that evaluates true if `weight` is greater than `50` and height is greater than `160`.

3.13 Write a Boolean expression that evaluates true if either `weight` is greater than `50` or height is greater than `160`, but not both.

Section 3.3 if Statements

3.14 Suppose x = 3 and y = 2; show the output, if any, of the following code. What is the output if x = 3 and y = 4? What is the output if x = 2 and y = 2? Draw a flow chart of the following code:

```
if (x > 2) {
  if (y > 2) {
    z = x + y;
    System.out.println("z is " + z);
  }
}
else
  System.out.println("x is " + x);
```

3.15 Which of the following statements are equivalent? Which ones are correctly indented?

```
if (i > 0) if
(j > 0)
x = 0; else
if (k > 0) y = 0;
else z = 0;
```

```
if (i > 0) {
  if (j > 0)
    x = 0;
  else if (k > 0)
    y = 0;
}
else
  z = 0;
```

```
if (i > 0)
  if (j > 0)
    x = 0;
  else if (k > 0)
    y = 0;
  else
    z = 0;
```

```
if (i > 0)
  if (j > 0)
    x = 0;
  else if (k > 0)
    y = 0;
else
  z = 0;
```

(a)   (b)   (c)   (d)

3.16 Suppose x = 2 and y = 3. Show the output, if any, of the following code. What is the output if x = 3 and y = 2? What is the output if x = 3 and y = 3? (*Hint*: Indent the statement correctly first.)

```
if (x > 2)
  if (y > 2) {
    int z = x + y;
    System.out.println("z is " + z);
  }
else
  System.out.println("x is " + x);
```

3.17 Are the following two statements equivalent?

```
if (income <= 10000)
  tax = income * 0.1;
else if (income <= 20000)
  tax = 1000 +
    (income - 10000) * 0.15;
```

```
if (income <= 10000)
  tax = income * 0.1;
else if (income > 10000 &&
         income <= 20000)
  tax = 1000 +
    (income - 10000) * 0.15;
```

3.18 Which of the following is a possible output from invoking `Math.random()`?

323.4, 0.5, 34, 1.0, 0.0, 0.234

3.19 How do you generate a random integer i such that $0 \le i < 20$? How do you generate a random integer i such that $10 \le i < 20$? How do you generate a random integer i such that $10 \le i \ge 50$?

3.20 Write an `if` statement that assigns 1 to x if y is greater than 0.

3.21 Write an `if` statement that increases `pay` by 3% if `score` is greater than `90`.

3.22 Write an `if` statement that increases `pay` by 3% if `score` is greater than `90`, otherwise increases `pay` by 1%.

3.23 Rewrite the following statement using a Boolean expression:

```
if (count % 10 == 0)
  newLine = true;
else
  newLine = false;
```

Section 3.4 `switch` Statements

3.24 What data types are required for a `switch` variable? If the keyword `break` is not used after a case is processed, what is the next statement to be executed? Can you convert a `switch` statement to an equivalent `if` statement, or vice versa? What are the advantages of using a `switch` statement?

3.25 What is `y` after the following `switch` statement is executed?

```
x = 3; y = 3;
switch (x + 3) {
  case 6:   y = 1;
  default: y += 1;
}
```

3.26 Use a `switch` statement to rewrite the following `if` statement and draw the flow chart for the `switch` statement:

```
if (a == 1)
  x += 5;
else if (a == 2)
  x += 10;
else if (a == 3)
  x += 16;
else if (a == 4)
  x += 34;
```

3.27 Write a `switch` statement that assigns a `String` variable `dayName` with Sunday, Monday, Tuesday, Wednesday, Thursday, Friday, Saturday, if `day` is 0, 1, 2, 3, 4, 5, 6, accordingly.

Section 3.5 Conditional Expressions

3.28 Rewrite the following `if` statement using the conditional operator:

```
if (count % 10 == 0)
  System.out.print(count + "\n");
else
  System.out.print(count + " ");
```

3.29 Rewrite the following statement using a conditional expression:

```
if (temperature > 90)
  pay = pay * 1.5;
else
  pay = pay * 1.1;
```

Section 3.6 Formatting Console Output

3.30 What are the specifiers for outputting a Boolean value, a character, a decimal integer, a floating-point number, and a string?

3.31 What is wrong in the following statements?

```
(a) System.out.printf("%5d %d", 1, 2, 3);
(b) System.out.printf("%5d %f", 1);
(c) System.out.printf("%5d %f", 1, 2);
```

3.32 Show the output of the following statements.

```
(a) System.out.printf("amount is %f %e\n", 32.32, 32.32);
(b) System.out.printf("amount is %5.4f %5.4e\n", 32.32, 32.32);
(c) System.out.printf("%6b\n", (1 > 2));
(d) System.out.printf("%6s\n", "Java");
(e) System.out.printf("%-6b%s\n", (1 > 2), "Java");
(f) System.out.printf("%6b%-s\n", (1 > 2), "Java");
```

3.33 How do you create a formatted string?

Section 3.7 Operator Precedence and Associativity

3.34 List the precedence order of the Boolean operators. Evaluate the following expressions:

```
true || true && false
true && true || false
```

3.35 True or false? All the binary operators except = are left associative.

3.36 Evaluate the following expressions:

```
2 * 2 - 3 > 2 && 4 - 2 > 5
2 * 2 - 3 > 2 || 4 - 2 > 5
```

Section 3.8 (GUI) Confirmation Dialogs

3.37 How do you display a confirmation dialog? What value is returned when invoking `JOptionPane.showConfirmDialog`?

PROGRAMMING EXERCISES

Pedagogical Note

think before coding

For each exercise, students should carefully analyze the problem requirements and design strategies for solving the problem before coding.

Pedagogical Note

document analysis and design

Instructors may ask students to document analysis and design for selected exercises. Students should use their own words to analyze the problem, including the input, output, and what needs to be computed, and describe how to solve the problem using English or pseudocode.

Debugging Tip

Before you ask for help, read and explain the program to yourself, and trace it using several representative inputs by hand or using an IDE debugger. You learn how to program by debugging your own mistakes.

learn from mistakes

Note

Do not use selection statements for Exercises 3.1–3.6.

Section 3.2 `boolean` Data Type and Operations

3.1* (*Validating triangles*) Write a program that reads three edges for a triangle and determines whether the input is valid. The input is valid if the sum of any two edges is greater than the third edge. Here are the sample runs of this program:

```
Enter three edges: 1 2 1  [↵Enter]
Can edges 1, 2, and 1 form a triangle? false
```

```
Enter three edges: 2 2 1  [↵Enter]
Can edges 2, 2, and 1 form a triangle? true
```

3.2 (*Checking whether a number is even*) Write a program that reads an integer and checks whether it is even. Here are the sample runs of this program:

```
Enter an integer: 25  [↵Enter]
Is 25 an even number? false
```

```
Enter an integer: 2000  [↵Enter]
Is 2000 an even number? true
```

3.3* (Using the **&&**, **||** and **∧** operators) Write a program that prompts the user to enter an integer and determines whether it is divisible by **5** and **6**, whether it is divisible by **5** or **6**, and whether it is divisible by **5** or **6**, but not both. Here is a sample run of this program:

```
Enter an integer: 10  [↵Enter]
Is 10 divisible by 5 and 6? false
Is 10 divisible by 5 or 6? true
Is 10 divisible by 5 or 6, but not both? true
```

3.4** (*Game: learning addition*) Write a program that generates two integers under **100** and prompts the user to enter the addition of these two integers. The program then reports true if the answer is correct, false otherwise. The program is similar to Listing 3.3.

3.5** (*Game: addition for three numbers*) The program in Listing 3.3 generates two integers and prompts the user to enter the addition of these two integers. Revise the program to generate three single-digit integers and prompt the user to enter the addition of these three integers.

3.6* (*Using the input dialog box*) Rewrite Listing 3.2, LeapYear.java, using the input dialog box.

Section 3.3 `if` Statements

3.7 (*Financial application: monetary units*) Modify Listing 2.8, ComputeChange.java, to display the nonzero denominations only, using singular words for single units like **1** dollar and **1** penny, and plural words for more than one unit like **2** dollars and **3** pennies. (Use input **23.67** to test your program.)

3.8* (*Sorting three integers*) Write a program that sorts three integers. The integers are entered from the input dialogs and stored in variables **num1**, **num2**, and **num3**, respectively. The program sorts the numbers so that *num1* ≤ *num2* ≤ *num3*.

Video Note
Sort three integers

3.9 (*Computing the perimeter of a triangle*) Write a program that reads three edges for a triangle and computes the perimeter if the input is valid. Otherwise, display that the input is invalid. The input is valid if the sum of any two edges is greater than the third edge. (Also see Exercise 3.1.)

3.10 (*Financial application: computing taxes*) Listing 3.7 gives the source code to compute taxes for single filers. Complete Listing 3.7 to give the complete source code.

3.11* (*Finding the number of days in a month*) Write a program that prompts the user to enter the month and year, and displays the number of days in the month. For example, if the user entered month 2 and year 2000, the program should display that February 2000 has 29 days. If the user entered month 3 and year 2005, the program should display that March 2005 has 31 days.

3.12 (*Checking a number*) Write a program that prompts the user to enter an integer and checks whether the number is divisible by both 5 and 6, or neither of them, or just one of them. Here are some sample outputs for inputs 10, 30, and 23.

```
10 is divisible by 5 or 6, but not both
30 is divisible by both 5 and 6
23 is not divisible by either 5 or 6
```

3.13* (*Game: addition quiz*) Listing 3.4, SubtractionQuiz.java, randomly generates a subtraction question. Revise the program to randomly generate an addition question with two integers less than 100.

3.14 (*Game: head or tail*) Write a program that lets the user guess the head or tail of a coin. The program randomly generates an integer 0 or 1, which represents the head or tail of a coin. The program prompts the user to enter a guess and reports whether the guess is correct or incorrect.

3.15* (*Game: lottery*) Revise Listing 3.5, Lottery.java, to generate a lottery of a three-digit number. The program prompts the user to enter a three-digit number and determines whether the user wins according to the following rule:

1. If the user input matches the lottery in exact order, the award is $10,000.
2. If the user input matches the lottery, the award is $3,000.
3. If one digit in the user input matches a digit in the lottery, the award is $1,000.

3.16 (*Random character*) Write a program that displays a random uppercase letter.

3.17* (*Game: scissor, rock, paper*) Write a program that plays the popular scissor-rock-paper game. The program randomly generates a number 0, 1, or 2 representing scissor, rock, and paper. The program prompts the user to enter a number 0, 1, or 2 and displays a message indicating whether the user or the computer wins or draws. Note that a scissor can cut a paper, a rock can knock a scissor, and a paper can wrap a rock.

3.18* (*Health application: BMI*) Revise Listing 3.6, ComputeBMI.java, to let the user enter weight, feet, and inches. For example, if a person is 5 feet and 10 inches, you will enter 5 for feet and 10 for inches.

3.19** (*Checking ISBN*) An **ISBN** (International Standard Book Number) consists of 10 digits $d_1d_2d_3d_4d_5d_6d_7d_8d_9d_{10}$. The last digit d_{10} is a checksum, which is calculated from the other nine digits using the following formula:

$$(d_1 \times 1 + d_2 \times 2 + d_3 \times 3 + d_4 \times 4 + d_5 \times 5 +$$

$$d_6 \times 6 + d_7 \times 7 + d_8 \times 8 + d_9 \times 9) \% 11$$

If the checksum is 10, the last digit is denoted X according to the ISBN convention. Write a program that prompts the user to enter the first 9 digits and displays the 10-digit ISBN (including leading zeros). Your program should read the input as an integer.

3.20* (*Science: wind chill temperature*) Exercise 2.17 gives a formula to compute the wind chill temperature. The formula is valid for the temperature in the range between $-58°F$ and above $41°F$ and wind speed greater than or equal to 2. Write a program that prompts the user to enter a temperature and a wind speed. The program displays the wind chill temperature if the input is valid, otherwise, displays a message that indicates whether the temperature and/or wind speed is invalid.

CHAPTER 4

LOOPS

Objectives

- To use `while`, `do-while`, and `for` loop statements to control the repetition of statements (§§4.2–4.4).

- To understand the flow of control in loop statements (§§4.2–4.4).

- To use Boolean expressions to control loop statements (§§4.2–4.4).

- To discover the similarities and differences between three types of loops (§4.5).

- To write nested loops (§4.6).

- To learn the techniques for minimizing numerical errors (§4.7).

- To learn loops from a variety of examples (§4.8).

- To implement program control with `break` and `continue` (§4.9).

- (GUI) To control a loop with a confirmation dialog (§4.10).

4.1 Introduction

Suppose that you need to print a string (e.g., `"Welcome to Java!"`) a hundred times. It would be tedious to have to write the following statement a hundred times:

```
System.out.println("Welcome to Java!");
```

problem
why loop?

So, how do you solve this problem?

Java provides a powerful control structure called a *loop* that controls how many times an operation or a sequence of operations is performed in succession. Using a loop statement, you simply tell the computer to print a string a hundred times without having to code the print statement a hundred times.

Loops are structures that control repeated executions of a block of statements. The concept of looping is fundamental to programming. Java provides three types of loop statements: `while` loops, `do-while` loops, and `for` loops.

4.2 The `while` Loop

The syntax for the `while` loop is as follows:

while loop

```
while (loop-continuation-condition) {
   // Loop body
   Statement(s);
}
```

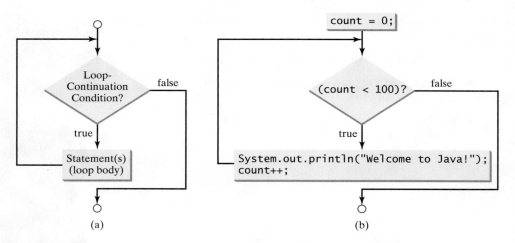

(a)   (b)

FIGURE 4.1   The `while` loop repeatedly executes the statements in the loop body when the `loop-continuation condition` evaluates to `true`.

The `while` loop flow chart is shown in Figure 4.1(a). The part of the loop that contains the statements to be repeated is called the *loop body*. A one-time execution of a loop body is referred to as an *iteration of the loop*. Each loop contains a loop-continuation condition, a Boolean expression that controls the execution of the body. It is evaluated each time to determine if the loop body is executed. If its evaluation is true, the loop body is executed; if its evaluation is false, the entire loop terminates and the program control turns to the statement that follows the `while` loop. For example, the following `while` loop prints `"Welcome to Java!"` a hundred times.

loop body
iteration

```
int count = 0;
while (count < 100) {
```

```
    System.out.println("Welcome to Java!");
    count++;
}
```

The flow chart of the preceding statement is shown in Figure 4.1(b). The variable `count` is initially `0`. The loop checks whether (`count < 100`) is true. If so, it executes the loop body to print the message `"Welcome to Java!"` and increments count by `1`. It repeatedly executes the loop body until (`count < 100`) becomes false. When (`count < 100`) is `false` (i.e., when `count` reaches `100`), the loop terminates and the next statement after the loop statement is executed.

Note

The `loop-continuation-condition` must always appear inside the parentheses. The braces enclosing the loop body can be omitted only if the loop body contains one or no statement.

Caution

Make sure that the `loop-continuation-condition` eventually becomes `false` so that the program will terminate. A common programming error involves *infinite loops*. That is, the program cannot terminate because of a mistake in the `loop-continuation-condition`. For instance, if you forgot to increase `count` (`count++`) in the code, the program would not stop.

infinite loop

4.2.1   Problem: Guessing Numbers

The problem is to guess what a number a computer has in mind. You will write a program that randomly generates an integer between `0` and `100`, inclusive. The program prompts the user to enter a number continuously until the number matches the randomly generated number. For each user input, the program tells the user whether the input is too low or too high, so the user can choose the next input intelligently. Here is a sample run:

```
Guess a magic number between 0 and 100

Enter your guess: 50  ↵Enter
Your guess is too high

Enter your guess: 25  ↵Enter
Your guess is too high

Enter your guess: 12  ↵Enter
Your guess is too high

Enter your guess:  6  ↵Enter
Your guess is too low

Enter your guess:  9  ↵Enter
Your guess is too high

Enter your guess:  7  ↵Enter
Your guess is too low

Enter your guess:  8  ↵Enter
Yes, the number is 8
```

The magic number is between `0` and `100`. To minimize the number of guesses, enter `50` first. If your guess is too high, the magic number is between `0` and `49`. If your guess is too low, the magic number is between `51` and `100`. So, you can eliminate half of the numbers from further consideration after one guess.

intelligent guess

think before coding

code incrementally

Video Note
Guess a number

How do you write this program? Do you immediately begin coding? No. It is important to *think before coding*. Think how you would solve the problem without writing a program. You need first to generate a random number between 0 and 100, inclusively, then to prompt the user to enter a guess, and then to compare the guess with the random number.

It is a good practice to *code incrementally* one step at a time. For programs involving loops, if you don't know how to write a loop right away, you may first write the code for executing the loop one time, and then figure out how to repeatedly execute the code in a loop. For this program, you may create an initial draft, as shown in Listing 4.1:

LISTING 4.1 GuessNumberOneTime.java

generate a number

enter a guess

correct guess?

too high?

too low?

```
1  import java.util.Scanner;
2
3  public class GuessNumberOneTime {
4    public static void main(String[] args) {
5      // Generate a random number to be guessed
6      int number = (int)(Math.random() * 101);
7
8      Scanner input = new Scanner(System.in);
9      System.out.println("Guess a magic number between 0 and 100");
10
11     // Prompt the user to guess the number
12     System.out.print("\nEnter your guess: ");
13     int guess = input.nextInt();
14
15     if (guess == number)
16       System.out.println("Yes, the number is " + number);
17     else if (guess > number)
18       System.out.println("Your guess is too high");
19     else
20       System.out.println("Your guess is too low");
21   }
22 }
```

When you run this program, it executes only once. You need to put the code in lines 11–20 in a loop. The loop ends when `guess == number` is true. The complete code is given in Listing 4.2.

LISTING 4.2 GuessNumber.java

generate a number

enter a guess

```
1  import java.util.Scanner;
2
3  public class GuessNumber {
4    public static void main(String[] args) {
5      // Generate a random number to be guessed
6      int number = (int)(Math.random() * 101);
7
8      Scanner input = new Scanner(System.in);
9      System.out.println("Guess a magic number between 0 and 100");
10
11     int guess = -1;
12     while (guess != number) {
13       // Prompt the user to guess the number
14       System.out.print("\nEnter your guess: ");
15       guess = input.nextInt();
16
17       if (guess == number)
18         System.out.println("Yes, the number is " + number);
```

```
19        else if (guess > number)
20          System.out.println("Your guess is too high");
21        else
22          System.out.println("Your guess is too low");
23      }
24    } // End of loop
25 }
```
too high?

too low?

The program generates the magic number in line 6 and prompts the user to enter a guess continuously in a loop (lines 12–23). For each guess, the program checks whether the guess is correct, too high, or too low (lines 17–22). When the guess is correct, the program exits the loop (line 12). Note that **guess** is initialized to **-1**. Initializing it to a value between **0** and **100** would be wrong, because that could be the number to be guessed.

4.2.2 Problem: An Advanced Math Learning Tool

The Math subtraction learning tool program in Listing 3.4, SubtractionQuiz.java, generates just one question for each run. You can use a loop to generate questions repeatedly. Listing 4.3 gives a program that generates five questions and, after a student answers all five, reports the number of correct answers. The program also displays the time spent on the test and lists all the questions.

LISTING 4.3 SubtractionQuizLoop.java

Video Note
Multiple subtraction quiz

```
 1 import java.util.Scanner;
 2
 3 public class SubtractionQuizLoop {
 4   public static void main(String[] args) {
 5     final int NUMBER_OF_QUESTIONS = 5; // Number of questions
 6     int correctCount = 0; // Count the number of correct answers
 7     int count = 0; // Count the number of questions
 8     long startTime = System.currentTimeMillis();
 9     String output = ""; // output string is initially empty
10     Scanner input = new Scanner(System.in);
11
12     while (count < NUMBER_OF_QUESTIONS) {
13       // 1. Generate two random single-digit integers
14       int number1 = (int)(Math.random() * 10);
15       int number2 = (int)(Math.random() * 10);
16
17       // 2. If number1 < number2, swap number1 with number2
18       if (number1 < number2) {
19         int temp = number1;
20         number1 = number2;
21         number2 = temp;
22       }
23
24       // 3. Prompt the student to answer "What is number1 - number2?"
25       System.out.print(
26         "What is " + number1 + " - " + number2 + "? ");
27       int answer = input.nextInt();
28
29       // 4. Grade the answer and display the result
30       if (number1 - number2 == answer) {
31         System.out.println("You are correct!");
32         correctCount++;
33       }
34       else
```

get start time

loop

display a question

grade an answer

increase correct count

```
35              System.out.println("Your answer is wrong.\n" + number1
36                + " - " + number2 + " should be " + (number1 - number2));
37
increase control variable 38      // Increase the count
39      count++;
40
prepare output 41      output += "\n" + number1 + "-" + number2 + "=" + answer +
42        ((number1 - number2 == answer) ? " correct" : " wrong");
end loop 43    }
44
get end time 45    long endTime = System.currentTimeMillis();
test time 46    long testTime = endTime - startTime;
47
display result 48    System.out.println("Correct count is " + correctCount +
49      "\nTest time is " + testTime / 1000 + " seconds\n" + output);
50  }
51 }
```

```
What is 9 − 2? 7  ↵Enter
You are correct!

What is 3 − 0? 3  ↵Enter
You are correct!

What is 3 − 2? 1  ↵Enter
You are correct!

What is 7 − 4? 4  ↵Enter
Your answer is wrong.
7 − 4 should be 3

What is 7 − 5? 4  ↵Enter
Your answer is wrong.
7 − 5 should be 2

Correct count is 3
Test time is 1021 seconds

9−2=7 correct
3−0=3 correct
3−2=1 correct
7−4=4 wrong
7−5=4 wrong
```

The program uses the control variable `count` to control the execution of the loop. `count` is initially `0` (line 7) and is increased by `1` in each iteration (line 39). A subtraction question is displayed and processed in each iteration. The program obtains the time before the test starts in line 8 and the time after the test ends in line 45, and computes the test time in line 46. The test time is in milliseconds and is converted to seconds in line 49.

4.2.3   Controlling a Loop with a Sentinel Value

sentinel value

Another common technique for controlling a loop is to designate a special value when reading and processing a set of values. This special input value, known as a *sentinel value*, signifies the end of the loop.

Listing 4.4 writes a program that reads and calculates the sum of an unspecified number of integers. The input `0` signifies the end of the input. Do you need to declare a new variable for each input value? No. Just use one variable named `data` (line 12) to store the input value and

use a variable named sum (line 15) to store the total. Whenever a value is read, assign it to
data and, if it is not zero, add it to sum (line 17).

LISTING 4.4 SentinelValue.java

```java
 1 import java.util.Scanner;
 2
 3 public class SentinelValue {
 4   /** Main method */
 5   public static void main(String[] args) {
 6     // Create a Scanner
 7     Scanner input = new Scanner(System.in);
 8
 9     // Read an initial data
10     System.out.print(
11       "Enter an int value (the program exits if the input is 0): ");
12     int data = input.nextInt();
13
14     // Keep reading data until the input is 0
15     int sum = 0;
16     while (data != 0) {
17       sum += data;
18
19       // Read the next data
20       System.out.print(
21         "Enter an int value (the program exits if the input is 0): ");
22       data = input.nextInt();
23     }
24
25     System.out.println("The sum is " + sum);
26   }
27 }
```

input

loop

end of loop

display result

```
Enter an int value (the program exits if the input is 0): 2  ↵Enter
Enter an int value (the program exits if the input is 0): 3  ↵Enter
Enter an int value (the program exits if the input is 0): 4  ↵Enter
Enter an int value (the program exits if the input is 0): 0  ↵Enter
The sum is 9
```

If data is not 0, it is added to sum (line 17) and the next item of input data is read (lines
20–22). If data is 0, the loop body is no longer executed and the while loop terminates. The
input value 0 is the sentinel value for this loop. Note that if the first input read is 0, the loop
body never executes, and the resulting sum is 0.

 Caution

Don't use floating-point values for equality checking in a loop control. Since floating-point values
are approximations for some values, using them could result in imprecise counter values and inaccurate results. This example uses int value for data. If a floating-point type value is used for
data, (data != 0) may be true even though data is exactly 0.
    Here is a good example provided by a reviewer of this book:

```java
// data should be zero
double data = Math.pow(Math.sqrt(2), 2) - 2;

if (data == 0)
  System.out.println("data is zero");
```

```
      else
        System.out.println("data is not zero");
```

numeric error

Like **pow**, **sqrt** is a method in the **Math** class for computing the square root of a number. The variable **data** in the above code should be zero, but it is not, because of rounding-off errors.

4.3 The **do-while** Loop

The **do-while** loop is a variation of the **while** loop. Its syntax is given below:

do-while loop

```
do {
  // Loop body;
  Statement(s);
} while (loop-continuation-condition);
```

Its execution flow chart is shown in Figure 4.2.

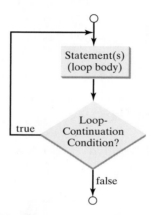

FIGURE 4.2 The **do-while** loop executes the loop body first, then checks the **loop-continuation-condition** to determine whether to continue or terminate the loop.

The loop body is executed first. Then the **loop-continuation-condition** is evaluated. If the evaluation is true, the loop body is executed again; if it is false, the **do-while** loop terminates. The difference between a **while** loop and a **do-while** loop is the order in which the **loop-continuation-condition** is evaluated and the loop body executed. The **while** loop and the **do-while** loop have equal expressive power. Sometimes one is a more convenient choice than the other. For example, you can rewrite the **while** loop in Listing 4.4 using a **do-while** loop, as shown in Listing 4.5:

LISTING 4.5 TestDoWhile.java

```
 1 import java.util.Scanner;
 2
 3 public class TestDoWhile {
 4   /** Main method */
 5   public static void main(String[] args) {
 6     int data;
 7     int sum = 0;
 8
 9     // Create a Scanner
10     Scanner input = new Scanner(System.in);
11
```

```
12      // Keep reading data until the input is 0
13      do {
14        // Read the next data
15        System.out.print(                                              loop
16          "Enter an int value (the program exits if the input is 0): ");
17        data = input.nextInt();
18
19        sum += data;
20      } while (data != 0);
21
22      System.out.println("The sum is " + sum);                          end loop
23    }
24 }
```

```
Enter an int value (the program exits if the input is 0): 3  ⏎Enter
Enter an int value (the program exits if the input is 0): 5  ⏎Enter
Enter an int value (the program exits if the input is 0): 6  ⏎Enter
Enter an int value (the program exits if the input is 0): 0  ⏎Enter
The sum is 14
```

Tip

Use the **do-while** loop if you have statements inside the loop that must be executed *at least once*, as in the case of the **do-while** loop in the preceding **TestDoWhile** program. These statements must appear before the loop as well as inside the loop if you use a **while** loop.

4.4 The **for** Loop

Often you write a loop in the following common form:

```
i = initialValue;  // Initialize loop control variable
while (i < endValue) {
  // Loop body
  ...
  i++; // Adjust loop control variable
}
```

A **for** loop can be used to simplify the proceding loop:

```
for (i = initialValue; i < endValue; i++) {
  // Loop body
  ...
}
```

In general, the syntax of a **for** loop is as shown below:

```
for (initial-action; loop-continuation-condition;                       for loop
     action-after-each-iteration) {
  // Loop body;
  Statement(s);
}
```

The flow chart of the **for** loop is shown in Figure 4.3(a).

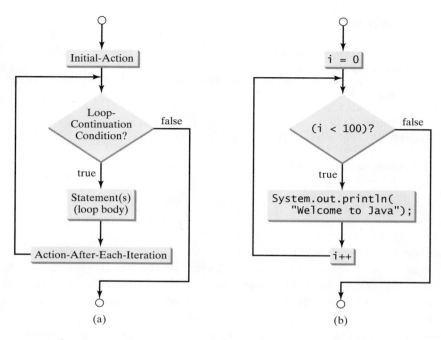

(a)   (b)

FIGURE 4.3   A `for` loop performs an initial action once, then repeatedly executes the statements in the loop body, and performs an action after an iteration when the `loop-continuation-condition` evaluates to `true`.

The `for` loop statement starts with the keyword `for`, followed by a pair of parentheses enclosing the control structure of the loop. This structure consists of `initial-action`, `loop-continuation-condition`, and `action-after-each-iteration`. The control structure is followed by the loop body enclosed inside braces. The `initial-action`, `loop-continuation-condition`, and `action-after-each-iteration` are separated by semicolons.

control variable

A `for` loop generally uses a variable to control how many times the loop body is executed and when the loop terminates. This variable is referred to as a *control variable*. The `initial-action` often initializes a control variable, the `action-after-each-iteration` usually increments or decrements the control variable, and the `loop-continuation-condition` tests whether the control variable has reached a termination value. For example, the following `for` loop prints `Welcome to Java!` a hundred times:

```java
int i;
for (i = 0; i < 100; i++) {
  System.out.println("Welcome to Java!");
}
```

The flow chart of the statement is shown in Figure 4.3(b). The `for` loop initializes `i` to `0`, then repeatedly executes the `println` statement and evaluates `i++` while `i` is less than `100`.

initial-action

The `initial-action`, i = 0, initializes the control variable, `i`. The `loop-continuation-condition`, i < 100, is a Boolean expression. The expression is evaluated at the beginning of each iteration. If this condition is true, execute the loop body. If it is false, the loop terminates and the program control turns to the line following the loop.

action-after-each-iteration

The `action-after-each-iteration`, i++, is a statement that adjusts the control variable. This statement is executed after each iteration. It increments the control variable. Eventually, the value of the control variable should force the `loop-continuation-condition` to become false. Otherwise the loop is infinite.

The loop control variable can be declared and initialized in the for loop. Here is an example:

```java
for (int i = 0; i < 100; i++) {
  System.out.println("Welcome to Java!");
}
```

If there is only one statement in the loop body, as in this example, the braces can be omitted.

omitting braces

Tip
The control variable must be declared inside the control structure of the loop or before the loop. If the loop control variable is used only in the loop, and not elsewhere, it is good programming practice to declare it in the `initial-action` of the for loop. If the variable is declared inside the loop control structure, it cannot be referenced outside the loop. In the preceding code, for example, you cannot reference `i` outside the for loop, because it is declared inside the for loop.

declare control variable

Note
The `initial-action` in a for loop can be a list of zero or more comma-separated variable declaration statements or assignment expressions. For example,

for loop variations

```java
for (int i = 0, j = 0; (i + j < 10); i++, j++) {
  // Do something
}
```

The `action-after-each-iteration` in a for loop can be a list of zero or more comma-separated statements. For example,

```java
for (int i = 1; i < 100; System.out.println(i), i++);
```

This example is correct, but it is not a good example, because it makes the code difficult to read. Normally, you declare and initialize a control variable as an initial action, and increment or decrement the control variable as an action after each iteration.

Note
If the `loop-continuation-condition` in a for loop is omitted, it is implicitly true. Thus the statement given below in (a), which is an infinite loop, is correct. Nevertheless, it is better to use the equivalent loop in (c) to avoid confusion:

```java
for ( ; ; ) {
  // Do something
}
```
(a)

Equivalent

```java
for ( ; true; ) {
  // Do something
}
```
(b)

Equivalent

This is better

```java
while (true) {
  // Do something
}
```
(c)

4.5 Which Loop to Use?

The `while` loop and `for` loop are called *pre-test loops* because the continuation condition is checked before the loop body is executed. The `do-while` loop is called a *post-test loop* because the condition is checked after the loop body is executed. The three forms of loop statements, `while`, `do-while`, and `for`, are expressively equivalent; that is, you can write a loop in any of these three forms. For example, a `while` loop in (a) in the following figure can always be converted into the `for` loop in (b):

pre-test loop
post-test loop

```
while (loop-continuation-condition) {
    // Loop body
}
```
(a)

Equivalent

```
for ( ; loop-continuation-condition; ) {
    // Loop body
}
```
(b)

A **for** loop in (a) in the next figure can generally be converted into the **while** loop in (b) except in certain special cases (see Review Question 4.13 for such a case):

```
for (initial-action;
     loop-continuation-condition;
     action-after-each-iteration) {
    // Loop body;
}
```
(a)

Equivalent

```
initial-action;
while (loop-continuation-condition) {
    // Loop body;
    action-after-each-iteration;
}
```
(b)

Use the loop statement that is most intuitive and comfortable for you. In general, a **for** loop may be used if the number of repetitions is known, as, for example, when you need to print a message a hundred times. A **while** loop may be used if the number of repetitions is not known, as in the case of reading the numbers until the input is 0. A **do-while** loop can be used to replace a **while** loop if the loop body has to be executed before the continuation condition is tested.

Caution

Adding a semicolon at the end of the **for** clause before the loop body is a common mistake, as shown below in (a). In (a), the semicolon signifies the end of the loop prematurely. The loop body is actually empty, as shown in (b). (a) and (b) are equivalent.

Error

```
for (int i = 0; i < 10; i++);
{
    System.out.println("i is " + i);
}
```
(a)

Empty Body

```
for (int i = 0; i < 10; i++)  { };
{
    System.out.println("i is " + i);
}
```
(b)

Similarly, the loop in (c) is also wrong. (c) is equivalent to (d).

Error

```
int i = 0;
while (i < 10);
{
    System.out.println("i is " + i);
    i++;
}
```
(c)

Empty Body

```
int i = 0;
while (i < 10) { };
{
    System.out.println("i is " + i);
    i++;
}
```
(d)

These errors often occur when you use the next-line block style. Using the end-of-line block style can avoid errors of this type.

In the case of the **do-while** loop, the semicolon is needed to end the loop.

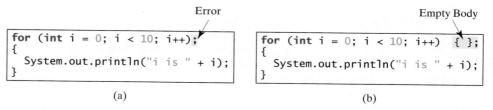

```
int i = 0;
do {
    System.out.println("i is " + i);
    i++;
} while (i < 10);
```
Correct

4.6 Nested Loops

Nested loops consist of an outer loop and one or more inner loops. Each time the outer loop is repeated, the inner loops are reentered, and started anew.

Listing 4.6 presents a program that uses nested **for** loops to print a multiplication table.

LISTING 4.6 `MultiplicationTable.java`

```
 1 public class MultiplicationTable {
 2    /** Main method */
 3    public static void main(String[] args) {
 4       // Display the table heading
 5       System.out.println("            Multiplication Table");          table title
 6
 7       // Display the number title
 8       System.out.print("    ");
 9       for (int j = 1; j <= 9; j++)
10          System.out.print("    " + j);
11
12       System.out.println("\n--------------------------------------");
13       String output = "";
14
15       // Print table body
16       for (int i = 1; i <= 9; i++) {                                   table body
17          output += i + " | ";
18          for (int j = 1; j <= 9; j++) {                               nested loop
19             // Display the product and align properly
20             if (i * j < 10)
21                output += "   " + i * j;
22             else
23                output += "  " + i * j;
24          }
25          output += "\n";
26       }
27
28       // Display result
29       System.out.println(output);
30    }
31 }
```

```
              Multiplication Table
         1   2   3   4   5   6   7   8   9

     -------------------------------------------
   1 |   1   2   3   4   5   6   7   8   9
   2 |   2   4   6   8  10  12  14  16  18
   3 |   3   6   9  12  15  18  21  24  27
   4 |   4   8  12  16  20  24  28  32  36
   5 |   5  10  15  20  25  30  35  40  45
   6 |   6  12  18  24  30  36  42  48  54
   7 |   7  14  21  28  35  42  49  56  63
   8 |   8  16  24  32  40  48  56  64  72
   9 |   9  18  27  36  45  54  63  72  81
```

The program displays a title (line 5) on the first line in the output. The first **for** loop (lines 9-10) displays the numbers 1 through 9 on the second line. A dash (-) line is displayed on the third line (line 12).

The next loop (lines 16–26) is a nested **for** loop with the control variable i in the outer loop and j in the inner loop. For each i, the product i * j is displayed on a line in the inner loop, with **j** being **1, 2, 3, ..., 9**. The **if** statement in the inner loop (lines 20–23) is used so that the product will be aligned properly. If the product is a single digit, it is displayed with an extra space before it.

Video Note
Minimize numeric errors

4.7 Minimizing Numeric Errors

Numeric errors involving floating-point numbers are inevitable. This section discusses how to minimize such errors through an example.

Listing 4.7 presents an example summing a series that starts with **0.01** and ends with **1.0**. The numbers in the series will increment by **0.01**, as follows: **0.01 + 0.02 + 0.03** and so on.

LISTING 4.7 TestSum.java

```
 1 public class TestSum {
 2   public static void main(String[] args) {
 3     // Initialize sum
 4     float sum = 0;
 5
 6     // Add 0.01, 0.02, ..., 0.99, 1 to sum
 7     for (float i = 0.01f; i <= 1.0f; i = i + 0.01f)
 8       sum += i;
 9
10     // Display result
11     System.out.println("The sum is " + sum);
12   }
13 }
```

loop

```
The sum is 50.499985
```

The **for** loop (lines 7-8) repeatedly adds the control variable **i** to **sum**. This variable, which begins with **0.01**, is incremented by **0.01** after each iteration. The loop terminates when **i** exceeds **1.0**.

The **for** loop initial action can be any statement, but it is often used to initialize a control variable. From this example, you can see that a control variable can be a **float** type. In fact, it can be any data type.

The exact **sum** should be **50.50**, but the answer is **50.499985**. The result is imprecise because computers use a fixed number of bits to represent floating-point numbers, and thus cannot represent some floating-point numbers exactly. If you change **float** in the program to **double**, as follows, you should see a slight improvement in precision, because a **double** variable takes 64 bits, whereas a **float** variable takes 32 bits.

double precision

```
// Initialize sum
double sum = 0;

// Add 0.01, 0.02, ..., 0.99, 1 to sum
for (double i = 0.01; i <= 1.0; i = i + 0.01)
  sum += i;
```

However, you will be stunned to see that the result is actually **49.50000000000003**. What went wrong? If you print out **i** for each iteration in the loop, you will see that the last **i** is slightly larger than **1** (not exactly **1**). This causes the last **i** not to be added into **sum**. The fundamental problem is that the floating-point numbers are represented by approximation. To fix the problem, use an integer count to ensure that all the numbers are added to **sum**. Here is the new loop:

numeric error

```java
double currentValue = 0.01;

for (int count = 0; count < 100; count++) {
  sum += currentValue;
  currentValue += 0.01;
}
```

After this loop, sum is 50.50000000000003. This loop adds the numbers from small to big. What happens if you add numbers from big to small (i.e., 1.0, 0.99, 0.98, ..., 0.02, 0.01 in this order) as follows:

```java
double currentValue = 1.0;

for (int count = 0; count < 100; count++) {
  sum += currentValue;
  currentValue -= 0.01;
}
```

After this loop, sum is 50.49999999999995. Adding from big to small is less accurate than adding from small to big. This phenomenon is an artifact of the finite-precision arithmetic. Adding a very small number to a very big number can have no effect if the true result requires more precision than the variable can store. For example, the inaccurate result of 100000000.0 + 0.000000001 is 100000000.0. To obtain more accurate results, carefully select the order of computation. Adding the smaller numbers before the big numbers is one way to minimize error.

avoiding numeric error

4.8 Case Studies

Loop are fundamental in programming. The ability to write loops is essential in learning Java programming. *If you can write programs using loops, you know how to program!* For this reason, this section presents three additional examples of solving problems using loops.

4.8.1 Problem: Finding the Greatest Common Divisor

The greatest common divisor of two integers 4 and 2 is 2. The greatest common divisor of two integers 16 and 24 is 8. How do you find the greatest common divisor? Let the two input integers be n1 and n2. You know that number 1 is a common divisor, but it may not be the greatest common divisor. So you can check whether k (for k = 2, 3, 4, and so on) is a common divisor for n1 and n2, until k is greater than n1 or n2. Store the common divisor in a variable named gcd. Initially, gcd is 1. Whenever a new common divisor is found, it becomes the new gcd. When you have checked all the possible common divisors from 2 up to n1 or n2, the value in variable gcd is the greatest common divisor. The idea can be translated into the following loop:

GCD

```java
int gcd = 1;
int k = 2;

while (k <= n1 && k <= n2) {
  if (n1 % k == 0 && n2 % k == 0)
    gcd = k;
  k++;
}

// After the loop, gcd is the greatest common divisor for n1 and n2
```

Listing 4.8 presents the program that prompts the user to enter two positive integers and finds their greatest common divisor.

LISTING 4.8 GreatestCommonDivisor.java

```java
 1 import java.util.Scanner;
 2
 3 public class GreatestCommonDivisor {
 4   /** Main method */
 5   public static void main(String[] args) {
 6     // Create a Scanner
 7     Scanner input = new Scanner(System.in);
 8
 9     // Prompt the user to enter two integers
10     System.out.print("Enter first integer: ");
11     int n1 = input.nextInt();
12     System.out.print("Enter second integer: ");
13     int n2 = input.nextInt();
14
15     int gcd = 1;
16     int k = 2;
17     while (k <= n1 && k <= n2) {
18       if (n1 % k == 0 && n2 % k == 0)
19         gcd = k;
20       k++;
21     }
22
23     System.out.println("The greatest common divisor for " + n1 +
24       " and " + n2 + " is " + gcd);
25   }
26 }
```

input *(line 11)*

input *(line 13)*

gcd *(line 15)*

check divisor *(line 18)*

output *(line 23)*

```
Enter first integer: 125  ↵Enter
Enter second integer: 2525  ↵Enter
The greatest common divisor for 125 and 2525 is 25
```

think before you type

How did you write this program? Did you immediately begin to write the code? No. It is important to *think before you type*. Thinking enables you to generate a logical solution for the problem without concern about how to write the code. Once you have a logical solution, type the code to translate the solution into a Java program. The translation is not unique. For example, you could use a **for** loop to rewrite the code as follows:

```java
for (int k = 2; k <= n1 && k <= n2; k++) {
  if (n1 % k == 0 && n2 % k == 0)
    gcd = k;
}
```

multiple solutions

A problem often has multiple solutions. The GCD problem can be solved in many ways. Exercise 4.15 suggests another solution. A more efficient solution is to use the classic Euclidean algorithm. See http://www.cut-the-knot.org/blue/Euclid.shtml for more information.

erroneous solutions

You might think that a divisor for a number **n1** cannot be greater than **n1 / 2**. So you would attempt to improve the program using the following loop:

```java
for (int k = 2; k <= n1 / 2 && k <= n2 / 2; k++) {
  if (n1 % k == 0 && n2 % k == 0)
    gcd = k;
}
```

This revision is wrong. Can you find the reason? See Review Question 4.10 for the answer.

4.8.2 Problem: Finding the Sales Amount

You have just started a sales job in a department store. Your pay consists of a base salary and a commission. The base salary is $5,000. The scheme shown below is used to determine the commission rate.

Sales Amount	Commission Rate
$0.01–$5,000	8 percent
$5,000.01–$10,000	10 percent
$10,000.01 and above	12 percent

Your goal is to earn $30,000 a year. This section writes a program that finds the minimum amount of sales you have to generate in order to make $30,000.

Since your base salary is $5,000, you have to make $25,000 in commissions to earn $30,000 a year. What is the sales amount for a $25,000 commission? If you know the sales amount, the commission can be computed as follows:

```
if (salesAmount >= 10000.01)
  commission =
    5000 * 0.08 + 5000 * 0.1 + (salesAmount - 10000) * 0.12;
else if (salesAmount >= 5000.01)
  commission = 5000 * 0.08 + (salesAmount - 5000) * 0.10;
else
  commission = salesAmount * 0.08;
```

This suggests that you can try to find the salesAmount to match a given commission through incremental approximation. For salesAmount of $0.01 (1 cent), find commission. If commission is less than $25,000, increment salesAmount by 0.01 and find commission again. If commission is still less than $25,000, repeat the process until it is greater than or equal to $25,000. This is a tedious job for humans, but it is exactly what a computer is good for. You can write a loop and let a computer execute it painlessly. The idea can be translated into the following loop:

```
Set COMMISSION_SOUGHT as a constant;
Set an initial salesAmount;

do {
  Increase salesAmount by 1 cent;
  Compute the commission from the current salesAmount;
} while (commission < COMMISSION_SOUGHT);
```

The complete program is given in Listing 4.9.

LISTING 4.9 FindSalesAmount.java

```
1 public class FindSalesAmount {
2   /** Main method */
3   public static void main(String[] args) {
4     // The commission sought
5     final double COMMISSION_SOUGHT = 25000;          constants
6     final double INITIAL_SALES_AMOUNT = 0.01;
7     double commission = 0;
8     double salesAmount = INITIAL_SALES_AMOUNT;
9
10    do {                                             loop
```

```
11        // Increase salesAmount by 1 cent
12        salesAmount += 0.01;
13
14        // Compute the commission from the current salesAmount;
15        if (salesAmount >= 10000.01)
16          commission =
17            5000 * 0.08 + 5000 * 0.1 + (salesAmount - 10000) * 0.12;
18        else if (salesAmount >= 5000.01)
19          commission = 5000 * 0.08 + (salesAmount - 5000) * 0.10;
20        else
21          commission = salesAmount * 0.08;
22      } while (commission < COMMISSION_SOUGHT);
23
24      // Display the sales amount
25      System.out.println(
26        "The sales amount $" + (int)(salesAmount * 100) / 100.0 +
27        "\nis needed to make a commission of $" + COMMISSION_SOUGHT);
28    }
29 }
```

compute commission (line 15)

end loop (line 22)

output (line 25)

```
The sales amount $210833.34
is needed to make a commission of $25000.0
```

The **do-while** loop (lines 10–22) is used to repeatedly compute **commission** for an incremental **salesAmount**. The loop terminates when **commission** is greater than or equal to a constant **COMMISSION_SOUGHT**.

In Exercise 4.17, you will rewrite this program to let the user enter **COMMISSION_SOUGHT** dynamically from an input dialog.

You can improve the performance of this program by estimating a higher **INITIAL_SALES_AMOUNT** (e.g., **25000**).

What is wrong if **salesAmount** is incremented after the commission is computed, as follows?

```
do {
  // Compute the commission from the current salesAmount;
  if (salesAmount >= 10000.01)
    commission =
      5000 * 0.08 + 5000 * 0.1 + (salesAmount - 10000) * 0.12;
  else if (salesAmount >= 5000.01)
    commission = 5000 * 0.08 + (salesAmount - 5000) * 0.10;
  else
    commission = salesAmount * 0.08;

  // Increase salesAmount by 1 cent
  salesAmount += 0.01;
} while (commission < COMMISSION_SOUGHT);
```

off-by-one error

The change is erroneous because, when the loop ends, **salesAmount** is **1** cent more than is needed for the commission. This is a common error in loops, known as the *off-by-one* error.

Tip

constants

This example uses constants **COMMISSION_SOUGHT** and **INITIAL_SALES_AMOUNT**. Using constants makes programs easy to read and maintain.

4.8.3 Problem: Displaying a Pyramid of Numbers

The problem is to write a program that prompts the user to enter an integer from 1 to 15 and displays a pyramid, as shown in the following sample output:

```
Enter the number of lines: 11  ⏎Enter
                            1
                         2  1  2
                      3  2  1  2  3
                   4  3  2  1  2  3  4
                5  4  3  2  1  2  3  4  5
             6  5  4  3  2  1  2  3  4  5  6
          7  6  5  4  3  2  1  2  3  4  5  6  7
       8  7  6  5  4  3  2  1  2  3  4  5  6  7  8
    9  8  7  6  5  4  3  2  1  2  3  4  5  6  7  8  9
 10  9  8  7  6  5  4  3  2  1  2  3  4  5  6  7  8  9  10
11 10  9  8  7  6  5  4  3  2  1  2  3  4  5  6  7  8  9  10  11
```

Your program receives the input for an integer (numberOfLines) that represents the total number of lines. It displays all the lines one by one. Each line has three parts. The first part comprises the spaces before the numbers; the second part, the leading numbers, such as 3 2 1 in line 3; and the last part, the ending numbers, such as 2 3 in line 3.

Each number occupies three spaces. Display an empty space before a double-digit number, and display two empty spaces before a single-digit number.

You can use an outer loop to control the lines. At the nth row, there are (numberOfLines – n) * 3 leading spaces, the leading numbers are n, n–1, ..., 1, and the ending numbers are 2, ..., n. You can use three separate inner loops to print each part.

Here is the algorithm for the problem:

```
Input numberOfLines;

for (int row = 1; row <= numberOfLines; row++) {
  Print (numberOfLines - row) * 3 leading spaces;
  Print leading numbers row, row - 1, ..., 1;
  Print ending numbers 2, 3, ..., row - 1, row;
  Start a new line;
}
```

The complete program is given in Listing 4.10.

LISTING 4.10 PrintPyramid.java

```java
 1 import java.util.Scanner;
 2
 3 public class PrintPyramid {
 4   public static void main(String[] args) {
 5     // Create a Scanner
 6     Scanner input = new Scanner(System.in);
 7
 8     // Prompt the user to enter the number of lines
 9     System.out.print("Enter the number of lines: ");
10     int numberOfLines = input.nextInt();
11
12     if (numberOfLines < 1 || numberOfLines > 15) {
13       System.out.println("You must enter a number from 1 to 15");
14       System.exit(0);
15     }
```

```
16
17      // Print lines
18      for (int row = 1; row <= numberOfLines; row++) {
19        // Print NUMBER_OF_LINES - row) leading spaces
20        for (int column = 1; column <= numberOfLines - row; column++)
21          System.out.print("   ");
22
23        // Print leading numbers row, row - 1, ..., 1
24        for (int num = row; num >= 1; num--)
25          System.out.print((num >= 10) ? " " + num : "  " + num);
26
27        // Print ending numbers 2, 3, ..., row - 1, row
28        for (int num = 2; num <= row; num++)
29          System.out.print((num >= 10) ? " " + num : "  " + num);
30
31        // Start a new line
32        System.out.println();
33      }
34    }
35 }
```

print lines

print spaces

print leading numbers

print ending numbers

a new line

The program uses the `print` method (lines 21, 25, and 29) to display a string to the console. The conditional expression (`num >= 10`) ? " "+ num : " " + num in lines 25 and 29 returns a string with a single empty space before the number if the number is greater than or equal to 10, and otherwise returns a string with two empty spaces before the number.

Printing patterns like this one and the ones in Exercises 4.18 and 4.19 are good exercise for practicing loop control statements. The key is to understand the pattern and to describe it using loop control variables.

The last line in the outer loop (line 32), `System.out.println()`, does not have any argument in the method. This call moves the cursor to the next line.

4.9 Keywords **break** and **continue**

Two keywords, break and continue, can be used in loop statements to provide additional control.

break

- **break** immediately ends the innermost loop that contains it. In other words, break breaks out of a loop.

continue

- **continue** ends only the current iteration. Program control goes to the end of the loop body. In other words, continue breaks out of an iteration.

You have already used the keyword break in a `switch` statement. You can also use break and continue in a loop. Normally, these two keywords are used with an `if` statement. Listings 4.11 and 4.12 present two programs to demonstrate the effect of the break and continue keywords in a loop.

The program in Listing 4.11 adds the integers from 1 to 20 in this order to sum until sum is greater than or equal to 100. Without the `if` statement (line 9), the program calculates the sum of the numbers from 1 to 20. But with the `if` statement, the loop terminates when sum becomes greater than or equal to 100.

LISTING 4.11 TestBreak.java

```
1 public class TestBreak {
2   public static void main(String[] args) {
3     int sum = 0;
4     int number = 0;
5
```

```
 6      while (number < 20) {
 7        number++;
 8        sum += number;
 9        if (sum >= 100) break;                               break
10      }
11
12      System.out.println("The number is " + number);
13      System.out.println("The sum is " + sum);
14    }
15 }
```

```
The number is 14
The sum is 105
```

If you changed the `if` statement as shown below,

```
if (sum == 100) break;
```

the output would be as follows:

```
The number is 20
The sum is 210
```

In this case, the `if` condition will never be true. Therefore, the `break` statement will never be executed.

The program in Listing 4.12 adds all the integers from 1 to 20 except 10 and 11 to sum. With the `if` statement in the program (line 8), the `continue` statement is executed when number becomes 10 or 11. The `continue` statement ends the current iteration so that the rest of the statement in the loop body is not executed; therefore, number is not added to sum when it is 10 or 11.

LISTING 4.12 TestContinue.java

```
 1 public class TestContinue {
 2   public static void main(String[] args) {
 3     int sum = 0;
 4     int number = 0;
 5
 6     while (number < 20) {
 7       number++;
 8       if (number == 10 || number == 11) continue;          continue
 9       sum += number;
10     }
11
12     System.out.println("The sum is " + sum);
13   }
14 }
```

```
The sum is 189
```

Without the `if` statement in the program, the output would be as follows:

```
The sum is 210
```

In this case, all of the numbers are added to sum, even when number is 10 or 11. Therefore, the result is 210, which is 21 more than it was with the if statement.

Note

The continue statement is always inside a loop. In the while and do-while loops, the loop-continuation-condition is evaluated immediately after the continue statement. In the for loop, the action-after-each-iteration is performed, then the loop-continuation-condition is evaluated immediately after the continue statement.

You can always write a program without using break or continue in a loop. See Review Question 4.14. In general, it is appropriate to use break and continue if their use simplifies coding and makes programs easier to read.

Listing 4.2 gives a program for guessing a number. You can rewrite it using a break statement, as shown in Listing 4.13.

LISTING 4.13   GuessNumberUsingBreak.java

```
1 import java.util.Scanner;
2
3 public class GuessNumberUsingBreak {
4   public static void main(String[] args) {
5     // Generate a random number to be guessed
6     int number = (int)(Math.random() * 101);
7
8     Scanner input = new Scanner(System.in);
9     System.out.println("Guess a magic number between 0 and 100");
10
11     while (true) {
12       // Prompt the user to guess the number
13       System.out.print("\nEnter your guess: ");
14       int guess = input.nextInt();
15
16       if (guess == number) {
17         System.out.println("Yes, the number is " + number);
18         break;
19       }
20       else if (guess > number)
21         System.out.println("Your guess is too high");
22       else
23         System.out.println("Your guess is too low");
24     } // End of loop
25   }
26 }
```

generate a number

loop continuously

enter a guess

break

Using the break statement makes the program simpler and easier to read.

Note

goto

Some programming languages have a goto statement. The goto statement would indiscriminately transfer the control to any statement in the program and execute it. Using it will make your program vulnerable to errors. The break and continue statements in Java are different from goto statements. They operate only in a loop or a switch statement. The break statement breaks out of the loop, and the continue statement breaks out of the current iteration in the loop.

4.9.1   Problem: Displaying Prime Numbers

An integer greater than 1 is *prime* if its only positive divisor is 1 or itself. For example, 2, 3, 5, and 7 are prime numbers, but 4, 6, 8, and 9 are not.

The problem is to display the first 50 prime numbers in five lines, each of which contains ten numbers. The problem can be broken into the following tasks:

- Determine whether a given number is prime.
- For number = 2, 3, 4, 5, 6, ..., test whether it is prime.
- Count the prime numbers.
- Print each prime number, and print ten numbers per line.

Obviously, you need to write a loop and repeatedly test whether a new number is prime. If the number is prime, increase the count by 1. The count is 0 initially. When it reaches 50, the loop terminates.

Here is the algorithm for the problem:

```
Set the number of prime numbers to be printed as
  a constant NUMBER_OF_PRIMES;
Use count to track the number of prime numbers and
  set an initial count to 0;
Set an initial number to 2;

while (count < NUMBER_OF_PRIMES) {
  Test if number is prime;

  if number is prime {
    Print the prime number and increase the count;
  }

  Increment number by 1;
}
```

To test whether a number is prime, check whether it is divisible by 2, 3, 4, up to number/2. If a divisor is found, the number is not a prime. The algorithm can be described as follows:

```
Use a boolean variable isPrime to denote whether
  the number is prime; Set isPrime to true initially;

for (int divisor = 2; divisor <= number / 2; divisor++) {
  if (number % divisor == 0) {
    Set isPrime to false
    Exit the loop;
  }
}
```

The complete program is given in Listing 4.14.

LISTING 4.14   PrimeNumber.java

```
1 public class PrimeNumber {
2   public static void main(String[] args) {
3     final int NUMBER_OF_PRIMES = 50; // Number of primes to display
4     final int NUMBER_OF_PRIMES_PER_LINE = 10; // Display 10 per line
5     int count = 0; // Count the number of prime numbers
6     int number = 2; // A number to be tested for primeness
7
```

```
 8        System.out.println("The first 50 prime numbers are \n");
 9
10        // Repeatedly find prime numbers
11        while (count < NUMBER_OF_PRIMES) {
12          // Assume the number is prime
13          boolean isPrime = true; // Is the current number prime?
14
15          // Test if number is prime
16          for (int divisor = 2; divisor <= number / 2; divisor++) {
17            if (number % divisor == 0) { // If true, number is not prime
18              isPrime = false; // Set isPrime to false
19              break; // Exit the for loop
20            }
21          }
22
23          // Print the prime number and increase the count
24          if (isPrime) {
25            count++; // Increase the count
26
27            if (count % NUMBER_OF_PRIMES_PER_LINE == 0) {
28              // Print the number and advance to the new line
29              System.out.println(number);
30            }
31            else
32              System.out.print(number + " ");
33          }
34
35          // Check if the next number is prime
36          number++;
37        }
38      }
39 }
```

count prime numbers

check primeness

exit loop

print if prime

```
The first 50 prime numbers are

2 3 5 7 11 13 17 19 23 29
31 37 41 43 47 53 59 61 67 71
73 79 83 89 97 101 103 107 109 113
127 131 137 139 149 151 157 163 167 173
179 181 191 193 197 199 211 223 227 229
```

subproblem

This is a complex program for novice programmers. The key to developing a programmatic solution to this problem, and to many other problems, is to break it into subproblems and develop solutions for each of them in turn. Do not attempt to develop a complete solution in the first trial. Instead, begin by writing the code to determine whether a given number is prime, then expand the program to test whether other numbers are prime in a loop.

To determine whether a number is prime, check whether it is divisible by a number between 2 and number/2 inclusive. If so, it is not a prime number; otherwise, it is a prime number. For a prime number, display it. If the count is divisible by 10, advance to a new line. The program ends when the count reaches 50.

The program uses the **break** statement in line 19 to exit the **for** loop as soon as the number is found to be a nonprime. You can rewrite the loop (lines 16-21) without using the **break** statement, as follows:

```
for (int divisor = 2; divisor <= number / 2 && isPrime;
     divisor++) {
```

```
      // If true, the number is not prime
      if (number % divisor == 0) {
        // Set isPrime to false, if the number is not prime
        isPrime = false;
      }
    }
```

However, using the **break** statement makes the program simpler and easier to read in this case.

4.10 (GUI) Controlling a Loop with a Confirmation Dialog

A sentinel-controlled loop can be implemented using a confirmation dialog. The answers *Yes* or *No* continue or terminate the loop. The template of the loop may look as follows:

    confirmation dialog

```
int option = 0;
while (option == JOptionPane.YES_OPTION) {
  System.out.println("continue loop");
  option = JOptionPane.showConfirmDialog(null, "Continue?");
}
```

Listing 4.15 rewrites Listing 4.4, SentinelValue.java, using a confirmation dialog box. A sample run is shown in Figure 4.4.

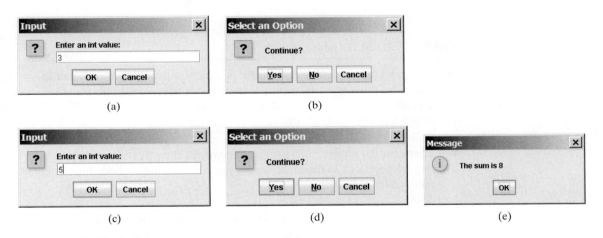

FIGURE 4.4 The user enters 3 in (a), clicks Yes in (b), enters 5 in (c), clicks No in (d), and the result is shown in (e).

LISTING 4.15 SentinelValueUsingConfirmationDialog.java

```
 1 import javax.swing.JOptionPane;
 2
 3 public class SentinelValueUsingConfirmationDialog {
 4   public static void main(String[] args) {
 5     int sum = 0;
 6
 7     // Keep reading data until the user answers No
 8     int option = 0;
 9     while (option == JOptionPane.YES_OPTION) {
10       // Read the next data
11       String dataString = JOptionPane.showInputDialog(
12         "Enter an int value: ");
13       int data = Integer.parseInt(dataString);
14
```

    confirmation option
    check option

    input dialog

confirmation dialog

message dialog

```
15        sum += data;
16
17        option = JOptionPane.showConfirmDialog(null, "Continue?");
18    }
19
20    JOptionPane.showMessageDialog(null, "The sum is " + sum);
21  }
22 }
```

A program displays an input dialog to prompt the user to enter an integer (line 11) and adds it to sum (line 15). Line 17 displays a confirmation dialog to let the user decide whether to continue the input. If the user clicks *Yes*, the loop continues; otherwise the loop exits. Finally the program displays the result in a message dialog box (line 20).

KEY TERMS

break statement 122
continue statement 122
loop control structure 113
infinite loop 105
iteration 104
labeled continue statement 123
loop 104

loop-continuation-condition 104
loop body 104
nested loop 115
off-by-one error 120
sentinel value 108

CHAPTER SUMMARY

■ Program control specifies the order in which statements are executed in a program. There are three types of control statements: sequence, selection, and repetition. The preceding chapters introduced sequence and selection statements. This chapter introduced repetition statements.

■ There are three types of repetition statements: the while loop, the do-while loop, and the for loop. In designing loops, you need to consider both the loop control structure and the loop body.

■ The while loop checks the loop-continuation-condition first. If the condition is true, the loop body is executed; if it is false, the loop terminates. The do-while loop is similar to the while loop, except that the do-while loop executes the loop body first and then checks the loop-continuation-condition to decide whether to continue or to terminate.

■ Since the while loop and the do-while loop contain the loop-continuation-condition, which is dependent on the loop body, the number of repetitions is determined by the loop body. The while loop and the do-while loop are often used when the number of repetitions is unspecified.

■ The for loop is generally used to execute a loop body a predictable number of times; this number is not determined by the loop body. The loop control has three parts. The first part is an initial action that often initializes a control variable. The second part, the loop-continuation-condition, determines whether the loop body is to be executed. The third part is executed after each iteration and is often used to adjust the control variable. Usually, the loop control variables are initialized and changed in the control structure.

■ Two keywords, `break` and `continue`, can be used in a loop. The keyword `break` breaks out of a loop. The keyword `continue` breaks out of an iteration.

REVIEW QUESTIONS

Sections 4.2–4.4

4.1 What is wrong if `guess` is initialized to 0 in line 11 in Listing 4.1?

4.2 How many times is the following loop body repeated? What is the printout of the loop?

```
int i = 1;
while (i > 10)
  if ((i++) % 2 == 0)
    System.out.println(i);
```
(a)

```
int i = 1;
while (i < 10)
  if ((i++) % 2 == 0)
    System.out.println(i);
```
(b)

4.3 What are the differences between a `while` loop and a `do-while` loop?

4.4 Do the following two loops result in the same value in `sum`?

```
for (int i = 0; i < 10; ++i) {
  sum += i;
}
```
(a)

```
for (int i = 0; i < 10; i++ ) {
  sum += i;
}
```
(b)

4.5 What are the three parts of a `for` loop control? Write a `for` loop that prints the numbers from 1 to 100.

4.6 What does the following statement do?

```
for ( ; ; ) {
  do something;
}
```

4.7 If a variable is declared in the `for` loop control, can it be used after the loop exits?

4.8 Can you convert a `for` loop to a `while` loop? List the advantages of using `for` loops.

4.9 Convert the following `for` loop statement to a `while` loop and to a `do-while` loop:

```
long sum = 0;
for (int i = 0; i <= 1000; i++)
  sum = sum + i;
```

4.10 Will the program work if `n1` and `n2` are replaced by `n1 / 2` and `n2 / 2` in line 15 in Listing 4.8?

Section 4.9 Keywords **break** and **continue**

4.11 What is the keyword `break` for? What is the keyword `continue` for? Will the following program terminate? If so, give the output.

```
int balance = 1000;
while (true) {
  if (balance < 9)
    break;
  balance = balance - 9;
}
System.out.println("Balance is "
  + balance);
```

(a)

```
int balance = 1000;
while (true) {
  if (balance < 9)
    continue;
  balance = balance - 9;
}
System.out.println("Balance is "
  + balance);
```

(b)

4.12 Can you always convert a `while` loop into a `for` loop? Convert the following `while` loop into a `for` loop.

```
int i = 1;
int sum = 0;
while (sum < 10000) {
  sum = sum + i;
  i++;
}
```

4.13 The `for` loop on the left is converted into the `while` loop on the right. What is wrong? Correct it.

```
for (int i = 0; i < 4; i++) {
  if (i % 3 == 0) continue;
  sum += i;
}
```

Converted
Wrong
conversion

```
int i = 0;
while (i < 4) {
  if(i % 3 == 0) continue;
  sum += i;
  i++;
}
```

4.14 Rewrite the programs `TestBreak` and `TestContinue` in Listings 4.9 and 4.10 without using `break` and `continue`.

4.15 After the `break` statement is executed in the following loop, which statement is executed? Show the output.

```
for (int i = 1; i < 4; i++) {
  for (int j = 1; j < 4; j++) {
    if (i * j > 2)
      break;

    System.out.println(i * j);
  }

  System.out.println(i);
}
```

4.16 After the `continue` statement is executed in the following loop, which statement is executed? Show the output.

```
for (int i = 1; i < 4; i++) {
  for (int j = 1; j < 4; j++) {
    if (i * j > 2)
      continue;

    System.out.println(i * j);
  }
```

```
          System.out.println(i);
        }
```

Comprehensive

4.17   Identify and fix the errors in the following code:

```
1 public class Test {
2    public void main(String[] args) {
3      for (int i = 0; i < 10; i++);
4        sum += i;
5
6      if (i < j);
7        System.out.println(i)
8      else
9        System.out.println(j);
10
11     while (j < 10);
12     {
13       j++;
14     };
15
16     do {
17       j++;
18     } while (j < 10)
19   }
20 }
```

4.18   What is wrong with the following programs?

```
1 public class ShowErrors {
2   public static void main(String[] args) {
3     int i;
4     int j = 5;
5
6     if (j > 3)
7       System.out.println(i + 4);
8   }
9 }
```
(a)

```
1 public class ShowErrors {
2   public static void main(String[] args) {
3     for (int i = 0; i < 10; i++);
4       System.out.println(i + 4);
5   }
6 }
```
(b)

4.19   Show the output of the following programs:

```
public class Test {
  /** Main method */
  public static void main(String[] args) {
    for (int i = 1; i < 5; i++) {
      int j = 0;
      while (j < i) {
        System.out.print(j + " ");
        j++;
      }
    }
  }
}
```
(a)

```
public class Test {
  /** Main method */
  public static void main(String[] args) {
    int i = 0;
    while (i < 5) {
      for (int j = i; j > 1; j--)
        System.out.print(j + " ");
      System.out.println("****");
      i++;
    }
  }
}
```
(b)

```java
public class Test {
  public static void main(String[] args) {
    int i = 5;
    while (i >= 1) {
      int num = 1;
      for (int j = 1; j <= i; j++) {
        System.out.print(num + "xxx");
        num *= 2;
      }

      System.out.println();
      i--;
    }
  }
}
```
(c)

```java
public class Test {
  public static void main(String[] args) {
    int i = 1;
    do {
      int num = 1;
      for (int j = 1; j <= i; j++) {
        System.out.print(num + "G");
        num += 2;
      }

      System.out.println();
      i++;
    } while (i <= 5);
  }
}
```
(d)

4.20 Reformat the following programs according to the programming style and documentation guidelines proposed in §2.13. Use the next-line brace style.

```java
public class Test {
  public static void main(String[] args) {
    int i = 0;
    if (i>0)
    i++;
    else
    i--;
    char grade;

    if (i >= 90)
     grade = 'A';
    else
      if (i >= 80)
       grade = 'B';

  }
}
```
(a)

```java
public class Test {
  public static void main(String[] args) {
    for (int i = 0; i<10; i++)
     if (i>0)
      i++;
     else
      i--;
    }
}
```
(b)

4.21 Count the number of iterations in the following loops.

```java
int count = 0;
while (count < n) {
  count++;
}
```
(a)

```java
for (int count = 0;
  count <= n; count++) {
}
```
(b)

```java
int count = 5;
while (count < n) {
  count++;
}
```
(c)

```java
int count = 5;
while (count < n) {
  count = count + 3;
}
```
(d)

PROGRAMMING EXERCISES

Pedagogical Note

A problem often can be solved in many different ways. Students are encouraged to explore various solutions.

explore solutions

Sections 4.2-4.7

4.1* (*Repeating additions*) Listing 4.1, SubtractionQuizLoop.java, generates ten random subtraction questions. Revise the program to generate ten random addition questions for two integers between 1 and 15. Display the correct count and test time.

4.2* (*Counting positive and negative numbers and computing the average of numbers*) Write a program that reads an unspecified number of integers, determines how many positive and negative values have been read, and computes the total and average of the input values, not counting zeros. Your program ends with the input 0. Display the average as a floating-point number. (For example, if you entered 1, 2, and 0, the average should be 1.5.)

4.3 (*Conversion from kilograms to pounds*) Write a program that displays the following table (note that 1 kilogram is 2.2 pounds):

Kilograms	Pounds
1	2.2
3	6.6
...	
197	433.4
199	437.8

4.4 (*Conversion from miles to kilometers*) Write a program that displays the following table (note that 1 mile is 1.609 kilometers):

Miles	Kilometers
1	1.609
2	3.218
...	
9	14.481
10	16.09

4.5 (*Conversion from kilograms to pounds*) Write a program that displays the following two tables side by side (note that 1 kilogram is 2.2 pounds):

Kilograms	Pounds	Pounds	Kilograms
1	2.2	20	9.09
3	6.6	25	11.36
...			
197	433.4	510	231.82
199	437.8	515	234.09

4.6 (*Conversion from miles to kilometers*) Write a program that displays the following two tables side by side (note that 1 mile is 1.609 kilometers):

Miles	Kilometers	Kilometers	Miles
1	1.609	20	12.430
2	3.218	25	15.538
...			
9	14.481	60	37.290
10	16.09	65	40.398

4.7** (*Financial application: computing future tuition*) Suppose that the tuition for a university is $10,000 this year and increases 5% every year. Write a program that uses a loop to compute the tuition in ten years. Write another program that computes the total cost of four years' worth of tuition starting ten years from now.

4.8 (*Finding the highest score*) Write a program that prompts the user to enter the number of students and each student's name and score, and finally displays the student with the highest score.

4.9* (*Finding the two highest scores*) Write a program that prompts the user to enter the number of students and each student's name and score, and finally displays the student with the highest score and the student with the second-highest score.

4.10 (*Finding numbers divisible by 5 and 6*) Write a program that displays all the numbers from 100 to 1000, ten per line, that are divisible by 5 and 6.

4.11 (*Finding numbers divisible by 5 or 6, but not both*) Write a program that displays all the numbers from 100 to 200, ten per line, that are divisible by 5 or 6, but not both.

4.12 (*Finding the smallest n such that $n^2 > 12,000$*) Use a `while` loop to find the smallest integer n such that n^2 is greater than 12,000.

4.13 (*Finding the largest n such that $n^3 < 12,000$*) Use a `while` loop to find the largest integer n such that n^3 is less than 12,000.

4.14* (*Displaying the ACSII character table*) Write a program that prints the characters in the ASCII character table from '!' to '~'. Print ten characters per line. The ASCII table is printed in Appendix B.

Section 4.8 Case Studies

4.15* (*Computing the greatest common divisor*) Another solution for Listing 4.8 to find the greatest common divisor of two integers n1 and n2 is as follows: First find d to be the minimum of n1 and n2, then check whether d, d-1, d-2, ..., 2, or 1 is a divisor for both n1 and n2 in this order. The first such common divisor is the greatest common divisor for n1 and n2. Write a program that prompts the user to enter two positive integers and displays the gcd.

4.16** (*Finding the factors of an integer*) Write a program that reads an integer and displays all its smallest factors in increasing order. For example, if the input integer is 120, the output should be as follows: 2, 2, 2, 3, 5.

4.17* (*Financial application: finding the sales amount*) Rewrite Listing 4.9, FindSalesAmount.java, as follows:

- Use a `for` loop instead of a `do-while` loop.

- Let the user enter COMMISSION_SOUGHT instead of fixing it as a constant.

4.18* (*Printing four patterns using loops*) Use nested loops that print the following patterns in four separate programs:

```
Pattern I        Pattern II       Pattern III      Pattern IV
1                1 2 3 4 5 6                1       1 2 3 4 5 6
1 2              1 2 3 4 5               2 1         1 2 3 4 5
1 2 3            1 2 3 4              3 2 1           1 2 3 4
1 2 3 4          1 2 3            4 3 2 1               1 2 3
1 2 3 4 5        1 2           5 4 3 2 1                 1 2
1 2 3 4 5 6      1           6 5 4 3 2 1                   1
```

4.19** (*Printing numbers in a pyramid pattern*) Write a nested `for` loop that prints the following output:

```
                        1
                    1   2   1
                1   2   4   2   1
            1   2   4   8   4   2   1
        1   2   4   8  16   8   4   2   1
      1   2   4   8  16  32  16   8   4   2   1
    1   2   4   8  16  32  64  32  16   8   4   2   1
  1   2   4   8  16  32  64 128  64  32  16   8   4   2   1
```

Hint: Here is the pseudocode solution:

```
for the row from 0 to 7 {
  Pad leading blanks in a row using a loop like this:
  for the column from 1 to 7-row
    System.out.print("    ");

  Print left half of the row for numbers 1, 2, 4, up to
    2^row using a look like this:
  for the column from 0 to row
    System.out.print("    " + (int)Math.pow(2, column));

  Print the right half of the row for numbers
    2^row-1, 2^row-2, ..., 1 using a loop like this:
  for (int column = row - 1; column >= 0; col--)
    System.out.print("    " + (int)Math.pow(2, column));

  Start a new line
  System.out.println();
}
```

You need to figure out how many spaces to print before the number. This depends on the number. If a number is a single digit, print four spaces. If a number has two digits, print three spaces. If a number has three digits, print two spaces.

The `Math.pow()` method was introduced in §2.12.1, "Problem: Computing Loan Payments." Can you write this program without using it?

4.20* (*Printing prime numbers between 2 and 1000*) Modify Listing 4.14 to print all the prime numbers between 2 and 1000, inclusively. Display eight prime numbers per line.

Comprehensive

4.21** (*Financial application: comparing loans with various interest rates*) Write a program that lets the user enter the loan amount and loan period in number of years and displays the monthly and total payments for each interest rate starting from 5% to 8%, with an increment of 1/8. Suppose you enter the loan amount 10,000 for five years; display a table as follows:

```
Loan Amount: 10000
Number of Years: 5
Interest Rate        Monthly Payment     Total Payment

5%                   188.71              11322.74
5.125%               189.28              11357.13
```

5.25%	189.85	11391.59
...		
7.85%	202.16	12129.97
8.0%	202.76	12165.83

Video Note

Display loan schedule

4.22** (*Financial application: loan amortization schedule*) The monthly payment for a given loan pays the principal and the interest. The monthly interest is computed by multiplying the monthly interest rate and the balance (the remaining principal). The principal paid for the month is therefore the monthly payment minus the monthly interest. Write a program that lets the user enter the loan amount, number of years, and interest rate, and displays the amortization schedule for the loan. Suppose you enter the loan amount 10,000 for one year with an interest rate of 7%, display a table as follows:

```
Loan Amount: 10000
Number of Years: 1
Annual Interest Rate: 7%

Monthly Payment: 865.26
Total Payment: 10383.21
```

Payment#	Interest	Principal	Balance
1	58.33	806.93	9193.07
2	53.62	811.64	8381.43
...			
11	10.0	855.26	860.27
12	5.01	860.25	0.01

Note

The balance after the last payment may not be zero. If so, the last payment should be the normal monthly payment plus the final balance.

Hint: Write a loop to print the table. Since monthly payment is the same for each month, it should be computed before the loop. The balance is initially the loan amount. For each iteration in the loop, compute the interest and principal, and update the balance. The loop may look like this:

```
for (i = 1; i <= numberOfYears * 12; i++) {
  interest = monthlyInterestRate * balance;
  principal = monthlyPayment - interest;
  balance = balance - principal;
  System.out.println(i + "\t\t" + interest
    + "\t\t" + principal + "\t\t" + balance);
}
```

4.23* (*Obtaining more accurate results*) In computing the following series, you will obtain more accurate results by computing from right to left rather than from left to right:

$$1 + \frac{1}{2} + \frac{1}{3} + \ldots + \frac{1}{n}$$

Write a program that compares the results of the summation of the preceding series, computing from left to right and from right to left with n = 50000.

4.24* (*Summing a series*) Write a program to sum the following series:

$$\frac{1}{3} + \frac{3}{5} + \frac{5}{7} + \frac{7}{9} + \frac{9}{11} + \frac{11}{13} + \ldots + \frac{95}{97} + \frac{97}{99}$$

4.25**(*Computing* π) You can approximate π by using the following series:

$$\pi = 4\left(1 - \frac{1}{3} + \frac{1}{5} - \frac{1}{7} + \frac{1}{9} - \frac{1}{11} + \frac{1}{13} - \cdots - \frac{1}{2i-1} + \frac{1}{2i+1}\right)$$

Write two separate programs. The first program displays the π value for $i =$ 10000, 20000, ..., and 100000. The second program finds out how many terms of this series you need to use before you first get 3.14159.

4.26**(*Computing* e) You can approximate e by using the following series:

$$e = 1 + \frac{1}{1!} + \frac{1}{2!} + \frac{1}{3!} + \frac{1}{4!} + \cdots + \frac{1}{i!}$$

Write a program that displays the e value for $i =$ 10000, 20000, ..., and 100000. (*Hint*: Since $i! = i \times (i-1) \times \cdots \times 2 \times 1$, $\frac{1}{i!}$ is $\frac{1}{i(i-1)!}$. Initialize e and item to be 1 and keep adding a new item to e. The new item is the previous item divided by i for i = 2, 3, 4, ...)

4.27**(*Displaying leap years*) Write a program that displays all the leap years, ten per line, in the twenty-first century (from 2001 to 2100).

4.28**(*Displaying the first days of each month*) Write a program that prompts the user to enter the year and first day of the year, and displays the first day of each month in the year on the console. For example, if the user entered the year 2005, and 6 for Saturday, January 1, 2005, your program should display the following output (Note that Sunday is 0):

```
January 1, 2005 is Saturday
...
December 1, 2005 is Thursday
```

4.29**(*Displaying calendars*) Write a program that prompts the user to enter the year and first day of the year, and displays the calendar table for the year on the console. For example, if the user entered the year 2005, and 6 for Saturday, January 1, 2005, your program should display the calendar for each month in the year, as follows:

January 2005

Sun	Mon	Tue	Wed	Thu	Fri	Sat
						1
2	3	4	5	6	7	8
9	10	11	12	13	14	15
16	17	18	19	20	21	22
23	24	25	26	27	28	29
30	31					

...

December 2005

Sun	Mon	Tue	Wed	Thu	Fri	Sat
				1	2	3
4	5	6	7	8	9	10
11	12	13	14	15	16	17
18	19	20	21	22	23	24
25	26	27	28	29	30	31

4.30* (*Financial application: compound value*) Suppose you save $100 *each* month into a savings account with the annual interest rate 5%. So, the monthly interest rate is 0.05 / 12 = 0.00417. After the first month, the value in the account becomes

$$100 * (1 + 0.00417) = 100.417$$

After the second month, the value in the account becomes

$$(100 + 100.417) * (1 + 0.00417) = 201.252$$

After the third month, the value in the account becomes

$$(100 + 201.252) * (1 + 0.00417) = 302.507$$

and so on.

Write a program that prompts the user to enter an amount (e.g., 100), the annual interest rate (e.g., 5), and the number of months (e.g., 6), and displays the amount in the savings account after the given month.

4.31* (*Financial application: computing CD value*) Suppose you put $10,000 into a CD with an annual percentage yield of 5.75%. After one month, the CD is worth

$$10000 + 10000 * 5.75 / 1200 = 10047.91$$

After two months, the CD is worth

$$10047.91 + 10047.91 * 5.75 / 1200 = 10096.06$$

After three months, the CD is worth

$$10096.06 + 10096.06 * 5.75 / 1200 = 10144.43$$

and so on.

Write a program that prompts the user to enter an amount (e.g., 10000), the annual percentage yield (e.g., 5.75), and the number of months (e.g., 18), and displays a table as shown in the sample output.

```
Enter the initial deposit amount: 10000  ⏎Enter
Enter annual percentage yield: 5.75  ⏎Enter
Enter maturity period (number of months): 18  ⏎Enter

Month          CD Value
1              10047.91
2              10096.06
...
17             10846.56
18             10898.54
```

4.32** (*Perfect number*) A positive integer is called a *perfect number* if it is equal to the sum of all of its positive divisors, excluding itself. For example, 6 is the first perfect number because 6 = 3 + 2 + 1. The next is 28 = 14 + 7 + 4 + 2 + 1. There are four perfect numbers less than 10000. Write a program to find all these four numbers.

4.33** (*Game: lottery*) Revise Listing 3.5, Lottery.java, to generate a lottery of a two-digit number. The two digits in the number are distinct. (*Hint*: Generate the first digit. Use a loop to continuously generate the second digit until it is different from the first digit.)

4.34*** (*Game: scissor, rock, paper*) Exercise 3.17 gives a program that plays the scissor-rock-paper game. Revise the program to let the user continuously play until either the user or the computer wins more than two times.

4.35* (*Summation*) You can prove that the following summation is 24.

$$\frac{1}{1 + \sqrt{2}} + \frac{1}{\sqrt{2} + \sqrt{3}} + \frac{1}{\sqrt{3} + \sqrt{4}} + \cdots + \frac{1}{\sqrt{624} + \sqrt{625}}$$

Write a program to verify your result.

4.36** (*Business application: checking ISBN*) Use loops to simplify Exercise 3.19.

4.37** (*Decimal to binary*) Write a program that prompts the user to enter a decimal integer and displays its corresponding binary value. Don't use Java's `Integer.toBinaryString(int)` in this program.

4.38** (*Decimal to hex*) Write a program that prompts the user to enter a decimal integer and displays its corresponding hexadecimal value. Don't use Java's `Integer.toHexString(int)` in this program.

CHAPTER 5

METHODS

Objectives

- ■ To define methods, invoke methods, and pass arguments to a method (§5.2–5.5).

- ■ To develop reusable code that is modular, easy to read, easy to debug, and easy to maintain (§5.6).

- ■ To use method overloading and understand ambiguous overloading (§5.7).

- ■ To determine the scope of variables (§5.8).

- ■ To solve mathematics problems using the methods in the Math class (§§5.9–5.10).

- ■ To apply the concept of method abstraction in software development (§5.11).

- ■ To design and implement methods using stepwise refinement (§5.11).

5.1 Introduction

A method is a construct for grouping statements together to perform a function. Using a method, you can write the code once for performing the function in a program and reuse it in many other programs. For example, often you need to find the maximum between two numbers. Whenever you need this function, you have to write the following code:

```java
int result;

if (num1 > num2)
  result = num1;
else
  result = num2;
```

If you define this function for finding a maximum number between any two numbers in a method, you don't have to repeatedly write the same code. You need to define it just once and reuse it in other programs.

In the preceding chapters, you have already used such methods as `System.out.println`, `JOptionPane.showMessageDialog`, `JOptionPane.showInputDialog`, `Integer.parseInt`, `Double.parseDouble`, `System.exit`, `Math.pow`, and `Math.random`. These methods are defined in the Java library. In this chapter, you will learn how to create your own methods and apply method abstraction to solve complex problems.

5.2 Defining a Method

The syntax for defining a method is as follows:

```java
modifier returnValueType methodName(list of parameters) {
  // Method body;
}
```

Let's take a look at a method created to find which of two integers is bigger. This method, named `max`, has two `int` parameters, `num1` and `num2`, the larger of which is returned by the method. Figure 5.1 illustrates the components of this method.

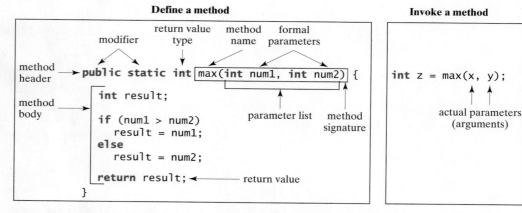

FIGURE 5.1 A method declaration consists of a method header and a method body.

The *method header* specifies the *modifiers*, *return value type*, *method name*, and *parameters* of the method. The static modifier is used for all the methods in this chapter. The reason for using it will be discussed in Chapter 7, "Objects and Classes."

A method may return a value. The `returnValueType` is the data type of the value the method returns. Some methods perform desired operations without returning a value. In this case, the `returnValueType` is the keyword `void`. For example, the `returnValueType` is `void` in the `main` method, as well as in `System.exit`, `System.out.println`, and `JOptionPane.showMessageDialog`. The method that returns a value is called a *value-returning method*, and the method that does not return a value is called a *void method*.

value-returning method
void method

The variables defined in the method header are known as *formal parameters* or simply *parameters*. A parameter is like a placeholder. When a method is invoked, you pass a value to the parameter. This value is referred to as an *actual parameter* or *argument*. The *parameter list* refers to the type, order, and number of the parameters of a method. The method name and the parameter list together constitute the *method signature*. Parameters are optional; that is, a method may contain no parameters. For example, the `Math.random()` method has no parameters.

parameter
argument
parameter list
method signature

The method body contains a collection of statements that define what the method does. The method body of the `max` method uses an `if` statement to determine which number is larger and return the value of that number. A return statement using the keyword `return` is *required* for a value-returning method to return a result. The method terminates when a return statement is executed.

Note

In certain other languages, methods are referred to as *procedures* and *functions*. A value-returning method is called a *function*; a void method is called a *procedure*.

Caution

You need to declare a separate data type for each parameter. For instance, `int num1, num2` should be replaced by `int num1, int num2`.

5.3 Calling a Method

In creating a method, you give a definition of what the method is to do. To use a method, you have to *call* or *invoke* it. There are two ways to call a method; the choice is based on whether the method returns a value or not.

If the method returns a value, a call to the method is usually treated as a value. For example,

```
int larger = max(3, 4);
```

calls `max(3, 4)` and assigns the result of the method to the variable `larger`. Another example of a call that is treated as a value is

```
System.out.println(max(3, 4));
```

which prints the return value of the method call `max(3, 4)`.

If the method returns `void`, a call to the method must be a statement. For example, the method `println` returns `void`. The following call is a statement:

```
System.out.println("Welcome to Java!");
```

Note

A value-returning method can also be invoked as a statement in Java. In this case, the caller simply ignores the return value. This is rare but is permissible if the caller is not interested in the return value.

When a program calls a method, program control is transferred to the called method. A called method returns control to the caller when its return statement is executed or when its method-ending closing brace is reached.

Listing 5.1 shows a complete program that is used to test the `max` method.

main method

invoke max

declare method

LISTING 5.1 TestMax.java

```java
1  public class TestMax {
2    /** Main method */
3    public static void main(String[] args) {
4      int i = 5;
5      int j = 2;
6      int k = max(i, j);
7      System.out.println("The maximum between " + i +
8        " and " + j + " is " + k);
9    }
10
11   /** Return the max between two numbers */
12   public static int max(int num1, int num2) {
13     int result;
14
15     if (num1 > num2)
16       result = num1;
17     else
18       result = num2;
19
20     return result;
21   }
22 }
```

```
The maximum between 5 and 2 is 5
```

main method

This program contains the `main` method and the `max` method. The `main` method is just like any other method except that it is invoked by the JVM.

The `main` method's header is always the same, like the one in this example, with the modifiers `public` and `static`, return value type `void`, method name `main`, and a parameter of the `String[]` type. `String[]` indicates that the parameter is an array of `String`, a subject addressed in Chapter 6, "Arrays."

The statements in `main` may invoke other methods that are defined in the class that contains the `main` method or in other classes. In this example, the `main` method invokes `max(i, j)`, which is defined in the same class with the `main` method.

max method

When the `max` method is invoked (line 6), variable `i`'s value 5 is passed to `num1`, and variable `j`'s value 2 is passed to `num2` in the `max` method. The flow of control transfers to the `max` method. The `max` method is executed. When the `return` statement in the `max` method is executed, the `max` method returns the control to its caller (in this case the caller is the `main` method). This process is illustrated in Figure 5.2.

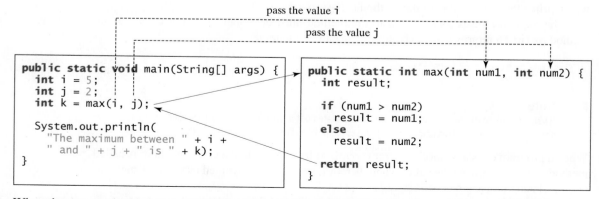

FIGURE 5.2 When the `max` method is invoked, the flow of control transfers to the `max` method. Once the `max` method is finished, it returns control back to the caller.

Caution

A `return` statement is required for a value-returning method. The method shown below in (a) is logically correct, but it has a compilation error because the Java compiler thinks it possible that this method does not return any value.

```java
public static int sign(int n) {
    if (n > 0)
        return 1;
    else if (n == 0)
        return 0;
    else if (n < 0)
        return -1;
}
```

Should be

```java
public static int sign(int n) {
    if (n > 0)
        return 1;
    else if (n == 0)
        return 0;
    else
        return -1;
}
```

(a) (b)

To fix this problem, delete *if (n < 0)* in (a), so that the compiler will see a `return` statement to be reached regardless of how the `if` statement is evaluated.

Note

reusing method

Methods enable code sharing and reuse. The `max` method can be invoked from any class besides `TestMax`. If you create a new class, you can invoke the `max` method using `ClassName.methodName` (i.e., `TestMax.max`).

5.3.1 Call Stacks

Each time a method is invoked, the system stores parameters and variables in an area of memory known as a *stack*, which stores elements in last-in, first-out fashion. When a method calls another method, the caller's stack space is kept intact, and new space is created to handle the new method call. When a method finishes its work and returns to its caller, its associated space is released.

stack

Understanding call stacks helps you to comprehend how methods are invoked. The variables defined in the `main` method are `i`, `j`, and `k`. The variables defined in the `max` method are `num1`, `num2`, and `result`. The variables `num1` and `num2` are defined in the method signature and are parameters of the method. Their values are passed through method invocation. Figure 5.3 illustrates the variables in the stack.

FIGURE 5.3 When the `max` method is invoked, the flow of control transfers to the `max` method. Once the `max` method is finished, it returns control back to the caller.

5.4 **void** Method Example

The preceding section gives an example of a value-returning method. This section shows how to declare and invoke a `void` method. Listing 5.2 gives a program that declares a method named `printGrade` and invokes it to print the grade for a given score.

Video Note
Use void method
main method
invoke **printGrade**

printGrade method

LISTING 5.2 TestVoidMethod.java

```java
1  public class TestVoidMethod {
2    public static void main(String[] args) {
3      System.out.print("The grade is ");
4      printGrade(78.5);
5    }
6
7    public static void printGrade(double score) {
8      if (score >= 90.0) {
9        System.out.println('A');
10     }
11     else if (score >= 80.0) {
12       System.out.println('B');
13     }
14     else if (score >= 70.0) {
15       System.out.println('C');
16     }
17     else if (score >= 60.0) {
18       System.out.println('D');
19     }
20     else {
21       System.out.println('F');
22     }
23   }
24 }
```

```
The grade is C
```

invoke void method

The `printGrade` method is a **void** method. It does not return any value. A call to a **void** method must be a statement. So, it is invoked as a statement in line 3 in the **main** method. This statement, like any Java statement, is terminated with a semicolon.

Note

return in void method

A **return** statement is not needed for a **void** method, but it can be used for terminating the method and returning to the method's caller. The syntax is simply

return;

This is rare but sometimes is useful for circumventing the normal flow of control in a **void** function. For example, the following code has a return statement to terminate the function when the score is invalid.

```java
public static void printGrade(double score) {
  if (score < 0 || score > 100) {
    System.out.println("Invalid score");
    return;
  }

  if (score >= 90.0) {
    System.out.println('A');
  }
  else if (score >= 80.0) {
    System.out.println('B');
  }
  else if (score >= 70.0) {
    System.out.println('C');
  }
```

```
        else if (score >= 60.0) {
            System.out.println('D');
        }
        else {
            System.out.println('F');
        }
    }
```

5.5 Passing Parameters by Values

The power of a method is its ability to work with parameters. You can use `println` to print any string and `max` to find the maximum between any two `int` values. When calling a method, you need to provide arguments, which must be given in the same order as their respective parameters in the method specification. This is known as *parameter order association*. For example, the following method prints a message `n` times:

parameter order association

```
public static void nPrintln(String message, int n) {
    for (int i = 0; i < n; i++)
        System.out.println(message);
}
```

You can use `nPrintln("Hello", 3)` to print `"Hello"` three times. The `nPrintln("Hello", 3)` statement passes the actual string parameter, `"Hello"`, to the parameter, `message`; passes `3` to `n`; and prints `"Hello"` three times. However, the statement `nPrintln(3, "Hello")` would be wrong. The data type of `3` does not match the data type for the first parameter, `message`, nor does the second parameter, `"Hello"`, match the second parameter, `n`.

Caution

The arguments must match the parameters in *order, number,* and *compatible type,* as defined in the method signature. Compatible type means that you can pass an argument to a parameter without explicit casting, such as passing an `int` value argument to a `double` value parameter.

When you invoke a method with a parameter, the value of the argument is passed to the parameter. This is referred to as *pass-by-value*. If the argument is a variable rather than a literal value, the value of the variable is passed to the parameter. The variable is not affected, regardless of the changes made to the parameter inside the method. As shown in Listing 5.3, the value of `x` (1) is passed to the parameter `n` to invoke the `increment` function (line 5). `n` is incremented by `1` in the function (line 10), but `x` is not changed no matter what the function does.

pass-by-value

LISTING 5.3 Increment.java

```
 1 public class Increment {
 2   public static void main(String[] args) {
 3     int x = 1;
 4     System.out.println("Before the call, x is " + x);
 5     increment(x);
 6     System.out.println("after the call, x is " + x);
 7   }
 8
 9   public static void increment(int n) {
10     n++;
11     System.out.println("n inside the function is " + n);
12   }
13 }
```

invoke increment

increment **n**

```
Before the call, x is 1
n inside the function is 2
after the call, x is 1
```

Listing 5.4 gives another program that demonstrates the effect of passing by value. The program creates a method for swapping two variables. The swap method is invoked by passing two arguments. Interestingly, the values of the arguments are not changed after the method is invoked.

LISTING 5.4 TestPassByValue.java

```
 1 public class TestPassByValue {
 2   /** Main method */
 3   public static void main(String[] args) {
 4     // Declare and initialize variables
 5     int num1 = 1;
 6     int num2 = 2;
 7
 8     System.out.println("Before invoking the swap method, num1 is " +
 9       num1 + " and num2 is " + num2);
10
11     // Invoke the swap method to attempt to swap two variables
12     swap(num1, num2);
13
14     System.out.println("After invoking the swap method, num1 is " +
15       num1 + " and num2 is " + num2);
16   }
17
18   /** Swap two variables */
19   public static void swap(int n1, int n2) {
20     System.out.println("\tInside the swap method");
21     System.out.println("\t\tBefore swapping n1 is " + n1
22       + " n2 is " + n2);
23
24     // Swap n1 with n2
25     int temp = n1;
26     n1 = n2;
27     n2 = temp;
28
29     System.out.println("\t\tAfter swapping n1 is " + n1
30       + " n2 is " + n2);
31   }
32 }
```

false swap

```
Before invoking the swap method, num1 is 1 and num2 is 2
  Inside the swap method
    Before swapping n1 is 1 n2 is 2
    After swapping n1 is 2 n2 is 1
After invoking the swap method, num1 is 1 and num2 is 2
```

Before the swap method is invoked (line 12), num1 is 1 and num2 is 2. After the swap method is invoked, num1 is still 1 and num2 is still 2. Their values are not swapped after the swap method is invoked. As shown in Figure 5.4, the values of the arguments num1 and num2 are passed to n1 and n2, but n1 and n2 have their own memory locations independent of num1 and num2. Therefore, changes in n1 and n2 do not affect the contents of num1 and num2.

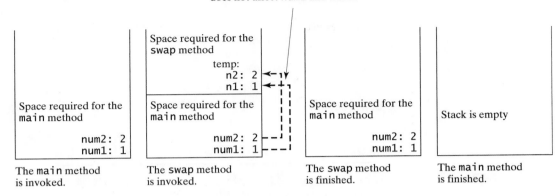

The values of **num1** and **num2** are passed to **n1** and **n2**. Executing swap does not affect **num1** and **num2**.

FIGURE 5.4 The values of the variables are passed to the parameters of the method.

Another twist is to change the parameter name **n1** in **swap** to **num1**. What effect does this have? No change occurs, because it makes no difference whether the parameter and the argument have the same name. The parameter is a variable in the method with its own memory space. The variable is allocated when the method is invoked, and it disappears when the method is returned to its caller.

Note

For simplicity, Java programmers often say *passing an argument x to a parameter y*, which actually means *passing the value of x to y*.

5.6 Modularizing Code

Methods can be used to reduce redundant code and enable code reuse. Methods can also be used to modularize code and improve the quality of the program.

Listing 4.8 gives a program that prompts the user to enter two integers and displays their greatest common divisor. You can rewrite the program using a method, as shown in Listing 5.5.

LISTING 5.5 GreatestCommonDivisorMethod.java

```
1  import java.util.Scanner;
2
3  public class GreatestCommonDivisorMethod {
4    /** Main method */
5    public static void main(String[] args) {
6      // Create a Scanner
7      Scanner input = new Scanner(System.in);
8
9      // Prompt the user to enter two integers
10     System.out.print("Enter first integer: ");
11     int n1 = input.nextInt();
12     System.out.print("Enter second integer: ");
13     int n2 = input.nextInt();
14
15     System.out.println("The greatest common divisor for " + n1 +
16       " and " + n2 + " is " + gcd(n1, n2));
17   }
18
19   /** Return the gcd of two integers */
```

Video Note
Modularize code

invoke **gcd**

compute gcd

```
20  public static int gcd(int n1, int n2) {
21    int gcd = 1; // Initial gcd is 1
22    int k = 2;    // Possible gcd
23
24    while (k <= n1 && k <= n2) {
25      if (n1 % k == 0 && n2 % k == 0)
26        gcd = k; // Update gcd
27      k++;
28    }
29
30    return gcd; // Return gcd
31  }
32 }
```

return gcd

```
Enter first integer: 45  ↵Enter
Enter second integer: 75  ↵Enter
The greatest common divisor for 45 and 75 is 15
```

By enclosing the code for obtaining the gcd in a method, this program has several advantages:

1. It isolates the problem for computing the gcd from the rest of the code in the main method. Thus, the logic becomes clear and the program is easier to read.

2. The errors on computing gcd are confined in the **gcd** method, which narrows the scope of debugging.

3. The **gcd** method now can be reused by other programs.

Listing 5.6 applies the concept of code modularization to improve Listing 4.14, PrimeNumber.java.

LISTING 5.6 PrimeNumberMethod.java

invoke **printPrimeNumbers**

printPrimeNumbers
method

invoke **isPrime**

```
1 public class PrimeNumberMethod {
2   public static void main(String[] args) {
3     System.out.println("The first 50 prime numbers are \n");
4     printPrimeNumbers(50);
5   }
6
7   public static void printPrimeNumbers(int numberOfPrimes) {
8     final int NUMBER_OF_PRIMES = 50; // Number of primes to display
9     final int NUMBER_OF_PRIMES_PER_LINE = 10; // Display 10 per line
10    int count = 0; // Count the number of prime numbers
11    int number = 2; // A number to be tested for primeness
12
13    // Repeatedly find prime numbers
14    while (count < numberOfPrimes) {
15      // Print the prime number and increase the count
16      if (isPrime(number)) {
17        count++; // Increase the count
18
19        if (count % NUMBER_OF_PRIMES_PER_LINE == 0) {
20          // Print the number and advance to the new line
21          System.out.printf("%-5s\n", number);
22        }
23        else
24          System.out.printf("%-5s", number);
25      }
```

```
26
27        // Check if the next number is prime
28        number++;
29    }
30  }
31
32  /** Check whether number is prime */
33  public static boolean isPrime(int number) {          isPrime method
34    for (int divisor = 2; divisor <= number / 2; divisor++) {
35      if (number % divisor == 0) { // If true, number is not prime
36        return false; // number is not a prime
37      }
38    }
39
40    return true; // number is prime
41  }
42 }
```

```
The first 50 prime numbers are

2    3    5    7    11   13   17   19   23   29
31   37   41   43   47   53   59   61   67   71
73   79   83   89   97   101  103  107  109  113
127  131  137  139  149  151  157  163  167  173
179  181  191  193  197  199  211  223  227  229
```

We divided a large problem into two subproblems. As a result, the new program is easier to read and easier to debug. Moreover, the methods printPrimeNumbers and isPrime can be reused by other programs.

5.7 Overloading Methods

The max method that was used earlier works only with the int data type. But what if you need to determine which of two floating-point numbers has the maximum value? The solution is to create another method with the same name but different parameters, as shown in the following code:

```
public static double max(double num1, double num2) {
  if (num1 > num2)
    return num1;
  else
    return num2;
}
```

If you call max with int parameters, the max method that expects int parameters will be invoked; if you call max with double parameters, the max method that expects double parameters will be invoked. This is referred to as *method overloading*; that is, two methods have the same name but different parameter lists within one class. The Java compiler determines which method is used based on the method signature.

method overloading

Listing 5.7 is a program that creates three methods. The first finds the maximum integer, the second finds the maximum double, and the third finds the maximum among three double values. All three methods are named max.

LISTING 5.7 TestMethodOverloading.java

```
1 public class TestMethodOverloading {
2   /** Main method */
3   public static void main(String[] args) {
```

```
4       // Invoke the max method with int parameters
5       System.out.println("The maximum between 3 and 4 is "
6         + max(3, 4));
7
8       // Invoke the max method with the double parameters
9       System.out.println("The maximum between 3.0 and 5.4 is "
10        + max(3.0, 5.4));
11
12      // Invoke the max method with three double parameters
13      System.out.println("The maximum between 3.0, 5.4, and 10.14 is "
14        + max(3.0, 5.4, 10.14));
15    }
16
17    /** Return the max between two int values */
18    public static int max(int num1, int num2) {
19      if (num1 > num2)
20        return num1;
21      else
22        return num2;
23    }
24
25    /** Find the max between two double values */
26    public static double max(double num1, double num2) {
27      if (num1 > num2)
28        return num1;
29      else
30        return num2;
31    }
32
33    /** Return the max among three double values */
34    public static double max(double num1, double num2, double num3) {
35      return max(max(num1, num2), num3);
36    }
37 }
```

overloaded **max** (line 18)

overloaded **max** (line 26)

overloaded **max** (line 34)

```
The maximum between 3 and 4 is 4
The maximum between 3.0 and 5.4 is 5.4
The maximum between 3.0, 5.4, and 10.14 is 10.14
```

When calling max(3, 4) (line 6), the max method for finding the maximum of two integers is invoked. When calling max(3.0, 5.4) (line 10), the max method for finding the maximum of two doubles is invoked. When calling max(3.0, 5.4, 10.14) (line 14), the max method for finding the maximum of three double values is invoked.

Can you invoke the max method with an int value and a double value, such as max(2, 2.5)? If so, which of the max methods is invoked? The answer to the first question is yes. The answer to the second is that the max method for finding the maximum of two double values is invoked. The argument value 2 is automatically converted into a double value and passed to this method.

You may be wondering why the method max(double, double) is not invoked for the call max(3, 4). Both max(double, double) and max(int, int) are possible matches for max(3, 4). The Java compiler finds the most specific method for a method invocation. Since the method max(int, int) is more specific than max(double, double), max(int, int) is used to invoke max(3, 4).

Tip
Overloading methods can make programs clearer and more readable. Methods that perform closely related tasks should be given the same name.

Note

Overloaded methods must have different parameter lists. You cannot overload methods based on different modifiers or return types.

Note

Sometimes there are two or more possible matches for an invocation of a method, but the compiler cannot determine the most specific match. This is referred to as *ambiguous invocation*. Ambiguous invocation causes a compilation error. Consider the following code:

ambiguous invocation

```
public class AmbiguousOverloading {
  public static void main(String[] args) {
    System.out.println(max(1, 2));
  }

  public static double max(int num1, double num2) {
    if (num1 > num2)
      return num1;
    else
      return num2;
  }

  public static double max(double num1, int num2) {
    if (num1 > num2)
      return num1;
    else
      return num2;
  }
}
```

Both `max(int, double)` and `max(double, int)` are possible candidates to match `max(1, 2)`. Since neither is more specific than the other, the invocation is ambiguous, resulting in a compilation error.

5.8 The Scope of Variables

The *scope of a variable* is the part of the program where the variable can be referenced. A variable defined inside a method is referred to as a *local variable*.

local variable

The scope of a local variable starts from its declaration and continues to the end of the block that contains the variable. A local variable must be declared and assigned a value before it can be used.

A parameter is actually a local variable. The scope of a method parameter covers the entire method.

A variable declared in the initial action part of a `for` loop header has its scope in the entire loop. But a variable declared inside a `for` loop body has its scope limited in the loop body from its declaration to the end of the block that contains the variable, as shown in Figure 5.5.

You can declare a local variable with the same name multiple times in different nonnested blocks in a method, but you cannot declare a local variable twice in nested blocks, as shown in Figure 5.6.

Caution

Do not declare a variable inside a block and then attempt to use it outside the block. Here is an example of a common mistake:

```
for (int i = 0; i < 10; i++) {
}

System.out.println(i);
```

The last statement would cause a syntax error because variable `i` is not defined outside of the `for` loop.

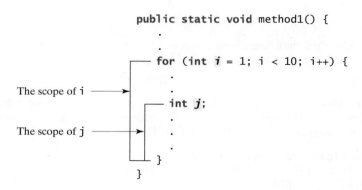

```
public static void method1() {
    .
    .
    for (int i = 1; i < 10; i++) {
        .
        int j;
        .
        .
    }
}
```

The scope of i

The scope of j

FIGURE 5.5 A variable declared in the initial action part of a `for` loop header has its scope in the entire loop.

It is fine to declare i in two nonnested blocks

```
public static void method1() {
    int x = 1;
    int y = 1;

    for (int i = 1; i < 10; i++) {
        x += i;
    }

    for (int i = 1; i < 10; i++) {
        y += i;
    }
}
```

It is wrong to declare i in two nested blocks

```
public static void method2() {

    int i = 1;
    int sum = 0;

    for (int i = 1; i < 10; i++)
        sum += i;
}
```

FIGURE 5.6 A variable can be declared multiple times in nonnested blocks, but can be declared only once in nested blocks.

5.9 The **Math** Class

The `Math` class contains the methods needed to perform basic mathematical functions. You have already used the `pow(a, b)` method to compute a^b in Listing 2.7, ComputeLoan.java, and the `Math.random()` method in Listing 3.3, AdditionQuiz.java. This section introduces other useful methods in the `Math` class. They can be categorized as *trigonometric methods*, *exponent methods*, and *service methods*. Besides methods, the `Math` class provides two useful `double` constants, `PI` and `E` (the base of natural logarithms). You can use these constants as `Math.PI` and `Math.E` in any program.

5.9.1　Trigonometric Methods

The `Math` class contains the following trigonometric methods:

```
public static double sin(double radians)
public static double cos(double radians)
public static double tan(double radians)
public static double asin(double radians)
public static double acos(double radians)
```

```
public static double atan(double radians)
public static double toRadians(double degree)
public static double toDegrees(double radians)
```

Each method has a single `double` parameter, and its return type is `double`. The parameter represents an angle in radians. One degree is equal to $\pi/180$ in radians. For example, `Math.sin(Math.PI)` returns the trigonometric sine of π. Since JDK 1.2, the `Math` class has also provided the method `toRadians(double angdeg)` for converting an angle in degrees to radians, and the method `toDegrees(double angrad)` for converting an angle in radians to degrees.

For example,

```
Math.sin(0) returns 0.0
Math.sin(Math.toRadians(270)) returns -1.0
Math.sin(Math.PI / 6) returns 0.5
Math.sin(Math.PI / 2) returns 1.0
Math.cos(0) returns 1.0
Math.cos(Math.PI / 6) returns 0.866
Math.cos(Math.PI / 2) returns 0
```

5.9.2 Exponent Methods

There are five methods related to exponents in the `Math` class:

```
/** Return e raised to the power of x (eˣ) */
public static double exp(double x)

/** Return the natural logarithm of x (ln(x) = logₑ(x)) */
public static double log(double x)

/** Return the base 10 logarithm of x (log₁₀(x)) */
public static double log10(double x)

/** Return a raised to the power of b (aᵇ) */
public static double pow(double a, double b)

/** Return the square root of x (√x) */
public static double sqrt(double x)
```

Note that the parameter in the `sqrt` method must not be negative.

For example,

```
Math.exp(1) returns 2.71828
Math.log(Math.E) returns 1.0
Math.log10(10) returns 1.0
Math.pow(2, 3) returns 8.0
Math.pow(3, 2) returns 9.0
Math.pow(3.5, 2.5) returns 22.91765
Math.sqrt(4) returns 2.0
Math.sqrt(10.5) returns 3.24
```

5.9.3 The Rounding Methods

The `Math` class contains five rounding methods:

```
/** x is rounded up to its nearest integer. This integer is
 * returned as a double value. */
public static double ceil(double x)
```

```
/** x is rounded down to its nearest integer. This integer is
 * returned as a double value. */
public static double floor(double x)

/** x is rounded to its nearest integer. If x is equally close
 * to two integers, the even one is returned as a double. */
public static double rint(double x)

/** Return (int)Math.floor(x + 0.5). */
public static int round(float x)

/** Return (long)Math.floor(x + 0.5). */
public static long round(double x)
```

For example,

```
Math.ceil(2.1) returns 3.0
Math.ceil(2.0) returns 2.0
Math.ceil(-2.0) returns -2.0
Math.ceil(-2.1) returns -2.0
Math.floor(2.1) returns 2.0
Math.floor(2.0) returns 2.0
Math.floor(-2.0) returns -2.0
Math.floor(-2.1) returns -3.0
Math.rint(2.1) returns 2.0
Math.rint(2.0) returns 2.0
Math.rint(-2.0) returns -2.0
Math.rint(-2.1) returns -2.0
Math.rint(2.5) returns 2.0
Math.rint(-2.5) returns -2.0
Math.round(2.6f) returns 3 // Returns int
Math.round(2.0) returns 2  // Returns long
Math.round(-2.0f) returns -2
Math.round(-2.6) returns -3
```

5.9.4 The min, max, and abs Methods

The min and max methods are overloaded to return the minimum and maximum numbers between two numbers (int, long, float, or double). For example, max(3.4, 5.0) returns 5.0, and min(3, 2) returns 2.

The abs method is overloaded to return the absolute value of the number (int, long, float, and double). For example,

```
Math.max(2, 3) returns 3
Math.max(2.5, 3) returns 3.0
Math.min(2.5, 3.6) returns 2.5
Math.abs(-2) returns 2
Math.abs(-2.1) returns 2.1
```

5.9.5 The random Method

The Math class also has a powerful method, random, which generates a random double value greater than or equal to 0.0 and less than 1.0 (0 <= Math.random() < 1.0). This method is very useful. Listing 3.4, SubtractQuiz.java, uses this method to generate a single-digit integer. You can use it to write a simple expression to generate random numbers in any range. For example,

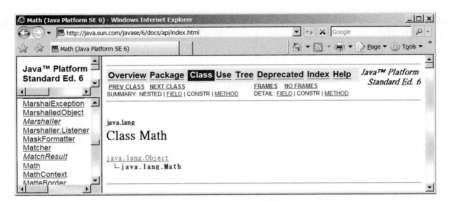

(`int`) (Math.random( ) * 10) $\longrightarrow$ Returns a random integer between 0 and 9

50 + (`int`) (Math.random( ) * 50) $\longrightarrow$ Returns a random integer between 50 and 99

In general,

a + Math.random( ) * b $\longrightarrow$ Returns a random number between a and a + b excluding a + b

Tip

You can view the complete documentation for the `Math` class online from http://java.sun.com/javase/6/docs/api/index.html, as shown in Figure 5.7.

FIGURE 5.7 You can view the documentation for Java API online.

Note

Not all classes need a `main` method. The `Math` class and `JOptionPane` class do not have `main` methods. These classes contain methods for other classes to use.

5.10 Case Study: Generating Random Characters

Computer programs process numerical data and characters. You have seen many examples that involve numerical data. It is also important to understand characters and how to process them. This section presents an example for generating random characters.

As introduced in §2.9, every character has a unique Unicode between 0 and FFFF in hexadecimal (65535 in decimal). To generate a random character is to generate a random integer between 0 and 65535 using the following expression (note that since 0 <= `Math.random()` < 1.0, you have to add 1 to 65535):

```
(int)(Math.random() * (65535 + 1))
```

Now let us consider how to generate a random lowercase letter. The Unicodes for lowercase letters are consecutive integers starting from the Unicode for `'a'`, then that for `'b'`, `'c'`, ..., and `'z'`. The Unicode for `'a'` is

```
(int)'a'
```

So a random integer between `(int)'a'` and `(int)'z'` is

$$(int)((int)'a' + Math.random() * ((int)'z' - (int)'a' + 1)$$

As discussed in §2.9.4, all numeric operators can be applied to the `char` operands. The `char` operand is cast into a number if the other operand is a number or a character. Thus the preceding expression can be simplified as follows:

$$'a' + Math.random() * ('z' - 'a' + 1)$$

and a random lowercase letter is

$$(char)('a' + Math.random() * ('z' - 'a' + 1))$$

To generalize the foregoing discussion, a random character between any two characters `ch1` and `ch2` with `ch1 < ch2` can be generated as follows:

$$(char)(ch1 + Math.random() * (ch2 - ch1 + 1))$$

This is a simple but useful discovery. Let us create a class named `RandomCharacter` in Listing 5.8 with five overloaded methods to get a certain type of character randomly. You can use these methods in your future projects.

LISTING 5.8 RandomCharacter.java

```java
 1 public class RandomCharacter {
 2    /** Generate a random character between ch1 and ch2 */
 3    public static char getRandomCharacter(char ch1, char ch2) {
 4       return (char)(ch1 + Math.random() * (ch2 - ch1 + 1));
 5    }
 6
 7    /** Generate a random lowercase letter */
 8    public static char getRandomLowerCaseLetter() {
 9       return getRandomCharacter('a', 'z');
10    }
11
12    /** Generate a random uppercase letter */
13    public static char getRandomUpperCaseLetter() {
14       return getRandomCharacter('A', 'Z');
15    }
16
17    /** Generate a random digit character */
18    public static char getRandomDigitCharacter() {
19       return getRandomCharacter('0', '9');
20    }
21
22    /** Generate a random character */
23    public static char getRandomCharacter() {
24       return getRandomCharacter('\u0000', '\uFFFF');
25    }
26 }
```

(margin labels: getRandomCharacter, getRandomLowerCaseLetter(), getRandomUpperCaseLetter(), getRandomDigitCharacter(), getRandomCharacter())

Listing 5.9 gives a test program that displays 175 random lowercase letters.

LISTING 5.9 TestRandomCharacter.java

```java
 1 public class TestRandomCharacter {
 2    /** Main method */
```

```
 3   public static void main(String[] args) {
 4     final int NUMBER_OF_CHARS = 175;                          constants
 5     final int CHARS_PER_LINE = 25;
 6
 7     // Print random characters between 'a' and 'z', 25 chars per line
 8     for (int i = 0; i < NUMBER_OF_CHARS; i++) {
 9       char ch = RandomCharacter.getRandomLowerCaseLetter() ;   lower-case letter
10       if ((i + 1) % CHARS_PER_LINE == 0)
11         System.out.println(ch);
12       else
13         System.out.print(ch);
14     }
15   }
16 }
```

5.11 Method Abstraction and Stepwise Refinement

The key to developing software is to apply the concept of abstraction. You will learn many levels of abstraction from this book. *Method abstraction* is achieved by separating the use of   method abstraction
a method from its implementation. The client can use a method without knowing how it is implemented. The details of the implementation are encapsulated in the method and hidden from the client who invokes the method. This is known as *information hiding* or *encapsulation*. If   information hiding
you decide to change the implementation, the client program will not be affected, provided that you do not change the method signature. The implementation of the method is hidden from the client in a "black box," as shown in Figure 5.8.

FIGURE 5.8   The method body can be thought of as a black box that contains the detailed implementation for the method.

You have already used the `System.out.print` method to display a string, the `JOptionPane.showInputDialog` method to read a string from a dialog box, and the `max` method to find the maximum number. You know how to write the code to invoke these methods in your program, but as a user of these methods, you are not required to know how they are implemented.

The concept of method abstraction can be applied to the process of developing programs. When writing a large program, you can use the *divide-and-conquer* strategy, also known as   divide and conquer
stepwise refinement, to decompose it into subproblems. The subproblems can be further decomposed into smaller, more manageable problems.   stepwise refinement

Suppose you write a program that displays the calendar for a given month of the year. The program prompts the user to enter the year and the month, and then displays the entire calendar for the month, as shown in the following sample output:

```
Enter full year (e.g., 2001): 2006  ↵Enter
Enter month in number between 1 and 12: 6  ↵Enter
            June 2006
    ─────────────────────────────
    Sun Mon Tue Wed Thu Fri Sat
                      1   2   3
      4   5   6   7   8   9  10
     11  12  13  14  15  16  17
     18  19  20  21  22  23  24
     25  26  27  28  29  30
```

Let us use this example to demonstrate the divide-and-conquer approach.

5.11.1   Top-Down Design

How would you get started on such a program? Would you immediately start coding? Beginning programmers often start by trying to work out the solution to every detail. Although details are important in the final program, concern for detail in the early stages may block the problem-solving process. To make problem solving flow as smoothly as possible, this example begins by using method abstraction to isolate details from design and only later implements the details.

For this example, the problem is first broken into two subproblems: get input from the user, and print the calendar for the month. At this stage, the creator of the program should be concerned with what the subproblems will achieve, not with how to get input and print the calendar for the month. You can draw a structure chart to help visualize the decomposition of the problem (see Figure 5.9(a)).

(a)   (b)

FIGURE 5.9   The structure chart shows that the `printCalendar` problem is divided into two subproblems, `readInput` and `printMonth`, and that `printMonth` is divided into two smaller subproblems, `printMonthTitle` and `printMonthBody`.

Use the `JOptionPane.showInputDialog` method to display input dialog boxes that prompt the user to enter the year and the month.

The problem of printing the calendar for a given month can be broken into two subproblems: print the month title, and print the month body, as shown in Figure 5.9(b). The month title consists of three lines: month and year, a dash line, and the names of the seven days of the week. You need to get the month name (e.g., January) from the numeric month (e.g., 1). This is accomplished in `getMonthName` (see Figure 5.10(a)).

(a)   (b)

FIGURE 5.10   (a) To `printMonthTitle`, you need `getMonthName`. (b) The `printMonthBody` problem is refined into several smaller problems.

In order to print the month body, you need to know which day of the week is the first day of the month (`getStartDay`) and how many days the month has (`getNumberOfDaysInMonth`), as shown in Figure 5.10(b). For example, December 2005 has 31 days, and the first of the month is Thursday.

How would you get the start day for the first date in a month? There are several ways to do so. The simplest approach is to use the `Calendar` class in §11.3, "Example: `Calendar` and `GregorianCalendar`." For now, an alternative approach is used. Assume you know that the start day (`startDay1800 = 3`) for Jan 1, 1800, was Wednesday. You could compute the total number of days (`totalNumberOfDays`) between Jan 1, 1800, and the first date of the calendar month. The start day for the calendar month is `(totalNumberOfDays + startDay1800) % 7`, since every week has seven days. So the `getStartDay` problem can be further refined as `getTotalNumberOfDays`, as shown in Figure 5.11(a).

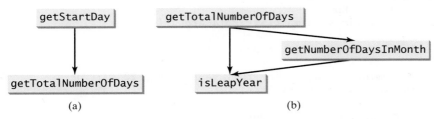

FIGURE 5.11 (a) To `getStartDay`, you need `getTotalNumberOfDays`. (b) The `getTotalNumberOfDays` problem is refined into two smaller problems.

To get the total number of days, you need to know whether the year is a leap year and the number of days in each month. So `getTotalNumberOfDays` is further refined into two subproblems: `isLeapYear` and `getNumberOfDaysInMonth`, as shown in Figure 5.11(b). The complete structure chart is shown in Figure 5.12.

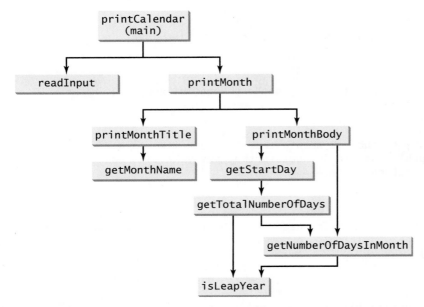

FIGURE 5.12 The structure chart shows the hierarchical relationship of the subproblems in the program.

5.11.2 Top-Down or Bottom-Up Implementation

Now we turn our attention to implementation. In general, a subproblem corresponds to a method in the implementation, although some are so simple that this is unnecessary. You would need to decide which modules to implement as methods and which to combine in other methods. Decisions of this kind should be based on whether the overall program will be easier to read as a result of your choice. In this example, the subproblem `readInput` can be simply implemented in the `main` method.

top-down approach

stub

You can use either a "top-down" approach or a "bottom-up" approach. The top-down approach implements one method in the structure chart at a time from the top to the bottom. Stubs can be used for the methods waiting to be implemented. A *stub* is a simple but incomplete version of a method. The use of stubs enables you to quickly build the framework of the program. Implement the `main` method first, and then use a stub for the `printMonth` method. For example, let `printMonth` display the year and the month in the stub. Thus, your program may begin like this:

```java
public class PrintCalendar {
  /** Main method */
  public static void main(String[] args) {
    // Prompt the user to enter year
    Scanner input = new Scanner(System.in);

    System.out.print("Enter full year (e.g., 2001): ");
    int year = input.nextInt();

    // Prompt the user to enter month
    System.out.print("Enter month as number between 1 and 12: ");
    int month = input.nextInt();

    // Print calendar for the month of the year
    printMonth(year, month);
  }

  /** A stub for printMonth may look like this */
  public static void printMonth(int year, int month) {
    System.out.print(month + " " + year);
  }

  /** A stub for printMonthTitle may look like this */
  public static void printMonthTitle(int year, int month) {
  }

  /** A stub for getMonthName may look like this */
  public static String getMonthName(int month) {
    return "January"; // A dummy value
  }

  /** A stub for getStartDay may look like this */
  public static int getStartDay(int year, int month) {
    return 1; // A dummy value
  }

  /** A stub for getNumberOfDaysInMonth may look like this */
  public static int getNumberOfDaysInMonth(int year, int month) {
    return 31; // A dummy value
  }

  /** A stub for getTotalNumberOfDays may look like this */
  public static int getTotalNumberOfDays(int year, int month) {
    return 10000; // A dummy value
  }
```

```
  /** A stub for getTotalNumberOfDays may look like this */
  public static boolean isLeapYear(int year) {
    return true; // A dummy value
  }
}
```

Compile and test the program, and fix any errors. You can now implement the `printMonth` method. For methods invoked from the `printMonth` method, you can again use stubs.

The bottom-up approach implements one method in the structure chart at a time from the bottom to the top. For each method implemented, write a test program to test it. The top-down and bottom-up approaches are both fine. Both approaches implement methods incrementally, help to isolate programming errors, and make debugging easy. Sometimes they can be used together.

bottom-up approach

5.11.3 Implementation Details

The `isLeapYear(int year)` method can be implemented using the following code:

```
return (year % 400 == 0 || (year % 4 == 0 && year % 100 != 0));
```

Use the following facts to implement `getTotalNumberOfDaysInMonth(int year, int month)`:

■ January, March, May, July, August, October, and December have 31 days.

■ April, June, September, and November have 30 days.

■ February has 28 days during a regular year and 29 days during a leap year. A regular year, therefore, has 365 days, a leap year 366 days.

To implement `getTotalNumberOfDays(int year, int month)`, you need to compute the total number of days (`totalNumberOfDays`) between January 1, 1800, and the first day of the calendar month. You could find the total number of days between the year 1800 and the calendar year and then figure out the total number of days prior to the calendar month in the calendar year. The sum of these two totals is `totalNumberOfDays`.

To print a body, first pad some space before the start day and then print the lines for every week.

The complete program is given in Listing 5.10.

LISTING 5.10 PrintCalendar.java

```java
 1 import java.util.Scanner;
 2
 3 public class PrintCalendar {
 4   /** Main method */
 5   public static void main(String[] args) {
 6     // Prompt the user to enter year
 7     Scanner input = new Scanner(System.in);
 8
 9     // Prompt the user to enter year
10     System.out.print("Enter full year (e.g., 2001): ");
11     int year = input.nextInt();
12
13     // Prompt the user to enter month
14     System.out.print("Enter month in number between 1 and 12: ");
15     int month = input.nextInt();
16
```

```
17     // Print calendar for the month of the year
18     printMonth(year, month);
19   }
20
21   /** Print the calendar for a month in a year */
22   static void printMonth(int year, int month) {
23     // Print the headings of the calendar
24     printMonthTitle(year, month);
25
26     // Print the body of the calendar
27     printMonthBody(year, month);
28   }
29
30   /** Print the month title, e.g., May, 1999 */
31   static void printMonthTitle(int year, int month) {
32     System.out.println("          " + getMonthName(month)
33       + " " + year);
34     System.out.println("-----------------------------");
35     System.out.println(" Sun Mon Tue Wed Thu Fri Sat");
36   }
37
38   /** Get the English name for the month */
39   static String getMonthName(int month) {
40     String monthName = null;
41     switch (month) {
42       case 1: monthName = "January"; break;
43       case 2: monthName = "February"; break;
44       case 3: monthName = "March"; break;
45       case 4: monthName = "April"; break;
46       case 5: monthName = "May"; break;
47       case 6: monthName = "June"; break;
48       case 7: monthName = "July"; break;
49       case 8: monthName = "August"; break;
50       case 9: monthName = "September"; break;
51       case 10: monthName = "October"; break;
52       case 11: monthName = "November"; break;
53       case 12: monthName = "December";
54     }
55
56     return monthName;
57   }
58
59   /** Print month body */
60   static void printMonthBody(int year, int month) {
61     // Get start day of the week for the first date in the month
62     int startDay = getStartDay(year, month);
63
64     // Get number of days in the month
65     int numberOfDaysInMonth = getNumberOfDaysInMonth(year, month);
66
67     // Pad space before the first day of the month
68     int i = 0;
69     for (i = 0; i < startDay; i++)
70       System.out.print("    ");
71
72     for (i = 1; i <= numberOfDaysInMonth; i++) {
73       if (i < 10)
74         System.out.print("    " + i);
75       else
76         System.out.print("   " + i);
```

printMonth

printMonthTitle

getMonthName

getMonthBody

```
77
78       if ((i + startDay) % 7 == 0)
79         System.out.println();
80     }
81
82     System.out.println();
83   }
84
85   /** Get the start day of month/1/year */
86   static int getStartDay(int year, int month) {                           getStartDay
87     final int START_DAY_FOR_JAN_1_1800 = 3;
88     // Get total number of days from 1/1/1800 to month/1/year
89     int totalNumberOfDays = getTotalNumberOfDays(year, month);
90
91     // Return the start day for month/1/year
92     return (totalNumberOfDays + START_DAY_FOR_JAN_1_1800) % 7;
93   }
94
95   /** Get the total number of days since January 1, 1800 */
96   static int getTotalNumberOfDays(int year, int month) {                   getTotalNumberOfDays
97     int total = 0;
98
99     // Get the total days from 1800 to 1/1/year
100    for (int i = 1800; i < year; i++)
101      if (isLeapYear(i))
102        total = total + 366;
103      else
104        total = total + 365;
105
106    // Add days from Jan to the month prior to the calendar month
107    for (int i = 1; i < month; i++)
108      total = total + getNumberOfDaysInMonth(year, i);
109
110    return total;
111  }
112
113  /** Get the number of days in a month */
114  static int getNumberOfDaysInMonth(int year, int month) {                 getNumberOfDaysInMonth
115    if (month == 1 || month == 3 || month == 5 || month == 7 ||
116      month == 8 || month == 10 || month == 12)
117      return 31;
118
119    if (month == 4 || month == 6 || month == 9 || month == 11)
120      return 30;
121
122    if (month == 2) return isLeapYear(year) ? 29 : 28;
123
124    return 0; // If month is incorrect
125  }
126
127  /** Determine if it is a leap year */
128  static boolean isLeapYear(int year) {                                    isLeapYear
129    return year % 400 == 0 || (year % 4 == 0 && year % 100 != 0);
130  }
131 }
```

The program does not validate user input. For instance, if the user enters either a month not in the range between 1 and 12 or a year before 1800, the program displays an erroneous calendar. To avoid this error, add an if statement to check the input before printing the calendar.

This program prints calendars for a month but could easily be modified to print calendars for a whole year. Although it can print months only after January 1800, it could be modified to trace the day of a month before 1800.

Note

Method abstraction modularizes programs in a neat, hierarchical manner. Programs written as collections of concise methods are easier to write, debug, maintain, and modify. This writing style also promotes method reusability.

Tip

incremental development and testing

When implementing a large program, use the top-down or bottom-up approach. Do not write the entire program at once. Using these approaches seems to take more development time (because you repeatedly compile and run the program), but it actually saves time and makes debugging easier.

KEY TERMS

actual parameter 143	method signature 143
argument 143	modifier 142
ambiguous invocation 153	pass-by-value 147
divide and conquer 159	parameter 142
formal parameter (i.e., parameter) 143	return type 142
information hiding 159	return value 142
method 142	scope of variable 153
method abstraction 159	stepwise refinement 159
method overloading 151	stub 162

CHAPTER SUMMARY

■ Making programs modular and reusable is one of the central goals in software engineering. Java provides many powerful constructs that help to achieve this goal. Methods are one such construct.

■ The method header specifies the *modifiers*, *return value type*, *method name*, and *parameters* of the method. The static modifier is used for all the methods in this chapter.

■ A method may return a value. The `returnValueType` is the data type of the value the method returns. If the method does not return a value, the `returnValueType` is the keyword `void`.

■ The *parameter list* refers to the type, order, and number of the parameters of a method. The method name and the parameter list together constitute the *method signature*. Parameters are optional; that is, a method may contain no parameters.

■ A return statement can also be used in a `void` method for terminating the method and returning to the method's caller. This is useful occasionally for circumventing the normal flow of control in a method.

■ The arguments that are passed to a method should have the same number, type, and order as the parameters in the method definition.

■ When a program calls a method, program control is transferred to the called method. A called method returns control to the caller when its return statement is executed or when its method-ending closing brace is reached.

■ A value-returning method can also be invoked as a statement in Java. In this case, the caller simply ignores the return value. In the majority of cases, a call to a method with return value is treated as a value. In some cases, however, the caller is not interested in the return value.

■ Each time a method is invoked, the system stores parameters and local variables in a space known as a *stack*. When a method calls another method, the caller's stack space is kept intact, and new space is created to handle the new method call. When a method finishes its work and returns to its caller, its associated space is released.

■ A method can be overloaded. This means that two methods can have the same name, as long as their method parameter lists differ.

■ The scope of a local variable is limited locally to a method. The scope of a local variable starts from its declaration and continues to the end of the block that contains the variable. A local variable must be declared before it can be used, and it must be initialized before it is referenced.

■ *Method abstraction* is achieved by separating the use of a method from its implementation. The client can use a method without knowing how it is implemented. The details of the implementation are encapsulated in the method and hidden from the client who invokes the method. This is known as *information hiding* or *encapsulation*.

■ Method abstraction modularizes programs in a neat, hierarchical manner. Programs written as collections of concise methods are easier to write, debug, maintain, and modify than would otherwise be the case. This writing style also promotes method reusability.

■ When implementing a large program, use the top-down or bottom-up coding approach. Do not write the entire program at once. These approaches seem to take more time for coding (because you are repeatedly compiling and running the program), but they actually save time and makes debugging easier.

REVIEW QUESTIONS

Sections 5.2–5.3

5.1 What are the benefits of using a method? How do you declare a method? How do you invoke a method?

5.2 What is the `return` type of a `main` method?

5.3 Can you simplify the `max` method in Listing 5.1 using the conditional operator?

5.4 True or false? A call to a method with a `void` return type is always a statement itself, but a call to a value-returning method is always a component of an expression.

5.5 What would be wrong with not writing a `return` statement in a value-returning method? Can you have a `return` statement in a `void` method, such as the following?

```java
public static void main(String[] args) {
  int i;
  while (true) {
    // Prompt the user to enter an integer
    String intString = JOptionPane.showInputDialog(
      "Enter an integer:");

    // Convert a string into int
    int i = Integer.parseInt(intString);
    if (i == 0)
      return;
    System.out.println("i = " + i);
  }
}
```

Does the **return** statement in the following method cause syntax errors?

```java
public static void xMethod(double x, double y) {
  System.out.println(x + y);
  return x + y;
}
```

5.6 Define the terms parameter, argument, and method signature.

5.7 Write method headers for the following methods:

- Computing a sales commission, given the sales amount and the commission rate.
- Printing the calendar for a month, given the month and year.
- Computing a square root.
- Testing whether a number is even, and returning **true** if it is.
- Printing a message a specified number of times.
- Computing the monthly payment, given the loan amount, number of years, and annual interest rate.
- Finding the corresponding uppercase letter, given a lowercase letter.

5.8 Identify and correct the errors in the following program:

```java
1  public class Test {
2    public static method1(int n, m) {
3      n += m;
4      xMethod(3.4);
5    }
6
7    public static int xMethod(int n) {
8      if (n > 0) return 1;
9      else if (n == 0) return 0;
10     else if (n < 0) return -1;
11   }
12 }
```

5.9 Reformat the following program according to the programming style and documentation guidelines proposed in §2.13, "Programming Style and Documentation." Use the next-line brace style.

```java
public class Test {
  public static double xMethod(double i,double j)
  {
  while (i<j) {
    j--;
  }
```

```
        return j;
      }
    }
```

Section 5.4 Passing Parameters

5.10 How is an argument passed to a method? Can the argument have the same name as its parameter?

5.11 What is pass-by-value? Show the result of the following programs:

```java
public class Test {
  public static void main(String[] args) {
    int max = 0;
    max(1, 2, max);
    System.out.println(max);
  }

  public static void max(
      int value1, int value2, int max) {
    if (value1 > value2)
      max = value1;
    else
      max = value2;
  }
}
```

(a)

```java
public class Test {
  public static void main(String[] args) {
    // Initialize times
    int times = 3;
    System.out.println("Before the call,"
      + " variable times is " + times);

    // Invoke nPrintln and display times
    nPrintln("Welcome to Java!", times);
    System.out.println("After the call,"
      + "variable times is " + times);
  }

  // Print the message n times
  public static void nPrintln(
      String message, int n) {
    while (n > 0) {
      System.out.println("n = " + n);
      System.out.println(message);
      n--;
    }
  }
}
```

(b)

```java
public class Test {
  public static void main(String[] args) {
    int i = 1;
    while (i <= 6) {
      xMethod(i, 2);
      i++;
    }
  }

  public static void xMethod(
      int i, int num) {
    for (int j = 1; j <= i; j++) {
      System.out.print(num + " ");
      num *= 2;
    }

    System.out.println();
  }
}
```

(c)

```java
public class Test {
  public static void main(String[] args) {
    int i = 0;
    while (i <= 4) {
      xMethod(i);
      i++;
    }

    System.out.println("i is " + i);
  }

  public static void xMethod(int i) {
    do {
      if (i % 3 != 0)
        System.out.print(i + " ");
      i--;
    }
    while (i >= 1);

    System.out.println();
  }
}
```

(d)

5.12 For (a) in the preceding question, show the contents of the stack just before the method `max` is invoked, just entering `max`, just before `max` is returned, and right after `max` is returned.

Section 5.7 Overloading Methods

5.13 What is method overloading? Is it permissible to define two methods that have the same name but different parameter types? Is it permissible to define two methods in a class that have identical method names and parameter lists but different return value types or different modifiers?

5.14 What is wrong in the following program?

```java
public class Test {
  public static void method(int x) {
  }

  public static int method(int y) {
    return y;
  }
}
```

Section 5.8 The Scope of Local Variables

5.15 Identify and correct the errors in the following program:

```java
 1 public class Test {
 2   public static void main(String[] args) {
 3     nPrintln("Welcome to Java!", 5);
 4   }
 5
 6   public static void nPrintln(String message, int n) {
 7     int n = 1;
 8     for (int i = 0; i < n; i++)
 9       System.out.println(message);
10   }
11 }
```

Section 5.9 The **Math** Class

5.16 True or false? The argument for trigonometric methods represents an angle in radians.

5.17 Write an expression that returns a random integer between `34` and `55`. Write an expression that returns a random integer between `0` and `999`. Write an expression that returns a random number between `5.5` and `55.5`. Write an expression that returns a random lowercase letter.

5.18 Evaluate the following method calls:

(a) Math.sqrt(4)
(b) Math.sin(2 * Math.PI)
(c) Math.cos(2 * Math.PI)
(d) Math.pow(2, 2)
(e) Math.log(Math.E)
(f) Math.exp(1)
(g) Math.max(2, Math.min(3, 4))
(h) Math.rint(− 2.5)
(i) Math.ceil(− 2.5)
(j) Math.floor(− 2.5)
(k) Math.round(− 2.5f)

(l)   Math.round(-2.5)
(m)   Math.rint(2.5)
(n)   Math.ceil(2.5)
(o)   Math.floor(2.5)
(p)   Math.round($2.5f$)
(q)   Math.round(2.5)
(r)   Math.round(Math.abs(-2.5))

PROGRAMMING EXERCISES

Sections 5.2–5.7

5.1   (*Converting an uppercase letter to lowercase*) Write a method that converts an uppercase letter to a lowercase letter. Use the following method header:

```
public static char upperCaseToLowerCase(char ch)
```

If the character is not an uppercase letter, the method simply returns the character itself. For example, `upperCaseToLowerCase('B')` returns `b` and `upperCaseToLowerCase('5')` returns `5`. See Exercise 2.7 on how to convert an uppercase letter to lowercase.

5.2*   (*Summing the digits in an integer*) Write a method that computes the sum of the digits in an integer. Use the following method header:

```
public static int sumDigits(long n)
```

For example, `sumDigits(234)` returns `9` ($2 + 3 + 4$).

Hint: Use the `%` operator to extract digits, and the `/` operator to remove the extracted digit. For instance, to extract `4` from `234`, use `234 % 10` (=4). To remove `4` from `234`, use `234 / 10` (=23). Use a loop to repeatedly extract and remove the digit until all the digits are extracted.

5.3*   (*Displaying an integer reversed*) Write the following method to display an integer in reverse order:

```
public static void reverse(int number)
```

For example, `reverse(3456)` displays `6543`.

5.4**   (*Returning an integer reversed*) Write the following method to return an integer reversed:

```
public static int reverse(int number)
```

For example, `reverse(3456)` returns `6543`.

5.5*   (*Sorting three numbers*) Write the following method to display three numbers in increasing order:

```
 public static void sort(double num1, double num2, double num3)
```

5.6*   (*Displaying patterns*) Write a method to display a pattern as follows:

```
        1
      2 1
    3 2 1
...
n n-1 ... 3 2 1
```

The method header is

```
public static void displayPattern(int n)
```

5.7* (*Financial application: computing the future investment value*) Write a method that computes future investment value at a given interest rate for a specified number of years. The future investment is determined using the formula in Exercise 2.9.
Use the following method header:

```
public static double futureInvestmentValue(
  double investmentAmount, double monthlyInterestRate, int
  years)
```

For example, `futureInvestmentValue(10000, 0.05/12, 5)` returns `12833.59`.
Write a test program that prompts the user to enter the investment amount (e.g., 1000) and the interest rate (e.g., 9%), and prints a table that displays future value for the years from 1 to 30, as shown below:

```
The amount invested: 1000
Annual interest rate: 9%
Years          Future Value
  1               1093.8
  2               1196.41
...
 29              13467.25
 30              14730.57
```

5.8 (*Conversions between Celsius and Fahrenheit*) Write a class that contains the following two methods:

```
/** Converts from Celsius to Fahrenheit */
public static double celsiusToFahrenheit(double celsius)


/** Converts from Fahrenheit to Celsius */
public static double fahrenheitToCelsius(double fahrenheit)
```

The formula for the conversion is:

```
fahrenheit = (9.0 / 5) * celsius + 32
```

Write a test program that invokes these methods to display the following tables:

Celsius	Fahrenheit	Fahrenheit	Celsius
40.0	104.0	120.0	48.89
39.0	102.2	110.0	43.33
...			
32.0	89.6	40.0	4.44
31.0	87.8	30.0	-1.11

5.9 (*Conversions between feet and meters*) Write a class that contains the following two methods:

```
/** Converts from feet to meters */
public static double footToMeter(double foot)

/** Converts from meters to feet */
public static double meterToFoot(double meter)
```

The formula for the conversion is:

```
meter = 0.305 * foot
```

Write a test program that invokes these methods to display the following tables:

Feet	Meters		Meters	Feet
1.0	0.305	|	20.0	65.574
2.0	0.61	|	25.0	81.967
...		|		
9.0	2.745	|	60.0	196.721
10.0	3.05	|	65.0	213.115

5.10 (*Using the* `isPrime` *Method*) Listing 5.6, PrimeNumberMethod.java, provides the `isPrime(int number)` method for testing whether a number is prime. Use this method to find the number of prime numbers less than **10000**.

5.11 (*Financial application: computing commissions*) Write a method that computes the commission, using the scheme in §4.8.2, "Problem: Finding the Sales Amount." The header of the method is as follows:

```
public static double computeCommission(double salesAmount)
```

Write a test program that displays the following table:

SalesAmount	Commission
10000	900.0
15000	1500.0
...	
95000	11100.0
100000	11700.0

5.12** (*Displaying characters*) Write a method that prints characters using the following header:

```
public static void printChars(char ch1, char ch2,
  int numberPerLine)
```

This method prints the characters between `ch1` and `ch2` with the specified numbers per line. Write a test program that prints ten characters per line from `'1'` to `'Z'`.

5.13* (*Summing series*) Write a method to compute the following series:

$$m(i) = \frac{1}{2} + \frac{2}{3} + \cdots + \frac{i}{i+1}$$

Write a test program that displays the following table:

i	m(i)
1	0.5
2	1.1667
...	
19	16.4023
20	17.3546

5.14* (*Computing series*) Write a method to compute the following series:

$$m(i) = 4\left(1 - \frac{1}{3} + \frac{1}{5} - \frac{1}{7} + \frac{1}{9} - \frac{1}{11} + \frac{1}{13} - \cdots + \frac{1}{2i-1} - \frac{1}{2i+1}\right)$$

5.15* (*Financial application: printing a tax table*) Listing 3.7 gives a program to compute tax. Write a method for computing tax using the following header:

```
public static double computetax(int status, double taxableIncome)
```

Use this method to write a program that prints a tax table for taxable income from $50,000 to $60,000 with intervals of $50 for all four statuses, as follows:

Taxable Income	Single	Married Joint	Married Separate	Head of a House
50000	9846	7296	10398	8506
50050	9859	7309	10411	8519
...				
59950	12532	9982	13190	11192
60000	12546	9996	13205	11206

5.16* (*Number of days in a year*) Write a method that returns the number of days in a year using the following header:

```
public static int numberOfDaysInAYear(int year)
```

Write a test program that displays the number of days in year 2000, ..., and 2010.

Section 5.9 The Math Class

5.17* (*Displaying matrix of 0s and 1s*) Write a method that displays an n-by-n matrix using the following header:

```
public static void printMatrix(int n)
```

Each element is 0 or 1, which is generated randomly. Write a test program that prints a 3-by-3 matrix that may look like this:

```
0 1 0
0 0 0
1 1 1
```

5.18 (*Using the Math.sqrt method*) Write a program that prints the following table using the sqrt method in the Math class.

Number	SquareRoot
0	0.0000
2	1.4142
...	
18	4.2426
20	4.4721

5.19* (*The MyTriangle class*) Create a class named MyTriangle that contains the following two methods:

```
/** Returns true if the sum of any two sides is
 *  greater than the third side. */
public static boolean isValid(
  double side1, double side2, double side3)

/** Returns the area of the triangle. */
public static double area(
  double side1, double side2, double side3)
```

The formula for computing the area is

$$s = (side1 + side2 + side3)/2;$$

$$area = \sqrt{s(s - side1)(s - side2)(s - side3)}$$

Write a test program that reads three sides for a triangle and computes the area if the input is valid. Otherwise, it displays that the input is invalid.

5.20 (*Using trigonometric methods*) Print the following table to display the `sin` value and `cos` value of degrees from 0 to 360 with increments of 10 degrees. Round the value to keep four digits after the decimal point.

Degree	Sin	Cos
0	0.0	1.0
10	0.1736	0.9848
...		
350	-0.1736	0.9848
360	0.0	1.0

5.21** (*Computing mean and standard deviation*) In business applications, you are often asked to compute the mean and standard deviation of data. The mean is simply the average of the numbers. The standard deviation is a statistic that tells you how tightly all the various data are clustered around the mean in a set of data. For example, what is the average age of the students in a class? How close are the ages? If all the students are the same age, the deviation is 0. Write a program that prompts the user to enter ten numbers, and displays the mean and standard deviations of these numbers using the following formula:

$$mean = \frac{\sum_{i=1}^{n} x_i}{n} = \frac{x_1 + x_2 + \dots + x_n}{n} \qquad deviation = \sqrt{\frac{\sum_{i=1}^{n} x_i^2 - \frac{\left(\sum_{i=1}^{n} x_i\right)^2}{n}}{n - 1}}$$

5.22** (*Approximating the square root*) Implement the `sqrt` method. The square root of a number, `num`, can be approximated by repeatedly performing a calculation using the following formula:

```
nextGuess = (lastGuess + (num / lastGuess)) / 2
```

When `nextGuess` and `lastGuess` are almost identical, `nextGuess` is the approximated square root.

The initial guess can be any positive value (e.g., `1`). This value will be the starting value for `lastGuess`. If the difference between `nextGuess` and `lastGuess` is less than a very small number, such as `0.0001`, you can claim that `nextGuess` is the approximated square root of `num`. If not, `nextGuess` becomes the `lastGuess` and continue the approximation process.

Sections 5.10–5.11

5.23* (*Generating random characters*) Use the methods in `RandomCharacter` in Listing 5.8 to print 100 uppercase letters and then 100 single digits, and print ten per line.

5.24** (*Displaying current date and time*) Listing 2.9, ShowCurrentTime.java, displays the current time. Improve this example to display the current date and time. The calendar example in Listing 5.10, PrintCalendar.java, should give you some ideas on how to find year, month, and day.

5.25**(*Converting milliseconds to hours, minutes, and seconds*) Write a method that converts milliseconds to hours, minutes, and seconds using the following header:

public static String convertMillis(**long** millis)

The method returns a string as hours:minutes:seconds. For example, convertMillis(5500) returns a string 0:0:5, convertMillis(100000) returns a string 0:1:40, and convertMillis(555550000) returns a string 154:19:10.

Comprehensive

Video Note
Find emirp prime

5.26**(*Emirp*) An *emirp* (prime spelled backward) is a prime number whose reversal is also a prime. For example, 17 is a prime and 71 is a prime. So 17 and 71 are emirps. Write a program that displays the first 100 emirps. Display 10 numbers per line and align the numbers properly, as follows:

```
    2    3    5    7   11   13   17   31   37   71
   73   79   97  101  107  113  131  149  151  157
. . .
```

5.27**(*Palindromic prime*) A *palindromic prime* is a prime number and also palindromic. For example, 131 is a prime and also a palindromic prime. So are 17 and 71. Write a program that displays the first 100 palindromic prime numbers. Display 10 numbers per line and align the numbers properly, as follows:

```
    2    3    5    7   11  101  131  151  181  191
  313  353  373  383  727  757  787  797  919  929
. . .
```

5.28**(*Mersenne prime*) A prime number is called a *Mersenne prime* if it can be written in the form $2^p - 1$ for some positive integer p. Write a program that finds all Mersenne primes with $p \le 31$ and displays the output as follows:

```
p        2^p - 1
2           3
3           7
5          31
. . .
```

5.29**(*Game: craps*) Craps is a popular dice game played in casinos. Write a program to play a variation of the game, as follows:

Roll two dice. Each die has six faces representing values 1, 2, ..., and 6, respectively. Check the sum of the two dice. If the sum is 2, 3, or 12 (called *craps*), you lose; if the sum is 7 or 11 (called *natural*), you win; if the sum is another value (i.e., 4, 5, 6, 8, 9, or 10), a *point* is established. Continue to roll the dice until either a 7 or the same point value is rolled. If 7 is rolled, you lose. Otherwise, you win.

Your program acts as a single player. Here are some sample runs.

```
You rolled 5 + 6 = 11
You win
```

```
You rolled 1 + 2 = 3
You lose
```

```
You rolled 4 + 4 = 8
point is 8
You rolled 6 + 2 = 8
You win
```

```
You rolled 3 + 2 = 5
point is 5
You rolled 2 + 5 = 7
You lose
```

5.30** (*Twin primes*) Twin primes are a pair of prime numbers that differ by 2. For example, 3 and 5 are twin primes, 5 and 7 are twin primes, and 11 and 13 are twin primes. Write a program to find all twin primes less than 1000. Display the output as follows:

```
(3, 5)
(5, 7)
...
```

5.31**(*Financial: credit card number validation*) Credit card numbers follow certain patterns. A credit card number must have between 13 and 16 digits. It must start with:

- 4 for Visa cards
- 5 for Master cards
- 37 for American Express cards
- 6 for Discover cards

In 1954, Hans Luhn of IBM proposed an algorithm for validating credit card numbers. The algorithm is useful to determine if a card number is entered correctly or if a credit card is scanned correctly by a scanner. Almost all credit card numbers are generated following this validity check, commonly known as the *Luhn check* or the *Mod 10 check*, which can be described as follows (for illustration, consider the card number 4388576018402625):

1. Double every second digit from right to left. If doubling of a digit results in a two-digit number, add up the two digits to get a single-digit number.

   $2 * 2 = 4$
   $2 * 2 = 4$
   $4 * 2 = 8$
   $1 * 2 = 2$
   $6 * 2 = 12 (1 + 2 = 3)$
   $5 * 2 = 10 (1 + 0 = 1)$
   $8 * 2 = 16 (1 + 6 = 7)$
   $4 * 2 = 8$

2. Now add all single-digit numbers from Step 1.
   $4 + 4 + 8 + 2 + 3 + 1 + 7 + 8 = 37$

3. Add all digits in the odd places from right to left in the card number.

   $5 + 6 + 0 + 8 + 0 + 7 + 8 + 3 = 37$

4. Sum the results from Step 2 and Step 3.

   $37 + 37 = 74$

5. If the result from Step 4 is divisible by 10, the card number is valid; otherwise, it is invalid. For example, the number 4388576018402625 is invalid, but the number 4388576018410707 is valid.

Write a program that prompts the user to enter a credit card number as a `long` integer. Display whether the number is valid. Design your program to use the following methods:

```java
/** Return true if the card number is valid */
public boolean isValid(long number)

/** Get the result from Step 2 */
public static int sumOfEvenPlace(long number)

/** Return this number if it is a single digit, otherwise, return
 * the sum of the two digits */
public static int getDigit(int number)

/** Return sum of odd place digits in number */
public static int sumOfOddPlace(long number)
```

5.32** (*Game: chance of winning at craps*) Revise Exercise 5.29 to run it 10000 times and display the number of winning games.

CHAPTER 6

ARRAYS

Objectives

- To describe why arrays are necessary in programming (§6.1).

- To learn the steps involved in using arrays: declaring array reference variables and creating arrays (§§6.2.1–6.2.2).

- To initialize the values in an array (§6.2.3).

- To access array elements using indexed variables (§6.2.4).

- To simplify programming using the for-each loops (§6.2.5).

- To declare, create, and initialize an array using an array initializer (§6.2.6).

- To copy contents from one array to another (§6.3).

- To develop and invoke methods with array arguments and return value (§6.4–6.5).

- To declare a method with variable-length argument list (§6.6).

- To search elements using the linear (§6.7.1) or binary (§6.7.2) search algorithm.

- To sort an array using the selection sort (§6.8.1)

- To sort an array using the insertion sort algorithm (§6.8.2).

- To use the methods in the `Arrays` class (§6.9).

- To declare and create two-dimensional arrays to solve interesting problems such as Sudoku (§6.10).

- To declare and create multidimensional arrays (§6.11).

6.1 Introduction

why array?

Often you will have to store a large number of values during the execution of a program. Suppose, for instance, that you need to read 100 numbers, compute their average, and find out how many numbers are above the average. Your program first reads the numbers and computes their average, and then compares each number with the average to determine whether it is above the average. The numbers must all be stored in variables in order to accomplish this task. You have to declare 100 variables and repeatedly write almost identical code one hundred times. From the standpoint of practicality, it is impossible to write a program this way. So, how do you solve this problem?

what is array?

An efficient, organized approach is needed. Java and most other high-level languages provide a data structure, the *array*, which stores a fixed-size sequential collection of elements of the same type. In this case, you can store all 100 numbers into an array and access the numbers through a single array variable.

6.2 Array Basics

An array is used to store a collection of data, but it is often more useful to think of an array as a collection of variables of the same type. Instead of declaring individual variables, such as `number0`, `number1`, ..., and `number99`, you declare one array variable such as `numbers` and use `numbers[0]`, `numbers[1]`, ..., and `numbers[99]` to represent individual variables. This section introduces how to declare array variables, create arrays, and process arrays using indexed variables.

6.2.1 Declaring Array Variables

To use an array in a program, you must declare a variable to reference the array and specify the type of array the variable can reference. Here is the syntax for declaring an array variable:

preferred syntax

```
dataType[] arrayRefVar;
```

For example, the following code snippets are examples of this syntax:

```
double[] myList;
```

Note

preferred syntax

You can also use `dataType arrayRefVar[]` to declare an array variable. This style comes from the C language and was adopted in Java to accommodate C programmers. The style `dataType[] arrayRefVar` is preferred

6.2.2 Creating Arrays

Unlike declarations for primitive data type variables, the declaration of an array variable does not allocate any space in memory for the array. It creates only a storage location for the reference to an array. If a variable does not contain a reference to an array, the value of the variable is `null`. You cannot assign elements to an array unless it has already been created. After an array variable is declared, you can create an array by using the `new` operator with the following syntax:

```
arrayRefVar = new dataType[arraySize];
```

This statement does two things: (1) it creates an array using `new dataType[arraySize];`   new operator
(2) it assigns the reference of the newly created array to the variable `arrayRefVar`.

Declaring an array variable, creating an array, and assigning the reference of the array to
the variable can be combined in one statement, as shown below:

```
dataType[] arrayRefVar = new dataType[arraySize];
```

or

```
dataType arrayRefVar[] = new dataType[arraySize];
```

Here is an example of such a statement:

```
double[] myList = newdouble[10];
```

This statement declares an array variable, `myList`, creates an array of ten elements of
`double` type, and assigns its reference to `myList`. To assign values to the elements, use the
syntax:

```
arrayRefVar[index] = value;
```

For example, the following code initializes the array.

```
myList[0] = 5.6;
myList[1] = 4.5;
myList[2] = 3.3;
myList[3] = 13.2;
myList[4] = 4.0;
myList[5] = 34.33;
myList[6] = 34.0;
myList[7] = 45.45;
myList[8] = 99.993;
myList[9] = 11123;
```

The array is pictured in Figure 6.1.

FIGURE 6.1   The array `myList` has ten elements of `double` type and `int` indices from 0 to 9.

array vs. array variable

Note

An array variable that appears to hold an array actually contains a reference to that array. Strictly speaking, an array variable and an array are different, but most of the time the distinction can be ignored. Thus it is all right to say, for simplicity, that `myList` is an array, instead of stating, at greater length, that `myList` is a variable that contains a reference to an array of ten double elements.

6.2.3 Array Size and Default Values

When space for an array is allocated, the array size must be given, to specify the number of elements that can be stored in it. The size of an array cannot be changed after the array is created. Size can be obtained using `arrayRefVar.length`. For example, `myList.length` is `10`.

array length

default values

When an array is created, its elements are assigned the default value of `0` for the numeric primitive data types, `'\u0000'` for `char` types, and `false` for `boolean` types.

6.2.4 Array Indexed Variables

0 based

The array elements are accessed through the index. Array indices are `0` based; that is, they start from `0` to `arrayRefVar.length-1`. In the example in Figure 6.1, `myList` holds ten `double` values, and the indices are from `0` to `9`.

indexed variables

Each element in the array is represented using the following syntax, known as an *indexed variable:*

```
arrayRefVar[index];
```

For example, `myList[9]` represents the last element in the array `myList`.

Caution

Some languages use parentheses to reference an array element, as in `myList(9)`. But Java uses brackets, as in `myList[9]`.

After an array is created, an indexed variable can be used in the same way as a regular variable. For example, the following code adds the values in `myList[0]` and `myList[1]` to `myList[2]`.

```
myList[2] = myList[0] + myList[1];
```

The following loop assigns `0` to `myList[0]`, `1` to `myList[1]`, ..., and `9` to `myList[9]`:

```
for (int i = 0; i < myList.length; i++) {
  myList[i] = i;
}
```

6.2.5 Array Initializers

Java has a shorthand notation, known as the *array initializer*, which combines in one statement declaring an array, creating an array, and initializing, using the following syntax:

```
dataType[] arrayRefVar = {value0, value1, ..., valuek};
```

For example,

```
double[] myList = {1.9, 2.9, 3.4, 3.5};
```

This statement declares, creates, and initializes the array `myList` with four elements, which is equivalent to the statements shown below:

```
double[] myList = new double[4];
myList[0] = 1.9;
myList[1] = 2.9;
myList[2] = 3.4;
myList[3] = 3.5;
```

Caution

The **new** operator is not used in the array initializer syntax. Using an array initializer, you have to declare, create, and initialize the array all in one statement. Splitting it would cause a syntax error. Thus the next statement is wrong:

```
double[] myList;
myList = {1.9, 2.9, 3.4, 3.5};
```

6.2.6 Processing Arrays

When processing array elements, you will often use a `for` loop—for two reasons:

- All of the elements in an array are of the same type. They are evenly processed in the same fashion by repeatedly using a loop.

- Since the size of the array is known, it is natural to use a `for` loop.

Here are some examples of processing arrays:

1. (*Initializing arrays with random values*) The following loop initializes the array `myList` with random values between `0.0` and `100.0`, but less than `100.0`.

```
for (int i = 0; i < myList.length; i++) {
   myList[i] = Math.random() * 100;
}
```

2. (*Printing arrays*) To print an array, you have to print each element in the array using a loop like the following:

```
for (int i = 0; i < myList.length; i++) {
   System.out.print(myList[i] + " ");
}
```

Tip

For an array of the `char[]` type, it can be printed using one print statement. For example, the following code displays `Dallas`:

print character array

```
char[] city = {'D', 'a', 'l', 'l', 'a', 's'};
System.out.println(city);
```

3. (*Summing all elements*) Use a variable named `total` to store the sum. Initially `total` is `0`. Add each element in the array to `total` using a loop like this:

```
double total = 0;
for (int i = 0; i < myList.length; i++) {
   total += myList[i];
}
```

4. (*Finding the largest element*) Use a variable named `max` to store the largest element. Initially `max` is `myList[0]`. To find the largest element in the array `myList`,

compare each element in `myList` with `max`, and update `max` if the element is greater than `max`.

```java
double max = myList[0];
for (int i = 1; i < myList.length; i++) {
  if (myList[i] > max) max = myList[i];
}
```

5. (*Finding the smallest index of the largest element*) Often you need to locate the largest element in an array. If an array has more than one largest element, find the smallest index of such an element. Suppose the array `myList` is {1, 5, 3, 4, 5, 5}. The largest element is 5 and the smallest index for 5 is 1. Use a variable named `max` to store the largest element and a variable named `indexOfMax` to denote the index of the largest element. Initially `max` is `myList[0]`, and `indexOfMax` is 0. Compare each element in `myList` with `max`, and update `max` and `indexOfMax` if the element is greater than `max`.

```java
double max = myList[0];
int indexOfMax = 0;
for (int i = 1; i < myList.length; i++) {
  if (myList[i] > max) {
    max = myList[i];
    indexOfMax = i;
  }
}
```

What is the consequence if `(myList[i] > max)` is replaced by `(myList[i] >= max)`?

6. (*Shifting elements*) Sometimes you need to shift the elements left or right. Here is an example to shift the elements one position to the left and fill the last element with the first element:

```java
double temp = myList[0]; // Retain the first element

// Shift elements left
for (int i = 1; i < myList.length; i++) {
  myList[i - 1] = myList[i];
}

// Move the first element to fill in the last position
myList[myList.length - 1] = temp;
```

myList

6.2.7 For-each Loops

JDK 1.5 introduced a new `for` loop, known as a *for-each loop* or *enhanced for loop*, which enables you to traverse the complete array sequentially without using an index variable. For example, the following code displays all the elements in the array `myList`:

```java
for (double element: myList) {
  System.out.println(element);
}
```

You can read the code as "for each element in `myList` do the following." Note that the variable, `element`, must be declared the same type as the elements in `myList`.

In general, the syntax for a `for-each` loop is

```java
for (elementType element: arrayRefVar) {
  // Process the element
}
```

You still have to use an index variable if you wish to traverse the array in a different order or change the elements in the array.

6.2.8 Problem: Analyzing Array Elements

The problem is to write a program that reads six integers, finds the largest of them, and counts its occurrences. Suppose that you entered 3, 5, 2, 5, 5, 5; the program finds that the largest is 5 and the occurrence count for 5 is 4.

An intuitive solution is to first read the numbers and store them in an array, then find the largest number in the array, and finally count the occurrences of the largest number in the array. The program is given in Listing 6.1.

LISTING 6.1 TestArray.java

```java
 1 import java.util.Scanner;
 2
 3 public class TestArray {
 4   /** Main method */
 5   public static void main(String[] args) {
 6     final int TOTAL_NUMBERS = 6;
 7     int[] numbers = new int[TOTAL_NUMBERS];
 8
 9     // Create a Scanner
10     Scanner input = new Scanner(System.in);
11
12     // Read all numbers
13     for (int i = 0; i < numbers.length; i++) {
14       System.out.print("Enter a number: ");
15
16       // Convert string into integer
17       numbers[i] = input.nextInt();
18     }
19
20     // Find the largest
21     int max = numbers[0];
22     for (int i = 1; i < numbers.length; i++) {
23       if (max < numbers[i])
24         max = numbers[i];
25     }
26
27     // Find the occurrence of the largest number
28     int count = 0;
29     for (int i = 0; i < numbers.length; i++) {
30       if (numbers[i] == max) count++;
31     }
32
33     // Prepare the result
34     String output = "The array is ";
35     for (int i = 0; i < numbers.length; i++) {
36       output += numbers[i] + " ";
37     }
38
39     output += "\nThe largest number is " + max;
40     output += "\nThe occurrence count of the largest number "
41       + "is " + count;
42
43     // Display the result
44     System.out.println(output);
45   }
46 }
```

create array

store numbers

update max

count occurrence

prepare output

output

```
Enter a number: 3 ↵ Enter
Enter a number: 5 ↵ Enter
Enter a number: 2 ↵ Enter
Enter a number: 5 ↵ Enter
Enter a number: 5 ↵ Enter
Enter a number: 5 ↵ Enter
The array is 3 5 2 5 5 5
The largest number is 5
The occurrence count of the largest number is 4
```

The program declares and creates an array of six integers (line 7). It finds the largest number in the array (lines 21–25), counts its occurrences (lines 28–31), and displays the result (lines 34–44). To display the array, you need to display each element in the array using a loop.

Without using the `numbers` array, you would have to declare a variable for each number entered, because all the numbers are compared to the largest number to count its occurrences after it is found.

Caution

Accessing an array out of bounds is a common programming error that throws a runtime `ArrayIndexOutOfBoundsException`. To avoid it, make sure that you do not use an index beyond `arrayRefVar.length - 1`.

Programmers often mistakenly reference the first element in an array with index `1`, but it should be `0`. This is called the *off-by-one error*.

margin notes:
**ArrayIndexOutOfBounds
Exception**

off-by-one error

6.2.9   Problem: Assigning Grades

The problem is to write a program that reads student scores, gets the best score, and then assigns grades based on the following scheme:

Grade is A if score is $>=$ best $-$ 10;

Grade is B if score is $>=$ best $-$ 20;

Grade is C if score is $>=$ best $-$ 30;

Grade is D if score is $>=$ best $-$ 40;

Grade is F otherwise.

The program prompts the user to enter the total number of students, then prompts the user to enter all of the scores, and concludes by displaying the grades.

The program reads the scores, then finds the best score, and finally assigns grades to the students based on the preceding scheme. Listing 6.2 gives the solution to the problem.

Video Note
Assign grades

LISTING 6.2   AssignGrade.java

```java
1  import java.util.Scanner;
2
3  public class AssignGrade {
4    /** Main method */
5    public static void main(String[] args) {
6      // Create a Scanner
7      Scanner input = new Scanner(System.in);
8
9      // Get number of students
10     System.out.print("Please enter number of students: ");
```

```
11      int numberOfStudents = input.nextInt();

12
13      int[] scores = new int[numberOfStudents]; // Array scores
14      int best = 0; // The best score
15      char grade; // The grade
16
17      // Read scores and find the best score
18      for (int i = 0; i < scores.length ; i++) {
19        System.out.print("Please enter a score: ");
20        scores[i] = input.nextInt();
21
22        if (scores[i] > best)
23          best = scores[i];
24      }
25
26      // Declare and initialize output string
27      String output = " ";
28
29      // Assign and display grades
30      for (int i = 0; i < scores.length ; i++) {
31        if (scores[i] >= best - 10)
32          grade = 'A';
33        else if (scores[i] >= best - 20)
34          grade = 'B';
35        else if (scores[i] >= best - 30)
36          grade = 'C';
37        else if (scores[i] >= best - 40)
38          grade = 'D';
39        else
40          grade = 'F';
41
42        output += "Student " + i + " score is " +
43          scores[i] + " and grade is " + grade + "\n";
44      }
45
46      // Display the result
47      System.out.println(output);
48    }
49 }
```

number of students

create array

get a score

update best

assign grade

display grade

```
Please enter number of students: 4  ↵Enter
Please enter a score: 40  ↵Enter
Please enter a score: 50  ↵Enter
Please enter a score: 60  ↵Enter
Please enter a score: 70  ↵Enter
Student 0 score is 40 and grade is C
Student 1 score is 50 and grade is B
Student 2 score is 60 and grade is A
Student 3 score is 70 and grade is A
```

The program declares and creates **scores** as an array of **int** type in order to store the students' scores (line 13), after the user enters the number of students into **numberOfStudents** in line 11. The size of the array is set at runtime; it cannot be changed once the array is created.

The array is not needed to find the best score, but it is needed to keep all of the scores so that grades can be assigned later on, and it is needed when scores are printed along with the students' grades.

6.3 Copying Arrays

Often, in a program, you need to duplicate an array or a part of an array. In such cases you could attempt to use the assignment statement (=), as follows:

```
list2 = list1;
```

copy reference

garbage collection

This statement does not copy the contents of the array referenced by `list1` to `list2`, but merely copies the reference value from `list1` to `list2`. After this statement, `list1` and `list2` reference to the same array, as shown in Figure 6.2. The array previously referenced by `list2` is no longer referenced; it becomes garbage, which will be automatically collected by the Java Virtual Machine.

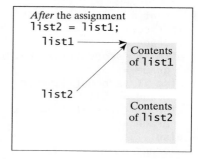

FIGURE 6.2 Before the assignment statement, `list1` and `list2` point to separate memory locations. After the assignment, the reference of the `list1` array is passed to `list2`.

In Java, you can use assignment statements to copy primitive data type variables, but not arrays. Assigning one array variable to another array variable actually copies one reference to another and makes both variables point to the same memory location.

There are three ways to copy arrays:

- Use a loop to copy individual elements one by one.

- Use the static `arraycopy` method in the `System` class.

- Use the `clone` method to copy arrays; this will be introduced in Chapter 10, "Inheritance and Polymorphism."

You can write a loop to copy every element from the source array to the corresponding element in the target array. The following code, for instance, copies `sourceArray` to `targetArray` using a `for` loop.

```java
int[] sourceArray = {2, 3, 1, 5, 10};
int[] targetArray = new int[sourceArray.length];
for (int i = 0; i < sourceArray.length; i++) {
  targetArray[i] = sourceArray[i];
}
```

arraycopy method

Another approach is to use the `arraycopy` method in the `java.lang.System` class to copy arrays instead of using a loop. The syntax for `arraycopy` is shown below:

```java
arraycopy(sourceArray, src_pos, targetArray, tar_pos, length);
```

The parameters `src_pos` and `tar_pos` indicate the starting positions in `sourceArray` and `targetArray`, respectively. The number of elements copied from `sourceArray` to `targetArray` is indicated by `length`. For example, you can rewrite the loop using the following statement:

```
System.arraycopy(sourceArray, 0, targetArray, 0, sourceArray.length);
```

The `arraycopy` method does not allocate memory space for the target array. The target array must have already been created with its memory space allocated. After the copying takes place, `targetArray` and `sourceArray` have the same content but independent memory locations.

Note

The `arraycopy` method violates the Java naming convention. By convention, this method should be named `arrayCopy` (i.e., with an uppercase C).

6.4 Passing Arrays to Methods

Just as you can pass primitive type values to methods, you can also pass arrays to methods. For example, the following method displays the elements in an `int` array.

```
public static void printArray(int[] array) {
  for (int i = 0; i < array.length; i++) {
    System.out.print(array[i] + " ");
  }
}
```

You can invoke it by passing an array. For example, the following statement invokes the `printArray` method to display 3, 1, 2, 6, 4, and 2.

```
printArray(new int[]{3, 1, 2, 6, 4, 2});
```

Note

The preceding statement creates an array using the following syntax:

```
new dataType[]{value0, value1, ..., valuek};
```

There is no explicit reference variable for the array. Such array is called an *anonymous array*.   anonymous arrays

Java uses *pass-by-value* to pass arguments to a method. There are important differences   pass-by-value
between passing the values of variables of primitive data types and passing arrays.

- For an argument of a primitive type, the argument's value is passed.

- For an argument of an array type, the value of the argument is a reference to an array; this reference value is passed to the method. Semantically, it can be best described as *pass-by-sharing*, i.e., the array in the method is the same as the array being passed. So   pass-by-sharing
  if you change the array in the method, you will see the change outside the method.

Take the following code, for example:

```
public class Test {
  public static void main(String[] args) {
    int x = 1; // x represents an int value
    int[] y = new int[10]; // y represents an array of int values

    m(x, y); // Invoke m with arguments x and y
```

```
        System.out.println("x is " + x);
        System.out.println("y[0] is " + y[0]);
  }

  public static void m(int number, int[] numbers) {
    number = 1001; // Assign a new value to number
    numbers[0] = 5555; // Assign a new value to numbers[0]
  }
}
```

You will see that after m is invoked, x remains 1, but y[0] is 5555. This is because y and numbers reference to the same array, although y and numbers are independent variables, as illustrated in Figure 6.3. When invoking m(x, y), the values of x and y are passed to number and numbers. Since y contains the reference value to the array, numbers now contains the same reference value to the same array.

FIGURE 6.3 The primitive type value in x is passed to number, and the reference value in y is passed to numbers.

 Note

The JVM stores the array in an area of memory called the *heap*, which is used for dynamic memory allocation where blocks of memory are allocated and freed in an arbitrary order.

heap

6.4.1 Passing Array Arguments

Listing 6.3 gives another program that shows the difference between passing a primitive data type value and an array reference variable to a method.

The program contains two methods for swapping elements in an array. The first method, named swap, fails to swap two int arguments. The second method, named swapFirstTwoInArray, successfully swaps the first two elements in the array argument.

LISTING 6.3 TestPassArray.java

```
 1 public class TestPassArray {
 2   /** Main method */
 3   public static void main(String[] args) {
 4     int[] a = {1, 2};
 5
 6     // Swap elements using the swap method
 7     System.out.println("Before invoking swap");
 8     System.out.println("array is {" + a[0] + ", " + a[1] + "}");
 9     swap(a[0], a[1]);
10     System.out.println("After invoking swap");
11     System.out.println("array is {" + a[0] + ", " + a[1] + "}");
12
```

false swap

```
13      // Swap elements using the swapFirstTwoInArray method
14      System.out.println("Before invoking swapFirstTwoInArray");
15      System.out.println("array is {" + a[0] + ", " + a[1] + "}");
16      swapFirstTwoInArray(a);
17      System.out.println("After invoking swapFirstTwoInArray");
18      System.out.println("array is {" + a[0] + ", " + a[1] + "}");
19    }
20
21    /** Swap two variables */
22    public static void swap(int n1, int n2) {
23      int temp = n1;
24      n1 = n2;
25      n2 = temp;
26    }
27
28    /** Swap the first two elements in the array */
29    public static void swapFirstTwoInArray(int[] array) {
30      int temp = array[0];
31      array[0] = array[1];
32      array[1] = temp;
33    }
34 }
```

swap array elements

```
Before invoking swap
array is {1,2}
After invoking swap
array is {1,2}
Before invoking swapFirstTwoInArray
array is {1,2}
After invoking swapFirstTwoInArray
array is {2,1}
```

As shown in Figure 6.4, the two elements are not swapped using the **swap** method. However, they are swapped using the **swapFirstTwoInArray** method. Since the parameters in the **swap** method are primitive type, the values of **a[0]** and **a[1]** are passed to **n1** and **n2** inside the method when invoking **swap(a[0], a[1])**. The memory locations for **n1** and **n2** are

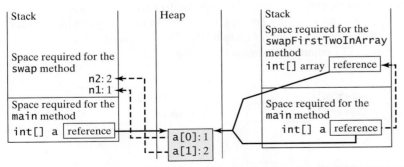

Invoke swap(int n1, int n2). The primitive type values in a[0] and a[1] are passed to the swap method.

The arrays are stored in a heap.

Invoke swapFirstTwoInArray(int[] array). The reference value in a is passed to the swapFirstTwoInArray method.

FIGURE 6.4 When passing an array to a method, the reference of the array is passed to the method.

independent of the ones for `a[0]` and `a[1]`. The contents of the array are not affected by this call.

The parameter in the `swapFirstTwoInArray` method is an array. As shown in Figure 6.4, the reference of the array is passed to the method. Thus the variables `a` (outside the method) and `array` (inside the method) both refer to the same array in the same memory location. Therefore, swapping `array[0]` with `array[1]` inside the method `swapFirst TwoInArray` is the same as swapping `a[0]` with `a[1]` outside of the method.

6.5 Returning an Array from a Method

You can pass arrays when invoking a method. A method may also return an array. For example, the method shown below returns an array that is the reversal of another array:

create array

```
1  public static int[] reverse(int[] list) {
2    int[] result = new int[list.length];
3
4    for (int i = 0, j = result.length - 1;
5         i < list.length; i++, j--) {
6      result[j] = list[i];
7    }
8
9    return result;
10 }
```

return array

Line 2 creates a new array `result`. Lines 4–7 copy elements from array `list` to array `result`. Line 9 returns the array. For example, the following statement returns a new array `list2` with elements 6, 5, 4, 3, 2, 1.

```
int[] list1 = {1, 2, 3, 4, 5, 6};
int[] list2 = reverse(list1);
```

6.5.1 Case Study: Counting the Occurrences of Each Letter

Listing 6.4 presents a program to count the occurrences of each letter in an array of characters. The program does the following:

1. Generate 100 lowercase letters randomly and assign them to an array of characters, as shown in Figure 6.5(a). You can obtain a random letter by using the `getRandomLowerCaseLetter()` method in the `RandomCharacter` class in Listing 5.8.

2. Count the occurrences of each letter in the array. To count the occurrences of each letter in the array, create an array, say `counts`, of 26 `int` values, each of which counts the occurrences of a letter, as shown in Figure 6.5(b). That is, `counts[0]` counts the number of `a`'s, `counts[1]` counts the number of `b`'s, and so on.

(a)   (b)

FIGURE 6.5 The `chars` array stores 100 characters, and the `counts` array stores 26 counts, each of which counts the occurrences of a letter.

LISTING 6.4 CountLettersInArray.java

```
 1 public class CountLettersInArray {
 2   /** Main method */
 3   public static void main(String[] args) {
 4     // Declare and create an array
 5     char[] chars = createArray();
 6
 7     // Display the array
 8     System.out.println("The lowercase letters are:");
 9     displayArray(chars);
10
11     // Count the occurrences of each letter
12     int[] counts = countLetters(chars);
13
14     // Display counts
15     System.out.println();
16     System.out.println("The occurrences of each letter are:");
17     displayCounts(counts);
18   }
19
20   /** Create an array of characters */
21   public static char[] createArray() {
22     // Declare an array of characters and create it
23     char[] chars = new char[100];
24
25     // Create lowercase letters randomly and assign
26     // them to the array
27     for (int i = 0; i < chars.length; i++)
28       chars[i] = RandomCharacter.getRandomLowerCaseLetter();
29
30     // Return the array
31     return chars;
32   }
33
34   /** Display the array of characters */
35   public static void displayArray(char[] chars) {
36     // Display the characters in the array 20 on each line
37     for (int i = 0; i < chars.length; i++) {
38       if ((i + 1) % 20 == 0)
39         System.out.println(chars[i] + " ");
40       else
41         System.out.print(chars[i] + " ");
42     }
43   }
44
45   /** Count the occurrences of each letter */
46   public static int[] countLetters(char[] chars) {
47     // Declare and create an array of 26 int
48     int[] counts = new int[26];
49
50     // For each lowercase letter in the array, count it
51     for (int i = 0; i < chars.length; i++)
52       counts[chars[i] - 'a']++;
53
54     return counts;
55   }
56
57   /** Display counts */
58   public static void displayCounts(int[] counts) {
```

create array

pass array

return array

pass array

count

```
59        for (int i = 0; i < counts.length; i++) {
60          if ((i + 1) % 10 == 0)
61            System.out.println(counts[i] + " " + (char)(i + 'a'));
62          else
63            System.out.print(counts[i] + " " + (char)(i + 'a') + " ");
64        }
65      }
66 }
```

```
The lowercase letters are:
e y l s r i b k j v j h a b z n w b t v
s c c k r d w a m p w v u n q a m p l o
a z g d e g f i n d x m z o u l o z j v
h w i w n t g x w c d o t x h y v z y z
q e a m f w p g u q t r e n n w f c r f

The occurrences of each letter are:
5 a 3 b 4 c 4 d 4 e 4 f 4 g 3 h 3 i 3 j
2 k 3 l 4 m 6 n 4 o 3 p 3 q 4 r 2 s 4 t
3 u 5 v 8 w 3 x 3 y 6 z
```

The **createArray** method (lines 21–32) generates an array of **100** random lowercase letters. Line 5 invokes the method and assigns the array to **chars**. What would be wrong if you rewrote the code as follows?

```
char[] chars = new char[100];
chars = createArray();
```

You would be creating two arrays. The first line would create an array by using **new char[100]**. The second line would create an array by invoking **createArray()** and assign the reference of the array to **chars**. The array created in the first line would be garbage because it is no longer referenced. Java automatically collects garbage behind the scenes. Your program would compile and run correctly, but it would create an array unnecessarily.

Invoking **getRandomLowerCaseLetter()** (line 28) returns a random lowercase letter. This method is defined in the **RandomCharacter** class in Listing 5.8.

The **countLetters** method (lines 46–55) returns an array of **26 int** values, each of which stores the number of occurrences of a letter. The method processes each letter in the array and increases its count by one. A brute-force approach to count the occurrences of each letter might be as follows:

```
for (int i = 0; i < chars.length; i++)
  if (chars[i] == 'a')
    counts[0]++;
  else if (chars[i] == 'b')
    counts[1]++;
  ...
```

But a better solution is given in lines 51–52.

```
for (int i = 0; i < chars.length; i++)
  counts[chars[i] - 'a']++;
```

If the letter (**chars[i]**) is **'a'**, the corresponding count is **counts['a' - 'a']** (i.e., **counts[0]**). If the letter is **'b'**, the corresponding count is **counts['b' - 'a']** (i.e., **counts[1]**) since the Unicode of **'b'** is one more than that of **'a'**. If the letter is **'z'**, the corresponding count is **counts['z' - 'a']** (i.e., **counts[25]**), since the Unicode of **'z'** is **25** more than that of **'a'**.

Figure 6.6 shows the call stack and heap *during* and *after* executing `createArray`. See Review Question 6.14 to show the call stack and heap for other methods in the program.

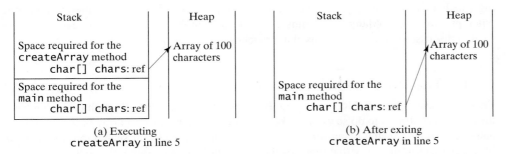

(a) Executing
createArray in line 5

(b) After exiting
createArray in line 5

FIGURE 6.6   (a) An array of 100 characters is created when executing `createArray`. (b) This array is returned and assigned to the variable `chars` in the `main` method.

6.6 Variable-Length Argument Lists

You can pass a variable number of arguments of the same type to a method. The parameter in the method is declared as follows:

```
typeName... parameterName
```

In the method declaration, you specify the type followed by an ellipsis (...). Only one variable-length parameter may be specified in a method, and this parameter must be the last parameter. Any regular parameters must precede it.

Java treats a variable-length parameter as an array. You can pass an array or a variable number of arguments to a variable-length parameter. When invoking a method with a variable number of arguments, Java creates an array and passes the arguments to it. Listing 6.5 contains a method that prints the maximum value in a list of an unspecified number of values.

LISTING 6.5 `VarArgsDemo.java`

```java
 1 public class VarArgsDemo {
 2   public static void main(String[] args) {
 3     printMax(34, 3, 3, 2, 56.5);                    pass variable-length arg list
 4     printMax(new double[]{1, 2, 3});                pass an array arg
 5   }
 6
 7   public static void printMax(double... numbers) {  a variable-length arg
 8     if (numbers.length == 0) {                          parameter
 9       System.out.println("No argument passed");
10       return;
11     }
12
13     double result = numbers[0];
14
15     for (int i = 1; i < numbers.length; i++)
16       if (numbers[i] > result)
17         result = numbers[i];
18
19     System.out.println("The max value is " + result);
20   }
21 }
```

Line 3 invokes the `printMax` method with a variable-length argument list passed to the array `numbers`. If no arguments are passed, the length of the array is `0` (line 8).

Line 4 invokes the `printMax` method with an array.

6.7 Searching Arrays

linear search
binary search

Searching is the process of looking for a specific element in an array—for example, discovering whether a certain score is included in a list of scores. Searching is a common task in computer programming. Many algorithms and data structures are devoted to searching. This section discusses two commonly used approaches, *linear search* and *binary search*.

6.7.1 The Linear Search Approach

The linear search approach compares the key element **key** sequentially with each element in the array. It continues to do so until the key matches an element in the array or the array is exhausted without a match being found. If a match is made, the linear search returns the index of the element in the array that matches the key. If no match is found, the search returns -1. The **linearSearch** method in Listing 6.6 gives the solution:

LISTING 6.6 LinearSearch.java

```
 1  public class LinearSearch {
 2    /** The method for finding a key in the list */
 3    public static int linearSearch(int[] list, int key) {
 4      for (int i = 0; i < list.length; i++) {
 5        if (key == list[i])
 6          return i;
 7      }
 8      return -1;
 9    }
10  }
```

```
          [0] [1] [2] ...
list
key  Compare key with list[i] for i = 0, 1, ...
```

To better understand this method, trace it with the following statements:

```
int[] list = {1, 4, 4, 2, 5, -3, 6, 2};
int i = linearSearch(list, 4);  // Returns 1
int j = linearSearch(list, -4); // Returns -1
int k = linearSearch(list, -3); // Returns 5
```

The linear search method compares the key with each element in the array. The elements in the array can be in any order. On average, the algorithm will have to compare half of the elements in an array before finding the key, if it exists. Since the execution time of a linear search increases linearly as the number of array elements increases, linear search is inefficient for a large array.

6.7.2 The Binary Search Approach

Binary search is the other common search approach for a list of values. For binary search to work, the elements in the array must already be ordered. Without loss of generality, assume that the array is in ascending order. The binary search first compares the key with the element in the middle of the array. Consider the following three cases:

■ If the key is less than the middle element, you need to continue to search for the key only in the first half of the array.

- If the key is equal to the middle element, the search ends with a match.

- If the key is greater than the middle element, you need to continue to search for the key only in the second half of the array.

Clearly, the binary search method eliminates half of the array after each comparison. Suppose that the array has n elements. For convenience, let n be a power of 2. After the first comparison, there are n/2 elements left for further search; after the second comparison, (n/2)/2 elements are left. After the kth comparison, $n/2^k$ elements are left for further search. When $k = \log_2 n$, only one element is left in the array, and you need only one more comparison. Therefore, in the worst case when using the binary search approach, you need $\log_2 n + 1$ comparisons to find an element in the sorted array. In the worst case for a list of 1024 (2^{10}) elements, binary search requires only 11 comparisons, whereas a linear search requires 1023 comparisons in the worst case.

The portion of the array being searched shrinks by half after each comparison. Let low and high denote, respectively, the first index and last index of the array that is currently being searched. Initially, low is 0 and high is list.length-1. Let mid denote the index of the middle element. So mid is (low + high)/2. Figure 6.7 shows how to find key 11 in the list {2, 4, 7, 10, 11, 45, 50, 59, 60, 66, 69, 70, 79} using binary search.

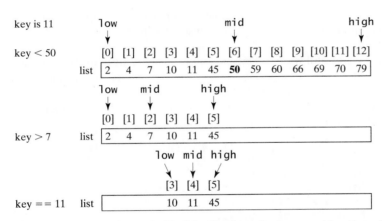

FIGURE 6.7 Binary search eliminates half of the list from further consideration after each comparison.

The binary search returns the index of the search key if it is contained in the list. Otherwise, it returns −(insertion point + 1) The insertion point is the point at which the key would be inserted into the list. For example, the insertion point for key 5 is 2, so the binary search returns −3; the insertion point for key 51 is 7, so the binary search returns −8.

You now know how the binary search works. The next task is to implement it in Java, as shown in Listing 6.7.

Listing 6.7 BinarySearch.java

```
1 public class BinarySearch {
2   /** Use binary search to find the key in the list */
3   public static int binarySearch(int[] list, int key) {
4     int low = 0;
```

```
5      int high = list.length - 1;
6
7      while (high >= low) {
8        int mid = (low + high) / 2;
9        if (key < list[mid])
10         high = mid - 1;
11       else if (key == list[mid])
12         return mid;
13       else
14         low = mid + 1;
15     }
16
17     return -low - 1; // Now high < low
18   }
19 }
```

first half

second half

You start by comparing the key with the middle element in the list whose `low` index is `0` and `high` index is `list.length-1`. If `key < list[mid]`, set the `high` index to `mid-1`; if `key == list[mid]`, a match is found and return `mid`; if `key > list[mid]`, set the `low` index to `mid+1`. Continue the search until `low > high` or a match is found. If `low > high`, return `-low - 1`, where `low` is the insertion point.

What happens if `(high >= low)` in line 7 is replaced by `(high > low)`? The search would miss a possible matching element. Consider a list with just one element. The search would miss the element.

Does the method still work if there are duplicate elements in the list? Yes, as long as the elements are sorted in increasing order in the list. The method returns the index of one of the matching elements if the element is in the list.

To better understand this method, trace it with the following statements and identify `low` and `high` when the method returns.

```
int[] list = {2, 4, 7, 10, 11, 45, 50, 59, 60, 66, 69, 70, 79};
int i = binarySearch(list, 2); // Returns 0
int j = binarySearch(list, 11); // Returns 4
int k = binarySearch(list, 12); // Returns -6
int l = binarySearch(list, 1); // Returns -1
int m = binarySearch(list, 3); // Returns -2
```

Here is the table that lists the `low` and `high` values when the method exits and the value returned from invoking the method.

Method	Low	High	Value Returned
binarySearch(list, 2)	0	1	0
binarySearch(list, 11)	3	5	4
binarySearch(list, 12)	5	4	−6
binarySearch(list, 1)	0	−1	−1
binarySearch(list, 3)	1	0	−2

why -low - 1?

If the key matches an element in the list, the method returns the index of the element. This index is a nonnegative integer (*including 0*). If the key is not in the list, `low` is the index where the element would be inserted. In this case, the method returns `-low - 1`. It would be more intuitive to return just `-low`. But this would be wrong. Suppose the key is smaller than `list[0]` (e.g., `binarySearch(list, 1)`). When the method exits, `low` is `0`. Returning

-low would be -0. There is no difference between -0 and 0. -0 would indicate that the element is not in the list, while 0 would indicate that the key matches the first element in the list (e.g., binarySearch(list, 2)). So, returning -low for a nonmatching case could conflict with returning 0 for the matching case on list[0]. For this reason, the method is designed to return -low - 1 for a nonmatching case.

Note

Linear search is useful for finding an element in a small array or an unsorted array, but it is inefficient for large arrays. Binary search is more efficient, but requires that the array be presorted.

binary search benefits

6.8 Sorting Arrays

Sorting, like searching, is a common task in computer programming. It would be used, for instance, if you wanted to display the grades from Listing 6.2, "Assigning Grades," in alphabetical order. Many different algorithms have been developed for sorting. This section introduces two simple, intuitive sorting algorithms: *selection sort* and *insertion sort*.

6.8.1 Selection Sort

Suppose that you want to sort a list in ascending order. Selection sort finds the largest number in the list and places it last. It then finds the largest number remaining and places it next to last, and so on until the list contains only a single number. Figure 6.8 shows how to sort a list {2, 9, 5, 4, 8, 1, 6} using selection sort.

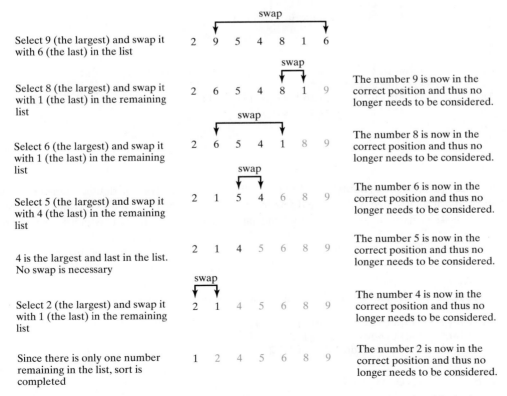

FIGURE 6.8 Selection sort repeatedly selects the largest number and swaps it with the last number in the list.

You know how the selection-sort approach works. The task now is to implement it in Java. Beginners find it difficult to develop a complete solution on the first attempt. Start by writing the code for the first iteration to find the largest element in the list and swap it with the last element, and then observe what would be different for the second iteration, the third, and so on. The insight this gives will enable you to write a loop that generalizes all the iterations.

The solution can be described as follows:

```
for (int i = list.length - 1; i >= 1; i−) {
    select the largest element in list[0..i];
    swap the largest with list[i], if necessary;
    // list[i] is in its correct position.
    // The next iteration apply on list[0..i-1]
}
```

Listing 6.8 implements the solution.

Video Note
Selection sort

LISTING 6.8   SelectionSort.java

```
 1  public class SelectionSort {
 2    /** The method for sorting the numbers */
 3    public static void selectionSort(double[] list) {
 4      for (int i = list.length - 1; i >= 1; i−−) {
 5        // Find the maximum in the list[0..i]
 6        double currentMax = list[0];
 7        int currentMaxIndex = 0;
 8
 9        for (int j = 1; j <= i; j++) {
10          if (currentMax < list[j]) {
11            currentMax = list[j];
12            currentMaxIndex = j;
13          }
14        }
15
16        // Swap list[i] with list[currentMaxIndex] if necessary;
17        if (currentMaxIndex != i) {
18          list[currentMaxIndex] = list[i];
19          list[i] = currentMax;
20        }
21      }
22    }
23  }
```

select

swap

The `selectionSort(double[] list)` method sorts any array of double elements. The method is implemented with a nested **for** loop. The outer loop (with the loop control variable `i`) (line 4) is iterated in order to find the largest element in the list, which ranges from `list[0]` to `list[i]`, and exchange it with the current last element, `list[i]`.

The variable `i` is initially `list.length-1`. After each iteration of the outer loop, `list[i]` is in the right place. Eventually, all the elements are put in the right place; therefore, the whole list is sorted.

To better understand this method, trace it with the following statements:

```
selectionSort(new double[]{2, 1});
selectionSort(new double[]{2, 3, 1});
selectionSort(new double[]{1, 2, 1});
```

6.8.2   Insertion Sort

Suppose that you want to sort a list in ascending order. The insertion-sort algorithm sorts a list of values by repeatedly inserting a new element into a sorted sublist until the whole list is sorted. Figure 6.9 shows how to sort the list {2, 9, 5, 4, 8, 1, 6} using insertion sort.

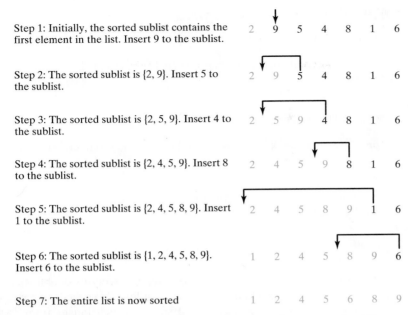

Step 1: Initially, the sorted sublist contains the first element in the list. Insert 9 to the sublist.

2 9 5 4 8 1 6

Step 2: The sorted sublist is {2, 9}. Insert 5 to the sublist.

2 9 5 4 8 1 6

Step 3: The sorted sublist is {2, 5, 9}. Insert 4 to the sublist.

2 5 9 4 8 1 6

Step 4: The sorted sublist is {2, 4, 5, 9}. Insert 8 to the sublist.

2 4 5 9 8 1 6

Step 5: The sorted sublist is {2, 4, 5, 8, 9}. Insert 1 to the sublist.

2 4 5 8 9 1 6

Step 6: The sorted sublist is {1, 2, 4, 5, 8, 9}. Insert 6 to the sublist.

1 2 4 5 8 9 6

Step 7: The entire list is now sorted

1 2 4 5 6 8 9

Figure 6.9 Insertion sort repeatedly inserts a new element into a sorted sublist.

The algorithm can be described as follows:

```
for (int i = 1; i < list.length; i++) {
  insert list[i] into a sorted sublist list[0..i-1] so that
  list[0..i] is sorted.
}
```

To insert `list[i]` into `list[0..i-1]`, save `list[i]` into a temporary variable, say `currentElement`. Move `list[i-1]` to `list[i]` if `list[i-1]` > `currentElement`, move `list[i-2]` to `list[i-1]` if `list[i-2]` > `currentElement`, and so on, until `list[i-k]` <= `currentElement` or k > i (we pass the first element of the sorted list). Assign `currentElement` to `list[i-k+1]`. For example, to insert 4 into {2, 5, 9} in Step 3 in Figure 6.10, move `list[2]` (9) to `list[3]` since 9 > 4, move `list[1]` (5) to `list[2]` since 5 > 4, Finally, move `currentElement` (4) to `list[1]`.

The algorithm can be expanded and implemented as in Listing 6.9.

```
        [0][1][2][3][4][5][6]
list     2  5  9  4              Step 1: Save 4 to a temporary variable currentElement

        [0][1][2][3][4][5][6]
list     2  5     9              Step 2: Move list[2] to list[3]

        [0][1][2][3][4][5][6]
list     2     5  9              Step 3: Move list[1] to list[2]

        [0][1][2][3][4][5][6]
list     2  4  5  9              Step 4: Assign currentElement to list[1]
```

Figure 6.10 A new element is inserted into a sorted sublist.

LISTING 6.9 InsertionSort.java

```
 1 public class InsertionSort {
 2   /** The method for sorting the numbers */
 3   public static void insertionSort(double[] list) {
 4     for (int i = 1; i < list.length; i++) {
 5       /** insert list[i] into a sorted sublist list[0..i-1] so that
 6             list[0..i] is sorted. */
 7       double currentElement = list[i];
 8       int k;
 9       for (k = i - 1; k >= 0 && list[k] > currentElement; k-) {
10         list[k + 1] = list[k];
11       }
12
13       // Insert the current element into list[k + 1]
14       list[k + 1] = currentElement;
15     }
16   }
17 }
```

shift

insert

The **insertionSort(double[] list)** method sorts any array of double elements. The method is implemented with a nested **for** loop. The outer loop (with the loop control variable **i**) (line 4) is iterated in order to obtain a sorted sublist, which ranges from **list[0]** to **list[i]**. The inner loop (with the loop control variable **k**) inserts **list[i]** into the sublist from **list[0]** to **list[i-1]**.

To better understand this method, trace it with the following statements:

```
insertionSort(new double[]{2, 1});
insertionSort(new double[]{2, 3, 1});
insertionSort(new double[]{1, 2, 1});
```

6.9 The **Arrays** Class

The **java.util.Arrays** class contains various static methods for sorting and searching arrays, comparing arrays, and filling array elements. These methods are overloaded for all primitive types.

sort

You can use the **sort** method to sort a whole array or a partial array. For example, the following code sorts an array of numbers and an array of characters.

```
double[] numbers = {6.0, 4.4, 1.9, 2.9, 3.4, 3.5};
java.util.Arrays.sort(numbers); // Sort the whole array

char[] chars = {'a', 'A', '4', 'F', 'D', 'P'};
java.util.Arrays.sort(chars, 1, 3); // Sort part of the array
```

Invoking **sort(numbers)** sorts the whole array **numbers**. Invoking **sort(chars, 1, 3)** sorts a partial array from **chars[1]** to **chars[3-1]**.

binarySearch

You can use the **binarySearch** method to search for a key in an array. The array must be presorted in increasing order. If the key is not in the array, the method returns **-(insertion point + 1)**. For example, the following code searches the keys in an array of integers and an array of characters.

```
int[] list = {2, 4, 7, 10, 11, 45, 50, 59, 60, 66, 69, 70, 79};
System.out.println("(1) Index is " +
  java.util.Arrays.binarySearch(list, 11));
System.out.println("(2) Index is " +
  java.util.Arrays.binarySearch(list, 12));
```

```
char[] chars = {'a', 'c', 'g', 'x', 'y', 'z'};
System.out.println("(3) Index is " +
  java.util.Arrays.binarySearch(chars, 'a'));
System.out.println("(4) Index is " +
  java.util.Arrays.binarySearch(chars, 't'));
```

The output of the preceding code is

(1) Index is 4
(2) Index is −6
(3) Index is 0
(4) Index is −4

You can use the `equals` method to check whether two arrays are equal. Two arrays are equal **equals**
if they have the same contents. In the following code, `list1` and `list2` are equal, but `list2`
and `list3` are not.

```
int[] list1 = {2, 4, 7, 10};
int[] list2 = {2, 4, 7, 10};
int[] list3 = {4, 2, 7, 10};
System.out.println(java.util.Arrays.equals(list1, list2)); // true
System.out.println(java.util.Arrays.equals(list2, list3)); // false
```

You can use the `fill` method to fill in all or part of the array. For example, the following code **fill**
fills `list1` with `5` and fills `8` into elements `list2[1]` and `list2[3-1]`.

```
int[] list1 = {2, 4, 7, 10};
int[] list2 = {2, 4, 7, 10};
java.util.Arrays.fill(list1, 5); // Fill 5 to the whole array
java.util.Arrays.fill(list2, 1, 3, 8); // Fill 8 to a partial array
```

6.10 Two-Dimensional Arrays

Thus far, you have used one-dimensional arrays to model linear collections of elements. You can
use a two-dimensional array to represent a matrix or a table. For example, the following table
that describes the distances between the cities can be represented using a two-dimensional array.

Distance Table (in miles)

	Chicago	Boston	New York	Atlanta	Miami	Dallas	Houston
Chicago	0	983	787	714	1375	967	1087
Boston	983	0	214	1102	1763	1723	1842
New York	787	214	0	888	1549	1548	1627
Atlanta	714	1102	888	0	661	781	810
Miami	1375	1763	1549	661	0	1426	1187
Dallas	967	1723	1548	781	1426	0	239
Houston	1087	1842	1627	810	1187	239	0

6.10.1 Declaring Variables of Two-Dimensional Arrays and Creating Two-Dimensional Arrays

Here is the syntax for declaring a two-dimensional array:

```
dataType[][] arrayRefVar;
```

or

```
dataType arrayRefVar[][]; // This style is allowed, but not preferred
```

As an example, here is how you would declare a two-dimensional array variable `matrix` of `int` values:

```
int[][] matrix;
```

or

```
int matrix[][]; // This style is allowed, but not preferred
```

You can create a two-dimensional array of 5 by 5 `int` values and assign it to `matrix` using this syntax:

```
matrix = new int[5][5];
```

Two subscripts are used in a two-dimensional array, one for the row, and the other for the column. As in a one-dimensional array, the index for each subscript is of the `int` type and starts from 0, as shown in Figure 6.11(a).

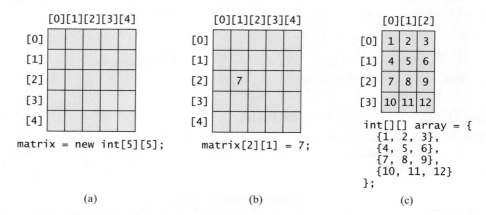

(a)   (b)   (c)

FIGURE 6.11 The index of each subscript of a two-dimensional array is an `int` value, starting from 0.

To assign the value 7 to a specific element at row 2 and column 1, as shown in Figure 6.11(b), you can use the following:

```
matrix[2][1] = 7;
```

 Caution

It is a common mistake to use `matrix[2, 1]` to access the element at row 2 and column 1. In Java, each subscript must be enclosed in a pair of square brackets.

You can also use an array initializer to declare, create, and initialize a two-dimensional array. For example, the following code in (a) creates an array with the specified initial values, as shown in Figure 6.11(c). This is equivalent to the code in (b).

```
int[][] array = {
  {1, 2, 3},
  {4, 5, 6},
  {7, 8, 9},
  {10, 11, 12}
};
```

Equivalent

```
int[][] array = new int[4][3];
array[0][0] = 1; array[0][1] = 2; array[0][2] = 3;
array[1][0] = 4; array[1][1] = 5; array[1][2] = 6;
array[2][0] = 7; array[2][1]  8; array[2][2] = 9;
array[3][0] = 10; array[3][1] = 11; array[3][2] = 12;
```

(a)   (b)

6.10.2 Obtaining the Lengths of Two-Dimensional Arrays

A two-dimensional array is actually an array in which each element is a one-dimensional array. The length of an array `x` is the number of elements in the array, which can be obtained using `x.length`. `x[0]`, `x[1]`, ..., and `x[x.length-1]` are arrays. Their lengths can be obtained using `x[0].length`, `x[1].length`, ..., and `x[x.length-1].length`.

For example, suppose `x = new int[3][4]`, `x[0]`, `x[1]`, and `x[2]` are one-dimensional arrays and each contains four elements, as shown in Figure 6.12. `x.length` is `3`, and `x[0].length`, `x[1].length`, and `x[2].length` are `4`.

FIGURE 6.12 A two-dimensional array is a one-dimensional array in which each element is another one-dimensional array.

6.10.3 Ragged Arrays

Each row in a two-dimensional array is itself an array. Thus the rows can have different lengths. An array of this kind is known as a *ragged array*. Here is an example of creating a ragged array:

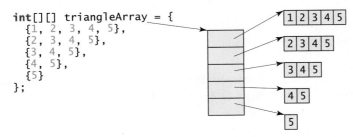

```
int[][] triangleArray = {
  {1, 2, 3, 4, 5},
  {2, 3, 4, 5},
  {3, 4, 5},
  {4, 5},
  {5}
};
```

As can be seen, `triangleArray[0].length` is 5, `triangleArray[1].length` is 4, `triangleArray[2].length` is 3, `triangleArray[3].length` is 2, and `triangleArray[4].length` is 1.

If you don't know the values in a ragged array in advance, but know the sizes, say the same as before, you can create a ragged array using the syntax that follows:

```
int[][] triangleArray = new int[5][];
triangleArray[0] = new int[5];
```

```
triangleArray[1] = new int[4];
triangleArray[2] = new int[3];
triangleArray[3] = new int[2];
triangleArray[4] = new int[1];
```

You can now assign values to the array. For example,

```
triangleArray[0][3] = 50;
triangleArray[4][0] = 45;
```

 Note

The syntax `new int[5][]` for creating an array requires the first index to be specified. The syntax `new int[][]` would be wrong.

6.10.4 Processing Two-Dimensional Arrays

Suppose an array `matrix` is declared as follows:

```
int[][] matrix = new int[10][10];
```

Here are some examples of processing two-dimensional arrays:

1. (*Initializing arrays with random values*) The following loop initializes the array with random values between 0 and 99:

```
for (int row = 0; row < matrix.length; row++) {
  for (int column = 0; column < matrix[row].length; column++) {
    matrix[row][column] = (int)(Math.random() * 100);
  }
}
```

2. (*Printing arrays*) To print a two-dimensional array, you have to print each element in the array using a loop like the following:

```
for (int row = 0; row < matrix.length; row++) {
  for (int column = 0; column < matrix[row].length; column++) {
    System.out.print(matrix[row][column] + " ");
  }

  System.out.println();
}
```

3. (*Summing all elements*) Use a variable named `total` to store the sum. Initially `total` is `0`. Add each element in the array to `total` using a loop like this:

```
int total = 0;
for (int row = 0; row < matrix.length; row++) {
  for (int column = 0; column < matrix[row].length; column++) {
    total += matrix[row][column];
  }
}
```

4. (*Summing elements by column*) For each column, use a variable named `total` to store its sum. Add each element in the column to `total` using a loop like this:

```
for (int column = 0; column < matrix[0].length; column++) {
  int total = 0;
```

```
  for (int row = 0; row < matrix.length; row++)
    total += matrix[row][column];
  System.out.println("Sum for column " + column + " is " + total);
}
```

5. (*Which row has the largest sum?*) Use variables `maxRow` and `indexOfMaxRow` to track the largest sum and index of the row. For each row, compute its sum and update `maxRow` and `indexOfMaxRow` if the new sum is greater.

```
int maxRow = 0;
int indexOfMaxRow = 0;

// Get sum of the first row in maxRow
for (int column = 0; column < matrix[0].length; column++) {
  maxRow += matrix[0][column];
}

for (int row = 1; row < matrix.length; row++) {
  int totalOfThisRow = 0;
  for (int column = 0; column < matrix[row].length; column++) {
    totalOfThisRow += matrix[row][column];
    if (totalOfThisRow > maxRow) {
      maxRow = totalOfThisRow;
      indexOfMaxRow = row;
    }
  }
}

System.out.println("Row " + indexOfMaxRow
  + " has the maximum sum" + " of " + maxRow);
```

6.10.5 Problem: Grading a Multiple-Choice Test

The problem is to write a program that grades multiple-choice tests. Suppose there are eight students and ten questions, and the answers are stored in a two-dimensional array. Each row records a student's answers to the questions. For example, the following array stores the test.

Students' Answers to the Questions:

	0	1	2	3	4	5	6	7	8	9
Student 0	A	B	A	C	C	D	E	E	A	D
Student 1	D	B	A	B	C	A	E	E	A	D
Student 2	E	D	D	A	C	B	E	E	A	D
Student 3	C	B	A	E	D	C	E	E	A	D
Student 4	A	B	D	C	C	D	E	E	A	D
Student 5	B	B	E	C	C	D	E	E	A	D
Student 6	B	B	A	C	C	D	E	E	A	D
Student 7	E	B	E	C	C	D	E	E	A	D

The key is stored in a one-dimensional array:

Key to the Questions:

	0	1	2	3	4	5	6	7	8	9
Key	D	B	D	C	C	D	A	E	A	D

Your program grades the test and displays the result. It compares each student's answers with the key, counts the number of correct answers, and displays it. Listing 6.10 gives the program.

LISTING 6.10 GradeExam.java

2-D array

1-D array

compare with key

```java
1 public class GradeExam {
2    /** Main method */
3    public static void main(String[] args) {
4      // Students' answers to the questions
5      char[][] answers = {
6        {'A', 'B', 'A', 'C', 'C', 'D', 'E', 'E', 'A', 'D'},
7        {'D', 'B', 'A', 'B', 'C', 'A', 'E', 'E', 'A', 'D'},
8        {'E', 'D', 'D', 'A', 'C', 'B', 'E', 'E', 'A', 'D'},
9        {'C', 'B', 'A', 'E', 'D', 'C', 'E', 'E', 'A', 'D'},
10       {'A', 'B', 'D', 'C', 'C', 'D', 'E', 'E', 'A', 'D'},
11       {'B', 'B', 'E', 'C', 'C', 'D', 'E', 'E', 'A', 'D'},
12       {'B', 'B', 'A', 'C', 'C', 'D', 'E', 'E', 'A', 'D'},
13       {'E', 'B', 'E', 'C', 'C', 'D', 'E', 'E', 'A', 'D'}};
14
15      // Key to the questions
16      char[] keys = {'D', 'B', 'D', 'C', 'C', 'D', 'A', 'E', 'A', 'D'};
17
18      // Grade all answers
19      for (int i = 0; i < answers.length; i++) {
20        // Grade one student
21        int correctCount = 0;
22        for (int j = 0; j < answers[i].length; j++) {
23          if (answers[i][j] == keys[j] )
24            correctCount++;
25        }
26
27        System.out.println("Student " + i + "'s correct count is " +
28          correctCount);
29      }
30    }
31 }
```

```
Student 0's correct count is 7
Student 1's correct count is 6
Student 2's correct count is 5
Student 3's correct count is 4
Student 4's correct count is 8
Student 5's correct count is 7
Student 6's correct count is 7
Student 7's correct count is 7
```

The statement in lines 5–13 declares, creates, and initializes a two-dimensional array of characters and assigns the reference to answers of the char[][] type.

The statement in line 16 declares, creates, and initializes an array of char values and assigns the reference to keys of the char[] type.

Each row in the array answers stores a student's answer, which is graded by comparing it with the key in the array keys. The result is displayed immediately after a student's answer is graded.

6.10.6 Problem: Finding a Closest Pair

The GPS navigation system is becoming increasingly popular. The system uses the graph and geometric algorithms to calculate distances and map a route. This section presents a geometric problem for finding a closest pair of points.

Given a set of points, the closest-pair problem is to find the two points that are nearest to each other. In Figure 6.13, for example, points (1, 1) and (2, 0.5) are closest to each other. There are several ways to solve this problem. An intuitive approach is to compute the distances between all pairs of points and find the one with the minimum distance, as implemented in Listing 6.11.

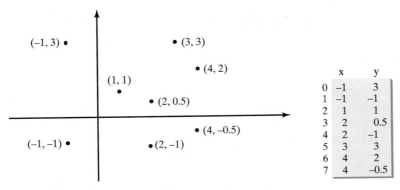

FIGURE 6.13 Points can be represented in a two-dimensional array.

LISTING 6.11 FindNearestPoints.java

```java
public class FindNearestPoints {
  public static void main(String[] args) {
    // Each row in points represents a point
    double[][] points = {{-1, 3}, {-1, -1}, {1, 1},
      {2, 0.5}, {2, -1}, {3, 3}, {4, 2}, {4, -0.5}};

    // p1 and p2 are the indices in the points array
    int p1 = 0, p2 = 1; // Initial two points
    double shortestDistances = distance(points[p1][0], points[p1][1],
      points[p2][0], points[p2][1]); // Initialize shortestDistances

    // Compute distance for every two points
    for (int i = 0; i < points.length; i++) {
      for (int j = i + 1; j < points.length; j++) {
        double distance = distance(points[i][0], points[i][1],
          points[j][0], points[j][1]); // Find distance

        if (shortestDistances > distance) {
          p1 = i; // Update p1
          p2 = j; // Update p2
          shortestDistances = distance; // Update shortestDistances
        }
      }
    }

    // Display result
```

2-D array

track two points
track **shortestDistance**

for each point **i**
for each point **j**
distance between **i** and **j**

update **shortestDistance**

```
27        System.out.println("The closest two points are " +
28          "(" + points[p1][0] + ", " + points[p1][1] + ") and (" +
29          points[p2][0] + ", " + points[p2][1] + ")");
30      }
31
32      /** Compute the distance between two points (x1, y1) and (x2, y2)*/
33      public static double distance(
34          double x1, double y1, double x2, double y2) {
35          return Math.sqrt((x2 - x1) * (x2 - x1) + (y2 - y1) * (y2 - y1));
36      }
37 }
```

distance between two points

The closest two points are (1.0, 1.0) and (2.0, 0.5)

The points are stored in a two-dimensional array named `points` (lines 4–5). The program uses variable `shortestDistances` (line 9) to store the distance between two nearest points, and the indices of these two points in the `points` array are stored in `p1` and `p2` (line 8).

For each point at index `i`, the program computes the distance between `points[i]` and `points[j]` for all `j > i` (lines 13–24). Whenever a shorter distance is found, the variable `shortestDistances`, `p1`, and `p2` are updated (lines 18–22).

The distance between two points `(x1, y1)` and `(x2, y2)` can be computed using the formula $\sqrt{(x_2 - x_1)^2 + (y_2 - y_1)^2}$ (lines 33–36).

The program assumes that the plain has at least two points. You can easily modify the program to handle the case if the plain has zero or one point.

Note that there might be more than one closest pair of points with the same minimum distance. The program finds one such pair.

6.10.7   Problem: Sudoku

Video Note
Solve Sudoku

This book teaches you how to program using a wide variety of problems with various levels of difficulty. This section presents an interesting problem of a sort that appears in the newspaper every day. It is a number-placement puzzle, commonly known as *Sudoku*. This is a challenge problem. Feel free to skip it if you wish.

The objective is to fill the grid (see Figure 6.14(a)) so that every row, every column, and every 3 × 3 box contains the numbers 1 to 9, as shown in Figure 6.14(b).

How do you write a program to solve this problem? Your program searches a solution for an input of a 9-by-9 grid Sudoku puzzle. Note that there may be multiple solutions for an input. The program will find one such solution if exists. The grid can be represented using a

(a) Input

(b) Output

FIGURE 6.14   (b) is the solution to the Sudoku puzzle in (a).

two-dimensional array. For example, the grid in Figure 6.14(a) can be represented as shown in Figure 6.15(a). The value 0 indicates a free cell whose value will be filled by the program.

```
int[][] grid =
  {{5, 3, 0, 0, 7, 0, 0, 0, 0},
   {6, 0, 0, 1, 9, 5, 0, 0, 0},
   {0, 9, 8, 0, 0, 0, 0, 6, 0},
   {8, 0, 0, 0, 6, 0, 0, 0, 3},
   {4, 0, 0, 8, 0, 3, 0, 0, 1},
   {7, 0, 0, 0, 2, 0, 0, 0, 6},
   {0, 6, 0, 0, 0, 0, 2, 8, 0},
   {0, 0, 0, 4, 1, 9, 0, 0, 5},
   {0, 0, 0, 0, 8, 0, 0, 7, 9}
  };
```

(a)

```
int[][] freeCellList =
  {{0, 2}, {0, 3}, {0, 5}, {0, 6}, {0, 7}, {0, 8},
   {1, 1}, {1, 2}, {1, 6}, {1, 7}, {1, 8},
   {2, 0}, {2, 3}, {2, 4}, {2, 5}, {2, 6}, {2, 8},
   {3, 1}, {3, 2}, {3, 3}, {3, 5}, {3, 6}, {3, 7},
   {4, 1}, {4, 2}, {4, 4}, {4, 6}, {4, 7},
   {5, 1}, {5, 2}, {5, 3}, {5, 5}, {5, 6}, {5, 7},
   {6, 0}, {6, 2}, {6, 3}, {6, 4}, {6, 5}, {6, 8},
   {7, 0}, {7, 1}, {7, 2}, {7, 6}, {7, 7},
   {8, 0}, {8, 1}, {8, 2}, {8, 3}, {8, 5}, {8, 6}
  };
```

(b)

FIGURE 6.15 (a) is a two-dimensional array representation for the grid; (b) is a two-dimensional array representation for the free cells.

To better facilitate search on free cells, the program stores free cells in a two-dimensional array, as shown 6.15(b). Each row in the array has two columns, which indicate the subscripts of the free cell in the grid. For example, {freeCellList[0][0], freeCellList[0][1]} (i.e., {0, 2}) is the subscript for the first free cell in the grid and {freeCellList[1][0], freeCellList[1][1]} (i.e., {0, 3}) is the subscript for the second free cell in the grid.

An intuitive approach to solve this problem is to start from the first free cell, then the second, and so on. Fill each free cell with the smallest value possible. For example, you can fill 1 into grid[0][2], 2 into grid[0][3], 4 into grid[0][5], 8 into grid[0][6], and 9 into grid[0][7], as shown in Figure 6.16(a).

FIGURE 6.16 The program attempts to fill in free cells.

Now look at grid[0][8]. There is no possible value to fill in this cell. You need to backtrack to the previous free cell at grid[0][7] and reset its value. Since grid[0][7] is already 9, no new value is possible. So you have to backtrack to its previous free cell at grid[0][6] and change its value to 9. Continue to move forward to set grid[0][7] to 8, as shown in Figure 6.16(b). Now there is still no possible value for grid[0][8]. Backtrack to grid[0][7], no possible new value for this cell. Backtrack to grid[0][6], no possible new value for this cell. Backtrack to grid[0][5] and change it to 6. Now continue to move forward.

backtrack

The search moves forward and backward continuously until one of the following two cases arises:

- All free cells are filled. A solution is found.

- The search is backtracked to the first free cell with no new possible value. The puzzle has no solution.

Listing 6.12 gives the solution to the program.

LISTING 6.12 Sudoku.java

```java
1  import java.util.Scanner;
2
3  public class Sudoku {
4    public static void main(String[] args) {
5      // Read a Sudoku puzzle
6      int[][] grid = readAPuzzle();
7
8      if (!isValid(grid))
9        System.out.println("Invalid input");
10     else if (search(grid)) {
11       System.out.println("The solution is found:");
12       printGrid(grid);
13     }
14     else
15       System.out.println("No solution");
16   }
17
18   /** Read a Sudoku puzzle from the keyboard */
19   public static int[][] readAPuzzle() {
20     // Create a Scanner
21     Scanner input = new Scanner(System.in);
22
23     System.out.println("Enter a Sudoku puzzle:");
24     int[][] grid = new int[9][9];
25     for (int i = 0; i < 9; i++)
26       for (int j = 0; j < 9; j++)
27         grid[i][j] = input.nextInt();
28
29     return grid;
30   }
31
32   /** Obtain a list of free cells from the puzzle */
33   public static int[][] getFreeCellList(int[][] grid) {
34     // Determine the number of free cells
35     int numberOfFreeCells = 0;
36     for (int i = 0; i < 9; i++)
37       for (int j = 0; j < 9; j++)
38         if (grid[i][j] == 0)
39           numberOfFreeCells++;
40
41     // Store free cell positions into freeCellList
42     int[][] freeCellList = new int[numberOfFreeCells][2];
43     int count = 0;
44     for (int i = 0; i < 9; i++)
45       for (int j = 0; j < 9; j++)
46         if (grid[i][j] == 0) {
47           freeCellList[count][0] = i;
48           freeCellList[count++][1] = j;
49         }
```

Margin notes:
read input
input valid?
search
print result
read input
return grid
get free-cell list
count free cells
create free-cell list

```
50
51      return freeCellList;
52  }
53
54  /** Print the values in the grid */
55  public static void printGrid(int[][] grid) {                    print grid
56    for (int i = 0; i < 9; i++) {
57      for (int j = 0; j < 9; j++)
58        System.out.print(grid[i][j] + " ");
59      System.out.println();
60    }
61  }
62
63  /** Search for a solution */
64  public static boolean search(int[][] grid) {                    search a solution
65    int[][] freeCellList = getFreeCellList(grid); // Free cells
66    int k = 0; // Start from the first free cell
67    boolean found = false; // Solution found?
68
69    while (!found) {                                              continuous search
70      int i = freeCellList[k][0];
71      int j = freeCellList[k][1];
72      if (grid[i][j] == 0)
73        grid[i][j] = 1; // Start with 1                          start with 1
74
75      if (isValid(i, j, grid)) {                                 is valid?
76        if (k + 1 == freeCellList.length) {  // No more free cells
77          found = true; // A solution is found                   found
78        }
79        else { // Move to the next free cell
80          k++;                                                   to next free cell
81        }
82      }
83      else if (grid[i][j] < 9) {
84        grid[i][j] = grid[i][j] + 1; // Check the next possible value   increase cell value
85      }
86      else {  // grid[i][j] is 9, backtrack
87        while (grid[i][j] == 9) {
88          grid[i][j] = 0; // Reset to free cell                  reset cell value
89          if (k == 0) {
90            return false; // No possible value                   no solution
91          }
92          k--; // Backtrack                                      backtrack
93          i = freeCellList[k][0];
94          j = freeCellList[k][1];
95        }
96
97        grid[i][j] = grid[i][j] + 1; // Check the next possible value
98      }
99    }
100
101   return true; // A solution is found
102 }
103
104 /** Check whether grid[i][j] is valid in the grid */
105 public static boolean isValid(int i, int j, int[][] grid) {     check valid
106   // Check whether grid[i][j] is valid at the i's row
107   for (int column = 0; column < 9; column++)                    check row
108     if (column != j && grid[i][column] == grid[i][j])
```

```
109        return false;
110
111   // Check whether grid[i][j] is valid at the j's column
112   for (int row = 0; row < 9; row++)
113     if (row != i && grid[row][j] == grid[i][j])
114       return false;
115
116   // Check whether grid[i][j] is valid in the 3 by 3 box
117   for (int row = (i / 3) * 3; row < (i / 3) * 3 + 3; row++)
118     for (int col = (j / 3) * 3; col < (j / 3) * 3 + 3; col++)
119       if (row != i && col != j && grid[row][col] == grid[i][j])
120         return false;
121
122   return true; // The current value at grid[i][j] is valid
123 }
124
125 /** Check whether the fixed cells are valid in the grid */
126 public static boolean isValid(int[][] grid) {
127   for (int i = 0; i < 9; i++)
128     for (int j = 0; j < 9; j++)
129       if (grid[i][j] != 0 && !isValid(i, j, grid)) return false;
130
131   return true; // The fixed cells are valid
132 }
133 }
```

check column

check box

valid grid?

```
Enter a puzzle:
0 6 0 1 0 4 0 5 0    ↵Enter
0 0 8 3 0 5 6 0 0    ↵Enter
2 0 0 0 0 0 0 0 1    ↵Enter
8 0 0 4 0 7 0 0 6    ↵Enter
0 0 6 0 0 0 3 0 0    ↵Enter
7 0 0 9 0 1 0 0 4    ↵Enter
5 0 0 0 0 0 0 0 2    ↵Enter
0 0 7 2 0 6 9 0 0    ↵Enter
0 4 0 5 0 8 0 7 0    ↵Enter

The solution is found:
9 6 3 1 7 4 2 5 8
1 7 8 3 2 5 6 4 9
2 5 4 6 8 9 7 3 1
8 2 1 4 3 7 5 9 6
4 9 6 8 5 2 3 1 7
7 3 5 9 6 1 8 2 4
5 8 9 7 1 3 4 6 2
3 1 7 2 4 6 9 8 5
6 4 2 5 9 8 1 7 3
```

The program invokes the `readAPuzzle()` method (line 6) to read a Sudoku puzzle and re-turn a two-dimensional array representing a Sudoku grid. There are three possible outputs from the program:

■ The input is invalid (line 9)

- A solution is found (line 11).

- No solution is found (line 15).

The `getFreeCellList(int[][] grid)` method returns a two-dimensional array storing the free cell positions. `freeCellList[i][j]` indicates a free cell at row index `i` and column index `j`. The method first counts the number of free cells (lines 35-39), then creates the array for storing free cell positions (lines 42-49).

The `search(int[][] grid)` method starts search from the first free cell with `k = 0` (line 66), where `k` points to the current free cell being considered, as shown below:

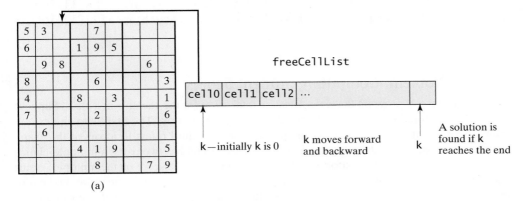

(a)

The value in a free cell starts with `1` (line 73). If the value is valid, the next cell is considered (line 80). If the value is not valid, its next value is considered (line 84). If the value is aready `9`, the search is backtracked (lines 87–95). All the backtracked cells become free again and their values are reset to `0` (line 88).

The `search` method returns `true` when no more free cells are left (lines 76–78) and returns `false` when the first cell has to be backtracked (lines 89–91).

The `isValid(i, j, grid)` method checks whether the current value at `grid[i][j]` is valid. It checks whether `grid[i][j]` appears more than once at row `i` (lines 107-109), at column `j` (lines 112–114), and in the 3 × 3 box (lines 117–120). Note that the starting row subscript and column subscript of the 3 × 3 box for `grid[i][j]` are `i / 3` and `j / 3`. This observation results in the short code in lines 117–120.

Tip
It is cumbersome to enter 81 numbers from the console. When you test the program, you may store the input in a file, say sudoku.txt, and run the program using the following command:　　　　input file

```
java Sudoku < sudoku.txt
```

Note
This program is not user friendly. You can improve it by providing a GUI interface. See Exercise 17.25.

6.11 Multidimensional Arrays

In the preceding section, you used a two-dimensional array to represent a matrix or a table. Occasionally, you will need to represent *n*-dimensional data structures. In Java, you can create *n*-dimensional arrays for any integer *n*.

The way to declare two-dimensional array variables and create two-dimensional arrays can be generalized to declare *n*-dimensional array variables and create *n*-dimensional arrays for

$n >= 3$. For example, the following syntax declares a three-dimensional array variable `scores`, creates an array, and assigns its reference to `scores`.

```java
double[][][] scores = new double[10][5][2];
```

A multidimensional array is actually an array in which each element is another array. A three-dimensional array consists of an array of two-dimensional arrays, each of which is an array of one-dimensional arrays. For example, suppose `x = new int[2][2][5]`, `x[0]` and `x[1]` are two-dimensional arrays. `X[0][0]`, `x[0][1]`, `x[1][0]`, and `x[1][1]` are one-dimensional arrays and each contains five elements. `x.length` is 2, `x[0].length` and `x[1].length` are 2, and `X[0][0].length`, `x[0][1].length`, `x[1][0].length`, and `x[1][1].length` are 5.

6.11.1 Problem: Computing Student Scores

Listing 6.13 gives a program that calculates the total score for the students in a class. Suppose the scores are stored in a three-dimensional array named `scores`. The first index in `scores` refers to a student, the second refers to an exam, and the third refers to a part of the exam. Suppose there are seven students, five exams, and each exam has two parts: a multiple-choice part and a programming part. `scores[i][j][0]` represents the score on the multiple-choice part for the `i`'s student on the `j`'s exam. `scores[i][j][1]` represents the score on the programming part for the `i`'s student on the `j`'s exam. The program processes the `scores` array for all the students. For each student, it adds the two scores from all exams to `totalScore` and displays `totalScore`. Your program displays the total score for each student, as shown in the sample output.

LISTING 6.13 TotalScore.java

3-D array

```java
1 public class TotalScore {
2   /** Main method */
3   public static void main(String[] args) {
4     double[][][] scores = {
5       {{7.5, 20.5}, {9.0, 22.5}, {15, 33.5}, {13, 21.5}, {15, 2.5}},
6       {{4.5, 21.5}, {9.0, 22.5}, {15, 34.5}, {12, 20.5}, {14, 9.5}},
7       {{6.5, 30.5}, {9.4, 10.5}, {11, 33.5}, {11, 23.5}, {10, 2.5}},
8       {{6.5, 23.5}, {9.4, 32.5}, {13, 34.5}, {11, 20.5}, {16, 7.5}},
9       {{8.5, 26.5}, {9.4, 52.5}, {13, 36.5}, {13, 24.5}, {16, 2.5}},
10      {{9.5, 20.5}, {9.4, 42.5}, {13, 31.5}, {12, 20.5}, {16, 6.5}},
11      {{1.5, 29.5}, {6.4, 22.5}, {14, 30.5}, {10, 30.5}, {16, 6.0}}};
12
13     // Calculate and display total score for each student
14     for (int i = 0; i < scores.length; i++) {
15       double totalScore = 0;
16       for (int j = 0; j < scores[i].length; j++)
17         for (int k = 0; k < scores[i][j].length; k++)
18           totalScore += scores[i][j][k];
19
20       System.out.println("Student " + i + "'s score is " +
21         totalScore);
22     }
23   }
24 }
```

```
Student 0's score is 160.0
Student 1's score is 163.0
Student 2's score is 147.4
Student 3's score is 174.4
Student 4's score is 201.4
Student 5's score is 181.4
Student 6's score is 165.9
```

To understand this program, it is essential to know how data in the three-dimensional array are interpreted. `scores[0]` is a two-dimensional array that stores all the exam scores for the first student. `scores[0][0]` is {7.5, 20.5}, a one-dimensional array, which stores two scores for the two parts of the first student's first exam. `scores[0][0][0]` is 7.5, which is the score for the first part of the first student's first exam. `scores[5]` is a two-dimensional array that stores all the exam scores for the sixth student. `scores[5][4]` is {16, 6.5}, a one-dimensional array, which stores two scores for the two parts of the sixth student's fifth exam. `scores[5][4][1]` is 6.5, which is the score for the second part of the sixth student's fifth exam.

The statement in lines 4–11 declares, creates, and initializes a three-dimensional array of `double` values and assigns the reference to `scores` of the `double[][][]` type.

The scores for each student are added in lines 16–18, and the result is displayed in lines 20–21. The `for` loop in line 14 process the scores for all the students.

6.11.2 Problem: Guessing Birth Dates

Listing 3.8, GuessBirthDate.java, gives a program that guesses a birth date. The program can be simplified by storing the numbers in five sets in a three-dimensional array, and it prompts the user for the answers using a loop, as shown in Listing 6.14. The sample run of the program can be the same as shown in Listing 3.8.

LISTING 6.14 GuessBirthDateUsingArray.java

```
 1 import java.util.Scanner;
 2
 3 public class GuessBirthDateUsingArray {
 4   public static void main(String[] args) {
 5     int date = 0; // Date to be determined
 6     int answer;
 7
 8     int[][][] dates = {                          three-dimensional array
 9       {{ 1,  3,  5,  7},
10        { 9, 11, 13, 15},
11        {17, 19, 21, 23},
12        {25, 27, 29, 31}},
13       {{ 2,  3,  6,  7},
14        {10, 11, 14, 15},
15        {18, 19, 22, 23},
16        {26, 27, 30, 31}},
17       {{ 4,  5,  6,  7},
18        {12, 13, 14, 15},
19        {20, 21, 22, 23},
20        {28, 29, 30, 31}},
21       {{ 8,  9, 10, 11},
22        {12, 13, 14, 15},
23        {24, 25, 26, 27},
24        {28, 29, 30, 31}},
25       {{16, 17, 18, 19},
26        {20, 21, 22, 23},
```

```
27              {24, 25, 26, 27},
28              {28, 29, 30, 31}}};
29
30       // Create a Scanner
31       Scanner input = new Scanner(System.in);
32
33       for (int i = 0; i < 5; i++) {
34         System.out.println("Is your birth date in Set" + (i + 1) + "?");
35         for (int j = 0; j < 4; j++) {
36           for (int k = 0; k < 4; k++)
37             System.out.print(dates[i][j][k] + "  ");
38           System.out.println();
39         }
40
41         System.out.print("\nEnter 0 for No and 1 for Yes: ");
42         answer = input.nextInt();
43
44         if (answer == 1)
45           date += dates[i][0][0] ;
46       }
47
48       System.out.println("Your birth date is " + date);
49     }
50 }
```

Set i (margin note for line 34)

add to Set i (margin note for line 45)

A three-dimensional array **dates** is created in Lines 8–28. This array stores five sets of numbers. Each set is a **4**-by-**4** two-dimensional array.

The loop starting from line 33 displays the numbers in each set and prompts the user to answer whether the date is in the set (lines 41–42). If the date is in the set, the first number (**dates[i][0][0]**) in the set is added to variable **date** (line 45).

KEY TERMS

anonymous array 189	indexed variable 182
array 180	insertion sort 200
array initializer 182	linear search 196
binary search 196	multidimensional array 215
garbage collection 188	ragged array 205
index 182	selection sort 199

CHAPTER SUMMARY

■ A variable is declared as an array type using the syntax `dataType[] arrayRefVar` or `dataType arrayRefVar[]`. The style `dataType[] arrayRefVar` is preferred, although `dataType arrayRefVar[]` is legal.

■ Unlike declarations for primitive data type variables, the declaration of an array variable does not allocate any space in memory for the array. An array variable is not a primitive data type variable. An array variable contains a reference to an array.

■ You cannot assign elements to an array unless it has already been created. You can create an array by using the `new` operator with the following syntax: `new dataType[arraySize]`.

■ Each element in the array is represented using the syntax `arrayRefVar[index]`. An index must be an integer or an integer expression.

■ After an array is created, its size becomes permanent and can be obtained using `arrayRefVar.length`. Since the index of an array always begins with 0, the last index is always `arrayRefVar.length` - 1. An out-of-bounds error will occur if you attempt to reference elements beyond the bounds of an array.

■ Programmers often mistakenly reference the first element in an array with index 1, but it should be 0. This is called the *index off-by-one error*.

■ When an array is created, its elements are assigned the default value of 0 for the numeric primitive data types, `'\u0000'` for char types, and `false` for `boolean` types.

■ Java has a shorthand notation, known as the *array initializer*, which combines in one statement declaring an array, creating an array, and initializing, using the syntax: `dataType[] arrayRefVar = {value0, value1, ..., valuek}`.

■ When you pass an array argument to a method, you are actually passing the reference of the array; that is, the called method can modify the elements in the caller's original array.

■ You can use arrays of arrays to form multidimensional arrays. For example, a two-dimensional array is declared as an array of arrays using the syntax `dataType[][] arrayRefVar` or `dataType arrayRefVar[][]`.

REVIEW QUESTIONS

Section 6.2 Array Basics

6.1 How do you declare and create an array?

6.2 How do you access elements of an array?

6.3 Is memory allocated for an array when it is declared? When is the memory allocated for an array? What is the printout of the following code?

```
int x = 30;
int[] numbers = new int[x];
x = 60;
System.out.println("x is " + x);
System.out.println("The size of numbers is " + numbers.length);
```

6.4 Indicate true or false for the following statements:

■ Every element in an array has the same type.
■ The array size is fixed after it is declared.
■ The array size is fixed after it is created.
■ The elements in an array must be of primitive data type.

6.5 Which of the following statements are valid array declarations?

```
int i = new int(30);
double d[] = new double[30];
char[] r = new char(1..30);
int i[] = (3, 4, 3, 2);
float f[] = {2.3, 4.5, 6.6};
char[] c = new char();
```

6.6 What is the array index type? What is the lowest index?

6.7 What is the representation of the third element in an array named a?

6.8 What happens when your program attempts to access an array element with an invalid index?

6.9 Identify and fix the errors in the following code:

```
1 public class Test {
2   public static void main(String[] args) {
3     double[100] r;
4
5     for (int i = 0; i < r.length(); i++);
6       r(i) = Math.random * 100;
7   }
8 }
```

Section 6.3 Copying Arrays

6.10 Use the arraycopy() method to copy the following array to a target array t:

```
int[] source = {3, 4, 5};
```

6.11 Once an array is created, its size cannot be changed. Does the following code resize the array?

```
int[] myList;
myList = new int[10];
// Some time later you want to assign a new array to myList
myList = new int[20];
```

Sections 6.4–6.5

6.12 When an array is passed to a method, a new array is created and passed to the method. Is this true?

6.13 Show the output of the following two programs:

```
public class Test {
  public static void main(String[] args) {
    int number = 0;
    int[] numbers = new int[1];

    m(number, numbers);

    System.out.println("number is " + number
      + " and numbers[0] is " + numbers[0]);
  }

  public static void m(int x, int[] y) {
    x = 3;
    y[0] = 3;
  }
}
```

(a)

```
public class Test {
  public static void main(String[] args) {
    int[] list = {1, 2, 3, 4, 5};
    reverse(list);
    for (int i = 0; i < list.length; i++)
      System.out.print(list[i] + " ");
  }

  public static void reverse(int[] list) {
    int[] newList = new int[list.length];

    for (int i = 0; i < list.length; i++)
      newList[i] = list[list.length - 1 - i];

    list = newList;
  }
}
```

(b)

6.14 Where are the arrays stored during execution? Show the contents of the stack and heap during and after executing createArray, displayArray, countLetters, displayCounts in Listing 6.4,

Section 6.6 Variable-Length Argument Lists

6.15 What is wrong in the following method declaration?

```
public static void print(String... strings, double... numbers)
public static void print(double... numbers, String name)
public static double... print(double d1, double d2)
```

6.16 Can you invoke the printMax method in Listing 6.5 using the following statements?

```
printMax(1, 2, 2, 1, 4);
printMax(new double[]{1, 2, 3});
printMax(new int[]{1, 2, 3});
```

Sections 6.7–6.8

6.17 Use Figure 6.7 as an example to show how to apply the binary search approach to a search for key 10 and key 12 in list {2, 4, 7, 10, 11, 45, 50, 59, 60, 66, 69, 70, 79}.

6.18 Use Figure 6.8 as an example to show how to apply the selection-sort approach to sort {3.4, 5, 3, 3.5, 2.2, 1.9, 2}.

6.19 Use Figure 6.9 as an example to show how to apply the insertion-sort approach to sort {3.4, 5, 3, 3.5, 2.2, 1.9, 2}.

6.20 How do you modify the selectionSort method in Listing 6.8 to sort numbers in decreasing order?

6.21 How do you modify the insertionSort method in Listing 6.9 to sort numbers in decreasing order?

Section 6.9 The Arrays Class

6.22 What types of array can be sorted using the java.util.Arrays.sort method? Does this sort method create a new array?

6.23 To apply java.util.Arrays.binarySearch(array, key), should the array be sorted in increasing order, in decreasing order, or neither?

6.24 Show the contents of the array after the execution of each line.

```
int[] list = {2, 4, 7, 10};
java.util.Arrays.fill(list, 7);
java.util.Arrays.fill(list, 1, 3, 8);
System.out.print(java.util.Arrays.equals(list, list));
```

Section 6.10 Two-Dimensional Arrays

6.25 Declare and create a 4-by-5 int matrix.

6.26 Can the rows in a two-dimensional array have different lengths?

6.27 What is the output of the following code?

```
int[][] array = new int[5][6];
int[] x = {1, 2};
array[0] = x;
System.out.println("array[0][1] is " + array[0][1]);
```

6.28 Which of the following statements are valid array declarations?

```
int[][] r = new int[2];
```

```
int[] x = new int[];
```

```
int[][] y = new int[3][];
```

6.29 True or false? Every valid Sudoku input has a solution. If false, give an example.

PROGRAMMING EXERCISES

Section 6.2 Array Basics

6.1   (*Analyzing input*) Write a program that reads ten numbers, computes their average, and finds out how many numbers are above the average.

6.2   (*Alternative solution to Listing 6.1, "Testing Arrays"*) The solution of Listing 6.1 counts the occurrences of the largest number by comparing *each number* with the largest. So you have to use an array to store all the numbers. Another way to solve the problem is to maintain two variables, `max` and `count`. `max` stores the current max number, and `count` stores its occurrences. Initially, assign the first number to `max` and `1` to `count`. Compare each subsequent number with `max`. If the number is greater than `max`, assign it to `max` and reset `count` to `1`. If the number is equal to `max`, increment `count` by `1`. Use this approach to rewrite Listing 6.1.

6.3   (*Reversing the numbers entered*) Write a program that reads ten integers and displays them in the reverse of the order in which they were read.

6.4   (*Analyzing scores*) Write a program that reads an unspecified number of scores and determines how many scores are above or equal to the average and how many scores are below the average. Enter a negative number to signify the end of the input. Assume that the maximum number of scores is `10`.

6.5**   (*Printing distinct numbers*) Write a program that reads in ten numbers and displays distinct numbers (i.e., if a number appears multiple times, it is displayed only once). (*Hint*: Read a number and store it to an array if it is new. If the number is already in the array, discard it. After the input, the array contains the distinct numbers.)

6.6*   (*Revising Listing 4.14, PrimeNumber.java*) Listing 4.14 determines whether a number `n` is prime by checking whether `2, 3, 4, 5, 6, ..., n/2` is a divisor. If a divisor is found, `n` is not prime. A more efficient approach to determine whether `n` is prime is to check whether any of the prime numbers less than or equal to $\sqrt{n}$ can divide `n` evenly. If not, `n` is prime. Rewrite Listing 4.14 to display the first 50 prime numbers using this approach. You need to use an array to store the prime numbers and later use them to check whether they are possible divisors for `n`.

6.7*   (*Counting single digits*) Write a program that generates `100` random integers between `0` and `9` and displays the count for each number. (*Hint*: Use `(int)(Math.random() * 10)` to generate a random integer between `0` and `9`. Use an array of ten integers, say `counts`, to store the counts for the number of `0`'s, `1`'s, ..., `9`'s.)

Sections 6.4–6.5

6.8   (*Averaging an array*) Write two overloaded methods that return the average of an array with the following headers:

```
public static int average(int[] array);
public static double average(double[] array);
```

Use {`1, 2, 3, 4, 5, 6`} and {`6.0, 4.4, 1.9, 2.9, 3.4, 3.5`} to test the methods.

6.9   (*Finding the smallest element*) Write a method that finds the smallest element in an array of integers. Use {`1, 2, 4, 5, 10, 100, 2, -22`} to test the method.

6.10   (*Finding the index of the smallest element*) Write a method that returns the index of the smallest element in an array of integers. If there are more than one such elements, return the smallest index. Use {`1, 2, 4, 5, 10, 100, 2, -22`} to test the method.

6.11* (*Computing deviation*) Exercise 5.21 computes the standard deviation of numbers. This exercise uses a different but equivalent formula to compute the standard deviation of n numbers.

$$mean = \frac{\sum_{i=1}^{n} x_i}{n} = \frac{x_1 + x_2 + \cdots + x_n}{n} \qquad deviation = \sqrt{\frac{\sum_{i=1}^{n} (x_i - mean)^2}{n-1}}$$

To compute deviation with this formula, you have to store the individual numbers using an array, so that they can be used after the mean is obtained. Use $\{1, 2, 3, 4, 5, 6, 7, 8, 9, 10\}$ to test the method.

Your program should contain the following methods:

```
/** Method for computing deviation of double values*/
public static double deviation(double[] x)

/** Method for computing deviation of int values*/
public static double deviation(int[] x)

/** Method for computing mean of an array of double values*/
public static double mean(double[] x)

/** Method for computing mean of an array of int values*/
public static double mean(int[] x)
```

6.12* (*Reversing an array*) The **reverse** method in §6.5 reverses an array by copying it to a new array. Rewrite the method without creating new arrays.

Section 6.6 Variable-Length Argument Lists

6.13* (*Random number chooser*) Write a method that returns a random number between 1 and 54, excluding the numbers passed in the argument. The method header is specified as follows:

```
public static int getRandom(int... numbers)
```

6.14 (*Computing gcd*) Write a method that returns the gcd of an unspecified number of integers. The method header is specified as follows:

```
public static int gcd(int... numbers)
```

Sections 6.7–6.9

6.15 (*Financial application: finding the sales amount*) Rewrite Listing 4.9, FindSalesAmount.cpp, using the binary search approach. Since the sales amount is between 1 and COMMISSION_SOUGHT/0.08, you can use a binary search to improve it.

6.16 (*Execution time*) Write a program that randomly generates an array of 100000 integers and a key. Estimate the execution time of invoking the **linearSearch** method in Listing 6.6. Sort the array and estimate the execution time of invoking the **binarySearch** method in Listing 6.7. You can use the following code template to obtain the execution time:

```
long startTime = System.currentTimeMillis();
perform the task;
long endTime = System.currentTimeMillis();
long executionTime = endTime - startTime;
```

6.17* (*Revising selection sort*) In §6.8.1, you used selection sort to sort an array. The selection sort method repeatedly finds the largest number in the current array and swaps it with the last number in the array. Rewrite this program by finding the smallest number and swapping it with the first number in the array.

6.18** (*Bubble sort*) Write a sort method that uses the bubble-sort algorithm. The bubble-sort algorithm makes several passes through the array. On each pass, successive neighboring pairs are compared. If a pair is in decreasing order, its values are swapped; otherwise, the values remain unchanged. The technique is called a *bubble sort* or *sinking sort* because the smaller values gradually "bubble" their way to the top and the larger values "sink" to the bottom. Use {6.0, 4.4, 1.9, 2.9, 3.4, 2.9, 3.5} to test the method.

6.19** (*Sorting students*) Write a program that prompts the user to enter the number of students, and student names and their scores, and prints student names in decreasing order of their scores.

Section 6.10 Two-dimensional Arrays

6.20* (*Summing all the numbers in a matrix*) Write a method that sums all the integers in a matrix of integers. Use {{1, 2, 4, 5}, {6, 7, 8, 9}, {10, 11, 12, 13}, {14, 15, 16, 17}} to test the method.

6.21* (*Summing the major diagonal in a matrix*) Write a method that sums all the integers in the major diagonal in an $n \times n$ matrix of integers. Use {{1, 2, 4, 5}, {6, 7, 8, 9}, {10, 11, 12, 13}, {14, 15, 16, 17}} to test the method.

6.22* (*Sorting students on grades*) Rewrite Listing 6.10, GradeExam.java, to display the students in increasing order of the number of correct answers.

6.23** (*Computing the weekly hours for each employee*) Suppose the weekly hours for all employees are stored in a two-dimensional array. Each row records an employee's seven-day work hours with seven columns. For example, the following array stores the work hours for eight employees. Write a program that displays employees and their total hours in decreasing order of the total hours.

	Su	M	T	W	H	F	Sa
Employee 0	2	4	3	4	5	8	8
Employee 1	7	3	4	3	3	4	4
Employee 2	3	3	4	3	3	2	2
Employee 3	9	3	4	7	3	4	1
Employee 4	3	5	4	3	6	3	8
Employee 5	3	4	4	6	3	4	4
Employee 6	3	7	4	8	3	8	4
Employee 7	6	3	5	9	2	7	9

6.24 (*Adding two matrices*) Write a method to add two matrices. The header of the method is as follows:

```
public static int[][] addMatrix(int[][] a, int[][] b)
```

In order to be added, the two matrices must have the same dimensions and the same or compatible types of elements. As shown below, two matrices are added by adding the two elements of the arrays with the same index:

$$\begin{pmatrix} a_{11} & a_{12} & a_{13} \\ a_{21} & a_{22} & a_{23} \\ a_{31} & a_{32} & a_{33} \end{pmatrix} + \begin{pmatrix} b_{11} & b_{12} & b_{13} \\ b_{21} & b_{22} & b_{23} \\ b_{31} & b_{32} & b_{33} \end{pmatrix} = \begin{pmatrix} a_{11} + b_{11} & a_{12} + b_{12} & a_{13} + b_{13} \\ a_{21} + b_{21} & a_{22} + b_{22} & a_{23} + b_{23} \\ a_{31} + b_{31} & a_{32} + b_{32} & a_{33} + b_{33} \end{pmatrix}$$

6.25** (*Multiplying two matrices*) Write a method to multiply two matrices. The header of the method is as follows:

```
public static int[][] multiplyMatrix(int[][] a, int[][] b)
```

To multiply matrix **a** by matrix **b**, the number of columns in **a** must be the same as the number of rows in **b**, and the two matrices must have elements of the same or compatible types. Let **c** be the result of the multiplication, and **a**, **b**, and **c** are denoted as follows:

$$\begin{pmatrix} a_{11} & a_{12} & a_{13} \\ a_{21} & a_{22} & a_{23} \\ a_{31} & a_{32} & a_{33} \end{pmatrix} \times \begin{pmatrix} b_{11} & b_{12} & b_{13} \\ b_{21} & b_{22} & b_{23} \\ b_{31} & b_{32} & b_{33} \end{pmatrix} = \begin{pmatrix} c_{11} & c_{12} & c_{13} \\ c_{21} & c_{22} & c_{23} \\ c_{31} & c_{32} & c_{33} \end{pmatrix}$$

where $c_{ij} = a_{i1} \times b_{1j} + a_{i2} \times b_{2j} + a_{i3} \times b_{3j}$.

6.26* (*Points nearest to each other*) Listing 6.11 gives a program that finds two points in a two-dimensional space nearest to other. Revise the program that finds two points in a three-dimensional space nearest to each other. Use a two-dimensional array to represent the points. Test the program using the following points:

Video Note
Find points nearest to each other

```
double[][] points = {{-1, 0, 3}, {-1, -1, -1}, {4, 1, 1},
  {2, 0.5, 9}, {3.5, 2, -1}, {3, 1.5, 3}, {-1.5, 4, 2},
  {5.5, 4, -0.5}};
```

The formula for computing the distance between two points (x1, y1, z1) and (x2, y2, z2) is $\sqrt{(x_2 - x_1)^2 + (y_2 - y_1)^2 + (z_2 - z_1)^2}$.

6.27** (*All closest pairs of points*) Revise Listing 6.11, FindNearestPoints.java, to find all closest pairs of points with same minimum distance.

Comprehensive

6.28* (*Game: TicTacToe board*) Write a program that randomly fills in 0s and 1s into a TicTacToe board, prints the board, and finds the rows, columns, or diagonals with all 0s or 1s. Use a two-dimensional array to represent a TicTacToe board. Here is a sample run of the program:

```
001
001
111
All 1's on row 2
All 1's on column 2
```

6.29*** (*Game: bean machine*) The bean machine, also known as a quincunx or the Galton box, is a device for statistic experiments named after English scientist Sir Francis Galton. It consists of an upright board with evenly spaced nails (or pegs) in a triangular form, as shown in Figure 6.17.

Balls are dropped from the opening of the board. Every time a ball hits a nail, it has a 50% of chance to fall to the left and a 50% of chance to fall to the right. The piles of balls are accumulated in the slots at the bottom of the board.

Write a program that simulates the bean machine. Your program should prompt the user to enter the number of the balls and the number of the slots in the machine. Simulate the falling of each ball by printing its path. For example, the path for the ball in Figure 6.17(b) is LLRRLLR and the path for the ball in Figure 6.17(c) is RLRRLRR. Display the final buildup of the balls in the slots in a histogram. Here is a sample run of the program:

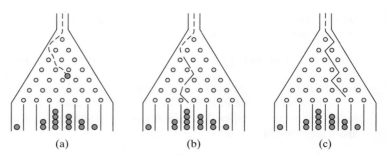

FIGURE 6.17 Each ball takes a random path and falls into a slot.

```
Enter the number of balls to drop: 5  ↵Enter
Enter the number of slots in the bean machine: 7  ↵Enter

LRLRLRR
RRLLLRR
LLRLLRR
RRLLLLL
LRLRRLR

        O
        O
      OOO
```

Hint: Create an array named `slots`. Each element in `slots` stores the number of balls in a slot. Each ball falls into a slot via a path. The number of R's in a path is the position of the slot where the ball falls. For example, for the path LRLRLRR, the ball falls into `slots[4]`, and for the path is RRLLLLL, the ball falls into `slots[2]`.

6.30* (*Game: playing a TicTacToe game*) In a game of TicTacToe, two players take turns marking an available cell in a 3 × 3 grid with their respective tokens (either X or O). When one player has placed three tokens in a horizontal, vertical, or diagonal row on the grid, the game is over and that player has won. A draw (no winner) occurs when all the cells on the grid have been filled with tokens and neither player has achieved a win. Create a program for playing TicTacToe, as follows:

1. The program prompts the first player to enter an X token, and then prompts the second player to enter an O token. Whenever a token is entered, the program refreshes the board and determines the status of the game (win, draw, or unfinished).
2. To place a token, display two dialog boxes to prompt the user to enter the row and the column for the token.

6.31** (*Game: nine heads and tails*) Nine coins are placed in a 3-by-3 matrix with some face up and some face down. You can represent the state of the coins using a 3-by-3 matrix with values 0 (head) and 1 (tail). Here are some examples:

```
0 0 0    1 0 1    1 1 0    1 0 1    1 0 0
0 1 0    0 0 1    1 0 0    1 1 0    1 1 1
0 0 0    1 0 0    0 0 1    1 0 0    1 1 0
```

Each state can also be represented using a binary number. For example, the preceding matrices correspond to the numbers

000010000 101001100 110100001 101110100 100111110

There are a total of **512** possibilities. So, you can use decimal numbers **0, 1, 2, 3, ...**, and **511** to represent all states of the matrix. Write a program that prompts the user to enter a number between **0** and **511** and displays the corresponding matrix with characters **H** and **T**. Here is a sample output:

```
Enter a number between 0 and 511: 7 ↵Enter
H H H
H H H
T T T
```

The user entered **7**, which corresponds to **000000111**. Since **0** stands for **H** and **1** for **T**, the output is correct.

6.32*   (*Financial application: computing tax*) Rewrite Listing 3.7, ComputeTax.java, using arrays. For each filing status, there are six tax rates. Each rate is applied to a certain amount of taxable income. For example, from the taxable income of $400,000 for a single filer, $6,000 is taxed at 10%, $(27,950 - 6,000)$ at 15%, $(67,700 - 27,950)$ at 27%, $(141,250 - 67,700)$ at 30%, $(307,050 - 141,250)$ at 35%, and $(400,000 - 307,050)$ at 38.6%. The six rates are the same for all filing statuses, which can be represented in the following array:

```
double[] rates = {0.10, 0.15, 0.27, 0.30, 0.35, 0.386};
```

The brackets for each rate for all the filing statuses can be represented in a two-dimensional array as follows:

```
int[][] brackets = {
  {6000, 27950, 67700, 141250, 307050},    // Single filer
  {12000, 46700, 112850, 171950, 307050},  // Married jointly
  {6000, 23350, 56425, 85975, 153525},     // Married separately
  {10000, 37450, 96700, 156600, 307050}    // Head of household
};
```

Suppose the taxable income is $400,000 for single filers. The tax can be computed as follows:

```
tax = brackets[0][0] * rates[0] +
  (brackets[0][1] - brackets[0][0]) * rates[1] +
  (brackets[0][2] - brackets[0][1]) * rates[2] +
  (brackets[0][3] - brackets[0][2]) * rates[3] +
  (brackets[0][4] - brackets[0][3]) * rates[4] +
  (400000 - brackets[0][4]) * rates[5]
```

6.33*   (*Game: locker puzzle*) A school has **100** lockers and **100** students. All lockers are closed on the first day of school. As the students enter, the first student, denoted S1, opens every locker. Then the second student, S2, begins with the second locker, denoted L2, and closes every other locker. Student S3 begins with the third locker and changes every third locker (closes it if it was open, and opens it if it was closed). Student S4 begins with locker L4 and changes every fourth locker. Student S5 starts with L5 and changes every fifth locker, and so on, until student S100 changes L100.

After all the students have passed through the building and changed the lockers, which lockers are open? Write a program to find your answer.

(*Hint*: Use an array of **100** elements, each of which stores the number of the times a locker has changed. If a locker changes an even number of times, it is closed; otherwise, it is open.)

6.34** (*Game: checker board*) Write a program that randomly fills in **0**s and **1**s into an 8 × 8 checker board, prints the board, and finds the rows, columns, or diagonals with all **0**s or **1**s. Use a two-dimensional array to represent a checker board. Here is a sample run of the program:

```
10101000
10100001
11100011
10100001
11100111
10000001
10100111
00100001
All 0's on subdiagonal
```

6.35*** (*Game: Eight Queens*) The classic Eight Queens puzzle is to place eight queens on a chessboard such that no two queens can attack each other (i.e., no two queens are on the same row, same column, or same diagonal). There are many possible solutions. Write a program that displays one such solution. A sample output is shown below:

```
|Q| | | | | | | |
| | | |Q| | | | |
| | | | | | |Q| |
| | | | |Q| | | |
| |Q| | | | | | |
| | | | | |Q| | |
| |Q| | | | | | |
| | | |Q| | | | |
```

6.36*** (*Game: multiple Sudoku solutions*) A Sudoku problem may have multiple solutions. Modify Listing 6.12, Sudoku.java, to display the total number of the solutions. Display two solutions if multiple solutions exist.

6.37*** (*Game: multiple Eight Queens solutions*) Exercise 6.35 finds one solution for the eight queens problem. Write a program to count all possible solutions for the eight queens problem and displays all solutions.

CHAPTER 7

OBJECTS AND CLASSES

Objectives

- To describe objects and classes, and use classes to model objects (§7.2).
- To use UML graphical notations to describe classes and objects (§7.2).
- To construct objects using constructors (§7.3).
- To access objects via object reference variables (§7.4).
- To define a reference variable using a reference type (§7.4.1).
- To access an object's data and methods (§7.4.2).
- To declare a class and create an object from a class (§7.4.3).
- To assign default values for an object's data fields (§7.4.4).
- To distinguish between object reference variables and primitive data type variables (§7.4.5).
- To use classes `Date`, `Random`, and `JFrame` in the Java library (§7.5).
- To distinguish between instance and static variables and methods (§7.6).
- To declare private data fields with appropriate `get` and `set` methods (§7.7).
- To encapsulate data fields to make classes easy to maintain (§7.8).
- To differentiate between primitive-type arguments and object-type arguments (§7.9).
- To develop methods with object arguments (§7.9).
- To store and process objects in arrays (§7.10).

7.1 Introduction

why OOP?

After learning the material in earlier chapters, you are able to solve many programming problems using selections, loops, methods, and arrays. However, these Java features are not sufficient for developing graphical user interfaces and large-scale software systems. Suppose you want to develop a GUI (graphical user interface, pronounced *goo-ee*) as shown in Figure 7.1. How do you program it?

FIGURE 7.1 The GUI component objects can be displayed.

This chapter begins the introduction of object-oriented programming, which will enable you to develop GUI and large-scale software systems effectively.

7.2 Defining Classes for Objects

object

Object-oriented programming (OOP) involves programming using objects. An *object* represents an entity in the real world that can be distinctly identified. For example, a student, a desk, a circle, a button, and even a loan can all be viewed as objects. An object has a unique identity, state, and behaviors.

state

■ The *state* of an object is represented by *data fields* (also known as *properties*) with their current values.

behavior

■ The *behavior* of an object is defined by a set of methods. To invoke a method on an object is to ask the object to perform a task.

A circle object, for example, has a data field, `radius`, which is the property that characterizes a circle. One behavior of a circle is that its area can be computed using the method `getArea()`.

instantiation
object
instance

Objects of the same type are defined using a common class. A class is a template or blueprint that defines what an object's data and methods will be. An object is an instance of a class. You can create many instances of a class. Creating an instance is referred to as *instantiation*. The terms *object* and *instance* are often interchangeable. The relationship between classes and objects is analogous to the-relationship between apple pie recipes and apple pies. You can make as many apple pies as you want from a single recipe. Figure 7.2 shows a class named `Circle` and its three objects.

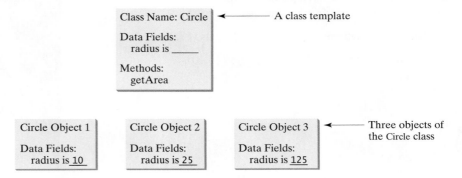

FIGURE 7.2 A class is a template for creating objects.

A Java class uses variables to define data fields and methods to define behaviors. Additionally, a class provides methods of a special type, known as *constructors*, which are invoked when a new object is created. A constructor is a special kind of method. A constructor can perform any action, but constructors are designed to perform initializing actions, such as initializing the data fields of objects. Figure 7.3 shows an example of the class for `Circle` objects.

class
data field
method
constructor

```
class Circle {
    /** The radius of this circle */
    double radius = 1.0;  ◄──────────────── Data field

    /** Construct a circle object */─┐
    Circle() {                       │
    }                                │
                                     ├─◄──── Constructors
    /** Construct a circle object */ │
    Circle(double newRadius) {       │
        radius = newRadius;          │
    }                                ┘

    /** Return the area of this circle */
    double getArea() {  ◄──────────────────── Method
        return radius * radius * Math.PI;
    }
}
```

FIGURE 7.3 A class is a construct that defines objects of the same type.

The `Circle` class is different from all of the other classes you have seen thus far. It does not have a `main` method and therefore cannot be run; it is merely a definition used to declare and create `Circle` objects. For convenience, the class that contains the `main` method will be referred to as the *main class* in this book.

main class

The illustration of class templates and objects in Figure 7.3 can be standardized using UML (Unified Modeling Language) notations. This notation, as shown in Figure 7.4, is called a *UML class diagram*, or simply a *class diagram*. In the class diagram, the data field is denoted as

class diagram

```
dataFieldName: dataFieldType
```

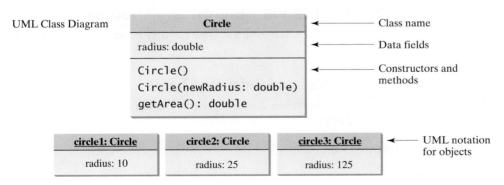

FIGURE 7.4 Classes and objects can be represented using UML notations.

The constructor is denoted as

```
ClassName(parameterName: parameterType)
```

The method is denoted as

```
methodName(parameterName: parameterType): returnType
```

7.3 Constructing Objects Using Constructors

overloaded constructors

Constructors are used to construct objects. The constructor has exactly the same name as the defining class. Like regular methods, constructors can be overloaded (i.e., multiple constructors with the same name but different signatures), making it easy to construct objects with different initial data values.

To construct an object from a class, invoke a constructor of the class using the **new** operator, as follows:

```
new ClassName(arguments);
```

For example, **new Circle()** creates an object of the **Circle** class using the first constructor defined in the **Circle** class, and **new Circle(5)** creates an object using the second constructor defined in the **Circle** class.

no-arg constructor

A class normally provides a constructor without arguments (e.g., **Circle()**). Such a constructor is referred to as a *no-arg* or *no-argument constructor*.

default constructor

A class may be declared without constructors. In this case, a no-arg constructor with an empty body is implicitly declared in the class. This constructor, called *a default constructor*, is provided automatically *only if no constructors are explicitly declared in the class*.

Constructors are a special kind of method, with three differences:

constructor's name

■ Constructors must have the same name as the class itself.

no return type

■ Constructors do not have a return type—not even **void**.

new operator

■ Constructors are invoked using the **new** operator when an object is created. Constructors play the role of initializing objects.

 Caution

It is a common mistake to put the **void** keyword in front of a constructor. For example,

```
public void Circle() {
}
```

In this case, **Circle()** is a method, not a constructor.

7.4 Accessing Objects via Reference Variables

Newly created objects are allocated in the memory. How can they be accessed? The answer is given in this section.

7.4.1 Reference Variables and Reference Types

reference variable

Objects are accessed via object *reference variables*, which contain references to the objects. Such variables are declared using the following syntax:

```
ClassName objectRefVar;
```

reference type

A class defines a type, known as a *reference type*. Any variable of the class type can reference an instance of the class. The following statement declares the variable **myCircle** to be of the **Circle** type:

```
Circle myCircle;
```

The variable **myCircle** can reference a **Circle** object. The next statement creates an object and assigns its reference to **myCircle**.

```
myCircle = new Circle();
```

Using the syntax shown below, you can write one statement that combines the declaration of an object reference variable, the creation of an object, and the assigning of an object reference to the variable.

```
ClassName objectRefVar = new ClassName();
```

Here is an example:

```
Circle myCircle = new Circle();
```

The variable `myCircle` holds a reference to a `Circle` object.

Note

An object reference variable that appears to hold an object actually contains a reference to that object. Strictly speaking, an object reference variable and an object are different, but most of the time the distinction can be ignored. So it is fine, for simplicity, to say that `myCircle` is a `Circle` object rather than use a more long-winded description that `myCircle` is a variable that contains a reference to a `Circle` object.

object vs. object reference variable

Note

Arrays are treated as objects in Java. Arrays are created using the `new` operator. An array variable is actually a variable that contains a reference to an array.

array object

7.4.2 Accessing an Object's Data and Methods

After an object is created, its data can be accessed and its methods invoked using the *dot operator* (`.`), also known as the *object member access operator*:

dot operator

- `objectRefVar.dataField` references a data field in the object.
- `objectRefVar.method(arguments)` invokes a method on the object.

For example, `myCircle.radius` references the radius in `myCircle`, and `myCircle.getArea()` invokes the `getArea` method on `myCircle`. Methods are invoked as operations on objects.

The data field `radius` is referred to as an *instance variable* because it is dependent on a specific instance. For the same reason, the method `getArea` is referred to as an *instance method*, because you can invoke it only on a specific instance. The object on which an instance method is invoked is called a *calling object*.

instance variable
instance method

calling object

Note

Most of the time, you create an object and assign it to a variable. Later you can use the variable to reference the object. Occasionally, an object does not need to be referenced later. In this case, you can create an object without explicitly assigning it to a variable, as shown below:

```
new Circle();
```

or

```
System.out.println("Area is " + new Circle(5).getArea());
```

The former statement creates a `Circle` object. The latter creates a `Circle` object and invokes its `getArea` method to return its area. An object created in this way is known as an *anonymous object*.

anonymous object

7.4.3 Example: Declaring Classes and Creating Objects

Listing 7.1 is a program that declares a circle class. To avoid a naming conflict with several improved versions of the `Circle` class introduced later in this book, the `Circle` class in this example is named `Circle1`.

The program constructs a circle object with radius 5 and an object with radius 1 and displays the radius and area of each of the two circles. Change the radius of the second object to 100 and display its new radius and area.

LISTING 7.1 TestCircle1.java

main class

main method

create object

create object

class **Circle1**

data field

no-arg constructor

second constructor

method

```java
1  public class TestCircle1 {
2    /** Main method */
3    public static void main(String[] args) {
4      // Create a circle with radius 5.0
5      Circle1 myCircle = new Circle1(5.0);
6      System.out.println("The area of the circle of radius "
7        + myCircle.radius + " is " + myCircle.getArea());
8
9      // Create a circle with radius 1
10     Circle1 yourCircle = new Circle1();
11     System.out.println("The area of the circle of radius "
12       + yourCircle.radius + " is " + yourCircle.getArea());
13
14     // Modify circle radius
15     yourCircle.radius = 100;
16     System.out.println("The area of the circle of radius "
17       + yourCircle.radius  + " is " + yourCircle.getArea() );
18   }
19 }
20
21 // Define the circle class with two constructors
22 class Circle1 {
23   double radius;
24
25   /** Construct a circle with radius 1 */
26   Circle1() {
27     radius = 1.0;
28   }
29
30   /** Construct a circle with a specified radius */
31   Circle1(double newRadius) {
32     radius = newRadius;
33   }
34
35   /** Return the area of this circle */
36   double getArea() {
37     return radius * radius * Math.PI;
38   }
39 }
```

```
The area of the circle of radius 5.0 is 78.53981633974483
The area of the circle of radius 1.0 is 3.141592653589793
The area of the circle of radius 100.0 is 31415.926535897932
```

The program contains two classes. The first class, TestCircle1, is the main class. Its sole purpose is to test the second class, Circle1. When you run the program, the Java runtime system invokes the main method in the main class.

You can put the two classes into one file, but only one class in the file can be a public class. Furthermore, the public class must have the same name as the file name. Therefore, the file name is TestCircle1.java since TestCircle1 is public.

The main class contains the **main** method (line 3) that creates two objects. The constructor **Circle1(5.0)** was used to create **myCircle** with a radius of **5.0** (line 5), and the constructor **Circle1()** was used to create **yourCircle** with a radius of **1.0** (line 10).

These two objects (referenced by **myCircle** and **yourCircle**) have different data but have the same methods. Therefore, you can compute their respective areas by using the **getArea()** method.

To write the **getArea** method in a procedural programming language like Pascal, you would pass radius as an argument to the method. But in object-oriented programming, **radius** and **getArea** are defined for the object. The **radius** is a data member in the object, which is accessible by the **getArea** method. In procedural programming languages, data and methods are separated, but in an object-oriented programming language, data and methods are coupled together.

The **getArea** method is an instance method that is always invoked by an instance in which the **radius** is specified.

There are many ways to write Java programs. For instance, you can combine the two classes in the example into one, as shown in Listing 7.2:

LISTING 7.2 Circle1.java

```
 1 public class Circle1 {
 2   /** Main method */
 3   public static void main(String[] args) {                        main method
 4     // Create a circle with radius 5.0
 5     Circle1 myCircle = new Circle1(5.0);
 6     System.out.println("The area of the circle of radius "
 7       + myCircle.radius + " is " + myCircle.getArea());
 8
 9     // Create a circle with radius 1
10     Circle1 yourCircle = new Circle1();
11     System.out.println("The area of the circle of radius "
12       + yourCircle.radius + " is " + yourCircle.getArea());
13
14     // Modify circle radius
15     yourCircle.radius = 100;
16     System.out.println("The area of the circle of radius "
17       + yourCircle.radius + " is " + yourCircle.getArea());
18   }
19
20   double radius;
21
22   /** Construct a circle with radius 1 */
23   Circle1() {                                                     no-arg constructor
24     radius = 1.0;
25   }
26
27   /** Construct a circle with a specified radius */
28   Circle1(double newRadius) {                                     second constructor
29     radius = newRadius;
30   }
31
32   /** Return the area of this circle */
33   double getArea() {                                              method
34     return radius * radius * Math.PI;
35   }
36 }
```

Since the combined class has a `main` method, it can be executed by the Java interpreter. The `main` method creates `myCircle` as a `Circle1` object and then displays radius and finds area in `myCircle`. This demonstrates that you can test a class by simply adding a `main` method in the same class.

Caution

invoking methods

Recall that you use `Math.methodName(arguments)` (e.g., `Math.pow(3, 2.5)`) to invoke a method in the `Math` class. Can you invoke `getArea()` using `Circle1.getArea()`? The answer is no. All the methods in the `Math` class are static methods, which are defined using the `static` keyword. However, `getArea()` is an instance method, and thus nonstatic. It must be invoked from an object using `objectRefVar.methodName(arguments)` (e.g., `myCircle.getArea()`). More explanations will follow in §7.6, "Static Variables, Constants, and Methods."

7.4.4 Reference Data Fields and the `null` Value

reference data fields

The data fields can be of reference types. For example, the following `Student` class contains a data field `name` of the `String` type. `String` is a predefined Java class.

```
class Student {
  String name; // name has default value null
  int age; // age has default value 0
  boolean isScienceMajor; // isScienceMajor has default value false
  char gender; // c has default value '\u0000'
}
```

`null` value

If a data field of a reference type does not reference any object, the data field holds a special Java value, `null`. `null` is a literal just like `true` and `false`. While `true` and `false` are Boolean literals, `null` is a literal for a reference type.

default field values

The default value of a data field is `null` for a reference type, `0` for a numeric type, `false` for a `boolean` type, and `'\u0000'` for a `char` type. However, Java assigns no default value to a local variable inside a method. The following code displays the default values of data fields `name`, `age`, `isScienceMajor`, and `gender` for a `Student` object:

```
class Test {
  public static void main(String[] args) {
    Student student = new Student();
    System.out.println("name? " + student.name );
    System.out.println("age? " + student.age);
    System.out.println("isScienceMajor? " + student.isScienceMajor);
    System.out.println("gender? " + student.gender);
  }
}
```

The following code has a compilation error because local variables `x` and `y` are not initialized:

```
class Test {
  public static void main(String[] args) {
    int x; // x has no default value
    String y; // y has no default value
    System.out.println("x is " + x);
    System.out.println("y is " + y);
  }
}
```

Caution

NullPointerException is a common runtime error. It happens when you invoke a method on a reference variable with **null** value. Make sure you assign an object reference to the variable before invoking the method through the reference variable.

NullPointerException

7.4.5 Differences Between Variables of Primitive Types and Reference Types

Every variable represents a memory location that holds a value. When you declare a variable, you are telling the compiler what type of value the variable can hold. For a variable of a primitive type, the value is of the primitive type. For a variable of a reference type, the value is a reference to where an object is located. For example, as shown in Figure 7.5, the value of **int** variable **i** is **int** value **1**, and the value of **Circle** object **c** holds a reference to where the contents of the **Circle** object are stored in the memory.

FIGURE 7.5 A variable of a primitive type holds a value of the primitive type, and a variable of a reference type holds a reference to where an object is stored in memory.

When you assign one variable to another, the other variable is set to the same value. For a variable of a primitive type, the real value of one variable is assigned to the other variable. For a variable of a reference type, the reference of one variable is assigned to the other variable. As shown in Figure 7.6, the assignment statement **i = j** copies the contents of **j** into **i** for primitive variables. As shown in Figure 7.7, the assignment statement **c1 = c2** copies the reference of **c2** into **c1** for reference variables. After the assignment, variables **c1** and **c2** refer to the same object.

Primitive type assignment i = j

Before: After:

i   1   i   2

j   2   j   2

FIGURE 7.6 Primitive variable **j** is copied to variable **i**.

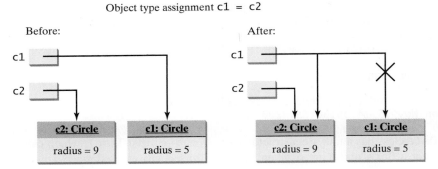

FIGURE 7.7 Reference variable **c2** is copied to variable **c1**.

garbage
garbage collection

Note

As shown in Figure 7.7, after the assignment statement **c1 = c2**, **c1** points to the same object referenced by **c2**. The object previously referenced by **c1** is no longer useful and therefore is now known as *garbage*. Garbage occupies memory space. The Java runtime system detects garbage and automatically reclaims the space it occupies. This process is called *garbage collection*.

Tip

If you know that an object is no longer needed, you can explicitly assign **null** to a reference variable for the object. The JVM will automatically collect the space if the object is not referenced by any reference variable.

7.5 Using Classes from the Java Library

Listing 7.1 declared the **Circle1** class and created objects from the class. You will frequently use the classes in the Java library to develop programs. This section gives some examples of the classes in the Java library.

7.5.1 The **Date** Class

In Listing 2.9, ShowCurrentTime.java, you learned how to obtain the current time using **System.currentTimeMillis()**. You used the division and remainder operators to extract current second, minute, and hour. Java provides a system-independent encapsulation of date and time in the **java.util.Date** class, as shown in Figure 7.8.

java.util.Date class

The + sign indicates public modifier ⟶

java.util.Date	
+Date()	Constructs a **Date** object for the current time.
+Date(elapseTime: long)	Constructs a **Date** object for a given time in milliseconds elapsed since January 1, 1970, GMT.
+toString(): String	Returns a string representing the date and time.
+getTime(): long	Returns the number of milliseconds since January 1, 1970, GMT.
+setTime(elapseTime: long): void	Sets a new elapse time in the object.

FIGURE 7.8 A **Date** object represents a specific date and time.

You can use the no-arg constructor in the **Date** class to create an instance for the current date and time, its **getTime()** method to return the elapsed time since January 1, 1970, GMT, and its **toString** method to return the date and time as a string. For example, the following code

create object

get elapsed time
invoke **toString**

```
java.util.Date date = new java.util.Date();
System.out.println("The elapsed time since Jan 1, 1970 is " +
  date.getTime() + " milliseconds");
System.out.println(date.toString());
```

displays the output like this:

```
The elapsed time since Jan 1, 1970 is 1100547210284 milliseconds
Mon Nov 15 14:33:30 EST 2004
```

The **Date** class has another constructor, **Date(long elapseTime)**, which can be used to construct a **Date** object for a given time in milliseconds elapsed since January 1, 1970, GMT.

7.5.2 The Random Class

You have used `Math.random()` to obtain a random double value between `0.0` and `1.0` (excluding `1.0`). Another way to generate random numbers is to use the `java.util.Random` class, as shown in Figure 7.9, which can generate a random `int`, `long`, `double`, `float`, and `boolean` value.

java.util.Random	
+Random()	Constructs a `Random` object with the current time as its seed.
+Random(seed: long)	Constructs a `Random` object with a specified seed.
+nextInt(): int	Returns a random `int` value.
+nextInt(n: int): int	Returns a random `int` value between 0 and n (exclusive).
+nextLong(): long	Returns a random `long` value.
+nextDouble(): double	Returns a random `double` value between `0.0` and `1.0` (exclusive).
+nextFloat(): float	Returns a random `float` value between `0.0F` and `1.0F` (exclusive).
+nextBoolean(): boolean	Returns a random `boolean` value.

FIGURE 7.9 A Random object can be used to generate random values.

When you create a Random object, you have to specify a seed or use the default seed. The no-arg constructor creates a Random object using the current elapsed time as its seed. If two Random objects have the same seed, they will generate identical sequences of numbers. For example, the following code creates two Random objects with the same seed, 3.

```java
Random random1 = new Random(3);
System.out.print("From random1: ");
for (int i = 0; i < 10; i++)
  System.out.print(random1.nextInt(1000) + " ");

Random random2 = new Random(3);
System.out.print("\nFrom random2: ");
for (int i = 0; i < 10; i++)
  System.out.print(random2.nextInt(1000) + " ");
```

The code generates the same sequence of random `int` values:

```
From random1: 734 660 210 581 128 202 549 564 459 961
From random2: 734 660 210 581 128 202 549 564 459 961
```

Note

The capability of generating the same sequence of random values is useful in software testing and many other applications. In software testing, you can test your program using a fixed sequence of numbers before using different sequences of random numbers.

same sequence

7.5.3 Displaying GUI Components

Pedagogical Note

Graphical user interface (GUI) components are good examples for teaching OOP. Simple GUI examples are introduced for this purpose. The complete introduction on GUI programming is covered starting from Chapter 13, "GUI Basics."

When you develop programs to create graphical user interfaces, you will use Java classes such as `JFrame`, `JButton`, `JRadioButton`, `JComboBox`, and `JList` to create frames, buttons, radio buttons, combo boxes, lists, and so on. Listing 7.3 is an example that creates two windows using the `JFrame` class. The output of the program is shown in Figure 7.10.

FIGURE 7.10 The program creates two windows using the JFrame class.

LISTING 7.3 TestFrame.java

```
1 import javax.swing.JFrame;
2
3 public class TestFrame {
4   public static void main(String[] args) {
5     JFrame frame1 = new JFrame();
6     frame1.setTitle("Window 1");
7     frame1.setSize(200, 150);
8     frame1.setLocation(200, 100);
9     frame1.setDefaultCloseOperation(JFrame.EXIT_ON_CLOSE);
10    frame1.setVisible(true);
11
12    JFrame frame2 = new JFrame();
13    frame2.setTitle("Window 2");
14    frame2.setSize(200, 150);
15    frame2.setLocation(410, 100);
16    frame2.setDefaultCloseOperation(JFrame.EXIT_ON_CLOSE);
17    frame2.setVisible(true);
18  }
19 }
```

create an object
invoke a method

create an object
invoke a method

This program creates two objects of the JFrame class (lines 5, 12) and then uses the methods setTitle, setSize, setLocation, setDefaultCloseOperation, and setVisible to set the properties of the objects. The setTitle method sets a title for the window (lines 6, 13). The setSize method sets the window's width and height (lines 7, 14). The setLocation method specifies the location of the window's upper-left corner (lines 8, 15). The setDefaultCloseOperation method terminates the program when the frame is closed (lines 8, 16). The setVisible method displays the window.

You can add graphical user interface components, such as buttons, labels, text fields, check boxes, and combo boxes to the window. The components are defined using classes. Listing 7.4 gives an example of creating a graphical user interface, as shown in Figure 7.1.

LISTING 7.4 GUIComponents.java

Video Note
Use classes

```
1 import javax.swing.*;
2
3 public class GUIComponents {
4   public static void main(String[] args) {
5     // Create a button with text OK
6     JButton jbtOK = new JButton("OK");
7
8     // Create a label with text "Enter your name: "
9     JLabel jlblName = new JLabel("Enter your name: ");
10
11    // Create a text field with text "Type Name Here"
12    JTextField jtfName = new JTextField("Type Name Here");
13
14    // Create a check box with text bold
15    JCheckBox jchkBold = new JCheckBox("Bold");
```

create a button

create a label

create a text field

create a check box

```
16
17      // Create a radio button with text red
18      JRadioButton jrbRed = new JRadioButton("Red");
19
20      // Create a combo box with choices red, green, and blue
21      JComboBox jcboColor = new JComboBox(new String[]{"Red",
22        "Green", "Blue"});
23
24      // Create a panel to group components
25      JPanel panel = new JPanel();
26      panel.add(jbtOK); // Add the button to the panel
27      panel.add(jlblName); // Add the label to the panel
28      panel.add(jtfName); // Add the text field to the panel
29      panel.add(jchkBold); // Add the check box to the panel
30      panel.add(jrbRed); // Add the radio button to the panel
31      panel.add(jcboColor); // Add the combo box to the panel
32
33      JFrame frame = new JFrame(); // Create a frame
34      frame.add(panel); // Add the panel to the frame
35      frame.setTitle("Show GUI Components");
36      frame.setSize(450, 100);
37      frame.setLocation(200, 100);
38      frame.setDefaultCloseOperation(JFrame.EXIT_ON_CLOSE);
39      frame.setVisible(true);
40    }
41 }
```

create a radio button

create a combo box

create a panel
add to panel

create a frame
add panel to frame

display frame

This program creates GUI objects using the classes `JButton`, `JLabel`, `JTextField`, `JCheckBox`, `JRadioButton`, and `JComboBox` (lines 6–22). It then creates a panel object using the `JPanel` class (line 25) and adds the button, label, text field, check box, radio button, and combo box to the panel (lines 26–31). The program then creates a frame and adds a panel to the frame (line 34). The frame is displayed in line 39.

7.6 Static Variables, Constants, and Methods

The data field `radius` in the circle class in Listing 7.1 is known as an *instance variable*. An instance variable is tied to a specific instance of the class; it is not shared among objects of the same class. For example, suppose that you create the following objects:

instance variable

```
Circle circle1 = new Circle();
Circle circle2 = new Circle(5);
```

The `radius` in `circle1` is independent of the `radius` in `circle2` and is stored in a different memory location. Changes made to `circle1`'s `radius` do not affect `circle2`'s `radius`, and vice versa.

If you want all the instances of a class to share data, use *static variables*, also known as *class variables*. Static variables store values for the variables in a common memory location. Because of this common location, all objects of the same class are affected if one object changes the value of a static variable. Java supports static methods as well as static variables. *Static methods* can be called without creating an instance of the class.

static variable

static method

Let us modify the `Circle` class by adding a static variable `numberOfObjects` to count the number of circle objects created. When the first object of this class is created, `numberOfObjects` is 1. When the second object is created, `numberOfObjects` becomes 2. The UML of the new circle class is shown in Figure 7.11. The `Circle` class defines the instance variable `radius` and the static variable `numberOfObjects`, the instance methods `getRadius`, `setRadius`, and `getArea`, and the static method `getNumberOfObjects`. (Note that static variables and functions are underlined in the UML class diagram.)

UML Notation:
underline: static variables or methods

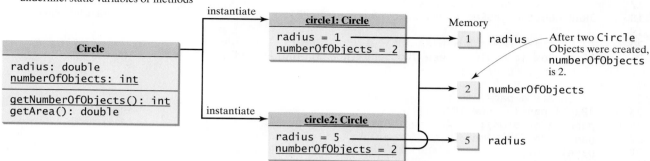

FIGURE 7.11 Instance variables belong to the instances and have memory storage independent of one another. Static variables are shared by all the instances of the same class.

To declare a static variable or a static method, put the modifier `static` in the variable or method declaration. The static variable `numberOfObjects` and the static method `getNumberOfObjects()` can be declared as follows:

declare static variable

```
static int numberOfObjects;
```

declare static method

```
static int getNumberObjects() {
  return numberOfObjects;
}
```

Constants in a class are shared by all objects of the class. Thus, constants should be declared `final static`. For example, the constant `PI` in the `Math` class is defined as:

declare constant

```
final static double PI = 3.14159265358979323846;
```

The new circle class, named `Circle2`, is declared in Listing 7.5:

Video Note
static vs. instance

LISTING 7.5 `Circle2.java`

static variable

increase by 1

increase by 1

static method

```
 1  public class Circle2 {
 2    /** The radius of the circle */
 3    double radius;
 4
 5    /** The number of objects created */
 6    static int numberOfObjects = 0;
 7
 8    /** Construct a circle with radius 1 */
 9    Circle2() {
10      radius = 1.0;
11      numberOfObjects++;
12    }
13
14    /** Construct a circle with a specified radius */
15    Circle2(double newRadius) {
16      radius = newRadius;
17      numberOfObjects++;
18    }
19
20    /** Return numberOfObjects */
21    static int getNumberOfObjects() {
22      return numberOfObjects;
23    }
```

```
24
25   /** Return the area of this circle */
26   double getArea() {
27     return radius * radius * Math.PI;
28   }
29 }
```

Method **getNumberOfObjects()** in **Circle2** is a static method. Other examples of static methods are **showMessageDialog** and **showInputDialog** in the **JOptionPane** class, and all the methods in the **Math** class. The **main** method is static, too.

Instance methods (e.g., **getArea()**) and instance data (e.g., **radius**) belong to instances and can be used only after the instances are created. They are accessed via a reference variable. Static methods (e.g., **getNumberOfObjects()**) and static data (e.g., **numberOfObjects**) can be accessed from a reference variable or from their class name.

The program in Listing 7.6 demonstrates how to use instance and static variables and methods, and illustrates the effects of using them.

LISTING 7.6 TestCircle2.java

```
 1 public class TestCircle2 {
 2   /** Main method */
 3   public static void main(String[] args) {
 4     // Create c1
 5     Circle2 c1 = new Circle2();
 6
 7     // Display c1 BEFORE c2 is created
 8     System.out.println("Before creating c2");
 9     System.out.println("c1 is : radius (" + c1.radius +
10       ") and number of Circle objects (" +
11       c1.numberOfObjects + ")");                              static variable
12
13     // Create c2
14     Circle2 c2 = new Circle2(5);
15
16     // Change the radius in c1
17     c1.radius = 9;                                            instance variable
18
19     // Display c1 and c2 AFTER c2 was created
20     System.out.println("\nAfter creating c2 and modifying " +
21       "c1's radius to 9");
22     System.out.println("c1 is : radius (" + c1.radius +
23       ") and number of Circle objects (" +
24       c1.numberOfObjects + ")");                              static variable
25     System.out.println("c2 is : radius (" + c2.radius +
26       ") and number of Circle objects (" +
27       c2.numberOfObjects + ")");                              static variable
28   }
29 }
```

```
Before creating c2
c1 is : radius (1.0) and number of Circle objects (1)

After creating c2 and modifying c1's radius to 9
c1 is : radius (9.0) and number of Circle objects (2)
c2 is : radius (5.0) and number of Circle objects (2)
```

The `main` method creates two circles, `c1` and `c2` (lines 5, 14). The instance variable `radius` in `c1` is modified to become `9` (line 17). This change does not affect the instance variable `radius` in `c2`, since these two instance variables are independent. The static variable `numberOfObjects` becomes `1` after `c1` is created (line 5), and it becomes `2` after `c2` is created (line 14).

Note that `PI` is a constant defined in `Math`, and `Math.PI` references the constant. `c.numberOfObjects` could be replaced by `Circle2.numberOfObjects`. This improves readability, because the reader can easily recognize the static variable. You can also replace `Circle2.numberOfObjects` by `Circle2.getNumberOfObjects()`.

use class name

Tip

Use `ClassName.methodName(arguments)` to invoke a static method and `ClassName.staticVariable`. This improves readability, because the user can easily recognize the static method and data in the class.

static import

Note

You can use a new JDK 1.5 feature to directly import static variables and methods from a class. The imported data and methods can be referenced or called without specifying a class. For example, you can use `PI` (instead of `Math.PI`), and `random()` (instead of `Math.random()`), if you have the following import statement in the class:

```
import static java.lang.Math.*;
```

Static variables and methods can be used from instance or static methods in the class. However, instance variables and methods can be used only from instance methods, not from static methods, since static variables and methods don't belong to a particular object. Thus the code given below is wrong.

```java
public class Foo {
  int i = 5;
  static int k = 2;

  public static void main(String[] args) {
    int j = i; // Wrong because i is an instance variable
    m1(); // Wrong because m1() is an instance method
  }

  public void m1() {
    // Correct since instance and static variables and methods
    // can be used in an instance method
    i = i + k + m2(i, k);
  }

  public static int m2(int i, int j) {
    return (int)(Math.pow(i, j));
  }
}
```

instance or static?

Design Guide

How do you decide whether a variable or method should be an instance one or a static one? A variable or method that is dependent on a specific instance of the class should be an instance variable or method. A variable or method that is not dependent on a specific instance of the class should be a static variable or method. For example, every circle has its own radius. Radius is dependent on a specific circle. Therefore, `radius` is an instance variable of the `Circle` class. Since the `getArea` method is dependent on a specific circle, it is an instance method. None of the methods in the `Math` class, such as `random`, `pow`, `sin`, and `cos`, is dependent on a specific instance. Therefore, these methods are static methods. The `main` method is static and can be invoked directly from a class.

Caution

It is a common design error to declare an instance method that should have been declared static. For example, the following method `factorial(int n)` should be declared static, because it is independent of any specific instance.

common design error

```
public class Test {
  public int factorial(int n) {
    int result = 1;
    for (int i = 1; i <= n; i++)
      result *= i;

    return result;
  }
}
```
(a) Wrong design

```
public class Test {
  public static int factorial(int n) {
    int result = 1;
    for (int i = 1; i <= n; i++)
      result *= i;

    return result;
  }
}
```
(b) Correct design

7.7 Visibility Modifiers

Java provides several modifiers that control access to data fields, methods, and classes. This section introduces the `public`, `private`, and default modifiers.

- `public` makes classes, methods, and data fields accessible from any class.
- `private` makes methods and data fields accessible only from within its own class.
- If `public` or `private` is not used, then by default the classes, methods, and data fields are accessible by any class in the same package. This is known as *package-private* or *package-access*.

public

private

package-private

Note

Packages can be used to organize classes. To do so, you need to add the following line as the first noncomment and nonblank statement in the program:

using packages

```
package packageName;
```

If a class is declared without the package statement, the class is said to be placed in the *default package*.

Java recommends that you place classes into packages rather using a default package. For simplicity, however, this book uses default packages. For more information on packages, see Supplement III.F, "Packages."

Figure 7.12 illustrates how a public, default, and private data field or method in class C1 can be accessed from a class C2 in the same package, and from a class C3 in a different package.

```
package p1;

public class C1 {
  public int x;
  int y;
  private int z;

  public void m1() {
  }
  void m2() {
  }
  private void m3() {
  }
}
```

```
public class C2 {
  void aMethod() {
    C1 o = new C1();
    can access o.x;
    can access o.y;
    cannot access o.z;

    can invoke o.m1();
    can invoke o.m2();
    cannot invoke o.m3();
  }
}
```

```
package p2;

public class C3 {
  void aMethod() {
    C1 o = new C1();
    can access o.x;
    cannot access o.y;
    cannot access o.z;

    can invoke o.m1();
    cannot invoke o.m2();
    cannot invoke o.m3();
  }
}
```

FIGURE 7.12 The private modifier restricts access to its defining class, the default modifier restricts access to a package, and the public modifier enables unrestricted access.

If a class is not declared public, it can be accessed only within the same package, as shown in Figure 7.13.

```
package p1;
    class C1 {          public class C2 {
        ...                 can access C1
    }                   }
```

```
package p2;
    public class C3 {
        cannot access C1;
        can access C2;
    }
```

FIGURE 7.13
A nonpublic class has package-access.

A visibility modifier specifies how data fields and methods in a class can be accessed from the outside of the class. There is no restriction on accessing data fields and methods from inside access | inside the class. As shown in Figure 7.14(b), an object foo of the Foo class cannot access its private members, because foo is in the Test class. As shown in Figure 7.14(a), an object foo of the Foo class can access its private members, because foo is declared inside its own class.

```
public class Foo {
    private boolean x;

    public static void main(String[] args) {
        Foo foo = new Foo();
        System.out.println(foo.x);
        System.out.println(foo.convert());
    }

    private int convert() {
        return x ? 1 : -1;
    }
}
```

```
public class Test {
    public static void main(String[] args) {
        Foo foo = new Foo();
        System.out.println(foo.x);
        System.out.println(foo.convert());
    }
}
```

(a) This is OK because object foo is used inside the Foo class   (b) This is wrong because x and convert are private in Foo.

FIGURE 7.14
An object can access its private members if it is declared in its own class.

Caution

The **private** modifier applies only to the members of a class. The **public** modifier can apply to a class or members of a class. Using modifiers **public** and **private** on local variables would cause a compile error.

Note

In most cases, the constructor should be public. However, if you want to prohibit the user from private constructor | creating an instance of a class, use a private constructor. For example, there is no reason to create an instance from the Math class, because all of its data fields and methods are static. To prevent the user from creating objects from the Math class, the constructor in java.lang.Math is defined as follows:

```
private Math() {
}
```

7.8 Data Field Encapsulation

The data fields `radius` and `numberOfObjects` in the `Circle2` class in Listing 7.5 can be modified directly (e.g., `myCircle.radius = 5` or `Circle2.numberOfObjects = 10`). This is not a good practice—for two reasons:

■ First, data may be tampered with. For example, `numberOfObjects` is to count the number of objects created, but it may be set to an arbitrary value (e.g., `Circle2.numberOfObjects = 10`).

■ Second, it makes the class difficult to maintain and vulnerable to bugs. Suppose you want to modify the `Circle2` class to ensure that the radius is nonnegative after other programs have already used the class. You have to change not only the `Circle2` class, but also the programs that use the `Circle2` class. Such programs are often referred to as *clients*. This is because the clients may have modified the radius directly (e.g., `myCircle.radius = -5`).

> client

To prevent direct modifications of data fields, you should declare the fields private, using the `private` modifier. This is known as *data field encapsulation*.

> data field encapsulation

A private data field cannot be accessed by an object through a direct reference outside the class that defines the private field. But often a client needs to retrieve and modify a data field. To make a private data field accessible, provide a *get* method to return the value of the data field. To enable a private data field to be updated, provide a *set* method to set a new value.

Note

Colloquially, a `get` method is referred to as a *getter* (or *accessor*), and a `set` method is referred to as a *setter* (or *mutator*).

> accessor
> mutator

A `get` method has the following signature:

```
public returnType getPropertyName()
```

If the `returnType` is `boolean`, the `get` method should be defined as follows by convention:

> boolean accessor

```
public boolean isPropertyName()
```

A `set` method has the following signature:

```
public void setPropertyName(dataType propertyValue)
```

Let us create a new circle class with a private data field radius and its associated accessor and mutator methods. The class diagram is shown in Figure 7.15. The new circle class, named `Circle3`, is declared in Listing 7.7:

Video Note
Data field encapsulation

> encapsulate **radius**

> encapsulate
> **numberOfObjects**

LISTING 7.7 `Circle3.java`

```java
 1 public class Circle3 {
 2   /** The radius of the circle */
 3   private double radius = 1;
 4
 5   /** The number of the objects created */
 6   private static int numberOfObjects = 0;
 7
 8   /** Construct a circle with radius 1 */
 9   public Circle3() {
10     numberOfObjects++;
11   }
12
```

```
13   /** Construct a circle with a specified radius */
14   public Circle3(double newRadius) {
15     radius = newRadius;
16     numberOfObjects++;
17   }
18
19   /** Return radius */
20   public double getRadius() {
21     return radius;
22   }
23
24   /** Set a new radius */
25   public void setRadius(double newRadius) {
26     radius = (newRadius >= 0) ? newRadius : 0;
27   }
28
29   /** Return numberOfObjects */
30   public static int getNumberOfObjects() {
31     return numberOfObjects;
32   }
33
34   /** Return the area of this circle */
35   public double getArea() {
36     return radius * radius * Math.PI;
37   }
38 }
```

access method — (lines 20)

mutator method — (line 25)

access method — (line 30)

FIGURE 7.15 The `Circle` class encapsulates circle properties and provides get/set and other methods.

The `getRadius()` method (lines 20–22) returns the radius, and the `setRadius(newRadius)` method (line 25–27) sets a new radius into the object. If the new radius is negative, `0` is set to the radius in the object. Since these methods are the only ways to read and modify radius, you have total control over how the `radius` property is accessed. If you have to change the implementation of these methods, you need not change the client programs. This makes the class easy to maintain.

Listing 7.8 gives a client program that uses the `Circle` class to create a `Circle` object and modifies the radius using the `setRadius` method.

LISTING 7.8 TestCircle3.java

```
1 public class TestCircle3 {
2   /** Main method */
3   public static void main(String[] args) {
4     // Create a Circle with radius 5.0
5     Circle3 myCircle = new Circle3(5.0);
```

```
 6        System.out.println("The area of the circle of radius "
 7          + myCircle.getRadius() + " is " + myCircle.getArea());
 8
 9        // Increase myCircle's radius by 10%
10        myCircle.setRadius(myCircle.getRadius() * 1.1);
11        System.out.println("The area of the circle of radius "
12          + myCircle.getRadius() + " is " + myCircle.getArea());
13      }
14    }
```

invoke instance method

invoke instance method

The data field `radius` is declared private. Private data can be accessed only within their defining class. You cannot use `myCircle.radius` in the client program. A compilation error would occur if you attempted to access private data from a client.

Since `numberOfObjects` is private, it cannot be modified. This prevents tampering. For example, the user cannot set `numberOfObjects` to `100`. The only way to make it `100` is to create 100 objects of the `Circle` class.

Suppose you combined `TestCircle` and `Circle` into one class by moving the `main` method in `TestCircle` into `Circle`. Could you use `myCircle.radius` in the `main` method? See Review Question 7.12 for the answer.

Note

When you compile `TestCircle3.java`, the Java compiler automatically compiles `Circle3.java` if it has not been compiled since the last change.

Design Guide

To prevent data from being tampered with and to make the class easy to maintain, declare data fields private.

7.9 Passing Objects to Methods

You can pass objects to methods. Like passing an array, passing an object is actually passing the reference of the object. The following code passes the `myCircle` object as an argument to the `printCircle` method:

```
 1 public class TestPassObject {
 2   public static void main(String[] args) {
 3     // Circle3 is defined in Listing 7.7
 4     Circle3 myCircle = new Circle3(5.0);
 5     printCircle(myCircle);
 6   }
 7
 8   public static void printCircle(Circle3 c) {
 9     System.out.println("The area of the circle of radius "
10       + c.getRadius() + " is " + c.getArea());
11   }
12 }
```

pass an object

Java uses exactly one mode of passing arguments: pass-by-value. In the preceding code, the value of `myCircle` is passed to the `printCircle` method. This value is a reference to a `Circle` object.

pass-by-value

Let us demonstrate the difference between passing a primitive type value and passing a reference value with the program in Listing 7.9:

LISTING 7.9 `TestPassObject.java`

```
1 public class TestPassObject {
2   /** Main method */
3   public static void main(String[] args) {
```

pass object

object parameter

```
4      // Create a Circle object with radius 1
5      Circle3 myCircle = new Circle3(1);
6
7      // Print areas for radius 1, 2, 3, 4, and 5.
8      int n = 5;
9      printAreas(myCircle, n);
10
11     // See myCircle.radius and times
12     System.out.println("\n" + "Radius is " + myCircle.getRadius());
13     System.out.println("n is " + n);
14   }
15
16   /** Print a table of areas for radius */
17   public static void printAreas(Circle3 c, int times) {
18     System.out.println("Radius \t\tArea");
19     while (times >= 1) {
20       System.out.println(c.getRadius() + "\t\t" + c.getArea());
21       c.setRadius(c.getRadius() + 1);
22       times--;
23     }
24   }
25 }
```

```
Radius                    Area
  1.0              3.141592653589793
  2.0              12.566370614359172
  3.0              29.274333882308138
  4.0              50.26548245743669
  5.0              79.53981633974483

Radius is 6.0
n is 5
```

The `Circle3` class is defined in Listing 7.7. The program passes a `Circle3` object `myCircle` and an integer value from `n` to invoke `printAreas(myCircle, n)` (line 9), which prints a table of areas for radii **1, 2, 3, 4**, as shown in the sample output.

Figure 7.16 shows the call stack for executing the methods in the program. Note that the objects are stored in a heap.

When passing an argument of a primitive data type, the value of the argument is passed. In this case, the value of `n` (5) is passed to `times`. Inside the `printAreas` method, the content of `times` is changed; this does not affect the content of `n`.

FIGURE 7.16 The value of `n` is passed to `times`, and the reference of `myCircle` is passed to `c` in the `printAreas` method.

When passing an argument of a reference type, the reference of the object is passed. In this case, `c` contains a reference for the object that is also referenced via `myCircle`. Therefore, changing the properties of the object through `c` inside the `printAreas` method has the same effect as doing so outside the method through the variable `myCircle`. Pass-by-value on references can be best described as *pass-by-sharing* semantically; i.e., the object referenced in the method is the same as the object being passed.

pass-by-sharing

7.10 Array of Objects

In Chapter 6, "Arrays," arrays of primitive type elements were created. You can also create arrays of objects. For example, the following statement declares and creates an array of ten `Circle` objects:

```
Circle[] circleArray = new Circle[10];
```

To initialize the `circleArray`, you can use a `for` loop like this one:

```
for (int i = 0; i < circleArray.length; i++) {
  circleArray[i] = new Circle();
}
```

An array of objects is actually an *array of reference variables*. So, invoking `circleArray[1].getArea()` involves two levels of referencing, as shown in Figure 7.17. `circleArray` references the entire array. `circleArray[1]` references a `Circle` object.

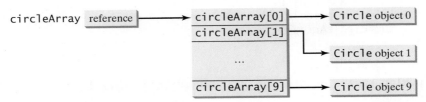

FIGURE 7.17 In an array of objects, an element of the array contains a reference to an object.

 Note
When an array of objects is created using the **new** operator, each element in the array is a reference variable with a default value of `null`.

Listing 7.10 gives an example that demonstrates how to use an array of objects. The program summarizes the areas of an array of circles. The program creates `circleArray`, an array composed of five `Circle` objects; it then initializes circle radii with random values, and displays the total area of the circles in the array.

LISTING 7.10 TotalArea.java

```
1 public class TotalArea {
2   /** Main method */
3   public static void main(String[] args) {
4     // Declare circleArray
5     Circle3[] circleArray;
6
7     // Create circleArray
8     circleArray = createCircleArray();
```

array of objects

```
 9
10      // Print circleArray and total areas of the circles
11      printCircleArray(circleArray);
12    }
13
14    /** Create an array of Circle objects */
15    public static Circle3[] createCircleArray() {
16      Circle3[] circleArray = new Circle3[5];
17
18      for (int i = 0; i < circleArray.length; i++) {
19        circleArray[i] = new Circle3(Math.random() * 100);
20      }
21
22      // Return Circle array
23      return circleArray;
24    }
25
26    /** Print an array of circles and their total area */
27    public static void printCircleArray(Circle3[] circleArray) {
28      System.out.println("Radius\t\t\t\t" + "Area");
29      for (int i = 0; i < circleArray.length; i++) {
30        System.out.print(circleArray[i].getRadius() + "\t\t" +
31          circleArray[i].getArea() + '\n');
32      }
33
34      System.out.println("------------------------------------------------");
35
36      // Compute and display the result
37      System.out.println("The total areas of circles is \t" +
38        sum(circleArray));
39    }
40
41    /** Add circle areas */
42    public static double sum(Circle3[] circleArray) {
43      // Initialize sum
44      double sum = 0;
45
46      // Add areas to sum
47      for (int i = 0; i < circleArray.length; i++)
48        sum += circleArray[i].getArea();
49
50      return sum;
51    }
52  }
```

return array of objects (line 15)
pass array of objects (line 27)
pass array of objects (line 42)

```
              Radius                               Area
      46.74450345121816                  6864.532638610253
      69.07475859903327                 14989.551008666382
       7.406606050399822                   172.34090289657104
      34.837951903312394                 3812.8972598630908
      69.54563440024302                 15194.612150185108
      ----------------------------------------------------------
      The total areas of circles is        41033.9339602214
```

The program invokes `createCircleArray()` (line 8) to create an array of five **Circle** objects. Several **Circle** classes were introduced in this chapter. This example uses the **Circle** class introduced in §7.8, "Data Field Encapsulation."

The circle radii are randomly generated using the `Math.random()` method (line 19). The `createCircleArray` method returns an array of `Circle` objects (line 23). The array is passed to the `printCircleArray` method, which displays the radius and area of each circle and the total area of the circles.

The sum of the areas of the circle is computed using the `sum` method (line 38), which takes the array of `Circle` objects as the argument and returns a `double` value for the total area.

KEY TERMS

accessor method (getter)   247
class   231
constructor   231
data field encapsulation   247
default constructor   232
dot operator (.)   233
instance   230
instance method   233
instance variable   233
instantiation   230
mutator method (setter)   247
`null`   236

no-arg constructor   237
object-oriented programming (OOP)   230
Unified Modeling Language (UML)   230
package-private (or package-access)   245
private   245
public   245
reference variable   232
reference type   232
static method   241
static variable   241

CHAPTER SUMMARY

■ A class is a template for objects. It defines the properties of objects, and provides constructors for creating objects and methods for manipulating them.

■ A class is also a data type. You can use it to declare object reference variables. An object reference variable that appears to hold an object actually contains a reference to that object. Strictly speaking, an object reference variable and an object are different, but most of the time the distinction can be ignored.

■ An object is an instance of a class. You use the `new` operator to create an object, and the dot (`.`) operator to access members of that object through its reference variable.

■ An instance variable or method belongs to an instance of a class. Its use is associated with individual instances. A static variable is a variable shared by all instances of the same class. A static method is a method that can be invoked without using instances.

■ Every instance of a class can access the class's static variables and methods. However, it is better to invoke static variables and methods using `ClassName.variable` and `ClassName.method` for clarity.

■ Modifiers specify how the class, method, and data are accessed. A `public` class, method, or data is accessible to all clients. A `private` method or data is only accessible inside the class.

■ You can provide a **get** method or a **set** method to enable clients to see or modify the data. Colloquially, a **get** method is referred to as a *getter* (or *accessor*), and a **set** method is referred to as a *setter* (or *mutator*).

■ A get method has the signature **public returnType getPropertyName()**. If the **returnType** is **boolean**, the get method should be defined as **public boolean isPropertyName()**. A set method has the signature **public void setPropertyName(dataType propertyValue)**.

■ All parameters are passed to methods using pass-by-value. For a parameter of a primitive type, the actual value is passed; for a parameter of a reference type, the reference for the object is passed.

■ A Java array is an object that can contain primitive type values or object type values. When an array of objects is created, its elements are assigned the default value of **null**.

REVIEW QUESTIONS

Sections 7.2–7.4

7.1 Describe the relationship between an object and its defining class. How do you declare a class? How do you declare an object reference variable? How do you create an object? How do you declare and create an object in one statement?

7.2 What are the differences between constructors and methods?

7.3 Is an array an object or a primitive type value? Can an array contain elements of an object type as well as a primitive type? Describe the default value for the elements of an array.

7.4 What is wrong with the following program?

```
1 public class ShowErrors {
2   public static void main(String[] args) {
3     ShowErrors t = new ShowErrors(5);
4   }
5 }
```

(a)

```
1 public class ShowErrors {
2   public static void main(String[] args) {
3     ShowErrors t = new ShowErrors();
4     t.x();
5   }
6 }
```

(b)

```
1 public class ShowErrors {
2   public void method1() {
3     Circle c;
4     System.out.println("What is radius "
5       + c.getRadius());
6     c = new Circle();
7   }
8 }
```

(c)

```
1 public class ShowErrors {
2   public static void main(String[] args) {
3     C c = new C(5.0);
4     System.out.println(c.value);
5   }
6 }
7
8 class C {
9   int value = 2;
10 }
```

(d)

7.5 What is wrong in the following code?

```
1 class Test {
2   public static void main(String[] args) {
3     A a = new A();
4     a.print();
5   }
6 }
7
8 class A {
9   String s;
10
11  A(String s) {
12    this.s = s;
13  }
14
15  public void print() {
16    System.out.print(s);
17  }
18 }
```

7.6 What is the printout of the following code?

```
public class Foo {
  private boolean x;

  public static void main(String[] args) {
    Foo foo = new Foo();
    System.out.println(foo.x);
  }
}
```

Section 7.5 Using Classes from the Java Library

7.7 How do you create a Date for the current time? How do you display the current time?

7.8 How do you create a JFrame, set a title in a frame, and display a frame?

7.9 Which packages contain the classes Date, JFrame, JOptionPane, System, and Math?

Section 7.6 Static Variables, Constants, and Methods

7.10 Suppose that the class Foo is defined in (a). Let f be an instance of Foo. Which of the statements in (b) are correct?

```
public class Foo {
  int i;
  static String s;

  void imethod() {
  }

  static void smethod() {
  }
}
```

```
System.out.println(f.i);
System.out.println(f.s);
f.imethod();
f.smethod();
System.out.println(Foo.i);
System.out.println(Foo.s);
Foo.imethod();
Foo.smethod();
```

       (a)   (b)

7.11 Add the static keyword in the place of ? if appropriate.

```
public class Test {
  private int count;

  public ? void main(String[] args) {
```

```
        ...
      }

      public ? int getCount() {
        return count;
      }

      public ? int factorial(int n) {
        int result = 1;
        for (int i = 1; i <= n; i++)
          result *= i;

        return result;
      }
    }
```

7.12 Can you invoke an instance method or reference an instance variable from a static method? Can you invoke a static method or reference a static variable from an instance method? What is wrong in the following code?

```
 1 public class Foo {
 2   public static void main(String[] args) {
 3     method1();
 4   }
 5
 6   public void method1() {
 7     method2();
 8   }
 9
10   public static void method2() {
11     System.out.println("What is radius " + c.getRadius());
12   }
13
14   Circle c = new Circle();
15 }
```

Sections 7.7–7.8

7.13 What is an accessor method? What is a mutator method? What are the naming conventions for accessor methods and mutator methods?

7.14 What are the benefits of data field encapsulation?

7.15 In the following code, radius is private in the Circle class, and myCircle is an object of the Circle class. Does the following highlighted code cause any problems? Explain why.

```
public class Circle {
  private double radius = 1.0;

  /** Find the area of this circle */
  double getArea() {
    return radius * radius * Math.PI;
  }

  public static void main(String[] args) {
    Circle myCircle = new Circle();
    System.out.println("Radius is " + myCircle.radius);
  }
}
```

Section 7.9 Passing Objects to Methods

7.16   Describe the difference between passing a parameter of a primitive type and passing a parameter of a reference type. Show the output of the following program:

```java
public class Test {
  public static void main(String[] args) {
    Count myCount = new Count();
    int times = 0;

    for (int i = 0; i < 100; i++)
      increment(myCount, times);

    System.out.println("count is " + myCount.count);
    System.out.println("times is " + times);
  }

  public static void increment(Count c, int times) {
    c.count++;
    times++;
  }
}
```

```java
public class Count {
  public int count;

  Count(int c) {
    count = c;
  }

  Count() {
    count = 1;
  }
}
```

7.17   Show the output of the following program:

```java
public class Test {
  public static void main(String[] args) {
    Circle circle1 = new Circle(1);
    Circle circle2 = new Circle(2);

    swap1(circle1, circle2);
    System.out.println("After swap1: circle1 = " +
      circle1.radius + " circle2 = " + circle2.radius);

    swap2(circle1, circle2);
    System.out.println("After swap2: circle1 = " +
      circle1.radius + " circle2 = " + circle2.radius);
  }

  public static void swap1(Circle x, Circle y) {
    Circle temp = x;
    x = y;
    y = temp;
  }

  public static void swap2(Circle x, Circle y) {
    double temp = x.radius;
    x.radius = y.radius;
    y.radius = temp;
  }
}

class Circle {
  double radius;
  Circle(double newRadius) {
    radius = newRadius;
  }
}
```

7.18 Show the printout of the following code:

```java
public class Test {
  public static void main(String[] args) {
    int[] a = {1, 2};
    swap(a[0], a[1]);
    System.out.println("a[0] = " + a[0]
      + " a[1] = " + a[1]);
  }

  public static void swap(int n1, int n2) {
    int temp = n1;
    n1 = n2;
    n2 = temp;
  }
}
```
(a)

```java
public class Test {
  public static void main(String[] args) {
    int[] a = {1, 2};
    swap(a);
    System.out.println("a[0] = " + a[0]
      + " a[1] = " + a[1]);
  }

  public static void swap(int[] a) {
    int temp = a[0];
    a[0] = a[1];
    a[1] = temp;
  }
}
```
(b)

```java
public class Test {
  public static void main(String[] args) {
    T t = new T();
    swap(t);
    System.out.println("e1 = " + t.e1
      + " e2 = " + t.e2);
  }

  public static void swap(T t) {
    int temp = t.e1;
    t.e1 = t.e2;
    t.e2 = temp;
  }
}

class T {
  int e1 = 1;
  int e2 = 2;
}
```
(c)

```java
public class Test {
  public static void main(String[] args) {
    T t1 = new T();
    T t2 = new T();
    System.out.println("t1's i = " +
      t1.i + " and j = " + t1.j);
    System.out.println("t2's i = " +
      t2.i + " and j = " + t2.j);
  }
}

class T {
  static int i = 0;
  int j = 0;

  T() {
    i++;
    j = 1;
  }
}
```
(d)

7.19 What is the output of the following program?

```java
import java.util.Date;

public class Test {
  public static void main(String[] args) {
    Date date = null;
    m1(date);
    System.out.println(date);
  }

  public static void m1(Date date) {
    date = new java.util.Date();
  }
}
```
(a)

```java
import java.util.Date;

public class Test {
  public static void main(String[] args) {
    Date date = new Date(1234567);
    m1(date);
    System.out.println(date.getTime());
  }

  public static void m1(Date date) {
    date = new java.util.Date(7654321);
  }
}
```
(b)

```java
import java.util.Date;

public class Test {
  public static void main(String[] args) {
    Date date = new Date(1234567);
    m1(date);
    System.out.println(date.getTime());
  }

  public static void m1(Date date) {
    date.setTime(7654321);
  }
}
```

(c)

```java
import java.util.Date;

public class Test {
  public static void main(String[] args) {
    Date date = new Date(1234567);
    m1(date);
    System.out.println(date.getTime());
  }

  public static void m1(Date date) {
    date = null;
  }
}
```

(d)

Section 7.10 Array of Objects

7.20 What is wrong in the following code?

```java
1 public class Test {
2   public static void main(String[] args) {
3     java.util.Date[] dates = new java.util.Date[10];
4     System.out.println(dates[0]);
5     System.out.println(dates[0].toString());
6   }
7 }
```

PROGRAMMING EXERCISES

Pedagogical Note

The exercises in Chapters 7–12 achieve three objectives: three objectives

- Design classes and draw UML class diagrams;
- Implement classes from the UML;
- Use classes to develop applications.

Solutions for the UML diagrams for the even-numbered exercises can be downloaded from the Student Web site and all others can be downloaded from the Instructor Web site.

7.1 (*The Rectangle class*) Design a class named `Rectangle` to represent a rectangle. The class contains:

- Two `double` data fields named `width` and `height` that specify the width and height of the rectangle. The default values are `1` for both `width` and `height`.
- A string data field named `color` that specifies the color of a rectangle. Hypothetically, assume that all rectangles have the same color. The default color is `white`.
- A no-arg constructor that creates a default rectangle.
- A constructor that creates a rectangle with the specified `width` and `height`.
- The accessor and mutator methods for all three data fields.
- A method named `getArea()` that returns the area of this rectangle.
- A method named `getPerimeter()` that returns the perimeter.

Draw the UML diagram for the class. Implement the class. Write a test program that creates two `Rectangle` objects. Assign width `4` and height `40` to the first object and width 3.5 and height 35.9 to the second object. Assign color red to all Rectangle objects. Display the properties of both objects and find their areas and perimeters.

Video Note
Fan class

7.2 (*The Fan class*) Design a class named Fan to represent a fan. The class contains:

- Three constants named SLOW, MEDIUM, and FAST with values 1, 2, and 3 to denote the fan speed.
- An int data field named speed that specifies the speed of the fan (default SLOW).
- A boolean data field named on that specifies whether the fan is on (default false).
- A double data field named radius that specifies the radius of the fan (default 5).
- A string data field named color that specifies the color of the fan (default blue).
- A no-arg constructor that creates a default fan.
- The accessor and mutator methods for all four data fields.
- A method named toString() that returns a string description for the fan. If the fan is on, the method returns the fan speed, color, and radius in one combined string. If the fan is not on, the method returns fan color and radius along with the string "fan is off" in one combined string.

Draw the UML diagram for the class. Implement the class. Write a test program that creates two Fan objects. Assign maximum speed, radius 10, color yellow, and turn it on to the first object. Assign medium speed, radius 5, color blue, and turn it off to the second object. Display the objects by invoking their toString method.

7.3 (*The Account class*) Design a class named Account that contains:

- An int data field named id for the account (default 0).
- A double data field named balance for the account (default 0).
- A double data field named annualInterestRate that stores the current interest rate (default 0).
- A Date data field named dateCreated that stores the date when the account was created.
- A no-arg constructor that creates a default account.
- The accessor and mutator methods for id, balance, and annualInterestRate.
- The accessor method for dateCreated.
- A method named getMonthlyInterestRate() that returns the monthly interest rate.
- A method named withdraw that withdraws a specified amount from the account.
- A method named deposit that deposits a specified amount to the account.

Draw the UML diagram for the class. Implement the class. Write a test program that creates an Account object with an account ID of 1122, a balance of $20,000, and an annual interest rate of 4.5%. Use the withdraw method to withdraw $2,500, use the deposit method to deposit $3,000, and print the balance, the monthly interest, and the date when this account was created.

7.4 (*The Stock class*) Design a class named Stock that contains:

- A string data field named symbol for the stock's symbol.
- A string data field named name for the stock's name.
- A double data field named previousClosingPrice that stores the stock price for the previous day.
- A double data field named currentPrice that stores the stock price for the current time.

■ A constructor that creates a stock with specified symbol and name.
■ The accessor methods for all data fields.
■ The mutator methods for `previousClosingPrice` and `currentPrice`.
■ A method named `getChangePercent()` that returns the percentage changed from `previousClosingPrice` to `currentPrice`.

Draw the UML diagram for the class. Implement the class. Write a test program that creates a `Stock` object with the stock symbol SUNW, the name Sun Microsystems Inc, and the previous closing price of `100`. Set a new current price to `90` and display the price-change percentage.

7.5* (*Using the GregorianCalendar class*) Java API has the `GregorianCalendar` class in the `java.util` package that can be used to obtain the year, month, and day of a date. The no-arg constructor constructs an instance for the current date, and the methods `get(GregorianCalendar.YEAR)`, `get(GregorianCalendar.MONTH)`, and `get(GregorianCalendar.DAY_OF_MONTH)` return the year, month, and day. Write a program to perform two tasks:

■ Display the current year, month, and day.
■ The `GregorianCalendar` class has the `setTimeInMillis(long)`, which can be used to set a specified elapsed time since January 1, 1970. Set the value to `1234567898765L` and display the year, month, and day.

7.6** (*Displaying calendars*) Rewrite the `PrintCalendar` class in §5.11, "Method Abstraction and Stepwise Refinement," to display calendars in a message dialog box. Since the output is generated from several static methods in the class, you may define a static `String` variable `output` for storing the output and display it in a message dialog box.

CHAPTER 8

STRINGS AND TEXT I/O

Objectives

- To use the `String` class to process fixed strings (§8.2).

- To use the `Character` class to process a single character (§8.3).

- To use the `StringBuilder`/`StringBuffer` class to process flexible strings (§8.4).

- To distinguish among the `String`, `StringBuilder`, and `StringBuffer` classes (§8.2–8.4).

- To learn how to pass arguments to the `main` method from the command line (§8.5).

- To discover file properties and to delete and rename files using the `File` class (§8.6).

- To write data to a file using the `PrintWriter` class (§8.7.1).

- To read data from a file using the `Scanner` class (§8.7.2).

- (GUI) To open files using a dialog box (§8.8).

8.1 Introduction

Often you encounter problems that involve string processing and file input and output. Suppose you need to write a program that replaces all occurrences of a word in a file with a new word. How do you solve this problem? This chapter introduces strings and text files, which will enable you to solve this type of problem. Another purpose of this chapter is to show how to program using the classes in the Java library.

8.2 The **String** Class

A *string* is a sequence of characters. In many languages, strings are treated as arrays of characters, but in Java a string is an object. The `String` class has 11 constructors and more than 40 methods for manipulating strings. The `String` class not only is very useful in programming but also is a good example for learning classes and objects.

8.2.1 Constructing a String

You can create a string object from a string value or from an array of characters. To create a string from a string literal, use a syntax like this one:

```
String newString = new String(stringLiteral);
```

The argument `stringLiteral` is a sequence of characters enclosed inside double quotes. The following statement creates a `String` object `message` for the string literal `"Welcome to Java"`:

```
String message = new String("Welcome to Java");
```

string literal object

Java treats a string literal as a `String` object. So the following statement is valid:

```
String message = "Welcome to Java";
```

You can also create a string from an array of characters. For example, the following statements create the string "Good Day".

```
char[] charArray = {'G', 'o', 'o', 'd', ' ', 'D', 'a', 'y'};
String message = new String(charArray);
```

Note

A `String` variable holds a reference to a `String` object that stores a string value. Strictly speaking, the terms *String* variable, *String* object, and *string value* are different, but most of the time the distinctions between them can be ignored. For simplicity, the term *string* will often be used to refer to `String` variable, `String` object, and string value.

string variable, string object, string value

8.2.2 Immutable Strings and Interned Strings

immutable

A `String` object is immutable; its contents cannot be changed. Does the following code change the contents of the string?

```
String s = "Java";
s = "HTML";
```

The answer is no. The first statement creates a `String` object with the content "Java" and assigns its reference to `s`. The second statement creates a new `String` object with the content "HTML" and assigns its reference to `s`. The first `String` object still exists after the assignment, but it can no longer be accessed, because variable `s` now points to the new object, as shown in Figure 8.1.

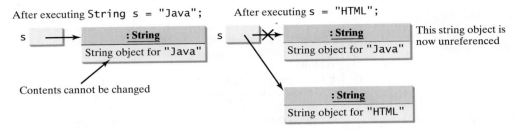

After executing `String s = "Java";` After executing `s = "HTML";`

This string object is now unreferenced

Contents cannot be changed

FIGURE 8.1 Strings are immutable; once created, their contents cannot be changed.

Since strings are immutable and are ubiquitous in programming, to improve efficiency and save memory, the JVM uses a unique instance for string literals with the same character sequence. Such an instance is called *interned*. For example, the following statements: *interned string*

```
String s1 = "Welcome to Java";

String s2 = new String("Welcome to Java");

String s3 = "Welcome to Java";

System.out.println("s1 == s2 is " + (s1 == s2));
System.out.println("s1 == s3 is " + (s1 == s3));
```

display

```
s1 == s2 is false
s1 == s3 is true
```

In the preceding statements, `s1` and `s3` refer to the same interned string "Welcome to Java", therefore `s1 == s3` is true. However, `s1 == s2` is false, because `s1` and `s2` are two different string objects, even though they have the same contents.

8.2.3 String Comparisons

The **String** class provides the methods for comparing strings, as shown in Figure 8.2.

How do you compare the contents of two strings? You might attempt to use the `==` operator,   `==`
as follows:

```
if (string1 == string2)
    System.out.println("string1 and string2 are the same object");
else
    System.out.println("string1 and string2 are different objects");
```

However, the `==` operator only checks whether `string1` and `string2` refer to the same object; it does not tell you whether `string1` and `string2` contain the same contents. Therefore, you cannot use the `==` operator to find out whether two string variables have the same contents. Instead, you should use the `equals` method for an equality comparison of the contents of objects. The code given below, for instance, can be used to compare two strings.

`string1.equals(string2)`

```
if (string1.equals(string2))
    System.out.println("string1 and string2 have the same contents");
else
    System.out.println("string1 and string2 are not equal");
```

java.lang.String	
+equals(s1: String): boolean	Returns true if this string is equal to string s1.
+equalsIgnoreCase(s1: String): boolean	Returns true if this string is equal to string s1 case insensitive.
+compareTo(s1: String): int	Returns an integer greater than 0, equal to 0, or less than 0 to indicate whether this string is greater than, equal to, or less than s1.
+compareToIgnoreCase(s1: String): int	Same as compareTo except that the comparison is case insensitive.
+regionMatches(toffset: int, s1: String, offset: int, len: int): boolean	Returns true if the specified subregion of this string exactly matches the specified subregion in string s1.
+regionMatches(ignoreCase: boolean, toffset: int, s1: String, offset: int, len: int): boolean	Same as the preceding method except that you can specify whether the match is case sensitive.
+startsWith(prefix: String): boolean	Returns true if this string starts with the specified prefix.
+endsWith(suffix: String): boolean	Returns true if this string ends with the specified suffix.

FIGURE 8.2 The String class contains the methods for comparing strings.

For example, the following statements display **true** and then **false**.

```
String s1 = new String("Welcome to Java");
String s2 = "Welcome to Java";
String s3 = "Welcome to C++";
System.out.println(s1.equals(s2)); // true
System.out.println(s1.equals(s3)); // false
```

The compareTo method can also be used to compare two strings. For example, consider the following code:

s1.compareTo(s2)

```
s1.compareTo(s2)
```

The method returns the value 0 if s1 is equal to s2, a value less than 0 if s1 is lexicographically (i.e., Unicode ordering) less than s2, and a value greater than 0 if s1 is lexicographically greater than s2.

The actual value returned from the compareTo method depends on the offset of the first two distinct characters in s1 and s2 from left to right. For example, suppose s1 is "abc" and s2 is "abg", and s1.compareTo(s2) returns -4. The first two characters (a vs. a) from s1 and s2 are compared. Because they are equal, the second two characters (b vs. b) are compared. Because they are also equal, the third two characters (c vs. g) are compared. Since the character c is 4 less than g, the comparison returns -4.

Caution

Syntax errors will occur if you compare strings by using comparison operators, such as >, >=, <, or <=. Instead, you have to use s1.compareTo(s2).

Note

The equals method returns true if two strings are equal, and false if they are not equal. The compareTo method returns 0, a positive integer, or a negative integer, depending on whether one string is equal to, greater than, or less than the other string.

The String class also provides equalsIgnoreCase, compareToIgnoreCase, and regionMatches methods for comparing strings. The equalsIgnoreCase and compareToIgnoreCase methods ignore the case of the letters when comparing two strings. The

regionMatches method compares portions of two strings for equality. You can also use **str.startsWith(prefix)** to check whether string **str** starts with a specified prefix, and **str.endsWith(suffix)** to check whether string **str** ends with a specified **suffix**.

8.2.4 String Length, Characters, and Combining Strings

The **String** class provides the methods for obtaining length, retrieving individual characters, and concatenating strings, as shown in Figure 8.3.

java.lang.String	
+length(): int	Returns the number of characters in this string.
+charAt(index: int): char	Returns the character at the specified index from this string.
+concat(s1: String): String	Returns a new string that concatenates this string with string s1.

FIGURE 8.3 The **String** class contains the methods for getting string length, individual characters, and combining strings.

You can get the length of a string by invoking its **length()** method. For example, **message.length()** returns the length of the string **message**.

length()

Caution
length is a method in the **String** class but is a property of an array object. So you have to use **s.length()** to get the number of characters in string **s**, and **a.length** to get the number of elements in array **a**.

length()

The **s.charAt(index)** method can be used to retrieve a specific character in a string **s**, where the index is between **0** and **s.length()-1**. For example, **message.charAt(0)** returns the character **W**, as shown in Figure 8.4.

charAt(index)

FIGURE 8.4 A **String** object is represented using an array internally.

Note
When you use a string, you often know its literal value. For convenience, Java allows you to use the string literal to refer directly to strings without creating new variables. Thus, **"Welcome to Java".charAt(0)** is correct and returns **W**.

string literal

Note
A string value is represented using a private array variable internally. The array cannot be accessed outside of the **String** class. The **String** class provides many public methods, such as **length()** and **charAt(index)**, to retrieve the array information. This is a good example of encapsulation: the detailed data structure of the class is hidden from the user through the private modifier, and thus the user cannot directly manipulate the internal data structure. If the array were not private, the user would be able to change the string content by modifying the array. This would violate the tenet that the **String** class is immutable.

encapsulating string

Caution

Attempting to access characters in a string `s` out of bounds is a common programming error. To
avoid it, make sure that you do not use an index beyond `s.length() - 1`. For example,
`s.charAt(s.length())` would cause a `StringIndexOutOfBoundsException`.

string index range

You can use the `concat` method to concatenate two strings. The statement shown below, for
example, concatenates strings `s1` and `s2` into `s3`:

`s1.concat(s2)`

```
String s3 = s1.concat(s2);
```

Since string concatenation is heavily used in programming, Java provides a convenient way to
accomplish it. You can use the plus (+) sign to concatenate two or more strings. So the above
statement is equivalent to

`s1 + s2`

```
String s3 = s1 + s2;
```

The following code combines the strings `message`, `" and "`, and `"HTML"` into one string:

```
String myString = message + " and " + "HTML";
```

Recall that the + sign can also concatenate a number with a string. In this case, the number is
converted into a string and then concatenated. Note that at least one of the operands must be a
string in order for concatenation to take place.

8.2.5 Obtaining Substrings

You can obtain a single character from a string using the `charAt` method. You can also obtain
a substring from a string using the `substring` method in the `String` class, as shown in
Figure 8.5.

java.lang.String
+substring(beginIndex: int): String	Returns this string's substring that begins with the character at the specified `beginIndex` and extends to the end of the string, as shown in Figure 8.6.
+substring(beginIndex: int, endIndex: int): String	Returns this string's substring that begins at the specified `beginIndex` and extends to the character at index `endIndex - 1`, as shown in Figure 8.6. Note that the character at `endIndex` is not part of the substring.

FIGURE 8.5 The `String` class contains the methods for obtaining substrings.

For example,

```
String message = "Welcome to Java".substring(0, 11) + "HTML";
```

The string `message` now becomes `"Welcome to HTML"`.

FIGURE 8.6 The `substring` method obtains a substring from a string.

Note
If `beginIndex` is `endIndex`, `substring(beginIndex, endIndex)` returns an empty string with length `0`. If `beginIndex > endIndex`, it would be a runtime error.

`beginIndex <= endIndex`

8.2.6 Converting, Replacing, and Splitting Strings

The `String` class provides the methods for converting, replacing, and splitting strings, as shown in Figure 8.7.

java.lang.String	
+toLowerCase(): String	Returns a new string with all characters converted to lowercase.
+toUpperCase(): String	Returns a new string with all characters converted to uppercase.
+trim(): String	Returns a new string with blank characters trimmed on both sides.
+replace(oldChar: char, newChar: char): String	Returns a new string that replaces all matching characters in this string with the new character.
+replaceFirst(oldString: String, newString: String): String	Returns a new string that replaces the first matching substring in this string with the new substring.
+replaceAll(oldString: String, newString: String): String	Returns a new string that replaces all matching substrings in this string with the new substring.
+split(delimiter: String): String[]	Returns an array of strings consisting of the substrings split by the delimiter.

FIGURE 8.7 The `String` class contains the methods for converting, replacing, and splitting strings.

Once a string is created, its contents cannot be changed. The methods `toLowerCase`, `toUpperCase`, `trim`, `replace`, `replaceFirst`, and `replaceAll` return a new string derived from the original string (without changing the original string!). The `toLowerCase` and `toUpperCase` methods return a new string by converting all the characters in the string to lowercase or uppercase. The `trim` method returns a new string by eliminating blank characters from both ends of the string. Several versions of the `replace` methods are provided to replace a character or a substring in the string with a new character or a new substring.

For example,

```
"Welcome".toLowerCase() returns a new string, welcome.
"Welcome".toUpperCase() returns a new string, WELCOME.
"  Welcome  ".trim() returns a new string, Welcome.
"Welcome".replace('e', 'A') returns a new string, WAlcomA.
"Welcome".replaceFirst("e", "AB") returns a new string, WABlcome.
"Welcome".replace("e", "AB") returns a new string, WABlcomAB.
"Welcome".replace("el", "AB") returns a new string, WABlcome.
```

`toLowerCase()`
`toUpperCase()`
`trim()`
`replace`
`replaceFirst`
`replace`
`replace`

The `split` method can be used to extract tokens from a string with the specified delimiters. `split` For example, the following code

```
String[] tokens = "Java#HTML#Perl".split("#", 0);
for (int i = 0; i < tokens.length; i++)
  System.out.print(tokens[i] + " ");
```

displays
Java HTML Perl

8.2.7 Matching, Replacing and Splitting by Patterns

regular expression

You can match, replace, or split a string by specifying a pattern. This is an extremely useful and powerful feature, commonly known as *regular expression*. Regular expressions seem complex to beginning students. For this reason, two simple patterns are used in this section. Please refer to Supplement III.F, "Regular Expressions," for further studies.

matches(regex)

Let us begin with the `matches` method in the `String` class. At first glance, the `matches` method is very similar to the `equals` method. For example, the following two statements both evaluate to `true`.

```
"Java".matches("Java");
"Java".equals("Java");
```

However, the `matches` method is more powerful. It can match not only a fixed string, but also a set of strings that follow a pattern. For example, the following statements all evaluate to `true`.

```
"Java is fun".matches("Java.*")
"Java is cool".matches("Java.*")
"Java is powerful".matches("Java.*")
```

`"Java.*"` in the preceding statements is a regular expression. It describes a string pattern that begins with Java followed by *any* zero or more characters. Here, the substring `.*` matches any zero or more characters.

The `replaceAll`, `replaceFirst`, and `split` methods can be used with a regular expression. For example, the following statement returns a new string that replaces $, +, or # in "a+b$#c" with the string NNN.

replaceAll(regex)

```
String s = "a+b$#c".replaceAll("[$+#]", "NNN");
System.out.println(s);
```

Here the regular expression `[$+#]` specifies a pattern that matches $, +, or #. So, the output is aNNNbNNNNNNc.

The following statement splits the string into an array of strings delimited by some punctuation marks.

split(regex)

```
String[] tokens = "Java,C?C#,C++".split("[.,:;?]");

for (int i = 0; i < tokens.length; i++)
  System.out.println(tokens[i]);
```

Here the regular expression `[.,:;?]` specifies a pattern that matches ., ,, :, ;, ?. Each of these characters is a delimiter for splitting the string. So, the string is split into Java, C, C#, and C++, which are stored into array tokens.

8.2.8 Finding a Character or a Substring in a String

The `String` class provides several overloaded `indexOf` and `lastIndexOf` methods to find a character or a substring in a string, as shown in Figure 8.8.

For example,

indexOf

```
"Welcome to Java".indexOf('W') returns 0.
"Welcome to Java".indexOf('o') returns 4.
"Welcome to Java".indexOf('o', 5) returns 8.
"Welcome to Java".indexOf("come") returns 3.
"Welcome to Java".indexOf("Java", 5) returns 11.
"Welcome to Java".indexOf("java", 5) returns -1.
```

java.lang.String	
+indexOf(ch: char): int	Returns the index of the first occurrence of ch in the string. Returns −1 if not matched.
+indexOf(ch: char, fromIndex: int): int	Returns the index of the first occurrence of ch after fromIndex in the string. Returns −1 if not matched.
+indexOf(s: String): int	Returns the index of the first occurrence of string s in this string. Returns −1 if not matched.
+indexOf(s: String, fromIndex: int): int	Returns the index of the first occurrence of string s in this string after fromIndex. Returns −1 if not matched.
+lastIndexOf(ch: int): int	Returns the index of the last occurrence of ch in the string. Returns −1 if not matched.
+lastIndexOf(ch: int, fromIndex: int): int	Returns the index of the last occurrence of ch before fromIndex in this string. Returns −1 if not matched.
+lastIndexOf(s: String): int	Returns the index of the last occurrence of string s. Returns −1 if not matched.
+lastIndexOf(s: String, fromIndex: int): int	Returns the index of the last occurrence of string s before fromIndex. Returns −1 if not matched.

FIGURE 8.8 The String class contains the methods for matching substrings.

```
"Welcome to Java".lastIndexOf('W') returns 0.
"Welcome to Java".lastIndexOf('o') returns 8.
"Welcome to Java".lastIndexOf('o', 5) returns 4.
"Welcome to Java".lastIndexOf("come") returns 3.
"Welcome to Java".lastIndexOf("Java", 5) returns −1.
"Welcome to Java".lastIndexOf("java", 5) returns −1.
```

lastIndexOf

8.2.9 Conversion between Strings and Arrays

Strings are not arrays, but a string can be converted into an array, and vice versa. To convert a string to an array of characters, use the **toCharArray** method. For example, the following statement converts the string "Java" to an array.

```
char[] chars = "Java".toCharArray();
```

toCharArray

So chars[0] is 'J', chars[1] is 'a', chars[2] is 'v', and chars[3] is 'a'.

You can also use the **getChars(int srcBegin, int srcEnd, char[] dst, int dstBegin)** method to copy a substring of the string from index srcBegin to index srcEnd-1 into a character array dst starting from index dstBegin. For example, the following code copies a substring "3720" in "CS3720" from index 2 to index 6−1 into the character array dst starting from index 4.

```
char[] dst = {'J', 'A', 'V', 'A', '1', '3', '0', '1'};
"CS3720".getChars(2, 6, dst, 4);
```

getChars

Thus dst becomes {'J', 'A', 'V', 'A', '3', '7', '2', '0'}.

To convert an array of characters into a string, use the **String(char[])** constructor or the **valueOf(char[])** method. For example, the following statement constructs a string from an array using the String constructor.

```
String str = new String(new char[]{'J', 'a', 'v', 'a'});
```

The next statement constructs a string from an array using the **valueOf** method.

```
String str = String.valueOf(new char[]{'J', 'a', 'v', 'a'});
```

valueOf

8.2.10 Converting Characters and Numeric Values to Strings

overloaded **valueOf**

The static `valueOf` method can be used to convert an array of characters into a string. There are several overloaded versions of the `valueOf` method that can be used to convert a character and numeric values to strings with different parameter types, `char`, `double`, `long`, `int`, and `float`, as shown in Figure 8.9.

java.lang.String	
+valueOf(c: char): String	Returns a string consisting of the character `c`.
+valueOf(data: char[]): String	Returns a string consisting of the characters in the array.
+valueOf(d: double): String	Returns a string representing the `double` value.
+valueOf(f: float): String	Returns a string representing the `float` value.
+valueOf(i: int): String	Returns a string representing the `int` value.
+valueOf(l: long): String	Returns a string representing the `long` value.

FIGURE 8.9 The `String` class contains the static methods for creating strings from primitive type values.

For example, to convert a double value `5.44` to a string, use `String.valueOf(5.44)`. The return value is a string consisting of the characters `'5'`, `'.'`, `'4'`, and `'4'`.

Note

Use `Double.parseDouble(str)` or `Integer.parseInt(str)` to convert a string to a `double` value or an `int` value.

8.2.11 Problem: Checking Palindromes

A string is a palindrome if it reads the same forward and backward. The words "mom," "dad," and "noon," for instance, are all palindromes.

The problem is to write a program that prompts the user to enter a string and reports whether the string is a palindrome. One solution is to check whether the first character in the string is the same as the last character. If so, check whether the second character is the same as the second-to-last character. This process continues until a mismatch is found or all the characters in the string are checked, except for the middle character if the string has an odd number of characters.

To implement this idea, use two variables, say `low` and `high`, to denote the position of two characters at the beginning and the end in a string `s`, as shown in Listing 8.1 (lines 22, 25). Initially, `low` is `0` and `high` is `s.length() - 1`. If the two characters at these positions match, increment `low` by `1` and decrement `high` by `1` (lines 31-32). This process continues until (`low >= high`) or a mismatch is found.

Video Note
Check palindrome

LISTING 8.1 CheckPalindrome.java

```java
1 import java.util.Scanner;
2
3 public class CheckPalindrome {
4   /** Main method */
5   public static void main(String[] args) {
6     // Create a Scanner
7     Scanner input = new Scanner(System.in);
8
9     // Prompt the user to enter a string
```

```
10      System.out.print("Enter a string: ");
11      String s = input.nextLine();
12
13      if (isPalindrome(s))
14        System.out.println(s + " is a palindrome");
15      else
16        System.out.println(s + " is not a palindrome");
17    }
18
19    /** Check if a string is a palindrome */
20    public static boolean isPalindrome(String s) {
21      // The index of the first character in the string
22      int low = 0;
23
24      // The index of the last character in the string
25      int high = s.length() - 1;
26
27      while (low < high) {
28        if (s.charAt(low) != s.charAt(high))
29          return false; // Not a palindrome
30
31        low++;
32        high--;
33      }
34
35      return true; // The string is a palindrome
36    }
37 }
```

input string

low index

high index

update indices

```
Enter a string: noon  ↵Enter
noon is a palindrome

Enter a string: moon  ↵Enter
moon is not a palindrome
```

The `nextLine()` method in the Scanner class (line 11) reads a line into s. `isPalindrome(s)` checks whether s is a palindrome (line 13).

8.3 The **Character** Class

Java provides a wrapper class for every primitive data type. These classes are Character, Boolean, Byte, Short, Integer, Long, Float, and Double for char, boolean, byte, short, int, long, float, and double. All these classes are in the java.lang package. They enable the primitive data values to be treated as objects. They also contain useful methods for processing primitive values. This section introduces the Character class. The other wrapper classes will be introduced in Chapter 11, "Abstract Classes and Interfaces."

The Character class has a constructor and several methods for determining a character's category (uppercase, lowercase, digit, etc.) and for converting characters from uppercase to lowercase, and vice versa, as shown in Figure 8.10.

You can create a Character object from a char value. For example, the following statement creates a Character object for the character 'a'.

```
Character character = new Character('a');
```

java.lang.Character	
+Character(value: char)	Constructs a character object with char value.
+charValue(): char	Returns the char value from this object.
+compareTo(anotherCharacter: Character): int	Compares this character with another.
+equals(anotherCharacter: Character): boolean	Returns true if this character is equal to another.
+isDigit(ch: char): boolean	Returns true if the specified character is a digit.
+isLetter(ch: char): boolean	Returns true if the specified character is a letter.
+isLetterOrDigit(ch: char): boolean	Returns true if the character is a letter or a digit.
+isLowerCase(ch: char): boolean	Returns true if the character is a lowercase letter.
+isUpperCase(ch: char): boolean	Returns true if the character is an uppercase letter.
+toLowerCase(ch: char): char	Returns the lowercase of the specified character.
+toUpperCase(ch: char): char	Returns the uppercase of the specified character.

FIGURE 8.10 The `Character` class provides the methods for manipulating a character.

The `charValue` method returns the character value wrapped in the `Character` object. The `compareTo` method compares this character with another character and returns an integer that is the difference between the Unicodes of this character and the other character. The `equals` method returns true if and only if the two characters are the same. For example, suppose `charObject` is `new Character('b')`:

```
charObject.compareTo(new Character('a')) returns 1
charObject.compareTo(new Character('b')) returns 0
charObject.compareTo(new Character('c')) returns -1
charObject.compareTo(new Character('d') returns -2
charObject.equals(new Character('b')) returns true
charObject.equals(new Character('d')) returns false
```

Most of the methods in the `Character` class are static methods. The `isDigit(char ch)` method returns true if the character is a digit. The `isLetter(char ch)` method returns true if the character is a letter. The `isLetterOrDigit(char ch)` method returns true if the character is a letter or a digit. The `isLowerCase(char ch)` method returns true if the character is a lowercase letter. The `isUpperCase(char ch)` method returns true if the character is an uppercase letter. The `toLowerCase(char ch)` method returns the lowercase letter for the character, and the `toUpperCase(char ch)` method returns the uppercase letter for the character.

8.3.1 Problem: Counting Each Letter in a String

The problem is to write a program that prompts the user to enter a string and counts the number of occurrences of each letter in the string regardless of case.

Here are the steps to solve this problem:

1. Convert all the uppercase letters in the string to lowercase using the `toLowerCase` method in the `String` class.

2. Create an array, say `counts` of `26 int` values, each of which counts the occurrences of a letter. That is, `counts[0]` counts the number of a's, `counts[1]` counts the number of b's, and so on.

3. For each character in the string, check whether it is a (lowercase) letter. If so, increment the corresponding count in the array.

LISTING 8.2 CountEachLetter.java

```java
1 import java.util.Scanner;
2
3 public class CountEachLetter {
4   /** Main method */
5   public static void main(String[] args) {
6     // Create a Scanner
7     Scanner input = new Scanner(System.in);
8
9     // Prompt the user to enter a string
10    System.out.print("Enter a string: ");
11    String s = input.nextLine();
12
13    // Invoke the countLetters method to count each letter
14    int[] counts = countLetters(s.toLowerCase());
15
16    // Display results
17    for (int i = 0; i < counts.length; i++) {
18      if (counts[i] != 0)
19        System.out.println((char)('a' + i) + " appears   " +
20          counts[i] + ((counts[i] == 1) ? " time" : " times"));
21    }
22  }
23
24  /** Count each letter in the string */
25  public static int[] countLetters(String s) {
26    int[] counts = new int[26];
27
28    for (int i = 0; i < s.length(); i++) {
29      if (Character.isLetter(s.charAt(i)))
30        counts[s.charAt(i) - 'a']++;
31    }
32
33    return counts;
34  }
35 }
```

input string

count letters

count a letter

```
Enter a string: abababx  ⏎Enter
a appears  3 times
b appears  3 times
x appears  1 time
```

The main method reads a line (line 11) and counts the number of occurrences of each letter in the string by invoking the **countLetters** method (line 14). Since the case of the letters is ignored, the program uses the **toLowerCase** method to convert the string into all lowercase and pass the new string to the **countLetters** method.

The **countLetters** method (lines 25–34) returns an array of **26** elements. Each element counts the number of occurrences of a letter in the string **s**. The method processes each character in the string. If the character is a letter, its corresponding count is increased by 1. For example, if the character (**s.charAr(i)**) is **'a'**, the corresponding count is **counts['a' - 'a']** (i.e., **counts[0]**). If the character is **'b'**, the corresponding count is **counts['b' - 'a']** (i.e., **counts[1]**), since the Unicode of **'b'** is **1** more than that of **'a'**. If the character is `'z'`, the corresponding count is `counts['z' - 'a']` (i.e., `counts[25]`), since the Unicode of `'z'` is `25` more than that of `'a'`.

8.4 The **StringBuilder/StringBuffer** Class

The `StringBuilder`/`StringBuffer` class is an alternative to the `String` class. In general, a `StringBuilder`/`StringBuffer` can be used wherever a string is used. `StringBuilder`/`StringBuffer` is more flexible than `String`. You can add, insert, or append new contents into a string builder or a string buffer, whereas the value of a `String` object is fixed, once the string is created.

StringBuilder

The `StringBuilder` class is similar to `StringBuffer` except that the methods for modifying buffer in `StringBuffer` are synchronized. Use `StringBuffer` if it may be accessed by multiple tasks concurrently. Using `StringBuilder` is more efficient if it is accessed by a single task. The constructors and methods in `StringBuffer` and `StringBuilder` are almost the same. This section covers `StringBuilder`. You may replace `StringBuilder` by `StringBuffer`. The program can compile and run without any other changes.

StringBuilder
constructors

The `StringBuilder` class has three constructors and more than 30 methods for managing the builder and modifying strings in the builder. You can create an empty string builder or a string builder from a string using the constructors, as shown in Figure 8.11.

java.lang.StringBuilder	
+StringBuilder()	Constructs an empty string builder with capacity 16.
+StringBuilder(capacity: int)	Constructs a string builder with the specified capacity.
+StringBuilder(s: String)	Constructs a string builder with the specified string.

FIGURE 8.11   The `StringBuilder` class contains the constructors for creating instances of `StringBuilder`.

8.4.1   Modifying Strings in the `StringBuilder`

You can append new contents at the end of a string builder, insert new contents at a specified position in a string builder, and delete or replace characters in a string builder, using the methods listed in Figure 8.12:

The `StringBuilder` class provides several overloaded methods to append `boolean`, `char`, `char array`, `double`, `float`, `int`, `long`, and `String` into a string builder. For example, the following code appends strings and characters into `stringBuilder` to form a new string, `"Welcome to Java"`.

```
StringBuilder stringBuilder = new StringBuilder();
```

append

```
stringBuilder.append("Welcome");
stringBuilder.append(' ');
stringBuilder.append("to");
stringBuilder.append(' ');
stringBuilder.append("Java");
```

The `StringBuilder` class also contains overloaded methods to insert `boolean`, `char`, `char array`, `double`, `float`, `int`, `long`, and `String` into a string builder. Consider the following code:

insert

```
stringBuilder.insert(11, "HTML and ");
```

Suppose `stringBuilder` contains `"Welcome to Java"` before the `insert()` method is applied. This code inserts `"HTML and "` at position 11 in `stringBuilder` (just before `J`). The new `stringBuilder` is `"Welcome to HTML and Java"`.

java.lang.StringBuilder	
+append(data: char[]): StringBuilder	Appends a char array into this string builder.
+append(data: char[], offset: int, len: int): StringBuilder	Appends a subarray in data into this string builder.
+append(v: *aPrimitiveType*): StringBuilder	Appends a primitive type value as a string to this builder.
+append(s: String): StringBuilder	Appends a string to this string builder.
+delete(startIndex: int, endIndex: int): StringBuilder	Deletes characters from startIndex to endIndex.
+deleteCharAt(index: int): StringBuilder	Deletes a character at the specified index.
+insert(index: int, data: char[], offset: int, len: int): StringBuilder	Inserts a subarray of the data in the array to the builder at the specified index.
+insert(offset: int, data: char[]): StringBuilder	Inserts data into this builder at the position offset.
+insert(offset: int, b: *aPrimitiveType*): StringBuilder	Inserts a value converted to a string into this builder.
+insert(offset: int, s: String): StringBuilder	Inserts a string into this builder at the position offset.
+replace(startIndex: int, endIndex: int, s: String): StringBuilder	Replaces the characters in this builder from startIndex to endIndex with the specified string.
+reverse(): StringBuilder	Reverses the characters in the builder.
+setCharAt(index: int, ch: char): void	Sets a new character at the specified index in this builder.

FIGURE 8.12 The StringBuilder class contains the methods for modifying string builders.

You can also delete characters from a string in the builder using the two delete methods, reverse the string using the reverse method, replace characters using the replace method, or set a new character in a string using the setCharAt method.

For example, suppose stringBuilder contains "Welcome to Java" before each of the following methods is applied.

stringBuilder.delete(8, 11) changes the builder to Welcome Java.   delete
stringBuilder.deleteCharAt(8) changes the builder to Welcome o Java.   deleteCharAt
stringBuilder.reverse() changes the builder to avaJ ot emocleW.   reverse
stringBuilder.replace(11, 15, "HTML") changes the builder to Welcome to HTML. replace
stringBuilder.setCharAt(0, 'w') sets the builder to welcome to Java.   setCharAt

All these modification methods except setCharAt do two things:

1. Change the contents of the string builder

2. Return the reference of the string builder

For example, the following statement

```
StringBuilder stringBuilder1 = stringBuilder.reverse();
```

reverses the string in the builder and assigns the reference of the builder to stringBuilder1. Thus, stringBuilder and stringBuilder1 both point to the same StringBuilder object. Recall that a value-returning method may be invoked as a statement, if you are not inter-   ignore return value
ested in the return value of the method. In this case, the return value is simply ignored. For example, in the following statement

```
stringBuilder.reverse();
```

the return value is ignored.

Tip

If a string does not require any change, use `String` rather than `StringBuilder`. Java can perform some optimizations for `String`, such as sharing interned strings.

8.4.2 The `toString`, `capacity`, `length`, `setLength`, and `charAt` Methods

The `StringBuilder` class provides the additional methods for manipulating a string builder and obtaining its properties, as shown in Figure 8.13.

java.lang.StringBuilder	
+toString(): String	Returns a string object from the string builder.
+capacity(): int	Returns the capacity of this string builder.
+charAt(index: int): char	Returns the character at the specified index.
+length(): int	Returns the number of characters in this builder.
+setLength(newLength: int): void	Sets a new length in this builder.
+substring(startIndex: int): String	Returns a substring starting at `startIndex`.
+substring(startIndex: int, endIndex: int): String	Returns a substring from `startIndex` to `endIndex-1`.
+trimToSize(): void	Reduces the storage size used for the string builder.

FIGURE 8.13 The `StringBuilder` class contains the methods for modifying string builders.

capacity()

The `capacity()` method returns the current capacity of the string builder. The capacity is the number of characters it is able to store without having to increase its size.

length()
setLength(int)

The `length()` method returns the number of characters actually stored in the string builder. The `setLength(newLength)` method sets the length of the string builder. If the `newLength` argument is less than the current length of the string builder, the string builder is truncated to contain exactly the number of characters given by the `newLength` argument. If the `newLength` argument is greater than or equal to the current length, sufficient null characters (`'\u0000'`) are appended to the string builder so that `length` becomes the `newLength` argument. The `newLength` argument must be greater than or equal to `0`.

charAt(int)

The `charAt(index)` method returns the character at a specific `index` in the string builder. The index is `0` based. The first character of a string builder is at index `0`, the next at index `1`, and so on. The `index` argument must be greater than or equal to `0`, and less than the length of the string builder.

Note

length and capacity

The length of the string is always less than or equal to the capacity of the builder. The length is the actual size of the string stored in the builder, and the capacity is the current size of the builder. The builder's capacity is automatically increased if more characters are added to exceed its capacity. Internally, a string builder is an array of characters, so the builder's capacity is the size of the array. If the builder's capacity is exceeded, the array is replaced by a new array. The new array size is `2 * (the previous array size + 1)`.

Tip

initial capacity

You can use `new StringBuilder(initialCapacity)` to create a `StringBuilder` with a specified initial capacity. By carefully choosing the initial capacity, you can make your program more efficient. If the capacity is always larger than the actual length of the builder, the JVM will never need to reallocate memory for the builder. On the other hand, if the capacity is too large, you will waste memory space. You can use the `trimToSize()` method to reduce the capacity to the actual size.

8.4.3 Problem: Ignoring Nonalphanumeric Characters When Checking Palindromes

Listing 8.1, "Checking Palindromes," considered all the characters in a string to check whether it was a palindrome. Write a new program that ignores nonalphanumeric characters in checking whether a string is a palindrome.

Here are the steps to solve the problem:

1. Filter the string by removing the nonalphanumeric characters. This can be done by creating an empty string builder, adding each alphanumeric character in the string to a string builder, and returning the string from the string builder. You can use the `isLetterOrDigit(ch)` method in the `Character` class to check whether character `ch` is a letter or a digit.

2. Obtain a new string that is the reversal of the filtered string. Compare the reversed string with the filtered string using the `equals` method.

The complete program is shown in Listing 8.3.

LISTING 8.3 PalindromeIgnoreNonAlphanumeric.java

```java
1  import java.util.Scanner;
2
3  public class PalindromeIgnoreNonAlphanumeric {
4    /** Main method */
5    public static void main(String[] args) {
6      // Create a Scanner
7      Scanner input = new Scanner(System.in);
8
9      // Prompt the user to enter a string
10     System.out.print("Enter a string: ");
11     String s = input.nextLine();
12
13     // Display result
14     System.out.println("Ignoring nonalphanumeric characters, \nis "
15       + s + " a palindrome? " + isPalindrome(s));
16   }
17
18   /** Return true if a string is a palindrome */
19   public static boolean isPalindrome(String s) {
20     // Create a new string by eliminating nonalphanumeric chars
21     String s1 = filter(s);
22
23     // Create a new string that is the reversal of s1
24     String s2 = reverse(s1);
25
26     // Compare if the reversal is the same as the original string
27     return s2.equals(s1);
28   }
29
30   /** Create a new string by eliminating nonalphanumeric chars */
31   public static String filter(String s) {
32     // Create a string builder
33     StringBuilder stringBuilder = new StringBuilder();
```

check palindrome

```
34
35      // Examine each char in the string to skip alphanumeric char
36      for (int i = 0; i < s.length(); i++) {
37        if (Character.isLetterOrDigit(s.charAt(i)) ) {
38          stringBuilder.append(s.charAt(i));
39        }
40      }
41
42      // Return a new filtered string
43      return stringBuilder.toString();
44    }
45
46    /** Create a new string by reversing a specified string */
47    public static String reverse(String s) {
48      StringBuilder stringBuilder = new StringBuilder(s);
49      stringBuilder.reverse(); // Use the reverse method
50      return stringBuilder.toString();
51    }
52  }
```

add letter or digit

```
Enter a string: ab<c>cb?a  ⏎Enter
Ignoring nonalphanumeric characters,
is ab<c>cb?a a palindrome? true

Enter a string: abcc><?cab  ⏎Enter
Ignoring nonalphanumeric characters,
is abcc><?cab a palindrome? false
```

The `filter(String s)` method (lines 31–44) examines each character in string `s` and copies it to a string builder if the character is a letter or a numeric character. The `filter` method returns the string in the builder. The `reverse(String s)` method (lines 47–51) creates a new string that reverses the specified string `s`. The `filter` and `reverse` methods both return a new string. The original string is not changed.

The program in Listing 8.1 checks whether a string is a palindrome by comparing pairs of characters from both ends of the string. Listing 8.3 uses the `reverse` method in the `StringBuilder` class to reverse the string, then compares whether the two strings are equal to determine whether the original string is a palindrome.

8.5 Command-Line Arguments

Perhaps you have already noticed the unusual declarations for the `main` method, which has parameter `args` of `String[]` type. It is clear that `args` is an array of strings. The `main` method is just like a regular method with a parameter. You can call a regular method by passing actual parameters. Can you pass arguments to `main`? Yes, of course you can. For example, the `main` method in class `B` is invoked by a method in `A`, as shown below:

```
public class A {
  public static void main(String[] args) {
    String[] strings = {"New York",
      "Boston", "Atlanta"};
    B.main(strings);
  }
}
```

```
public class B {
  public static void main(String[] args) {
    for (int i = 0; i < args.length; i++)
      System.out.println(args[i]);
  }
}
```

A main method is just a regular method. Furthermore, you can pass arguments from the command line.

8.5.1 Passing Strings to the `main` Method

You can pass strings to a `main` method from the command line when you run the program. The following command line, for example, starts the program `TestMain` with three strings: `arg0`, `arg1`, and `arg2`:

```
java TestMain arg0 arg1 arg2
```

`arg0`, `arg1`, and `arg2` are strings, but they don't have to appear in double quotes on the command line. The strings are separated by a space. A string that contains a space must be enclosed in double quotes. Consider the following command line:

```
java TestMain "First num" alpha 53
```

It starts the program with three strings: `"First num"`, `alpha`, and `53`, a numeric string. Since `"First num"` is a string, it is enclosed in double quotes. Note that `53` is actually treated as a string. You can use `"53"` instead of `53` in the command line.

When the `main` method is invoked, the Java interpreter creates an array to hold the command-line arguments and pass the array reference to `args`. For example, if you invoke a program with n arguments, the Java interpreter creates an array like this one:

```
args = new String[n];
```

The Java interpreter then passes `args` to invoke the `main` method.

Note

If you run the program with no strings passed, the array is created with `new String[0]`. In this case, the array is empty with length `0`. `args` references to this empty array. Therefore, `args` is not `null`, but `args.length` is `0`.

8.5.2 Problem: Calculator

Suppose you are to develop a program that performs arithmetic operations on integers. The program receives three arguments: an integer followed by an operator and another integer. For example, to add two integers, use this command:

```
java Calculator 2 + 3
```

The program will display the following output:

```
2 + 3 = 5
```

Figure 8.14 shows sample runs of the program.

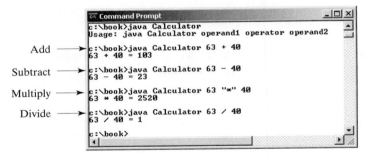

FIGURE 8.14 The program takes three arguments (operand1 operator operand2) from the command line and displays the expression and the result of the arithmetic operation.

The strings passed to the main program are stored in `args`, which is an array of strings. The first string is stored in `args[0]`, and `args.length` is the number of strings passed. Here are the steps in the program:

1. Use `args.length` to determine whether three arguments have been provided in the command line. If not, terminate the program using `System.exit(0)`.

2. Perform a binary arithmetic operation on the operands `args[0]` and `args[2]` using the operator specified in `args[1]`.

The program is shown in Listing 8.4.

Video Note
Command-line argument

LISTING 8.4 Calculator.java

```java
 1 public class Calculator {
 2   /** Main method */
 3   public static void main(String[] args) {
 4     // Check number of strings passed
 5     if (args.length != 3) {
 6       System.out.println(
 7         "Usage: java Calculator operand1 operator operand2");
 8       System.exit(0);
 9     }
10
11     // The result of the operation
12     int result = 0;
13
14     // Determine the operator
15     switch (args[1].charAt(0)) {
16       case '+': result = Integer.parseInt(args[0]) +
17                          Integer.parseInt(args[2]);
18               break;
19       case '-': result = Integer.parseInt(args[0]) -
20                          Integer.parseInt(args[2]);
21               break;
22       case '*': result = Integer.parseInt(args[0]) *
23                          Integer.parseInt(args[2]);
24               break;
25       case '/': result = Integer.parseInt(args[0]) /
26                          Integer.parseInt(args[2]);
27     }
28
29     // Display result
30     System.out.println(args[0] + ' ' + args[1] + ' ' + args[2]
31       + " = " + result);
32   }
33 }
```

check operator

`Integer.parseInt(args[0])` (line 15) converts a digital string into an integer. The string must consist of digits. If not, the program will terminate abnormally.

Note

special * character

In the sample run, "*" had to be used instead of * for the command

`java Calculator 63 "*" 40`

In JDK 1.1 and above, the * symbol refers to all the files in the current directory when it is used on a command line. Therefore, in order to specify the multiplication operator, the * must be enclosed in quote marks in the command line. The following program displays all the files in the current directory when issuing the command `java Test *`:

```java
public class Test {
  public static void main(String[] args) {
    for (int i = 0; i < args.length; i++)
      System.out.println(args[i]);
  }
}
```

8.6 The **File** Class

Data stored in variables, arrays, and objects are temporary; they are lost when the program terminates. To permanently store the data created in a program, you need to save them in a file on a disk or a CD. The file can be transported and can be read later by other programs. Since data are stored in files, this section introduces how to use the `File` class to obtain file properties and to delete and rename files. The next section introduces how to read/write data from/to text files. why file?

Every file is placed in a directory in the file system. An *absolute file name* contains a file name with its complete path and drive letter. For example, **c:\book\Welcome.java** is the absolute file name for the file **Welcome.java** on the Windows operating system. Here **c:\book** is referred to as the *directory path* for the file. Absolute file names are machine dependent. On the Unix platform, the absolute file name may be **/home/liang/book/Welcome.java**, where **/home/liang/book** is the directory path for the file **Welcome.java**. absolute file name
directory path

The `File` class is intended to provide an abstraction that deals with most of the machine-dependent complexities of files and path names in a machine-independent fashion. The `File` class contains the methods for obtaining file properties and for renaming and deleting files, as shown in Figure 8.15. However, *the `File` class does not contain the methods for reading and writing file contents*.

The file name is a string. The `File` class is a wrapper class for the file name and its directory path. For example, `new File("c:\\book")` creates a `File` object for the directory **c:\book**, and `new File("c:\\book\\test.dat")` creates a `File` object for the file **c:\\book\\test.dat**, both on Windows. You can use the `File` class's `isDirectory()` method to check whether the object represents a directory, and the `isFile()` method to check whether the object represents a file.

Caution

The directory separator for Windows is a backslash (\). The backslash is a special character in Java and should be written as \\ in a string literal (see Table 2.5). \ in file names

Note

Constructing a `File` instance does not create a file on the machine. You can create a `File` instance for any filename regardless whether it exists or not. You can invoke the `exists()` method on a `File` instance to check whether the file exists.

Do not use absolute file names in your program. If you use a file name such as `"c:\\book\\Welcome.java"`, it will work on Windows but not on other platforms. You should use a file name relative to the current directory. For example, you may create a `File` object using `new File("Welcome.java")` for the file **Welcome.java** in the current directory. You may create a `File` object using `new File("image/us.gif")` for the file **us.gif** under the **image** directory in the current directory. The forward slash (/) is the Java directory separator, which is the same as on Unix. The statement `new File("image/us.gif")` works on Windows, Unix, or any other platform. relative file name

Java directory separator (/)

java.io.File	
+File(pathname: String)	Creates a File object for the specified path name. The path name may be a directory or a file.
+File(parent: String, child: String)	Creates a File object for the child under the directory parent. The child may be a file name or a subdirectory.
+File(parent: File, child: String)	Creates a File object for the child under the directory parent. The parent is a File object. In the preceding constructor, the parent is a string.
+exists(): boolean	Returns true if the file or the directory represented by the File object exists.
+canRead(): boolean	Returns true if the file represented by the File object exists and can be read.
+canWrite(): boolean	Returns true if the file represented by the File object exists and can be written.
+isDirectory(): boolean	Returns true if the File object represents a directory.
+isFile(): boolean	Returns true if the File object represents a file.
+isAbsolute(): boolean	Returns true if the File object is created using an absolute path name.
+isHidden(): boolean	Returns true if the file represented in the File object is hidden. The exact definition of *hidden* is system dependent. On Windows, you can mark a file hidden in the File Properties dialog box. On Unix systems, a file is hidden if its name begins with a period character '.'.
+getAbsolutePath(): String	Returns the complete absolute file or directory name represented by the File object.
+getCanonicalPath(): String	Returns the same as getAbsolutePath() except that it removes redundant names, such as "." and "..", from the path name, resolves symbolic links (on Unix platforms), and converts drive letters to standard uppercase (on Win32 platforms).
+getName(): String	Returns the last name of the complete directory and file name represented by the File object. For example, new File("c:\\book\\test.dat").getName() returns test.dat.
+getPath(): String	Returns the complete directory and file name represented by the File object. For example, new File("c:\\book\\test.dat").getPath() returns c:\book\test.dat.
+getParent(): String	Returns the complete parent directory of the current directory or the file represented by the File object. For example, new File("c:\\book\\test.dat").getParent() returns c:\book.
+lastModified(): long	Returns the time that the file was last modified.
+length(): long	Returns the size of the file, or 0 if it does not exist or if it is a directory.
+listFile(): File[]	Returns the files under the directory for a directory File object.
+delete(): boolean	Deletes this file. The method returns true if the deletion succeeds.
+renameTo(dest: File): boolean	Renames this file. The method returns true if the operation succeeds.

FIGURE 8.15 The File class can be used to obtain file and directory properties and to delete and rename files.

Listing 8.5 demonstrates how to create a File object and use the methods in the File class to obtain its properties. The program creates a File object for the file **us.gif**. This file is stored under the **image** directory in the current directory.

LISTING 8.5 TestFileClass.java

```
 1 public class TestFileClass {
 2   public static void main(String[] args) {
 3     java.io.File file = new java.io.File("image/us.gif");
 4     System.out.println("Does it exist? " + file.exists());
 5     System.out.println("The file has " + file.length() + " bytes");
 6     System.out.println("Can it be read? " + file.canRead());
 7     System.out.println("Can it be written? " + file.canWrite());
 8     System.out.println("Is it a directory? " + file.isDirectory());
 9     System.out.println("Is it a file? " + file.isFile());
10     System.out.println("Is it absolute? " + file.isAbsolute());
11     System.out.println("Is it hidden? " + file.isHidden());
12     System.out.println("Absolute path is " +
13       file.getAbsolutePath());
```

create a File
exists()
length()
canRead()
canWrite()
isDirectory()
isFile()
isAbsolute()
isHidden()

getAbsolutePath()

```
14      System.out.println("Last modified on " +
15          new java.util.Date(file.lastModified()));
16  }
17 }
```

`lastModified()`

The `lastModified()` method returns the date and time when the file was last modified, measured in milliseconds since the beginning of Unix time (00:00:00 GMT, January 1, 1970). The `Date` class is used to display it in a readable format in lines 14–15.

Figure 8.16(a) shows a sample run of the program on Windows, and Figure 8.16(b), a sample run on Unix. As shown in the figures, the path-naming conventions on Windows are different from those on Unix.

(a) On Windows　　　　　(b) On Unix

FIGURE 8.16 The program creates a `File` object and displays file properties.

8.7 File Input and Output

A `File` object encapsulates the properties of a file or a path, but does not contain the methods for reading/writing data from/to a file. In order to perform I/O, you need to create objects using appropriate Java I/O classes. The objects contain the methods for reading/writing data from/to a file. This section introduces how to read/write strings and numeric values from/to a text file using the `Scanner` and `PrintWriter` classes.

8.7.1 Writing Data Using `PrintWriter`

The `java.io.PrintWriter` class can be used to write data to a text file. First, you have to create a `PrintWriter` object for a text file as follows:

```
PrintWriter output = new PrintWriter(filename);
```

Then, you can invoke the `print`, `println`, and `printf` methods on the `PrintWriter` object to write data to a file. Figure 8.17 summarizes frequently used methods in `PrintWriter`.

Listing 8.6 gives an example that creates an instance of `PrintWriter` and writes two lines to the file "scores.txt". Each line consists of first name (a string), middle name initial (a character), last name (a string), and score (an integer).

LISTING 8.6 WriteData.java

```
1 public class WriteData {
2   public static void main(String[] args) throws Exception {
3     java.io.File file = new java.io.File("scores.txt");
```

Video Note
Write/read data to/from files

throws an exception
create **File** object

file exist?

```
 4    if (file.exists()) {
 5      System.out.println("File already exists");
 6      System.exit(0);
 7    }
 8
 9    // Create a file
10    java.io.PrintWriter output = new java.io.PrintWriter(file);
11
12    // Write formatted output to the file
13    output.print("John T Smith ");
14    output.println(90);
15    output.print("Eric K Jones ");
16    output.println(85);
17
18    // Close the file
19    output.close();
20  }
21 }
```

create **PrintWriter**

print data

close file

```
John T Smith 90   scores.txt
Eric K Jones 85
```

java.io.PrintWriter	
+PrintWriter(filename: String)	Creates a PrintWriter object for the specified file.
+print(s: String): void	Writes a string.
+print(c: char): void	Writes a character.
+print(cArray: char[]): void	Writes an array of characters.
+print(i: int): void	Writes an int value.
+print(l: long): void	Writes a long value.
+print(f: float): void	Writes a float value.
+print(d: double): void	Writes a double value.
+print(b: boolean): void	Writes a boolean value.
Also contains the overloaded println methods.	A println method acts like a print method; additionally it prints a line separator. The line separator string is defined by the system. It is \r\n on Windows and \n on Unix.
Also contains the overloaded printf methods.	The printf method was introduced in §3.6, "Formatting Console Output."

FIGURE 8.17 The PrintWriter class contains the methods for writing data to a text file.

Lines 3–7 check whether the file scores.txt exists. If so, exit the program (line 6).

create a file

Invoking the constructor *new PrintWriter(String filename)* will create a new file if the file does not exist. If the file already exists, the current content in the file will be discarded.

Invoking the constructor *new PrintWriter(String filename)* may throw an I/O exception. Java forces you to write the code to deal with this type of exception. You will learn how to handle it in Chapter 19, "Exception Handling." For now, simply declare *throws Exception* in the method declaration (line 2).

throws Exception

print method

You have used the System.out.print and System.out.println methods to write text to the console. System.out is a standard Java object for the console. You can create objects for writing text to any file using print, println, and printf (lines 13–16).

close file

The close() method must be used to close the file. If this method is not invoked, the data may not be saved properly in the file.

8.7.2 Reading Data Using Scanner

The java.util.Scanner class was used to read strings and primitive values from the console in §2.11, "Console Input Using the Scanner Class." A Scanner breaks its input into tokens delimited by whitespace characters. To read from the keyboard, you create a Scanner for System.in, as follows:

```
Scanner input = new Scanner(System.in);
```

To read from a file, create a Scanner for a file, as follows:

```
Scanner input = new Scanner(new File(filename));
```

Figure 8.18 summarizes frequently used methods in Scanner.

java.util.Scanner	
+Scanner(source: File)	Creates a scanner that produces values scanned from the specified file.
+Scanner(source: String)	Creates a scanner that produces values scanned from the specified string.
+close()	Closes this scanner.
+hasNext(): boolean	Returns true if this scanner has more data to be read.
+next(): String	Returns next token as a string delimited by a white space.
+nextline(): String	Returns a line ending with the line separator.
+nextByte(): byte	Returns next token as a byte.
+nextShort(): short	Returns next token as a short.
+nextInt(): int	Returns next token as an int.
+nextLong(): long	Returns next token as a long.
+nextFloat(): float	Returns next token as a float.
+nextDouble(): double	Returns next token as a double.
+useDelimiter(pattern: String): Scanner	Sets this scanner's delimiting pattern.

FIGURE 8.18 The Scanner class contains the methods for scanning data.

Listing 8.7 gives an example that creates an instance of Scanner and reads data from the file "scores.txt".

LISTING 8.7 ReadData.java

```java
 1 import java.util.Scanner;
 2
 3 public class ReadData {
 4   public static void main(String[] args) throws Exception {
 5     // Create a File instance                                    create a File
 6     java.io.File file = new java.io.File("scores.txt");
 7
 8     // Create a Scanner for the file
 9     Scanner input = new Scanner(file);                           create a Scanner
10
11     // Read data from a file                    scores.txt
12     while (input.hasNext()) {                                    has next?
13       String firstName = input.next();    John T Smith 90        read items
14       String mi = input.next();           Eric K Jones 85
15       String lastName = input.next();
16       int score = input.nextInt();
17       System.out.println(
18         firstName + " " + mi + " " + lastName + " " + score);
19     }
20
21     // Close the file                                            close file
22     input.close();
23   }
24 }
```

File class

Note that `new Scanner(String)` creates a `Scanner` for a given string. To create a `Scanner` to read data from a file, you have to use the `java.io.File` class to create an instance of the `File` using the constructor *new File(filename)* (line 6), and use `new Scanner(File)` to create a `Scanner` for the file (line 9).

throws Exception

Invoking the constructor *new Scanner(File)* may throw an I/O exception. So the `main` method declares *throws Exception* in line 6.

Each iteration in the `while` loop reads first name, mi, last name, and score from the text file (lines 12–19). The file is closed in line 22.

close file

It is not necessary to close the input file (line 22), but it is a good practice to do so to release the resources occupied by the file.

8.7.3   How Does Scanner Work?

token-reading method
change delimiter

The `nextByte()`, `nextShort()`, `nextInt()`, `nextLong()`, `nextFloat()`, `nextDouble()`, and `next()` methods are known as *token-reading methods*, because they read tokens separated by delimiters. By default, the delimiters are whitespace. You can use the `useDelimiter(String regex)` method to set a new pattern for delimiters.

How does an input method work? A token-reading method first skips any delimiters (whitespace by default), then reads a token ending at a delimiter. The token is then automatically converted into a value of the `byte`, `short`, `int`, `long`, `float`, or `double` type for `nextByte()`, `nextShort()`, `nextInt()`, `nextLong()`, `nextFloat()`, and `nextDouble()`, respectively. For the `next()` method, no conversion is performed. If the token does not match the expected type, a runtime exception `java.util.InputMismatchException` will be thrown.

InputMismatchException
next() vs. nextLine()

Both methods `next()` and `nextLine()` read a string. The `next()` method reads a string delimited by delimiters, but `nextLine()` reads a line ending with a line separator. Recall that the line separator is platform dependent. It is `\r\n` on Windows and `\n` on Unix.

Note

The line separator string is defined by the system. It is `\r\n` on Windows and `\n` on Unix. To get the line separator on a particular platform, use

line separator

```
String lineSeparator = System.getProperty("line.separator");
```

If you enter input from a keyboard, a line ends with the ENTER key, which corresponds to the `\n` character.

behavior of nextLine()

The token-reading method does not read the delimiter after the token. If the `nextLine()` is invoked after a token-reading method, the method reads characters that start from this delimiter and end with the line separator. The line separator is read, but is not part of the string returned by `nextLine()`.

input from file

Suppose a text file named test.txt contains a line

```
34 567
```

After the following code is executed,

```
Scanner input = new Scanner(new File("test.txt"));
int intValue = input.nextInt();
String line = input.nextLine();
```

`intValue` contains `34` and `line` contains characters `' '`, `'5'`, `'6'`, `'7'`.

What happens if the input is *entered from the keyboard*? Suppose you enter `34`, the ENTER key, `567`, and the ENTER key for the following code:

```
Scanner input = new Scanner(System.in);
int intValue = input.nextInt();
String line = input.nextLine();
```

You will get 34 in `intValue`, and an empty string in `line`. Why? Here is the reason. The token-reading method `nextInt()` reads in 34 and stops at the delimiter, which is a line separator (the ENTER key) in this case. The `nextLine()` method ends after reading the line separator and returns the string read before the line separator. Since there are no characters before the line separator, `line` is empty.

input from keyboard

8.7.4 Problem: Replacing Text

Suppose you are to write a program named `ReplaceText` that replaces all occurrence of a string in a text file with a new string. The file name and strings are passed as command-line arguments as follows:

```
java ReplaceText sourceFile targetFile oldString newString
```

For example, invoking

```
java ReplaceText FormatString.java t.txt StringBuilder StringBuffer
```

replaces all the occurrences of `StringBuilder` by `StringBuffer` in FormatString.java and saves the new file in t.txt.

Listing 8.8 gives the solution to the problem. The program checks the number of arguments passed to the `main` method (lines 7–11), checks whether the source and target files exist (lines 14–25), creates a `Scanner` for the source file (line 28), creates a `PrintWriter` for the target file, and repeatedly reads a line from the source file (line 33), replaces the text (line 33), and writes a new line to the target file (line 34). You must close the output file (line 38) to ensure that data is saved to the file properly.

LISTING 8.8 ReplaceText.java

```
1  import java.io.*;
2  import java.util.*;
3
4  public class ReplaceText {
5    public static void main(String[] args) throws Exception {
6      // Check command line-parameter usage
7      if (args.length != 4) {
8        System.out.println(
9          "Usage: java ReplaceText sourceFile targetFile oldStr newStr");
10       System.exit(0);
11     }
12
13     // Check if source file exists
14     File sourceFile = new File(args[0]);
15     if (!sourceFile.exists()) {
16       System.out.println("Source file " + args[0] + " does not exist");
17       System.exit(0);
18     }
19
20     // Check if target file exists
21     File targetFile = new File(args[1]);
22     if (targetFile.exists()) {
23       System.out.println("Target file " + args[1] + " already exists");
24       System.exit(0);
25     }
26
27     // Create input and output files
28     Scanner input = new Scanner(sourceFile);
29     PrintWriter output = new PrintWriter(targetFile);
```

check command usage

source file exists?

target file exists?

create a **Scanner**
create a **PrintWriter**

has next?
read a line

close file

```
30
31   while (input.hasNext()) {
32     String s1 = input.nextLine();
33     String s2 = s1.replaceAll(args[2], args[3]);
34     output.println(s2);
35   }
36
37   input.close();
38   output.close();
39 }
40 }
```

8.8 (GUI) File Dialogs

Java provides the `javax.swing.JFileChooser` class for displaying a file dialog, as shown in Figure 8.19. From this dialog box, the user can choose a file.

FIGURE 8.19 `JFileChooser` can be used to display a file dialog for opening a file.

Listing 8.9 gives a program that prompts the user to choose a file and displays the contents of the file on the console.

LISTING 8.9 `ReadFileUsingJFileChooser.java`

create a **JFileChooser**
display file chooser
check status

getSelectedFile

```
1 import java.util.Scanner;
2 import javax.swing.JFileChooser;
3
4 public class ReadFileUsingJFileChooser {
5   public static void main(String[] args) throws Exception {
6     JFileChooser fileChooser = new JFileChooser();
7     if (fileChooser.showOpenDialog(null)
8         == JFileChooser.APPROVE_OPTION ) {
9       // Get the selected file
10      java.io.File file = fileChooser.getSelectedFile();
11
12      // Create a Scanner for the file
13      Scanner input = new Scanner(file);
14
15      // Read text from the file
16      while (input.hasNext()) {
17        System.out.println(input.nextLine());
18      }
19
```

```
20        // Close the file
21        input.close();
22      }
23      else {
24        System.out.println("No file selected");
25      }
26    }
27 }
```

The program creates a `JFileChooser` in line 6. The `showOpenDialog(null)` method displays a dialog box, as shown in Figure 8.19. The method returns an `int` value, either `APPROVE_OPTION` or `CANCEL_OPTION`, which indicates whether the *Open* button or the *Cancel* button was clicked.

    The `getSelectedFile()` method (line 10) returns the selected file from the file dialog box. Line 13 creates a scanner for the file. The program continuously reads the lines from the file and displays them to the console (lines 16-18).

`showOpenDialog`

`APPROVE_OPTION`

`getSelectedFile`

CHAPTER SUMMARY

- Strings are objects encapsulated in the `String` class. A string can be constructed using one of the 11 constructors or using a string literal shorthand initializer.

- A `String` object is immutable; its contents cannot be changed. To improve efficiency and save memory, the JVM stores string literals in a unique object if two literal strings have the same character sequence. This unique object is called an interned string object.

- You can get the length of a string by invoking its `length()` method, retrieve a character at the specified `index` in the string using the `charAt(index)` method, and use the `indexOf` and `lastIndexOf` methods to find a character or a substring in a string.

- You can use the `concat` method to concatenate two strings, or the plus (+) sign to concatenate two or more strings.

- You can use the `substring` method to obtain a substring from the string.

- You can use the `equals` and `compareTo` methods to compare strings. The `equals` method returns `true` if two strings are equal, and `false` if they are not equal. The `compareTo` method returns `0`, a positive integer, or a negative integer, depending on whether one string is equal to, greater than, or less than the other string.

- The `Character` class is a wrapper class for a single character. The `Character` class provides useful static methods to determine whether a character is a letter (`isLetter(char)`), a digit (`isDigit(char)`), uppercase (`isUpperCase(char)`), or lowercase (`isLowerCase(char)`).

- The `StringBuilder`/`StringBuffer` class can be used to replace the `String` class. The `String` object is immutable, but you can add, insert, or append new contents into a `StringBuilder`/`StringBuffer` object. Use `String` if the string contents do not require any change, and use `StringBuilder`/`StringBuffer` if they change.

- You can pass strings to the `main` method from the command line. Strings passed to the `main` program are stored in `args`, which is an array of strings. The first string is represented by `args[0]`, and `args.length` is the number of strings passed.

- The `File` class is used to obtain file properties and manipulate files. It does not contain the methods for reading/writing data from/to a file.

- You can use `Scanner` to read string and primitive data values from a text file and use `PrintWriter` to write data to a text file.

- The `JFileChooser` class can be used to display files graphically.

REVIEW QUESTIONS

Section 8.2 The String Class

8.1　Suppose that `s1`, `s2`, `s3`, and `s4` are four strings, given as follows:

```
String s1 = "Welcome to Java";
String s2 = s1;
String s3 = new String("Welcome to Java");
String s4 = s3.intern();
```

What are the results of the following expressions?

(1) s1 == s2	(13) s1.length()
(2) s2 == s3	(14) s1.substring(5)
(3) s1.equals(s2)	(15) s1.substring(5, 11)
(4) s2.equals(s3)	(16) s1.startsWith("Wel")
(5) s1.compareTo(s2)	(17) s1.endsWith("Java")
(6) s2.compareTo(s3)	(18) s1.toLowerCase()
(7) s1 == s4	(19) s1.toUpperCase()
(8) s1.charAt(0)	(20) " Welcome ".trim()
(9) s1.indexOf('j')	(21) s1.replace('o', 'T')
(10) s1.indexOf("to")	(22) s1.replaceAll("o", "T")
(11) s1.lastIndexOf('a')	(23) s1.replaceFirst("o", "T")
(12) s1.lastIndexOf("o", 15)	(24) s1.toCharArray()

To create a string `"Welcome to Java"`, you may use a statement like this:

```
String s = "Welcome to Java";
```

Or

```
String s = new String("Welcome to Java);
```

Which one is better? Why?

8.2　Suppose that `s1` and `s2` are two strings. Which of the following statements or expressions are incorrect?

```
String s = new String("new string");
String s3 = s1 + s2;
String s3 = s1 - s2;
s1 == s2;
s1 >= s2;
s1.compareTo(s2);
int i = s1.length();
char c = s1(0);
char c = s1.charAt(s1.length());
```

8.3 What is the printout of the following code?

```
String s1 = "Welcome to Java";
String s2 = s1.replace("o", "abc");
System.out.println(s1);
System.out.println(s2);
```

8.4 Let `s1` be " Welcome " and `s2` be " welcome ". Write the code for the following statements:

- Check whether `s1` is equal to `s2` and assign the result to a Boolean variable `isEqual`.
- Check whether `s1` is equal to `s2` ignoring case and assign the result to a Boolean variable `isEqual`.
- Compare `s1` with `s2` and assign the result to an `int` variable `x`.
- Compare `s1` with `s2` ignoring case and assign the result to an `int` variable `x`.
- Check whether `s1` has prefix `"AAA"` and assign the result to a Boolean variable `b`.
- Check whether `s1` has suffix `"AAA"` and assign the result to a Boolean variable `b`.
- Assign the length of `s1` to an `int` variable `x`.
- Assign the first character of `s1` to a `char` variable `x`.
- Create a new string `s3` that combines `s1` with `s2`.
- Create a substring of `s1` starting from index `1`.
- Create a substring of `s1` from index `1` to index `4`.
- Create a new string `s3` that converts `s1` to lowercase.
- Create a new string `s3` that converts `s1` to uppercase.
- Create a new string `s3` that trims blank spaces on both ends of `s1`.
- Replace all occurrences of character `e` with `E` in `s1` and assign the new string to `s3`.
- Split `"Welcome to Java and HTML"` into an array `tokens` delimited by a space.
- Assign the index of the first occurrence of character `e` in `s1` to an `int` variable `x`.
- Assign the index of the last occurrence of string `abc` in `s1` to an `int` variable `x`.

8.5 Does any method in the `String` class change the contents of the string?

8.6 Suppose string `s` is created using `new String()`; what is `s.length()`?

8.7 How do you convert a `char`, an array of characters, or a number to a string?

8.8 Why does the following code cause a `NullPointerException`?

```
 1 public class Test {
 2   private String text;
 3
 4   public Test(String s) {
 5     String text = s;
 6   }
 7
 8   public static void main(String[] args) {
 9     Test test = new Test("ABC");
10     System.out.println(test.text.toLowerCase());
11   }
12 }
```

8.9 What is wrong in the following program?

```
1 public class Test  {
2   String text;
3
4   public void Test(String s) {
5     this.text  = s;
6   }
7
8   public static void main(String[] args) {
9     Test test = new Test("ABC");
10    System.out.println(test);
11  }
12 }
```

Section 8.3 The **Character** Class

8.10 How do you determine whether a character is in lowercase or uppercase?

8.11 How do you determine whether a character is alphanumeric?

Section 8.4 The **StringBuilder/StringBuffer** Class

8.12 What is the difference between **StringBuilder** and **StringBuffer**?

8.13 How do you create a string builder for a string? How do you get the string from a string builder?

8.14 Write three statements to reverse a string **s** using the **reverse** method in the **StringBuilder** class.

8.15 Write a statement to delete a substring from a string **s** of **20** characters, starting at index **4** and ending with index **10**. Use the **delete** method in the **StringBuilder** class.

8.16 What is the internal structure of a string and a string builder?

8.17 Suppose that **s1** and **s2** are given as follows:

```
StringBuilder s1 = new StringBuilder("Java");
StringBuilder s2 = new StringBuilder("HTML");
```

Show the value of **s2** after each of the following statement. Assume that the statements are independent.

```
(1) s1.append(" is fun");    (7) s1.deleteCharAt(3);
(2) s1.append(s2);           (8) s1.delete(1, 3);
(3) s1.insert(2, "is fun");  (9) s1.reverse();
(4) s1.insert(1, s2);        (10) s1.replace(1, 3, "Computer");
(5) s1.charAt(2);            (11) s1.substring(1, 3);
(6) s1.length();             (12) s1.substring(2);
```

8.18 Show the output of the following program:

```
public class Test {
  public static void main(String[] args) {
    String s = "Java";
    StringBuilder builder = new StringBuilder(s);
    change(s, builder);

    System.out.println(s);
```

```
      System.out.println(builder);
    }

    private static void change(String s, StringBuilder builder) {
      s = s + " and HTML";
      builder.append(" and HTML");
    }
  }
```

Section 8.5 Command-Line Arguments

8.19 This book declares the `main` method as

```
public static void main(String[] args)
```

Can it be replaced by one of the following lines?

```
public static void main(String args[])
public static void main(String[] x)
public static void main(String x[])
static void main(String x[])
```

8.20 Show the output of the following program when invoked using

1. **java Test I have a dream**
2. **java Test "1 2 3"**
3. **java Test**
4. **java Test "*"**
5. **java Test ***

```
public class Test {
  public static void main(String[] args) {
    System.out.println("Number of strings is " + args.length);
    for (int i = 0; i < args.length; i++)
      System.out.println(args[i]);
  }
}
```

Section 8.6 The File Class

8.21 What is wrong about creating a `File` object using the following statement?

```
new File("c:\book\test.dat");
```

8.22 How do you check whether a file already exists? How do you delete a file? How do you rename a file? Can you find the file size (the number of bytes) using the `File` class?

8.23 Can you use the `File` class for I/O? Does creating a `File` object create a file on the disk?

Section 8.7 File Input and Output

8.24 How do you create a `PrintWriter` to write data to a file? What is the reason to declare `throws Exception` in the main method in Listing 8.6, WriteData.java. What would happen if the `close()` method were not invoked in Listing 8.6.

8.25 Show the contents of the file temp.txt after the following program is executed.

```
public class Test {
  public static void main(String[] args) throws Exception {
```

```
          java.io.PrintWriter output = new
            java.io.PrintWriter("temp.txt");
          output.printf("amount is %f %e\r\n", 32.32, 32.32);
          output.printf("amount is %5.4f %5.4e\r\n", 32.32, 32.32);
          output.printf("%6b\r\n", (1 > 2));
          output.printf("%6s\r\n", "Java");
          output.close();
      }
  }
```

8.26 How do you create a Scanner to read data from a file? What is the reason to declare throws Exception in the main method in Listing 8.7, ReadData.java? What would happen if the close() method were not invoked in Listing 8.7.

8.27 What will happen if you attempt to create a Scanner for a nonexistent file? What will happen if you attempt to create a PrintWriter for an existing file?

8.28 Is the line separator the same on all platforms? What is the line separator on Windows?

8.29 Suppose you enter 45 57.8 789, then press the ENTER key. Show the contents of the variables after the following code is executed.

```
Scanner input = new Scanner(System.in);
int intValue = input.nextInt();
double doubleValue = input.nextDouble();
String line = input.nextLine();
```

8.30 Suppose you enter 45, the ENTER key, 57.8, the ENTER key, 789, the ENTER key. Show the contents of the variables after the following code is executed.

```
Scanner input = new Scanner(System.in);
int intValue = input.nextInt();
double doubleValue = input.nextDouble();
String line = input.nextLine();
```

PROGRAMMING EXERCISES

Sections 8.2–8.3

8.1* (*Checking SSN*) Write a program that prompts the user to enter a social security number in the format DDD-DD-DDDD, where D is a digit. The program displays "valid SSN" for a correct social security number and "invalid SSN" otherwise.

8.2** (*Checking substrings*) You can check whether a string is a substring of another string by using the indexOf method in the String class. Write your own method for this function. Write a program that prompts the user to enter two strings, and check whether the first string is a substring of the second.

8.3** (*Checking password*) Some Web sites impose certain rules for passwords. Write a method that checks whether a string is a valid password. Suppose the password rule is as follows:

- A password must have at least eight characters.
- A password consists of only letters and digits.
- A password must contain at least two digits.

Write a test program that prompts the user to enter a password and displays "Valid Password" if the rule is followed or "Invalid Password" otherwise.

8.4 (*Occurrences of a specified character*) Write a method that finds the number of occurrences of a specified character in the string using the following header:

```
public static int count(String str, char a)
```

For example, `count("Welcome", 'e')` returns `2`.

8.5** (*Occurrences of each digit in a string*) Write a method that counts the occurrences of each digit in a string using the following header:

```
public static int[] count(String s)
```

The method counts how many times a digit appears in the string. The return value is an array of ten elements, each of which holds the count for a digit. For example, after executing `int[] counts = count("12203AB3")`, `counts[0]` is `1`, `counts[1]` is `1`, `counts[2]` is `2`, `counts[3]` is `2`.

Write a `main` method to display the count for `"SSN is 343 32 4545 and ID is 434 34 4323"`.

8.6* (*Counting the letters in a string*) Write a method that counts the number of letters in the string using the following header:

```
public static int countLetters(String s)
```

Write a `main` method to invoke `countLetters("Java in 2008")` and display its return value.

8.7* (*Hex to decimal*) Write a method that parses a hex number as a string into a decimal integer. The method header is as follows:

```
public static int parseHex(String hexString)
```

For example, `hexString` A5 is 165 ($10 \times 16 + 5 = 165$) and FAA is 4010 ($15 \times 16^2 + 10 \times 16 + 10 = 4010$). So `parseHex("A5")` returns `165`, and `parseHex("FAA")` returns `4010`. Use hex strings ABC and 10A to test the method. Note that `Integer.parseInt("FAA", 16)` parses a hex string to a decimal value. Do not use this method in this exercise.

8.8* (*Binary to decimal*) Write a method that parses a binary number as a string into a decimal integer. The method header is as follows:

```
public static int parseBinary(String binaryString)
```

For example, `binaryString` 10001 is 17 ($1 \times 2^4 + 0 \times 2^3 + 0 \times 2^2 + 0 \times 2 + 1 = 17$). So, `parseBinary("10001")` returns `17`. Use binary string 11111111 to test the method. Note that `Integer.parseInt("10001", 2)` parses a binary string to a decimal value. Do not use this method in this exercise.

Section 8.4 The `StringBuilder/StringBuffer` Class

8.9** (*Decimal to hex*) Write a method that parses a decimal number into a hex number as a string. The method header is as follows:

```
public static String convertDecimalToHex(int value)
```

See §1.5, "Number Systems," for converting a decimal into a hex. Use decimal 298 and 9123 to test the method.

8.10** (*Decimal to binary*) Write a method that parses a decimal number into a binary number as a string. The method header is as follows:

```
public static String convertDecimalToBinary(int value)
```

Video Note
Convert a decimal number into a binary number

See §1.5, "Number Systems," for converting a decimal into a binary. Use decimal 298 and 9123 to test the method.

8.11** (*Sorting characters in a string*) Write a method that returns a sorted string using the following header:

```java
public static String sort(String s)
```

For example, sort("acb") returns abc.

8.12** (*Anagrams*) Write a method that checks whether two words are anagrams. Two words are anagrams if they contain the same letters in any order. For example, "silent" and "listen" are anagrams. The header of the method is as follows:

```java
public static boolean isAnagram(String s1, String s2)
```

Write a main method to invoke isAnagram("silent", "listen"), isAnagram("garden", "ranged"), and isAnagram("split", "lisp").

Section 8.5 Command-Line Arguments

8.13* (*Passing a string to check palindromes*) Rewrite Listing 8.1 by passing the string as a command-line argument.

8.14* (*Summing integers*) Write two programs. The first program passes an unspecified number of integers as separate strings to the main method and displays their total. The second program passes an unspecified number of integers delimited by one space in a string to the main method and displays their total. Name the two programs Exercise8_14a and Exercise8_14b, as shown in Figure 8.20.

FIGURE 8.20 The program adds all the numbers passed from the command line.

8.15* (*Finding the number of uppercase letters in a string*) Write a program that passes a string to the main method and displays the number of uppercase letters in a string.

Sections 8.7–8.8

8.16** (*Reformatting Java source code*) Write a program that converts the Java source code from the next-line brace style to the end-of-line brace style. For example, the following Java source in (a) uses the next-line brace style. Your program converts it to the end-of-line brace style in (b).

```java
public class Test
{
  public static void main(String[] args)
  {
    // Some statements
  }
}
```

(a) Next-line brace style

```java
public class Test {
  public static void main(String[] args) {
    // Some statements
  }
}
```

(b) End-of-line brace style

Your program can be invoked from the command line with the Java source-code file as the argument. It converts the Java source code to a new format. For example, the following command converts the Java source code file **Test.java** to the end-of-line brace style.

```
java Exercise8_16 Test.java
```

8.17* (*Counting characters, words, and lines in a file*) Write a program that will count the number of characters (excluding control characters '\r' and '\n'), words, and lines, in a file. Words are separated by spaces, tabs, carriage return, or line-feed characters. The file name should be passed as a command-line argument, as shown in Figure 8.21.

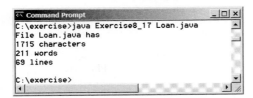

FIGURE 8.21   The program displays the number of characters, words, and lines in the given file.

8.18* (*Processing scores in a text file*) Suppose that a text file **Exercise8_18.txt** contains an unspecified number of scores. Write a program that reads the scores from the file and displays their total and average. Scores are separated by blanks.

8.19* (*Writing/Reading data*) Write a program to create a file named **Exercise8_19.txt** if it does not exist. Write 100 integers created randomly into the file using text I/O. Integers are separated by spaces in the file. Read the data back from the file and display the sorted data.

8.20** (*Replacing text*) Listing 8.8, ReplaceText.java, gives a program that replaces text in a source file and saves the change into a new file. Revise the program to save the change into the original file. For example, invoking

```
java Exercise8_20 file oldString newString
```

replaces oldString in the source file with newString.

8.21** (*Removing text*) Write a program that removes all the occurrences of a specified string from a text file. For example, invoking

```
java Exercise8_21 John filename
```

removes string John from the specified file.

Comprehensive

8.22** (*Guessing the capitals*) Write a program that repeatedly prompts the user to enter a capital for a state, as shown in Figure 8.22(a). Upon receiving the user input, the program reports whether the answer is correct, as shown in Figure 8.22(b). Assume that 50 states and their capitals are stored in a two-dimensional array, as

FIGURE 8.22 The program prompts the user to enter the capital in (a) and reports the correctness of the answer.

shown in Figure 8.23. The program prompts the user to answer all ten states' capitals and displays the total correct count.

```
Alabama      Montgomery
Alaska       Juneau
Arizona      Phoenix
...          ...
...          ...
```

FIGURE 8.23 A two-dimensional array stores states and their capitals.

8.23**(*Implementing the String class*) The String class is provided in the Java library. Provide your own implementation for the following methods (name the new class MyString1):

```
public MyString1(char[] chars);
public char charAt(int index);
public int length();
public MyString1 substring(int begin, int end);
public char[] toChars();
public MyString1 toLowerCase();
public boolean equals(MyString1 s);
public static MyString1 valueOf(int i);
```

8.24**(*Implementing the String class*) The String class is provided in the Java library. Provide your own implementation for the following methods (name the new class MyString2):

```
public MyString2(char[] chars);
public int compare(String s);
public MyString2 substring(int begin);
public MyString2 toUpperCase();
public char[] toChars();
public static MyString2 valueOf(boolean b);
```

8.25 (*Implementing the Character class*) The Character class is provided in the Java library. Provide your own implementation for this class. Name the new class MyCharacter.

8.26**(*Implementing the StringBuilder class*) The `StringBuilder` class is provided in the Java library. Provide your own implementation for the following methods (name the new class `MyStringBuilder1`):

```java
public MyStringBuilder1();
public MyStringBuilder1(char[] chars);
public MyStringBuilder1(String s);
public MyStringBuilder1 append(MyStringBuilder1 s);
public MyStringBuilder1 append(int i);
public int length();
public char charAt(int index);
public MyStringBuilder1 toLowerCase();
public MyStringBuilder1 substring(int begin, int end);
public String toString();
```

8.27**(*Implementing the StringBuilder class*) The `StringBuilder` class is provided in the Java library. Provide your own implementation for the following methods (name the new class `MyStringBuilder2`):

```java
public MyStringBuilder2();
public MyStringBuilder2(char[] chars);
public MyStringBuilder2(String s);
public MyStringBuilder2 insert(int offset, MyStringBuilder2 s);
public MyStringBuilder2 reverse();
public MyStringBuilder2 substring(int begin);
public MyStringBuilder2 toUpperCase();
```

8.28* (*Common prefix*) Write a method that returns the common prefix of two strings. For example, the common prefix of `"distance"` and `"disinfection"` is `"dis"`. The header of the method is as follows:

```java
public static String prefix(String s1, String s2)
```

If the two strings have no common prefix, the method returns an empty string.
 Write a `main` method that prompts the user to enter two strings and display their common prefix.

8.29**(*New string split method*) The `split` method in the `String` class returns an array of strings consisting of the substrings split by the delimiters. However, the delimiters are not returned. Implement the following new method that returns an array of strings consisting of the substrings split by the matches, including the matches.

```java
public static String[] split(String s, String regex)
```

For example, `split("ab#12#453", "#")` returns `ab`, `#`, `12`, `#`, `453` in an array of `String`, and `split("a?b?gf#e", "[?#]")` returns `a`, `b`, `?`, `b`, `gf`, `#`, and `e` in an array of `String`.

8.30**(*Financial: credit card number validation*) Rewrite Exercise 5.31 using a string input for credit card number. Redesign the program using the following method:

```java
/** Get the result from Step 2 */
public static int sumOfEvenPlace(String cardNumber)
```

```
/** Return this number if it is a single digit, otherwise,
    return the sum of the two digits */
public static int getDigit(int number)

/** Return sum of odd place digits in number */
public static int sumOfOddPlace(String cardNumber)
```

8.31** (*Checking ISBN*) Use string operations to simplify Exercise 3.19. Enter the first 9-digit of an ISBN number as a string.

CHAPTER 9

THINKING IN OBJECTS

Objectives

- To create immutable objects from immutable classes to protect the contents of objects (§9.2).

- To determine the scope of variables in the context of a class (§9.3).

- To use the keyword **this** to refer to the calling object itself (§9.4).

- To apply class abstraction to develop software (§9.5).

- To explore the differences between the procedural paradigm and object-oriented paradigm (§9.6).

- To design programs using the object-oriented paradigm (§§9.7–9.9).

9.1 Introduction

The preceding two chapters introduced the concept of objects and classes. You learned how to program using objects from several classes in the Java API (e.g., **Date**, **Random**, **JFrame**, **String**, **StringBuilder**, **File**, **Scanner**, **PrintWriter**). This chapter focuses on class design. Several examples will illustrate the advantages of object-oriented programming. To begin, we will introduce some language features supporting these examples.

9.2 Immutable Objects and Classes

immutable object
immutable class

Normally, you create an object and allow its contents to be changed later. Occasionally, it is desirable to create an object whose contents cannot be changed once the object is created. We call such an object an *immutable object* and its class an *immutable class*. The **String** class, for example, is immutable. If you deleted the **set** method in the **Circle** class in Listing 7.7, the class would be immutable because radius is private and cannot be changed without a **set** method.

A class with all private data fields and no mutators is not necessarily immutable. An example is the class **Student**.

Student class

```
 1  public class Student {
 2    private int id;
 3    private String name;
 4    private java.util.Date dateCreated;
 5
 6    public Student(int ssn, String newName) {
 7      id = ssn;
 8      name = newName;
 9      dateCreated = new java.util.Date();
10    }
11
12    public int getId() {
13      return id;
14    }
15
16    public String getName() {
17      return name;
18    }
19
20    public java.util.Date getDateCreated() {
21      return dateCreated;
22    }
23  }
```

As shown in the following code, the data field **dateCreated** is returned using the **getDateCreated()** method. This is a reference to a **Date** object. Through this reference, the content for **dateCreated** can be changed.

```
public class Test {
  public static void main(String[] args) {
    Student student = new Student(111223333, "John");
    java.util.Date dateCreated = student.getDateCreated();
    dateCreated.setTime(200000); // Now dateCreated field is changed!
  }
}
```

For a class to be immutable, it must meet the following requirements:

- Declare all data fields private;

- Provide no mutator methods;

- Provide no accessor method that returns a reference to a data field that is mutable.

9.3 The Scope of Variables

Chapter 5, "Methods," discussed local variables and their scope rules. Local variables are declared and used inside a method locally. This section discusses the scope rules of all the variables in the context of a class.

Instance and static variables in a class are referred to as the *class's variables* or *data fields*. A variable defined inside a method is referred to as a local variable. The scope of a class's variables is the entire class, regardless of where the variables are declared. A class's variables and methods can be declared in any order in the class, as shown in Figure 9.1(a). The exception is when a data field is initialized based on a reference to another data field. In such cases, the other data field must be declared first, as shown in Figure 9.1(b). For consistency, this book declares data fields at the beginning of the class.

```
public class Circle {
  public double findArea() {
    return radius * radius * Math.PI;
  }
  private double radius = 1;
}
```

```
public class Foo {
  private int i;
  private int j = i + 1;
}
```

(a) Variable `radius` and method `findArea()` can be declared in any order.

(b) i has to be declared before j because j's initial value is dependent on i.

FIGURE 9.1 Members of a class can be declared in any order, with one exception.

You can declare a class's variable only once, but you can declare the same variable name in a method many times in different nonnesting blocks.

If a local variable has the same name as a class's variable, the local variable takes precedence and the class's variable with the same name is *hidden*. For example, in the following program, x is defined as an instance variable and as a local variable in the method.

```
class Foo {
  int x = 0; // Instance variable
  int y = 0;

  Foo() {
  }

  void p() {
    int x = 1; // Local variable
    System.out.println("x = " + x);
    System.out.println("y = " + y);
  }
}
```

What is the printout for `f.p()`, where f is an instance of Foo? The printout for `f.p()` is 1 for x and 0 for y. Here is why:

- x is declared as a data field with the initial value of 0 in the class, but is also defined in the method p() with an initial value of 1. The latter x is referenced in the `System.out.println` statement.

- y is declared outside the method p(), but is accessible inside it.

Tip
To avoid confusion and mistakes, do not use the names of instance or static variables as local variable names, except for method parameters.

9.4 The **this** Reference

The **this** keyword is the name of a reference that refers to a calling object itself. One common use of the **this** keyword is to reference a class's *hidden data fields*. For example, a property name is often used as the parameter name in a **set** method for the property. In this case, you need to reference the hidden property name in the method in order to set a new value to it. A hidden static variable can be accessed simply by using the `ClassName.StaticVariable` reference. A hidden instance variable can be accessed by using the keyword **this**, as shown in Figure 9.2(a).

hidden data fields

```
public class Foo {
  int i = 5;
  static double k = 0;

  void setI(int i) {
    this.i = i;
  }

  static void setK(double k) {
    Foo.k = k;
  }
}
```

(a)

```
Suppose that f1 and f2 are two objects of Foo.

Invoking f1.setI(10) is to execute
    this.i = 10, where this refers f1

Invoking f2.setI(45) is to execute
    this.i = 45, where this refers f2
```

(b)

FIGURE 9.2 The keyword **this** refers to the calling object that invokes the method.

The line `this.i = i` means "assign the value of parameter `i` to the data field `i` of the calling object." The keyword **this** refers to the object that invokes the instance method `setI`, as shown in Figure 9.2(b). The line `Foo.k = k` means that the value in parameter `k` is assigned to the static data field `k` of the class, which is shared by all the objects of the class.

call another constructor

Another common use of the **this** keyword is to enable a constructor to invoke another constructor of the same class. For example, you can redefine the `Circle` class as follows:

```
public class Circle {
  private double radius;

  public Circle(double radius) {
    this.radius = radius;
  }

  public Circle() {
    this(1.0);
  }

  public double getArea() {
    return this.radius * this.radius * Math.PI;
  }
}
```

`this` must be explicitly used to reference the data field radius of the object being constructed

`this` is used to invoke another constructor

Every instance variable belongs to an instance represented by `this`, which is normally omitted

The line `this(1.0)` in the second constructor invokes the first constructor with a `double` value argument.

Tip

If a class has multiple constructors, it is better to implement them using `this(arg-list)` as much as possible. In general, a constructor with no or fewer arguments can invoke the constructor with more arguments using `this(arg-list)`. This often simplifies coding and makes the class easier to read and to maintain.

Note

Java requires that the `this(arg-list)` statement appear first in the constructor before any other statements.

9.5 Class Abstraction and Encapsulation

In Chapter 5, "Methods," you learned about method abstraction and used it in program development. Java provides many levels of abstraction. *Class abstraction* is the separation of class implementation from the use of a class. The creator of a class describes it and lets the user know how it can be used. The collection of methods and fields that are accessible from outside the class, together with the description of how these members are expected to behave, serves as the *class's contract*. As shown in Figure 9.3, the user of the class does not need to know how the class is implemented. The details of implementation are encapsulated and hidden from the user. This is known as *class encapsulation*. For example, you can create a `Circle` object and find the area of the circle without knowing how the area is computed.

class abstraction

class encapsulation

FIGURE 9.3 Class abstraction separates class implementation from the use of the class.

Class abstraction and encapsulation are two sides of the same coin. There are many real-life examples that illustrate the concept of class abstraction. Consider building a computer system, for instance. Your personal computer is made up of many components, such as a CPU, CD-ROM, floppy disk, motherboard, fan, and so on. Each component can be viewed as an object that has properties and methods. To get the components to work together, all you need to know is how each component is used and how it interacts with the others. You don't need to know how they work internally. The internal implementation is encapsulated and hidden from you. You can build a computer without knowing how a component is implemented.

The computer-system analogy precisely mirrors the object-oriented approach. Each component can be viewed as an object of the class for the component. For example, you might have a class that models all kinds of fans for use in a computer, with properties like fan size and speed, and methods like start, stop, and so on. A specific fan is an instance of this class with specific property values.

As another example, consider getting a loan. A specific loan can be viewed as an object of a `Loan` class. Interest rate, loan amount, and loan period are its data properties, and computing monthly payment and total payment are its methods. When you buy a car, a loan object is created by instantiating the class with your loan interest rate, loan amount, and loan period. You can then use the methods to find the monthly payment and total payment of your loan. As a user of the `Loan` class, you don't need to know how these methods are implemented.

Listing 2.7, ComputeLoan.java, presented a program for computing loan payments. The program cannot be reused in other programs. One way to fix this problem is to define static

Video Note
Loan class

methods for computing monthly payment and total payment. However, this solution has limitations. Suppose you wish to associate a date with the loan. The ideal way is to create an object that ties the properties for loan information and date together. Figure 9.4 shows the UML class diagram for the Loan class.

Loan
-annualInterestRate: double
-numberOfYears: int
-loanAmount: double
-loanDate: java.util.Date
+Loan()
+Loan(annualInterestRate: double, numberOfYears: int,loanAmount: double)
+getAnnualInterestRate(): double
+getNumberOfYears(): int
+getLoanAmount(): double
+getLoanDate(): java.util.Date
+setAnnualInterestRate(annualInterestRate: double): void
+setNumberOfYears(numberOfYears: int): void
+setLoanAmount(loanAmount: double): void
+getMonthlyPayment(): double
+getTotalPayment(): double

The annual interest rate of the loan (default: 2.5).
The number of years for the loan (default: 1).
The loan amount (default: 1000).
The date this loan was created.

Constructs a default Loan object.
Constructs a loan with specified interest rate, years, and loan amount.

Returns the annual interest rate of this loan.
Returns the number of the years of this loan.
Returns the amount of this loan.
Returns the date of the creation of this loan.
Sets a new annual interest rate to this loan.

Sets a new number of years to this loan.

Sets a new amount for this loan.

Returns the monthly payment of this loan.
Returns the total payment of this loan.

FIGURE 9.4 The Loan class models the properties and behaviors of loans.

The UML diagram in Figure 9.4 serves as the contract for the Loan class. Throughout the book, you will play the role of both class user and class writer. The user can use the class without knowing how the class is implemented. Assume that the Loan class is available. Let us begin by writing a test program that uses the Loan class in Listing 9.1.

LISTING 9.1 TestLoanClass.java

```java
1  import java.util.Scanner;
2
3  public class TestLoanClass {
4    /** Main method */
5    public static void main(String[] args) {
6      // Create a Scanner
7      Scanner input = new Scanner(System.in);
8
9      // Enter yearly interest rate
10     System.out.print(
11       "Enter yearly interest rate, for example, 8.25: ");
12     double annualInterestRate = input.nextDouble();
13
14     // Enter number of years
15     System.out.print("Enter number of years as an integer: ");
16     int numberOfYears = input.nextInt();
17
18     // Enter loan amount
19     System.out.print("Enter loan amount, for example, 120000.95: ");
```

```
20      double loanAmount =  input.nextDouble();
21
22      // Create Loan object
23      Loan loan =
24        new Loan(annualInterestRate, numberOfYears, loanAmount);      create Loan object
25
26      // Format to keep two digits after the decimal point
27      double monthlyPayment =
28        (int)(loan.getMonthlyPayment () * 100) / 100.0;               invoke instance method
29      double totalPayment =
30        (int)(loan.getTotalPayment () * 100) / 100.0;                 invoke instance method
31
32      // Display results
33      System.out.println("The loan was created on " +
34        loan.getLoanDate().toString() + "\nThe monthly payment is " +
35        monthlyPayment + "\nThe total payment is " + totalPayment);
36  }
37 }
```

```
Enter yearly interest rate, for example, 8.25: 2.5  ↵Enter
Enter number of years as an integer: 5  ↵Enter
Enter loan amount, for example, 120000.95: 1000  ↵Enter
The loan was created on Sat Jun 10 21:12:50 EDT 2006
The monthly payment is 17.74
The total payment is 1064.84
```

The `main` method reads interest rate, payment period (in years), and loan amount; creates a `Loan` object; and then obtains the monthly payment (lines 27–28) and total payment (lines 29–30) using the instance methods in the `Loan` class.

The `Loan` class can be implemented as in Listing 9.2.

LISTING 9.2 Loan.java

```
 1 public class Loan {
 2   private double annualInterestRate;
 3   private int numberOfYears;
 4   private double loanAmount;
 5   private java.util.Date loanDate;
 6
 7   /** Default constructor */
 8   public Loan() {                                                    no-arg constructor
 9     this(2.5, 1, 1000);
10   }
11
12   /** Construct a loan with specified annual interest rate,
13       number of years and loan amount */
14   public Loan(double annualInterestRate, int numberOfYears,         constructor
15       double loanAmount) {
16     this.annualInterestRate = annualInterestRate;
17     this.numberOfYears = numberOfYears;
18     this.loanAmount = loanAmount;
19     loanDate = new java.util.Date();
20   }
21
22   /** Return annualInterestRate */
23   public double getAnnualInterestRate() {
```

```
24       return annualInterestRate;
25     }
26
27     /** Set a new annualInterestRate */
28     public void setAnnualInterestRate(double annualInterestRate) {
29       this.annualInterestRate = annualInterestRate;
30     }
31
32     /** Return numberOfYears */
33     public int getNumberOfYears() {
34       return numberOfYears;
35     }
36
37     /** Set a new numberOfYears */
38     public void setNumberOfYears(int numberOfYears) {
39       this.numberOfYears = numberOfYears;
40     }
41
42     /** Return loanAmount */
43     public double getLoanAmount() {
44       return loanAmount;
45     }
46
47     /** Set a newloanAmount */
48     public void setLoanAmount(double loanAmount) {
49       this.loanAmount = loanAmount;
50     }
51
52     /** Find monthly payment */
53     public double getMonthlyPayment() {
54       double monthlyInterestRate = annualInterestRate / 1200;
55       double monthlyPayment = loanAmount * monthlyInterestRate / (1 -
56         (Math.pow(1 / (1 + monthlyInterestRate), numberOfYears * 12)));
57       return monthlyPayment;
58     }
59
60     /** Find total payment */
61     public double getTotalPayment() {
62       double totalPayment = getMonthlyPayment() * numberOfYears * 12;
63       return totalPayment;
64     }
65
66     /** Return loan date */
67     public java.util.Date getLoanDate() {
68       return loanDate;
69     }
70 }
```

From a class developer's perspective, a class is designed for use by many different customers. In order to be useful in a wide range of applications, a class should provide a variety of ways for customization through constructors, properties, and methods.

The Loan class contains two constructors, four get methods, three set methods, and the methods for finding monthly payment and total payment. You can construct a Loan object by using the no-arg constructor or the one with three parameters: annual interest rate, number of years, and loan amount. When a loan object is created, its date is stored in the loanDate field. The getLoanDate method returns the date. The three get methods, getAnnualInterest, getNumberOfYears, and getLoanAmount, return annual interest rate, payment years, and loan amount, respectively. All the data properties and methods in this class are tied to a specific instance of the Loan class. Therefore, they are instance variables or methods.

Important Pedagogical TIP

The UML diagram for the Loan class is shown in Figure 9.4. Students should begin by writing a test program that uses the Loan class even though they don't know how the Loan class is implemented. This has three benefits:

- It demonstrates that developing a class and using a class are two separate tasks.
- It enables you to skip the complex implementation of certain classes without interrupting the sequence of the book.
- It is easier to learn how to implement a class if you are familiar with the class through using it.

For all the examples from now on, you may first create an object from the class and try to use its methods and then turn your attention to its implementation.

9.6 Object-Oriented Thinking

Chapters 1–6 introduced fundamental programming techniques for problem solving using loops, methods, and arrays. The study of these techniques lays a solid foundation for object-oriented programming. Classes provide more flexibility and modularity for building reusable software. This section improves the solution for a problem introduced in Chapter 3 using the object-oriented approach. From the improvements, you will gain insight on the differences between the procedural programming and object-oriented programming and see the benefits of developing reusable code using objects and classes.

Listing 3.6, ComputeBMI.java, presented a program for computing body mass index. The program cannot be reused in other programs. To make the code reusable, define a static method to compute body mass index as follows:

```
public static double getBMI(double weight, double height)
```

This method is useful for computing body mass index for a specified weight and height. However, it has limitations. Suppose you need to associate the weight and height with a person's name and birth date. You may declare separate variables to store these values. But these values are not tightly coupled. The ideal way to couple them is to create an object that contains them. Since these values are tied to individual objects, they should be stored in instance data fields. You can declare a class named BMI, as shown in Figure 9.5.

Video Note
BMI class

The get methods for these data fields are provided in the class, but omitted in the UML diagram for brevity.

BMI	
-name: String	The name of the person.
-age: int	The age of the person.
-weight: double	The weight of the person in pounds.
-height: double	The height of the person in inches.
+BMI(name: String, age: int, weight: double, height: double)	Creates a BMI object with the specified name, age, weight, and height.
+BMI(name: String, weight: double, height: double)	Creates a BMI object with the specified name, weight, height, and a default age 20.
+getBMI(): double	Returns the BMI
+getStatus(): String	Returns the BMI status (e.g., normal, overweight, etc.)

FIGURE 9.5 The BMI class encapsulates BMI information.

Assume that the BMI class is available. Listing 9.3 gives a test program that uses this class.

LISTING 9.3 UseBMIClass.java

```
1 public class UseBMIClass {
2   public static void main(String[] args) {
3     BMI bmi1 = new BMI("John Doe", 18, 145, 70);
4     System.out.println("The BMI for " + bmi1.getName() + " is "
5       + bmi1.getBMI() + " " + bmi1.getStatus());
6
7     BMI bmi2 = new BMI("Peter King", 215, 70);
8     System.out.println("The BMI for " + bmi2.getName() + " is "
9       + bmi2.getBMI() + " " + bmi2.getStatus());
10  }
11 }
```

create object (line 3)
invoke instance method (line 4)

create object (line 7)
invoke instance method (line 8)

```
The BMI for John Doe is 20.81 normal weight
The BMI for Peter King is 30.85 seriously overweight
```

Line 3 creates an object bmi1 for John Doe and line 7 creates an object bmi2 for Peter King. You can use the instance methods getName(), getBMI(), and getStatus() to return the BMI information in a BMI object.

The BMI class can be implemented as in Listing 9.4.

LISTING 9.4 BMI.java

```
1 public class BMI {
2   private String name;
3   private int age;
4   private double weight; // in pounds
5   private double height; // in inches
6   public final double KILOGRAMS_PER_POUND = 0.45359237;
7   public final double METERS_PER_INCH = 0.0254;
8
9   public BMI(String name, int age, double weight, double height) {
10    this.name = name;
11    this.age = age;
12    this.weight = weight;
13    this.height = height;
14  }
15
16  public BMI(String name, double weight, double height) {
17    this(name, 20, weight, height);
18  }
19
20  public double getBMI() {
21    double bmi = weight * KILOGRAMS_PER_POUND /
22      ((height * METERS_PER_INCH) * (height * METERS_PER_INCH));
23    return Math.round(bmi * 100) / 100.0;
24  }
25
26  public String getStatus() {
27    double bmi = getBMI();
28    if (bmi < 16)
```

constructor (line 9)

constructor (line 16)

getBMI (line 20)

getStatus (line 26)

```
29        return "seriously underweight";
30      else if (bmi < 18)
31        return "underweight";
32      else if (bmi < 24)
33        return "normal weight";
34      else if (bmi < 29)
35        return "overweight";
36      else if (bmi < 35)
37        return "seriously overweight";
38      else
39        return "gravely overweight";
40    }
41
42    public String getName() {
43      return name;
44    }
45
46    public int getAge() {
47      return age;
48    }
49
50    public double getWeight() {
51      return weight;
52    }
53
54    public double getHeight() {
55      return height;
56    }
57 }
```

The mathematic formula for computing the BMI using weight and height is given in §3.3.6. The instance method **getBMI()** returns the BMI. Since the weight and height are instance data fields in the object, the **getBMI()** method can use these properties to compute the BMI for the object.

The instance method **getStatus()** returns a string that interprets the BMI. The interpretation is also given in §3.3.6.

This example demonstrates the advantages of using the object-oriented paradigm over the procedural paradigm. The procedural paradigm focuses on designing methods. The object-oriented paradigm couples data and methods together into objects. Software design using the object-oriented paradigm focuses on objects and operations on objects. The object-oriented approach combines the power of the procedural paradigm with an added dimension that integrates data with operations into objects.

Procedural vs. Object-Oriented Paradigms

In procedural programming, data and operations on the data are separate, and this methodology requires sending data to methods. Object-oriented programming places data and the operations that pertain to them within a single entity called an *object*; this approach solves many of the problems inherent in procedural programming. The object-oriented programming approach organizes programs in a way that mirrors the real world, in which all objects are associated with both attributes and activities. Using objects improves software reusability and makes programs easier to develop and easier to maintain. Programming in Java involves thinking in terms of objects; a Java program can be viewed as a collection of cooperating objects.

9.7 Designing the **Course** Class

The philosophy of this book is *teaching by example and learning by doing*. To this extent, the book provides a wide variety of examples to demonstrate object-oriented programming. The following three sections offer additional examples on designing classes.

Suppose you need to process course information. Each course has a name and students who take the course. You should be able to add/drop a student to/from the course. You can use a class to model the courses, as shown in Figure 9.6.

Course	
-courseName: String	The name of the course.
-students: String[]	An array to store the students for the course.
-numberOfStudents: int	The number of students (default: 0).
+Course(courseName: String)	Creates a course with the specified name.
+getCourseName(): String	Returns the course name.
+addStudent(student: String): void	Adds a new student to the course.
+addStudent(student: String): void	Drops a student from the course.
+getStudents(): String[]	Returns the students for the course.
+getNumberOfStudents(): int	Returns the number of students for the course.

FIGURE 9.6   The Course class models the courses.

A Course object can be created using the constructor Course(String name) by passing a course name. You can add students to the course using the addStudent(String student) method, drop a student from the course using the dropStudent (String student) method, and return all the students for the course using the getStudents() method. Suppose the class is available; Listing 9.5 gives a test class that creates two courses and adds students to them.

LISTING 9.5   TestCourse.java

create a course

add a student

number of students
return students

```java
 1 public class TestCourse {
 2   public static void main(String[] args) {
 3     Course course1 = new Course("Data Structures");
 4     Course course2 = new Course("Database Systems");
 5
 6     course1.addStudent("Peter Jones");
 7     course1.addStudent("Brian Smith");
 8     course1.addStudent("Anne Kennedy");
 9
10     course2.addStudent("Peter Jones");
11     course2.addStudent("Steve Smith");
12
13     System.out.println("Number of students in course1: "
14       + course1.getNumberOfStudents());
15     String[] students = course1.getStudents();
16     for (int i = 0; i < course1.getNumberOfStudents() ; i++)
17       System.out.print(students[i] + ", ");
18
19     System.out.println();
20     System.out.print("Number of students in course2: "
21       + course2.getNumberOfStudents());
22   }
23 }
```

```
Number of students in course1: 3
Peter Jones, Brian Smith, Anne Kennedy,
Number of students in course2: 2
```

The **Course** class is implemented in Listing 9.6. It uses an array to store the students for the course. For simplicity, assume that the maximum course enrollment is **100**. The array is created using **new String[100]** in line 3. The **addStudent** method (line 10) adds a student to the array. Whenever a new student is added to the course, **numberOfStudents** is increased (line 11). The **getStudents** method returns the array. The **dropStudent** method (line 27) is left as an exercise.

LISTING 9.6 Course.java

```
 1 public class Course {
 2    private String courseName;
 3    private String[] students = new String[100];          create students
 4    private int numberOfStudents;
 5
 6    public Course(String courseName) {                     add a course
 7       this.courseName = courseName;
 8    }
 9
10    public void addStudent(String student) {
11       students[numberOfStudents] = student;
12       numberOfStudents++;
13    }
14
15    public String[] getStudents() {                        return students
16       return students;
17    }
18
19    public int getNumberOfStudents() {                     number of students
20       return numberOfStudents;
21    }
22
23    public String getCourseName() {
24       return courseName;
25    }
26
27    public void dropStudent(String student) {
28       // Left as an exercise in Exercise 9.9
29    }
30 }
```

The array size is fixed to be **100** (line 3) in Listing 9.6. You can improve it to automatically increase the array size in Exercise 9.9.

When you create a **Course** object, an array object is created. A **Course** object contains a reference to the array. For simplicity, you can say that the **Course** object contains the array.

The user can create a **Course** and manipulate it through the public methods **addStudent**, **dropStudent**, **getNumberOfStudents**, and **getStudents**. However, the user doesn't need to know how these methods are implemented. The **Course** class encapsulates the internal implementation. This example uses an array to store students. You may use a different data structure to store students. The program that uses **Course** does not need to change as long as the contract of the public methods remains unchanged.

9.8 Designing a Class for Stacks

Recall that a stack is a data structure that holds objects in a last-in, first-out fashion, as shown in Figure 9.7.

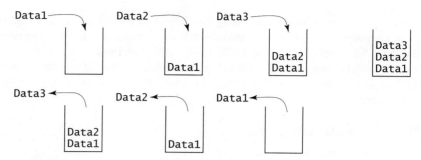

FIGURE 9.7 A stack holds objects in a last-in, first-out fashion.

stack

Stacks have many applications. For example, the compiler uses a stack to process method invocations. When a method is invoked, its parameters and local variables are pushed into a stack. When a method calls another method, the new method's parameters and local variables are pushed into the stack. When a method finishes its work and returns to its caller, its associated space is released from the stack.

You can define a class to model stacks. For simplicity, assume the stack holds the **int** values. So, name the stack class **StackOfIntegers**. The UML diagram for the class is shown in Figure 9.8.

StackOfIntegers	
-elements: int[]	An array to store integers in the stack.
-size: int	The number of integers in the stack.
+StackOfIntegers()	Constructs an empty stack with a default capacity of 16.
+StackOfIntegers(capacity: int)	Constructs an empty stack with a specified capacity.
+empty(): boolean	Returns true if the stack is empty.
+peek(): int	Returns the integer at the top of the stack without removing it from the stack.
+push(value: int): int	Stores an integer into the top of the stack.
+pop(): int	Removes the integer at the top of the stack and returns it.
+getSize(): int	Returns the number of elements in the stack.

FIGURE 9.8 The **StackOfIntegers** class encapsulates the stack storage and provides the operations for manipulating the stack.

Suppose that the class is available. Let us write a test program in Listing 9.7 that uses the class to create a stack (line 3), stores ten integers 0, 1, 2, ..., and 9 (line 6), and displays them in reverse order (line 9).

LISTING 9.7 TestStackOfIntegers.java

create a stack

```
1 public class TestStackOfIntegers {
2   public static void main(String[] args) {
3     StackOfIntegers stack = new StackOfIntegers();
```

```
4
5      for (int i = 0; i < 10; i++)
6        stack.push(i);                                    push to stack
7
8      while (!stack.empty())
9        System.out.print(stack.pop() + " ");              pop from stack
10   }
11 }
```

```
9 8 7 6 5 4 3 2 1 0
```

How do you implement the **StackOfIntegers** class? The elements in the stack are stored in an array named **elements**. When you create a stack, the array is also created. The no-arg constructor creates an array with the default capacity of **16**. The variable **size** counts the number of elements in the stack, and **size – 1** is the index of the element at the top of the stack, as shown in Figure 9.9. For an empty stack, **size** is **0**.

Video Note
StackOfInteger class

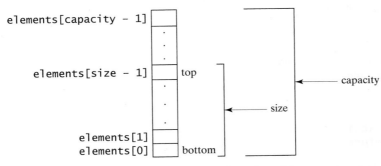

FIGURE 9.9 The **StackOfIntegers** class encapsulates the stack storage and provides the operations for manipulating the stack.

The **StackOfIntegers** class is implemented in Listing 9.8. The methods **empty()**, **peek()**, **pop()**, and **getSize()** are easy to implement. To implement **push(int value)**, assign **value** to **elements[size]** if **size < capacity** (line 24). If the stack is full (i.e., **size >= capacity**), create a new array of twice the current capacity (line 19), copy the contents of the current array to the new array (line 20), and assign the reference of the new array to the current array in the stack (line 21). Now you can add the new value to the array (line 24).

LISTING 9.8 StackOfIntegers.java

```
1 public class StackOfIntegers {
2    private int[] elements;
3    private int size;
4    public static final int DEFAULT_CAPACITY = 16;        max capacity 16
5
6    /** Construct a stack with the default capacity 16 */
7    public StackOfIntegers() {
8      this(DEFAULT_CAPACITY);
9    }
10
11   /** Construct a stack with the specified maximum capacity */
12   public StackOfIntegers(int capacity) {
```

```
13      elements = new int[capacity];
14    }
15
16    /** Push a new integer into the top of the stack */
17    public int push(int value) {
18      if (size >= elements.length) {
19        int[] temp = new int[elements.length * 2];
20        System.arraycopy(elements, 0, temp, 0, elements.length);
21        elements = temp;
22      }
23
24      return elements[size++] = value;
25    }
26
27    /** Return and remove the top element from the stack */
28    public int pop() {
29      return elements[-size];
30    }
31
32    /** Return the top element from the stack */
33    public int peek() {
34      return elements[size - 1];
35    }
36
37    /** Test whether the stack is empty */
38    public boolean empty() {
39      return size == 0;
40    }
41
42    /** Return the number of elements in the stack */
43    public int getSize() {
44      return size;
45    }
46 }
```

double the capacity

add to stack

9.9 Designing the GuessDate Class

Listing 3.8, GuessBirthDate.java, and Listing 6.14, GuessBirthDateUsingArray.java, present-ed two programs for guessing birth dates. Both programs use the same data developed with the procedural paradigm. The majority of code in these two programs is to define the five sets of data. You cannot reuse the code in these two programs. To make the code reusable, design a class to encapsulate the data, as defined in Figure 9.10.

GuessDate
-dates: int[][][]
+getValue(setNo: int, row: int, column: int): int

The static array to hold dates.

Returns a date at the specified row and column in a given set.

Figure 9.10 The GuessDate class defines data for guessing birth dates.

Note that getValue is defined as a static method because it is not dependent on a specific object of the GuessDate class. The GuessDate class encapsulates dates as a private mem-ber. The user of this class does not need to know how dates is implemented and does not even need to know the existence of the dates field in the class. All that the user needs to know is how to use this method to access dates. Suppose this class is available. As shown in Figure 3.4, there are five sets of dates. Invoking `getValue(setNo, row, column)` returns the date at the specified row and column in the given set. For example, `getValue(1, 0, 0)` returns `16`.

Assume that the `GuessDate` class is available. Listing 9.9 gives a test program that uses this class.

LISTING 9.9 UseGuessDateClass.java

```java
 1 import java.util.Scanner;
 2
 3 public class UseGuessDateClass {
 4   public static void main(String[] args) {
 5     int date = 0; // Date to be determined
 6     int answer;
 7
 8     // Create a Scanner
 9     Scanner input = new Scanner(System.in);
10
11     for (int i = 0; i < 5; i++) {
12       System.out.println("Is your birth date in Set" + (i + 1) + "?");
13       for (int j = 0; j < 4; j++) {
14         for (int k = 0; k < 4; k++)
15           System.out.print(GuessDate.getValue(i, j, k) + " ");     invoke static method
16         System.out.println();
17       }
18
19       System.out.print("\nEnter 0 for No and 1 for Yes: ");
20       answer = input.nextInt();
21
22       if (answer == 1)
23         date + = GuessDate.getValue(i, 0, 0);     invoke static method
24     }
25
26     System.out.println("Your birth date is " + date);
27   }
28 }
```

```
Is your birth date in Set1?
1   3   5   7
9   11  13  15
17  19  21  23
25  27  29  31
Enter 0 for No and 1 for Yes: 0  [↵ Enter]

Is your birth date in Set2?
2   3   6   7
10  11  14  15
18  19  22  23
26  27  30  31
Enter 0 for No and 1 for Yes: 1  [↵ Enter]

Is your birth date in Set3?
4   5   6   7
12  13  14  15
20  21  22  23
28  29  30  31
Enter 0 for No and 1 for Yes: 0  [↵ Enter]
```

```
Is your birth date in Set4?
 8   9  10  11
12  13  14  15
24  25  26  27
28  29  30  31
Enter 0 for No and 1 for Yes: 1  [↵ Enter]

Is your birth date in Set5?
16  17  18  19
20  21  22  23
24  25  26  27
28  29  30  31
Enter 0 for No and 1 for Yes: 1  [↵ Enter]

Your birth date is 26
```

Since **getValue** is a static method, you don't need to create an object in order to invoke it. **GuessDate.getValue(i, j, k)** (line 15) returns the date at row **i** and column **k** in Set **i**. The **GuessDate** class can be implemented in Listing 9.10.

LISTING 9.10 GuessDate.java

static field

private constructor

static method

```
 1  public class GuessDate {
 2    private final static int[][][] dates = {
 3      {{ 1,  3,  5,  7},
 4       { 9, 11, 13, 15},
 5       {17, 19, 21, 23},
 6       {25, 27, 29, 31}},
 7      {{ 2,  3,  6,  7},
 8       {10, 11, 14, 15},
 9       {18, 19, 22, 23},
10       {26, 27, 30, 31}},
11      {{ 4,  5,  6,  7},
12       {12, 13, 14, 15},
13       {20, 21, 22, 23},
14       {28, 29, 30, 31}},
15      {{ 8,  9, 10, 11},
16       {12, 13, 14, 15},
17       {24, 25, 26, 27},
18       {28, 29, 30, 31}},
19      {{16, 17, 18, 19},
20       {20, 21, 22, 23},
21       {24, 25, 26, 27},
22       {28, 29, 30, 31}}};
23
24    /** Prevent the user from creating objects from GuessDate */
25    private GuessDate() {
26    }
27
28    /** Return a date at the specified row and column in a given set */
29    public static int getValue(int setNo, int k, int j) {
30      return dates[setNo][k][j];
31    }
32  }
```

This class uses a three-dimensional array to store dates (lines 2–22). You may use a different data structure (i.e., five two-dimensional arrays for representing five sets of numbers). The implementation of the `getValue` method will change, but the program that uses `GuessDate` does not need to change as long as the contract of the public method `getValue` remains unchanged. This shows the benefit of data encapsulation.

The class defines a private no-arg constructor (line 25) to prevent the user from creating objects for this class. Since all methods are static in this class, there is no need to create objects from this class.

benefit of data encapsulation
private constructor

KEY TERMS

immutable class 307	stack 307
immutable object 307	`this` keyword 305

CHAPTER SUMMARY

- An immutable object cannot be modified once it is created. To prevent users from modifying an object, you may declare immutable classes.

- The scope of instance and static variables is the entire class, regardless of where the variables are declared. Instance and static variables can be declared anywhere in the class. For consistency, they are declared at the beginning of the class.

- The keyword `this` can be used to refer to the calling object. It can also be used inside a constructor to invoke another constructor of the same class.

- The procedural paradigm focuses on designing methods. The object-oriented paradigm couples data and methods together into objects. Software design using the object-oriented paradigm focuses on objects and operations on objects. The object-oriented approach combines the power of the procedural paradigm with an added dimension that integrates data with operations into objects.

REVIEW QUESTIONS

Section 9.2 Immutable Objects and Classes

9.1   If a class contains only private data fields and no set methods, is the class immutable?

9.2   If all the data fields in a class are private and primitive type, and the class contains no `set` methods, is the class immutable?

9.3   Is the following class immutable?

```
class A {
  private int[] values;
  public int[] getValues() {
    return values;
  }
}
```

9.4   If you redefine the `Loan` class in the preceding chapter without `set` methods, is the class immutable?

Section 9.3 The Scope of Variables

9.5   What is the output of the following program?

```java
public class Foo {
  static int i = 0;
  static int j = 0;

  public static void main(String[] args) {
    int i = 2;
    int k = 3;

    {
      int j = 3;
      System.out.println("i + j is " + i + j);
    }

    k = i + j;
    System.out.println("k is " + k);
    System.out.println("j is " + j);
  }
}
```

Section 9.4 The **this** Reference

9.6   Describe the role of the `this` keyword. What is wrong in the following code?

```java
 1 public class C {
 2   int p;
 3
 4   public C() {
 5     System.out.println("C's no-arg constructor invoked");
 6     this(0);
 7   }
 8
 9   public C(int p) {
10     p = p;
11   }
12
13   public void setP(int p) {
14     p = p;
15   }
16 }
```

PROGRAMMING EXERCISES

9.1*   (*The Time class*) Design a class named `Time`. The class contains:

  ■ Data fields `hour`, `minute`, and `second` that represent a time.
  ■ A no-arg constructor that creates a `Time` object for the current time. (The data fields value will represent the current time.)
  ■ A constructor that constructs a `Time` object with a specified elapsed time since midnight, Jan 1, 1970, in milliseconds. (The data fields value will represent this time.)
  ■ Three `get` methods for the data fields `hour`, `minute`, and `second`, respectively.

Draw the UML diagram for the class. Implement the class. Write a test program that creates two `Time` objects (using `new Time()` and `new Time(555550000)`) and display their hour, minute, and second.

(*Hint*: The current time can be obtained using `System.currentTime()`, as shown in Listing 2.9, ShowCurrentTime.java. The other constructor sets the hour, minute, and second for the specified elapsed time. For example, if the elapsed time is `555550000` milliseconds, the hour is `10`, the minute is `19`, and the second is `10`.)

9.2 (*The BMI class*) Add the following new constructor in the BMI class:

```
/** Construct a BMI with the specified name, age, weight,
 * feet and inches
 */
public BMI(String name, int age, double weight, int feet,
  int inches)
```

9.3 (*The MyInteger class*) Design a class named MyInteger. The class contains:

- An int data field named value that stores the int value represented by this object.
- A constructor that creates a MyInteger object for the specified int value.
- A get method that return the int value.
- Methods isEven(), isOdd(), and isPrime() that return true if the value is even, odd, or prime, respectively.
- Static methods isEven(int), isOdd(int), and isPrime(int) that return true if the specified value is even, odd, or prime, respectively.
- Static methods isEven(MyInteger), isOdd(MyInteger), and isPrime-(MyInteger) that return true if the specified value is even, odd, or prime, respectively.
- Methods equals(int) and equals(MyInteger) that return true if the value in the object is equal to the specified value.
- A static method parseInt(char[]) that converts an array of numeric characters to an int value.

Draw the UML diagram for the class. Implement the class. Write a client program that tests all methods in the class.

9.4 (*The MyPoint class*) Design a class named MyPoint to represent a point with x- and y-coordinates. The class contains:

Video Note
Design and implement
MyPoint class

- Two data fields x and y that represent the coordinates with get methods.
- A no-arg constructor that creates a point (0, 0).
- A constructor that constructs a point with specified coordinates.
- Two get methods for data fields x and y, respectively.
- A method named distance that returns the distance from this point to another point of the MyPoint type.
- A method named distance that returns the distance from this point to another point with specified -x and y-coordinates.

Draw the UML diagram for the class. Implement the class. Write a test program that creates two points (0, 0) and (10, 30.5) and displays the distance between them.

9.5* (*Displaying the prime factors*) Write a program that receives a positive integer and displays all its smallest factors in decreasing order. For example, if the integer is 120, the smallest factors are displayed as 5, 3, 2, 2, 2. Use the StackOfIntegers class to store the factors (e.g., 2, 2, 2, 3, 5) and retrieve and display them in reverse order.

9.6* (*Displaying the prime numbers*) Write a program that displays all the prime numbers less than 120 in decreasing order. Use the StackOfIntegers class to store the prime numbers (e.g., 2, 3, 5, ...) and retrieve and display them in reverse order.

9.7** (*Game: ATM machine*) Use the Account class created in Exercise 7.3 to simulate an ATM machine. Create ten accounts in an array with id 0, 1, ..., 9, and initial balance $100. The system prompts the user to enter an id. If the id is entered incorrectly, ask the user to enter a correct id. Once an id is accepted, the main menu is displayed as shown in the sample output. You can enter a choice 1 for viewing the current balance, 2 for withdrawing money, 3 for depositing money, and 4 for exiting the main menu. Once you exit, the system will prompt for an id again. So, once the system starts, it will not stop.

```
Enter an id: 4 ↵Enter
Main menu
1: check balance
2: withdraw
3: deposit
4: exit
Enter a choice: 1 ↵Enter
The balance is 100.0

Main menu
1: check balance
2: withdraw
3: deposit
4: exit
Enter a choice: 2 ↵Enter
Enter an amount to withdraw: 3 ↵Enter

Main menu
1: check balance
2: withdraw
3: deposit
4: exit
Enter a choice: 1 ↵Enter
The balance is 97.0

Main menu
1: check balance
2: withdraw
3: deposit
4: exit
Enter a choice: 3 ↵Enter
Enter an amount to deposit: 10 ↵Enter

Main menu
1: check balance
2: withdraw
3: deposit
4: exit
Enter a choice: 1 ↵Enter
The balance is 107.0

Main menu
1: check balance
2: withdraw
3: deposit
4: exit
Enter a choice: 4 ↵Enter

Enter an id:
```

9.8*** (*Financial: the Tax class*) Exercise 6.32 writes a program for computing taxes using arrays. Design a class named `Tax` to contain the following instance data fields:

- **int filingStatus**: One of the four tax filing statuses: 0—single filer, 1—married filing jointly, 2—married filing separately, and 3—head of household. Use the public static constants `SINGLE_FILER` (0), `MARRIED_JOINTLY` (1), `MARRIED_SEPARATELY` (2), `HEAD_OF_HOUSEHOLD` (3) to represent the status.
- **int[][] brackets**: Stores the tax brackets for each filing status.
- **double[] rates**: Stores tax rates for each bracket.
- **double taxableIncome**: Stores the taxable income.

Provide the `get` and `set` methods for each data field and the `getTax()` method that returns the tax. Also provide a no-arg constructor and the constructor `Tax(filingStatus, brackets, rates, taxableIncome)`.

Draw the UML diagram for the class. Implement the class. Write a test program that uses the `Tax` class to print the 2001 and 2002 tax tables for taxable income from $50,000 to $60,000 with intervals of $1,000 for all four statuses. The tax rates for the year 2002 were given in Table 3.7. The tax rates for 2001 are shown in Table 9.1.

TABLE 9.1   2001 United States Federal Personal Tax Rates

Tax rate	Single filers	Married filing jointly or qualifying widow(er)	Married filing separately	Head of household
15%	Up to $27,050	Up to $45,200	Up to $22,600	Up to $36,250
27.5%	$27,051–$65,550	$45,201–$109,250	$22,601–$54,625	$36,251–$93,650
30.5%	$65,551–$136,750	$109,251–$166,500	$54,626–$83,250	$93,651–$151,650
35.5%	$136,751–$297,350	$166,501–$297,350	$83,251–$148,675	$151,651–$297,350
39.1%	$297,351 or more	$297,351 or more	$148,676 or more	$297,351 or more

9.9** (*The Course class*) Revise the `Course` class as follows:

- The array size is fixed in Listing 9.6. Improve it to automatically increase the array size by creating a new larger array and copying the contents of the current array to it.
- Implement the `dropStudent` method.
- Add a new method named `clear()` that removes all students from the course.

Write a test program that creates a course, adds three students, removes one, and displays the students in the course.

9.10* (*Game: The GuessDate class*) Modify the `GuessDate` class in Listing 9.10. Instead of representing dates in a three-dimensional array, use five two-dimensional arrays to represent the five sets of numbers. So you need to declare:

```
private static int[][] set1 = {{ 1,  3,  5,  7}, ... };
private static int[][] set2 = {{ 2,  3,  6,  7}, ... };
private static int[][] set3 = {{ 4,  5,  6,  7}, ... };
private static int[][] set4 = {{ 8,  9, 10, 11}, ... };
private static int[][] set5 = {{16, 17, 18, 19}, ... };
```

9.11* (*Geometry: The Circle2D class*) Define the Circle2D class that contains:

- Two **double** data fields named x and y that specify the center of the circle with **get** methods.
- A data field **radius** with a **get** method.
- A no-arg constructor that creates a default circle with (0, 0) for (x, y) and 1 for **radius**.
- A constructor that creates a circle with the specified x, y, and **radius**.
- A method **getArea()** that returns the area of the circle.
- A method **getPerimeter()** that returns the perimeter of the circle.
- A method **contains(double x, double y)** that returns **true** if the specified point (x, y) is inside this circle. See Figure 9.11(a).
- A method **contains(Circle2D circle)** that returns **true** if the specified circle is inside this circle. See Figure 9.11(b).
- A method **overlaps(Circle2D circle)** that returns **true** if the specified circle overlaps with this circle. See Figure 9.11(c).

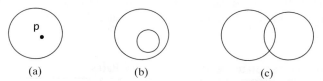

(a) (b) (c)

FIGURE 9.11 (a) A point is inside the circle. (b) A circle is inside another circle. (c) A circle overlaps another circle.

Draw the UML diagram for the class. Implement the class. Write a test program that creates a Circle2D object c1 (new Circle2D(2, 2, 5.5)), displays its area and perimeter, and displays the result of c1.contains(3, 3), c1.contains(new Circle2D(4, 5, 10.5)), and c1.overlaps(new Circle2D(3, 5, 2.3)).

9.12* (*Geometry: The Rectangle2D class*) Define the Rectangle2D class that contains:

- Two **double** data fields named x and y that specify the center of the rectangle with **get** and **set** methods. (Assume that the rectangle sides are parallel to x- or y- axes.)
- The data fields **width** and **height** with **get** and **set** methods.
- A no-arg constructor that creates a default rectangle with (0, 0) for (x, y) and 1 for both **width** and **height**.
- A constructor that creates a rectangle with the specified x, y, and **radius**.
- A method **getArea()** that returns the area of the rectangle.
- A method **getPerimeter()** that returns the perimeter of the rectangle.
- A method **contains(double x, double y)** that returns **true** if the specified point (x, y) is inside this rectangle. See Figure 9.12(a).
- A method **contains(Rectangle2D r)** that returns **true** if the specified rectangle is inside this rectangle. See Figure 9.12(b).
- A method **overlaps(Rectangle2D r)** that returns **true** if the specified rectangle overlaps with this rectangle. See Figure 9.12(c).

(a)   (b)   (c)

FIGURE 9.12   (a) A point is inside the rectangle. (b) A rectangle is inside another rectangle.
(c) A rectangle overlaps another rectangle.

Draw the UML diagram for the class. Implement the class. Write a test program that creates a `Rectangle2D` objects `r1` (new `Rectangle2D(2, 2, 5.5,  4.9)`), displays its area and perimeter, and displays the result of `r1.contains(3, 3)`, `r1.contains(new Rectangle2D(4, 5, 10.5, 3.2))`, and `r1.overlaps(new Rectangle2D(3, 5, 2.3, 5.4))`.

9.13*** (*Geometry: The `Triangle2D` class*) Define the `Triangle2D` *class that contains:*

- Three points named `p1`, `p2`, and `p3` with the type `MyPoint` with `get` and `set` methods. `MyPoint` is defined in Exercise 9.4.
- A no-arg constructor that creates a default triangle with points (0, 0), (1, 1), and (2, 5).
- A constructor that creates a triangle with the specified points.
- A method `getArea()` that returns the area of the triangle.
- A method `getPerimeter()` that returns the perimeter of the triangle.
- A method `contains(MyPoint p)` that returns `true` if the specified point `p` is inside this triangle. See Figure 9.13(a).
- A method `contains(Triangle2D t)` that returns `true` if the specified triangle is inside this triangle. See Figure 9.13(b).
- A method `overlaps(Triangle2D t)` that returns `true` if the specified triangle overlaps with this triangle. See Figure 9.13(c).

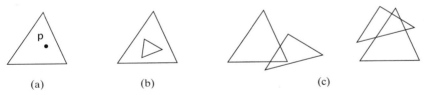

(a)   (b)   (c)

FIGURE 9.13   (a) A point is inside the triangle. (b) A triangle is inside another triangle.
(c) A triangle overlaps another triangle.

Draw the UML diagram for the class. Implement the class. Write a test program that creates a `Triangle2D` objects `t1` (new `Triangle2D(new MyPoint(2.5, 2)`, new `MyPoint(4.2, 3)`, `MyPoint(5, 3.5))`), displays its area and perimeter, and displays the result of `t1.contains(3, 3)`, `r1.contains(new Triangle2D(new MyPoint(2.9, 2)`, new `MyPoint(4, 1)`, `MyPoint(1, 3.4)))`, and `t1.overlaps(new Triangle2D(new MyPoint(2, 5.5)`, new `MyPoint(4, -3)`, `MyPoint(2, 6.5)))`.

(*Hint*: For the formula to compute the area of a triangle, see Exercise 5.19. Use the `java.awt.geo.Line2D` class in the Java API to implement the `contains` and `overlaps` methods. The `Line2D` class contains the methods for checking whether two line segments intersect and whether a line contains a point, etc. Please see the Java API for more information on **Line2D**. To detect whether a point is inside a triangle, draw three dashed lines, as shown in Figure 9.14. If the point is inside a triangle, each dashed line should intersect a side only once. If a dashed line intersects a side twice, then the point must be outside the triangle.)

(a)   (b)

FIGURE 9.14   (a) A point is inside the triangle. (b) A point is outside the triangle.

CHAPTER 10

INHERITANCE AND POLYMORPHISM

Objectives

- To develop a subclass from a superclass through inheritance (§10.2).

- To illustrate inheritance by creating a custom frame that extends `JFrame` (§10.3).

- To invoke the superclass's constructors and methods using the `super` keyword (§10.4).

- To override instance methods in the subclass (§10.5).

- To distinguish differences between overriding and overloading (§10.6).

- To explore the methods `toString()` and `equals(Object)` in the `Object` class (§10.7).

- To discover polymorphism, dynamic binding, and generic programming (§10.8).

- To describe casting and explain why explicit downcasting is necessary (§10.9).

- To store, retrieve, and manipulate objects in an `ArrayList` (§10.10).

- To implement a `Stack` class using `ArrayList` (§10.11).

- To restrict access to data and methods to subclasses using the `protected` visibility modifier (§10.12).

- To prevent class extending and method overriding using the `final` modifier (§10.13).

10.1 Introduction

Object-oriented programming allows you to derive new classes from existing classes. This is called *inheritance*. Inheritance is an important and powerful feature in Java for reusing software. In fact, every class you define in Java is inherited from an existing class, either explicitly or implicitly. The classes you created in the preceding chapters were all extended implicitly from the `java.lang.Object` class.

Suppose you are to define classes to model circles, rectangles, and triangles. These classes have many common features. What is the best way to design these classes so to avoid redundancy? The answer is to use inheritance.

Recall that you create an instance of `JFrame` and add components into the frame in Listing 7.4 GUIComponents.java. Suppose you wish to display two identical frames with the same components in each, as shown in Figure 10.1. Do you have to write the same code repeatedly for creating two frames and adding the same type of components to each frame? There are several ways to solve this problem. An effective way is to use inheritance.

FIGURE 10.1 The program displays two windows with the same components.

This chapter introduces inheritance, which will enable you to solve these problems effectively.

10.2 Superclasses and Subclasses

In Java terminology, a class `C1` extended from another class `C2` is called a *subclass*, and `C2` is called a *superclass*. A superclass is also referred to as a *parent class,* or a *base class*, and a subclass as a *child class*, an *extended class*, or a *derived class*. A subclass inherits accessible data fields and methods from its superclass, and may also add new data fields and methods.

Consider geometric objects. Suppose you want to design the classes to model geometric objects such as circles and rectangles. Geometric objects have many common properties and behaviors. They can be drawn in a certain color, filled or unfilled. Thus a general class `GeometricObject` can be used to model all geometric objects. This class contains the properties `color` and `filled` and their appropriate get and set methods. Assume that this class also contains the `dateCreated` property and the `getDateCreated()` and `toString()` methods. The `toString()` method returns a string representation for the object. Since a circle is a special type of geometric object, it shares common properties and methods with other geometric objects. Thus it makes sense to define the `Circle` class that extends the `GeometricObject` class. Likewise, `Rectangle` can also be declared as a subclass of `GeometricObject`. Figure 10.2 shows the relationship among these classes. An arrow pointing to the superclass is used to denote the inheritance relationship between the two classes involved.

The `Circle` class inherits all accessible data fields and methods from the `Geometric-Object` class. In addition, it has a new data field, `radius`, and its associated `get` and `set` methods. It also contains the `getArea()`, `getPerimeter()`, and `getDiameter()` methods for returning the area, perimeter, and diameter of the circle.

The `Rectangle` class inherits all accessible data fields and methods from the `GeometricObject` class. In addition, it has the data fields `width` and `height`, and the associated `get` and `set` methods. It also contains the `getArea()` and `getPerimeter()` methods for returning the area and perimeter of the rectangle.

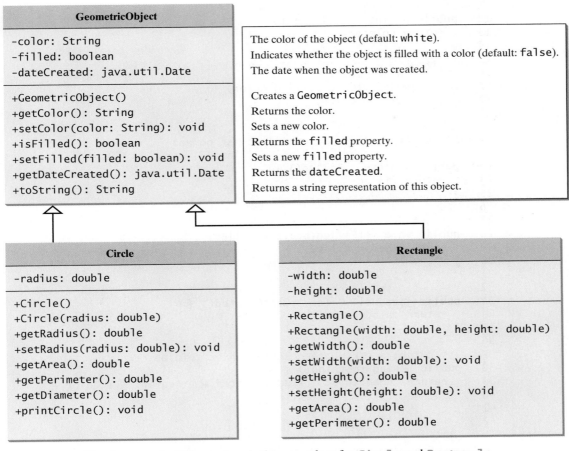

FIGURE 10.2 The GeometricObject class is the superclass for Circle and Rectangle.

The GeometricObject, Circle, and Rectangle classes are shown in Listings 10.1, 10.2, and 10.3.

 Note

To avoid naming conflict with the improved GeometricObject, Circle, and Rectangle classes introduced in the next chapter, name these classes GeometricObject1, Circle4, and Rectangle1 in this chapter. For convenience, we will still refer to them in the text as GeometricObject, Circle, and Rectangle classes. The best way to avoid naming conflict would be to place these classes in a different package. However, for simplicity and consistency, all classes in this book are placed in the default package.

avoid naming conflict

LISTING 10.1 GeometricObject1.java

```
1 public class GeometricObject1 {
2   private String color = "white";
3   private boolean filled;
4   private java.util.Date dateCreated;
5
6   /** Construct a default geometric object */
7   public GeometricObject1() {
8     dateCreated = new java.util.Date();
9   }
10
```

data fields

constructor
date constructed

methods

```
11    /** Return color */
12    public String getColor() {
13      return color;
14    }
15
16    /** Set a new color */
17    public void setColor(String color) {
18      this.color = color;
19    }
20
21    /** Return filled. Since filled is boolean,
22      its get method is named isFilled */
23    public boolean isFilled() {
24      return filled;
25    }
26
27    /** Set a new filled */
28    public void setFilled(boolean filled) {
29      this.filled = filled;
30    }
31
32    /** Get dateCreated */
33    public java.util.Date getDateCreated() {
34      return dateCreated;
35    }
36
37    /** Return a string representation of this object */
38    public String toString() {
39      return "created on " + dateCreated + "\ncolor: " + color +
40        " and filled: " + filled;
41    }
42 }
```

LISTING 10.2 Circle4.java

data fields

constructor

methods

```
1 public class Circle4 extends GeometricObject1 {
2    private double radius;
3
4    public Circle4() {
5    }
6
7    public Circle4(double radius) {
8      this.radius = radius;
9    }
10
11    /** Return radius */
12    public double getRadius() {
13      return radius;
14    }
15
16    /** Set a new radius */
17    public void setRadius(double radius) {
18      this.radius = radius;
19    }
20
21    /** Return area */
22    public double getArea() {
23      return radius * radius * Math.PI;
24    }
25
```

```
26   /** Return diameter */
27   public double getDiameter() {
28     return 2 * radius;
29   }
30
31   /** Return perimeter */
32   public double getPerimeter() {
33     return 2 * radius * Math.PI;
34   }
35
36   /* Print the circle info */
37   public void printCircle() {
38     System.out.println("The circle is created " + getDateCreated() +
39       " and the radius is " + radius);
40   }
41 }
```

LISTING 10.3   Rectangle1.java

```
1 public class Rectangle1 extends GeometricObject1 {
2     private double width;                                    data fields
3     private double height;
4
5     public Rectangle1() {                                    constructor
6     }
7
8     public Rectangle1(double width, double height) {
9       this.width = width;
10      this.height = height;
11    }
12
13    /** Return width */                                      methods
14    public double getWidth() {
15      return width;
16    }
17
18    /** Set a new width */
19    public void setWidth(double width) {
20      this.width = width;
21    }
22
23    /** Return height */
24    public double getHeight() {
25      return height;
26    }
27
28    /** Set a new height */
29    public void setHeight(double height) {
30      this.height = height;
31    }
32
33    /** Return area */
34    public double getArea() {
35      return width * height;
36    }
37
38    /** Return perimeter */
39    public double getPerimeter() {
40      return 2 * (width + height);
41    }
42 }
```

The `Circle` class extends the `GeometricObject` class. The reserved word `extends` (line 1) tells the compiler that the `Circle` class extends the `GeometricObject` class, thus inheriting the methods `getColor`, `setColor`, `isFilled`, `setFilled`, and `toString`.

The following code in Listing 10.4 creates objects of `Circle` and `Rectangle` and invokes the methods on these objects.

LISTING 10.4 TestCircleRectangle.java

Circle object
invoke **toString**

Rectangle object
invoke **toString**

```java
 1 public class TestCircleRectangle {
 2   public static void main(String[] args) {
 3     Circle4 circle = new Circle4(1);
 4     System.out.println("A circle " + circle.toString());
 5     System.out.println("The radius is " + circle.getRadius());
 6     System.out.println("The area is " + circle.getArea());
 7     System.out.println("The diameter is " + circle.getDiameter());
 8
 9     Rectangle1 rectangle = new Rectangle1(2, 4);
10     System.out.println("\nA rectangle " + rectangle.toString());
11     System.out.println("The area is " + rectangle.getArea());
12     System.out.println("The perimeter is " +
13       rectangle.getPerimeter());
14   }
15 }
```

```
A circle created on Fri Dec 22 10:07:02 CST 2006
color: white and filled: false
The radius is 1.0
The area is 3.141592653589793
The diameter is 2.0

A rectangle created on Fri Dec 22 10:07:02 CST 2006
color: white and filled: false
The area is 8.0
The perimeter is 12.0
```

The following points regarding inheritance are worthwhile to note:

more in subclass

- Contrary to the conventional interpretation, a subclass is not a subset of its superclass. In fact, a subclass usually contains more information and functions than its superclass.

nonextensible is-a

- Not all is-a relationships should be modeled using inheritance. For example, a square is a rectangle, but you should not declare a `Square` class to extend a `Rectangle` class, because there is nothing to extend (or supplement) from a rectangle to a square. Rather you should declare a `Square` class to extend the `GeometricObject` class. For class A to extend class B, A should contain more detailed information than B.

no blind extension

- Inheritance is used to model the *is-a* relationship. Do not blindly extend a class just for the sake of reusing methods. For example, it makes no sense for a `Tree` class to extend a `Person` class, even though they share common properties such as height and weight, etc. A subclass and its superclass must have the is-a relationship.

multiple inheritance

- Some programming languages allow you to derive a subclass from several classes. This capability is known as *multiple inheritance*. Java, however, does not allow multiple inheritance. A Java class may inherit directly from only one superclass.

This restriction is known as *single inheritance*. If you use the **extends** keyword to define a subclass, it allows only one parent class. Nevertheless, multiple inheritance can be achieved through interfaces, which will be introduced in §11.4, "Interfaces."

single inheritance

10.3 Extending the **JFrame** Class

In the introduction of this chapter, we proposed the problem of creating two identical windows that contain the same components. This problem can be effectively solved using inheritance. You can declare a custom frame class by extending the `JFrame` class, as shown in Listing 10.5.

Video Note
Extend **JFrame**

Listing 10.5 UseCustomFrame.java

```java
1 import javax.swing.*;
2
3 public class UseCustomFrame {
4   public static void main(String[] args) {
5     JFrame frame1 = new CustomFrame(); // Create a frame
6     frame1.setTitle("Window 1"); // Set frame title
7     frame1.setLocation(200, 100); // Set frame location
8     frame1.setVisible(true); // Display frame
9
10    JFrame frame2 = new CustomFrame(); // Create another frame
11    frame2.setTitle("Window 2"); // Set frame title
12    frame2.setLocation(200, 300); // Set frame location
13    frame2.setVisible(true); // Display frame
14  }
15 }
16
17 class CustomFrame extends JFrame {
18   public CustomFrame() {
19     // Create a button with text OK
20     JButton jbtOK = new JButton("OK");
21
22     // Create a label with text "Enter your name: "
23     JLabel jlblName = new JLabel("Enter your name: ");
24
25     // Create a text field with text "Type Name Here"
26     JTextField jtfName = new JTextField("Type Name Here");
27
28     // Create a check box with text bold
29     JCheckBox jchkBold = new JCheckBox("Bold");
30
31     // Create a radio button with text red
32     JRadioButton jrbRed = new JRadioButton("Red");
33
34     // Create a combo box with choices red, green, and blue
35     JComboBox jcboColor = new JComboBox(new String[]{"Red",
36       "Green", "Blue"});
37
38     // Create a panel to group components
39     JPanel panel = new JPanel();
40     panel.add(jbtOK); // Add the button to the panel
41     panel.add(jlblName); // Add the label to the panel
42     panel.add(jtfName); // Add the text field to the panel
43     panel.add(jchkBold); // Add the check box to the panel
44     panel.add(jrbRed); // Add the radio button to the panel
45     panel.add(jcboColor); // Add the combo box to the panel
46
```

create frame

create frame

custom frame class
frame constructor

```
47        add(panel); // Add the panel to the frame
48        setSize(450, 70); // Set frame's size
49        setDefaultCloseOperation(JFrame.EXIT_ON_CLOSE);
50    }
51 }
```

The CustomFrame class extends JFrame (line 17) to inherit all accessible methods from JFrame. CustomFrame is also a JFrame. The methods such as add, setSize, setDefaultCloseOperation, and setVisible defined in JFrame can also be invoked from CustomFrame. The program invokes the JFrame's add method to add the panel to the frame (line 47), invokes the setSize method to set the frame's size (line 48), and invokes the setDefaultCloseOperation method to terminate the program when the frame is closed (line 49).

In the main method, two instances frame1 and frame2 of CustomFrame are created by invoking new CustomFrame() (lines 5, 10). frame1 and frame2 are instances of CustomFrame and also instances of JFrame. frame1 can invoke all the accessible methods defined in JFrame. So frame1 can invoke setLocation(200, 100) to set the location for frame1 (line 7) and invoke setVisible(true) to display the frame (line 8).

10.4 Using the **super** Keyword

A subclass inherits accessible data fields and methods from its superclass. Does it inherit constructors? Can superclass constructors be invoked from subclasses? This section addresses these questions and their ramification.

§9.4, "The this Reference," introduced the use of the keyword this to reference the calling object. The keyword super refers to the superclass of the class in which super appears. It can be used in two ways:

- To call a superclass constructor.

- To call a superclass method.

10.4.1 Calling Superclass Constructors

The syntax to call a superclass constructor is:

```
super(), or super(parameters);
```

The statement super() invokes the no-arg constructor of its superclass, and the statement super(arguments) invokes the superclass constructor that matches the arguments. The statement super() or super(arguments) must appear in the first line of the subclass constructor; this is the only way to invoke a superclass constructor.

Caution

You must use the keyword super to call the superclass constructor, and the call must be the first statement in the constructor. Invoking a superclass constructor's name in a subclass causes a syntax error.

Note

A constructor is used to construct an instance of a class. Unlike properties and methods, the constructors of a superclass are not inherited in the subclass. They can only be invoked from the constructors of the subclasses, using the keyword super.

10.4.2   Constructor Chaining

A constructor may invoke an overloaded constructor or its superclass's constructor. If neither of them is invoked explicitly, the compiler puts `super()` as the first statement in the constructor. For example,

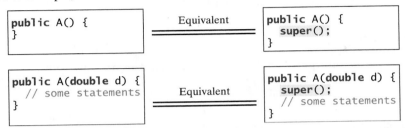

```
public A() {
}
```
Equivalent
```
public A() {
   super();
}
```

```
public A(double d) {
   // some statements
}
```
Equivalent
```
public A(double d) {
   super();
   // some statements
}
```

In any case, constructing an instance of a class invokes the constructors of all the superclasses along the inheritance chain. A superclass's constructor is called before the subclass's constructor. This is called *constructor chaining*. Consider the following code:

constructor chaining

```
 1 public class Faculty extends Employee {
 2   public static void main(String[] args) {
 3     new Faculty();
 4   }
 5
 6   public Faculty() {
 7     System.out.println("(4) Invoke Faculty's no-arg constructor");
 8   }
 9 }
10
11 class Employee extends Person {
12   public Employee() {
13     this("(2) Invoke Employee's overloaded constructor");
14     System.out.println("(3) Invoke Employee's no-arg constructor");
15   }
16
17   public Employee(String s) {
18     System.out.println(s);
19   }
20 }
21
22 class Person {
23   public Person() {
24     System.out.println("(1) Invoke Person's no-arg constructor");
25   }
26 }
```

invoke overloaded
constructor

```
(1) Invoke Person's no-arg constructor
(2) Invoke Employee's overloaded constructor
(3) Invoke Employee's no-arg constructor
(4) Invoke Faculty's no-arg constructor
```

The program produces the preceding output. Why? Let us discuss the reason. In line 3, new Faculty() invokes Faculty's no-arg constructor. Since Faculty is a subclass of Employee, Employee's no-arg constructor is invoked before any statements in Faculty's constructor are executed. Employee's no-arg constructor invokes Employee's second constructor (line 12). Since Employee is a subclass of Person, Person's no-arg constructor is invoked before any statements in Employee's second constructor are executed.

no-arg constructor

Caution

If a class is designed to be extended, it is better to provide a no-arg constructor to avoid programming errors. Consider the following code:

```java
public class Apple extends Fruit {
}

class Fruit {
  public Fruit(String name) {
    System.out.println("Fruit's constructor is invoked");
  }
}
```

Since no constructor is explicitly defined in `Apple`, `Apple`'s default no-arg constructor is declared implicitly. Since `Apple` is a subclass of `Fruit`, `Apple`'s default constructor automatically invokes `Fruit`'s no-arg constructor. However, `Fruit` does not have a no-arg constructor because `Fruit` has an explicit constructor defined. Therefore, the program cannot be compiled.

no-arg constructor

Design Guide

It is better to provide a no-arg constructor (if desirable) for every class to make the class easy to extend and to avoid errors.

10.4.3   Calling Superclass Methods

The keyword **super** can also be used to reference a method other than the constructor in the superclass. The syntax is like this:

```java
super.method(parameters);
```

You could rewrite the **printCircle()** method in the **Circle** class as follows:

```java
public void printCircle() {
  System.out.println("The circle is created " +
    super.getDateCreated() + " and the radius is " + radius);
}
```

It is not necessary to put **super** before **getDateCreated()** in this case, however, because **getDateCreated** is a method in the **GeometricObject** class and is inherited by the **Circle** class. Nevertheless, in some cases, as shown in the next section, the keyword **super** is needed.

no multiple **super**s

Caution

You can use **super.p()** to invoke the method **p()** defined in the superclass. Suppose **A** extends **B**, and **B** extends **C**, and a method **p()** is defined in **C**. Can you invoke **super.super.p()** from **A**? The answer is no. It is illegal to have such a chain of **super**s in Java.

10.5 Overriding Methods

method overriding

A subclass inherits methods from a superclass. Sometimes it is necessary for the subclass to modify the implementation of a method defined in the superclass. This is referred to as *method overriding*.

The **toString** method in the **GeometricObject** class returns the string representation for a geometric object. This method can be overridden to return the string representation for a circle. To override it, add the following new method in Listing 10.2, Circle4.java:

```java
1 public class Circle4 extends GeometricObject1 {
2   // Other methods are omitted
3
```

```
4    /** Override the toString method defined in GeometricObject */
5    public String toString() {
6      return super.toString() + "\nradius is " + radius;
7    }
8  }
```

The `toString()` method is defined in the `GeometricObject` class and modified in the `Circle` class. Both methods can be used in the `Circle` class. To invoke the `toString` method defined in the `GeometricObject` class from the `Circle` class, use `super.toString()` (line 6).

Can a subclass of `Circle` access the `toString` method defined in the `GeometricObject` class using a syntax such as `super.super.toString()`? No. This is a syntax error.

Several points are worth noting:

no super.super.
methodName()

- Private data fields in a superclass are not accessible outside the class. Therefore, they cannot be used directly in a subclass. They can, however, be accessed/mutated through public accessor/mutator if defined in the superclass.

private data fields

- An instance method can be overridden only if it is accessible. Thus a private method cannot be overridden, because it is not accessible outside its own class. If a method defined in a subclass is private in its superclass, the two methods are completely unrelated.

override accessible instance method

- Like an instance method, a static method can be inherited. However, a static method cannot be overridden. If a static method defined in the superclass is redefined in a subclass, the method defined in the superclass is hidden. The hidden static methods can be invoked using the syntax `SuperClassName.staticMethodName`.

cannot override static method

10.6 Overriding vs. Overloading

You have learned about overloading methods in §5.7, "Overloading Methods." Overloading a method is a way to provide more than one method with the same name but with different signatures to distinguish them. To override a method, the method must be defined in the subclass using the same signature and same return type as in its superclass.

same signature
same return type

Let us use an example to show the differences between overriding and overloading. In (a), the method `p(int i)` in class `A` overrides the same method defined in class `B`. However, in (b), the method `p(double i)` in class `A` and the method `p(int i)` in class `B` are two overloaded methods. The method `p(int i)` in class `B` is inherited in `A`.

```
public class Test {
  public static void main(String[] args) {
    A a = new A();
    a.p(10);
  }
}

class B {
  public void p(int i) {
  }
}

class A extends B {
  // This method overrides the method in B
  public void p(int i) {
    System.out.println(i);
  }
}
```

(a)

```
public class Test {
  public static void main(String[] args) {
    A a = new A();
    a.p(10);
  }
}

class B {
  public void p(int i) {
  }
}

class A extends B {
  // This method overloads the method in B
  public void p(double i) {
    System.out.println(i);
  }
}
```

(b)

When you run the Test class in (a), a.p(10) invokes the p(int i) method defined in class A, so the program displays 10. When you run the Test class in (b), a.p(10) invokes the p(int i) method defined in class B, so nothing is printed.

10.7 The Object Class and Its Methods

Every class in Java is descended from the java.lang.Object class. If no inheritance is specified when a class is defined, the superclass of the class is Object by default. For example, the following two class declarations are the same:

```public class Circle {``` ``` ...``` ```}```	Equivalent
	```public class Circle extends Object {``` ``` ...``` ```}```

Classes like String, StringBuffer, Loan, and GeometricObject are implicitly subclasses of Object (as are all the main classes you have seen in this book so far). It is important to be familiar with the methods provided by the Object class so that you can use them in your classes. Two methods in the Object class to be discussed here are toString and equals.

toString()

The signature of the toString() method is

```
public String toString()
```

string representation

Invoking toString() on an object returns a string that describes the object. By default, it returns a string consisting of a class name of which the object is an instance, an at sign (@), and the object's memory address in hexadecimal. For example, consider the following code for the Loan class defined in Listing 9.2:

```
Loan loan = new Loan();
System.out.println(loan.toString());
```

The code displays something like Loan@15037e5. This message is not very helpful or informative. Usually you should override the toString method so that it returns a descriptive string representation of the object. For example, the toString method in the Geometric Object class in Listing 10.1 was overridden as follows:

```
public String toString() {
  return "color: " + color + "and is filled: " + filled;
}
```

print object

> **Note**
> You can also pass an object to invoke System.out.println(object) or System.out.print(object). This is equivalent to invoking System.out.println(object.toString()) or System.out.print(object.toString()). So you could replace System.out.println(loan.toString()) with System.out.println(loan).

equals(Object)

The signature of the equals method is

```
public boolean equals(Object o)
```

This method tests whether two objects are equal. The syntax for invoking it is:

```
object1.equals(object2);
```

The default implementation of the `equals` method in the `Object` class is:

```java
public boolean equals(Object obj) {
  return (this == obj);
}
```

This implementation checks whether two reference variables point to the same object using the `==` operator. You should override this method in your custom class to test whether two distinct objects have the same content.

You have already used the `equals` method to compare two strings in §9.2, "The `String` Class." The `equals` method in the `String` class is inherited from the `Object` class and is modified in the `String` class to test whether two strings are identical in content. You can override the `equals` method in the `Circle` class to compare whether two circles are equal based on their radius as follows:

```java
public boolean equals(Object o) {
  if (o instanceof Circle) {
    return radius == ((Circle)o).radius;
  }
  else
    return false;
}
```

Note

The `==` comparison operator is used for comparing two primitive data type values or for determining whether two objects have the same references. The `equals` method is intended to test whether two objects have the same contents, provided that the method is modified in the defining class of the objects. The `==` operator is stronger than the `equals` method, in that the `==` operator checks whether the two reference variables refer to the same object.

== vs. equals

Caution

Using the signature `equals(SomeClassName obj)` (e.g., `equals(Circle c)` to override the `equals` method in a subclass is a common mistake. You should use `equals(Object obj)`. See Review Question 10.12.

equals(Object)

10.8 Polymorphism, Dynamic Binding, and Generic Programming

The three pillars of object-oriented programming are encapsulation, inheritance, and polymorphism. You have already learned the first two. This section introduces polymorphism.

Before getting into the detail, let us define two useful terms: subtype and supertype. A class defines a type. A type defined by a subclass is called a *subtype* and a type defined by its superclass is called a *supertype*. A variable must be declared a type. The type of a variable is called its *declared type*. A variable of a reference type can hold a `null` value or a reference to an object. An object is an instance of a class.

subtype
supertype
declared type

The inheritance relationship enables a subclass to inherit features from its superclass with additional new features. A subclass is a specialization of its superclass; every instance of a subclass is an instance of its superclass, but not vice versa. For example, every circle is an object, but not every object is a circle. Therefore, you can always pass an instance of a subclass to a parameter of its superclass type. Consider the code in Listing 10.6:

LISTING 10.6 PolymorphismDemo.java

```java
1 public class PolymorphismDemo {
2   public static void main(String[] args) {
```

polymorphic call

```
 3      m(new GraduateStudent());
 4      m(new Student());
 5      m(new Person());
 6      m(new Object());
 7    }
 8
 9    public static void m(Object x) {
10      System.out.println(x.toString());
11    }
12  }
13
14  class GraduateStudent extends Student {
15  }
16
17  class Student extends Person {
18    public String toString() {
19      return "Student";
20    }
21  }
22
23  class Person extends Object {
24    public String toString() {
25      return "Person";
26    }
27  }
```

dynamic binding

override **toString()**

override **toString()**

```
Student
Student
Person
java.lang.Object@130c19b
```

The program produces the preceding output. Why? Let us discuss the reason. Method m (line 9) takes a parameter of the `Object` type. You can invoke m with any object (e.g., `new Graduate-Student()`, `new Student()`, `new Person()`, and `new Object()`)in lines 3-6). An object of a subclass can be used wherever its superclass object is required. This is commonly known as *polymorphism* (from a Greek word meaning "many forms"). In simple terms, polymorphism means that a variable of supertype can refer to a subtype object.

polymorphism

When the method `m(Object x)` is executed, the argument x's `toString` method is invoked. x may be an instance of `GraduateStudent`, `Student`, `Person`, or `Object`. Classes `GraduateStudent`, `Student`, `Person`, and `Object` have their own implementations of the `toString` method. Which implementation is used will be determined dynamically by the Java Virtual Machine at runtime. This capability is known as *dynamic binding*.

dynamic binding

Dynamic binding works as follows: Suppose an object o is an instance of classes C_1, C_2, ..., C_{n-1}, and C_n, where C_1 is a subclass of C_2, C_2 is a subclass of C_3, ..., and C_{n-1} is a subclass of C_n, as shown in Figure 10.3. That is, C_n is the most general class, and C_1 is the most specific class. In Java, C_n is the `Object` class. If o invokes a method p, the JVM searches the implementation for the method p in C_1, C_2, ..., C_{n-1}, and C_n, in this order, until it is found. Once

$$C_n \longleftarrow C_{n-1} \longleftarrow \quad \cdots \cdots \quad \longleftarrow C_2 \longleftarrow C_1$$

java.lang.Object

If o is an instance of C_1, o is also an instance of C_2, C_3, ..., C_{n-1}, and C_n

FIGURE 10.3 The method to be invoked is dynamically bound at runtime.

an implementation is found, the search stops and the first-found implementation is invoked. For example, when `m(new GraduateStudent())` is invoked in line 3, the `toString` method defined in the `Student` class is used.

Matching a method signature and binding a method implementation are two separate issues. The *declared type* of the reference variable decides which method to match at compile time. The compiler finds a matching method according to parameter type, number of parameters, and order of the parameters at compile time. A method may be implemented in several subclasses. The JVM dynamically binds the implementation of the method at runtime, decided by the *actual class* of the object referenced by the variable. *matching vs. binding*

Dynamic binding enables new classes to be loaded on the fly without recompilation. There is no need for developers to create, and for users to install, major new software versions. New features can be incorporated transparently as needed. For example, suppose you have placed the classes `Test`, `GraduateStudent`, `Student`, `Person` in four separate files. If you change `GraduateStudent` as follows: *benefits of dynamic binding*

```
class GraduateStudent extends Student {
  public String toString() {
    return "Graduate Student";
  }
}
```

you have a new version of `GraduateStudent` with a new `toString` method, but you don't have to recompile the classes `Test`, `Student`, and `Person`. When you run `Test`, the JVM dynamically binds the new `toString` method for the object of `GraduateStudent` when executing `m(new GraduateStudent())`.

Polymorphism allows methods to be used generically for a wide range of object arguments. This is known as *generic programming*. If a method's parameter type is a superclass (e.g., `Object`), you may pass to this method an object of any of the parameter's subclasses (e.g., `Student` or `String`). When an object (e.g., a `Student` object or a `String` object) is used in the method, the particular implementation of the method of the object invoked (e.g., `toString`) is determined dynamically. *generic programming*

10.9 Casting Objects and the `instanceof` Operator

You have already used the casting operator to convert variables of one primitive type to another. Casting can also be used to convert an object of one class type to another within an inheritance hierarchy. In the preceding section, the statement

```
m(new Student());
```

assigns the object `new Student()` to a parameter of the `Object` type. This statement is equivalent to

```
Object o = new Student(); // Implicit casting
m(o);
```

The statement `Object o = new Student()`, known as *implicit casting*, is legal because an instance of `Student` is automatically an instance of `Object`. *implicit casting*

Suppose you want to assign the object reference `o` to a variable of the `Student` type using the following statement:

```
Student b = o;
```

In this case a compilation error would occur. Why does the statement `Object o  = new Student()` work when `Student b = o` doesn't? The reason is that a `Student` object is

explicit casting

always an instance of `Object`, but an `Object` is not necessarily an instance of `Student`. Even though you can see that `o` is really a `Student` object, the compiler is not clever enough to know it. To tell the compiler that `o` is a `Student` object, use an *explicit casting*. The syntax is similar to the one used for casting among primitive data types. Enclose the target object type in parentheses and place it before the object to be cast, as follows:

```
Student b = (Student)o; // Explicit casting
```

upcasting
downcasting

ClassCastException

instanceof

It is always possible to cast an instance of a subclass to a variable of a superclass (known as *upcasting*), because an instance of a subclass is *always* an instance of its superclass. When casting an instance of a superclass to a variable of its subclass (known as *downcasting*), explicit casting must be used to confirm your intention to the compiler with the (`SubclassName`) cast notation. For the casting to be successful, you must make sure that the object to be cast is an instance of the subclass. If the superclass object is not an instance of the subclass, a runtime *`ClassCastException`* occurs. For example, if an object is not an instance of `Student`, it cannot be cast into a variable of `Student`. It is a good practice, therefore, to ensure that the object is an instance of another object before attempting a casting. This can be accomplished by using the `instanceof` operator. Consider the following code:

```
Object myObject = new Circle();
... // Some lines of code
/** Perform casting if myObject is an instance of Circle */
if (myObject instanceof Circle) {
  System.out.println("The circle diameter is " +
    ((Circle)myObject).getDiameter());
  ...
}
```

You may be wondering why casting is necessary. Variable `myObject` is declared `Object`. The *declared type* decides which method to match at compile time. Using `myObject.-getDiameter()` would cause a compilation error, because the `Object` class does not have the `getDiameter` method. The compiler cannot find a match for `myObject.getDiameter()`. It is necessary to cast `myObject` into the `Circle` type to tell the compiler that `myObject` is also an instance of `Circle`.

Why not declare `myObject` as a `Circle` type in the first place? To enable generic programming, it is a good practice to declare a variable with a supertype, which can accept a value of any subtype.

lowercase keywords

Note

`instanceof` is a Java keyword. Every letter in a Java keyword is in lowercase.

casting analogy

Tip

To help understand casting, you may also consider the analogy of fruit, apple, and orange with the `Fruit` class as the superclass for `Apple` and `Orange`. An apple is a fruit, so you can always safely assign an instance of `Apple` to a variable for `Fruit`. However, a fruit is not necessarily an apple, so you have to use explicit casting to assign an instance of `Fruit` to a variable of `Apple`.

Listing 10.7 demonstrates polymorphism and casting. The program creates two objects (lines 5-6), a circle and a rectangle, and invokes the `displayObject` method to display them (lines 9-10). The `displayObject` method displays the area and diameter if the object is a circle (line 15), and the area if the object is a rectangle (line 21).

LISTING 10.7   `TestPolymorphismCasting.java`

```
1 public class TestPolymorphismCasting {
2   /** Main method */
```

```
 3    public static void main(String[] args) {
 4      // Declare and initialize two objects
 5      Object object1 = new Circle4(1);
 6      Object object2 = new Rectangle1(1, 1);
 7
 8      // Display circle and rectangle
 9      displayObject(object1);
10      displayObject(object2);
11    }
12
13    /** A method for displaying an object */
14    public static void displayObject(Object object) {
15      if (object instanceof Circle4) {
16        System.out.println("The circle area is " +
17          ((Circle4)object).getArea());
18        System.out.println("The circle diameter is " +
19          ((Circle4)object).getDiameter());
20      }
21      else if (object instanceof Rectangle1) {
22        System.out.println("The rectangle area is " +
23          ((Rectangle1)object).getArea());
24      }
25    }
26  }
```

polymorphic call

polymorphic call

```
The circle area is 3.141592653589793
The circle diameter is 2.0
The rectangle area is 1.0
```

The `displayObject(Object object)` method is an example of generic programming. It can be invoked by passing any instance of `Object`.

The program uses implicit casting to assign a `Circle` object to `object1` and a `Rectangle` object to `object2` (lines 5–6), and then invokes the `displayObject` method to display the information on these objects (lines 9–10).

In the `displayObject` method (lines 14–25), explicit casting is used to cast the object to `Circle` if the object is an instance of `Circle`, and the methods `getArea` and `getDiameter` are used to display the area and diameter of the circle.

Casting can be done only when the source object is an instance of the target class. The program uses the `instanceof` operator to ensure that the source object is an instance of the target class before performing a casting (line 15).

Explicit casting to `Circle` (lines 17, 19) and to `Rectangle` (line 23) is necessary because the `getArea` and `getDiameter` methods are not available in the `Object` class.

Caution

The object member access operator (.) precedes the casting operator. Use parentheses to ensure that casting is done before the . operator, as in

. precedes casting

```
((Circle)object).getArea());
```

10.10 The ArrayList Class

You can create an array to store objects. But, once the array is created, the array's size is fixed. Java provides the `ArrayList` class that can be used to store an unlimited number of objects. Figure 10.4 shows some methods in `ArrayList`.

Video Note
ArrayList class

java.util.ArrayList	
+ArrayList()	Creates an empty list.
+add(o: Object): void	Appends a new element o at the end of this list.
+add(index: int, o: Object): void	Adds a new element o at the specified index in this list.
+clear(): void	Removes all the elements from this list.
+contains(o: Object): boolean	Returns true if this list contains the element o.
+get(index: int): Object	Returns the element from this list at the specified index.
+indexOf(o: Object): int	Returns the index of the first matching element in this list.
+isEmpty(): boolean	Returns true if this list contains no elements.
+lastIndexOf(o: Object): int	Returns the index of the last matching element in this list.
+remove(o: Object): boolean	Removes the element o from this list.
+size(): int	Returns the number of elements in this list.
+remove(index: int): boolean	Removes the element at the specified index.
+set(index: int, o: Object): Object	Sets the element at the specified index.

FIGURE 10.4 An ArrayList stores an unlimited number of objects.

Listing 10.8 is an example of using ArrayList. The program creates an ArrayList using its no-arg constructor (line 4). The **add** method adds any instance of Object into the list. Since **String** is a subclass of Object, strings can be added to the list. The **add** method (lines 7-17) adds an object to the end of list. So, after cityList.add("London") (line 7), the list contains

[London]

add(Object)

After cityList.add("New York") (line 9), the list contains

[London, New York]

After adding Paris, Toronto, Hong Kong, and Singapore (lines 11-17), the list would contain

[London, New York, Paris, Toronto, Hong Kong, Singapore]

size()

Invoking size() (line 21) returns the size of the list, which is currently 6. Invoking contains("Toronto") (line 23) checks whether the object is in the list. In this case, it returns true, since Toronto is in the list. Invoking indexOf("New York") (line 25) returns the index of the object in the list, which is 1. If the object is not in the list, it returns -1. The isEmpty() method (line 27) checks whether the list is empty. It returns false, since the list is not empty.

add(index, Object)

The statement cityList.add(2, "Beijing") (line 30) inserts an object to the list at the specified index. After this statement, the list becomes

[London, New York, Beijing, Paris, Toronto, Hong Kong, Singapore]

remove(Object)

The statement cityList.remove("Toronto") (line 35) removes the object from the list. After this statement, the list becomes

[London, New York, Beijing, Paris, Hong Kong, Singapore]

remove(index)

The statement cityList.remove(1) (line 40) removes the object at the specified index from the list. After this statement, the list becomes

[London, Beijing, Paris, Hong Kong, Singapore]

The statement in line 44 is same as

```
System.out.println(cityList);
```

The toString() method returns a string representation for the list in the form of [e0.toString(), e1.toString(), ..., ek.toString()], where e0, e1, ..., and ek are the elements in the list.

    The get(index) method (line 48) returns the object at the specified index.

toString()

getIndex()

LISTING 10.8 TestArrayList.java

```java
 1  public class TestArrayList {
 2    public static void main(String[] args) {
 3      // Create a list to store cities
 4      java.util.ArrayList cityList = new java.util.ArrayList();
 5
 6      // Add some cities in the list
 7      cityList.add("London");
 8      // cityList now contains [London]
 9      cityList.add("New York");
10      // cityList now contains [London, New York]
11      cityList.add("Paris");
12      // cityList now contains [London, New York, Paris]
13      cityList.add("Toronto");
14      // cityList now contains [London, New York, Paris, Toronto]
15      cityList.add("Hong Kong");
16      // contains [London, New York, Paris, Toronto, Hong Kong]
17      cityList.add("Singapore");
18      // contains [London, New York, Paris, Toronto,
19      //           Hong Kong, Singapore]
20
21      System.out.println("List size? " + cityList.size());
22      System.out.println("Is Toronto in the list? " +
23        cityList.contains("Toronto"));
24      System.out.println("The location of New York in the list? "
25        + cityList.indexOf("New York"));
26      System.out.println("Is the list empty? " +
27        cityList.isEmpty()); // Print false
28
29      // Insert a new city at index 2
30      cityList.add(2, "Beijing");
31      // contains [London, New York, Beijing, Paris, Toronto,
32      //           Hong Kong, Singapore]
33
34      // Remove a city from the list
35      cityList.remove("Toronto");
36      // contains [London, New York, Beijing, Paris,
37      //           Hong Kong, Singapore]
38
39      // Remove a city at index 1
40      cityList.remove(1);
41      // contains [London, Beijing, Paris, Hong Kong, Singapore]
42
43      // Display the contents in the list
44      System.out.println(cityList.toString());
45
46      // Display the contents in the list in reverse order
47      for (int i = cityList.size() - 1; i> = 0; i--)
48        System.out.print(cityList.get(i) + " ");
49      System.out.println();
```

create **ArrayList**

add element

list size

contains element?

element index

is empty?

remove element

remove element

toString()

get element

create **ArrayList**

```
50
51    // Create a list to store two circles
52    java.util.ArrayList list = new java.util.ArrayList();
53
54    // Add two circles
55    list.add(new Circle4(2));
56    list.add(new Circle4(3));
57
58    // Display the area of the first circle in the list
59    System.out.println("The area of the circle? " +
60      ((Circle4)list.get(0)).getArea());
61  }
62 }
```

```
List size? 6
Is Toronto in the list? True
The location of New York in the list? 1
Is the list empty? false
[London, Beijing, Paris, Hong Kong, Singapore]
Singapore Hong Kong Paris Beijing London
The area of the circle? 12.566370614359172
```

Note

compiler warning

You will get the following warning when compiling this program from the command prompt:

```
Note: TestArrayList.java uses unchecked or unsafe operations.
Note: Recompile with –Xlint:unchecked for details.
```

This warning can be eliminated using generic types discussed in Chapter 21, "Generics." For now, ignore it. Despite the warning, the program will be compiled just fine to produce a .class file.

array vs. **ArrayList**

`ArrayList` objects can be used like arrays, but there are many differences. Table 10.1 lists their similarities and differences.

TABLE 10.1 Differences and Similarities between Arrays and `ArrayList`

Operation	Array	ArrayList
Creating an array/ArrayList	Object[] a = new Object[10]	ArrayList list = new ArrayList();
Accessing an element	a[index]	list.get(index);
Updating an element	a[index] = "London";	list.set(index, "London");
Returning size	a.length	list.size();
Adding a new element		list.add("London");
Inserting a new element		list.add(index, "London");
Removing an element		list.remove(index);
Removing an element		list.remove(Object);
Removing all elements		list.clear();

Once an array is created, its size is fixed. You can access an array element using the square bracket notation (e.g., `a[index]`). When an `ArrayList` is created, its size is `0`. You cannot use the `get` and `set` methods if the element is not in the list. It is easy to add, insert, and remove elements in a list, but it is rather complex to add, insert, and remove elements in an array. You have to write the code to manipulate the array in order to perform these operations.

Note

java.util.Vector is also a class for storing objects, which is very similar to the ArrayList class. All the methods in ArrayList are also available in Vector. The Vector class was introduced in JDK 1.1. The ArrayList class introduced in JDK 1.2 was intended to replace the Vector class.

Vector class

10.11 A Custom Stack Class

"Designing a Class for Stacks" in §9.8 presented a stack class for storing int values. This section introduces a stack class to store objects. You can use an ArrayList to implement Stack, as shown in Listing 10.9. The UML diagram for the class is shown in Figure 10.5.

MyStack	
-list: ArrayList	A list to store elements.
+isEmpty(): boolean	Returns true if this stack is empty.
+getSize(): int	Returns the number of elements in this stack.
+peek(): Object	Returns the top element in this stack.
+pop(): Object	Returns and removes the top element in this stack.
+push(o: Object): Object	Adds a new element to the top of this stack.
+search(o: Object): int	Returns the position of the first element in the stack from the top that matches the specified element.

FIGURE 10.5 The MyStack class encapsulates the stack storage and provides the operations for manipulating the stack.

LISTING 10.9 MyStack.java

```
 1  public class MyStack {
 2    private java.util.ArrayList list = new java.util.ArrayList();    array list
 3
 4    public boolean isEmpty() {                                       stack empty?
 5      return list.isEmpty();
 6    }
 7
 8    public int getSize() {                                           get stack size
 9      return list.size();
10    }
11
12    public Object peek() {                                           peek stack
13      return list.get(getSize() - 1);
14    }
15
16    public Object pop() {                                            remove
17      Object o = list.get(getSize() - 1);
18      list.remove(getSize() - 1);
19      return o;
20    }
21
22    public Object push(Object o) {                                   add
23      list.add(o);
24      return o;
25    }
26
```

search

```
27  public int search(Object o) {
28    return list.lastIndexOf(o);
29  }
30
31  /** Override the toString in the Object class */
32  public String toString() {
33    return "stack: " + list.toString();
34  }
35 }
```

An array list is created to store the elements in the stack (line 2). The `isEmpty()` method (lines 4-6) is the same as `list.isEmpty()`. The `getSize()` method (lines 8-10) is the same as `list.size()`. The `peek()` method (lines 12-14) looks at the element at the top of the stack without removing it. The end of the list is the top of the stack. The `pop()` method (lines 16-20) removes the top element from the stack and returns it. The `push(Object element)` method (lines 22-25) adds the specified element to the stack. The `search(Object element)` method checks whether the specified element is in the stack, and returns the index of first-matching element in the stack from the top by invoking `list.lastIndexOf(o)`. The `toString()` method (lines 32-34) defined in the `Object` class is overridden to display the contents of the stack by invoking `list.toString()`. The `toString()` method implemented in `ArrayList` returns a string representation of all the elements in an array list.

Design Guide

In Listing 10.9, `MyStack` contains `ArrayList`. The relationship between `MyStack` and `ArrayList` is called *composition*. While inheritance models an is-a relationship, composition models a has-a relationship. You may also implement `MyStack` as a subclass of `ArrayList` (see Exercise 10.4). Using composition is better, however, because it enables you to declare a completely new stack class without inheriting the unnecessary and inappropriate methods from `ArrayList`.

composition

has-a

is-a

10.12 The **protected** Data and Methods

The modifier `protected` can be applied to data and methods in a class. A protected datum or a protected method in a public class can be accessed *by any class in the same package or its subclasses*, even if the subclasses are in different packages.

The modifiers `private`, `protected`, and `public` are known as *visibility* or *accessibility modifiers* because they specify how class and class members are accessed. The visibility of these modifiers increases in this order:

Visibility increases

⟶

private, none (if no modifier is used), protected, public

Table 10.2 summarizes the accessibility of the members in a class. Figure 10.6 illustrates how a public, protected, default, and private datum or method in class `C1` can be accessed from a class `C2` in the same package, from a subclass `C3` in the same package, from a subclass `C4` in a different package, and from a class `C5` in a different package.

TABLE 10.2 Data and Methods Visibility

Modifier on members in a class	Accessed from the same class	Accessed from the same package	Accessed from a subclass	Accessed from a different package
Public	✓	✓	✓	✓
Protected	✓	✓	✓	–
(default)	✓	✓	–	–
private	✓	–	–	–

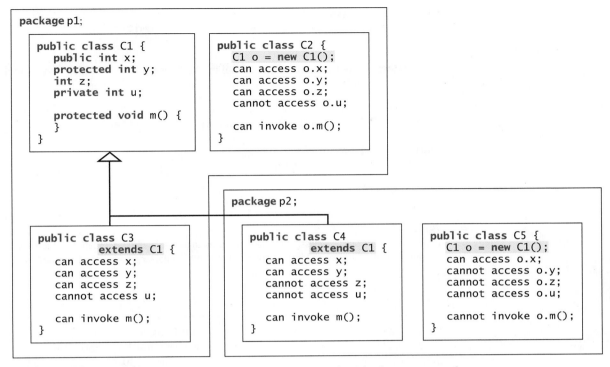

FIGURE 10.6   Visibility modifiers are used to control how data and methods are accessed.

Use the `private` modifier to hide the members of the class completely so that they cannot be accessed directly from outside the class. Use no modifiers in order to allow the members of the class to be accessed directly from any class within the same package but not from other packages. Use the `protected` modifier to enable the members of the class to be accessed by the subclasses in any package or classes in the same package. Use the `public` modifier to enable the members of the class to be accessed by any class.

Your class can be used in two ways: for creating instances of the class, and for creating subclasses by extending the class. Make the members `private` if they are not intended for use from outside the class. Make the members `public` if they are intended for the users of the class. Make the fields or methods `protected` if they are intended for the extenders of the class but not the users of the class.

The `private` and `protected` modifiers can be used only for members of the class. The `public` modifier and the default modifier (i.e., no modifier) can be used on members of the class as well on the class. A class with no modifier (i.e., not a public class) is not accessible by classes from other packages.

Note

A subclass may override a protected method in its superclass and change its visibility to public. However, a subclass cannot weaken the accessibility of a method defined in the superclass. For example, if a method is defined as public in the superclass, it must be defined as public in the subclass.

change visibility

10.13 Preventing Extending and Overriding

You may occasionally want to prevent classes from being extended. In such cases, use the `final` modifier to indicate that a class is final and cannot be a parent class. The `Math` class, introduced in Chapter 5, "Methods," is a final class. The `String`, `StringBuilder`, and `StringBuffer` classes, introduced in Chapter 8, "Strings and Text I/O," are also final classes. For example, the following class is final and cannot be extended.

```
public final class C {
  // Data fields, constructors, and methods omitted
}
```

You also can define a method to be final; a final method cannot be overridden by its subclasses. For example, the following method is final and cannot be overridden.

```
public class Test {
  // Data fields, constructors, and methods omitted

  public final void m() {
    // Do something
  }
}
```

 Note

The modifiers are used on classes and class members (data and methods), except that the `final` modifier can also be used on local variables in a method. A final local variable is a constant inside a method.

KEY TERMS

array list   345
casting objects   343
composition   350
constructor chaining   337
dynamic binding   342
final   351
generic programming   343
has-a relationship   350
inheritance   330

instanceof   344
is-a relationship   350
override   339
polymorphism   342
protected   350
subclass   330
subtype   341
superclass   330
supertype   341

CHAPTER SUMMARY

■   You can derive a new class from an existing class. This is known as *class inheritance*. The new class is called a *subclass*, *child class,* or *extended class*. The existing class is called a *superclass*, *parent class*, or *base class*.

■   A constructor is used to construct an instance of a class. Unlike properties and methods, the constructors of a superclass are not inherited in the subclass. They can be invoked only from the constructors of the subclasses, using the keyword `super`.

■   A constructor may invoke an overloaded constructor or its superclass's constructor. The call must be the first statement in the constructor. If none of them is invoked explicitly, the compiler puts `super()` as the first statement in the constructor.

■   To override a method, the method must be defined in the subclass using the same signature as in its superclass.

■   An instance method can be overridden only if it is accessible. Thus a private method cannot be overridden, because it is not accessible outside its own class. If a method defined in a subclass is private in its superclass, the two methods are completely unrelated.

■   Like an instance method, a static method can be inherited. However, a static method cannot be overridden. If a static method defined in the superclass is redefined in a subclass, the method defined in the superclass is hidden.

■ Every class in Java is descended from the `java.lang.Object` class. If no inheritance is specified when a class is defined, its superclass is `Object`.

■ If a method's parameter type is a superclass (e.g., `Object`), you may pass an object to this method of any of the parameter's subclasses (e.g., `Circle` or `String`). When an object (e.g., a `Circle` object or a `String` object) is used in the method, the particular implementation of the method of the object that is invoked (e.g., `toString`) is determined dynamically.

■ It is always possible to cast an instance of a subclass to a variable of a superclass, because an instance of a subclass is *always* an instance of its superclass. When casting an instance of a superclass to a variable of its subclass, explicit casting must be used to confirm your intention to the compiler with the (`SubclassName`) cast notation.

■ You can override an instance method, but you cannot override a field (instance or static) or a static method. If you declare a field or a static method in a subclass with the same name as one in the superclass, the one in the superclass is hidden, but it still exists. You can reference the hidden field or static method using the `super` keyword in the subclass. The hidden field or method can also be accessed via a reference variable of the superclass's type.

■ When invoking an instance method from a reference variable, the *actual class of the object* referenced by the variable decides which implementation of the method is used *at runtime*. When accessing a field or a static method, the *declared type* of the reference variable decides which method is used *at compile time*.

■ You can use `obj instanceof AClass` to check whether an object is an instance of a class.

■ You can use the **protected** modifier to prevent the data and methods from being accessed by nonsubclasses from a different package.

■ You can use the `final` modifier to indicate that a class is final and cannot be a parent class.

REVIEW QUESTIONS

Sections 10.2–10.6

10.1 What is the printout of running the class `C` in (a)? What problem arises in compiling the program in (b)?

```
class A {
  public A() {
    System.out.println(
      "A's no-arg constructor is invoked");
  }
}

class B extends A {
}

public class C {
  public static void main(String[] args) {
    B b = new B();
  }
}
```

(a)

```
class A {
  public A(int x) {
  }
}

class B extends A {
  public B() {
  }
}

public class C {
  public static void main(String[] args) {
    B b = new B();
  }
}
```

(b)

10.2 True or false?

1. A subclass is a subset of a superclass.
2. When invoking a constructor from a subclass, its superclass's no-arg constructor is always invoked.
3. You can override a private method defined in a superclass.
4. You can override a static method defined in a superclass.

10.3 Identify the problems in the following classes:

```
 1 public class Circle {
 2   private double radius;
 3
 4   public Circle(double radius) {
 5     radius = radius;
 6   }
 7
 8   public double getRadius() {
 9     return radius;
10   }
11
12   public double getArea() {
13     return radius * radius * Math.PI;
14   }
15 }
16
17 class B extends Circle {
18   private double length;
19
20   B(double radius, double length) {
21     Circle(radius);
22     length = length;
23   }
24
25   /** Override getArea() */
26   public double getArea() {
27     return getArea() * length;
28   }
29 }
```

10.4 How do you explicitly invoke a superclass's constructor from the subclass?

10.5 How do you invoke an overridden superclass method from the subclass?

10.6 Explain the difference between method overloading and method overriding.

10.7 If a method in a subclass has the same signature as a method in its superclass with the same return type, is the method overridden or overloaded?

10.8 If a method in a subclass has the same signature as a method in its superclass with a different return type, will this be a problem?

10.9 If a method in a subclass has the same name as a method in its superclass with different parameter types, is the method overridden or overloaded?

Section 10.7 The Object Class and Its Methods

10.10 Does every class have a toString method and an equals method? Where do they come from? How are they used? Is it appropriate to override these methods?

10.11 Show the output of following program:

```
1 public class Test {
2   public static void main(String[] args) {
```

```
3      A a = new A(3);
4    }
5 }
6
7 class A extends B {
8    public A(int t) {
9        System.out.println("A's constructor is invoked");
10   }
11 }
12
13 class B {
14   public B() {
15       System.out.println("B's constructor is invoked");
16   }
17 }
```

Is the no-arg constructor of `Object` invoked when `new A(3)` is invoked?

10.12 When overriding the `equals` method, a common mistake is mistyping its signature in the subclass. For example, the `equals` method is incorrectly written as `equals(Circle circle)`, as shown in (a) in the following code; instead, it should be `equals(Object circle)`, as shown in (b). Show the output of running class `Test` with the `Circle` class in (a) and in (b), respectively.

```
public class Test {
  public static void main(String[] args) {
    Object circle1 = new Circle();
    Object circle2 = new Circle();
    System.out.println(circle1.equals(circle2));
  }
}
```

```
class Circle {
  double radius;

  public boolean equals(Circle circle) {
    return this.radius == circle.radius;

  }
}
```

```
class Circle {
  double radius;

  public boolean equals(Object circle) {
    return this.radius ==
           ((Circle)circle).radius;
  }
}
```

(a)   (b)

Sections 10.8–10.9

10.13 For the `GeometricObject` and `Circle` classes in Listings 10.1 and 10.2, answer the following questions:

(a) Are the following Boolean expressions true or false?

```
Circle circle = new Circle(1);
GeometricObject object1 = new GeometricObject();
(circle instanceof GeometricObject)
(object1 instanceof GeometricObject)
(circle instanceof Circle)
(object1 instanceof Circle)
```

(b) Can the following statements be compiled?

```
Circle circle = new Circle(5);
GeometricObject object = circle;
```

(c) Can the following statements be compiled?

```
GeometricObject object = new GeometricObject();
Circle circle = (Circle)object;
```

10.14 Suppose that `Fruit`, `Apple`, `Orange`, `Golden Delicious Apple`, and `Macintosh Apple` are declared, as shown in Figure 10.7.

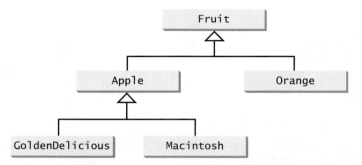

FIGURE 10.7 `GoldenDelicious` and `Macintosh` are subclasses of `Apple`, `Apple` and `Orange` are subclasses of `Fruit`.

Assume that the following declaration is given:

```
Fruit fruit = new GoldenDelicious();
Orange orange = new Orange();
```

Answer the following questions:

(1) Is `fruit instanceof Fruit`?
(2) Is `fruit instanceof Orange`?
(3) Is `fruit instanceof Apple`?
(4) Is `fruit instanceof GoldenDelicious`?
(5) Is `fruit instanceof Macintosh`?
(6) Is `orange instanceof Orange`?
(7) Is `orange instanceof Fruit`?
(8) Is `orange instanceof Apple`?
(9) Suppose the method `makeApple` is defined in the `Apple` class. Can `fruit` invoke this method? Can `orange` invoke this method?
(10) Suppose the method `makeOrangeJuice` is defined in the `Orange` class. Can `orange` invoke this method? Can `fruit` invoke this method?
(11) Is the statement `Orange p = new Apple()` legal?
(12) Is the statement `Macintosh p = new Apple()` legal?
(13) Is the statement `Apple p = new Macintosh()` legal?

10.15 What is wrong in the following code?

```
1 public class Test {
2   public static void main(String[] args) {
3     Object fruit = new Fruit();
4     Object apple = (Apple)fruit;
5   }
6 }
7
8 class Apple extends Fruit {
9 }
10
11 class Fruit {
12 }
```

Section 10.10 The ArrayList Class

10.16 How do you create an ArrayList? How do you append an object to a list? How do you insert an object at the beginning of a list? How do you find the number of objects in a list? How do you remove a given object from a list? How do you re-move the last object from the list? How do you check whether a given object is in a list? How do you retrieve an object at a specified index from a list?

10.17 There are three errors in the following code. Identify them.

```
ArrayList list = new ArrayList();
list.add("New York");
list.add("Austin");
list.add(new java.util.Date());
String city = list.get(0);
list.set(3, "Dallas");
System.out.println(list.get(3));
```

Sections 10.12-10.13

10.18 What modifier should you use on a class so that a class in the same package can access it, but a class in a different package cannot access it?

10.19 What modifier should you use so that a class in a different package cannot access the class, but its subclasses in any package can access it?

10.20 In the following code, classes A and B are in the same package. If the question marks are replaced by blanks, can class B be compiled? If the question marks are replaced by private, can class B be compiled? If the question marks are replaced by protected, can class B be compiled?

```
package p1;

public class A {
    ?    int i;
    ?    void m() {
        ...
    }
}
```
(a)

```
package p1;

public class B extends A {
    public void m1(String[] args) {
        System.out.println(i);
        m();
    }
}
```
(b)

10.21 In the following code, classes A and B are in different packages. If the question marks are replaced by blanks, can class B be compiled? If the question marks are replaced by private, can class B be compiled? If the question marks are replaced by protected, can class B be compiled?

```
package p1;

public class A {
    ?    int i;
    ?    void m() {
        ...
    }
}
```
(a)

```
package p2;

public class B extends A {
    public void m1(String[] args) {
        System.out.println(i);
        m();
    }
}
```
(b)

10.22 How do you prevent a class from being extended? How do you prevent a method from being overridden?

Comprehensive

10.23 Define the following terms: inheritance, superclass, subclass, the keywords `super` and `this`, casting objects, the modifiers `protected` and `final`.

10.24 Indicate true or false for the following statements:

- A protected datum or method can be accessed by any class in the same package.
- A protected datum or method can be accessed by any class in different packages.
- A protected datum or method can be accessed by its subclasses in any package.
- A final class can have instances.
- A final class can be extended.
- A final method can be overridden.
- You can always successfully cast an instance of a subclass to a superclass.
- You can always successfully cast an instance of a superclass to a subclass.

10.25 Describe the difference between method matching and method binding.

10.26 What is polymorphism? What is dynamic binding? What is generic programming? What are the advantages of dynamic binding?

PROGRAMMING EXERCISES

Sections 10.2–10.5

10.1 (*The Triangle class*) Design a class named `Triangle` that extends `GeometricObject`. The class contains:

- Three `double` data fields named `side1`, `side2`, and `side3` with default values `1.0` to denote three sides of the triangle.
- A no-arg constructor that creates a default triangle.
- A constructor that creates a triangle with the specified `side1`, `side2`, and `side3`.
- The accessor methods for all three data fields.
- A method named `getArea()` that returns the area of this triangle.
- A method named `getPerimeter()` that returns the perimeter of this triangle.
- A method named `toString()` that returns a string description for the triangle.

For the formula to compute the area of a triangle, see Exercise 5.19. The `toString()` method is implemented as follows:

```
return "Triangle: side1 = " + side1 + " side2 = " + side2 +
    " side3 = " + side3;
```

Draw the UML diagram that involves the classes `Triangle` and `Geometric Object`. Implement the class. Write a test program that creates a `Triangle` object with sides `1`, `1.5`, `1`, setting color `yellow` and filled `true`, and displaying the area, perimeter, color, and whether filled or not.

Sections 10.6–10.9

10.2 (*The Person, Student, Employee, Faculty, and Staff classes*) Design a class named `Person` and its two subclasses named `Student` and `Employee`. Make `Faculty` and `Staff` subclasses of `Employee`. A person has a name, address, phone number, and email address. A student has a class status (freshman, sophomore, junior, or senior). Define the status as a constant. An employee has an office, salary, and date-hired. Define a class named `MyDate` that contains the fields year, month, and day. A faculty member has office hours and a rank. A staff member has a title. Override the toString method in each class to display the class name and the person's name.

Draw the UML diagram for the classes. Implement the classes. Write a test program that creates a Person, Student, Employee, Faculty, and Staff, and invokes their toString() methods.

10.3   (*Subclasses of Account*) In Exercise 7.3, the Account class was created to model a bank account. An account has the properties account number, balance, annual interest rate, and date created, and methods to deposit and withdraw. Create two subclasses for checking and saving accounts. A checking account has an overdraft limit, but a savings account cannot be overdrawn.

Draw the UML diagram for the classes. Implement the classes. Write a test program that creates objects of Account, SavingsAccount, and CheckingAccount and invokes their toString() methods.

10.4   (*Implementing MyStack using inheritance*) In Listing 10.9, MyStack is implemented using composition. Create a new stack class that extends ArrayList.

Video Note
Implement **MyStack** using inheritance

Draw the UML diagram for the classes. Implement MyStack. Write a test program that prompts the user to enter five strings and displays them in reverse order.

10.5   (*The Course class*) Rewrite the Course class in Listing 9.8. Use an ArrayList to replace an array to store students.

10.6   (*Using ArrayList*) Write a program that creates an ArrayList and adds a Loan object, a Date object, a string, a JFrame object, and a Circle object to the list, and use a loop to display all the elements in the list by invoking the object's toString() method.

10.7***   (*Implementing ArrayList*) ArrayList is implemented in the Java API. Implement ArrayList and the methods defined in Figure 10.4. (*Hint*: Use an array to store the elements in ArrayList. If the size of the ArrayList exceeds the capacity of the current array, create a new array that doubles the size of the current array and copy the contents of the current to the new array.)

CHAPTER 11

ABSTRACT CLASSES AND INTERFACES

Objectives

- To design and use abstract classes (§11.2).

- To process a calendar using the `Calendar` and `GregorianCalendar` classes (§11.3).

- To specify common behavior for objects using interfaces (§11.4).

- To define interfaces and declare classes that implement interfaces (§11.4).

- To define a natural order using the `Comparable` interface (§11.5).

- To enable objects to listen for action events using the `ActionListener` interface (§11.6).

- To make objects cloneable using the `Cloneable` interface (§11.7).

- To explore the similarities and differences between an abstract class and an interface (§11.8).

- To create objects for primitive values using the wrapper classes (`Byte`, `Short`, `Integer`, `Long`, `Float`, `Double`, `Character`, and `Boolean`) (§11.9).

- To create a generic sort method (§11.10).

- To simplify programming using automatic conversion between primitive types and wrapper class types (§11.11).

- To use the `BigInteger` and `BigDecimal` classes for computing very large numbers with arbitrary precisions (§11.12).

11.1 Introduction

problem

You have learned how to write simple programs to create and display GUI components. Can you write the code to respond to user actions, such as clicking a button? As shown in Figure 11.1, when a button is clicked, a message is displayed on the console.

FIGURE 11.1 The program responds to button-clicking action events.

In order to write such code, you have to know interfaces. An interface is for defining common behavior for classes. Before discussing interfaces, we introduce a closely related subject: abstract classes.

11.2 Abstract Classes

abstract class

In the inheritance hierarchy, classes become more specific and concrete *with each new subclass*. If you move from a subclass back up to a superclass, the classes become more general and less specific. Class design should ensure that a superclass contains common features of its subclasses. Sometimes a superclass is so abstract that it cannot have any specific instances. Such a class is referred to as an *abstract class*.

In Chapter 10, `GeometricObject` was declared as the superclass for `Circle` and `Rectangle`. `GeometricObject` models common features of geometric objects. Both `Circle` and `Rectangle` contain the `getArea()` and `getPerimeter()` methods for computing the area and perimeter of a circle and a rectangle. Since you can compute areas and perimeters for all geometric objects, it is better to declare the `getArea()` and `getPerimeter()` methods in the `GeometricObject` class. However, these methods cannot be implemented in the `GeometricObject` class, because their implementation depends on the specific type of geometric object. Such methods are referred to as *abstract methods* and are denoted using the *abstract* *modifier* in the method header. After you declare the methods in `GeometricObject`, it becomes an abstract class. Abstract classes are denoted using the **abstract** modifier in the class header. In UML graphic notation, the names of abstract classes and their abstract methods are italicized, as shown in Figure 11.2. Listing 11.1 gives the source code for the new `GeometricObject` class.

abstract method
abstract modifier

abstract class

Video Note
Abstract
GeometricObject class

LISTING 11.1 GeometricObject.java

```java
1  public abstract class GeometricObject {
2    private String color = "white";
3    private boolean filled;
4    private java.util.Date dateCreated;
5
6    /** Construct a default geometric object */
7    protected GeometricObject() {
8      dateCreated = new java.util.Date();
9    }
10
11   /** Return color */
12   public String getColor() {
13     return color;
14   }
15
```

```
16   /** Set a new color */
17   public void setColor(String color) {
18     this.color = color;
19   }
20
21   /** Return filled. Since filled is boolean,
22    *  the get method is named isFilled */
23   public boolean isFilled() {
24     return filled;
25   }
26
27   /** Set a new filled */
28   public void setFilled(boolean filled) {
29     this.filled = filled;
30   }
31
32   /** Get dateCreated */
33   public java.util.Date getDateCreated() {
34     return dateCreated;
35   }
36
37   /** Return a string representation of this object */
38   public String toString() {
39     return "created on " + dateCreated + "\ncolor: " + color +
40       " and filled: " + filled;
41   }
42
43   /** Abstract method getArea */
44   public abstract double getArea();                              abstract method
45
46   /** Abstract method getPerimeter */
47   public abstract double getPerimeter();                         abstract method
48 }
```

Abstract classes are like regular classes with data fields and methods, but you cannot create instances of abstract classes using the **new** operator. An abstract method is a method signature without implementation. Its implementation is provided by the subclasses. A class that contains abstract methods must be declared abstract.

The constructor in the abstract class is declared protected, because it is used only by subclasses. When you create an instance of a concrete subclass, the subclass's parent class constructor is invoked to initialize data fields defined in the parent class.

The `GeometricObject` abstract class provides the common features (data and methods) for geometric objects. Because you don't know how to compute areas and perimeters of geometric objects, `getArea` and `getPerimeter` are defined as abstract methods. These methods are implemented in the subclasses. The implementation of `Circle` and `Rectangle` is the same as in Listings 10.2 and 10.3, except that they extend the `GeometricObject` class defined in this chapter, as follows:

why protected constructor?

implementing **Circle**
implementing **Rectangle**

LISTING 11.2 Circle.java

```
1 public class Circle extends GeometricObject {
2   // Same as lines 2-40 in Listing 10.2, so omitted
3 }
```

extends **GeometricObject**

LISTING 11.3 Rectangle.java

```
1 public class Rectangle extends GeometricObject {
2   // Same as lines 2-41 in Listing 10.3, so omitted
3 }
```

extends **GeometricObject**

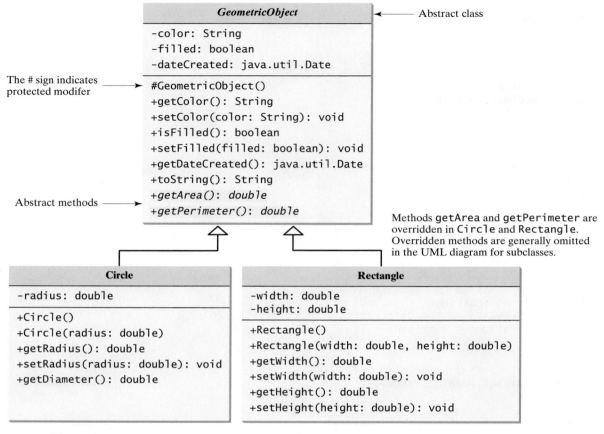

The # sign indicates protected modifer

Abstract methods

Methods getArea and getPerimeter are overridden in Circle and Rectangle. Overridden methods are generally omitted in the UML diagram for subclasses.

FIGURE 11.2 The new GeometricObject class contains abstract methods.

11.2.1 Why Abstract Methods?

You may be wondering what advantage is gained by defining the methods getArea and getPerimeter as abstract in the GeometricObject class instead of defining them only in each subclass. The following example shows the benefits of retaining them in the GeometricObject class.

The example in Listing 11.4 creates two geometric objects, a circle and a rectangle, invokes the equalArea method to check whether the two objects have equal areas, and invokes the displayGeometricObject method to display the objects.

LISTING 11.4 TestGeometricObject.java

```
1 public class TestGeometricObject {
2   /** Main method */
3   public static void main(String[] args) {
4     // Declare and initialize two geometric objects
5     GeometricObject geoObject1 = new Circle(5);
6     GeometricObject geoObject2 = new Rectangle(5, 3);
7
8     System.out.println("The two objects have the same area? " +
9       equalArea(geoObject1, geoObject2) );
10
11     // Display circle
12     displayGeometricObject(geoObject1);
13
```

create a circle
create a rectangle

```
14      // Display rectangle
15      displayGeometricObject(geoObject2);
16    }
17
18    /** A method for comparing the areas of two geometric objects */
19    public static boolean equalArea(GeometricObject object1,                    equalArea
20        GeometricObject object2) {
21      return object1.getArea() == object2.getArea();
22    }
23
24    /** A method for displaying a geometric object */
25    public static void displayGeometricObject(GeometricObject object) {         displayGeometricObject
26      System.out.println();
27      System.out.println("The area is " + object.getArea());
28      System.out.println("The perimeter is " + object.getPerimeter());
29    }
30  }
```

```
The two objects have the same area? false

The area is 78.53981633974483
The perimeter is 31.41592653589793

The area is 15.0
The perimeter is 16.0
```

The methods getArea() and getPerimeter() defined in the GeometricObject class are overridden in the Circle class and the Rectangle class. The statements (lines 5–6)

```
GeometricObject geoObject1 = new Circle(5);
GeometricObject geoObject2 = new Rectangle(5, 3);
```

create a new circle and rectangle and assign them to the variables geoObject1 and geoObject2. These two variables are of the GeometricObject type.

When invoking equalArea(geoObject1, geoObject2) (line 9), the getArea method defined in the Circle class is used for object1.getArea(), since geoObject1 is a circle, and the getArea method defined in the Rectangle class is used for object2.getArea(), since geoObject2 is a rectangle.

Similarly, when invoking displayGeometricObject(geoObject1) (line 12), the methods getArea and getPerimeter defined in the Circle class are used, and when invoking displayGeometricObject(geoObject2) (line 15), the methods getArea and getPerimeter defined in the Rectangle class are used. The JVM dynamically determines which of these methods to invoke at runtime, depending on the type of object.

Note that if the getArea and getPerimeter methods were not defined in GeometricObject, you cannot define the equalArea and displayObject methods in this program. So, you now see the benefits of defining the abstract methods in GeometricObject.

why abstract methods?

11.2.2 Interesting Points on Abstract Classes

The following points on abstract classes are worth noting:

- An abstract method cannot be contained in a nonabstract class. If a subclass of an abstract superclass does not implement all the abstract methods, the subclass must be declared abstract. In other words, in a nonabstract subclass extended from an abstract class, all the abstract methods must be implemented, even if they are not used in the subclass. Also note that abstract methods are nonstatic.

abstract method in abstract class

object cannot be created from
  abstract class

- An abstract class cannot be instantiated using the **new** operator, but you can still define its constructors, which are invoked in the constructors of its subclasses. For instance, the constructors of `GeometricObject` are invoked in the `Circle` class and the `Rectangle` class.

abstract class without abstract
  method

- A class that contains abstract methods must be abstract. However, it is possible to declare an abstract class that contains no abstract methods. In this case, you cannot create instances of the class using the **new** operator. This class is used as a base class for defining a new subclass.

superclass of abstract class
  may be concrete

- A subclass can be abstract even if its superclass is concrete. For example, the `Object` class is concrete, but its subclasses, such as `GeometricObject`, may be abstract.

concrete method overridden
  to be abstract

- A subclass can override a method from its superclass to declare it **abstract**. This is *very unusual*, but is useful when the implementation of the method in the superclass becomes invalid in the subclass. In this case, the subclass must be declared abstract.

abstract class as type

- You cannot create an instance from an abstract class using the **new** operator, but an abstract class can be used as a data type. Therefore, the following statement, which creates an array whose elements are of the `GeometricObject` type, is correct.

```
GeometricObject[] objects = new GeometricObject[10];
```

Video Note
Calendar and
GregorianCalendar
classes

abstract **add** method

11.3 Example: `Calendar` and `GregorianCalendar`

An instance of `java.util.Date` represents a specific instant in time with millisecond precision. `java.util.Calendar` is an abstract base class for extracting detailed calendar information, such as year, month, date, hour, minute, and second. Subclasses of `Calendar` can implement specific calendar systems, such as the Gregorian calendar, the lunar calendar, and the Jewish calendar. Currently, `java.util.GregorianCalendar` for the Gregorian calendar is supported in Java, as shown in Figure 11.3. The **add** method is abstract in the `Calendar` class, because its implementation is dependent on a concrete calendar system.

java.util.Calendar	
`#Calendar()`	Constructs a default calendar.
`+get(field: int): int`	Returns the value of the given calendar field.
`+set(field: int, value: int): void`	Sets the given calendar to the specified value.
`+set(year: int, month: int,` `  dayOfMonth: int): void`	Sets the calendar with the specified year, month, and date. The month parameter is 0 based; that is, 0 is for January.
`+getActualMaximum(field: int): int`	Returns the maximum value that the specified calendar field could have.
`+add(field: int, amount: int): void`	Adds or subtracts the specified amount of time to the given calendar field.
`+getTime(): java.util.Date`	Returns a `Date` object representing this calendar's time value (million second offset from the Unix epoch).
`+setTime(date: java.util.Date): void`	Sets this calendar's time with the given `Date` object.

java.util.GregorianCalendar	
`+GregorianCalendar()`	Constructs a `GregorianCalendar` for the current time.
`+GregorianCalendar(year: int,` `  month: int, dayOfMonth: int)`	Constructs a `GregorianCalendar` for the specified year, month, and day of month.

`+GregorianCalendar(year: int,`
`  month: int, dayOfMonth: int,`
`  hour:int, minute: int, second: int)`
	Constructs a `GregorianCalendar` for the specified year, month, day of month, hour, minute, and second. The month parameter is 0 based; that is, 0 is for January.

FIGURE 11.3   The abstract `Calendar` class defines common features of various calendars.

You can use `new GregorianCalendar()` to construct a default `GregorianCalendar` with the current time and `new GregorianCalendar(year, month, date)` to construct a `GregorianCalendar` with the specified `year`, `month`, and `date`. The `month` parameter is `0` based—that is, `0` is for January.

constructing calendar

The `get(int field)` method defined in the `Calendar` class is useful for extracting the date and time information from a `Calendar` object. The fields are defined as constants, as shown in Table 11.1.

get(field)

TABLE 11.1   Field constants in the `Calendar` class

Constant	Description
YEAR	The year of the calendar.
MONTH	The month of the calendar with 0 for January.
DATE	The day of the calendar.
HOUR	The hour of the calendar (12-hour notation).
HOUR_OF_DAY	The hour of the calendar (24-hour notation).
MINUTE	The minute of the calendar.
SECOND	The second of the calendar.
DAY_OF_WEEK	The day number within the week with 1 for Sunday.
DAY_OF_MONTH	Same as DATE.
DAY_OF_YEAR	The day number in the year with 1 for the first day of the year.
WEEK_OF_MONTH	The week number within the month.
WEEK_OF_YEAR	The week number within the year.
AM_PM	Indicator for AM or PM (0 for AM and 1 for PM).

Listing 11.5 gives an example that displays the date and time information for the current time.

LISTING 11.5   TestCalendar.java

```
 1 import java.util.*;
 2
 3 public class TestCalendar {
 4   public static void main(String[] args) {
 5     // Construct a Gregorian calendar for the current date and time
 6     Calendar calendar = new GregorianCalendar();
 7     System.out.println("Current time is " + new Date());
 8     System.out.println("YEAR:\t" + calendar.get(Calendar.YEAR));
 9     System.out.println("MONTH:\t" + calendar.get(Calendar.MONTH));
10     System.out.println("DATE:\t" + calendar.get(Calendar.DATE));
11     System.out.println("HOUR:\t" + calendar.get(Calendar.HOUR));
12     System.out.println("HOUR_OF_DAY:\t" +
13       calendar.get(Calendar.HOUR_OF_DAY));
14     System.out.println("MINUTE:\t" + calendar.get(Calendar.MINUTE));
15     System.out.println("SECOND:\t" + calendar.get(Calendar.SECOND));
16     System.out.println("DAY_OF_WEEK:\t" +
17       calendar.get(Calendar.DAY_OF_WEEK));
18     System.out.println("DAY_OF_MONTH:\t" +
19       calendar.get(Calendar.DAY_OF_MONTH));
20     System.out.println("DAY_OF_YEAR: " +
```

calendar for current time

extract fields in calendar

```
21            calendar.get(Calendar.DAY_OF_YEAR));
22        System.out.println("WEEK_OF_MONTH: " +
23          calendar.get(Calendar.WEEK_OF_MONTH));
24        System.out.println("WEEK_OF_YEAR: " +
25          calendar.get(Calendar.WEEK_OF_YEAR));
26        System.out.println("AM_PM: " + calendar.get(Calendar.AM_PM));
27
28        // Construct a calendar for September 11, 2001
29        Calendar calendar1 = new GregorianCalendar(2001, 8, 11);
30        System.out.println("September 11, 2001 is a " +
31          dayNameOfWeek(calendar1.get(Calendar.DAY_OF_WEEK)));
32      }
33
34      public static String dayNameOfWeek(int dayOfWeek) {
35        switch (dayOfWeek) {
36          case 1: return "Sunday";
37          case 2: return "Monday";
38          case 3: return "Tuesday";
39          case 4: return "Wednesday";
40          case 5: return "Thursday";
41          case 6: return "Friday";
42          case 7: return "Saturday";
43          default: return null;
44        }
45      }
46    }
```

create a calendar (line 29)

```
Current time is Sun Sep 09 21:23:59 EDT 2007
YEAR:           2007
MONTH:          8
DATE:           9
HOUR:           9
HOUR_OF_DAY:    21
MINUTE:         23
SECOND:         59
DAY_OF_WEEK:    1
DAY_OF_MONTH:   9
DAY_OF_YEAR:    252
WEEK_OF_MONTH:  3
WEEK_OF_YEAR:   37
AM_PM:          1
September 11, 2001 is a Tuesday
```

set(field, value)

The set(int field, value) method defined in the Calendar class can be used to set a field. For example, you can use calendar.set(Calendar.DAY_OF_MONTH, 1) to set the calendar to the first day of the month.

add(field, amount)

The add(field, value) method adds or subtracts the specified amount to a given field. For example, to subtract five days from the current time of the calendar, you must call add(Calendar.DAY_OF_MONTH, -5).

getActualMaximum(field)

To obtain the number of days in a month, use calendar.getActualMaximum-(Calendar.DAY_OF_MONTH). For example, if the calendar were for March, this method would return 31.

setTime(Date)
getTime()

You can set a time represented in a Date object for the calendar by invoking calendar.setTime(date) and retrieve the time by invoking calendar.getTime().

11.4 Interfaces

An interface is a classlike construct that contains only constants and abstract methods. In many ways an interface is similar to an abstract class, but the intent of an interface is to specify common behavior for objects. For example, using appropriate interfaces, you can specify that the objects are comparable, edible, and cloneable.

Video Note
The concept of interface

To distinguish an interface from a class, Java uses the following syntax to declare an interface:

```
modifier interface InterfaceName {
  /** Constant declarations */
  /** Method signatures */
}
```

Here is an example of an interface:

```
public interface Edible {
  /** Describe how to eat */
  public abstract String howToEat();
}
```

An interface is treated like a special class in Java. Each interface is compiled into a separate bytecode file, just like a regular class. As with an abstract class, you cannot create an instance from an interface using the `new` operator, but in most cases you can use an interface more or less the same way you use an abstract class. For example, you can use an interface as a data type for a variable, as the result of casting, and so on.

You can now use the `Edible` interface to specify whether an object is edible. This is accomplished by letting the class for the object implement this interface using the `implements` keyword. For example, the classes `Chicken` and `Fruit` in Listing 11.6 (lines 14, 23) implement the `Edible` interface. The relationship between the class and the interface is known as *interface inheritance*. Since interface inheritance and class inheritance are essentially the same, we will simply refer to both as inheritance.

interface inheritance

LISTING 11.6 TestEdible.java

```
 1 public class TestEdible {
 2   public static void main(String[] args) {
 3     Object[] objects = {new Tiger(), new Chicken(), new Apple()};
 4     for (int i = 0; i < objects.length; i++)
 5       if (objects[i] instanceof Edible)
 6         System.out.println(((Edible)objects[i]).howToEat());
 7   }
 8 }
 9
10 class Animal {
11   // Data fields, constructors, and methods omitted here
12 }
13
14 class Chicken extends Animal implements Edible {
15   public String howToEat() {
16     return "Chicken: Fry it";
17   }
18 }
19
20 class Tiger extends Animal {
21 }
22
23 abstract class Fruit implements Edible {
```

Animal class

implements Edible
howToEat()

Tiger class

implements Edible

Apple class

```
24   // Data fields, constructors, and methods omitted here
25 }
26
27 class Apple extends Fruit {
28   public String howToEat() {
29     return "Apple: Make apple cider";
30   }
31 }
32
```

Orange class

```
33 class Orange extends Fruit {
34   public String howToEat() {
35     return "Orange: Make orange juice";
36   }
37 }
```

```
Chicken: Fry it
Apple: Make apple cider
```

The `Chicken` class extends `Animal` and implements `Edible` to specify that chickens are edible. When a class implements an interface, it implements all the methods defined in the interface with the exact signature and return type. The `Chicken` class provides the implementation for the `howToEat` method (lines 15–17).

The `Fruit` class implements `Edible`. Since it does not implement the `howToEat` method, `Fruit` must be denoted `abstract` (line 23). The concrete subclasses of `Fruit` must provide implementation for the `howToEach` method. The `Apple` and `Orange` classes implement the `howToEat` method (lines 28, 34).

The main method creates an array with three objects for `Tiger`, `Chicken`, and `Apple` (line 3) and invokes the `howToEat` method if the element is edible.

Note

omitting modifiers

Since all data fields are *public final static* and all methods are *public abstract* in an interface, Java allows these modifiers to be omitted. Therefore the following declarations are equivalent:

```
public interface T {
  public static  final int K = 1;

  public abstract  void p();
}
```

Equivalent

```
public interface T {
  int K = 1;

  void p();
}
```

Tip

accessing constants

A constant defined in an interface can be accessed using the syntax `InterfaceName.CONSTANT_NAME` (e.g., `T.K`).

11.5 Example: The **Comparable** Interface

Suppose you want to design a generic method to find the larger of two objects. The objects can be students, circles, rectangles, or squares. Since compare methods are different for different types of objects, you need to define a generic compare method to determine the order of the two objects. Then you can tailor the method to compare students, circles, or rectangles. For example, you can use student ID as the key for comparing students, radius as the key for comparing circles, and area as the key for comparing rectangles. You can use an interface to define a generic compareTo method, as follows:

java.lang.Comparable

```java
// Interface for comparing objects, defined in java.lang
package java.lang;

public interface Comparable {
  public int compareTo(Object o);
}
```

The compareTo method determines the order of this object with the specified object o, and returns a negative integer, zero, or a positive integer if this object is less than, equal to, or greater than the specified object o.

Many classes in the Java library (e.g., String and Date) implement Comparable to define a natural order for the objects. If you examine the source code of these classes, you will see the keyword implements used in the classes, as shown below:

```java
public class String extends Object
     implements Comparable  {
   // class body omitted
}
```

```java
public class Date extends Object
     implements Comparable  {
   // class body omitted
}
```

Thus, strings are comparable, and so are dates. Let s be a String object and d be a Date object. All the following expressions are true.

```
s instanceof String
s instanceof Object
s instanceof Comparable
```

```
d instanceof java.util.Date
d instanceof Object
d instanceof Comparable
```

A generic max method for finding the larger of two objects can be declared, as shown in (a) or (b):

```java
// Max.java: Find a maximum object
public class Max {
   /** Return the maximum of two objects */
   public static Comparable max
      (Comparable o1, Comparable o2) {
    if (o1.compareTo(o2) > 0)
      return o1;
    else
      return o2;
   }
}
```

```java
// Max.java: Find a maximum object
public class Max {
   /** Return the maximum of two objects */
   public static Object max
      (Object o1, Object o2) {
    if (((Comparable)o1).compareTo(o2) > 0)
      return o1;
    else
      return o2;
   }
}
```

(a)   (b)

The max method in (a) is simpler than the one in (b). In the Max class in (b), o1 is declared as Object, and (Comparable)o1 tells the compiler to cast o1 into Comparable so that the compareTo method can be invoked from o1. However, no casting is needed in the Max class in (a), since o1 is declared as Comparable.

(a) is simpler

The max method in (a) is more robust than the one in (b). You must invoke the max method with two comparable objects. Suppose you invoke max with two noncomparable objects:

(a) is more robust

```java
Max.max(anyObject1, anyObject2);
```

The compiler will detect the error using the max method in (a), because anyObject1 is not an instance of Comparable. Using the max method in (b), this line of code will compile fine but will have a runtime `ClassCastException`, because `anyObject1` is not an instance of `Comparable` and cannot be cast into `Comparable`.

From now on, assume that the `max` method in (a) is in the text. Since strings are comparable and dates are comparable, you can use the `max` method to find the larger of two instances of `String` or `Date`. Here is an example:

```
String s1 = "abcdef";
String s2 = "abcdee";
String s3 = (String)Max.max(s1, s2);
```

```
Date d1 = new Date();
Date d2 = new Date();
Date d3 = (Date)Max.max(d1, d2);
```

The `return` value from the `max` method is of the `Comparable` type. So you need to cast it to `String` or `Date` explicitly.

You cannot use the `max` method to find the larger of two instances of `Rectangle`, because `Rectangle` does not implement `Comparable`. However, you can declare a new rectangle class that implements `Comparable`. The instances of this new class are comparable. Let this new class be named `ComparableRectangle`, as shown in Listing 11.7.

LISTING 11.7 ComparableRectangle.java

implements **Comparable**

implement **compareTo**

```
 1  public class ComparableRectangle extends Rectangle
 2      implements Comparable {
 3    /** Construct a ComparableRectangle with specified properties */
 4    public ComparableRectangle(double width, double height) {
 5      super(width, height);
 6    }
 7
 8    /** Implement the compareTo method defined in Comparable */
 9    public int compareTo(Object o) {
10      if (getArea() > ((ComparableRectangle)o).getArea())
11        return 1;
12      else if (getArea() < ((ComparableRectangle)o).getArea())
13        return -1;
14      else
15        return 0;
16    }
17  }
```

`ComparableRectangle` extends `Rectangle` and implements `Comparable`, as shown in Figure 11.4. The keyword `implements` indicates that `ComparableRectangle` inherits all the constants from the `Comparable` interface and implements the methods in the interface. The `compareTo` method compares the areas of two rectangles. An instance of `ComparableRectangle` is also an instance of `Rectangle`, `GeometricObject`, `Object`, and `Comparable`.

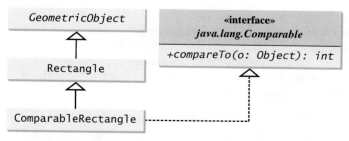

Notation:
The interface name and the method names are italicized. The dashed lines and hollow triangles are used to point to the interface.

FIGURE 11.4 `ComparableRectangle` extends `Rectangle` and implements `Comparable`.

You can now use the `max` method to find the larger of two objects of `ComparableRectangle`. Here is an example:

```
ComparableRectangle rectangle1 = new ComparableRectangle(4, 5);
ComparableRectangle rectangle2 = new ComparableRectangle(3, 6);
System.out.println(Max.max(rectangle1, rectangle2));
```

An interface provides another form of generic programming. It would be difficult to use a generic `max` method to find the maximum of the objects without using an interface in this example, because multiple inheritance would be necessary to inherit `Comparable` and another class, such as `Rectangle`, at the same time.

The `Object` class contains the `equals` method, which is intended for the subclasses of the `Object` class to override in order to compare whether the contents of the objects are the same. Suppose that the `Object` class contains the `compareTo` method, as defined in the `Comparable` interface; the new `max` method can be used to compare a list of *any* objects. Whether a `compareTo` method should be included in the `Object` class is debatable. Since the `compareTo` method is not defined in the `Object` class, the `Comparable` interface is created in Java to enable objects to be compared if they are instances of the `Comparable` interface. It is strongly recommended (though not required) that `compareTo` should be consistent with `equals`. That is, for two objects `o1` and `o2`, `o1.compareTo(o2) == 0` if and only if `o1.equals(o2)` is `true`.

11.6 Example: The **ActionListener** Interface

Now you are ready to write a simple program to address the problem proposed in the introduction of this chapter. The program displays two buttons in the frame, as shown in Figure 11.1. To respond to a button click, you need to write the code to process the clicking button action. The button is a *source object* where the action originates. You need to create an object capable of handling the action event on a button. This object is called a *listener*. Not all objects can be listeners for an action event. To be a listener, two requirements must be met:

1. The object must be an instance of the `ActionListener` interface. The `ActionListener` interface contains the `actionPerformed` method for processing the event.

    ActionListener interface

2. The `ActionListener` object `listener` must be registered with the source using the method `source.addActionListener(listener)`.

    addActionListener (listener)

Listing 11.8 gives the code that processes the `ActionEvent` on the two buttons. When you click the *OK* button, the message "OK button clicked" is displayed. When you click the *Cancel* button, the message "Cancel button clicked" is displayed, as shown in Figure 11.1.

LISTING 11.8 `HandleEvent.java`

```
 1 import javax.swing.*;
 2 import java.awt.event.*;
 3
 4 public class HandleEvent extends JFrame {
 5   public HandleEvent() {
 6     // Create two buttons
 7     JButton jbtOK = new JButton("OK");
 8     JButton jbtCancel = new JButton("Cancel");
 9
10     // Create a panel to hold buttons
11     JPanel panel = new JPanel();
12     panel.add(jbtOK);
```

```
13        panel.add(jbtCancel);
14
15        add(panel); // Add panel to the frame
16
17        // Register listeners
18        OKListenerClass listener1 = new OKListenerClass();
19        CancelListenerClass listener2 = new CancelListenerClass();
20        jbtOK.addActionListener(listener1);
21        jbtCancel.addActionListener(listener2);
22      }
23
24      public static void main(String[] args) {
25        JFrame frame = new HandleEvent();
26        frame.setTitle("Handle Event");
27        frame.setSize(200, 150);
28        frame.setLocation(200, 100);
29        frame.setDefaultCloseOperation(JFrame.EXIT_ON_CLOSE);
30        frame.setVisible(true);
31      }
32    }
33
34    class OKListenerClass implements ActionListener {
35      public void actionPerformed(ActionEvent e) {
36        System.out.println("OK button clicked");
37      }
38    }
39
40    class CancelListenerClass implements ActionListener {
41      public void actionPerformed(ActionEvent e) {
42        System.out.println("Cancel button clicked");
43      }
44    }
```

create listener (line 18)
register listener (line 20)
listener class / *process event* (lines 34–38)
listener class / *process event* (lines 40–44)

Two listener classes are declared in lines 34–44. Each listener class implements `ActionListener` to process `ActionEvent`. The object `listener1` is an instance of `OKListenerClass` (line 18), which is registered with the button `jbtOK` (line 20). When the OK button is clicked, the `actionPerformed(ActionEvent)` method (line 36) in `OKListenerClass` is invoked to process the event. The object `listener2` is an instance of `CancelListenerClass` (line 19), which is registered with the button `jbtCancel` in line 21. When the OK button is clicked, the `actionPerformed(ActionEvent)` method (line 42) in `CancelListenerClass` is invoked to process the event. More discussions on how to process events will be covered in Chapter 15, "Event-driven Programming."

11.7 Example: The **Cloneable** Interface

Often it is desirable to create a copy of an object. You need to use the `clone` method and understand the `Cloneable` interface, which is the subject of this section.

An interface contains constants and abstract methods, but the `Cloneable` interface is a special case. The `Cloneable` interface in the `java.lang` package is defined as follows:

java.lang.Cloneable

```
package java.lang;

public interface Cloneable {
}
```

marker interface

This interface is empty. An interface with an empty body is referred to as a *marker interface*. A marker interface does not contain constants or methods. It is used to denote that a class possesses certain desirable properties. A class that implements the `Cloneable` interface is marked cloneable, and its objects can be cloned using the clone() method defined in the Object class.

Many classes in the Java library (e.g., Date, Calendar, and ArrayList) implement Cloneable. Thus, the instances of these classes can be cloned. For example, the following code

```
Calendar calendar = new GregorianCalendar(2003, 2, 1);
Calendar calendarCopy = (Calendar)calendar.clone();
System.out.println("calendar == calendarCopy is " +
  (calendar == calendarCopy));
System.out.println("calendar.equals(calendarCopy) is " +
  calendar.equals(calendarCopy));
```

displays

```
calendar == calendarCopy is false
calendar.equals(calendarCopy) is true
```

To declare a custom class that implements the Cloneable interface, the class must override the clone() method in the Object class. Listing 11.9 declares a class named House that implements Cloneable and Comparable.

how to implement Cloneable

Listing 11.9 House.java

```
 1 public class House implements Cloneable, Comparable {
 2    private int id;
 3    private double area;
 4    private java.util.Date whenBuilt;
 5
 6    public House(int id, double area) {
 7      this.id = id;
 8      this.area = area;
 9      whenBuilt = new java.util.Date();
10    }
11
12    public double getId() {
13      return id;
14    }
15
16    public double getArea() {
17      return area;
18    }
19
20    public java.util.Date getWhenBuilt() {
21      return whenBuilt;
22    }
23
24    /** Override the protected clone method defined in the Object
25       class, and strengthen its accessibility */
26    public Object clone() throws CloneNotSupportedException {
27      return super.clone();
28    }
29
30    /** Implement the compareTo method defined in Comparable */
31    public int compareTo(Object o) {
32      if (area > ((House)o).area)
33        return 1;
34      else if (area < ((House)o).area)
35        return -1;
```

This exception is thrown if **House** does not implement **Cloneable**

```
36      else
37        return 0;
38    }
39 }
```

The House class implements the clone method (lines 26-28) defined in the Object class. The definition is:

```
protected native Object clone() throws CloneNotSupportedException;
```

The keyword native indicates that this method is not written in Java, but is implemented in the JVM for the native platform. The keyword protected restricts the method to be accessed in the same package or in a subclass. For this reason, the House class must override the method and change the visibility modifier to public so that the method can be used in any package. Since the clone method implemented for the native platform in the Object class performs the task of cloning objects, the clone method in the House class simply invokes super.clone(). The clone method defined in the Object class may throw CloneNotSupportedException.

CloneNotSupported-Exception

The House class implements the compareTo method (lines 31-38) defined in the Comparable interface. The method compares the areas of two houses.

You can now create an object of the House class and create an identical copy from it, as follows:

```
House house1 = new House(1, 1750.50);
House house2 = (House)house1.clone();
```

house1 and house2 are two different objects with identical contents. The clone method in the Object class copies each field from the original object to the target object. If the field is of a primitive type, its value is copied. For example, the value of area (double type) is copied from house1 to house2. If the field is of an object, the reference of the field is copied. For example, the field whenBuilt is of the Date class, so its reference is copied into house2, as shown in Figure 11.5. Therefore, house1.whenBuilt == house2.whenBuilt is true, although house1 == house2 is false. This is referred to as a *shallow copy* rather than a *deep copy*, meaning that if the field is of an object, the reference of the field is copied rather than its contents.

shallow copy

deep copy

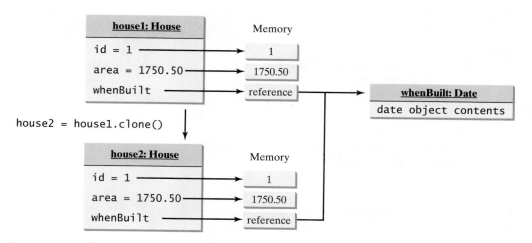

Figure 11.5 The clone method copies the values of primitive type fields and the references of object type fields.

If you want to perform a deep copy, you can override the `clone` method with custom cloning operations after invoking `super.clone()`. See Exercise 11.4.

Note

You learned how to use the `arraycopy` method to copy arrays in Chapter 6, "Arrays." This method provides shallow copies. It works fine for arrays of primitive data type elements, but not for arrays of object type elements. To support a deep copy, you have to deal with how to copy individual object elements in the array.

Caution

If the `House` class does not override the `clone()` method, the program will receive a syntax error, because `clone()` is protected in `java.lang.Object`. If `House` does not implement `java.lang.Cloneable`, invoking `super.clone()` (line 28) in House.java would cause a `CloneNotSupportedException`. Thus, to enable cloning an object, the class for the object must override the `clone()` method and implement `Cloneable`.

11.8 Interfaces vs. Abstract Classes

An interface can be used the same way as an abstract class, but declaring an interface is different from declaring an abstract class. Table 11.2 summarizes the differences.

TABLE 11.2 Interfaces vs. Abstract Classes

	Variables	Constructors	Methods
Abstract class	No restrictions	Constructors are invoked by subclasses through constructor chaining. An abstract class cannot be instantiated using the new operator.	No restrictions.
Interface	All variables must be `public static final`.	No constructors. An interface cannot be instantiated using the new operator.	All methods must be public abstract instance methods

Java allows only *single inheritance* for class extension, but multiple extensions for interfaces. For example,

```
public class NewClass extends BaseClass
    implements Interface1, ..., InterfaceN {
  ...
}
```

An interface can inherit other interfaces using the `extends` keyword. Such an interface is called a *subinterface*. For example, `NewInterface` in the following code is a subinterface of `Interface1, ...,` and `InterfaceN`.

subinterface

```
public interface NewInterface extends Interface1, ..., InterfaceN {
  // constants and abstract methods
}
```

A class implementing `NewInterface` must implement the abstract methods defined in `NewInterface, Interface1, ...,` and `InterfaceN`. An interface can extend other interfaces, but not classes. A class can extend its superclass and implement *multiple interfaces*.

All classes share a single root, the `Object` class, but there is no single root for interfaces. Like a class, an interface also defines a type. A variable of an interface type can reference any instance of the class that implements the interface. If a class implements an interface, the interface is like a superclass for the class. You can use an interface as a data type and cast a variable of an interface type to its subclass, and vice versa. For example, suppose that `c` is an instance of `Class2` in Figure 11.6. `c` is also an instance of `Object`, `Class1`, `Interface1`, `Interface1_1`, `Interface1_2`, `Interface2_1`, and `Interface2_2`.

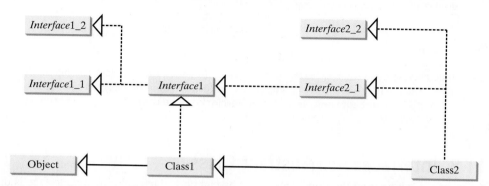

FIGURE 11.6 `Class1` implements `Interface1`; `Interface1` extends `Interface1_1` and `Interface1_2`. `Class2` extends `Class1` and implements `Interface2_1` and `Interface2_2`.

Note

naming convention

Class names are nouns. Interface names may be adjectives or nouns. For example, both `java.lang.Comparable` and `java.awt.event.ActionListener` are interfaces. `Comparable` is an adjective, and `ActionListener` is a noun.

Design Guide

Abstract classes and interfaces can both be used to specify common behaviour of objects. How do you decide whether to use an interface or a class? In general, a *strong is-a relationship* that clearly describes a parent-child relationship should be modeled using classes. For example, Gregorian calendar is a calendar, so the relationship between the class `java.util.GregorianCalendar` and `java.util.Calendar` is modeled using class inheritance. A *weak is-a relationship*, also known as an *is-kind-of relationship*, indicates that an object possesses a certain property. A weak is-a relationship can be modeled using interfaces. For example, all strings are comparable, so the `String` class implements the `Comparable` interface.

is-a relationship

is-kind-of relationship

interface preferred

In general, interfaces are preferred over classes because an interface can represent a common supertype for unrelated classes. Interfaces are more flexible than classes. Consider the `Animal` class. Suppose the `howToEat` method is defined in the `Animal` class, as follows:

Animal class

```
abstract class Animal {
  public String howToEat();
}
```

Two subclasses of `Animal` are defined as follows:

Chicken class

```
class Chicken extends Animal {
  public String howToEat() {
    return "Fry it";
  }
}
```

```
class Duck extends Animal {
  public String howToEat() {
    return "Roast it";
  }
}
```
Duck class

Given this inheritance hierarchy, polymorphism enables you to hold a reference to a Chicken object or a Duck object in a variable of type Animal, as in the following code:

```
public static void main(String[] args) {
  Animal animal = new Chicken();
  eat(animal);

  animal = new Duck();
  eat(animal);
}

public static void eat(Animal animal) {
  animal.howToEat();
}
```

The JVM dynamically decides which howToEat method to invoke based on the actual object that invokes the method.

You can add another subclass (e.g., Turkey) to the animal family. However, there is a restriction. The subclass must be for another animal.

Interfaces don't have this restriction. Interfaces give you more flexibility than classes, because you don't have make everything fit into one type of class. You may define the howToEat() method in an interface and let it serve as a common supertype for other classes. For example,

```
public static void main(String[] args) {
  Edible stuff = new Chicken();
  eat(stuff);

  stuff = new Duck();
  eat(stuff);

  stuff = new Broccoli();
  eat(stuff);
}

public static void eat(Edible stuff) {
  stuff.howToEat();
}

interface Edible {
  public String howToEat() ;
}

class Chicken implements Edible {
  public String howToEat() {
    return "Fry it";
  }
}

class Duck implements Edible {
  public String howToEat() {
    return "Roast it";
  }
}

class Broccoli implements Edible {
  public String howToEat() {
    return "Stir-fry it";
  }
}
```
Edible interface

Chicken class

Duck class

Broccoli class

To define a class that represents edible objects, simply let the class implement the `Edible` interface. The class is now a subtype of the `Edible` type. Any `Edible` object can be passed to invoke the `eat` method.

11.9 Processing Primitive Data Type Values as Objects

Owing to performance considerations, primitive data types are not used as objects in Java. Because of the overhead of processing objects, the language's performance would be adversely affected if primitive data types were treated as objects. However, many Java methods require the use of objects as arguments. For example, the `add(object)` method in the `ArrayList` class adds an object to an `ArrayList`. Java offers a convenient way to incorporate, or wrap, a primitive data type into an object (e.g., wrapping `int` into the `Integer` class, and wrapping `double` into the `Double` class). The corresponding class is called a *wrapper class*. By using a wrapper object instead of a primitive data type variable, you can take advantage of generic programming.

wrapper class
why wrapper class?

Java provides `Boolean`, `Character`, `Double`, `Float`, `Byte`, `Short`, `Integer`, and `Long` wrapper classes for primitive data types. These classes are grouped in the `java.lang` package. Their inheritance hierarchy is shown in Figure 11.7.

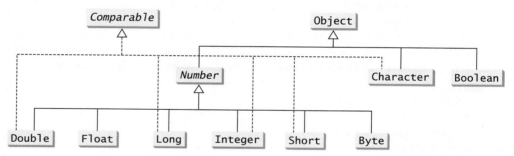

FIGURE 11.7 The `Number` class is an abstract superclass for `Double`, `Float`, `Long`, `Integer`, `Short`, and `Byte`.

naming convention

 Note
Most wrapper class names for a primitive type are the same as the primitive data type name with the first letter capitalized. The exceptions are `Integer` and `Character`.

Each numeric wrapper class extends the abstract `Number` class, which contains the methods `doubleValue()`, `floatValue()`, `intValue()`, `longValue()`, `shortValue()`, and `byteValue()`. These methods "convert" objects into primitive type values. Each wrapper class overrides the `toString`, and `equals`, methods defined in the `Object` class. Since all the numeric wrapper classes and the `Character` class implement the `Comparable` interface, the `compareTo` method is implemented in these classes.

Wrapper classes are very similar to each other. The `Character` class was introduced in Chapter 8, "Strings and Text I/O." The `Boolean` class wraps a Boolean value `true` or `false`. This section uses `Integer` and `Double` as examples to introduce the numeric wrapper classes. The key features of `Integer` and `Double` are shown in Figure 11.8.

constructors

You can construct a wrapper object either from a primitive data type value or from a string representing the numeric value—for example, `new Double(5.0)`, `new Double("5.0")`, `new Integer(5)`, and `new Integer("5")`.

no no-arg constructor
immutable

The wrapper classes do not have no-arg constructors. The instances of all wrapper classes are immutable; this means that, once the objects are created, their internal values cannot be changed.

FIGURE 11.8 The wrapper classes provide constructors, constants, and conversion methods for manipulating various data types.

Each numeric wrapper class has the constants MAX_VALUE and MIN_VALUE. MAX_VALUE represents the maximum value of the corresponding primitive data type. For Byte, Short, Integer, and Long, MIN_VALUE represents the minimum byte, short, int, and long values. For Float and Double, MIN_VALUE represents the minimum *positive float* and double values. The following statements display the maximum integer (2,147,483,647), the minimum positive float (1.4E-45), and the maximum double floating-point number (1.79769313486231570e+308d).

    constants

```
System.out.println("The maximum integer is " + Integer.MAX_VALUE);
System.out.println("The minimum positive float is " +
  Float.MIN_VALUE);
System.out.println(
  "The maximum double precision floating-point number is " +
  Double.MAX_VALUE);
```

Each numeric wrapper class implements the abstract methods doubleValue(), floatValue(), intValue(), longValue(), and shortValue(), which are defined in the Number class. These methods return a double, float, int, long, or short value for the wrapper object.

    conversion methods

The numeric wrapper classes have a useful static method, valueOf(String s). This method creates a new object initialized to the value represented by the specified string. For example,

    static valueOf methods

```
Double doubleObject = Double.valueOf("12.4");
Integer integerObject = Integer.valueOf("12");
```

You have used the parseInt method in the Integer class to parse a numeric string into an int value and the parseDouble method in the Double class to parse a numeric string into a double value. Each numeric wrapper class has two overloaded parsing methods to parse a numeric string into an appropriate numeric value based on 10 (decimal) or any specified

    static parsing methods

radix (e.g., 2 for binary, 8 for octal, and 16 for hexadecimal). These methods are shown below:

```
// These two methods are in the Byte class
public static byte parseByte(String s)
public static byte parseByte(String s, int radix)

// These two methods are in the Short class
public static short parseShort(String s)
public static short parseShort(String s, int radix)

// These two methods are in the Integer class
public static int parseInt(String s)
public static int parseInt(String s, int radix)

// These two methods are in the Long class
public static long parseLong(String s)
public static long parseLong(String s, int radix)

// These two methods are in the Float class
public static float parseFloat(String s)
public static float parseFloat(String s, int radix)

// These two methods are in the Double class
public static double parseDouble(String s)
public static double parseDouble(String s, int radix)
```

For example,

```
Integer.parseInt("11", 2) returns 3;
Integer.parseInt("12", 8) returns 10;
Integer.parseInt("13", 10) returns 13;
Integer.parseInt("1A", 16) returns 26;
```

`Integer.parseInt("12", 2)` would raise a runtime exception because 12 is not a binary number.

11.10 Sorting an Array of Objects

This example presents a static generic method for sorting an array of comparable objects. The objects are instances of the `Comparable` interface, and they are compared using the `compareTo` method. The method can be used to sort an array of any objects as long as their classes implement the `Comparable` interface.

To test the method, the program sorts an array of integers, an array of double numbers, an array of characters, and an array of strings. The program is shown in Listing 11.10.

LISTING 11.10 GenericSort.java

```java
 1 public class GenericSort {
 2   public static void main(String[] args) {
 3     // Create an Integer array
 4     Integer[] intArray = {new Integer(2), new Integer(4),
 5       new Integer(3)};
 6
 7     // Create a Double array
 8     Double[] doubleArray = {new Double(3.4), new Double(1.3),
 9       new Double(-22.1)};
10
11     // Create a Character array
12     Character[] charArray = {new Character('a'),
13       new Character('J'), new Character('r')};
14
```

```
15      // Create a String array
16      String[] stringArray = {"Tom", "John", "Fred"};
17
18      // Sort the arrays
19      sort(intArray);
20      sort(doubleArray);
21      sort(charArray);
22      sort(stringArray);
23
24      // Display the sorted arrays
25      System.out.print("Sorted Integer objects: ");
26      printList(intArray);
27      System.out.print("Sorted Double objects: ");
28      printList(doubleArray);
29      System.out.print("Sorted Character objects: ");
30      printList(charArray);
31      System.out.print("Sorted String objects: ");
32      printList(stringArray);
33    }
34
35    /** Sort an array of comparable objects */
36    public static void sort(Comparable[] list) {
37      Comparable currentMax;
38      int currentMaxIndex;
39
40      for (int i = list.length - 1; i >= 1; i--) {
41        // Find the maximum in the list[0..i]
42        currentMax = list[i];
43        currentMaxIndex = i;
44
45        for (int j = i - 1; j >= 0; j--) {
46          if (currentMax.compareTo(list[j]) < 0) {
47            currentMax = list[j];
48            currentMaxIndex = j;
49          }
50        }
51
52        // Swap list[i] with list[currentMaxIndex] if necessary;
53        if (currentMaxIndex != i) {
54          list[currentMaxIndex] = list[i];
55          list[i] = currentMax;
56        }
57      }
58    }
59
60    /** Print an array of objects */
61    public static void printList(Object[] list) {
62      for (int i = 0; i < list.length; i++)
63        System.out.print(list[i] + " ");
64      System.out.println();
65    }
66 }
```

sort **Integer** objects
sort **Double** objects
sort **Character** objects
sort **String** objects

generic sort method

compareTo

```
Sorted Integer objects: 2 3 4
Sorted Double objects: -22.1 1.3 3.4
Sorted Character objects: J a r
Sorted String objects: Fred John Tom
```

The algorithm for the `sort` method is the same as in §6.8.1, "Selection Sort." The `sort` method in §6.8.1 sorts an array of double values. The `sort` method in this example can sort an array of any object type, provided that the objects are also instances of the `Comparable` interface. This is another example of *generic programming*, a subject discussed in §10.8, "Polymorphism, Dynamic Binding, and Generic Programming." Generic programming enables a method to operate on arguments of generic types, making it reusable with multiple types.

`Integer`, `Double`, `Character`, and `String` implement `Comparable`, so the objects of these classes can be compared using the `compareTo` method. The sort method uses the `compareTo` method to determine the order of the objects in the array.

`Arrays.sort` method

Tip

Java provides a static `sort` method for sorting an array of any object type in the `java.util.Arrays` class, provided that the elements in the array are comparable. Thus you can use the following code to sort arrays in this example:

```
java.util.Arrays.sort(intArray);
java.util.Arrays.sort(doubleArray);
java.util.Arrays.sort(charArray);
java.util.Arrays.sort(stringArray);
```

Note

Arrays are objects. An array is an instance of the `Object` class. Furthermore, if `A` is a subtype of `B`, every instance of `A[]` is an instance of `B[]`. Therefore, the following statements are all true:

```
new int[10] instanceof Object
new Integer[10] instanceof Object
new Integer[10] instanceof Comparable[]
new Integer[10] instanceof Number[]
new Number[10] instanceof Object[]
```

Caution

Although an `int` value can be assigned to a `double` type variable, `int[]` and `double[]` are two incompatible types. Therefore, you cannot assign an `int[]` array to a variable of `double[]` or `Object[]` type.

11.11 Automatic Conversion between Primitive Types and Wrapper Class Types

Java allows primitive types and wrapper classes to be converted automatically. For example, the following statement in (a) can be simplified as in (b) due to autoboxing:

	Equivalent	
`Integer intObject = new Integer(2);`	══════	`Integer intObject = 2;`
(a)		autoboxing (b)

boxing
unboxing

Converting a primitive value to a wrapper object is called *boxing*. The reverse conversion is called *unboxing*. The compiler will automatically box a primitive value that appears in a context requiring an object, and will unbox an object that appears in a context requiring a primitive value. Consider the following example:

```
1 Integer[] intArray = {1, 2, 3};
2 System.out.println(intArray[0] + intArray[1] + intArray[2]);
```

In line 1, primitive values 1, 2, and 3 are automatically boxed into objects `new Integer(1)`, `new Integer(2)`, and `new Integer(3)`. In line 2, objects `intArray[0]`, `intArray[1]`, and `intArray[2]` are automatically converted into `int` values that are added together.

11.12 The `BigInteger` and `BigDecimal` Classes

If you need to compute with very large integers or high-precision floating-point values, you can use the `BigInteger` and `BigDecimal` classes in the `java.math` package. Both are *immutable*. Both extend the `Number` class and implement the `Comparable` interface. The largest integer of the `long` type is `Long.MAX_VALUE` (i.e., 9223372036854775807). An instance of `BigInteger` can represent an integer of any size. You can use `new BigInteger(String)` and `new BigDecimal(String)` to create an instance of `BigInteger` and `BigDecimal`, use the `add`, `subtract`, `multiple`, `divide`, and `remainder` methods to perform arithmetic operations, and use the `compareTo` method to compare two big numbers. For example, the following code creates two `BigInteger` objects and multiplies them.

immutable

```java
BigInteger a = new BigInteger("9223372036854775807");
BigInteger b = new BigInteger("2");
BigInteger c = a.multiply(b); // 9223372036854775807 * 2
System.out.println(c);
```

The output is 18446744073709551614.

There is no limit to the precision of a `BigDecimal` object. The `divide` method may throw an `ArithmeticException` if the result cannot be terminated. However, you can use the overloaded `divide(BigDecimal d, int scale, int roundingMode)` method to specify a scale and a rounding mode to avoid this exception, where `scale` is the minimum number of digits after the decimal point. For example, the following code creates two `BigDecimal` objects and performs division with scale 20 and rounding mode `BigDecimal.ROUND_UP`.

```java
BigDecimal a = new BigDecimal(1.0);
BigDecimal b = new BigDecimal(3);
BigDecimal c = a.divide(b, 20, BigDecimal.ROUND_UP);
System.out.println(c);
```

The output is 0.33333333333333333334.

Note that the factorial of an integer can be very large. Listing 11.11 gives a method that can return the factorial of any integer.

LISTING 11.11 `LargeFactorial.java`

```java
 1  import java.math.*;
 2
 3  public class LargeFactorial {
 4    public static void main(String[] args) {
 5      System.out.println("50! is \n" + factorial(50));
 6    }
 7
 8    public static BigInteger factorial(long n) {
 9      BigInteger result = BigInteger.ONE;
10      for (int i = 1; i <= n; i++)
11        result = result.multiply(new BigInteger(i + ""));
12
13      return result;
14    }
15  }
```

constant
multiply

```
50! is
30414093201713378043612608166064768844377641568960512000000000000
```

`BigInteger.ONE` (line 9) is a constant defined in the `BigInteger` class. `BigInteger.ONE` is same as `new BigInteger("1")`.

A new result is obtained by invoking the `multiply` method (line 11).

KEY TERMS

abstract class 362	multiple inheritance 373
abstract method 362	subinterface 377
deep copy 376	shallow copy 376
interface 369	single inheritance 377
marker interface 374	wrapper class 380

CHAPTER SUMMARY

- Abstract classes are like regular classes with data and methods, but you cannot create instances of abstract classes using the `new` operator.

- An abstract method cannot be contained in a nonabstract class. If a subclass of an abstract superclass does not implement all the inherited abstract methods of the superclass, the subclass must be declared abstract.

- A class that contains abstract methods must be abstract. However, it is possible to declare an abstract class that contains no abstract methods.

- A subclass can be abstract even if its superclass is concrete.

- An interface is a classlike construct that contains only constants and abstract methods. In many ways, an interface is similar to an abstract class, but an abstract class can contain constants and abstract methods as well as variables and concrete methods.

- An interface is treated like a special class in Java. Each interface is compiled into a separate bytecode file, just like a regular class.

- The `java.lang.Comparable` interface defines the `compareTo` method. Many classes in the Java library implement `Comparable`.

- The `java.lang.Cloneable` interface is a marker interface. An object of the class that implements the `Cloneable` interface is cloneable.

- A class can extend only one superclass but can implement one or more interfaces.

- An interface can extend one or more interfaces.

- Many Java methods require the use of objects as arguments. Java offers a convenient way to incorporate, or wrap, a primitive data type into an object (e.g., wrapping `int` into the `Integer` class, and wrapping `double` into the `Double` class).

The corresponding class is called a *wrapper class*. By using a wrapper object instead of a primitive data type variable, you can take advantage of generic programming.

■ Java can automatically convert a primitive type value to its corresponding wrapper object in the context and vice versa.

■ The `BigInteger` class is useful to compute and process integers of any size. The `BigDecimal` class can be used to compute and process floating-point numbers with any arbitrary precision.

REVIEW QUESTIONS

Section 11.2 Abstract Classes

11.1 Which of the following class definitions defines a legal abstract class?

```
class A {
  abstract void unfinished() {
  }
}
```
(a)

```
public class abstract A {
  abstract void unfinished();
}
```
(d)

```
class A {
  abstract void unfinished();
}
```
(b)

```
abstract class A {
  protected void unfinished();
}
```
(e)

```
abstract class A {
  abstract void unfinished();
}
```
(c)

```
abstract class A {
  abstract int unfinished();
}
```
(f)

11.2 The `getArea` and `getPerimeter` methods may be removed from the `GeometricObject` class. What are the benefits of defining `getArea` and `getPerimeter` as abstract methods in the `GeometricObject` class?

11.3 True or false? An abstract class can be used just like a nonabstract class except that you cannot use the `new` operator to create an instance from the abstract class.

Sections 11.4–11.8

11.4 Which of the following is a correct interface?

```
interface A {
  void print() { };
}
```
(a)

```
abstract interface A extends I1, I2 {
  abstract void print() { };
}
```
(c)

```
abstract interface A {
  print();
}
```
(b)

```
interface A {
  void print();
}
```
(d)

11.5 True or false? If a class implements Comparable, the object of the class can invoke the compareTo method.

11.6 Two max methods are defined in §11.5. Explain why the max with the signature max(Comparable, Comparable) is better than the one with the signature max(Object, Object).

11.7 You can define the compareTo method in a class without implementing the Comparable interface. What are the benefits of implementing the Comparable interface?

11.8 True or false? If a class implements java.awt.event.ActionListener, the object of the class can invoke the actionPerformed method.

11.9 Can you invoke the clone() method to clone an object if the class for the object does not implement the java.lang.Cloneable? Does the Date class implement Cloneable?

11.10 What would happen if the House class (defined in Listing 11.9) did not override the clone() method or if House did not implement java.lang.Cloneable?

11.11 Show the printout of the following code:

```java
java.util.Date date = new java.util.Date();
java.util.Date date1 = (java.util.Date)(date.clone());
System.out.println(date == date1);
System.out.println(date.equals(date1));
```

11.12 Show the printout of the following code:

```java
java.util.ArrayList list = new java.util.ArrayList();
list.add("New York"); list.add(new java.util.Date());
  java.util.ArrayList list1 =
(java.util.ArrayList)(list.clone());
System.out.println(list == list1);
System.out.println(list.get(0) == list1.get(0));
System.out.println(list.get(1) == list1.get(1));
```

11.13 What is wrong in the following code?

```java
public class Test {
  public static void main(String[] args) {
    GeometricObject x = new Circle(3);
    GeometricObject y = x.clone();
    System.out.println(x == y);
  }
}
```

Section 11.9 Processing Primitive Data Type Values as Objects

11.14 Describe primitive-type wrapper classes. Why do you need these wrapper classes?

11.15 Can each of the following statement be compiled?

```java
Integer i = new Integer("23");
Integer i = new Integer(23);
Integer i = Integer.valueOf("23");
Integer i = Integer.parseInt("23", 8);
Double d = new Double();
Double d = Double.valueOf("23.45");
int i = (Integer.valueOf("23")).intValue();
double d = (Double.valueOf("23.4")).doubleValue();
```

```
int i = (Double.valueOf("23.4")).intValue();
String s = (Double.valueOf("23.4")).toString();
```

11.16 How do you convert an integer into a string? How do you convert a numeric string into an integer? How do you convert a double number into a string? How do you convert a numeric string into a double value?

11.17 Why do the following two lines of code compile but cause a runtime error?

```
Number numberRef = new Integer(0);
Double doubleRef = (Double)numberRef;
```

11.18 Why do the following two lines of code compile but cause a runtime error?

```
Number[] numberArray = new Integer[2];
numberArray[0] = new Double(1.5);
```

11.19 What is wrong in the following code?

```
public class Test {
  public static void main(String[] args) {
    Number x = new Integer(3);
    System.out.println(x.intValue());
    System.out.println(x.compareTo(new Integer(4)));
  }
}
```

11.20 What is wrong in the following code?

```
public class Test {
  public static void main(String[] args) {
    Number x = new Integer(3);
    System.out.println(x.intValue());
    System.out.println((Integer)x.compareTo(new Integer(4)));
  }
}
```

11.21 What is output of the following code?

```
public class Test {
  public static void main(String[] args) {
    System.out.println(Integer.parseInt("10"));
    System.out.println(Integer.parseInt("10", 10));
    System.out.println(Integer.parseInt("10", 16));
  }
}
```

Sections 11.10–11.12

11.22 What are the autoboxing and autounboxing features? Are the following statements correct?

```
Number x = 3;
Integer x = 3;
Double x = 3;
Double x = 3.0;
int x = new Integer(3);
int x = new Integer(3) + new Integer(4);
double y = 3.4;
```

```
    y.intValue();
    JOptionPane.showMessageDialog(null, 45.5);
```

11.23 Can you assign `new int[10]`, `new String[100]`, `new Object[50]`, or `new Calendar[20]` into a variable of `Object[]` type?

11.24 What is the output of the following code?

```
public class Test {
  public static void main(String[] args) {
    java.math.BigInteger x = new java.math.BigInteger("3");
    java.math.BigInteger y = new java.math.BigInteger("7");
    x.add(y);
    System.out.println(x);
  }
}
```

Comprehensive

11.25 Define the following terms: abstract classes, interfaces. What are the similarities and differences between abstract classes and interfaces?

11.26 Indicate true or false for the following statements:

■ An abstract class can have instances created using the constructor of the abstract class.
■ An abstract class can be extended.
■ An interface is compiled into a separate bytecode file.
■ A subclass of a nonabstract superclass cannot be abstract.
■ A subclass cannot override a concrete method in a superclass to declare it abstract.
■ An abstract method must be nonstatic.
■ An interface can have static methods.
■ An interface can extend one or more interfaces.
■ An interface can extend an abstract class.
■ An abstract class can extend an interface.

PROGRAMMING EXERCISES

Sections 11.1–11.7

11.1* (*Enabling GeometricObject comparable*) Modify the `GeometricObject` class to implement the `Comparable` interface, and define a static `max` method in the `GeometricObject` class for finding the larger of two `GeometricObject` objects. Draw the UML diagram and implement the new `GeometricObject` class. Write a test program that uses the `max` method to find the larger of two circles and the larger of two rectangles.

11.2* (*The ComparableCircle class*) Create a class named `ComparableCircle` that extends `Circle` and implements `Comparable`. Draw the UML diagram and implement the `compareTo` method to compare the circles on the basis of area. Write a test class to find the larger of two instances of `ComparableCircle` objects.

11.3* (*The Colorable interface*) Design an interface named `Colorable` with a void method named `howToColor()`. Every class of a colorable object must implement the `Colorable` interface. Design a class named `Square` that extends `GeometricObject` and implements `Colorable`. Implement `howToColor` to display a message on how to color the square.

Draw a UML diagram that involves Colorable, Square, and Geometric-Object. Write a test program that creates an array of five GeometricObject. For each object in the array, invoke its howToColor method if it is colorable.

11.4* (*Revising the House class*) Rewrite the House class in Listing 11.9 to perform a deep copy on the whenBuilt field.

11.5* (*Enabling Circle comparable*) Rewrite the Circle class in Listing 10.2 to extend GeometricObject and implement the Comparable interface. Override the equals method in the Object class. Two Circle objects are equal if their radii are the same. Draw the UML diagram that involves Circle, GeometricObject, and Comparable.

11.6* (*Enabling Rectangle comparable*) Rewrite the Rectangle class in Listing 10.3 to extend GeometricObject and implement the Comparable interface. Override the equals method in the Object class. Two Rectangle objects are equal if their areas are the same. Draw the UML diagram that involves Rectangle, GeometricObject, and Comparable.

Video Note
Redesign the **Rectangle** class

11.7* (*The Octagon class*) Write a class named Octagon that extends GeometricObject and implements the Comparable and Cloneable interfaces. Assume that all eight sides of the octagon are of equal size. The area can be computed using the following formula:

$$area = \left(2 + 4/\sqrt{2}\right)side*side$$

Draw the UML diagram that involves Octagon, GeometricObject, Comparable, and Cloneable. Write a test program that creates an Octagon object with side value 5 and displays its area and perimeter. Create a new object using the clone method and compare the two objects using the compareTo method.

11.8* (*Summing the areas of geometric objects*) Write a method that sums the areas of all the geometric objects in an array. The method signature is:

```
public static double sumArea(GeometricObject[] a)
```

Write a test program that creates an array of four objects (two circles and two rectangles) and computes their total area using the sumArea method.

11.9* (*Finding the largest object*) Write a method that returns the largest object in an array of objects. The method signature is:

```
public static Object max(Comparable[] a)
```

All the objects are instances of the Comparable interface. The order of the objects in the array is determined using the compareTo method.

Write a test program that creates an array of ten strings, an array of ten integers, and an array of ten dates, and finds the largest string, integer, and date in the arrays.

11.10** (*Displaying calendars*) Rewrite the PrintCalendar class in Listing 5.10 to display a calendar for a specified month using the Calendar and GregorianCalendar classes. Your program receives the month and year from the command line. For example:

```
java Exercise11_10 1 2007
```

This displays the calendar shown in Figure 11.9.

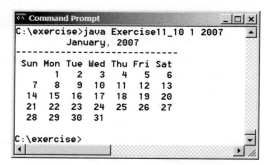

FIGURE 11.9 The program displays a calendar for *January 2007*.

You also can run the program without the year. In this case, the year is the current year. If you run the program without specifying a month and a year, the month is the current month.

Section 11.12 The `BigInteger` and `BigDecimal` Classes

11.11** (*Divisible by 5 or 6*) Find the first ten numbers (greater than `Long.MAX_VALUE`) that are divisible by 5 or 6.

11.12** (*Divisible by 2 or 3*) Find the first ten numbers with 50 decimal digits that are divisible by 2 or 3.

11.13** (*Square numbers*) Find the first ten square numbers that are greater than `Long.MAX_VALUE`. A square number is a number in the form of n^2.

11.14** (*Large prime numbers*) Write a program that finds five prime numbers larger than `long.MAX_VALUE`.

11.15** (*Mersenne prime*) A prime number is called a *Mersenne prime* if it can be written in the form $2^p - 1$ for some positive integer p. Write a program that finds all Mersenne primes with $p \leq 100$ and displays the output as shown below. (You have to use `BigInteger` to store the number, because it is too big to be stored in `long`. Your program may take several hours to complete.)

p	2^p - 1
2	3
3	7
5	31
...	

OBJECT-ORIENTED DESIGN AND PATTERNS

Objectives

- To describe the software life cycle (§12.2).

- To discover classes and determine responsibilities of each class (§12.3).

- To describe relationship types: association, aggregation, composition, dependency, strong inheritance, and weak inheritance (§12.4).

- To declare classes to represent the relationships (§12.4).

- To design systems by identifying the classes and discovering the relationships among these classes (§12.5).

- To implement the `Rational` class and process rational numbers using this class (§12.6).

- To design classes that follow the class-design guidelines (§12.7).

- To explain the concept of framework-based programming using the Java API (§12.8).

- To apply design patterns for developing sound software systems (§12.9).

12.1 Introduction

The preceding chapters introduced objects, classes, class inheritance, and interfaces. You learned the concepts of object-oriented programming. This chapter focuses on the analysis and design of software systems using the object-oriented approach. You will learn class-design guidelines and the techniques and patterns for designing reusable classes.

12.2 Software Life Cycle

Developing a software project is an engineering process. Software products, no matter how large or how small, have the same life cycle: requirements specification, analysis, design, implementation, testing, deployment, and maintenance, as shown in Figure 12.1.

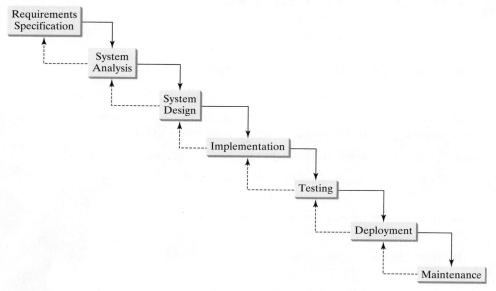

FIGURE 12.1 Developing a project involves requirements specification, system analysis, system design, implementation, testing, deployment, and maintenance.

requirements specification *Requirements specification* is a formal process that seeks to understand the problem and to document in detail what the software system needs to do. This phase involves close interaction between users and developers. Most of the examples in this book are simple, and their requirements are clearly stated. In the real world, however, problems are not well defined. You need to work closely with your customer and study a problem carefully to identify its requirements.

system analysis *System analysis* seeks to analyze the business process in terms of data flow, and to identify the system's input and output. Part of the analysis entails modeling the system's behavior. The model is intended to capture the essential elements of the system and to define services to the system.

system design *System design* is the process of designing the system's components. This phase involves the use of many levels of abstraction to decompose the problem into manageable components, identify classes and interfaces, and establish relationships among the classes and interfaces.

implementation *Implementation* is translating the system design into programs. Separate programs are written for each component and put to work together. This phase requires the use of a programming language like Java. The implementation involves coding, testing, and debugging.

testing *Testing* ensures that the code meets the requirements specification and weeds out bugs. An independent team of software engineers not involved in the design and implementation of the project usually conducts such testing.

Deployment makes the project available for use. For a Java applet, this means installing it on a Web server; for a Java application, installing it on the client's computer. A project usually consists of many classes. An effective approach for deployment is to package all the classes into a Java archive file, as described in Supplement III.Q, "Packaging and Deploying Java Projects."

deployment

Maintenance is concerned with changing and improving the product. A software product must continue to perform and improve in a changing environment. This requires periodic upgrades of the product to fix newly discovered bugs and incorporate changes.

maintenance

This chapter is concerned mainly with object-oriented design. While there are many object-oriented methodologies, UML has become the industry-standard notation for object-oriented modeling, and itself leads to a methodology. The process of designing classes calls for identifying the classes and discovering the relationships among them.

12.3 Discovering Classes

The key to object-oriented programming is to model the application in terms of cooperative objects. Careful design of classes is critical when a project is being developed.

There are many levels of abstraction in system design. You have learned method abstraction and have applied it to the development of large programs. Methods are means to group statements. Classes extend abstraction to a higher level and provide a means of grouping methods. Classes do more than just group methods, however; they also contain data fields. Methods and data fields together describe the properties and behaviors of classes.

The power of classes is further extended by inheritance. Inheritance enables a class to extend the contract and the implementation of an existing class without knowing the details of the existing class. In the development of a Java program, class abstraction is applied to decompose the problem into a set of related classes, and method abstraction is applied to design individual classes.

Your first task is to identify classes and determine the responsibilities of each class. There are many strategies for identifying classes in a system, one of which is to study how the system works and select a number of use cases, or scenarios. A simple rule is to look for nouns in the problem description. For example, to design an information system for a university, obviously you will identify student, faculty, and courses as classes.

Once the classes are identified, you will determine the responsibilities of each class, i.e., the methods carried out by the objects of the class. A simple rule is to look for verbs in the problem description and match the verbs to appropriate objects. For example, in the information system for a university, a student registers for a course. Obviously, registering for courses is the responsibility of the **Student** class. The **Course** class is involved in this operation, which is known as a *collaborator* for the operation.

One popular way of facilitating the discovery process is by creating CRC cards. CRC stands for *classes*, *responsibilities*, and *collaborators*. Use an index card for each class, as shown in Figure 12.2.

CRC cards

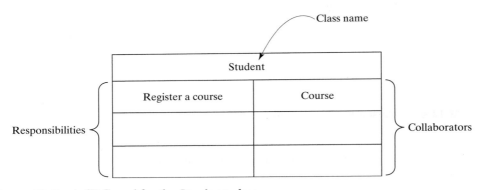

FIGURE 12.2 A CRC card for the **Student** class.

At the top of the card, write the class name. Each row has two columns. Write a responsibility in the left column. If the responsibility involves a collaborator class, write it in the corresponding right column.

12.4 Discovering Class Relationships

The common relationships among classes are: *association*, *aggregation*, *composition*, *dependency*, and *inheritance*.

12.4.1 Association

association

Association is a general binary relationship that describes an activity between two classes. For example, a student taking a course is an association between the Student class and the Course class, and a faculty member teaching a course is an association between the Faculty class and the Course class. These associations can be represented in UML graphical notation, as shown in Figure 12.3.

FIGURE 12.3   A student may take any number of courses, and a faculty member teaches at most three courses. A course may have from five to 60 students and is taught by only one faculty member.

An association is illustrated by a solid line between two classes with an optional label that describes the relationship. In Figure 12.3, the labels are *Take* and *Teach*. Each relationship may have an optional small black triangle that indicates the direction of the relationship. In Figure 12.3, the direction indicates that a student takes a course, as opposed to a course taking a student.

Each class involved in the relationship may have a role name that describes the role it plays in the relationship. In Figure 12.3, *teacher* is the role name for Faculty.

Each class involved in an association may specify a *multiplicity*. A multiplicity could be a number or an interval that specifies how many objects of the class are involved in the relationship. The character * means an unlimited number of objects, and the interval m..n means that the number of objects should be between m and n, inclusive. In Figure 12.3, each student may take any number of courses, and each course must have at least five students and at most 60 students. Each course is taught by only one faculty member, and a faculty member may teach from zero to three courses per semester.

Association may exist between objects of the same class. For example, a person may have a supervisor. This is illustrated in Figure 12.4.

FIGURE 12.4   A person may have a supervisor.

In Java code, an association can be implemented using data fields and methods. For example, the relationships in Figure 12.3 may be implemented in the following classes:

```
public class Student {
    private Course[]
        courseList;

    public void addCourse(
        Course s)
}
```

```
public class Course {
    private Student[]
        classList;
    private Faculty faculty;

    public void addStudent(
        Student s)

    public void setFaculty(
        Faculty faculty)
}
```

```
public class Faculty {
    private Course[]
        courseList;

    public void addCourse(
        Course c)
}
```

Note

There are many possible ways to implement relationships. For example, the student and faculty information in the `Course` class can be omitted, since they are already in the `Student` and `Faculty` class. Likewise, if you don't need to know the courses a student takes or a faculty member teaches, the data field `courseList` and the `addCourse` method in `Student` or `Faculty` can be omitted.

many possible implementations

12.4.2 Aggregation and Composition

Aggregation is a special form of association that represents an ownership relationship between two objects. Aggregation models *has-a* relationships. The owner object is called an *aggregating object*, and its class an *aggregating class*. The subject object is called an *aggregated object*, and its class an *aggregated class*. The association "a person has a supervisor" in Figure 12.4 is actually an aggregation.

aggregation
aggregating object
aggregated object

An object may be owned by several other aggregating objects. If an object is exclusively owned by an aggregating object, the relationship between the object and its aggregating object is referred to as *composition*. For example, "a student has a name" is a composition relationship between the `Student` class and the `Name` class, whereas "a student has an address" is an aggregation relationship between the `Student` class and the `Address` class, since an address may be shared by several students. In UML, a filled diamond is attached to an aggregating class (e.g., `Student`) to denote the composition relationship with an aggregated class (e.g., `Name`), and an empty diamond is attached to an aggregating class (e.g., `Student`) to denote the aggregation relationship with an aggregated class (e.g., `Address`), as shown in Figure 12.5.

composition

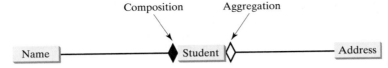

FIGURE 12.5 A student has a name and an address.

An aggregation relationship is usually represented as a data field in the aggregating class. For example, the relationship in Figure 12.5 can be represented as follows:

```
public class Name {
    ...
}
```

```
public class Person {
    private Name name;
    private Address address;

    ...
}
```

```
public class Address {
    ...
}
```

Aggregated class   Aggregating class   Aggregated class

In the relationship "a person has a supervisor," as shown in Figure 12.4, a supervisor can be represented as a data field in the **Person** class, as follows:

```java
public class Person {
    // The type for the data is the class itself
    private Person supervisor;

    ...
}
```

If a person has several supervisors, as shown in Figure 12.6, you may use an array or an **ArrayList** to store the supervisors.

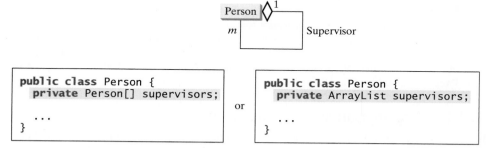

```java
public class Person {
    private Person[] supervisors;

    ...
}
```
or
```java
public class Person {
    private ArrayList supervisors;

    ...
}
```

FIGURE 12.6   A person may have several supervisors.

Note

For simplicity, since aggregation and composition relationships are translated into the same class template, both are called composition.

aggregation or composition

12.4.3 Dependency

client
supplier

A *dependency* describes a relationship between two classes where one (called **client**) uses the other (called *supplier*). In UML, draw a dashed line with an arrow from the client class to the supplier class. For example, the **ArrayList** class uses **Object** because you can add objects to an **ArrayList**. The relationship between **ArrayList** and **Object** can be described using dependency, as shown in Figure 12.7(a). The **Calendar** class uses **Date** because you can set a calendar with a specified **Date** object. The relationship between **Calendar** and **Date** can be described using dependency, as shown in Figure 12.7(b).

FIGURE 12.7   (a) **ArrayList** uses **Object**. (b) **Calendar** uses **Date**.

In Java code, a dependency can be implemented using a method in the client class. The method contains a parameter of the supplier class type. For example, the **ArrayList** class has the **add(Object)** method that adds an object to the **ArrayList**. The **Calendar** class has the **setTime(Date)** method that sets a new time in the calendar.

```java
public class ArrayList {
    public void add(Object o)

    ...
}
```

```java
public abstract class Calendar {
    public void setTime(Date d)

    ...
}
```

12.4.4 Comparing Dependency, Association, Aggregation, and Composition

Dependency, association, aggregation, and composition all describe dependent relationships between two classes. The difference is the degree of *coupling* with composition being the strongest, followed by aggregation, association, and dependency in this order.

coupling increases

dependency, association, aggregation, composition

If class A contains a method with a parameter whose type is class B, as shown in Figure 12.8(a), A is said to be dependent on B. If class A contains a data field whose type is class B, as shown in Figure 12.8(b), the relationship between the classes is association.

```
public class A {
   public void aMethod(B b)
      ...
}
```

```
public class A {
   private B b;
      ...
}
```

(a) Dependency

(b) Association

FIGURE 12.8 Association is stronger than dependency.

Association can be viewed as a special case of dependency. Aggregation is a special case of association where it describes a has-a relationship. Composition is a special case of aggregation where it describes an exclusive has-a relationship.

12.4.5 Inheritance

Inheritance models the *is-a* relationship between two classes. A strong is-a relationship describes a direct inheritance relationship between two classes. A weak is-a relationship conveys that a class has certain properties. A strong is-a relationship can be represented using class inheritance. For example, the relationship "a faculty member is a person" (shown in Figure 12.9(a)) is a strong is-a relationship and can be represented using the class in Figure 12.9(b).

strong is-a
weak is-a

Person ◁——Faculty

```
public class Faculty extends Person {
   ...
}
```

(a)

(b)

FIGURE 12.9 **Faculty** extends **Person**.

A weak is-a relationship is better represented using interfaces. For example, the weak is-a relationship "students are comparable based on their grades" (shown in Figure 12.10(a)) can be represented by implementing the Comparable interface, as shown in Figure 12.10(b).

(a)   (b)

FIGURE 12.10 Student extends Person and implements Comparable.

Video Note
Object-oriented design

12.5 Case Study: Object-Oriented Design

This case study models borrowing loans to demonstrate how to identify classes, discover the relationships between classes, and apply class abstraction in object-oriented program development.

For simplicity, the example does not attempt to build a complete system for storing, processing, and manipulating loans for borrowers; instead it focuses on modeling borrowers and the loans for the borrowers. The following steps are usually involved in building an object-oriented system:

1. Identify classes for the system.

2. Establish relationships among classes.

3. Describe the attributes and methods in each class.

4. Implement the classes.

identify classes

The first step is to identify classes for the system. Since a borrower is a person who obtains a loan, and a person has a name and an address, you can identify the following classes: Person, Name, Address, Borrower, and Loan.

Identifying objects is not easy for novice programmers. How do you find the right objects? There is no unique solution, even for simple problems. Software development is more an art than a science. The quality of a program ultimately depends on the programmer's intuition, experience, and knowledge. This example identifies five classes: Name, Address, Person, Borrower, and Loan. There are several alternatives. One would combine Name, Address, Person, and Borrower into one class. This design is not good because it would put unrelated entities into one class. Is there a good justification for combining name with person into the Person class? Yes, but separating them makes Name reusable. The many ways to design classes have different advantages. You need to consider trade-offs to choose one.

establish relationships

The second step is to establish relationships among the classes. The relationship is derived from the system analysis. The first two steps are intertwined. When you identify classes, you also think about the relationships among them. Establishing relationships among objects helps you understand the interactions among them. An object-oriented system consists of a collection of interrelated cooperative objects. The relationships for the classes in this example are illustrated in Figure 12.11.

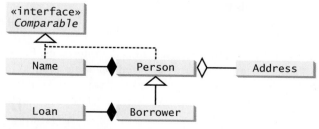

FIGURE 12.11 A borrower is a person who has a loan.

The third step is to describe the attributes and methods in each of the classes you have identified. The `Name` class has the properties `firstName`, `mi`, and `lastName`, their associated `get`
and `set` methods, and the `getFullName` method for returning the full name. You can compare
names in alphabetical order of last name, first name, and mi. The `Address` class has the properties `street`, `city`, `state`, and `zip`, their associated `get` and `set` methods, and the
`getAddress` method for returning the full address. The `Loan` class, presented in Listing 9.2,
has the properties `annualInterestRate`, `numberOfYears`, and `loanAmount`, their associated `get` and `set` methods, and `getMonthlyPayment` and `getTotalPayment` methods. The
`Person` class has the properties `name` and `address`, their associated `get` and `set` methods,
and the `toString` method for displaying complete information about the person. `Borrower` is
a subclass of `Person`. Additionally, `Borrower` has the `loan` property and its associated `get`
and `set` methods, and the `toString` method for displaying the person and the loan payments.
You can compare persons according to their names. Figure 12.11 is expanded to Figure 12.12.

describe attributes

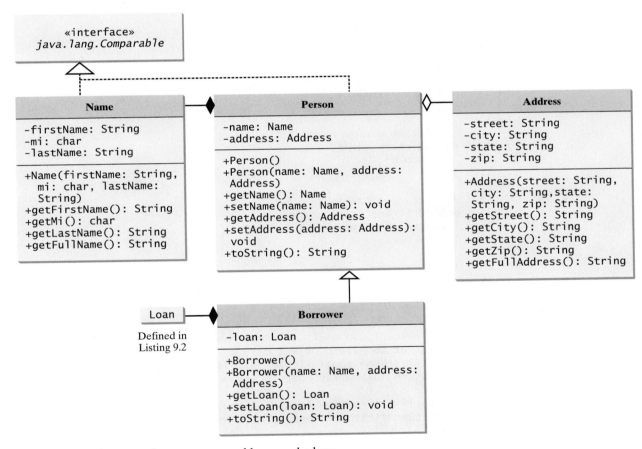

FIGURE 12.12   A borrower has a name, an address, and a loan.

 Note
The first three steps are often *intertwined*. For example, when you discover a class, you think of
its responsibilities. You may identify new classes as collaborators. You will discover the relationships among these classes.

steps intertwined

The fourth step is to write the code for the classes. The program is long, but most of the
coding is for the `get` and `set` methods. Once an object is identified, its properties and methods

coding

can be defined by analyzing the requirements and scenarios of the system. It is a good practice to provide complete **get** and **set** methods. These may not be needed for your current project, but they will be useful in other projects, because your classes are designed for reuse in future projects. Listings 12.1, 12.2, 12.3, and 12.4 give the **Name**, **Address**, **Person**, and **Borrower** classes.

LISTING 12.1 Name.java

Name class

```java
1  public final class Name implements Comparable {
2    private String firstName;
3    private char mi;
4    private String lastName;
5
6    /** Construct a name with firstName, mi, and lastName */
7    public Name(String firstName, char mi, String lastName) {
8      this.firstName = firstName;
9      this.mi = mi;
10      this.lastName = lastName;
11    }
12
13    /** Return firstName */
14    public String getFirstName() {
15      return firstName;
16    }
17
18    /** Return middle name initial */
19    public char getMi() {
20      return mi;
21    }
22
23    /** Return lastName */
24    public String getLastname() {
25      return lastName;
26    }
27
28    /** Obtain full name */
29    public String getFullName() {
30      return firstName + ' ' + mi + ' ' + lastName;
31    }
32
33    /** Implement compareTo in the Comparable interface */
34    public int compareTo(Object o) {
35      if (!lastName.equals(((Name)o).lastName)) {
36        return lastName.compareTo(((Name)o).lastName);
37      }
38      else if (!firstName.equals(((Name)o).firstName)) {
39        return firstName.compareTo(((Name)o).firstName);
40      }
41      else {
42        return mi - ((Name)o).mi;
43      }
44    }
45  }
```

constructor

LISTING 12.2 Address.java

Address class

```java
1  public final class Address {
2    private String street;
3    private String city;
4    private String state;
```

```
 5    private String zip;
 6
 7    /** Create an address with street, city, state, and zip */
 8    public Address(String street, String city,
 9      String state, String zip) {
10      this.street = street;
11      this.city = city;
12      this.state = state;
13      this.zip = zip;
14    }
15
16    /** Return street */
17    public String getStreet() {
18      return street;
19    }
20
21    /** Return city */
22    public String getCity() {
23      return city;
24    }
25
26    /** Return state */
27    public String getState() {
28      return state;
29    }
30
31    /** Return zip */
32    public String getZip() {
33      return zip;
34    }
35
36    /** Get full address */
37    public String getFullAddress() {
38      return street + '\n' + city + ", " + state + ' ' + zip + '\n';
39    }
40 }
```

constructor

Note

To avoid naming conflict with the **Person** class defined in Chapter 10, name the class **Person1** here.

LISTING 12.3 Person1.java

```
 1 public class Person1 implements Comparable {
 2    private Name name;
 3    private Address address;
 4
 5    /** Construct a person with default properties */
 6    public Person1() {
 7      this(new Name("Jill", 'S', "Barr"),
 8        new Address("100 Main", "Savannah", "GA", "31411"));
 9    }
10
11    /** Construct a person with specified name and address */
12    public Person1(Name name, Address address) {
13      this.name = name;
14      this.address = address;
15    }
16
17    /** Return name */
```

Person class

constructor

constructor

```
18    public Name getName() {
19      return name;
20    }
21
22    /** Set a new name */
23    public void setName(Name name) {
24      this.name = name;
25    }
26
27    /** Return address */
28    public Address getAddress() {
29      return address;
30    }
31
32    /** Set a new address */
33    public void setAddress(Address address) {
34      this.address = address;
35    }
36
37    /** Override the toString method */
38    public String toString() {
39      return '\n' + name.getFullName() + '\n' +
40        address.getFullAddress() + '\n';
41    }
42
43    /** Implement compareTo in the Comparable interface */
44    public int compareTo(Object o) {
45      return name.compareTo((((Person1)o).name);
46    }
47 }
```

LISTING 12.4 Borrower.java

Borrower class

```
1  public class Borrower extends Person1 {
2    private Loan loan;
3
4    /** Construct a borrower with default properties */
5    public Borrower() {
6      super();
7    }
8
9    /** Create a borrower with specified name and address */
10   public Borrower(Name name, Address address) {
11     super(name, address);
12   }
13
14   /** Return loan */
15   public Loan getLoan() {
16     return loan;
17   }
18
19   /** Set a new loan */
20   public void setLoan(Loan loan) {
21     this.loan = loan;
22   }
23
24   /** String representation for borrower */
25   public String toString() {
26     return super.toString() +
```

```
27          "Monthly payment is " + loan.getMonthlyPayment() + '\n' +
28          "Total payment is " + loan.getTotalPayment();
29   }
30 }
```

Listing 12.5 is a test program that uses the classes Name, Address, Borrower, and Loan.

LISTING 12.5 BorrowLoan.java

```
 1 public class BorrowLoan {
 2   /** Main method */
 3   public static void main(String[] args) {
 4     // Create a name
 5     Name name = new Name("John", 'D', "Smith");
 6
 7     // Create an address
 8     Address address = new Address("100 Main Street", "Savannah",
 9       "GA", "31419");
10
11     // Create a loan
12     Loan loan = new Loan(5.5, 15, 250000);
13
14     // Create a borrower
15     Borrower borrower = new Borrower(name, address);
16
17     borrower.setLoan(loan);
18
19     // Display loan information
20     System.out.println(borrower);
21   }
22 }
```

BorrowLoan class

```
John D Smith
100 Main Street
Savannah, GA 31419

Monthly payment is 2042.7086365528232
Total payment is 367687.5545795082
```

12.6 Case Study: The **Rational** Class

Video Note
Rational class

A rational number has a numerator and a denominator in the form a/b, where a is the numerator and b is the denominator. For example, 1/3, 3/4, and 10/4 are rational numbers.

A rational number cannot have a denominator of 0, but a numerator of 0 is fine. Every integer a is equivalent to a rational number a/1. Rational numbers are used in exact computations involving fractions—for example, $1/3 = 0.33333\ldots$. This number cannot be precisely represented in floating-point format using data type double or float. To obtain the exact result, we must use rational numbers.

Java provides data types for integers and floating-point numbers, but not for rational numbers. This section shows how to design a class to represent rational numbers.

Since rational numbers share many common features with integers and floating-point numbers, and Number is the root class for numeric wrapper classes, it is appropriate to define Rational as a subclass of Number. Since rational numbers are comparable, the Rational class should also implement the Comparable interface. Figure 12.13 illustrates the Rational class and its relationship to the Number class and the Comparable interface.

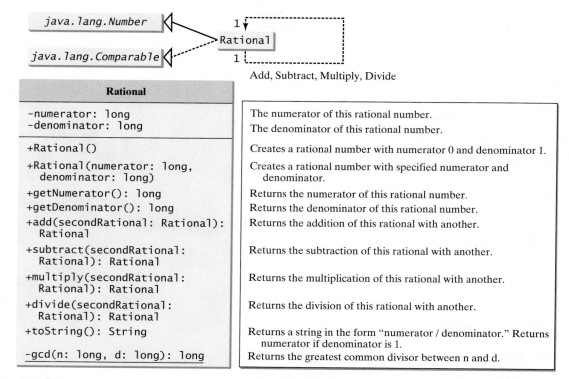

FIGURE 12.13 The properties, constructors, and methods of the Rational class are illustrated in UML.

A rational number consists of a numerator and a denominator. There are many equivalent rational numbers—for example, $1/3 = 2/6 = 3/9 = 4/12$. The numerator and the denominator of 1/3 have no common divisor except 1, so 1/3 is said to be in lowest terms.

To reduce a rational number to its lowest terms, you need to find the greatest common divisor (GCD) of the absolute values of its numerator and denominator, and then divide both numerator and denominator by this value. You can use the method for computing the GCD of two integers n and d, as suggested in Listing 4.8, GreatestCommonDivisor.java. The numerator and denominator in a Rational object are reduced to their lowest terms.

As usual, let us first write a test program to create two Rational objects and test its methods. Listing 12.6 is a test program.

LISTING 12.6 TestRationalClass.java

```
 1 public class TestRationalClass {
 2   /** Main method */
 3   public static void main(String[] args) {
 4     // Create and initialize two rational numbers r1 and r2.
 5     Rational r1 = new Rational(4, 2);
 6     Rational r2 = new Rational(2, 3);
 7
 8     // Display results
 9     System.out.println(r1 + " + " + r2 + " = " + r1.add(r2) );
10     System.out.println(r1 + " - " + r2 + " = " + r1.subtract(r2));
11     System.out.println(r1 + " * " + r2 + " = " + r1.multiply(r2));
12     System.out.println(r1 + " / " + r2 + " = " + r1.divide(r2) );
13     System.out.println(r2 + " is " + r2.doubleValue());
14   }
15 }
```

create a Rational
create a Rational

add

```
2 + 2/3 = 8/3
2 - 2/3 = 4/3
2 * 2/3 = 4/3
2 / 2/3 = 3
2/3 is 0.6666666666666666
```

The `main` method creates two rational numbers, `r1` and `r2` (lines 5–6), and displays the results of `r1 + r2`, `r1 - r2`, `r1 x r2`, and `r1 / r2` (lines 9–12). To perform `r1 + r2`, invoke `r1.add(r2)` to return a new `Rational` object. Similarly, `r1.subtract(r2)` is for `r1 - r2`, `r1.multiply(r2)` for `r1 x r2`, and `r1.divide(r2)` for `r1 / r2`.

The `doubleValue()` method displays the double value of `r2` (line 13). The `doubleValue()` method is defined in `java.lang.Number` and overridden in `Rational`.

Note that when a string is concatenated with an object using the plus sign (+), the object's string representation from the `toString()` method is used to concatenate with the string. So `r1 + " + " + r2 + " = " + r1.add(r2)` is equivalent to `r1.toString() + " + " + r2.toString() + " = " + r1.add(r2).toString()`.

The `Rational` class is implemented in Listing 12.7.

LISTING 12.7 Rational.java

```java
 1 public class Rational extends Number implements Comparable {
 2   // Data fields for numerator and denominator
 3   private long numerator = 0;
 4   private long denominator = 1;
 5
 6   /** Construct a rational with default properties */
 7   public Rational() {
 8     this(0, 1);
 9   }
10
11   /** Construct a rational with specified numerator and denominator */
12   public Rational(long numerator, long denominator) {
13     long gcd = gcd(numerator, denominator);
14     this.numerator = ((denominator > 0) ? 1 : -1) * numerator / gcd;
15     this.denominator = Math.abs(denominator) / gcd;
16   }
17
18   /** Find GCD of two numbers */
19   private static long gcd(long n, long d) {
20     long n1 = Math.abs(n);
21     long n2 = Math.abs(d);
22     int gcd = 1;
23
24     for (int k = 1; k <= n1 && k <= n2; k++) {
25       if (n1 % k == 0 && n2 % k == 0)
26         gcd = k;
27     }
28
29     return gcd;
30   }
31
32   /** Return numerator */
33   public long getNumerator() {
34     return numerator;
35   }
36
37   /** Return denominator */
```

$$\frac{a}{b} + \frac{c}{d} = \frac{ad + bc}{bd}$$

$$\frac{a}{b} - \frac{c}{d} = \frac{ad - bc}{bd}$$

$$\frac{a}{b} \times \frac{c}{d} = \frac{ac}{bd}$$

$$\frac{a}{b} \div \frac{c}{d} = \frac{ad}{bc}$$

```java
38    public long getDenominator() {
39      return denominator;
40    }
41
42    /** Add a rational number to this rational */
43    public Rational add(Rational secondRational) {
44      long n = numerator * secondRational.getDenominator() +
45        denominator * secondRational.getNumerator();
46      long d = denominator * secondRational.getDenominator();
47      return new Rational(n, d);
48    }
49
50    /** Subtract a rational number from this rational */
51    public Rational subtract(Rational secondRational) {
52      long n = numerator * secondRational.getDenominator()
53        - denominator * secondRational.getNumerator();
54      long d = denominator * secondRational.getDenominator();
55      return new Rational(n, d);
56    }
57
58    /** Multiply a rational number to this rational */
59    public Rational multiply(Rational secondRational) {
60      long n = numerator * secondRational.getNumerator();
61      long d = denominator * secondRational.getDenominator();
62      return new Rational(n, d);
63    }
64
65    /** Divide a rational number from this rational */
66    public Rational divide(Rational secondRational) {
67      long n = numerator * secondRational.getDenominator();
68      long d = denominator * secondRational.numerator;
69      return new Rational(n, d);
70    }
71
72    /** Override the toString() method */
73    public String toString() {
74      if (denominator == 1)
75        return numerator + "";
76      else
77        return numerator + "/" + denominator;
78    }
79
80    /** Override the equals method in the Object class */
81    public boolean equals(Object parm1) {
82      if ((this.subtract((Rational)(parm1))).getNumerator() == 0)
83        return true;
84      else
85        return false;
86    }
87
88    /** Implement the abstract intValue method in java.lang.Number */
89    public int intValue() {
90      return (int)doubleValue();
91    }
92
93    /** Implement the abstract floatValue method in java.lang.Number */
94    public float floatValue() {
```

```
95        return (float)doubleValue();
96    }
97
98    /** Implement the doubleValue method in java.lang.Number */
99    public double doubleValue() {
100       return numerator * 1.0 / denominator;
101   }
102
103   /** Implement the abstract longValue method in java.lang.Number */
104   public long longValue() {
105       return (long)doubleValue();
106   }
107
108   /** Implement the compareTo method in java.lang.Comparable */
109   public int compareTo(Object o) {
110       if ((this.subtract((Rational)o)).getNumerator() > 0)
111           return 1;
112       else if ((this.subtract((Rational)o)).getNumerator() < 0)
113           return -1;
114       else
115           return 0;
116   }
117 }
```

The rational number is encapsulated in a `Rational` object. Internally, a rational number is represented in its lowest terms (line 13), and the numerator determines its sign (line 14). The denominator is always positive (line 15).

The `gcd()` method (lines 19–30 in the `Rational` class) is private; it is not intended for use by clients. The `gcd()` method is only for internal use by the `Rational` class. The `gcd()` method is also static, since it is not dependent on any particular `Rational` object.

The `abs(x)` method (lines 20–21 in the `Rational` class) is defined in the `Math` class that returns the absolute value of `x`.

Two `Rational` objects can interact with each other to perform add, subtract, multiply, and divide operations. These methods return a new `Rational` object (lines 43–70).

The methods `toString` and `equals` in the `Object` class are overridden in the `Rational` class (lines 73–91). The `toString()` method returns a string representation of a `Rational` object in the form `numerator/denominator`, or simply `numerator` if `denominator` is 1. The `equals(Object other)` method returns true if this rational number is equal to the other rational number.

The abstract methods `intValue`, `longValue`, `floatValue`, and `doubleValue` in the `Number` class are implemented in the `Rational` class (lines 88–106). These methods return `int`, `long`, `float`, and `double` value for this rational number.

The `compareTo(Object other)` method in the `Comparable` interface is implemented in the `Rational` class (lines 109–117) to compare this rational number to the other rational number.

 Tip

The `get` methods for the properties `numerator` and `denominator` are provided in the `Rational` class, but the `set` methods are not provided, so, once a `Rational` object is created, its contents cannot be changed. The `Rational` class is immutable. A well-known example   immutable
of an immutable class is the `String` class. The wrapper classes introduced in §11.9, "Processing Primitive Data Type Values as Objects," are also immutable.

encapsulation

Tip
The numerator and denominator are represented using two variables. It is possible to use an array of two integers to represent the numerator and denominator. See Exercise 12.4. The signatures of the public methods in the `Rational` class are not changed, although the internal representation of a rational number is changed. This is a good example to illustrate the idea that the data fields of a class should be kept private so as to encapsulate the implementation of the class from the use of the class.

overflow

The `Rational` class has serious limitations. It can easily overflow. For example, the following code will display an incorrect result, because the denominator is too large.

```java
public class Test {
  public static void main(String[] args) {
    Rational r1 = new Rational(1, 123456789);
    Rational r2 = new Rational(1, 123456789);
    Rational r3 = new Rational(1, 123456789);
    System.out.println("r1 * r2 * r3 is " +
      r1.multiply(r2.multiply(r3)));
  }
}
```

```
r1 * r2 * r3 is -1/2204193661661244627
```

To fix it, you may implement the `Rational` class using the `BigInteger` for numerator and denominator (see Exercises 12.3 and 12.5).

12.7 Class Design Guidelines

You have learned how to design classes from the preceding two examples and from many other examples in the preceding chapters. Here are some guidelines.

12.7.1 Cohesion

coherent purpose

A class should describe a single entity, and all the class operations should logically fit together to support a coherent purpose. You can use a class for students, for example, but you should not combine students and staff in the same class, because students and staff have different entities.

separating responsibilities

A single entity with too many responsibilities can be broken into several classes to separate responsibilities. The classes `String`, `StringBuilder`, and `StringBuffer` all deal with strings, for example, but have different responsibilities. The `String` class deals with immutable strings, the `StringBuilder` class is for creating mutable strings, and the `StringBuffer` class is similar to `StringBuilder` except that `StringBuffer` contains synchronized methods for updating strings.

The `Date`, `Calendar`, and `GregorianCalendar` classes all deal with date and time, but have different responsibilities. The `Date` class represents a specific time. `Calendar` is an abstract class for extracting detailed calendar information from a specific time. `GregorianCalendar` implements a concrete calendar system.

12.7.2 Consistency

naming conventions

Follow standard Java programming style and naming conventions. Choose informative names for classes, data fields, and methods. A popular style is to place the data declaration before the constructor, and place constructors before methods.

Choose names consistently. It is not a good practice to choose different names for similar operations. For example, the `length()` method returns the size of a `String`, a `StringBuilder`, and a `StringBuffer`. But the `size()` method is used to return the size of an `ArrayList`. For consistency it would be better to use the same name.

naming consistency

In general, you should consistently provide a public no-arg constructor for constructing a default instance. If a class does not support a no-arg constructor, document the reason. If no constructors are defined explicitly, a public default no-arg constructor with an empty body is assumed. If a constructor does not invoke an overloaded constructor or its superclass's constructor, it invokes its superclass no-arg constructor by default.

no-arg constructor

If you want to prevent users from creating an object for a class, you may declare a private constructor in the class, as is the case for the `Math` class. The constructors in abstract classes should always be declared `protected`.

12.7.3 Encapsulation

A class should use the `private` modifier to hide its data from direct access by clients. This makes the class easy to maintain.

encapsulating data fields

Provide a `get` method only if you want the field to be readable, and provide a `set` method only if you want the field to be updateable. For example, the `Rational` class provides `get` methods for numerator and denominator, but no `set` methods, because `Rational` is an immutable class.

A class should also hide methods not intended for client use. The `gcd` method in the `Rational` class in the preceding section is private, for example, because it is only for internal use within the class.

A class can present two contracts: one for the users of the class, and one for the extenders of the class. Make the fields `private` and the accessor and mutator methods `public` if they are intended for the users of the class. Make the fields or methods `protected` if they are intended for extenders of the class. The contract for extenders encompasses the contract for users. The extended class may increase the visibility of an instance method from `protected` to `public`, or may change its implementation, but you should never change the implementation in a way that violates the contract.

private vs. protected

12.7.4 Clarity

Cohesion, consistency, and encapsulation are good guidelines for achieving design clarity. Additionally, a class should have a clear contract that is easy to explain and easy to understand.

easy to explain

Users can incorporate classes in many different combinations, orders, and environments. Therefore, you should design a class that imposes no restrictions on what or when the user can do with it, design the properties in a way that lets the user set them in any order and with any combination of values, and design methods that function independently of their order of occurrence. For example, the `Loan` class contains the properties `loanAmount`, `numberOfYears`, and `annualInterestRate`. The values of these properties can be set in any order.

independent methods

Methods should be defined intuitively without generating confusion. For example, the `substring(int beginIndex, int endIndex)` method in the `String` class is somehow confusing. The method returns a substring from `beginIndex` to `endIndex - 1`, rather than `endIndex`.

intuitive meaning

You should not declare a data field that can be derived from other data fields. For example, the following `Person` class has two data fields: `birthDate` and `age`. Since `age` can be derived from `birthDate`, age should not be declared as a data field.

independent properties

```java
public class Person {
  private java.util.Date birthDate;
  int age;

  ...
}
```

12.7.5   Completeness

Classes are designed for use by many different customers. In order to be useful in a wide range of applications, a class should provide a variety of ways for customization through properties and methods. For example, the `String` class contains more than 50 methods that are useful for a variety of applications. The `Calendar` class defines many time fields as constants, such as YEAR, MONTH, DATE, HOUR, HOUR_OF_DAY, MINUTE, SECOND, and DAY_OF_WEEK, and provides many methods for extracting date and time and for setting a new date and time in the calendar.

12.7.6   Instance vs. Static

A variable or method that is dependent on a specific instance of the class should be an instance variable or method. A variable that is shared by all the instances of a class should be declared static. For example, the variable `numberOfObjects` in `Circle3` in Listing 7.7, is shared by all the objects of the `SimpleCircle1` class, and therefore is declared static. A method that is not dependent on a specific instance should be declared as a static method. For instance, the `getNumberOfObjects` method in `Circle3` and the `gcd` method in `Rational` are not tied to any specific instance, and therefore are declared as static methods.

Always reference static variables and methods from a class name (rather than a reference variable) to improve readability and avoid errors.

Do not pass a parameter from a constructor to initialize a static data field. It is better to use a `set` method to change the static data field. The class in (a) below is better replaced by (b).

```
public class SomeThing {
  int t1;
  static int t2;

  public SomeThing(int t1, int t2) {
    ...
  }
}
```

```
public class SomeThing {
  int t1;
  static int t2;

  public SomeThing(int t1) {
    ...
  }

  public static void setT2(int t2) {
    SomeThing.t2 = t2;
  }
}
```

(a)   (b)

Instance and static are integral parts of object-oriented programming. A data field or method is either instance or static. Do not mistakenly overlook static data fields or methods. It is a common design error to declare an instance method that should have been declared static. For example, the `factorial(int n)` method for computing the factorial of n should be declared static, because it is independent of any specific instance.

A constructor is always instance, because it is used to create a specific instance. A static variable or method can be invoked from an instance method, but an instance variable or method cannot be invoked from a static method.

common design error

12.7.7   Inheritance vs. Aggregation

The difference between inheritance and aggregation is the difference between an is-a and a has-a relationship. For example, an apple is a fruit; thus, you would use inheritance to model the relationship between the classes `Apple` and `Fruit`. A person has a name; thus, you would use aggregation to model the relationship between the classes `Person` and `Name`.

12.7.8 Interfaces vs. Abstract Classes

Both interfaces and abstract classes can be used to specify common behaviour for objects. How do you decide whether to use an interface or a class? In general, a *strong is-a relationship* that clearly describes a parent-child relationship should be modeled using classes. For example, since an orange is a fruit, their relationship should be modeled using class inheritance. A *weak is-a relationship*, also known as an *is-kind-of relationship*, indicates that an object possesses a certain property. A weak is-a relationship can be modeled using interfaces. For example, all strings are comparable, so the `String` class implements the `Comparable` interface. A circle or a rectangle is a geometric object, so `Circle` can be designed as a subclass of `GeometricObject`. Circles are different and comparable based on their radii, so `Circle` can implement the `Comparable` interface.

Interfaces are more flexible than abstract classes, because a subclass can extend only one superclass but can implement any number of interfaces. However, interfaces cannot contain concrete methods. The virtues of interfaces and abstract classes can be combined by creating an interface with an abstract class that implements it. Then you can use the interface or the abstract class, whichever is convenient. For this reason, such classes are known as *convenience classes*. For example, in the Java Collections Framework, introduced in Chapter 22, the `AbstractCollection` class is a convenience class for the `Collection` interface, and the `AbstractSet` class is a convenience class for the `Set` interface.

12.8 Framework-Based Programming Using Java API

The Java *API* (*Application Program Interface*) consists of numerous classes and interfaces grouped into more than a dozen packages, as shown in Table 12.1.

API

TABLE 12.1 Some Java API packages

Package	Description
`java.lang`	contains core Java classes and interfaces (e.g., `System`, `Math`, `Object`, `String`, `StringBuffer`, `Number`, `Character`, `Boolean`, `Byte`, `Short`, `Integer`, `Long`, `Float`, `Double`, `Comparable`, and `Cloneable`). This package is implicitly imported to every Java program.
`javax.swing`	contains the lightweight graphical user interface components (e.g., `JOptionPane`, `JFrame`, `JButton`) for developing Swing GUI programs.
`java.util`	contains utility classes and interfaces, such as `Scanner`, `Arrays`, `ArrayList`, `Date`, `Calendar`, and `GregorianCalendar`.
`java.io`	contains classes and interfaces for IO, such as `File` and `PrintWriter`.
`java.math`	contains classes `BigInteger` for performing arbitrary-precision integer arithmetic and `BigDecimal` for performing arbitrary-precision decimal arithmetic.
`java.net`	contains classes for network programming.
`java.applet`	contains classes for supporting applets.
`java.awt`	contains classes for supporting GUI programming.

You have used several classes and interfaces in the `java.lang`, `javax.swing`, `java.util`, and `java.io` packages. These are just a few of the classes and interfaces you have learned. To create comprehensive projects, you have to use more classes and interfaces in the Java API. The classes and interfaces in the Java API establish a framework for programmers to develop applications using Java. For example, the classes and interfaces in the Java GUI API establish a framework for developing GUI programs. You have to use these classes and interfaces and follow their conventions and rules to create applications. This is referred to as *framework-based programming*.

framework-based programming

Once you understand the concept of Java and object-oriented programming, the most important lesson from now on is learning how to use the API to develop useful programs. The most effective way to achieve this is to imitate good examples. The book provides many carefully designed examples to demonstrate the concept of framework-based programming using the Java API. You will learn the Java GUI programming framework in Chapters 13–17, the Java exception–handling framework in Chapter 18, and the Java I/O framework in Chapter 19.

12.9 Design Patterns

reuse code

One important benefit of object-oriented programming is to *reuse code*. For example, to create a button, you simply use the `JButton` class to create an instance of `JButton`. The `JButton` class is already defined in the Java API, so you can use it without having to reinvent the wheel. Design patterns are proven sound software strategies for designing classes. Applying design patterns is like *reusing experience*. You can apply successful patterns to develop new software without reinventing new solution strategies.

reuse experience

The formal recognition of design patterns was presented in a groundbreaking book, *Design Patterns: Elements of Reusable Object-Oriented Software*, by Erich Gamma, Richard Helm, Ralph Johnson, and John Vlissides. The book profoundly influenced object-oriented software development. The authors are respectfully nicknamed the "*Gang of Four*" and their book is commonly known as the *gang-of-four book*.

the gang-of-four book

The gang-of-four book argues that expert designers do not solve every problem from scratch. Rather, they reuse solutions that have worked for them in the past. When they find a good solution, they use it over and over again. Design patterns can speed up the development process by providing almost ready-made solutions that have been used earlier and proved to be effective and efficient. The gang-of-four book records experiences in designing object-oriented software as design patterns, documenting 23 of them.

23 design patterns

To apply design patterns effectively, you need to familiarize yourself with the most popular and effective ones. The best way to learn these patterns is by examples. We will illustrate design patterns throughout the book with concrete examples.

learn design patterns

Singleton pattern

As an example, this section introduces the *Singleton pattern*. This pattern declares a class that can be used to instantiate a unique instance. Occasionally, it is desirable to restrict instantiation of a class to exactly one object. For example, there may be many printers in a system, but there should be only one printer spooler. So, your system should ensure that only one printer spooler object is created.

The Singleton pattern can be implemented by creating a class with a private constructor and a static constant that references an instance of the class. Listing 12.8 shows an example of such class.

LISTING 12.8 Singleton.java

create object

private constructor

```
1 public final class Singleton {
2   private static final Singleton uniqueInstance = new Singleton();
3
4   private Singleton() {
5   }
6
```

```
 7   public static Singleton getInstance() {          access point
 8      return uniqueInstance;
 9   }
10 }
```

An object of the `Singleton` class is created in line 2. Since the constructor is private (line 4), it prevents the client from creating objects using `new Singleton()`. The only way to access the object is through the `getInstance()` method (line 7), which returns the reference of the object (line 8). For example, the following code displays `true`, since `object1` and `object2` refer to the same object.

```
Singleton object1 = Singleton.getInstance();
Singleton object2 = Singleton.getInstance();
System.out.println(object1 == object2);
```

KEY TERMS

aggregated object   397
aggregation   397
aggregating object   397
Application Program Interface
   (API)   413
association   396

composition   397
CRC cards   395
dependency   398
design pattern   414
framework-based
   programming   414

CHAPTER SUMMARY

- Software life cycle involves *requirements specification, system analysis, system design, implementation, testing, deployment,* and *maintenance.*

- The process of designing classes calls for identifying the classes and discovering the relationships among them.

- The common relationships among classes are *association*, *aggregation*, *composition*, *dependency*, and *inheritance*.

- Some guidelines for class design are *cohesion*, *consistency*, *encapsulation*, *clarity*, and *completeness*.

- A property shared by all the instances of a class should be declared as a static property. Don't mistakenly overlook static data fields or methods. A method not tied to a specific instance should be declared static.

- The difference between inheritance and aggregation is the difference between an is-a and a has-a relationship.

- Both interfaces and abstract classes can be used to specify common behavior of objects. How do you decide whether to use an interface or a class? In general, a *strong is-a relationship* that clearly describes a parent-child relationship should be modeled using classes. A weak is-a relationship can be modeled using interfaces.

- Interfaces are more flexible than abstract classes, because a subclass can extend only one superclass but can implement any number of interfaces. However, interfaces cannot contain concrete methods.

■ Design patterns are proven sound software strategies for designing classes. Applying design patterns is like *reusing experience*. You can apply successful patterns to develop new software without reinventing new solution strategies.

REVIEW QUESTIONS

Section 12.3 Discovering Relationships among Objects

12.1 What are the common types of relationships among classes? Describe the graphical notations for modeling the relationships among classes.

12.2 What relationship is appropriate for the following classes? Draw the relationships using UML diagrams.

- Company and Employee
- Course and Faculty
- Student and Person
- House and Window
- Account and Savings Account
- The `JOptionPane` class and the `String` class
- The `Loan` class and the `Date` class

Section 12.6 The `Rational` Class

12.3 Show the output of the following code:

```java
public class Test {
  public static void main(String[] args) {
    Rational r1 = new Rational(1, 3);
    Rational r2 = new Rational(2, 4);
    System.out.println(r1 + " + " + r2 + " = " + r1.add(r2));
    System.out.println(r2 + " + " + r1 + " = " + r2.add(r1));
    System.out.println(r1 + " - " + r2 + " = " +
      r1.subtract(r2));
    System.out.println(r2 + " - " + r1 + " = " +
      r2.subtract(r1));
    System.out.println(r1 + " * " + r2 + " = " +
      r1.multiply(r2));
    System.out.println(r2 + " * " + r1 + " = " +
      r2.multiply(r1));
    System.out.println(r1 + " / " + r2 + " = " +
      r1.divide(r2));
    System.out.println(r2 + " / " + r1 + " = " +
      r2.divide(r1));
    System.out.println(r1 + " = " + r1.doubleValue());
    System.out.println(r2 + " = " + r2.doubleValue());
  }
}
```

12.4 What is wrong in the following code?

```java
Number r = new Rational();
System.out.println(r);
System.out.println(r.doubleValue());
System.out.println(r.add(new Rational()));
System.out.println((Rational)r.add(new Rational()));
System.out.println(((Rational)r).add(new Rational()));
```

12.5 What is wrong in the following code?

```
Number r = new Number();
System.out.println(r);
```

12.6 Is the following code correct?

```
Comparable r = new Rational();
System.out.println(r);
```

(a)

```
Comparable r = new Rational();
System.out.println(
  r.compareTo(new Rational()));
```

(b)

Section 12.7 Class Design Guidelines

12.7 What is cohesion? Give examples of cohesive class design.

12.8 What is consistency? Give examples of inconsistent class design.

12.9 What is encapsulation? What are the benefits of data field encapsulation?

12.10 When is it appropriate to use the `protected` modifier?

12.11 Which of the following is poor design?

- A data field is derived from other data fields in the same class.
- A method must be invoked after/before invoking another method in the same class.
- A method is an instance method, but it does not reference any instance data fields or invoke instance methods.
- A parameter is passed from a constructor to initialize a static data field.

12.12 Which of the following is incorrect?

- A static method may reference instance data fields or invoke instance methods.
- An instance method may reference static data fields or invoke static methods.
- A constructor may be static.
- A constructor may be private.
- A constructor may invoke a static method.
- A constructor may invoke an overloaded constructor.
- A constructor invokes its superclass no-arg constructor by default if it does not invoke an overloaded constructor or its superclass's constructor.
- An abstract class contains constructors.
- The constructors in an abstract class are public.
- The constructors in an abstract class are private.
- You may declare a final abstract class.
- An interface may contain constructors.
- An interface may contain instance data fields.
- An interface may contain static methods.

PROGRAMMING EXERCISES

12.1* (*Multiple loans*) For the case study in §12.5, suppose that a borrower may have multiple loans. Redesign the system and redraw the UML diagrams to reflect the change. Use an array list to store multiple loans. You need a method that adds a new loan, a method that removes an existing loan, and a method that returns all loans in a list. Implement the new design and write a test program that creates a borrower with three loans, and display borrower and loan information.

Video Note

Design/implement classes
for **Person** and **Student**

12.2** (*The Person and Student classes*) Design the **Student** class that extends **Person**. Implement the **compareTo** method in the **Person** class to compare persons in alphabetical order of their last name. Implement the **compareTo** method to compare students in alphabetical order of their major and last name. Draw a UML diagram that involves **Person**, **Student**, **Comparable**, and **Name**.

Write a program with the following four methods:

```
/** Sort an array of comparable objects  */
public static void sort(Comparable[] list)

/** Pirnt an array of objects */
public static void printList(Object[] object)

/** Return the max object in an array of comparable objects */
public static Comparable max(Comparable[] list)
```

main method: Test the **sort**, **printList**, and **max** methods using an array of four students, an array of four strings, an array of 100 random rationals, and an array of 100 random integers.

12.3 (*Using the Rational class*) Write a program that will compute the following summation series using the **Rational** class:

$$\frac{1}{2} + \frac{2}{3} + \frac{3}{4} + \ldots + \frac{98}{99} + \frac{99}{100}$$

You will discover that output is incorrect because of integer overflow (too large). To fix this problem, see Exercise 12.5.

12.4* (*Demonstrating the benefits of encapsulation*) Rewrite the **Rational** class in §12.6 using a new internal representation for numerator and denominator. Declare an array of two integers as follows:

```
private long[] r = new long[2];
```

Use **r[0]** to represent the numerator and **r[1]** to represent the denominator. The signatures of the methods in the **Rational** class are not changed, so a client application that uses the previous **Rational** class can continue to use this new **Rational** class without being recompiled.

12.5** (*Using BigInteger for the Rational class*) Redesign and implement the **Rational** class in §12.6 using **BigInteger** for numerator and denominator.

12.6* (*Creating a rational number calculator*) Write a program similar to Listing 8.4, Calculator.java. Instead of using integers, use rationals, as shown in Figure 12.14. You will need to use the **split** method in the **String** class, introduced in §8.2.6, "Converting, Replacing, and Splitting Strings," to retrieve the numerator string and denominator string, and convert strings into integers using the **Integer.parseInt** method.

Figure 12.14   The program takes three arguments (operand1, operator, and operand2) from the command line and displays the expression and the result of the arithmetic operation.

CHAPTER 13

GUI BASICS

Objectives

- To distinguish between Swing and AWT (§13.2).

- To describe the Java GUI API hierarchy (§13.3).

- To create user interfaces using frames, panels, and simple GUI components (§13.4).

- To understand the role of layout managers (§13.5).

- To use the `FlowLayout`, `GridLayout`, and `BorderLayout` managers to layout components in a container (§13.5).

- To specify colors and fonts using the `Color` and `Font` classes (§§13.6–13.7).

- To use `JPanel` as subcontainers (§13.8).

- To apply common features such as borders, tool tips, fonts, and colors on Swing components (§13.9).

- To use borders to visually group user-interface components (§13.9).

- To create image icons using the `ImageIcon` class (§13.10).

13.1 Introduction

The design of the API for Java GUI programming is an excellent example of how the object-oriented principle is applied. In the preceding chapters, we used simple GUI examples to demonstrate OOP. In the chapters that follow, you will learn the framework of Java GUI API and use the GUI components to develop user-friendly interfaces for applications and applets.

This chapter introduces the basics of Java GUI programming. Specifically, it discusses GUI components and their relationships, containers and layout managers, colors, fonts, borders, image icons, and tool tips.

13.2 Swing vs. AWT

Why do the GUI component classes have the prefix *J*? Instead of `JButton`, why not name it simply `Button`? In fact, there is a class already named `Button` in the `java.awt` package.

When Java was introduced, the GUI classes were bundled in a library known as the Abstract Windows Toolkit (AWT). For every platform on which Java runs, the AWT components are automatically mapped to the platform-specific components through their respective agents, known as *peers*. AWT is fine for developing simple graphical user interfaces, but not for developing comprehensive GUI projects. Besides, AWT is prone to platform-specific bugs, because its peer-based approach relies heavily on the underlying platform. With the release of Java 2, the AWT user-interface components were replaced by a more robust, versatile, and flexible library known as *Swing components*. Swing components are painted directly on canvases using Java code, except for components that are subclasses of `java.awt.Window` or `java.awt.Panel`, which must be drawn using native GUI on a specific platform. Swing components are less dependent on the target platform and use less of the native GUI resource. For this reason, Swing components that don't rely on native GUI are referred to as *lightweight components,* and AWT components are referred to as *heavyweight components*.

To distinguish new Swing component classes from their AWT counterparts, the names of Swing GUI component classes begin with a prefixed *J*. Although AWT components are still supported in Java 2, it is better to learn to how program using Swing components, because the AWT user-interface components will eventually fade away. This book uses Swing GUI components exclusively.

Swing components

lightweight
heavyweight

why prefix J?

13.3 The Java GUI API

The GUI API contains the essential classes listed below. Their hierarchical relationships are shown in Figures 13.1 and 13.2.

The GUI classes can be classified into three groups: *container classes*, *component classes,* and *helper classes*. The container classes, such as `JFrame`, `JPanel`, and `JApplet`, are used to contain other components. The GUI component classes, such as `JButton`, `JTextField`, `JTextArea`, `JComboBox`, `JList`, `JRadioButton`, and `JMenu`, are subclasses of `JComponent`. The helper classes, such as `Graphics`, `Color`, `Font`, `FontMetrics`, and `Dimension`, are used to support GUI components.

Note

The `JFrame`, `JApplet`, `JDialog`, and `JComponent` classes and their subclasses are grouped in the `javax.swing` package. All the other classes in Figure 13.1 are grouped in the `java.awt` package.

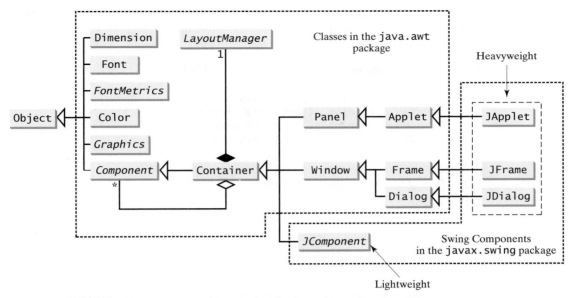

FIGURE 13.1 Java GUI programming utilizes the classes shown in this hierarchical diagram.

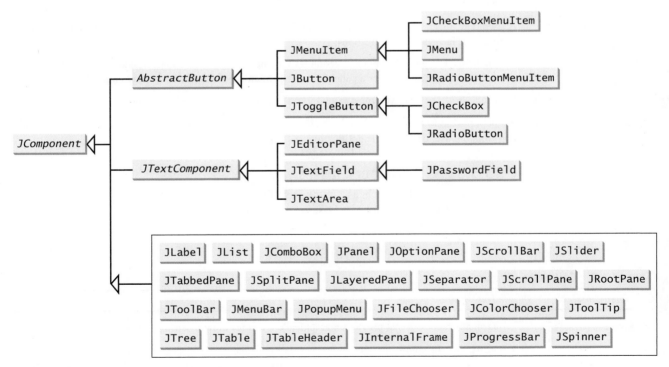

FIGURE 13.2 JComponent and its subclasses are the basic elements for building graphical user interfaces.

13.3.1 Swing GUI Components

Component is a superclass of all the user-interface classes, and JComponent is a superclass of all the lightweight Swing components, Since JComponent is an abstract class, you cannot use new JComponent() to create an instance of JComponent. However, you can use the constructors of concrete subclasses of `JComponent` to create `JComponent` instances. It is important to become familiar with the class inheritance hierarchy. For example, the following statements all display true.

```
JButton jbtOK = new JButton("OK");
System.out.println(jbtOK instanceof JButton);
System.out.println(jbtOK instanceof AbstractButton);
System.out.println(jbtOK instanceof JComponent);
System.out.println(jbtOK instanceof Container);
System.out.println(jbtOK instanceof Component);
System.out.println(jbtOK instanceof Object);
```

13.3.2 Container Classes

Container classes are GUI components that are used to contain other GUI components. `Window`, `Panel`, `Applet`, `Frame`, and `Dialog` are the container classes for AWT components. To work with Swing components, use `Container`, `JFrame`, `JDialog`, `JApplet`, and `JPanel`, as described in Table 13.1.

TABLE 13.1 GUI Container Classes

Container Class	Description
`java.awt.Container`	is used to group components. Frames, panels, and applets are its subclasses.
`javax.swing.JFrame`	is a window not contained inside another window. It is the container that holds other Swing user-interface components in Java GUI applications.
`javax.swing.JPanel`	is an invisible container that holds user-interface components. Panels can be nested. You can place panels inside a container that includes a panel. `JPanel` is often used as a canvas to draw graphics.
`javax.swing.JApplet`	is a subclass of `Applet`. You must extend `JApplet` to create a Swing-based Java applet.
`javax.swing.JDialog`	is a popup window or message box generally used as a temporary window to receive additional information from the user or to provide notification that an event has occurred.

13.3.3 GUI Helper Classes

The helper classes, such as `Graphics`, `Color`, `Font`, `FontMetrics`, `Dimension`, and `LayoutManager`, are not subclasses of `Component`. They are used to describe the properties of GUI components, such as graphics context, colors, fonts, and dimension, as described in Table 13.2.

TABLE 13.2 GUI Helper Classes

Container Class	Description
`java.awt.Graphics`	is an abstract class that provides a graphical context for drawing strings, lines, and simple shapes.
`java.awt.Color`	deals with the colors of GUI components. For example, you can specify background or foreground colors in components like `JFrame` and `JPanel`, or you can specify colors of lines, shapes, and strings in drawings.
`java.awt.Font`	specifies fonts for the text and drawings on GUI components. For example, you can specify the font type (e.g., SansSerif), style (e.g., bold), and size (e.g., 24 points) for the text on a button.
`java.awt.FontMetrics`	is an abstract class used to get the properties of the fonts.
`java.awt.Dimension`	encapsulates the width and height of a component (in integer precision) in a single object.
`java.awt.LayoutManager`	is an interface, whose instances specify how components are arranged in a container.

Note

The helper classes are in the `java.awt` package. The Swing components do not replace all the classes in AWT, only the AWT GUI component classes (e.g., `Button`, `TextField`, `TextArea`). The AWT helper classes remain unchanged.

13.4 Frames

To create a user interface, you need to create either a frame or an applet to hold the user-interface components. Creating Java applets will be introduced in Chapter 17, "Applets and Multimedia." This section introduces frames.

13.4.1 Creating a Frame

To create a frame, use the `JFrame` class, as shown in Figure 13.3.

javax.swing.JFrame	
+JFrame()	Creates a default frame with no title.
+JFrame(title: String)	Creates a frame with the specified title.
+setSize(width: int, height: int): void	Specifies the size of the frame.
+setLocation(x: int, y: int): void	Specifies the upper-left-corner location of the frame.
+setVisible(visible: boolean): void	Sets true to display the frame.
+setDefaultCloseOperation(mode: int): void	Specifies the operation when the frame is closed.
+setLocationRelativeTo(c: Component): void	Sets the location of the frame relative to the specified component. If the component is null, the frame is centered on the screen.
+pack(): void	Automatically sets the frame size to hold the components in the frame.

FIGURE 13.3 Frame is a top-level container to hold GUI components.

The program in Listing 13.1 creates a frame:

LISTING 13.1 MyFrame.java

```
 1  import javax.swing.*;                                                    import package
 2
 3  public class MyFrame {
 4    public static void main(String[] args) {
 5      JFrame frame = new JFrame("MyFrame"); // Create a frame        create frame
 6      frame.setSize(400, 300); // Set the frame size                 set size
 7      frame.setLocationRelativeTo(null); // New since JDK 1.4        center frame
 8      frame.setDefaultCloseOperation(JFrame.EXIT_ON_CLOSE);          close upon exit
 9      frame.setVisible(true); // Display the frame                   display the frame
10    }
11  }
```

The frame is not displayed *until* the `frame.setVisible(true)` method is invoked. `frame.setSize(400, 300)` specifies that the frame is `400` pixels wide and `300` pixels high. If the `setSize` method is not used, the frame will be sized to display just the title bar. Since the `setSize` and `setVisible` methods are both defined in the `Component` class, they are inherited by the `JFrame` class. Later you will see that these methods are also useful in many other subclasses of `Component`.

When you run the `MyFrame` program, a window will be displayed on-screen (see Figure 13.4(a)).

Title bar

Content pane

Title bar

Content pane

FIGURE 13.4 (a) The program creates and displays a frame with the title MyFrame. (b) An OK button is added to the frame.

Invoking `setLocationRelativeTo(null)` (line 7) centers the frame on the screen. Invoking `setDefaultCloseOperation(JFrame.EXIT_ON_CLOSE)` (line 8) tells the program to terminate when the frame is closed. If this statement is not used, the program does not terminate when the frame is closed. In that case, you have to stop the program by pressing Ctrl+C at the DOS prompt window in Windows or stop the process by using the kill command in Unix.

pixel and resolution

Note
Recall that a pixel is the smallest unit of space available for drawing on the screen. You can think of a pixel as a small rectangle and think of the screen as paved with pixels. The *resolution* specifies the number of pixels per square inch. The more pixels the screen has, the higher the screen's resolution. The higher the resolution, the finer the detail you can see.

setSize before centering

Note
You should invoke `setSize(w, h)` method before invoking `setLocationRelativeTo(null)` to center the frame.

13.4.2 Adding Components to a Frame

The frame shown in Figure 13.4(a) is empty. Using the **add** method, you can add components into the frame, as in Listing 13.2.

LISTING 13.2 MyFrameWithComponents.java

```
1 import javax.swing.*;
2
3 public class MyFrameWithComponents {
4   public static void main(String[] args) {
5     JFrame frame = new JFrame("MyFrameWithComponents");
6
7     // Add a button into the frame
8     JButton jbtOK = new JButton("OK");
9     frame.add(jbtOK);
10
11    frame.setSize(400, 300);
12    frame.setDefaultCloseOperation(JFrame.EXIT_ON_CLOSE);
13    frame.setLocationRelativeTo(null); // Center the frame
14    frame.setVisible(true);
15  }
16 }
```

create a button
add to frame

set size
exit upon closing window
center the frame
set visible

Each `JFrame` contains a content pane. A content pane is an instance of `java.awt.Container`. The GUI components such as buttons are placed in the content pane in a frame. Prior to JDK 1.5, you had to use the `getContentPane` method in the `JFrame` class to return the content pane of the frame, and then invoke the content pane's add method to place a component into the content pane, as follows:

```
java.awt.Container container = frame.getContentPane();
container.add(jbtOK);
```

This was cumbersome. JDK 1.5 allows you to place components to the content pane by invoking a frame's add method, as follows:

```
frame.add(jbtOK);
```

This new feature is called *content pane delegation*. Strictly speaking, a component is added into the content pane of a frame. For simplicity we say that a component is added to a frame.

content pane delegation

An object of JButton was created using new JButton("OK"), and this object was added to the content pane of the frame (line 9).

The add(Component comp) method defined in the Container class adds an instance of Component to the container. Since JButton is a subclass of Component, an instance of JButton is also an instance of Component. To remove a component from a container, use the remove method. The following statement removes the button from the container:

```
container.remove(jbtOK);
```

When you run the program MyFrameWithComponents, the window will be displayed as in Figure 13.4(b). The button is always centered in the frame and occupies the entire frame no matter how you resize it. This is because components are put in the frame by the content pane's layout manager, and the default layout manager for the content pane places the button in the center. In the next section, you will use several different layout managers to place components in other locations as desired.

13.5 Layout Managers

In many other window systems, the user-interface components are arranged by using hard-coded pixel measurements. For example, put a button at location (10, 10) in the window. Using hard-coded pixel measurements, the user interface might look fine on one system but be unusable on another. Java's layout managers provide a level of abstraction that automatically maps your user interface on all window systems.

The Java GUI components are placed in containers, where they are arranged by the container's layout manager. In the preceding program, you did not specify where to place the OK button in the frame, but Java knows where to place it because the layout manager works behind the scenes to place components in the correct locations. A layout manager is created using a layout manager class. Every layout manager class implements the LayoutManager interface.

Layout managers are set in containers using the setLayout(LayoutManager) method. For example, you can use the following statements to create an instance of XLayout and set it in a container:

```
LayoutManager layoutManager = new XLayout();
container.setLayout(layoutManager);
```

This section introduces three basic layout managers: FlowLayout, GridLayout, and BorderLayout.

13.5.1 FlowLayout

FlowLayout is the simplest layout manager. The components are arranged in the container from left to right in the order in which they were added. When one row is filled, a new row is started. You can specify the way the components are aligned by using one of three constants:

FlowLayout.RIGHT, FlowLayout.CENTER, or FlowLayout.LEFT. You can also specify the gap between components in pixels. The constructors and methods in FlowLayout are shown in Figure 13.5.

FIGURE 13.5 FlowLayout lays out components row by row.

Listing 13.3 gives a program that demonstrates flow layout. The program adds three labels and text fields into the frame with a FlowLayout manager, as shown in Figure 13.6.

(a)   (b)

FIGURE 13.6 The components are added by the FlowLayout manager to fill in the rows in the container one after another.

Video Note
Test layout managers

LISTING 13.3 ShowFlowLayout.java

extends JFrame

set layout

add label
add text field

```java
 1  import javax.swing.JLabel;
 2  import javax.swing.JTextField;
 3  import javax.swing.JFrame;
 4  import java.awt.FlowLayout;
 5
 6  public class ShowFlowLayout extends JFrame {
 7    public ShowFlowLayout() {
 8      // Set FlowLayout, aligned left with horizontal gap 10
 9      // and vertical gap 20 between components
10      setLayout(new FlowLayout(FlowLayout.LEFT, 10, 20));
11
12      // Add labels and text fields to the frame
13      add(new JLabel("First Name"));
14      add(new JTextField(8));
15      add(new JLabel("MI"));
16      add(new JTextField(1));
17      add(new JLabel("Last Name"));
18      add(new JTextField(8));
19    }
20
```

```
21    /** Main method */
22    public static void main(String[] args) {
23      ShowFlowLayout frame = new ShowFlowLayout();
24      frame.setTitle("ShowFlowLayout");
25      frame.setSize(200, 200);
26      frame.setLocationRelativeTo(null); // Center the frame
27      frame.setDefaultCloseOperation(JFrame.EXIT_ON_CLOSE);
28      frame.setVisible(true);
29    }
30  }
```

create frame

set visible

This example creates a program using a style different from the programs in the preceding section, where frames were created using the JFrame class. This example creates a class named ShowFlowLayout that extends the JFrame class (line 6). The main method in this program creates an instance of ShowFlowLayout (line 23). The constructor of ShowFlowLayout constructs and places the components in the frame. This is the preferred style of creating GUI applications—for three reasons:

■ Creating a GUI application means creating a frame, so it is natural to define a frame to extend JFrame.

■ The frame may be further extended to add new components or functions.

■ The class can be easily reused. For example, you can create multiple frames by creating multiple instances of the class.

Using one style consistently makes programs easy to read. From now on, most of the GUI main classes will extend the JFrame class. The constructor of the main class constructs the user interface. The main method creates an instance of the main class and then displays the frame.

In this example, the FlowLayout manager is used to place components in a frame. If you resize the frame, the components are automatically rearranged to fit in it. In Figure 13.6(a), the first row has three components, but in Figure 13.6(b), the first row has four components, because the width has been increased.

If you replace the setLayout statement (line 10) with setLayout(new FlowLayout(FlowLayout.RIGHT, 0, 0)), all the rows of buttons will be right-aligned with no gaps.

An anonymous FlowLayout object was created in the statement (line 10):

```
setLayout(new FlowLayout(FlowLayout.LEFT, 10, 20));
```

which is equivalent to:

```
FlowLayout layout = new FlowLayout(FlowLayout.LEFT, 10, 20);
setLayout(layout);
```

This code creates an explicit reference to the object layout of the FlowLayout class. The explicit reference is not necessary, because the object is not directly referenced in the ShowFlowLayout class.

The setTitle method (line 24) is defined in the java.awt.Frame class. Since JFrame is a subclass of Frame, you can use it to set a title for an object of JFrame.

Suppose you add the same button into the container ten times, will ten buttons appear in the container? No, only the last one will be displayed.

Caution
Do not forget to put the new operator before a layout manager class when setting a layout style—for example, setLayout(new FlowLayout()).

Note

The constructor `ShowFlowLayout()` does not explicitly invoke the constructor `JFrame()`, but the constructor `JFrame()` is invoked implicitly. See §10.4.2, "Constructor Chaining."

13.5.2 GridLayout

The `GridLayout` manager arranges components in a grid (matrix) formation with the number of rows and columns defined by the constructor. The components are placed in the grid from left to right, starting with the first row, then the second, and so on, in the order in which they are added. The constructors and methods in `GridLayout` are shown in Figure 13.7.

The get and set methods for these data fields are provided in the class, but omitted in the UML diagram for brevity.

java.awt.GridLayout	
-rows: int	The number of rows in this layout manager (default: 1).
-columns: int	The number of columns in this layout manager (default: 1).
-hgap: int	The horizontal gap of this layout manager (default: 0).
-vgap: int	The vertical gap of this layout manager (default: 0).
+GridLayout()	Creates a default `GridLayout` manager.
+GridLayout(rows: int, columns: int)	Creates a `GridLayout` with a specified number of rows and columns.
+GridLayout(rows: int, columns: int, hgap: int, vgap: int)	Creates a `GridLayout` manager with a specified number of rows and columns, horizontal gap, and vertical gap.

FIGURE 13.7 `GridLayout` lays out components in equal-sized cells on a grid.

You can specify the number of rows and columns in the grid. The basic rule is as follows:

■ The number of rows or the number of columns can be zero, but not both. If one is zero and the other is nonzero, the nonzero dimension is fixed, while the zero dimension is determined dynamically by the layout manager. For example, if you specify zero rows and three columns for a grid that has ten components, `GridLayout` creates three fixed columns of four rows, with the last row containing one component. If you specify three rows and zero columns for a grid that has ten components, `GridLayout` creates three fixed rows of four columns, with the last row containing two components.

■ If both the number of rows and the number of columns are nonzero, the number of rows is the dominating parameter; that is, the number of rows is fixed, and the layout manager dynamically calculates the number of columns. For example, if you specify three rows and three columns for a grid that has ten components, `GridLayout` creates three fixed rows of four columns, with the last row containing two components.

Listing 13.4 gives a program that demonstrates grid layout. The program is similar to the one in Listing 13.3. It adds three labels and three text fields to the frame of `GridLayout` instead of `FlowLayout`, as shown in Figure 13.8.

FIGURE 13.8 The `GridLayout` manager divides the container into grids; then the components are added to fill in the cells row by row.

LISTING 13.4 ShowGridLayout.java

```
1  import javax.swing.JLabel;
2  import javax.swing.JTextField;
3  import javax.swing.JFrame;
4  import java.awt.GridLayout;
5
6  public class ShowGridLayout extends JFrame {
7    public ShowGridLayout() {
8      // Set GridLayout, 3 rows, 2 columns, and gaps 5 between
9      // components horizontally and vertically
10     setLayout(new GridLayout(3, 2, 5, 5));          set layout
11
12     // Add labels and text fields to the frame
13     add(new JLabel("First Name"));                  add label
14     add(new JTextField(8));                         add text field
15     add(new JLabel("MI"));
16     add(new JTextField(1));
17     add(new JLabel("Last Name"));
18     add(new JTextField(8));
19   }
20
21   /** Main method */
22   public static void main(String[] args) {
23     ShowGridLayout frame = new ShowGridLayout();
24     frame.setTitle("ShowGridLayout");
25     frame.setSize(200, 125);
26     frame.setLocationRelativeTo(null); // Center the frame    create a frame
27     frame.setDefaultCloseOperation(JFrame.EXIT_ON_CLOSE);
28     frame.setVisible(true);                         set visible
29   }
30 }
```

If you resize the frame, the layout of the buttons remains unchanged (i.e., the number of rows and columns does not change, and the gaps don't change either).

All components are given equal size in the container of GridLayout.

Replacing the setLayout statement (line 8) with setLayout(new GridLayout(3, 10)) would still yield three rows and *two* columns. The columns parameter is ignored because the rows parameter is nonzero. The actual number of columns is calculated by the layout manager.

What would happen if the setLayout statement (line 10) were replaced with setLayout(new GridLayout(4, 2)) or with setLayout(new GridLayout(2, 2))? Please try it yourself.

 Note

In FlowLayout and GridLayout, the order in which the components are added to the container is important. It determines the location of the components in the container.

13.5.3 BorderLayout

The BorderLayout manager divides the window into five areas: East, South, West, North, and Center. Components are added to a BorderLayout by using add(Component, index), where index is a constant BorderLayout.EAST, BorderLayout.SOUTH, BorderLayout.WEST, BorderLayout.NORTH, or BorderLayout.CENTER. The constructors and methods in BorderLayout are shown in Figure 13.9.

The components are laid out according to their preferred sizes and where they are placed in the container. The North and South components can stretch horizontally; the East and West

The get and set methods for these data fields are provided in the class, but omitted in the UML diagram for brevity.

java.awt.BorderLayout
-hgap: int
-vgap: int
+BorderLayout()
+BorderLayout(hgap: int, vgap: int)

The horizontal gap of this layout manager (default: 0).

The vertical gap of this layout manager (default: 0).

Creates a default BorderLayout manager.

Creates a BorderLayout manager with a specified number of horizontal gap, and vertical gap.

FIGURE 13.9 BorderLayout lays out components in five areas.

components can stretch vertically; the Center component can stretch both horizontally and vertically to fill any empty space.

Listing 13.5 gives a program that demonstrates border layout. The program adds five buttons labeled East, South, West, North, and Center into the frame with a BorderLayout manager, as shown in Figure 13.10.

FIGURE 13.10 BorderLayout divides the container into five areas, each of which can hold a component.

LISTING 13.5 ShowBorderLayout.java

```
1  import javax.swing.JButton;
2  import javax.swing.JFrame;
3  import java.awt.BorderLayout;
4
5  public class ShowBorderLayout extends JFrame {
6    public ShowBorderLayout() {
7      // Set BorderLayout with horizontal gap 5 and vertical gap 10
8      setLayout(new BorderLayout(5, 10));
9
10     // Add buttons to the frame
11     add(new JButton("East"), BorderLayout.EAST);
12     add(new JButton("South"), BorderLayout.SOUTH);
13     add(new JButton("West"), BorderLayout.WEST);
14     add(new JButton("North"), BorderLayout.NORTH);
15     add(new JButton("Center"), BorderLayout.CENTER);
16   }
17
18   /** Main method */
19   public static void main(String[] args) {
20     ShowBorderLayout frame = new ShowBorderLayout();
21     frame.setTitle("ShowBorderLayout");
22     frame.setSize(300, 200);
23     frame.setLocationRelativeTo(null); // Center the frame
```

set layout

add buttons

create a frame

```
24        frame.setDefaultCloseOperation(JFrame.EXIT_ON_CLOSE);
25        frame.setVisible(true);
26    }
27 }
```

set visible

The buttons are added to the frame (lines 11–15). Note that the **add** method for BorderLayout is different from the one for FlowLayout and GridLayout. With BorderLayout you specify where to put the components.

It is unnecessary to place components to occupy all the areas. If you remove the East button from the program and rerun it, you will see that the center stretches rightward to occupy the East area.

Note

BorderLayout interprets the absence of an index specification as BorderLayout.CENTER. For example, add(component) is the same as add(Component, BorderLayout.CEN-TER). If you add two components into a container of BorderLayout, as follows,

```
container.add(component1);
container.add(component2);
```

only the last component is displayed.

13.5.4   Properties of Layout Managers

Layout managers have properties that can be changed dynamically. FlowLayout has alignment, hgap, and vgap properties. You can use the setAlignment, setHgap, and setVgap methods to specify the alignment and the horizontal and vertical gaps. GridLayout has the rows, columns, hgap, and vgap properties. You can use the setRows, setColumns, setHgap, and setVgap methods to specify the number of rows, the number of columns, and the horizontal and vertical gaps. BorderLayout has the hgap and vgap properties. You can use the setHgap and setVgap methods to specify the horizontal and vertical gaps.

In the preceding sections, an anonymous layout manager is used because the properties of a layout manager do not change, once it is created. If you have to change the properties of a layout manager dynamically, the layout manager must be explicitly referenced by a variable. You can then change the properties of the layout manager through the variable. For example, the following code creates a layout manager and sets its properties:

```
// Create a layout manager
FlowLayout flowLayout = new FlowLayout();

// Set layout properties
flowLayout.setAlignment(FlowLayout.RIGHT);
flowLayout.setHgap(10);
flowLayout.setVgap(20);
```

13.5.5   The `validate` and `doLayout` Methods

A container can have only one layout manager at a time. You can change its layout manager by using the setLayout(aNewLayout) method and then use the validate() method to force the container to again lay out the components in the container using the new layout manager.

validate()

If you use the same layout manager but change its properties, you need to use the doLayout() method to force the container to re-lay out the components using the new properties of the layout manager.

doLayout()

13.6 The **Color** Class

You can set colors for GUI components by using the `java.awt.Color` class. Colors are made of red, green, and blue components, each represented by an unsigned byte value that describes its intensity, ranging from `0` (darkest shade) to `255` (lightest shade). This is known as the *RGB model*.

You can create a color using the following constructor:

```
public Color(int r, int g, int b);
```

in which `r`, `g`, and `b` specify a color by its red, green, and blue components. For example,

```
Color color = new Color(128, 100, 100);
```

IllegalArgumentException

Note
The arguments `r`, `g`, `b` are between `0` and `255`. If a value beyond this range is passed to the argument, an `IllegalArgumentException` will occur.

You can use the `setBackground(Color c)` and `setForeground(Color c)` methods defined in the `java.awt.Component` class to set a component's background and foreground colors. Here is an example of setting the background and foreground of a button:

```
JButton jbtOK = new JButton();
jbtOK.setBackground(color);
jbtOK.setForeground(new Color(100, 1, 1));
```

Alternatively, you can use one of the 13 standard colors (`black`, `blue`, `cyan`, `darkGray`, `gray`, `green`, `lightGray`, `magenta`, `orange`, `pink`, `red`, `white`, `yellow`) defined as constants in `java.awt.Color`. The following code, for instance, sets the foreground color of a button to red:

```
jbtOK.setForeground(Color.red);
```

color constants

Note
The standard color names are constants, but they are named as variables with lowercase for the first word and uppercase for the first letters of subsequent words. Thus the color names violate the Java naming convention. Since JDK 1.4, you can also use the new constants `BLACK`, `BLUE`, `CYAN`, `DARK_GRAY`, `GRAY`, `GREEN`, `LIGHT_GRAY`, `MAGENTA`, `ORANGE`, `PINK`, `RED`, `WHITE`, and `YELLOW`.

13.7 The **Font** Class

You can create a font using the `java.awt.Font` class and set fonts for the components using the `setFont` method in the `Component` class.

The constructor for `Font` is:

```
public Font(String name, int style, int size);
```

You can choose a font name from `SansSerif`, `Serif`, `Monospaced`, `Dialog`, or `DialogInput`, choose a style from `Font.PLAIN` (0), `Font.BOLD` (1), `Font.ITALIC` (2), and `Font.BOLD + Font.ITALIC` (3), and specify a font size of any positive integer. For example, the following statements create two fonts and set one font to a button.

```
Font font1 = new Font("SansSerif", Font.BOLD, 16);
Font font2 = new Font("Serif", Font.BOLD + Font.ITALIC, 12);
```

```java
JButton jbtOK = new JButton("OK");
jbtOK.setFont(font1);
```

Tip

If your system supports other fonts, such as "Times New Roman," you can use it to create a `Font` object. To find the fonts available on your system, you need to create an instance of `java.awt.GraphicsEnvironment` using its static method `getLocalGraphicsEn-vironment()`. `GraphicsEnvironment` is an abstract class that describes the graphics environment on a particular system. You can use its `getAllFonts()` method to obtain all the available fonts on the system, and its `getAvailableFontFamilyNames()` method to obtain the names of all the available fonts. For example, the following statements print all the available font names in the system:

find available fonts

```java
GraphicsEnvironment e =
  GraphicsEnvironment.getLocalGraphicsEnvironment();
String[] fontnames = e.getAvailableFontFamilyNames();

for (int i = 0; i < fontnames.length; i++)
  System.out.println(fontnames[i]);
```

13.8 Using Panels as Subcontainers

Video Note
Organize components using panels

Suppose that you want to place ten buttons and a text field in a frame. The buttons are placed in grid formation, but the text field is placed on a separate row. It is difficult to achieve the desired look by placing all the components in a single container. With Java GUI programming, you can divide a window into panels. Panels act as subcontainers to group user-interface components. You add the buttons in one panel, and then add the panel into the frame.

The Swing version of panel is `JPanel`. You can use `new JPanel()` to create a panel with a default `FlowLayout` manager or `new JPanel(LayoutManager)` to create a panel with the specified layout manager. Use the `add(Component)` method to add a component to the panel. For example, the following code creates a panel and adds a button to it:

```java
JPanel p = new JPanel();
p.add(new JButton("OK"));
```

Panels can be placed inside a frame or inside another panel. The following statement places panel `p` into frame `f`:

```java
f.add(p);
```

Listing 13.6 gives an example that demonstrates using panels as subcontainers. The program creates a user interface for a microwave oven, as shown in Figure 13.11.

FIGURE 13.11   The program uses panels to organize components.

LISTING 13.6 TestPanels.java

```
 1 import java.awt.*;
 2 import javax.swing.*;
 3
 4 public class TestPanels extends JFrame {
 5   public TestPanels() {
 6     // Create panel p1 for the buttons and set GridLayout
 7     JPanel p1 = new JPanel();
 8     p1.setLayout(new GridLayout(4, 3));
 9
10     // Add buttons to the panel
11     for (int i = 1; i <= 9; i++) {
12       p1.add(new JButton("" + i));
13     }
14
15     p1.add(new JButton("" + 0));
16     p1.add(new JButton("Start"));
17     p1.add(new JButton("Stop"));
18
19     // Create panel p2 to hold a text field and p1
20     JPanel p2 = new JPanel(new BorderLayout());
21     p2.add(new JTextField("Time to be displayed here"),
22       BorderLayout.NORTH);
23     p2.add(p1, BorderLayout.CENTER);
24
25     // add contents into the frame
26     add(p2, BorderLayout.EAST);
27     add(new JButton("Food to be placed here"),
28       BorderLayout.CENTER);
29   }
30
31   /** Main method */
32   public static void main(String[] args) {
33     TestPanels frame = new TestPanels();
34     frame.setTitle("The Front View of a Microwave Oven");
35     frame.setSize(400, 250);
36     frame.setLocationRelativeTo(null); // Center the frame
37     frame.setDefaultCloseOperation(JFrame.EXIT_ON_CLOSE);
38     frame.setVisible(true);
39   }
40 }
```

panel p1 *(line 7–8)*

panel p2 *(line 20)*

add p2 to frame *(line 26)*

The setLayout method is defined in java.awt.Container. Since JPanel is a subclass of Container, you can use setLayout to set a new layout manager in the panel (line 8). Lines 7–8 can be replaced by JPanel p1 = new JPanel(new GridLayout(4, 3)).

To achieve the desired layout, the program uses panel p1 of GridLayout to group the number buttons, the *Stop* button, and the *Start* button, and panel p2 of BorderLayout to hold a text field in the north and p1 in the center. The button representing the food is placed in the center of the frame, and p2 is placed in the east of the frame.

The statement (lines 21–23)

```
p2.add(new JTextField("Time to be displayed here"),
  BorderLayout.NORTH);
```

creates an instance of JTextField and adds it to p2. JTextField is a GUI component that can be used for user input as well as to display values.

Note

It is worthwhile to note that the `Container` class is the superclass for GUI component classes, such as `JButton`. Every GUI component is a container. In theory, you could use the `setLayout` method to set the layout in a button and add components into a button, because all the public methods in the `Container` class are inherited into `JButton`, but for practical reasons you should not use buttons as containers.

superclass **Container**

13.9 Common Features of Swing GUI Components

You have used several GUI components (e.g., `JFrame`, `Container`, `JPanel`, `JButton`, `JLabel`, `JTextField`) in this chapter. Many more GUI components will be introduced in this book. It is important to understand the common features of Swing GUI components. The `Component` class is the root for all GUI components and containers. All Swing GUI components (except `JFrame`, `JApplet`, and `JDialog`) are subclasses of `JComponent`, as shown in Figures 13.1 and 13.2. Figure 13.12 lists some frequently used methods in `Component`, `Container`, and `JComponent` for manipulating properties like font, color, size, tool tip text, and border.

Video Note
Swing common properties

Component
Container
JComponent

---

java.awt.Component

-font: java.awt.Font	The font of this component.
-background: java.awt.Color	The background color of this component.
-foreground: java.awt.Color	The foreground color of this component.
-preferredSize: java.awt.Dimension	The preferred size of this component.
-visible: boolean	Indicates whether this component is visible.
+getWidth(): int	Returns the width of this component.
+getHeight(): int	Returns the height of this component.
+getX(): int	getX() and getY() return the coordinate of the
+getY(): int	component's upper-left corner within its parent component.

The get and set methods for these data fields are provided in the class, but omitted in the UML diagram for brevity.

java.awt.Container

+add(comp: Component): Component	Adds a component to the container.
+add(comp: Component, index: int): Component	Adds a component to the container with the specified index.
+remove(comp: Component): void	Removes the component from the container.
+getLayout(): LayoutManager	Returns the layout manager for this container.
+setLayout(l: LayoutManager): void	Sets the layout manager for this container.
+paintComponents(g: Graphics): void	Paints each of the components in this container.

javax.swing.JComponent

| -toolTipText: String | The tool tip text for this component. Tool tip text is displayed when the mouse points on the component without clicking. |
| -border: javax.swing.border.Border | The border for this component. |

The get and set methods for these data fields are provided in the class, but omitted in the UML diagram for brevity.

FIGURE 13.12 All the Swing GUI components inherit the public methods from `Component`, `Container`, and `JComponent`.

A *tool tip* is text displayed on a component when you move the mouse on the component. It is often used to describe the function of a component.

You can set a border on any object of the `JComponent` class. Swing has several types of borders. To create a titled border, use `new TitledBorder(String title)`. To create a line border, use `new LineBorder(Color color, int width)`, where `width` specifies the thickness of the line.

Listing 13.7 is an example to demonstrate Swing common features. The example creates a panel `p1` to hold three buttons (line 8) and a panel `p2` to hold two labels (line 25) as shown in Figure 13.13. The background of the button `jbtLeft` is set to white (line 12) and the foreground of the button `jbtCenter` is set to green (line 13). The tool tip of the button `jbtRight` is set in line 14. Titled borders are set on panels `p1` and `p2` (lines 18, 36) and line borders are set on the labels (lines 32-33).

LISTING 13.7 TestSwingCommonFeatures.java

```java
1  import java.awt.*;
2  import javax.swing.*;
3  import javax.swing.border.*;
4
5  public class TestSwingCommonFeatures extends JFrame {
6    public TestSwingCommonFeatures() {
7      // Create a panel to group three buttons
8      JPanel p1 = new JPanel(new FlowLayout(FlowLayout.LEFT, 2, 2));
9      JButton jbtLeft = new JButton("Left");
10     JButton jbtCenter = new JButton("Center");
11     JButton jbtRight = new JButton("Right");
12     jbtLeft.setBackground(Color.WHITE);
13     jbtCenter.setForeground(Color.GREEN);
14     jbtRight.setToolTipText("This is the Right button");
15     p1.add(jbtLeft);
16     p1.add(jbtCenter);
17     p1.add(jbtRight);
18     p1.setBorder(new TitledBorder("Three Buttons"));
19
20     // Create a font and a line border
21     Font largeFont = new Font("TimesRoman", Font.BOLD, 20);
22     Border lineBorder = new LineBorder(Color.BLACK, 2);
23
24     // Create a panel to group two labels
25     JPanel p2 = new JPanel(new GridLayout(1, 2, 5, 5));
26     JLabel jlblRed = new JLabel("Red");
27     JLabel jlblOrange = new JLabel("Orange");
28     jlblRed.setForeground(Color.RED);
29     jlblOrange.setForeground(Color.ORANGE);
30     jlblRed.setFont(largeFont);
31     jlblOrange.setFont(largeFont);
32     jlblRed.setBorder(lineBorder);
33     jlblOrange.setBorder(lineBorder);
34     p2.add(jlblRed);
35     p2.add(jlblOrange);
36     p2.setBorder(new TitledBorder("Two Labels"));
37
38     // Add two panels to the frame
39     setLayout(new GridLayout(2, 1, 5, 5));
40     add(p1);
41     add(p2);
42   }
43
```

Margin annotations:
- set background (line 12)
- set foreground (line 13)
- set tool tip text (line 14)
- set titled border (line 18)
- create a font (line 21)
- create a border (line 22)
- set foreground (line 28)
- set font (line 30)
- set line border (line 32)
- set titled border (line 36)

```
44   public static void main(String[] args) {
45     // Create a frame and set its properties
46     JFrame frame = new TestSwingCommonFeatures();
47     frame.setTitle("TestSwingCommonFeatures");
48     frame.setSize(300, 150);
49     frame.setLocationRelativeTo(null); // Center the frame
50     frame.setDefaultCloseOperation(JFrame.EXIT_ON_CLOSE);
51     frame.setVisible(true);
52   }
53 }
```

Titled border

Titled border
Line border

Having the mouse cursor
over the Right button
displays the tool tip text

FIGURE 13.13   The font, color, border, and tool tip text are set in the message panel.

Note

The same property may have different default values in different components. For example, the `visible` property in `JFrame` is `false` by default, but it is `true` in every instance of `JComponent` (e.g., `JButton` and `JLabel`) by default. To display a `JFrame`, you have to invoke `setVisible(true)` to set the `visible` property `true`, but you don't have to set this property for a `JButton` or a `JLabel`, because it is already `true`. To make a `JButton` or a `JLabel` invisible, you may invoke `setVisible(false)` on. Please run the program and see the effect after inserting the following two statements in line 37.

property default values

```
jbtLeft.setVisible(false);
jlblRed.setVisible(false);
```

13.10 Image Icons

An icon is a fixed-size picture; typically it is small and used to decorate components. Images are normally stored in image files. Java currently supports three image formats: GIF (Graphics Interchange Format), JPEG (Joint Photographic Experts Group), and PNG (Portable Network Graphics). The image filenames for these types end with .gif, .jpg, and .png, respectively. If you have a bitmap file or image files in other formats, you can use image-processing utilities to convert them into GIF, JPEG, or PNG format for use in Java.

image file format

To display an image icon, first create an `ImageIcon` object using `new javax.swing.ImageIcon(filename)`. For example, the following statement creates an icon from an image file `us.gif` in the `image` directory under the current class path:

new

```
ImageIcon icon = new ImageIcon("image/us.gif");
```

create **ImageIcon**

"`image/us.gif`" is located in "`c:\book\image\us.gif`." The back slash (\) is the Windows file path notation. In Unix, the forward slash (/) should be used. In Java, the forward slash (/) is used to denote a relative file path under the Java classpath (e.g., `image/left.gif`, as in this example).

file path character

naming files consistently

Tip

File names are not case sensitive in Windows but are case sensitive in Unix. To enable your programs to run on all platforms, name all the image files consistently, using lowercase.

An image icon can be displayed in a label or a button using new JLabel(imageIcon) or new JButton(imageIcon). Listing 13.8 demonstrates displaying icons in labels and buttons. The example creates two labels and two buttons with icons, as shown in Figure 13.14.

LISTING 13.8 TestImageIcon.java

```java
1  import javax.swing.*;
2  import java.awt.*;
3
4  public class TestImageIcon extends JFrame {
5    private ImageIcon usIcon = new ImageIcon("image/us.gif");
6    private ImageIcon myIcon = new ImageIcon("image/my.jpg");
7    private ImageIcon frIcon = new ImageIcon("image/fr.gif");
8    private ImageIcon ukIcon = new ImageIcon("image/uk.gif");
9
10   public TestImageIcon() {
11     setLayout(new GridLayout(1, 4, 5, 5));
12     add(new JLabel(usIcon));
13     add(new JLabel(myIcon));
14     add(new JButton(frIcon));
15     add(new JButton(ukIcon));
16   }
17
18   /** Main method */
19   public static void main(String[] args) {
20     TestImageIcon frame = new TestImageIcon();
21     frame.setTitle("TestImageIcon");
22     frame.setSize(200, 200);
23     frame.setLocationRelativeTo(null); // Center the frame
24     frame.setDefaultCloseOperation(JFrame.EXIT_ON_CLOSE);
25     frame.setVisible(true);
26   }
27 }
```

create image icons

a label with image

a button with image

FIGURE 13.14 The image icons are displayed in labels and buttons.

Note

GUI components cannot be shared by containers, because one GUI component can appear in only one container at a time. Therefore, the relationship between a component and a container is the composition denoted by a solid diamond, as shown in Figure 13.1.

Note

Borders and icons can be shared. Thus you can create a border or icon and use it to set the **border** or **icon** property for any GUI component. For example, the following statements set a border **b** for two panels **p1** and **p2**:

sharing borders and icons

```java
p1.setBorder(b);
p2.setBorder(b);
```

The following statements set an icon in two buttons `jbt1` and `jbt2`:

```
jbt1.setIcon(icon);
jbt2.setIcon(icon);
```

Tip

A *splash screen* is an image that is displayed while the application is starting up. If your program takes a long time to load, you may display a splash screen to alert the user. For example, the following command:

splash screen

```
java -splash:image/us.gif TestImageIcon
```

displays an image while the program `TestImageIcon` is being loaded.

KEY TERMS

AWT   420
heavyweight component   420
lightweight component   420

Swing   420
splash screen   439

CHAPTER SUMMARY

- Every container has a layout manager that is used to position and place components in the container in the desired locations. Three simple and frequently-used layout managers are `FlowLayout`, `GridLayout`, and `BorderLayout`.

- You can use a `JPanel` as a subcontainer to group components to achieve a desired layout.

- Use the `add` method to place components to a `JFrame` or a `JPanel`. By default, the frame's layout is `BorderLayout`, and the `JPanel`'s layout is `FlowLayout`.

- You can set colors for GUI components by using the `java.awt.Color` class. Colors are made of red, green, and blue components, each of which is represented by an unsigned byte value that describes its intensity, ranging from 0 (darkest shade) to 255 (lightest shade). This is known as the *RGB model*.

- The syntax to create a `Color` object is `Color color = new Color(r, g, b)`, in which `r`, `g`, and `b` specify a color by its red, green, and blue components. Alternatively, you can use one of the 13 standard colors (`BLACK`, `BLUE`, `CYAN`, `DARK_GRAY`, `GRAY`, `GREEN`, `LIGHT_GRAY`, `MAGENTA`, `ORANGE`, `PINK`, `RED`, `WHITE`, `YELLOW`) defined as constants in `java.awt.Color`.

- Every Swing GUI component is a subclass of `javax.swing.JComponent`, and `JComponent` is a subclass of `java.awt.Component`. The properties `font`, `background`, `foreground`, `height`, `width`, and `preferredSize` in `Component` are inherited in these subclasses, as are `toolTipText` and `border` in `JComponent`.

- You can use borders on any Swing components. You can create an image icon using the `ImageIcon` class and display it in a label and a button. Icons and borders can be shared.

REVIEW QUESTIONS

Sections 13.3–13.4

13.1 Which class is the root of the Java GUI component classes? Is a container class a subclass of Component? Which class is the root of the Swing GUI component classes?

13.2 Explain the difference between AWT GUI components, such as java.awt.Button, and Swing components, such as javax.swing.JButton.

13.3 How do you create a frame? How do you set the size for a frame? How do you get the size of a frame? How do you add components to a frame? What would happen if the statements frame.setSize(400, 300) and frame.setVisible(true) were swapped in the MyFrameWithComponents class in §13.4.2, "Adding Components to a Frame"?

13.4 Determine whether the following statements are true or false:

■ You can add a button to a frame.
■ You can add a frame to a panel.
■ You can add a panel to a frame.
■ You can add any number of components to a panel or a frame.
■ You can derive a class from JButton, JPanel, JFrame, or JApplet.

13.5 The following program is supposed to display a button in a frame, but nothing is displayed. What is the problem?

```
1 public class Test extends javax.swing.JFrame {
2   public Test() {
3     add(new javax.swing.JButton("OK"));
4   }
5
6   public static void main(String[] args) {
7     javax.swing.JFrame frame = new javax.swing.JFrame();
8     frame.setSize(100, 200);
9     frame.setVisible(true);
10   }
11 }
```

13.6 Which of the following statements have syntax errors?

```
Component c1 = new Component();
JComponent c2 = new JComponent();
Component c3 = new JButton();
JComponent c4 = new JButton();
Container c5 = new JButton();
c5.add(c4);
Object c6 = new JButton();
c5.add(c6);
```

Section 13.5 Layout Managers

13.7 Why do you need to use layout managers? What is the default layout manager for a frame? How do you add a component to a frame?

13.8 Describe FlowLayout. How do you create a FlowLayout manager? How do you add a component to a FlowLayout container? Is there a limit to the number of components that can be added to a FlowLayout container?

13.9 Describe GridLayout. How do you create a GridLayout manager? How do you add a component to a GridLayout container? Is there a limit to the number of components that can be added to a GridLayout container?

13.10 Describe BorderLayout. How do you create a BorderLayout manager? How do you add a component to a BorderLayout container?

Sections 13.6–13.7

13.11 How do you create a color? What is wrong about creating a Color using new Color(400, 200, 300)? Which of two colors is darker, new Color(10, 0, 0) or new Color(200, 0, 0)?

13.12 How do you create a font? How do you find all available fonts on your system?

Section 13.8 Using Panels as Subcontainers

13.13 How do you create a panel with a specified layout manager?

13.14 What is the default layout manager for a JPanel? How do you add a component to a JPanel?

13.15 Can you use the setTitle method in a panel? What is the purpose of using a panel?

13.16 Since a GUI component class such as JButton is a subclass of Container, can you add components into a button?

Sections 13.9–13.10

13.17 How do you set background color, foreground color, font, and tool tip text on a Swing GUI component? Why is the tool tip text not displayed in the following code?

```
1 import javax.swing.*;
2
3 public class Test extends JFrame {
4   private JButton jbtOK = new JButton("OK");
5
6   public static void main(String[] args) {
7     // Create a frame and set its properties
8     JFrame frame = new Test();
9     frame.setTitle("Logic Error");
10    frame.setSize(200, 100);
11    frame.setDefaultCloseOperation(JFrame.EXIT_ON_CLOSE);
12    frame.setVisible(true);
13  }
14
15  public Test() {
16    jbtOK.setToolTipText("This is a button");
17    add(new JButton("OK"));
18  }
19 }
```

13.18 Show the output of the following code:

```
import javax.swing.*;

public class Test {
  public static void main(String[] args) {
    JButton jbtOK = new JButton("OK");
    System.out.println(jbtOK.isVisible());
    JFrame frame = new JFrame();
    System.out.println(frame.isVisible());
  }
}
```

13.19 How do you create an ImageIcon from the file image/us.gif in the class directory?

13.20 What happens if you add a button to a container several times, as shown below? Does it cause syntax errors? Does it cause runtime errors?

```
JButton jbt = new JButton();
JPanel panel = new JPanel();
panel.add(jbt);
panel.add(jbt);
panel.add(jbt);
```

13.21 Will the following code display three buttons? Will the buttons display the same icon?

```
1 import javax.swing.*;
2 import java.awt.*;
3
4 public class Test extends JFrame  {
5   public static void main(String[] args) {
6     // Create a frame and set its properties
7     JFrame frame = new Test();
8     frame.setTitle("ButtonIcons");
9     frame.setSize(200, 100);
10     frame.setDefaultCloseOperation(JFrame.EXIT_ON_CLOSE);
11     frame.setVisible(true);
12   }
13
14   public Test() {
15     ImageIcon usIcon = new ImageIcon("image/usIcon.gif");
16     JButton jbt1 = new JButton(usIcon);
17     JButton jbt2 = new JButton(usIcon);
18
19     JPanel p1 = new JPanel();
20     p1.add(jbt1);
21
22     JPanel p2 = new JPanel();
23     p2.add(jbt2);
24
25     JPanel p3 = new JPanel();
26     p2.add(jbt1);
27
28     add(p1, BorderLayout.NORTH);
29     add(p2, BorderLayout.SOUTH);
30     add(p3, BorderLayout.CENTER);
31   }
32 }
```

13.22 Can a border or an icon be shared by GUI components?

PROGRAMMING EXERCISES

Section 13.5 Layout Managers

13.1 (*Using the* FlowLayout *manager*) Write a program that meets the following requirements (see Figure 13.15):

- Create a frame and set its layout to FlowLayout.
- Create two panels and add them to the frame.
- Each panel contains three buttons. The panel uses FlowLayout.

FIGURE 13.15 Exercise 13.1 places the first three buttons in one panel and the other three buttons in another panel.

13.2 (*Using the `BorderLayout` manager*) Rewrite the preceding program to create the same user interface, but instead of using `FlowLayout` for the frame, use `BorderLayout`. Place one panel in the south of the frame, and the other panel in the center.

13.3 (*Using the `GridLayout` manager*) Rewrite the preceding program to create the same user interface. Instead of using `FlowLayout` for the panels, use a `GridLayout` of two rows and three columns.

13.4 (*Using `JPanel` to group buttons*) Rewrite the preceding program to create the same user interface. Instead of creating buttons and panels separately, define a class that extends the `JPanel` class. Place three buttons in your panel class, and create two panels from the user-defined panel class.

13.5 (*Displaying labels*) Write a program that displays four lines of text in four labels, as shown in Figure 13.16(a). Add a line border on each label.

(a)   (b)   (c)

FIGURE 13.16 (a) Exercise 13.5 displays four labels. (b) Exercise 13.6 displays four icons. (c) A TicTacToe board is displayed with image icons in labels.

13.6 (*Displaying icons*) Write a program that displays four icons in four labels, as shown in Figure 13.16(b). Add a line border on each label. (Use any images of your choice or the ones in the book, which can be obtained along with the book's source code.)

13.7** (*Game: displaying a TicTacToe board*) Display a frame that contains nine labels. A label may display an image icon for X, an image icon for O, or nothing, as shown in Figure 13.16(c). What to display is randomly decided. Use the `Math.random()` method to generate an integer `0`, `1`, or `2`, which corresponds to displaying a cross image icon, a not image icon, or nothing. The cross and not images are in the files `x.gif` and `o.gif`, which are under the `image` directory in www.cs.armstrong.edu/liang/intro7e/evennumberedexercise.zip).

13.8* (*Swing common features*) Display a frame that contains six labels. Set the background of the labels to white. Set the foreground of the labels to black, blue, cyan, green, magenta, and orange, respectively, as shown in Figure 13.17(a). Set the border of each label to a line border with the yellow color. Set the font of each label to TimesRoman, bold, and 20 pixels. Set the text and tool tip text of each label to the name of its foreground color.

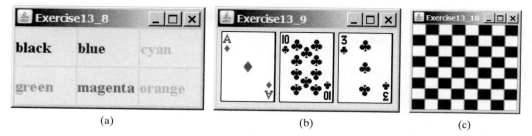

(a)   (b)   (c)

FIGURE 13.17 (a) Six labels are placed in the frame. (b) Three cards are randomly selected (c) A checkerboard is displayed using buttons.

13.9* (*Game: displaying four cards*) Display a frame that contains three labels. Each label displays a card, as shown in Figure 13.17(b). The card image files are named 1.png, 2.png, ..., 54.png, and stored in the `image/card` directory. All three cards are distinct and selected randomly. The image files can be obtained from www.cs.armstrong.edu/liang/intro7e/evennumberedexercise.zip.

Video Note
Display a checker board

13.10* (*Game: displaying a checkerboard*) Write a program that displays a checkerboard in which each white and black cell is a `JButton` with a background black or white, as shown in Figure 13.17(c).

CHAPTER 14

GRAPHICS

Objectives

- To describe Java coordinate systems in a GUI component (§14.2).
- To draw things using the methods in the Graphics class (§14.3).
- To explain how and when a Graphics object is created (§14.3).
- To override the paintComponent method to draw things on a GUI component (§14.4).
- To use a panel as a canvas to draw things (§14.5).
- To draw strings, lines, rectangles, ovals, arcs, and polygons (§§14.6, 14.8–14.9).
- To obtain font properties using FontMetrics and know how to center a message (§14.10).
- To display an image in a GUI component (§14.13).
- To develop reusable GUI components FigurePanel, MessagePanel, StillClock, and ImageViewer (§§14.7, 14.11, 14.12, 14.14).

14.1 Introduction

If you want to draw shapes such as a bar chart, a clock, or a stop sign, as shown in Figure 14.1, how can you do so?

    (a)   (b)   (c)

FIGURE 14.1 You can draw shapes using the drawing methods in the **Graphics** class.

You can accomplish the task using the **Graphics** class. This chapter describes how to draw strings, lines, rectangles, ovals, arcs, polygons, and images, and how to develop reusable GUI components.

14.2 Graphical Coordinate Systems

To paint, you need to specify where to paint. Each component has its own coordinate system with the origin $(0, 0)$ at the upper-left corner of the component. The x coordinate increases to the right, and the y coordinate increases downward. Note that the Java coordinate system differs from the conventional coordinate system, as shown in Figure 14.2.

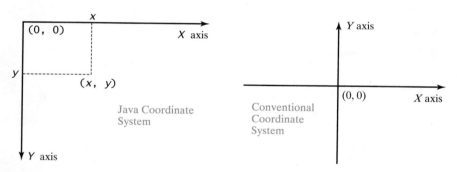

FIGURE 14.2 The Java coordinate system is measured in pixels, with $(0, 0)$ at its upper-left corner.

The location of the upper-left corner of a component **c1** (e.g., a button) inside its parent component **c2** (e.g., a panel) can be located using **c1.getX()** and **c1.getY()**. As shown in Figure 14.3, **(x1, y1) = (c1.getX(), c1.getY())**, **(x2, y2) = (c2.getX(), c2.getY())**, and **(x3, y3) = (c3.getX(), c3.getY())**.

14.3 The **Graphics** Class

You can draw strings, lines, rectangles, ovals, arcs, polygons, and polylines, using the methods in the **Graphics** class, as shown in Figure 14.4.

The **Graphics** class is an abstract class that provides a device-independent graphics interface for displaying figures and images on the screen on different platforms. Whenever a component (e.g., a button, a label, a panel) is displayed, the JVM automatically creates a **Graphics**

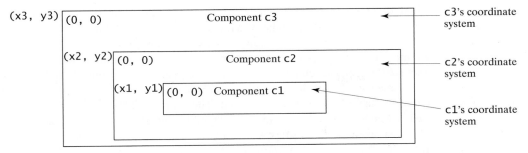

FIGURE 14.3 Each GUI component has its own coordinate system.

java.awt.Graphics	
+setColor(color: Color): void	Sets a new color for subsequent drawings.
+setFont(font: Font): void	Sets a new font for subsequent drawings.
+drawString(s: String, x: int, y: int): void	Draws a string starting at point (x, y).
+drawLine(x1: int, y1: int, x2: int, y2: int): void	Draws a line from (x1, y1) to (x2, y2).
+drawRect(x:int, y: int, w: int, h: int): void	Draws a rectangle with specified upper-left corner point at (x,y) and width w and height h.
+fillRect(x: int, y: int, w: int, h: int): void	Draws a filled rectangle with specified upper-left corner point at (x, y) and width w and height h.
+drawRoundRect(x: int, y: int, w: int, h: int, aw: int, ah: int): void	Draws a round-cornered rectangle with specified arc width aw and arc height ah.
+fillRoundRect(x: int, y: int, w: int, h: int, aw: int, ah: int): void	Draws a filled round-cornered rectangle with specified arc width aw and arc height ah.
+draw3DRect(x: int, y: int, w: int, h: int, raised: boolean): void	Draws a 3-D rectangle raised above the surface or sunk into the surface.
+fill3DRect(x: int, y: int, w: int, h: int, raised: boolean): void	Draws a filled 3-D rectangle raised above the surface or sunk into the surface.
+drawOval(x: int, y: int, w: int, h: int): void	Draws an oval bounded by the rectangle specified by the parameters x, y, w, and h.
+fillOval(x: int, y: int, w: int, h: int): void	Draws a filled oval bounded by the rectangle specified by the parameters x, y, w, and h.
+drawArc(x: int, y: int, w: int, h: int, startAngle: int, arcAngle: int): void	Draws an arc conceived as part of an oval bounded by the rectangle specified by the parameters x, y, w, and h.
+fillArc(x: int, y: int, w: int, h: int, startAngle: int, arcAngle: int): void	Draws a filled arc conceived as part of an oval bounded by the rectangle specified by the parameters x, y, w, and h.
+drawPolygon(xPoints: int[], yPoints: int[], nPoints: int): void	Draws a closed polygon defined by arrays of x- and y-coordinates. Each pair of (x[i], y[i]) coordinates is a point.
+fillPolygon(xPoints: int[], yPoints: int[], nPoints: int): void	Draws a filled polygon defined by arrays of x- and y-coordinates. Each pair of (x[i], y[i])-coordinates is a point.
+drawPolygon(g: Polygon): void	Draws a closed polygon defined by a Polygon object.
+fillPolygon(g: Polygon): void	Draws a filled polygon defined by a Polygon object.
+drawPolyline(xPoints: int[], yPoints: int[], nPoints: int): void	Draws a polyline defined by arrays of x- and y-coordinates. Each pair of (x[i], y[i])-coordinates is a point.

FIGURE 14.4 The Graphics class contains the methods for drawing strings and shapes.

object for the component on the native platform. This object can be obtained using the getGraphics() method. For example, the Graphics object for a label jlblBanner can be obtained using

```
Graphics graphics = jlblBanner.getGraphics();
```

Think of a GUI component as a piece of paper and the Graphics object as a pencil or paint-brush. You can apply the methods in the Graphics class to draw things on a GUI component.

To help understand the Graphics class, we first present an intuitive, but not practical, example in Listing 14.1. The program creates a label in line 5. When the main method is executed, the constructor TestGetGraphics is executed (line 13) and the label is added to the frame (line 8). At this time, the Graphics object for the label has not been created because the label has not been displayed. Therefore, jlblBanner.getGraphics() returns null (line 9). After the frame is displayed in line 18, all the components in the frame are also displayed. The Graphics object for the label is obtained in line 21. A line is drawn from (0, 0) to (50, 50) on the label, as shown in Figure 14.5.

LISTING 14.1 TestGetGraphics.java

```
 1 import javax.swing.*;
 2 import java.awt.Graphics;
 3
 4 public class TestGetGraphics extends JFrame {
 5     private JLabel jlblBanner = new JLabel("Banner");
 6
 7     public TestGetGraphics() {
 8         add(jlblBanner);
 9         System.out.println(jlblBanner.getGraphics());
10     }
11
12     public static void main(String[] args) {
13         TestGetGraphics frame = new TestGetGraphics();
14         frame.setTitle("TestGetGraphics");
15         frame.setSize(200, 100);
16         frame.setLocationRelativeTo(null); // Center the frame
17         frame.setDefaultCloseOperation(JFrame.EXIT_ON_CLOSE);
18         frame.setVisible(true);
19         JOptionPane.showMessageDialog(null,
20             "Delay on purpose\nClick OK to dismiss the dialog");
21         Graphics graphics = frame.jlblBanner.getGraphics();
22         graphics.drawLine(0, 0, 50, 50);
23     }
24 }
```

create a label — (line 5)

add a label — (line 8)

create a frame — (line 13)

display frame — (line 18)
for delay purpose — (line 19)

get graphics — (line 21)
draw line — (line 22)

FIGURE 14.5 A line is drawn on a label, and the label is placed inside the frame.

When you run this program, the frame is displayed (line 18), then a message dialog box is displayed (line 19). What is the purpose of having a message dialog box in this program? It is to delay the execution of lines 21 and 22. Without the delay, you might not see the line (line 22). The reason will be discussed in the next section.

When you create a label with a text such as new JLabel("Banner"), you see the text on the label when the label is displayed. The text is actually painted on the label using the drawString method in the Graphics class internally.

Every GUI component has a Graphics object that can be obtained using getGraphics() after the component is displayed. You may rewrite this example using a button, a text field, or a text area rather a label. Note that jlblBanner.getGraphics() returns null in line 9, because `jlblBanner` has not been displayed yet. It is displayed when the frame is set visible in line 18.

In line 11, `jlblBanner.getGraphics()` is used to return a `Graphics` object. In line 21, why do you have to use `frame.jlblBanner.getGraphics()` in the `main` method? This is because `jlblBanner` is an instance variable, and it cannot be referenced directly in a static method.

14.4 The **paintComponent** Method

The program in Listing 14.1 has two problems:

1. If you resize the frame, the line disappears.

2. It is awkward to program because you have to make sure that the component is displayed before obtaining its `Graphics` object using the `getGraphics()` method. For this reason, lines 21 and 22 are placed after the frame is displayed in line 18.

Because of these two problems, you should avoid programming using the `getGraphics()` method. To fix the first problem, you need to know its cause. When you resize the frame, the JVM automatically invokes the `paintComponent` method of a Swing component (e.g., a `JLabel`) to redisplay the graphics on the component. Since you did not draw a line in the `paintComponent` method, the line is gone when the frame is resized. To permanently display the line, you need to draw the line in the `paintComponent` method. The signature of the `paintComponent` method is as follows:

```
protected void paintComponent(Graphics g)
```

This method, defined in the `JComponent` class, is invoked whenever a component is first displayed or redisplayed. The `Graphics` object `g` is created automatically by the JVM for every visible GUI component. The JVM obtains the `Graphics` object and passes it to invoke `paintComponent`.

In order to draw things on a component (e.g., a `JLabel`) consistently, you need to declare a class that extends a Swing GUI component class and overrides its `paintComponent` method to specify what to draw. The program in Listing 14.1 can be rewritten as shown in Listing 14.2. The output is the same as shown in Figure 14.5. When you resize the frame, the JVM invokes the `paintComponent` method to repaint the line and the text.

LISTING 14.2 TestPaintComponent.java

```java
 1 import javax.swing.*;
 2 import java.awt.Graphics;
 3
 4 public class TestPaintComponent extends JFrame {
 5   public TestPaintComponent() {
 6     add(new NewLabel("Banner"));         create a label
 7   }
 8
 9   public static void main(String[] args) {
10     TestPaintComponent frame = new TestPaintComponent();
11     frame.setTitle("TestPaintComponent");
12     frame.setSize(200, 100);
13     frame.setLocationRelativeTo(null); // Center the frame
14     frame.setDefaultCloseOperation(JFrame.EXIT_ON_CLOSE);
15     frame.setVisible(true);
16   }
17 }
18
```

new label class

```
19  class NewLabel extends JLabel {
20    public NewLabel(String text) {
21      super(text);
22    }
23
```

override **paintComponent**
draw things in the superclass
draw line

```
24    protected void paintComponent(Graphics g) {
25      super.paintComponent(g);
26      g.drawLine(0, 0, 50, 50);
27    }
28  }
```

The `paintComponent` method is automatically invoked to paint graphics when the component is first displayed or whenever the component needs to be redisplayed. The text "banner" is drawn in the `paintComponent` method defined in the `JLabel` class. Invoking `super.paintComponent(g)` (line 25) displays the text in the label, and invoking the `drawLine` method (line 26) draws a line.

The JVM invokes `paintComponent` to draw things on a component. The user should never invoke `paintComponent` directly. For this reason, the protected visibility is sufficient for `paintComponent`.

14.5 Drawing Graphics on Panels

Panels are invisible and are used as small containers that group components to achieve a desired layout. Another important use of `JPanel` is for drawing. You can draw things on any Swing GUI component, but normally you should use a `JPanel` as a canvas upon which to draw things.

To draw in a `JPanel`, you create a new class that extends `JPanel` and overrides the `paintComponent` method to tell the panel how to draw things. Listing 14.3 is an example to demonstrate drawings on a panel. The example declares the `NewPanel` class, which extends `JPanel` and overrides the `paintComponent` method to draw a line (line 22) and a string (line 23), as shown in Figure 14.6.

LISTING 14.3 TestPanelDrawing.java

```
1  import javax.swing.*;
2  import java.awt.Graphics;
3
4  public class TestPanelDrawing extends JFrame {
5    public TestPanelDrawing() {
6      add(new NewPanel());
7    }
8
9    public static void main(String[] args) {
10     TestPanelDrawing frame = new TestPanelDrawing();
11     frame.setTitle("TestPanelDrawing");
12     frame.setSize(200, 100);
13     frame.setLocationRelativeTo(null); // Center the frame
14     frame.setDefaultCloseOperation(JFrame.EXIT_ON_CLOSE);
15     frame.setVisible(true);
16   }
17 }
18
19 class NewPanel extends JPanel {
20   protected void paintComponent(Graphics g) {
21     super.paintComponent(g);
22     g.drawLine(0, 0, 50, 50);
```

create a label

new panel class
override **paintComponent**
draw things in the superclass
draw line

```
23        g.drawString("Banner", 0, 40);
24   }
25 }
```

FIGURE 14.6   A line and a string are drawn on a panel.

All the drawing methods have parameters that specify the locations of the subjects to be drawn. All measurements in Java are made in pixels. The string "Banner" is drawn at location (0, 40).

Note

Invoking `super.paintComponent(g)` (line 23) is necessary to ensure that the viewing area is cleared before a new drawing is displayed.

`super.paint-`
`Component(g)`

Tip

Some textbooks declare a canvas class by subclassing `JComponent`. The problem is that you have to write the code to paint the background color if you wish to set a background in the canvas. A simple `setBackground(Color color)` method will not set a background color in a `JComponent`.

`extends JComponent`?

14.6 Drawing Strings, Lines, Rectangles, and Ovals

The `drawString(String s, int x, int y)` method draws a string starting at the point (x, y), as shown in Figure 14.7(a).

`drawString`

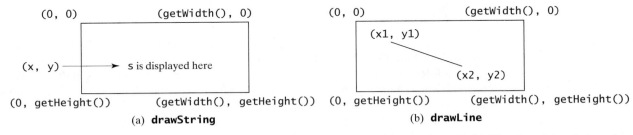

(a) **drawString**   (b) **drawLine**

FIGURE 14.7   (a) The `drawString(s, x, y)` method draws a string starting at (x, y). (b) The `drawLine(x1, y1, x2, y2)` method draws a line between two specified points.

The `drawLine(int x1, int y1, int x2, int y2)` method draws a straight line from point (x1, y1) to point (x2, y2), as shown in Figure 14.7(b).

`drawLine`

Java provides six methods for drawing rectangles in outline or filled with color. You can draw or fill plain rectangles, round-cornered rectangles, or three-dimensional rectangles.

The `drawRect(int x, int y, int w, int h)` method draws a plain rectangle and the `fillRect(int x, int y, int w, int h)` method draws a filled rectangle. The parameters x and y represent the upper-left corner of the rectangle, and w and h are its width and height (see Figure 14.8).

`drawRect`
`fillRect`

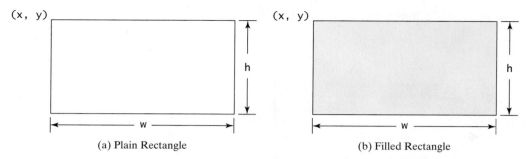

(a) Plain Rectangle   (b) Filled Rectangle

FIGURE 14.8 (a) The `drawRect(x, y, w, h)` method draws a rectangle. (b) The `fillRect(x, y, w, h)` method draws a filled rectangle.

drawRoundRect
fillRoundRect

    The `drawRoundRect(int x, int y, int w, int h, int aw, int ah)` method draws a round-cornered rectangle, and the `fillRoundRect(int x, int y, int w, int h, int aw, int ah)` method draws a filled round-cornered rectangle. Parameters `x`, `y`, `w`, and `h` are the same as in the `drawRect` method, parameter `aw` is the horizontal diameter of the arcs at the corner, and `ah` is the vertical diameter of the arcs at the corner (see Figure 14.9(a)). In other words, `aw` and `ah` are the width and the height of the oval that produces a quarter-circle at each corner.

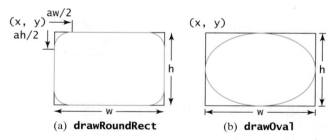

(a) **drawRoundRect**   (b) **drawOval**

FIGURE 14.9 (a) The `drawRoundRect(x, y, w, h, aw, ah)` method draws a round-cornered rectangle. (b) The `drawOval(x, y, w, h)` method draws an oval based on its bounding rectangle.

draw3DRect
fill3DRect

    The `draw3DRect(int x, int y, int w, int h, boolean raised)` method draws a 3D rectangle and the `fill3DRect(int x, int y, int w, int h, boolean raised)` method draws a filled 3D rectangle. The parameters `x`, `y`, `w`, and `h` are the same as in the `drawRect` method. The last parameter, a Boolean value, indicates whether the rectangle is raised above the surface or sunk into the surface.

drawOval
fillOval

    Depending on whether you wish to draw an oval in outline or filled solid, you can use either the `drawOval(int x, int y, int w, int h)` method or the `fillOval(int x, int y, int w, int h)` method. An oval is drawn based on its bounding rectangle. Parameters `x` and `y` indicate the top-left corner of the bounding rectangle, and `w` and `h` indicate the width and height, respectively, of the bounding rectangle, as shown in Figure 14.9(b).

Video Note
FigurePanel class

14.7 Case Study: The **FigurePanel** Class

This example develops a useful class for displaying various figures. The class enables the user to set the figure type and specify whether the figure is filled, and displays the figure on a panel. The UML diagram for the class is shown in Figure 14.10. The panel can display lines,

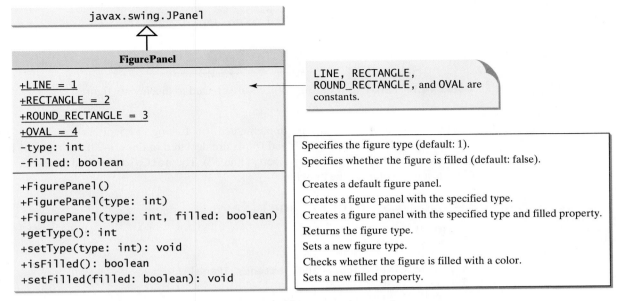

FIGURE 14.10 FigurePanel displays various types of figures on the panel.

rectangles, round-cornered rectangles, and ovals. Which figure to display is decided by the type property. If the filled property is true, the rectangle, round-cornered rectangle, and oval are filled in the panel.

The UML diagram serves as the contract for the FigurePanel class. The user can use the class without knowing how the class is implemented. Let us begin by writing a program in Listing 14.4 that uses the class to display six figure panels, as shown in Figure 14.11.

LISTING 14.4 TestFigurePanel.java

```
1  import java.awt.*;
2  import javax.swing.*;
3
4  public class TestFigurePanel extends JFrame {
5    public TestFigurePanel() {
6      setLayout(new GridLayout(2, 3, 5, 5));
7      add(new FigurePanel(FigurePanel.LINE));                          create figures
8      add(new FigurePanel(FigurePanel.RECTANGLE));
9      add(new FigurePanel(FigurePanel.ROUND_RECTANGLE));
10     add(new FigurePanel(FigurePanel.OVAL));
11     add(new FigurePanel(FigurePanel.RECTANGLE, true));
12     add(new FigurePanel(FigurePanel.ROUND_RECTANGLE, true));
13   }
14
15   public static void main(String[] args) {
16     TestFigurePanel frame = new TestFigurePanel();
17     frame.setSize(400, 200);
18     frame.setTitle("TestFigurePanel");
19     frame.setLocationRelativeTo(null); // Center the frame
20     frame.setDefaultCloseOperation(JFrame.EXIT_ON_CLOSE);
21     frame.setVisible(true);
22   }
23 }
```

FIGURE 14.11 Six `FigurePanel` objects are created to display six figures.

The `FigurePanel` class is implemented in Listing 14.5. Four constants, `LINE`, `RECTANGLE`, `ROUND_RECTANGLE`, and `OVAL`, are declared in lines 6–9. Four types of figures are drawn according to the `type` property (line 37). The `setColor` method (lines 39, 44, 53, 62) sets a new color for the drawing.

LISTING 14.5 FigurePanel.java

```
 1  import java.awt.*;
 2  import javax.swing.JPanel;
 3
 4  public class FigurePanel extends JPanel {
 5    // Define constants
 6    public static final int LINE = 1;
 7    public static final int RECTANGLE = 2;
 8    public static final int ROUND_RECTANGLE = 3;
 9    public static final int OVAL = 4;
10
11    private int type = 1;
12    private boolean filled = false;
13
14    /** Construct a default FigurePanel */
15    public FigurePanel() {
16    }
17
18    /** Construct a FigurePanel with the specified type */
19    public FigurePanel(int type) {
20      this.type = type;
21    }
22
23    /** Construct a FigurePanel with the specified type and filled */
24    public FigurePanel(int type, boolean filled) {
25      this.type = type;
26      this.filled = filled;
27    }
28
29    /** Draw a figure on the panel */
30    protected void paintComponent(Graphics g) {
31      super.paintComponent(g);
32
33      // Get the appropriate size for the figure
34      int width = getSize().width;
35      int height = getSize().height;
36
37      switch (type) {
38        case LINE: // Display two cross lines
39          g.setColor(Color.BLACK);
40          g.drawLine(10, 10, width - 10, height - 10);
41          g.drawLine(width - 10, 10, 10, height - 10);
42          break;
43        case RECTANGLE: // Display a rectangle
44          g.setColor(Color.BLUE);
```

constants

override
  paintComponent(g)

check type

draw lines

```
45          if (filled)
46            g.fillRect((int)(0.1 * width), (int)(0.1 * height),
47              (int)(0.8 * width), (int)(0.8 * height));
48          else
49            g.drawRect((int)(0.1 * width), (int)(0.1 * height),
50              (int)(0.8 * width), (int)(0.8 * height));
51          break;
52        case ROUND_RECTANGLE: // Display a round-cornered rectangle
53          g.setColor(Color.RED);
54          if (filled)
55            g.fillRoundRect((int)(0.1 * width), (int)(0.1 * height),
56              (int)(0.8 * width), (int)(0.8 * height), 20, 20);
57          else
58            g.drawRoundRect((int)(0.1 * width), (int)(0.1 * height),
59              (int)(0.8 * width), (int)(0.8 * height), 20, 20);
60          break;
61        case OVAL: // Display an oval
62          g.setColor(Color.BLACK);
63          if (filled)
64            g.fillOval((int)(0.1 * width), (int)(0.1 * height),
65              (int)(0.8 * width), (int)(0.8 * height));
66          else
67            g.drawOval((int)(0.1 * width), (int)(0.1 * height),
68              (int)(0.8 * width), (int)(0.8 * height));
69      }
70    }
71
72    /** Set a new figure type */
73    public void setType(int type) {
74      this.type = type;
75      repaint();
76    }
77
78    /** Return figure type */
79    public int getType() {
80      return type;
81    }
82
83    /** Set a new filled property */
84    public void setFilled(boolean filled) {
85      this.filled = filled;
86      repaint();
87    }
88
89    /** Check if the figure is filled */
90    public boolean isFilled() {
91      return filled;
92    }
93
94    /** Specify preferred size */
95    public Dimension getPreferredSize() {
96      return new Dimension(80, 80);
97    }
98  }
```

- fill a rectangle (lines 46–47)
- draw a rectangle (lines 49–50)
- fill round-cornered rect (lines 55–56)
- draw round-cornered rect (lines 58–59)
- fill an oval (lines 64–65)
- draw an oval (lines 67–68)
- repaint panel (line 75)
- repaint panel (line 86)
- override **getPreferredSize()** (line 95)

The **repaint** method (lines 75, 86) is defined in the **Component** class. Invoking **repaint** causes the **paintComponent** method to be called. The **repaint** method is invoked to refresh the viewing area. Typically, you call it if you have new things to display.

Caution

don't invoke
paintComponent

The paintComponent method should never be invoked directly. It is invoked either by the JVM whenever the viewing area changes or by the repaint method. You should override the paintComponent method to tell the system how to paint the viewing area, but never override the repaint method.

Note

request repaint using
repaint()

The repaint method lodges a request to update the viewing area and returns immediately. Its effect is asynchronous, meaning that it is up to the JVM to execute the paintComponent method.

getPreferredSize()

The getPreferredSize() method (lines 95–97), defined in Component, is overridden in FigurePanel to specify the preferred size for the layout manager to consider when laying out a FigurePanel object. This property may or may not be considered by the layout manager, depending on its rules. For example, a component uses its preferred size in a container with a FlowLayout manager, but its preferred size may be ignored if it is placed in a container with a GridLayout manager. It is a good practice to override getPreferredSize() in a subclass of JPanel to specify a preferred size, because the default preferred size for a JPanel is 0 by 0.

14.8 Drawing Arcs

An arc is conceived as part of an oval bounded by a rectangle. The methods to draw or fill an arc are as follows:

```
drawArc(int x, int y, int w, int h, int startAngle, int arcAngle);
fillArc(int x, int y, int w, int h, int startAngle, int arcAngle);
```

Parameters x, y, w, and h are the same as in the drawOval method; parameter startAngle is the starting angle; arcAngle is the spanning angle (i.e., the angle covered by the arc). Angles are measured in degrees and follow the usual mathematical conventions (i.e., 0 degrees is in the easterly direction, and positive angles indicate counterclockwise rotation from the easterly direction); see Figure 14.12.

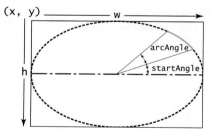

FIGURE 14.12 The drawArc method draws an arc based on an oval with specified angles.

Listing 14.6 is an example of how to draw arcs; the output is shown in Figure 14.13.

LISTING 14.6 DrawArcs.java

```
1 import javax.swing.JFrame;
2 import javax.swing.JPanel;
3 import java.awt.Graphics;
4
5 public class DrawArcs extends JFrame {
6   public DrawArcs() {
```

```
 7        setTitle("DrawArcs");
 8        add(new ArcsPanel());                                          add a panel
 9      }
10
11      /** Main method */
12      public static void main(String[] args) {
13        DrawArcs frame = new DrawArcs();
14        frame.setSize(250, 300);
15        frame.setLocationRelativeTo(null); // Center the frame
16        frame.setDefaultCloseOperation(JFrame.EXIT_ON_CLOSE);
17        frame.setVisible(true);
18      }
19    }
20
21    // The class for drawing arcs on a panel
22    class ArcsPanel extends JPanel {
23      // Draw four blades of a fan
24      protected void paintComponent(Graphics g) {                      override paintComponent
25        super.paintComponent(g);
26
27        int xCenter = getWidth() / 2;
28        int yCenter = getHeight() / 2;
29        int radius = (int)(Math.min(getWidth(), getHeight()) * 0.4);
30
31        int x = xCenter - radius;
32        int y = yCenter - radius;
33
34        g.fillArc(x, y, 2 * radius, 2 * radius, 0, 30);                 30° arc from 0°
35        g.fillArc(x, y, 2 * radius, 2 * radius, 90, 30);               30° arc from 90°
36        g.fillArc(x, y, 2 * radius, 2 * radius, 180, 30);              30° arc from 180°
37        g.fillArc(x, y, 2 * radius, 2 * radius, 270, 30);             30° arc from 270°
38      }
39    }
```

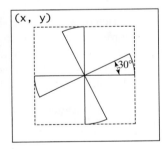

FIGURE 14.13   The program draws four filled arcs.

Angles may be negative. A negative starting angle sweeps clockwise from the easterly   negative degrees
direction, as shown in Figure 14.14. A negative spanning angle sweeps clockwise from the
starting angle. The following two statements draw the same arc:

```
g.fillArc(x, y, 2 * radius, 2 * radius, -30, -20);
g.fillArc(x, y, 2 * radius, 2 * radius, -50, 20);
```

The first statement uses negative starting angle -30 and negative spanning angle -20, as
shown in Figure 14.14(a). The second statement uses negative starting angle -50 and positive
spanning angle 20, as shown in Figure 14.14(b).

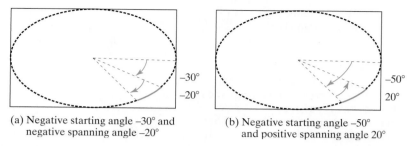

(a) Negative starting angle –30° and
negative spanning angle –20°

(b) Negative starting angle –50°
and positive spanning angle 20°

FIGURE 14.14 Angles may be negative.

14.9 Drawing Polygons and Polylines

To draw a polygon, first create a `Polygon` object using the `Polygon` class, as shown in Figure 14.15.

java.awt.Polygon	
+xpoints: int[]	x-coordinates of all points in the polygon.
+ypoints: int[]	y-coordinates of all points in the polygon.
+npoints: int	The number of points in the polygon.
+Polygon()	Creates an empty polygon.
+Polygon(xpoints: int[], ypoints: int[], npoints: int)	Creates a polygon with the specified points.
+addPoint(x: int, y: int)	Appends a point to the polygon.

FIGURE 14.15 The `Polygon` class models a polygon.

A polygon is a closed two-dimensional region. This region is bounded by an arbitrary number of line segments, each of which is one side (or edge) of the polygon. A polygon comprises a list of (x, y)-coordinate pairs in which each pair defines a vertex of the polygon, and two successive pairs are the endpoints of a line that is a side of the polygon. The first and final pairs of (x, y) points are joined by a line segment that closes the polygon.

Here is an example of creating a polygon and adding points into it:

```
Polygon polygon = new Polygon();
polygon.addPoint(40, 20);
polygon.addPoint(70, 40);
polygon.addPoint(60, 80);
polygon.addPoint(45, 45);
polygon.addPoint(20, 60);
```

After these points are added, xpoints is { 40, 70, 60, 45, 20}, ypoints is { 20, 40, 80, 45, 60}, and npoints is 5. xpoints, ypoints, and npoints are public data fields in Polygon, which is a bad design. In principle, all data fields should be kept private.

To draw or fill a polygon, use one of the following methods in the Graphics class:

```
drawPolygon(Polygon polygon);

fillPolygon(Polygon polygon);

drawPolygon(int[] xpoints, int[] ypoints, int npoints);

fillPolygon(int[] xpoints, int[] ypoints, int npoints);
```

For example:

```
int x[] = {40, 70, 60, 45, 20};
int y[] = {20, 40, 80, 45, 60};
g.drawPolygon(x, y, x.length);
```

The drawing method opens the polygon by drawing lines between point (x[i], y[i]) and point (x[i+1], y[i+1]) for i = 0, ... , x.length-1; it closes the polygon by drawing a line between the first and last points (see Figure 14.16(a)).

(a) Polygon

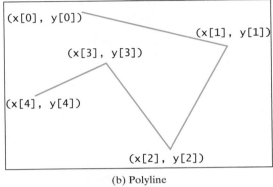

(b) Polyline

FIGURE 14.16 The drawPolygon method draws a polygon, and the polyLine method draws a polyline.

To draw a polyline, use the drawPolyline(int[] x, int[] y, int nPoints) method, which draws a sequence of connected lines defined by arrays of x- and y-coordinates. For example, the following code draws the polyline, as shown in Figure 14.16(b).

```
int x[] = {40, 70, 60, 45, 20};
int y[] = {20, 40, 80, 45, 60};
g.drawPolygon(x, y, x.length);
```

Listing 14.7 is an example of how to draw a hexagon, with the output shown in Figure 14.17.

LISTING 14.7 DrawPolygon.java

```
 1 import javax.swing.JFrame;
 2 import javax.swing.JPanel;
 3 import java.awt.Graphics;
 4 import java.awt.Polygon;
 5
 6 public class DrawPolygon extends JFrame {
 7   public DrawPolygon() {
 8     setTitle("DrawPolygon");
 9     add(new PolygonsPanel());                          add a panel
10   }
11
12   /** Main method */
13   public static void main(String[] args) {
14     DrawPolygon frame = new DrawPolygon();
15     frame.setSize(200, 250);
16     frame.setLocationRelativeTo(null); // Center the frame
17     frame.setDefaultCloseOperation(JFrame.EXIT_ON_CLOSE);
18     frame.setVisible(true);
19   }
20 }
21
```

paintComponent

```
22  // Draw a polygon in the panel
23  class PolygonsPanel extends JPanel {
24    protected void paintComponent(Graphics g) {
25      super.paintComponent(g);
26
27      int xCenter = getWidth() / 2;
28      int yCenter = getHeight() / 2;
29      int radius = (int)(Math.min(getWidth(), getHeight()) * 0.4);
30
31      // Create a Polygon object
32      Polygon polygon = new Polygon();
33
34      // Add points to the polygon in this order
35      polygon.addPoint(xCenter + radius, yCenter);
36      polygon.addPoint((int)(xCenter + radius *
37        Math.cos(2 * Math.PI / 6)), (int)(yCenter - radius *
38        Math.sin(2 * Math.PI / 6)));
39      polygon.addPoint((int)(xCenter + radius *
40        Math.cos(2 * 2 * Math.PI / 6)), (int)(yCenter - radius *
41        Math.sin(2 * 2 * Math.PI / 6)));
42      polygon.addPoint((int)(xCenter + radius *
43        Math.cos(3 * 2 * Math.PI / 6)), (int)(yCenter - radius *
44        Math.sin(3 * 2 * Math.PI / 6)));
45      polygon.addPoint((int)(xCenter + radius *
46        Math.cos(4 * 2 * Math.PI / 6)), (int)(yCenter - radius *
47        Math.sin(4 * 2 * Math.PI / 6)));
48      polygon.addPoint((int)(xCenter + radius *
49        Math.cos(5 * 2 * Math.PI / 6)), (int)(yCenter - radius *
50        Math.sin(5 * 2 * Math.PI / 6)));
51
52      // Draw the polygon
53      g.drawPolygon(polygon);
54    }
55  }
```

add a point (line 35)

draw polygon (line 53)

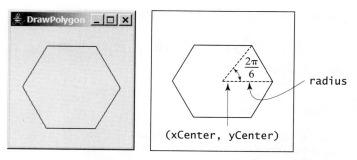

FIGURE 14.17 The program uses the drawPolygon method to draw a polygon.

14.10 Centering a String Using the **FontMetrics** Class

You can display a string at any location in a panel. Can you display it centered? To do so, you need to use the FontMetrics class to measure the exact width and height of the string for a particular font. FontMetrics can measure the following attributes for a given font (see Figure 14.18):

- **Leading,** pronounced *ledding,* is the amount of space between lines of text.

- **Ascent** is the distance from the baseline to the ascent line. The top of most characters in the font will be under the ascent line, but some may extend above the ascent line.

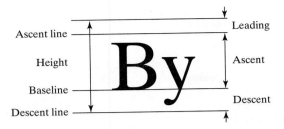

FIGURE 14.18 The FontMetrics class can be used to determine the font properties of characters for a given font.

- **Descent** is the distance from the baseline to the descent line. The bottom of most descending characters (e.g., *j*, *y*, and *g*) in the font will be above the descending line, but some may extend below the descending line.

- **Height** is the sum of leading, ascent, and descent.

FontMetrics is an abstract class. To get a FontMetrics object for a specific font, use the following getFontMetrics methods defined in the Graphics class:

- **public** FontMetrics getFontMetrics(Font font)
  Returns the font metrics of the specified font.

- **public** FontMetrics getFontMetrics()
  Returns the font metrics of the current font.

You can use the following instance methods in the FontMetrics class to obtain the attributes of a font and the width of a string when it is drawn using the font:

```
public int getAscent() // Return the ascent
public int getDescent() // Return the descent
public int getLeading() // Return the leading
public int getHeight() // Return the height
public int stringWidth(String str) // Return the width of the string
```

Listing 14.8 gives an example that displays a message in the center of the panel, as shown in Figure 14.19.

LISTING 14.8 TestCenterMessage.java

```
 1 import javax.swing.*;
 2 import java.awt.*;
 3
 4 public class TestCenterMessage extends JFrame {
 5   public TestCenterMessage() {
 6     CenterMessage messagePanel = new CenterMessage();
 7     add(messagePanel);
 8     messagePanel.setBackground(Color.WHITE);
 9     messagePanel.setFont(new Font("Californian FB", Font.BOLD, 30));
10   }
11
12   /** Main method */
13   public static void main(String[] args) {
14     TestCenterMessage frame = new TestCenterMessage();
15     frame.setSize(300, 150);
16     frame.setLocationRelativeTo(null); // Center the frame
```

create a message panel
add a message panel
set background
set font

```
17        frame.setDefaultCloseOperation(JFrame.EXIT_ON_CLOSE);
18        frame.setVisible(true);
19   }
20 }
21
22 class CenterMessage extends JPanel {
23   /** Paint the message */
24   protected void paintComponent(Graphics g) {
25     super.paintComponent(g);
26
27     // Get font metrics for the current font
28     FontMetrics fm = g.getFontMetrics();
29
30     // Find the center location to display
31     int stringWidth = fm.stringWidth("Welcome to Java");
32     int stringAscent = fm.getAscent();
33
34     // Get the position of the leftmost character in the baseline
35     int xCoordinate = getWidth() / 2 - stringWidth / 2;
36     int yCoordinate = getHeight() / 2 + stringAscent / 2;
37
38     g.drawString("Welcome to Java", xCoordinate, yCoordinate);
39   }
40 }
```

override **paintComponent**

get **FontMetrics**

This is a MessagePanel object

FIGURE 14.19 The program uses the FontMetrics class to measure the string width and height, and displays it at the center of the panel.

The methods getWidth() and getHeight() (lines 35–36) defined in the Component class, return the component's width and height, respectively.

yCoordinate is the height of the baseline for the first character of the string to be displayed. Since the message is centered, yCoordinate should be getHeight() / 2 + h / 2, where h is the ascent of the string.

xCoordinate is the width of the baseline for the first character of the string to be displayed. Since the message is centered, xCoordinate should be getWidth() / 2 − stringWidth / 2.

Video Note
MessagePanel class

14.11 Case Study: The **MessagePanel** Class

This case study develops a useful class that displays a message in a panel. The class enables the user to set the location of the message, center the message, and move the message with the specified interval. The contract of the class is shown in Figure 14.20.

FIGURE 14.20 MessagePanel displays a message on the panel.

Let us first write a test program in Listing 14.9 that uses the MessagePanel class to display four message panels, as shown in Figure 14.21.

LISTING 14.9 TestMessagePanel.java

```
1 import java.awt.*;
2 import javax.swing.*;
3
4 public class TestMessagePanel extends JFrame {
5   public TestMessagePanel() {
6     MessagePanel messagePanel1 = new MessagePanel("Wecome to Java");     create message panel
7     MessagePanel messagePanel2 = new MessagePanel("Java is fun");
8     MessagePanel messagePanel3 = new MessagePanel("Java is cool");
9     MessagePanel messagePanel4 = new MessagePanel("I love Java");
10    messagePanel1.setFont(new Font("SansSerif", Font.ITALIC, 20));       set font
11    messagePanel2.setFont(new Font("Courie", Font.BOLD, 20));
12    messagePanel3.setFont(new Font("Times", Font.ITALIC, 20));
13    messagePanel4.setFont(new Font("Californian FB", Font.PLAIN, 20));
14    messagePanel1.setBackground(Color.red);                              set background
15    messagePanel2.setBackground(Color.cyan);
16    messagePanel3.setBackground(Color.green);
17    messagePanel4.setBackground(Color.white);
18    messagePanel1.setCentered(true);
19
20    setLayout(new GridLayout(2, 2));
21    add(messagePanel1);                                                  add message panel
22    add(messagePanel2);
23    add(messagePanel3);
```

```
24      add(messagePanel4);
25    }
26
27    public static void main(String[] args) {
28      TestMessagePanel frame = new TestMessagePanel();
29      frame.setSize(300, 200);
30      frame.setTitle("TestMessagePanel");
31      frame.setLocationRelativeTo(null); // Center the frame
32      frame.setDefaultCloseOperation(JFrame.EXIT_ON_CLOSE);
33      frame.setVisible(true);
34    }
35  }
```

FIGURE 14.21 `TestMessagePanel` uses `MessagePanel` to display four message panels.

skip implementation?

The rest of this section explains how to implement the `MessagePanel` class. Since you can use the class without knowing how it is implemented, you may skip the implementation if you wish.

The `MessagePanel` class is implemented in Listing 14.10. The program seems long but is actually simple, because most of the methods are `get` and `set` methods, and each method is relatively short and easy to read.

LISTING 14.10 MessagePanel.java

```
1  import java.awt.FontMetrics;
2  import java.awt.Dimension;
3  import java.awt.Graphics;
4  import javax.swing.JPanel;
5
6  public class MessagePanel extends JPanel {
7    /** The message to be displayed */
8    private String message = "Welcome to Java";
9
10   /** The x-coordinate where the message is displayed */
11   private int xCoordinate = 20;
12
13   /** The y-coordinate where the message is displayed */
14   private int yCoordinate = 20;
15
16   /** Indicate whether the message is displayed in the center */
17   private boolean centered;
18
19   /** The interval for moving the message horizontally and vertically */
20   private int interval = 10;
21
22   /** Construct with default properties */
23   public MessagePanel() {
24   }
25
```

```
26    /** Construct a message panel with a specified message */
27    public MessagePanel(String message) {
28      this.message = message;
29    }
30
31    /** Return message */
32    public String getMessage() {
33      return message;
34    }
35
36    /** Set a new message */
37    public void setMessage(String message) {
38      this.message = message;
39      repaint();                                              repaint panel
40    }
41
42    /** Return xCoordinator */
43    public int getXCoordinate() {
44      return xCoordinate;
45    }
46
47    /** Set a new xCoordinator */
48    public void setXCoordinate(int x) {
49      this.xCoordinate = x;
50      repaint();                                              repaint panel
51    }
52
53    /** Return yCoordinator */
54    public int getYCoordinate() {
55      return yCoordinate;
56    }
57
58    /** Set a new yCoordinator */
59    public void setYCoordinate(int y) {
60      this.yCoordinate = y;
61      repaint();                                              repaint panel
62    }
63
64    /** Return centered */
65    public boolean isCentered() {
66      return centered;
67    }
68
69    /** Set a new centered */
70    public void setCentered(boolean centered) {
71      this.centered = centered;
72      repaint();                                              repaint panel
73    }
74
75    /** Return interval */
76    public int getInterval() {
77      return interval;
78    }
79
80    /** Set a new interval */
81    public void setInterval(int interval) {
82      this.interval = interval;
83      repaint();                                              repaint panel
84    }
85
```

override **paintComponent**

check centered

```
86    /** Paint the message */
87    protected void paintComponent(Graphics g) {
88      super.paintComponent(g);
89
90      if (centered) {
91        // Get font metrics for the current font
92        FontMetrics fm = g.getFontMetrics();
93
94        // Find the center location to display
95        int stringWidth = fm.stringWidth(message);
96        int stringAscent = fm.getAscent();
97        // Get the position of the leftmost character in the baseline
98        xCoordinate = getWidth() / 2 - stringWidth / 2;
99        yCoordinate = getHeight() / 2 + stringAscent / 2;
100     }
101
102     g.drawString(message, xCoordinate, yCoordinate);
103   }
104
105   /** Move the message left */
106   public void moveLeft() {
107     xCoordinate -= interval;
108     repaint();
109   }
110
111   /** Move the message right */
112   public void moveRight() {
113     xCoordinate += interval;
114     repaint();
115   }
116
117   /** Move the message up */
118   public void moveUp() {
119     yCoordinate -= interval;
120     repaint();
121   }
122
123   /** Move the message down */
124   public void moveDown() {
125     yCoordinate += interval;
126     repaint();
127   }
128
```

override
getPreferredSize

```
129   /** Override get method for preferredSize */
130   public Dimension getPreferredSize() {
131     return new Dimension(200, 30);
132   }
133 }
```

The `paintComponent` method displays the message centered, if the `centered` property is true (line 90). `message` is initialized to "Welcome to Java" in line 8. If it is not initialized, a `NullPointerException` runtime error would occur when you create a `MessagePanel` using the no-arg constructor, because `message` would be `null` in line 102.

 Caution

The `MessagePanel` class uses the properties `xCoordinate` and `yCoordinate` to specify the position of the message displayed on the panel. Do not use the property names `x` and `y`, because they are already defined in the `Component` class to return the position of the component in the parent's coordinate system using `getX()` and `getY()`.

Note
The Component class has the setBackground, setForeground, and setFont methods. These methods are for setting colors and fonts for the entire component. Suppose you want to draw several messages in a panel with different colors and fonts; you have to use the setColor and setFont methods in the Graphics class to set the color and font for the current drawing.

Note
One of the key features of Java programming is the reuse of classes. Throughout the book, reusable classes are developed and later reused. MessagePanel is an example of this, as are Loan in §9.5 and FigurePanel in §14.7. It can be reused whenever you need to display a message on a panel. To make your class reusable in a wide range of applications, you should provide a variety of ways to use it. MessagePanel provides many properties and methods that will be used in several examples in the book. §14.12 presents another useful and reusable class for displaying a clock on a panel graphically.

design classes for reuse

14.12 Case Study: The **StillClock** Class

This case study develops a class that displays a clock on a panel. The contract of the class is shown in Figure 14.22.

Video Note
StillClock class

FIGURE 14.22 StillClock displays an analog clock.

Let us first write a test program in Listing 14.11 that uses the StillClock class to display an analog clock and uses the MessagePanel class to display the hour, minute, and second in a panel, as shown in Figure 14.23(a).

LISTING 14.11 DisplayClock.java

```
1 import java.awt.*;
2 import javax.swing.*;
3
4 public class DisplayClock extends JFrame {
5   public DisplayClock() {
6     // Create an analog clock for the current time
7     StillClock clock = new StillClock();
8
9     // Display hour, minute, and seconds in the message panel
```

create a clock

create a message panel

```
10    MessagePanel messagePanel = new MessagePanel(clock.getHour() +
11      ":" + clock.getMinute() + ":" + clock.getSecond());
12    messagePanel.setCentered(true);
13    messagePanel.setForeground(Color.blue);
14    messagePanel.setFont(new Font("Courie", Font.BOLD, 16));
15
16    // Add the clock and message panel to the frame
17    add(clock);
18    add(messagePanel, BorderLayout.SOUTH);
19  }
20
21  public static void main(String[] args) {
22    DisplayClock frame = new DisplayClock();
23    frame.setTitle("DisplayClock");
24    frame.setSize(300, 350);
25    frame.setLocationRelativeTo(null); // Center the frame
26    frame.setDefaultCloseOperation(JFrame.EXIT_ON_CLOSE);
27    frame.setVisible(true);
28  }
29 }
```

add a clock
add a message panel

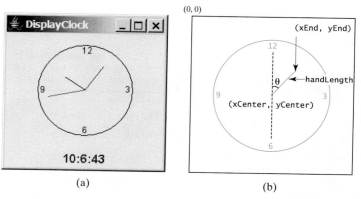

(a)   (b)

FIGURE 14.23 (a) The DisplayClock program displays a clock that shows the current time. (b) The end point of a clock hand can be determined given the spanning angle, the hand length, and the center point.

skip implementation?

The rest of this section explains how to implement the StillClock class. Since you can use the class without knowing how it is implemented, you may skip the implementation if you wish.

implementation

To draw a clock, you need to draw a circle and three hands for second, minute, and hour. To draw a hand, you need to specify the two ends of the line. As shown in Figure 14.23(b), one end is the center of the clock at (xCenter, yCenter); the other end, at (xEnd, yEnd), is determined by the following formula:

```
xEnd = xCenter + handLength × sin(θ)
yEnd = yCenter - handLength × cos(θ)
```

Since there are sixty seconds in one minute, the angle for the second hand is

```
second × (2π/60)
```

The position of the minute hand is determined by the minute and second. The exact minute value combined with seconds is minute + second/60. For example, if the time is 3 minutes and 30 seconds, the total minutes are 3.5. Since there are sixty minutes in one hour, the angle for the minute hand is

(minute + second/60) × (2π/60)

Since one circle is divided into twelve hours, the angle for the hour hand is

(hour + minute/60 + second/(60 × 60)) × (2π/12)

For simplicity, you can omit the seconds in computing the angles of the minute hand and the hour hand, because they are very small and can be neglected. Therefore, the end points for the second hand, minute hand, and hour hand can be computed as:

```
xSecond = xCenter + secondHandLength × sin(second × (2π/60))
ySecond = yCenter - secondHandLength × cos(second × (2π/60))
xMinute = xCenter + minuteHandLength × sin(minute × (2π/60))
yMinute = yCenter - minuteHandLength × cos(minute × (2π/60))
xHour = xCenter + hourHandLength × sin((hour + minute/60) × (2π/60))
yHour = yCenter - hourHandLength × cos((hour + minute/60) × (2π/60))
```

The StillClock class is implemented in Listing 14.12.

LISTING 14.12 StillClock.java

```java
1  import java.awt.*;
2  import javax.swing.*;
3  import java.util.*;
4
5  public class StillClock extends JPanel {
6    private int hour;
7    private int minute;
8    private int second;
9
10   /** Construct a default clock with the current time*/
11   public StillClock() {
12     setCurrentTime();
13   }
14
15   /** Construct a clock with specified hour, minute, and second */
16   public StillClock(int hour, int minute, int second) {
17     this.hour = hour;
18     this.minute = minute;
19     this.second = second;
20   }
21
22   /** Return hour */
23   public int getHour() {
24     return hour;
25   }
26
27   /** Set a new hour */
28   public void setHour(int hour) {
29     this.hour = hour;
30     repaint();                                           repaint panel
31   }
32
33   /** Return minute */
34   public int getMinute() {
35     return minute;
36   }
37
```

repaint panel

repaint panel

override **paintComponent**

```
38   /** Set a new minute */
39   public void setMinute(int minute) {
40     this.minute = minute;
41     repaint();
42   }
43
44   /** Return second */
45   public int getSecond() {
46     return second;
47   }
48
49   /** Set a new second */
50   public void setSecond(int second) {
51     this.second = second;
52     repaint();
53   }
54
55   /** Draw the clock */
56   protected void paintComponent(Graphics g) {
57     super.paintComponent(g);
58
59     // Initialize clock parameters
60     int clockRadius =
61       (int)(Math.min(getWidth(), getHeight()) * 0.8 * 0.5);
62     int xCenter = getWidth() / 2;
63     int yCenter = getHeight() / 2;
64
65     // Draw circle
66     g.setColor(Color.black);
67     g.drawOval(xCenter - clockRadius, yCenter - clockRadius,
68       2 * clockRadius, 2 * clockRadius);
69     g.drawString("12", xCenter - 5, yCenter - clockRadius + 12);
70     g.drawString("9", xCenter - clockRadius + 3, yCenter + 5);
71     g.drawString("3", xCenter + clockRadius - 10, yCenter + 3);
72     g.drawString("6", xCenter - 3, yCenter + clockRadius - 3);
73
74     // Draw second hand
75     int sLength = (int)(clockRadius * 0.8);
76     int xSecond = (int)(xCenter + sLength *
77       Math.sin(second * (2 * Math.PI / 60)));
78     int ySecond = (int)(yCenter - sLength *
79       Math.cos(second * (2 * Math.PI / 60)));
80     g.setColor(Color.red);
81     g.drawLine(xCenter, yCenter, xSecond, ySecond);
82
83     // Draw minute hand
84     int mLength = (int)(clockRadius * 0.65);
85     int xMinute = (int)(xCenter + mLength *
86       Math.sin(minute * (2 * Math.PI / 60)));
87     int yMinute = (int)(yCenter - mLength *
88       Math.cos(minute * (2 * Math.PI / 60)));
89     g.setColor(Color.blue);
90     g.drawLine(xCenter, yCenter, xMinute, yMinute);
91
92     // Draw hour hand
93     int hLength = (int)(clockRadius * 0.5);
94     int xHour = (int)(xCenter + hLength *
95       Math.sin((hour % 12 + minute / 60.0) * (2 * Math.PI / 12)));
96     int yHour = (int)(yCenter - hLength *
97       Math.cos((hour % 12 + minute / 60.0) * (2 * Math.PI / 12)));
```

```
 98        g.setColor(Color.green);
 99        g.drawLine(xCenter, yCenter, xHour, yHour);
100    }
101
102    public void setCurrentTime() {
103        // Construct a calendar for the current date and time
104        Calendar calendar = new GregorianCalendar();
105
106        // Set current hour, minute and second
107        this.hour = calendar.get(Calendar.HOUR_OF_DAY);
108        this.minute = calendar.get(Calendar.MINUTE);
109        this.second = calendar.get(Calendar.SECOND);
110    }
111
112    public Dimension getPreferredSize() {
113        return new Dimension(200, 200);
114    }
115 }
```

get current time

override
getPreferredSize

The program enables the clock size to adjust as the frame resizes. Every time you resize the frame, the `paintComponent` method is automatically invoked to paint the new frame. The `paintComponent` method displays the clock in proportion to the panel width (`getWidth()`) and height (`getHeight()`) (lines 60–63 in `StillClock`).

14.13 Displaying Images

You learned how to create image icons and display them in labels and buttons in §13.10, "Image Icons." For example, the following statements create an image icon and display it in a label:

```
ImageIcon icon = new ImageIcon("image/us.gif");
JLabel jlblImage = new JLabel(imageIcon);
```

An image icon displays a fixed-size image. To display an image in a flexible size, you need to use the `java.awt.Image` class. An image can be created from an image icon using the `getImage()` method as follows:

```
Image image = imageIcon.getImage();
```

Using a label as an area for displaying images is simple and convenient, but you don't have much control over how the image is displayed. A more flexible way to display images is to use the `drawImage` method of the `Graphics` class on a panel. Four versions of the `drawImage` method are shown in Figure 14.24.

`ImageObserver` is an asynchronous update interface that receives notifications of image information as the image is constructed. The `Component` class implements `ImageObserver`. Therefore, every GUI component is an instance of `ImageObserver`. To draw images using the `drawImage` method in a Swing component, such as `JPanel`, override the `paintComponent` method to tell the component how to display the image in the panel.

Listing 14.13 gives the code that displays an image from `image/us.gif`. The file `image/us.gif` (line 20) is under the class directory. An `Image` object is obtained in line 21. The `drawImage` method displays the image to fill in the whole panel, as shown in Figure 14.25.

java.awt.Graphics	
+drawImage(image: Image, x: int, y: int, bgcolor: Color, observer: ImageObserver): void	Draws the image in a specified location. The image's top-left corner is at (x, y) in the graphics context's coordinate space. Transparent pixels in the image are drawn in the specified color bgcolor. The observer is the object on which the image is displayed. The image is cut off if it is larger than the area it is being drawn on.
+drawImage(image: Image, x: int, y: int, observer: ImageObserver): void	Same as the preceding method except that it does not specify a background color.
+drawImage(image: Image, x: int, y: int, width: int, height: int, observer: ImageObserver): void	Draws a scaled version of the image that can fill all of the available space in the specified rectangle.
+drawImage(image: Image, x: int, y: int, width: int, height: int, bgcolor: Color, observer: ImageObserver): void	Same as the preceding method except that it provides a solid background color behind the image being drawn.

FIGURE 14.24 You can apply the drawImage method on a Graphics object to display an image in a GUI component.

LISTING 14.13 DisplayImage.java

```java
1  import java.awt.*;
2  import javax.swing.*;
3
4  public class DisplayImage extends JFrame {
5    public DisplayImage() {
6      add(new ImagePanel());
7    }
8
9    public static void main(String[] args) {
10     JFrame frame = new DisplayImage();
11     frame.setTitle("DisplayImage");
12     frame.setSize(300, 300);
13     frame.setLocationRelativeTo(null); // Center the frame
14     frame.setDefaultCloseOperation(JFrame.EXIT_ON_CLOSE);
15     frame.setVisible(true);
16   }
17
18   // Inner class: Define the panel for showing an image
19   static class ImagePanel extends JPanel {
20     ImageIcon imageIcon = new ImageIcon("image/us.gif");
21     Image image = imageIcon.getImage();
22
23     /** Draw image on the panel */
24     public void paintComponent(Graphics g) {
25       super.paintComponent(g);
26
27       if (image != null)
28         g.drawImage(image, 0, 0, getWidth(), getHeight(), this);
29     }
30   }
31 }
```

add panel

inner class
create image icon
get image

override **paintComponent**

draw image

FIGURE 14.25 An image is displayed in a panel.

14.14 Case Study: The **ImageViewer** Class

Displaying an image is a common task in Java programming. This case study develops a reusable component named ImageViewer that displays an image on a panel. The class contains the properties image, stretched, xCoordinate, and yCoordinate, with associated accessor and mutator methods, as shown in Figure 14.26.

FIGURE 14.26 The ImageViewer class displays an image on a panel.

You can use images in Swing components like JLabel and JButton, but these images are not stretchable. The image in an ImageViewer can be stretched.   stretchable image

Let us write a test program in Listing 14.14 that displays six images using the ImageViewer class. Figure 14.27 shows a sample run of the program.

LISTING 14.14 SixFlags.java

```java
1 import javax.swing.*;
2 import java.awt.*;
3
4 public class SixFlags extends JFrame {
5   public SixFlags() {
6     Image image1 = new ImageIcon("image/us.gif").getImage();
7     Image image2 = new ImageIcon("image/ca.gif").getImage();
8     Image image3 = new ImageIcon("image/india.gif").getImage();
9     Image image4 = new ImageIcon("image/uk.gif").getImage();
10    Image image5 = new ImageIcon("image/china.gif").getImage();
11    Image image6 = new ImageIcon("image/norway.gif").getImage();
12
13    setLayout(new GridLayout(2, 0, 5, 5));
14    add(new ImageViewer(image1));
15    add(new ImageViewer(image2));
16    add(new ImageViewer(image3));
17    add(new ImageViewer(image4));
18    add(new ImageViewer(image5));
19    add(new ImageViewer(image6));
20  }
21
22  public static void main(String[] args) {
23    SixFlags frame = new SixFlags();
24    frame.setTitle("SixFlags");
25    frame.setSize(400, 320);
26    frame.setLocationRelativeTo(null); // Center the frame
27    frame.setDefaultCloseOperation(JFrame.EXIT_ON_CLOSE);
28    frame.setVisible(true);
29  }
30 }
```

create image

create image viewer

FIGURE 14.27 Six images are displayed in six `ImageViewer` components.

implementation

skip implementation?

The `ImageViewer` class is implemented in Listing 14.15. (*Note: You may skip the implementation.*) The accessor and mutator methods for the properties `image`, `stretched`, `xCoordinate`, and `yCoordinate` are easy to implement. The `paintComponent` method (lines 26–35) displays the image on the panel. Line 29 ensures that the image is not `null` before displaying it. Line 30 checks whether the image is stretched or not.

LISTING 14.15 `ImageViewer.java`

properties

constructor

constructor

image null?

stretched

non-stretched

```
1  import java.awt.*;
2  import javax.swing.*;
3
4  public class ImageViewer extends JPanel {
5    /** Hold value of property image. */
6    private java.awt.Image image;
7
8    /** Hold value of property stretched. */
9    private boolean stretched = true;
10
11   /** Hold value of property xCoordinate. */
12   private int xCoordinate;
13
14   /** Hold value of property yCoordinate. */
15   private int yCoordinate;
16
17   /** Construct an empty image viewer */
18   public ImageViewer() {
19   }
20
21   /** Construct an image viewer for a specified Image object */
22   public ImageViewer(Image image) {
23     this.image = image;
24   }
25
26   protected void paintComponent(Graphics g) {
27     super.paintComponent(g);
28
29     if (image != null)
30       if (isStretched())
31         g.drawImage(image, xCoordinate, yCoordinate,
32           getSize().width, getSize().height, this);
33       else
34         g.drawImage(image, xCoordinate, yCoordinate, this);
35   }
36
37   /** Return value of property image */
38   public java.awt.Image getImage() {
39     return image;
40   }
41
```

```
42    /** Set a new value for property image */
43    public void setImage(java.awt.Image image) {
44      this.image = image;
45      repaint();
46    }
47
48    /** Return value of property stretched */
49    public boolean isStretched() {
50      return stretched;
51    }
52
53    /** Set a new value for property stretched */
54    public void setStretched(boolean stretched) {
55      this.stretched = stretched;
56      repaint();
57    }
58
59    /** Return value of property xCoordinate */
60    public int getXCoordinate() {
61      return xCoordinate;
62    }
63
64    /** Set a new value for property xCoordinate */
65    public void setXCoordinate(int xCoordinate) {
66      this.xCoordinate = xCoordinate;
67      repaint();
68    }
69
70    /** Return value of property yCoordinate */
71    public int getYCoordinate() {
72      return yCoordinate;
73    }
74
75    /** Set a new value for property yCoordinate */
76    public void setYCoordinate(int yCoordinate) {
77      this.yCoordinate = yCoordinate;
78      repaint();
79    }
80 }
```

CHAPTER SUMMARY

■ Each component has its own coordinate system with the origin (0, 0) at the upper-left corner of the window. The *x*-coordinate increases to the right, and the *y*-coordinate increases downward.

■ The Graphics class is an abstract class for displaying figures and images on the screen on different platforms. The Graphics class is implemented on the native platform in the JVM. When you use the paintComponent(g) method to paint on a GUI component, this g is an instance of a concrete subclass of the abstract Graphics class for the specific platform. The Graphics class encapsulates the platform details and enables you to draw things uniformly without concern for the specific platform.

■ Invoking super.paintComponent(g) is necessary to ensure that the viewing area is cleared before a new drawing is displayed. The user can request the component to be redisplayed by invoking the repaint() method defined in the Component class. Invoking repaint() causes paintComponent to be invoked by the JVM. The user should never invoke `paintComponent` directly. For this reason, the `protected` visibility is sufficient for `paintComponent`.

■ Normally you use `JPanel` as a canvas. To draw on a `JPanel`, you create a new class that extends `JPanel` and overrides the `paintComponent` method to tell the panel how to draw things.

■ You can set fonts for the components or subjects you draw, and use font metrics to measure font size. Fonts and font metrics are encapsulated in the classes `Font` and `FontMetrics`. `FontMetrics` can be used to compute the exact length and width of a string, which is helpful for measuring the size of a string in order to display it in the right position.

■ The `Component` class has the `setBackground`, `setForeground`, and `setFont` methods. These methods are used to set colors and fonts for the entire component. Suppose you want to draw several messages in a panel with different colors and fonts; you have to use the `setColor` and `setFont` methods in the `Graphics` class to set the color and font for the current drawing.

■ To display an image, first create an image icon. You can then use `ImageIcon`'s `getImage()` method to get an `Image` object for the image and draw the image using the `drawImage` method in the `java.awt.Graphics` class.

REVIEW QUESTIONS

Sections 14.2–14.3

14.1 Suppose that you want to draw a new message below an existing message. Should the x-coordinate, y-coordinate, or both increase or decrease?

14.2 Why does `jlblBanner.getGraphics()` in line 9 in Listing 14.1 return `null`? What is the reason for showing the message dialog box in line 19 in Listing 14.1? In line 9, `jlblBanner.getGraphics()` is used to return a `Graphics` object. In line 21, why do you have to use `frame.jlblBanner.getGraphics()` in the main method?

Sections 14.4–14.5

14.3 Describe the `paintComponent` method. Where is it defined? How is it invoked? Can it be directly invoked? How can the program cause this method be invoked?

14.4 Why is the `paintComponent` method `protected`? What happens if you change it to `public` or `private` in a subclass? Why is `super.paintComponent(g)` invoked in line 25 in Listing 14.2 and in line 21 in Listing 14.3?

14.5 Can you draw things on any Swing GUI component? Why should you use a panel as a canvas for drawings rather than a label or a button?

Sections 14.6–14.9

14.6 Describe the methods for drawing strings, lines, rectangles, round-cornered rectangles, 3D rectangles, ovals, arcs, polygons, and polylines.

14.7 Describe the methods for filling rectangles, round-cornered rectangle, ovals, arcs, and polygons.

14.8 How do you get and set colors and fonts in a `Graphics` object?

14.9   Write a statement to draw the following shapes:

- Draw a thick line from (10, 10) to (70, 30). You can draw several lines next to each other to create the effect of one thick line.
- Draw/fill a rectangle of width 100 and height 50 with the upper-left corner at (10, 10).
- Draw/fill a round-cornered rectangle with width 100, height 200, corner horizontal diameter 40, and corner vertical diameter 20.
- Draw/fill a circle with radius 30.
- Draw/fill an oval with width 50 and height 100.
- Draw the upper half of a circle with radius 50.
- Draw/fill a polygon connecting the following points: (20, 40), (30, 50), (40, 90), (90, 10), (10, 30).

Sections 14.10–14.12

14.10   How do you find the leading, ascent, descent, and height of a font? How do you find the exact length in pixels of a string in a `Graphics` object?

14.11   If `message` is not initialized in line 8 in Listing 14.10, MessagePanel.java, what will happen when you create a `MessagePanel` using its no-arg constructor?

14.12   The following program is supposed to display a message on the panel, but nothing is displayed. There are problems in lines 2 and 14. Correct them.

```
 1 public class TestDrawMessage extends javax.swing.JFrame {
 2   public void TestDrawMessage() {
 3     add(new DrawMessage());
 4   }
 5
 6   public static void main(String[] args) {
 7     javax.swing.JFrame frame = new TestDrawMessage();
 8     frame.setSize(100, 200);
 9     frame.setVisible(true);
10   }
11 }
12
13 class DrawMessage extends javax.swing.JPanel {
14   protected void PaintComponent(java.awt.Graphics g) {
15     super.paintComponent(g);
16     g.drawString("Welcome to Java", 20, 20);
17   }
18 }
```

Sections 14.13–14.14

14.13   How do you create an `Image` object from the `ImageIcon` object?

14.14   How do you create an `ImageIcon` object from an `Image` object?

14.15   Describe the `drawImage` method in the `Graphics` class.

14.16   Explain the differences between displaying images in a `JLabel` and in a `JPanel`.

14.17   Which package contains `ImageIcon`, and which contains `Image`?

PROGRAMMING EXERCISES

Sections 14.2–14.9

14.1* (*Displaying a* 3 × 3 *grid*) Write a program that displays a 3 × 3 grid, as shown in Figure 14.28(a). Use red color for vertical lines and blue color for horizontal lines.

(a)   (b)   (c)

FIGURE 14.28 (a) Exercise 14.1 displays a grid. (b) Exercise 14.2 displays two objects of OvalButton. (c) Exercise 14.3 displays a checkerboard.

14.2** (*Creating a custom button class*) Develop a custom button class named OvalButton that extends JButton and displays the button text inside an oval. Figure 14.28(b) shows two buttons created using the OvalButton class.

14.3* (*Displaying a checkerboard*) Exercise 13.10 displays a checkerboard in which each white and black cell is a JButton. Rewrite a program that draws a checkerboard on a JPanel using the drawing methods in the Graphics class, as shown in Figure 14.28(c).

14.4* (*Displaying a multiplication table*) Write a program that displays a multiplication table in a panel using the drawing methods, as shown in Figure 14.29(a).

(a)   (b)

FIGURE 14.29 (a) Exercise 14.4 displays a multiplication table. (b) Exercise 14.5 displays numbers in a triangle formation.

14.5** (*Displaying numbers in a triangular pattern*) Write a program that displays numbers in a triangular pattern, as shown in Figure 14.29(b). The number of lines in the display changes to fit the window as the window resizes.

14.6** (*Improving FigurePanel*) The FigurePanel class in Listing 14.5 can display lines, rectangles, round-cornered rectangles, and ovals. Add appropriate new code in the class to display arcs and polygons. Write a test program to display the shapes as shown in Figure 14.30(a) using the new FigurePanel class.

(a)   (b)   (c)

FIGURE 14.30 (a) Four panels of geometric figures are displayed in a frame of `GridLayout`. (b) `TicTacToe` cells display X, O, or nothing randomly. (c) Exercise 14.8 draws an octagon.

14.7** (*Displaying a TicTacToe board*) Create a custom panel that displays X, O, or nothing. What to display is randomly decided whenever a panel is repainted. Use the `Math.random()` method to generate an integer 0, 1, or 2, which corresponds to displaying X, O, or nothing. Create a frame that contains nine custom panels, as shown in Figure 14.30(b).

14.8** (*Drawing an octagon*) Write a program that draws an octagon, as shown in Figure 14.30(c).

14.9* (*Creating four fans*) Write a program that places four fans in a frame of `GridLayout` with two rows and two columns, as shown in Figure 14.31(a).

(a)   (b)   (c)

FIGURE 14.31 (a) Exercise 14.9 draws four fans. (b) Exercise 14.10 draws a cylinder. (c) Exercise 14.11 draws a diagram for function $f(x) = x^2$.

14.10* (*Creating a cylinder*) Write a program that draws a cylinder, as shown in Figure 14.31(b).

14.11** (*Plotting the square function*) Write a program that draws a diagram for the function $f(x) = x^2$ (see Figure 14.31(c)).

Hint: Add points to a polygon p using the following loop:

```
double scaleFactor = 0.1;

for (int x = -100; x <= 100; x++) {
   p.addPoint(x + 200, 200 - (int)(scaleFactor * x * x));
}
```

Connect the points using `g.drawPolyline(p.xpoints, p.ypoints, p.npoints)` for a `Graphics` object g. `p.xpoints` returns an array of x-coordinates, `p.ypoints` returns an array of y-coordinates, and `p.npoints` returns the number of points in `Polygon` object p.

14.12** (*Plotting the sine function*) Write a program that draws a diagram for the sine function, as shown in Figure 14.32(a).

(a)   (b)

FIGURE 14.32 (a) Exercise 14.12 draws a diagram for function $f(x) = sin(x)$. (b) Exercise 14.13 draws the sine and cosine functions.

Hint: The Unicode for π is \u03c0. To display -2π, use `g.drawString("-2\-u03c0", x, y)`. For a trigonometric function like `sin(x)`, `x` is in radians. Use the following loop to add the points to a polygon `p`:

```
for (intx = -100; x <= 100; x++) {
  p.addPoint(x + 200,
    100 - (int)(50 * Math.sin((x / 100.0) * 2 * Math.PI)));
}
```

-2π is at ($100, 100$), the center of the axis is at ($200, 100$), and 2π is at ($300, 100$). Use the `drawPolyline` method in the `Graphics` class to connect the points.

14.13** (*Plotting functions using abstract methods*) Write an abstract class that draws the diagram for a function. The class is defined as follows:

```
public abstract class AbstractDrawFunction extends JPanel {
  /** Polygon to hold the points */
  private Polygon p = new Polygon();

  protected AbstractDrawFunction () {
    drawFunction();
  }

  /** Return the y-coordinate */
  abstract double f(double x);

  /** Obtain points for x-coordinates 100, 101, ..., 300 */
  public void drawFunction() {
    for (int x = -100; x <= 100; x++) {
      p.addPoint(x + 200, 200 - (int)f(x));
    }
  }

  /** Implement paintComponent to draw axes, labels, and
   *  connecting points
   */
  protected void paintComponent(Graphics g) {
    // To be completed by you
  }
}
```

Test the class with the following functions:

```
f(x) = x²;
f(x) = sin(x);
f(x) = cos(x);
f(x) = tan(x);
f(x) = cos(x) + 5sin(x);
f(x) = 5cos(x) + sin(x);
f(x) = log(x) + x²;
```

For each function, create a class that extends the `AbstractDrawFunction` class and implements the `f` method. Figure 14.32(b) displays the drawings for the sine function and the cosine function.

14.14** (*Displaying a bar chart*) Write a program that uses a bar chart to display the percentages of the overall grade represented by projects, quizzes, midterm exams, and the final exam, as shown in Figure 14.1(a). Suppose that projects take **20** percent and are displayed in red, quizzes take **10** percent and are displayed in blue, midterm exams take **30** percent and are displayed in green, and the final exam takes **40** percent and is displayed in orange.

14.15** (*Displaying a pie chart*) Write a program that uses a pie chart to display the percentages of the overall grade represented by projects, quizzes, midterm exams, and the final exam, as shown in Figure 14.33(a). Suppose that projects take **20** percent and are displayed in red, quizzes take **10** percent and are displayed in blue, midterm exams take **30** percent and are displayed in green, and the final exam takes **40** percent and is displayed in orange.

(a) (b) (c)

FIGURE 14.33   (a) Exercise 14.15 uses a pie chart to show the percentages of projects, quizzes, midterm exams, and final exam in the overall grade. (b) Exercise 14.16 displays font properties in a tool tip text. (c) Exercise 14.17 uses `MessagePanel` to display four strings.

14.16 (*Obtaining font information*) Write a program that displays the message "Java is fun" in a panel. Set the panel's font to `TimesRoman`, `bold`, and `20` pixel. Display the font's leading, ascent, descent, height, and the string width as a tool tip text for the panel, as shown in Figure 14.33(b).

14.17 (*Using the `MessagePanel` class*) Write a program that displays four messages, as shown in Figure 14.33(c).

14.18 (*Using the `StillClock` class*) Write a program that displays two clocks. The hour, minute, and second values are 4, 20, 45 for the first clock, and 22, 46, 15 for the second clock, as shown in Figure 14.34(a).

14.19* (*Random time*) Modify the `StillClock` class with three new Boolean properties: `hourHandVisible`, `minuteHandVisible`, and `secondHandVisible`, and their associated accessor and mutator methods. You can use the `set` methods to make a hand visible or invisible. Write a test program that displays only the hour

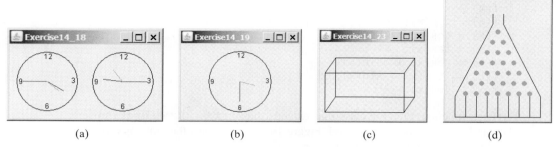

FIGURE 14.34 (a) Exercise 14.18 displays two clocks. (b) Exercise 14.19 displays a clock with random hour and minute values. (c) Exercise 14.23 displays a rectanguloid. (d) Exercise 14.24 simulates a bean machine.

and minute hands. The hour and minute values are randomly generated. The hour is between 0 and 11, and the minute is either 0 or 30, as shown in Figure 14.34(b).

14.20** (*Drawing a detailed clock*) Modify the StillClock class in §14.12, "Case Study: The StillClock Class," to draw the clock with more details on the hours and minutes, as shown in Figure 14.1(b).

14.21** (*Displaying a TicTacToe board with images*) Rewrite Exercise 13.7 to display an image in a JPanel instead of displaying an image icon in a JLabel.

14.22* (*Displaying a STOP sign*) Write a program that displays a STOP sign, as shown in Figure 14.1(c). The hexagon is in red and the sign is in white. (*Hint*: See Listing 14.7, DrawPolygon.java, and Listing 14.8, TestCenterMessage.java.)

14.23 (*Displaying a rectanguloid*) Write a program that displays a rectanguloid, as shown in Figure 14.34(c). The cube should grow and shrink as the frame grows or shrinks.

14.24 (*Game: bean machine*) Write a program that displays a bean machine introduced in Exercise 6.29. The bean machine should be centered in a resizable panel, as shown in Figure 14.34(d).

CHAPTER 15

EVENT-DRIVEN PROGRAMMING

Objectives

- To describe events, event sources, and event classes (§15.2).
- To declare listener classes, register listener objects with the source object, and write the code to handle events (§15.3).
- To declare listener classes using inner classes (§15.3.1).
- To declare listener classes using anonymous inner classes (§15.3.2).
- To write programs to deal with `ActionEvent` (§15.3.3).
- To write programs to deal with `WindowEvent` (§15.3.4).
- To simplify coding for listener classes using listener interface adapters (§15.3.5).
- To write programs to deal with `MouseEvent` (§15.4).
- To write programs to deal with `KeyEvent` (§15.5).
- To use the `javax.swing.Timer` class to control animations (§15.6).

15.1 Introduction

problem

Suppose you wish to write a program that animates a rising flag, as shown in Figure 15.1. How do you accomplish the task? There are several solutions to this problem. An effective way to solve it is to use event-driven programming, which is the subject of this chapter.

FIGURE 15.1 A flag is rising upward.

event-driven programming

All the programs so far execute in a procedural order. This chapter introduces *event-driven programming*, in which code is executed when an event occurs (e.g., a button click, or a mouse movement).

§11.6, "Example: The `ActionListener` Interface," gave you a taste of event-driven programming. You probably have many questions, such as why a listener class is declared to implement the `ActionListener` interface. This chapter will give you all the answers.

15.2 Event and Event Source

When you run Java GUI programs, the program interacts with the user, and the events drive its execution. An *event* can be defined as a signal to the program that something has happened. Events are triggered either by external user actions, such as mouse movements, button clicks, and keystrokes, or by internal program activities, such as a timer. The program can choose to respond to or ignore an event.

event

fire event
source object

The component on which an event is *fired* or *generated* is called the *source object* or *source component*. For example, a button is the source object for a button-clicking action event. An event is an instance of an event class. The root class of the event classes is `java.util.EventObject`. The hierarchical relationships of some event classes are shown in Figure 15.2.

getSource()

An event object contains whatever properties are pertinent to the event. You can identify the source object of an event using the `getSource()` instance method in the `EventObject` class. The subclasses of `EventObject` deal with special types of events, such as action events, window events, component events, mouse events, and key events. Table 15.1 lists external user actions, source objects, and event types fired.

```
EventObject ◁── AWTEvent ◁── ActionEvent        ContainerEvent
                            AdjustmentEvent      FocusEvent        MouseEvent
                            ComponentEvent ◁──   InputEvent ◁──
                            ItemEvent            PaintEvent        KeyEvent
                            TextEvent            WindowEvent
                ListSelectionEvent
```

FIGURE 15.2 An event is an object of the `EventObject` class.

TABLE 15.1   User Action, Source Object, and Event Type

User Action	Source Object	Event Type Fired
Click a button	`JButton`	`ActionEvent`
Press return on a text field	`JTextField`	`ActionEvent`
Select a new item	`JComboBox`	`ItemEvent`, `ActionEvent`
Select item(s)	`JList`	`ListSelectionEvent`
Click a check box	`JCheckBox`	`ItemEvent`, `ActionEvent`
Click a radio button	`JRadioButton`	`ItemEvent`, `ActionEvent`
Select a menu item	`JMenuItem`	`ActionEvent`
Move the scroll bar	`JScrollBar`	`AdjustmentEvent`
Window opened, closed, iconified, deiconified, or closing	`Window`	`WindowEvent`
Mouse pressed, released, clicked, entered, or exited	`Component`	`MouseEvent`
Mouse moved or dragged	`Component`	`MouseEvent`
Key released or pressed	`Component`	`KeyEvent`
Component added or removed from the container	`Container`	`ContainerEvent`
Component moved, resized, hidden, or shown	`Component`	`ComponentEvent`
Component gained or lost focus	`Component`	`FocusEvent`

Note

If a component can fire an event, any subclass of the component can fire the same type of event. For example, every GUI component can fire `MouseEvent`, `KeyEvent`, `FocusEvent`, and `ComponentEvent`, since `Component` is the superclass of all GUI components.

Note

All the event classes in Figure 15.2 are included in the `java.awt.event` package except `ListSelectionEvent`, which is in the `javax.swing.event` package. AWT events were originally designed for AWT components, but many Swing components fire them.

15.3 Listeners, Registrations, and Handling Events

Java uses a delegation-based model for event handling: a source object fires an event, and an object interested in the event handles the event. The latter object is called a *listener*. For an object to be a listener for an event on a source object, two things are needed, as shown in Figure 15.3.

  1. The listener object must be an instance of the corresponding event-listener interface to ensure that the listener has the correct method for processing the event. Java provides a listener interface for every type of GUI event. The listener interface is usually named *X*`Listener` for *X*`Event`, with the exception of `MouseMotionListener`. For example,

listener

listener interface

*X*Listener/*X*Event

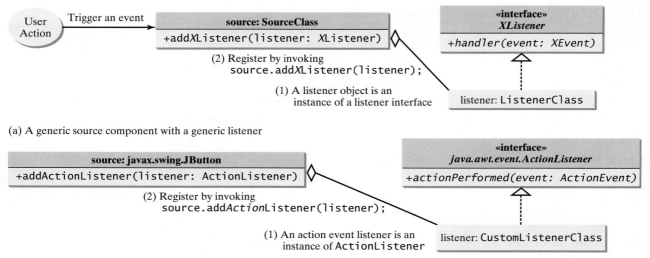

(a) A generic source component with a generic listener

(b) A JButton source component with an ActionListener

FIGURE 15.3 A listener must be an instance of a listener interface and must be registered with a source component.

ActionEvent/ActionListener

the corresponding listener interface for **ActionEvent** is **ActionListener**; each listener for **ActionEvent** should implement the **ActionListener** interface. Table 15.2 lists event types, the corresponding listener interfaces, and the methods defined in the listener interfaces. The listener interface contains the method(s), known as the *handler(s)*, invoked by the source object to process the event.

handler

2. The listener object must be registered by the source object. Registration methods are dependent on the event type. For **ActionEvent**, the method is **add-ActionListener**. In general, the method is named **add***X***Listener** for *X***Event**. A source object may fire several types of events. For each event, the source object maintains a list of listeners and notifies all the registered listeners by invoking the *handler* on the listener object to respond to the event, as shown in Figure 15.4. (Figure 15.4 shows the internal implementation of a source class. You don't have to know how a source class like **JButton** is implemented in order to use it. Nevertheless, knowing this will help you to understand the Java event-driven programming framework and is the first step in being able to develop custom source components in the future).

register listener

Let's revisit Listing 11.8, HandleEvent.java. Since a **JButton** object fires **ActionEvent**, a listener object for **ActionEvent** must be an instance of **ActionListener**, so the listener class implements **ActionListener** in line 34. The source object invokes **addActionListener(listener)** to register a listener, as follows:

create source object
create listener object
register listener

```java
JButton jbtOK = new JButton("OK"); // Line 7 in Listing 11.8
ActionListener listener1 = new OKListener(); // Line 18 in Listing 11.8
jbtOK.addActionListener(listener1); // Line 20 in Listing 11.8
```

TABLE 15.2   Events, Event Listeners, and Listener Methods

Event Class (Handlers)	Listener Interface	Listener Methods
ActionEvent	ActionListener	actionPerformed(ActionEvent)
ItemEvent	ItemListener	itemStateChanged(ItemEvent)
MouseEvent	MouseListener	mousePressed(MouseEvent)
		mouseReleased(MouseEvent)
		mouseEntered(MouseEvent)
		mouseExited(MouseEvent)
		mouseClicked(MouseEvent)
	MouseMotionListener	mouseDragged(MouseEvent)
		mouseMoved(MouseEvent)
KeyEvent	KeyListener	keyPressed(KeyEvent)
		keyReleased(KeyEvent)
		keyTyped(KeyEvent)
WindowEvent	WindowListener	windowClosing(WindowEvent)
		windowOpened(WindowEvent)
		windowIconified(WindowEvent)
		windowDeiconified (WindowEvent)
		windowClosed(WindowEvent)
		windowActivated(WindowEvent)
		windowDeactivated(WindowEvent)
ContainerEvent	ContainerListener	componentAdded(ContainerEvent)
		componentRemoved(ContainerEvent)
ComponentEvent	ComponentListener	componentMoved(ComponentEvent)
		componentHidden(ComponentEvent)
		componentResized(ComponentEvent)
		componentShown(ComponentEvent)
FocusEvent	FocusListener	focusGained(FocusEvent)
		focusLost(FocusEvent)
AdjustmentEvent	AdjustmentListener	adjustmentValueChanged(AdjustmentEvent)

When you click the button, the `JButton` object fires an `ActionEvent` and passes it to invoke the listener's `actionPerformed` method to handle the event.

The event object contains information pertinent to the event, which can be obtained using the methods, as shown in Figure 15.5. For example, you can use `e.getSource()` to obtain the source object in order to determine whether it is a button, a check box, or a radio button. For an action event, you can use `e.getWhen()` to obtain the time when the event occurs.

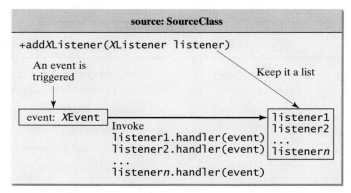

(a) Internal function of a generic source object

(b) Internal function of a JButton object

FIGURE 15.4 The source object notifies the listeners of the event by invoking the handler of the listener object.

FIGURE 15.5 You can obtain useful information from an event object.

Listing 15.1 gives an example that uses the event object in the handler. This example displays two buttons, *OK* and *Cancel*, in a frame. A message is displayed on the console to indicate which button is clicked and when, as shown in Figure 15.6.

LISTING 15.1 SimpleEventDemo.java

Video Note
Create source and listener

```
1  import javax.swing.*;
2  import java.awt.event.*;
3
4  public class SimpleEventDemo extends JFrame {
5    public SimpleEventDemo() {
6      // Create two buttons
7      JButton jbtOK = new JButton("OK");
8      JButton jbtCancel = new JButton("Cancel");
9
10     // Create a panel to hold buttons
11     JPanel panel = new JPanel();
12     panel.add(jbtOK);
13     panel.add(jbtCancel);
14
15     add(panel); // Add panel to the frame
16
17     // Register listeners
18     ListenerClass listener = new ListenerClass();
19     jbtOK.addActionListener(listener);
20     jbtCancel.addActionListener(listener);
21   }
22
23   public static void main(String[] args) {
24     JFrame frame = new SimpleEventDemo();
25     frame.setTitle("Handle Event");
26     frame.setSize(200, 150);
27     frame.setLocation(200, 100);
28     frame.setDefaultCloseOperation(JFrame.EXIT_ON_CLOSE);
29     frame.setVisible(true);
30   }
31 }
32
33 class ListenerClass implements ActionListener {
34   public void actionPerformed(ActionEvent e) {
35     System.out.println("The " + e.getActionCommand() + " button "
36       + "is clicked at\n " + new java.util.Date(e.getWhen()));
37   }
38 }
```

create listener
register listener

listener class
handle event

FIGURE 15.6   The program responds to the button action events.

The program creates a listener from `ListenerClass` (line 18). The listener is registered with both the *OK* button and the *Cancel* button (lines 19–20).

The button objects `jbtOK` and `jbtCancel` are the source of `ActionEvent`. Clicking a button causes the `actionPerformed` method in the listener to be invoked. The `e.getActionCommand()` method returns the action command from the button (line 35). By default, a button's action command is the label of the button.

The `e.getWhen()` method returns the time of the action in milliseconds since January 1, 1970, 00:00:00 GMT. The `Date` class converts the time to year, month, date, hours, minutes, and seconds (line 36).

15.3.1 Inner Class Listeners

A listener class is designed specifically to create a listener object for a GUI component (e.g., a button). The listener class will not be shared by other applications and therefore is appropriately defined inside the frame class as an inner class.

inner class

An *inner class*, or *nested class,* is a class defined within the scope of another class. The code in Figure 15.7(a) declares two separate classes, `Test` and `A`. The code in Figure 15.7(b) declares `A` as an inner class in `Test`.

```
public class Test {
  ...
}

public class A {
  ...
}
```
(a)

```
public class Test {
  ...
  // Inner class
  public class A {
    ...
  }
}
```
(b)

```
// OuterClass.java: inner class demo
public class OuterClass {
  private int data;

  /** A method in the outer class */
  public void m() {
    // Do something
  }

  // An inner class
  class InnerClass {
    /** A method in the inner class */
    public void mi() {
      // Directly reference data and method
      // defined in its outer class
      data++;
      m();
    }
  }
}
```
(c)

FIGURE 15.7 Inner classes combine dependent classes into the primary class.

The class `InnerClass` defined inside `OuterClass` in Figure 15.6(c) is another example of an inner class. An inner class may be used just like a regular class. Normally, you declare a class an inner class if it is used only by its outer class. An inner class has the following features:

- An inner class is compiled into a class named `OuterClassName$InnerClassName.class`. For example, the inner class `A` in `Test` is compiled into `Test$A.class` in Figure 15.6(b).

- An inner class can reference the data and methods defined in the outer class in which it nests, so you do not need to pass the reference of an object of the outer class to the constructor of the inner class. For this reason, inner classes can make programs simple and concise.

- An inner class can be declared with a visibility modifier subject to the same visibility rules applied to a member of the class.

- An inner class can be declared `static`. A `static` inner class can be accessed using the outer class name. A `static` inner class cannot access nonstatic members of the outer class.

- Objects of an inner class are often created in the outer class. But you can also create an object of an inner class from another class. If the inner class is nonstatic, you must first create an instance of the outer class, then use the following syntax to create an object for the inner class:

```
OuterClass.InnerClass innerObject = outerObject.new InnerClass();
```

■ If the inner class is static, use the following syntax to create an object for it:

```
OuterClass.InnerClass innerObject = new OuterClass.InnerClass();
```

Tip
A simple use of inner classes is to combine dependent classes into a primary class. This reduces the number of source files. It also makes class files easy to organize, since all the class files are named with the primary class as the prefix. For example, rather than creating two source files, Test.java and A.java, in Figure 15.6(a), you can combine class **A** into class **Test** and create just one source file Test.java in Figure 15.6(b). The resulting class files are Test.class and Test$A.class.

Listing 15.2 modifies Listing 15.1 using an inner class.

LISTING 15.2 SimpleEventDemoInnerClass.java

```java
 1 import javax.swing.*;
 2 import java.awt.event.*;
 3
 4 public class SimpleEventDemoInnerClass extends JFrame {
 5   public SimpleEventDemoInnerClass() {
 6     // Create two buttons
 7     JButton jbtOK = new JButton("OK");
 8     JButton jbtCancel = new JButton("Cancel");
 9
10     // Create a panel to hold buttons
11     JPanel panel = new JPanel();
12     panel.add(jbtOK);
13     panel.add(jbtCancel);
14
15     add(panel); // Add panel to the frame
16
17     // Register listeners
18     ListenerClass listener = new ListenerClass();
19     jbtOK.addActionListener(listener);
20     jbtCancel.addActionListener(listener);
21   }
22
23   /** Main method */
24   public static void main(String[] args) {
25     JFrame frame = new SimpleEventDemoInnerClass();
26     frame.setTitle("SimpleEventDemoInnerClass");
27     frame.setLocationRelativeTo(null); // Center the frame
28     frame.setDefaultCloseOperation(JFrame.EXIT_ON_CLOSE);
29     frame.setSize(220, 80);
30     frame.setVisible(true);
31   }
32
33   private static class ListenerClass implements ActionListener {
34     public void actionPerformed(ActionEvent e) {
35       System.out.println("The " + e.getActionCommand() + " button "
36         + "is clicked at\n  " + new java.util.Date(e.getWhen()));
37     }
38   }
39 }
```

create listener
register listener

listener class
handle event

Listing 15.2 is the same as Listing 15.1 except that `ListenerClass` is now an inner class. Since the listener class will not be used by applications outside the frame class, it is declared `private`. Since `ListenerClass` does not refer to any instance members of the outer class, it is declared as a static inner class (line 33).

15.3.2 Anonymous Class Listeners

anonymous inner class

Inner classes can be shortened using anonymous inner classes. An *anonymous inner class* is an inner class without a name. It combines declaring an inner class and creating an instance of the class in one step. An anonymous inner class is declared as follows:

```
new SuperClassName/InterfaceName() {
  // Implement or override methods in superclass or interface

  // Other methods if necessary
}
```

Since an anonymous inner class is a special kind of inner class, it is treated like an inner class with the following features:

- An anonymous inner class must always extend a superclass or implement an interface, but it cannot have an explicit `extends` or `implements` clause.

- An anonymous inner class must implement all the abstract methods in the superclass or in the interface.

- An anonymous inner class always uses the no-arg constructor from its superclass to create an instance. If an anonymous inner class implements an interface, the constructor is `Object()`.

- An anonymous inner class is compiled into a class named `OuterClassName$n.class`. For example, if the outer class `Test` has two anonymous inner classes, they are compiled into `Test$1.class` and `Test$2.class`.

Listing 15.3 gives an example that handles the events from four buttons, as shown in Figure 15.8.

LISTING 15.3 AnonymousListenerDemo.java

```
1  import javax.swing.*;
2  import java.awt.event.*;
3
4  public class AnonymousListenerDemo extends JFrame {
5    public AnonymousListenerDemo() {
6      // Create four buttons
7      JButton jbtNew = new JButton("New");
8      JButton jbtOpen = new JButton("Open");
9      JButton jbtSave = new JButton("Save");
10     JButton jbtPrint = new JButton("Print");
11
12     // Create a panel to hold buttons
13     JPanel panel = new JPanel();
14     panel.add(jbtNew);
15     panel.add(jbtOpen);
16     panel.add(jbtSave);
17     panel.add(jbtPrint);
18
19     add(panel);
20
21     // Create and register anonymous inner class listener
22     jbtNew.addActionListener(new ActionListener() {
```

anonymous listener

```
23      public void actionPerformed(ActionEvent e) {                          handle event
24        System.out.println("Process New");
25      }
26    });
27
28    jbtOpen.addActionListener(new ActionListener() {
29      public void actionPerformed(ActionEvent e) {
30        System.out.println("Process Open");
31      }
32    });
33
34    jbtSave.addActionListener(new ActionListener() {
35      public void actionPerformed(ActionEvent e) {
36        System.out.println("Process Save");
37      }
38    });
39
40    jbtPrint.addActionListener(new ActionListener() {
41      public void actionPerformed(ActionEvent e) {
42        System.out.println("Process Print");
43      }
44    });
45  }
46
47  /** Main method */
48  public static void main(String[] args) {
49    JFrame frame = new AnonymousListenerDemo();
50    frame.setTitle("AnonymousListenerDemo");
51    frame.setLocationRelativeTo(null); // Center the frame
52    frame.setDefaultCloseOperation(JFrame.EXIT_ON_CLOSE);
53    frame.pack();
54    frame.setVisible(true);
55  }
56 }
```

FIGURE 15.8 The program handles the events from four buttons.

The program creates four listeners using anonymous inner classes (lines 22–44). Without using anonymous inner classes, you would have to create four separate classes. An anonymous listener works the same way as an inner class listener. The program is condensed using an anonymous inner class.

Anonymous inner classes are compiled into OuterClassName$#.class, where # starts at 1 and is incremented for each anonymous class encountered by the compiler. In this example, the anonymous inner class is compiled into AnonymousListenerDemo$1.class, AnonymousListenerDemo$2.class, AnonymousListenerDemo$3.class, and AnonymousListenerDemo$4.class.

Instead of using the setSize method to set the size for the frame, the program uses the pack() method (line 53), which automatically sizes up the frame according to the size of the components placed in it.

pack()

Pedagogical Note

Handing events using anonymous inner classes has become a standard in Java. From here on, this book will use anonymous inner classes to implement listeners.

Video Note

Enlarge and shrink a ball

15.3.3 Example: Enlarging or Shrinking a Circle

This example presents a program in Listing 15.4 that uses two buttons to control the size of a circle, as shown in Figure 15.9.

LISTING 15.4 ControlBall.java

```
 1  import javax.swing.*;
 2  import java.awt.*;
 3  import java.awt.event.*;
 4
 5  public class ControlBall extends JFrame {
 6    private JButton jbtEnlarge = new JButton("Enlarge");
 7    private JButton jbtShrink = new JButton("Shrink");
 8    private BallCanvas canvas = new BallCanvas();
 9
10    public ControlBall() {
11      JPanel panel = new JPanel(); // Use the panel to group buttons
12      panel.add(jbtEnlarge);
13      panel.add(jbtShrink);
14
15      this.add(canvas, BorderLayout.CENTER); // Add canvas to center
16      this.add(panel, BorderLayout.SOUTH); // Add buttons to the frame
17
18      jbtEnlarge.addActionListener(new ActionListener() {
19        public void actionPerformed(ActionEvent e) {
20          canvas.enlarge();
21        }
22      });
23
24      jbtShrink.addActionListener(new ActionListener() {
25        public void actionPerformed(ActionEvent e) {
26          canvas.shrink();
27        }
28      });
29    }
30
31    /** Main method */
32    public static void main(String[] args) {
33      JFrame frame = new ControlBall();
34      frame.setTitle("ControlBall");
35      frame.setLocationRelativeTo(null); // Center the frame
36      frame.setDefaultCloseOperation(JFrame.EXIT_ON_CLOSE);
37      frame.setSize(200, 200);
38      frame.setVisible(true);
39    }
40
41    public static class BallCanvas extends JPanel {
42      private int radius = 5; // Default ball radius
43
44      /** Enlarge the ball */
45      public void enlarge() {
46        radius += 1;
47        repaint();
```

buttons

ball canvas

button listener

button listener

BallCanvas inner class

enlarge radius

```
48      }
49
50      /** Shrink the ball */
51      public void shrink() {
52        radius -= 1;
53        repaint();
54      }
55
56      /** Repaint the ball */
57      protected void paintComponent(Graphics g) {
58        super.paintComponent(g);
59        g.drawOval(getWidth() / 2 - radius, getHeight() / 2 - radius,
60          2 * radius, 2 * radius);
61      }
62    }
63 }
```

shrink radius (line 51)

paint the ball (line 59)

FIGURE 15.9   The user clicks the *Enlarge* and *Shrink* buttons to enlarge and shrink the size of the circle.

The `BallCanvas` class extends `JPanel` to display a ball centered in the panel (lines 59–60). Since `BallCanvas` does not refer to any instance members of `BallControl`, it is declared as a static inner class in `ControlBall` (line 41).

When the *Enlarge* button is clicked, it invokes the `BallCanvas`'s `enlarge` method (line 20), which enlarges the radius of the ball by 1 (line 46).

When the *Shrink* button is clicked, it invokes the `BallCanvas`'s `shrink` method (line 26), which shrinks the radius of the ball by 1 (line 52).

15.3.4   Example: Handling Window Events

This example writes a program that demonstrates handling window events. Any subclass of the `Window` class can fire the following window events: window opened, closing, closed, activated, deactivated, iconified, and deiconified. The program in Listing 15.5 creates a frame, listens to the window events, and displays a message to indicate the occurring event. Figure 15.10 shows a sample run of the program.

LISTING 15.5   TestWindowEvent.java

```java
 1 import java.awt.event.*;
 2 import javax.swing.JFrame;
 3
 4 public class TestWindowEvent extends JFrame {
 5   public static void main(String[] args) {
 6     TestWindowEvent frame = new TestWindowEvent();
 7     frame.setSize(220, 80);
 8     frame.setLocationRelativeTo(null); // Center the frame
 9     frame.setDefaultCloseOperation(JFrame.EXIT_ON_CLOSE);
10     frame.setTitle("TestWindowEvent");
```

```
11        frame.setVisible(true);
12      }
13
14      public TestWindowEvent() {
15        addWindowListener(new WindowListener() {
16          /**
17           * Handler for window deiconified event
18           * Invoked when a window is changed from a minimized
19           * to a normal state.
20           */
21          public void windowDeiconified(WindowEvent event) {
22            System.out.println("Window deiconified");
23          }
24
25          /**
26           * Handler for window iconified event
27           * Invoked when a window is changed from a normal to a
28           * minimized state. For many platforms, a minimized window
29           * is displayed as the icon specified in the window's
30           * iconImage property.
31           */
32          public void windowIconified(WindowEvent event) {
33            System.out.println("Window iconified");
34          }
35
36          /**
37           * Handler for window activated event
38           * Invoked when the window is set to be the user's
39           * active window, which means the window (or one of its
40           * subcomponents) will receive keyboard events.
41           */
42          public void windowActivated(WindowEvent event) {
43            System.out.println("Window activated");
44          }
45
46          /**
47           * Handler for window deactivated event
48           * Invoked when a window is no longer the user's active
49           * window, which means that keyboard events will no longer
50           * be delivered to the window or its subcomponents.
51           */
52          public void windowDeactivated(WindowEvent event) {
53            System.out.println("Window deactivated");
54          }
55
56          /**
57           * Handler for window opened event
58           * Invoked the first time a window is made visible.
59           */
60          public void windowOpened(WindowEvent event) {
61            System.out.println("Window opened");
62          }
63
64          /**
65           * Handler for window closing event
66           * Invoked when the user attempts to close the window
67           * from the window's system menu.  If the program does not
68           * explicitly hide or dispose the window while processing
```

implement handler (line 21)

implement handler (line 32)

implement handler (line 42)

implement handler (line 52)

```
69        * this event, the window close operation will be cancelled.
70        */
71       public void windowClosing(WindowEvent event) {          implement handler
72         System.out.println("Window closing");
73       }
74
75       /**
76        * Handler for window closed event
77        * Invoked when a window has been closed as the result
78        * of calling dispose on the window.
79        */
80       public void windowClosed(WindowEvent event) {           implement handler
81         System.out.println("Window closed");
82       }
83     });
84   }
85 }
```

FIGURE 15.10 The window events are displayed on the console when you run the program from the command prompt.

The `WindowEvent` can be fired by the `Window` class or by any subclass of `Window`. Since `JFrame` is a subclass of `Window`, it can fire `WindowEvent`.

`TestWindowEvent` extends `JFrame` and implements `WindowListener`. The `WindowListener` interface defines several abstract methods (`windowActivated`, `windowClosed`, `windowClosing`, `windowDeactivated`, `windowDeiconified`, `windowIconified`, `windowOpened`) for handling window events when the window is activated, closed, closing, deactivated, deiconified, iconified, or opened.

When a window event, such as activation, occurs, the `windowActivated` method is triggered. Implement the `windowActivated` method with a concrete response if you want the event to be processed.

15.3.5 Listener Interface Adapters

Because the methods in the `WindowListener` interface are abstract, you must implement all of them even if your program does not care about some of the events. For convenience, Java provides support classes, called *convenience adapters*, which provide default implementations for all the methods in the listener interface. The default implementation is simply an empty body. Java provides convenience listener adapters for every AWT listener interface with multiple handlers. A *convenience listener adapter* is named *X*Adapter for *X*Listener. For example, `WindowAdapter` is a convenience listener adapter for `WindowListener`. Table 15.3 lists the convenience adapters.

convenience adapter

Using `WindowAdapter`, the preceding example can be simplified as shown in Listing 15.6, if you are interested only in the window activated event. The `WindowAdapter` class is used to create an anonymous listener instead of `WindowListener` (line 15). The `windowActivated` handler is implemented in line 16.

TABLE 15.3 Convenience Adapters

Adapter	Interface
WindowAdapter	WindowListener
MouseAdapter	MouseListener
MouseMotionAdapter	MouseMotionListener
KeyAdapter	KeyListener
ContainerAdapter	ContainerListener
ComponentAdapter	ComponentListener
FocusAdapter	FocusListener

LISTING 15.6 AdapterDemo.java

```java
1  import java.awt.event.*;
2  import javax.swing.JFrame;
3
4  public class AdapterDemo extends JFrame {
5    public static void main(String[] args) {
6      AdapterDemo frame = new AdapterDemo();
7      frame.setSize(220, 80);
8      frame.setLocationRelativeTo(null); // Center the frame
9      frame.setDefaultCloseOperation(JFrame.EXIT_ON_CLOSE);
10     frame.setTitle("AdapterDemo");
11     frame.setVisible(true);
12   }
13
14   public AdapterDemo() {
15     addWindowListener(new WindowAdapter() {
16       public void windowActivated(WindowEvent event) {
17         System.out.println("Window activated");
18       }
19     });
20   }
21 }
```

register listener
implement handler

15.4 Mouse Events

A mouse event is fired whenever a mouse is pressed, released, clicked, moved, or dragged on a component. The mouse-event object captures the event, such as the number of clicks associated with it or the location (x- and y-coordinates) of the mouse, as shown in Figure 15.11.

Since the MouseEvent class inherits InputEvent, you can use the methods defined in the InputEvent class on a MouseEvent object.

The java.awt.Point class represents a point on a component. The class contains two public variables, x and y, for coordinates. To create a Point, use the following constructor:

Point class

```java
Point(int x, int y)
```

This constructs a Point object with the specified x- and y-coordinates. Normally, the data fields in a class should be private. This class has two public data fields, which is not a good practice.

Java provides two listener interfaces, MouseListener and MouseMotionListener, to handle mouse events, as shown in Figure 15.12. Implement the MouseListener interface to listen for such actions as pressing, releasing, entering, exiting, or clicking the mouse, and

java.awt.event.InputEvent	
+getWhen(): long	Returns the timestamp when this event occurred.
+isAltDown(): boolean	Returns true if the Alt key is pressed on this event.
+isControlDown(): boolean	Returns true if the Control key is pressed on this event.
+isMetaDown(): boolean	Returns true if the Meta mouse button is pressed on this event.
+isShiftDown(): boolean	Returns true if the Shift key is pressed on this event.

java.awt.event.MouseEvent	
+getButton(): int	Indicates which mouse button has been clicked.
+getClickCount(): int	Returns the number of mouse clicks associated with this event.
+getPoint():java.awt.Point	Returns a Point object containing the x- and y-coordinates.
+getX(): int	Returns the x-coordinate of the mouse point.
+getY(): int	Returns the y-coordinate of the mouse point.

FIGURE 15.11 The MouseEvent class encapsulates information for mouse events.

«interface» java.awt.event.MouseListener	
+mousePressed(e: MouseEvent): void	Invoked after the mouse button has been pressed on the source component.
+mouseReleased(e: MouseEvent): void	Invoked after the mouse button has been released on the source component.
+mouseClicked(e: MouseEvent): void	Invoked after the mouse button has been clicked (pressed and released) on the source component.
+mouseEntered(e: MouseEvent): void	Invoked after the mouse enters the source component.
+mouseExited(e: MouseEvent): void	Invoked after the mouse exits the source component.

«interface» java.awt.event.MouseMotionListener	
+mouseDragged(e: MouseEvent): void	Invoked after a mouse button is moved with a button pressed.
+mouseMoved(e: MouseEvent): void	Invoked after a mouse button is moved without a button pressed.

FIGURE 15.12 The MouseListener interface handles mouse pressed, released, clicked, entered, and exited events. The MouseMotionListener interface handles mouse dragged and moved events.

implement the MouseMotionListener interface to listen for such actions as dragging or moving the mouse.

15.4.1 Example: Moving a Message on a Panel Using a Mouse

This example writes a program that displays a message in a panel, as shown in Listing 15.7. You can use the mouse to move the message. The message moves as the mouse drags and is always displayed at the mouse point. A sample run of the program is shown in Figure 15.13.

Video Note
Move message using
the mouse

LISTING 15.7 MoveMessageDemo.java

```java
1  import java.awt.*;
2  import java.awt.event.*;
3  import javax.swing.*;
4
5  public class MoveMessageDemo extends JFrame {
6    public MoveMessageDemo() {
7      // Create a MovableMessagePanel instance for moving a message
8      MovableMessagePanel p = new MovableMessagePanel("Welcome to Java");
9
10     // Place the message panel in the frame
11     setLayout(new BorderLayout());
12     add(p);
13   }
14
15   /** Main method */
16   public static void main(String[] args) {
17     MoveMessageDemo frame = new MoveMessageDemo();
18     frame.setTitle("MoveMessageDemo");
19     frame.setSize(200, 100);
20     frame.setLocationRelativeTo(null); // Center the frame
21     frame.setDefaultCloseOperation(JFrame.EXIT_ON_CLOSE);
22     frame.setVisible(true);
23   }
24
25   // Inner class: MovableMessagePanel draws a message
26   static class MovableMessagePanel extends JPanel {
27     private String message = "Welcome to Java";
28     private int x = 20;
29     private int y = 20;
30
31     /** Construct a panel to draw string s */
32     public MovableMessagePanel(String s) {
33       message = s;
34       addMouseMotionListener(new MouseMotionAdapter() {
35         /** Handle mouse dragged event */
36         public void mouseDragged(MouseEvent e) {
37           // Get the new location and repaint the screen
38           x = e.getX();
39           y = e.getY();
40           repaint();
41         }
42       });
43     }
44
45     /** Paint the component */
46     protected void paintComponent(Graphics g) {
47       super.paintComponent(g);
48       g.drawString(message, x, y);
49     }
50   }
51 }
```

create a panel

inner class

set a new message
anonymous listener

override handler

new location

repaint

FIGURE 15.13   You can move the message by dragging the mouse.

The `MovableMessagePanel` class extends `JPanel` to draw a message (line 26). Additionally, it handles redisplaying the message when the mouse is dragged. This class is declared as an inner class inside the main class because it is used only in this class. Furthermore, the inner class is declared static because it does not reference any instance members of the main class.

The `MouseMotionListener` interface contains two handlers, `mouseMoved` and `mouse-Dragged`, for handling mouse-motion events. When you move the mouse with the button pressed, the `mouseDragged` method is invoked to repaint the viewing area and display the message at the mouse point. When you move the mouse without pressing the button, the `mouseMoved` method is invoked.

Because the listener is interested only in the mouse dragged event, the anonymous inner class listener extends `MouseMotionAdapter` to override the `mouseDragged` method. If the inner class implemented the `MouseMotionListener` interface, you would have to implement all of the handlers, even if your listener did not care about some of the events.

The `mouseDragged` method is invoked when you move the mouse with a button pressed. This method obtains the mouse location using `getX` and `getY` methods (lines 38–39) in the `MouseEvent` class. This becomes the new location for the message. Invoking the `repaint()` method (line 40) causes `paintComponent` to be invoked (line 46), which displays the message in a new location.

15.5 Key Events

Key events enable the use of the keys to control and perform actions or get input from the keyboard. A key event is fired whenever a key is pressed, released, or typed on a component. The `KeyEvent` object describes the nature of the event (namely, that a key has been pressed, released, or typed) and the value of the key, as shown in Figure 15.14. Java provides the `KeyListener` to handle key events, as shown in Figure 15.15.

FIGURE 15.14 The `KeyEvent` class encapsulates information about key events.

FIGURE 15.15 The `KeyListener` interface handles key pressed, released, and typed events.

The `keyPressed` handler is invoked when a key is pressed, the `keyReleased` handler is invoked when a key is released, and the `keyTyped` handler is invoked when a Unicode character is entered. If a key does not have a Unicode (e.g., function keys, modifier keys, action keys, and control keys), the `keyTyped` handler will be not be invoked.

Every key event has an associated key character or key code that is returned by the `getKeyChar()` or `getKeyCode()` method in `KeyEvent`. The key codes are constants defined in Table 15.4. For a key of the Unicode character, the key code is the same as the

TABLE 15.4 Key Constants

Constant	Description	Constant	Description
VK_HOME	The Home key	VK_SHIFT	The Shift key
VK_END	The End key	VK_BACK_SPACE	The Backspace key
VK_PGUP	The Page Up key	VK_CAPS_LOCK	The Caps Lock key
VK_PGDN	The Page Down key	VK_NUM_LOCK	The Num Lock key
VK_UP	The up-arrow key	VK_ENTER	The Enter key
VK_DOWN	The down-arrow key	VK_UNDEFINED	The keyCode unknown
VK_LEFT	The left-arrow key	VK_F1 to VK_F12	The function keys from F1 to F12
VK_RIGHT	The right-arrow key		
VK_ESCAPE	The Esc key	VK_0 to VK_9	The number keys from 0 to 9
VK_TAB	The Tab key	VK_A to VK_Z	The letter keys from A to Z
VK_CONTROL	The Control key		

Unicode value. For the key pressed and key released events, `getKeyCode()` returns the value as defined in the table. For the key typed event, `getKeyCode()` returns `VK_UNDEFINED`.

The program in Listing 15.8 displays a user-input character. The user can move the character up, down, left, and right, using the arrow keys `VK_UP`, `VK_DOWN`, `VK_LEFT`, and `VK_RIGHT`. Figure 15.16 contains a sample run of the program.

FIGURE 15.16 The program responds to key events by displaying a character and moving it up, down, left, or right.

LISTING 15.8 KeyEventDemo.java

```
1  import java.awt.*;
2  import java.awt.event.*;
3  import javax.swing.*;
4
5  public class KeyEventDemo extends JFrame {
6    private KeyboardPanel keyboardPanel = new KeyboardPanel();
7
8    /** Initialize UI */
9    public KeyEventDemo() {
10     // Add the keyboard panel to accept and display user input
11     add(keyboardPanel);
12
13     // Set focus
14     keyboardPanel.setFocusable(true);
15   }
16
17   /** Main method */
18   public static void main(String[] args) {
19     KeyEventDemo frame = new KeyEventDemo();
```

create a panel

focusable

```
20      frame.setTitle("KeyEventDemo");
21      frame.setSize(300, 300);
22      frame.setLocationRelativeTo(null); // Center the frame
23      frame.setDefaultCloseOperation(JFrame.EXIT_ON_CLOSE);
24      frame.setVisible(true);
25    }
26
27    // Inner class: KeyboardPanel for receiving key input
28    static class KeyboardPanel extends JPanel {
29      private int x = 100;
30      private int y = 100;
31      private char keyChar = 'A'; // Default key
32
33      public KeyboardPanel() {
34        addKeyListener(new KeyAdapter() {
35          public void keyPressed(KeyEvent e) {
36            switch (e.getKeyCode()) {
37              case KeyEvent.VK_DOWN: y += 10; break;
38              case KeyEvent.VK_UP: y -= 10; break;
39              case KeyEvent.VK_LEFT: x -= 10; break;
40              case KeyEvent.VK_RIGHT: x += 10; break;
41              default: keyChar = e.getKeyChar();
42            }
43
44            repaint();
45          }
46        });
47      }
48
49      /** Draw the character */
50      protected void paintComponent(Graphics g) {
51        super.paintComponent(g);
52
53        g.setFont(new Font("TimesRoman", Font.PLAIN, 24));
54        g.drawString(String.valueOf(keyChar), x, y);
55      }
56    }
57 }
```

inner class

register listener
override handler

get the key pressed

repaint

redraw character

The **KeyboardPanel** class extends **JPanel** to display a character (line 28). This class is declared as an inner class inside the main class, because it is used only in this class. Furthermore, the inner class is declared static, because it does not reference any instance members of the main class.

Because the program gets input from the keyboard, it listens for **KeyEvent** and extends **KeyAdapter** to handle key input (line 34).

When a key is pressed, the **keyPressed** handler is invoked. The program uses **e.getKeyCode()** to obtain the key code and **e.getKeyChar()** to get the character for the key. When a nonarrow key is pressed, the key is displayed (line 41). When an arrow key is pressed, the character moves in the direction indicated by the arrow key (lines 37–40).

Only a focused component can receive **KeyEvent**. To make a component focusable, set its **isFocusable** property to **true** (line 14).

focusable

Every time the component is repainted, a new font is created for the **Graphics** object in line 53. This is not efficient. It is better to create the font once as a data field.

efficient?

15.6 Animation Using the **Timer** Class

Not all source objects are GUI components. The `javax.swing.Timer` class is a source component that fires an **ActionEvent** at a predefined rate. Figure 15.17 lists some of the methods in the class.

Video Note
Animate a clock

javax.swing.Timer	
+Timer(delay: int, listener: ActionListener)	Creates a Timer object with a specified delay in milliseconds and an ActionListener.
+addActionListener(listener: ActionListener): void	Adds an ActionListener to the timer.
+start(): void	Starts this timer.
+stop(): void	Stops this timer.
+setDelay(delay: int): void	Sets a new delay value for this timer.

FIGURE 15.17 A Timer object fires an ActionEvent at a fixed rate.

A Timer object serves as the source of an ActionEvent. The listeners must be instances of ActionListener and registered with a Timer object. You create a Timer object using its sole constructor with a delay and a listener, where delay specifies the number of milliseconds between two action events. You can add additional listeners using the addActionListener method, and adjust the delay using the setDelay method. To start the timer, invoke the start() method. To stop the timer, invoke the stop() method.

The Timer class can be used to control animations. For example, you can use it to display a moving message, as shown in Figure 15.18, with the code in Listing 15.9.

FIGURE 15.18 A message moves in the panel.

LISTING 15.9 AnimationDemo.java

```
1  import java.awt.*;
2  import java.awt.event.*;
3  import javax.swing.*;
4
5  public class AnimationDemo extends JFrame {
6    public AnimationDemo() {
7      // Create a MovingMessagePanel for displaying a moving message
8      add(new MovingMessagePanel("message moving?"));
9    }
10
11   /** Main method */
12   public static void main(String[] args) {
13     AnimationDemo frame = new AnimationDemo();
14     frame.setTitle("AnimationDemo");
15     frame.setSize(280, 100);
16     frame.setLocationRelativeTo(null); // Center the frame
17     frame.setDefaultCloseOperation(JFrame.EXIT_ON_CLOSE);
18     frame.setVisible(true);
19   }
20
21   // Inner class: Displaying a moving message
22   static class MovingMessagePanel extends JPanel {
23     private String message = "Welcome to Java";
24     private int xCoordinate = 0;
25     private int yCoordinate = 20;
26
```

create panel

```
27    public MovingMessagePanel(String message) {
28      this.message = message;
29
30      // Create a timer
31      Timer timer = new Timer(1000, new TimerListener());
32      timer.start();
33    }
34
35    /** Paint message */
36    protected void paintComponent(Graphics g) {
37      super.paintComponent(g);
38
39      if (xCoordinate > getWidth()) {
40        xCoordinate = -20;
41      }
42      xCoordinate += 5;
43      g.drawString(message, xCoordinate, yCoordinate);
44    }
45
46    class TimerListener implements ActionListener {
47      /** Handle ActionEvent */
48      public void actionPerformed(ActionEvent e) {
49        repaint();
50      }
51    }
52  }
53 }
```

set message

create timer
start timer

reset x-coordinate

move message

listener class

event handler
repaint

The MovingMessagePanel class extends JPanel to display a message (line 22). This class is declared as an inner class inside the main class, because it is used only in this class. Furthermore, the inner class is declared static, because it does not reference any instance members of the main class.

An inner class listener is declared in line 46 to listen for ActionEvent. Line 31 creates a Timer for the listener. The timer is started in line 32. The timer fires an ActionEvent every second, and the listener responds in line 49 to repaint the panel. When a panel is painted, its x-coordinate is increased (line 42), so the message is displayed to the right. When the x-coordinate exceeds the bound of the panel, it is reset to -20 (line 40), so the message continues moving from left to right.

In §14.12, "Case Study: The StillClock Class," you drew a StillClock to show the current time. The clock does not tick after it is displayed. What can you do to make the clock display a new current time every second? The key to making the clock tick is to repaint it every second with a new current time. You can use a timer to control the repainting of the clock with the code in Listing 15.10.

LISTING 15.10 ClockAnimation.java

```
1 import java.awt.event.*;
2 import javax.swing.*;
3
4 public class ClockAnimation extends StillClock {
5   public ClockAnimation() {
6     // Create a timer with delay 1000 ms
7     Timer timer = new Timer(1000, new TimerListener());
8     timer.start();
9   }
10
11   private class TimerListener implements ActionListener {
12     /** Handle the action event */
```

create timer
start timer

listener class

implement handler

set new time
repaint

```
13     public void actionPerformed(ActionEvent e) {
14       // Set new time and repaint the clock to display current time
15       setCurrentTime();
16       repaint();
17     }
18   }
19
20   /** Main method */
21   public static void main(String[] args) {
22     JFrame frame = new JFrame("ClockAnimation");
23     ClockAnimation clock = new ClockAnimation();
24     frame.add(clock);
25     frame.setSize(200, 200);
26     frame.setLocationRelativeTo(null); // Center the frame
27     frame.setDefaultCloseOperation(JFrame.EXIT_ON_CLOSE);
28     frame.setVisible(true);
29   }
30 }
```

The program displays a running clock, as shown in Figure 15.19. `ClockAnimation` extends `StillClock` and repaints the clock every 1 second triggered by a timer. Line 7 creates a `Timer` for a `ClockAnimation`. The timer is started in line 8 when a `ClockAnimation` is constructed. The timer fires an `ActionEvent` every second, and the listener responds in line 15 to set a new time and repaint the clock. The `setCurrentTime()` method defined in `StillClock` sets the current time in the clock.

FIGURE 15.19 A live clock is displayed in the panel.

KEY TERMS

anonymous inner class   492
convenience listener adapter   497
event   484
event delegation   485
event handler   486
event listener   485

event listener interface   485
event object   484
event registration   486
event source (source object)   485
event-driven programming   484
inner class   490

CHAPTER SUMMARY

■ The root class of the event classes is `java.util.EventObject`. The subclasses of `EventObject` deal with special types of events, such as action events, window events, component events, mouse events, and key events. You can identify the source object of an event using the `getSource()` instance method in the `EventObject` class. If a component can fire an event, any subclass of the component can fire the same type of event.

- The listener object's class must implement the corresponding event-listener interface. Java provides a listener interface for every event class. The listener interface is usually named `XListener` for `XEvent`, with the exception of `MouseMotionListener`. For example, the corresponding listener interface for `ActionEvent` is `ActionListener`; each listener for `ActionEvent` should implement the `ActionListener` interface. The listener interface contains the method(s), known as the *handler(s)*, which process the events.

- The listener object must be registered by the source object. Registration methods are dependent on the event type. For `ActionEvent`, the method is `addActionListener`. In general, the method is named `addXListener` for `XEvent`.

- An *inner class*, or *nested class,* is a class defined within the scope of another class. An inner class can reference the data and methods defined in the outer class in which it nests, so you need not pass the reference of the outer class to the constructor of the inner class.

- Convenience adapters are support classes that provide default implementations for all the methods in the listener interface. Java provides convenience listener adapters for every AWT listener interface with multiple handlers. A convenience listener adapter is named *X*Adapter for *X*Listener.

- A source object may fire several types of events. For each event, the source object maintains a list of listeners and notifies all the registered listeners by invoking the *handler* on the listener object to process the event.

- A mouse event is fired whenever a mouse is clicked, released, moved, or dragged on a component. The mouse event object captures the event, such as the number of clicks associated with it or the location (`x`- and `y`-coordinates) of the mouse point.

- Java provides two listener interfaces, `MouseListener` and `MouseMotionListener`, to handle mouse events, implement the `MouseListener` interface to listen for such actions as mouse pressed, released, clicked, entered, or exited, and implement the `MouseMotionListener` interface to listen for such actions as mouse dragged or moved.

- A `KeyEvent` object describes the nature of the event (namely, that a key has been pressed, released, or typed) and the value of the key.

- The `keyPressed` handler is invoked when a key is pressed, the `keyReleased` handler is invoked when a key is released, and the `keyTyped` handler is invoked when a Unicode character key is entered. If a key does not have a Unicode (e.g., function keys, modifier keys, action keys, and control keys), the `keyTyped` handler will be not be invoked.

- You can use the `Timer` class to control Java animations. A timer fires an `ActionEvent` at a fixed rate. The listener updates the painting to simulate an animation.

REVIEW QUESTIONS

Sections 15.2–15.3

15.1 Can a button fire a `WindowEvent`? Can a button fire a `MouseEvent`? Can a button fire an `ActionEvent`?

15.2 Why must a listener be an instance of an appropriate listener interface? Explain how to register a listener object and how to implement a listener interface.

15.3 Can a source have multiple listeners? Can a listener listen on multiple sources? Can a source be a listener for itself?

15.4 How do you implement a method defined in the listener interface? Do you need to implement all the methods defined in the listener interface?

15.5 Can an inner class be used in a class other than the class in which it nests?

15.6 Can the modifiers `public`, `private`, and `static` be used on inner classes?

15.7 If class A is an inner class in class B, what is the .class file for A? If class B contains two anonymous inner classes, what are the .class file names for these two classes?

15.8 What is wrong in the following code?

```java
import java.swing.*;
import java.awt.*;

public class Test extends JFrame {
  public Test() {
    JButton jbtOK = new JButton("OK");
    add(jbtOK);
  }

  private class Listener
      implements ActionListener {
    public void actionPerform
        (ActionEvent e) {
      System.out.println
        (jbtOK.getActionCommand());
    }
  }

  /** Main method omitted */
}
```

(a)

```java
import java.awt.event.*;
import javax.swing.*;

public class Test extends JFrame {
  public Test() {
    JButton jbtOK = new JButton("OK");
    add(jbtOK);
    jbtOK.addActionListener(
      new ActionListener() {
        public void actionPerformed
            (ActionEvent e) {
          System.out.println
            (jbtOK.getActionCommand());
        }
    } // Something missing here
  }

  /** Main method omitted */
}
```

(b)

15.9 What is the difference between the `setSize(width, height)` method and the `pack()` method in `JFrame`?

Sections 15.4–15.5

15.10 What method do you use to get the source of an event? What method do you use to get the timestamp for an action event, a mouse event, or a key event? What method do you use to get the mouse point position for a mouse event? What method do you use to get the key character for a key event?

15.11 What is the listener interface for mouse pressed, released, clicked, entered, and exited? What is the listener interface for mouse moved and dragged?

15.12 Does every key in the keyboard have a Unicode? Is a key code in the `KeyEvent` class equivalent to a Unicode?

15.13 Is the `keyPressed` handler invoked after a key is pressed? Is the `keyReleased` handler invoked after a key is released? Is the `keyTyped` handler invoked after *any* key is typed?

Section 15.6 Animation Using the **Timer** Class

15.14 How do you create a timer? How do you start a timer? How do you stop a timer?

15.15 Does the `Timer` class have a no-arg constructor? Can you add multiple listeners to a timer?

PROGRAMMING EXERCISES

Sections 15.2–15.3

15.1   (*Finding which button has been clicked on the console*) Add the code to Exercise 13.1 that will display a message on the console indicating which button has been clicked.

15.2   (*Using ComponentEvent*) Any GUI component can fire a ComponentEvent. The ComponentListener defines the componentMoved, componentResized, componentShown, and componentHidden methods for processing component events. Write a test program to demonstrate ComponentEvent.

15.3*   (*Moving the ball*) Write a program that moves the ball in a panel. You should define a panel class for displaying the ball and provide the methods for moving the button left, right, up, and down, as shown in Figure 15.20(a).

(a)

(b)

(c)

FIGURE 15.20   (a) Exercise 15.3 displays which button is clicked on a message panel. (b) Exercise 15.4 displays the mouse position. (c) Exercise 15.9 uses the arrow keys to draw the lines.

Section 15.4 Mouse Events

15.4*   (*Displaying the mouse position*) Write two programs, such that one displays the mouse position when the mouse is clicked (see Figure 15.20(b)) and the other displays the mouse position when the mouse is pressed and ceases to display it when the mouse is released.

15.5*   (*Setting background color using a mouse*) Write a program that displays the background color of a panel as black when the mouse is pressed and as white when the mouse is released.

15.6** (*Alternating two messages*) Write a program to rotate two messages "Java is fun" and "Java is powerful" displayed on a panel with a mouse click.

Section 15.5 Key Events

15.7** (*Entering and displaying a string*) Write a program that receives a string from the keyboard and displays it on a panel. The *Enter* key signals the end of a string. Whenever a new string is entered, it is displayed on the panel.

15.8*   (*Displaying a character*) Write a program to get a character input from the keyboard and display the character where the mouse points.

15.9*   (*Drawing lines using the arrow keys*) Write a program that draws line segments using the arrow keys. The line starts from the center of the frame and draws toward east, north, west, or south when the right-arrow key, up-arrow key, left-arrow key, or down-arrow key is clicked, as shown in Figure 15.20(c).

Section 15.6 Animation Using the Timer Class

15.10* (*Displaying a flashing label*) Write a program that displays a flashing label.

(*Hint*: To make the label flash, you need to repaint the panel alternately with the label and without it (blank screen) at a fixed rate. Use a boolean variable to control the alternation.)

15.11* (*Controlling a moving label*) Modify Listing 15.9, AnimationDemo.java, to control a moving label using the mouse. The label freezes when the mouse is pressed, and moves again when the button is released.

15.12* (*Displaying a running fan*) Listing 14.6, DrawArcs.java, displays a motionless fan. Write a program that displays a running fan.

15.13* (*Slide show*) Twenty-five slides are stored as image files (slide0.jpg, slide1.jpg, ..., slide24.jpg) in the image directory downloadable along with the source code in the book. The size of each image is 800 × 600. Write a Java application that automatically displays the slides repeatedly. Each slide is shown for a second. The slides are displayed in order. When the last slide finishes, the first slide is redisplayed, and so on. (*Hint*: Place a label in the frame and set a slide as an image icon in the label.)

Video Note
Animate a rising flag

15.14* (*Raising flag*) Write a Java program that animates raising a flag, as shown in Figure 15.1. (See §14.13, "Displaying Images," on how to display images.)

15.15* (*Racing car*) Write a Java program that simulates car racing, as shown in Figure 15.21(a). The car moves from left to right. When it hits the right end, it restarts from the left and continues the same process. You can use a timer to control animation. Redraw the car with a new base coordinates (x, y), as shown in Figure 15.21(b).

(a) (b)

FIGURE 15.21 (a) Exercise 15.15 displays a moving car. (b) You can redraw a car with a new base point.

15.16* (*Moving a circle using keys*) Write a program that moves a circle up, down, left, or right using the arrow keys.

15.17* (*Moving a circle using mouse*) Write a program that displays a circle with radius **10** pixels. You can point the mouse inside the circle and drag (i.e., move with mouse pressed) the circle wherever the mouse goes, as shown in Figure 15.22(b).

(a) (b) (c) (d)

FIGURE 15.22 (a)–(b) You can point, drag, and move the circle. (c) When you click a circle, a new circle is displayed at a random location. (d) After 20 circles are clicked, the time spent in the panel is displayed.

15.18*** (*Game: eye-hand coordination*) Write a program that displays a circle of radius 10 pixels filled with a random color at a random location on a panel, as shown in Figure 15.22(c). When you click the circle, it is gone and a new random-colored circle is displayed at another random location. After twenty circles are clicked, display the time spent in the panel, as shown in Figure 15.22(d).

15.19** (*Geometry: inside a circle?*) Write a program that draws a fixed circle centered at (100, 60) with radius 50. Whenever a mouse is moved, display the message indicating whether the mouse point is inside the circle, as shown in Figure 15.23(a).

(a)   (b)   (c)

FIGURE 15.23 Detect whether a point is inside a circle, a rectangle, or a triangle.

15.20** (*Geometry: inside a rectangle?*) Write a program that draws a fixed rectangle centered at (100, 60) with width 100 and height 40. Whenever a mouse is moved, display the message indicating whether the mouse point is inside the rectangle, as shown in Figure 15.23(b). To detect whether a point is inside a rectangle, use the `Rectangle2D` class defined in Exercise 9.12.

15.21** (*Geometry: inside a triangle?*) Write a program that draws a fixed triangle with three vertices at (20, 20), (100, 100), and (140, 40). Whenever a mouse is moved, display the message indicating whether the mouse point is inside the triangle, as shown in Figure 15.23(c). To detect whether a point is inside a triangle, use the `Triangle2D` class defined in Exercise 9.13.

15.22*** (*Game: bean machine animation*) Write a program that animates a bean machine introduced in Exercise 14.24. The animation terminates after ten balls are dropped, as shown in Figure 15.24.

FIGURE 15.24 The balls are dropped to the bean machine.

15.23*** (*Geometry: closest pair of points*) Write a program that lets the user click on the panel to dynamically create points. Initially, the panel is empty. When a panel has two or more points, highlight the pair of closest points. Whenever a new point is created, a new pair of closest points is highlighted. Display the points using small circles and highlight the points using filled circles, as shown in Figure 15.25(a–c). (*Hint:* store the points in an `ArrayList`.)

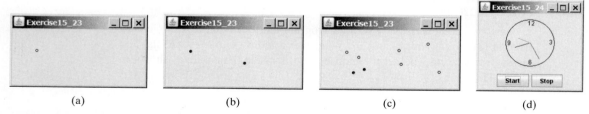

(a)   (b)   (c)   (d)

FIGURE 15.25 (a)–(c) Exercise15.23 allows the user to create new points with a mouse click and highlights the pair of the closest points. (d) Exercise15.24 allows the user to start and stop a clock.

15.24* (*Controlling a clock*) Modify Listing 15.10 ClockAnimation.java to add two methods `start()` and `stop()` to start and stop the clock. Write a program that lets the user control the clock with the *Start* and *Stop* buttons, as shown in Figure 15.25(d).

15.25*** (*Game: hitting balloons*) Write a program that displays a balloon in a random position in a panel (Figure 15.26(a)). Use the left and right arrow keys to point the gun left or right to aim at the balloon (Figure 15.26(b)). Press the up arrow key to fire a small ball from the gun (Figure 15.26(c)). Once the ball hits the balloon, the debris is displayed (Figure 15.26(e)) and a new balloon is displayed in a random location (Figure 15.26(f)). If the ball misses the balloon, the ball disappears once it hits the boundary of the panel. You can then press the up arrow key to fire another ball. Whenever you press the left or the right arrow key, the gun turns 5 degrees left or right. (Instructors may modify the game as follows: 1. display the number of the balloons destroyed; 2. display a countdown timer (e.g., 60 seconds) and terminate the game once the time expires; 3. allow the balloon to rise dynamically.)

(a)   (b)   (c)

(d)   (e)   (f)

FIGURE 15.26 (a) A balloon is displayed in a random location; (b) Press the left/right arrow keys to aim the balloon; (c) Press the up arrow key to fire a ball; (d) The ball moves straight toward the balloon; (e) The ball hits the balloon; (f) A new balloon is displayed in a random position.

CHAPTER 16

CREATING USER INTERFACES

Objectives

- To create graphical user interfaces with various user-interface components: `JButton`, `JCheckBox`, `JRadioButton`, `JLabel`, `JTextField`, `JTextArea`, `JComboBox`, `JList`, `JScrollBar`, and `JSlider` (§§16.2–16.11).

- To create listeners for various types of events (§§16.2–16.11).

- To explore `JButton` (§16.2)

- To explore `JCheckBox` (§16.3)

- To explore `JRadioButton` (§16.4)

- To explore `JLabel` (§16.5)

- To explore `JTextField` (§16.6)

- To explore `JTextArea` (§16.7)

- To explore `JComboBox` (§16.8)

- To explore `JList` (§16.9)

- To explore `JScrollBar` (§16.10)

- To explore `JSlider` (§16.11)

- To display multiple windows in an application (§16.12).

16.1 Introduction

GUI

A graphical user interface (GUI) makes a system user-friendly and easy to use. Creating a GUI requires creativity and knowledge of how GUI components work. Since the GUI components in Java are very flexible and versatile, you can create a wide assortment of useful user interfaces.

Many Java IDEs provide tools for visually designing and developing GUI interfaces. This enables you to rapidly assemble the elements of a user interface (UI) for a Java application or applet with minimum coding. Tools, however, cannot do everything. You have to modify the programs they produce. Consequently, before you begin to use the visual tools, you must understand the basic concepts of Java GUI programming.

Previous chapters briefly introduced several GUI components. This chapter introduces the frequently used GUI components in detail (see Figure 16.1). Since there are no new concepts introduced in this chapter, instructors may assign this chapter for students to study on their own.

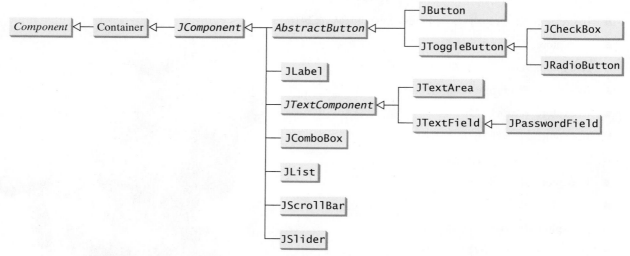

FIGURE 16.1 These Swing GUI components are frequently used to create user interfaces.

Note

naming convention for components

Throughout this book, the prefixes `jbt`, `jchk`, `jrb`, `jlbl`, `jtf`, `jpf`, `jta`, `jcbo`, `jlst`, `jscb`, and `jsld` are used to name reference variables for `JButton`, `JCheckBox`, `JRadioButton`, `JLabel`, `JTextField`, `JPasswordField`, `JTextArea`, `JComboBox`, `JList`, `JScrollBar`, and `JSlider`.

16.2 Buttons

AbstractButton

A *button* is a component that triggers an action event when clicked. Swing provides regular buttons, toggle buttons, check box buttons, and radio buttons. The common features of these buttons are represented in `javax.swing.AbstractButton`, as shown in Figure 16.2.

FIGURE 16.2 `AbstractButton` defines common features of different types of buttons.

This section introduces the regular buttons defined in the `JButton` class. `JButton` inherits `AbstractButton` and provides several constructors to create buttons, as shown in Figure 16.3.

JButton

FIGURE 16.3 `JButton` defines a regular push button.

16.2.1 Icons, Pressed Icons, and Rollover Icons

A regular button has a default icon, a pressed icon, and a rollover icon. Normally, you use the default icon. The other icons are for special effects. A pressed icon is displayed when a button is pressed, and a rollover icon is displayed when the mouse is over the button but not pressed. For example, Listing 16.1 displays the American flag as a regular icon, the Canadian flag as a pressed icon, and the British flag as a rollover icon, as shown in Figure 16.4.

LISTING 16.1 TestButtonIcons.java

```
 1  import javax.swing.*;
 2
 3  public class TestButtonIcons extends JFrame  {
 4    public static void main(String[] args) {
 5      // Create a frame and set its properties
 6      JFrame frame = new TestButtonIcons();
 7      frame.setTitle("ButtonIcons");
 8      frame.setSize(200, 100);
 9      frame.setLocationRelativeTo(null); // Center the frame
10      frame.setDefaultCloseOperation(JFrame.EXIT_ON_CLOSE);
11      frame.setVisible(true);
12    }
13
14    public TestButtonIcons() {
15      ImageIcon usIcon = new ImageIcon("image/usIcon.gif");
16      ImageIcon caIcon = new ImageIcon("image/caIcon.gif");
17      ImageIcon ukIcon = new ImageIcon("image/ukIcon.gif");
18
19      JButton jbt = new JButton("Click it", usIcon);
20      jbt.setPressedIcon(caIcon);
21      jbt.setRolloverIcon(ukIcon);
22
23      add(jbt);
24    }
25  }
```

create icons — lines 15–17

regular icon — line 19
pressed icon — line 20
rollover icon — line 21

add a button — line 23

(a) Default icon (b) Pressed icon (c) Rollover icon

FIGURE 16.4 A button can have several types of icons.

16.2.2 Alignments

horizontal alignment

Horizontal alignment specifies how the icon and text are placed horizontally on a button. You can set the horizontal alignment using **setHorizontalAlignment(int)** with one of the five constants **LEADING**, **LEFT**, **CENTER**, **RIGHT**, **TRAILING**, as shown in Figure 16.5. At present, **LEADING** and **LEFT** are the same, and **TRAILING** and **RIGHT** are the same. Future implementation may distinguish them. The default horizontal alignment is **SwingConstants.TRAILING**.

Horizontally left   Horizontally center   Horizontally right

FIGURE 16.5 You can specify how the icon and text are placed on a button horizontally.

vertical alignment

Vertical alignment specifies how the icon and text are placed vertically on a button. You can set the vertical alignment using **setVerticalAlignment(int)** with one of the three constants **TOP**, **CENTER**, **BOTTOM**, as shown in Figure 16.6. The default vertical alignment is **SwingConstants.CENTER**.

Vertically top   Vertically center   Vertically bottom

FIGURE 16.6 You can specify how the icon and text are placed on a button vertically.

16.2.3 Text Positions

Horizontal text position specifies the horizontal position of the text relative to the icon. You can set the horizontal text position using `setHorizontalTextPosition(int)` with one of the five constants `LEADING`, `LEFT`, `CENTER`, `RIGHT`, `TRAILING`, as shown in Figure 16.7. At present, `LEADING` and `LEFT` are the same, and `TRAILING` and `RIGHT` are the same. Future implementation may distinguish them. The default horizontal text position is `SwingConstants.RIGHT`. horizontal text position

Text positioned left   Text positioned center   Text positioned right

FIGURE 16.7 You can specify the horizontal position of the text relative to the icon.

Vertical text position specifies the vertical position of the text relative to the icon. You can set the vertical text position using `setVerticalTextPosition(int)` with one of the three constants `TOP`, `CENTER`, `BOTTOM`, as shown in Figure 16.8. The default vertical text position is `SwingConstants.CENTER`. vertical text position

Text positioned top   Text positioned vertically center   Text positioned bottom

FIGURE 16.8 You can specify the vertical position of the text relative to the icon.

Note

The constants `LEFT`, `CENTER`, `RIGHT`, `LEADING`, `TRAILING`, `TOP`, and `BOTTOM` used in `AbstractButton` are also used in many other Swing components. These constants are centrally defined in the `javax.swing.SwingConstants` interface. Since all Swing GUI components implement `SwingConstants`, you can reference the constants through `SwingConstants` or a GUI component. For example, `SwingConstants.CENTER` is the same as `JButton.CENTER`. **SwingConstants**

`JButton` can generate many types of events, but often you need to respond to an `ActionEvent`. When a button is pressed, it generates an `ActionEvent`.

16.2.4 Using Buttons

This section presents a program, shown in Listing 16.2, that displays a message on a panel and uses two buttons, <= and => to move the message on the panel to the left or right. The layout of the UI and the output of the program are shown in Figure 16.9.

FIGURE 16.9 Clicking the <= and => buttons causes the message on the panel to move to the left and right, respectively.

Here are the major steps in the program:

1. Create the user interface.
   Create a `MessagePanel` object to display the message. The `MessagePanel` class was created in Listing 14.10, MessagePanel.java. Place it in the center of the frame. Create two buttons, <= and =>, on a panel. Place the panel in the south of the frame.

2. Process the event.
   Create and register listeners for processing the action event to move the message left or right according to whether the left or right button was clicked.

LISTING 16.2 ButtonDemo.java

```java
1  import java.awt.*;
2  import java.awt.event.ActionListener;
3  import java.awt.event.ActionEvent;
4  import javax.swing.*;
5
6  public class ButtonDemo extends JFrame {
7    // Create a panel for displaying message
8    protected MessagePanel messagePanel
9      = new MessagePanel("Welcome to Java");
10
11   // Declare two buttons to move the message left and right
12   private JButton jbtLeft = new JButton("<=");
13   private JButton jbtRight = new JButton("=>");
14
15   public static void main(String[] args) {
16     ButtonDemo frame = new ButtonDemo();
17     frame.setTitle("ButtonDemo");
18     frame.setSize(250, 100);
19     frame.setLocationRelativeTo(null); // Center the frame
20     frame.setDefaultCloseOperation(JFrame.EXIT_ON_CLOSE);
21     frame.setVisible(true);
22   }
23
24   public ButtonDemo() {
25     // Set the background color of messagePanel
26     messagePanel.setBackground(Color.white);
27
28     // Create Panel jpButtons to hold two Buttons "<=" and "right =>"
29     JPanel jpButtons = new JPanel();
```

create frame

create UI

```
┌─────────────┐
│   JFrame    │
└─────────────┘
       ▲
       │
┌─────────────┐
│ CheckBoxDemo│
└─────────────┘
```

```
30      jpButtons.setLayout(new FlowLayout());
31      jpButtons.add(jbtLeft);
32      jpButtons.add(jbtRight);
33
34      // Set keyboard mnemonics
35      jbtLeft.setMnemonic('L');                                          mnemonic
36      jbtRight.setMnemonic('R');
37
38      // Set icons and remove text
39      // jbtLeft.setIcon(new ImageIcon("image/left.gif"));
40      // jbtRight.setIcon(new ImageIcon("image/right.gif"));
41      // jbtLeft.setText(null);
42      // jbtRight.setText(null);
43
44      // Set tool tip text on the buttons
45      jbtLeft.setToolTipText("Move message to left");                    tool tip
46      jbtRight.setToolTipText("Move message to right");
47
48      // Place panels in the frame
49      setLayout(new BorderLayout());
50      add(messagePanel, BorderLayout.CENTER);
51      add(jpButtons, BorderLayout.SOUTH);
52
53      // Register listeners with the buttons
54      jbtLeft.addActionListener(new ActionListener() {                   register listener
55        public void actionPerformed(ActionEvent e) {
56          messagePanel.moveLeft();
57        }
58      });
59      jbtRight.addActionListener(new ActionListener() {                  register listener
60        public void actionPerformed(ActionEvent e) {
61          messagePanel.moveRight();
62        }
63      });
64    }
65 }
```

`messagePanel` (line 10) is deliberately declared `protected` so that it can be referenced by a subclass in future examples.

You can set an icon image on the button by using the `setIcon` method. If you uncomment the following code in lines 39–42:

```
// jbtLeft.setIcon(new ImageIcon("image/left.gif"));
// jbtRight.setIcon(new ImageIcon("image/right.gif"));
// jbtLeft.setText(null);
// jbtRight.setText(null);
```

the texts are replaced by the icons, as shown in Figure 16.10(a). `"image/left.gif"` is located in `"c:\book\image\left.gif"`. Note that the back slash is the Windows file path notation. In Java, the forward slash should be used.

You can set text and an icon on a button at the same time, if you wish, as shown in Figure 16.10(b). By default, the text and icon are centered horizontally and vertically.

The button can also be accessed by using the keyboard mnemonics. Pressing ALT+L is equivalent to clicking the <= button, since you set the mnemonic property to `'L'` in the left button (line 35). If you change the left button text to `"Left"` and the right button to `"Right"`, the `L` and `R` in the captions of these buttons will be underlined, as shown in Figure 16.10(b).

Each button has a tool-tip text (lines 45–46), which appears when the mouse is set on the button without clicking, as shown in Figure 16.10(c).

(a)   (b)   (c)

FIGURE 16.10   You can set an icon on a `JButton` and access a button using mnemonic keys.

locating **MessagePanel**

> 🏺 **Note**
>
> Since `MessagePanel` is not in the Java API, you should place MessagePanel.java in the same directory with ButtonDemo.java.

16.3 Check Boxes

toggle button

A *toggle button* is a two-state button like a light switch. `JToggleButton` inherits `AbstractButton` and implements a toggle button. Often `JToggleButton`'s subclasses `JCheckBox` and `JRadioButton` are used to enable the user to toggle a choice on or off. This section introduces `JCheckBox`. `JRadioButton` will be introduced in the next section.

`JCheckBox` inherits all the properties from `AbstractButton`, such as `text`, `icon`, `mnemonic`, `verticalAlignment`, `horizontalAlignment`, `horizontalTextPosition`, `verticalTextPosition`, and `selected`, and provides several constructors to create check boxes, as shown in Figure 16.11.

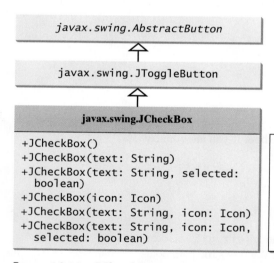

FIGURE 16.11   `JCheckBox` defines a check box button.

Here is an example of a check box with text Student, red foreground, white background, mnemonic key `'S'`, and initially selected.

```
JCheckBox jchk = new JCheckBox("Student", true);
jchk.setForeground(Color.RED);
jchk.setBackground(Color.WHITE);
jchk.setMnemonic('S');
```

When a check box is clicked (checked or unchecked), it fires an `ItemEvent` and then an `ActionEvent`. To see if a check box is selected, use the `isSelected()` method.

Listing 16.3 gives a program that adds three check boxes named *Centered*, *Bold*, and *Italic* to the preceding example to let the user specify whether the message is centered, bold, or italic, as shown in Figure 16.12.

JPanel with GridLayout for three check boxes

FIGURE 16.12 Three check boxes are added to specify how the message is displayed.

There are at least two approaches to writing this program. The first is to revise the preceding **ButtonDemo** class to insert the code for adding the check boxes and processing their events. The second is to create a subclass that extends **ButtonDemo**. Please implement the first approach as an exercise. Listing 16.3 gives the code to implement the second approach.

Video Note
Use check boxes

LISTING 16.3 CheckBoxDemo.java

```java
1 import java.awt.*;
2 import java.awt.event.*;
3 import javax.swing.*;
4
5 public class CheckBoxDemo extends ButtonDemo {
6   // Create three check boxes to control the display of message
7   private JCheckBox jchkCentered = new JCheckBox("Centered");
8   private JCheckBox jchkBold = new JCheckBox("Bold");
9   private JCheckBox jchkItalic = new JCheckBox("Italic");
10
11  public static void main(String[] args) {
12    CheckBoxDemo frame = new CheckBoxDemo();
13    frame.setTitle("CheckBoxDemo");
14    frame.setSize(500, 200);
15    frame.setLocationRelativeTo(null); // Center the frame
16    frame.setDefaultCloseOperation(JFrame.EXIT_ON_CLOSE);
17    frame.setVisible(true);
18  }
19
20  public CheckBoxDemo() {
21    // Set mnemonic keys
22    jchkCentered.setMnemonic('C');
23    jchkBold.setMnemonic('B');
24    jchkItalic.setMnemonic('I');
25
26    // Create a new panel to hold check boxes
27    JPanel jpCheckBoxes = new JPanel();
28    jpCheckBoxes.setLayout(new GridLayout(3, 1));
29    jpCheckBoxes.add(jchkCentered);
30    jpCheckBoxes.add(jchkBold);
31    jpCheckBoxes.add(jchkItalic);
32    add(jpCheckBoxes, BorderLayout.EAST);
33
34    // Register listeners with the check boxes
35    jchkCentered.addActionListener(new ActionListener() {
```

JFrame
↑
ButtonDemo
↑
CheckBoxDemo

create frame

create UI

register listener

register listener

set a new font

```
36       public void actionPerformed(ActionEvent e) {
37          messagePanel.setCentered(jchkCentered.isSelected());
38       }
39    });
40    jchkBold.addActionListener(new ActionListener() {
41       public void actionPerformed(ActionEvent e) {
42          setNewFont();
43       }
44    });
45    jchkItalic.addActionListener(new ActionListener() {
46       public void actionPerformed(ActionEvent e) {
47          setNewFont();
48       }
49    });
50  }
51
52  private void setNewFont() {
53    // Determine a font style
54    int fontStyle = Font.PLAIN;
55    fontStyle += (jchkBold.isSelected() ? Font.BOLD : Font.PLAIN);
56    fontStyle += (jchkItalic.isSelected() ? Font.ITALIC : Font.PLAIN);
57
58    // Set font for the message
59    Font font = messagePanel.getFont();
60    messagePanel.setFont(
61      new Font(font.getName(), fontStyle, font.getSize()));
62  }
63 }
```

CheckBoxDemo extends ButtonDemo and adds three check boxes to control how the message is displayed. When a CheckBoxDemo is constructed (line 12), its superclass's no-arg constructor is invoked, so you don't have to rewrite the code that is already in the constructor of ButtonDemo.

When a check box is checked or unchecked, the listener's actionPerformed method is invoked to process the event. When the *Centered* check box is checked or unchecked, the centered property of the MessagePanel class is set to true or false.

The current font name and size used in MessagePanel are obtained from messagePanel.getFont() using the getName() and getSize() methods. The font styles (Font.BOLD and Font.ITALIC) are specified in the check boxes. If no font style is selected, the font style is Font.PLAIN. Font styles are combined by adding together the selected integers representing the fonts.

The keyboard mnemonics *C*, *B*, and *I* are set on the check boxes *Centered*, *Bold*, and *Italic*, respectively (lines 22–24). You can use a mouse gesture or a shortcut key to select a check box.

The setFont method (line 60) defined in the Component class is inherited in the MessagePanel class. This method automatically invokes the repaint method. Invoking setFont in messagePanel automatically repaints the message.

A check box fires an ActionEvent and an ItemEvent when it is clicked. You could process either the ActionEvent or the ItemEvent to redisplay the message. The example processes the ActionEvent. If you wished to process the ItemEvent, you could create a listener for ItemEvent and register it with a check box, as shown below:

```
public class CheckBoxDemoUsingItemEvent extends ButtonDemo {
  ... // Same as in CheckBoxDemo.java, so omitted

  public CheckBoxDemoUsingItemEvent() {
    ... // Same as in CheckBoxDemo.java, so omitted
```

```
// TO listen for ItemEvent
jchkCentered.addItemListener(new ItemListener() {
  /** Handle ItemEvent */
  public void itemStateChanged(ItemEvent e) {
    messagePanel.setCentered(jchkCentered.isSelected());
  }
});
  }
}
```

16.4 Radio Buttons

Radio buttons, also known as *option buttons*, enable you to choose a single item from a group of choices. In appearance radio buttons resemble check boxes, but check boxes display a square that is either checked or blank, whereas radio buttons display a circle that is either filled (if selected) or blank (if not selected).

JRadioButton inherits AbstractButton and provides several constructors to create radio buttons, as shown in Figure 16.13. These constructors are similar to the constructors for JCheckBox.

FIGURE 16.13 JRadioButton defines a radio button.

Here is an example of a radio button with text Student, RED foreground, WHITE background, mnemonic key 'S', and initially selected.

```
JRadioButton jrb = new JRadioButton("Student", true);
jrb.setForeground(Color.RED);
jrb.setBackground(Color.WHITE);
jrb.setMnemonic('S');
```

To group radio buttons, you need to create an instance of java.swing.ButtonGroup and use the add method to add them to it, as follows:

```
ButtonGroup group = new ButtonGroup();
group.add(jrb1);
group.add(jrb2);
```

This code creates a radio button group for radio buttons jrb1 and jrb2 so that jrb1 and jrb2 are selected mutually exclusively. Without grouping, jrb1 and jrb2 would be independent.

Note

ButtonGroup is not a subclass of java.awt.Component, so a ButtonGroup object cannot be added to a container.

When a radio button is changed (selected or deselected), it fires an ItemEvent and then an ActionEvent. To see if a radio button is selected, use the isSelected() method.

Listing 16.4 gives a program that adds three radio buttons named *Red*, *Green*, and *Blue* to the preceding example to let the user choose the color of the message, as shown in Figure 16.14.

FIGURE 16.14 Three radio buttons are added to specify the color of the message.

Again there are at least two approaches to writing this program. The first is to revise the preceding CheckBoxDemo class to insert the code for adding the radio buttons and processing their events. The second is to create a subclass that extends CheckBoxDemo. Listing 16.4 gives the code to implement the second approach.

LISTING 16.4 RadioButtonDemo.java

Video Note
Use radio buttons

create frame

create UI

```
1  import java.awt.*;
2  import java.awt.event.*;
3  import javax.swing.*;
4
5  public class RadioButtonDemo extends CheckBoxDemo {
6    // Declare radio buttons
7    private JRadioButton jrbRed, jrbGreen, jrbBlue;
8
9    public static void main(String[] args) {
10     RadioButtonDemo frame = new RadioButtonDemo();
11     frame.setSize(500, 200);
12     frame.setLocationRelativeTo(null); // Center the frame
13     frame.setDefaultCloseOperation(JFrame.EXIT_ON_CLOSE);
14     frame.setTitle("RadioButtonDemo");
15     frame.setVisible(true);
16   }
17
18   public RadioButtonDemo() {
19     // Create a new panel to hold check boxes
20     JPanel jpRadioButtons = new JPanel();
21     jpRadioButtons.setLayout(new GridLayout(3, 1));
22     jpRadioButtons.add(jrbRed = new JRadioButton("Red"));
23     jpRadioButtons.add(jrbGreen = new JRadioButton("Green"));
```

```
24      jpRadioButtons.add(jrbBlue = new JRadioButton("Blue"));
25      add(jpRadioButtons, BorderLayout.WEST);
26
27      // Create a radio button group to group three buttons
28      ButtonGroup group = new ButtonGroup();                       group buttons
29      group.add(jrbRed);
30      group.add(jrbGreen);
31      group.add(jrbBlue);
32
33      // Set keyboard mnemonics
34      jrbRed.setMnemonic('E');
35      jrbGreen.setMnemonic('G');
36      jrbBlue.setMnemonic('U');
37
38      // Register listeners for check boxes
39      jrbRed.addActionListener(new ActionListener() {              register listener
40        public void actionPerformed(ActionEvent e) {
41          messagePanel.setForeground(Color.red);
42        }
43      });
44      jrbGreen.addActionListener(new ActionListener() {            register listener
45        public void actionPerformed(ActionEvent e) {
46          messagePanel.setForeground(Color.green);
47        }
48      });
49      jrbBlue.addActionListener(new ActionListener() {             register listener
50        public void actionPerformed(ActionEvent e) {
51          messagePanel.setForeground(Color.blue);
52        }
53      });
54
55      // Set initial message color to blue
56      jrbBlue.setSelected(true);
57      messagePanel.setForeground(Color.blue);
58    }
59 }
```

RadioButtonDemo extends CheckBoxDemo and adds three radio buttons to specify the message color. When a radio button is clicked, the radio button's action event listener sets the corresponding foreground color in messagePanel.

The keyboard mnemonics 'R' and 'B' are already set for the Right button and Bold check box. To avoid conflict, the keyboard mnemonics 'E', 'G', and 'U' are set on the radio buttons *Red*, *Green*, and *Blue*, respectively (lines 34–36).

The program creates a ButtonGroup and puts three JRadioButton instances (jrbRed, jrbGreen, and jrbBlue) in the group (lines 28–31).

A radio button fires an ActionEvent and an ItemEvent when it is selected or deselected. You could process either the ActionEvent or the ItemEvent to choose a color. The example processes the ActionEvent. Please rewrite the code using the ItemEvent as an exercise.

16.5 Labels

A *label* is a display area for a short text, an image, or both. It is often used to label other components (usually text fields). Figure 16.15 lists the constructors and methods in JLabel.

FIGURE 16.15 JLabel displays text or an icon, or both.

JLabel inherits all the properties from JComponent and has many properties similar to the ones in JButton, such as text, icon, horizontalAlignment, verticalAlignment, horizontalTextPosition, verticalTextPosition, and iconTextGap. For example, the following code displays a label with text and an icon:

```
// Create an image icon from an image file
ImageIcon icon = new ImageIcon("image/grapes.gif");

// Create a label with a text, an icon,
// with centered horizontal alignment
JLabel jlbl = new JLabel("Grapes", icon, SwingConstants.CENTER);

//Set label's text alignment and gap between text and icon
jlbl.setHorizontalTextPosition(SwingConstants.CENTER);
jlbl.setVerticalTextPosition(SwingConstants.BOTTOM);
jlbl.setIconTextGap(5);
```

16.6 Text Fields

A *text field* can be used to enter or display a string. JTextField is a subclass of JTextComponent. Figure 16.16 lists the constructors and methods in JTextField.

JTextField inherits JTextComponent, which inherits JComponent. Here is an example of creating a non-editable text field with red foreground color and right horizontal alignment:

```
JTextField jtfMessage = new JTextField("T-Strom");
jtfMessage.setEditable(false);
jtfMessage.setForeground(Color.RED);
jtfMessage.setHorizontalAlignment(SwingConstants.RIGHT);
```

When you move the cursor in the text field and press the *Enter* key, it fires an ActionEvent.

Listing 16.5 gives a program that adds a text field to the preceding example to let the user set a new message, as shown in Figure 16.17.

The **get** and **set** methods for these data fields are provided in the class, but omitted in the UML diagram for brevity.

The text contained in this text component.
Indicates whether this text component is editable (default: true).

The number of columns in this text field.
The horizontal alignment of this text field (default: LEFT).

Creates a default empty text field with number of columns set to 0.
Creates an empty text field with a specified number of columns.
Creates a text field initialized with the specified text.
Creates a text field initialized with the specified text and columns.

FIGURE 16.16 `JTextField` enables you to enter or display a string.

FIGURE 16.17 A label and a text field are added to set a new message.

Listing 16.5 creates a subclass that extends `RadioButtonDemo`.

LISTING 16.5 `TextFieldDemo.java`

```java
1  import java.awt.*;
2  import java.awt.event.*;
3  import javax.swing.*;
4
5  public class TextFieldDemo extends RadioButtonDemo {
6    private JTextField jtfMessage = new JTextField(10);
7
8    /** Main method */
9    public static void main(String[] args) {
10     TextFieldDemo frame = new TextFieldDemo();
11     frame.pack();
12     frame.setTitle("TextFieldDemo");
13     frame.setLocationRelativeTo(null); // Center the frame
14     frame.setDefaultCloseOperation(JFrame.EXIT_ON_CLOSE);
15     frame.setVisible(true);
16   }
17
18   public TextFieldDemo() {
19     // Create a new panel to hold label and text field
20     JPanel jpTextField = new JPanel();
21     jpTextField.setLayout(new BorderLayout(5, 0));
22     jpTextField.add(
23       new JLabel("Enter a new message"), BorderLayout.WEST);
24     jpTextField.add(jtfMessage, BorderLayout.CENTER);
```

Video Note
Use labels and text fields

create frame
pack frame

create UI

```
25        add(jpTextField, BorderLayout.NORTH);
26
27        jtfMessage.setHorizontalAlignment(JTextField.RIGHT);
28
29        // Register listener
30        jtfMessage.addActionListener(new ActionListener() {
31          /** Handle ActionEvent */
32          public void actionPerformed(ActionEvent e) {
33            messagePanel.setMessage(jtfMessage.getText());
34            jtfMessage.requestFocusInWindow();
35          }
36        });
37      }
38    }
```

listener

TextFieldDemo extends RadioButtonDemo and adds a label and a text field to let the user enter a new message. After you set a new message in the text field and press the *Enter* key, a new message is displayed. Pressing the *Enter* key on the text field triggers an action event. The listener sets a new message in messagePanel (line 33).

pack()

The pack() method (line 11) automatically sizes up the frame according to the size of the components placed in it.

requestFocusInWindow()

The requestFocusInWindow() method (line 34) defined in the Component class requests the component to receive input focus. Thus, jtfMessage.requestFocusInWindow() requests the input focus on jtfMessage. You will see the cursor on jtfMessage after the actionPerformed method is invoked.

Note

JPasswordField

If a text field is used for entering a password, use JPasswordField to replace JTextField. JPasswordField extends JTextField and hides the input text with echo charaters (e.g., ******). By default, the echo character is *. You can specify a new echo character using the setEchoChar(char) method.

16.7 Text Areas

If you want to let the user enter multiple lines of text, you have to create several instances of JTextField. A better alternative is to use JTextArea, which enables the user to enter multiple lines of text. Figure 16.18 lists the constructors and methods in JTextArea.

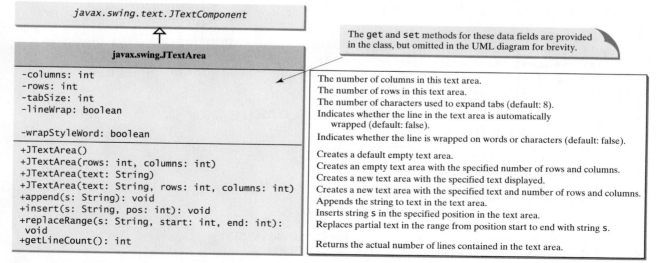

FIGURE 16.18 JTextArea enables you to enter or display multiple lines of characters.

Like `JTextField`, `JTextArea` inherits `JTextComponent`, which contains the methods `getText`, `setText`, `isEditable`, and `setEditable`. Here is an example of creating a text area with five rows and 20 columns, line-wrapped on words, `red` foreground color, and `Courier` font, **bold**, 20 pixels.

```
JTextArea jtaNote = new JTextArea("This is a text area", 5, 20);
jtaNote.setLineWrap(true);                                          wrap line
jtaNote.setWrapStyleWord(true);                                     wrap word
jtaNote.setForeground(Color.RED);
jtaNote.setFont(new Font("Courier", Font.BOLD, 20));
```

`JTextArea` does not handle scrolling, but you can create a `JScrollPane` object to hold an instance of `JTextArea` and let `JScrollPane` handle scrolling for `JTextArea`, as follows:

```
// Create a scroll pane to hold text area
JScrollPane scrollPane = new JScrollPane(jta = new JTextArea());
add(scrollPane, BorderLayout.CENTER);
```

Listing 16.7 gives a program that displays an image and a text in a label, and a text in a text area, as shown in Figure 16.19.

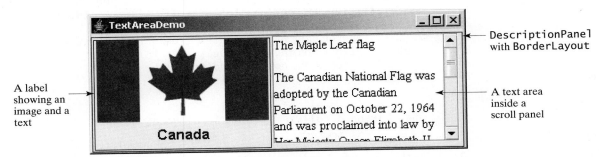

FIGURE 16.19   The program displays an image in a label, a title in a label, and a text in the text area.

Here are the major steps in the program:

1. Create a class named `DescriptionPanel` that extends `JPanel`, as shown in Listing 16.6. This class contains a text area inside a scroll pane, and a label for displaying an image icon and a title. This class is used in the present example and will be reused in later examples.

2. Create a class named `TextAreaDemo` that extends `JFrame`, as shown in Listing 16.7. Create an instance of `DescriptionPanel` and add it to the center of the frame. The relationship between `DescriptionPanel` and `TextAreaDemo` is shown in Figure 16.20.

FIGURE 16.20   `TextAreaDemo` uses `DescriptionPanel` to display an image, title, and text description of a national flag.

LISTING 16.6 DescriptionPanel.java

```
1  import javax.swing.*;
2  import java.awt.*;
3
4  public class DescriptionPanel extends JPanel {
5    /** Label for displaying an image icon and a text */
6    private JLabel jlblImageTitle = new JLabel();
7
8    /** Text area for displaying text */
9    private JTextArea jtaDescription = new JTextArea();
10
11   public DescriptionPanel() {
12     // Center the icon and text and place the text under the icon
13     jlblImageTitle.setHorizontalAlignment(JLabel.CENTER);
14     jlblImageTitle.setHorizontalTextPosition(JLabel.CENTER);
15     jlblImageTitle.setVerticalTextPosition(JLabel.BOTTOM);
16
17     // Set the font in the label and the text field
18     jlblImageTitle.setFont(new Font("SansSerif", Font.BOLD, 16));
19     jtaDescription.setFont(new Font("Serif", Font.PLAIN, 14));
20
21     // Set lineWrap and wrapStyleWord true for the text area
22     jtaDescription.setLineWrap(true);
23     jtaDescription.setWrapStyleWord(true);
24     jtaDescription.setEditable(false);
25
26     // Create a scroll pane to hold the text area
27     JScrollPane scrollPane = new JScrollPane(jtaDescription);
28
29     // Set BorderLayout for the panel, add label and scrollpane
30     setLayout(new BorderLayout(5, 5));
31     add(scrollPane, BorderLayout.CENTER);
32     add(jlblImageTitle, BorderLayout.WEST);
33   }
34
35   /** Set the title */
36   public void setTitle(String title) {
37     jlblImageTitle.setText(title);
38   }
39
40   /** Set the image icon */
41   public void setImageIcon(ImageIcon icon) {
42     jlblImageTitle.setIcon(icon);
43   }
44
45   /** Set the text description */
46   public void setDescription(String text) {
47     jtaDescription.setText(text);
48   }
49 }
```

label

text area

label properties

wrap line
wrap word
read only

scroll pane

The text area is inside a **JScrollPane** (line 27), which provides scrolling functions for the text area. Scroll bars automatically appear if there is more text than the physical size of the text area, and disappear if the text is deleted and the remaining text does not exceed the text area size.

The **lineWrap** property is set to **true** (line 21) so that the line is automatically wrapped when the text cannot fit in one line. The **wrapStyleWord** property is set to **true** (line 23) so that the line is wrapped on words rather than characters. The text area is set non-editable (line 24), so you cannot edit the description in the text area.

It is not necessary to create a separate class for `DescriptionPanel` in this example. Nevertheless, this class was created for reuse in the next example, where you will use it to display a description panel for various images.

LISTING 16.7 `TextAreaDemo.java`

```
 1  import java.awt.*;
 2  import javax.swing.*;
 3
 4  public class TextAreaDemo extends JFrame {
 5    // Declare and create a description panel
 6    private DescriptionPanel descriptionPanel = new DescriptionPanel();     create descriptionPanel
 7
 8    public static void main(String[] args) {
 9      TextAreaDemo frame = new TextAreaDemo();                              create frame
10      frame.pack();
11      frame.setLocationRelativeTo(null); // Center the frame
12      frame.setDefaultCloseOperation(JFrame.EXIT_ON_CLOSE);
13      frame.setTitle("TextAreaDemo");
14      frame.setVisible(true);
15    }
16
17    public TextAreaDemo() {
18      // Set title, text and image in the description panel              create UI
19      descriptionPanel.setTitle("Canada");
20      String description = "The Maple Leaf flag \n\n" +
21        "The Canadian National Flag was adopted by the Canadian " +
22        "Parliament on October 22, 1964 and was proclaimed into law " +
23        "by Her Majesty Queen Elizabeth II (the Queen of Canada) on " +
24        "February 15, 1965. The Canadian Flag (colloquially known " +
25        "as The Maple Leaf Flag) is a red flag of the proportions " +
26        "two by length and one by width, containing in its center a " +
27        "white square, with a single red stylized eleven-point " +
28        "mapleleaf centered in the white square.";
29      descriptionPanel.setDescription(description);
30      descriptionPanel.setImageIcon(new ImageIcon("image/ca.gif"));
31
32      // Add the description panel to the frame
33      setLayout(new BorderLayout());
34      add(descriptionPanel, BorderLayout.CENTER);                         add descriptionPanel
35    }
36  }
```

`TextAreaDemo` simply creates an instance of `DescriptionPanel` (line 6), and sets the title (line 19), image (line 30), and text in the description panel (line 29). `DescriptionPanel` is a subclass of `JPanel`. `DescriptionPanel` contains a label for displaying an image icon and a text title, and a text area for displaying a description of the image.

16.8 Combo Boxes

A *combo box*, also known as a *choice list* or *drop-down list*, contains a list of items from which the user can choose. It is useful in limiting a user's range of choices and avoids the cumbersome validation of data input. Figure 16.21 lists several frequently used constructors and methods in `JComboBox`.

The following statements create a combo box with four items, red foreground, white background, and the second item selected.

```
JComboBox jcb = new JComboBox(new Object[]
    {"Item 1", "Item 2", "Item 3", "Item 4"});
jcb.setForeground(Color.RED);
jcb.setBackground(Color.WHITE);
jcb.setSelectedItem("Item 2");
```

FIGURE 16.21   JComboBox enables you to select an item from a set of items.

JComboBox can generate **ActionEvent** and **ItemEvent**, among many other events. Whenever an item is selected, an **ActionEvent** is fired. Whenever a new item is selected, JComboBox generates **ItemEvent** twice, once for deselecting the previously selected item, and the other for selecting the currently selected item. Note that no **ItemEvent** is fired if the current item is reselected. To respond to an **ItemEvent**, you need to implement the **itemStateChanged(ItemEvent e)** handler for processing a choice. To get data from a JComboBox menu, you can use **getSelectedItem()** to return the currently selected item, or **e.getItem()** method to get the item from the **itemStateChanged(ItemEvent e)** handler.

Listing 16.8 gives a program that lets users view an image and a description of a country's flag by selecting the country from a combo box, as shown in Figure 16.22.

FIGURE 16.22   A country's info, including a flag image and a description of the flag, is displayed when the country is selected in the combo box.

Here are the major steps in the program:

1. Create the user interface.

    Create a combo box with country names as its selection values. Create a **DescriptionPanel** object. The **DescriptionPanel** class was introduced in the preceding example. Place the combo box in the north of the frame and the description panel in the center of the frame.

2. Process the event.
Create a listener to implement the `itemStateChanged` handler to set the flag title, image, and text in the description panel for the selected country name.

LISTING 16.8 ComboBoxDemo.java

```java
1  import java.awt.*;
2  import java.awt.event.*;
3  import javax.swing.*;
4
5  public class ComboBoxDemo extends JFrame {
6    // Declare an array of Strings for flag titles
7    private String[] flagTitles = {"Canada", "China", "Denmark",            country
8      "France", "Germany", "India", "Norway", "United Kingdom",
9      "United States of America"};
10
11   // Declare an ImageIcon array for the national flags of 9 countries
12   private ImageIcon[] flagImage = {                                        image icon
13     new ImageIcon("image/ca.gif"),
14     new ImageIcon("image/china.gif"),
15     new ImageIcon("image/denmark.gif"),
16     new ImageIcon("image/fr.gif"),
17     new ImageIcon("image/germany.gif"),
18     new ImageIcon("image/india.gif"),
19     new ImageIcon("image/norway.gif"),
20     new ImageIcon("image/uk.gif"),
21     new ImageIcon("image/us.gif")
22   };
23
24   // Declare an array of strings for flag descriptions
25   private String[] flagDescription = new String[9];                        description
26
27   // Declare and create a description panel
28   private DescriptionPanel descriptionPanel = new DescriptionPanel();
29
30   // Create a combo box for selecting countries
31   private JComboBox jcbo = new JComboBox(flagTitles);                      combo box
32
33   public static void main(String[] args) {
34     ComboBoxDemo frame = new ComboBoxDemo();
35     frame.pack();
36     frame.setTitle("ComboBoxDemo");
37     frame.setLocationRelativeTo(null); // Center the frame
38     frame.setDefaultCloseOperation(JFrame.EXIT_ON_CLOSE);
39     frame.setVisible(true);
40   }
41
42   public ComboBoxDemo() {
43     // Set text description
44     flagDescription[0] = "The Maple Leaf flag \n\n" +
45       "The Canadian National Flag was adopted by the Canadian " +
46       "Parliament on October 22, 1964 and was proclaimed into law " +
47       "by Her Majesty Queen Elizabeth II (the Queen of Canada) on " +
48       "February 15, 1965. The Canadian Flag (colloquially known " +
49       "as The Maple Leaf Flag) is a red flag of the proportions " +
50       "two by length and one by width, containing in its center a " +
51       "white square, with a single red stylized eleven-point " +
52       "mapleleaf centered in the white square.";
53     flagDescription[1] = "Description for China ... ";
```

```
54     flagDescription[2] = "Description for Denmark ... ";
55     flagDescription[3] = "Description for France ... ";
56     flagDescription[4] = "Description for Germany ... ";
57     flagDescription[5] = "Description for India ... ";
58     flagDescription[6] = "Description for Norway ... ";
59     flagDescription[7] = "Description for UK ... ";
60     flagDescription[8] = "Description for US ... ";
61
62     // Set the first country (Canada) for display
63     setDisplay(0);
64
65     // Add combo box and description panel to the list
66     add(jcbo, BorderLayout.NORTH);
67     add(descriptionPanel, BorderLayout.CENTER);
68
69     // Register listener
70     jcbo.addItemListener(new ItemListener() {
71       /** Handle item selection */
72       public void itemStateChanged(ItemEvent e) {
73         setDisplay(jcbo.getSelectedIndex());
74       }
75     });
76   }
77
78   /** Set display information on the description panel */
79   public void setDisplay(int index) {
80     descriptionPanel.setTitle(flagTitles[index]);
81     descriptionPanel.setImageIcon(flagImage[index]);
82     descriptionPanel.setDescription(flagDescription[index]);
83   }
84 }
```

(margin note: create UI, at line 66)
(margin note: listener, at line 70)

The listener listens to `ItemEvent` from the combo box and implements `ItemListener` (lines 70–75). Instead of using `ItemEvent`, you may rewrite the program to use `ActionEvent` for handling combo box item selection.

The program stores the flag information in three arrays: `flagTitles`, `flagImage`, and `flagDescription` (lines 7–25). The array `flagTitles` contains the names of nine countries, the array `flagImage` contains images of the nine countries' flags, and the array `flagDescription` contains descriptions of the flags.

The program creates an instance of `DescriptionPanel` (line 28), which was presented in Listing 16.6, TextAreasDemo.java. The program creates a combo box with initial values from `flagTitles` (line 31). When the user selects an item in the combo box, the `ItemStateChanged` handler is executed, finds the selected index, and sets its corresponding flag title, flag image, and flag description on the panel.

16.9 Lists

A *list* is a component that basically performs the same function as a combo box but enables the user to choose a single value or multiple values. The Swing `JList` is very versatile. Figure 16.23 lists several frequently used constructors and methods in `JList`.

`selectionMode` is one of the three values (`SINGLE_SELECTION`, `SINGLE_INTERVAL_SELECTION`, `MULTIPLE_INTERVAL_SELECTION`) defined in `javax.swing.ListSelectionModel` that indicate whether a single item, single-interval item, or multiple-interval item can be selected. Single selection allows only one item to be selected. Single-interval selection allows multiple selections, but the selected items must be contiguous. Multiple-interval selection allows selections of multiple contiguous items without restrictions, as shown in Figure 16.24. The default value is `MULTIPLE_INTERVAL_SELECTION`.

FIGURE 16.23 `JList` enables you to select multiple items from a set of items.

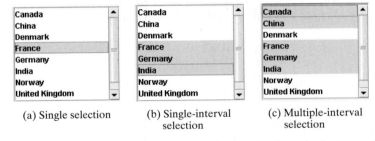

(a) Single selection   (b) Single-interval
                            selection   (c) Multiple-interval
                                            selection

FIGURE 16.24 `JList` has three selection modes: single selection, single-interval selection, and multiple-interval selection.

The following statements create a list with six items, `red` foreground, `white` background, `pink` selection foreground, `black` selection background, and visible row count `4`.

```
JList jlst = new JList(new Object[]
  {"Item 1", "Item 2", "Item 3", "Item 4", "Item 5", "Item 6"});
jlst.setForeground(Color.RED);
jlst.setBackground(Color.WHITE);
jlst.setSelectionForeground(Color.PINK);
jlst.setSelectionBackground(Color.BLACK);
jlst.setVisibleRowCount(4);
```

Lists do not scroll automatically. To make a list scrollable, create a scroll pane and add the list to it. Text areas are made scrollable in the same way.

`JList` generates `javax.swing.event.ListSelectionEvent` to notify the listeners of the selections. The listener must implement the `valueChanged` handler in the `javax.swing.event.ListSelectionListener` interface to process the event.

Listing 16.9 gives a program that lets users select countries in a list and display the flags of the selected countries in the labels. Figure 16.25 shows a sample run of the program.

FIGURE 16.25 When the countries in the list are selected, corresponding images of their flags are displayed in the labels.

Here are the major steps in the program:

1. Create the user interface.
   Create a list with nine country names as selection values, and place the list inside a scroll pane. Place the scroll pane in the west of the frame. Create nine labels to be used to display the countries' flag images. Place the labels in the panel, and place the panel in the center of the frame.

2. Process the event.
   Create a listener to implement the `valueChanged` method in the `ListSelection-Listener` interface to set the selected countries' flag images in the labels.

LISTING 16.9 `ListDemo.java`

```java
1 import java.awt.*;
2 import javax.swing.*;
3 import javax.swing.event.*;
4
5 public class ListDemo extends JFrame {
6   final int NUMBER_OF_FLAGS = 9;
7
8   // Declare an array of Strings for flag titles
9   private String[] flagTitles = {"Canada", "China", "Denmark",
10    "France", "Germany", "India", "Norway", "United Kingdom",
11    "United States of America"};
12
13   // The list for selecting countries
14   private JList jlst = new JList(flagTitles);
15
16   // Declare an ImageIcon array for the national flags of 9 countries
17   private ImageIcon[] imageIcons = {
18     new ImageIcon("image/ca.gif"),
19     new ImageIcon("image/china.gif"),
20     new ImageIcon("image/denmark.gif"),
21     new ImageIcon("image/fr.gif"),
22     new ImageIcon("image/germany.gif"),
23     new ImageIcon("image/india.gif"),
24     new ImageIcon("image/norway.gif"),
25     new ImageIcon("image/uk.gif"),
26     new ImageIcon("image/us.gif")
27   };
28
29   // Arrays of labels for displaying images
30   private JLabel[] jlblImageViewer = new JLabel[NUMBER_OF_FLAGS];
31
```

```
32    public static void main(String[] args) {
33      ListDemo frame = new ListDemo();
34      frame.setSize(650, 500);
35      frame.setTitle("ListDemo");
36      frame.setLocationRelativeTo(null); // Center the frame
37      frame.setDefaultCloseOperation(JFrame.EXIT_ON_CLOSE);
38      frame.setVisible(true);
39    }
40
41    public ListDemo() {
42      // Create a panel to hold nine labels
43      JPanel p = new JPanel(new GridLayout(3, 3, 5, 5));
44
45      for (int i = 0; i < NUMBER_OF_FLAGS; i++) {
46        p.add(jlblImageViewer[i] = new JLabel());
47        jlblImageViewer[i].setHorizontalAlignment
48          (SwingConstants.CENTER);
49      }
50
51      // Add p and the list to the frame
52      add(p, BorderLayout.CENTER);
53      add(new JScrollPane(jlst), BorderLayout.WEST);
54
55      // Register listeners
56      jlst.addListSelectionListener(new ListSelectionListener() {
57        /** Handle list selection */
58        public void valueChanged(ListSelectionEvent e) {
59          // Get selected indices
60          int[] indices = jlst.getSelectedIndices();
61
62          int i;
63          // Set icons in the labels
64          for (i = 0; i < indices.length; i++) {
65            jlblImageViewer[i].setIcon(imageIcons[indices[i]]);
66          }
67
68          // Remove icons from the rest of the labels
69          for (; i < NUMBER_OF_FLAGS; i++) {
70            jlblImageViewer[i].setIcon(null);
71          }
72        }
73      });
74    }
75  }
```

create frame

create UI

event handler

The anonymous inner class listener listens to **ListSelectionEvent** for handling the selection of country names in the list (lines 56–73). **ListSelectionEvent** and **List-SelectionListener** are defined in the **javax.swing.event** package, so this package is imported in the program (line 3).

The program creates an array of nine labels for displaying flag images for nine countries. The program loads the images of the nine countries into an image array (lines 17–27) and creates a list of the nine countries in the same order as in the image array (lines 9–11). Thus the index **0** of the image array corresponds to the first country in the list.

The list is placed in a scroll pane (line 53) so that it can be scrolled when the number of items in the list extends beyond the viewing area.

By default, the selection mode of the list is multiple-interval, which allows the user to select multiple items from different blocks in the list. When the user selects countries in the list, the **valueChanged** handler (lines 58–72) is executed, which gets the indices of the selected item and sets their corresponding image icons in the label to display the flags.

16.10 Scroll Bars

`JScrollBar` is a component that enables the user to select from a range of values, as shown in Figure 11.26.

FIGURE 16.26 A scroll bar represents a range of values graphically.

Normally, the user changes the value of the scroll bar by making a gesture with the mouse. For example, the user can drag the scroll bar's bubble up and down, or click in the scroll bar's unit-increment or block-increment areas. Keyboard gestures can also be mapped to the scroll bar. By convention, the Page Up and Page Down keys are equivalent to clicking in the scroll bar's block-increment and block-decrement areas.

 Note

The width of the scroll bar's track corresponds to `maximum + visibleAmount`. When a scroll bar is set to its maximum value, the left side of the bubble is at `maximum`, and the right side is at `maximum + visibleAmount`.

`JScrollBar` has the following properties, as shown in Figure 16.27.

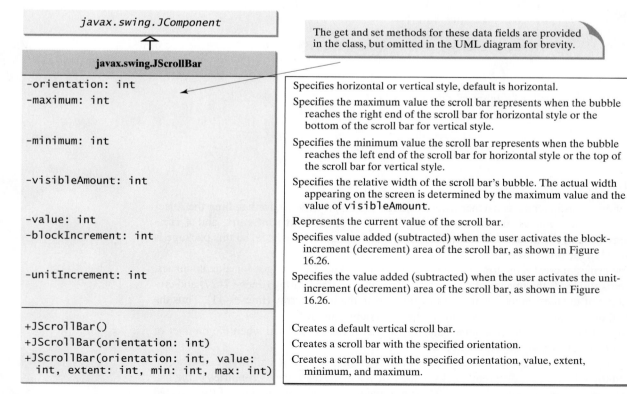

FIGURE 16.27 `JScrollBar` enables you to select from a range of values.

When the user changes the value of the scroll bar, the scroll bar generates an instance of `AdjustmentEvent`, which is passed to every registered listener. An object that wishes to be notified of changes to the scroll bar's value must implement the `adjustmentValueChanged` method in the `AdjustmentListener` interface defined in the package `java.awt.event`.

Listing 16.10 gives a program that uses horizontal and vertical scroll bars to control a message displayed on a panel. The horizontal scroll bar is used to move the message to the left or the right, and the vertical scroll bar to move it up and down. A sample run of the program is shown in Figure 16.28.

FIGURE 16.28 The scroll bars move the message on a panel horizontally and vertically.

Here are the major steps in the program:

1. Create the user interface.
   Create a `MessagePanel` object and place it in the center of the frame. Create a vertical scroll bar and place it in the east of the frame. Create a horizontal scroll bar and place it in the south of the frame.

2. Process the event.
   Create a listener to implement the `adjustmentValueChanged` handler to move the message according to the bar movement in the scroll bars.

LISTING 16.10 ScrollBarDemo.java

```java
1  import java.awt.*;
2  import java.awt.event.*;
3  import javax.swing.*;
4
5  public class ScrollBarDemo extends JFrame {
6    // Create horizontal and vertical scroll bars
7    private JScrollBar jscbHort =
8      new JScrollBar(JScrollBar.HORIZONTAL);
9    private JScrollBar jscbVert =
10     new JScrollBar(JScrollBar.VERTICAL);
11
12   // Create a MessagePanel
13   private MessagePanel messagePanel =
14     new MessagePanel("Welcome to Java");
15
16   public static void main(String[] args) {
17     ScrollBarDemo frame = new ScrollBarDemo();
18     frame.setTitle("ScrollBarDemo");
19     frame.setLocationRelativeTo(null); // Center the frame
20     frame.setDefaultCloseOperation(JFrame.EXIT_ON_CLOSE);
21     frame.pack();
```

horizontal scroll bar

vertical scroll bar

create frame

```
22        frame.setVisible(true);
23    }
24
25    public ScrollBarDemo() {
26        // Add scroll bars and message panel to the frame
27        setLayout(new BorderLayout());
28        add(messagePanel, BorderLayout.CENTER);
29        add(jscbVert, BorderLayout.EAST);
30        add(jscbHort, BorderLayout.SOUTH);
31
32        // Register listener for the scroll bars
33        jscbHort.addAdjustmentListener(new AdjustmentListener() {
34            public void adjustmentValueChanged(AdjustmentEvent e) {
35                // getValue() and getMaximumValue() return int, but for better
36                // precision, use double
37                double value = jscbHort.getValue();
38                double maximumValue = jscbHort.getMaximum();
39                double newX = (value * messagePanel.getWidth() /
40                    maximumValue);
41                messagePanel.setXCoordinate((int)newX);
42            }
43        });
44        jscbVert.addAdjustmentListener(new AdjustmentListener() {
45            public void adjustmentValueChanged(AdjustmentEvent e) {
46                // getValue() and getMaximumValue() return int, but for better
47                // precision, use double
48                double value = jscbVert.getValue();
49                double maximumValue = jscbVert.getMaximum();
50                double newY = (value * messagePanel.getHeight() /
51                    maximumValue);
52                messagePanel.setYCoordinate((int)newY);
53            }
54        });
55    }
56 }
```

create UI (line 27)

add scroll bar (lines 29-30)

adjustment listener (line 33)

adjustment listener (line 44)

The program creates two scroll bars (`jscbVert` and `jscbHort`) (lines 7–10) and an instance of `MessagePanel` (`messagePanel`) (lines 13–14). `messagePanel` is placed in the center of the frame; `jscbVert` and `jscbHort` are placed in the east and south sections of the frame (lines 29–30), respectively.

You can specify the orientation of the scroll bar in the constructor or use the `setOrientation` method. By default, the property value is `100` for `maximum`, `0` for `minimum`, `10` for `blockIncrement`, and `10` for `visibleAmount`.

When the user drags the bubble, or clicks the increment or decrement unit, the value of the scroll bar changes. An instance of `AdjustmentEvent` is generated and passed to the listener by invoking the `adjustmentValueChanged` handler. The listener for the vertical scroll bar moves the message up and down (lines 33–43), and the listener for the horizontal bar moves the message to right and left (lines 44–54).

The maximum value of the vertical scroll bar corresponds to the height of the panel, and the maximum value of the horizontal scroll bar corresponds to the width of the panel. The ratio between the current and maximum values of the horizontal scroll bar is the same as the ratio between the x value and the width of the message panel. Similarly, the ratio between the current and maximum values of the vertical scroll bar is the same as the ratio between the y value and the height of the message panel. The x-coordinate and y-coordinate are set in response to the scroll bar adjustments (lines 39, 49).

16.11 Sliders

JSlider is similar to JScrollBar, but JSlider has more properties and can appear in many forms. Figure 16.29 shows two sliders.

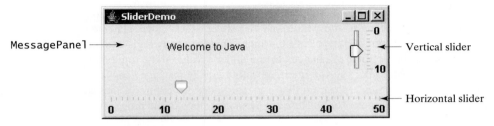

MessagePanel → ... Welcome to Java ... ← Vertical slider

← Horizontal slider

FIGURE 16.29 The sliders move the message on a panel horizontally and vertically.

JSlider lets the user graphically select a value by sliding a knob within a bounded interval. The slider can show both major tick marks and minor tick marks between them. The number of pixels between the tick marks is controlled by the majorTickSpacing and minorTickSpacing properties. Sliders can be displayed horizontally or vertically, with or without ticks, and with or without labels. The frequently used constructors and properties in JSlider are shown in Figure 16.30.

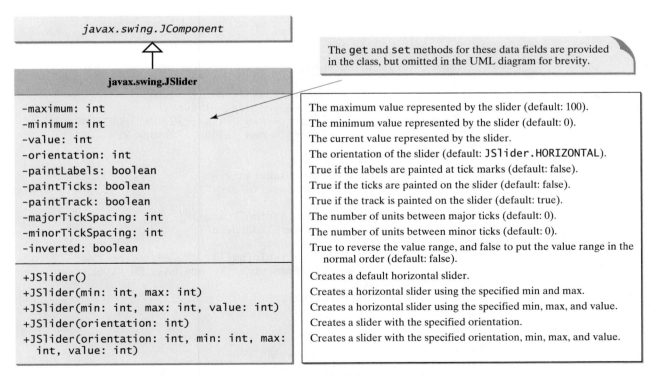

The get and set methods for these data fields are provided in the class, but omitted in the UML diagram for brevity.

javax.swing.JComponent

javax.swing.JSlider

-maximum: int	The maximum value represented by the slider (default: 100).
-minimum: int	The minimum value represented by the slider (default: 0).
-value: int	The current value represented by the slider.
-orientation: int	The orientation of the slider (default: JSlider.HORIZONTAL).
-paintLabels: boolean	True if the labels are painted at tick marks (default: false).
-paintTicks: boolean	True if the ticks are painted on the slider (default: false).
-paintTrack: boolean	True if the track is painted on the slider (default: true).
-majorTickSpacing: int	The number of units between major ticks (default: 0).
-minorTickSpacing: int	The number of units between minor ticks (default: 0).
-inverted: boolean	True to reverse the value range, and false to put the value range in the normal order (default: false).
+JSlider()	Creates a default horizontal slider.
+JSlider(min: int, max: int)	Creates a horizontal slider using the specified min and max.
+JSlider(min: int, max: int, value: int)	Creates a horizontal slider using the specified min, max, and value.
+JSlider(orientation: int)	Creates a slider with the specified orientation.
+JSlider(orientation: int, min: int, max: int, value: int)	Creates a slider with the specified orientation, min, max, and value.

FIGURE 16.30 JSlider enables you to select from a range of values.

 Note
The values of a vertical scroll bar increase from top to bottom, but the values of a vertical slider decrease from top to bottom.

Note

By convention, the **get** method for a Boolean property is named *is<PropertyName>()*. In the **JSlider** class, the **get** methods for **paintLabels**, **paintTicks**, **paintTrack**, and **inverted** are **getPaintLabels()**, **getPaintTicks()**, **getPaintTrack()**, and **getInverted()**, which violate the naming convention.

When the user changes the value of the slider, the slider generates an instance of **javax.swing.event.ChangeEvent**, which is passed to any registered listeners. Any object that wishes to be notified of changes to the slider's value must implement **stateChanged** method in the **ChangeListener** interface defined in the package **javax.swing.event**.

Listing 16.11 writes a program that uses the sliders to control a message displayed on a panel, as shown in Figure 16.29. Here are the major steps in the program:

1. Create the user interface.
   Create a **MessagePanel** object and place it in the center of the frame. Create a vertical slider and place it in the east of the frame. Create a horizontal slider and place it in the south of the frame.

2. Process the event.
   Create a listener to implement the **stateChanged** handler in the **ChangeListener** interface to move the message according to the knot movement in the slider.

LISTING 16.11 SliderDemo.java

```
1  import java.awt.*;
2  import javax.swing.*;
3  import javax.swing.event.*;
4
5  public class SliderDemo extends JFrame {
6    // Create horizontal and vertical sliders
7    private JSlider jsldHort = new JSlider(JSlider.HORIZONTAL);
8    private JSlider jsldVert = new JSlider(JSlider.VERTICAL);
9
10   // Create a MessagePanel
11   private MessagePanel messagePanel =
12     new MessagePanel("Welcome to Java");
13
14   public static void main(String[] args) {
15     SliderDemo frame = new SliderDemo();
16     frame.setTitle("SliderDemo");
17     frame.setLocationRelativeTo(null); // Center the frame
18     frame.setDefaultCloseOperation(JFrame.EXIT_ON_CLOSE);
19     frame.pack();
20     frame.setVisible(true);
21   }
22
23   public SliderDemo() {
24     // Add sliders and message panel to the frame
25     setLayout(new BorderLayout(5, 5));
26     add(messagePanel, BorderLayout.CENTER);
27     add(jsldVert, BorderLayout.EAST);
28     add(jsldHort, BorderLayout.SOUTH);
29
30     // Set properties for sliders
31     jsldHort.setMaximum(50);
32     jsldHort.setPaintLabels(true);
33     jsldHort.setPaintTicks(true);
```

horizontal slider
vertical slider

create frame

create UI

slider properties

```
34      jsldHort.setMajorTickSpacing(10);
35      jsldHort.setMinorTickSpacing(1);
36      jsldHort.setPaintTrack(false);
37      jsldVert.setInverted(true);
38      jsldVert.setMaximum(10);
39      jsldVert.setPaintLabels(true);
40      jsldVert.setPaintTicks(true);
41      jsldVert.setMajorTickSpacing(10);
42      jsldVert.setMinorTickSpacing(1);
43
44      // Register listener for the sliders
45      jsldHort.addChangeListener(new ChangeListener() {          listener
46        /** Handle scroll bar adjustment actions */
47        public void stateChanged(ChangeEvent e) {
48          // getValue() and getMaximumValue() return int, but for better
49          // precision, use double
50          double value = jsldHort.getValue();
51          double maximumValue = jsldHort.getMaximum();
52          double newX = (value * messagePanel.getWidth() /
53            maximumValue);
54          messagePanel.setXCoordinate((int)newX);
55        }
56      });
57      jsldVert.addChangeListener(new ChangeListener() {          listener
58        /** Handle scroll bar adjustment actions */
59        public void stateChanged(ChangeEvent e) {
60          // getValue() and getMaximumValue() return int, but for better
61          // precision, use double
62          double value = jsldVert.getValue();
63          double maximumValue = jsldVert.getMaximum();
64          double newY = (value * messagePanel.getHeight() /
65            maximumValue);
66          messagePanel.setYCoordinate((int) newY);
67        }
68      });
69    }
70 }
```

`JSlider` is similar to `JScrollBar` but has more features. As shown in this example, you can specify maximum, labels, major ticks, and minor ticks on a `JSlider` (lines 31–35). You can also choose to hide the track (line 36). Since the values of a vertical slider decrease from top to bottom, the `setInverted` method reverses the order (line 37).

`JSlider` fires `ChangeEvent` when the slider is changed. The listener needs to implement the `stateChanged` handler in `ChangeListener` (lines 45–68). Note that `JScrollBar` fires `AdjustmentEvent` when the scroll bar is adjusted.

16.12 Creating Multiple Windows

Occasionally, you may want to create multiple windows in an application. The application opens a new window to perform a specified task. The new windows are called *subwindows*, and the main frame is called the *main window*.

To create a subwindow from an application, you need to create a subclass of `JFrame` that defines the task and tells the new window what to do. You can then create an instance of this subclass in the application and launch the new window by setting the frame instance to be visible.

Listing 16.12 gives a program that creates a main window with a text area in the scroll pane and a button named *Show Histogram*. When the user clicks the button, a new window appears that displays a histogram to show the occurrences of the letters in the text area. Figure 16.31 contains a sample run of the program.

FIGURE 16.31 The histogram is displayed in a separate frame.

Here are the major steps in the program:

1. Create a main class for the frame named `MultipleWindowsDemo` in Listing 16.12. Add a text area inside a scroll pane, and place the scroll pane in the center of the frame. Create a button "Show Histogram" and place it in the south of the frame.

2. Create a subclass of `JPanel` named `Histogram` in Listing 16.13. The class contains a data field named `count` of the `int[]` type, which counts the occurrences of `26` letters. The values in `count` are displayed in the histogram.

3. Implement the `actionPerformed` handler in `MultipleWindowsDemo`, as follows:

   a. Create an instance of `Histogram`. Count the letters in the text area and pass the count to the `Histogram` object.

   b. Create a new frame and place the `Histogram` object in the center of frame. Display the frame.

LISTING 16.12 `MultipleWindowsDemo.java`

```
1  import java.awt.*;
2  import java.awt.event.*;
3  import javax.swing.*;
4
5  public class MultipleWindowsDemo extends JFrame {
6    private JTextArea jta;
7    private JButton jbtShowHistogram = new JButton("Show Histogram");
8    private Histogram histogram = new Histogram();
9
10   // Create a new frame to hold the histogram panel
11   private JFrame histogramFrame = new JFrame();
12
13   public MultipleWindowsDemo() {
14     // Store text area in a scroll pane
15     JScrollPane scrollPane = new JScrollPane(jta = new JTextArea());
16     scrollPane.setPreferredSize(new Dimension(300, 200));
17     jta.setWrapStyleWord(true);
18     jta.setLineWrap(true);
19
20     // Place scroll pane and button in the frame
21     add(scrollPane, BorderLayout.CENTER);
22     add(jbtShowHistogram, BorderLayout.SOUTH);
23
24     // Register listener
25     jbtShowHistogram.addActionListener(new ActionListener() {
26       /** Handle the button action */
27       public void actionPerformed(ActionEvent e) {
28         // Count the letters in the text area
```

create subframe (line 8)

create subframe (line 11)

create UI (line 13)

```
29            int[] count = countLetters();
30
31            // Set the letter count to histogram for display
32            histogram.showHistogram(count);
33
34            // Show the frame
35            histogramFrame.setVisible(true);                    display subframe
36          }
37        });
38
39      // Create a new frame to hold the histogram panel
40      histogramFrame.add(histogram);
41      histogramFrame.pack();
42      histogramFrame.setTitle("Histogram");
43    }
44
45    /** Count the letters in the text area */
46    private int[] countLetters() {
47      // Count for 26 letters
48      int[] count = new int[26];
49
50      // Get contents from the text area
51      String text = jta.getText();
52
53      // Count occurrence of each letter (case insensitive)
54      for (int i = 0; i < text.length(); i++) {
55        char character = text.charAt(i);
56
57        if ((character >= 'A') && (character <= 'Z')) {
58          count[character - 'A']++;
59        }
60        else if ((character >= 'a') && (character <= 'z')) {
61          count[character - 'a']++;
62        }
63      }
64
65      return count; // Return the count array
66    }
67
68    public static void main(String[] args) {
69      MultipleWindowsDemo frame = new MultipleWindowsDemo();    create main frame
70      frame.setLocationRelativeTo(null); // Center the frame
71      frame.setDefaultCloseOperation(JFrame.EXIT_ON_CLOSE);
72      frame.setTitle("MultipleWindowsDemo");
73      frame.pack();
74      frame.setVisible(true);
75    }
76 }
```

LISTING 16.13 Histogram.java

```
1 import javax.swing.*;
2 import java.awt.*;
3
4 public class Histogram extends JPanel {
5   // Count the occurrence of 26 letters
6   private int[] count;
7
8   /** Set the count and display histogram */
9   public void showHistogram(int[] count) {
10    this.count = count;
```

paint histogram

```
11      repaint();
12    }
13
14    /** Paint the histogram */
15    protected void paintComponent(Graphics g) {
16      if (count == null) return; // No display if count is null
17
18      super.paintComponent(g);
19
20      // Find the panel size and bar width and interval dynamically
21      int width = getWidth();
22      int height = getHeight();
23      int interval = (width - 40) / count.length;
24      int individualWidth = (int)(((width - 40) / 24) * 0.60);
25
26      // Find the maximum count. The maximum count has the highest bar
27      int maxCount = 0;
28      for (int i = 0; i < count.length; i++) {
29        if (maxCount < count[i])
30          maxCount = count[i];
31      }
32
33      // x is the start position for the first bar in the histogram
34      int x = 30;
35
36      // Draw a horizontal base line
37      g.drawLine(10, height - 45, width - 10, height - 45);
38      for (int i = 0; i < count.length; i++) {
39        // Find the bar height
40        int barHeight =
41          (int)(((double)count[i] / (double)maxCount) * (height - 55));
42
43        // Display a bar (i.e. rectangle)
44        g.drawRect(x, height - 45 - barHeight, individualWidth,
45          barHeight);
46
47        // Display a letter under the base line
48        g.drawString((char)(65 + i) + "", x, height - 30);
49
50        // Move x for displaying the next character
51        x += interval;
52      }
53    }
54
55    /** Override getPreferredSize */
56    public Dimension getPreferredSize() {
57      return new Dimension(300, 300);
58    }
59 }
```

preferredSize

The program contains two classes: MultipleWindowsDemo and Histogram. Their relationship is shown in Figure 16.32.

MultipleWindowsDemo is a frame that holds a text area in a scroll pane and a button. Histogram is a subclass of JPanel that displays a histogram for the occurrences of letters in the text area.

When the user clicks the *Show Histogram* button, the handler counts the occurrences of letters in the text area. Letters are counted regardless of their case. Nonletter characters are not counted. The count is stored in an int array of twenty-six elements. The first element stores the count for letter '*a*' or '*A*', and the last element in the array stores the count for letter '*z*' or

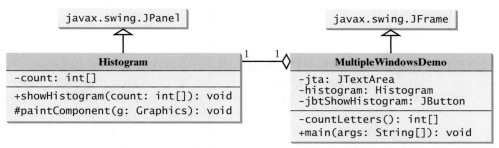

FIGURE 16.32 `MultipleWindowsDemo` uses `Histogram` to display a histogram of the occurrences of the letters in a text area in the frame.

'Z'. The `count` array is passed to the histogram for display. The `MultipleWindowsDemo` class contains a `main` method. The `main` method creates an instance of `Multiple-WindowsDemo` and displays the frame. The `MultipleWindowsDemo` class also contains an instance of `JFrame`, named `histogramFrame`, which holds an instance of `Histogram`. When the user clicks the *Show Histogram* button, `histogramFrame` is set visible to display the histogram.

The height and width of the bars in the histogram are determined dynamically according to the window size of the histogram.

You cannot add an instance of `JFrame` to a container. For example, adding `his-togramFrame` to the main frame would cause a runtime exception. However, you can create a frame instance and set it visible to launch a new window.

CHAPTER SUMMARY

- You learned how to create graphical user interfaces using Swing GUI components `JButton`, `JCheckBox`, `JRadioButton`, `JLabel`, `JTextField`, `JTextArea`, `JComboBox`, `JList`, `JScrollBar`, and `JSlider`. You also learned how to handle events on these components.

- You can display a text and icon on buttons (`JButton`, `JCheckBox`, `JRadioButton`) and labels `Jlabel`).

REVIEW QUESTIONS

Sections 16.2–16.4

16.1   How do you create a button labeled OK? How do you change text on a button? How do you set an icon, pressed icon, and rollover icon in a button?

16.2   Given a `JButton` object `jbtOK`, write statements to set the button's foreground to `red`, background to `yellow`, mnemonic to `'K'`, tool tip text to `"Click OK to proceed"`, horizontal alignment to `RIGHT`, vertical alignment to `BOTTOM`, horizontal text position to `LEFT`, vertical text position to `TOP`, and icon text gap to 5.

16.3   How do you create a check box? How do you create a check box with the box checked initially? How do you determine whether a check box is selected?

16.4   What is wrong if the statement `super.actionPerformed(e)` in Listing 16.3, `CheckBoxDemo.java`, is omitted?

16.5   How do you create a radio button? How do you create a radio button with the button selected initially? How do you group the radio buttons together? How do you determine whether a radio button is selected?

Sections 16.5–16.9

16.6 How do you create a label named `"Address"`? How do you change the name on a label? How do you set an icon in a label?

16.7 Given a `JLabel` object `jlblMap`, write statements to set the label's foreground to `red`, background to `yellow`, mnemonic to `'K'`, tool tip text to `"Map image"`, horizontal alignment to `RIGHT`, vertical alignment to `BOTTOM`, horizontal text position to `LEFT`, vertical text position to `TOP`, and icon text gap to `5`.

16.8 How do you create a text field with ten columns and the default text `"Welcome to Java"`? How do you write the code to check whether a text field is empty?

16.9 How do you create a text area with 10 rows and `20` columns? How do you insert three lines into the text area? How do you create a scrollable text area?

16.10 How do you create a combo box, add three items to it, and retrieve a selected item?

16.11 How do you create a list with an array of strings?

Sections 16.10–16.12

16.12 How do you create a horizontal scroll bar? What event can a scroll bar generate?

16.13 How do you create a vertical slider? What event can a slider generate?

16.14 Explain how to create and show multiple frames in an application.

PROGRAMMING EXERCISES

Pedagogical Note

Instructors may assign txercises 17.5–17.27 from the next chapter as exercises for this chapter. Instead of writing Java applets, ask students to write Java applications.

additional exercises

Sections 16.2–16.5

16.1* (*Revising Listing 16.2,* `ButtonDemo.java`) Rewrite Listing 16.2 to add a group of radio buttons to select background colors. The available colors are red, yellow, white, gray, and green (see Figure 16.33).

FIGURE 16.33 The `<=` and `=>` buttons move the message on the panel, and you can also set the background color for the message.

16.2* (*Selecting geometric figures*) Write a program that draws various figures, as shown in Figure 16.34. The user selects a figure from a radio button and specifies

FIGURE 16.34 The program displays lines, rectangles, and ovals when you select a shape type.

whether it is filled in a check box. (*Hint*: Use the `FigurePanel` class introduced in §14.7 to display a figure.)

16.3** (*Traffic lights*) Write a program that simulates a traffic light. The program lets the user select one of three lights: red, yellow, or green. When a radio button is selected, the light is turned on, and only one light can be on at a time (see Figure 16.35). No light is on when the program starts.

FIGURE 16.35 The radio buttons are grouped to let you select only one color in the group to control a traffic light.

Sections 16.6–16.10

16.4* (*Creating a simple calculator*) Write a program to perform add, subtract, multiply, and divide operations (see Figure 16.36).

FIGURE 16.36 The program performs addition, subtraction, multiplication, and division on double numbers.

16.5* (*Creating a miles/kilometers converter*) Write a program that converts miles and kilometers, as shown in Figure 16.37. If you enter a value in the Mile text field and press the *Enter* key, the corresponding kilometer is displayed in the Kilometer text field. Likewise, if you enter a value in the Kilometer text field and press the *Enter* key, the corresponding mile is displayed in the Mile text field.

FIGURE 16.37 The program converts miles to kilometers, and vice versa.

16.6* (*Creating an investment value calculator*) Write a program that calculates the future value of an investment at a given interest rate for a specified number of years. The formula for the calculation is as follows:

```
futureValue = investmentAmount * (1 + monthlyInterestRate)^(years*12)
```

Use text fields for interest rate, investment amount, and years. Display the future amount in a text field when the user clicks the *Calculate* button, as shown in Figure 16.38.

Panel with GridLayout of 4 rows and 2 columns

Panel with FlowLayout

FIGURE 16.38 The user enters the investment amount, years, and interest rate to compute future value.

16.7* (*Setting clock time*) Write a program that displays a clock time and sets the clock time with the input from three text fields, as shown in Figure 16.39. Use the **StillClock** in §14.12, "Case Study: The **StillClock** Class."

StillClock

Panel with FlowLayout

FIGURE 16.39 The program displays the time specified in the text fields.

16.8** (*Selecting a font*) Write a program that can dynamically change the font of a message to be displayed on a panel. The message can be displayed in bold and italic at the same time, or can be displayed in the center of the panel. You can select the font name or font size from combo boxes, as shown in Figure 16.40. The available font names can be obtained using **getAvailableFontFamilyNames()** in **GraphicsEnvironment** (§13.7, "The **Font** Class"). The combo box for font size is initialized with numbers from 1 to 100.

Panel with BorderLayout →

Panel with BorderLayout →

Panel with BorderLayout

FIGURE 16.40 You can dynamically set the font for the message.

16.9** (*Demonstrating JLabel properties*) Write a program to let the user dynamically set the properties **horizontalAlignment**, **verticalAlignment**, **horizontalTextAlignment**, and **verticalTextAlignment**, as shown in Figure 16.41.

Panel with BorderLayout → Panel with GridLayout

Panel with GridLayout → Panel with BorderLayout

Panel with GridLayout for two combo boxes

Panel with GridLayout for two combo boxes   Panel with GridLayout for two labels

FIGURE 16.41   You can set the alignment and text-position properties of a button dynamically.

16.10*   (*Adding new features into Listing 16.2,* `ButtonDemo.java` *incrementally*) Improve Listing 16.2 incrementally, as follows (see Figure 16.42):

1.   Add a text field labeled `"Enter a new message"` in the same panel with the buttons. Upon typing a new message `in` the text field and pressing the Enter key, the new message is displayed in the message panel.
2.   Add a combo box labeled `"Select an interval"` in the same panel with the buttons. The combo box enables the user to select a new interval for moving the message. The selection values range from `5` to `100` with interval `5`. The user can also type a new interval in the combo box.
3.   Add three radio buttons that enable the user to select the foreground color for the message as `Red`, `Green`, and `Blue`. The radio buttons are grouped in a panel, and the panel is placed in the north of the frame's content pane.
4.   Add three check boxes that enable the user to center the message and display it in italic or bold. Place the check boxes in the same panel with the radio buttons.
5.   Add a border titled `"Message Panel"` on the message panel, add a border titled `"South Panel"` on the panel for buttons, and add a border titled `"North Panel"` on the panel for radio buttons and check boxes.

Panel with FlowLayout

MessagePanel

Panel with FlowLayout

FIGURE 16.42   The program uses buttons, labels, text fields, combo boxes, radio buttons, check boxes, and borders.

16.11*   (*Demonstrating* `JTextField` *properties*) Write a program that sets the horizontal-alignment and column-size properties of a text field dynamically, as shown in Figure 16.43.

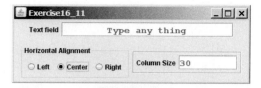

FIGURE 16.43 You can set the horizontal-alignment and column-size properties of a text field dynamically.

Video Note
Use text areas

16.12* (*Demonstrating JTextArea properties*) Write a program that demonstrates the wrapping styles of the text area. The program uses a check box to indicate whether the text area is wrapped. In the case where the text area is wrapped, you need to specify whether it is wrapped by characters or by words, as shown in Figure 16.44.

FIGURE 16.44 You can set the options to wrap a text area by characters or by words dynamically.

16.13* (*Comparing loans with various interest rates*) Rewrite Exercise 4.21 to create a user interface, as shown in Figure 16.45. Your program should let the user enter the loan amount and loan period in number of years from a text field, and should display the monthly and total payments for each interest rate starting from **5** percent to **8** percent, with increments of one-eighth, in a text area.

FIGURE 16.45 The program displays a table for monthly payments and total payments on a given loan based on various interest rates.

16.14* (*Using JComboBox and JList*) Write a program that demonstrates selecting items in a list. The program uses a combo box to specify a selection mode, as shown in Figure 16.46. When you select items, they are displayed in a label below the list.

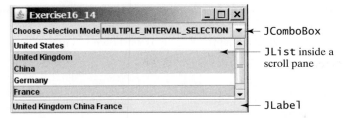

FIGURE 16.46   You can choose single selection, single-interval selection, or multiple-interval selection in a list.

Sections 16.11–16.13

16.15** (*Using `JScrollBar`*) Write a program that uses scroll bars to select the foreground color for a label, as shown in Figure 16.47. Three horizontal scroll bars are used for selecting the red, green, and blue components of the color. Use a title border on the panel that holds the scroll bars.

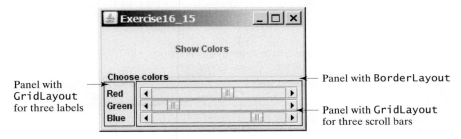

FIGURE 16.47   The foreground color changes in the label as you adjust the scroll bars.

16.16** (Using *`JSlider`*) Revise the preceding exercise using sliders.

16.17***(*Displaying a calendar*) Write a program that displays the calendar for the current month, as shown in Figure 16.48. Use labels, and set texts on the labels to display the calendar. Use the `GregorianCalendar` class in §11.3, "Example: `Calendar` and `GregorianCalendar`" to obtain the information about month, year, first day of the month, and number of days in the month.

Exercise16_17						
			2/2008			
Sunday	Monday	Tuesday	Wednesday	Thursday	Friday	Saturday
					1	2
3	4	5	6	7	8	9
10	11	12	13	14	15	16
17	18	19	20	21	22	23
24	25	26	27	28	29	

FIGURE 16.48   The program displays the calendar for the current month.

16.18* (*Revising Listing 16.12, MultipleWindowsDemo.java*) Instead of displaying the occurrences of the letters using the `Histogram` component in Listing 16.13, use a bar chart, so that the display is as shown in Figure 16.49.

FIGURE 16.49 The number of occurrences of each letter is displayed in a bar chart.

The following exercises involing text I/O using **Scanner**

16.19** (*Text Viewer*) Write a program that displays a text file in a text area, as shown in Figure 16.50. The user enters a file name in a text field and clicks the *View* button; the file is then displayed in a text area.

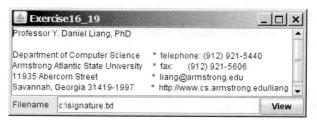

FIGURE 16.50 The program displays the text from a file to a text area.

16.20** (*Displaying country flag and flag description*) Listing 16.8, ComboBoxDemo.java, gives a program that lets users view a country's flag image and description by selecting the country from a combo box. The description is a string coded in the program. Rewrite the program to read the **text** description from a file. Suppose that the descriptions are stored in the file **description0.txt**, ..., and **description8.txt** under the text directory for the nine countries Canada, China, Denmark, France, Germany, India, Norway, the United Kingdom, and the United States, in this order.

16.21** (*Creating a histogram for occurrences of letters*) In Listing 16.12, MultipleWindowsDemo.java, you developed a program that displays a histogram to show the occurrences of each letter in a text area. Reuse the `Histogram` class created in Listing 16.12 to write a program that will display a histogram on a panel. The histogram should show the occurrences of each letter in a text file, as shown in Figure 16.51. Assume that the letters are not case sensitive.

FIGURE 16.51 The program displays a histogram that shows the occurrences of each letter in the file.

- Place a panel that will display the histogram in the center of the frame.
- Place a label and a text field in a panel, and put the panel in the south side of the frame. The text file will be entered from this text field.
- Pressing the *Enter* key on the text field causes the program to count the occurrences of each letter and display the count in a histogram.

16.22** (*Slide show*) Exercise 15.13 developed slides show using images. Rewrite Exercise 15.13 to develop a slide show using text files. Suppose ten text files named `slide0.txt`, `slide1.txt`, ..., and `slide9.txt` are stored in the `text` directory. Each slide displays the text from one file. Each slide is shown for a second. The slides are displayed in order. When the last slide finishes, the first slide is redisplayed, and so on. Use a text area to display the slide.

CHAPTER 17

APPLETS AND MULTIMEDIA

Objectives

- To explain how the Web browser controls and executes applets (§17.2).
- To describe the `init`, `start`, `stop`, and `destroy` methods in the `Applet` class (§§17.2.1–17.2.4).
- To develop Swing applets using the `JApplet` class (§17.3).
- To embed applets in Web pages (§17.4).
- To run applets from the appletviewer and from Web browsers (§§17.4.1–17.4.2).
- To write a Java program that can run as both an application and an applet (§17.5).
- To pass string values to applets from HTML (§17.6).
- To locate resources (images and audio) using the `URL` class (§17.9).
- To play audio in any Java program (§17.10).

17.1 Introduction

When browsing the Web, often the graphical user interface and animation you see are developed by the use of Java. The programs used are called Java applets. Suppose you want to develop a Java applet for the Sudoku game, as shown in Figure 17.1. How do you write this program?

In this chapter, you will learn how to write Java applets, explore the relationship between applets and the Web browser, and discover the similarities and differences between applications and applets. You will also learn how to create multimedia Java applications and applets with images and audio.

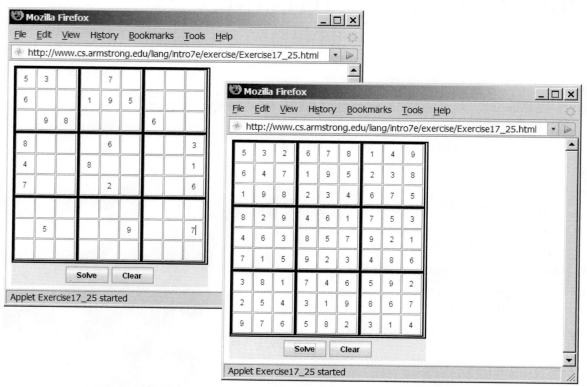

FIGURE 17.1   The Sudoku game is displayed in a Web browser.

17.2 The **Applet** Class

So far, you have used only Java applications. Everything you have learned about writing applications, however, applies also to writing applets. Applications and applets share many common programming features, although they differ slightly in some respects. For example, every application must have a **main** method, which is invoked by the Java interpreter. Java applets, on the other hand, do not need a **main** method. They run in the Web browser environment. Because applets are invoked from a Web page, Java provides special features that enable applets to run from a Web browser.

The **Applet** class provides the essential framework that enables applets to be run from a Web browser. While every Java application has a **main** method that is executed when the application starts, applets do not have a **main** method. Instead they depend on the browser to call the methods in the **Applet** class. Every applet is a subclass of `java.applet.Applet`, as outlined below:

subclass of **Applet**

```
public class MyApplet extends java.applet.Applet {
    ...
    /** The no-arg constructor is called by the browser when the Web
     *  page containing this applet is initially loaded, or reloaded
```

no-arg constructor required

```
   */
public MyApplet() {
  ...
}

/** Called by the browser after the applet is loaded
 */
public void init() {
  ...
}

/** Called by the browser after the init() method, or
 *  every time the Web page is visited
 */
public void start() {
  ...
}

/** Called by the browser when the page containing this
 *  applet becomes inactive
 */
public void stop() {
  ...
}

/** Called by the browser when the Web browser exits */
public void destroy() {
  ...
}

/** Other methods if necessary... */
}
```

When the applet is loaded, the Web browser creates an instance of the applet by invoking the applet's no-arg constructor. So the applet must have a no-arg constructor declared either explicitly or implicitly. The browser uses the `init`, `start`, `stop`, and `destroy` methods to control the applet. By default, these methods do nothing. To perform specific functions, they need to be modified in the user's applet so that the browser can call the code properly. Figure 17.2(a) shows how the browser calls these methods, and Figure 17.2(b) illustrates the flow of control of an applet using a statechart diagram.

no-arg constructor

17.2.1 The `init` Method

The `init` method is invoked after the applet is created. If a subclass of `Applet` has an initialization to perform, it should override this method. The functions usually implemented in this method include setting up user-interface components, loading resources such as images and audio, and getting string parameter values from the `<applet>` tag in the HTML page.

init()

17.2.2 The `start` Method

The `start` method is invoked after the `init` method. It is also called when the user returns to the Web page containing the applet after surfing other pages.

A subclass of `Applet` overrides this method if it has any operation that needs to be performed whenever the Web page containing the applet is visited. An applet with animation, for example, might start the timer to resume animation.

start()

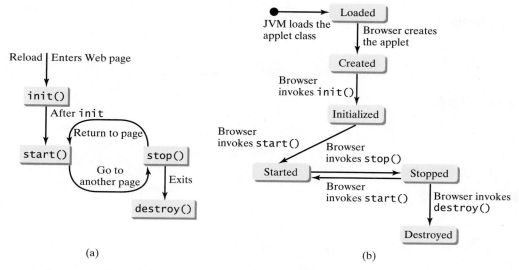

FIGURE 17.2 The Web browser uses the `init`, `start`, `stop`, and `destroy` methods to control the applet.

17.2.3 The `stop` Method

`stop()`

The `stop` method is the opposite of the `start` method. The `start` method is called when the user moves back to the page that contains the applet. The `stop` method is invoked when the user leaves the page.

A subclass of `Applet` overrides this method if it has any operation to be performed each time the Web page containing the applet is no longer visible. An applet with animation, for example, might stop the timer to pause animation.

17.2.4 The `destroy` Method

`destroy()`

The `destroy` method is invoked when the browser exits normally to inform the applet that it is no longer needed and should release any resources it has allocated. The `stop` method is always called before the `destroy` method.

A subclass of `Applet` overrides this method if it has any operation to be performed before it is destroyed. Usually, you won't need to override this method unless you wish to release specific resources that the applet created.

17.3 The `JApplet` Class

The `Applet` class is an AWT class and is not designed to work with Swing components. To use Swing components in Java applets, you need to create a Java applet that extends `javax.swing.JApplet`, which is a subclass of `java.applet.Applet`. `JApplet` inherits all the methods from the `Applet` class. In addition, it provides support for laying out Swing components.

To add a component to an applet, you add it to the applet's content pane, which is similar to adding a component to the content pane of a frame. By default, the content pane of `JApplet` uses `BorderLayout`. Here is an example of a simple applet that uses `JLabel` to display a message.

Video Note
First applet

```
// WelcomeApplet.java: Applet for displaying a message
import javax.swing.*;

public class WelcomeApplet extends JApplet {
  /** Initialize the applet */
```

```java
  public void init() {
    add (new JLabel("Welcome to Java", JLabel.CENTER));
  }
}
```

add a label in applet

Note

The content pane delegation feature in JDK 1.5 allows you to invoke the **add** method from an applet to add components to the content pane of an applet. Strictly speaking, a component is added to an applet's content pane, but for simplicity we say that a component is added to an applet.

content pane delegation

You cannot run this applet standalone, because it does not have a **main** method. You have to create an HTML file with the applet tag that references the applet. When you write Java GUI applications, you must create a frame to hold graphical components, set the frame size, and make the frame visible. Applets are run from the Web browser. The Web browser automatically places the applet inside the frame and makes it visible. The following section shows how to create HTML files for applets.

Note

You may rewrite the **WelcomeApplet** by moving the code in the **init** method to the no-arg constructor, as follows:

alternative coding

```java
// WelcomeApplet.java: Applet for displaying a message
import javax.swing.*;

public class WelcomeApplet extends JApplet {
  /** Construct the applet */
  public WelcomeApplet() {
    add (new JLabel("Welcome to Java", JLabel.CENTER));
  }
}
```

17.4 The HTML File and the <applet> Tag

HTML is a markup language that presents static documents on the Web. It uses tags to instruct the Web browser how to render a Web page and contains a tag called <applet> that incorporates applets into a Web page.

The following HTML file named WelcomeApplet.html invokes the **WelcomeApplet.class**:

```html
<html>
  <head>
    <title>Welcome Java Applet</title>
  </head>
  <body>
    <applet
      code = "WelcomeApplet.class"
      width = 350
      height = 200>
    </applet>
  </body>
</html>
```

applet class

A *tag* is an instruction to the Web browser. The browser interprets the tag and decides how to display or otherwise treat the subsequent contents of the HTML document. Tags are enclosed inside brackets. The first word in a tag, called the *tag name*, describes tag functions. A tag can have additional attributes, sometimes with values after an equals sign, which further define the tag's action. For example, in the preceding HTML file, <applet> is the tag name, and code, width, and height are attributes. The width and height attributes specify the rectangular viewing area of the applet.

Most tags have a *start tag* and a corresponding *end tag*. The tag has a specific effect on the region between the start tag and the end tag. For example, `<applet...>...</applet>` tells the browser to display an applet. An end tag is always the start tag's name preceded by a slash.

HTML tag

An HTML document begins with the `<html>` tag, which declares that the document is written in HTML. Each document has two parts, a *head* and a *body*, defined by `<head>` and `<body>` tags, respectively. The head part contains the document title, including the `<title>` tag and other information the browser can use when rendering the document, and the body part contains the actual contents of the document. The header is optional. For more information, refer to Supplement V.A, "HTML and XHTML Tutorial."

`<applet>` tag

The complete syntax of the `<applet>` tag is as follows:

```
<applet
  [codebase = applet_url]
  code = classfilename.class
  width = applet_viewing_width_in_pixels
  height = applet_viewing_height_in_pixels
  [archive = archivefile]
  [vspace = vertical_margin]
  [hspace = horizontal_margin]
  [align = applet_alignment]
  [alt = alternative_text]
>
<param name = param_name1 value = param_value1>
<param name = param_name2 value = param_value2>
...
<param name = param_name3 value = param_value3>
</applet>
```

`<param>` tag

The `code`, `width`, and `height` attributes are required; all the others are optional. The `<param>` tag is introduced in §17.6, "Passing Strings to Applets." The other attributes are explained below.

codebase attribute

■ **codebase** specifies a base where your classes are loaded. If this attribute is not used, the Web browser loads the applet from the directory in which the HTML page is located. If your applet is located in a different directory from the HTML page, you must specify the `applet_url` for the browser to load the applet. This attribute enables you to load the class from anywhere on the Internet. The classes used by the applet are dynamically loaded when needed.

archive attribute

■ **archive** instructs the browser to load an archive file that contains all the class files needed to run the applet. Archiving allows the Web browser to load all the classes from a single compressed file at one time, thus reducing loading time and improving performance. To create archives, see Supplement lll.Q, "Packaging and Deploying Java Projects."

■ **vspace** and **hspace** specify the size, in pixels, of the blank margin to pad around the applet vertically and horizontally.

■ **align** specifies how the applet will be aligned in the browser. One of nine values is used: `left`, `right`, `top`, `texttop`, `middle`, `absmiddle`, `baseline`, `bottom`, or `absbottom`.

■ **alt** specifies the text to be displayed in case the browser cannot run Java.

17.4.1 Viewing Applets Using the Applet Viewer Utility

appletviewer

You can test the applet using the applet viewer utility, which can be invoked from the DOS prompt using the **appletviewer** command from **c:\book**, as shown in Figure 17.3(a). Its output is shown in Figure 17.3(b).

(a)   (b)

FIGURE 17.3   The appletviewer command runs a Java applet in the applet viewer utility.

17.4.2   Viewing Applets from a Web Browser

Applets are eventually displayed in a Web browser. Using the applet viewer, you do not need to start a Web browser. The applet viewer functions as a browser. It is convenient for testing applets during development. However, you should also test the applets from a Web browser before deploying them on a Web site. To display an applet from a Web browser, open the applet's HTML file (e.g., WelcomeApplet.html). Its output is shown in Figure 17.4.

FIGURE 17.4   The WelcomeApplet program (from a Web server and from a local host) is displayed in a browser.

To make your applet accessible on the Web, you need to store the WelcomeApplet.class and WelcomeApplet.html on a Web server. You can view the applet from an appropriate URL. For example, I have uploaded these two files on Web server www.cs.armstrong.edu/. As shown in Figure 17.4, you can access the applet from www.cs.armstrong.edu/liang/intro7e/book/WelcomeApplet.html.

17.4.3 Problem: Creating a Loan Applet

This section presents an applet that computes loan payments. It enables the user to enter the interest rate, the number of years, and the loan amount. Clicking the *Compute Payment* button displays the monthly payment and the total payment, as shown in Figure 17.5. The applet is given in Listing 17.1.

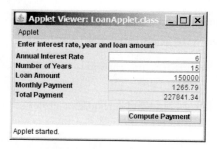

FIGURE 17.5 The applet computes the monthly payment and the total payment when provided with the interest rate, number of years, and loan amount.

LISTING 17.1 LoanApplet.java

```java
1  import java.awt.*;
2  import java.awt.event.*;
3  import javax.swing.*;
4  import javax.swing.border.TitledBorder;
5
6  public class LoanApplet extends JApplet {
7    // Declare and create text fields for interest rate
8    // year, loan amount, monthly payment, and total payment
9    private JTextField jtfAnnualInterestRate = new JTextField();
10   private JTextField jtfNumberOfYears = new JTextField();
11   private JTextField jtfLoanAmount = new JTextField();
12   private JTextField jtfMonthlyPayment = new JTextField();
13   private JTextField jtfTotalPayment = new JTextField();
14
15   // Declare and create a Compute Payment button
16   private JButton jbtComputeLoan = new JButton("Compute Payment");
17
18   /** Initialize user interface */
19   public void init() {
20     // Set properties on the text fields
21     jtfMonthlyPayment.setEditable(false);
22     jtfTotalPayment.setEditable(false);
23
24     // Right align text fields
25     jtfAnnualInterestRate.setHorizontalAlignment(JTextField.RIGHT);
26     jtfNumberOfYears.setHorizontalAlignment(JTextField.RIGHT);
27     jtfLoanAmount.setHorizontalAlignment(JTextField.RIGHT);
28     jtfMonthlyPayment.setHorizontalAlignment(JTextField.RIGHT);
29     jtfTotalPayment.setHorizontalAlignment(JTextField.RIGHT);
30
31     // Panel p1 to hold labels and text fields
32     JPanel p1 = new JPanel(new GridLayout(5, 2));
33     p1.add(new JLabel("Annual Interest Rate"));
34     p1.add(jtfAnnualInterestRate);
```

create text fields

create a button

create UI

```
35      p1.add(new JLabel("Number of Years"));
36      p1.add(jtfNumberOfYears);
37      p1.add(new JLabel("Loan Amount"));
38      p1.add(jtfLoanAmount);
39      p1.add(new JLabel("Monthly Payment"));
40      p1.add(jtfMonthlyPayment);
41      p1.add(new JLabel("Total Payment"));
42      p1.add(jtfTotalPayment);
43      p1.setBorder(new
44        TitledBorder("Enter interest rate, year and loan amount"));
45
46      // Panel p2 to hold the button
47      JPanel p2 = new JPanel(new FlowLayout(FlowLayout.RIGHT));
48      p2.add(jbtComputeLoan);
49
50      // Add the components to the applet
51      add(p1, BorderLayout.CENTER);
52      add(p2, BorderLayout.SOUTH);
53
54      // Register listener
55      jbtComputeLoan.addActionListener(new ButtonListener());
56    }
57
58    /** Handle the Compute Payment button */
59    private class ButtonListener implements ActionListener {
60      public void actionPerformed(ActionEvent e) {
61        // Get values from text fields
62        double interest =
63          Double.parseDouble(jtfAnnualInterestRate.getText());
64        int year =
65          Integer.parseInt(jtfNumberOfYears.getText());
66        double loanAmount =
67          Double.parseDouble(jtfLoanAmount.getText());
68
69        // Create a loan object
70        Loan loan = new Loan(interest, year, loanAmount);
71
72        // Display monthly payment and total payment
73        jtfMonthlyPayment.setText(String.format("%.2f",
74          loan.getMonthlyPayment()));
75        jtfTotalPayment.setText(String.format("%.2f",
76          loan.getTotalPayment()));
77      }
78    }
79 }
```

titled border (lines 43–44)

add to applet (lines 50–52)

listener class (lines 58–59)

create Loan object (line 70)

You need to use the `public` modifier (line 6) for the `LoanApplet`; otherwise, the Web browser cannot load it.   *public applet*

The `init` method initializes the user interface (lines 19–56). The program overrides this method to create user-interface components (labels, text fields, and a button), and places them in the applet.

The only event handled is the *Compute Payment* button. When this button is clicked, the `actionPerformed` method gets the interest rate, number of years, and loan amount from the text fields. It then creates a `Loan` object (line 70) to obtain the monthly payment and the total payment. Finally, it displays the monthly and total payments in their respective text fields. The `Loan` class is responsible for computing the payments. This class was introduced in Listing 9.2, Loan.java.

To run the applet, embed it in the HTML file, as shown in Listing 17.2.

LISTING 17.2   LoanApplet.html

```html
<!-- HTML code, this code is separated from the preceding Java code-->
<html>
  <head>
    <title>Loan Applet</title>
  </head>
  <body>
    This is a loan calculator. Enter your input for interest, year,
    and loan amount. Click the "Compute Payment" button, you will
    get the payment information. <p>
    <applet
      code = "LoanApplet.class"
      width = 300
      height = 150
      alt = "You must have a Java 2-enabled browser to view the applet">
    </applet>
  </body>
</html>
```

Applet demos

Tip

Many interesting applets are included in the JDK demo. To run them, change the directory to

```
c:\Program Files\Java\jdk1.6.0\demo\applets
```

Use the **dir** command to list the contents in the directory, as shown in Figure 17.6(a). Change to a subdirectory (e.g., using the command **cd Animator**). There are one or several .html files in that directory for executing applets (e.g., **example1.html**). In the command window, type the following to run the applet, as shown in Figure 17.6(b).

```
appletviewer example1.html
```

(a)   (b)

FIGURE 17.6   You can find applet examples in the JDK demo directory.

17.5 Enabling Applets to Run as Applications

Video Note
Run applets standalone

Despite some differences, the `JFrame` class and the `JApplet` class have a lot in common. Since they both are subclasses of the `Container` class, all their user-interface components, layout managers, and event-handling features are the same. Applications, however, are invoked from the static `main` method by the Java interpreter, and applets are run by the Web browser. The Web browser creates an instance of the applet using the applet's no-arg constructor and controls and executes the applet through the `init`, `start`, `stop`, and `destroy` methods.

For security reasons, the restrictions listed below are imposed on applets to prevent destructive programs from damaging the system on which the browser is running.

- Applets are not allowed to read from, or write to, the file system of the computer. Otherwise, they could damage the files and spread viruses.

- Applets are not allowed to run programs on the browser's computer. Otherwise, they might call destructive local programs and damage the local system on the user's computer.

- Applets are not allowed to establish connections between the user's computer and any other computer, except for the server where the applets are stored. This restriction prevents the applet from connecting the user's computer to another computer without the user's knowledge.

Note

A new security protocol was introduced in Java 2 to allow *trusted applets* to circumvent the security restrictions. See http://www.developer.com/java/ent/article.php/3303561 for detailed instructions on how to create trusted applets.

trusted applet

In general, an applet can be converted to an application without loss of functionality. An application can be converted to an applet as long as it does not violate the security restrictions imposed on applets. You can implement a `main` method in an applet to enable the applet to run as an application. This feature has both theoretical and practical implications. Theoretically, it blurs the difference between applets and applications. You can write a class that is both an applet and an application. From the standpoint of practicality, it is convenient to be able to run a program in two ways.

It is not difficult to write such programs on your own. Suppose you have an applet named `MyApplet`. To enable it to run as an application, all you need to do is add a `main` method in the applet with the implementation, as follows:

```java
public static void main(String[] args) {
    // Create a frame
    JFrame frame = new JFrame("Applet is in the frame");

    // Create an instance of the applet
    MyApplet applet = new MyApplet();

    // Add the applet to the frame
    frame.add(applet, BorderLayout.CENTER);

    // Invoke init and start
    applet.init();
    applet.start();

    // Display the frame
    frame.setSize(300, 300);
    frame.setLocationRelativeTo(null); // Center the frame
    frame.setDefaultCloseOperation(JFrame.EXIT_ON_CLOSE);
    frame.setVisible(true);
}
```

create frame

create applet

add applet

init()
start()

show frame

You can revise the LoanApplet class in Listing 17.1 to enable LoanApplet to run stand-alone by adding a main method in Listing 17.3.

The main method creates a frame to hold an applet (line 12). When the applet is run from a Web browser, the Web browser invokes the init and start methods of the applet. When the applet is run standalone, you have to manually invoke the init and start methods in order to perform the operations in these methods.

LISTING 17.3 New LoanApplet.java With a **main** Method

```
1 import java.awt.*;
2 import java.awt.event.*;
3 import javax.swing.*;
4 import javax.swing.border.TitledBorder;
5
6 public class LoanApplet extends JApplet {
7   // Same code in Listing 17.1 from line 7 to line 78
8   ...
9
10  public static void main(String[] args) {
11    // Create a frame
12    JFrame frame = new JFrame("Applet is in the frame");
13
14    // Create an instance of the applet
15    LoanApplet applet = new LoanApplet();
16
17    // Add the applet to the frame
18    frame.add(applet, BorderLayout.CENTER);
19
20    // Invoke applet's init method
21    applet.init();
22
23    // Display the frame
24    frame.setSize(300, 300);
25    frame.setLocationRelativeTo(null); // Center the frame
26    frame.setDefaultCloseOperation(JFrame.EXIT_ON_CLOSE);
27    frame.setVisible(true);
28  }
29 }
```

code omitted

new main method

17.6 Passing Strings to Applets

In §8.5, "Command-Line Arguments," you learned how to pass strings to Java applications from a command line. Strings are passed to the main method as an array of strings. When the application starts, the main method can use these strings. There is no main method in an applet, however, and applets are not run from the command line by the Java interpreter.

How, then, can applets accept arguments? In this section, you will learn how to pass strings to Java applets. To be passed to an applet, a parameter must be declared in the HTML file and must be read by the applet when it is initialized. Parameters are declared using the <param> tag. The <param> tag must be embedded in the <applet> tag and has no end tag. The syntax for the <param> tag is given below:

```
<param name = parametername value = stringvalue />
```

This tag specifies a parameter and its corresponding string value.

Note
No comma separates the parameter name from the parameter value in the HTML code. The
HTML parameter names are not case sensitive.

Suppose you want to write an applet to display a message. The message is passed as a parameter. In addition, you want the message to be displayed at a specific location with x-
coordinate and y-coordinate, which are passed as two parameters. The parameters and their
values are listed in Table 17.1.

TABLE 17.1   Parameter Names and Values for the
DisplayMessage Applet

Parameter Name	Parameter Value
MESSAGE	"Welcome to Java"
X	20
Y	30

The HTML source file is given in Listing 17.4:

LISTING 17.4 DisplayMessage.html

```
<html>
  <head>
    <title>Passing Strings to Java Applets</title>
  </head>
  <body>
    <p>This applet gets a message from the HTML
       page and displays it.</p>
    <applet
      code = "DisplayMessage.class"
      width = 200
      height = 50
      alt = "You must have a Java 2-enabled browser to view the
        applet"
    >
      <param name = MESSAGE value = "Welcome to Java" />
      <param name = X value = 20 />
      <param name = Y value = 30 />
    </applet>
  </body>
</html>
```

To read the parameter from the applet, use the following method defined in the `Applet` class:

```
public String getParameter(String parametername);
```

This returns the value of the specified parameter.
    The applet is given in Listing 17.5. A sample run of the applet is shown in Figure 17.7.

LISTING 17.5 DisplayMessage.java

```
1 import javax.swing.*;
2
3 public class DisplayMessage extends JApplet {
```

getParameter

add to applet

```
 4  /** Initialize the applet */
 5  public void init() {
 6    // Get parameter values from the HTML file
 7    String message = getParameter("MESSAGE");
 8    int x = Integer.parseInt(getParameter("X"));
 9    int y = Integer.parseInt(getParameter("Y"));
10
11    // Create a message panel
12    MessagePanel messagePanel = new MessagePanel(message);
13    messagePanel.setXCoordinate(x);
14    messagePanel.setYCoordinate(y);
15
16    // Add the message panel to the applet
17    add(messagePanel);
18  }
19 }
```

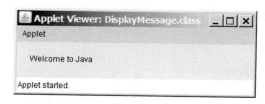

FIGURE 17.7 The applet displays the message `Welcome to Java` passed from the HTML page.

The program gets the parameter values from the HTML in the `init` method. The values are strings obtained using the `getParameter` method (lines 7–9). Because `x` and `y` are `int`, the program uses `Integer.parseInt(string)` to parse a digital string into an `int` value.

If you change *Welcome to Java* in the HTML file to *Welcome to HTML*, and reload the HTML file in the Web browser, you should see *Welcome to HTML* displayed. Similarly, the `x` and `y` values can be changed to display the message in a desired location.

 Caution

The `Applet`'s `getParameter` method can be invoked only after an instance of the applet is created. Therefore, this method cannot be invoked in the constructor of the applet class. You should invoke it from the `init` method.

You can add a main method to enable this applet to run standalone. The applet takes the parameters from the HTML file when it runs as an applet and takes the parameters from the command line when it runs standalone. The program, as shown in Listing 17.6, is identical to `DisplayMessage` except for the addition of a new `main` method and of a variable named `isStandalone` to indicate whether it is running as an applet or as an application.

LISTING 17.6 DisplayMessageApp.java

```
1 import javax.swing.*;
2 import java.awt.Font;
3 import java.awt.BorderLayout;
4
5 public class DisplayMessageApp extends JApplet {
6   private String message = "A default message"; // Message to display
```

```
 7   private int x = 20; // Default x-coordinate
 8   private int y = 20; // Default y-coordinate
 9
10   /** Determine if it is application */
11   private boolean isStandalone = false;                              isStandalone
12
13   /** Initialize the applet */
14   public void init() {
15     if (!isStandalone) {
16       // Get parameter values from the HTML file
17       message = getParameter("MESSAGE");                             applet params
18       x = Integer.parseInt(getParameter("X"));
19       y = Integer.parseInt(getParameter("Y"));
20     }
21
22     // Create a message panel
23     MessagePanel messagePanel = new MessagePanel(message);
24     messagePanel.setFont(new Font("SansSerif", Font.BOLD, 20));
25     messagePanel.setXCoordinate(x);
26     messagePanel.setYCoordinate(y);
27
28     // Add the message panel to the applet
29     add(messagePanel);
30   }
31
32   /** Main method to display a message
33      @param args[0] x-coordinate
34      @param args[1] y-coordinate
35      @param args[2] message
36   */
37   public static void main(String[] args) {
38     // Create a frame
39     JFrame frame = new JFrame("DisplayMessageApp");
40
41     // Create an instance of the applet
42     DisplayMessageApp applet = new DisplayMessageApp();
43
44     // It runs as an application
45     applet.isStandalone = true;                                      standalone
46
47     // Get parameters from the command line
48     applet.getCommandLineParameters(args);                           command params
49
50     // Add the applet instance to the frame
51     frame.add(applet, BorderLayout.CENTER);
52
53     // Invoke applet's init method
54     applet.init();
55     applet.start();
56
57     // Display the frame
58     frame.setSize(300, 300);
59     frame.setLocationRelativeTo(null); // Center the frame
60     frame.setDefaultCloseOperation(JFrame.EXIT_ON_CLOSE);
61     frame.setVisible(true);
62   }
63
64   /** Get command-line parameters */
65   private void getCommandLineParameters(String[] args) {
```

```
66      // Check usage and get x, y and message
67      if (args.length != 3) {
68        System.out.println(
69          "Usage: java DisplayMessageApp x y message");
70        System.exit(0);
71      }
72      else {
73        x = Integer.parseInt(args[0]);
74        y = Integer.parseInt(args[1]);
75        message = args[2];
76      }
77    }
78  }
```

When you run the program as an applet, the `main` method is ignored. When you run it as an application, the `main` method is invoked. Sample runs of the program as an application and as an applet are shown in Figure 17.8.

FIGURE 17.8   The `DisplayMessageApp` class can run as an application and as an applet.

The `main` method creates a `JFrame` object `frame` and creates a `JApplet` object `applet`, then places the applet `applet` into the frame `frame` and invokes its `init` method. The application runs just like an applet.

The `main` method sets `isStandalone true` (line 45) so that it does not attempt to retrieve HTML parameters when the `init` method is invoked.

The `setVisible(true)` method (line 61) is invoked *after* the components are added to the applet, and the applet is added to the frame to ensure that the components will be visible. Otherwise, the components are not shown when the frame starts.

Important Pedagogical Note

omitting main method

From now on, all the GUI examples will be created as applets with a `main` method. Thus you will be able to run the program either as an applet or as an application. For brevity, the `main` method is not listed in the text.

Video Note
TicTacToe

17.7 Case Study: TicTacToe

You have learned about objects, classes, arrays, class inheritance, GUI, event-driven programming, and applets from the many examples in this chapter and the preceding chapters. Now it is time to put what you have learned to work in developing comprehensive projects. In this section, you will develop a Java applet with which to play the popular game of TicTacToe.

Two players take turns marking an available cell in a 3 × 3 grid with their respective tokens (either X or O). When one player has placed three tokens in a horizontal, vertical, or diagonal row on the grid, the game is over and that player has won. A draw (no winner) occurs when all the cells on the grid have been filled with tokens and neither player has achieved a win. Figure 17.9 shows two representative sample runs of the example.

All the examples you have seen so far show simple behaviors that are easy to model with classes. The behavior of the TicTacToe game is somewhat more complex. To create classes that model the behavior, you need to study and understand the game.

(a) The X player won the game   (b) Draw—no winners

FIGURE 17.9 Two players play a TicTacToe game.

Assume that all the cells are initially empty, and that the first player takes the X token, the second player the O token. To mark a cell, the player points the mouse to the cell and clicks it. If the cell is empty, the token (X or O) is displayed. If the cell is already filled, the player's action is ignored.

From the preceding description, it is obvious that a cell is a GUI object that handles the mouse-click event and displays tokens. Such an object could be either a button or a panel. Drawing on panels is more flexible than on buttons, because the token (X or O) can be drawn on a panel in any size, but on a button it can be displayed only as a text label. Therefore, a panel should be used to model a cell. How do you know the state of the cell (empty, X, or O)? You use a property named `token` of `char` type in the `Cell` class. The `Cell` class is responsible for drawing the token when an empty cell is clicked. So you need to write the code for listening to the `MouseEvent` and for painting the shapes for tokens X and O. The `Cell` class can be defined as shown in Figure 17.10.

FIGURE 17.10 The `Cell` class paints the token on a cell.

The TicTacToe board consists of nine cells, declared using `new Cell[3][3]`. To determine which player's turn it is, you can introduce a variable named `whoseTurn` of `char` type. `whoseTurn` is initially X, then changes to O, and subsequently changes between X and O whenever a new cell is occupied. When the game is over, set `whoseTurn` to `' '`.

How do you know whether the game is over, whether there is a winner, and who the winner, if any, is? You can create a method named `isWon(char token)` to check whether a specified token has won and a method named `isFull()` to check whether all the cells are occupied.

Clearly, two classes emerge from the foregoing analysis. One is the `Cell` class, which handles operations for a single cell; and the other is the `TicTacToe` class, which plays the whole game and deals with all the cells. The relationship between these two classes is shown in Figure 17.11.

FIGURE 17.11 The TicTacToe class contains nine cells.

Since the Cell class is only to support the TicTacToe class, it can be defined as an inner class in TicTacToe. The complete program is given in Listing 17.7:

LISTING 17.7 TicTacToe.java

```
1  import java.awt.*;
2  import java.awt.event.*;
3  import javax.swing.*;
4  import javax.swing.border.LineBorder;
5
6  public class TicTacToe extends JApplet {
7    // Indicate which player has a turn; initially it is the X player
8    private char whoseTurn = 'X';
9
10   // Create and initialize cells
11   private Cell[][] cells =  new Cell[3][3];
12
13   // Create and initialize a status label
14   private JLabel jlblStatus = new JLabel("X's turn to play");
15
16   /** Initialize UI */
17   public TicTacToe() {
18     // Panel p to hold cells
19     JPanel p = new JPanel(new GridLayout(3, 3, 0, 0));
20     for (int i = 0; i < 3; i++)
21       for (int j = 0; j < 3; j++)
22         p.add(cells[i][j] = new Cell());
23
24     // Set line borders on the cells panel and the status label
25     p.setBorder(new LineBorder(Color.red, 1));
26     jlblStatus.setBorder(new LineBorder(Color.yellow, 1));
27
28     // Place the panel and the label to the applet
29     add(p, BorderLayout.CENTER);
30     add(jlblStatus, BorderLayout.SOUTH);
31   }
32
33   /** Determine if the cells are all occupied */
34   public boolean isFull() {
```

main class TicTacToe

check isFull

```
35      for (int i = 0; i < 3; i++)
36        for (int j = 0; j < 3; j++)
37          if (cells[i][j].getToken() == ' ')
38            return false;
39
40      return true;
41  }
42
43  /** Determine if the player with the specified token wins */
44  public boolean isWon(char token) {
45      for (int i = 0; i < 3; i++)
46        if ((cells[i][0].getToken() == token)
47            && (cells[i][1].getToken() == token)
48            && (cells[i][2].getToken() == token)) {
49          return true;
50        }
51
52      for (int j = 0; j < 3; j++)
53        if ((cells[0][j].getToken() ==  token)
54            && (cells[1][j].getToken() == token)
55            && (cells[2][j].getToken() == token)) {
56          return true;
57        }
58
59      if ((cells[0][0].getToken() == token)
60          && (cells[1][1].getToken() == token)
61          && (cells[2][2].getToken() == token)) {
62        return true;
63      }
64
65      if ((cells[0][2].getToken() == token)
66          && (cells[1][1].getToken() == token)
67          && (cells[2][0].getToken() == token)) {
68        return true;
69      }
70
71      return false;
72  }
73
74  // An inner class for a cell
75  public class Cell extends JPanel {
76      // Token used for this cell
77      private char token = ' ';
78
79      public Cell() {
80        setBorder(new LineBorder(Color.black, 1)); // Set cell's border
81        addMouseListener(new MyMouseListener()); // Register listener
82      }
83
84      /** Return token */
85      public char getToken() {
86        return token;
87      }
88
89      /** Set a new token */
90      public void setToken(char c) {
91        token = c;
92        repaint();
93      }
94
```

check rows

check columns

check major diagonal

check subdiagonal

inner class Cell

register listener

paint cell

```
 95    /** Paint the cell */
 96    protected void paintComponent(Graphics g) {
 97      super.paintComponent(g);
 98
 99      if (token == 'X') {
100        g.drawLine(10, 10, getWidth() - 10, getHeight() - 10);
101        g.drawLine(getWidth() - 10, 10, 10, getHeight() - 10);
102      }
103      else if (token == 'O') {
104        g.drawOval(10, 10, getWidth() - 20, getHeight() - 20);
105      }
106    }
107
```

listener class

```
108    private class MyMouseListener extends MouseAdapter {
109      /** Handle mouse click on a cell */
110      public void mouseClicked(MouseEvent e) {
111        // If cell is empty and game is not over
112        if (token == ' ' && whoseTurn != ' ') {
113          setToken(whoseTurn); // Set token in the cell
114
115          // Check game status
116          if (isWon(whoseTurn)) {
117            jlblStatus.setText(whoseTurn + " won! The game is over");
118            whoseTurn = ' '; // Game is over
119          }
120          else if (isFull()) {
121            jlblStatus.setText("Draw! The game is over");
122            whoseTurn = ' '; // Game is over
123          }
124          else {
125            // Change the turn
126            whoseTurn = (whoseTurn == 'X') ? 'O': 'X';
127            // Display whose turn
128            jlblStatus.setText(whoseTurn + "'s turn");
129          }
130        }
131      }
132    }
133  }
```

main method omitted

```
134 }
```

The TicTacToe class initializes the user interface with nine cells placed in a panel of GridLayout (lines 19–22). A label named jlblStatus is used to show the status of the game (line 14). The variable whoseTurn (line 8) is used to track the next type of token to be placed in a cell. The methods isFull (lines 34–41) and isWon (lines 44–72) are for checking the status of the game.

Since Cell is an inner class in TicTacToe, the variable (whoseTurn) and methods (isFull and isWon) defined in TicTacToe can be referenced from the Cell class. The inner class makes programs simple and concise. If Cell were not declared as an inner class of TicTacToe, you would have to pass an object of TicTacToe to Cell in order for the variables and methods in TicTacToe to be used in Cell. You will rewrite the program without using an inner class in Exercise 17.6.

The listener for MouseEvent is registered for the cell (line 81). If an empty cell is clicked and the game is not over, a token is set in the cell (line 113). If the game is over, whoseTurn is set to ' ' (lines 118, 122). Otherwise, whoseTurn is alternated to a new turn (line 126).

Tip
Use an incremental approach in developing and testing a Java project of this kind. The foregoing
program can be divided into five steps:

incremental development and
testing

1. Lay out the user interface and display a fixed token X on a cell.
2. Enable the cell to display a fixed token X upon a mouse click.
3. Coordinate between the two players so as to display tokens X and O alternately.
4. Check whether a player wins, or whether all the cells are occupied without a winner.
5. Implement displaying a message on the label upon each move by a player.

17.8 Case Study: Bouncing Ball

This section presents an applet that displays a ball bouncing in a panel. Use two buttons to
suspend and resume the movement, and use a scroll bar to control the bouncing speed, as
shown in Figure 17.12.

FIGURE 17.12   The ball's movement is controlled by the *Suspend* and *Resume* buttons and
the scroll bar.

Here are the major steps to complete this example:

1. Create a subclass of `JPanel` named `Ball` to display a ball bouncing, as shown in
   Listing 17.8.

2. Create a subclass of `JPanel` named `BallControl` to contain the ball with a scroll bar
   and two control buttons *Suspend* and *Resume*, as shown in Listing 17.9.

3. Create an applet named `BounceBallApp` to contain an instance of `BallControl` and
   enable the applet to run standalone, as shown in Listing 17.10.

The relationship among these classes is shown in Figure 17.13.

LISTING 17.8 Ball.java

```java
1 import javax.swing.Timer;
2 import java.awt.*;
3 import javax.swing.*;
4 import java.awt.event.*;
5
6 public class Ball extends JPanel {
7   private int delay = 10;
8
9   // Create a timer with delay 1000 ms
10  private Timer timer = new Timer(delay, new TimerListener());
11
12  private int x = 0; private int y = 0; // Current ball position
13  private int radius = 5; // Ball radius
14  private int dx = 2; // Increment on ball's x-coordinate
```

timer delay

create timer

<table>
<tr><td>start timer</td><td></td></tr>
</table>

start timer

timer listener

repaint ball

paint ball

```
15    private int dy = 2; // Increment on ball's y-coordinate
16
17    public Ball() {
18      timer.start();
19    }
20
21    private class TimerListener implements ActionListener {
22      /** Handle the action event */
23      public void actionPerformed(ActionEvent e) {
24        repaint();
25      }
26    }
27
28    protected void paintComponent(Graphics g) {
29      super.paintComponent(g);
30
31      g.setColor(Color.red);
32
33      // Check boundaries
34      if (x < radius) dx = Math.abs(dx);
35      if (x > getWidth() - radius) dx = -Math.abs(dx);
36      if (y < radius) dy = Math.abs(dy);
37      if (y > getHeight() - radius) dy = -Math.abs(dy);
38
39      // Adjust ball position
40      x += dx;
41      y += dy;
42      g.fillOval(x - radius, y - radius, radius * 2, radius * 2);
43    }
44
45    public void suspend() {
46      timer.stop(); // Suspend timer
47    }
48
49    public void resume() {
50      timer.start(); // Resume timer
51    }
52
53    public void setDelay(int delay) {
54      this.delay = delay;
55      timer.setDelay(delay);
56    }
57  }
```

Using Timer to control animation was introduced in §15.6, "Animation Using The Timer Class." Ball extends JPanel to display a moving ball. The timer listener implements ActionListener to listen for ActionEvent (line 21). Line 10 creates a Timer for a Ball. The timer is started in line 18 when a Ball is constructed. The timer fires an ActionEvent at a fixed rate. The listener responds in line 24 to repaint the ball to animate ball movement. The center of the ball is at (x, y), which changes to (x + dx, y + dy) on the next display (lines 40–41). The suspend and resume methods (lines 45–51) can be used to stop and start the timer. The setDelay(int) method (lines 53–56) sets a new delay.

LISTING 17.9 BallControl.java

```
1 import javax.swing.*;
2 import java.awt.event.*;
3 import java.awt.*;
4
```

```
 5 public class BallControl extends JPanel {
 6   private Ball ball = new Ball();
 7   private JButton jbtSuspend = new JButton("Suspend");
 8   private JButton jbtResume = new JButton("Resume");
 9   private JScrollBar jsbDelay = new JScrollBar();
10
11   public BallControl() {
12     // Group buttons in a panel
13     JPanel panel = new JPanel();
14     panel.add(jbtSuspend);
15     panel.add(jbtResume);
16
17     // Add ball and buttons to the panel
18     ball.setBorder(new javax.swing.border.LineBorder(Color.red));
19     jsbDelay.setOrientation(JScrollBar.HORIZONTAL);
20     ball.setDelay(jsbDelay.getMaximum());
21     setLayout(new BorderLayout());
22     add(jsbDelay, BorderLayout.NORTH);
23     add(ball, BorderLayout.CENTER);
24     add(panel, BorderLayout.SOUTH);
25
26     // Register listeners
27     jbtSuspend.addActionListener(new ActionListener() {
28       public void actionPerformed(ActionEvent e) {
29         ball.suspend();
30       }
31     });
32     jbtResume.addActionListener(new ActionListener() {
33       public void actionPerformed(ActionEvent e) {
34         ball.resume();
35       }
36     });
37     jsbDelay.addAdjustmentListener(new AdjustmentListener() {
38       public void adjustmentValueChanged(AdjustmentEvent e) {
39         ball.setDelay(jsbDelay.getMaximum() - e.getValue());
40       }
41     });
42   }
43 }
```

button

scroll bar

create UI

register listener

suspend

register listener

resume

register listener

new delay

The `BallControl` class extends `JPanel` to display the ball with a scroll bar and two control buttons. When the *Suspend* button is clicked, the ball's **suspend()** method is invoked to suspend the ball movement (line 29). When the *Resume* button is clicked, the ball's **resume()** method is invoked to resume the ball movement (line 34). The bouncing speed can be changed using the scroll bar.

LISTING 17.10 BounceBallApp.java

```
1 import java.awt.*;
2 import javax.swing.*;
3
4 public class BounceBallApp extends JApplet {
5   public BounceBallApp() {
6     add(new BallControl());
7   }
8 }
```

add **BallControl**

main method omitted

The `BounceBallApp` class simply places an instance of `BallControl` in the applet. The `main` method is provided in the applet (not displayed in the listing for brevity) so that you can also run it standalone.

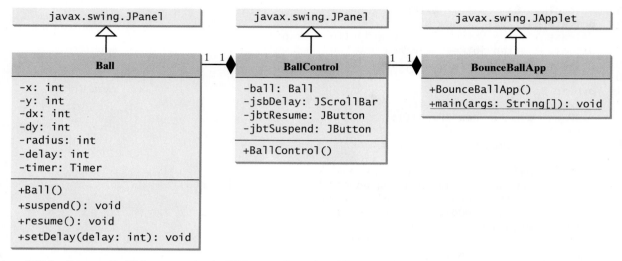

FIGURE 17.13 `BounceBallApp` contains `BallControl`, and `BallControl` contains `Ball`.

Video Note
Audio and image in applets
and application

17.9 Locating Resources Using the **URL** Class

You have used the `ImageIcon` class to create an icon from an image file and used the `setIcon` method or the constructor to place the icon in a GUI component, such as a button or a label. For example, the following statements create an `ImageIcon` and set it on a `JLabel` object `jlbl`:

```
ImageIcon imageIcon = new ImageIcon("c:\\book\\image\\us.gif");
jlbl.setIcon(imageIcon);
```

This approach presents a problem. The file location is fixed, because it uses the absolute file path on the Windows platform. As a result, the program cannot run on other platforms and cannot run as an applet. Assume that `image/us.gif` is under the class directory. You can circumvent this problem by using a relative path as follows:

```
ImageIcon imageIcon = new ImageIcon("image/us.gif");
```

This works fine with Java applications on all platforms but not with Java applets, because applets cannot load local files. To enable it to work with both applications and applets, you need to locate the file using the `URL` class.

why URL class?

The `java.net.URL` class can be used to identify files (image, audio, text, etc.) on the Internet. In general, a URL (Uniform Resource Locator) is a pointer to a "resource" on the World Wide Web on a local machine or a remote host. A resource can be something as simple as a file or a directory.

A URL for a file can also be accessed by class code in a way that is independent of the location of the file, as long as the file is located in the class directory. Recall that the class directory is where the class (i.e., the .class file) is stored. For example, all the classes in this book are stored in `c:\book`. So the class directory is `c:\book`.

To obtain the URL of a file in the class directory, use

```
URL url = getClass().getResource(filename);
```

The `getClass()` method returns an instance of the `java.lang.Class` class. This instance is automatically created by the JVM when the class file is loaded into the memory. This instance, also known as a *meta object*, contains the information about the class file such as class

meta object

name, constructors, methods, etc. You can obtain the URL of a file in the class path by invoking the `getResource(filename)` method on the meta object. For example, if the class file is in `c:\book`, the following statements create a URL for `c:\book\image\us.gif`.

```
Class metaObject = this.getClass(); // this. can be omitted
URL url = metaObject.getResource("image/us.gif");
```

You can now create an `ImageIcon` using

```
ImageIcon imageIcon = new ImageIcon(url);
```

Listing 17.11 gives the code that displays an image from `image/us.gif` in the class directory. The file `image/us.gif` is under the class directory, and its URL is obtained using the `getResource` method (line 5). A label with an image icon is created in line 6. The image icon is obtained from the URL.

LISTING 17.11 DisplayImageWithURL.java

```
1 import javax.swing.*;
2
3 public class DisplayImageWithURL extends JApplet {
4   public DisplayImageWithURL() {
5     java.net.URL url = this.getClass().getResource("image/us.gif");   get image URL
6     add(new JLabel(new ImageIcon(url) ));                             create a label
7   }
8 }                                                                    main method omitted
```

If you replace the code in lines 5–6 with the following code,

```
add(new JLabel(new ImageIcon("image/us.gif")));
```

you can still run the program standalone, but not from a browser.

17.10 Playing Audio in Any Java Program

There are several formats for audio files. Java programs can play audio files in the WAV, AIFF, MIDI, AU, and RMF formats.

To play an audio file in Java (application or applet), first create an *audio clip object* for the file. The audio clip is created once and can be played repeatedly without reloading the file. To create an audio clip, use the static method `newAudioClip()` in the `java.applet.Applet` class:

```
AudioClip audioClip = Applet.newAudioClip(url);
```

Audio originally can be played only from Java applets. For this reason, the `AudioClip` interface is in the `java.applet` package. Since Java 2, audio can be played in any Java program.

The following statements, for example, create an `AudioClip` for the `beep.au` audio file in the class directory:

```
Class metaObject = this.getClass();
URL url = metaObject.getResource("beep.au");
AudioClip audioClip = Applet.newAudioClip(url);
```

To manipulate a sound for an audio clip, use the `play()`, `loop()`, and `stop()` methods in `java.applet.AudioClip`, as shown in Figure 17.14.

Listing 17.12 gives the code that displays the Danish flag and plays the Danish national anthem repeatedly. The image file `image/denmark.gif` and audio file `audio/denmark.mid` are stored under the class directory. Line 12 obtains the audio file URL. Line 13 creates an audio clip for the file. Line 14 repeatedly plays the audio.

FIGURE 17.14 The `AudioClip` interface provides the methods for playing sound.

LISTING 17.12 `DisplayImagePlayAudio.java`

```
 1 import javax.swing.*;
 2 import java.net.URL;
 3 import java.applet.*;
 4
 5 public class DisplayImagePlayAudio extends JApplet {
 6   private AudioClip audioClip;
 7
 8   public DisplayImagePlayAudio() {
 9     URL urlForImage = getClass().getResource("image/denmark.gif");
10     add(new JLabel(new ImageIcon(urlForImage)));
11
12     URL urlForAudio = getClass().getResource("audio/denmark.mid");
13     audioClip = Applet.newAudioClip(urlForAudio);
14     audioClip.loop();
15   }
16
17   public void start() {
18     if (audioClip != null) audioClip.loop();
19   }
20
21   public void stop() {
22     if (audioClip != null) audioClip.stop();
23   }
24 }
```

get image URL
create a label

get audio URL
create an audio clip
play audio repeatedly

start audio

stop audio

main method omitted

The `stop` method (lines 21–23) stops the audio when the applet is not displayed, and the `start` method (lines 17–19) restarts the audio when the applet is redisplayed. Try to run this applet from a browser and observe the effect without the `stop` and `start` methods.

Run this program standalone from the main method and from a Web browser to test it. Recall that, for brevity, the main method in all applets in this text is not printed in the text.

17.11 Case Study: Multimedia Animations

This case study presents a multimedia animation with images and audio. The images are for seven national flags, named `flag0.gif`, `flag1.gif`, ..., `flag6.gif` for Denmark, Germany, China, India, Norway, U.K., and U.S. They are stored under the `image` directory in the class path. The audio consists of national anthems for these seven nations, named `anthem0.mid`, `anthem1.mid`, ..., and `anthem6.mid`. They are stored under the `audio` directory in the class path.

The program presents the nations, starting from the first one. For each nation, it displays its flag and plays its anthem. When the audio for a nation finishes, the next nation is presented, and so on. After the last nation is presented, the program starts to present all the nations again. You may suspend animation by clicking the *Suspend* button and resume it by clicking the *Resume* button, as shown in Figure 17.15. You can also directly select a nation from a combo box.

FIGURE 17.15   The applet displays a sequence of images and plays audio.

The program is given in Listing 17.13. A timer is created to control the animation (line 15). The timer delay for each presentation is the play time for the anthem. You can find the play time for an audio file using RealPlayer or Windows Media on Windows. The delay times are stored in an array named `delays` (lines 13–14). The delay time for the first audio file (the Danish anthem) is 48 seconds.

LISTING 17.13   ImageAudioAnimation.java

```
1  import java.awt.*;
2  import java.awt.event.*;
3  import javax.swing.*;
4  import java.applet.*;
5
6  public class ImageAudioAnimation extends JApplet {
7    private final static int NUMBER_OF_NATIONS = 7;
8    private int current = 0;
9    private ImageIcon[] icons = new ImageIcon[NUMBER_OF_NATIONS];       image icons
10   private AudioClip[] audioClips = new AudioClip[NUMBER_OF_NATIONS];   audio clips
11   private AudioClip currentAudioClip;                                 current audio clip
12
13   private int[] delays =                                              audio play time
14     {48000, 54000, 59000, 54000, 59000, 31000, 68000};
15   private Timer timer = new Timer(delays[0], new TimerListener());    timer
16
17   private JLabel jlblImageLabel = new JLabel();                       GUI components
18   private JButton jbtResume = new JButton("Resume");
19   private JButton jbtSuspend = new JButton("Suspend");
20   private JComboBox jcboNations = new JComboBox(new Object[]
21     {"Denmark", "Germany", "China", "India", "Norway", "UK", "US"});
22
23   public ImageAudioAnimation() {
24     // Load image icons and audio clips
25     for (int i = 0; i < NUMBER_OF_NATIONS; i++) {
26       icons[i] = new ImageIcon(getClass().getResource(              create icons
27         "image/flag" + i + ".gif"));
28       audioClips[i] = Applet.newAudioClip(                          create audio clips
29         getClass().getResource("audio/anthem" + i + ".mid"));
30     }
31
32     JPanel panel = new JPanel();                                    create UI
33     panel.add(jbtResume);
34     panel.add(jbtSuspend);
35     panel.add(new JLabel("Select"));
36     panel.add(jcboNations);
37     add(jlblImageLabel, BorderLayout.CENTER);
38     add(panel, BorderLayout.SOUTH);
39
```

```
40      jbtResume.addActionListener(new ActionListener() {
41        public void actionPerformed(ActionEvent e) {
42          start();
43        }
44      });
45      jbtSuspend.addActionListener(new ActionListener() {
46        public void actionPerformed(ActionEvent e) {
47          stop();
48        }
49      });
50      jcboNations.addActionListener(new ActionListener() {
51        public void actionPerformed(ActionEvent e) {
52          stop();
53          current = jcboNations.getSelectedIndex();
54          presentNation(current);
55          timer.start();
56        }
57      });
58
59      timer.start();
60      jlblImageLabel.setIcon(icons[0]);
61      jlblImageLabel.setHorizontalAlignment(JLabel.CENTER);
62      currentAudioClip = audioClips[0];
63      currentAudioClip.play();
64    }
65
66    private class TimerListener implements ActionListener {
67      public void actionPerformed(ActionEvent e) {
68        current = (current + 1) % NUMBER_OF_NATIONS;
69        presentNation(current);
70      }
71    }
72
73    private void presentNation(int index) {
74      jlblImageLabel.setIcon(icons[index]);
75      jcboNations.setSelectedIndex(index);
76      currentAudioClip = audioClips[index];
77      currentAudioClip.play();
78      timer.setDelay(delays[index]);
79    }
80
81    public void start() {
82      timer.start();
83      currentAudioClip.play();
84    }
85
86    public void stop() {
87      timer.stop();
88      currentAudioClip.stop();
89    }
90 }
```

Margin notes:
- register listener (line 40)
- start animation (line 42)
- register listener (line 45)
- stop animation (line 47)
- register listener (line 50)
- select a nation (line 53)
- present a nation (line 54)
- set a new delay (line 78)
- stop audio clip (line 88)
- main method omitted (line 90)

A label is created in line 17 to display a flag image. An array of flag images for seven nations is created in lines 26–27. An array of audio clips is created in lines 28–29. Each audio clip is created for an audio file through the URL of the current class. The audio files are stored in the same directory with the applet class file.

The combo box for country names is created in lines 20–21. When a new country name in the combo box is selected, the current presentation is stopped and a new selected nation is presented (lines 52–55).

The `presentNation(index)` method (lines 73–79) presents a nation with the specified index. It sets a new image in the label (line 74), synchronizes with the combo box by setting the selected index (line 75), plays the new audio, and sets a new delay time (line 78).

The applet's `start` and `stop` methods are overridden to resume and suspend the animation (lines 81–89).

KEY TERMS

applet   558
HTML   561
.html or .htm   561

tag   561
archive   562

CHAPTER SUMMARY

- The Web browser controls and executes applets through the `init`, `start`, `stop`, and `destroy` methods in the `Applet` class. Applets always extend the `Applet` class and implement these methods, if necessary.

- `JApplet` is a subclass of `Applet`. It should be used for developing Java applets with Swing components.

- The applet bytecode must be specified, using the `<applet>` tag in an HTML file to tell the Web browser where to find the applet. The applet can accept string parameters from HTML using the `<param>` tag.

- When an applet is loaded, the Web browser creates an instance of it by invoking its no-arg constructor. The `init` method is invoked after the applet is created. The `start` method is invoked after the `init` method. It is also called whenever the applet becomes active again after the page containing the applet is revisited. The `stop` method is invoked when the applet becomes inactive.

- The `destroy` method is invoked when the browser exits normally to inform the applet that it is no longer needed and should release any resources it has allocated. The `stop` method is always called before the `destroy` method.

- The procedures for writing applications and writing applets are very similar. An applet can easily be converted into an application, and vice versa. Moreover, an applet can be written with the additional capability of running as an application.

- You can pass arguments to an applet using the `param` attribute in the applet's tag in HTML. To retrieve the value of the parameter, invoke the `getParameter(paramName)` method.

- The `Applet`'s `getParameter` method can be invoked only after an instance of the applet is created. Therefore, this method cannot be invoked in the constructor of the applet class. You should invoke this method from the `init` method.

- You learned how to incorporate images and audio in Java applications and applets. To load audio and images for Java applications and applets, you have to create a URL for the audio and image. You can create a `URL` from a file under the class directory or from an Internet source.

- To play an audio, create an audio clip from the `URL` for the audio source. You can use the `AudioClip`'s `play()` method to play it once, the `loop()` method to play it repeatedly, and the `stop()` method to stop it.

REVIEW QUESTIONS

Sections 17.2–17.4

17.1 Is every applet an instance of `java.applet.Applet`? Is every applet an instance of `javax.swing.JApplet`?

17.2 Describe the `init()`, `start()`, `stop()`, and `destroy()` methods in the `Applet` class.

17.3 How do you add components to a `JApplet`? What is the default layout manager of the content pane of `JApplet`?

17.4 Why does the applet in (a) display nothing? Why does the applet in (b) have a run-time `NullPointerException` on the highlighted line?

```java
import javax.swing.*;

public class WelcomeApplet extends JApplet {
  public void WelcomeApplet() {
    JLabel jlblMessage =
      new JLabel("It is Java");
  }
}
```

(a)

```java
import javax.swing.*;

public class WelcomeApplet extends JApplet {
  private JLabel jlblMessage;

  public WelcomeApplet() {
    JLabel jlblMessage =
      new JLabel("It is Java");
  }

  public void init() {
    add(jlblMessage);
  }
}
```

(b)

Sections 17.5–17.6

17.5 Describe the `<applet>` HTML tag. How do you pass parameters to an applet?

17.6 Where is the `getParameter` method defined?

17.7 What is wrong if the `DisplayMessage` applet is revised as follows?

```java
public class DisplayMessage extends JApplet {
  /** Initialize the applet */
  public DisplayMessage() {
    // Get parameter values from the HTML file
    String message = getParameter("MESSAGE");
    int x =
      Integer.parseInt(getParameter("X"));
    int y =
      Integer.parseInt(getParameter("Y"));

    // Create a message panel
    MessagePanel messagePanel =
      new MessagePanel(message);
    messagePanel.setXCoordinate(x);
    messagePanel.setYCoordinate(y);

    // Add the message panel to the applet
    getContentPane().add(messagePanel);
  }
}
```

(a) Revision 1

```java
public class DisplayMessage extends JApplet {
  private String message;
  private int x;
  private int y;

  /** Initialize the applet */
  public void init() {
    // Get parameter values from the HTML file
    message = getParameter("MESSAGE");
    x = Integer.parseInt(getParameter("X"));
    y = Integer.parseInt(getParameter("Y"));
  }

  public DisplayMessage() {
    // Create a message panel
    MessagePanel messagePanel =
      new  MessagePanel(message);
    messagePanel.setXCoordinate(x);
    messagePanel.setYCoordinate(y);

    // Add the message panel to the applet
    getContentPane().add(messagePanel);
  }
}
```

(b) Revision 2

17.8 What are the differences between applications and applets? How do you run an application, and how do you run an applet? Is the compilation process different for applications and applets? List some security restrictions on applets.

17.9 Can you place a frame in an applet?

17.10 Can you place an applet in a frame?

17.11 Delete `super.paintComponent(g)` on line 97 in TicTacToe.java in Listing 17.5 and run the program to see what happens.

Sections 17.8–17.9

17.12 How do you create a URL object for the file www.cs.armstrong.edu/liang/anthem/us.gif on the Internet? How do you create a URL object for the file image/us.gif in the class directory?

17.13 How do you create an `ImageIcon` from the file image/us.gif in the class directory? How do you create an `ImageIcon` from www.cs.armstrong.edu/liang/anthem/us.gif?

Section 17.10 Playing Audio

17.14 What types of audio files are used in Java?

17.15 How do you create an audio clip from a file anthem/us.mid in the class directory? How do you create an audio clip from www.cs.armstrong.edu/liang/anthem/us.mid?

17.16 How do you play, repeatedly play, and stop an audio clip?

PROGRAMMING EXERCISES

Note:
For every applet in the exercise, add a main method to enable it to run standalone.   run standalone

Sections 17.2–17.4

17.1 (*Converting applications to applets*) Convert Listing 16.2, ButtonDemo.java, into an applet.

Sections 17.5–17.6

17.2* (*Passing strings to applets*) Rewrite Listing 17.5, DisplayMessage.java, to display a message with a standard color, font, and size. The `message`, `x`, `y`, `color`, `fontname`, and `fontsize` are parameters in the `<applet>` tag, as shown below:

```
<applet
  code = "Exercise17_2.class"
  width = 200
  height = 50
  alt = "You must have a Java-enabled browser to view the applet"
>
    <param name = MESSAGE value = "Welcome to Java" />
    <param name = X value = 40 />
    <param name = Y value = 50 />
    <param name = COLOR value = "red" />
    <param name = FONTNAME value = "Monospaced" />
    <param name = FONTSIZE value = 20 />
</applet>
```

17.3 (*Enabling applets to run standalone*) Rewrite the `LoanApplet` in Listing 17.1, LoanApplet.java, to enable it to run as an application as well as an applet.

17.4* (*Creating multiple windows from an applet*) Write an applet that contains two buttons called *Investment Calculator* and *Loan Calculator*. When you click *Investment*

Calculator, a frame appears in a new window for calculating future investment values. When you click *Loan Calculator*, a frame appears in a separate new window for computing loan payments (see Figure 17.16).

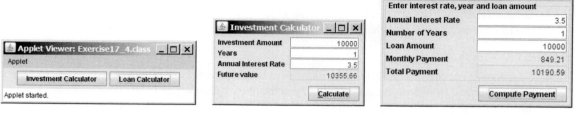

FIGURE 17.16 You can show frames in the applets.

17.5** (*Game: a clock learning tool*) Develop a clock applet to show a first-grade student how to read a clock. Modify Exercise 14.19 to display a detailed clock with an hour hand and minute hand in an applet, as shown in Figure 17.17(a). The hour and minute values are randomly generated. The hour is between 0 and 11, and the minute is 0, 15, 30, or 45. Upon a mouse click, a new random time is displayed on the clock.

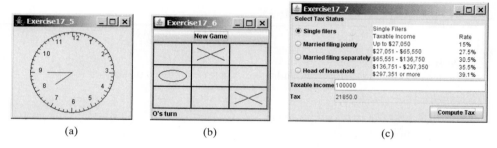

(a)   (b)   (c)

FIGURE 17.17 (a) Upon a mouse click on the clock, the clock time is randomly displayed. (b) The *New Game* button starts a new game. (c) The tax calculator computes the tax for the specified taxable income and tax status.

17.6** (*Game: TicTacToe*) Rewrite the program in §17.7, "Case Study: TicTacToe," with the following modifications:

- Declare `Cell` as a separate class rather than an inner class.
- Add a button named *New Game*, as shown in Figure 17.17(b). The *New Game* button starts a new game.

17.7** (*Financial application: tax calculator*) Create an applet to compute tax, as shown in Figure 17.17(c). The applet lets the user select the tax status and enter the taxable income to compute the tax based on the 2001 federal tax rates, as shown in Exercise 9.8.

17.8*** (*Creating a calculator*) Use various panels of `FlowLayout`, `GridLayout`, and `BorderLayout` to lay out the following calculator and to implement addition (+), subtraction (−), division (/), square root (`sqrt`), and modulus (%) functions (see Figure 17.18(a)).

(a)   (b)

FIGURE 17.18 (a) Exercise 17.8 is a Java implementation of a popular calculator. (b) Exercise 17.9 converts between decimal, hex, and binary numbers.

17.9* (*Converting numbers*) Write an applet that converts between decimal, hex, and binary numbers, as shown in Figure 17.18(b). When you enter a decimal value on the decimal value text field and press the Enter key, its corresponding hex and binary numbers are displayed in the other two text fields. Likewise, you can enter values in the other fields and convert them accordingly.

17.10** (*Repainting a partial area*) When you repaint the entire viewing area of a panel, sometimes only a tiny portion of the viewing area is changed. You can improve the performance by repainting only the affected area, but do not invoke `super.paintComponent(g)` when repainting the panel, because this will cause the entire viewing area to be cleared. Use this approach to write an applet to display the temperatures of each hour during the last 24 hours in a histogram. Suppose that temperatures between 50 and 90 degrees Fahrenheit are obtained randomly and are updated every hour. The temperature of the current hour needs to be redisplayed, while the others remain unchanged. Use a unique color to highlight the temperature for the current hour (see Figure 17.19(a)).

(a)   (b)

FIGURE 17.19 (a) The histogram displays the average temperature of every hour in the last 24 hours. (b) The program simulates a running fan.

17.11** (*Simulation: a running fan*) Write a Java applet that simulates a running fan, as shown in Figure 17.19(b). The buttons *Start*, *Stop*, and *Reverse* control the fan. The scrollbar controls the fan's speed. Create a class named `Fan`, a subclass of `JPanel`, to display the fan. This class also contains the methods to suspend and resume the fan, set its speed, and reverse its direction. Create a class named `FanControl` that contains a fan, and three buttons and a scroll bar to control the fan. Create a Java applet that contains an instance of `FanControl`.

17.12** (*Controlling a group of fans*) Write a Java applet that displays three fans in a group, with control buttons to start and stop all of them, as shown in Figure 17.20. Use the `FanControl` to control and display a single fan.

FIGURE 17.20 The program runs and controls a group of fans.

17.13*** (*Creating an elevator simulator*) Write an applet that simulates an elevator going up and down (see Figure 17.21). The buttons on the left indicate the floor where the passenger is now located. The passenger must click a button on the left to request that the elevator come to his or her floor. On entering the elevator, the passenger clicks a button on the right to request that it go to the specified floor.

FIGURE 17.21 The program simulates elevator operations.

Video Note
Control a group of clocks

17.14* (*Controlling a group of clocks*) Write a Java applet that displays three clocks in a group, with control buttons to start and stop all of them, as shown in Figure 17.22. Use the `ClockControl` to control and display a single clock.

FIGURE 17.22 Three clocks run independently with individual control and group control.

Section 17.9 Displaying Images

17.15* (*Enlarging and shrinking an image*) Write an applet that will display a sequence of images from a single image file in different sizes. Initially, the viewing area for this image has a width of 300 and a height of 300. Your program should continuously shrink the viewing area by 1 in width and 1 in height until it reaches a width of 50 and a height of 50. At that point, the viewing area should continuously enlarge by 1 in width and 1 in height until it reaches a width of 300 and a height of 300. The viewing area should shrink and enlarge (alternately) to create animation for the single image.

17.16*** (*Simulating a stock ticker*) Write a Java applet that displays a stock index ticker (see Figure 17.23). The stock index information is passed from the `<param>` tag in the HTML file. Each index has four parameters: Index Name (e.g., S&P 500), Current Time (e.g., 15:54), the index from the previous day (e.g., 919.01), and Change (e.g., 4.54).

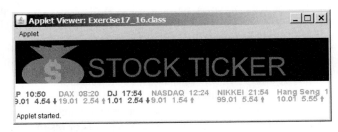

FIGURE 17.23   The program displays a stock index ticker.

Use at least five indexes, such as Dow Jones, S&P 500, NASDAQ, NIKKEI, and Gold & Silver Index. Display positive changes in green, and negative changes in red. The indexes move from right to left in the applet's viewing area. The applet freezes the ticker when the mouse button is pressed; it moves again when the mouse button is released.

17.17** (*Racing cars*) Write an applet that simulates four cars racing, as shown in Figure 17.24(a). You can set the speed for each car, with 1 being the highest.

| (a) | (b) |

FIGURE 17.24   (a) You can set the speed for each car. (b) This applet shows each country's flag, name, and description, one after another, and reads the description that is currently shown.

17.18** (*Showing national flags*) Write an applet that introduces national flags, one after the other, by presenting each one's photo, name, and description (see Figure 17.24(b)) along with audio that reads the description.

Suppose your applet displays the flags of eight countries. Assume that the photo image files, named **flag0.gif**, **flag1.gif**, and so on, up to **flag7.gif**, are stored in a subdirectory named **image** in the applet's directory. The length of each audio is less than 10 seconds. Assume that the name and description of each country's flag are passed from the HTML using the parameters `name0`, `name1`, ..., `name7`, and `description0`, `description1`, ..., and `description7`. Pass the number of countries as an HTML parameter using `numberOfCountries`. Here is an example:

```
<param name="numberOfCountries" value=8>
<param name="name0" value="Canada">
<param name="description0" value=
"The Maple Leaf flag
The Canadian National Flag was adopted by the Canadian
Parliament on October 22, 1964 and was proclaimed into law
by Her Majesty Queen Elizabeth II (the Queen of Canada) on
February 15, 1965. The Canadian Flag (colloquially known
as The Maple Leaf Flag) is a red flag of the proportions
two by length and one by width, containing in its center a
white square, with a single red stylized eleven-point
maple leaf centered in the white square.">
```

Hint: Use the `DescriptionPanel` class to display the image, name, and the text. The `DescriptionPanel` class was introduced in Listing 16.6.

17.19*** (*Bouncing balls*) The example in §17.8 simulates a bouncing ball. Extend the example to allow multiple balls, as shown in Figure 17.25(a). You may use the *+1* or *−1* button to increase or decrease the number of the balls, and use the *Suspend* and *Resume* buttons to freeze the balls or resume bouncing.

(a)　　　　　　　　　　　(b)

FIGURE 17.25 (a) The applet allows you to add or remove bouncing balls. (b) Click *Play* to play an audio clip once, click *Loop* to play an audio repeatedly, and click *Stop* to terminate playing.

Section 17.12 Playing Audio

17.20* (*Playing, looping, and stopping a sound clip*) Write an applet that meets the following requirements:

- Get an audio file. The file is in the class directory.
- Place three buttons labeled *Play*, *Loop*, and *Stop*, as shown in Figure 17.25(b).
- If you click the *Play* button, the audio file is played once. If you click the *Loop* button, the audio file keeps playing repeatedly. If you click the *Stop* button, the playing stops.
- The applet can run as an application.

17.21** (*Creating an alarm clock*) Write an applet that will display a digital clock with a large display panel that shows hour, minute, and second. This clock should allow the user to set an alarm. Figure 17.26(a) shows an example of such a clock. To turn on the alarm, check the *Alarm* check box. To specify the alarm time, click the *Set alarm* button to display a new frame, as shown in Figure 17.26(b). You can set the alarm time in the frame.

(a)   (b)

FIGURE 17.26 The program displays current hour, minute, and second, and enables you to set an alarm.

17.22** (*Creating an image animator with audio*) Create animation using the applet (see Figure 17.27) to meet the following requirements:

■ Allow the user to specify the animation speed. The user can enter the speed in a text field.
■ Get the number of frames and the image file-name prefix from the user. For example, if the user enters **n** for the number of frames and **L** for the image prefix, then the files are **L1**, **L2**, and so on, to **L***n*. Assume that the images are stored in the **image** directory, a subdirectory of the applet's directory.
■ Allow the user to specify an audio file name. The audio file is stored in the same directory as the applet. The sound is played while the animation runs.

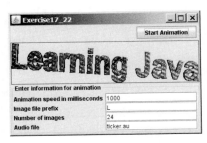

FIGURE 17.27 This applet lets the user select image files, audio file, and animation speed.

17.23** (*Simulation: raising flag and playing anthem*) Create an applet that displays a flag rising up, as shown in Figure 15.1. As the national flag rises, play the national anthem. (You may use a flag image and anthem audio file from Listing 17.13.)

17.24** (*Game: guessing birth dates*) Listing 3.8, GuessBirthDate.java, gives a program for guessing a birth date. Create an applet for guessing birth dates as shown in Figure 17.28. The applet prompts the user to check whether the date is in any of the five sets. The date is displayed in the text field upon clicking the *Guess Birth Date* button.

FIGURE 17.28 This applet guesses the birth dates.

17.25*** (*Game: Sudoku*) Listing 6.12, Sudoku.java, gives a program that prompts the user to enter a Sudoku puzzle from the console. Write a program that lets the user enter the input from the text fields in an applet, as shown in Figure 17.1. Clicking the *Solve* button displays the result.

17.26*** (*Game: Math quiz*) Listing 3.3, AdditionQuiz.java, and Listing 3.4, SubtractionQuiz.java, generate and grade Math quizzes. Write an applet that allows the user to select a question type and difficulty level, as shown in Figure 17.29(a). When the user clicks the *Start* button, the program begins to generate a question, after the user enters an answer with the *Enter* key, a new question is displayed. When the user clicks the *Start* button, the elapse time is displayed. The time is updated every second until the *Stop* button is clicked. The correct count is updated whenever a correct answer is made.

(a) Before a session starts

(b) After a session is started

FIGURE 17.29 The applet tests Math skills.

17.27*** (*Simulation: traffic control*) Exercise 16.3 uses the radio buttons to change the traffic lights. Revise the program that simulates traffic control at an intersection, as shown in Figure 17.30. When the light turns red, the traffic flows vertically; when the light turns green, the traffic flows horizontally. The light changes automatically every one minute. Before the light changes to red from green, it first changes to yellow for a brief five seconds.

(a) The traffic flows vertically

(b) The traffic flows horizontally

FIGURE 17.30 The applet simulates traffic control.

17.28** (*Geometry: two circles intersect?*) The `Circle2D` class was created in Exercise 9.11. Write an applet that enables the user to specify the location and size of the circles and displays whether the two circles intersect, as shown in Figure 17.31(a).

(a)

(b)

(c)

FIGURE 17.31 Check whether two circles, two rectangles, and two triangles are overlapping.

17.29** (*Geometry: two rectangles intersect?*) The `Rectangle2D` class was created in Exercise 9.12. Write an applet that enables the user to specify the location and size of the rectangles and displays whether the two rectangles intersect, as shown in Figure 17.31(b).

17.30** (*Geometry: two circles intersect?*) The `Triangle2D` class was created in Exercise 9.13. Write an applet that enables the user to specify the location of the two triangles and displays whether the two triangles intersect, as shown in Figure 17.31(c).

17.31*** (*Game: bean machine animation*) Write an applet that animates a bean machine introduced in Exercise 15.22. The applet lets you set the number of slots, as shown in Figure 17.32. Click *Start* to start or restart the animation and click *Stop* to stop.

FIGURE 17.32 The applet controls a bean machine animation.

CHAPTER 18

EXCEPTION HANDLING

Objectives

- To get an overview of exceptions and exception handling (§18.2).

- To explore the advantages of using exception handling (§18.3).

- To distinguish exception types: `Error` (fatal) vs. `Exception` (nonfatal), and checked vs. unchecked (§18.4).

- To declare exceptions in a method header (§18.5.1).

- To throw exceptions in a method (§18.5.2).

- To write a `try-catch` block to handle exceptions (§18.5.3).

- To explain how an exception is propagated (§18.5.3).

- To use the `finally` clause in a `try-catch` block (§18.6).

- To use exceptions only for unexpected errors (§18.7).

- To rethrow exceptions in a `catch` block (§18.8).

- To create chained exceptions (§18.9).

- To declare custom exception classes (§18.10).

18.1 Introduction

When a program encounters a runtime error, it terminates abnormally. How can you handle the runtime error so that the program can continue to run or else terminate gracefully? This is the subject we will introduce in this chapter.

18.2 Exception-Handling Overview

Video Note
Exception handling advantage

To demonstrate exception handling, we begin with an example in Listing 18.1 that reads in two integers and displays their quotient.

LISTING 18.1 Quotient.java

```
 1 import java.util.Scanner;
 2
 3 public class Quotient {
 4   public static void main(String[] args) {
 5     Scanner input = new Scanner(System.in);
 6
 7     // Prompt the user to enter two integers
 8     System.out.print("Enter two integers: ");
 9     int number1 = input.nextInt();
10     int number2 = input.nextInt();
11
12     System.out.println(number1 + " / " + number2 + " is " +
13       (number1 / number2 ));
14   }
15 }
```

reads two integers

integer division

```
Enter two integers: 5 2 ↵Enter
5 / 2 is 2
```

```
Enter two integers: 3 0 ↵Enter
Exception in thread "main" java.lang.ArithmeticException: / by zero
                    at Quotient.main(Quotient.java:11)
```

If you entered 0 for the second number, a runtime error would occur, because you cannot divide an integer by 0. (*Recall that a floating-point number divided by 0 does not raise an exception.*) A simple way to fix the error is to add an `if` statement to test the second number, as shown in Listing 18.2.

LISTING 18.2 QuotientWithIf.java

```
 1 import java.util.Scanner;
 2
 3 public class QuotientWithIf {
 4   public static void main(String[] args) {
 5     Scanner input = new Scanner(System.in);
 6
 7     // Prompt the user to enter two integers
 8     System.out.print("Enter two integers: ");
 9     int number1 = input.nextInt();
10     int number2 = input.nextInt();
11
12     if (number2 != 0)
```

reads two integers

test number2

```
13        System.out.println(number1 + " / " + number2 + " is " +
14          (number1 / number2));
15      else
16        System.out.println("Divisor cannot be zero ");
17   }
18 }
```

```
Enter two integers: 5 0 ↵Enter
Divisor cannot be zero
```

Listing 18.2 can be rewritten using exception handling, as shown in Listing 18.3. Note that, since Listing 18.2 is simpler than Listing 18.3, you should not actually use exception handling in this situation. The purpose of Listing 18.3 is to give a simple example to demonstrate the concept of exception handling. Later you will see the practical advantages of using exception handling.

LISTING 18.3 QuotientWithException.java

```
1 import java.util.Scanner;
2
3 public class QuotientWithException {
4   public static void main(String[] args) {
5     Scanner input = new Scanner(System.in);
6
7     // Prompt the user to enter two integers
8     System.out.print("Enter two integers: ");
9     int number1 = input.nextInt();                          reads two integers
10    int number2 = input.nextInt();
11
12    try {                                                   try block
13      if (number2 == 0)
14        throw new ArithmeticException("Divisor cannot be zero");
15
16      System.out.println(number1 + " / " + number2 + " is " +
17        (number1 / number2));
18    }
19    catch (ArithmeticException ex) {                        catch block
20      System.out.println("Exception: an integer " +
21        "cannot be divided by zero ");
22    }
23
24    System.out.println("Execution continues ...");
25  }
26 }
```

```
Enter two integers: 5 3 ↵Enter
5 / 3 is 1
Execution continues ...
```

```
Enter two integers: 5 0 ↵Enter
Exception: an integer cannot be divided by zero
Execution continues ...
```

The program contains a `try` block and a `catch` block. The `try` block (lines 12–18) contains the code that is executed in normal circumstances. The `catch` block (lines 19–22)

throw statement

contains the code that is executed when `number2` is `0`. In this event the program throws an exception by executing

```
throw new ArithmeticException("Divisor cannot be zero");
```

exception
throwing exception

The value thrown, in this case `new ArithmeticException("Divisor cannot be zero")`, is called an *exception*. The execution of a throw statement is called *throwing an exception*. The exception is an object created from an exception class. In this case, the exception class is `java.lang.ArithmeticException`.

handle exception

When an exception is thrown, the normal execution flow is interrupted. As the name suggests, "throw exception" is to pass the exception from one place to another. The exception is caught by the `catch` block. The code in the `catch` block is executed to *handle the exception*. Afterward, the statement (line 23) after the `catch` block is executed.

The `throw` statement is analogous to a method call, but instead of calling a method, it calls a `catch` block. In this sense, a `catch` block is like a method definition with a parameter that matches the type of the value being thrown. Unlike a method, after executing the `catch` block, the program control does not return back to the `throw` statement; instead, it executes the next statement after the `catch` block.

The identifier `ex` in the catch block header

```
catch (ArithmeticException ex)
```

catch block parameter

acts very much like a parameter in a method. So this parameter is referred to as a `catch` block parameter. The type (e.g., `ArithmeticException`) preceding `ex` specifies what kind of exception the `catch` block can catch. Once the exception is caught, you can access the thrown value from this parameter in the body of a catch block.

In summary, a template for a `try-throw-catch` block may look like this:

```
try {
  Code to try;
  Throw an exception with a throw statement or
    from method if necessary;
  More code to try;
}
catch (type ex) {
  Code to process the exception;
}
```

An exception may be thrown directly using a `throw` statement in a `try` block, or from invoking a method that may throw an exception.

18.3 Exception-Handling Advantages

Listing 18.3 provides a simple example to demonstrate the concept of exception handling. This section uses methods to demonstrate the advantages of using exception handling.

Listing 18.4 rewrites Listing 18.3 to compute a quotient using a method.

LISTING 18.4 QuotientWithMethod.cpp

```
1 import java.util.Scanner;
2
3 public class QuotientWithMethod {
4   public static int quotient(int number1, int number2) {
5     if (number2 == 0)
```

quotient method

```
6        throw new ArithmeticException("Divisor cannot be zero");
7
8      return number1 / number2;
9    }
10
11   public static void main(String[] args) {
12     Scanner input = new Scanner(System.in);
13
14     // Prompt the user to enter two integers
15     System.out.print("Enter two integers: ");
16     int number1 = input.nextInt();
17     int number2 = input.nextInt();
18
19     try {
20       int result = quotient(number1, number2);
21       System.out.println(number1 + " / " + number2 + " is "
22         + result);
23     }
24     catch (ArithmeticException ex) {
25       System.out.println("Exception: an integer " +
26         "cannot be divided by zero ");
27     }
28
29     System.out.println("Execution continues ...");
30   }
31 }
```

throw exception

reads two integers

try block
invoke method

catch block

```
Enter two integers: 5 3 [↵Enter]
5 / 3 is 1
Execution continues ...
```

```
Enter two integers: 5 0 [↵Enter]
Exception: an integer cannot be divided by zero
Execution continues ...
```

Method `quotient` (lines 4–9) returns the quotient of two integers. If `number2` is `0`, it cannot return a value. So, an exception is thrown in line 6.

The main method invokes `quotient` (line 20). If the quotient method executes normally, it returns a value to the caller. If the `quotient` method encounters an exception, it throws the exception back to its caller. The caller's `catch` block handles the exception.

Now you see the *advantages* of using exception handling. It enables a method to throw an exception to its caller. Without this capability, a method must handle the exception or terminate the program.

advantage

18.4 Exception Types

The `catch` block parameter in the preceding section is of the `ArithmeticException` type. Are there any other types you can use? Yes. You can use the `Throwable` class or any subclass of `Throwable`. `ArithmeticException` is a subtype of `Throwable`.

The `Throwable` class is contained in the `java.lang` package, and subclasses of `Throwable` are contained in various packages. Errors related to GUI components are included in the `java.awt` package; numeric exceptions are included in the `java.lang` package, because they are related to the `java.lang.Number` class. You can create your own exception classes by extending `Throwable` or a subclass of `Throwable`. Figure 18.1 shows some of Java's predefined exception classes.

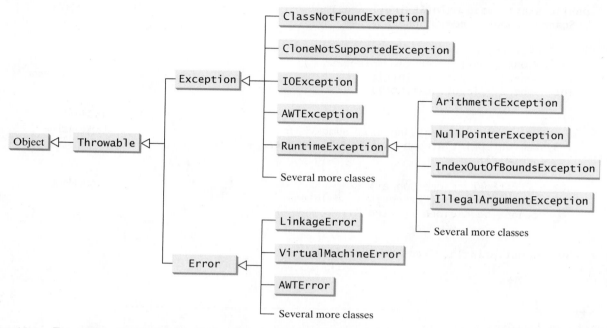

FIGURE 18.1   Exceptions thrown are instances of the classes shown in this diagram, or of subclasses of one of these classes.

 Note

The class names `Error`, `Exception`, and `RuntimeException` are somewhat confusing. All three of these classes are exceptions, and all of the errors discussed here occur at runtime.

The exception classes can be classified into three major types: system errors, exceptions, and runtime exceptions.

system error

- *System errors* are thrown by the JVM and represented in the `Error` class. The `Error` class describes internal system errors. Such errors rarely occur. If one does, there is little you can do beyond notifying the user and trying to terminate the program gracefully. Examples of subclasses of `Error` are listed in Table 18.1.

exception

- *Exceptions* are represented in the `Exception` class, which describes errors caused by your program and by external circumstances. These errors can be caught and

TABLE 18.1   Examples of Subclasses of **Error**

Class	Possible Reason for Exception
LinkageError	A class has some dependency on another class, but the latter class has changed incompatibly after the compilation of the former class.
VirtualMachineError	The JVM is broken or has run out of the resources necessary for it to continue operating.
AWTError	A fatal error in the GUI runtime system.

handled by your program. Examples of subclasses of `Exception` are listed in Table 18.2.

TABLE 18.2 Examples of Subclasses of **Exception**

Class	Possible Reason for Exception
`ClassNotFoundException`	Attempt to use a class that does not exist. This exception would occur, for example, if you tried to run a nonexistent class using the **java** command, or if your program were composed of, say, three class files, only two of which could be found.
`CloneNotSupportedException`	Attempt to clone an object whose defining class does not implement the `Cloneable` interface. Cloning objects were introduced in Chapter 11, "Abstract Classes and Interfaces."
`IOException`	Related to input/output operations, such as invalid input, reading past the end of a file, and opening a nonexistent file. Examples of subclasses of `IOException` are `InterruptedIOException`, `EOFException` (EOF is short for End Of File), and `FileNotFoundException`.
`AWTException`	Exceptions in GUI components.

- *Runtime exceptions* are represented in the `RuntimeException` class, which describes programming errors, such as bad casting, accessing an out-of-bounds array, and numeric errors. Runtime exceptions are generally thrown by the JVM. Examples of subclasses are listed in Table 18.3.

runtime exception

TABLE 18.3 Examples of Subclasses of **RuntimeException**

Class	Possible Reason for Exception
`ArithmeticException`	Dividing an integer by zero. Note that floating-point arithmetic does not throw exceptions. See Appendix E, "Special Floating-Point Values."
`NullPointerException`	Attempt to access an object through a `null` reference variable.
`IndexOutOfBoundsException`	Index to an array is out of range.
`IllegalArgumentException`	A method is passed an argument that is illegal or inappropriate.

`RuntimeException`, `Error`, and their subclasses are known as *unchecked exceptions*. All other exceptions are known as *checked exceptions*, meaning that the compiler forces the programmer to check and deal with them.

unchecked exception
checked exception

In most cases, unchecked exceptions reflect programming logic errors that are not recoverable. For example, a `NullPointerException` is thrown if you access an object through a reference variable before an object is assigned to it; an `IndexOutOfBoundsException` is thrown if you access an element in an array outside the bounds of the array. These are logic errors that should be corrected in the program. Unchecked exceptions can occur anywhere in a program. To avoid cumbersome overuse of try-catch blocks, Java does not mandate that you write code to catch or declare unchecked exceptions.

integer overflow/underflow

Caution

At present, Java does not throw integer overflow or underflow exceptions. The following statement adds **1** to the maximum integer.

```
int number = Integer.MAX_VALUE + 1;
System.out.println(number);
```

It displays **-2147483648**, which is logically incorrect. The cause of this problem is overflow; that is, the result exceeds the maximum for an **int** value.

A future version of Java may fix this problem by throwing an overflow exception.

BigInteger

Tip

For processing large integral values, use the **BigInteger** class, introduced in §11.12, "The **BigInteger** and **BigDecimal** Classes."

18.5 Understanding Exception Handling

Java's exception-handling model is based on three operations: *declaring an exception*, *throwing an exception*, and *catching an exception*, as shown in Figure 18.2.

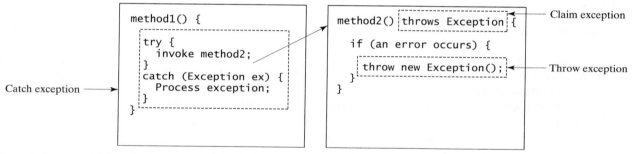

FIGURE 18.2 Exception handling in Java consists of declaring exceptions, throwing exceptions, and catching and processing exceptions.

18.5.1 Declaring Exceptions

In Java, the statement currently being executed belongs to a method. The Java interpreter invokes the **main** method for a Java application, and the Web browser invokes the applet's no-arg constructor and then the **init** method for a Java applet. Every method must state the types of checked exceptions it might throw. This is known as *declaring exceptions*. Because system errors and runtime errors can happen to any code, Java does not require that you declare **Error** and **RuntimeException** (unchecked exceptions) explicitly in the method. However, all other exceptions thrown by the method must be explicitly declared in the method declaration so that the caller of the method is informed of the exception.

declare exception

To declare an exception in a method, use the **throws** keyword in the method declaration, as in this example:

```
public void myMethod() throws IOException
```

The **throws** keyword indicates that **myMethod** might throw an **IOException**. If the method might throw multiple exceptions, add a list of the exceptions, separated by commas, after **throws**:

```
public void myMethod()
  throws Exception1, Exception2, ..., ExceptionN
```

Note

If a method does not declare exceptions in the superclass, you cannot override it to declare exceptions in the subclass.

18.5.2 Throwing Exceptions

A program that detects an error can create an instance of an appropriate exception type and throw it. This is known as *throwing an exception*. Here is an example: Suppose the program detects that an argument passed to the method violates the method contract (e.g., the argument must be nonnegative, but a negative argument is passed); the program can create an instance of `IllegalArgumentException` and throw it, as follows:

throw exception

```
IllegalArgumentException ex =
  new IllegalArgumentException("Wrong Argument");
throw ex;
```

Or, if you prefer, you can use the following:

```
throw new IllegalArgumentException("Wrong Argument");
```

Note

`IllegalArgumentException` is an exception class in the Java API. In general, each exception class in the Java API has at least two constructors: a no-arg constructor, and a constructor with a `String` argument that describes the exception. This argument is called the *exception message*, which can be obtained using `getMessage()`.

exception message

Tip

The keyword to declare an exception is **throws**, and the keyword to throw an exception is **throw**.

throws and **throw**

18.5.3 Catching Exceptions

You now know how to declare an exception and how to throw an exception. When an exception is thrown, it can be caught and handled in a try-catch block, as follows:

catch exception

```
try {
  statements;   // Statements that may throw exceptions
}
catch (Exception1 exVar1) {
  handler for exception1;
}
catch (Exception2 exVar2) {
  handler for exception2;
}
...
catch (ExceptionN exVar3) {
  handler for exceptionN;
}
```

If no exceptions arise during the execution of the **try** block, the **catch** blocks are skipped.

If one of the statements inside the **try** block throws an exception, Java skips the remaining statements in the try block and starts the process of finding the code to handle the exception. The code that handles the exception is called the *exception handler*; it is found by propagating the exception backward through a chain of method calls, starting from the current method. Each **catch** block is examined in turn, from first to last, to see whether the type of the exception object is an instance of the exception class in the **catch** block. If so, the exception object is assigned to the variable declared, and the code in the **catch**

exception handler

block is executed. If no handler is found, Java exits this method, passes the exception to the method that invoked the method, and continues the same process to find a handler. If no handler is found in the chain of methods being invoked, the program terminates and prints an error message on the console. The process of finding a handler is called *catching an exception*.

Suppose the `main` method invokes `method1`, `method1` invokes `method2`, `method2` invokes `method3`, and an exception occurs in `method3`, as shown in Figure 18.3. Consider the following scenario:

- If `method3` cannot handle the exception, `method3` is aborted and the control is returned to `method2`. If the exception type is `Exception3`, it is caught by the `catch` block for handling exception `ex3` in `method2`. `statement5` is skipped, and `statement6` is executed.

- If the exception type is `Exception2`, `method2` is aborted, the control is returned to `method1`, and the exception is caught by the `catch` block for handling exception `ex2` in `method1`. `statement3` is skipped, and `statement4` is executed.

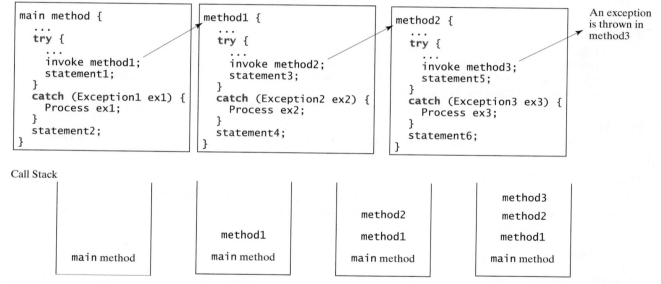

FIGURE 18.3 If an exception is not caught in the current method, it is passed to its caller. The process is repeated until the exception is caught or passed to the `main` method.

- If the exception type is `Exception1`, `method1` is aborted, the control is returned to the `main` method, and the exception is caught by the `catch` block for handling exception `ex1` in the `main` method. `statement1` is skipped, and `statement2` is executed.

- If the exception type is not `Exception1`, `Exception2`, or `Exception3`, the exception is not caught and the program terminates. `statement1` and `statement2` are not executed.

Note

catch block

Various exception classes can be derived from a common superclass. If a `catch` block catches exception objects of a superclass, it can catch all the exception objects of the subclasses of that superclass.

Note

The order in which exceptions are specified in `catch` blocks is important. A compilation error will result if a catch block for a superclass type appears before a catch block for a subclass type. For example, the ordering in (a) below is erroneous, because `RuntimeException` is a subclass of `Exception`. The correct ordering should be as shown in (b).

order of exception handlers

```
try {
  ...
}
catch (Exception ex) {
  ...
}
catch (RuntimeException ex) {
  ...
}
```

(a) Wrong order

```
try {
  ...
}
catch (RuntimeException ex) {
  ...
}
catch (Exception ex) {
  ...
}
```

(b) Correct order

Note

Java forces you to deal with checked exceptions. If a method declares a checked exception (i.e., an exception other than `Error` or `RuntimeException`), you must invoke it in a `try-catch` block or declare to throw the exception in the calling method. For example, suppose that method **p1** invokes method **p2** and **p2** may throw a checked exception (e.g., `IOException`); you have to write the code as shown in (a) or (b).

catch or declare checked exceptions

```
void p1() {
  try {
    p2();
  }
  catch (IOException ex) {
    ...
  }
}
```

(a) Catch exception

```
void p1() throws IOException {

  p2();

}
```

(b) Throw exception

18.5.4 Getting Information from Exceptions

An exception object contains valuable information about the exception. You may use the following instance methods in the `java.lang.Throwable` class to get information regarding the exception, as shown in Figure 18.4. The `printStackTrace()` method prints stack trace information on the console. The `getStackTrace()` method provides programmatic access to the stack trace information printed by `printStackTrace()`.

*methods in **Throwable***

java.lang.Throwable	
+getMessage(): String	Returns the message of this object.
+toString(): String	Returns the concatenation of three strings: (1) the full name of the exception class; (2) ":" (a colon and a space); (3) the getMessage() method.
+printStackTrace(): void	Prints the Throwable object and its call stack trace information on the console.
+getStackTrace(): StackTraceElement[]	Returns an array of stack trace elements representing the stack trace pertaining to this throwable.

FIGURE 18.4 `Throwable` is the root class for all exception objects.

Listing 18.5 gives an example that uses the methods in `Throwable` to display exception information. Line 4 invokes the `sum` method to return the sum of all the elements in the array. There is an error in line 23 that causes the `ArrayIndexOutOfBoundsException`, a subclass of `IndexOutOfBoundsException`. This exception is caught in the try-catch block. Lines 7, 8, 9 display the stack trace, exception message, and exception object and message using the `printStackTrace()`, `getMessage()`, and `toString()` methods, as shown in Figure 18.5. Line 10 brings stack trace elements into an array. Each element represents a method call. You can obtain the method (line 12), class name (line 13), and exception line number (line 14) for each element.

LISTING 18.5 `TestException.java`

```
1  public class TestException  {
2    public static void main(String[] args) {
3      try {
4        System.out.println(sum(new int[] {1, 2, 3, 4, 5}));
5      }
6      catch (Exception ex) {
7        ex.printStackTrace();
8        System.out.println("\n" + ex.getMessage());
9        System.out.println("\n" + ex.toString());
10
11        System.out.println("\nTrace Info Obtained from getStackTrace");
12        StackTraceElement[] traceElements = ex.getStackTrace();
13        for (int i = 0; i < traceElements.length; i++) {
14          System.out.print("method " + traceElements[i].getMethodName());
15          System.out.print("(" + traceElements[i].getClassName() + ":");
16          System.out.println(traceElements[i].getLineNumber() + ")");
17        }
18      }
19    }
20
21    private static int sum(int[] list) {
22      int result = 0;
23      for (int i = 0; i <= list.length; i++)
24        result += list[i];
25      return result;
26    }
27  }
```

invoke sum (line 4 annotation)

printStackTrace()
getMessage()
toString() (lines 7-9 annotation)

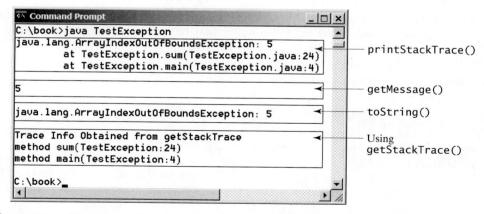

FIGURE 18.5 You can use the `printStackTrace()`, `getMessage()`, `toString()`, and `getStackTrace()` methods to obtain information from exception objects.

18.5.5 Example: Declaring, Throwing, and Catching Exceptions

This example demonstrates declaring, throwing, and catching exceptions by modifying the `setRadius` method in Listing 7.7, Circle3.java. The new `setRadius` method throws an exception if the radius is negative.

Rename the circle class given in Listing 18.6 as `CircleWithException`, which is the same as `Circle3` except that the `setRadius(double newRadius)` method throws an `IllegalArgumentException` if the argument `newRadius` is negative.

LISTING 18.6 CircleWithException.java

```java
 1 public class CircleWithException {
 2   /** The radius of the circle */
 3   private double radius;
 4
 5   /** The number of the objects created */
 6   private static int numberOfObjects = 0;
 7
 8   /** Construct a circle with radius 1 */
 9   public CircleWithException() {
10     this(1.0);
11   }
12
13   /** Construct a circle with a specified radius */
14   public CircleWithException(double newRadius) {
15     setRadius(newRadius);
16     numberOfObjects++;
17   }
18
19   /** Return radius */
20   public double getRadius() {
21     return radius;
22   }
23
24   /** Set a new radius */
25   public void setRadius(double newRadius)
26       throws IllegalArgumentException  {
27     if (newRadius >= 0)
28       radius =  newRadius;
29     else
30       throw new IllegalArgumentException(
31         "Radius cannot be negative");
32   }
33
34   /** Return numberOfObjects */
35   public static int getNumberOfObjects() {
36     return numberOfObjects;
37   }
38
39   /** Return the area of this circle */
40   public double findArea() {
41     return radius * radius * 3.14159;
42   }
43 }
```

declare exception

throw exception

A test program that uses the new `Circle` class is given in Listing 18.7.

LISTING 18.7 TestCircleWithException.java

try

catch

```
 1 public class TestCircleWithException {
 2   /** Main method */
 3   public static void main(String[] args) {
 4     try {
 5       CircleWithException c1 = new CircleWithException(5);
 6       CircleWithException c2 = new CircleWithException(-5);
 7       CircleWithException c3 = new CircleWithException(0);
 8     }
 9     catch (IllegalArgumentException ex) {
10       System.out.println(ex);
11     }
12
13     System.out.println("Number of objects created: " +
14       CircleWithException.getNumberOfObjects());
15   }
16 }
```

```
java.lang.IllegalArgumentException: Radius cannot be negative
Number of objects created: 1
```

The original `Circle3` class remains intact except that the class name is changed to `CircleWithException`, a new constructor `CircleWithException(newRadius)` is added, and the `setRadius` method now declares an exception and throws it if the radius is negative.

The `setRadius` method declares to throw `IllegalArgumentException` in the method declaration (lines 25–32 in CircleWithException.java). The `CircleWithException` class would still compile if the `throws IllegalArgumentException` clause were removed from the method declaration, since it is a subclass of `RuntimeException` and every method can throw `RuntimeException` (unchecked exception) regardless of whether it is declared in the method header.

The test program creates three `CircleWithException` objects, `c1`, `c2`, and `c3`, to test how to handle exceptions. Invoking `new CircleWithException(-5)` (line 5 in Listing 18.7) causes the `setRadius` method to be invoked, which throws an `Illegal-ArgumentException`, because the radius is negative. In the `catch` block, the type of the object `ex` is `IllegalArgumentException`, which matches the exception object thrown by the `setRadius` method. So, this exception is caught by the `catch` block.

The exception handler prints a short message, `ex.toString()` (line 10), about the exception, using `System.out.println(ex)`.

Note that the execution continues in the event of the exception. If the handlers had not caught the exception, the program would have abruptly terminated.

The test program would still compile if the `try` statement were not used, because the method throws an instance of `IllegalArgumentException`, a subclass of `Runtime-Exception` (unchecked exception). If a method throws an exception other than `RuntimeException` and `Error`, the method must be invoked within a `try-catch` block.

Note

As you will learn in Chapter 29, "Multithreading," Java supports multithreading. One program can have many threads. Methods are executed on threads. If an exception occurs on a thread, the thread is terminated if the exception is not caught. If a program has only one thread, an uncaught exception will cause the program to terminate. If a program has multiple threads, an uncaught exception will terminate only the thread where the exception occurred. However, since certain threads may rely on the terminated thread, terminating a thread may affect the rest of the program.

multiple threads

18.6 The **finally** Clause

Occasionally, you may want some code to be executed regardless of whether an exception occurs or is caught. Java has a **finally** clause that can be used to accomplish this objective. The syntax for the **finally** clause might look like this:

```
try {
  statements;
}
catch (TheException ex) {
  handling ex;
}
finally {
  finalStatements;
}
```

The code in the **finally** block is executed under all circumstances, regardless of whether an exception occurs in the **try** block or is caught. Consider three possible cases:

- If no exception arises in the **try** block, **finalStatements** is executed, and the next statement after the **try** statement is executed.

- If one of the statements causes an exception in the **try** block that is caught in a **catch** block, the other statements in the **try** block are skipped, the **catch** block is executed, and the **finally** clause is executed. If the **catch** block does not rethrow an exception, the next statement after the **try** statement is executed. If it does, the exception is passed to the caller of this method.

- If one of the statements causes an exception that is not caught in any **catch** block, the other statements in the **try** block are skipped, the **finally** clause is executed, and the exception is passed to the caller of this method.

- The **finally** block executes even if there is a **return** statement prior to reaching the **finally** block.

Note

The **catch** block may be omitted when the **finally** clause is used.

omitting catch block

A common use of the **finally** clause is in I/O programming. To ensure that a file is closed under all circumstances, you may place a file closing statement in the **finally** block, as shown in Listing 18.8.

LISTING 18.8 FinallyDemo.java

```
 1 public class FinallyDemo {
 2   public static void main(String[] args) {
 3     java.io.PrintWriter output = null;
 4
 5     try {
 6       // Create a file
 7       output = new java.io.PrintWriter("text.txt");
 8
 9       // Write formatted output to the file
10       output.println("Welcome to Java");
11     }
12     catch (java.io.IOException ex) {
13       ex.printStackTrace();
14     }
15     finally {
```

try

catch

finally

```
16          // Close the file
17          if (output != null) output.close();
18      }
19    }
20 }
```

The statements in lines 7 and 10 may throw an `IOException`, so they are placed inside a `try` block. The statement `output.close()` closes the `PrintWriter` object output in the `finally` block. This statement is executed regardless of whether an exception occurs in the `try` block or is caught.

18.7 When to Use Exceptions

The `try` block contains the code that is executed in normal circumstances. The `catch` block contains the code that is executed in exceptional circumstances. Exception handling separates error-handling code from normal programming tasks, thus making programs easier to read and to modify. Be aware, however, that exception handling usually requires more time and resources, because it requires instantiating a new exception object, rolling back the call stack, and propagating the exception through the chain of methods invoked to search for the handler.

An exception occurs in a method. If you want the exception to be processed by its caller, you should create an exception object and throw it. If you can handle the exception in the method where it occurs, there is no need to throw or use exceptions.

In general, common exceptions that may occur in multiple classes in a project are candidates for exception classes. Simple errors that may occur in individual methods are best handled locally without throwing exceptions.

When should you use a `try-catch` block in the code? Use it when you have to deal with unexpected error conditions. Do not use a try-catch block to deal with simple, expected situations. For example, the following code

```
try {
  System.out.println(refVar.toString());
}
catch (NullPointerException ex) {
  System.out.println("refVar is null");
}
```

is better replaced by

```
if (refVar != null)
  System.out.println(refVar.toString());
else
  System.out.println("refVar is null");
```

Which situations are exceptional and which are expected is sometimes difficult to decide. The point is not to abuse exception handling as a way to deal with a simple logic test.

18.8 Rethrowing Exceptions

Java allows an exception handler to rethrow the exception if the handler cannot process the exception or simply wants to let its caller be notified of the exception. The syntax may look like this:

```
try {
  statements;
}
```

```
catch (TheException ex) {
  perform operations before exits;
  throw ex;
}
```

The statement `throw ex` rethrows the exception so that other handlers get a chance to process the exception `ex`.

18.9 Chained Exceptions

In the preceding section, the catch block rethrows the original exception. Sometimes, you may need to throw a new exception (with additional information) along with the original exception. This is called *chained exceptions*. Listing 18.9 illustrates how to create and throw chained exceptions.

LISTING 18.9 ChainedExceptionDemo.java

```
 1 public class ChainedExceptionDemo {
 2   public static void main(String[] args) {
 3     try {
 4       method1();
 5     }
 6     catch (Exception ex) {
 7       ex.printStackTrace();                                     stack trace
 8     }
 9   }
10
11   public static void method1() throws Exception {
12     try {
13       method2();
14     }
15     catch (Exception ex) {
16       throw new Exception("New info from method1", ex);        chained exception
17     }
18   }
19
20   public static void method2() throws Exception {
21     throw new Exception("New info from method2");              throw exception
22   }
23 }
```

```
java.lang.Exception: New info from method1
        at ChainedExceptionDemo.method1(ChainedExceptionDemo.java:16)
        at ChainedExceptionDemo.main(ChainedExceptionDemo.java:4)
Caused by: java.lang.Exception: New info from method2
        at ChainedExceptionDemo.method2(ChainedExceptionDemo.java:21)
        at ChainedExceptionDemo.method1(ChainedExceptionDemo.java:13)
        ... 1 more
```

The `main` method invokes `method1` (line 4), `method1` invokes `method2` (line 13), and `method2` throws an exception (line 21). This exception is caught in the catch block in `method1` and is wrapped in a new exception in line 16. The new exception is thrown and caught in the catch block in the `main` method in line 4. The sample output shows the output from the `printStackTrace()` method in line 7. The new exception thrown from `method1` is displayed first, followed by the original exception thrown from `method2`.

Video Note
Create custom exception classes

18.10 Creating Custom Exception Classes

Java provides quite a few exception classes. Use them whenever possible instead of creating your own exception classes. However, if you run into a problem that cannot be adequately described by the predefined exception classes, you can create your own exception class, derived from Exception or from a subclass of Exception, such as IOException.

In Listing 18.6, CircleWithException.java, the setRadius method throws an exception if the radius is negative. Suppose you wish to pass the radius to the handler. In that case, you may create a custom exception class, as shown in Listing 18.10.

LISTING 18.10 InvalidRadiusException.java

extends **Exception**

```
1  public class InvalidRadiusException extends Exception {
2    private double radius;
3
4    /** Construct an exception */
5    public InvalidRadiusException(double radius) {
6      super("Invalid radius " + radius);
7      this.radius = radius;
8    }
9
10   /** Return the radius */
11   public double getRadius() {
12     return radius;
13   }
14 }
```

Exception constructors

This custom exception class extends java.lang.Exception (line 1). The Exception class extends java.lang.Throwable. All the methods (e.g., getMessage(), toString(), and printStackTrace()) in Exception are inherited from Throwable. The Exception class contains four constructors. Among them, the following two constructors are often used:

java.lang.Exception	
+Exception()	Constructs an exception with no message.
+Exception(message: String)	Constructs an exception with the specified message.

Line 6 invokes the superclass's constructor with a message. This message will be set in the exception object and can be obtained by invoking getMessage() on the object.

 Tip
Most exception classes in the Java API contain two constructors: a no-arg constructor and a constructor with a message parameter.

To create an InvalidRadiusException, you have to pass a radius. So the setRadius method in Listing 18.6 can be modified as follows:

```
/** Set a new radius */
public void setRadius(double newRadius)
    throws InvalidRadiusException {
  if (newRadius >= 0)
    radius = newRadius;
  else
    throw new InvalidRadiusException(newRadius);
}
```

The following code creates a circle object and sets its radius to -5.

```
try {
  CircleWithException1 c = new CircleWithException1(4);
  c.setRadius(-5);
}
catch (InvalidRadiusException ex) {
  System.out.println("The invalid radius is " + ex.getRadius());
}
```

Invoking `setRadius(-5)` throws an `InvalidRadiusException`, which is caught by the handler. The handler displays the radius in the exception object `ex`.

Tip

Can you declare a custom exception class by extending `RuntimeException`? Yes, but it is not a good way to go, because it makes your custom exception unchecked. It is better to make a custom exception checked so that the complier can force these exceptions to be caught in your program.

checked custom exception

KEY TERMS

chained exception 613	exception propagation 605
checked exception 603	throw exception 601
declare exception 604	unchecked exception 603
exception 600	

CHAPTER SUMMARY

- When an exception occurs, Java creates an object that contains the information for the exception. You can use the information to handle the exception.

- A Java exception is an instance of a class derived from `java.lang.Throwable`. Java provides a number of predefined exception classes, such as `Error`, `Exception`, `RuntimeException`, `ClassNotFoundException`, `NullPointerException`, and `ArithmeticException`. You can also define your own exception class by extending `Exception`.

- Exceptions occur during the execution of a method. `RuntimeException` and `Error` are unchecked exceptions; all other exceptions are checked.

- When declaring a method, you have to declare a checked exception if the method might throw it, thus telling the compiler what can go wrong.

- The keyword for declaring an exception is `throws`, and the keyword for throwing an exception is `throw`.

- To invoke the method that declares checked exceptions, you must enclose the method call in a `try` statement. When an exception occurs during the execution of the method, the `catch` block catches and handles the exception.

- If an exception is not caught in the current method, it is passed to its caller. The process is repeated until the exception is caught or passed to the `main` method.

- Various exception classes can be derived from a common superclass. If a `catch` block catches the exception objects of a superclass, it can also catch all the exception objects of the subclasses of that superclass.

- The order in which exceptions are specified in a `catch` block is important. A compilation error will result if you do not specify an exception object of a class before an exception object of the superclass of that class.

- When an exception occurs in a method, the method exits immediately if it does not catch the exception. If the method is required to perform some task before exiting, you can catch the exception in the method and then rethrow it to the real handler.

- The code in the `finally` block is executed under all circumstances, regardless of whether an exception occurs in the `try` block or is caught.

- Exception handling separates error-handling code from normal programming tasks, thus making programs easier to read and to modify.

- Exception handling should not be used to replace simple tests. You should test simple exceptions whenever possible, and reserve exception handling for dealing with situations that cannot be handled with `if` statements.

REVIEW QUESTIONS

Sections 18.1–18.13

18.1   Describe the Java `Throwable` class, its subclasses, and the types of exceptions. What `RunTimeException` will the following programs throw, if any?

```java
public class Test {
  public static void main(String[] args) {
    System.out.println(1 / 0);
  }
}
```
(a)

```java
public class Test {
  public static void main(String[] args) {
    int[] list = new int[5];
    System.out.println(list[5]);
  }
}
```
(b)

```java
public class Test {
  public static void main(String[] args) {
    String s = "abc";
    System.out.println(s.charAt(3));
  }
}
```
(c)

```java
public class Test {
  public static void main(String[] args) {
    Object o = new Object();
    String d = (String)o;
  }
}
```
(d)

```java
public class Test {
  public static void main(String[] args) {
    Object o = null;
    System.out.println(o.toString());
  }
}
```
(e)

```java
public class Test {
  public static void main(String[] args) {
    System.out.println(1.0 / 0);
  }
}
```
(f)

18.2 Show the output of the following code.

```
public class Test {
  public static void main(String[] args) {
    for (int i = 0; i < 2; i++) {
      System.out.print(i + " ");
      try {
        System.out.println(1 / 0);
      }
      catch (Exception ex) {
      }
    }
  }
}
```
(a)

```
public class Test {
  public static void main(String[] args) {
    try {
      for (int i = 0; i < 2; i++) {
        System.out.print(i + " ");
        System.out.println(1 / 0);
      }
    }
    catch (Exception ex) {
    }
  }
}
```
(b)

18.3 Point out the problem in the following code. Does the code throw any exceptions?

```
long value = Long.MAX_VALUE + 1;
System.out.println(value);
```

18.4 What is the purpose of declaring exceptions? How do you declare an exception, and where? Can you declare multiple exceptions in a method declaration?

18.5 What is a checked exception, and what is an unchecked exception?

18.6 How do you throw an exception? Can you throw multiple exceptions in one throw statement?

18.7 What is the keyword throw used for? What is the keyword throws used for?

18.8 What does the JVM do when an exception occurs? How do you catch an exception?

18.9 What is the printout of the following code?

```
public class Test {
  public static void main(String[] args) {
    try {
      int value = 30;
      if (value < 40)
        throw new Exception("value is too small");
    }
    catch (Exception ex) {
      System.out.println(ex.getMessage());
    }
    System.out.println("Continue after the catch block");
  }
}
```

What would be the printout if the line

```
int value = 30;
```

were changed to

```
int value = 50;
```

18.10 Suppose that statement2 causes an exception in the following try-catch block:

```
try {
  statement1;
  statement2;
```

```
      statement3;
    }
    catch (Exception1 ex1) {
    }
    catch (Exception2 ex2) {
    }

    statement4;
```

Answer the following questions:

■ Will statement3 be executed?
■ If the exception is not caught, will statement4 be executed?
■ If the exception is caught in the catch block, will statement4 be executed?
■ If the exception is passed to the caller, will statement4 be executed?

18.11 What is displayed when the following program is run?

```java
public class Test {
  public static void main(String[] args) {
    try {
      int[] list = new int[10];
      System.out.println("list[10] is " + list[10]);
    }
    catch (ArithmeticException ex) {
      System.out.println("ArithmeticException");
    }
    catch (RuntimeException ex) {
      System.out.println("RuntimeException");
    }
    catch (Exception ex) {
      System.out.println("Exception");
    }
  }
}
```

18.12 What is displayed when the following program is run?

```java
public class Test {
  public static void main(String[] args) {
    try {
      method();
      System.out.println("After the method call");
    }
    catch (ArithmeticException ex) {
      System.out.println("ArithmeticException");
    }
    catch (RuntimeException ex) {
      System.out.println("RuntimeException");
    }
    catch (Exception e) {
      System.out.println("Exception");
    }
  }

  static void method() throws Exception {
    System.out.println(1 / 0);
  }
}
```

18.13 What is displayed when the following program is run?

```java
public class Test {
  public static void main(String[] args) {
    try {
      method();
      System.out.println("After the method call");
    }
    catch (RuntimeException ex) {
      System.out.println("RuntimeException in main");
    }
    catch (Exception ex) {
      System.out.println("Exception in main");
    }
  }

  static void method() throws Exception {
    try {
      String s ="abc";
      System.out.println(s.charAt(3));
    }
    catch (RuntimeException ex) {
      System.out.println("RuntimeException in method()");
    }
    catch (Exception ex) {
      System.out.println("Exception in method()");
    }
  }
}
```

18.14 If an exception is not caught in a non-GUI application, what will happen? If an exception is not caught in a GUI application, what will happen?

18.15 What does the method `printStackTrace` do?

18.16 Does the presence of a `try-catch` block impose overhead when no exception occurs?

18.17 Correct a compilation error in the following code:

```java
public void m(int value) {
  if (value < 40)
    throw new Exception("value is too small");
}
```

Sections 18.4–18.7

18.18 Suppose that `statement2` causes an exception in the following statement:

```java
try {
  statement1;
  statement2;
  statement3;
}
catch (Exception1 ex1) {
}
catch (Exception2 ex2) {
}
catch (Exception3 ex3) {
  throw ex3;
}
finally {
  statement4;
};
statement5;
```

Answer the following questions:

■ Will statement5 be executed if the exception is not caught?
■ If the exception is of type Exception3, will statement4 be executed, and will statement5 be executed?

18.19 Suppose the setRadius method throws the RadiusException declared in §18.7. What is displayed when the following program is run?

```java
public class Test {
  public static void main(String[] args) {
    try {
      method();
      System.out.println("After the method call");
    }
    catch (RuntimeException ex) {
      System.out.println("RuntimeException in main");
    }
    catch (Exception ex) {
      System.out.println("Exception in main");
    }
  }

  static void method() throws Exception {
    try {
      Circle c1 = new Circle(1);
      c1.setRadius(-1);
      System.out.println(c1.getRadius());
    }
    catch (RuntimeException ex) {
      System.out.println("RuntimeException in method()");
    }
    catch (Exception ex) {
      System.out.println("Exception in method()");
      throw ex;
    }
  }
}
```

18.20 The following method checks whether a string is a numeric string:

```java
public static boolean isNumeric(String token) {
  try {
    Double.parseDouble(token);
    return true;
  }
  catch (java.lang.NumberFormatException ex) {
    return false;
  }
}
```

Is it correct? Rewrite it without using exceptions.

PROGRAMMING EXERCISES

Sections 18.2–18.4

18.1* (*NumberFormatException*) Listing 8.4, Calculator.java, is a simple command-line calculator. Note that the program terminates if any operand is nonnumeric. Write a program with an exception handler that deals with nonnumeric operands;

then write another program without using an exception handler to achieve the same objective. Your program should display a message that informs the user of the wrong operand type before exiting (see Figure 18.6).

FIGURE 18.6   The program performs arithmetic operations and detects input errors.

18.2* (*ArithmeticException* and *NumberFormatException*) Write a program that creates a user interface to perform integer divisions, as shown in Figure 18.7. The user enters two numbers in the text fields, **Number 1** and **Number 2**. The division of **Number 1** and **Number 2** is displayed in the Result field when the Divide button is clicked. If **Number 1** or **Number 2** were not an integer, the program would throw a **NumberFormatException**. If **Number 2** were zero, the program would throw an **ArithmeticException**. Display the exception in a message dialog box, as shown in Figure 18.7.

FIGURE 18.7   The program displays an error message in the dialog box if the number is not well formatted.

18.3* (*ArrayIndexOutBoundsException*) Write a program that meets the following requirements:

■ Create an array with 100 randomly chosen integers.
■ Create a text field to enter an array index and another text field to display the array element at the specified index (see Figure 18.8).
■ Create a *Show Element* button to cause the array element to be displayed. If the specified index is out of bounds, display the message **Out of Bound**.

FIGURE 18.8   The program displays the array element at the specified index or displays the message **Out of Bound** if the index is out of bounds.

18.4* (*IllegalArgumentException*) Modify the Loan class in Listing 9.2 to throw IllegalArgumentException if the loan amount, interest rate, or number of years is less than or equal to zero.

18.5* (*IllegalTriangleException*) Exercise 10.1 defined the Triangle class with three sides. In a triangle, the sum of any two sides is greater than the other side. The Triangle class must adhere to this rule. Create the IllegalTriangleException class, and modify the constructor of the Triangle class to throw an IllegalTriangleException object if a triangle is created with sides that violate the rule, as follows:

```
/** Construct a triangle with the specified sides */
public Triangle(double side1, double side2, double side3)
  throws IllegalTriangleException {
  // Implement it
}
```

18.6* (*NumberFormatException*) Exercise 8.7 specifies the parseHex(String hexString) method, which converts a hex string into a decimal number. Implement the parseHex method to throw a NumberFormatException if the string is not a hex string.

18.7* (*NumberFormatException*) Exercise 8.8 specifies the parseBinary(String binaryString) method, which converts a binary string into a decimal number. Implement the parseBinary method to throw a NumberFormatException if the string is not a binary string.

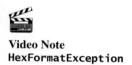

Video Note
HexFormatException

18.8* (*HexFormatException*) Exercise 18.6 implements the parseHex method to throw a NumberFormatException if the string is not a hex string. Define a custom exception called HexFormatException. Implement the parseHex method to throw a HexFormatException if the string is not a hex string.

18.9* (*BinaryFormatException*) Exercise 18.7 implements the parseBinary method to throw a BinaryFormatException if the string is not a binary string. Define a custom exception called BinaryFormatException. Implement the parseBinary method to throw a BinaryFormatException if the string is not a binary string.

CHAPTER 19

BINARY I/O

Objectives

- To discover how I/O is processed in Java (§19.2).

- To distinguish between text I/O and binary I/O (§19.3).

- To read and write bytes using **FileInputStream** and **FileOutputStream** (§19.4.1).

- To filter data using base classes **FilterInputStream** / **FilterOutputStream** (§19.4.2).

- To read and write primitive values and strings using **DataInputStream**/ **DataOutputStream** (§19.4.3).

- To store and restore objects using **ObjectOutputStream** and **ObjectInputStream**, and to understand how objects are serialized and what kind of objects can be serialized (§19.6).

- To implement the **Serializable** interface to make objects serializable (§19.6.1).

- To serialize arrays (§19.6.2).

- To read and write files using the **RandomAccessFile** class (§19.7).

19.1 Introduction

text file
binary file

Data stored in a text file are represented in human-readable form. Data stored in a binary file are represented in binary form. You cannot read binary files. They are designed to be read by programs. For example, Java source programs are stored in text files and can be read by a text editor, but Java classes are stored in binary files and are read by the JVM. The advantage of binary files is that they are more efficient to process than text files.

Although it is not technically precise and correct, you can envision a text file as consisting of a sequence of characters and a binary file as consisting of a sequence of bits. For example, the decimal integer 199 is stored as the sequence of three characters, '1', '9', '9', in a text file, and the same integer is stored as a byte-type value C7 in a binary file, because decimal 199 equals hex C7 ($199 = 12 \times 16^1 + 7$).

text I/O
binary I/O

Java offers many classes for performing file input and output. These can be categorized as *text I/O classes* and *binary I/O classes.* You learned how to read/write strings and numeric values from/to a text file using Scanner and PrintWriter in §8.7, "File Input and Output." This section introduces the classes for performing binary I/O.

19.2 How is I/O Handled in Java?

Recall that a File object encapsulates the properties of a file or a path, but does not contain the methods for reading/writing data from/to a file. In order to perform I/O, you need to create objects using appropriate Java I/O classes. The objects contain the methods for reading/writing data from/to a file. For example, to write text to a file named temp.txt, you may create an object using the PrintWriter class as follows:

```
PrintWriter output = new PrintWriter("temp.txt");
```

You can now invoke the print method from the object to write a string into the file. For example, the following statement writes "Java 101" to the file.

```
output.print("Java 101");
```

The next statement closes the file.

```
output.close();
```

There are many I/O classes for various purposes. In general, these can be classified as input classes and output classes. An input class contains the methods to read data, and an output class contains the methods to write data. PrintWriter is an example of an output class, and Scanner is an example of an input class. The following code creates an input object for the file **temp.txt** and reads data from the file.

```
Scanner input = new Scanner(new File("temp.txt"));
System.out.println(input.nextLine());
```

If **temp.txt** contains "Java 101", input.nextLine() returns string "Java 101".

Figure 19.1 illustrates Java I/O programming. An input object reads a stream of data from a file, and an output object writes a stream of data to a file. An input object is also called an *input stream* and an output object an *output stream*.

input stream
output stream

19.3 Text I/O vs. Binary I/O

Computers do not differentiate binary files and text files. All files are stored in binary format, and thus all files are essentially binary files. Text I/O is built upon binary I/O to provide a level of abstraction for character encoding and decoding, as shown in Figure 19.2(a). Encoding and decoding are automatically performed for text I/O. The JVM converts a Unicode

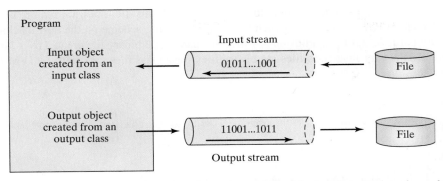

FIGURE 19.1 The program receives data through an input object and sends data through an output object.

to a file-specific encoding when writing a character and converts a file-specific encoding to a Unicode when reading a character. For example, suppose you write string **"199"** using text I/O to a file. Each character is written to the file. Since the Unicode for character **'1'** is **0x0031**, the Unicode **0x0031** is converted to a code that depends on the encoding scheme for the file. (Note that the prefix **0x** denotes a hex number.) In the United States, the default encoding for text files on Windows is ASCII. The ASCII code for character **'1'** is **49** (**0x31** in hex) and for character **'9'** is **57** (**0x39** in hex). So to write the characters **"199"**, three bytes, **0x31**, **0x39**, and **0x39**, are sent to the output, as shown in Figure 19.2(a).

Note

JDK 1.5 supports supplementary Unicode. For simplicity, however, this book considers only the original Unicode from **0** to **FFFF**.

supplementary Unicode

Binary I/O does not require conversions. If you write a numeric value to a file using binary I/O, the exact value in the memory is copied into the file. For example, a byte-type value **199** is represented as **0xC7** ($199 = 12 \times 16^1 + 7$) in the memory and appears exactly as **0xC7** in the file, as shown in Figure 19.2(b). When you read a byte using binary I/O, one byte value is read from the input.

In general, you should use text input to read a file created by a text editor or a text output program, and use binary input to read a file created by a Java binary output program.

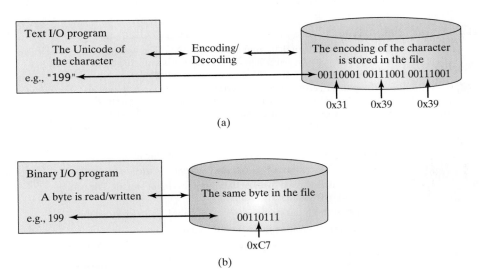

FIGURE 19.2 Text I/O requires encoding and decoding, whereas binary I/O does not.

Binary I/O is more efficient than text I/O, because binary I/O does not require encoding and decoding. Binary files are independent of the encoding scheme on the host machine and thus are portable. Java programs on any machine can read a binary file created by a Java program. This is why Java class files are binary files. Java class files can run on a JVM on any machine.

Note

.txt and .dat

For consistency, this book uses the extension `.txt` to name text files and `.dat` to name binary files.

19.4 Binary I/O Classes

The design of the Java I/O classes is a good example of applying inheritance, where common operations are generalized in superclasses, and subclasses provide specialized operations. Figure 19.3 lists some of the classes for performing binary I/O. `InputStream` is the root for binary input classes, and `OutputStream` is the root for binary output classes. Figures 19.4 and 19.5 list all the methods in `InputStream` and `OutputStream`.

FIGURE 19.3 `InputStream`, `OutputStream`, and their subclasses are for binary I/O.

java.io.InputStream	
+read(): int	Reads the next byte of data from the input stream. The value byte is returned as an `int` value in the range 0 to 255. If no byte is available because the end of the stream has been reached, the value –1 is returned.
+read(b: byte[]): int	Reads up to `b.length` bytes into array `b` from the input stream and returns the actual number of bytes read. Returns –1 at the end of the stream.
+read(b: byte[], off: int, len: int): int	Reads bytes from the input stream and stores them in `b[off]`, `b[off+1]`, . . ., `b[off+len–1]`. The actual number of bytes read is returned. Returns –1 at the end of the stream.
+available(): int	Returns the number of bytes that can be read from the input stream.
+close(): void	Closes this input stream and releases any system resources occupied with it.
+skip(n: long): long	Skips over and discards `n` bytes of data from this input stream. The actual number of bytes skipped is returned.
+markSupported(): boolean	Tests whether this input stream supports the `mark` and `reset` methods.
+mark(readlimit: int): void	Marks the current position in this input stream.
+reset(): void	Repositions this stream to the position at the time the `mark` method was last called on this stream.

FIGURE 19.4 The abstract `InputStream` class defines the methods for the input stream of bytes.

java.io.OutputStream	
+write(int b): void	Writes the specified byte to this output stream. The parameter b is an `int` value. `(byte)b` is written to the output stream.
+write(b: byte[]): void	Writes all the bytes in array b to the output stream.
+write(b: byte[], off: int, len: int): void	Writes b[off], b[off+1],. . . ., b[off+len-1] into the output stream.
+close(): void	Closes this output stream and releases any system resources occupied by it.
+flush(): void	Flushes this output stream and forces any buffered output bytes to be written out.

FIGURE 19.5 The abstract `OutputStream` class defines the methods for the output stream of bytes.

Note

All the methods in the binary I/O classes are declared to throw `java.io.IOException` or a subclass of `java.io.IOException`.   **throws IOException**

19.4.1 FileInputStream/FileOutputStream

`FileInputStream/FileOutputStream` is for reading/writing bytes from/to files. All the methods in these classes are inherited from `InputStream` and `OutputStream`. `FileInputStream/FileOutputStream` does not introduce new methods. To construct a `FileInputStream`, use the following constructors, as shown in Figure 19.6:

java.io.InputStream	
javo.io.FileInputStream	
+FileInputStream(file: File)	Creates a `FileInputStream` from a `File` object.
+FileInputStream(filename: String)	Creates a `FileInputStream` from a file name.

FIGURE 19.6 `FileInputStream` inputs stream of bytes from a file.

A `java.io.FileNotFoundException` will occur if you attempt to create a   **FileNotFoundException** `FileInputStream` with a nonexistent file.

To construct a `FileOutputStream`, use the constructors shown in Figure 19.7.

java.io.OutputStream	
java.io.FileOutputStream	
+FileOutputStream(file: File)	Creates a `FileOutputStream` from a `File` object.
+FileOutputStream(filename: String)	Creates a `FileOutputStream` from a file name.
+FileOutputStream(file: File, append: boolean)	If append is true, data are appended to the existing file.
+FileOutputStream(filename: String, append: boolean)	If append is true, data are appended to the existing file.

FIGURE 19.7 `FileOutputStream` outputs stream of bytes to a file.

If the file does not exist, a new file will be created. If the file already exists, the first two constructors will delete the current content of the file. To retain the current content and append new data into the file, use the last two constructors by passing **true** to the **append** parameter.

IOException

Almost all the methods in the I/O classes throw `java.io.IOException`. Therefore you have to declare `java.io.IOException` to throw in the method or place the code in a try-catch block, as shown below:

Declaring exception in the method

```
public static void main(String[] args)
    throws IOException {
  // Perform I/O operations
}
```

Using try-catch block

```
public static void main(String[] args) {
  try {
    // Perform I/O operations
  }
  catch (IOException ex) {
    ex.printStackTrace();
  }
}
```

Listing 19.1 uses binary I/O to write ten byte values from 1 to 10 to a file named **temp.dat** and reads them back from the file.

LISTING 19.1   TestFileStream.java

import

output stream

output

input stream

input

```
 1 import java.io.*;
 2
 3 public class TestFileStream {
 4   public static void main(String[] args) throws IOException {
 5     // Create an output stream to the file
 6     FileOutputStream output = new FileOutputStream("temp.dat");
 7
 8     // Output values to the file
 9     for (int i = 1; i <= 10; i++)
10       output.write(i);
11
12     // Close the output stream
13     output.close();
14
15     // Create an input stream for the file
16     FileInputStream input = new FileInputStream("temp.dat");
17
18     // Read values from the file
19     int value;
20     while ((value = input.read()) != -1)
21       System.out.print(value + " ");
22
23     // Close the output stream
24     input.close();
25   }
26 }
```

```
 1 2 3 4 5 6 7 8 9 10
```

A `FileOutputStream` is created for file **temp.dat** in line 6. The `for` loop writes ten byte values into the file (lines 9–10). Invoking `write(i)` is the same as invoking `write((byte)i)`. Line 13 closes the output stream. Line 16 creates a `FileInputStream` for file **temp.dat**. Values are read from the file and displayed on the console in lines 19–21. The expression `((value = input.read()) != -1)` (line 20) reads a byte from `input.read()`, assigns it to `value`, and checks whether it is `-1`. The input value of `-1` signifies the end of a file.

end of a file

The file **temp.dat** created in this example is a binary file. It can be read from a Java program but not from a text editor, as shown in Figure 19.8.

Binary data →

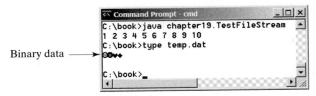

FIGURE 19.8 A binary file cannot be displayed in text mode.

Tip

When a stream is no longer needed, always close it using the `close()` method. Not closing streams may cause data corruption in the output file, or other programming errors.

close stream

Note

The root directory for the file is the classpath directory. For the example in this book, the root directory is **c:\book**. So the file **temp.dat** is located at **c:\book**. If you wish to place **temp.dat** in a specific directory, replace line 8 by

where is the file?

```
FileOutputStream output =
    new FileOutputStream("directory/temp.dat");
```

Note

An instance of `FileInputStream` can be used as an argument to construct a `Scanner`, and an instance of `FileOutputStream` can be used as an argument to construct a `PrintWriter`. You can create a `PrintWriter` to append text into a file using

appending to text file

```
new PrintWriter(new FileOutputStream("temp.txt", true));
```

If **temp.txt** does not exist, it is created. If **temp.txt** already exists, new data are appended to the file.

19.4.2 FilterInputStream/FilterOutputStream

Filter streams are streams that filter bytes for some purpose. The basic byte input stream provides a read method that can be used only for reading bytes. If you want to read integers, doubles, or strings, you need a filter class to wrap the byte input stream. Using a filter class enables you to read integers, doubles, and strings instead of bytes and characters. `FilterInputStream` and `FilterOutputStream` are the base classes for filtering data. When you need to process primitive numeric types, use `DataInputStream` and `DataOutputStream` to filter bytes.

19.4.3 DataInputStream/DataOutputStream

`DataInputStream` reads bytes from the stream and converts them into appropriate primitive type values or strings. `DataOutputStream` converts primitive type values or strings into bytes and outputs the bytes to the stream.

`DataInputStream` extends `FilterInputStream` and implements the `DataInput` interface, as shown in Figure 19.9. `DataOutputStream` extends `FilterOutputStream` and implements the `DataOutput` interface, as shown in Figure 19.10.

`DataInputStream` implements the methods defined in the `DataInput` interface to read primitive data type values and strings. `DataOutputStream` implements the methods defined in the `DataOutput` interface to write primitive data type values and strings. Primitive values

FIGURE 19.9 `DataInputStream` filters an input stream of bytes into primitive data type values and strings.

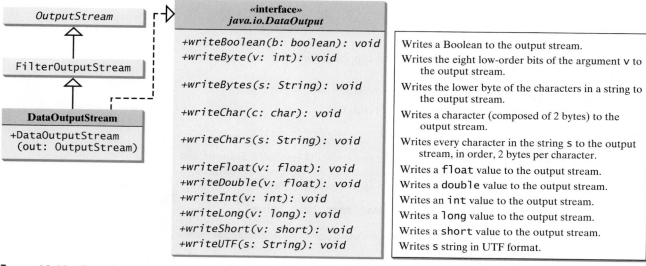

FIGURE 19.10 `DataOutputStream` enables you to write primitive data type values and strings into an output stream.

are copied from memory to the output without any conversions. Characters in a string may be written in several ways, as discussed in the next section.

Characters and Strings in Binary I/O

A Unicode consists of two bytes. The `writeChar(char c)` method writes the Unicode of character `c` to the output. The `writeChars(String s)` method writes the Unicode for each character in the string `s` to the output. The `writeBytes(String s)` method writes the lower byte of the Unicode for each character in the string `s` to the output. The high byte of the Unicode is discarded. The `writeBytes` method is suitable for strings that consist of ASCII characters, since an ASCII code is stored only in the lower byte of a Unicode. If a string consists of non-ASCII characters, you have to use the `writeChars` method to write the string.

The `writeUTF(String s)` method writes two bytes of length information to the output stream, followed by the `modified UTF-8` representation of every character in the string s. UTF-8 is a coding scheme that allows systems to operate with both ASCII and Unicode. Most operating systems use ASCII. Java uses Unicode. The ASCII character set is a subset of the Unicode character set. Since most applications need only the ASCII character set, it is a waste to represent an 8-bit ASCII character as a 16-bit Unicode character. The modified UTF-8 scheme stores a character using one, two, or three bytes. Characters are coded in one byte if their code is less than or equal to 0x7F, in two bytes if their code is greater than 0x7F and less than or equal to 0x7FF, in three bytes if their code is greater than 0x7FF.

The initial bits of a UTF-8 character indicate whether a character is stored in one byte, two bytes, or three bytes. If the first bit is 0, it is a one-byte character. If the first bits are 110, it is the first byte of a two-byte sequence. If the first bits are 1110, it is the first byte of a three-byte sequence. The information that indicates the number of characters in a string is stored in the first two bytes preceding the UTF-8 characters. For example, writeUTF("ABCDEF") actually writes eight bytes (i.e., 00 06 41 42 43 44 45 46) to the file, because the first two bytes store the number of characters in the string.

UTF-8 scheme

The writeUTF(String s) method converts a string into a series of bytes in the UTF-8 format and writes them into a binary stream. The readUTF() method reads a string that has been written using the writeUTF method.

The UTF-8 format has the advantage of saving a byte for each ASCII character, because a Unicode character takes up two bytes and an ASCII character in UTF-8 only one byte. If most of the characters in a long string are regular ASCII characters, using UTF-8 is efficient.

Using DataInputStream/DataOutputStream

Data streams are used as wrappers on existing input and output streams to filter data in the original stream. They are created using the following constructors (see Figure 19.9 and Figure 19.10):

```java
public DataInputStream(InputStream instream)
public DataOutputStream(OutputStream outstream)
```

The statements given below create data streams. The first statement creates an input stream for file **in.dat**; the second statement creates an output stream for file **out.dat**.

```java
DataInputStream input =
  new DataInputStream(new FileInputStream("in.dat"));
DataOutputStream ouput =
  new DataOutputStream(new FileOutputStream("out.dat"));
```

Listing 19.2 writes student names and scores to a file named **temp.dat** and reads the data back from the file.

LISTING 19.2 TestDataStream.java

```java
1 import java.io.*;
2
3 public class TestDataStream {
4   public static void main(String[] args) throws IOException {
5     // Create an output stream for file temp.dat
6     DataOutputStream output =
7       new DataOutputStream(new FileOutputStream("temp.dat"));
8
9     // Write student test scores to the file
10    output.writeUTF("John");
11    output.writeDouble(85.5);
12    output.writeUTF("Jim");
13    output.writeDouble(185.5);
14    output.writeUTF("George");
15    output.writeDouble(105.25);
16
17    // Close output stream
18    output.close();
19
```

output stream

output

close stream

input stream

```
20      // Create an input stream for file temp.dat
21      DataInputStream input =
22        new DataInputStream(new FileInputStream("temp.dat"));
23
24      // Read student test scores from the file
```

input

```
25      System.out.println(input.readUTF() + " " + input.readDouble());
26      System.out.println(input.readUTF() + " " + input.readDouble());
27      System.out.println(input.readUTF() + " " + input.readDouble());
28    }
29 }
```

```
John 85.5
Jim 185.5
George 105.25
```

A `DataOutputStream` is created for file **temp.dat** in lines 6–7. Student names and scores are written to the file in lines 10–15. Line 18 closes the output stream. A `DataInputStream` is created for the same file in lines 21–22. Student names and scores are read back from the file and displayed on the console in lines 25–27.

`DataInputStream` and `DataOutputStream` read and write Java primitive type values and strings in a machine-independent fashion, thereby enabling you to write a data file on one machine and read it on another machine that has a different operating system or file structure. An application uses a data output stream to write data that can later be read by a program using a data input stream.

Caution

You have to read data in the same order and format in which they are stored. For example, since names are written in UTF-8 using `writeUTF`, you must read names using `readUTF`.

Tip

If you keep reading data at the end of a `DataInputStream`, an `EOFException` will occur. How, then, do you check the end of a file? Use `input.available()` to check it. `input.available() == 0` indicates the end of a file.

19.4.4 BufferedInputStream/BufferedOutputStream

`BufferedInputStream`/`BufferedOutputStream` can be used to speed up input and output by reducing the number of reads and writes. `BufferedInputStream`/`BufferedOutputStream` does not contain new methods. All the methods in `BufferedInputStream`/`BufferedOutputStream` are inherited from the `InputStream`/`OutputStream` classes. `BufferedInputStream`/`BufferedOutputStream` adds a buffer in the stream for storing bytes for efficient processing.

You may wrap a `BufferedInputStream`/`BufferedOutputStream` on any `InputStream`/`OutputStream` using the constructors shown in Figures 19.11 and 19.12.

If no buffer size is specified, the default size is `512` bytes. A buffered input stream reads as many data as possible into its buffer in a single read call. By contrast, a buffered output stream calls the write method only when its buffer fills up or when the `flush()` method is called.

You can improve the performance of the `TestDataStream` program in the preceding example by adding buffers in the stream in lines 6–7 and 21–22, as follows:

```
DataOutputStream output = new DataOutputStream(
  new BufferedOutputStream (new FileOutputStream("temp.dat")));
```

```
DataInputStream input = new DataInputStream(
  new BufferedInputStream (new FileInputStream("temp.dat")));
```

FIGURE 19.11   `BufferedInputStream` buffers input stream.

FIGURE 19.12   `BufferedOutputStream` buffers output stream.

   Tip

You should always use buffered IO to speed up input and output. For small files, you may not notice performance improvements. However, for large files—over 100 MB—you will see substantial improvements using buffered IO.

19.5 Problem: Copying Files

Video Note
Copy file

This section develops a program that copies files. The user needs to provide a source file and a target file as command-line arguments using the following command:

java Copy source target

The program copies a source file to a target file and displays the number of bytes in the file. If the source does not exist, tell the user that the file has not been found. If the target file already exists, tell the user that the file exists. A sample run of the program is shown in Figure 19.13.

To copy the contents from a source to a target file, it is appropriate to use a binary input stream to read bytes from the source file and a binary output stream to send bytes to the target file, regardless of the contents of the file. The source file and the target file are specified from the command line. Create an `InputFileStream` for the source file and an `OutputFileStream` for the target file. Use the `read()` method to read a byte from the input stream, and then use the `write(b)` method to write the byte to the output stream. Use `BufferedInputStream` and `BufferedOutputStream` to improve the performance. Listing 19.3 gives the solution to the problem.

File exists

Delete file

Copy

Source does not exist

FIGURE 19.13 The program copies a file.

LISTING 19.3 Copy.java

```java
1  import java.io.*;
2
3  public class Copy {
4    /** Main method
5       @param args[0] for sourcefile
6       @param args[1] for target file
7     */
8    public static void main(String[] args) throws IOException {
9      // Check command-line parameter usage
10     if (args.length != 2) {
11       System.out.println(
12         "Usage: java CopyFile sourceFile targetfile");
13       System.exit(0);
14     }
15
16     // Check if source file exists
17     File sourceFile = new File(args[0]);
18     if (!sourceFile.exists()) {
19       System.out.println("Source file " + args[0] + " not exist");
20       System.exit(0);
21     }
22
23     // Check if target file exists
24     File targetFile = new File(args[1]);
25     if (targetFile.exists()) {
26       System.out.println("Target file " + args[1] + " already exists");
27       System.exit(0);
28     }
29
30     // Create an input stream
31     BufferedInputStream input =
32       new BufferedInputStream(new FileInputStream(sourceFile));
33
34     // Create an output stream
35     BufferedOutputStream output =
36       new BufferedOutputStream(new FileOutputStream(targetFile));
37
38     // Display the file size
39     System.out.println("The file " + args[0] + " has "+
```

check usage

source file

target file

input stream

output stream

```
40          input.available() + " bytes");
41
42      // Continuously read a byte from input and write it to output
43      int r;
44      while ((r = input.read()) != -1)                          read
45        output.write((byte)r);                                  write
46
47      // Close streams
48      input.close();                                            close stream
49      output.close();
50
51      System.out.println("Copy done!");
52    }
53 }
```

- The program first checks whether the user has passed two required arguments from the command line in lines 10–14.

- The program uses the `File` class to check whether the source file and target file exist. If the source file does not exist (lines 18–21) or if the target file already exists, exit the program.

- An input stream is created using `BufferedInputStream` wrapped on `File-InputStream` in lines 31–32, and an output stream is created using `Buffered-OutputStream` wrapped on `FileOutputStream` in lines 35–36.

- The `available()` method (line 40) defined in the `InputStream` class returns the number of bytes remaining in the input stream.

- The expression `((r = input.read()) != -1)` (line 44) reads a byte from `input.read()`, assigns it to `r`, and checks whether it is `-1`. The input value of `-1` signifies the end of a file. The program continuously reads bytes from the input stream and sends them to the output stream until all of the bytes have been read.

19.6 Object I/O

Video Note
Object I/O

`DataInputStream`/`DataOutputStream` enables you to perform I/O for primitive type values and strings. `ObjectInputStream`/`ObjectOutputStream` enables you to perform I/O for objects in addition to primitive type values and strings. Since `ObjectInput-Stream`/`ObjectOutputStream` contains all the functions of `DataInputStream`/`Data-OutputStream`, you can replace `DataInputStream`/`DataOutputStream` completely with `ObjectInputStream`/`ObjectOutputStream`.

`ObjectInputStream` extends `InputStream` and implements `ObjectInput` and `ObjectStreamConstants`, as shown in Figure 19.14. `ObjectInput` is a subinterface of `DataInput`. `DataInput` is shown in Figure 19.9. `ObjectStreamConstants` contains the constants to support `ObjectInputStream`/`ObjectOutputStream`.

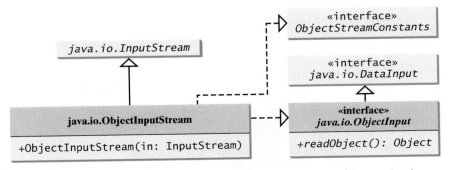

FIGURE 19.14 `ObjectInputStream` can read objects, primitive type values, and strings.

`ObjectOutputStream` extends `OutputStream` and implements `ObjectOutput` and `ObjectStreamConstants`, as shown in Figure 19.15. `ObjectOutput` is a subinterface of `DataOutput`. `DataOutput` is shown in Figure 19.10.

FIGURE 19.15 `ObjectOutputStream` can write objects, primitive type values, and strings.

You may wrap an `ObjectInputStream`/`ObjectOutputStream` on any `InputStream`/`OutputStream` using the following constructors:

```
// Create an ObjectInputStream
public ObjectInputStream(InputStream in)

// Create an ObjectOutputStream
public ObjectOutputStream(OutputStream out)
```

Listing 19.4 writes student names, scores, and current date to a file named **object.dat**.

LISTING 19.4 TestObjectOutputStream.java

```
 1 import java.io.*;
 2
 3 public class TestObjectOutputStream {
 4   public static void main(String[] args) throws IOException {
 5     // Create an output stream for file object.dat
 6     ObjectOutputStream output =
 7       new ObjectOutputStream(new FileOutputStream("object.dat"));
 8
 9     // Write a string, double value, and object to the file
10     output.writeUTF("John");
11     output.writeDouble(85.5);
12     output.writeObject(new java.util.Date());
13
14     // Close output stream
15     output.close();
16   }
17 }
```

output stream

output

An `ObjectOutputStream` is created to write data into file **object.dat** in lines 6–7. A string, a double value, and an object are written to the file in lines 10–12. To improve performance, you may add a buffer in the stream using the following statement to replace lines 6–7:

```
ObjectOutputStream output = new ObjectOutputStream(
  new BufferedOutputStream(new FileOutputStream("object.dat")));
```

Multiple objects or primitives can be written to the stream. The objects must be read back from the corresponding `ObjectInputStream` with the same types and in the same order as they were written. Java's safe casting should be used to get the desired type. Listing 19.5 reads data back from object.dat.

LISTING 19.5 `TestObjectInputStream.java`

```java
 1  import java.io.*;
 2
 3  public class TestObjectInputStream {
 4    public static void main(String[] args)
 5      throws ClassNotFoundException, IOException {
 6      // Create an input stream for file object.dat
 7      ObjectInputStream input =
 8        new ObjectInputStream(new FileInputStream("object.dat"));
 9
10      // Write a string, double value, and object to the file
11      String name = input.readUTF();
12      double score = input.readDouble();
13      java.util.Date date = (java.util.Date)(input.readObject());
14      System.out.println(name + " " + score + " " + date);
15
16      // Close output stream
17      input.close();
18    }
19  }
```

input stream

input

```
John 85.5 Mon Jun 26 17:17:29 EDT 2006
```

The `readObject()` method may throw `java.lang.ClassNotFoundException`. The reason is that when the JVM restores an object, it first loads the class for the object if the class has not been loaded. Since `ClassNotFoundException` is a checked exception, the `main` method declares to throw it in line 5. An `ObjectInputStream` is created to read input from **object.dat** in lines 7–8. You have to read the data from the file in the same order and format as they were written to the file. A string, a double value, and an object are read in lines 11–13. Since `readObject()` returns an `Object`, it is cast into `Date` and assigned to a `Date` variable in line 13.

ClassNotFoundException

19.6.1 The `Serializable` Interface

Not every object can be written to an output stream. Objects that can be written to an object stream are said to be *serializable*. A serializable object is an instance of the `java.io.Serializable` interface, so the class of a serializable object must implement `Serializable`.

serializable

The `Serializable` interface is a marker interface. Since it has no methods, you don't need to add additional code in your class that implements `Serializable`. Implementing this interface enables the Java serialization mechanism to automate the process of storing objects and arrays.

To appreciate this automation feature and understand how an object is stored, consider what you otherwise need to do in order to store an object. Suppose you want to store a `JButton` object. To do this you need to store all the current values of the properties (e.g., color, font, text, alignment) in the object. Since `JButton` is a subclass of `AbstractButton`, the property values of `AbstractButton` have to be stored as well as the properties of all the superclasses of `AbstractButton`. If a property is of an object type (e.g., `background` of the `Color` type), storing it requires storing all the property values inside this object. As you can see, this is a very tedious process. Fortunately, you don't have to go through it manually. Java provides a built-in mechanism to automate the process of writing objects. This process is referred to as *object serialization*, which is implemented in `ObjectOutputStream`. In contrast, the process of reading objects is referred to as *object deserialization*, which is implemented in `ObjectInputStream`.

Many classes in the Java API implement `Serializable`. The utility classes, such as `java.util.Date`, and all the Swing GUI component classes implement `Serializable`. Attempting to store an object that does not support the `Serializable` interface would cause a `NotSerializableException`.

When a serializable object is stored, the class of the object is encoded; this includes the class name and the signature of the class, the values of the object's instance variables, and the closure of any other objects referenced from the initial object. The values of the object's static variables are not stored.

Note

If an object is an instance of `Serializable` but contains nonserializable instance data fields, can it be serialized? The answer is no. To enable the object to be serialized, mark these data fields with the `transient` keyword to tell the JVM to ignore them when writing the object to an object stream. Consider the following class:

```java
public class Foo implements java.io.Serializable {
  private int v1;
  private static double v2;
  private transient A v3 = new A();
}

class A { } // A is not serializable
```

When an object of the `Foo` class is serialized, only variable `v1` is serialized. Variable `v2` is not serialized because it is a static variable, and variable `v3` is not serialized because it is marked `transient`. If `v3` were not marked `transient`, a `java.io.NotSerializableException` would occur.

Note

If an object is written to an object stream more than once, will it be stored in multiple copies? No, it will not. When an object is written for the first time, a serial number is created for it. The JVM writes the complete content of the object along with the serial number into the object stream. After the first time, only the serial number is stored if the same object is written again. When the objects are read back, their references are the same, since only one object is actually created in the memory.

19.6.2 Serializing Arrays

An array is serializable if all its elements are serializable. An entire array can be saved using `writeObject` into a file and later can be restored using `readObject`. Listing 19.6 stores an array of five `int` values and an array of three strings, and reads them back to display on the console.

LISTING 19.6 `TestObjectStreamForArray.java`

```java
1 import java.io.*;
2
3 public class TestObjectStreamForArray {
4   public static void main(String[] args)
5       throws ClassNotFoundException, IOException {
6     int[] numbers = {1, 2, 3, 4, 5};
7     String[] strings = {"John", "Jim", "Jake"};
8
```

Margin notes:

serialization
deserialization

`NotSerializable-Exception`

nonserializable fields

transient

duplicate objects

```
 9      // Create an output stream for file array.dat
10      ObjectOutputStream output =
11        new ObjectOutputStream(new FileOutputStream("array.dat", true));
12
13      // Write arrays to the object output stream
14      output.writeObject(numbers);
15      output.writeObject(strings);
16
17      // Close the stream
18      output.close();
19
20      // Create an input stream for file array.dat
21      ObjectInputStream input =
22        new ObjectInputStream(new FileInputStream("array.dat"));
23
24      int[] newNumbers = (int[])(input.readObject());
25      String[] newStrings = (String[])(input.readObject());
26
27      // Display arrays
28      for (int i = 0; i < newNumbers.length; i++)
29        System.out.print(newNumbers[i] + " ");
30      System.out.println();
31
32      for (int i = 0; i < newStrings.length; i++)
33        System.out.print(newStrings[i] + " ");
34    }
35 }
```

output stream

store array

input stream

restore array

```
1 2 3 4 5
John Jim Jake
```

Lines 14–15 write two arrays into file **array.dat**. Lines 24–25 read three arrays back in the same order they were written. Since `readObject()` returns `Object`, casting is used to cast the objects into `int[]` and `String[]`.

19.7 Random Access Files

All of the streams you have used so far are known as *read-only* or *write-only* streams. The external files of these streams are *sequential* files that cannot be updated without creating a new file. It is often necessary to modify files or to insert new records into files. Java provides the `RandomAccessFile` class to allow a file to be read from and written to at random locations.

read-only
write-only
sequential

The `RandomAccessFile` class implements the `DataInput` and `DataOutput` interfaces, as shown in Figure 19.16. The `DataInput` interface shown in Figure 19.9 defines the methods (e.g., `readInt`, `readDouble`, `readChar`, `readBoolean`, `readUTF`) for reading primitive type values and strings, and the `DataOutput` interface shown in Figure 19.10 defines the methods (e.g., `writeInt`, `writeDouble`, `writeChar`, `writeBoolean`, `writeUTF`) for writing primitive type values and strings.

When creating a `RandomAccessFile`, you can specify one of two modes ("r" or "rw"). Mode "r" means that the stream is read-only, and mode "rw" indicates that the stream allows both read and write. For example, the following statement creates a new stream, `raf`, that allows the program to read from and write to the file **test.dat**:

```
RandomAccessFile raf = new RandomAccessFile("test.dat", "rw");
```

If **test.dat** already exists, `raf` is created to access it; if **test.dat** does not exist, a new file named **test.dat** is created, and `raf` is created to access the new file. The method `raf.length()`

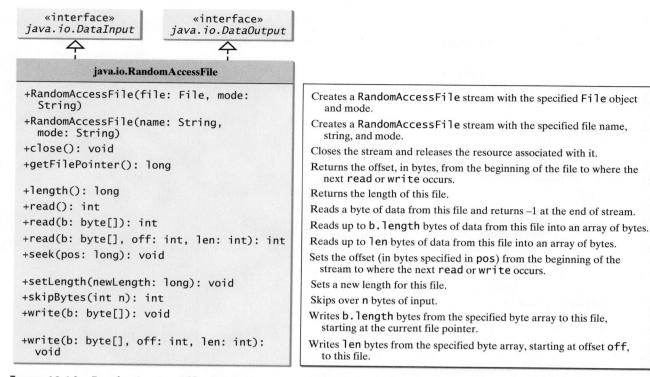

FIGURE 19.16 RandomAccessFile implements the DataInput and DataOutput interfaces with additional methods to support random access.

returns the number of bytes in **test.dat** at any given time. If you append new data into the file, raf.length() increases.

Tip
Open the file with the "r" mode if the file is not intended to be modified. This prevents unintentional modification of the file.

file pointer

A random access file consists of a sequence of bytes. A special marker called a *file pointer* is positioned at one of these bytes. A read or write operation takes place at the location of the file pointer. When a file is opened, the file pointer is set at the beginning of the file. When you read or write data to the file, the file pointer moves forward to the next data item. For example, if you read an int value using readInt(), the JVM reads 4 bytes from the file pointer, and now the file pointer is 4 bytes ahead of the previous location, as shown in Figure 19.17.

For a RandomAccessFile raf, you can use the raf.seek(position) method to move the file pointer to a specified position. raf.seek(0) moves it to the beginning of the file, and

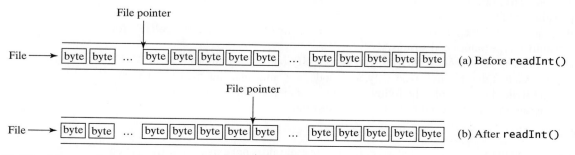

FIGURE 19.17 After reading an int value, the file pointer is moved 4 bytes ahead.

`raf.seek(raf.length())` moves it to the end of the file. Listing 19.7 demonstrates RandomAccessFile.

LISTING 19.7 TestRandomAccessFile.java

```java
 1 import java.io.*;
 2
 3 public class TestRandomAccessFile {
 4   public static void main(String[] args) throws IOException {
 5     // Create a random access file
 6     RandomAccessFile inout = new RandomAccessFile("inout.dat", "rw");    RandomAccessFile
 7
 8     // Clear the file to destroy the old contents if exists
 9     inout.setLength(0);                                                  empty file
10
11     // Write new integers to the file
12     for (int i = 0; i < 200; i++)
13       inout.writeInt(i);                                                 write
14
15     // Display the current length of the file
16     System.out.println("Current file length is " + inout.length());
17
18     // Retrieve the first number
19     inout.seek(0); // Move the file pointer to the beginning             move pointer
20     System.out.println("The first number is " + inout.readInt());        read
21
22     // Retrieve the second number
23     inout.seek(1 * 4); // Move the file pointer to the second number
24     System.out.println("The second number is " + inout.readInt());
25
26     // Retrieve the tenth number
27     inout.seek(9 * 4); // Move the file pointer to the tenth number
28     System.out.println("The tenth number is " + inout.readInt());
29
30     // Modify the eleventh number
31     inout.writeInt(555);
32
33     // Append a new number
34     inout.seek(inout.length()); // Move the file pointer to the end
35     inout.writeInt(999);
36
37     // Display the new length
38     System.out.println("The new length is " + inout.length());
39
40     // Retrieve the new eleventh number
41     inout.seek(10 * 4); // Move the file pointer to the eleventh number
42     System.out.println("The eleventh number is " + inout.readInt());
43
44     inout.close();                                                       close file
45   }
46 }
```

```
Current file length is 800
The first number is 0
The second number is 1
The tenth number is 9
The new length is 804
The eleventh number is 555
```

A `RandomAccessFile` is created for the file named **inout.dat** with mode "`rw`" to allow both read and write operations in line 6.

`inout.setLength(0)` sets the length to `0` in line 9. This, in effect, destroys the old contents of the file.

The `for` loop writes `200 int` values from `0` to `199` into the file in lines 12–13. Since each `int` value takes `4` bytes, the total length of the file returned from `inout.length()` is now `800` (line 16), as shown in sample output.

Invoking `inout.seek(0)` in line 19 sets the file pointer to the beginning of the file. `inout.readInt()` reads the first value in line 20 and moves the file pointer to the next number. The second number is read in line 23.

`inout.seek(9 * 4)` (line 27) moves the file pointer to the tenth number. `inout.readInt()` reads the tenth number and moves the file pointer to the eleventh number in line 28. `inout.write(555)` writes a new eleventh number at the current position (line 31). The previous eleventh number is destroyed.

`inout.seek(inout.length())` moves the file pointer to the end of the file (line 34). `inout.writeInt(999)` writes a `999` to the file. Now the length of the file is increased by `4`, so `inout.length()` returns `804` (line 38).

`inout.seek(10 * 4)` moves the file pointer to the eleventh number in line 41. The new eleventh number, `555`, is displayed in line 42.

Video Note
Address book

19.8 Problem: Creating an Address Book

Now let us use `RandomAccessFile` to create a useful project for storing and viewing an address book. The user interface of the program is shown in Figure 19.18. The *Add* button stores a new address at the end of the file. The *First*, *Next*, *Previous*, and *Last* buttons retrieve the first, next, previous, and last addresses from the file, respectively.

FIGURE 19.18 `AddressBook` stores and retrieves addresses from a file.

fixed-length record

Random access files are often used to process files of records. For convenience, fixed-length records are used in random access files so that a record can be located easily, as shown in Figure 19.19. A record consists of a fixed number of fields. A field can be a string or a primitive data type. A string in a fixed-length record has a maximum size. If a string is smaller than the maximum size, the rest of the string is padded with blanks.

FIGURE 19.19 Random access files are often used to process files of fixed-length records.

Let **address.dat** be the file to store addresses. A RandomAccessFile for both read and write can be created using

```
RandomAccessFile raf = new RandomAccessFile("address.dat", "rw");
```

Let each address consist of a name (32 characters), street (32 characters), city (20 characters), state (2 characters), and zip (5 characters). If the actual size of a field (e.g., name) is less than the fixed maximum size, fill it with blank characters. If the actual size of a field is greater than the fixed maximum size, truncate the string. Thus the total size of an address is 32 + 32 + 20 + 2 + 5 = 91 characters. Since each character occupies two bytes, one address takes 2 * 91 = 182 bytes. After an address record is read, the file pointer is 182 bytes ahead of the previous file pointer.

For convenience, Listing 19.8 contains two methods for reading and writing a fixed-length string.

LISTING 19.8 FixedLengthStringIO.java

```java
1  import java.io.*;
2
3  public class FixedLengthStringIO {
4    /** Read fixed number of characters from a DataInput stream */
5    public static String readFixedLengthString(int size,
6        DataInput in) throws IOException {
7      // Declare an array of characters
8      char[] chars = new char[size];
9
10     // Read fixed number of characters to the array
11     for (int i = 0; i < size; i++)
12       chars[i] = in.readChar();                           read characters
13
14     return new String(chars);
15   }
16
17   /** Write fixed number of characters to a DataOutput stream */
18   public static void writeFixedLengthString(String s, int size,
19       DataOutput out) throws IOException {
20     char[] chars = new char[size];
21
22     // Fill an array of characters from the string
23     s.getChars(0, Math.min(s.length(), size), chars, 0);    fill string
24
25     // Fill in blank characters in the rest of the array
26     for (int i = Math.min(s.length(), size); i < chars.length; i++)
27       chars[i] = ' ';                                       fill blank
28
29     // Create and write a new string padded with blank characters
30     out.writeChars(new String(chars));                     write string
31   }
32 }
```

The writeFixedLengthString(String s, int size, DataOutput out) method writes a string in a fixed size to a DataOutput stream. If the string is longer than the specified size, it is truncated (line 23); if it is shorter than the specified size, blanks are padded into it (lines 26–27). In any case, a new fixed-length string is written to a specified output stream. Since RandomAccessFile implements DataOutput, this method can be used to write a string to a RandomAccessFile. For example, invoking writeFixedLengthString-("John", 2, raf) actually writes "Jo" to the RandomAccessFile raf, since the size is 2. Invoking writeFixedLengthString("John", 6, raf) actually writes "John " to the RandomAccessFile raf, since the size is 6.

The readFixedLengthString(int size, InputOutput in) method reads a fixed number of characters from an InputStream and returns as a string. Since Random-AccessFile implements InputOutput, this method can be used to read a string from a writeFixedLengthString(String s, int size, DataOutput out).

The rest of the work can be summarized in the following steps:

1. Create the user interface.

2. Add a record to the file.

3. Read a record from the file.

4. Write the code to implement the button actions.

The program is shown in Listing 19.9.

LISTING 19.9 AddressBook.java

```java
1  import java.io.*;
2  import java.awt.*;
3  import java.awt.event.*;
4  import javax.swing.*;
5  import javax.swing.border.*;
6
7  public class AddressBook extends JFrame {
8    // Specify the size of five string fields in the record
9    final static int NAME_SIZE = 32;
10   final static int STREET_SIZE = 32;
11   final static int CITY_SIZE = 20;
12   final static int STATE_SIZE = 2;
13   final static int ZIP_SIZE = 5;
14   final static int RECORD_SIZE =
15     (NAME_SIZE + STREET_SIZE + CITY_SIZE + STATE_SIZE + ZIP_SIZE);
16
17   // Access address.dat using RandomAccessFile
18   private RandomAccessFile raf;
19
20   // Text fields
21   private JTextField jtfName = new JTextField(NAME_SIZE);
22   private JTextField jtfStreet = new JTextField(STREET_SIZE);
23   private JTextField jtfCity = new JTextField(CITY_SIZE);
24   private JTextField jtfState = new JTextField(STATE_SIZE);
25   private JTextField jtfZip = new JTextField(ZIP_SIZE);
26
27   // Buttons
28   private JButton jbtAdd = new JButton("Add");
29   private JButton jbtFirst = new JButton("First");
30   private JButton jbtNext = new JButton("Next");
31   private JButton jbtPrevious = new JButton("Previous");
32   private JButton jbtLast = new JButton("Last");
33
34   public AddressBook() {
35     // Open or create a random access file
36     try {
37       raf = new RandomAccessFile("address.dat", "rw");
38     }
39     catch(IOException ex) {
40       System.out.print("Error: " + ex);
41       System.exit(0);
42     }
```

constant

raf

GUI component

open file

```
43
44      // Panel p1 for holding labels Name, Street, and City          create UI
45      JPanel p1 = new JPanel();
46      p1.setLayout(new GridLayout(3, 1));
47      p1.add(new JLabel("Name"));
48      p1.add(new JLabel("Street"));
49      p1.add(new JLabel("City"));
50
51      // Panel jpState for holding state
52      JPanel jpState = new JPanel();
53      jpState.setLayout(new BorderLayout());
54      jpState.add(new JLabel("State"), BorderLayout.WEST);
55      jpState.add(jtfState, BorderLayout.CENTER);
56
57      // Panel jpZip for holding zip
58      JPanel jpZip = new JPanel();
59      jpZip.setLayout(new BorderLayout());
60      jpZip.add(new JLabel("Zip"), BorderLayout.WEST);
61      jpZip.add(jtfZip, BorderLayout.CENTER);
62
63      // Panel p2 for holding jpState and jpZip
64      JPanel p2 = new JPanel();
65      p2.setLayout(new BorderLayout());
66      p2.add(jpState, BorderLayout.WEST);
67      p2.add(jpZip, BorderLayout.CENTER);
68
69      // Panel p3 for holding jtfCity and p2
70      JPanel p3 = new JPanel();
71      p3.setLayout(new BorderLayout());
72      p3.add(jtfCity, BorderLayout.CENTER);
73      p3.add(p2, BorderLayout.EAST);
74
75      // Panel p4 for holding jtfName, jtfStreet, and p3
76      JPanel p4 = new JPanel();
77      p4.setLayout(new GridLayout(3, 1));
78      p4.add(jtfName);
79      p4.add(jtfStreet);
80      p4.add(p3);
81
82      // Place p1 and p4 into jpAddress
83      JPanel jpAddress = new JPanel(new BorderLayout());
84      jpAddress.add(p1, BorderLayout.WEST);
85      jpAddress.add(p4, BorderLayout.CENTER);
86
87      // Set the panel with line border
88      jpAddress.setBorder(new BevelBorder(BevelBorder.RAISED));
89
90      // Add buttons to a panel
91      JPanel jpButton = new JPanel();
92      jpButton.add(jbtAdd);
93      jpButton.add(jbtFirst);
94      jpButton.add(jbtNext);
95      jpButton.add(jbtPrevious);
96      jpButton.add(jbtLast);
97
98      // Add jpAddress and jpButton to the frame
99      add(jpAddress, BorderLayout.CENTER);
100     add(jpButton, BorderLayout.SOUTH);
101
```

```
                                102    jbtAdd.addActionListener(new ActionListener() {
register listener              103      public void actionPerformed(ActionEvent e) {
add address                    104        writeAddress();
                               105      }
                               106    });
register listener              107    jbtFirst.addActionListener(new ActionListener() {
                               108      public void actionPerformed(ActionEvent e) {
                               109        try {
first record                   110          if (raf.length() > 0) readAddress(0);
                               111        }
                               112        catch (IOException ex) {
                               113          ex.printStackTrace();
                               114        }
                               115      }
                               116    });
register listener              117    jbtNext.addActionListener(new ActionListener() {
                               118      public void actionPerformed(ActionEvent e) {
                               119        try {
                               120          long currentPosition = raf.getFilePointer();
                               121          if (currentPosition < raf.length())
next address                   122            readAddress(currentPosition);
                               123        }
                               124        catch (IOException ex) {
                               125          ex.printStackTrace();
                               126        }
                               127      }
                               128    });
                               129    jbtPrevious.addActionListener(new ActionListener() {
                               130      public void actionPerformed(ActionEvent e) {
                               131        try {
                               132          long currentPosition = raf.getFilePointer();
                               133          if (currentPosition - 2 * RECORD_SIZE > 0)
                               134            // Why 2 * 2 * RECORD_SIZE? See the follow-up remarks
                               135            readAddress(currentPosition - 2 * 2 * RECORD_SIZE);
                               136          else
                               137            readAddress(0);
                               138        }
                               139        catch (IOException ex) {
                               140          ex.printStackTrace();
                               141        }
                               142      }
                               143    });
register listener              144    jbtLast.addActionListener(new ActionListener() {
                               145      public void actionPerformed(ActionEvent e) {
                               146        try {
                               147          long lastPosition = raf.length();
                               148          if (lastPosition > 0)
                               149            // Why 2 * RECORD_SIZE? See the follow-up remarks
last address                   150            readAddress(lastPosition - 2 * RECORD_SIZE);
                               151        }
                               152        catch (IOException ex) {
                               153          ex.printStackTrace();
                               154        }
                               155      }
                               156    });
                               157
                               158    // Display the first record if exists
                               159    try {
first address                  160      if (raf.length() > 0) readAddress(0);
                               161    }
```

```
162        catch (IOException ex) {
163          ex.printStackTrace();
164        }
165    }
166
167    /** Write a record at the end of the file */
168    public void writeAddress() {
169      try {
170        raf.seek(raf.length());
171        FixedLengthStringIO.writeFixedLengthString(
172          jtfName.getText(), NAME_SIZE, raf);
173        FixedLengthStringIO.writeFixedLengthString(
174          jtfStreet.getText(), STREET_SIZE, raf);
175        FixedLengthStringIO.writeFixedLengthString(
176          jtfCity.getText(), CITY_SIZE, raf);
177        FixedLengthStringIO.writeFixedLengthString(
178          jtfState.getText(), STATE_SIZE, raf);
179        FixedLengthStringIO.writeFixedLengthString(
180          jtfZip.getText(), ZIP_SIZE, raf);
181      }
182      catch (IOException ex) {
183        ex.printStackTrace();
184      }
185    }
186
187    /** Read a record at the specified position */
188    public void readAddress(long position) throws IOException {
189      raf.seek(position);
190      String name = FixedLengthStringIO.readFixedLengthString(
191        NAME_SIZE, raf);
192      String street = FixedLengthStringIO.readFixedLengthString(
193        STREET_SIZE, raf);
194      String city = FixedLengthStringIO.readFixedLengthString(
195        CITY_SIZE, raf);
196      String state = FixedLengthStringIO.readFixedLengthString(
197        STATE_SIZE, raf);
198      String zip = FixedLengthStringIO.readFixedLengthString(
199        ZIP_SIZE, raf);
200
201      jtfName.setText(name);
202      jtfStreet.setText(street);
203      jtfCity.setText(city);
204      jtfState.setText(state);
205      jtfZip.setText(zip);
206    }
207
208    public static void main(String[] args) {
209      AddressBook frame = new AddressBook();
210      frame.pack();
211      frame.setTitle("AddressBook");
212      frame.setDefaultCloseOperation(JFrame.EXIT_ON_CLOSE);
213      frame.setVisible(true);
214    }
215 }
```

A random access file, **address.dat**, is created to store address information if the file does not yet exist (line 37). If it already exists, the file is opened. A random file object, raf, is used for both write and read operations. The size of each field in the record is fixed and therefore defined as a constant in lines 9–15.

The user interface is created in lines 44–100. The listeners are registered in lines 102–156. When the program starts, it displays the first record, if it exists, in lines 159–164.

The `writeAddress()` method sets the file pointer to the end of the file (line 170) and writes a new record to the file (lines 171–180).

The `readAddress()` method sets the file pointer at the specified position (line 189) and reads a record from the file (lines 190–199). The record is displayed in lines 201–205.

To add a record, you need to collect the address information from the user interface and write the address into the file (line 104).

The code to process button events is implemented in lines 102–156. For the *First* button, read the record from position `0` (line 110). For the *Next* button, read the record from the current file pointer (line 122). When a record is read, the file pointer is moved `2 * RECORD_SIZE` number of bytes ahead of the previous file pointer. For the *Previous* button, you need to display the record prior to the one being displayed now. You have to move the file pointer two records before the current file pointer (line 135). For the *Last* button, read the record from the position at `raf.length() - 2 * RECORD_SIZE.`

KEY TERMS

binary I/O 624	sequential access file 639
deserialization 638	serialization 638
file pointer 640	stream 624
random access file 639	text I/O 624

CHAPTER SUMMARY

■ I/O can be classified into text I/O and binary I/O. Text I/O interprets data in sequences of characters. Binary I/O interprets data as raw binary values. How text is stored in a file depends on the encoding scheme for the file. Java automatically performs encoding and decoding for text I/O.

■ The `InputStream` and `OutputStream` classes are the roots of all binary I/O classes. `FileInputStream`/`FileOutputStream` associates a file for binary input/output. `BufferedInputStream`/`BufferedOutputStream` can be used to wrap on any binary I/O stream to improve performance. `DataInputStream`/`DataOutputStream` can be used to read/write primitive values and strings.

■ `ObjectInputStream`/`ObjectOutputStream` can be used to read/write objects in addition to primitive values and strings. To enable object serialization, the object's defining class must implement the `java.io.Serializable` marker interface.

■ The `RandomAccessFile` class enables you to read and write data to a file. You can open a file with the "`r`" mode to indicate that it is read-only, or with the "`rw`" mode to indicate that it is updateable. Since the `RandomAccessFile` class implements `DataInput` and `DataOutput` interfaces, many methods in `RandomAccessFile` are the same as those in `DataInputStream` and `DataOutputStream`.

REVIEW QUESTIONS

Sections 19.1–19.2

19.1 What is a text file, and what is a binary file? Can you view a text file or a binary file using a text editor?

19.2 How do you read or write data in Java? What is a stream?

Section 19.3 Text I/O vs. Binary I/O

19.3 What are the differences between text I/O and binary I/O?

19.4 How is a Java character represented in the memory, and how is a character represented in a text file?

19.5 If you write string "ABC" to an ASCII text file, what values are stored in the file?

19.6 If you write string "100" to an ASCII text file, what values are stored in the file? If you write a numeric byte-type value 100 using binary I/O, what values are stored in the file?

19.7 What is the encoding scheme for representing a character in a Java program? By default, what is the encoding scheme for a text file on Windows?

Section 19.4 Binary I/O Classes

19.8 Why do you have to declare to throw IOException in the method or use a try-catch block to handle IOException for Java IO programs?

19.9 Why should you always close streams?

19.10 InputStream reads bytes. Why does the read() method return an int instead of a byte? Find the abstract methods in InputStream and OutputStream.

19.11 Does FileInputStream/FileOutputStream introduce any new methods? How do you create a FileInputStream/FileOutputStream?

19.12 What will happen if you attempt to create an input stream on a nonexistent file? What will happen if you attempt to create an output stream on an existing file? Can you append data to an existing file?

19.13 How do you append data to an existing text file using java.io.PrintWriter?

19.14 Suppose input is a DataInputStream, and input.available() returns 100. After invoking read(), what is input.available()? After invoking readInt(), what is input.available()? After invoking readChar(), what is input.-available()? After invoking readDouble(), what is input.available()?

19.15 What is written to a file using writeByte(91) on a FileOutputStream?

19.16 How do you check the end of a file in a binary input stream (FileInputStream, DataInputStream)?

19.17 What is wrong in the following code?

```java
import java.io.*;

public class Test {
  public static void main(String[] args) {
    try {
      FileInputStream fis = new FileInputStream("test.dat");
    }
```

```
        catch (IOException ex) {
          ex.printStackTrace();
        }
        catch (FileNotFoundException ex) {
          ex.printStackTrace();
        }
      }
    }
```

19.18 Suppose you run the program on Windows using the default ASCII encoding. After the program is finished, how many bytes are in the file **t.txt**? Show the contents of each byte.

```java
public class Test {
  public static void main(String[] args) throws
      java.io.IOException {
    java.io.PrintWriter output = new
      java.io.PrintWriter("t.txt");
    output.printf("%s", "1234");
    output.printf("%s", "5678");
    output.close();
  }
}
```

19.19 After the program is finished, how many bytes are in the file **t.dat**? Show the contents of each byte.

```java
import java.io.*;

public class Test {
  public static void main(String[] args) throws IOException {
    DataOutputStream output = new DataOutputStream(
      new FileOutputStream("t.dat"));
    output.writeInt(1234);
    output.writeInt(5678);
    output.close();
  }
}
```

19.20 For each of the following statements on a DataOutputStream out, how many bytes are sent to the output?

```java
output.writeChar('A');
output.writeChars("BC");
output.writeUTF("DEF");
```

19.21 What are the advantages of using buffered streams? Are the following statements correct?

```java
BufferedInputStream input1 =
  new BufferedInputStream(new FileInputStream("t.dat"));

DataInputStream input2 = new DataInputStream(
  new BufferedInputStream(new FileInputStream("t.dat")));

ObjectInputStream input3 = new ObjectInputStream(
  new BufferedInputStream(new FileInputStream("t.dat")));
```

Section 19.6 Object I/O

19.22 What types of objects can be stored using the `ObjectOutputStream`? What is the method for writing an object? What is the method for reading an object? What is the return type of the method that reads an object from `ObjectInputStream`?

19.23 If you serialize two objects of the same type, will they take the same amount of space?

19.24 Is it true that any instance of `java.io.Serializable` can be successfully serialized? Are the static variables in an object serialized? How do you mark an instance variable not to be serialized?

19.25 Can you write an array to an `ObjectOutputStream`?

19.26 Is it true that `DataInputStream`/`DataOutputStream` can always be replaced by `ObjectInputStream`/`ObjectOutputStream`?

19.27 What will happen when you attempt to run the following code?

```java
import java.io.*;

public class Test {
  public static void main(String[] args) throws IOException {
    ObjectOutputStream output =
      new ObjectOutputStream(new FileOutputStream("object.dat"));

    output.writeObject(new A());
  }
}

class A implements Serializable {
  B b = new B();
}

class B {
}
```

Section 19.7 Random Access Files

19.28 Can `RandomAccessFile` streams read and write a data file created by `DataOutputStream`? Can `RandomAccessFile` streams read and write objects?

19.29 Create a `RandomAccessFile` stream for the file **address.dat** to allow the updating of student information in the file. Create a `DataOutputStream` for the file **address.dat**. Explain the differences between these two statements.

19.30 What happens if the file **test.dat** does not exist when you attempt to compile and run the following code?

```java
import java.io.*;

public class Test {
  public static void main(String[] args) {
    try {
      RandomAccessFile raf =
        new RandomAccessFile("test.dat", "r");
      int i = raf.readInt();
    }
    catch (IOException ex) {
      System.out.println("IO exception");
    }
  }
}
```

Programming Exercises

Section 19.3 Text I/O vs. Binary I/O

19.1* (*Creating a text file*) Write a program to create a file named **Exercise19_1.txt** if it does not exist. Append new data to it. Write 100 integers created randomly into the file using text I/O. Integers are separated by a space.

Section 19.4 Binary I/O Classes

19.2* (*Creating a binary data file*) Write a program to create a file named **Exercise19_2.dat** if it does not exist. Append new data to it. Write 100 integers created randomly into the file using binary I/O.

19.3* (*Summing all the integers in a binary data file*) Suppose a binary data file named **Exercise19_3.dat** has been created using `writeInt(int)` in `Data-OutputStream`. The file contains an unspecified number of integers. Write a program to find the sum of integers.

19.4* (*Converting a text file into UTF*) Write a program that reads lines of characters from a text and writes each line as a UTF-8 string into a binary file. Display the sizes of the text file and the binary file. Use the following command to run the program:

java Exercise19_4 Welcome.java Welcome.utf

Section 19.6 Object I/O

19.5* (*Storing objects and arrays into a file*) Write a program that stores an array of five `int` values **1**, **2**, **3**, **4** and **5**, a `Date` object for current time, and a `double` value **5.5** into the file named **Exercise19_5.dat**.

19.6* (*Storing* *Loan* *objects*) The `Loan` class, in Listing 9.2, does not implement `Serializable`. Rewrite the `Loan` class to implement `Serializable`. Write a program that creates five `Loan` objects and stores them in a file named **Exercise19_6.dat**.

19.7* (*Restoring objects from a file*) Suppose a file named **Exercise19_7.dat** has been created using the `ObjectOutputStream`. The file contains `Loan` objects. The `Loan` class, in Listing 9.2, does not implement `Serializable`. Rewrite the `Loan` class to implement `Serializable`. Write a program that reads the `Loan` objects from the file and computes the total loan amount. Suppose you don't know how many `Loan` objects are in the file. Use `EOFException` to end the loop.

Section 19.7 Random Access Files

19.8* (*Updating count*) Suppose you want to track how many times a program has been executed. You may store an `int` to count the file. Increase the count by **1** each time this program is executed. Let the program be **Exercise19_8** and store the count in **Exercise19_8.dat**.

19.9** (*Updating address*) Modify `AddressBook` in Listing 19.9, AddressBook.java, to add an *Update* button, as shown in Figure 19.20, to enable the user to modify an address that is being displayed.

Figure 19.20 You can update the address record that is currently displayed.

Comprehensive

19.10* (*Splitting files*) Suppose you wish to back up a huge file (e.g., a 10-GB AVI file) to a CD-R. You can achieve it by splitting the file into smaller pieces and backing up these pieces separately. Write a utility program that splits a large file into smaller ones using the following command:

Video Note
Split a large file

java Exercise19_10 SourceFile numberOfPieces

The command creates files SourceFile.1, SourceFile.2, ..., SourceFile.n, where `n` is `numberOfPieces` and the output files are about the same size.

19.11** (*Splitting files GUI*) Rewrite Exercise 19.10 with a GUI, as shown in Figure 19.21(a).

(a)   (b)

FIGURE 19.21   (a) The program splits a file. (b) The program combines files into a new file.

19.12* (*Combining files*) Write a utility program that combines the files together into a new file using the following command:

java Exercise19_12 SourceFile1 ... SoureFilen TargetFile

The command combines SourceFile1, ..., and SourceFilen into TargetFile.

19.13* (*Combining files GUI*) Rewrite Exercise 19.12 with a GUI, as shown in Figure 19.21(b).

19.14 (*Encrypting files*) Encode the file by adding 5 to every byte in the file. Write a program that prompts the user to enter an input file name and an output file name and saves the encrypted version of the input file to the output file.

19.15 (*Decrypting files*) Suppose a file is encrypted using the scheme in Exercise 19.14. Write a program to decode an encrypted file. Your program should prompt the user to enter an input file name and an output file name and should save the unencrypted version of the input file to the output file.

CHAPTER 20

RECURSION

Objectives

- To describe what a recursive method is and the benefits of using recursion (§20.1).
- To develop recursive methods for recursive mathematical functions (§§20.2–20.3).
- To explain how recursive method calls are handled in a call stack (§§20.2–20.3).
- To use an overloaded helper method to derive a recursive method (§20.5).
- To solve selection sort using recursion (§20.5.1).
- To solve binary search using recursion (§20.5.2).
- To get the directory size using recursion (§20.6).
- To solve the Towers of Hanoi problem using recursion (§20.7).
- To draw fractals using recursion (§20.8).
- To solve the Eight Queens problem (§20.9).
- To discover the relationship and difference between recursion and iteration (§20.10).

20.1 Introduction

Suppose you want to find all the files under a directory that contain a particular word. How do you solve this problem? There are several ways to do so. An intuitive and effective solution is to use recursion by searching the files in the subdirectories recursively.

The classic Eight Queens puzzle is to place eight queens on a chessboard such that no two can attack each other (i.e., no two queens are on the same row, same column, or same diagonal), as shown in Figure 20.1. How do you write a program to solve this problem? A good approach is to use recursion.

FIGURE 20.1   The Eight Queens problem can be solved using recursion.

To use recursion is to program using *recursive methods*—methods that directly or indirectly invoke themselves. Recursion is a useful programming technique. In some cases, it enables you to develop a natural, straightforward, simple solution to an otherwise difficult problem. This chapter introduces the concepts and techniques of recursive programming and illustrates by examples how to "think recursively."

20.2 Problem: Computing Factorials

Many mathematical functions are defined using recursion. We begin with a simple example that illustrates recursion. The factorial of a number n can be recursively defined as follows:

```
0! = 1;
n! = n × (n - 1) × ... × 2 × 1 = n × (n - 1)!; n > 0
```

How do you find n! for a given n? To find 1! is easy, because you know that 0! is 1, and 1! is 1×0!. Assuming that you know (n - 1)!, you can obtain n! immediately using n × (n - 1)!. Thus, the problem of computing n! is reduced to computing (n - 1)!. When computing (n - 1)!, you can apply the same idea recursively until n is reduced to 0.

Let factorial(n) be the method for computing n!. If you call the method with n = 0, it immediately returns the result. The method knows how to solve the simplest case, which is referred to as the *base case* or the *stopping condition*. If you call the method with n > 0, it reduces the problem into a subproblem for computing the factorial of n - 1. The subproblem is essentially the same as the original problem, but is simpler or smaller. Because the subproblem has the same property as the original, you can call the method with a different argument,

which is referred to as a *recursive call*.

The recursive algorithm for computing factorial(n) can be simply described as follows:

```
if (n == 0)
  return 1;
else
  return n * factorial(n - 1);
```

A recursive call can result in many more recursive calls, because the method keeps on dividing a subproblem into new subproblems. For a recursive method to terminate, the problem must eventually be reduced to a stopping case, at which point the method returns a result to its caller. The caller then performs a computation and returns the result to its own caller. This process continues until the result is passed back to the original caller. The original problem can now be solved by multiplying `n` by the result of `factorial(n - 1)`.

Listing 20.1 gives a complete program that prompts the user to enter a nonnegative integer and displays the factorial for the number.

LISTING 20.1 ComputeFactorial.java

```
 1 import java.util.Scanner;
 2
 3 public class ComputeFactorial {
 4   /** Main method */
 5   public static void main(String[] args) {
 6     // Create a Scanner
 7     Scanner input = new Scanner(System.in);
 8     System.out.print("Enter a nonnegative integer: ");
 9     int n =input.nextInt();
10
11     // Display factorial
12     System.out.println("Factorial of " + n + " is " + factorial(n));
13   }
14
15   /** Return the factorial for a specified number */
16   public static long factorial(int n) {
17     if (n == 0) // Base case                          base case
18       return 1;
19     else
20       return n * factorial(n - 1); // Recursive call   recursion
21   }
22 }
```

```
Enter a nonnegative integer: 4  ↵Enter
Factorial of 4 is 24
```

```
Enter a nonnegative integer: 10  ↵Enter
Factorial of 10 is 3628800
```

The `factorial` method (lines 16–21) is essentially a direct translation of the recursive mathematical definition for the factorial into Java code. The call to `factorial` is recursive because it calls itself. The parameter passed to `factorial` is decremented until it reaches the base case of `0`.

Figure 20.2 illustrates the execution of the recursive calls, starting with n = 4. The use of stack space for recursive calls is shown in Figure 20.3.

Caution

If recursion does not reduce the problem in a manner that allows it to eventually converge into the base case, *infinite recursion* can occur. For example, suppose you mistakenly write the `factorial` method as follows:

infinite recursion

```
public static long factorial(int n) {
  return n * factorial(n - 1);
}
```

The method runs infinitely and causes a `StackOverflowError`.

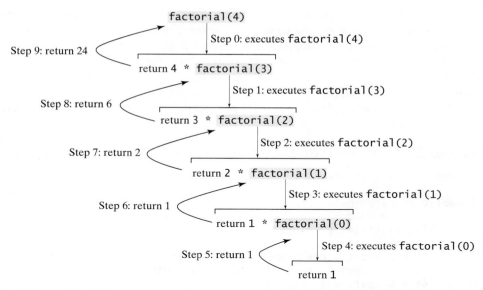

FIGURE 20.2 Invoking `factorial(4)` spawns recursive calls to `factorial`.

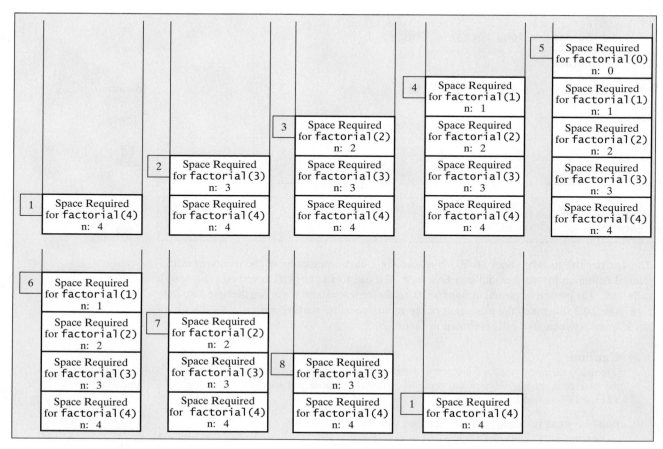

FIGURE 20.3 When `factorial(4)` is being executed, the `factorial` method is called recursively, causing memory space to dynamically change.

Pedagogical Note

It is simpler and more efficient to implement the `factorial` method using a loop. However, we use the recursive `factorial` method here to demonstrate the concept of recursion. Later in this chapter, we will present some problems that are inherently recursive and are difficult to solve without using recursion.

20.3 Problem: Computing Fibonacci Numbers

The `factorial` method in the preceding section could easily be rewritten without using recursion. In some cases, however, using recursion enables you to give a natural, straightforward, simple solution to a program that would otherwise be difficult to solve. Consider the well-known Fibonacci series problem:

The series:	0	1	1	2	3	5	8	13	21	34	55	89 ...
indices:	0	1	2	3	4	5	6	7	8	9	10	11

The Fibonacci series begins with 0 and 1, and each subsequent number is the sum of the preceding two. The series can be recursively defined as follows:

```
fib(0) = 0;
fib(1) = 1;
fib(index) = fib(index - 2) + fib(index - 1); index >= 2
```

The Fibonacci series was named for Leonardo Fibonacci, a medieval mathematician, who originated it to model the growth of the rabbit population. It can be applied in numeric optimization and in various other areas.

How do you find `fib(index)` for a given `index`? It is easy to find `fib(2)`, because you know `fib(0)` and `fib(1)`. Assuming that you know `fib(index - 2)` and `fib(index - 1)`, you can obtain `fib(index)` immediately. Thus, the problem of computing `fib(index)` is reduced to computing `fib(index - 2)` and `fib(index - 1)`. When computing `fib(index - 2)` and `fib(index - 1)`, you apply the idea recursively until `index` is reduced to 0 or 1.

The base case is `index = 0` or `index = 1`. If you call the method with `index = 0` or `index = 1`, it immediately returns the result. If you call the method with `index >= 2`, it divides the problem into two subproblems for computing `fib(index - 1)` and `fib(index - 2)` using recursive calls. The recursive algorithm for computing `fib(index)` can be simply described as follows:

```
if (index == 0)
  return 0;
else if (index == 1)
  return 1;
else
  return fib(index - 1) + fib(index - 2);
```

Listing 20.2 gives a complete program that prompts the user to enter an index and computes the Fibonacci number for the index.

LISTING 20.2 ComputeFibonacci.java

```
1 import java.util.Scanner;
2
3 public class ComputeFibonacci {
4   /** Main method */
5   public static void main(String args[]) {
6     // Create a Scanner
7     Scanner input = new Scanner(System.in);
```

```
 8       System.out.print("Enter an index for the Fibonacci number: ");
 9       int index = input.nextInt();
10
11       // Find and display the Fibonacci number
12       System.out.println(
13         "Fibonacci number at index " + index + " is " + fib(index));
14     }
15
16     /** The method for finding the Fibonacci number */
17     public static long fib(long index) {
18       if (index == 0) // Base case
19         return 0;
20       else if (index == 1) // Base case
21         return 1;
22       else  // Reduction and recursive calls
23         return fib(index - 1) + fib(index - 2);
24     }
25   }
```

base case (line 18)
base case (line 20)
recursion (line 23)

```
Enter an index for the Fibonacci number: 1
Fibonacci number at index 1 is 1
```

```
Enter an index for the Fibonacci number: 6 ↵Enter
Fibonacci number at index 6 is 8
```

```
Enter an index for the Fibonacci number: 7 ↵Enter
Fibonacci number at index 7 is 13
```

The program does not show the considerable amount of work done behind the scenes by the computer. Figure 20.4, however, shows successive recursive calls for evaluating fib(4). The original method, fib(4), makes two recursive calls, fib(3) and fib(2), and then returns fib(3) + fib(2). But in what order are these methods called? In Java, operands are

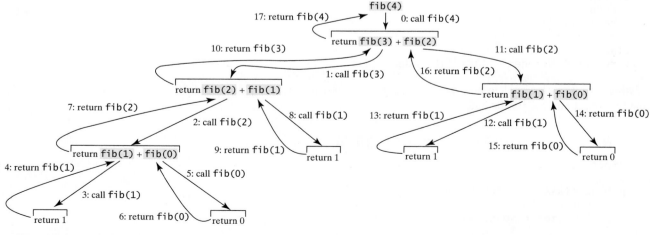

FIGURE 20.4 Invoking fib(4) spawns recursive calls to fib.

evaluated from left to right. `fib(2)` is called after `fib(3)` is completely evaluated. The labels in Figure 20.4 show the order in which methods are called.

As shown in Figure 20.4, there are many duplicated recursive calls. For instance, `fib(2)` is called twice, `fib(1)` is called three times, and `fib(0)` is called twice. In general, computing `fib(index)` requires roughly twice as many recursive calls as are needed for computing `fib(index - 1)`. As you try larger index values, the number of calls substantially increases.

Besides the large number of recursive calls, the computer requires more time and space to run recursive methods.

Pedagogical Note

The recursive implementation of the `fib` method is very simple and straightforward, but not efficient. See Exercise 20.2 for an efficient solution using loops. Though it is not practical, the recursive `fib` method is a good example of how to write recursive methods.

20.4 Problem Solving Using Recursion

The preceding sections presented two classic recursion examples. All recursive methods have the following characteristics:

- The method is implemented using an `if-else` or a `switch` statement that leads to different cases.

- One or more base cases (the simplest case) are used to stop recursion.

- Every recursive call reduces the original problem, bringing it increasingly closer to a base case until it becomes that case.

recursion characteristics

if-else

base cases

reduction

In general, to solve a problem using recursion, you break it into subproblems. Each subproblem is almost the same as the original problem but smaller in size. You can apply the same approach to each subproblem to solve it recursively.

Let us consider the simple problem of printing a message **n** times. You can break the problem into two subproblems: one is to print the message one time and the other is to print it **n - 1** times. The second problem is the same as the original problem but smaller in size. The base case for the problem is **n == 0**. You can solve this problem using recursion as follows:

```
public static void nPrintln(String message, int times) {
  if (times >= 1) {
    System.out.println(message);
    nPrintln(message, times - 1);
  } // The base case is times == 0
}
```

recursive call

Note that the `fib` method in the preceding example returns a value to its caller, but the `nPrintln` method is `void` and does not return a value to its caller.

If you *think recursively*, you can use recursion to solve many of the problems presented in earlier chapters of this book. Consider the palindrome problem in Listing 8.1. Recall that a string is a palindrome if it reads the same from the left and from the right. For example, mom and dad are palindromes, but uncle and aunt are not. The problem to check whether a string is a palindrome can be divided into two subproblems:

think recursively

- Check whether the first character and the last character of the string are equal.

- Ignore the two end characters and check whether the rest of the substring is a palindrome.

The second subproblem is the same as the original problem but smaller in size. There are two base cases: (1) the two end characters are not same; (2) the string size is 0 or 1. In case 1, the string is not a palindrome; and in case 2, the string is a palindrome. The recursive method for this problem can be implemented as shown in Listing 20.3.

LISTING 20.3 RecursivePalindromeUsingSubstring.java

method header
base case

base case

recursive call

```
 1 public class RecursivePalindromeUsingSubstring {
 2   public static boolean isPalindrome(String s) {
 3     if (s.length() <= 1) // Base case
 4       return true;
 5     else if (s.charAt(0) != s.charAt(s.length() - 1)) // Base case
 6       return false;
 7     else
 8       return isPalindrome(s.substring(1, s.length() - 1));
 9   }
10
11   public static void main(String[] args) {
12     System.out.println("Is moon a palindrome? "
13       + isPalindrome("moon"));
14     System.out.println("Is noon a palindrome? "
15       + isPalindrome("noon"));
16     System.out.println("Is a a palindrome? " + isPalindrome("a"));
17     System.out.println("Is aba a palindrome? " +
18       isPalindrome("aba"));
19     System.out.println("Is ab a palindrome? " + isPalindrome("ab"));
20   }
21 }
```

```
Is moon a palindrome? false
Is noon a palindrome? true
Is a a palindrome? true
Is aba a palindrome? true
Is ab a palindrome? false
```

The `substring` method in line 8 creates a new string that is the same as the original string except without the first and last characters in the original string. Checking whether a string is a palindrome is equivalent to checking whether the substring is a palindrome if the two end characters in the original string are the same.

20.5 Recursive Helper Methods

The preceding recursive `isPalindrome` method is not efficient, because it creates a new string for every recursive call. To avoid creating new strings, you can use the low and high indices to indicate the range of the substring. These two indices must be passed to the recursive method. Since the original method is `isPalindrome(String s)`, you have to create a new method `isPalindrome(String s, int low, int high)` to accept additional information on the string, as shown in Listing 20.4.

LISTING 20.4 RecursivePalindrome.java

helper method
base case

base case

```
 1 public class RecursivePalindrome {
 2   public static boolean isPalindrome(String s) {
 3     return isPalindrome(s, 0, s.length() - 1);
 4   }
 5
 6   public static boolean isPalindrome(String s, int low, int high) {
 7     if (high <= low) // Base case
 8       return true;
 9     else if (s.charAt(low) != s.charAt(high)) // Base case
10       return false;
```

```
11    else
12      return isPalindrome(s, low + 1, high - 1);
13  }
14
15  public static void main(String[] args) {
16    System.out.println("Is moon a palindrome? "
17      + isPalindrome("moon"));
18    System.out.println("Is noon a palindrome? "
19      + isPalindrome("noon"));
20    System.out.println("Is a a palindrome? " + isPalindrome("a"));
21    System.out.println("Is aba a palindrome? " +
22      isPalindrome("aba"));
23    System.out.println("Is ab a palindrome? " + isPalindrome("ab"));
24  }
25 }
```

Two overloaded `isPalindrome` methods are declared. The first, `isPalindrome(String s)`, checks whether a string is a palindrome, and the second, `isPalindrome(String s, int low, int high)`, checks whether a substring `s(low..high)` is a palindrome. The first method passes the string `s` with `low = 0` and `high = s.length() – 1` to the second method. The second method can be invoked recursively to check a palindrome in an ever-shrinking substring. It is a common design technique in recursive programming to declare a second method that receives additional parameters. Such a method is known as a *recursive helper method*.

recursive helper method

Helper methods are very useful in designing recursive solutions for problems involving strings and arrays. The sections that follow give two more examples.

20.5.1 Selection Sort

Selection sort was introduced in §6.8.1, "Selection Sort." Recall that it finds the largest number in the list and places it last. It then finds the largest number remaining and places it next to last, and so on until the list contains only a single number. The problem can be divided into two subproblems:

- Find the largest number in the list and swap it with the last number.
- Ignore the last number and sort the remaining smaller list recursively.

The base case is that the list contains only one number. Listing 20.5 gives the recursive sort method.

LISTING 20.5 RecursiveSelectionSort.java

```
1 public class RecursiveSelectionSort {
2   public static void sort(double[] list) {
3     sort(list, list.length - 1);
4   }
5
6   public static void sort(double[] list, int high) {
7     if (high > 0) {
8       // Find the largest number and its index
9       int indexOfMax = 0;
10      double max = list[0];
11      for (int i = 1; i <= high; i++) {
12        if (list[i] > max) {
13          max = list[i];
14          indexOfMax = i;
15        }
16      }
17
```

helper method
base case

```
18          // Swap the largest with the last number in the list
19          list[indexOfMax] = list[high];
20          list[high] = max;
21
22          // Sort the remaining list
23          sort(list, high - 1);
24      }
25    }
26 }
```

recursive call (margin note, line 23)

Two overloaded **sort** methods are declared. The first method, **sort(double[] list)**, sorts an array in **list[0..list.length - 1]** and the second method **sort(double[] list, int high)** sorts an array in **list[0..high]**. The second method can be invoked recursively to sort an ever-shrinking subarray.

Video Note
Binary search

20.5.2 Binary Search

Binary search was introduced in §6.7.2. For binary search to work, the elements in the array must already be ordered. The binary search first compares the key with the element in the middle of the array. Consider the following three cases:

- Case 1: If the key is less than the middle element, recursively search the key in the first half of the array.

- Case 2: If the key is equal to the middle element, the search ends with a match.

- Case 3: If the key is greater than the middle element, recursively search the key in the second half of the array.

Case 1 and Case 3 reduce the search to a smaller list. Case 2 is a base case when there is a match. Another base case is that the search is exhausted without a match. Listing 20.6 gives a clear, simple solution for the binary search problem using recursion.

LISTING 20.6 Recursive Binary Search Method

```
 1 public class RecursiveBinarySearch {
 2   public static int recursiveBinarySearch(int[] list, int key) {
 3     int low = 0;
 4     int high = list.length - 1;
 5     return recursiveBinarySearch(list, key, low, high);
 6   }
 7
 8   public static int recursiveBinarySearch(int[] list, int key,
 9       int low, int high) {
10     if (low > high)   // The list has been exhausted without a match
11       return -low - 1;
12
13     int mid = (low + high) / 2;
14     if (key < list[mid])
15       return recursiveBinarySearch(list, key, low, mid - 1);
16     else if (key == list[mid])
17       return mid;
18     else
19       return recursiveBinarySearch(list, key, mid + 1, high);
20   }
21 }
```

helper method (margin note, line 8)
base case (margin note, line 10)
recursive call (margin note, line 15)
base case (margin note, line 17)
recursive call (margin note, line 19)

The first method finds a key in the whole list. The second method finds a key in the list with index from **low** to **high**.

The first `binarySearch` method passes the initial array with `low = 0` and `high = list.length - 1` to the second `binarySearch` method. The second method is invoked recursively to find the key in an ever-shrinking subarray.

20.6 Problem: Finding the Directory Size

Video Note
Directory size

The preceding examples can easily be solved without using recursion. This section presents a problem that is difficult to solve without using recursion. The problem is to find the size of a directory. The size of a directory is the sum of the sizes of all files in the directory. A directory d may contain subdirectories. Suppose a directory contains files $f_1, f_2, \ldots, f_m$, and subdirectories $d_1, d_2, \ldots, d_n$, as shown in Figure 20.5.

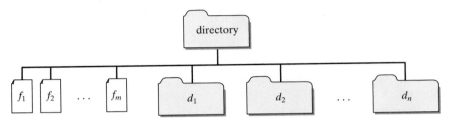

FIGURE 20.5 A directory contains files and subdirectories.

The size of the directory can be defined recursively as follows:

$$size(d) = size(f_1) + size(f_2) + \cdots + size(f_m) + size(d_1) + size(d_2) + \cdots + size(d_n)$$

The `File` class, introduced in §8.6, can be used to represent a file or a directory and obtain the properties for files and directories. Two methods in the `File` class are useful for this problem:

- The `length()` method returns the size of a file.

- The `listFiles()` method returns an array of `File` objects under a directory.

Listing 20.7 gives a program that prompts the user to enter a directory or a file and displays its size.

LISTING 20.7 DirectorySize.java

```
 1 import java.io.File;
 2 import java.util.Scanner;
 3
 4 public class DirectorySize {
 5   public static void main(String[] args) {
 6     // Prompt the user to enter a directory or a file
 7     System.out.print("Enter a directory or a file: ");
 8     Scanner input = new Scanner(System.in);
 9     String directory = input.nextLine();
10
11     // Display the size
12     System.out.println(getSize(new File(directory)) + " bytes");
13   }
14
15   public static long getSize(File file) {
16     long size = 0; // Store the total size of all files
17
18     if (file.isDirectory()) {
19       File[] files =file.listFiles(); // All files and subdirectories
```

invoke method

getSize method

is directory?
all subitems

```
20          for (int i = 0; i < files.length; i++) {
21            size += getSize(files[i]); // Recursive call
22          }
23        }
24      else { // Base case
25        size += file.length();
26      }
27
28      return size;
29    }
30 }
```

recursive call

base case

```
Enter a directory or a file: c:\book  ↵Enter
48619631 bytes
```

```
Enter a directory or a file: c:\book\Welcome.java  ↵Enter
172 bytes
```

```
Enter a directory or a file: c:\book\NonExistentFile  ↵Enter
0 bytes
```

If the `file` object represents a directory (line 18), each subitem (file or subdirectory) in the directory is recursively invoked to obtain its size (line 21). If the `file` object represents a file (line 24), the file size is obtained (line 25).

What happens if an incorrect or a nonexistent directory is entered? The program will detect that it is not a directory and invoke `file.length()` (line 25), which returns `0`. So, in this case, the `getSize` method will return `0`.

Tip

testing base cases

To avoid mistakes, it is a good practice to test base cases. For example, you should trace the program for an input of file, an empty directory, a nonexistent directory, and a nonexistent file.

20.7 Problem: Tower of Hanoi

The Tower of Hanoi problem is a classic recursion example. The problem can be solved easily using recursion, but is difficult to solve otherwise.

The problem involves moving a specified number of disks of distinct sizes from one tower to another while observing the following rules:

■ There are n disks labeled 1, 2, 3, ..., n, and three towers labeled A, B, and C.

■ No disk can be on top of a smaller disk at any time.

■ All the disks are initially placed on tower A.

■ Only one disk can be moved at a time, and it must be the top disk on the tower.

The objective of the problem is to move all the disks from A to B with the assistance of C. For example, if you have three disks, the steps to move all of the disks from A to B are shown in Figure 20.6.

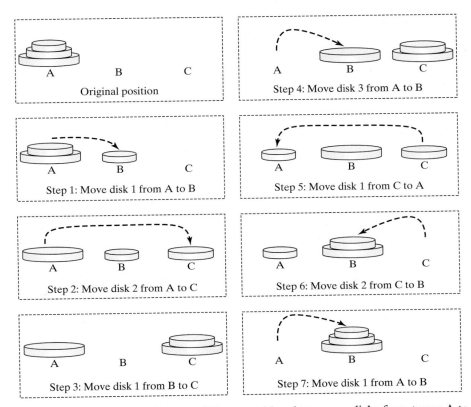

FIGURE 20.6 The goal of the Towers of Hanoi problem is to move disks from tower A to tower B without breaking the rules.

 Note

The Towers of Hanoi is a classic computer-science problem, to which many Web sites are devoted. One of them worth seeing is www.cut-the-knot.com/recurrence/hanoi.html.

In the case of three disks, you can find the solution manually. For a larger number of disks, however—even for four—the problem is quite complex. Fortunately, the problem has an inherently recursive nature, which leads to a straightforward recursive solution.

The base case for the problem is n = 1. If n == 1, you could simply move the disk from A to B. When n > 1, you could split the original problem into three subproblems and solve them sequentially.

1. Move the first n - 1 disks from A to C with the assistance of tower B, as shown in Step 1 in Figure 20.7.

2. Move disk n from A to B, as shown in Step 2 in Figure 20.7.

3. Move n - 1 disks from C to B with the assistance of tower A, as shown in Step 3 in Figure 20.7.

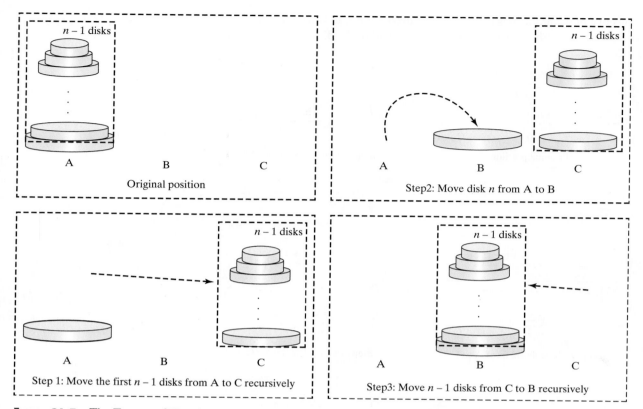

FIGURE 20.7 The Towers of Hanoi problem can be decomposed into three subproblems.

The following method moves *n* disks from the `fromTower` to the `toTower` with the assistance of the `auxTower`:

```
void moveDisks(int n, char fromTower, char toTower, char auxTower)
```

The algorithm for the method can be described as follows:

```
if (n == 1) // Stopping condition
  Move disk 1 from the fromTower to the toTower;
else {
  moveDisks(n - 1, fromTower, auxTower, toTower);
  Move disk n from the fromTower to the toTower;
  moveDisks(n - 1, auxTower, toTower, fromTower);
}
```

Listing 20.8 gives a program that prompts the user to enter the number of disks and invokes the recursive method `moveDisks` to display the solution for moving the disks.

LISTING 20.8 TowersOfHanoi.java

```
1 import java.util.Scanner;
2
3 public class TowersOfHanoi {
```

```
 4   /** Main method */
 5   public static void main(String[] args) {
 6     // Create a Scanner
 7     Scanner input = new Scanner(System.in);
 8     System.out.print("Enter number of disks: ");
 9     int n = input.nextInt();
10
11     // Find the solution recursively
12     System.out.println("The moves are:");
13     moveDisks(n, 'A', 'B', 'C');
14   }
15
16   /** The method for finding the solution to move n disks
17       from fromTower to toTower with auxTower */
18   public static void moveDisks(int n, char fromTower,
19       char toTower, char auxTower) {
20     if (n == 1) // Stopping condition                              base case
21       System.out.println("Move disk " + n + " from " +
22         fromTower + " to " + toTower);
23     else {
24       moveDisks(n - 1, fromTower, auxTower, toTower);              recursion
25       System.out.println("Move disk " + n + " from " +
26         fromTower + " to " + toTower);
27       moveDisks(n - 1, auxTower, toTower, fromTower);              recursion
28     }
29   }
30 }
```

```
Enter number of disks: 4  ⏎Enter
The moves are:
Move disk 1 from A to C
Move disk 2 from A to B
Move disk 1 from C to B
Move disk 3 from A to C
Move disk 1 from B to A
Move disk 2 from B to C
Move disk 1 from A to C
Move disk 4 from A to B
Move disk 1 from C to B
Move disk 2 from C to A
Move disk 1 from B to A
Move disk 3 from C to B
Move disk 1 from A to C
Move disk 2 from A to B
Move disk 1 from C to B
```

This problem is inherently recursive. Using recursion makes it possible to find a natural, simple solution. It would be difficult to solve the problem without using recursion.

Consider tracing the program for n = 3. The successive recursive calls are shown in Figure 20.8. As you can see, writing the program is easier than tracing the recursive calls. The system uses stacks to trace the calls behind the scenes. To some extent, recursion provides a level of abstraction that hides iterations and other details from the user.

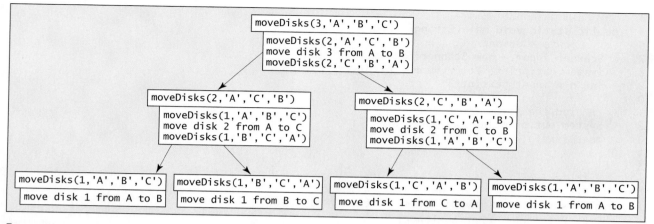

FIGURE 20.8 Invoking `moveDisks(3, 'A', 'B', 'C')` spawns calls to `moveDisks` recursively.

20.8 Problem: Fractals

A *fractal* is a geometrical figure, but unlike triangles, circles, and rectangles, fractals can be divided into parts, each of which is a reduced-size copy of the whole. There are many interesting examples of fractals. This section introduces a simple fractal, the *Sierpinski triangle*, named after a famous Polish mathematician.

A Sierpinski triangle is created as follows:

1. Begin with an equilateral triangle, which is considered to be a Sierpinski fractal of order (or level) 0, as shown in Figure 20.9(a).

2. Connect the midpoints of the sides of the triangle of order 0 to create a Sierpinski triangle of order 1 (Figure 20.9(b)).

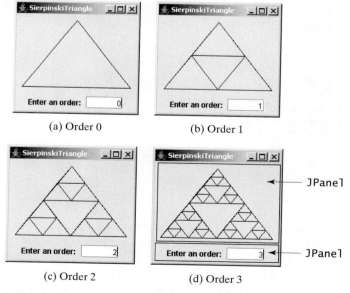

(a) Order 0

(b) Order 1

(c) Order 2

(d) Order 3

FIGURE 20.9 A Sierpinski triangle is a pattern of triangles.

3. Leave the center triangle intact. Connect the midpoints of the sides of the three other triangles to create a Sierpinski triangle of order 2 (Figure 20.9(c)).

4. You can repeat the same process recursively to create a Sierpinski triangle of order 3, 4, ..., and so on (Figure 20.9(d)).

The problem is inherently recursive. How do you develop a recursive solution for it? Consider the base case when the order is 0. It is easy to draw a Sierpinski triangle of order 0. How do you draw a Sierpinski triangle of order 1? The problem can be reduced to drawing three Sierpinski triangles of order 0. How do you draw a Sierpinski triangle of order 2? The problem can be reduced to drawing three Sierpinski triangles of order 1. So the problem of drawing a Sierpinski triangle of order n can be reduced to drawing three Sierpinski triangles of order $n - 1$.

Listing 20.9 gives a Java applet that displays a Sierpinski triangle of any order, as shown in Figure 20.8. You can enter an order in a text field to display a Sierpinski triangle of the specified order.

LISTING 20.9 SierpinskiTriangle.java

```java
1  import javax.swing.*;
2  import java.awt.*;
3  import java.awt.event.*;
4
5  public class SierpinskiTriangle extends JApplet {
6    private JTextField jtfOrder = new JTextField(5); // To hold order
7    private SierpinskiTrianglePanel trianglePanel =
8      new SierpinskiTrianglePanel(); // To display the pattern
9
10   public SierpinskiTriangle() {
11     // Panel to hold label, text field, and a button
12     JPanel panel = new JPanel();
13     panel.add(new JLabel("Enter an order: "));
14     panel.add(jtfOrder);
15     jtfOrder.setHorizontalAlignment(SwingConstants.RIGHT);
16
17     // Add a Sierpinski Triangle panel to the applet
18     add(trianglePanel);
19     add(panel, BorderLayout.SOUTH);
20
21     // Register a listener
22     jtfOrder.addActionListener(new ActionListener() {          listener
23       public void actionPerformed(ActionEvent e) {
24         trianglePanel.setOrder(Integer.parseInt(jtfOrder.getText()));  set a new order
25       }
26     });
27   }
28
29   static class SierpinskiTrianglePanel extends JPanel {
30     private int order = 0;
31
32     /** Set a new order */
33     public void setOrder(int order) {
34       this.order = order;
35       repaint();
36     }
37
```

```
38     protected void paintComponent(Graphics g) {
39       super.paintComponent(g);
40
41       // Select three points in proportion to the panel size
42       Point p1 = new Point(getWidth() / 2, 10);
43       Point p2 = new Point(10, getHeight() - 10);
44       Point p3 = new Point(getWidth() - 10, getHeight() - 10);
45
46       displayTriangles(g, order, p1, p2, p3);
47     }
48
49     private static void displayTriangles(Graphics g, int order,
50         Point p1, Point p2, Point p3) {
51       if (order >= 0) {
52         // Draw a triangle to connect three points
53         g.drawLine(p1.x, p1.y, p2.x, p2.y);
54         g.drawLine(p1.x, p1.y, p3.x, p3.y);
55         g.drawLine(p2.x, p2.y, p3.x, p3.y);
56
57         // Get three midpints in the triangle
58         Point midBetweenP1P2 = midpoint(p1, p2);
59         Point midBetweenP2P3 = midpoint(p2, p3);
60         Point midBetweenP3P1 = midpoint(p3, p1);
61
62         // Recursively display three triangles
63         displayTriangles(g, order - 1,
64           p1, midBetweenP1P2, midBetweenP3P1);
65         displayTriangles(g, order - 1,
66           midBetweenP1P2, p2, midBetweenP2P3);
67         displayTriangles(g, order - 1,
68           midBetweenP3P1, midBetweenP2P3, p3);
69       }
70     }
71
72     private static Point midpoint(Point p1, Point p2) {
73       return new Point((p1.x + p2.x) / 2, (p1.y + p2.y) / 2);
74     }
75   }
76 }
```

The margin notes from left to right are:

three initial points (lines 42–44)

draw a triangle (lines 53–55)

top subtriangle (line 63)

left subtriangle (line 65)

right subtriangle (line 67)

main method omitted (line 76)

The initial triangle has three points set in proportion to the panel size (lines 42–44). The displayTriangles(g, order, p1, p2, p3) method performs the following tasks if order >= 0:

1. Display a triangle to connect three points p1, p2, and p3 in lines 53–55.

2. Obtain a midpoint between p1 and p2 (line 58), a midpoint between p2 and p3 (line 59), and a midpoint between p3 and p1 (line 60), as shown in Figure 20.10.

3. Recursively invoke displayTriangles with a reduced order to display three smaller triangles (lines 63–68).

A Sierpinski triangle is displayed in a SierpinskiTrianglePanel. The order property in the inner class SierpinskiTrianglePanel specifies the order for the Sierpinski triangle. The Point class, introduced in §15.4, "Mouse Events," represents a point on a component. The midpoint(Point p1, Point p2) method returns the midpoint between p1 and p2 (lines 72–74).

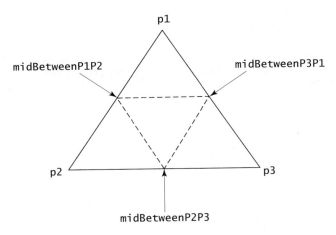

FIGURE 20.10 Three small triangles are created.

20.9 Problem: Eight Queens

This section gives a recursive solution to the Eight Queens problem presented at the beginning of this chapter. The task is to find a solution to place a queen in each row on a chessboard such that no two queens can attack each other. You may use a two-dimensional array to represent a chess board. However, since each row can have only one queen, it is sufficient to use a one-dimensional array to denote the position of the queen in the row. So, you may declare array **queens** as follows:

```java
int[] queens = new int[8];
```

Assign **j** to **queens[i]** to denote that a queen is placed in row **i** and column **j**. Figure 20.11(a) shows the contents of array **queens** for the chessboard in Figure 20.11(b).

Listing 20.10 gives the program that displays a solution for the Eight Queens problem.

LISTING 20.10 EightQueens.java

```java
 1 import java.awt.*;
 2 import javax.swing.*;
 3
 4 public class EightQueens extends JApplet {
 5   public static final int SIZE = 8; // The size of the chess board
 6   private int[] queens = new int[SIZE]; // Queen positions
 7
 8   public EightQueens() {
 9     search(0); // Search for a solution from row 0          search for solution
10     add(new ChessBoard(), BorderLayout.CENTER);
11   }
12
13   /** Check if a queen can be placed at row i and column j */
14   private boolean isValid(int row, int column) {          check if valid
15     for (int i = 1; i <= row; i++)
16       if (queens[row - i] == column // Check column
17         || queens[row - i] == column - i // Check upper left diagonal
18         || queens[row - i] == column + i) // Check upright diagonal
19         return false; // There is a conflict
20     return true; // No conflict
21   }
22
23   /** Search for a solution starting from a specified row */
```

search this row

search columns

search next row

found

main method omitted

```
24   private boolean search(int row) {
25     if (row < SIZE) {
26       for (int column = 0; column < SIZE; column++) {
27         queens[row] = column; // Place a queen at (row, column)
28         if (isValid(row, column) && search(row + 1))
29           return true; // Found, thus return true to exit the loop
30       }
31     }
32     else {
33       return true; // A solution found
34     }
35
36     return false; // No solution
37   }
38
39   class ChessBoard extends JPanel {
40     private Image queenImage =
41       new ImageIcon("image/queen.jpg").getImage();
42
43     ChessBoard() {
44       this.setBorder(BorderFactory.createLineBorder(Color.BLACK, 2));
45     }
46
47     protected void paintComponent(Graphics g) {
48       super.paintComponent(g);
49
50       // Paint the queens
51       for (int i = 0; i < SIZE; i++) {
52         int j = queens[i]; // The position of the queen in row i
53         g.drawImage(queenImage, j * getWidth() / SIZE,
54           i * getHeight() / SIZE, getWidth() / SIZE,
55           getHeight() / SIZE, this);
56       }
57
58       // Draw the horizontal and vertical lines
59       for (int i = 1; i < SIZE; i++) {
60         g.drawLine(0, i * getHeight() / SIZE,
61           getWidth(), i * getHeight() / SIZE);
62         g.drawLine(i * getWidth() / SIZE, 0,
63           i * getWidth() / SIZE, getHeight());
64       }
65     }
66   }
67 }
```

queens[0]	0
queens[1]	4
queens[2]	7
queens[3]	5
queens[4]	2
queens[5]	6
queens[6]	1
queens[7]	3

(a)   (b)   (c)

Figure 20.11 queens[i] denotes the position of the queen in row i.

The program invokes `search(0)` (line 9) to start a search for a solution at row `0`, which recursively invokes `search(1)`, `search(2)`,..., and `search(7)` (line 26).

The `search(row)` method checks whether a queen can be placed in column `0`, `1`, `2`, ..., and `7` in a `for` loop (line 26). Place a queen in the column (line 25). If the placement is valid, recursively search for the next row (line 28). If search is successful, return `true` (line 29) to exit the `for` loop. In this case, there is no need to look for the next column in the row.

The `isValid(row, column)` method checks whether placing a queen at the specified position causes a conflict with the queens placed before this row. It ensures that no queen is placed in the same column (line 16), no queen is placed in the upper left diagonal (line 17), and no queen is placed in the upper right diagonal (line 18), as shown in Figure 20.11(c).

20.10 Recursion versus Iteration

Recursion is an alternative form of program control. It is essentially repetition without a loop control. When you use loops, you specify a loop body. The repetition of the loop body is controlled by the loop-control structure. In recursion, the method itself is called repeatedly. A selection statement must be used to control whether to call the method recursively or not.

Recursion bears substantial overhead. Each time the program calls a method, the system must assign space for all of the method's local variables and parameters. This can consume considerable memory and requires extra time to manage the additional space.

recursion overhead

Any problem that can be solved recursively can be solved nonrecursively with iterations. Recursion has some negative aspects: it uses up too much time and too much memory. Why, then, should you use it? In some cases, using recursion enables you to specify a clear, simple solution for an inherent recursive problem that would otherwise be difficult to obtain. Examples are the directory-size problem, the Towers of Hanoi problem, and the fractal problem, which are rather difficult to solve without using recursion.

recursion advantages

The decision whether to use recursion or iteration should be based on the nature of, and your understanding of, the problem you are trying to solve. The rule of thumb is to use whichever approach can best develop an intuitive solution that naturally mirrors the problem. If an iterative solution is obvious, use it. It will generally be more efficient than the recursive option.

recursion or iteration?

Note

Your recursive program could run out of memory, causing a `StackOverflowError`.

`StackOverflowError`

Tip

If you are concerned about your program's performance, avoid using recursion, because it takes more time and consumes more memory than iteration.

performance concern

KEY TERMS

base case   656
infinite recursion   657
recursive method   656

recursive helper method   663
stopping condition   656

CHAPTER SUMMARY

■ A recursive method is one that directly or indirectly invokes itself. For a recursive method to terminate, there must be one or more base cases.

■ Recursion is an alternative form of program control. It is essentially repetition without a loop control. It can be used to specify simple, clear solutions for inherently recursive problems that would otherwise be difficult to solve.

■ Sometimes the original method needs to be modified to receive additional parameters in order to be invoked recursively. A recursive helper method can be declared for this purpose.

■ Recursion bears substantial overhead. Each time the program calls a method, the system must assign space for all of the method's local variables and parameters. This can consume considerable memory and requires extra time to manage the additional space.

REVIEW QUESTIONS

Sections 20.1–20.3

20.1 What is a recursive method? Describe the characteristics of recursive methods. What is an infinite recursion?

20.2 Write a recursive mathematical definition for computing 2^n for a positive integer n.

20.3 Write a recursive mathematical definition for computing x^n for a positive integer n and a real number x.

20.4 Write a recursive mathematical definition for computing $1 + 2 + 3 + \cdots + n$ for a positive integer.

20.5 How many times is the `factorial` method in Listing 20.1 invoked for `factorial(6)`?

20.6 How many times is the `fib` method in Listing 20.2 invoked for `fib(6)`?

Sections 20.4–20.6

20.7 Show the call stack for `isPalindrome("abcba")` using the methods declared in Listing 20.3 and Listing 20.4, respectively.

20.8 Show the call stack for `selectionSort(new double[]{2, 3, 5, 1})` using the method declared in Listing 20.5.

20.9 What is a recursive helper method?

Section 20.7 Towers of Hanoi

20.10 How many times is the `moveDisks` method in Listing 20.8 invoked for `moveDisks(5, 'A', 'B', 'C')`?

Section 20.9 Recursion versus Iteration

20.11 Which of the following statements are true?

■ Any recursive method can be converted into a nonrecursive method.
■ Recursive methods take more time and memory to execute than nonrecursive methods.
■ Recursive methods are *always* simpler than nonrecursive methods.
■ There is always a condition statement in a recursive method to check whether a base case is reached.

20.12 What is the cause for the stack overflow exception?

Comprehensive

20.13 Show the output of the following program:

```java
public class Test {
  public static void main(String[] args) {
    System.out.println(
      "Sum is " + xMethod(5));
  }

  public static int xMethod(int n) {
    if (n == 1)
      return 1;
    else
      return n + xMethod(n - 1);
  }
}
```

```java
public class Test {
  public static void main(String[] args) {
    xMethod(1234567);
  }

  public static void xMethod(int n) {
    if (n > 0) {
      System.out.print(n % 10);
      xMethod(n / 10);
    }
  }
}
```

20.14 Show the output of the following two programs:

```java
public class Test {
  public static void main(String[] args) {
    xMethod(5);
  }

  public static void xMethod(int n) {
    if (n > 0) {
      System.out.print(n + " ");
      xMethod(n - 1);
    }
  }
}
```

```java
public class Test {
  public static void main(String[] args) {
    xMethod(5);
  }

  public static void xMethod(int n) {
    if (n > 0) {
      xMethod(n - 1);
      System.out.print(n + " ");
    }
  }
}
```

20.15 What is wrong in the following method?

```java
public class Test {
  public static void main(String[] args) {
    xMethod(1234567);
  }

  public static void xMethod(double n) {
    if (n != 0) {
      System.out.print(n);
      xMethod(n / 10);
    }
  }
}
```

```java
public class Test {
  public static void main(String[] args) {
    Test test = new Test();
    System.out.println(test.toString());
  }

  public Test() {
    Test test = new Test();
  }
}
```

PROGRAMMING EXERCISES

Sections 20.2–20.3

20.1** (*Factorial*) Using the `BigInteger` class introduced in §11.12, you can find the factorial for a large number (e.g., `100!`). Write a program that prompts the user to enter an integer and displays its factorial. Implement the method using recursion.

20.2* (*Fibonacci numbers*) Rewrite the `fib` method in Listing 20.2 using iterations.

Hint: To compute `fib(n)` without recursion, you need to obtain `fib(n - 2)` and `fib(n - 1)` first. Let f0 and f1 denote the two previous Fibonacci numbers. The current Fibonacci number would then be `f0 + f1`. The algorithm can be described as follows:

```
f0 = 0; // For fib(0)
f1 = 1; // For fib(1)

for (int i = 1; i <= n; i++) {
  currentFib = f0 + f1;
  f0 = f1;
  f1 = currentFib;
}

// After the loop, currentFib is fib(n)
```

20.3* (*Computing greatest common divisor using recursion*) The `gcd(m, n)` can also be defined recursively as follows:

■ If `m % n` is `0`, `gcd (m, n)` is `n`.
■ Otherwise, `gcd(m, n)` is `gcd(n, m % n)`.

Write a recursive method to find the GCD. Write a test program that computes `gcd(24, 16)` and `gcd(255, 25)`.

20.4 (*Summing series*) Write a recursive method to compute the following series:

$$m(i) = 1 + \frac{1}{2} + \frac{1}{3} + \cdots + \frac{1}{i}$$

20.5 (*Summing series*) Write a recursive method to compute the following series:

$$m(i) = \frac{1}{3} + \frac{2}{5} + \frac{3}{7} + \frac{4}{9} + \frac{5}{11} + \frac{6}{13} + \cdots + \frac{i}{2i + 1}$$

20.6* (*Summing series*) Write a recursive method to compute the following series:

$$m(i) = \frac{1}{2} + \frac{2}{3} + \cdots + \frac{i}{i + 1}$$

20.7* (*Fibonacci series*) Modify Listing 20.2, ComputeFibonacci.java, so that the program finds the number of times the `fib` method is called.

(*Hint*: Use a static variable and increment it every time the method is called.)

Section 20.4 Problem Solving Using Recursion

20.8* (*Printing the digits in an integer reversely*) Write a recursive method that displays an `int` value reversely on the console using the following header:

public static void reverseDisplay(**int** value)

For example, `reverseDisplay(12345)` displays `54321`.

20.9* (*Printing the characters in a string reversely*) Write a recursive method that displays a string reversely on the console using the following header:

public static void reverseDisplay(String value)

For example, `reverseDisplay("abcd")` displays `dcba`.

20.10* (*Occurrences of a specified character in a string*) Write a recursive method that finds the number of occurrences of a specified letter in a string using the following method header.

```
public static int count(String str, char a)
```

For example, count("Welcome", 'e') returns 2.

20.11* (*Summing the digits in an integer using recursion*) Write a recursive method that computes the sum of the digits in an integer. Use the following method header:

```
public static int sumDigits(long n)
```

For example, sumDigits(234) returns 2 + 3 + 4 = 9.

Section 20.5 Recursive Helper Methods

20.12** (*Printing the characters in a string reversely*) Rewrite Exercise 20.9 using a helper method to pass the substring high index to the method. The helper method header is:

```
public static void reverseDisplay(String value, int high)
```

20.13* (*Finding the largest number in an array*) Write a recursive method that returns the largest integer in an array.

20.14* (*Finding the number of uppercase letters in a string*) Write a recursive method to return the number of uppercase letters in a string.

20.15* (*Occurrences of a specified character in a string*) Rewrite Exercise 20.10 using a helper method to pass the substring high index to the method. The helper method header is:

```
public static int count(String str, char a, int high)
```

20.16* (*Finding the number of uppercase letters in an array*) Write a recursive method to return the number of uppercase letters in an array of characters. You need to declare the following two methods. The second one is a recursive helper method.

```
public static int count(char[] chars)
public static int count(char[] chars, int high)
```

20.17* (*Occurrences of a specified character in an array*) Write a recursive method that finds the number of occurrences of a specified character in an array. You need to declare the following two methods. The second one is a recursive helper method.

```
public static int count(char[] chars, char ch)
public static int count(char[] chars, char ch, int high)
```

Sections 20.6 Tower of Hanoi

20.18* (*Towers of Hanoi*) Modify Listing 20.8, TowersOfHanoi.java, so that the program finds the number of moves needed to move *n* disks from tower A to tower B.

(*Hint*: Use a static variable and increment it every time the method is called.)

20.19* (*Sierpinski triangle*) Revise Listing 20.9 to develop an applet that lets the user use the *Increase* and *Decrease* buttons to increase or decrease the current order by 1, as shown in Figure 20.12(a). The initial order is 0. If the current order is 0, the *Decrease* button is ignored.

(a)   (b)

FIGURE 20.12 (a) Exercise 20.19 uses the *Increase* and *Decrease* buttons to increase or decrease the current order by 1. (b) Exercise 20.10 draws ovals using a recursive method.

20.20* (*Displaying circles*) Write a Java applet that displays ovals, as shown in Figure 20.12(b). The ovals are centered in the panel. The gap between two adjacent ovals is **10** pixels, and the gap between the panel and the largest oval is also **10**.

Comprehensive

20.21* (*Decimal to binary*) Write a recursive method that converts a decimal number into a binary number as a string. The method header is as follows:

```
public static String convertDecimalToBinary(int value)
```

20.22* (*Decimal to hex*) Write a recursive method that converts a decimal number into a hex number as a string. The method header is as follows:

```
public static String convertDecimalToHex(int value)
```

20.23* (*Binary to decimal*) Write a recursive method that parses a binary number as a string into a decimal integer. The method header is as follows:

```
public static int parseBinary(String binaryString)
```

20.24* (*Hex to decimal*) Write a recursive method that parses a hex number as a string into a decimal integer. The method header is as follows:

```
public static int parseHex(String hexString)
```

20.25** (*String permutation*) Write a recursive method to print all the permutations of a string. For example, for a string **abc**, the printout is

```
abc
acb
bac
bca
cab
cba
```

(*Hint*: Declare the following two methods. The second is a helper method.)

```
public static void displayPermuation(String s)
public static void displayPermuation(String s1, String s2)
```

The first method simply invokes `displayPermuation("", s)`. The second method uses a loop to move a character from `s2` to `s1` and recursively invoke it with a new `s1` and `s2`. The base case is that `s2` is empty and prints `s1` to the console.

20.26** (*Creating a maze*) Write an applet that will find a path in a maze, as shown in Figure 20.13(a). The applet should also run as an application. The maze is represented by an 8×8 board. The path must meet the following conditions:

- The path is between the upper-left corner cell and the lower-right corner cell in the maze.
- The applet enables the user to insert or remove a mark on a cell. A path consists of adjacent unmarked cells. Two cells are said to be adjacent if they are horizontal or vertical neighbors, but not if they are diagonal neighbors.
- The path does not contain cells that form a square. The path in Figure 20.13(b), for example, does not meet this condition. (The condition makes a path easy to identify on the board.)

(a) Correct path   (b) Illegal path

FIGURE 20.13 The program finds a path from the upper-left corner to the bottom-right corner.

20.27** (*Koch snowflake fractal*) The text presented the Sierpinski triangle fractal. In this exercise, you will write an applet to display another fractal, called the *Koch snowflake*, named after a famous Swedish mathematician. A Koch snowflake is created as follows:

1. Begin with an equilateral triangle, which is considered to be the Koch fractal of order (or level) 0, as shown in Figure 20.14(a).
2. Divide each line in the shape into three equal line segments and draw an outward equilateral triangle with the middle line segment as the base to create a Koch fractal of order 1, as shown in Figure 20.14(b).
3. Repeat step 2 to create a Koch fractal of order 2, 3, . . . , and so on, as shown in Figure 20.14(c).

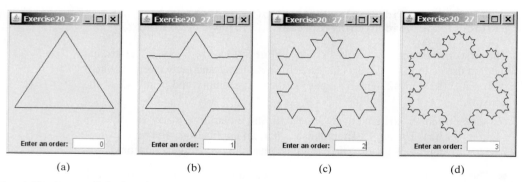

(a)   (b)   (c)   (d)

FIGURE 20.14   A Koch snowflake is a fractal starting with a triangle.

20.28**   (*Nonrecursive directory size*) Rewrite Listing 20.7, DirectorySize.java, without using recursion.

20.29*   (*Number of files in a directory*) Write a program that prompts the user to enter a directory and displays the number of files in the directory.

Video Note
Search a string in a directory

20.30**   (*Finding words*) Write a program that finds all occurrences of a word in all the files under a directory, recursively. Pass the parameters from the command line as follows:

```
java Exercise20_30 dirName word
```

20.31**   (*Replacing words*) Write a program that replaces all occurrences of a word with a new word in all the files under a directory, recursively. Pass the parameters from the command line as follows:

```
java Exercise20_31 dirName oldWord newWord
```

Don't modify the file if it does not contain the oldWord.

20.32***   (*Game: Knight's Tour*) The Knight's Tour is an ancient puzzle. The objective is to move a knight, starting from any square on a chessboard, to every other square once, as shown in Figure 20.15(a). Note that the knight makes only L-shape moves (two spaces in one direction and one space in a perpendicular direction). As shown in Figure 20.15(b), the knight can move to eight squares. Write a program that displays the moves for the knight in an applet, as shown in Figure 20.15(b).

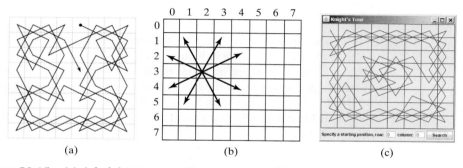

(a)   (b)   (c)

FIGURE 20.15   (a) A knight traverses all squares once. (b) A knight makes an L-shape move. (c) An applet displays a knight tour path.

(*Hint*: A brute-force approach for this problem is to move the knight from one square to another available square arbitrarily. Using such an approach, your program will take a long time to finish. A better approach is to employ some heuristics. A knight has two, three, four, six, or eight possible moves, depending on its location. Intuitively, you should attempt to move the knight to the least accessible squares first and leave those more accessible squares open, so there will be a better chance of success in the end of the search.)

20.33*** (*Game: Knight's Tour animation*) Write an applet for the Knight's Tour problem. Your applet should let the user move a knight to any starting square and click the *Solve* button to animate a knight moving along the path, as shown in Figure 20.16.

FIGURE 20.16 A knight traverses along the path.

20.34** (*Game: Sudoku*) Rewrite Listing 6.12, Sudoku.java, using recursion.

20.35** (*H-tree fractal*) An H-tree is a fractal defined as follows:

1. Begin with a letter H. The three lines of the H are of the same length, as shown in Figure 20.17(a).
2. The letter H has four endpoints. Draw an H centered at each of the four endpoints to an H-tree of order 1, as shown in Figure 20.17(b). These H's are half the size of the H that contains the four endpoints.
3. Repeat step 2 to create a H-tree of order 2, 3, ..., and so on, as shown in Figure 20.17(c).

     (a)   (b)   (c)   (d)

FIGURE 20.17 An H-tree is a fractal starting with three lines of equal length in an H-shape.

The H-tree is used in VLSI design as a clock distribution network for routing timing signals to all parts of a chip with equal propagation delays. Write an applet that draws an H-tree, as shown in Figure 20.17.

20.36*** (*Game: all Sudoku solutions*) Rewrite Exercise 20.34 to find all possible solutions to a Sudoku problem.

20.37*** (*Game: multiple Eight Queens solution*) Write an applet to display all possible solutions for the Eight Queens puzzle in a scroll pane, as shown in Figure 20.18. For each solution, put a label to denote the solution number.

FIGURE 20.18 All solutions are placed in a scroll pane.

CHAPTER 21

GENERICS

Objectives

- To describe the benefits of generics (§21.1).

- To use generic classes and interfaces (§21.2).

- To declare generic classes and interfaces (§21.3).

- To explain why generic types can improve reliability and readability (§21.3).

- To declare and use generic methods and bounded generic types (§21.4).

- To use raw types for backward compatibility (§21.5).

- To explain why wildcard generic types are necessary (§21.6).

- To describe generic type erasure and list certain restrictions and limitations on generic types caused by type erasure (§21.7).

- To design and implement generic matrix classes (§21.8).

21.1 Introduction

Generics is the capability to parameterize types. With this capability, you can define a class or a method with generic types that can be substituted using concrete types by the compiler. For example, you may define a generic stack class that stores the elements of a generic type. From this generic class, you may create a stack object for holding strings and a stack object for holding numbers. Here, strings and numbers are concrete types that replace the generic type.

The key benefit of generics is to enable errors to be detected at compile time rather than at runtime. A generic class or method permits you to specify allowable types of objects that the class or method may work with. If you attempt to use the class or method with an incompatible object, the compiler can detect the errors.

This chapter explains how to declare and use generic classes, interfaces, and methods, and demonstrates how generics can be used to improve software reliability and readability. This chapter can be intertwined with Chapter 11, "Abstract Classes and Interfaces."

21.2 Motivations and Benefits

Since JDK 1.5, Java allows you to declare generic classes, interfaces, and methods. Several interfaces and classes in the Java API are modified using generics. For example, prior to JDK 1.5 the `java.lang.Comparable` interface was declared as shown in Figure 21.1(a), but in JDK 1.5 is modified as shown in Figure 21.1(b).

```
package java.lang;

public interface Comparable {
   public int compareTo(Object o)
}
```
(a) Prior to JDK 1.5

```
package java.lang;

public interface Comparable<T> {
   public int compareTo(T o)
}
```
(b) JDK 1.5

FIGURE 21.1 The `java.lang.Comparable` interface is redefined in JDK 1.5 with a generic type.

Here, `<T>` represents a *formal generic type*, which can be replaced later with an *actual concrete type*. Replacing a generic type is called a *generic instantiation*. By convention, a single capital letter such as `E` or `T` is used to denote a formal generic type.

To see the benefits of using generics, let us examine the code in Figures 21.2. The statement in Figure 21.2(a) declares that `c` is a reference variable whose type is `Comparable` and invokes the `compareTo` method to compare a `Date` object with a string. The code compiles fine, but has a runtime error because a string cannot be compared with a date.

```
Comparable c = new Date();
System.out.println(c.compareTo("red"));
```
(a) Prior to JDK 1.5

```
Comparable<Date> c = new Date();
System.out.println(c.compareTo("red"));
```
(b) JDK 1.5

FIGURE 21.2 The new generic type detects possible errors at compile time.

The statement in Figure 21.2(b) declares that `c` is a reference variable whose type is `Comparable<Date>` and invokes the `compareTo` method to compare a `Date` object with a string. The code has a compile error, because the argument passed to the `compareTo` method must be of the `Date` type. Since the errors can be detected at compile time rather than at runtime, the generic type makes the program more reliable.

ArrayList was introduced in §10.10, "The ArrayList Class." This class is a generic class in JDK 1.5. Figure 21.3 shows the class diagram for ArrayList prior to JDK 1.5 and in JDK 1.5, respectively.

java.util.ArrayList
+ArrayList()
+add(o: Object): void
+add(index: int, o: Object): void
+clear(): void
+contains(o: Object):boolean
+get(index:int): Object
+indexOf(o: Object): int
+isEmpty(): boolean
+lastIndexOf(o: Object): int
+remove(o: Object): boolean
+size(): int
+remove(index: int): boolean
+set(index: int, o: Object): Object

(a) ArrayList before JDK 1.5

java.util.ArrayList<E>
+ArrayList()
+add(o: E): void
+add(index: int, o: E): void
+clear(): void
+contains(o: Object): boolean
+get(index:int): E
+indexOf(o: Object): int
+isEmpty(): boolean
+lastIndexOf(o: Object): int
+remove(o: Object): boolean
+size(): int
+remove(index: int): boolean
+set(index: int, o: E): E

(b) ArrayList in JDK 1.5

FIGURE 21.3 ArrayList is a generic class in JDK 1.5.

For example, the following statement creates a list for strings:

```
ArrayList<String> list = new ArrayList<String>();
```

You can now add *only strings* into the list. For example,

only string allowed

```
list.add("Red");
```

If you attempt to add a nonstring, a compile error will occur. For example, the following statement is now illegal, because list can contain only strings.

```
list.add(new Integer(1));
```

Generic types must be reference types. You cannot replace a generic type with a primitive type such as int, double, or char. For example, the following statement is wrong:

generic reference type

```
ArrayList<int> intList = new ArrayList<int>();
```

To create an ArrayList object for int values, you have to use:

```
ArrayList<Integer> intList = new ArrayList<Integer>();
```

You can add an int value to intList. For example,

```
intList.add(5);
```

Java automatically wraps 5 into new Integer(5). This is called *autoboxing*, as introduced in §11.11, "Automatic Conversion between Primitive Types and Wrapper Class Types."

autoboxing

Casting is not needed to retrieve a value from a list with a specified element type, because the compiler already knows the element type. For example, the following statements create a list that contains strings, add strings to the list, and retrieve strings from the list.

no casting needed

```
1 ArrayList<String> list = new ArrayList<String>();
2 list.add("Red");
3 list.add("White");
4 String s = list.get(0); // No casting is needed
```

Prior to JDK 1.5, without using generics, you would have to cast the return value to **String** as follows:

```
String s = (String)(list.get(0)); // Casting needed prior to JDK 1.5
```

If the elements are of wrapper types, such as **Integer**, **Double**, and **Character**, you can directly assign an element to a primitive type variable. This is called *autounboxing*, as introduced in §11.11. For example, see the following code:

autounboxing

```
1 ArrayList<Double> list = new ArrayList<Double>();
2 list.add(5.5); // 5.5 is automatically converted to new Double(5.5)
3 list.add(3.0); // 3.0 is automatically converted to new Double(3.0)
4 Double doubleObject = list.get(0); // No casting is needed
5 double d = list.get(1);  // Automatically converted to double
```

In lines 2 and 3, **5.5** and **3.0** are automatically converted into **Double** objects and added to **list**. In line 4, the first element in **list** is assigned to a **Double** variable. No casting is necessary, because list is declared for **Double** objects. In line 5, the second element in **list** is assigned to a **double** variable. The object in **list.get(1)** is automatically converted into a primitive type value.

21.3 Declaring Generic Classes and Interfaces

Video Note
Design generic class

Let us revise the stack class in §10.11, "A Custom Stack Class," to generalize the element type with a generic type. The new stack class, named **GenericStack**, is shown in Figure 21.4 and is implemented in Listing 21.1.

GenericStack\<E>	
-list: java.util.ArrayList \<E>	An array list to store elements.
+GenericStack()	Creates an empty stack.
+getSize(): int	Returns the number of elements in this stack.
+peek(): E	Returns the top element in this stack.
+pop(): E	Returns and removes the top element in this stack.
+push(o: E): E	Adds a new element to the top of this stack.
+isEmpty(): boolean	Return true if the stack is empty.

FIGURE 21.4 The **GenericStack** class encapsulates the stack storage and provides the operations for manipulating the stack.

LISTING 21.1 GenericStack.java

generic type **E** declared
generic array list

getSize

```
1 public class GenericStack<E> {
2   private java.util.ArrayList<E> list = new java.util.ArrayList<E>();
3
4   public int getSize() {
5     return list.size();
6   }
7
```

```
 8    public E peek() {                                              peek
 9      return list.get(getSize() - 1);
10    }
11
12    public E push(E o) {                                           push
13      list.add(o);
14      return o;
15    }
16
17    public E pop() {                                               pop
18      E o = list.get(getSize() - 1);
19      list.remove(getSize() - 1);
20      return o;
21    }
22
23    public boolean isEmpty() {                                     isEmpty
24      return list.isEmpty();
25    }
26 }
```

Here is an example that creates a stack to hold strings and adds three strings to the stack:

```
GenericStack<String> stack1 = new GenericStack<String>();
stack1.push("London");
stack1.push("Paris");
stack1.push("Berlin");
```

Here is another example that creates a stack to hold integers and adds three integers to the stack:

```
GenericStack<Integer> stack2 = new GenericStack<Integer>();
stack2.push(1); // auto boxing 1 to new Integer(1)
stack2.push(2);
stack2.push(3);
```

Instead of using a generic type, you could simply make the type element `Object`, which can accommodate any object type. However, using generic types can improve software reliability and readability, because certain errors can be detected at compile time rather than at runtime. For example, since `stack1` is declared `GenericStack-<String>`, only strings can be added to the stack. It would be a compile error if you attempted to add an integer to `stack1`.

benefits of using generic types

Caution

To create a stack of strings, you use `new GenericStack<String>()`. This could mislead you into thinking that the constructor of `GenericStack` should be declared as

generic class constructor

```
public GenericStack<E>()
```

This is wrong. It should be declared

```
public GenericStack()
```

Note

Occasionally, a generic class may have more than one parameter. In this case, place the parameters together inside the brackets, separated by commas, such as `<E1, E2, E3>`.

multiple generic parameters

inheritance with generics

Note

You can declare a class or an interface as a subtype of a generic class or interface. For example, the `java.lang.String` class is declared to implement the `Comparable` interface in the Java API as follows:

```
public class String implements Comparable<String>
```

21.4 Generic Methods

You can declare generic interfaces (e.g., the `Comparable` interface in Figure 21.1(b)) and classes (e.g., the `GenericStack` class in Listing 21.1). You can also use generic types to declare generic methods. For example, Listing 21.2 declares a generic method `print` (lines 10–14) to print an array of objects. Line 6 passes an array of integer objects to invoke the generic `print` method. Line 7 invokes `print` with an array of strings.

LISTING 21.2 GenericMethodDemo.java

```
 1 public class GenericMethodDemo {
 2   public static void main(String[] args ) {
 3     Integer[] integers = {1, 2, 3, 4, 5};
 4     String[] strings = {"London", "Paris", "New York", "Austin"};
 5
 6     GenericMethodDemo.<Integer>print(integers);
 7     GenericMethodDemo.<String>print(strings);
 8   }
 9
10   public static <E> void print(E[] list) {
11     for (int i = 0; i < list.length; i++)
12       System.out.print(list[i] + " ");
13     System.out.println();
14   }
15 }
```

generic method

invoke generic method

To invoke a generic method, prefix the method name with the actual type in angle brackets. For example,

```
GenericMethodDemo.<Integer>print(integers);
GenericMethodDemo.<String>print(strings);
```

A generic type can be bounded. For example, Listing 21.3 revises the `equalArea` method in Listing 11.4, TestGeometricObject.java, to test whether two geometric objects have the same area. The bounded generic type `<E extends GeometricObject>` (line 7) specifies that E is a generic subtype of `GeometricObject`. You must invoke `equalArea` by passing two instances of `GeometricObject`.

bounded generic type

Video Note
Bounded types and raw types

Rectangle in Listing 11.2
Circle in Listing 11.3

LISTING 21.3 BoundedTypeDemo.java

```
 1 public class BoundedTypeDemo {
 2   public static void main(String[] args ) {
 3     Rectangle rectangle = new Rectangle(2, 2);
 4     Circle circle = new Circle(2);
 5
 6     System.out.println("Same area? " +
 7       BoundedTypeDemo.<GeometricObject>equalArea(rectangle, circle));
 8   }
 9
10   public static <E extends GeometricObject> boolean equalArea(
11       E object1, E object2) {
```

```
12        return object1.getArea() == object2.getArea();
13    }
14 }
```

bounded type

Note

An unbounded generic type `<E>` is the same as `<E extends Object>`.

Note

To declare a generic type for a class, place the generic type after the class name, such as `GenericStack<E>`. To declare a generic type for a method, place the generic type before the method return type, such as `<E> void max(E o1, E o2)`.

generic class parameter vs. generic method parameter

21.5 Raw Type and Backward Compatibility

You may use a generic class without specifying a concrete type like this:

```
GenericStack stack = new GenericStack(); // raw type
```

This is roughly equivalent to

```
GenericStack<Object> stack = new GenericStack<Object>();
```

A class such as `GenericStack` used without a type parameter is called a *raw type*. Use of raw type is allowed for backward compatibility with the earlier versions of JDK. For example, generic type is used in `java.lang.Comparable`, since JDK 1.5, but a lot of code still uses the raw type `Comparable`, as shown in Listing 21.4 (also see the `Max` class in §11.5, "Example: The `Comparable` Interface"):

raw type
backward compatibility

LISTING 21.4 Max.java

```
1 public class Max {
2    /** Return the maximum between two objects */
3    public static Comparable max(Comparable o1, Comparable o2) {
4      if (o1.compareTo(o2) > 0)
5        return o1;
6      else
7        return o2;
8    }
9 }
```

raw type

`Comparable o1` and `Comparable o2` are raw type declarations. *Raw type is unsafe*. For example, you might invoke the `max` method using

```
Max.max("Welcome", 23); // 23 is autoboxed into new Integer(23)
```

This would cause a runtime error, because you cannot compare a string with an integer object. The new JDK 1.5 compiler displays a warning on line 3 when compiled with the option *–Xlint:unchecked*, as shown in Figure 21.5.

Xlint:unchecked

```
Command Prompt                                            _|□|x|
C:\book>javac -Xlint:unchecked Max.java
Max.java:6: warning: [unchecked] unchecked call to compareTo(T) as a member of t
he raw type java.lang.Comparable
    if (o1.compareTo(o2) > 0)

1 warning

C:\book>_
```

FIGURE 21.5 The unchecked warnings are displayed using the compiler option *–Xlint:unchecked*.

A better way to write the `max` method is to use a generic type, as shown in Listing 21.5.

LISTING 21.5 Max1.java

bounded type

```
1 public class Max1 {
2   /** Return the maximum between two objects */
3   public static <E extends Comparable<E>> E max(E o1, E o2) {
4     if (o1.compareTo(o2) > 0)
5       return o1;
6     else
7       return o2;
8   }
9 }
```

If you invoke the `max` method using

```
Max1.max("Welcome", 23); // 23 is autoboxed into new Integer(23)
```

a compile error will be displayed, because two arguments of the `max` method in `Max1` must have the same type (e.g., two strings or two integer objects). Furthermore, the type `E` must be a subtype of `Comparable<E>`.

As another example, in the following code you may declare a raw type `stack` in line 1, assign `new GenericStack<String>` to it in line 2, and push a string and an integer object to the stack in lines 3 and 4.

```
1 GenericStack stack;
2 stack = new GenericStack<String>();
3 stack.push("Welcome to Java");
4 stack.push(new Integer(2));
```

Line 4 is unsafe because the stack is intended to store strings, but an `Integer` object is added into the stack. Line 3 should be OK, but the compiler will show warnings on both line 3 and line 4, because it cannot follow the semantic meaning of the program. All the compiler knows is that stack is a raw type, and it is unsafe to perform certain operations. Therefore, warnings are displayed to alert potential programs.

Tip
Since raw types are unsafe, this book will not use them from here on.

21.6 Wildcard Generic Types

What are wildcard generic types? Listing 21.6 gives an example to demonstrate the needs. The example declares a generic `max` method for finding the maximum in a stack of numbers (lines 12–22). The main method creates a stack of integer objects, adds three integers to the stack, and invokes the `max` method to find the maximum number in the stack.

LISTING 21.6 WildCardDemo1.java

GenericStack <Integer>
type

```
1 public class WildCardDemo1 {
2   public static void main(String[] args ) {
3     GenericStack<Integer> intStack = new GenericStack<Integer>();
4     intStack.push(1); // 1 is autoboxed into new Integer(1)
5     intStack.push(2);
6     intStack.push(-2);
7
8     System.out.print("The max number is " + max(intStack));
9   }
```

```
10
11      /** Find the maximum in a stack of numbers */
12      public static double max(GenericStack<Number> stack) {
13        double max = stack.pop().doubleValue(); // Initialize max
14
15        while (!stack.isEmpty()) {
16          double value = stack.pop().doubleValue();
17          if (value > max)
18            max = value;
19        }
20
21        return max;
22      }
23    }
```

GenericStack<Number>
type

The program in Listing 21.6 has a compile error in line 8 because `intStack` is not an instance of `GenericStack<Number>`. So you cannot invoke `max(intStack)`.

The fact is that `Integer` is a subtype of `Number`, but `GenericStack<Integer>` is not a subtype of `GenericStack<Number>`. To circumvent this problem, use wildcard generic types. A wildcard generic type has three forms—`?`, `? extends T`, or `? super T`, where `T` is a generic type.

The first form, `?`, called an *unbounded wildcard*, is the same as `? extends Object`. The second form, `? extends T`, called a *bounded wildcard*, represents `T` or an unknown subtype of `T`. The third form, `? super T`, called a *lower-bound wildcard*, denotes `T` or an unknown supertype of `T`.

unbounded wildcard
bounded wildcard
lower bound wildcard

You can fix the error by replacing line 12 in Listing 21.6 as follows:

```
public static double max(GenericStack<? extends Number> stack) {
```

`<? extends Number>` is a wildcard type that represents `Number` or a subtype of `Number`. So it is legal to invoke `max(new GenericStack<Integer>())` or `max(new GenericStack<Double>())`.

Listing 21.7 shows an example of using the `?` wildcard in the `print` method that prints objects in a stack and empties the stack. `<?>` is a wildcard that represents any object type. It is equivalent to `<? Extends Object>`. What happens if you replace `GenericStack <?>` by `GenericStack <Object>`? It would be wrong to invoke `print(intStack)`, because `instack` is not an instance of `GenericStack<Object>`. Please note that `GenericStack<Integer>` is not a subtype of `GenericStack<Object>`, although `Integer` is a subtype of `Object`.

LISTING 21.7 WildCardDemo2.java

```
1  public class WildCardDemo2 {
2    public static void main(String[] args ) {
3      GenericStack<Integer> intStack = new GenericStack<Integer>();
4      intStack.push(1); // 1 is autoboxed into new Integer(1)
5      intStack.push(2);
6      intStack.push(-2);
7
8      print(intStack);
9    }
10
11     /** Prints objects and empties the stack */
12     public static void print(GenericStack<?> stack) {
13       while (!stack.isEmpty()) {
14         System.out.print(stack.pop() + " ");
15       }
16     }
17   }
```

GenericStack<Integer>
type

wild card type

why **<? Super T>**

When is the wildcard <? super T> needed? Consider the example in Listing 21.8. The example creates a stack of strings in **stack1** (line 3) and a stack of objects in **stack2** (line 4) and invokes **add(stack1, stack2)** (line 8) to add the strings in **stack1** into **stack2**. **GenericStack <? super T>** is used to declare **stack2** in line 13. If **<? super T>** is replaced by **<T>**, a compile error will occur on **add(stack1, stack2)** in line 8, because **stack1**'s type is **GenericStack<String>** and **stack2**'s type is **GenericStack<Object>**. **<? super T>** represents type **T** or a supertype of **T**. **GenericStack<Object>** is a subtype of **GenericStack <? super String>**.

LISTING 21.8 WildCardDemo3.java

GenericStack<Integer>
type

```
 1  public class WildCardDemo3 {
 2    public static void main(String[] args) {
 3      GenericStack<String> stack1 = new GenericStack<String>();
 4      GenericStack<Object> stack2 = new GenericStack<Object>();
 5      stack2.push("Java");
 6      stack2.push(2);
 7      stack1.push("Sun");
 8      add(stack1, stack2);
 9      WildCardDemo2.print(stack2);
10    }
11
12    public static <T> void add(GenericStack<T> stack1,
13        GenericStack<? super T> stack2) {
14      while (!stack1.isEmpty())
15        stack2.push(stack1.pop());
16    }
17  }
```

GenericStack<?> type

The inheritance relationship involving generic types and wildcard types is summarized in Figure 21.6. In this figure, **A** and **B** represent classes or interfaces, and **E** is a generic type parameter.

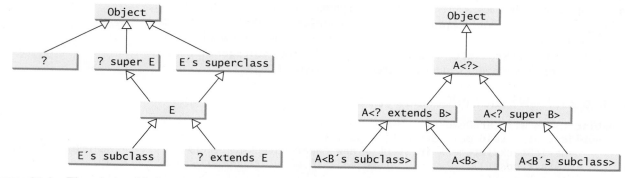

FIGURE 21.6 The relationship between generic types and wildcard types.

21.7 Erasure and Restrictions on Generics

type erasure

Generics are implemented using an approach called *type erasure*. The compiler uses the generic type information to compile the code, but erases it afterward. So the generic information is not available at runtime. This approach enables the generic code to be backward compatible with the legacy code that uses raw types.

erase generics

The generics are present at compile time. Once the compiler confirms that a generic type is used safely, it converts it to a raw type. For example, the compiler checks whether generics is used correctly for the following code in (a) and translates it into the equivalent code in (b) for runtime use. The code in (b) uses the raw type.

```
ArrayList<String> list = new ArrayList<String> ();
list.add("Oklahoma");
String state = list.get(0);
```

(a)

```
ArrayList list = new ArrayList();
list.add("Oklahoma");
String state = (String)(list.get(0));
```

(b)

When generic classes, interfaces, and methods are compiled, the compiler replaces the generic type with the `Object` type. For example, the compiler would convert the following method in (a) into (b).

replace generic type

```
public static <E> void print(E[] list) {
  for (int i = 0; i < list.length; i++)
    System.out.print(list[i] + " ");
  System.out.println();
}
```

(a)

```
public static Object void print(Object[] list) {
  for (int i = 0; i < list.length; i++)
    System.out.print(list[i] + " ");
  System.out.println();
}
```

(b)

If a generic type is bounded, the compiler replaces the generic type with the bounded type. For example, the compiler would convert the following method in (a) into (b).

replace bounded type

```
public static <E extends GeometricObject>
    boolean equalArea(
      E object1,
      E object2) {
  return object1.getArea() ==
    object2.getArea();
}
```

(a)

```
public static GeometricObject
    boolean equalArea(
      GeometricObject object1,
      GeometricObject object2) {
  return object1.getArea() ==
    object2.getArea();
}
```

(b)

It is important to note that a generic class is shared by all its instances regardless of its actual concrete type. Suppose `list1` and `list2` are created as follows:

important fact

```
ArrayList<String> list1 = new ArrayList<String>();
ArrayList<Integer> list2 = new ArrayList<Integer>();
```

Although `ArrayList<String>` and `ArrayList<Integer>` are two types at compile time, only one `ArrayList` class is loaded into the JVM at runtime. `list1` and `list2` are both instances of `ArrayList`. So the following statements display true.

```
System.out.println(list1 instanceof ArrayList);
System.out.println(list2 instanceof ArrayList);
```

But the expression `list1 instanceof ArrayList<String>` is wrong. Since `ArrayList<String>` is not stored as a separate class in the JVM, using it at runtime makes no sense.

Because generic types are erased at runtime, there are certain restrictions on how generic types can be used. Here are some of the restrictions:

Restriction 1: Cannot Create an Instance of a Generic Type

You cannot create an instance using a generic type parameter. For example, the following statement is wrong.

```
E object = new E();
```

no **new** E()

The reason is that `new E()` is executed at runtime, but the generic type E is not available at runtime.

Restriction 2: Generic Array Creation Is Not Allowed

You cannot create an array using a generic type parameter. For example, the following statement is wrong.

no **new E[5]**

```
E[] elements = new E[capacity];
```

You can circumvent this limitation by creating an array of the `Object` type and then casting it to `E[]`, as follows:

```
E[] elements = (E[]) new Object[capacity];
```

unavoidable compile warning

However, casting to `(E[])` causes an unchecked compile warning. The warning occurs because the compiler is not certain that casting will succeed at runtime. For example, if E is `String` and `new Object[]` is an array of `Integer` objects, `(String[])(new Object[])` would cause a `ClassCastException`. This type of compile warning is the limitation of Java generics and is unavoidable.

Generic array creation using a generic class is not allowed, either. For example, the following code is wrong:

```
ArrayList<String>[] list = new ArrayList<String>[10];
```

You can use the following code to circumvent this restriction:

```
ArrayList<String>[] list = (ArrayList<String>[]) new ArrayList[10];
```

You will get a compile warning.

Restriction 3: A Generic Type Parameter of a Class Is Not Allowed in a Static Context

Since all instances of a generic class have the same runtime class, the static variables and methods of a generic class are shared by all its instances. Therefore, it is illegal to refer to a generic type parameter for a class in a static method, field, or initializer. For example, the following code is illegal:

```
public class Test<E> {
  public static void m(E o1) { // Illegal
  }

  public static E o1; // Illegal

  static {
    E o2; // Illegal
  }
}
```

Restriction 4: Exception Classes Cannot be Generic

A generic class may not extend `java.lang.Throwable`, so the following class declaration would be illegal:

```
public class MyException<T> extends Exception {

}
```

Why? If it were allowed, you would have a `catch` clause for `MyException<T>` as follows:

```
try {
    ...
}
catch (MyException<T> ex) {
    ...
}
```

The JVM has to check the exception thrown from the `try` clause to see if it matches the type specified in a `catch` clause. This is impossible, because the type information is not present at runtime.

21.8 Case Study: Generic Matrix Class

This section presents a case study on designing classes for matrix operations using generic types. The addition and multiplication operations for all matrices are similar except that their element types differ. Therefore, you can design a superclass that describes the common operations shared by matrices of all types regardless of their element types, and you can create subclasses tailored to specific types of matrices. This case study gives implementations for two types: `int` and `Rational`. For the `int` type, the wrapper class `Integer` should be used to wrap an `int` value into an object, so that the object is passed in the methods for operations.

The class diagram is shown in Figure 21.7. The methods `addMatrix` and `multiplyMatrix` add and multiply two matrices of a generic type `E[][]`. The static method `printResult` displays the matrices, the operations, and their result. The methods `add`, `multiply`, and `zero` are abstract, because their implementations depend on the specific type of the array elements. For example, the `zero()` method returns `0` for the `Integer` type and `0/1` for the `Rational` type. These methods will be implemented in the subclasses in which the matrix element type is specified.

FIGURE 21.7 The `GenericMatrix` class is an abstract superclass for `IntegerMatrix` and `RationalMatrix`.

`IntegerMatrix` and `RationalMatrix` are concrete subclasses of `GenericMatrix`. These two classes implement the `add`, `multiply`, and `zero` methods defined in the `GenericMatrix` class.

Listing 21.9 implements the `GenericMatrix` class. `<E extends Number>` in line 3 specifies that the generic type is a subtype of `Number`. Three abstract methods `add`, `multiply`, and `zero` are defined in lines 3, 6, and 9. These methods are abstract because we cannot implement them without knowing the exact type of the elements. The `addMaxtrix` (lines 12–30) and `multiplyMatrix` (lines 33–57) methods implement the methods for adding and multiplying two matrices. All these methods must be nonstatic, because they use generic type `E`. The `printResult` method (lines 59–84) is static because it is not tied to specific instances.

The matrix element type is generic. This enables you to use an object of any class as long as you can implement the abstract **add**, **multiply**, and **zero** methods in subclasses.

The **addMatrix** and **multiplyMatrix** methods (lines 12–56) are concrete methods. They are ready to use as long as the **add**, **multiply**, and **zero** methods are implemented in the subclasses.

The **addMatrix** and **multiplyMatrix** methods check the bounds of the matrices before performing operations. If the two matrices have incompatible bounds, the program throws an exception (lines 17, 37).

LISTING 21.9 GenericMatrix.java

```java
 1  public abstract class GenericMatrix<E extends Number> {
 2    /** Abstract method for adding two elements of the matrices */
 3    protected abstract E add(E o1, E o2);
 4
 5    /** Abstract method for multiplying two elements of the matrices */
 6    protected abstract E multiply(E o1, E o2);
 7
 8    /** Abstract method for defining zero for the matrix element */
 9    protected abstract E zero();
10
11    /** Add two matrices */
12    public E[][] addMatrix(E[][] matrix1, E[][] matrix2) {
13      // Check bounds of the two matrices
14      if ((matrix1.length != matrix2.length) ||
15          (matrix1[0].length != matrix2.length)) {
16        throw new RuntimeException(
17          "The matrices do not have the same size");
18      }
19
20      E[][] result =
21        (E[][])new Number[matrix1.length][matrix1[0].length];
22
23      // Perform addition
24      for (int i = 0; i < result.length; i++)
25        for (int j = 0; j < result[i].length; j++) {
26          result[i][j] = add(matrix1[i][j], matrix2[i][j]);
27        }
28
29      return result;
30    }
31
32    /** Multiply two matrices */
33    public E[][] multiplyMatrix(E[][] matrix1, E[][] matrix2){
34      // Check bounds
35      if (matrix1[0].length != matrix2.length) {
36        throw new RuntimeException(
37          "The matrices do not have compatible size");
38      }
39
40      // Create result matrix
41      E[][] result =
42        (E[][])new Number[matrix1.length][matrix2[0].length];
43
44      // Perform multiplication of two matrices
45      for (int i = 0; i < result.length; i++) {
46        for (int j = 0; j < result[0].length; j++) {
47          result[i][j] = zero();
48
```

Margin notes:
- bounded generic type (line 1)
- abstract method (line 3)
- abstract method (line 6)
- abstract method (line 9)
- add two matrices (line 12)
- multiply two matrices (line 33)

```
49              for (int k = 0; k < matrix1[0].length; k++) {
50                result[i][j] = add(result[i][j],
51                  multiply(matrix1[i][k], matrix2[k][j]));
52              }
53          }
54        }
55
56        return result;
57    }
58
59    /** Print matrices, the operator, and their operation result */
60    public static void printResult(
61          Number[][] m1, Number[][] m2, Number[][] m3, char op) {
62      for (int i = 0; i < m1.length; i++) {
63        for (int j = 0; j < m1[0].length; j++)
64          System.out.print(" " + m1[i][j]);
65
66        if (i == m1.length / 2)
67          System.out.print( "  " + op + "  " );
68        else
69          System.out.print( "    " );
70
71        for (int j = 0; j < m2.length; j++)
72          System.out.print(" " + m2[i][j]);
73
74        if (i == m1.length / 2)
75          System.out.print( "  =  " );
76        else
77          System.out.print( "    " );
78
79        for (int j = 0; j < m3.length; j++)
80          System.out.print(m3[i][j] + " ");
81
82        System.out.println();
83      }
84    }
85 }
```

display result

Listing 21.10 implements the `IntegerMatrix` class. The class extends `GenericMatrix-<Integer>` in line 3. After the generic instantiation, the `add` method in `GenericMatrix-<Integer>` is now `Integer add(Integer o1, Integer o2)`. The `add`, `multiply` and `zero` methods are implemented for `Integer` objects. These methods are still protected, because they are invoked only by the `addMatrix` and `multiplyMatrix` methods.

LISTING 21.10 IntegerMatrix.java

```
1 public class IntegerMatrix extends GenericMatrix<Integer> {
2   /** Implement the add method for adding two matrix elements */
3   protected Integer add(Integer o1, Integer o2) {
4     return new Integer(o1.intValue() + o2.intValue());
5   }
6
7   /** Implement the multiply method for multiplying two
8       matrix elements */
9   protected Integer multiply(Integer o1, Integer o2) {
10    return new Integer(o1.intValue() * o2.intValue());
11  }
12
```

extends generic type

implement add

implement multiply

implement zero

```
13   /** Implement the zero method to specify zero for Integer */
14   protected Integer zero() {
15     return new Integer(0);
16   }
17 }
```

Listing 21.11 implements the `RationalMatrix` class. The `Rational` class was introduced in §12.6, "Case Study: The `Rational` Class." `Rational` is a subtype of `Number`. The `RationalMatrix` class extends `GenericMatrix<Rational>` in line 1. After the generic instantiation, the `add` method in `GenericMatrix<Rational>` is now `Rational add(Rational o1, Rational o2)`. The `add`, `multiply`, and `zero` methods are implemented for `Rational` objects. These methods are still protected, because they are invoked only by the `addMatrix` and `multiplyMatrix` methods.

LISTING 21.11 RationalMatrix.java

extends generic type

implement add

implement multiply

implement zero

```
1 public class RationalMatrix extends GenericMatrix<Rational> {
2    /** Implement the add method for adding two rational elements */
3    protected Rational add(Rational r1, Rational r2) {
4      return r1.add(r2);
5    }
6
7    /** Implement the multiply method for multiplying
8        two rational elements */
9    protected Rational multiply(Rational r1, Rational r2) {
10     return r1.multiply(r2);
11   }
12
13   /** Implement the zero method to specify zero for Rational */
14   protected Rational zero() {
15     return new Rational(0,1);
16   }
17 }
```

Listing 21.12 gives a program that creates two `Integer` matrices (lines 4–5) and an `IntegerMatrix` object (line 8), and adds and multiplies two matrices in lines 12 and 16.

LISTING 21.12 TestIntegerMatrix.java

create matrices

create **IntegerMatrix**

add two matrices

multiply two matrices

```
1 public class TestIntegerMatrix {
2   public static void main(String[] args) {
3     // Create Integer arrays m1, m2
4     Integer[][] m1 = new Integer[][]{{1, 2, 3}, {4, 5, 6}, {1, 1, 1}};
5     Integer[][] m2 = new Integer[][]{{1, 1, 1}, {2, 2, 2}, {0, 0, 0}};
6
7     // Create an instance of IntegerMatrix
8     IntegerMatrix integerMatrix = new IntegerMatrix();
9
10    System.out.println("\nm1 + m2 is ");
11    GenericMatrix.printResult(
12      m1, m2, integerMatrix.addMatrix(m1, m2), '+');
13
14    System.out.println("\nm1 * m2 is ");
15    GenericMatrix.printResult(
16      m1, m2, integerMatrix.multiplyMatrix(m1, m2), '*');
17   }
18 }
```

```
m1 + m2 is
 1 2 3      1 1 1      2 3 4
 4 5 6  +   2 2 2  =   6 7 8
 1 1 1      0 0 0      1 1 1

m1 * m2 is
 1 2 3      1 1 1      5  5  5
 4 5 6  *   2 2 2  =  14 14 14
 1 1 1      0 0 0      3  3  3
```

Listing 21.13 gives a program that creates two **Rational** matrices (lines 4–10) and a **RationalMatrix** object (line 13), and adds and multiplies two matrices in lines 17 and 21.

LISTING 21.13 `TestRationalMatrix.java`

```java
 1 public class TestRationalMatrix {
 2   public static void main(String[] args) {
 3     // Create two Rational arrays m1 and m2
 4     Rational[][] m1 = new Rational[3][3];
 5     Rational[][] m2 = new Rational[3][3];
 6     for (int i = 0; i < m1.length; i++)
 7       for (int j = 0; j < m1[0].length; j++) {
 8         m1[i][j] = new Rational(i + 1, j + 5);
 9         m2[i][j] = new Rational(i + 1, j + 6);
10       }
11
12     // Create an instance of RationalMatrix
13     RationalMatrix rationalMatrix = new RationalMatrix();
14
15     System.out.println("\nm1 + m2 is ");
16     GenericMatrix.printResult(
17       m1, m2, rationalMatrix.addMatrix(m1, m2), '+');
18
19     System.out.println("\nm1 * m2 is ");
20     GenericMatrix.printResult(
21       m1, m2, rationalMatrix.multiplyMatrix(m1, m2), '*');
22   }
23 }
```

create matrices

create **RationalMatrix**

add two matrices

multiply two matrices

```
m1 + m2 is
 1/5 1/6 1/7     1/6 1/7 1/8     11/30 13/42 15/56
 2/5 1/3 2/7  +  1/3 2/7 1/4  =  11/15 13/21 15/28
 3/5 1/2 3/7     1/2 3/7 3/8     11/10 13/14 45/56

m1 * m2 is
 1/5 1/6 1/7     1/6 1/7 1/8     101/630 101/735 101/840
 2/5 1/3 2/7  *  1/3 2/7 1/4  =  101/315 202/735 101/420
 3/5 1/2 3/7     1/2 3/7 3/8     101/210 101/245 101/280
```

KEY TERMS

actual concrete type   686
bounded generic type   690
formal generic type   686
generic instantiation   686

raw type   691
<?> type   693
<? extends E> type   693
<? super E> type   693

Review Questions

Sections 21.2–21.4

21.1   Are there any compile errors in (a) and (b)?

```
ArrayList dates = new ArrayList();
dates.add(new Date());
dates.add(new String());
```

(a)

```
ArrayList<Date> dates =
   new ArrayList<Date>();
dates.add(new Date());
dates.add(new String());
```

(b)

21.2   What is wrong in (a)? Is the code in (b) correct?

```
ArrayList dates = new ArrayList();
dates.add(new Date());
Date date = dates.get(0);
```
Date date = (Date)dates.get(0);

(a)

```
ArrayList<Date> dates =
   new ArrayList<Date>();
dates.add(new Date());
Date date = dates.get(0);
```

(b)

21.3   What are the benefits of using generic types?

21.4   Write the generic declaration for `java.lang.Comparable`.

21.5   Since you create an instance of `ArrayList` of strings using `new ArrayList-<String>()`, should the constructor in the `ArrayList` class be declared as

   `public ArrayList<E>()`

21.6   Can a generic class have multiple generic parameters?

21.7   How do you declare a generic type in a class? How do you declare a generic type in a method?

21.8   What is a bounded generic type?

Sections 21.5–21.6

21.9   What is a raw type? Is `GenericStack` the same as `GenericStack<Object>`?

21.10   What are an unbounded wildcard, a bounded wildcard, and a lower bounded wildcard?

21.11   What happens if lines 12–13 in Listing 21.8 are changed to

   ```
   public static <T> void add(GenericStack<T> stack1,
         GenericStack<T> stack2)
   ```

21.12   What happens if lines 12–13 in Listing 21.8 are changed to

   ```
   public static <T> void add(GenericStack<? extends T> stack1,
         GenericStack<T> stack2)
   ```

Section 21.7 Erasure and Restrictions on Generics

21.13   What is erasure? Why is Java generics implemented using erasure?

21.14   If your program uses `ArrayList<String>` and `ArrayList<Date>`, does the JVM load both of them?

21.15   Can you create an instance using `new E()` for a generic type `E`? Why?

21.16   Can a method that uses a generic class parameter be static? Why?

21.17   Can you declare a custom generic exception class? Why?

PROGRAMMING EXERCISES

21.1   (*Revising Listing 21.1*) Revise the `GenericStack` class in Listing 21.1 to implement it using an array rather than an `ArrayList`. You should check the array size before adding a new element to the stack. If the array is full, create a new array that doubles the current array size and copy the elements from the current array to the new array.

21.2   (*Generic binary search*) Implement the following method using binary search.

```
public static <E extends Comparable<E>>
  int binarySearch(E[] list, E key)
```

21.3   (*Generic selection sort*) Implement the following method using selection sort.

```
public static <E extends Comparable<E>>
  void selectionSort(E[] list)
```

21.4   (*Generic insertion sort*) Implement the following method using insertion sort.

```
public static <E extends Comparable<E>>
  void selectionSort(E[] list)
```

21.5   (*Maximum element in an array*) Implement the following method that returns the maximum element in an array.

```
public static <E extends Comparable<E>> E max(E[] list)
```

21.6   (*Maximum element in a two-dimensional array*) Write a generic method that returns the maximum element in a two-dimensional array.

```
public static <E extends Comparable<E>> E max(E[][] list)
```

Video Note
Develop a generic method for
finding the largest element in
a 2-d array

CHAPTER 22

JAVA COLLECTIONS FRAMEWORK

Objectives

- To describe the Java Collections Framework hierarchy (§22.1).
- To use the common methods defined in the `Collection` interface for operating sets and lists (§22.2).
- To use the `Iterator` interface to traverse a collection (§22.3).
- To use the for-each loop to simplify traversing a collection (§22.3).
- To explore how and when to use `HashSet`, `LinkedHashSet`, or `TreeSet` to store elements (§22.3).
- To compare elements using the `Comparable` interface and the `Comparator` interface (§22.4).
- To explore how and when to use `ArrayList` or `LinkedList` to store elements (§22.5).
- To use the static utility methods in the `Collections` class for sorting, searching, shuffling lists, and finding the largest and smallest element in collections (§22.6).
- To compare performance of sets and lists (§22.7).
- To distinguish between `Vector` and `ArrayList`, and to use the `Stack` class for creating stacks (§22.8).
- To explore the relationships among `Collection`, `Queue`, `LinkedList`, and `PriorityQueue` and to create priority queues using the `PriorityQueue` class (§22.9).
- To tell the differences between `Collection` and `Map`, and describe when and how to use `HashMap`, `LinkedHashMap`, and `TreeMap` to store values associated with keys (§22.10).
- To obtain singleton sets, lists, and maps, and unmodifiable sets, lists, and maps, using the static methods in the `Collections` class (§22.11).

22.1 Introduction

A *data structure* is a collection of data organized in some fashion. The structure not only stores data but also supports operations for accessing and manipulating the data. You have learned `ArrayList`, which is a data structure to store elements in a list. Java provides several more data structures that can be used to organize and manipulate data efficiently. These data structures are commonly known as *Java Collections Framework*.

In object-oriented thinking, a data structure, also known as a *collection*, is an object that stores other objects, referred to as data or elements. Some people refer to data structures as *container objects* or *collection objects*. To define a data structure is essentially to declare a class. The class for a data structure should use data fields to store data and provide methods to support such operations as search, insertion, and deletion. To create a data structure is therefore to create an instance from the class. You can then apply the methods on the instance to manipulate the data structure, such as inserting an element into or deleting an element from the data structure.

The Java Collections Framework supports three major types of collections: *set*, *list*, and *map*. They are defined in the interfaces `Set`, `List`, and `Map`. An instance of `Set` stores a group of nonduplicate elements. An instance of `List` stores an ordered collection of elements. An instance of `Map` stores a group of objects, each associated with a key. The relationships of the interfaces and classes in the Java Collections Framework are shown in Figures 22.1 and 22.2. These interfaces and classes provide a unified API for efficiently storing and processing a collection of objects. You will learn how to use them in this chapter.

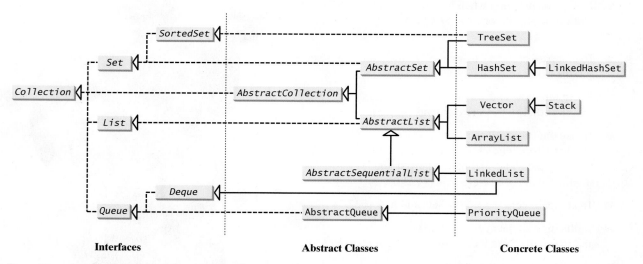

FIGURE 22.1 A collection is a container that stores objects.

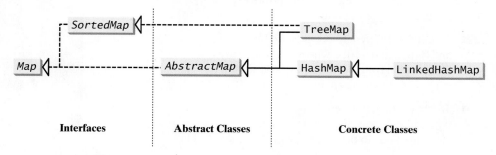

FIGURE 22.2 A map stores key/value pairs.

Note

All the interfaces and classes defined in the Java Collections Framework are grouped in the `java.util` package.

Design Guide

The design of the Java Collections Framework is a good example of using interfaces, abstract classes, and concrete classes. The interfaces define the framework. The abstract classes provide partial implementation for convenience. The concrete classes implement the interfaces with concrete data structures.

Note

All the concrete classes in the Java Collections Framework implement the `Cloneable` and `Serializable` interfaces. Thus their instances can be cloned and serialized.

`Cloneable`
`Serializable`

22.2 The `Collection` Interface and the `AbstractCollection` Class

The `Collection` interface is the root interface for manipulating a collection of objects. Its public methods are listed in Figure 22.3. The `AbstractCollection` class is a convenience class that provides partial implementation for the `Collection` interface. It implements all the methods in `Collection` except the `size` and `iterator` methods. These are implemented in appropriate subclasses.

«interface» *java.util.Collection<E>*	
+add(o: E): boolean	Adds a new element o to this collection.
+addAll(c: Collection<? extends E): boolean	Adds all the elements in the collection c to this collection.
+clear(): void	Removes all the elements from this collection.
+contains(o: Object): boolean	Returns true if this collection contains the element o.
+containsAll(c: Collection<?>): boolean	Returns true if this collection contains all the elements in c.
+equals(o: Object): boolean	Returns true if this collection is equal to another collection o.
+hashCode(): int	Returns the hash code for this collection.
+isEmpty(): boolean	Returns true if this collection contains no elements.
+iterator(): Iterator<E>	Returns an iterator for the elements in this collection.
+remove(o: Object): boolean	Removes the element o from this collection.
+removeAll(c: Collection<?>): boolean	Removes all the elements in c from this collection.
+retainAll(c: Collection<?>): boolean	Retains the elements that are both in c and in this collection.
+size(): int	Returns the number of elements in this collection.
+toArray(): Object[]	Returns an array of `Object` for the elements in this collection.

«interface» *java.util.Iterator<E>*	
+hasNext(): boolean	Returns true if this iterator has more elements to traverse.
+next(): E	Returns the next element from this iterator.
+remove(): void	Removes the last element obtained using the next method.

FIGURE 22.3 The `Collection` interface contains the methods for manipulating the elements in a collection, and each collection object contains an iterator for traversing elements in the collection.

basic operations

The `Collection` interface provides the basic operations for adding and removing elements in a collection. The `add` method adds an element to the collection. The `addAll` method adds all the elements in the specified collection to this collection. The `remove` method removes an element from the collection. The `removeAll` method removes the elements from this collection that are present in the specified collection. The `retainAll` method retains the elements in this collection that are also present in the specified collection. All these methods return `boolean`. The return value is true if the collection is changed as a result of the method execution. The `clear()` method simply removes all the elements from the collection.

 Note

set operations

The methods `addAll`, `removeAll`, and `retainAll` are similar to the set union, difference, and intersection operations.

query operations

The `Collection` interface provides various query operations. The `size` method returns the number of elements in the collection. The `contains` method checks whether the collection contains the specified element. The `containsAll` method checks whether the collection contains all the elements in the specified collection. The `isEmpty` method returns `true` if the collection is empty.

The `Collection` interface provides the `toArray()` method that returns an array representation for the collection.

iterator

A collection may be a set or a list. The `Iterator` interface provides a uniform way for traversing elements in various types of collections. The `iterator` method in the `Collection` interface returns an instance of the `Iterator` interface, as shown in Figure 22.3, which provides sequential access to the elements in the collection using the `next()` method. You can also use the `hasNext()` method to check whether there are more elements in the iterator, and the `remove()` method to remove the last element returned by the iterator.

 Design Note

Unsupported Operations

Some of the methods in the `Collection` interface cannot be implemented in the concrete subclass. In this case, the method would throw `java.lang.UnsupportedOperationException`, a subclass of `RuntimeException`. This is a good design that you can use in your project. If a method has no meaning in the subclass, you can implement it as follows:

```java
public void someMethod() {
  throw new UnsupportedOperationException
    ("Method not supported");
}
```

22.3 Sets

no duplicates

The `Set` interface extends the `Collection` interface. It does not introduce new methods or constants, but it stipulates that an instance of `Set` contains no duplicate elements. The concrete classes that implement `Set` must ensure that no duplicate elements can be added to the set. That is, no two elements `e1` and `e2` can be in the set such that `e1.equals(e2)` is true.

The `AbstractSet` class is a convenience class that extends `AbstractCollection` and implements `Set`. The `AbstractSet` class provides concrete implementations for the `equals` method and the `hashCode` method. The hash code of a set is the sum of the hash codes of all the elements in the set. Since the `size` method and `iterator` method are not implemented in the `AbstractSet` class, `AbstractSet` is an abstract class.

Three concrete classes of `Set` are `HashSet`, `LinkedHashSet`, and `TreeSet`, as shown in Figure 22.4.

FIGURE 22.4 The Java Collections Framework provides three concrete set classes.

22.3.1 HashSet

The **HashSet** class is a concrete class that implements **Set**. You can create an empty hash set using its no-arg constructor or create a hash set from an existing collection. By default, the initial capacity is **16** and load factor is **0.75**. If you know the size of your set, you may specify the initial capacity and load factor in the constructor. Otherwise, use the default setting. Load factor is a value between **0.0** and **1.0**.

Load factor measures how full the set is allowed to be before its capacity is increased. When the number of elements exceeds the product of the capacity and load factor, the capacity is automatically doubled. For example, if the capacity is **16** and load factor is **0.75**, the capacity will be doubled to **32** when the size reaches **12** (16 * 0.75 = 12). Higher load factor decreases the space costs but increases the search time. Generally, the default load factor **0.75** is a good trade-off between time and space costs.

A **HashSet** can be used to store *duplicate-free* elements. For efficiency, objects added to a hash set need to implement the **hashCode** method in a manner that properly disperses the hash code. Recall that **hashCode** is defined in the **Object** class. The hash codes of two objects must be the same if the two objects are equal. Two unequal objects may have the same hash code, but you should implement the **hashCode** method to avoid too many such cases. Most of the classes in the Java API implement the **hashCode** method. For example, the **hashCode** in the **Integer** class returns its **int** value. The **hashCode** in the **Character** class returns the Unicode of the character. The **hashCode** in the **String** class returns $s_0*31^{(n-1)} + s_1*31^{(n-2)} + \ldots + s_{n-1}$, where s_i is **s.charAt(i)**.

Listing 22.1 gives a program that creates a hash set to store strings and uses an iterator to traverse the elements in the set.

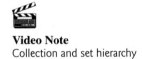

Video Note
Collection and set hierarchy

load factor

hashCode()

LISTING 22.1 TestHashSet.java

```
 1 import java.util.*;
 2
 3 public class TestHashSet {
 4   public static void main(String[] args) {
 5     // Create a hash set
 6     Set<String> set = new HashSet<String>();
 7
 8     // Add strings to the set
 9     set.add("London");
10     set.add("Paris");
11     set.add("New York");
12     set.add("San Francisco");
13     set.add("Beijing");
14     set.add("New York");
15
16     System.out.println(set);
17
18     // Obtain an iterator for the hash set
19     Iterator<String> iterator = set.iterator();
20
21     // Display the elements in the hash set
22     while (iterator.hasNext()) {
23       System.out.print(iterator.next() + " ");
24     }
25   }
26 }
```

create set

add element

get iterator

traverse iterator

```
[Paris, Beijing, London, San Francisco, New York]
Paris Beijing London San Francisco New York
```

The strings are added to the set (lines 9–14). "New York" is added to the set more than once, but only one is stored, because a set does not allow duplicates.

As shown in the output, the strings are not stored in the order in which they are inserted into the set. There is no particular order for the elements in a hash set. To impose an order on them, you need to use the LinkedHashSet class, which is introduced in the next section.

Tip
You can simplify the code in lines 21–26 using a JDK 1.5 for-each loop without using an iterator, as follows:

JDK 1.5 for-each loop

```
for (Object element: set)
  System.out.print(element);
```

This loop is read as "for each element in the set, do the following." The for-each loop can be used for arrays (see §6.2.7) as well as any instance of Collection.

Since a set is an instance of Collection, all methods defined in Collection can be used for sets. Listing 22.2 gives an example that explores the methods in the Collection interface.

LISTING 22.2 TestMethodsInCollection.java

```
1 public class TestMethodsInCollection {
2   public static void main(String[] args) {
3     // Create set1
4     java.util.Set<String> set1 = new java.util.HashSet<String>();
5
```

create a set

```
6      // Add strings to set1
7      set1.add("London");                                                    add element
8      set1.add("Paris");
9      set1.add("New York");
10     set1.add("San Francisco");
11     set1.add("Beijing");
12
13     System.out.println("set1 is " + set1);
14     System.out.println(set1.size() + " elements in set1");                  set size
15
16     // Delete a string from set1
17     set1.remove("London");                                                  remove element
18     System.out.println("\nset1 is " + set1);
19     System.out.println(set1.size() + " elements in set1");
20
21     // Create set2
22     java.util.Set<String> set2 = new java.util.HashSet<String>();           create a set
23
24     // Add strings to set2
25     set2.add("London");                                                     add element
26     set2.add("Shanghai");
27     set2.add("Paris");
28     System.out.println("\nset2 is " + set2);
29     System.out.println(set2.size() + " elements in set2");
30
31     System.out.println("\nIs Taipei in set2? "
32       + set2.contains("Taipei"));                                           contains element?
33
34     set1.addAll(set2);                                                      addAll
35     System.out.println("\nAfter adding set2 to set1, set1 is "
36       + set1);
37
38     set1.removeAll(set2);                                                   removeAll
39     System.out.println("After removing set2 from set1, set1 is "
40       + set1);
41
42     set1.retainAll(set2);                                                   retainAll
43     System.out.println("After removing common elements in set2 "
44       + "from set1, set1 is " + set1);
45   }
46 }
```

```
set1 is [San Francisco, New York, Paris, Beijing, London]
5 elements in set1

set1 is [San Francisco, New York, Paris, Beijing]
4 elements in set1

set2 is [Shanghai, Paris, London]
3 elements in set2

Is Taipei in set2? false

After adding set2 to set1, set1 is
  [San Francisco, New York, Shanghai, Paris, Beijing, London]

After removing set2 from set1, set1 is
  [San Francisco, New York, Beijing]

After removing common elements in set2 from set1, set1 is []
```

The program creates two sets (lines 4, 22). The `size()` method returns the number of the elements in a set (line 14). Line 17

```
set1.remove("London");
```

removes "London" from set1.

The contains method (line 32) checks whether an element is in the set. Line 34

```
set1.addAll(set2);
```

adds set2 to set1. So, set1 becomes [San Francisco, New York, Shanghai, Paris, Beijing, London].

Line 38

```
set1.removeAll(set2);
```

removes set2 from set1. So, set1 becomes [San Francisco, New York, Beijing].

Line 42

```
set1.retainAll(set2);
```

retains the common elements in set1. Since set1 and set2 have no common elements, set1 becomes empty.

22.3.2 LinkedHashSet

LinkedHashSet was added in JDK 1.4. It extends HashSet with a linked-list implementation that supports an ordering of the elements in the set. The elements in a HashSet are not ordered, but the elements in a LinkedHashSet can be retrieved in the order in which they were inserted into the set. A LinkedHashSet can be created by using one of its four constructors, as shown in Figure 22.4. These constructors are similar to the constructors for HashSet.

Listing 22.3 gives a test program for LinkedHashSet. The program simply replaces HashSet by LinkedHashSet in Listing 22.1.

LISTING 22.3 TestLinkedHashSet.java

```
 1 import java.util.*;
 2
 3 public class TestLinkedHashSet {
 4   public static void main(String[] args) {
 5     // Create a hash set
 6     Set<String> set = new LinkedHashSet<String>();
 7
 8     // Add strings to the set
 9     set.add("London");
10     set.add("Paris");
11     set.add("New York");
12     set.add("San Francisco");
13     set.add("Beijing");
14     set.add("New York");
15
16     System.out.println(set);
17
18     // Display the elements in the hash set
19     for (Object element: set)
20       System.out.print(element.toString() + " ");
21   }
22 }
```

create linked hash set

add element

display elements

```
[London, Paris, New York, San Francisco, Beijing]
London Paris New York San Francisco Beijing
```

A `LinkedHashSet` is created in line 6. As shown in the output, the strings are stored in the order in which they are inserted. Since `LinkedHashSet` is a set, it does not store duplicate elements.

The `LinkedHashSet` maintains the order in which the elements are inserted. To impose a different order (e.g., increasing or decreasing order), you can use the `TreeSet` class introduced in the next section.

Tip
If you don't need to maintain the order in which the elements are inserted, use `HashSet`, which is more efficient than `LinkedHashSet`.

22.3.3 TreeSet

`SortedSet` is a subinterface of `Set`, which guarantees that the elements in the set are sorted. Additionally, it provides the methods `first()` and `last()` for returning the first and last elements in the set, and `headSet(toElement)` and `tailSet(fromElement)` for returning a portion of the set whose elements are less than `toElement` and greater than or equal to `fromElement`.

`TreeSet` is a concrete class that implements the `SortedSet` interface. To create a `TreeSet`, use one of its three constructors, as shown in Figure 22.4. You can add objects into a tree set as long as they can be compared with each other. There are two ways to compare objects.

- Use the `Comparable` interface. Since the objects added to the set are instances of `Comparable`, they can be compared using the `compareTo` method. The `Comparable` interface was introduced in §11.5. Several classes in the Java API, such as `String`, `Date`, `Calendar`, and all the wrapper classes for the primitive types, implement the `Comparable` interface. This approach is referred to as *natural order*.   Comparable   natural order

- If the class for the elements does not implement the `Comparable` interface, or if you don't want to use the `compareTo` method in the class that implements the `Comparable` interface, specify a comparator for the elements in the set. This approach is referred to as *order by comparator*. It will be introduced in §22.4, "The `Comparator` Interface."   order by comparator

Listing 22.4 gives an example of ordering elements using the `Comparable` interface. The preceding example in Listing 22.3 displays all the strings in their insertion order. This example rewrites the preceding example to display the strings in alphabetical order using the `TreeSet` class.

LISTING 22.4 TestTreeSet.java

```
1 import java.util.*;
2
3 public class TestTreeSet {
4   public static void main(String[] args) {
5     // Create a hash set
6     Set<String> set = new HashSet<String>();
7
8     // Add strings to the set
9     set.add("London");
10    set.add("Paris");
```
create hash set

```
11      set.add("New York");
12      set.add("San Francisco");
13      set.add("Beijing");
14      set.add("New York");
15
16      Set<String> treeSet = new TreeSet<String>(set);
17      System.out.println(treeSet);
18
19      // Display the elements in the hash set
20      for (Object element: set)
21          System.out.print(element.toString() + " ");
22   }
23 }
```

create tree set

display elements

```
[Beijing, London, New York, Paris, San Francisco]
Paris Beijing London San Francisco New York
```

The example creates a hash set filled with strings, and then creates a tree set for the same strings. The strings are sorted in the tree set using the compareTo method in the Comparable interface.

The elements in the set are sorted once you create a TreeSet object from a HashSet object using new TreeSet(hashSet) (line 16). You may rewrite the program to create an instance of TreeSet using its no-arg constructor, and add the strings into the TreeSet object. Then, every time a string is added to the TreeSet object, the elements in it will be re-ordered. The approach used in the example is generally more efficient because it requires only a one-time sorting.

Note

All the concrete classes in Java Collections Framework (see Figure 22.1) have at least two constructors. One is the no-arg constructor that constructs an empty collection. The other constructs instances from a collection. Thus the TreeSet class has the constructor TreeSet(Collection c) for constructing a TreeSet from a collection c. In this example, new TreeSet(hashSet) creates an instance of TreeSet from the collection hashSet.

Tip

If you don't need to maintain a sorted set when updating a set, you should can use a hash set, because it takes less time to insert and remove elements in a hash set. When you need a set to be sorted, you can convert it into a tree set.

22.4 The **Comparator** Interface

Sometimes you want to insert elements into a tree set. The elements may not be instances of java.lang.Comparable. You can define a comparator to compare these elements. To do so, create a class that implements the java.util.Comparator interface. The Comparator interface has two methods, compare and equals.

■ **public int** compare(Object element1, Object element2)
  Returns a negative value if element1 is less than element2, a positive value if element1 is greater than element2, and zero if they are equal.

■ **public boolean** equals(Object element)
  Returns true if the specified object is also a comparator and imposes the same ordering as this comparator.

The `equals` method is also defined in the `Object` class. Therefore, you will not get a compile error even if you don't implement the `equals` method in your custom comparator class. However, in some cases implementing this method may improve performance by allowing programs to determine quickly whether two distinct comparators impose the same order.

Listing 22.5 declares a `Comparator` for geometric objects. The `GeometricObject` class was introduced in §11.2, "Abstract Classes." Line 2 implements `Comparator<GeometricObject>`. Line 3 overrides the `compare` method to compare two geometric objects. The comparator class also implements `Serializable`. It is generally a good idea for comparators to implement `Serializable`, as they may be used as ordering methods in serializable data structures such as `TreeSet`. In order for the data structure to serialize successfully, the comparator (if provided) must implement `Serializable`.

LISTING 22.5 GeometricObjectComparator.java

```java
1 import java.util.Comparator;
2
3 public class GeometricObjectComparator
4     implements Comparator<GeometricObject>, java.io.Serializable {
5   public int compare(GeometricObject o1, GeometricObject o2) {
6     double area1 = o1.getArea();
7     double area2 = o2.getArea();
8
9     if (area1 < area2)
10       return -1;
11     else if (area1 == area2)
12       return 0;
13     else
14       return 1;
15   }
16 }
```

implements **Comparator**
implements **compare**

If you create a `TreeSet` using its no-arg constructor, the `compareTo` method is used to compare the elements in the set, assuming that the class of the elements implements the `Comparable` interface. To use a comparator, you have to use the constructor `TreeSet(Comparator comparator)` to create a sorted set that uses the `compare` method in the comparator to order the elements in the set.

Listing 22.6 gives a program that demonstrates how to sort elements in a tree set using the `Comparator` interface. The example creates a tree set of geometric objects in lines 6–11. The geometric objects are sorted using the `compare` method in the `Comparator` interface.

LISTING 22.6 TestTreeSetWithComparator.java

```java
1 import java.util.*;
2
3 public class TestTreeSetWithComparator {
4   public static void main(String[] args) {
5     // Create a tree set for geometric objects using a comparator
6     Set<GeometricObject> set =
7       new TreeSet<GeometricObject>(new GeometricObjectComparator());
8     set.add(new Rectangle(4, 5));
9     set.add(new Circle(40));
10     set.add(new Circle(40));
11     set.add(new Rectangle(4, 1));
12
13     // Display geometric objects in the tree set
14     System.out.println("A sorted set of geometric objects");
```

tree set

display elements

```
15    for (GeometricObject element: set)
16       System.out.println("area = " + element.getArea());
17    }
18 }
```

A sorted set of geometric objects
area = 4.0
area = 20.0
area = 5022.548245743669

The `Circle` and `Rectangle` classes were defined in §11.2, "Abstract Classes." They are all subclasses of `GeometricObject`.

Two circles of the same radius are added to the set in the tree set (lines 9–11), but only one is stored, because the two circles are equal and the set does not allow duplicates.

Comparable vs. **Comparator**

Note

`Comparable` is used to compare the objects of the class that implement `Comparable`. `Comparator` can be used to compare the objects of the class that doesn't implement `Comparable`.

Video Note
Collection and list hierarchy

22.5 Lists

A set stores nonduplicate elements. To allow duplicate elements to be stored in a collection, you need to use a list. A list can not only store duplicate elements but also allow the user to specify where they are stored. The user can access elements by an index. The `List` interface extends `Collection` to define an ordered collection with duplicates allowed. The `List` interface adds position-oriented operations, as well as a new list iterator that enables the user to traverse the list bidirectionally. The new methods in the `List` interface are shown in Figure 22.5.

The `add(index, element)` method is used to insert an element at a specified index, and the `addAll(index, collection)` method to insert a collection at a specified index. The

«interface» *java.util.Collection\<E>*

«interface» *java.util.List\<E>*	
+add(index: int, element: E): boolean	Adds a new element at the specified index.
+addAll(index: int, c: Collection<? extends E>) : boolean	Adds all the elements in c to this list at the specified index.
+get(index: int): E	Returns the element in this list at the specified index.
+indexOf(element: Object): int	Returns the index of the first matching element.
+lastIndexOf(element: Object): int	Returns the index of the last matching element.
+listIterator(): ListIterator\<E>	Returns the list iterator for the elements in this list.
+listIterator(startIndex: int): ListIterator\<E>	Returns the iterator for the elements from startIndex.
+remove(index: int): E	Removes the element at the specified index.
+set(index: int, element: E): E	Sets the element at the specified index.
+subList(fromIndex: int, toIndex: int): List\<E>	Returns a sublist from fromIndex to toIndex.

FIGURE 22.5 The `List` interface stores elements in sequence, permitting duplicates.

`remove(index)` method is used to remove an element at the specified index from the list. A new element can be set at the specified index using the `set(index, element)` method.

The `indexOf(element)` method is used to obtain the index of the specified element's first occurrence in the list, and the `lastIndexOf(element)` method to obtain the index of its last occurrence. A sublist can be obtained by using the `subList(fromIndex, toIndex)` method.

The `listIterator()` or `listIterator(startIndex)` method returns an instance of `ListIterator`. The `ListIterator` interface extends the `Iterator` interface to add bidirectional traversal of the list. The methods in `ListIterator` are listed in Figure 22.6.

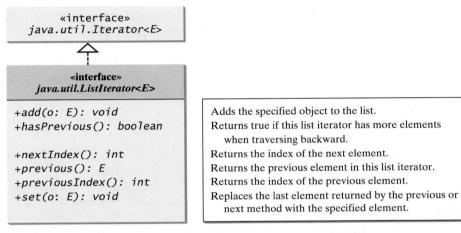

FIGURE 22.6 `ListIterator` enables traversal of a list bidirectionally.

The `add(element)` method inserts the specified element into the list. The element is inserted immediately before the next element that would be returned by the `next()` method defined in the `Iterator` interface, if any, and after the element that would be returned by the `previous()` method, if any. If the list contains no elements, the new element becomes the sole element on the list. The `set(element)` method can be used to replace the last element returned by the `next` method or the `previous` method with the specified element.

The `hasNext()` method defined in the `Iterator` interface is used to check whether the iterator has more elements when traversed in the forward direction, and the `hasPrevious()` method to check whether the iterator has more elements when traversed in the backward direction.

The `next()` method defined in the `Iterator` interface returns the next element in the iterator, and the `previous()` method returns the previous element in the iterator. The `nextIndex()` method returns the index of the next element in the iterator, and the `previousIndex()` returns the index of the previous element in the iterator.

The `AbstractList` class provides a partial implementation for the `List` interface. The `AbstractSequentialList` class extends `AbstractList` to provide support for linked lists.

22.5.1 The `ArrayList` and `LinkedList` Classes

The `ArrayList` class (introduced in §10.10) and the `LinkedList` class are two concrete implementations of the `List` interface. `ArrayList` stores elements in an array. The array is dynamically created. If the capacity of the array is exceeded, a larger new array is created and all the elements from the current array are copied to the new array. `LinkedList` stores elements in a linked list. Which of the two classes you use depends on your specific needs. If you need to support random access through an index without inserting or removing elements except at the end, `ArrayList` offers the most efficient collection. If, however, your application requires the insertion or deletion of elements anywhere in the list, you should choose `LinkedList`. A list can grow or shrink dynamically. An array is fixed once it is created. If your application does not require the insertion or deletion of elements, an array is the most efficient data structure.

`ArrayList` is a resizable-array implementation of the `List` interface. It also provides methods for manipulating the size of the array used internally to store the list, as shown in Figure 22.7. Each `ArrayList` instance has a capacity, which is the size of the array used to store the elements in the list. It is always at least as large as the list size. As elements are added to an `ArrayList`, its capacity grows automatically. An `ArrayList` does not automatically shrink. You can use the `trimToSize()` method to reduce the array capacity to the size of the list. An `ArrayList` can be constructed using its no-arg constructor, `ArrayList(Collection)`, or `ArrayList(intialCapacity)`.

trimToSize()

FIGURE 22.7 `ArrayList` implements `List` using an array.

`LinkedList` is a linked list implementation of the `List` interface. In addition to implementing the `List` interface, this class provides the methods for retrieving, inserting, and removing elements from both ends of the list, as shown in Figure 22.8. A `LinkedList` can be constructed using its no-arg constructor or `LinkedList(Collection)`.

FIGURE 22.8 `LinkedList` provides methods for adding and inserting elements at both ends of the list.

Listing 22.7 gives a program that creates an array list filled with numbers and inserts new elements into specified locations in the list. The example also creates a linked list from the array list, and inserts and removes elements from the list. Finally, the example traverses the list forward and backward.

LISTING 22.7 TestArrayAndLinkedList.java

```java
1 import java.util.*;
2
3 public class TestArrayAndLinkedList {
4   public static void main(String[] args) {
5     List<Integer> arrayList = new ArrayList<Integer>();        array list
6     arrayList.add(1); // 1 is autoboxed to new Integer(1)
7     arrayList.add(2);
8     arrayList.add(3);
9     arrayList.add(1);
10    arrayList.add(4);
11    arrayList.add(0, 10);
12    arrayList.add(3, 30);
13
14    System.out.println("A list of integers in the array list:");
15    System.out.println(arrayList);
16
17    LinkedList<Object> linkedList = new LinkedList<Object>(arrayList);   linked list
18    linkedList.add(1, "red");
19    linkedList.removeLast();
20    linkedList.addFirst("green");
21
22    System.out.println("Display the linked list forward:");
23    ListIterator<Object> listIterator = linkedList.listIterator();    list iterator
24    while (listIterator.hasNext()) {
25      System.out.print(listIterator.next() + " ");
26    }
27    System.out.println();
28
29    System.out.println("Display the linked list backward:");
30    listIterator = linkedList.listIterator(linkedList.size());    list iterator
31    while (listIterator.hasPrevious()) {
32      System.out.print(listIterator.previous() + " ");
33    }
34  }
35 }
```

```
A list of integers in the array list:
[10, 1, 2, 30, 3, 1, 4]
Display the linked list forward:
green 10 red 1 2 30 3 1
Display the linked list backward:
1 3 30 2 1 red 10 green
```

A list can hold identical elements. Integer 1 is stored twice in the list (lines 6, 9). ArrayList and LinkedList are operated similarly. The critical difference between them pertains to internal implementation, which affects their performance. ArrayList is efficient for retrieving elements, and for inserting and removing elements from the end of the list. LinkedList is efficient for inserting and removing elements anywhere in the list.

`Arrays.asList(T... a)`
method

Tip

Java provides the static `asList` method for creating a list from a variable-length argument list of a generic type. Thus you can use the following code to create a list of strings and a list of integers:

```
List<String> list1 = Arrays.asList("red", "green", "blue");
List<Integer> list2 = Arrays.asList(10, 20, 30, 40, 50);
```

22.6 Static Methods for Lists and Collections

You can use `TreeSet` to store sorted elements in a set. But there is no sorted list. However, the Java Collections Framework provides static methods in the `Collections` class that can be used to sort a list. The `Collections` class also contains the `binarySearch`, `reverse`, `shuffle`, `copy`, and `fill` methods on lists, and `max`, `min`, `disjoint`, and `frequency` methods on collections, as shown in Figure 22.9.

java.util.Collections	
+sort(list: List): void	Sorts the specified list.
+sort(list: List, c: Comparator): void	Sorts the specified list with the comparator.
+binarySearch(list: List, key: Object): int	Searches the key in the sorted list using binary search.
+binarySearch(list: List, key: Object, c: Comparator): int	Searches the key in the sorted list using binary search with the comparator.
+reverse(list: List): void	Reverses the specified list.
+reverseOrder(): Comparator	Returns a comparator with the reverse ordering.
+shuffle(list: List): void	Shuffles the specified list randomly.
+shuffle(list: List, rmd: Random): void	Shuffles the specified list with a random object.
+copy(des: List, src: List): void	Copies from the source list to the destination list.
+nCopies(n: int, o: Object): List	Returns a list consisting of *n* copies of the object.
+fill(list: List, o: Object): void	Fills the list with the object.
+max(c: Collection): Object	Returns the `max` object in the collection.
+max(c: Collection, c: Comparator): Object	Returns the `max` object using the comparator.
+min(c: Collection): Object	Returns the `min` object in the collection.
+min(c: Collection, c: Comparator): Object	Returns the `min` object using the comparator.
+disjoint(c1: Collection, c2: Collection): boolean	Returns true if `c1` and `c2` have no elements in common.
+frequency(c: Collection, o: Object): int	Returns the number of occurrences of the specified element in the collection.

List — (rows from sort to fill)
Collection — (rows from max to frequency)

FIGURE 22.9 The `Collections` class contains static methods for manipulating lists and collections.

sort list

You can sort the comparable elements in a list in its natural order through the `compareTo` method in the `Comparable` interface. You may also specify a comparator to sort elements. For example, the following code sorts strings in a list.

```
List<String> list = Arrays.asList("red", "green", "blue");
Collections.sort(list);
System.out.println(list);
```

The output is `[blue, green, red]`.

ascending order
descending order

The preceding code sorts a list in ascending order. To sort it in descending order, you may simply use the `Collections.reverseOrder()` method to return a `Comparator` object that orders the elements in reverse order. For example, the following code sorts a list of strings in descending order.

```
List<String> list = Arrays.asList("yellow", "red", "green", "blue");
Collections.sort(list, Collections.reverseOrder());
System.out.println(list);
```

The output is `[yellow, red, green, blue]`.

You can use the **binarySearch** method to search for a key in a list. The list must be presorted in increasing order. If the key is not in the list, the method returns –*(insertion point + 1)*. Recall that the insertion point is where the item would fall in the list if it were present. For example, the following code searches the keys in a list of integers and a list of strings.

binarySearch

```
List<Integer> list1 =
  Arrays.asList(2, 4, 7, 10, 11, 45, 50, 59, 60, 66);
System.out.println("(1) Index: " + Collections.binarySearch(list1, 7));
System.out.println("(2) Index: " + Collections.binarySearch(list1, 9));

List<String> list2 = Arrays.asList("blue", "green", "red");
System.out.println("(3) Index: " +
  Collections.binarySearch(list2, "red"));
System.out.println("(4) Index: " +
  Collections.binarySearch(list2, "cyan"));
```

The output of the preceding code is

```
(1) Index: 2
(2) Index: −4
(3) Index: 2
(4) Index: −2
```

You can use the **reverse** method to reverse the elements in a list. For example, the following code displays `[blue, green, red, yellow]`.

reverse

```
List<String> list = Arrays.asList("yellow", "red", "green", "blue");
Collections.reverse(list);
System.out.println(list);
```

You can use the **shuffle(List)** method to randomly reorder the elements in a list. For example, the following code shuffles the elements in `list`.

shuffle

```
List<String> list = Arrays.asList("yellow", "red", "green", "blue");
Collections.shuffle(list);
System.out.println(list);
```

You can also use the **shuffle(List, Random)** method to randomly reorder the elements in a list with a specified **Random** object. Using a specified **Random** object is useful to generate a list with identical sequences of elements for the same original list. For example, the following code shuffles the elements in `list`.

```
List<String> list1 = Arrays.asList("yellow", "red", "green", "blue");
List<String> list2 = Arrays.asList("yellow", "red", "green", "blue");
Collections.shuffle(list1, new Random(20));
Collections.shuffle(list2, new Random(20));
System.out.println(list1);
System.out.println(list2);
```

You will see that `list1` and `list2` have the same sequence of elements before and after the shuffling.

copy

You can use the `copy(det, src)` method to copy all the elements from a source list to a destination list on the same index. The destination must be as long as the source list. If it is longer, the remaining elements in the source list are not affected. For example, the following code copies `list2` to `list1`.

```
List<String> list1 = Arrays.asList("yellow", "red", "green", "blue");
List<String> list2 = Arrays.asList("white", "black");
Collections.copy(list1, list2);
System.out.println(list1);
```

The output for `list1` is [white, black, green, blue]. The `copy` method performs a shallow copy. Only the references of the elements from the source list are copied.

nCopies

You can use the `nCopies(int n, Object o)` method to create an immutable list that consists of `n` copies of the specified object. For example, the following code creates a list with five `Calendar` objects.

```
List<GregorianCalendar> list1 = Collections.nCopies
  (5, new GregorianCalendar(2005, 0, 1));
```

The list created from the `nCopies` method is immutable, so you cannot add, remove, or update elements in the list. All the elements have the same references.

fill

You can use the `fill(List list, Object o)` method to replace all the elements in the list with the specified element. For example, the following code displays [black, black, black].

```
List<String> list = Arrays.asList("red", "green", "blue");
Collections.fill(list, "black");
System.out.println(list);
```

max and **min** methods

You can use the `max` and `min` methods for finding the maximum and minimum elements in a collection. The elements must be comparable using the `Comparable` interface or the `Comparator` interface. For example, the following code displays the largest and smallest strings in a collection.

```
Collection<String> collection = Arrays.asList("red", "green", "blue");
System.out.println(Collections.max(collection));
System.out.println(Collections.min(collection));
```

disjoint method

The `disjoint(collection1, collection2)` method returns `true` if the two collections have no elements in common. For example, in the following code, `disjoint(collection1, collection2)` returns `false`, but `disjoint(collection1, collection3)` returns `true`.

```
Collection<String> collection1 = Arrays.asList("red", "cyan");
Collection<String> collection2 = Arrays.asList("red", "blue");
Collection<String> collection3 = Arrays.asList("pink", "tan");
System.out.println(Collections.disjoint(collection1, collection2));
System.out.println(Collections.disjoint(collection1, collection3));
```

frequency method

The `frequency(collection, element)` method finds the number of occurrences of the element in the collection. For example, `frequency(collection, "red")` returns 2 in the following code.

```
Collection<String> collection = Arrays.asList("red", "cyan", "red");
System.out.println(Collections.frequency(collection, "red"));
```

22.7 Performance of Sets and Lists

We now conduct an interesting experiment to test the performance of sets and lists. Listing 22.8 gives a program that shows the execution time of adding and removing elements in a hash set, linked hash set, tree set, array list, and linked list.

LISTING **22.8** `SetListPerformanceTest.java`

```java
1  import java.util.*;
2
3  public class SetListPerformanceTest {
4    public static void main(String[] args) {
5      // Create a hash set, and test its performance
6      Collection<Integer> set1 = new HashSet<Integer>();
7      System.out.println("Time for hash set is " +
8        getTestTime(set1, 500000)   + " milliseconds");
9
10     // Create a linked hash set, and test its performance
11     Collection<Integer> set2 = new LinkedHashSet<Integer>();
12     System.out.println("Time for linked hash set is " +
13       getTestTime(set2, 500000) + " milliseconds");
14
15     // Create a tree set, and test its performance
16     Collection<Integer> set3 = new TreeSet<Integer>();
17     System.out.println("Time for tree set is " +
18       getTestTime(set3, 500000) + " milliseconds");
19
20     // Create an array list, and test its performance
21     Collection<Integer> list1 = new ArrayList<Integer>();
22     System.out.println("Time for array list is " +
23       getTestTime(list1, 60000) + " milliseconds");
24
25     // Create a linked list, and test its performance
26     Collection<Integer> list2 = new LinkedList<Integer>();
27     System.out.println("Time for linked list is " +
28       getTestTime(list2, 60000) + " milliseconds");
29   }
30
31   public static long getTestTime(Collection<Integer> c, int size) {
32     long startTime = System.currentTimeMillis();
33
34     // Add numbers 0, 1, 2, ..., size - 1 to the array list
35     List<Integer> list = new ArrayList<Integer>();
36     for (int i = 0; i < size; i++)
37       list.add(i);
38
39     Collections.shuffle(list); // Shuffle the array list
40
41     // Add the elements to the container
42     for (int element: list)
43       c.add(element);
44
45     Collections.shuffle(list); // Shuffle the array list
46
47     // Remove the element from the container
48     for (int element: list)
49       c.remove(element);
50
51     long endTime = System.currentTimeMillis();
```

Annotations (right margin):
- a hash set (line 6)
- a linked hash set (line 11)
- a tree set (line 16)
- an array list (line 21)
- a linked list (line 26)
- start time (line 32)
- shuffle (line 39)
- add to container (line 43)
- shuffle (line 45)
- remove from container (line 49)
- end time (line 51)

return elapsed time

```
52      return endTime - startTime; // Return the execution time
53    }
54 }
```

```
Time for hash set is 1437 milliseconds
Time for linked hash set is 1891 milliseconds
Time for tree set is 2891 milliseconds
Time for array list is 13797 milliseconds
Time for linked list is 15344 milliseconds
```

The `getTestTime` method creates a list of distinct integers from `0` to `size - 1` (lines 35–37), shuffles the list (line 39), adds the elements from the list to a container `c` (lines 42–43), shuffles the list again (line 45), removes the elements from the container (lines 48–49), and finally returns the execution time (line 52).

The program creates a hash set (line 6), a linked hash set (line 11), a tree set (line 16), an array list (line 21), and a linked list (line 26). The program obtains the execution time for adding and removing **500000** elements in the three sets and adding and removing **60000** elements in the two lists.

sets are better

As you see, sets are much more efficient than lists. If sets are sufficient for your application, use sets. Furthermore, if no particular order is needed for your application, choose hash sets.

The program tested general remove operation for array lists and linked lists. Their complexity is about the same. Please note that linked lists are more efficient than array lists for insertion and deletion anywhere in the list except at the end.

22.8 The **Vector** and **Stack** Classes

The Java Collections Framework was introduced with Java 2. Several data structures were supported earlier, among them the **Vector** and **Stack** classes. These classes were redesigned to fit into the Java Collections Framework, but all their old style methods are retained for compatibility.

Vector is the same as **ArrayList**, except that it contains synchronized methods for accessing and modifying the vector. Synchronized methods can prevent data corruption when a vector is accessed and modified by two or more threads concurrently. For the many applications that do not require synchronization, using **ArrayList** is more efficient than using **Vector**.

The **Vector** class implements the **List** interface. It also has the methods contained in the original **Vector** class defined prior to Java 2, as shown in Figure 22.10.

Most of the additional methods in the **Vector** class listed in the UML diagram in Figure 22.10 are similar to the methods in the **List** interface. These methods were introduced before the Java Collections Framework. For example, `addElement(Object element)` is the same as the `add(Object element)` method, except that `addElement` method is synchronized. Use the **ArrayList** class if you don't need synchronization. It works much faster than **Vector**.

Note

The `elements()` method returns an **Enumeration**. The **Enumeration** interface was introduced prior to Java 2 and was superseded by the **Iterator** interface.

Note

Vector is widely used in Java programming because it was the Java resizable array implementation before Java 2. Many of the Swing data models use vectors.

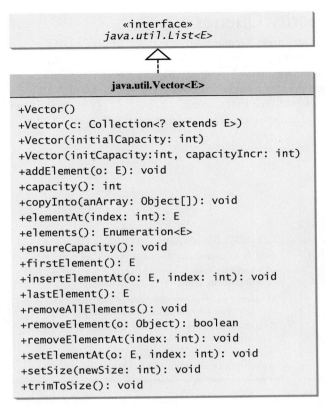

«interface» *java.util.List<E>*

java.util.Vector<E>
+Vector() +Vector(c: Collection<? extends E>) +Vector(initialCapacity: int) +Vector(initCapacity:int, capacityIncr: int) +addElement(o: E): void +capacity(): int +copyInto(anArray: Object[]): void +elementAt(index: int): E +elements(): Enumeration<E> +ensureCapacity(): void +firstElement(): E +insertElementAt(o: E, index: int): void +lastElement(): E +removeAllElements(): void +removeElement(o: Object): boolean +removeElementAt(index: int): void +setElementAt(o: E, index: int): void +setSize(newSize: int): void +trimToSize(): void

Creates a default empty vector with initial capacity 10.
Creates a vector from an existing collection.
Creates a vector with the specified initial capacity.
Creates a vector with the specified initial capacity and increment.
Appends the element to the end of this vector.
Returns the current capacity of this vector.
Copies the elements in this vector to the array.
Returns the object at the specified index.
Returns an enumeration of this vector.
Increases the capacity of this vector.
Returns the first element in this vector.
Inserts o to this vector at the specified index.
Returns the last element in this vector.
Removes all the elements in this vector.
Removes the first matching element in this vector.
Removes the element at the specified index.
Sets a new element at the specified index.
Sets a new size in this vector.
Trims the capacity of this vector to its size.

FIGURE 22.10 The `Vector` class in Java 2 implements `List` and also retains all the methods in the original `Vector` class.

In the Java Collections Framework, `Stack` is implemented as an extension of `Vector`, as illustrated in Figure 22.11.

The `Stack` class was introduced prior to Java 2. The methods shown in Figure 22.11 were used before Java 2. The `empty()` method is the same as `isEmpty()`. The `peek()` method looks at the element at the top of the stack without removing it. The `pop()` method removes the top element from the stack and returns it. The `push(Object element)` method adds the specified element to the stack. The `search(Object element)` method checks whether the specified element is in the stack.

java.util.Vector<E>

java.util.Stack<E>
+Stack() +empty(): boolean +peek(): E +pop(): E +push(o: E): E +search(o: Object): int

Creates an empty stack.
Returns true if this stack is empty.
Returns the top element in this stack.
Returns and removes the top element in this stack.
Adds a new element to the top of this stack.
Returns the position of the specified element in this stack.

FIGURE 22.11 The `Stack` class extends `Vector` to provide a last-in, first-out data structure.

22.9 Queues and Priority Queues

A queue is a first-in, first-out data structure. Elements are appended to the end of the queue and are removed from the beginning of the queue. In a priority queue, elements are assigned priorities. When accessing elements, the element with the highest priority is removed first. This section introduces queues and priority queues in the Java API.

Queue interface

JDK 1.5 introduced the `Queue` interface that extends `java.util.Collection` with additional insertion, extraction, and inspection operations, as shown in Figure 22.12.

FIGURE 22.12   The `Queue` interface extends `Collection` to provide additional insertion, extraction, and inspection operations.

queue operations

The `offer` method is used to add an element to the queue. This method is similar to the **add** method in the `Collection` interface, but the `offer` method is preferred for queues. The `poll` and `remove` methods are similar except that `poll()` returns `null` if the queue is empty, whereas `remove()` throws an exception. The `peek` and `element` methods are similar except that `peek()` returns `null` if the queue is empty, whereas `element()` throws an exception.

22.9.1   `Deque` and `LinkedList`

In JDK 1.5, the `LinkedList` class implements the `Deque` interface, which extends the `Queue` interface, as shown in Figure 22.13. So you can use `LinkedList` to create a queue.

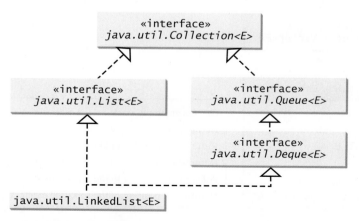

FIGURE 22.13   `LinkedList` implements `List` and `Deque`.

Deque supports element insertion and removal at both ends. The name *deque* is short for "double ended queue" and is usually pronounced "deck". The **Deque** interface extends **Queue** with additional methods for inserting and removing elements from the both ends of the queue. The methods **addFirst(e)**, **removeFirst()**, **addLast(e)**, **removeLast()**, **getFirst()**, and **getLast()** are defined in the **Deque** interface.

Listing 22.9 shows an example of using a queue to store strings. Line 4 creates a queue using **LinkedList**. Four strings are added to the queue in lines 5–8. The **size()** method defined in the **Collection** interface returns the number of elements in the queue (line 10). The **remove()** method retrieves and removes the element at the head of the queue (line 11).

LISTING 22.9 `TestQueue.java`

```
 1 public class TestQueue {
 2   public static void main(String[] args) {
 3     java.util.Queue<String> queue = new
 4       java.util.LinkedList<String>();
 5     queue.offer("Oklahoma");
 6     queue.offer("Indiana");
 7     queue.offer("Georgia");
 8     queue.offer("Texas");
 9
10     while (queue.size() > 0)
11       System.out.print(queue.remove() + " ");
12   }
13 }
```

- creates a queue
- inserts an element
- queue size
- remove element

```
Oklahoma Indiana Georgia Texas
```

The **PriorityQueue** class in JDK 1.5 implements a priority queue, as shown in Figure 22.14. By default, the priority queue orders its elements according to their natural ordering using **Comparable**. The element with the least value is assigned the highest priority, and thus is removed from the queue first. If there are several elements with the same highest priority, the tie is broken arbitrarily. You can also specify an ordering using **Comparator** in the constructor **PriorityQueue(initialCapacity, comparator)**.

PriorityQueue class

Listing 22.10 shows an example of using a priority queue to store strings. Line 5 creates a priority queue for strings using its no-arg constructor. This priority queue orders the strings using their

«interface» *java.util.Queue\<E>*

java.util.PriorityQueue\<E>
+PriorityQueue()
+PriorityQueue(initialCapacity: int)
+PriorityQueue(c: Collection\<? extends E>)
+PriorityQueue(initialCapacity: int, comparator: Comparator\<? super E>)

- Creates a default priority queue with initial capacity 11.
- Creates a default priority queue with the specified initial capacity.
- Creates a priority queue with the specified collection.
- Creates a priority queue with the specified initial capacity and the comparator.

FIGURE 22.14 The **PriorityQueue** class implements a priority queue.

natural order, so the strings are removed from the queue in increasing order. Lines 16–17 create a priority queue using the comparator obtained from `Collections.reverseOrder()`, which orders the elements in reverse order, so the strings are removed from the queue in decreasing order.

LISTING 22.10 PriorityQueueDemo.java

a default queue
inserts an element

a queue with comparator

comparator

```
 1 import java.util.*;
 2
 3 public class PriorityQueueDemo {
 4   public static void main(String[] args) {
 5     PriorityQueue<String> queue1 = new PriorityQueue<String>();
 6     queue1.offer("Oklahoma");
 7     queue1.offer("Indiana");
 8     queue1.offer("Georgia");
 9     queue1.offer("Texas");
10
11     System.out.println("Priority queue using Comparable:");
12     while (queue1.size() > 0) {
13       System.out.print(queue1.remove() + " ");
14     }
15
16     PriorityQueue<String> queue2 = new PriorityQueue<String>(
17       4, Collections.reverseOrder());
18     queue2.offer("Oklahoma");
19     queue2.offer("Indiana");
20     queue2.offer("Georgia");
21     queue2.offer("Texas");
22
23     System.out.println("\nPriority queue using Comparator:");
24     while (queue2.size() > 0) {
25       System.out.print(queue2.remove() + " ");
26     }
27   }
28 }
```

```
Priority queue using Comparable:
Georgia Indiana Oklahoma Texas
Priority queue using Comparator:
Texas Oklahoma Indiana Georgia
```

Video Note
Maps

22.10 Maps

The `Collection` interface represents a collection of elements stored in a set or a list. The `Map` interface maps keys to the elements. The keys are like indexes. In `List`, the indexes are integers. In `Map`, the keys can be any objects. A map cannot contain duplicate keys. Each key maps to one value. A key and its corresponding value form an entry, which is actually stored in a map, as shown in Figure 22.15.

The `Map` interface provides the methods for querying, updating, and obtaining a collection of values and a set of keys, as shown in Figure 22.16.

update methods

The *update methods* include `clear`, `put`, `putAll`, and `remove`. The `clear()` method removes all entries from the map. The `put(K key, V value)` method associates a value with a key in the map. If the map formerly contained a mapping for this key, the old value associated with the key is returned. The `putAll(Map m)` method adds the specified map to this map. The `remove(Object key)` method removes the map elements for the specified key from the map.

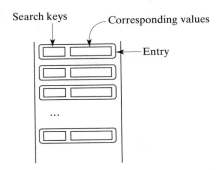

FIGURE 22.15 The entries consisting of key and values pairs are stored in a map.

«interface» *java.util.Map<K,V>*	
+clear(): void	Removes all mappings from this map.
+containsKey(key: Object): boolean	Returns true if this map contains a mapping for the specified key.
+containsValue(value: Object): boolean	Returns true if this map maps one or more keys to the specified value.
+entrySet(): Set<Map.Entry<K,V>>	Returns a set consisting of the entries in this map.
+get(key: Object): V	Returns the value for the specified key in this map.
+isEmpty(): boolean	Returns true if this map contains no mappings.
+keySet(): Set<K>	Returns a set consisting of the keys in this map.
+put(key: K, value: V): V	Puts a mapping in this map.
+putAll(m: Map<? extends K,? extends V>): void	Adds all the mappings from m to this map.
+remove(key: Object): V	Removes the mapping for the specified key.
+size(): int	Returns the number of mappings in this map.
+values(): Collection<V>	Returns a collection consisting of the values in this map.

FIGURE 22.16 The Map interface maps keys to values.

The *query methods* include containsKey, containsValue, isEmpty, and size. The containsKey(Object key) method checks whether the map contains a mapping for the specified key. The containsValue(Object value) method checks whether the map contains a mapping for this value. The isEmpty() method checks whether the map contains any mappings. The size() method returns the number of mappings in the map.

You can obtain a set of the keys in the map using the keySet() method, and a collection of the values in the map using the values() method. The entrySet() method returns a set of objects that implement the Map.Entry<K, V> interface, where Entry is an inner interface for the Map interface, as shown in Figure 22.17. Each object in the set is a specific key/value pair in the underlying map.

The AbstractMap class is a convenience class that implements all the methods in the Map interface except the entrySet() method.

query methods

keySet()
values()
entrySet()

AbstractMap

«interface» *java.util.Map.Entry<K,V>*	
+getKey(): K	Returns the key corresponding to this entry.
+getValue(): V	Returns the value corresponding to this entry.
+setValue(value: V): void	Replaces the value in this entry with a new value.

FIGURE 22.17 The Map.Entry interface operates on an entry in the map.

The `SortedMap` interface extends the `Map` interface to maintain the mapping in ascending order of keys with additional methods `firstKey()` and `lastKey()` for returning the lowest and highest key, `headMap(toKey)` for returning the portion of the map whose keys are less than `toKey`, and `tailMap(fromKey)` for returning the portion of the map whose keys are greater than or equal to `fromKey`.

concrete implementation

The `HashMap`, `LinkedHashMap`, and `TreeMap` classes are three *concrete implementations* of the `Map` interface, as shown in Figure 22.18.

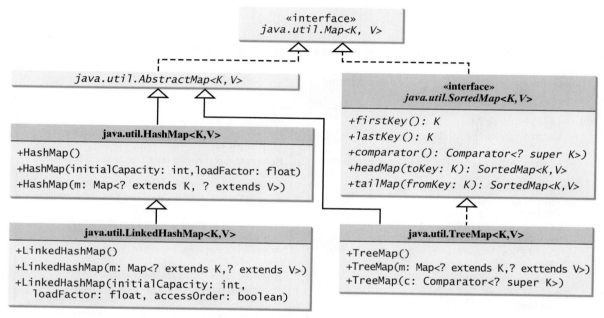

FIGURE 22.18 The Java Collections Framework provides three concrete map classes.

HashMap

The `HashMap` class is efficient for locating a value, inserting a mapping, and deleting a mapping.

LinkedHashMap

`LinkedHashMap` was introduced in JDK 1.4. It extends `HashMap` with a linked-list implementation that supports an ordering of the entries in the map. The entries in a `HashMap` are not ordered, but the entries in a `LinkedHashMap` can be retrieved either in the order in which they were inserted into the map (known as the *insertion order*) or in the order in which they were last accessed, from least recently accessed to most recently accessed (*access order*). The no-arg constructor constructs a `LinkedHashMap` with the insertion order. To construct a `LinkedHashMap` with the access order, use the `LinkedHashMap(initialCapacity, loadFactor, true)`.

insertion order
access order

TreeMap

The `TreeMap` class, implementing `SortedMap`, is efficient for traversing the keys in a sorted order. The keys can be sorted using the `Comparable` interface or the `Comparator` interface. If you create a `TreeMap` using its no-arg constructor, the `compareTo` method in the `Comparable` interface is used to compare the elements in the set, assuming that the class of the elements implements the `Comparable` interface. To use a comparator, you have to use the `TreeMap(Comparator comparator)` constructor to create a sorted map that uses the `compare` method in the comparator to order the elements in the map based on the keys.

 Note

Prior to JDK 1.2, `java.util.Hashtable` was used for mapping keys with elements. `Hashtable` was redesigned to fit into the Java Collections Framework with all its methods retained for compatibility. `Hashtable` implements the `Map` interface and is used in the same way as `HashMap` except that `Hashtable` is synchronized.

Hashtable

Listing 22.11 gives an example that creates a hash map, a linked hash map, and a tree map that map students to ages. The program first creates a hash map with the student's name as its key and the age as its value. The program then creates a tree map from the hash map and displays the mappings in ascending order of the keys. Finally, the program creates a linked hash map, adds the same entries to the map, and displays the entries.

LISTING 22.11 TestMap.java

```java
 1 import java.util.*;
 2
 3 public class TestMap {
 4   public static void main(String[] args) {
 5     // Create a HashMap
 6     Map<String, Integer> hashMap = new HashMap<String, Integer>();
 7     hashMap.put("Smith", 30);
 8     hashMap.put("Anderson", 31);
 9     hashMap.put("Lewis", 29);
10     hashMap.put("Cook", 29);
11
12     System.out.println("Display entries in HashMap");
13     System.out.println(hashMap);
14
15     // Create a TreeMap from the previous HashMap
16     Map<String, Integer> treeMap = new TreeMap<String,
17       Integer>(hashMap);
18     System.out.println("Display entries in ascending order of key");
19     System.out.println(treeMap + "\n");
20
21     // Create a LinkedHashMap
22     Map<String, Integer> linkedHashMap =
23       new LinkedHashMap<String, Integer>(16, 0.75f, true);
24     linkedHashMap.put("Smith", 30);
25     linkedHashMap.put("Anderson", 31);
26     linkedHashMap.put("Lewis", 29);
27     linkedHashMap.put("Cook", 29);
28
29     // Display the age for Lewis
30     System.out.println("The age for " + "Lewis is " +
31       linkedHashMap.get("Lewis").intValue());
32
33     System.out.println("\nDisplay entries in LinkedHashMap");
34     System.out.println(linkedHashMap);
35   }
36 }
```

create map
add entry

tree map

linked hash map

```
Display entries in HashMap
{Cook=29, Smith=30, Lewis=29, Anderson=31}

Display entries in ascending order of key
{Anderson=31, Cook=29, Lewis=29, Smith=30}
The age for Lewis is 29

Display entries in LinkedHashMap
{Smith=30, Anderson=31, Cook=29, Lewis=29}
```

As shown in the output, the entries in the `HashMap` are in random order. The entries in the `TreeMap` are in increasing order of the keys. The entries in the `LinkedHashMap` are in the order of their access, from least recently accessed to most recently.

All the concrete classes that implement the `Map` interface have at least two constructors. One is the no-arg constructor that constructs an empty map, and the other constructs a map from an instance of `Map`. Thus `new TreeMap<String, Integer>(hashMap)` (lines 16–17) constructs a tree map from a hash map.

You can create an insertion-ordered or access-ordered linked hash map. An access-ordered linked hash map is created in lines 22–23. The most recently accessed entry is placed at the end of the map. The entry with the key Lewis is last accessed in line 31, so it is displayed last in line 34.

Tip

If you don't need to maintain an order in a map when updating it, use a `HashMap`, because less time is needed than to insert and remove mappings. When you need to maintain the insertion order or access order in the map, use a `LinkedHashMap`. When you need the map to be sorted on keys, convert it to a tree map.

22.10.1 Case Study: Occurrences of Words

This case study writes a program that counts the occurrences of words in a text and displays the words and their occurrences in alphabetical order of words. The program uses a `TreeMap` to store an entry consisting of a word and its count. For each word, check whether it is already a key in the map. If not, add an entry with the word as the key and value 1 to the map. Otherwise, increase the value for the word (key) by 1 in the map. Assume the words are case insensitive; e.g., Good is treated same as good.

Listing 22.12 gives the solution to the problem.

LISTING 22.12 CountOccurrenceOfWords.java

```
 1  import java.util.*;
 2
 3  public class CountOccurrenceOfWords {
 4    public static void main(String[] args) {
 5      // Set text in a string
 6      String text = "Good morning. Have a good class. " +
 7        "Have a good visit. Have fun!";
 8
 9      // Create a TreeMap to hold words as key and count as value
10      TreeMap<String, Integer> map = new TreeMap<String, Integer>();
11
12      String[] words = text.split("[ \n\t\r.,;:!?(){}]");
13      for (int i = 0; i < words.length; i++) {
14        String key = words[i].toLowerCase();
15
16        if (words[i].length() > 1) {
17          if (map.get(key) == null) {
18            map.put(key, 1);
19          }
20          else {
21            int value = map.get(key).intValue();
22            value++;
23            map.put(key, value);
24          }
25        }
26      }
27
28      // Get all entries into a set
```

tree map — line 10

split string — line 12

add entry — line 18

add entry — line 23

```
29    Set<Map.Entry<String, Integer>> entrySet = map.entrySet();
30
31    // Get key and value from each entry
32    for (Map.Entry<String, Integer> entry: entrySet)
33      System.out.println(entry.getValue() + "\t" + entry.getKey());
34  }
35 }
```

entry set

display entry

```
1    class
1    fun
3    good
3    have
1    morning
1    visit
```

The program creates a `TreeMap` (line 10) to store pairs of words and their occurrence counts. The words serve as the keys. Since all elements in the map must be stored as objects, the count is wrapped in an `Integer` object.

The program extracts a word from a text using the `split` method (line 12) in the `String` class. For each word extracted, the program checks whether it is already stored as a key in the map (line 17). If not, a new pair consisting of the word and its initial count (`1`) is stored to the map (line 18). Otherwise, the count for the word is incremented by `1` (lines 21–23).

The program obtains the entries of the map in a set (line 29), and traverses the set to display the count and the key in each entry (lines 32–33).

Since the map is a tree map, the entries are displayed in increasing order of words. To display them in ascending order of the occurrence counts, see Exercise 22.8.

22.11 Singleton and Unmodifiable Collections and Maps

The `Collections` class contains the static methods for lists and collections. It also contains the methods for creating singleton sets, lists, and maps, and for creating unmodifiable sets, lists, and maps, as shown in Figure 22.19.

The `Collections` class defines three constants: one for an empty set, one for an empty list, and one for an empty map (`EMPTY_SET`, `EMPTY_LIST`, and `EMPTY_MAP`). The class also

java.util.Collections	
+singleton(o: Object): Set	Returns a singleton set containing the specified object.
+singletonList(o: Object): List	Returns a singleton list containing the specified object.
+singletonMap(key: Object, value: Object): Map	Returns a singleton map with the key and value pair.
+unmodifiedCollection(c: Collection): Collection	Returns an unmodified collection.
+unmodifiableList(list: List): List	Returns an unmodified list.
+unmodifiableMap(m: Map): Map	Returns an unmodified map.
+unmodifiableSet(s: Set): Set	Returns an unmodified set.
+unmodifiableSortedMap(s: SortedMap): SortedMap	Returns an unmodified sorted map.
+unmodifiableSortedSet(s: SortedSet): SortedSet	Returns an unmodified sorted set.

FIGURE 22.19 The `Collections` class contains the static methods for creating singleton and unmodifiable sets, lists, and maps.

provides the `singleton(Object o)` method for creating an immutable set containing only a single item, the `singletonList(Object o)` method for creating an immutable list containing only a single item, and the `singletonMap(Object key, Object value)` method for creating an immutable map containing only a single mapping.

The `Collections` class also provides six static methods for creating read-only collections: `unmodifiableCollection(Collection c)`, `unmodifiableList(List list)`, `unmodifiableMap(Map m)`, `unmodifiableSet(Set set)`, `unmodifiableSortedMap(SortedMap m)`, and `unmodifiableSortedSet(SortedSet s)`. The read-only collections prevent the data in the collections from being modified, and, as well, offer better performance for read-only operations.

KEY TERMS

collection 706	linked list 717
comparator 713	list 716
data structure 706	map 728
dynamic data structure 706	priority queue 726
hash map 730	queue 726
hash set 709	set 708
linked hash map 731	tree map 730
linked hash set 712	tree set 715

CHAPTER SUMMARY

■   The Java Collections Framework supports three types of collections: *sets*, *lists*, and *maps*. They are defined in the interfaces `Set`, `List`, and `Map`. A *set* stores a group of nonduplicate elements. A *list* stores an ordered collection of elements. A *map* stores a group of objects, each associated with a key.

■   A set stores nonduplicate elements. To allow duplicate elements to be stored in a collection, you need to use a list. A list not only can store duplicate elements but also allows the user to specify where they are stored. The user can access elements by an index.

■   Three types of sets are supported: `HashSet`, `LinkedHashSet`, and `TreeSet`. `HashSet` stores elements in an unpredictable order. `LinkedHashSet` stores elements in the order they were inserted. `TreeSet` stores elements sorted. All the methods in `HashSet`, `LinkedHashSet`, and `TreeSet` are inherited from the `Collection` interface.

■   Two types of lists are supported: `ArrayList` and `LinkedList`. `ArrayList` is a resizable-array implementation of the `List` interface. All the methods in `ArrayList` are defined in `List`. `LinkedList` is a linked-list implementation of the `List` interface. In addition to implementing the `List` interface, this class provides the methods for retrieving, inserting, and removing elements from both ends of the list.

■   The `Vector` class implements the `List` interface. In Java 2, `Vector` is the same as `ArrayList`, except that it contains synchronized methods for accessing and modifying the vector. The `Stack` class extends the `Vector` class and provides several methods for manipulating the stack.

■   The `Collection` interface represents a collection of elements stored in a set or a list. The `Map` interface maps keys to the elements. The keys are like indexes. In `List`, the indexes are integers. In `Map`, the keys can be any objects. A map cannot contain duplicate keys. Each key can map to at most one value. The `Map` interface provides the methods for querying, updating, and obtaining a collection of values and a set of keys.

■ The `Queue` interface represents a queue. The `PriorityQueue` class implements `Queue` for a priority queue.

■ Three types of maps are supported: `HashMap`, `LinkedHashMap`, and `TreeMap`. `HashMap` is efficient for locating a value, inserting a mapping, and deleting a mapping. `LinkedHashMap` supports ordering of the entries in the map. The entries in a `HashMap` are not ordered, but the entries in a `LinkedHashMap` can be retrieved either in the order in which they were inserted into the map (known as the *insertion order*) or in the order in which they were last accessed, from least recently accessed to most recently (*access order*). `TreeMap` is efficient for traversing the keys in a sorted order. The keys can be sorted using the `Comparable` interface or the `Comparator` interface.

REVIEW QUESTIONS

Sections 22.1–22.2

22.1 Describe the Java Collections Framework. List the interfaces, convenience abstract classes, and concrete classes.

22.2 Can a collection object be cloned and serialized?

22.3 The `hashCode` method and the `equals` method are defined in the `Object` class. Why are they redefined in the `Collection` interface?

22.4 Find the default implementation for the `equals` method and the `hashCode` method in the `Object` class from the source code of Object.java.

Section 22.3 Sets

22.5 How do you create an instance of `Set`? How do you insert a new element in a set? How do you remove an element from a set? How do you find the size of a set?

22.6 What are the differences between `HashSet`, `LinkedHashSet`, and `TreeSet`?

22.7 How do you traverse the elements in a set? Can you traverse the elements in a set in an arbitrary order?

22.8 How do you sort the elements in a set using the `compareTo` method in the `Comparable` interface? How do you sort the elements in a set using the `Comparator` interface? What would happen if you added an element that cannot be compared with the existing elements in a tree set?

22.9 Suppose that `set1` is a set that contains the strings `"red"`, `"yellow"`, `"green"`, and that `set2` is another set that contains the strings `"red"`, `"yellow"`, `"blue"`. Answer the following questions:

   ■ What are `set1` and `set2` after executing `set1.addAll(set2)`?
   ■ What are `set1` and `set2` after executing `set1.add(set2)`?
   ■ What are `set1` and `set2` after executing `set1.removeAll(set2)`?
   ■ What are `set1` and `set2` after executing `set1.remove(set2)`?
   ■ What are `set1` and `set2` after executing `set1.retainAll(set2)`?
   ■ What is `set1` after executing `set1.clear()`?

Section 22.4 The `Comparator` Interface

22.10 What are the differences between the `Comparable` interface and the `Comparator` interface? Which package is `Comparable` in, and which package is `Comparator` in?

22.11 The `Comparator` interface contains the `equals` method. Why is the method not implemented in the `GeometricObjectComparator` class in this section?

Section 22.5 Lists

22.12 How do you add and remove elements from a list? How do you traverse a list in both directions?

22.13 Suppose that `list1` is a list that contains the strings `"red"`, `"yellow"`, `"green"`, and that `list2` is another list that contains the strings `"red"`, `"yellow"`, `"blue"`. Answer the following questions:

- What are `list1` and `list2` after executing `list1.addAll(list2)`?
- What are `list1` and `list2` after executing `list1.add(list2)`?
- What are `list1` and `list2` after executing `list1.removeAll(list2)`?
- What are `list1` and `list2` after executing `list1.remove(list2)`?
- What are `list1` and `list2` after executing `list1.retainAll(list2)`?
- What is `list1` after executing `list1.clear()`?

22.14 What are the differences between `ArrayList` and `LinkedList`? Are all the methods in `ArrayList` also in `LinkedList`? What methods are in `LinkedList` but not in `ArrayList`?

22.15 How do you create a set or a list from an array of objects?

Section 22.6 Static Methods for Lists and Collections

22.16 Are all the methods in the `Collections` class static?

22.17 Which of the following static methods in the `Collections` class are for lists, and which are for collections?

```
sort, binarySearch, reverse, shuffle, max, min, disjoint,
  frequency
```

22.18 Show the printout of the following code.

```java
import java.util.*;

public class Test {
  public static void main(String[] args) {
    List<String> list =
      Arrays.asList("yellow", "red", "green", "blue");
    Collections.reverse(list);
    System.out.println(list);
    List<String> list1 =
      Arrays.asList("yellow", "red", "green", "blue");
    List<String> list2 = Arrays.asList("white", "black");
    Collections.copy(list1, list2);
    System.out.println(list1);

    Collection<String> collection1 = Arrays.asList("red",
      "cyan");
    Collection<String> collection2 = Arrays.asList("red",
      "blue");
    Collection<String> collection3 = Arrays.asList("pink",
      "tan");
    System.out.println(Collections.disjoint(collection1,
      collection2));
    System.out.println(Collections.disjoint(collection1,
      collection3));

    Collection<String> collection =
      Arrays.asList("red", "cyan", "red");
    System.out.println(Collections.frequency(collection,
      "red"));
  }
}
```

22.19 Which method can you use to sort the elements in an `ArrayList` or a `LinkedList`? Which method can you use to sort an array of strings?

22.20 Which method can you use to perform binary search for elements in an `ArrayList` or a `LinkedList`? Which method can you use to perform binary search for an array of strings?

22.21 Write a statement to find the largest element in an array of comparable objects.

Section 22.8 Vectors and Stacks

22.22 How do you create an instance of `Vector`? How do you add or insert a new element into a vector? How do you remove an element from a vector? How do you find the size of a vector?

22.23 How do you create an instance of `Stack`? How do you add a new element into a stack? How do you remove an element from a stack? How do you find the size of a stack?

22.24 Does Listing 22.1, TestHashSet.java, compile and run if line 7 (`Set set = new HashSet()`) is replaced by one of the following statements?

```
Collection set = new LinkedHashSet();
Collection set = new TreeSet();
Collection set = new ArrayList();
Collection set = new LinkedList();
Collection set = new Vector();
Collection set = new Stack();
```

Section 22.9 Queues and Priority Queues

22.25 Is `java.util.Queue` a subinterface of `java.util.Collection`, `java.util.Set`, or `java.util.List`? Does `LinkedList` implement `Queue`?

22.26 How do you create a priority queue for integers? By default, how are elements ordered in a priority queue? Is the element with the least value assigned the highest priority in a priority queue?

22.27 How do you create a priority queue that reverses the natural order of the elements?

Section 22.10 Maps

22.28 How do you create an instance of `Map`? How do you add an entry consisting of an element and a key into a map? How do you remove an entry from a map? How do you find the size of a map? How do you traverse entries in a map?

22.29 Describe and compare `HashMap`, `LinkedHashMap`, and `TreeMap`.

22.30 Show the printout of the following code:

```java
public class Test {
  public static void main(String[] args) {
    Map map = new LinkedHashMap();
    map.put("123", "John Smith");
    map.put("111", "George Smith");
    map.put("123", "Steve Yao");
    map.put("222", "Steve Yao");
    System.out.println("(1) " + map);
    System.out.println("(2) " + new TreeMap(map));
  }
}
```

PROGRAMMING EXERCISES

Section 22.3 Sets

22.1 (*Performing set operations on hash sets*) Create two hash sets {"George", "Jim", "John", "Blake", "Kevin", "Michael"} and {"George", "Katie", "Kevin", "Michelle", "Ryan"} and find their union, difference, and intersection. (You may clone the sets to preserve the original sets from being changed by these set methods.)

22.2 (*Displaying nonduplicate words in ascending order*) Write a program that reads words from a text file and displays all the nonduplicate words in ascending order. The text file is passed as a command-line argument.

22.3** (*Counting the keywords in Java source code*) Write a program that reads a Java source-code file and reports the number of keywords in the file. Pass the Java file name from the command line.

Hint: Create a set to store all the Java keywords.

Section 22.4 Lists

22.4 (*Performing set operations on array lists*) Create two array lists {"George", "Jim", "John", "Blake", "Kevin", "Michael"} and {"George", "Katie", "Kevin", "Michelle", "Ryan"} and find their union, difference, and intersection. (You may clone the lists to preserve the original lists from being changed by these methods.)

22.5* (*Displaying words in ascending alphabetical order*) Write a program that reads words from a text file and displays all the words (duplicates allowed) in ascending alphabetical order. The text file is passed as a command-line argument.

Section 22.6 Static Methods for Lists and Collections

22.6* (*Storing numbers in a linked list*) Write a program that lets the user enter numbers from a graphical user interface and display them in a text area, as shown in Figure 22.20. Use a linked list to store the numbers. Do not store duplicate numbers. Add the buttons *Sort*, *Shuffle*, and *Reverse* to sort, shuffle, and reverse the list.

FIGURE 22.20 The program stores numbers in a list.

Section 22.10 Maps

22.7* (*Counting the occurrences of numbers entered*) Write a program that reads an unspecified number of integers and finds the one that has the most occurrences. Your input ends when the input is 0. For example, if you entered 2 3 40 3 5 4 −3 3 3 2 0, the number 3 occurred most often. Please enter one number at a time. If not one but several numbers have the most occurrences, all of them should be reported. For example, since 9 and 3 appear twice in the list 9 30 3 9 3 2 4, both occurrences should be reported.

Video Note
Count occurrences of words in ascending order

22.8** (*Revising Listing 22.12, CountOccurrenceOfWords.java*) Rewrite Listing 22.12 to display the words in ascending order of occurrence counts.

Hint: Create a class named `WordOccurrence` that implements the `Comparable` interface. The class contains two fields, `word` and `count`. The `compareTo` method compares the counts. For each pair in the hash set in Listing 22.12, create an instance of `WordOccurrence` and store it in an array list. Sort the array list using the `Collections.sort` method. What would be wrong if you stored the instances of `WordOccurrence` in a tree set?

22.9** (*Counting the occurrences of words in a text file*) Rewrite Listing 22.12 to read the text from a text file. The text file is passed as a command-line argument. Words are delimited by whitespace, punctuations (`,;.:?`), quotation marks (`'"`), and parentheses. Count words in case-insensitive fashion (e.g., consider Good and good to be the same word). Don't count the word if the first character is not a letter. Display the output in alphabetical order of words with each word preceded by its occurrence count.

22.10*** (*Syntax highlighting*) Write a program that converts a Java file into an HTML file. In the HTML file, the keywords, comments, and literals are displayed in bold navy, green, and blue, respectively. Use the command line to pass a Java file and an HTML file. For example, the following command

```
java Exercise22_10 ComputeArea.java ComputeArea.HTML
```

converts ComputeArea.java into ComputeArea.HTML. Figure 22.21(a) shows a Java file. The corresponding HTML file is shown in Figure 22.21(b).

(a)

(b)

FIGURE 22.21 The Java code in plain text in (a) is displayed in HTML with syntax highlighted in (b).

22.11* (*Guessing the capitals*) Rewrite Exercise 8.22 so that the questions are randomly displayed.

22.12* (*Sort points in a plain*) Write a program that meets the following requirements:

- Define a class named **Point** with two data fields **x** and **y** to represent a point's **x** and **y** coordinates. Implement the **Comparable** interface for comparing the points on x-coordinates and on y-coordinates if x-coordinates are identical.
- Define a class named **CompareY** that implements **Comparator<Point>**. Implement the **compare** method to compare two points on their y-coordinates and on their x-coordinates if y-coordinates are identical.
- Randomly create **100** points and apply the **Arrays.sort** method to display the points in increasing order of their x-coordinates and display the points in increasing order of their y-coordinates, respectively.

22.13** (*Game: lottery*) Revise Exercise 3.15 to add an additional $2,000 award if two digits from the user input are in the lottery number.

(*Hint*: Sort the three digits for lottery and for user input in two lists and use the **Collection**'s **containsAll** method to check whether the two digits in the user input are in the lottery.)

CHAPTER 23

ALGORITHM EFFICIENCY

Objectives

- To estimate algorithm efficiency using the Big O notation (§23.2).

- To explain growth rates and why constants and nondominating terms can be ignored in the estimation (§23.2).

- To determine the complexity of various types of algorithms (§23.3).

- To analyze the binary search algorithm (§23.4).

- To analyze the selection sort algorithm (§23.5).

- To analyze the insertion sort algorithm (§23.6).

- To analyze the Towers of Hanoi algorithm (§23.7).

- To describe common growth functions (constant, logarithmic, log-linear, quadratic, cubic, exponential) (§23.8).

- To design efficient algorithms for finding Fibonacci numbers (§23.9).

- To design efficient algorithms for finding GCD (§23.10).

- To design efficient algorithms for finding prime numbers (§23.11).

- To design efficient algorithms for finding a closest pair of points (§23.12).

23.1 Introduction

execution time

Suppose two algorithms perform the same task, such as search (linear search vs. binary search) or sort (selection sort vs. insertion sort). Which one is better? To answer this question, we might implement these algorithms in Java and run the programs to get execution time. But there are two problems with this approach:

1. First, many tasks run concurrently on a computer. The execution time of a particular program depends on the system load.

2. Second, the execution time depends on specific input. Consider, for example, linear search and binary search. If an element to be searched happens to be the first in the list, linear search will find the element quicker than binary search.

It is very difficult to compare algorithms by measuring their execution time. To overcome these problems, a theoretical approach was developed to analyze algorithms independent of computers and specific input. This approach approximates the effect of a change on the size of the input. In this way, you can see how fast an algorithm's execution time increases as the input size increases, so you can compare two algorithms by examining their *growth rates*.

growth rate

Video Note
Big O notation

23.2 Big O Notation

Big *O* notation

Consider linear search. The linear search algorithm compares the key with the elements in the array sequentially until the key is found or the array is exhausted. If the key is not in the array, it requires n comparisons for an array of size n. If the key is in the array, it requires $n/2$ comparisons on average. The algorithm's execution time is proportional to the size of the array. If you double the size of the array, you will expect the number of comparisons to double. The algorithm grows at a linear rate. The growth rate has an order of magnitude of n. Computer scientists use the Big *O* notation to represent "order of magnitude." Using this notation, the complexity of the linear search algorithm is $O(n)$, pronounced as *"order of n."*

best-case
worst-case

For the same input size, an algorithm's execution time may vary, depending on the input. An input that results in the shortest execution time is called the *best-case* input, and an input that results in the longest execution time is called the *worst-case* input. Best case and worst case are not representative, but worst-case analysis is very useful. You can be assured that the algorithm will never be slower than the worst case. An average-case analysis attempts to determine the average amount of time among all possible inputs of the same size. Average-case analysis is ideal, but difficult to perform, because for many problems it is hard to determine the relative probabilities and distributions of various input instances. Worst-case analysis is easier to perform, so the analysis is generally conducted for the worst case.

average-case

The linear search algorithm requires n comparisons in the worst-case and $n/2$ comparisons in the average case. Using the Big *O* notation, both cases require $O(n)$ time. The multiplicative constant (1/2) can be omitted. Algorithm analysis is focused on growth rate. The multiplicative constants have no impact on growth rates. The growth rate for $n/2$ or $100n$ is the same as for n; i.e., $O(n) = O(n/2) = O(100n)$.

ignoring multiplicative constants

Consider the algorithm for finding the maximum number in an array of n elements. To find the maximum number if n is 2, it takes one comparison; if n is 3, two comparisons. In general, it takes $n - 1$ comparisons to find maximum number in a list of n elements. Algorithm analysis is for large input size. If the input size is small, there is no significance in estimating an algorithm's efficiency. As n grows larger, the n part in the expression $n - 1$ dominates the complexity. The Big *O* notation allows you to ignore the nondominating part (e.g., -1 in the expression $n - 1$) and highlight the important part (e.g., n in the expression $n - 1$). So, the complexity of this algorithm is $O(n)$.

large input size
ignoring nondominating terms

The Big *O* notation estimates the execution time of an algorithm in relation to the input size. If the time is not related to the input size, the algorithm is said to take *constant*

constant time

time with the notation $O(1)$. For example, a method that retrieves an element at a given index in an array takes constant time, because the time does not grow as the size of the array increases.

The following mathematical summations are often useful in algorithm analysis: useful summations

$$1 + 2 + 3 + \cdots + (n - 1) + n = \frac{n(n + 1)}{2}$$

$$a^0 + a^1 + a^2 + a^3 + \cdots + a^{(n-1)} + a^n = \frac{a^{n+1} - 1}{a - 1}$$

$$2^0 + 2^1 + 2^2 + 2^3 + \cdots + 2^{(n-1)} + 2^n = \frac{2^{n+1} - 1}{2 - 1} = 2^{n+1} - 1$$

23.3 Examples: Determining Big *O*

This section gives several examples of determining Big *O* for repetition, sequence, and selection statements.

Example 1

Consider the time complexity for the following loop:

```
for (i = 1; i = n; i++) {
  k = k + 5;
}
```

It is a constant time, c, for executing

```
k = k + 5;
```

Since the loop is executed n times, the time complexity for the loop is

$$T(n) = (\text{a constant } c) * n = O(n).$$

Example 2

What is the time complexity for the following loop?

```
for (i = 1; i <= n; i++) {
  for (j = 1; j <= n; j++) {
    k = k + i + j;
  }
}
```

It is a constant time, c, for executing

```
k = k + i + j;
```

The outer loop executes n times. For each iteration in the outer loop, the inner loop is executed n times. So, the time complexity for the loop is

$$T(n) = (\text{a constant } c) * n * n = O(n^2)$$

An algorithm with the $O(n^2)$ time complexity is called a *quadratic algorithm*. The qua- quadratic time
dratic algorithm grows quickly as the problem size increases. If you double the input size, the time for the algorithm is quadrupled. Algorithms with a nested loop are often quadratic.

Example 3

Consider the following loop:

```
for (i = 1; i <= n; i++) {
  for (j = 1; j <= i; j++) {
    k = k + i + j;
  }
}
```

The outer loop executes n times. For $i = 1, 2, \ldots$, the inner loop is executed one time, two times, and n times. So, the time complexity for the loop is

$$T(n) = c + 2c + 3c + 4c + \cdots + nc = cn(n + 1)/2 = (c/2)n + (c/2)n = O(n^2)$$

Example 4

Consider the following loop:

```
for (i = 1; i <= n; i++) {
  for (j = 1; j <= 20; j++) {
    k = k + i + j;
  }
}
```

The inner loop executes 20 times, and the outer loop executes n times. So, the time complexity for the loop is

$$T(n) = 20 * c * n = O(n)$$

Example 5

Consider the following sequences:

```
for (j = 1; j <= 10; j++) {
  k = k + 4;
}

for (i = 1; i <= n; i++) {
  for (j = 1; j <= 20; j++) {
    k = k + i + j;
  }
}
```

The first loop executes 10 times, and the second loop executes $20 * n$ times. So, the time complexity for the loop is

$$T(n) = 10 * c + 20 * c * n = O(n)$$

Example 6

Consider the following selection statement:

```
if (list.contains(e)) {
  System.out.println(e);
}
else
  for (Object t: list) {
    System.out.println(t);
  }
```

Suppose the list contains n elements. The execution time for `list.contains(e)` is $O(n)$. The loop in the `else` clause takes $O(n)$ time. So, the time complexity for the entire statement is

$T(n) = $ if test time $+$ worst-case time (if clause, else clause) $= O(n) + O(n) = O(n)$

Example 7

Consider the computation of a^n for an integer n. A simple algorithm would multiply a n times, as follows:

```
result = 1;
for (int i = 1; i <= n; i++)
  result *= a;
```

The algorithm takes $O(n)$ time. Without loss of generality, assume $n = 2^k$. You can improve the algorithm using the following scheme:

```
result = a;
for (int i = 1; i <= k; i++)
  result = result * result;
```

The algorithm takes $O(\log n)$ time. For an arbitrary n, you can revise the algorithm and prove that the complexity is still $O(\log n)$ (Review Question 23.7).

Note

For simplicity, since $O(\log n) = O(\log_2 n) = O(\log_a n)$, the constant base is omitted.   omitting base

23.4 Analyzing Binary Search

The binary search algorithm presented in Listing 6.7, BinarySearch.java, searches a key in a sorted array. Each iteration in the algorithm contains a fixed number of operations, denoted by c. Let $T(n)$ denote the time complexity for a binary search on a list of n elements. Without loss of generality, assume n is a power of 2 and $k = \log n$. Since binary search eliminates half of the input after two comparisons,

$$T(n) = T\left(\frac{n}{2}\right) + c = T\left(\frac{n}{2^2}\right) + c + c = T\left(\frac{n}{2^k}\right) + kc$$
$$= T(1) + c\log n = 1 + (\log n)c$$
$$= O(\log n)$$

Ignoring constants and nondominating terms, the complexity of the binary search algorithm is $O(\log n)$. An algorithm with the $O(\log n)$ time complexity is called a *logarithmic algorithm*. The base of the log is 2, but the base does not affect a logarithmic growth rate, so it can be   logarithmic time
omitted. The logarithmic algorithm grows slowly as the problem size increases. If you square the input size, you only double the time for the algorithm.

23.5 Analyzing Selection Sort

The selection sort algorithm presented in Listing 6.8, SelectionSort.java, finds the largest number in the list and places it last. It then finds the largest number remaining and places it next to last, and so on until the list contains only a single number. The number of comparisons is $n - 1$ for the first iteration, $n - 2$ for the second iteration, and so on. Let $T(n)$ denote the complexity for selection sort and c denote the total number of other operations such as assignments and additional comparisons in each iteration. So,

$$T(n) = (n - 1) + c + (n - 2) + c + \cdots + 2 + c + 1 + c$$
$$= \frac{(n - 1)(n - 1 + 1)}{2} + c(n - 1) = \frac{n^2}{2} - \frac{n}{2} + cn - c$$
$$= O(n^2)$$

Therefore, the complexity of the selection sort algorithm is $O(n^2)$.

23.6 Analyzing Insertion Sort

The insertion sort algorithm presented in Listing 6.9, InsertionSort.java, sorts a list of values by repeatedly inserting a new element into a sorted partial array until the whole array is sorted. At the k th iteration, to insert an element into an array of size k, it may take k comparisons to find the insertion position, and k moves to insert the element. Let $T(n)$ denote the complexity for insertion sort and c denote the total number of other operations such as assignments and additional comparisons in each iteration. So,

$$T(n) = (2 + c) + (2 \times 2 + c) + \cdots + (2 \times (n - 1) + c)$$
$$= 2(1 + 2 + \cdots + n - 1) + c(n - 1)$$
$$= 2\frac{(n - 1)n}{2} + cn - c = n^2 - n + cn - c$$
$$= O(n^2)$$

Therefore, the complexity of the insertion sort algorithm is $O(n^2)$. So, the selection sort and insertion sort are of the same time complexity.

23.7 Analyzing the Towers of Hanoi Problem

The Towers of Hanoi problem presented in Listing 20.8, TowersOfHanoi.java, moves n disks from tower A to tower B with the assistance of tower C recursively as follows:

1. Move the first $n-1$ disks from A to C with the assistance of tower B.

2. Move disk n from A to B.

3. Move $n-1$ disks from C to B with the assistance of tower A.

Let $T(n)$ denote the complexity for the algorithm that moves n disks and c denote the constant time to move one disk; i.e., $T(1)$ is c. So,

$$T(n) = T(n - 1) + c + T(n - 1)$$
$$= 2T(n - 1) + c$$
$$= 2(2T(n - 2) + c) + c$$
$$= 2(2(2T(n - 3) + c) + c) + c$$
$$= 2^{n-1}T(1) + 2^{n-2}c + \cdots + 2c + c$$
$$= 2^{n-1}c + 2^{n-2}c + \cdots + 2c + c = (2^n - 1)c = O(2^n)$$

$O(2^n)$
exponential time

An algorithm with $O(2^n)$ time complexity is called an *exponential algorithm*. As the input size increases, the time for the exponential algorithm grows exponentially. Exponential algorithms are not practical for large input size.

23.8 Comparing Common Growth Functions

The preceding sections analyzed the complexity of several algorithms. Table 23.1 lists some common growth functions and shows how growth rates change as the input size doubles from $n = 25$ to $n = 50$.

TABLE 23.1 Change of Growth Rates

Function	Name	$n = 25$	$n = 50$	$f(50)/f(25)$
$O(1)$	Constant time	1	1	1
$O(\log n)$	Logarithmic time	4.64	5.64	1.21
$O(n)$	Linear time	25	50	2
$O(n \log n)$	Log-linear time	116	282	23.431
$O(n^2)$	Quadratic time	625	2500	4
$O(n^3)$	Cubic time	15625	125000	8
$O(2^n)$	Exponential time	3.36×10^7	1.27×10^{15}	3.35×10^7

These functions are ordered as follows, as illustrated in Figure 23.1.

$$O(1) < O(\log n) < O(n) < O(n \log n) < O(n^2) < O(n^3) < O(2^n)$$

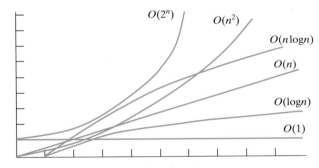

FIGURE 23.1 As the size n increases, the function grows.

23.9 Case Studies: Finding Fibonacci Numbers

§20.3, "Example: Fibonacci Numbers," gave a recursive method for finding the Fibonacci number, as follows:

```
/** The method for finding the Fibonacci number */
public static long fib(long index) {
  if (index == 0) // Base case
    return 0;
  else if (index == 1) // Base case
    return 1;
  else  // Reduction and recursive calls
    return fib(index - 1) + fib(index - 2);
}
```

We can now prove that the complexity of this algorithm is $O(2^n)$. For convenience, let the index be n. Let $T(n)$ denote the complexity for the algorithm that finds fib(n) and c denote the constant time for comparing index with 0 and 1; i.e., $T(1)$ is c. So,

$$T(n) = T(n - 1) + T(n - 2) + c$$
$$\leq 2T(n - 1) + c$$
$$\leq 2(2T(n - 2) + c) + c$$
$$= 2^2 T(n - 2) + 2c + c$$

Similar to the analysis of the Towers of Hanoi problem, we can show that $T(n)$ is $O(2^n)$.

This algorithm is not efficient. Is there an efficient algorithm for finding a Fibonacci number? The trouble in the recursive `fib` method is that the method is invoked redundantly with the same arguments. For example, to compute `fib(4)`, `fib(3)` and `fib(2)` are invoked. To compute `fib(3)`, `fib(2)` and `fib(1)` are invoked. Note that `fib(2)` is redundantly invoked. We can improve it by avoiding repeated calling of the `fib` method with the same argument. Note that a new Fibonacci number is obtained by adding the preceding two numbers in the sequence. If you use two variables `f0` and `f1` to store the two preceding numbers, the new number can be immediately obtained by adding `f0` with `f1`. Now you should update `f0` and `f1` by assigning `f1` to `f0` and assigning the new number to `f1`. The new method is presented in Listing 23.1.

LISTING 23.1 ImprovedFibonacci.java

```java
 1 import java.util.Scanner;
 2
 3 public class ImprovedFibonacci {
 4   /** Main method */
 5   public static void main(String args[]) {
 6     // Create a Scanner
 7     Scanner input = new Scanner(System.in);
 8     System.out.print("Enter an index for the Fibonacci number: ");
 9     int index = input.nextInt();
10
11     // Find and display the Fibonacci number
12     System.out.println(
13       "Fibonacci number at index " + index + " is " + fib(index));
14   }
15
16   /** The method for finding the Fibonacci number */
17   public static long fib(long n) {
18     if (n == 0 || n == 1)
19       return n;
20
21     long f0 = 0; // For fib(0)
22     long f1 = 1; // For fib(1)
23     long currentFib = 1; // For fib(2)
24
25     for (int i = 2; i <= n; i++) {
26       currentFib = f0 + f1;
27       f0 = f1;
28       f1 = currentFib;
29     }
30
31     return currentFib;
32   }
33 }
```

input

invoke fib

simple case

f0
f1

get a new fib

```
Enter an index for the Fibonacci number:  6  ⏎ Enter
Fibonacci number at index 6 is 8
```

```
Enter an index for the Fibonacci number:  7  ⏎ Enter
Fibonacci number at index 7 is 13
```

$O(n)$

Obviously, the complexity of this new algorithm is $O(n)$. This is a tremendous improvement over the recursive $O(2^n)$ algorithm.

23.10 Case Studies: Finding Greatest Common Divisors

Video Note
Algorithms for finding
GCD

This section presents several algorithms in the search for an efficient algorithm for finding the greatest common divisor between two integers.

The greatest common divisor of two integers is the largest number that can evenly divide both integers. Listing 4.8, GreatestCommonDivisor.java, presented a brute-force algorithm for finding the greatest common divisor (GCD) of two integers m and n. The algorithm checks whether k (for k = 2, 3, 4, and so on) is a common divisor for n1 and n2, until k is greater than n1 or n2. The algorithm can be described as follows:

```java
public static int gcd(int m, int n) {
  int gcd = 1;

  for (int k = 2; k <= m && k <= n; k++) {
    if (m % k == 0 && n % k == 0)
      gcd = k;
  }

  return gcd;
}
```

Assume $m \geq n$, the complexity of this algorithm is obviously $O(n)$.

Is there any better algorithm for finding the gcd? Rather than searching a possible divisor from 1 up, it is more efficient to search from n down. Once a divisor is found, the divisor is the GCD. So you can improve the algorithm using the following loop:

assume $m \geq n$

$O(n)$

improved solutions

```java
for (int k = n; k >= 1; k--) {
  if (m % k == 0 && n % k == 0) {
    gcd = k;
    break;
  }
}
```

This algorithm is better than the preceding one, but its worst-case time complexity is still $O(n)$.

A divisor for a number m cannot be greater than m / 2. So you can further improve the algorithm using the following loop:

```java
for (int k = n / 2; k >= 1; k--) {
  if (m % k == 0 && n % k == 0) {
    gcd = k;
    break;
  }
}
```

However, this algorithm is incorrect, because m can be a divisor for m itself. This revision does not work for the case when m is equal to n. The correct algorithm is shown in Listing 23.2.

LISTING 23.2 GCD1.java

```java
1 import java.util.Scanner;
2
3 public class GCD1 {
4   /** Find gcd for integers m and n */
5   public static int gcd(int m, int n) {
6     int gcd = 1;
7
8     if (m == n) return m;
9
```

check divisor

```
10      for (int k = n / 2; k >= 1; k--) {
11        if (m % k == 0 && n % k == 0) {
12          gcd = k;
13          break;
14        }
15      }
16
17      return gcd;
18    }
19
20    /** Main method */
21    public static void main(String[] args) {
22      // Create a Scanner
23      Scanner input = new Scanner(System.in);
24
25      // Prompt the user to enter two integers
26      System.out.print("Enter first integer: ");
27      int m = input.nextInt();
28      System.out.print("Enter second integer: ");
29      int n = input.nextInt();
30
31      System.out.println("The greatest common divisor for " + m +
32        " and " + n + " is " + gcd(m, n));
33    }
34 }
```

gcd found

input

input

```
Enter first integer: 2525  ↵Enter
Enter second integer: 125  ↵Enter
The greatest common divisor for 2525 and 125 is 25
```

```
Enter first integer:  3  ↵Enter
Enter second integer:  3  ↵Enter
The greatest common divisor for 3 and 3 is 3
```

O(n)

Assuming $m \geq n$, the **for** loop is executed at most n / 2 times, which cuts the time by half from the previous algorithm. The time complexity of this algorithm is still $O(n)$, but practically, it is much faster than the algorithm in Listing 4.8.

Note

The Big *O* notation provides a good theoretical estimate of algorithm efficiency. However, two algorithms of the same time complexity are not necessarily equally efficient. As shown in the preceding example, both algorithms in Listings 4.8 and 23.2 have the same complexity, but in terms of practically the one in Listing 23.2 is obviously better.

practical consideration

improved solutions

A more efficient algorithm for finding gcd was discovered by Euclid around 300 B.C. This is one of the oldest known algorithms. The algorithm can be defined recursively as follows: Let gcd(m, n) denote the gcd for integers m and n:

- If m % n is 0, gcd (m, n) is n.

- Otherwise, gcd(m, n) is gcd(n, m % n).

It is not difficult to prove the correctness of the algorithm. Suppose m % n = r. So, m = qn + r, where q is the quotient of m / n. Any number that is divisible by m and n must also be divisible by r. Therefore, gcd(m, n) is same as gcd(n, r), where r = m % n. The algorithm can be implemented as in Listing 23.3.

LISTING 23.3 GCD2.java

```
1 import java.util.Scanner;
2
3 public class GCD2 {
4   /** Find gcd for integers m and n */
5   public static int gcd(int m, int n) {
6     if (m % n == 0)
7       return n;
8     else
9       return gcd(n, m % n);
10  }
11
12  /** Main method */
13  public static void main(String[] args) {
14    // Create a Scanner
15    Scanner input = new Scanner(System.in);
16
17    // Prompt the user to enter two integers
18    System.out.print("Enter first integer: ");
19    int m = input.nextInt();
20    System.out.print("Enter second integer: ");
21    int n = input.nextInt();
22
23    System.out.println("The greatest common divisor for " + m +
24      " and " + n + " is " + gcd(m, n));
25  }
26 }
```

base case

reduction

input

input

```
Enter first integer: 2525 ↵Enter
Enter second integer: 125 ↵Enter
The greatest common divisor for 2525 and 125 is 25
```

```
Enter first integer: 3 ↵Enter
Enter second integer: 3 ↵Enter
The greatest common divisor for 3 and 3 is 3
```

In the best case when m % n is 0, the algorithm takes just one step to find the gcd. It is difficult to analyze the average case. However, we can prove that the worst-case time complexity is $O(\log n)$.

best case
average case
worst case

Assuming $m \geq n$, we can show that m % n < m / 2, as follows:

- If n <= m / 2, m % n < m / 2, since the remainder of *m* divided by *n* is always less than *n*.

- If n > m / 2, m % n = m − n < m / 2. Therefore, m % n < m / 2.

The Euclid's algorithm recursively invokes the gcd method. It first calls gcd(m, n), then calls gcd(n, m % n), and gcd(m % n, n % (m % n)), and so on, as follows:

```
  gcd(m, n)
= gcd(n, m % n)
= gcd(m % n, n % (m % n))
= ...
```

Since m % n < m / 2 and n % (m % n) < n / 2, the argument passed to the gcd method is reduced by half after every two iterations. After invoking gcd two times, the second parameter is less than *n*/2. After invoking gcd four times, the second parameter is less than *n*/4.

After invoking gcd six times, the second parameter is less than $\frac{n}{2^3}$. Let k be the number of times the gcd method is invoked. After invoking gcd k times, the second parameter is less than $\frac{n}{2^{(k/2)}}$, which is greater than or equal to 1. That is,

$$\frac{n}{2^{(k/2)}} \geq 1 \quad => \quad n \geq 2^{(k/2)} \quad => \quad \log n \geq k/2 \quad => \quad k \leq 2 \log n$$

Therefore, $k \leq 2 \log n$. So, the time complexity of the gcd method is $O(\log n)$.

The worst case occurs when the two numbers result in most divisions. It turns out that two successive Fibonacci numbers will result in most divisions. Recall that the Fibonacci series begins with 0 and 1, and each subsequent number is the sum of the preceding two numbers in the series, such as:

$$0 \quad 1 \quad 1 \quad 2 \quad 3 \quad 5 \quad 8 \quad 13 \quad 21 \quad 34 \quad 55 \quad 89 \ldots$$

The series can be recursively defined as

```
fib(0) = 0;
fib(1) = 1;
fib(index) = fib(index - 2) + fib(index - 1); index >= 2
```

For two successive Fibonacci numbers `fib(index)` and `fib(index -1)`,

```
gcd(fib(index), fib(index -1))
= gcd(fib(index -1), fib(index -2))
= gcd(fib(index -2), fib(index -3))
= gcd(fib(index -3), fib(index -4))
= ...
= gcd(fib(2), fib(1))
= 1
```

For example,

```
gcd(21, 13)
= gcd(13, 8)
= gcd(8, 5)
= gcd(5, 3)
= gcd(3, 2)
= gcd(2, 1)
= 1
```

So, the number of times the gcd method is invoked is the same as the index. We can prove that $index \leq 1.44 \log n$, where $n = \text{fib}(index - 1)$. This is a tighter bound than $index \leq 2 \log n$. The proof is given at www.cs.armstrong.edu/liang/javads/euclides.html.

Table 23.2 summarizes the complexity of three algorithms for finding the gcd:

TABLE 23.2 Comparisons of GCD Algorithms

	Listing 4.8	Listing 23.2	Listing 23.3
Complexity	$O(n)$	$O(n)$	$O(\log n)$

23.11 Case Studies: Finding Prime Numbers

A $100,000 award awaits the first individual or group who discovers a prime number with at least 10,000,000 decimal digits (www.eff.org/awards/coop.php). This section presents several algorithms in the search for an efficient algorithm for finding the prime numbers.

An integer greater than 1 is *prime* if its only positive divisor is 1 or itself. For example, 2, 3, 5, and 7 are prime numbers, but 4, 6, 8, and 9 are not.

what is prime?

How do you determine whether a number n is prime? Listing 4.14 presented a brute-force algorithm for finding prime numbers. The algorithm checks whether 2, 3, 4, 5, ..., or n - 1 is divisible by n. If not, n is prime. This algorithm takes $O(n)$ time to check whether n is prime. Note that you only need to check whether 2, 3, 4, 5, ..., and n/2 is divisible by n. If not, n is prime. The algorithm is slightly improved, but it is still of the order of $O(n)$.

In fact, we can prove that if n is not a prime, n must have a factor that is greater than 1 and less than or equal to $\sqrt{n}$. Here is the proof. Since n is not a prime, there exists two numbers p and q such that n = pq with $1 \leq p \leq q$. Note that $n = \sqrt{n}\sqrt{n}$. p must be less than or equal to $\sqrt{n}$. Hence, you only need to check whether 2, 3, 4, 5, ..., or $\sqrt{n}$ is divisible by n. If not, n is prime. This significantly reduces the time complexity of the algorithm to $O(\sqrt{n})$.

Now consider the algorithm for finding all the prime numbers up to n. A straightforward implementation is to check whether i is prime for i = 2, 3, 4, ..., n. The program is given in Listing 23.4.

LISTING 23.4 PrimeNumbers.java

```java
1  import java.util.Scanner;
2
3  public class PrimeNumbers {
4    public static void main(String[] args) {
5      Scanner input = new Scanner(System.in);
6      System.out.print("Find all prime numbers <= n, enter n: ");
7      int n = input.nextInt();
8
9      final int NUMBER_PER_LINE = 10; // Display 10 per line
10     int count = 0; // Count the number of prime numbers
11     int number = 2; // A number to be tested for primeness
12
13     System.out.println("The prime numbers are:");
14
15     // Repeatedly find prime numbers
16     while (number <= n) {
17       // Assume the number is prime
18       boolean isPrime = true; // Is the current number prime?
19
20       // Test if number is prime
21       for (int divisor = 2; divisor <= (int)(Math.sqrt(number));
22            divisor++) {
23         if (number % divisor == 0) { // If true, number is not prime
24           isPrime = false; // Set isPrime to false
25           break; // Exit the for loop
26         }
27       }
28
29       // Print the prime number and increase the count
30       if (isPrime) {
31         count++; // Increase the count
32
33         if (count % NUMBER_PER_LINE == 0) {
34           // Print the number and advance to the new line
35           System.out.printf("%7d\n", number);
36         }
37         else
38           System.out.printf("%7d", number);
39     }
40
```

check prime

increase count

check next number

```
41      // Check if the next number is prime
42        number++;
43    }
44
45      System.out.println("\n" + count + " number of primes <= " + n);
46  }
47 }
```

```
Find all prime numbers <= n, enter n: 1000 ⏎Enter
The prime numbers are:
      2      3      5      7     11     13     17     19     23     29
     31     37     41     43     47     53     59     61     67     71
 ...
 ...
 168 number of primes <= 1000
```

The program is not efficient if you have to compute `Math.sqrt(number)` for every iteration of the for loop (line 21). A good compiler should evaluate `Math.sqrt(number)` only once for the entire for loop. To ensure this happens, you may explicitly replace line 21 by the following two lines:

```
int squareRoot = (int)(Math.sqrt(number));
for (int divisor = 2; divisor <= squareRoot; divisor++) {
```

In fact, there is no need to actually compute `Math.sqrt(number)` for every `number`. You need only look for the perfect squares such as **4, 9, 16, 25, 36, 49**, and so on. Note that for all the numbers between **36** and **48**, their `(int)(Math.sqrt(number))` is **6**. With this insight, you can replace the code in lines 16–27 with the following code:

```
...
int squareRoot = 1;

// Repeatedly find prime numbers
while (number <= n) {
  // Assume the number is prime
  boolean isPrime = true; // Is the current number prime?

  if (squareRoot * squareRoot < number) squareRoot++;

  // Test if number is prime
  for (int k = 0; k < list.size() && list.get(k) <= squareRoot; k++) {
    if (number % list.get(k) == 0) { // If true, number is not prime
      isPrime = false; // Set isPrime to false
      break; // Exit the for loop
    }
  }
}
...
```

Now we turn our attention to analyzing the complexity of this program. Since it takes $\sqrt{i}$ steps in the for loop (lines 21–26) to check whether number i is prime, the algorithm takes $\sqrt{2} + \sqrt{3} + \sqrt{4} + \cdots + \sqrt{n}$ steps to find all the prime numbers less than or equal to n. Observe that

$$\sqrt{2} + \sqrt{3} + \sqrt{4} + \cdots + \sqrt{n} \leq n\sqrt{n}$$

Therefore, the time complexity for this algorithm is $O(n\sqrt{n})$.

To determine whether i is prime, the algorithm checks whether **2, 3, 4, 5**, ..., and $\sqrt{i}$ is divisible by i. This algorithm can be further improved. In fact, you only need to check whether the prime numbers from 2 to $\sqrt{i}$ are possible divisors for i.

We can prove that if i is not prime, there must exist a prime number p such that $i = pq$ and $p \leq q$. Here is the proof. Assume that i is not prime; let p be the smallest factor of i. p must be prime, otherwise, p has a factor k with $2 \leq k < p$. k is also a factor of i, which contradicts that p be the smallest factor of i. Therefore, if i is not prime, you can find a prime number from 2 to $\sqrt{i}$ that is divisible by i. This leads to a more efficient algorithm for finding all prime numbers up to n, as shown in Listing 23.5.

LISTING 23.5 EfficientPrimeNumbers.java

```java
1 import java.util.Scanner;
2
3 public class EfficientPrimeNumbers {
4   public static void main(String[] args) {
5     Scanner input = new Scanner(System.in);
6     System.out.print("Find all prime numbers <= n, enter n: ");
7     int n = input.nextInt();
8
9     // A list to hold prime numbers
10    java.util.List<Integer> list =
11      new java.util.ArrayList<Integer>();
12
13    final int NUMBER_PER_LINE = 10; // Display 10 per line
14    int count = 0; // Count the number of prime numbers
15    int number = 2; // A number to be tested for primeness
16    int squareRoot = 1; // Check whether number <= squareRoot
17
18    System.out.println("The prime numbers are \n");
19
20    // Repeatedly find prime numbers
21    while (number <= n) {
22      // Assume the number is prime
23      boolean isPrime = true; // Is the current number prime?
24
25      if (squareRoot * squareRoot < number) squareRoot++;
26
27      // Test if number is prime
28      for (int k = 0; k < list.size()                            check prime
29                      && list.get(k) <= squareRoot; k++) {
30        if (number % list.get(k) == 0) { // If true, not prime
31          isPrime = false; // Set isPrime to false
32          break; // Exit the for loop
33        }
34      }
35
36      // Print the prime number and increase the count
37      if (isPrime) {
38        count++; // Increase the count                          increase count
39        list.add(number); // Add a new prime to the list
40        if (count % NUMBER_PER_LINE == 0) {
41          // Print the number and advance to the new line
42          System.out.println(number);
43        }
44        else
45          System.out.print(number + " ");
46      }
47
48      // Check if the next number is prime
49      number++;                                                 check next number
50    }
51
```

```
52        System.out.println("\n" + count + " number of primes <= " + n);
53  }
54 }
```

```
Find all prime numbers <= n, enter n: 1000  ↵Enter
The prime numbers are:
         2      3      5      7     11     13     17     19     23     29
        31     37     41     43     47     53     59     61     67     71
...
...
168 number of primes <= 1000
```

Let $\pi(i)$ denote the number of prime numbers less than or equal to i. The primes under **20** are **2, 3, 5, 7, 11, 13, 17,** and **19**. So, $\pi(2)$ is **1**, $\pi(3)$ is **2**, $\pi(6)$ is **3**, and $\pi(20)$ is **8**. It has been proved that $\pi(i)$ is approximately $\dfrac{i}{\log i}$ (see primes.utm.edu/howmany.shtml).

For each number i, the algorithm checks whether a prime number less than or equal to $\sqrt{i}$ is divisible by i. The number of the prime numbers less than or equal to $\sqrt{i}$ is $\dfrac{\sqrt{i}}{\log \sqrt{i}} = \dfrac{2\sqrt{i}}{\log i}$. Thus, the complexity for finding all prime numbers up to **n** is

$$\frac{2\sqrt{2}}{\log 2} + \frac{2\sqrt{3}}{\log 3} + \frac{2\sqrt{4}}{\log 4} + \frac{2\sqrt{5}}{\log 5} + \frac{2\sqrt{6}}{\log 6} + \frac{2\sqrt{7}}{\log 7} + \frac{2\sqrt{8}}{\log 8} + \cdots + \frac{2\sqrt{n}}{\log n}$$

Since $\dfrac{\sqrt{i}}{\log i} < \dfrac{\sqrt{n}}{\log n}$ for $i < n$ and $n \geq 16$,

$$\frac{2\sqrt{2}}{\log 2} + \frac{2\sqrt{3}}{\log 3} + \frac{2\sqrt{4}}{\log 4} + \frac{2\sqrt{5}}{\log 5} + \frac{2\sqrt{6}}{\log 6} + \frac{2\sqrt{7}}{\log 7} + \frac{2\sqrt{8}}{\log 8} + \cdots + \frac{2\sqrt{n}}{\log n} < \frac{2n\sqrt{n}}{\log n}$$

Therefore, the complexity of this algorithm is $O\left(\dfrac{n\sqrt{n}}{\log n}\right)$.

Is there any algorithm better than $O\left(\dfrac{n\sqrt{n}}{\log n}\right)$? Let us examine the well-known Eratosthenes algorithm for finding prime numbers. Eratosthenes (276–194 B.C.) was a Greek mathematician who devised a clever algorithm, known as the *Sieve of Eratosthenes*, for finding all prime numbers $\leq n$. His algorithm is to use an array named `primes` of n Boolean values. Initially, all elements in `primes` are set `true`. Since the multiples of **2** are not prime, set `primes[2 * i]` to `false` for all $2 \leq i \leq n/2$, as shown in Figure 23.2. Since we don't care about `primes[0]` and `primes[1]`, these values are marked × in the figure.

Sieve of Eratosthenes

primes array

```
index  0  1  2  3  4  5  6  7  8  9 10 11 12 13 14 15 16 17 18 19 20 21 22 23 24 25 26 27
initial × ×  T  T  T  T  T  T  T  T  T  T  T  T  T  T  T  T  T  T  T  T  T  T  T  T  T  T
k = 2   × ×  T  T  F  T  F  T  F  T  F  T  F  T  F  T  F  T  F  T  F  T  F  T  F  T  F  T
k = 3   × ×  T  T  F  T  F  T  F  F  F  T  F  T  F  F  F  T  F  T  F  F  F  T  F  T  F  F
k = 5   × ×  Ⓣ Ⓣ  F  Ⓣ  F  Ⓣ  F  F  F  Ⓣ  F  Ⓣ  F  F  F  Ⓣ  F  Ⓣ  F  F  F  Ⓣ  F  F  F
```

FIGURE 23.2 The values in `primes` are changed with each prime number k.

Since the multiples of 3 are not prime, set `primes[3 * i]` to `false` for all $3 \leq i \leq n/3$. Since the multiples of 5 are not prime, set `primes[5 * i]` to `false` for all $5 \leq i \leq n/5$. Note that you don't need to consider the multiples of 4, because the multiples of 4 are also the multiples of 2, which have already been considered. Similarly, multiples of 6, 8, 9 need not be considered. You only need to consider the multiples of a prime number $k = 2, 3, 5, 7, 11, \ldots$, and set the corresponding element in `primes` to `false`. Afterward, if `primes[i]` is still true, then `i` is a prime number. As shown in Figure 23.2, 2, 3, 5, 7, 11, 13, 17, 19, 23 are prime numbers. Listing 23.6 gives the program for finding the prime numbers using the *Sieve of Eratosthenes* algorithm.

LISTING 23.6 SieveOfEratosthenes.java

```java
1 import java.util.Scanner;
2
3 public class SieveOfEratosthenes {
4   public static void main(String[] args) {
5     Scanner input = new Scanner(System.in);
6     System.out.print("Find all prime numbers <= n, enter n: ");
7     int n = input.nextInt();
8
9     boolean[] primes = new boolean[n + 1]; // Prime number sieve
10
11     // Initialize primes[i] to true
12     for (int i = 0; i < primes.length; i++) {
13       primes[i] = true;
14     }
15
16     for (int k = 2; k <= n / k; k++) {
17       if (primes[k]) {
18         for (int i = k; i <= n / k; i++) {
19           primes[k * i] = false; // k * i is not prime
20         }
21       }
22     }
23
24     final int NUMBER_PER_LINE = 10; // Display 10 per line
25     int count = 0; // Count the number of prime numbers found so far
26     // Print prime numbers
27     for (int i = 2; i < primes.length; i++) {
28       if (primes[i]) {
29         count++;
30         if (count % 10 == 0)
31           System.out.printf("%7d\n", i);
32         else
33           System.out.printf("%7d", i);
34       }
35     }
36
37     System.out.println("\n" + count + " number of primes <= " + n);
38   }
39 }
```

sieve

initialize sieve

nonprime

```
Find all prime numbers <= n, enter n: 1000 ↵Enter
The prime numbers are:
    2      3      5      7     11     13     17     19     23     29
   31     37     41     43     47     53     59     61     67     71
...

...
168 number of primes <= 1000
```

Note that $k \leq n / k$ (line 16). Otherwise, $k * i$ would be greater than n (line 19). What is the time complexity of this algorithm?

For each prime number k (line 17), the algorithm sets `primes[k * i]` to `false` (line 19). This is performed $n / k - k + 1$ times in the for loop (line 18). Thus, the complexity for finding all prime numbers up to n is

$$\frac{n}{2} - 2 + 1 + \frac{n}{3} - 3 + 1 + \frac{n}{5} - 5 + 1 + \frac{n}{7} - 7 + 1 + \frac{n}{11} - 11 + 1 \dots$$

$$= O\left(\frac{n}{2} + \frac{n}{3} + \frac{n}{5} + \frac{n}{7} + \frac{n}{11} + \cdots\right) < O(n \pi (n))$$

$$= O\left(n \frac{\sqrt{n}}{\log n}\right)$$

This upper bound $O\left(\dfrac{n\sqrt{n}}{\log n}\right)$ is very loose. The actual time complexity is much better than $O\left(\dfrac{n\sqrt{n}}{\log n}\right)$. The Sieve of Eratosthenes algorithm is good for a small n such that the array `primes` can fit in the memory.

Table 23.3 summarizes the complexity of three algorithms for finding all prime numbers up to n:

TABLE 23.3   Comparisons of Prime Number Algorithms

	Listing 4.14	Listing 23.4	Listing 23.5	Listing 23.6
Complexity	$O(n^2)$	$O(n\sqrt{n})$	$O\left(\dfrac{n\sqrt{n}}{\log n}\right)$	$O\left(\dfrac{n\sqrt{n}}{\log n}\right)$

23.12 Case Studies: Closest Pair of Points

Given a set of points, the closest pair problem is to find the two points that are nearest to each other. §6.10.6, "Problem: Finding a Closest Pair," presented an intuitive algorithm for finding a closest pair of points. The algorithm computes the distances between all pairs of points and finds the one with the minimum distance. Clearly, the algorithm takes $O(n^2)$ time. Can you beat this algorithm?

One way to beat this algorithm is to use a divide-and-conquer approach, as described in Listing 23.7.

LISTING 23.7 Algorithm for Finding a Closest Pair

Step 1: Sort the points in increasing order of x-coordinates. For the points with the same x-coordinates, sort on y-coordinates. This results in a sorted list S of points.

Step 2: Divide S into two subsets S_1 and S_2 of the equal size using the mid point in the sorted list. Recursively find the closest pair in S_1 and S_2. Let d_1 and d_2 denote the distance of the closest pairs in the two subsets, respectively.

Step 3: Find the closest pair between a point in S_1 and a point in S_2 and denote their distance to be d_3. The closest pair is the one with the distance $\min(d_1, d_2, d_3)$.

Selection sort and insertion sort take $O(n^2)$ time. In Chapter 26, we will introduce merge sort and heap sort. These sorting algorithms take $O(n \log n)$ time. So, Step 1 can be done in $O(n \log n)$ time.

Step 3 can be done in $O(n)$ time. Let $d = \min(d_1, d_2)$. We already know that the closest pair distance cannot be larger than d. For a point in S_1 and a point in S_2 to form a closest pair in S, the left point must be in `stripL` and the right point must be in `stripR`, as pictured in Figure 23.3(a).

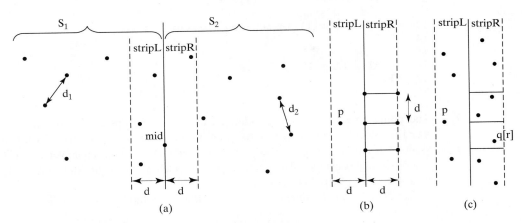

FIGURE 23.3   The mid point divides the points into two sets of equal size.

Further, for a point p in `stripL`, you only need to consider a right point within the $d \times 2d$ rectangle, as shown in 23.2(b). Any right point outside the rectangle cannot form a closest pair with p. Since the closest pair distance in S_2 is greater than or equal to d, there can be at most six points in the rectangle. So for each point in `stripL`, at most six points in `stripR` need to be considered.

For each point p in `stripL`, how do you locate the points in the corresponding $d \times 2d$ rectangle area in `stripR`? This can be done efficiently if the points in `stripL` and `stripR` are sorted in increasing order of their y-coordinates. Let `pointsOrderedOnY` be the list of the points sorted in increasing order of y-coordinates. `pointsOrderedOnY` can be obtained beforehand in the algorithm. `stripL` and `stripR` can be obtained from `pointsOrderedOnY` in Step 3 as described in Listing 23.8.

LISTING 23.8 Algorithm for obtaining `stripL` and `stripR`

```
1 for each point p in pointsOrderedOnY
2   if (p is in S1 and mid.x - p.x <= d)
3     append p to stripL;                          stripL
4   else if (p is in S2 and p.x - mid.x <= d)
5     append p to stripR;                          stripR
```

Let the points in `stripL` and `stripR` be $\{p_0, p_1, \ldots, p_k\}$ and $\{q_0, q_1, \ldots, q_t\}$. A closest pair between a point in `stripL` and a point in `stripR` can be found using the algorithm described in Listing 23.9.

LISTING 23.9 Algorithm for Finding a Closest Pair in Step 3

```
1 d = min(d1, d2);
2 r = 0; // r is the index in stripR
3 for (each point p in stripL) {
4   // Skip the points below the rectangle area
5   while (r < stripR.length && q[r].y <= p.y - d)
```

```
 6      r++;
 7
 8   let r1 = r;
 9   while (r1 < stripR.length && |q[r1].y - p.y| <= d) {
10     // Check if (p, q[r1]) is a possible closest pair
11     if (distance(p, q[r1]) < d) {
12       d = distance(p, q[r1]);
13       (p, q[r1]) is now the current closed pair;
14     }
15
16     r1 = r1 + 1;
17   }
18 }
```

update closest pair

The points in `stripL` are considered from $p_0, p_1, \ldots, p_k$ in this order. For a point **p** in `stripL`, skip the points in `stripR` that are below **p.y** − **d** (lines 5-6). Once a point is skipped, it will no longer be considered. The `while` loop (lines 9-17) checks if **(p, q[r1])** is a possible closest pair. There are at most six such **q[r1]**'s. So, the complexity for findings a closest pair in Step 3 is $O(n)$.

Let $T(n)$ denote the time complexity for the algorithm. So,

$$T(n) = 2T(n/2) + O(n) = O(n \log n)$$

Therefore, a closest pair of points can be found in $O(n \log n)$ time. The complete implementation of this algorithm is left as an exercise (see Exercise 23.9).

23.13 Preview of Other Algorithms

The examples in this chapter demonstrated how to analyze and design efficient algorithms for several well-known problems. Chapter 24 will introduce efficient algorithms for implementing lists, stacks, and queues. Chapter 25 will introduce efficient algorithms for implementing trees, heaps, and priority queues. Chapter 26 will introduce efficient algorithms for internal and external sorting. Chapter 27 will introduce efficient algorithms and data structures for graph problems. Chapter 28 will introduce efficient algorithms and data structures for weighted graph problems.

For the algorithms in Chapters 24–28, we will also analyze their complexities. Recurrence relations are a useful tool for analyzing algorithm complexity. Table 23.4 summarizes the common recurrence relations.

TABLE 23.4 Common Recurrence Functions

Recurrence Relation	Result	Example
$T(n) = T(n/2) + O(1)$	$T(n) = O(\log n)$	Binary search, Euclid's GCD
$T(n) = T(n - 1) + O(1)$	$T(n) = O(n)$	Linear search
$T(n) = 2T(n/2) + O(1)$	$T(n) = O(n)$	
$T(n) = 2T(n/2) + O(n)$	$T(n) = O(n \log n)$	Merge sort (Chapter 26)
$T(n) = 2T(n/2) + O(n \log n)$	$T(n) = O(n \log^2 n)$	
$T(n) = T(n - 1) + O(n)$	$T(n) = O(n^2)$	Selection sort, insertion sort
$T(n) = 2T(n - 1) + O(1)$	$T(n) = O(2^n)$	Towers of Hanoi
$T(n) = T(n - 1) + T(n - 2) + O(1)$	$T(n) = O(2^n)$	Recursive Fibonacci algorithm

KEY TERMS

average-time analysis   742
best-time analysis   742
Big *O* notation   742
constant time   742
exponential time   746

growth rate   742
logarithmic time   745
quadratic time   743
worst-time analysis   742

CHAPTER SUMMARY

- The Big *O* notation is a theoretical approach for analyzing the performance of the algorithm. It estimates how fast an algorithm's execution time increases as the input size increases. So you can compare two algorithms by examining their *growth rates*.

- An input that results in the shortest execution time is called the *best-case* input and an input that results in the longest execution time is called the *worst-case* input. Best case and worst case are not representative, but worst-case analysis is very useful. You can be assured that the algorithm will never be slower than the worst case.

- An average-case analysis attempts to determine the average amount of time among all possible input of the same size. Average-case analysis is ideal, but difficult to perform, because for many problems it is hard to determine the relative probabilities and distributions of various input instances.

- If the time is not related to the input size, the algorithm is said to take *constant time* with the notation $O(1)$.

- Linear search takes $O(n)$ time. An algorithm with the $O(n)$ time complexity is called a *linear algorithm*. Binary search takes $O(\log n)$ time. An algorithm with the $O(\log n)$ time complexity is called a *logarithmic algorithm*.

- The worst-time complexity for selection sort and insertion sort is $O(n^2)$. An algorithm with the $O(n^2)$ time complexity is called a *quadratic algorithm*.

- The time complexity for the Towers of Hanoi problem is $O(2^n)$. An algorithm with the $O(2^n)$ time complexity is called an *exponential algorithm*.

- A Fibonacci number at a given index can be found in $O(n)$ time.

- The Euclid's GCD algorithm takes $O(\log n)$ time.

- All prime numbers less than or equal to n can be found in $O\left(\dfrac{n\sqrt{n}}{\log n}\right)$ time.

REVIEW QUESTIONS

Sections 23.2 Estimating Algorithm Efficiency

23.1   Put the following growth functions in order:

$$\frac{5n^3}{4032}, \quad 44\log n, \quad 10n\log n, \quad 500, \quad 2n^2, \quad \frac{2^n}{45}, \quad 3n$$

23.2 Count the number of iterations in the following loops.

```
int count = 1;
while (count < 30) {
    count = count * 2;
}
```
(a)

```
int count = 15;
while (count < 30) {
    count = count * 3;
}
```
(b)

```
int count = 1;
while (count < n) {
    count = count * 2;
}
```
(c)

```
int count = 15;
while (count < n) {
    count = count * 3;
}
```
(d)

23.3 How many stars are displayed in the following code if **n** is 10? How many if **n** is 20? Use the Big O notation to estimate the time complexity.

```
for (int i = 0; i < n; i++) {
    System.out.print('*');
}
```

```
for (int i = 0; i < n; i++) {
    for (int j = 0; j < n; j++) {
        System.out.print('*');
    }
}
```

```
for (int k = 0; k < n; k++) {
    for (int i = 0; i < n; i++) {
        for (int j = 0; j < n; j++) {
            System.out.print('*');
        }
    }
}
```

```
for (int k = 0; k < 10; k++) {
    for (int i = 0; i < n; i++) {
        for (int j = 0; j < n; j++) {
            System.out.print('*');
        }
    }
}
```

23.4 Use the Big O notation to estimate the time complexity of the following methods:

```
public static void mA(int n) {
    for (int i = 0; i < n; i++) {
        System.out.print(Math.random());
    }
}
```

```
public static void mB(int n) {
    for (int i = 0; i < n; i++) {
        for (int j = 0; j < i; j++)
            System.out.print(Math.random());
    }
}
```

```
public static void mC(int[] m) {
    for (int i = 0; i < m.length; i++) {
        System.out.print(m[i]);
    }

    for (int i = m.length - 1; i >= 0; )
    {
        System.out.print(m[i]);
        i--;
    }
}
```

```
public static void mD(int[] m) {
    for (int i = 0; i < m.length; i++) {
        for (int j = 0; j < i; j++)
            System.out.print(m[i] * m[j]);
    }
}
```

23.5 Estimate the time complexity for adding two $n \times m$ matrices, and for multiplying a $n \times m$ matrix with a $m \times k$ matrix.

23.6 Analyze the following sorting algorithm:

```
for (int i = 0; i < list.length; i++) {
  if (list[i] > list[i + 1]) {
    swap list[i] with list[i + 1];
    i = 0;
  }
}
```

23.7 The Example 7 in §23.3, assumes $n = 2^k$. Revise the algorithm for an arbitrary n and prove that the complexity is still $O(\log n)$.

PROGRAMMING EXERCISES

23.1* (*Maximum consecutive sorted substring*) Write an efficient algorithm to find the maximum consecutive sorted substring in a string. For example, the maximum consecutive sorted substring in "abacdefkabfh" is acdefk. Analyze the time complexity of your algorithm.

23.2** (*Maximum sorted subsequence*) Write an efficient algorithm to find the maximum sorted subsequence in a string. For example, the maximum sorted subsequence in "abacdefkabfhxy" is acdefkxy. Analyze the time complexity of your algorithm.

23.3* (*Pattern matching*) Write an efficient algorithm to check whether a string is in a text. *Suppose all characters in the string are distinct.* Analyze the time complexity of your algorithm. For simplicity, assume the text is stored in a string, too.

23.4* (*Pattern matching*) Write an efficient algorithm to check whether a string is in a text. Analyze the time complexity of your algorithm. For simplicity, assume the text is stored in a string, too.

Video Note
Pattern matching

23.5* (*Execution time for GCD*) Write a program that obtains the execution time for finding the GCD of every two consecutive Fibonacci numbers from the index 40 to index 45 using the algorithms in Listings 23.2 and 20.3. Your program should print a table like this:

	40	41	42	43	44	45
Listing 23.2 GCD1						
Listing 23.2 GCD2						

Hint: You can use the following code template to obtain the execution time:

```
long startTime = System.currentTimeMillis();
perform the task;
long endTime = System.currentTimeMillis();
long executionTime = endTime - startTime;
```

23.6** (*Execution time for prime numbers*) Write a program that obtains the execution time for finding all the prime numbers less than 8,000,000, 10,000,000, 12,000,000, 14,000,000, 16,000,000, and 18,000,000 using the algorithms in Listings 23.4–23.6. Your program should print a table like this:

	8000000	10000000	12000000	14000000	16000000	18000000
Listing 23.5						
Listing 23.6						

23.7**   (*All prime numbers up to* 10,000,000,000) Write a program that finds all prime numbers up to 10,000,000,000. There are approximately 455,052,511 such prime numbers. Your program should meet the following requirements:

- Your program should store the prime numbers in a binary data file, named Exercise23_7.dat. When a new prime number is found, the number is appended to the file.

- To find whether a new number is prime, your program should load the prime numbers from the file to an array of the **long** type of size **10000**. If no number in the array is a divisor for the new number, continue to read the next **10000** prime numbers from the data file, until a divisor is found or all numbers in the file are read. If no divisor is found, the new number is prime.

- Since this program takes a long time to finish, you should run it as a batch job from a UNIX machine. If the machine is shut down and rebooted, your program should resume by using the prime numbers stored in the binary data file rather than start over from the scratch.

23.8   (*Number of prime numbers*) The preceding exercise stores the prime numbers in a file named Exercise23_7.dat. Write a program that finds the number of the prime numbers less than or equal to 10, 100, 1,000, 10,000, 100,000, 1,000,000, 10,000,000, 100,000,000, 1,000,000,000, and 10,000,000,000. Your program should read the data from Exercise23_7.dat. Note that the data file may continue to grow as more prime numbers are stored to the file.

23.9***   (*Closest pair of points*) §23.12 introduced an algorithm for finding a closest pair of points using a divide-and-conquer approach. Implement the algorithm to meet the following requirements:

- Define the classes **Point** and **CompareY** in the same way as in Exercise 22.12.

- Define a class named **Pair** with data fields **p1** and **p2** to represent two points, and a method named **getDistance()** that returns the distance of the two points.

- Implement the following methods:

```
/** Return the distance of the closest pair of points */
public static Pair getClosestPair(double[][] points)

/** Return the distance of the closest pair of points */
public static Pair getClosestPair(Point[] points)

/** Return the distance of the closest pair of points
  * in pointsOrderedOnX[low..high]. This is a recursive
  * method. pointsOrderedOnX and pointsOrderedOnY are
  * not changed in the subsequent recursive calls.
  */
```

```
public static Pair distance(Point[] pointsOrderedOnX,
    int low, int high, Point[] pointsOrderedOnY)

/** Compute the distance between two points p1 and p2 */
public static double distance(Point p1, Point p2)

/** Compute the distance between points (x1, y1) and (x2, y2) */
public static double distance(double x1, double y1,
    double x2, double y2)
```

23.10 (*Last 100 prime numbers*) Exercise 23.7 stores the prime numbers in a file named Exercise23_7.dat. Write an efficient program that reads the last 100 numbers in the file.

(*Hint*: Don't read all numbers from the file. Skip all numbers before the last 100 numbers in the file.)

CHAPTER 24

LISTS, STACKS, AND QUEUES

Objectives

- To design common features of list in an interface and provide skeleton implementation in an abstract class (§24.2).

- To design and implement a dynamic list using an array (§24.3).

- To design and implement a dynamic list using a linked structure (§24.4).

- To explore variations of linked lists (§24.5).

- To design and implement a stack using an array list (§24.5).

- To design and implement a queue using a linked list (§24.6).

- To evaluate expressions using stacks (§24.7).

24.1 Introduction

Lists, stacks, and queues are classic data structures typically covered in a data structures course. These data structures are supported in the Java API, and their uses were presented in Chapter 22, "Java Collections Framework." This chapter will examine how these data structures are implemented under the hood and give an interesting application on evaluating expressions using stacks. Implementation of sets and maps is covered in Supplement VI, "Data Structures."

24.2 Common Features for Lists

A list is a popular data structure for storing data in sequential order—for example, a list of students, a list of available rooms, a list of cities, a list of books. The operations listed below are typical of most lists:

- Retrieve an element from a list.

- Insert a new element to a list.

- Delete an element from a list.

- Find how many elements are in a list.

- Find whether an element is in a list.

- Find whether a list is empty.

Video Note
Implement **ArrayList**

There are two ways to implement a list. One is to use an *array* to store the elements. Arrays are dynamically created. If the capacity of the array is exceeded, create a new, larger array and copy all the elements from the current array to the new array. The other approach is to use a *linked structure*. A linked structure consists of nodes. Each node is dynamically created to hold an element. All the nodes are linked together to form a list. Thus you can declare two classes for lists. For convenience, let's name these two classes `MyArrayList` and `MyLinkedList`. These two classes have common operations but different implementations.

abstract class for interface

 Design Guide

The common operations can be generalized in an interface or an abstract class. A good strategy is to combine the virtues of interfaces and abstract classes by providing both an interface and an abstract class in the design so that the user can use either of them, whichever is convenient. The abstract class provides a skeletal implementation of the interface, which minimizes the effort required to implement the interface.

Let us name the interface `MyList` and the convenience class `MyAbstractList`. Figure 24.1 shows the relationship of `MyList`, `MyAbstractList`, `MyArrayList`, and `MyLinkedList`. The methods in `MyList` and the methods implemented in `MyAbstractList` are shown in Figure 24.2. Listing 24.1 gives the source code for `MyList`.

FIGURE 24.1   `MyList` defines a common interface for `MyAbstractList`, `MyArrayList`, and `MyLinkedList`.

FIGURE 24.2 List supports many methods for manipulating a list. MyAbstractList provides a partial implementation of the List interface.

LISTING 24.1 MyList.java

```java
1  public interface MyList<E> {
2    /** Add a new element at the end of this list */
3    public void add(E e);                                          add(e)
4
5    /** Add a new element at the specified index in this list */
6    public void add(int index, E e);                               add(index, e)
7
8    /** Clear the list */
9    public void clear();                                           clear()
10
11   /** Return true if this list contains the element */
12   public boolean contains(E e);                                  contains(e)
13
14   /** Return the element from this list at the specified index */
15   public E get(int index);                                       get(index)
16
17   /** Return the index of the first matching element in this list.
18    *  Return -1 if no match. */
19   public int indexOf(E e);                                       indexOf(e)
20
21   /** Return true if this list contains no elements */
22   public boolean isEmpty();                                      isEmpty(e)
23
```

```
24    /** Return the index of the last matching element in this list
25     *   Return -1 if no match. */
26    public int lastIndexOf(E e);
27
28    /** Remove the first occurrence of the element o from this list.
29     *   Shift any subsequent elements to the left.
30     *   Return true if the element is removed. */
31    public boolean remove(E e);
32
33    /** Remove the element at the specified position in this list
34     *   Shift any subsequent elements to the left.
35     *   Return the element that was removed from the list. */
36    public E remove(int index);
37
38    /** Replace the element at the specified position in this list
39     *   with the specified element and return the new set. */
40    public Object set(int index, E e);
41
42    /** Return the number of elements in this list */
43    public int size();
44 }
```

lastIndexOf(e) — line 26
remove(e) — line 31
remove(index) — line 36
set(index, e) — line 40
size(e) — line 43

MyAbstractList declares variable size to indicate the number of elements in the list. The methods isEmpty and size can be implemented in the class in Listing 24.2.

LISTING 24.2 MyAbstractList.java

```
1  public abstract class MyAbstractList<E> implements MyList<E> {
2    protected int size = 0; // The size of the list
3
4    /** Create a default list */
5    protected MyAbstractList() {
6    }
7
8    /** Create a list from an array of objects */
9    protected MyAbstractList(E[] objects) {
10     for (int i = 0; i < objects.length; i++)
11       add(objects[i]);
12   }
13
14   /** Add a new element at the end of this list */
15   public void add(E e) {
16     add(size, e);
17   }
18
19   /** Return true if this list contains no elements */
20   public boolean isEmpty() {
21     return size == 0;
22   }
23
24   /** Return the number of elements in this list */
25   public int size() {
26     return size;
27   }
28
29   /** Remove the first occurrence of the element o from this list.
30    *   Shift any subsequent elements to the left.
31    *   Return true if the element is removed. */
32   public boolean remove(E e) {
33     if (indexOf(e) >= 0) {
```

size — line 2
no-arg constructor — line 5
constructor — line 9
implement add — line 15
implement isEmpty() — line 20
implement size() — line 25
implement remove(E e) — line 32

```
34          remove(indexOf(e));
35          return true;
36      }
37      else
38          return false;
39  }
40 }
```

The following sections give the implementation for `MyArrayList` and `MyLinkedList`, respectively.

Design Guide

Protected data fields are rarely used. However, making `size` a protected data field in the `MyAbstractList` class is a good choice. The subclass of `MyAbstractList` can access `size`, but nonsubclasses of `MyAbstractList` in different packages cannot access it. As a general rule, you may declare protected data fields in abstract classes.

protected data field

24.3 Array Lists

Array is a fixed-size data structure. Once an array is created, its size cannot be changed. Nevertheless, you can still use arrays to implement dynamic data structures. The trick is to create a larger new array to replace the current array, if the current array cannot hold new elements in the list.

Initially, an array, say `data` of `E[]` type, is created with a default size. When inserting a new element into the array, first make sure that there is enough room in the array. If not, create a new array twice as large as the current one. Copy the elements from the current array to the new array. The new array now becomes the current array. Before inserting a new element at a specified index, shift all the elements after the index to the right and increase the list size by `1`, as shown in Figure 24.3.

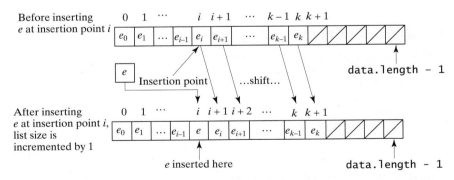

FIGURE 24.3 Inserting a new element into the array requires that all the elements after the insertion point be shifted one position to the right, so that the new element can be inserted at the insertion point.

Note

The data array is of type `E[]`. Each cell in the array actually stores the reference of an object.

To remove an element at a specified index, shift all the elements after the index to the left by one position and decrease the list size by `1`, as shown in Figure 24.4.

`MyArrayList` uses an array to implement `MyAbstractList`, as shown in Figure 24.5. Its implementation is given in Listing 24.3.

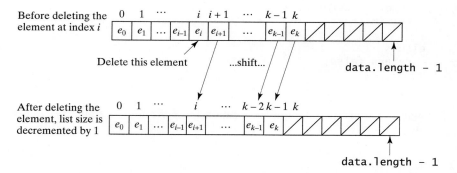

FIGURE 24.4 Deleting an element from the array requires that all the elements after the deletion point be shifted one position to the left.

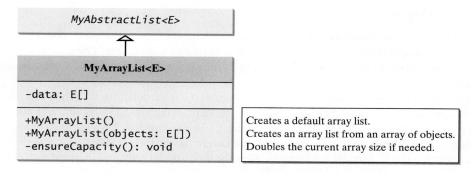

FIGURE 24.5 `MyArrayList` implements a list using an array.

LISTING 24.3 `MyArrayList.java`

```
 1  public class MyArrayList<E> extends MyAbstractList<E> {
 2    public static final int INITIAL_CAPACITY = 16;
 3    private E[] data = (E[])new Object[INITIAL_CAPACITY];
 4
 5    /** Create a default list */
 6    public MyArrayList() {
 7    }
 8
 9    /** Create a list from an array of objects */
10    public MyArrayList(E[] objects) {
11      for (int i = 0; i < objects.length; i++)
12        add(objects[i]);
13    }
14
15    /** Add a new element at the specified index in this list */
16    public void add(int index, E e) {
17      ensureCapacity();
18
19      // Move the elements to the right after the specified index
20      for (int i = size - 1; i >= index; i--)
21        data[i + 1] = data[i];
22
```

initial capacity

array

no-arg constructor

constructor

add

```
23       // Insert new element to data[index]
24       data[index] = e;
25
26       // Increase size by 1
27       size++;
28     }
29
30     /** Create a new larger array, double the current size */
31     private void ensureCapacity() {                                    ensureCapacity
32       if (size >= data.length) {
33         E[] newData = (E[])(new Object[data.length * 2]);             double capacity
34         System.arraycopy(data, 0, newData, 0, data.length);
35         data = newData;
36       }
37     }
38
39     /** Clear the list */
40     public void clear() {                                              clear
41       data = (E[])new Object[INITIAL_CAPACITY];
42       size = 0;
43     }
44
45     /** Return true if this list contains the element */
46     public boolean contains(E e) {                                     contains
47       for (int i = 0; i < size; i++)
48         if (e.equals(data[i])) return true;
49
50       return false;
51     }
52
53     /** Return the element from this list at the specified index */
54     public E get(int index) {                                          get
55       return data[index];
56     }
57
58     /** Return the index of the first matching element in this list.
59      *  Return -1 if no match. */
60     public int indexOf(E e) {                                          indexOf
61       for (int i = 0; i < size; i++)
62         if (e.equals(data[i])) return i;
63
64       return -1;
65     }
66
67     /** Return the index of the last matching element in this list
68      *  Return -1 if no match. */
69     public int lastIndexOf(E e) {                                      lastIndexOf
70       for (int i = size - 1; i >= 0; i--)
71         if (e.equals(data[i])) return i;
72
73       return -1;
74     }
75
76     /** Remove the element at the specified position in this list
77      *  Shift any subsequent elements to the left.
78      *  Return the element that was removed from the list. */
79     public E remove(int index) {                                       remove
80       E e = data[index];
81
```

```
82      // Shift data to the left
83      for (int j = index; j < size - 1; j++)
84        data[j] = data[j + 1];
85
86      data[size - 1] = null; // This element is now null
87
88      // Decrement size
89      size--;
90
91      return e;
92    }
93
94    /** Replace the element at the specified position in this list
95     *  with the specified element. */
96    public E set(int index, E e) {
97      E old = data[index];
98      data[index] = e;
99      return old;
100   }
101
102   /** Override toString() to return elements in the list */
103   public String toString() {
104     StringBuilder result = new StringBuilder("[");
105
106     for (int i = 0; i < size; i++) {
107       result.append(data[i]);
108       if (i < size - 1) result.append(", ");
109     }
110
111     return result.toString() + "]";
112   }
113 }
```

set (line 96)

toString (line 103)

The constant `INITIAL_CAPACITY` (line 2) is used to create an initial array `data` (line 3). Owing to generics type erasure, you cannot create a generic array using the syntax `new e[INITIAL_CAPACITY]`. To circumvent this limitation, an array of the `Object` type is created in line 3 and cast into `E[]`.

The `add(int index, E e)` method (lines 16–28) adds element `e` at the specified `index` in the array. This method first invokes `ensureCapacity()` (line 17), which ensures that there is a space in the array for the new element. It then shifts all the elements after the index one position to the right before inserting the element (lines 20–21). After the element is added, `size` is incremented by 1 (line 27). Note that variable `size` is defined as `protected` in `MyAbstractList`, so it can be accessed in `MyArrayList`.

The `ensureCapacity()` method (lines 31–37) checks whether the array is full. If so, create a new array that doubles the current array size, copy the current array to the new array using the `System.arraycopy` method, and set the new array as the current array.

The `clear()` method (lines 40–43) creates a brand-new array with initial capacity.

The `contains(E e)` method (lines 46–51) checks whether element `e` is contained in the array by comparing `e` with each element in the array using the `equals` method.

The `get(int index)` method (lines 54–56) simply returns `data[index]`. The implementation of this method is simple and efficient.

The `indexOf(E e)` method (lines 60–65) compares element `e` with the elements in the array, starting from the first one. If a match is found, the index of the element is returned; otherwise, it returns –1.

The `lastIndexOf(E e)` method (lines 69–74) compares element `e` with the elements in the array, starting from the last one. If a match is found, the index of the element is returned; otherwise, it returns –1.

The `remove(int index)` method (lines 79–92) shifts all the elements before the index one position to the left and decrements `size` by 1.

The `set(int index, E e)` method (lines 96–100) simply assigns `e` to `data[index]` to replace the element at the specified index with element `e`.

The `toString()` method (lines 103–112) overrides the `toString` method in the `Object` class to return a string representing all the elements in the list.

Listing 24.4 gives an example that creates a list using `MyArrayList`. It uses the `add` method to add strings to the list and the `remove` method to remove strings from the list.

LISTING 24.4 TestList.java

```java
 1 public class TestList {
 2   public static void main(String[] args) {
 3     // Create a list
 4     MyList<String> list = new MyArrayList<String>();        create a list
 5
 6     // Add elements to the list
 7     list.add("America"); // Add it to the list           add to list
 8     System.out.println("(1) " + list);
 9
10     list.add(0, "Canada"); // Add it to the beginning of the list
11     System.out.println("(2) " + list);
12
13     list.add("Russia"); // Add it to the end of the list
14     System.out.println("(3) " + list);
15
16     list.add("France"); // Add it to the end of the list
17     System.out.println("(4) " + list);
18
19     list.add(2, "Germany"); // Add it to the list at index 2
20     System.out.println("(5) " + list);
21
22     list.add(5, "Norway"); // Add it to the list at index 5
23     System.out.println("(6) " + list);
24
25     // Remove elements from the list
26     list.remove("Canada"); // Same as list.remove(0) in this case    remove from list
27     System.out.println("(7) " + list);
28
29     list.remove(2); // Remove the element at index 2
30     System.out.println("(8) " + list);
31
32     list.remove(list.size() - 1); // Remove the last element
33     System.out.println("(9) " + list);
34   }
35 }
```

```
(1) [America]
(2) [Canada, America]
(3) [Canada, America, Russia]
(4) [Canada, America, Russia, France]
(5) [Canada, America, Germany, Russia, France]
(6) [Canada, America, Germany, Russia, France, Norway]
(7) [America, Germany, Russia, France, Norway]
```

```
(8) [America, Germany, France, Norway]
(9) [America, Germany, France]
```

24.4 Linked Lists

Since `MyArrayList` is implemented using an array, the methods `get(int index)` and `set(int index, Object o)` for accessing and modifying an element through an index and the `add(Object o)` for adding an element at the end of the list are efficient. However, the methods `add(int index, Object o)` and `remove(int index)` are inefficient, because they require shifting a potentially large number of elements. You can use a linked structure to implement a list to improve efficiency for adding and removing an element anywhere in a list.

24.4.1 Nodes

In a linked list, each element is contained in a structure, called the *node*. When a new element is added to the list, a node is created to contain the element. Each node is linked to its next neighbor, as shown in Figure 24.6.

FIGURE 24.6 A linked list consists of any number of nodes chained together.

A node can be defined as a class, as follows:

```java
class Node<E> {
  E element;
  Node<E> next;

  public Node(E e) {
    element = e;
  }
}
```

The variable `head` refers to the first node in the list, and the variable `tail` refers to the last node in the list. If the list is empty, both `head` and `tail` are `null`. For example, you can create three nodes to store three strings in a list, as follows:

Step 1: Declare `head` and `tail`:

```
Node<String> head = null;        The list is empty now
Node<String> tail = null;
```

Step 2: Create the first node and insert it to the list:

```
head = new Node<String>("Chicago");   After the first node is inserted
last = head;
```

head → "Chicago"
tail → next: null

Step 3: Create the second node and insert it into the list:

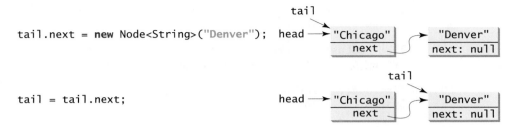

Step 4: Create the third node and insert it to the list:

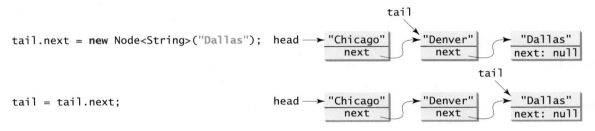

Each node contains the element and a data field named *next* that points to the next element. If the node is the last in the list, its pointer data field `next` contains the value `null`. You can use this property to detect the last node. For example, you may write the following loop to traverse all the nodes in the list.

```
1 Node<String> current = head;
2 while (current != null) {
3    System.out.println(current.element);
4    current = current.next;
5 }
```

current pointer
check last node

next node

The variable `current` points to the first node in the list initially (line 1). In the loop, the element of the current node is retrieved (line 3), and then `current` points to the next node (line 4). The loop continues until the current node is `null`.

24.4.2 The `LinkedList` Class

`MyLinkedList` uses a linked structure to implement a dynamic list. It extends `MyAbstractList`. In addition, it provides the methods `addFirst`, `addLast`, `removeFirst`, `removeLast`, `getFirst`, and `getLast`, as shown in Figure 24.7.

Assume the class has been implemented. Listing 24.5 gives a test program that uses the class.

LISTING 24.5 TestLinkedList.java

```
1 public class TestLinkedList {
2    /** Main method */
3    public static void main(String[] args) {
4       // Create a list for strings
5       MyLinkedList<String> list = new MyLinkedList<String>();
6
7       // Add elements to the list
8       list.add("America"); // Add it to the list
9       System.out.println("(1) " + list);
10
11      list.add(0, "Canada"); // Add it to the beginning of the list
12      System.out.println("(2) " + list);
13
```

create list

append element
print list

insert element

append element

```
14        list.add("Russia"); // Add it to the end of the list
15        System.out.println("(3) " + list);
16
```

append element

```
17        list.addLast("France"); // Add it to the end of the list
18        System.out.println("(4) " + list);
19
```

insert element

```
20        list.add(2, "Germany"); // Add it to the list at index 2
21        System.out.println("(5) " + list);
22
```

insert element

```
23        list.add(5, "Norway"); // Add it to the list at index 5
24        System.out.println("(6) " + list);
25
```

insert element

```
26        list.add(0, "Poland"); // Same as list.addFirst("Poland")
27        System.out.println("(7) " + list);
28
```

```
29        // Remove elements from the list
```

remove element

```
30        list.remove(0); // Same as list.remove("Australia") in this case
31        System.out.println("(8) " + list);
32
```

remove element

```
33        list.remove(2); // Remove the element at index 2
34        System.out.println("(9) " + list);
35
```

remove element

```
36        list.remove(list.size() - 1); // Remove the last element
37        System.out.println("(10) " + list);
38    }
39 }
```

```
(1) [America]
(2) [Canada, America]
(3) [Canada, America, Russia]
(4) [Canada, America, Russia, France]
(5) [Canada, America, Germany, Russia, France]
(6) [Canada, America, Germany, Russia, France, Norway]
(7) [Poland, Canada, America, Germany, Russia, France, Norway]
(8) [Canada, America, Germany, Russia, France, Norway]
(9) [Canada, America, Russia, France, Norway]
(10) [Canada, America, Russia, France]
```

FIGURE 24.7 `MyLinkedList` implements a list using a linked list of nodes.

24.4.3   Implementing `MyLinkedList`

Now let us turn our attention to implementing the `MyLinkedList` class. We will discuss how to implement methods `addFirst`, `addLast`, `add(index, e)`, `removeFirst`, `removeLast`, and `remove(index)` and leave other methods in the `MyLinkedList` class as exercises.

24.4.3.1   Implementing **addFirst(e)**

The `addFirst(e)` method creates a new node for holding element `e`. The new node becomes the first node in the list. It can be implemented as follows:

```
1 public void addFirst(E e) {
2   Node<E> newNode = new Node<E>(e); // Create a new node          create a node
3   newNode.next = head; // link the new node with the head         link with head
4   head = newNode;  // head points to the new node                 head to new node
5   size++; // Increase list size                                   increase size
6
7   if (tail == null) // the new node is the only node in list      was empty?
8     tail = head;
9 }
```

The `addFirst(e)` method creates a new node to store the element (line 2) and insert the node to the beginning of the list (line 3). After the insertion, **head** should point to this new element node (line 4), as shown in Figure 24.8(b).

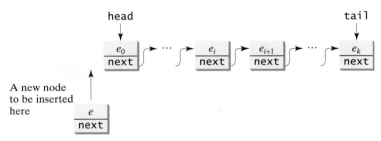

(a) Before a new node is inserted.

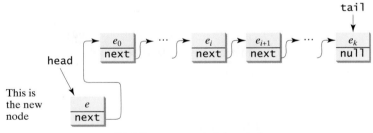

(b) After a new node is inserted.

FIGURE 24.8   A new element is added to the beginning of the list.

If the list is empty (line 7), both **head** and **tail** will point to this new node (line 8). After the node is created, **size** should be increased by 1 (line 5).

24.4.3.2   Implementing **addLast(e)**

The `addLast(e)` method creates a node to hold the element and appends the node at the end of the list. It can be implemented as follows:

```
1 public void addLast(E e) {
2   Node<E> newNode = new Node<E>(e); // Create a new for element e     create a node
```

```
 3
 4    if (tail == null) {
 5      head = tail = newNode; // The only node in list
 6    }
 7    else {
 8      tail.next = newNode; // Link the new with the last node
 9      tail = tail.next; // tail now points to the last node
10    }
11
12    size++; // Increase size
13 }
```

increase size

The **addLast(e)** method creates a new node to store the element (line 2) and appends it to the end of the list (line 3). Consider two cases:

1. If the list is empty (line 4), both **head** and **tail** will point to this new node (line 5);

2. Otherwise, link the node with the last node in the list (line 8). **tail** should now point to this new node (line 9), as shown in Figure 24.9(b).

In any case, after the node is created, the size should be increased by **1** (line 12).

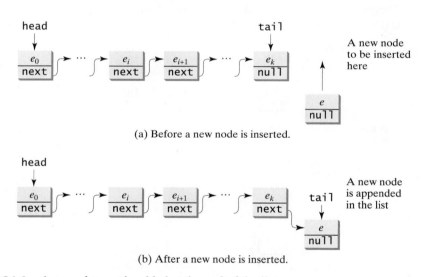

(a) Before a new node is inserted.

(b) After a new node is inserted.

FIGURE 24.9 A new element is added at the end of the list.

24.4.3.3 Implementing **add(index, e)**

The **add(index, e)** method inserts an element into the list at the specified index. It can be implemented as follows:

insert first
insert last

```
1 public void add(int index, E e) {
2    if (index == 0) addFirst(e); // Insert first
3    else if (index >= size) addLast(e); // Insert last
4    else { // Insert in the middle
5      Node<E> current = head;
6      for (int i = 1; i < index; i++)
7        current = current.next;
8      Node<E> temp = current.next;
9      current.next = new Node<E>(e);
```

create a node

```
10        (current.next).next = temp;
11        size++;
12    }
13 }
```
increase size

There are three cases when inserting an element into the list:

1. If `index` is `0`, invoke `addFirst(e)` (line 2) to insert the element at the beginning of the list;

2. If `index` is greater than or equal to `size`, invoke `addLast(e)` (line 3) to insert the element at the end of the list;

3. Otherwise, create a new node to store the new element and locate where to insert it. As shown in Figure 24.10(b), the new node is to be inserted between the nodes `current` and `temp`. The method assigns the new node to `current.next` and assigns `temp` to the new node's `next`. The size is now increased by `1` (line 11).

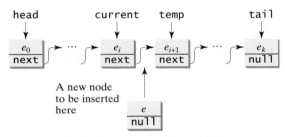

(a) Before a new node is inserted.

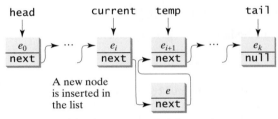

(b) After a new node is inserted.

FIGURE 24.10   A new element is inserted in the middle of the list.

24.4.3.4   Implementing `removeFirst()`

The `removeFirst()` method is to remove the first element from the list. It can be implemented as follows:

```
 1 public E removeFirst() {
 2   if (size == 0) return null; // Nothing to delete
 3   else {
 4     Node<E> temp = head; // Keep the first node temporarily
 5     head = head.next; // Move head to point the next node
 6     size--; // Reduce size by 1
 7     if (head == null) tail = null; // List becomes empty
 8     return temp.element; // Return the deleted element
 9   }
10 }
```

nothing to remove

keep old head
new head
decrease **size**
destroy the node

Consider two cases:

1. If the list is empty, there is nothing to delete, so return **null** (line 2);

2. Otherwise, remove the first node from the list by pointing **head** to the second node, as shown in Figure 24.11. The size is reduced by 1 after the deletion (line 6). If there is one element, after removing the element, **tail** should be set to **null** (line 7).

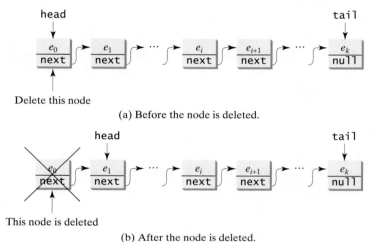

(a) Before the node is deleted.

(b) After the node is deleted.

FIGURE 24.11 The first node is deleted from the list.

24.4.3.5 Implementing **removeLast()**

The **removeLast()** method removes the last element from the list. It can be implemented as follows:

```
1 public E removeLast() {
2    if (size == 0) return null; // Nothing to remove
3    else if (size == 1) // Only one element in the list
4    {
5        Node<E> temp = head;
6        head = tail = null;   // list becomes empty
7        size = 0;
8        return temp.element;
9    }
10   else
11   {
12       Node<E> current = head;
13
14       for (int i = 0; i < size - 2; i++)
15           current = current.next;
16
17       Node<E> temp = tail;
18       tail = current;
19       tail.next = null;
20       size--;
21       return temp.element;
22   }
23 }
```

empty?
size 1?

head and tail null
size is 0
return element

size > 1?

move tail

reduce size
return element

Consider three cases:

1. If the list is empty, return `null` (line 2);

2. If the list contains only one node, this node is destroyed; `head` and `tail` both become `null` (line 6);

3. Otherwise, the last node is destroyed (line 18) and the `tail` is repositioned to point to the second-to-last node, as shown in Figure 24.12(a). For the last two cases, the size is reduced by 1 after the deletion (lines 7, 20) and the element value of the deleted node is returned (lines 8, 21).

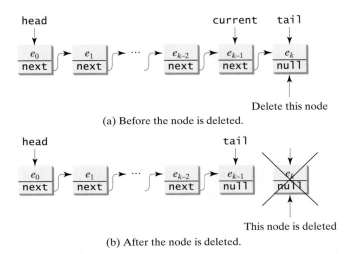

(a) Before the node is deleted.

(b) After the node is deleted.

FIGURE 24.12 The last node is deleted from the list.

24.4.3.6 Implementing `remove(index)`

The `remove(index)` method finds the node at the specified index and then removes it. It can be implemented as follows:

```
1 public E remove(int index) {
2   if (index < 0 || index >= size) return null; // Out of range
3   else if (index == 0) return removeFirst(); // Remove first
4   else if (index == size - 1) return removeLast(); // Remove last
5   else {
6     Node<E> previous = head;
7
8     for (int i = 1; i < index; i++) {
9       previous = previous.next;
10    }
11
12    Node<E> current = previous.next;
13    previous.next = current.next;
14    size--;
15    return current.element;
16  }
17 }
```

out of range
remove first
remove last

locate previous

locate current
remove from list
reduce size
return element

Consider four cases:

1. If `index` is beyond the range of the list (i.e., `index < 0 || index >= size`), return `null` (line 2);

2. If `index` is `0`, invoke `removeFirst()` to remove the first node (line 3);

3. If `index` is `size - 1`, invoke `removeLast()` to remove the last node (line 4);

4. Otherwise, locate the node at the specified `index`. Let `current` denote this node and `previous` denote the node before this node, as shown in Figure 24.13(a). Assign `current.next` to `previous.next` to eliminate the current node, as shown in Figure 24.13(b).

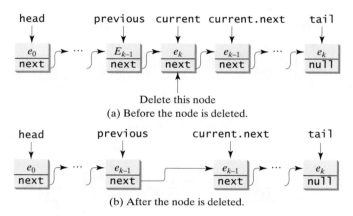

(a) Before the node is deleted.

(b) After the node is deleted.

FIGURE 24.13 A node is deleted from the list.

Listing 24.6 gives the implementation of `MyLinkedList`. The implementation of `get(index)`, `indexOf(e)`, `lastIndexOf(e)`, `contains(e)`, and `set(index, e)` is omitted and left as an exercise.

LISTING 24.6 MyLinkedList.java

head, tail

no-arg constructor

constructor

getFirst

```java
1  public class MyLinkedList<E> extends MyAbstractList<E> {
2    private Node<E> head, tail;
3
4    /** Create a default list */
5    public MyLinkedList() {
6    }
7
8    /** Create a list from an array of objects */
9    public MyLinkedList(E[] objects) {
10     super(objects);
11   }
12
13   /** Return the head element in the list */
14   public E getFirst() {
15     if (size == 0) {
16       return null;
17     }
18     else {
19       return head.element;
20     }
21   }
22
```

```
23    /** Return the last element in the list */
24    public E getLast() {                                           getLast
25      if (size == 0) {
26        return null;
27      }
28      else {
29        return tail.element;
30      }
31    }
32
33    /** Add an element to the beginning of the list */
34    public void addFirst(E e) {                                    addFirst
35      // Implemented in §24.4.3.1, so omitted here
36    }
37
38    /** Add an element to the end of the list */
39    public void addLast(E e) {                                     addLast
40      // Implemented in §24.4.3.2, so omitted here
41    }
42
43    /** Add a new element at the specified index in this list
44     * The index of the head element is 0 */
45    public void add(int index, E e) {                              add
46      // Implemented in §24.4.3.3, so omitted here
47    }
48
49    /** Remove the head node and
50     *  return the object that is contained in the removed node. */
51    public E removeFirst() {                                       removeFirst
52      // Implemented in §24.4.3.4, so omitted here
53    }
54
55    /** Remove the last node and
56     * return the object that is contained in the removed node. */
57    public E removeLast() {                                        removeLast
58      // Implemented in §24.4.3.5, so omitted here
59    }
60
61    /** Remove the element at the specified position in this list.
62     *  Return the element that was removed from the list. */
63    public E remove(int index) {                                   remove
64      // Implemented in §24.4.3.6, so omitted here
65    }
66
67    /** Override toString() to return elements in the list */
68    public String toString() {                                     toString
69      StringBuilder result = new StringBuilder("[");
70
71      Node<E> current = head;
72      for (int i = 0; i < size; i++) {
73        result.append(current.element);
74        current = current.next;
75        if (current != null) {
76          result.append(", "); // Separate two elements with a comma
77        }
78        else {
79          result.append("]"); // Insert the closing ] in the string
80        }
81      }
82
```

```
83        return result.toString();
84      }
85
86      /** Clear the list */
87      public void clear() {
88        head = tail = null;
89      }
90
91      /** Return true if this list contains the element o */
92      public boolean contains(E e) {
93        System.out.println("Implementation left as an exercise");
94        return true;
95      }
96
97      /** Return the element from this list at the specified index */
98      public E get(int index) {
99        System.out.println("Implementation left as an exercise");
100       return null;
101     }
102
103     /** Return the index of the head matching element in this list.
104      *   Return -1 if no match. */
105     public int indexOf(E e) {
106       System.out.println("Implementation left as an exercise");
107       return 0;
108     }
109
110     /** Return the index of the last matching element in this list
111      *   Return -1 if no match. */
112     public int lastIndexOf(E e) {
113       System.out.println("Implementation left as an exercise");
114       return 0;
115     }
116
117     /** Replace the element at the specified position in this list
118      *   with the specified element. */
119     public E set(int index, E e) {
120       System.out.println("Implementation left as an exercise");
121       return null;
122     }
123
124     private static class Node<E> {
125       E element;
126       Node<E> next;
127
128       public Node(E element) {
129         this.element = element;
130       }
131     }
132   }
```

Margin labels: clear (line 87), contains (line 92), get (line 98), indexOf (line 105), lastIndexOf (line 112), set (line 119), **Node** inner class (line 124).

24.4.4 MyArrayList vs. MyLinkedList

Both MyArrayList and MyLinkedList can be used to store a list. MyArrayList is implemented using an array and MyLinkedList is implemented using a linked list. The overhead of MyArrayList is smaller than that of MyLinkedList. However, MyLinkedList is more efficient if you need to insert and delete the elements from anywhere in the list. Table 24.1 summarizes the complexity of the methods in MyArrayList and MyLinkedList.

TABLE 24.1   Time Complexities for Methods in `MyArrayList` and `MyLinkedList`

Methods	MyArrayList	MyLinkList
add(e: E)	$O(1)$	$O(1)$
add(index: int, e: E)	$O(n)$	$O(n)$
clear()	$O(1)$	$O(1)$
contains(e: E)	$O(n)$	$O(n)$
get(index: int)	$O(n)$	$O(n)$
indexOf(e: E)	$O(n)$	$O(n)$
isEmpty()	$O(1)$	$O(1)$
lastIndexOf(e: E)	$O(n)$	$O(n)$
remove(e: E)	$O(n)$	$O(n)$
size()	$O(1)$	$O(1)$
remove(index: int)	$O(n)$	$O(n)$
set(index: int, e: E)	$O(n)$	$O(n)$
addFirst(e: E)	$O(n)$	$O(1)$
removeFirst()	$O(n)$	$O(1)$

24.5 Variations of Linked Lists

The linked list introduced in the preceding section is known as a *singly linked list*. It contains a pointer to the list's first node, and each node contains a pointer to the next node sequentially. Several variations of the linked list are useful in certain applications.

A *circular, singly linked list* is like a singly linked list, except that the pointer of the last node points back to the first node, as shown in Figure 24.14(a).

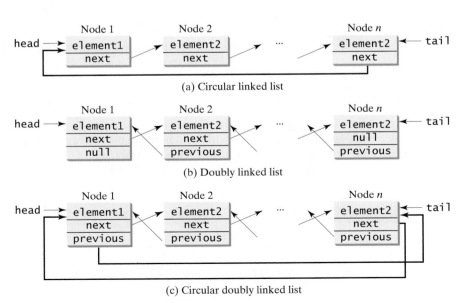

FIGURE 24.14   Linked lists may appear in various forms.

A *doubly linked list* contains the nodes with two pointers. One points to the next node and the other points to the previous node, as shown in Figure 24.14(b). These two pointers are conveniently called *a forward pointer* and *a backward pointer*. So, a doubly linked list can be traversed forward and backward.

A *circular*, *doubly linked list* is a doubly linked list, except that the forward pointer of the last node points to the first node and the backward pointer of the first pointer points to the last node, as shown in Figure 24.14(c).

The implementation of these linked lists is left as exercises.

24.6 Stacks and Queues

A stack can be viewed as a special type of list whose elements are accessed, inserted, and deleted only from the end (top) of the stack, as shown in Figure 9.7. A queue represents a waiting list. A queue can be viewed as a special type of list whose elements are inserted into the end (tail) of the queue, and are accessed and deleted from the beginning (head) of the queue, as shown in Figure 24.15.

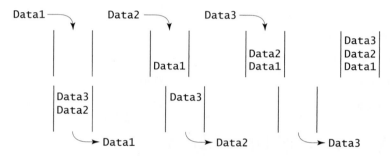

FIGURE 24.15 A queue holds objects in a first-in first-out fashion.

Since the insertion and deletion operations on a stack are made only at the end of the stack, it is more efficient to implement a stack with an array list than with a linked list. Since deletions are made at the beginning of the list, it is more efficient to implement a queue using a linked list than an array list. This section implements a stack class using an array list and a queue using a linked list. There are two ways to design the stack and queue classes:

inheritance

- Using inheritance: You can declare a stack class by extending `MyArrayList`, and a queue class by extending `MyLinkedList`, as shown in Figure 24.16(a).

composition

- Using composition: You can declare an array list as a data field in the stack class, and a linked list as a data field in the queue class, as shown in Figure 24.16(b).

Both designs are fine, but using composition is better because it enables you to declare a completely new stack class and queue class without inheriting the unnecessary and inappropriate methods from the array list and linked list. The implementation of the stack class using the composition approach was given in Listing 10.9, `MyStack.java`. Listing 24.7

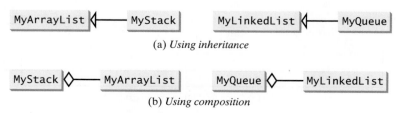

(a) *Using inheritance*

(b) *Using composition*

FIGURE 24.16 `MyStack` and `MyQueue` may be implemented using inheritance or composition.

implements the queue class using the composition approach. Figure 24.17 shows the UML of the class.

LISTING 24.7 MyQueue.java

```
1  public class MyQueue<E> {
2    private MyLinkedList<E> list = new MyLinkedList<E>();          linked list
3
4    public void enqueue(E e) {                                     enqueue
5      list.addLast(e);
6    }
7
8    public E dequeue() {                                           dequeue
9      return list.removeFirst();
10   }
11
12   public int getSize() {                                         getSize
13     return list.size();
14   }
15
16   public String toString() {                                     toString
17     return "Queue: " + list.toString();
18   }
19 }
```

```
                MyQueue<E>

-list: MyLinkedList<E>

+enqueue(e: E): void           Adds an element to this queue.
+dequeue(): E                  Removes an element from this queue.
+getSize(): int                Returns the number of elements from this queue.
```

FIGURE 24.17 MyQueue uses a linked list to provide a first-in, first-out data structure.

A linked list is created to store the elements in a queue (line 2). The **enqueue(e)** method (lines 4–6) adds element **e** into the tail of the queue. The **dequeue()** method (lines 8–10) removes an element from the head of the queue and returns the removed element. The **getSize()** method (lines 12–14) returns the number of elements in the queue.

Listing 24.8 gives an example that creates a stack using MyStack and a queue using MyQueue. It uses the **push** (**enqueue**) method to add strings to the stack (queue) and the **pop** (**dequeue**) method to remove strings from the stack (queue).

LISTING 24.8 TestStackQueue.java

```
1  public class TestStackQueue {
2    public static void main(String[] args) {
3      // Create a stack
4      GenericStack<String> stack = new GenericStack<String>();
5
6      // Add elements to the stack
7      stack.push("Tom"); // Push it to the stack
8      System.out.println("(1) " + stack);
9
10     stack.push("John"); // Push it to the the stack
11     System.out.println("(2) " + stack);
12
13     stack.push("George"); // Push it to the stack
```

```
14        stack.push("Michael"); // Push it to the stack
15        System.out.println("(3) " + stack);
16
17        // Remove elements from the stack
18        System.out.println("(4) " + stack.pop());
19        System.out.println("(5) " + stack.pop());
20        System.out.println("(6) " + stack);
21
22        // Create a queue
23        MyQueue<String> queue = new MyQueue<String>();
24
25        // Add elements to the queue
26        queue.enqueue("Tom"); // Add it to the queue
27        System.out.println("(7) " + queue);
28
29        queue.enqueue("John"); // Add it to the queue
30        System.out.println("(8) " + queue);
31
32        queue.enqueue("George"); // Add it to the queue
33        queue.enqueue("Michael"); // Add it to the queue
34        System.out.println("(9) " + queue);
35
36        // Remove elements from the queue
37        System.out.println("(10) " + queue.dequeue());
38        System.out.println("(11) " + queue.dequeue());
39        System.out.println("(12) " + queue);
40    }
41 }
```

```
(1) stack: [Tom]
(2) stack: [Tom, John]
(3) stack: [Tom, John, George, Michael]
(4) Michael
(5) George
(6) stack: [Tom, John]
(7) Queue: [Tom]
(8) Queue: [Tom, John]
(9) Queue: [Tom, John, George, Michael]
(10) Tom
(11) John
(12) Queue: [George, Michael]
```

For a stack, the `push(e)` method adds an element to the top of the stack, and the `pop()` method removes the top element from the stack and returns the removed element. It is easy to see that the time complexity for the **push** and **pop** methods is $O(1)$.

For a queue, the `enqueue(o)` method adds an element to the tail of the queue, and the `dequeue()` method removes the element from the head of the queue. It is easy to see that the time complexity for the **enqueue** and **dequeue** methods is $O(1)$.

Stack time complexity

Queue time complexity

24.7 Case Study: Evaluating Expressions

Listing 8.4, Calculator.java, gives a program that evaluates a simple expression with one operator and two operands (e.g., 2 + 3). This section presents a program that evaluates a *compound expression* with multiple operators and parentheses (e.g., (1 + 2) * 3 − 2). For simplicity, assume that the operands are integers and operators are of four types: +, −, *, and /.

The problem can be easily solved with stacks. The program uses two stacks, named `operandStack` and `operatorStack`, for storing operands and operators, respectively.

compound expression

Video Note
Applications of stacks

Operands and operators are pushed into the stacks before they are processed. When an *operator is processed*, it is popped from operatorStack and applied on the first two operands from operandStack (the two operands are popped from operandStack). The resultant value is pushed back to operandStack.

process an operator

The algorithm takes two phases:

Phase 1: Scanning expression
The program scans the expression from left to right to extract operands, operators, and the parentheses.

■ If the extracted item is an operand, push it to operandStack.

■ If the extracted item is a + or – operator, process all the operators at the top of operatorStack with higher or equal precedence (i.e., +, –, *, /), push the extracted operator to operatorStack.

■ If the extracted item is a * or / operator, process all the operators at the top of operatorStack with higher or equal precedence (i.e., *, /), push the extracted operator to operatorStack.

■ If the extracted item is a (symbol, push it to operatorStack.

■ If the extracted item is a) symbol, repeatedly process the operators from the top of operatorStack until seeing the (symbol on the stack.

Phase 2: Clearing stack
Repeatedly process the operators from the top of operatorStack until operatorStack is empty.

The following diagram shows how the algorithm is applied to evaluate the expression (1 + 2) * 4 - 3.

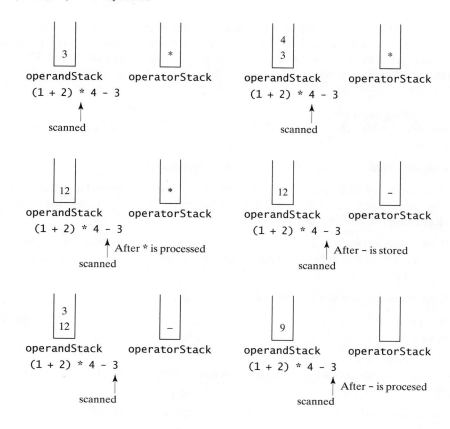

Listing 24.9 gives the program. Figure 24.18 gives some sample output.

LISTING 24.9 EvaluateExpression.java

```
 1 public class EvaluateExpression {
 2   public static void main(String[] args) {
 3     // Check number of arguments passed
 4     if (args.length < 1) {
 5       System.out.println(
 6         "Usage: java EvaluateExpression expression");
 7       System.exit(0);
 8     }
 9
10     String expression = "";
11     for (int i = 0; i < args.length; i++)
12       expression += args[i];
13
14     try {
15       System.out.println(evaluateExpression(expression));
16     }
17     catch (Exception ex) {
18       System.out.println("Wrong expression");
19     }
20   }
21
22   /** Evaluate an expression */
23   public static int evaluateExpression(String expression) {
24     // Create operandStack to store operands
```

check usage

concatenate arguments

evaluate expression

exception

```java
25    GenericStack<Integer> operandStack
26      = new GenericStack<Integer>();
27
28    // Create operatorStack to store operators
29    GenericStack<Character> operatorStack
30      = new GenericStack<Character>();
31
32    // Extract operands and operators
33    java.util.StringTokenizer tokens =
34      new java.util.StringTokenizer(expression, "()+-/*", true);
35
36    // Phase 1: Scan tokens
37    while (tokens.hasMoreTokens()) {
38      String token = tokens.nextToken().trim(); // Extract a token
39      if (token.length() == 0)  // Blank space
40        continue; // Back to the while loop to extract the next token
41      else if (token.charAt(0) == '+' || token.charAt(0) == '-') {
42        // Process all +, -, *, / in the top of the operator stack
43        while (!operatorStack.isEmpty() &&
44          (operatorStack.peek().equals('+') ||
45           operatorStack.peek().equals('-') ||
46           operatorStack.peek().equals('*') ||
47           operatorStack.peek().equals('/')
48          )) {
49          processAnOperator(operandStack, operatorStack);
50        }
51
52        // Push the + or - operator into the operator stack
53        operatorStack.push(new Character(token.charAt(0)));
54      }
55      else if (token.charAt(0) == '*' || token.charAt(0) == '/') {
56        // Process all *, / in the top of the operator stack
57        while (!operatorStack.isEmpty() &&
58          (operatorStack.peek().equals('*') ||
59           operatorStack.peek().equals('/')
60          )) {
61          processAnOperator(operandStack, operatorStack);
62        }
63
64        // Push the * or / operator into the operator stack
65        operatorStack.push(new Character(token.charAt(0)));
66      }
67      else if (token.trim().charAt(0) == '(') {
68        operatorStack.push(new Character('(')); // Push '(' to stack
69      }
70      else if (token.trim().charAt(0) == ')') {
71        // Process all the operators in the stack until seeing '('
72        while (!operatorStack.peek().equals('(')) {
73          processAnOperator(operandStack, operatorStack);
74        }
75
76        operatorStack.pop(); // Pop the '(' symbol from the stack
77      }
78      else { // An operand scanned
79        // Push an operand to the stack
80        operandStack.push(new Integer(token));
81      }
82    }
83
84    // Phase 2: process all the remaining operators in the stack
```

operandStack

operatorStack

extract tokens

more tokens?

+ or - scanned

* or / scanned

(scanned

) scanned

an operand scanned

clear **operatorStack**

```
85      while (!operatorStack.isEmpty()) {
86        processAnOperator(operandStack, operatorStack);
87      }
88
89      // Return the result
90      return ((Integer)(operandStack.pop())).intValue();
91    }
92
93    /** Process one operator: Take an operator from operatorStack and
94     *  apply it on the operands in the operandStack */
95    public static void processAnOperator(
96        GenericStack<Integer> operandStack,
97        GenericStack<Character> operatorStack) {
98      if (operatorStack.peek().equals('+')) {
99        operatorStack.pop();
100       int op1 = ((Integer)(operandStack.pop())).intValue();
101       int op2 = ((Integer)(operandStack.pop())).intValue();
102       operandStack.push(new Integer(op2 + op1));
103     }
104     else if (operatorStack.peek().equals('-')) {
105       operatorStack.pop();
106       int op1 = ((Integer)(operandStack.pop())).intValue();
107       int op2 = ((Integer)(operandStack.pop())).intValue();
108       operandStack.push(new Integer(op2 - op1));
109     }
110     else if (operatorStack.peek().equals('*')) {
111       operatorStack.pop();
112       int op1 = ((Integer)(operandStack.pop())).intValue();
113       int op2 = ((Integer)(operandStack.pop())).intValue();
114       operandStack.push(new Integer(op2 * op1));
115     }
116     else if (operatorStack.peek().equals('/')) {
117       operatorStack.pop();
118       int op1 = ((Integer)(operandStack.pop())).intValue();
119       int op2 = ((Integer)(operandStack.pop())).intValue();
120       operandStack.push(new Integer(op2 / op1));
121     }
122   }
123 }
```

return result (line 90)

process + (line 98)

process − (line 104)

process * (line 110)

process / (line 116)

```
Command Prompt                                            _□×

C:\book>java EvaluateExpression 1 × 2
Wrong expression

C:\book>java EvaluateExpression 1 "×" 2
2

C:\book>java EvaluateExpression (1 + 2 "×" 4 - 3) "×" (7 / 5 "×" 6)
36
```

FIGURE 24.18   The program takes an expression as command-line arguments.

The program takes an expression as command-line arguments and concatenates all arguments into a string (lines 11–12). The `evaluateExpression` method creates two stacks `operandStack` and `operatorStack` (lines 25, 29) and uses `StringTokenizer` to extract tokens with operators and parentheses as delimiters (lines 33–34). The `StringTokenizer` class is introduced in Supplement III.Z, "The `StringTokenizer` Class." Normally, you use the split method in the `String` class to separate and extract tokens, ignoring delimiters from a string, but `StringTokenizer` is useful to extract tokens including delimiters.

The program scans each token in the `while` loop (lines 37–82). If a token is empty, skip it (line 39). If a token is an operand, push it to `operandStack` (line 80). If a token is a + or − operator (line 41), process all the operators from the top of `operatorStack` if any (lines 43–49) and push the newly scanned operator to the stack (line 53). If a token is a * or / operator (line 55), process all the * and / operators from the top of `operatorStack` if any (lines 57–62) and push the newly scanned operator to the stack (line 65). If a token is a (symbol (line 67), push it to `operatorStack`. If a token is a) symbol (line 70), process all the operators from the top of `operatorStack` until seeing the) symbol (lines 72–74) and pop the) symbol from the stack.

After all tokens are considered, the program processes the remaining operators in `operatorStack` (lines 85–87).

The `processAnOperator` method (lines 95–122) processes an operator. To process an operator is to pop the operator from `operatorStack` (line 99), pop two operands from `operandStack` (lines 100–101), apply the operator on the operands, and push the result back to `operandStack` (line 102).

Recall that the * character has special meaning when passed as a command-line argument (see the Note after Listing 8.4 Calculator.java). You have to use `"*"` to replace *, as shown in Figure 24.18.

special * character

KEY TERMS

array list   768
linked list   768
list   768

queue   788
stack   788

CHAPTER SUMMARY

■ You have learned the concept of object-oriented data structures and how to implement lists, stacks, and queues using the object-oriented approach.

■ To define a data structure is essentially to declare a class. The class for a data structure should use data fields to store data and provide methods to support such operations as insertion and deletion.

■ To create a data structure is to create an instance from the class. You can then apply the methods on the instance to manipulate the data structure, such as inserting an element into the data structure or deleting an element from the data structure.

■ Stacks can be applied to evaluate expressions.

REVIEW QUESTIONS

Sections 24.1–24.2

24.1 What is a data structure? What is an object-oriented data structure?

24.2 What are the limitations of the array data type?

24.3 `MyArrayList` is implemented using an array, and an array is a fixed-size data structure. Why is `MyArrayList` considered a dynamic data structure?

24.4 What are the benefits of defining both the `MyList` interface and the `MyAbstractList` class? What is a convenience class?

24.5 What is wrong in the following code?

```
MyArrayList list = new MyArrayList();
list.add(100);
```

24.6 What is wrong if lines 11–12 in MyArrayList.java

```
for (int i = 0; i < objects.length; i++)
  add(objects[i]);
```

are replaced by

```
super(objects);
```

or

```
data = objects;
size = objects.length;
```

24.7 If the number of elements in the program is fixed, what data structure should you use? If the number of elements in the program changes, what data structure should you use?

24.8 If you have to add or delete the elements anywhere in a list, should you use ArrayList or LinkedList?

Section 24.3 Stacks and Queues

24.9 You can use inheritance or composition to design the data structures for stacks and queues. Discuss the pros and cons of these two approaches.

24.10 Which lines of the following code are wrong?

```
MyList list = new MyArrayList();
list.add("Tom");
list = new MyLinkedList();
list.add("Tom");
list = new MyStack();
list.add("Tom");
```

PROGRAMMING EXERCISES

Section 24.2 Lists

24.1 (*Adding set operations in MyAbstractList*) Add and implement the following methods in MyAbstractList:

```
/** Adds the elements in otherList to this list.
 * Returns true if this list changed as a result of the call */
public boolean addAll(MyList otherList)

/** Removes all the elements in otherList from this list
 * Returns true if this list changed as a result of the call */
public boolean removeAll(MyList otherList)

/** Retains the elements in this list that are also in otherList
 * Returns true if this list changed as a result of the call */
public boolean retainAll(MyList otherList)
```

Write a test program that creates two `MyArrayList`s, `list1` and `list2`, with the initial values `{"Tom", "George", "Peter", "Jean", "Jane"}` and `{"Tom", "George", "Michael", "Michelle", "Daniel"}`, then invokes `list1.addAll(list2)`, `list1.removeAll(list2)`, and `list1.retain-All(list2)`, and displays the resulting new `list1`.

24.2* (*Completing the implementation of* `MyLinkedList`) The implementations of methods `clear()`, `contains(Object o)`, `get(int index)`, `indexOf-(Object o)`, `lastIndexOf(Object o)`, and `set(int index, Object o)` are omitted in the text. Implement these methods.

24.3* (*Creating a two-way linked list*) The `MyLinkedList` class used in Listing 24.6 is a one-way directional linked list that enables one-way traversal of the list. Modify the `Node` class to add the new field name `previous` to refer to the previous node in the list, as follows:

```java
public class Node {
  Object element;
  Node next;
  Node previous;

  public Node(Object o) {
    element = o;
  }
}
```

Simplify the implementation of the `add(Object element, int index)` and `remove(int index)` methods to take advantage of the bidirectional linked list.

Section 24.6 Stacks and Queues

24.4 (*Using the* `Stack` *class*) Write a program that displays the first 50 prime numbers in descending order. Use a stack to store prime numbers.

24.5 (*Implementing* `MyQueue` *using inheritance*) In §24.6, "Stacks and Queues," `MyQueue` is implemented using composition. Create a new queue class that extends `MyLinkedList`.

24.6* (*Matching grouping symbols*) A Java program contains various pairs of grouping symbols, such as:

- Parentheses: (and).
- Braces: { and }.
- Brackets: [and].

Video Note
Match grouping symbols

Note that the grouping symbols cannot overlap. For example, `(a{b)}` is illegal. Write a program to check whether a Java source-code file has correct pairs of grouping symbols. Pass the source-code file name as a command-line argument.

24.7** (*Game: the 24-card game*) The 24-card game is to pick any four cards from 52 cards, as shown in Figure 24.19. Note that two Jokers are excluded. Each card represents a number. A King, Queen, and Jack represent 13, 12, and 11, respectively. Enter an expression that uses the four numbers for the selected cards. Each number must be used once and only once. You can use the operators (addition, subtraction, multiplication, and division) and parentheses in the expression. The expression must evaluate to 24. After entering the expression, click the *Verify* button to check whether the numbers in the expression are currently selected and whether the result of the expression is correct. Display the verification in a dialog box. Note that it is possible that such an expression does not exist. In this case, click the *Refresh* button to get another set of four cards. Assume that images are stored in files named 1.png, 2.png, ..., 52.png, in the order of spades, hearts, diamonds, and clubs. So, the first 13 images are for spades 1, 2, 3, ..., and 13.

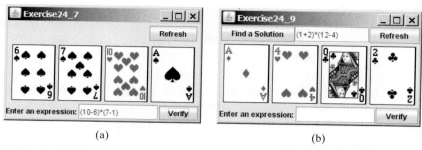

(a)   (b)

FIGURE 24.19 (a) The user enters an expression consisting of the numbers in the cards. (b) The program can automatically find a solution if one exists.

24.8** (*Postfix notation*) Postfix notation is a way of writing expressions without using parentheses. For example, the expression (1 + 2) * 3 would be written as 1 2 + 3 *. A postfix expression is evaluated using a stack. Scan a postfix expression from left to right. A variable or constant is pushed to the stack. When an operator is encountered, apply the operator with the top two operands in the stack and replace the two operands with the result. The following diagram shows how to evaluate 1 2 + 3 *.

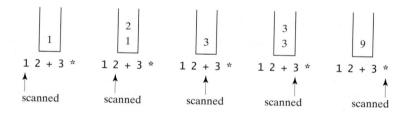

Write a program to evaluate postfix expressions. Pass the expression as command-line arguments.

24.9*** (*Game: the 24-card game*) Improve Exercise 24.7 to enable the computer to display the expression if one exists, as shown in Figure 24.19(b). Otherwise, report that the expression does not exist.

24.10** (*Converting infix to postfix*) Write a method that converts an infix expression into a postfix expression using the following header.

```
public static String infixToPostfix(String expression)
```

For example, the method should convert the infix expression (1 + 2) * 3 to 1 2 + 3 * and 2 * (1 + 3) to 2 1 3 + *.

24.11** (*Implementing MyArrayList*) Implement `MyArrayList` by extending `java.util.AbstractList`. Please study the Java API to learn the details of `java.util.AbstractList`.

24.12** (*Implementing MyLinkedList*) Implement `MyLinkedList` by extending `java.util.AbstractSequentialList`. Please study the Java API to learn the details of `java.util.AbstractSequentialList`.

CHAPTER 25

TREES, ITERATORS, HEAPS, AND PRIORITY QUEUES

Objectives

- To design and implement a binary search tree (§25.2).
- To represent binary trees using linked data structures (§25.2.1).
- To search an element in binary search tree (§25.2.2).
- To insert an element into a binary search tree (§25.2.3).
- To traverse elements in a binary tree (§25.2.4).
- To delete elements from a binary search tree (§25.3).
- To display binary tree graphically (§25.4).
- To create iterators for traversing a binary tree (§25.5).
- To design and implement a heap (§25.6).
- To design and implement a priority queue (§25.7).

25.1 Introduction

A tree is a classic data structure with many important applications. A tree provides a hierarchical organization in which data are stored in the nodes. A *heap* is a special type of binary tree that provides efficient operation for insertion, deletion, and retrieval operations. A heap is often used to implement a priority queue.

This chapter introduces trees, heaps, and priority queues. You have used iterators in the Java collections framework. This chapter will also demonstrate how to implement iterators for traversing elements in a binary tree.

25.2 Binary Search Trees

Recall that a list, stack, or queue is a linear structure that consists of a sequence of elements. A binary tree is a hierarchical structure. It either is empty or consists of an element, called the *root*, and two distinct binary trees, called the *left subtree* and *right subtree*, either or both of which may be empty. Examples of binary trees are shown in Figure 25.1.

root
left subtree
right subtree

Video Note
Binary search tree

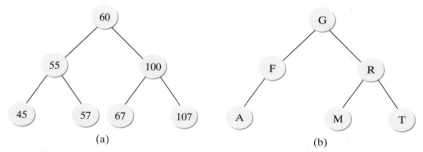

FIGURE 25.1 Each node in a binary tree has zero, one, or two subtrees.

length
depth
level
sibling
leaf
height

The *length* of a path is the number of the edges in the path. The *depth* of a node is the length of the path from the root to the node. The set of all nodes at a given depth is sometimes called a *level* of the tree. *Siblings* are nodes that share the same parent node. The root of a left (right) subtree of a node is called a *left (right) child* of the node. A node without children is called a *leaf*. The *height* of a tree is the length of the path from the root node to its furthest leaf. Consider the tree in Figure 25.1(a). The length for the path from node 60 to 45 is **2**. The depth of node 60 is **0**, the depth of node 55 is **1**, and the depth of node 45 is **2**. The height of the tree is **2**. Nodes 45 and 57 are siblings. Nodes 45, 57, 67, and 107 are in the same level.

binary search tree

A special type of binary tree called a *binary search tree* (BST) is often useful. A BST (with no duplicate elements) has the property that for every node in the tree, the value of any node in its left subtree is less than the value of the node, and the value of any node in its right subtree is greater than the value of the node. The binary trees in Figure 25.1 are all BSTs. This section is concerned with BSTs.

binary tree animation

Pedagogical Note
Follow the link www.cs.armstrong.edu/liang/intro7e/exercise/Exercise25_15.html to see how a BST works, as shown in Figure 25.2.

25.2.1 Representing Binary Search Trees

A binary tree can be represented using a set of linked nodes. Each node contains a value and two links named *left* and *right* that reference the left child and right child, respectively, as shown in Figure 25.3.

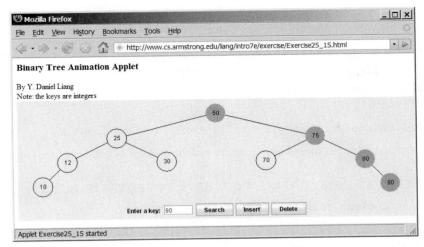

FIGURE 25.2 The animation tool enables you to insert, delete, and search elements visually.

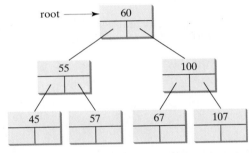

FIGURE 25.3 A binary tree can be represented using a set of linked nodes.

A node can be defined as a class, as follows:

```
class TreeNode<E> {
  E element;
  TreeNode<E> left;
  TreeNode<E> right;

  public TreeNode(E e) {
    element = e;
  }
}
```

The variable **root** refers to the root node of the tree. If the tree is empty, **root** is **null**. The following code creates the first three nodes of the tree in Figure 25.3.

```
// Create the root node
TreeNode<Integer> root = new TreeNode<Integer>(new Integer(60));

// Create the left child node
root.left = new TreeNode<Integer>(new Integer(55));

// Create the right child node
root.right = new TreeNode<Integer>(new Integer(100));
```

25.2.2 Searching for an Element

To search for an element in the BST, you start from the root and scan down from the root until a match is found or you arrive at an empty subtree. The algorithm is described in Listing 25.1.

Let `current` point to the root (line 2). Repeat the following steps until `current` is `null` (line 4) or the element matches `element` (line 12) matches `current.element`.

- If `element` is less than `current.element`, assign `current.left` to `current` (line 6).

- If `element` is greater than `current.element`, assign `current.right` to `current` (line 9).

- If `element` is equal to `current.element`, return true (line 12).

If the `current` is `null`, the subtree is empty and the element is not in the tree (line 14).

LISTING 25.1 Searching for an Element in a BST

```
1  public boolean search(E element) {
2    TreeNode<E> current = root; // Start from the root
3
4    while (current != null)
5      if (element < current.element) {
6        current = current.left; // Go left
7      }
8      else if (element > current.element) {
9        current = current.right; // Go right
10     }
11     else // Element matches current.element
12       return true; // Element is found
13
14   return false; // Element is not in the tree
15 }
```

start from root

left subtree

right subtree

found

not found

25.2.3 Inserting an Element into a BST

To insert an element into a BST, you need to locate where to insert the element in the tree. The key idea is to locate the parent for the new node. Listing 25.2 gives the algorithm.

LISTING 25.2 Inserting an Element into a BST

```
1  boolean insert(E e) {
2    if (tree is empty)
3      // Create the node for e as the root;
4    else {
5      // Locate the parent node
6      parent = current = root;
7      while (current != null)
8        if (e < the value in current.element) {
9          parent = current;  // Keep the parent
10         current = current.left; // Go left
11       }
12       else if (e > the value in current.element) {
13         parent = current; // Keep the parent
14         current = current.right; // Go right
15       }
16       else
17         return false; // Duplicate node not inserted
18
19     // Create a new node for e and attach it to parent
20
21     return true; // Element inserted
22   }
23 }
```

create a new node

locate parent

left child

right child

If the tree is empty, create a root node with the new element (lines 2–3). Otherwise, locate the parent node for the new element node (lines 4–17). Create a new node for the element and link this node to its parent node. If the new element is less than the parent element, the node for the new element will be the left child of the parent. If the new element is greater than the parent element, the node for the new element will be the right child of the parent.

For example, to insert 101 into the tree in Figure 25.3, after the `while` loop finishes in the algorithm, `parent` points to the node for 107, as shown in Figure 25.4(a). The new node for 101 becomes the left child of the parent. To insert 59 into the tree, after the `while` finishes in the algorithm, the parent points to the node for 57, as shown in Figure 25.4(b). The new node for 59 becomes the right child of the parent.

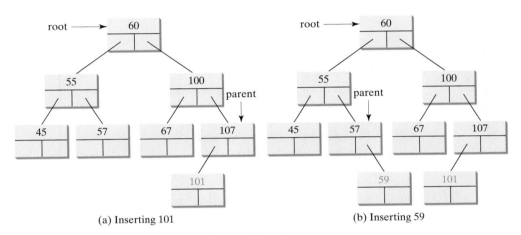

(a) Inserting 101   (b) Inserting 59

FIGURE 25.4 Two new elements are inserted into the tree.

25.2.4 Tree Traversal

Tree traversal is the process of visiting each node in the tree exactly once. There are several ways to traverse a tree. This section presents *inorder, preorder, postorder, depth-first, and breadth-first* traversals.

With inorder traversal, the left subtree of the current node is visited first, then the current node, and finally the right subtree of the current node. The inorder traversal displays all the nodes in a BST in increasing order.   inorder

With postorder traversal, the left subtree of the current node is visited first, then the right subtree of the current node, and finally the current node itself.   postorder

With preorder traversal, the current node is visited first, then the left subtree of the current node, and finally the right subtree of the current node. Depth-first traversal is the same as preorder traversal.   preorder   depth-first

With breadth-first traversal, the nodes are visited level by level. First the root is visited, then all the children of the root from left to right, then the grandchildren of the root from left to right, and so on.   breadth-first

For example, in the tree in Figure 25.4(b), the inorder is

```
45 55 57 59 60 67 100 101 107
```

The postorder is

```
45 59 57 55 67 101 107 100 60
```

The preorder is

    60 55 45 57 59 100 67 107 101

The breadth-first traversal is

    60 55 100 45 57 67 107 59 101

25.2.5 The `BinaryTree` Class

Following the design pattern for the Java collections framework API, we use an interface named `Tree` to define all common operations for trees and provide an abstract class named `AbstractTree` that partially implements `Tree`, as shown in Figure 25.5. A concrete `BinaryTree` class can be defined to extend `AbstractTree`, as shown in Figure 25.6.

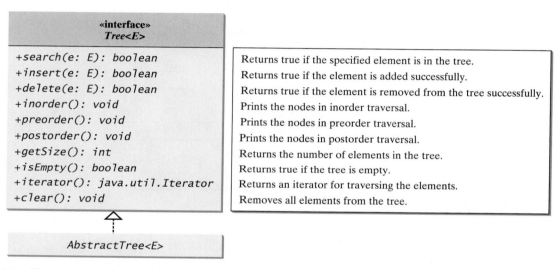

FIGURE 25.5 The `Tree` interface defines common operations for trees, and the `AbstractTree` class partially implements `Tree`.

FIGURE 25.6 The `BinaryTree` class defines a concrete BST.

Listings 25.3, 25.4, and 25.5 give the implementation for Tree, AbstractTree, and BinaryTree.

LISTING 25.3 Tree.java

```java
 1 public interface Tree<E extends Comparable<E>> {
 2   /** Return true if the element is in the tree */
 3   public boolean search(E e);
 4
 5   /** Insert element o into the binary tree
 6    * Return true if the element is inserted successfully */
 7   public boolean insert(E e);
 8
 9   /** Delete the specified element from the tree
10    * Return true if the element is deleted successfully */
11   public boolean delete(E e);
12
13   /** Inorder traversal from the root*/
14   public void inorder();
15
16   /** Postorder traversal from the root */
17   public void postorder();
18
19   /** Preorder traversal from the root */
20   public void preorder();
21
22   /** Get the number of nodes in the tree */
23   public int getSize();
24
25   /** Return true if the tree is empty */
26   public boolean isEmpty();
27
28   /** Return an iterator to traverse elements in the tree */
29   public java.util.Iterator iterator();
30 }
```

interface

search

insert

delete

inorder

postorder

preorder

getSize

isEmpty

iterator

LISTING 25.4 AbstractTree.java

```java
 1 public abstract class AbstractTree<E extends Comparable<E>>
 2     implements Tree<E> {
 3   /** Inorder traversal from the root*/
 4   public void inorder() {
 5   }
 6
 7   /** Postorder traversal from the root */
 8   public void postorder() {
 9   }
10
11   /** Preorder traversal from the root */
12   public void preorder() {
13   }
14
15   /** Return true if the tree is empty */
16   public boolean isEmpty() {
17     return getSize() == 0;
18   }
19
20   /** Return an iterator to traverse elements in the tree */
21   public java.util.Iterator iterator() {
```

abstract class

default **inorder**
  implementation

default **postorder**
  implementation

default **preorder**
  implementation

isEmpty implementation

default **iterator**
  implementation

```
22        return null;
23    }
24 }
```

LISTING 25.5 BinaryTree.java

BinaryTree class
root
size

no-arg constructor

constructor

search

compare objects

insert

new root

compare objects

```
 1 public class BinaryTree<E extends Comparable<E>>
 2       extends AbstractTree<E> {
 3   protected TreeNode<E> root;
 4   protected int size = 0;
 5
 6   /** Create a default binary tree */
 7   public BinaryTree() {
 8   }
 9
10   /** Create a binary tree from an array of objects */
11   public BinaryTree(E[] objects) {
12     for (int i = 0; i < objects.length; i++)
13       insert(objects[i]);
14   }
15
16   /** Returns true if the element is in the tree */
17   public boolean search(E e) {
18     TreeNode<E> current = root; // Start from the root
19
20     while (current != null) {
21       if (e.compareTo(current.element) < 0) {
22         current = current.left;
23       }
24       else if (e.compareTo(current.element) > 0) {
25         current = current.right;
26       }
27       else // element matches current.element
28         return true; // Element is found
29     }
30
31     return false;
32   }
33
34   /** Insert element o into the binary tree
35    * Return true if the element is inserted successfully */
36   public boolean insert(E e) {
37     if (root == null)
38       root = createNewNode(e); // Create a new root
39     else {
40       // Locate the parent node
41       TreeNode<E> parent = null;
42       TreeNode<E> current = root;
43       while (current != null)
44         if (e.compareTo(current.element) < 0) {
45           parent = current;
46           current = current.left;
47         }
48         else if (e.compareTo(current.element) > 0) {
49           parent = current;
50           current = current.right;
51         }
52         else
53           return false; // Duplicate node not inserted
54
```

```
55        // Create the new node and attach it to the parent node
56        if (e.compareTo(parent.element) < 0)                    link to parent
57          parent.left = createNewNode(e);
58        else
59          parent.right = createNewNode(e);
60      }
61
62      size++;                                                   increase size
63      return true; // Element inserted
64    }
65
66    protected TreeNode<E> createNewNode(E e) {                  create new node
67      return new TreeNode<E>(e);
68    }
69
70    /** Inorder traversal from the root*/
71    public void inorder() {                                     inorder
72      inorder(root);
73    }
74
75    /** Inorder traversal from a subtree */
76    protected void inorder(TreeNode<E> root) {                  recursive helper method
77      if (root == null) return;
78      inorder(root.left);
79      System.out.print(root.element + " ");
80      inorder(root.right);
81    }
82
83    /** Postorder traversal from the root */
84    public void postorder() {                                   postorder
85      postorder(root);
86    }
87
88    /** Postorder traversal from a subtree */
89    protected void postorder(TreeNode<E> root) {                recursive helper method
90      if (root == null) return;
91      postorder(root.left);
92      postorder(root.right);
93      System.out.print(root.element + " ");
94    }
95
96    /** Preorder traversal from the root */
97    public void preorder() {                                    preorder
98      preorder(root);
99    }
100
101   /** Preorder traversal from a subtree */
102   protected void preorder(TreeNode<E> root) {                 recursive helper method
103     if (root == null) return;
104     System.out.print(root.element + " ");
105     preorder(root.left);
106     preorder(root.right);
107   }
108
109   /** Inner class tree node */
110   public static class TreeNode<E extends Comparable<E>> {      inner class
111     E element;
112     TreeNode<E> left;
113     TreeNode<E> right;
114
```

```
115      public TreeNode(E e) {
116        element = e;
117      }
118    }
119
120    /** Get the number of nodes in the tree */
121    public int getSize() {
122      return size;
123    }
124
125    /** Returns the root of the tree */
126    public TreeNode getRoot() {
127      return root;
128    }
129
130    /** Returns a path from the root leading to the specified element */
131    public java.util.ArrayList<TreeNode<E>> path(E e) {
132      java.util.ArrayList<TreeNode<E>> list =
133        new java.util.ArrayList<TreeNode<E>>();
134      TreeNode<E> current = root; // Start from the root
135
136      while (current != null) {
137        list.add(current); // Add the node to the list
138        if (e.compareTo(current.element) < 0) {
139          current = current.left;
140        }
141        else if (e.compareTo(current.element) > 0) {
142          current = current.right;
143        }
144        else
145          break;
146      }
147
148      return list; // Return an array of nodes
149    }
150
151    /** Delete an element from the binary tree.
152     * Return true if the element is deleted successfully
153     * Return false if the element is not in the tree */
154    public boolean delete(E e) {
155      // Locate the node to be deleted and also locate its parent node
156      TreeNode<E> parent = null;
157      TreeNode<E> current = root;
158      while (current != null) {
159        if (e.compareTo(current.element) < 0) {
160          parent = current;
161          current = current.left;
162        }
163        else if (e.compareTo(current.element) > 0) {
164          parent = current;
165          current = current.right;
166        }
167        else
168          break; // Element is in the tree pointed by current
169      }
170
171      if (current == null)
172        return false; // Element is not in the tree
173
```

Margin labels:
getSize (line 121)
getRoot (line 126)
path (line 131)
delete (line 154)
locate **parent** (line 156)
locate **current** (line 157)
current found (line 168)
not found (line 171)

```
174      // Case 1: current has no left children
175      if (current.left == null) {                              Case 1
176        // Connect the parent with the right child of the current node
177        if (parent == null) {
178          root = current.right;
179        }
180        else {
181          if (e.compareTo(parent.element) < 0)
182            parent.left = current.right;                       reconnect parent
183          else
184            parent.right = current.right;                      reconnect parent
185        }
186      }
187      else {
188        // Case 2: The current node has a left child            Case 2
189        // Locate the rightmost node in the left subtree of
190        // the current node and also its parent
191        TreeNode<E> parentOfRightMost = current;               locate parentOfRightMost
192        TreeNode<E> rightMost = current.left;                  locate rightMost
193
194        while (rightMost.right != null) {
195          parentOfRightMost = rightMost;
196          rightMost = rightMost.right; // Keep going to the right
197        }
198
199        // Replace the element in current by the element in rightMost
200        current.element = rightMost.element;                   replace current
201
202        // Eliminate rightmost node
203        if (parentOfRightMost.right == rightMost)
204          parentOfRightMost.right = rightMost.left;
205        else                                                   reconnect
206          // Special case: parentOfRightMost == current          parentOfRightMost
207          parentOfRightMost.left = rightMost.left;
208      }
209
210      size--;                                                  reduce size
211      return true; // Element inserted                         successful deletion
212    }
213
214    /** Obtain an iterator. Use inorder. */
215    public java.util.Iterator iterator() {                     default iterator
216      return inorderIterator();
217    }
218
219    /** Obtain an inorder iterator */
220    public java.util.Iterator inorderIterator() {              inorder iterator
221      return new InorderIterator();
222    }
223
224    // Inner class InorderIterator
225    class InorderIterator implements java.util.Iterator {      inner class
226      // Store the elements in a list
227      private java.util.ArrayList<E> list =                    internal list
228        new java.util.ArrayList<E>();
229      private int current = 0; // Point to the current element in list   current position
230
231      public InorderIterator() {
232        inorder(); // Traverse binary tree and store elements in list
233      }
```

obtain inorder list

```
234
235     /** Inorder traversal from the root*/
236     private void inorder() {
237       inorder(root);
238     }
239
240     /** Inorder traversal from a subtree */
241     private void inorder(TreeNode<E> root) {
242       if (root == null)return;
243       inorder(root.left);
244       list.add(root.element);
245       inorder(root.right);
246     }
247
```

hasNext in iterator?

```
248     /** Next element for traversing? */
249     public boolean hasNext() {
250       if (current < list.size())
251         return true;
252
253       return false;
254     }
255
```

get next element

```
256     /** Get the current element and move cursor to the next */
257     public Object next() {
258       return list.get(current++);
259     }
260
```

remove the current

refresh list

```
261     /** Remove the current element and refresh the list */
262     public void remove() {
263       delete(list.get(current)); // Delete the current element
264       list.clear(); // Clear the list
265       inorder(); // Rebuild the list
266     }
267   }
268
269   /** Remove all elements from the tree */
270   public void clear() {
271     root = null;
272     size = 0;
273   }
274 }
```

The `insert(E e)` method (lines 36–64) creates a node for element `e` and inserts it into the tree. If the tree is empty, the node becomes the root. Otherwise, the method finds an appropriate parent for the node to maintain the order of the tree. If the element is already in the tree, the method returns false; otherwise it returns true.

The `inorder()` method (lines 71–81) invokes `inorder(root)` to traverse the entire tree. The method `inorder(TreeNode root)` traverses the tree with the specified root. This is a recursive method. It recursively traverses the left subtree, then the root, and finally the right subtree. The traversal ends when the tree is empty.

The `postorder()` method (lines 84–94) and the `preorder()` method (lines 97–107) are implemented similarly using recursion.

The `path(E e)` method (lines 131–149) returns a path of the nodes as an array list. The path starts from the root leading to the element. The element may not be in the tree. For example, in Figure 25.4(a), `path(45)` contains the nodes for elements 60, 55, and 45, and `path(58)` contains the nodes for elements 60, 55, and 57.

The implementation of `delete()` and `iterator()` (lines 151–267) will be discussed in §25.3 and §25.4.

Listing 25.6 gives an example that creates a binary tree using `BinaryTree` (line 4). The program adds strings into the tree (lines 5–11), traverses the tree in inorder, postorder, and preorder (lines 14–20), searches an element (line 24), and obtains a path from the node containing `Peter` to the root (lines 28–31).

LISTING 25.6 TestBinaryTree.java

```java
1 public class TestBinaryTree {
2   public static void main(String[] args) {
3     // Create a BinaryTree
4     BinaryTree<String> tree = new BinaryTree<String>();
5     tree.insert("George");
6     tree.insert("Michael");
7     tree.insert("Tom");
8     tree.insert("Adam");
9     tree.insert("Jones");
10    tree.insert("Peter");
11    tree.insert("Daniel");
12
13    // Traverse tree
14    System.out.print("Inorder (sorted): ");
15    tree.inorder();
16    System.out.print("\nPostorder: ");
17    tree.postorder();
18    System.out.print("\nPreorder: ");
19    tree.preorder();
20    System.out.print("\nThe number of nodes is " + tree.getSize());
21
22    // Search for an element
23    System.out.print("\nIs Peter in the tree? " +
24      tree.search("Peter"));
25
26    // Get a path from the root to Peter
27    System.out.print("\nA path from the root to Peter is: ");
28    java.util.ArrayList path = tree.path("Peter");
29    for (int i = 0; path != null && i < path.size(); i++)
30      System.out.print(((BinaryTree.TreeNode)(path.get(i))).element
31        + " ");
32  }
33 }
```

create tree
insert

inorder

postorder

preorder
getSize

search

```
Inorder (sorted): Adam Daniel George Jones Michael Peter Tom
Postorder: Daniel Adam Jones Peter Tom Michael George
Preorder: George Adam Daniel Michael Jones Tom Peter
The number of nodes is 7
Is Peter in the tree? true
A path from the root to Peter is: George Michael Tom Peter
```

The program checks `path != null` in line 29 to ensure that the path is not `null` before invoking `path.get(i)`. This is an example of defensive programming to avoid potential runtime errors.

After all the elements are inserted, the tree should appear as shown in Figure 25.7.

If the elements are inserted in a different order (e.g., Daniel, Adam, Jones, Peter, Tom, Michael, George), the tree will look different. However, the inorder traversal prints elements in the same order as long as the set of elements is the same. The inorder traversal displays a sorted list.

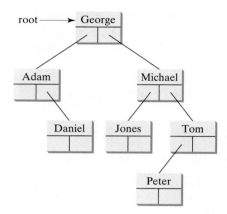

FIGURE 25.7 The BST is pictured here after line 10 is executed.

25.3 Deleting Elements in a BST

The `insert(element)` method was presented in §25.2.3. Often you need to delete an element from a binary tree. Deleting an element from a binary tree is far more complex than adding an element into a binary tree.

locating element

To delete an element from a binary tree, you need to first locate the node that contains the element and also its parent node. Let `current` point to the node that contains the element in the binary tree and `parent` point to the parent of the `current` node. The `current` node may be a left child or a right child of the `parent` node. There are two cases to consider:

Case 1: The current node does not have a left child, as shown in Figure 25.8(a). Simply connect the parent with the right child of the current node, as shown in Figure 25.8(b).

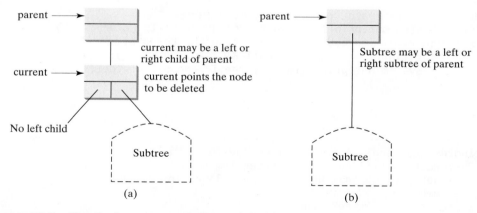

FIGURE 25.8 Case 1: the current node has no left child.

For example, to delete node 10 in Figure 25.9(a). Connect the parent of node 10 with the right child of node 10, as shown in Figure 25.9(b).

 Note

delete a leaf

If the current node is a leaf, it falls into Case 1. For example, to delete element 16 in Figure 25.9(a), connect its right child to the parent of node 16. In this case, the right child of node 16 is `null`.

Case 2: The `current` node has a left child. Let `rightMost` point to the node that contains the largest element in the left subtree of the `current` node and `parentOfRightMost` point to

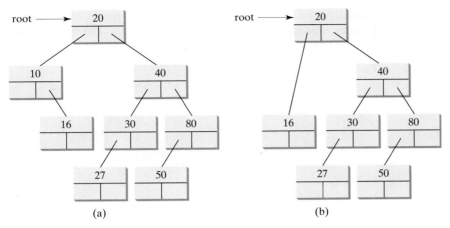

FIGURE 25.9 Case 1: deleting node 20 from (a) results in (b).

the parent node of the `rightMost` node, as shown in Figure 25.10(a). Note that the `rightMost` node cannot have a right child, but may have a left child. Replace the element value in the `current` node with the one in the `rightMost` node, connect the `parentOfRightMost` node with the left child of the `rightMost` node, and delete the `rightMost` node, as shown in Figure 25.10(b).

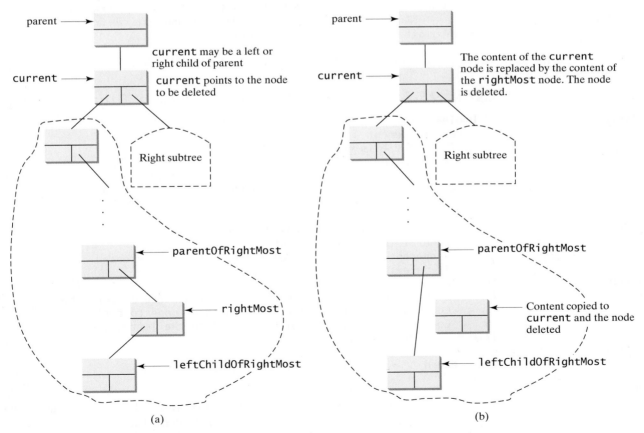

FIGURE 25.10 Case 2: the current node has a left child.

For example, consider deleting node **20** in Figure 25.11(a). The `rightMost` node has the element value **16**. Replace the element value **20** with **16** in the **current** node and make node **10** the parent for node **14**, as shown in Figure 25.11(b).

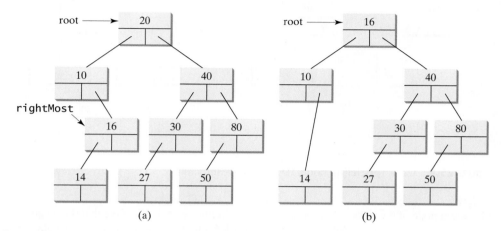

FIGURE 25.11 Case 2: deleting node **20** from (a) results in (b).

Note

If the left child of **current** does not have a right child, **current.left** points to the large element in the left subtree of **current**. In this case, **rightMost** is **current.left** and **parentOfRightMost** is **current**. You have to take care of this special case to reconnect the right child of **rightMost** with **parentOfRightMost**.

special case

The algorithm for deleting an element from a binary tree can be described as follows:

LISTING 25.7 Deleting an Element from a Binary Tree

delete method

not in the tree

locate parent

no left child

has a left child

```
 1 boolean delete(E e) {
 2   Locate element e in the tree;
 3   if element e is not found
 4     return true;
 5
 6   Let current be the node that contains e and parent be
 7     the parent of current;
 8
 9   if (current has no left child) // Case 1
10     Connect the right child of
11       current with parent; now current is not referenced, so
12     it is eliminated;
13   else // Case 2
14     Locate the rightmost node in the left subtree of current.
15     Copy the element value in the rightmost node to current.
16     Connect the parent of the rightmost to the left child
17       of rightmost;
18
19   return true; // Element deleted
20 }
```

The complete implementation of the **delete** method is given in lines 154–212 in Listing 25.5. The method locates the node (named **current**) to be deleted and also locates its parent (named `parent`) in lines 158–169. If `current` is `null`, the element is not in tree. So, the method returns `false` (line 172). Please note that if `current` is `root`, `parent` is `null`. If the tree is empty, both `current` and `parent` are `null`.

Case 1 of the algorithm is covered in lines 175–186. In this case, the `current` node has no left child (i.e., `current.left == null`). If `parent` is `null`, assign `current.right` to `root` (lines 177–179). Otherwise, assign `current.right` to `parent.left` or `parent.right`, depending on whether `current` is a left or right child of `parent` (181–184).

Case 2 of the algorithm is covered in lines 187–208. In this case, the `current` has a left child. The algorithm locates the rightmost node (named `rightMost`) in the left subtree of the current node and also its parent (named `parentOfRightMost`) (lines 194–197). Replace the element in `current` by the element in `rightMost` (line 200); assign `rightMost.left` to `parentOfRightMost.right` or `parentOfRightMost.right` (lines 203–207), depending on whether `rightMost` is a right or left child of `parentOfRightMost`.

Listing 25.8 gives a test program that deletes the elements from the binary tree.

LISTING 25.8 TestBinaryTreeDelete.java

```java
 1 public class TestBinaryTreeDelete {
 2   public static void main(String[] args) {
 3     BinaryTree<String> tree = new BinaryTree<String>();
 4     tree.insert("George");
 5     tree.insert("Michael");
 6     tree.insert("Tom");
 7     tree.insert("Adam");
 8     tree.insert("Jones");
 9     tree.insert("Peter");
10     tree.insert("Daniel");
11     printTree(tree);
12
13     System.out.println("\nAfter delete George:");
14     tree.delete("George");                              delete an element
15     printTree(tree);
16
17     System.out.println("\nAfter delete Adam:");
18     tree.delete("Adam");                                delete an element
19     printTree(tree);
20
21     System.out.println("\nAfter delete Michael:");
22     tree.delete("Michael");                             delete an element
23     printTree(tree);
24   }
25
26   public static void printTree(BinaryTree tree) {
27     // Traverse tree
28     System.out.print("Inorder (sorted): ");
29     tree.inorder();
30     System.out.print("\nPostorder: ");
31     tree.postorder();
32     System.out.print("\nPreorder: ");
33     tree.preorder();
34     System.out.print("\nThe number of nodes is " + tree.getSize());
35     System.out.println();
36   }
37 }
```

```
Inorder (sorted): Adam Daniel George Jones Michael Peter Tom
Postorder: Daniel Adam Jones Peter Tom Michael George
Preorder: George Adam Daniel Michael Jones Tom Peter
The number of nodes is 7

After delete George:
Inorder (sorted): Adam Daniel Jones Michael Peter Tom
Postorder: Adam Jones Peter Tom Michael Daniel
Preorder: Daniel Adam Michael Jones Tom Peter
The number of nodes is 6

After delete Adam:
Inorder (sorted): Daniel Jones Michael Peter Tom
Postorder: Jones Peter Tom Michael Daniel
Preorder: Daniel Michael Jones Tom Peter
The number of nodes is 5

After delete Michael:
Inorder (sorted): Daniel Jones Peter Tom
Postorder: Peter Tom Jones Daniel
Preorder: Daniel Jones Tom Peter
The number of nodes is 4
```

Figures 25.11–25.14 show how the tree evolves as the elements are deleted from it.

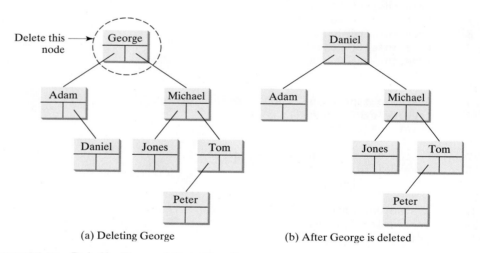

(a) Deleting George   (b) After George is deleted

FIGURE 25.12 Deleting George falls in Case 2.

Note

It is obvious that the time complexity for the inorder, preorder, and postorder is $O(n)$, since each node is traversed only once. The time complexity for search, insertion and deletion is the height of the tree. In the worst case, the height of the tree is $O(n)$.

binary tree time complexity

Video Note
Tree visualization

25.4 Tree Visualization

One challenge facing the data structure course is to motivate students. To display a binary tree graphically will not only help students understand the working of a binary tree, but also stimulates their interest in programming. Students can apply visualization techniques in other

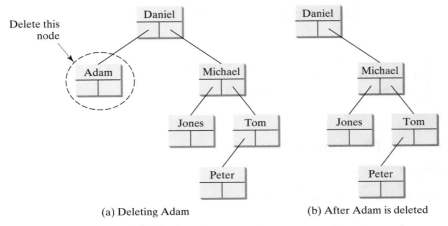

(a) Deleting Adam   (b) After Adam is deleted

FIGURE 25.13 Deleting Adam falls in Case 1.

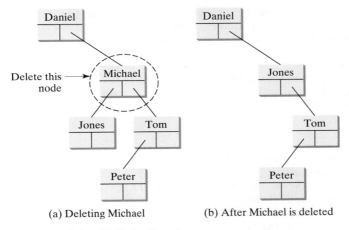

(a) Deleting Michael   (b) After Michael is deleted

FIGURE 25.14 Deleting Michael falls in Case 2.

projects. How do you display a binary tree? A binary tree is a recursive structure. You can simply display the root, and then display the two subtrees recursively. The techniques for displaying the Sierpinski triangle (Listing 20.9 SierpinskiTriangle.java) can be applied to display a binary tree. You can display a binary tree using recursion. For simplicity, we assume the keys are positive integers less than **100**. Listings 25.9 and 25.10 give the program, and Figure 25.15 shows some sample runs of the program.

(a) Inserting 50, 25, 35, 30, and 60   (b) After 50 is deleted

FIGURE 25.15 A binary tree is displayed graphically.

LISTING 25.9 DisplayBinaryTree.java

```
1  import javax.swing.*;
2
3  public class DisplayBinaryTree extends JApplet {
4    public DisplayBinaryTree() {
5      add(new BinaryTreeView(new BinaryTree<Integer>()));
6    }
7  }
```

create a view

main method omitted

LISTING 25.10 BinaryTreeView.java

```
1  import java.awt.*;
2  import java.awt.event.*;
3  import javax.swing.*;
4
5  public class BinaryTreeView extends JPanel {
6    private BinaryTree<Integer> tree; // A binary tree to be displayed
7    private JTextField jtfKey = new JTextField(5);
8    private PaintTree paintTree = new PaintTree();
9    private JButton jbtInsert = new JButton("Insert");
10   private JButton jbtDelete = new JButton("Delete");
11
12   /** Construct a view for a binary tree */
13   public BinaryTreeView(BinaryTree<Integer> tree) {
14     this.tree = tree; // Set a binary tree to be displayed
15     setUI();
16   }
17
18   /** Initialize UI for binary tree */
19   private void setUI() {
20     this.setLayout(new BorderLayout());
21     add(paintTree, BorderLayout.CENTER);
22     JPanel panel = new JPanel();
23     panel.add(new JLabel("Enter a key: "));
24     panel.add(jtfKey);
25     panel.add(jbtInsert);
26     panel.add(jbtDelete);
27     add(panel, BorderLayout.SOUTH);
28
29     // Listener for the Insert button
30     jbtInsert.addActionListener(new ActionListener() {
31       public void actionPerformed(ActionEvent e) {
32         int key = Integer.parseInt(jtfKey.getText());
33         if (tree.search(key)) { // key is in the tree already
34           JOptionPane.showMessageDialog(null,
35             key + " is already in the tree");
36         }
37         else {
38           tree.insert(key); // Insert a new key
39           paintTree.repaint(); // Redisplay the tree
40         }
41       }
42     });
43
44     // Listener for the Delete button
45     jbtDelete.addActionListener(new ActionListener() {
46       public void actionPerformed(ActionEvent e) {
47         int key = Integer.parseInt(jtfKey.getText());
48         if (!tree.search(key)) { // key is not in the tree
```

binary tree

paint tree

create UI

insert button listener

insert key
repaint the tree

delete button listener

```
49              JOptionPane.showMessageDialog(null,
50                 key + " is not in the tree");
51           }
52         else {
53             tree.delete(key); // Delete a key                          delete key
54             paintTree.repaint(); // Redisplay the tree                 repaint the tree
55         }
56       }
57     });
58   }
59
60   // Inner class PaintTree for displaying a tree on a panel
61   class PaintTree extends JPanel {                                     PaintTree class
62     private int radius = 20; // Tree node radius
63     private int vGap = 50; // Gap between two levels in a tree
64
65     protected void paintComponent(Graphics g) {
66       super.paintComponent(g);
67
68       if (tree.getRoot() != null) {
69         // Display tree recursively
70         displayTree(g, tree.getRoot(), getWidth() / 2, 30,            display tree
71           getWidth() / 4);
72       }
73     }
74
75     /** Display a subtree rooted at position (x, y) */
76     private void displayTree(Graphics g, BinaryTree.TreeNode root,
77         int x, int y, int hGap) {
78       // Display the root
79       g.drawOval(x - radius, y - radius, 2 * radius, 2 * radius);     paint a node
80       g.drawString(root.element + "", x - 6, y + 4);
81
82       if (root.left != null) {
83         // Draw a line to the left node
84         connectLeftChild(g, x - hGap, y + vGap, x, y);               connect two nodes
85         // Draw the left subtree recursively
86         displayTree(g, root.left, x - hGap, y + vGap, hGap / 2);     draw left subtree
87       }
88
89       if (root.right != null) {
90         // Draw a line to the right node
91         connectRightChild(g, x + hGap, y + vGap, x, y);              connect two nodes
92         // Draw the right subtree recursively
93         displayTree(g, root.right, x + hGap, y + vGap, hGap / 2);    draw right subtree
94       }
95     }
96
97     /** Connect a parent at (x2, y2) with
98      * its left child at (x1, y1) */
99     private void connectLeftChild(Graphics g,
100         int x1, int y1, int x2, int y2) {
101       double d = Math.sqrt(vGap * vGap + (x2 - x1) * (x2 - x1));
102       int x11 = (int)(x1 + radius * (x2 - x1) / d);
103       int y11 = (int)(y1 - radius * vGap / d);
104       int x21 = (int)(x2 - radius * (x2 - x1) / d);
105       int y21 = (int)(y2 + radius * vGap / d);
106       g.drawLine(x11, y11, x21, y21);
107     }
108
```

```
109      /** Connect a parent at (x2, y2) with
110       * its right child at (x1, y1) */
111      private void connectRightChild(Graphics g,
112          int x1, int y1, int x2, int y2) {
113        double d = Math.sqrt(vGap * vGap + (x2 - x1) * (x2 - x1));
114        int x11 = (int)(x1 - radius * (x1 - x2) / d);
115        int y11 = (int)(y1 - radius * vGap / d);
116        int x21 = (int)(x2 + radius * (x1 - x2) / d);
117        int y21 = (int)(y2 + radius * vGap / d);
118        g.drawLine(x11, y11, x21, y21);
119      }
120    }
121  }
```

After a new key is inserted into the tree (line 38), the tree is repainted (line 39) to reflect the change. After a key is deleted (line 53), the tree is repainted (line 54) to reflect the change.

The node is displayed as a circle with **radius 20** (line 62). The distance between two levels in the tree is defined in **vGap 50** (line 63). **hGap** (line 77) defines the distance between two nodes horizontally. This value is reduced by half (**hGap / 2**) in the next level when the **displayTree** method is called recursively (lines 86, 93). Note that **vGap** is not changed in the tree.

Invoking **connectLeftChild** connects a parent with its left child. You need to find the two end points (**x11, y11**) and (**x21, y21**) in order to connect the two nodes, as shown in Figure 25.16. The mathematical calculation for finding the two ends is illustrated in Figure 25.16.

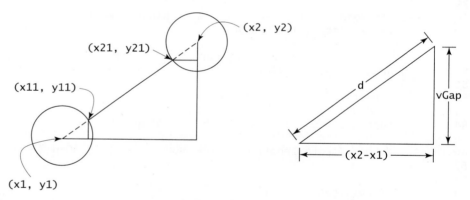

FIGURE 25.16 You need to find the position of the end points to connect to nodes.

Invoking **connectRightChild** connects a parent with its right child. The mathematical calculation for the two ends of the line is similar to the case for connecting a parent with its left child.

The program assumes that the keys are integers. You can easily modify the program with a generic type to display keys of characters or short strings.

25.5 Iterators

The methods **inorder()**, **preorder()**, and **postorder()** display the elements in **inorder**, **preorder**, and **postorder** in a binary tree. These methods are limited to displaying the elements in a tree. If you wish to process the elements in a binary tree rather than displaying them, these methods cannot be used. A more useful approach is to provide an iterator. An *iterator* is an object that provides a uniform way of traversing the elements in a container, such as a set, list, binary tree, etc.

iterator

Java provides the `java.util.Iterator` interface (see Figure 22.17), which defines the common features of iterators. All the containers (set, list, and map) in the collections framework support iterators.

«interface» *java.util.Iterator*	
+hasNext(): boolean	Returns true if the iterator has more elements.
+next(): Object	Returns the next element in the iterator.
+remove(): void	Removes from the underlying container the last element returned by the iterator (optional operation).

FIGURE 25.17 The `Iterator` interface defines a uniform way of traversing the elements in a container.

To enable the iterator to be used in a wide range of applications, you should define your iterator class as a subtype of `java.util.Iterator`. You can traverse a binary tree in inorder, preorder, or postorder. So, you may define three iterator classes, named `InorderIterator`, `PreorderIterator`, and `PostorderIterator`. Since these classes are dependent on the `BinaryTree` class, it is appropriate to define them as inner classes in `BinaryTree`. Also it is convenient to add three methods named `inorderIterator()`, `preorderIterator()`, and `postorderIterator()` to return the iterator objects.

how to create iterator

The implementation of `inorderIterator()` is shown in lines in Listing 25.5. The implementation of `preorderIterator()` and `postorderIterator()` is left as an exercise.

The `InorderIterator` constructor invokes the `inorder` method. The `inorder(root)` method (lines 241–246) stores all the elements from the tree in `list`. The elements are traversed in `inorder`.

Once an `Iterator` object is created, its `current` value is initialized to `0` (line 229), which points to the first element in the list. Invoking the `next()` method returns the current element and moves current to point to the next element in the list (line 258).

The `hasNext()` method checks whether current is still in the range of `list` (line 250).

The `remove()` method removes the current element from the tree (line 262). Afterward, a new list is created (lines 263–265). Note that `current` does not need to be changed.

Listing 25.11 gives a test program that stores the strings in a BST and displays all strings in uppercase.

LISTING 25.11 `TestBinaryTreeWithIterator.java`

```java
1  public class TestBinaryTreeWithIterator {
2    public static void main(String[] args) {
3      BinaryTree<String> tree = new BinaryTree<String>();
4      tree.insert("George");
5      tree.insert("Michael");
6      tree.insert("Tom");
7      tree.insert("Adam");
8      tree.insert("Jones");
9      tree.insert("Peter");
10     tree.insert("Daniel");
11
12     java.util.Iterator iterator = tree.inorderIterator();
13     while (iterator.hasNext()) {
14       System.out.println(((String)(iterator.next())).toUpperCase());
15     }
16   }
17 }
```

get an iterator
hasNext?
get current element

```
ADAM
DANIEL
GEORGE
JONES
MICHAEL
PETER
TOM
```

The program constructs an iterator (line 12), which enables you to process all elements in the tree (lines 13–15).

Design Guide

iterator pattern
advantages of iterators

Iterator is an important software design pattern. It provides a uniform way of traversing the elements in a container, while hiding the container's structural details. By implementing the same interface `java.util.Iterator`, you can write a program that traverses the elements of all containers in the same way.

Note

variations of iterators

`java.util.Iterator` defines a forward iterator, which traverses the element in the iterator in a forward direction, and each element can be traversed only once. Java API also provides the `java.util.ListIterator`, which supports traversing in both forward and backward directions. If your data structure warrants flexible traversing, you may define iterator classes as a subtype of `java.util.ListIterator`.

25.6 Heaps

heap

Heaps are a useful data structure for designing efficient sorting algorithms and priority queues. A *heap* is a binary tree with the following properties:

- It is a complete binary tree.

- Each node is greater than or equal to any of its children.

complete binary tree

Video Note
Heaps

A binary tree is *complete* if every level of the tree is full except that the last level may not be full and all the leaves on the last level are placed leftmost. For example, in Figure 25.18, the binary trees in (a) and (b) are complete, but the binary trees in (c) and (d) are not complete. Further, the binary tree in (a) is a heap, but the binary tree in (b) is not a heap, because the root (39) is less than its right child (42).

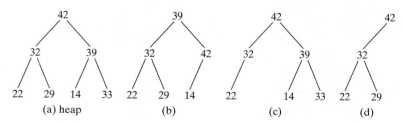

FIGURE 25.18 A heap is a special complete binary tree.

Pedagogical Note

binary tree animation

A heap can be implemented efficiently for inserting keys and for deleting the root. Follow the link www.cs.armstrong.edu/liang/intro7e/exercise/Exercise25_20.html to see how a heap works, as shown in Figure 25.19.

FIGURE 25.19 The animation tool enables you to insert a key and delete the root visually.

25.6.1 Representing a Heap

A heap is a binary tree, so it can be represented using a binary tree data structure. However, a more efficient representation for a heap is an array, or an `ArrayList`. The heap in Figure 25.20(a) can be represented using the array in Figure 25.20(b). The root is at position 0, and its two children are at positions 1 and 2. For a node at position i, its left child is at position $2i + 1$, its right child is at position $2i + 2$, and its parent is $(i - 1)/2$. For example, the node for element 39 is at position 4, so its left child (element 14) is at 9 ($2 \times 4 + 1$), its right child (element 33) is at 10 ($2 \times 4 + 2$), and its parent (element 42) is at 1 (($(4-1)/2$).

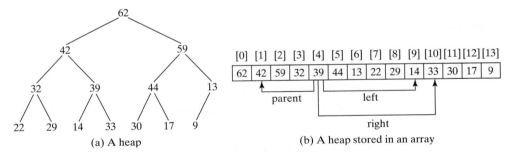

(a) A heap (b) A heap stored in an array

FIGURE 25.20 A binary heap can be implemented using an array.

25.6.2 Adding a New Node

To add a new node to the heap, first add it to the end of the heap and then rebuild the tree as follows:

```
Let the last node be the current node;
while (the current node is greater than its parent) {
    Swap the current node with its parent;
    Now the current node is one level up;
}
```

Suppose the heap is initially empty. The heap is shown in Figure 25.21, after adding numbers 3, 5, 1, 19, 11, and 22 in this order.

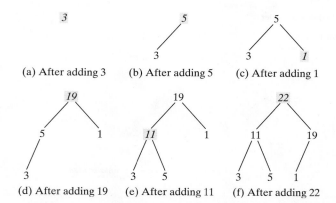

(a) After adding 3   (b) After adding 5   (c) After adding 1

(d) After adding 19   (e) After adding 11   (f) After adding 22

FIGURE 25.21 Elements 3, 5, 1, 19, 11, and 22 are inserted into the heap.

Now consider adding 88 into the heap. Place the new node 88 at the end of the tree, as shown in Figure 25.22(a). Swap 88 with 19, as shown in Figure 25.17(b). Swap 88 with 22, as shown in Figure 25.22(c).

(a) Add 88 to a heap   (b) After swapping 88 with 19   (c) After swapping 88 with 22

FIGURE 25.22 Rebuild the heap after adding a new node.

25.6.3   Removing the Root

Often you need to remove the max element which is the root in a heap. After the root is removed, the tree must be rebuilt to maintain the heap property. The algorithm for rebuilding the tree can be described as follows:

```
Move the last node to replace the root;
Let the root be the current node;
while (the current node has children and the current node is
        smaller than one of its children) {
  Swap the current node with the larger of its children;
  Now the current node is one level down;
}
```

Figure 25.23 shows the process of rebuilding a heap after the root 62 is removed from Figure 25.20(a). Move the last node 9 to the root, as shown in Figure 25.23(a). Swap 9 with 59 as shown in Figure 25.23(b). Swap 9 with 44 as shown in Figure 25.23(c). Swap 9 with 30 as shown in Figure 25.23(d).

Figure 25.24 shows the process of rebuilding a heap after the root 59 is removed from Figure 25.23(d). Move the last node 17 to the root, as shown in Figure 25.24(a). Swap 17 with 44 as shown in Figure 25.24(b). Swap 17 with 30 as shown in Figure 25.24(c).

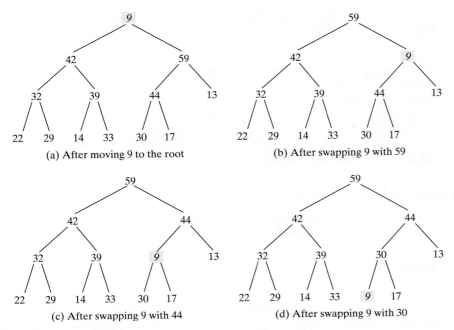

FIGURE 25.23 Rebuild the heap after the root 62 is removed.

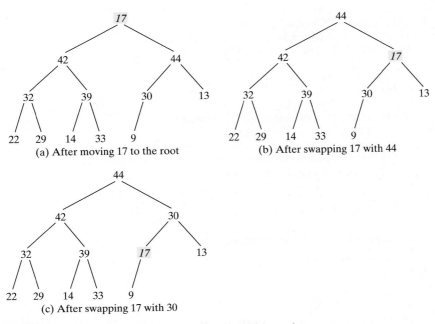

FIGURE 25.24 Rebuild the heap after the root 59 is removed.

25.6.4 The Heap Class

Now you are ready to design and implement the Heap class. The class diagram is shown in Figure 25.25. Its implementation is given in Listing 25.12.

Heap\<E>
-list: java.util.ArrayList\<E>
+Heap() +Heap(objects: E[]) +add(newObject: E): void +remove(): E +getSize(): int

Creates a default empty heap.
Creates a heap with the specified objects.
Adds a new object to the heap.
Removes the root from the heap and returns it.
Returns the size of the heap.

FIGURE 25.25 **Heap** provides operations for manipulating a heap.

LISTING 25.12 Heap.java

```
 1 public class Heap<E extends Comparable> {
 2   private java.util.ArrayList<E> list = new java.util.ArrayList<E>();
 3
 4   /** Create a default heap */
 5   public Heap() {
 6   }
 7
 8   /** Create a heap from an array of objects */
 9   public Heap(E[] objects) {
10     for (int i = 0; i < objects.length; i++)
11       add(objects[i]);
12   }
13
14   /** Add a new object into the heap */
15   public void add(E newObject) {
16     list.add(newObject); // Append to the heap
17     int currentIndex = list.size() - 1; // The index of the last node
18
19     while (currentIndex > 0) {
20       int parentIndex = (currentIndex - 1) / 2;
21       // Swap if the current object is greater than its parent
22       if (list.get(currentIndex).compareTo(
23           list.get(parentIndex)) > 0) {
24         E temp = list.get(currentIndex);
25         list.set(currentIndex, list.get(parentIndex));
26         list.set(parentIndex, temp);
27       }
28       else
29         break; // the tree is a heap now
30
31       currentIndex = parentIndex;
32     }
33   }
34
35   /** Remove the root from the heap */
36   public E remove() {
37     if (list.size() == 0) return null;
38
39     E removedObject = list.get(0);
40     list.set(0, list.get(list.size() - 1));
41     list.remove(list.size() - 1);
42
43     int currentIndex = 0;
44     while (currentIndex < list.size()) {
45       int leftChildIndex = 2 * currentIndex + 1;
46       int rightChildIndex = 2 * currentIndex + 2;
```

internal heap representation

no-arg constructor

constructor

add a new object
append the object

swap with parent

heap now

remove the root
empty heap

root
new root
remove the last

adjust the tree

```
47
48      // Find the maximum between two children
49      if (leftChildIndex >= list.size()) break; // The tree is a heap
50      int maxIndex = leftChildIndex;
51      if (rightChildIndex < list.size()) {
52        if (list.get(maxIndex).compareTo(                          compare two children
53              list.get(rightChildIndex)) < 0) {
54          maxIndex = rightChildIndex;
55        }
56      }
57
58      // Swap if the current node is less than the maximum
59      if (list.get(currentIndex).compareTo(
60            list.get(maxIndex)) < 0) {
61        E temp = list.get(maxIndex);                                swap with the larger child
62        list.set(maxIndex, list.get(currentIndex));
63        list.set(currentIndex, temp);
64        currentIndex = maxIndex;
65      }
66      else
67        break; // The tree is a heap
68    }
69
70    return removedObject;
71  }
72
73  /** Get the number of nodes in the tree */
74  public int getSize() {
75    return list.size();
76  }
77 }
```

A heap is represented using an array list internally (line 2). You may change it to other data structures, but the Heap class contract will remain unchanged.

The add(E newObject) method (lines 15–33) appends the object to the tree and then swaps it with its parent if it is greater than its parent. This process continues until the new object becomes the root or is not greater than its parent.

The remove() method (lines 36–71) removes and returns the root. To maintain the heap property, the method moves the last object to the root position and swaps it with its larger child if it is less than the larger child. This process continues until the last object becomes a leaf or is not less than its children.

Listing 25.13 gives an example of using a heap to sort numbers. Line 1 creates a heap from an array of integers. The loop in lines 6–7 displays all the elements in the heap in decreasing order.

LISTING 25.13 TestHeap.java

```
1 public class TestHeap {
2   public static void main(String[] args) {
3     Heap<Integer> heap =                                          create a heap
4       new Heap<Integer>(new Integer[]{8, 9, 2, 3, 4, 1, 5, 6, 7});
5
6     while (heap.getSize() > 0)                                     heap not empty?
7       System.out.print(heap.remove() + " ");                      remove the root
8   }
9 }
```

```
9 8 7 6 5 4 3 2 1
```

25.6.5 Heap Time Complexity

height of a heap

Let us turn our attention to analyzing the time complexity for the insertion and deletion operations. Let h denote the height for a heap of n elements. Since a heap is a complete binary tree, the top level 0 has 1 node, the next level 1 has 2 nodes, the level k has 2^k nodes, the level $h - 1$ has 2^{h-1} nodes, and the last level h has at least one node and at most 2^h nodes. Therefore,

$$1 + 2 + \ldots + 2^{h-1} < n \le 1 + 2 + \ldots + 2^{h-1} + 2^h$$

i.e.,

$$2^h - 1 < n \le 2^{h+1} - 1$$
$$2^h < n + 1 \le 2^{h+1}$$
$$h < \log(n + 1) \le h + 1$$

Thus, $h < \log(n + 1)$ and $\log(n + 1) - 1 \le h$. Therefore, $\log(n + 1) - 1 \le h < \log(n + 1)$. Hence, the height of the heap is $O(\log n)$.

Since the **add** method traces a path from a leaf to a root, it takes at most h steps to add a new element to the heap. Since the **remove** method traces a path from a root to a leaf, it takes at most h steps to rebuild a heap after removing the root from the heap. So, the time complexity for both insertion and deletion operations is $O(\log n)$.

$O(\log n)$ worst-case time

25.7 Priority Queues

An ordinary queue is a first-in, first-out data structure. Elements are appended to the end of the queue and are removed from the beginning of the queue. In a priority queue, elements are assigned with priorities. When accessing elements, the element with the highest priority is removed first. A priority queue has a largest-in, first-out behavior. For example, the emergency room in a hospital assigns priority numbers to patients; the patient with the highest priority is treated first.

A priority queue can be implemented using a heap, where the root is the object with the highest priority in the queue. The class diagram for the priority queue is shown in Figure 25.26. Its implementation is given in Listing 25.14.

MyPriorityQueue\<E>
-heap: Heap\<E>
+enqueue(element: E): void +dequeue(): E +getSize(): int

> Adds an element to this queue.
> Removes an element from this queue.
> Returns the number of elements from this queue.

FIGURE 25.26 `MyPriorityQueue` uses a heap to provide a largest-in, first-out data structure.

LISTING 25.14 MyPriorityQueue.java

heap for priority queue

enqueue

dequeue

```
1  public class MyPriorityQueue<E extends Comparable> {
2    private Heap<E> heap = new Heap<E>();
3
4    public void enqueue(E newObject) {
5      heap.add(newObject);
6    }
7
8    public E dequeue() {
9      return heap.remove();
10   }
```

```
11
12   public int getSize() {
13     return heap.getSize();
14   }
15 }
```

getsize

Listing 25.15 gives an example of using a priority queue for patients. The `Patient` class is declared in lines 18–34. Four patients are created with associated priority values in lines 3–6. Line 8 creates a priority queue. The patients are enqueued in lines 9–12. Line 15 dequeues a patient from the queue.

LISTING 25.15   `TestPriorityQueue.java`

```
 1 public class TestPriorityQueue {
 2   public static void main(String[] args) {
 3     Patient patient1 = new Patient("John", 2);
 4     Patient patient2 = new Patient("Jim", 1);
 5     Patient patient3 = new Patient("Tim", 5);
 6     Patient patient4 = new Patient("Cindy", 7);
 7
 8     MyPriorityQueue priorityQueue = new MyPriorityQueue();
 9     priorityQueue.enqueue(patient1);
10     priorityQueue.enqueue(patient2);
11     priorityQueue.enqueue(patient3);
12     priorityQueue.enqueue(patient4);
13
14     while (priorityQueue.getSize() > 0)
15       System.out.print(priorityQueue.dequeue() + " ");
16   }
17
18   static class Patient implements Comparable {
19     private String name;
20     private int priority;
21
22     public Patient(String name, int priority) {
23       this.name = name;
24       this.priority = priority;
25     }
26
27     public String toString() {
28       return name + "(priority:" + priority + ")";
29     }
30
31     public int compareTo(Object o) {
32       return this.priority - ((Patient)o).priority;
33     }
34   }
35 }
```

create a patient

create a priority queue
add to queue

remove from queue

inner class **Patient**

compareTo

```
Cindy(priority:7) Tim(priority:5) John(priority:2) Jim(priority:1)
```

KEY TERMS

binary search tree	800	heap	822
binary tree	800	inorder traversal	803

postorder traversal   803

preorder traversal   803

priority queue   828

tree traversal   803

CHAPTER SUMMARY

■ A BST is a hierarchical data structure. You learned how to define and implement a BST class. You learned how to insert and delete elements to/from a BST. You learned how to traverse a BST using inorder, postorder, preorder, depth-first, and breadth-first search.

■ An iterator is an object that provides a uniform way of traversing the elements in a container, such as a set, list, binary tree, etc. You learned how to define and implement iterator classes for traversing the elements in a binary tree.

■ Heaps are a useful data structure for designing efficient sorting algorithms and priority queues. You learned how to define and implement a heap class, and how to insert and delete elements to/from a heap.

■ You learned how to implement a priority queue using a heap.

REVIEW QUESTIONS

Section 25.2 Binary Search Trees

25.1   Show the result of inserting 44 into Figure 25.4(b).

25.2   Show the inorder, preorder, and postorder of traversing the elements in the binary tree, as shown in Figure 25.1(b).

25.3   If a set of the same elements is inserted into a BST in two different orders, will the two corresponding BSTs look the same? Will the inorder traversal be the same? Will the postorder traversal be the same? Will the preorder traversal be the same?

25.4   What is the time complexity of inserting an element into a BST?

Section 25.3 Deleting Elements from a BST

25.5   Show the result of deleting 55 from the tree in Figure 25.4(b).

25.6   Show the result of deleting 60 from the tree in Figure 25.4(b).

25.7   What is the time complexity of deleting an element from a BST?

25.8   Is the algorithm correct if lines 202–207 in Case 2 of the `delete()` method are replaced by the following code?

```
parentOfRightMost.right = rightMost.left;
```

Section 25.4 Iterators

25.9   What is an iterator?

25.10 Why should you define an interator class to be a subtype of `java.util.Iterator`?

Section 25.6 Heaps

25.11 What is a complete binary tree? What is a heap? Describe how to remove the root from a heap and how to add a new object to a heap.

25.12 What is the returned value from invoking the `remove` method if the heap is empty?

25.13 Add the elements 4, 5, 1, 2, 9, 3 into a heap in this order. Draw the diagrams to show the heap after each element is added.

25.14 Show the heap after the root in the heap in Figure 25.24(c) is removed.

25.15 What is the time complexity of inserting a new element into a heap and what is the time complexity of deleting an element from a heap?

Section 25.7 Priority Queues

25.16 What is a priority queue?

PROGRAMMING EXERCISES

Section 25.2 Binary Search Trees

25.1* (*Adding new methods in* `BinaryTree`) Add the following new methods in `BinaryTree`.

```
/** Displays the nodes in breadth-first traversal */
public void breadthFirstTraversal()

/** Returns the depth of this binary tree. Depth is the
  * number of the nodes in the longest path of the tree */
public int depth()
```

25.2** (*Implementing inorder without using recursion*) Implement the `inorder` method in `BinaryTree` using a stack instead of recursion.

25.3** (*Implementing preorder without using recursion*) Implement the `preorder` method in `BinaryTree` using a stack instead of recursion.

25.4** (*Implementing postorder without using recursion*) Implement the `postorder` method in `BinaryTree` using a stack instead of recursion.

25.5** (*Finding the leaves*) Add a method in the `BinaryTree` class to return the number of the leaves as follows:

```
/** Displays the leaf nodes */
public int countLeaves()
```

25.6** (*Finding the nonleaves*) Add a method in the `BinaryTree` class to return the number of the nonleaves as follows:

```
/** Displays the non-leaf nodes */
public int countNonLeaves()
```

Section 25.4 Iterators

25.7** (*Implementing iterator on* `MyArrayList`) Define an inner class named `MyArrayListIterator` in `MyArrayList` for traversing the elements on `MyArrayList`. `MyArrayListIterator` should implement `java.util.Iterator`. Add a method `iterator()` that returns an instance of `MyArrayListIterator` in the `MyArrayList` class.

25.8** (*Implementing iterator on* `MyLinkedList`) Define an inner class named `MyLinkedListIterator` in `MyLinkedList` for traversing the elements on `MyLinkedList`. `MyLinkedListIterator` should implement `java.util.Iterator`. Add a method `iterator()` that returns an instance of `MyLinkedListIterator` in the `MyLinkedList` class.

25.9*** (*Implementing bidirectional iterator*) The `java.util.Iterator` interface defines a forward iterator. The Java API also provides the `java.util.ListIterator` interface that defines a bidirectional iterator. Study `ListIterator` and create a bidirectional iterator for the `BinaryTree` class.

Section 25.6 Heaps

25.10 (*Min-heap*) The heap presented in the text is also known as a *max-heap*, in which each node is greater than or equal to any of its children. A *min-heap* is a heap in which each node is less than or equal to any of its children. Revise the `Heap` class in Listing 25.12 to implement a min-heap.

25.11* (*Sorting using a heap*) Implement the following `sort` method using a heap.

```
public static <E extends Comparable<E>> void sort(E[] list)
```

Comprehensive

25.12** (*Binary tree search visualization*) Write a Java applet that displays a search path, as shown in Figure 25.27(a). The applet allows the user to enter a key. If the key is not in the tree, a message dialog box is displayed. Otherwise, the nodes in the path from the root leading to the key are displayed in green.

(a)   (b)

FIGURE 25.27   (a) The search path is highlighted in green. (b) The applet animates how an insertion is performed.

25.13** (*Binary tree search animation*) The preceding exercise simply highlights a search path. Write a Java applet that animates how search is performed. First you see the root is searched, and then a subtree is searched recursively. When a node is searched, the node is highlighted in green. The search stops when a key is found in the tree, or displays that a key is not in the tree.

25.14** (*Binary tree insert animation*) Add an *Insert* button to the preceding exercise to animate how insertion is performed, as shown in Figure 25.27(b). When the *Insert* button is clicked, the applet first animates a search. If the key is already in the tree, display a dialog box. Otherwise, insert the key and repaint the tree.

25.15** (*Binary tree animation*) Write a Java applet that animates the binary tree `insert`, `delete`, and `search` methods, as shown in Figure 25.2.

25.16* (*Generic BinaryTree using Comparator*) Revise `BinaryTree` in Listing 25.5, using a generic parameter and a `Comparator` for comparing objects. Define a new constructor with a `Comparator` as its argument as follows:

```
BinaryTree(Comparator<? super E> comparator)
```

25.17* (*Generic Heap* using Comparator) Revise Heap in Listing 25.12, using a generic parameter and a Comparator for comparing objects. Define a new constructor with a Comparator as its argument as follows:

```
Heap(Comparator<? super E> comparator)
```

25.18* (*Generic PriorityQueue* using Comparator) Revise MyPriorityQueue in Listing 25.14, using a generic parameter for comparing objects. Define a new constructor with a Comparator as its argument as follows:

```
PriorityQueue(Comparator<? super E> comparator)
```

25.19* (*Parent reference for BinaryTree*) Redefine TreeNode by adding a reference to a node's parent, as shown below:

```
BinaryTree.TreeNode<E>

#element: E
#left: TreeNode<E>
#right: TreeNode<E>
#parent: TreeNode<E>
```

Add the following two new methods in BinaryTree:

```
public TreeNode<E> getParent(TreeNode<E> node)
```

Returns the parent for the specified node.

```
public ArrayList<TreeNode<E>> getPath(TreeNode<E> node)
```

Returns the path from the specified node to the root in an array list.

Write a test program that adds numbers 1, 2, ..., 100 to the tree and displays the paths for all leaf nodes.

25.20** (*Heap visualization*) Write a Java applet that displays a heap graphically, as shown in Figure 25.19. The applet lets you insert and delete an element from the heap.

Video Note
Heap visualization

25.21** (*Tree clone and equals*) Implement the clone and equals method in the BinaryTree class.

25.22** (*Heap clone and equals*) Implement the clone and equals method in the Heap class.

CHAPTER 26

SORTING

Objectives

- To study and analyze time efficiency of various sorting algorithms (§§26.2–26.7).
- To design, implement, and analyze bubble sort (§26.2).
- To design, implement, and analyze merge sort (§26.3).
- To design, implement, and analyze quick sort (§26.4).
- To design, implement, and analyze heap sort (§26.5).
- To design, implement, and analyze bucket sort and radix sort (§26.6).
- To design, implement, and analyze external sort for large data in a file (§26.7).

26.1 Introduction

why study sorting?

Sorting is a classic subject in computer science. There are three reasons for studying sorting algorithms. First, sorting algorithms illustrate many creative approaches to problem solving, and these approaches can be applied to solve other problems. Second, sorting algorithms are good for practicing fundamental programming techniques using selection statements, loops, methods, and arrays. Third, sorting algorithms are excellent examples to demonstrate algorithm performance.

what data to sort?

The data to be sorted might be integers, doubles, characters, or objects. §6.8, "Sorting Arrays," presented selection sort and insertion sort for numeric values. The selection sort algorithm was extended to sort an array of objects in §11.10, "Sorting an Array of Objects." The Java API contains several overloaded sort methods for sorting primitive type values and objects in the `java.util.Arrays` and `java.util.Collections` class. For simplicity, this section assumes:

1. data to be sorted are integers,

2. data are stored in an array, and

3. data are sorted in ascending order.

The programs can be easily modified to sort other types of data, to sort in descending order, or to sort data in an `ArrayList` or a `LinkedList`.

There are many algorithms for sorting. You have already learned selection sort and insertion sort. This chapter introduces bubble sort, merge sort, quick sort, bucket sort, radix sort, and external sort.

Note

The whole chapter is optional. No chapter in the book depends on this chapter.

26.2 Bubble Sort

The bubble sort algorithm makes several passes through the array. On each pass, successive neighboring pairs are compared. If a pair is in decreasing order, its values are swapped; otherwise, the values remain unchanged. The technique is called a *bubble sort* or *sinking sort* because the smaller values gradually "bubble" their way to the top and the larger values sink to the bottom. After first pass, the last element becomes the largest in the array. After the second pass, the second-to-last element becomes the second largest in the array. This process is continued until all elements are sorted.

bubble sort illustration

Figure 26.1(a) shows the first pass of a bubble sort of an array of six elements (2 9 5 4 8 1). Compare the elements in the first pair (2 and 9), and no swap is needed because they are already in order. Compare the elements in the second pair (9 and 5), and swap 9 with 5 because 9 is greater than 5. Compare the elements in the third pair (9 and 4), and swap 9 with 4. Compare the elements in the fourth pair (9 and 8), and swap 9 with 8. Compare the elements in the fifth pair (9 and 1), swap 9 with 1. The pairs being compared are highlighted and the numbers that are already sorted are italicized.

2 9 5 4 8 1	2 5 4 8 1 9	2 4 5 1 8 9	2 4 1 5 8 9	1 2 4 5 8 9
2 5 9 4 8 1	2 4 5 8 1 9	2 4 5 1 8 9	2 1 4 5 8 9	
2 5 4 9 8 1	2 4 5 8 1 9	2 4 1 5 8 9		
2 5 4 8 9 1	2 4 5 1 8 9			
2 5 4 8 1 9				
(a) 1st pass	(b) 2nd pass	(c) 3rd pass	(d) 4th pass	(e) 5th pass

FIGURE 26.1 Each pass compares and orders the pairs of elements sequentially.

The first pass places the largest number (9) as the last in the array. In the second pass, as shown in Figure 26.1(b), you compare and order pairs of elements sequentially. There is no need to consider the last pair, because the last element in the array is already the largest. In the third pass, as shown in Figure 26.1(c), you compare and order pairs of elements sequentially except the last two elements, because they are already ordered. So in the kth pass, you don't need to consider the last $k - 1$ elements, because they are already ordered.

The algorithm for bubble sort can be described in Listing 26.1.

algorithm

LISTING 26.1 Bubble Sort Algorithm

```
1 for (int k = 1; k < list.length; k++) {
2   // Perform the kth pass
3   for (int i = 0; i < list.length - k; i++) {
4     if (list[i] > list[i + 1])
5       swap list[i] with list[i + 1];
6   }
7 }
```

Note that if no swap takes place in a pass, there is no need to perform the next pass, because all the elements are already sorted. You may improve the preceding algorithm by utilizing this property as in Listing 26.2.

LISTING 26.2 Improved Bubble Sort Algorithm

```
1 boolean needNextPass = true;
2 for (int k = 1; k < list.length && needNextPass; k++) {
3   // Array may be sorted and next pass not needed
4   needNextPass = false;
5   // Perform the kth pass
6   for (int i = 0; i < list.length - k; i++) {
7     if (list[i] > list[i + 1]) {
8       swap list[i] with list[i + 1];
9       needNextPass = true; // Next pass still needed
10    }
11  }
12 }
```

The algorithm can be implemented in Listing 26.3.

LISTING 26.3 BubbleSort.java

```
1 public class BubbleSort {
2   /** The method for sorting the numbers */
3   public static void bubbleSort(int[] list) {
4     boolean needNextPass = true;
5
6     for (int k = 1; k < list.length && needNextPass; k++) {
7       // Array may be sorted and next pass not needed
8       needNextPass = false;
9       for (int i = 0; i < list.length - k; i++) {
10        if (list[i] > list[i + 1]) {
11          // Swap list[i] with list[i + 1]
12          int temp = list[i];
13          list[i] = list[i + 1];
14          list[i + 1] = temp;
15
16          needNextPass = true; // Next pass still needed
17        }
18      }
```

perform one pass

```
19     }
20   }
21 }
```

26.2.1 Bubble Sort Time

In the best-case, the bubble sort algorithm needs just the first pass to find out that the array is already sorted. No next pass is needed. Since the number of comparisons is $n - 1$ in the first pass, the best-case time for bubble sort is $O(n)$.

In the worst case, the bubble sort algorithm requires $n - 1$ passes. The first pass takes $n - 1$ comparisons; the second pass takes $n - 2$ comparisons; and so on; the last pass takes 1 comparison. So, the total number of comparisons is:

$$(n - 1) + (n - 2) + \ldots + 2 + 1$$

$$= \frac{(n - 1)n}{2} = \frac{n^2}{2} - \frac{n}{2} = O(n^2)$$

Therefore, the worst-case time for bubble sort is $O(n^2)$.

26.3 Merge Sort

Video Note
Merge sort

The merge sort algorithm can be described recursively as follows: The algorithm divides the array into two halves and applies merge sort on each half recursively. After the two halves are sorted, merge them. The algorithm is given in Listing 26.4.

LISTING 26.4 Merge Sort Algorithm

base condition
sort first half
sort second half
merge two halves

```
1 public static void mergeSort(int[] list) {
2   if (list.length > 1) {
3     mergeSort(list[0 ... list.length / 2]);
4     mergeSort(list[list.length / 2 + 1 ... list.length]);
5     merge list[0 ... list.length / 2] with
6       list[list.length / 2 + 1 ... list.length];
7   }
8 }
```

merge sort illustration

Figure 26.2 illustrates a merge sort of an array of eight elements (2 9 5 4 8 1 6 7). The original array is split into (2 9 5 4) and (8 1 6 7). Apply merge sort on these two subarrays recursively

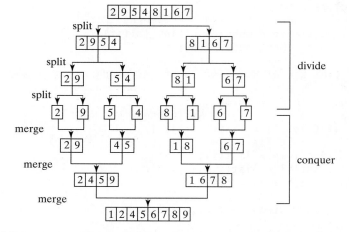

FIGURE 26.2 Merge sort employs a divide-and-conquer approach to sort the array.

to split (1 9 5 4) into (1 9) and (5 4) and (8 1 6 7) into (8 1) and (6 7). This process continues until the subarray contains only one element. For example, array (2 9) is split into subarrays (2) and (9). Since array (2) contains a single element, it cannot be further split. Now merge (2) with (9) into a new sorted array (2 9), merge (5) with (4) into a new sorted array (4 5). Merge (2 9) with (4 5) into a new sorted array (2 4 5 9), and finally merge (2 4 5 9) with (1 6 7 8) into a new sorted array (1 2 4 5 6 7 8 9).

The recursive call continues dividing the array into subarrays until each subarray contains only one element. The algorithm then merges these small subarrays into larger sorted subarrays until one sorted array results. The method for merging two sorted arrays is given in Listing 26.5.

LISTING 26.5 Method for Merging Two Arrays

```
1 private static int[] merge(int[] list1, int[] list2) {
2   int[] temp = new int[list1.length + list2.length];    create a new array
3
4   int current1 = 0; // Index in list1
5   int current2 = 0; // Index in list2
6   int current3 = 0; // Index in temp
7
8   while (current1 < list1.length && current2 < list2.length) {
9     if (list1[current1] < list2[current2])
10        temp[current3++] = list1[current1++];             move to temp
11    else
12        temp[current3++] = list2[current2++];
13  }
14
15  while (current1 < list1.length)
16    temp[current3++] = list1[current1++];
17
18  while (current2 < list2.length)
19    temp[current3++] = list2[current2++];
20
21  return temp;                                            temp is sorted
22 }
```

This method merges arrays `list1` and `list2` into a temporary array `temp`. So, `temp.length` is `list1.length + list2.length` (line 2). `current1` and `current2` point to the current element to be considered in `list1` and `list2` (lines 4–5). The method repeatedly compares the current elements from `list1` and `list2` and moves the smaller one to `temp`. `current1` is increased by 1 (line 10) if the smaller one is in `list1` and `current2` is increased by 1 (line 12) if the smaller one is in `list2`. Finally, all the elements in one of the lists are moved to `temp`. If there are still unmoved elements in `list1`, copy them to `temp` (lines 15–16). If there are still unmoved elements in `list2`, copy them to `temp` (lines 18–19). The method returns `temp` as the new sorted array in line 21.

Figure 26.3 illustrates how to merge two arrays `list1` (2 4 5 9) and `list2` (1 6 7 8). Initially the current elements to be considered in the arrays are 2 and 1. Compare them and move the smaller element 1 to `temp`, as shown in Figure 26.3(a). `current2` and `current3` are increased by 1. Continue to compare the current elements in the two arrays and move the smaller one to `temp` until one of the arrays is completely moved. As shown in Figure 26.3(b), all the elements in `list2` are moved to `temp` and `current1` points to element 9 in `list1`. Copy 9 to `temp`, as shown in Figure 26.3(c).

The merge sort algorithm is implemented in Listing 26.6.

LISTING 26.6 MergeSort.java

```
1 public class MergeSort {
2   /** The method for sorting the numbers */
```

base case

sort first half

sort second half

merge two halves
copy to original array

```
3   public static void mergeSort(int[] list) {
4     if (list.length > 1) {
5       // Merge sort the first half
6       int[] firstHalf = new int[list.length / 2];
7       System.arraycopy(list, 0, firstHalf, 0, list.length / 2);
8       mergeSort(firstHalf);
9
10      // Merge sort the second half
11      int secondHalfLength = list.length - list.length / 2;
12      int[] secondHalf = new int[secondHalfLength];
13      System.arraycopy(list, list.length / 2,
14        secondHalf, 0, secondHalfLength);
15      mergeSort(secondHalf);
16
17      // Merge firstHalf with secondHalf
18      int[] temp = merge(firstHalf, secondHalf);
19      System.arraycopy(temp, 0, list, 0, temp.length);
20    }
21  }
22
23  private static int[] merge(int[] list1, int[] list2) {
24    // Same as in Listing 26.5, so omitted
25  }
26 }
```

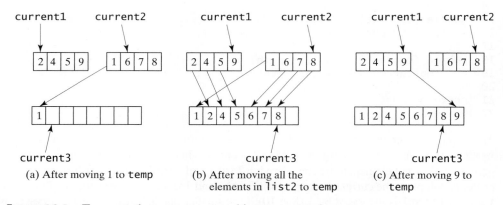

FIGURE 26.3 Two sorted arrays are merged into one sorted array.

The algorithm creates a new array firstHalf, which is a copy of the first half of list (line 7). The algorithm invokes mergeSort recursively on firstHalf (line 8). The length of the firstHalf is list.length / 2 and the length of the secondHalf is list.length - list.length / 2. The new array secondHalf was created to contain the second part of the original array list. The algorithm invokes mergeSort recursively on secondHalf (line 15). After firstHalf and secondHalf are sorted, they are merged to become a new sorted array in temp (line 18). Finally, temp is assigned to the original array list (line 19). So, array list is now sorted.

26.3.1 Merge Sort Time

time analysis

Let $T(n)$ denote the time required for sorting an array of n elements using merge sort. Without loss of generality, assume n is a power of 2. The merge sort algorithm splits the array into two subarrays, sorts the subarrays using the same algorithm recursively, and then merges the subarrays. So,

$$T(n) = T\left(\frac{n}{2}\right) + T\left(\frac{n}{2}\right) + mergetime$$

The first $T\left(\frac{n}{2}\right)$ is the time for sorting the first half of the array and the second $T\left(\frac{n}{2}\right)$ is the time for sorting the second half. To merge two subarrays, it takes at most $n - 1$ comparisons to compare the elements from the two subarrays and n moves to move elements to the temporary array. So, the total time is $2n - 1$. Therefore,

$$T(n) = T\left(\frac{n}{2}\right) + T\left(\frac{n}{2}\right) + mergetime$$

$$= 2T\left(\frac{n}{2}\right) + 2n - 1$$

$$= 2\left(2T\left(\frac{n}{4}\right) + 2\frac{n}{2} - 1\right) + 2n - 1$$

$$= 2\left(2\left(2T\left(\frac{n}{8}\right) + 2\frac{n}{4} - 1\right) + 2\frac{n}{2} - 1\right) + 2n - 1$$

$$= 2\left(2\left(2T\left(\frac{n}{2^3}\right) + 2\frac{n}{2^2} - 1\right) + 2\frac{n}{2^1} - 1\right) + 2n - 1$$

$$= 2^kT\left(\frac{n}{2^k}\right) + 2n - 2^{k-1} + \ldots + 2n - 2 + 2n - 1$$

$$= 2^kT\left(\frac{n}{2^k}\right) + \overbrace{2n + 2n + \ldots + 2n}^{k} - 2^{k-1} + \ldots - 2 - 1$$

$$= 2^kT\left(\frac{n}{2^k}\right) + 2nk - (2^k - 1)$$

$$= 2^{\log n}T(1) + 2n(\log n) - (2^{\log n} - 1)$$

$$= n + 2n \log n - n + 1$$

$$= 2n \log n + 1 = O(n \log n)$$

The complexity of merge sort is $O(n \log n)$. This algorithm is better than selection sort, insertion sort, and bubble sort. The **sort** method in the **java.util.Arrays** class is implemented using a variation of the merge sort algorithm.

$O(n \log n)$ merge sort

26.4 Quick Sort

Quick sort, developed by C. A. R. Hoare (1962), works as follows: The algorithm selects an element, called the *pivot*, in the array. Divide the array into two parts such that all the elements in the first part are less than or equal to the pivot and all the elements in the second part are

Video Note
Quick sort

greater than the pivot. Recursively apply the quick sort algorithm to the first part and then the second part. The algorithm is described in Listing 26.7.

LISTING 26.7 Quick Sort Algorithm

base condition
select the pivot
partition the list

sort first part
sort second part

```
 1 public static void quickSort(int[] list) {
 2   if (list.length > 1) {
 3     select a pivot;
 4     partition list into list1 and list2 such that
 5       all elements in list1 <= pivot and all elements
 6       in list2 > pivot;
 7     quickSort(list1);
 8     quickSort(list2);
 9   }
10 }
```

how to partition

Each partition places the pivot in the right place. The selection of the pivot affects the performance of the algorithm. Ideally, you should choose the pivot that divides the two parts evenly. For simplicity, assume the first element in the array is chosen as the pivot. Exercise 26.4 proposes an alternative strategy for selecting the pivot.

quick sort illustration

Figure 26.4 illustrates how to sort an array (5 2 9 3 8 4 0 1 6 7) using quick sort. Choose the first element 5 as the pivot. The array is partitioned into two parts, as shown in Figure 26.4(b). The highlighted pivot is placed in the right place in the array. Apply quick sort on two partial arrays (4 2 1 3 0) and then (8 9 6 7). The pivot 4 partitions (4 2 1 3 0) into just one partial array (0 2 1 3), as shown in Figure 26.4(c). Apply quick sort on (0 2 1 3). The pivot 0 partitions it to just one partial array (2 1 3), as shown in Figure 26.4(d). Apply quick sort on (2 1 3). The pivot 2 partitions it to (1) and (3), as shown in Figure 26.4(e). Apply quick sort on (1). Since the array contains just one element, no further partition is needed.

FIGURE 26.4 The quick sort algorithm is recursively applied to partial arrays.

Now we turn our attention to partition. To partition an array or a partial array, search for the first element from left forward in the array that is greater than the pivot, then search for the first element from right backward in the array that is less than or equal to the pivot. Swap these two elements. Repeat the same search and swap operations until all the elements are searched. Listing 26.8 gives a method that partitions a partial array `list[first..last]`. The first element in the partial array is chosen as the pivot (line 3). Initially `low` points to the second element in the partial array and `high` points to the last element in the partial array. The method returns the new index for the pivot that divides the partial array into two parts.

LISTING 26.8 Partition Method

```
 1  /** Partition the array list[first..last] */
 2  private static int partition(int[] list, int first, int last) {
 3    int pivot = list[first]; // Choose the first element as the pivot
 4    int low = first + 1; // Index for forward search
 5    int high = last; // Index for backward search
 6
 7    while (high > low) {
 8      // Search forward from left
 9      while (low <= high && list[low] <= pivot)
10        low++;                                                          forward
11
12      // Search backward from right
13      while (low <= high && list[high] > pivot)
14        high--;                                                         backward
15
16      // Swap two elements in the list
17      if (high > low) {
18        int temp = list[high];                                         swap
19        list[high] = list[low];
20        list[low] = temp;
21      }
22    }
23
24    while (high > first && list[high] >= pivot)                        place pivot
25      high--;
26
27    // Swap pivot with list[high]
28    if (pivot > list[high]) {
29      list[first] = list[high];
30      list[high] = pivot;
31      return high;                                                     pivot's new index
32    }
33    else {
34      return first;                                                    pivot's new index
35    }
36  }
```

Figure 26.5 illustrates how to partition an array (5 2 9 3 8 4 0 1 6 7). Choose the first element 5 as the pivot. Initially `low` is the index that points to element 2 and `high` points to element 7, as shown in Figure 26.5(a). Advance index `low` forward to search for the first element (9) that is greater than the pivot and move index `high` backward to search for the first element (1) that is less than or equal to the pivot, as shown in Figure 26.5(b). Swap 9 with 1, as shown in Figure 26.5(c). Continue the search and move `low` to point to element 8 and `high` to point to element 0, as shown in Figure 26.5(d). Swap element 8 with 0, as shown in Figure 26.5(e). Continue to move `low` until it passes `high`, as shown in Figure 26.5(f). Now all the elements are examined. Swap the pivot with element 4 at index `high`. The final partition is shown in Figure 26.5(g). The index of the pivot is returned when the method is finished.   partition illustration

The quick sort algorithm is implemented in Listing 26.9. There are two overloaded `quickSort` methods in the class. The first method (line 2) is used to sort an array. The second is a helper method (line 6) that sorts a partial array with a specified range.

LISTING 26.9 QuickSort.java

sort method

helper method

recursive call

```java
1 public class QuickSort {
2   public static void quickSort(int[] list) {
3     quickSort(list, 0, list.length - 1);
4   }
5
6   private static void quickSort(int[] list, int first, int last) {
7     if (last > first) {
8       int pivotIndex = partition(list, first, last);
9       quickSort(list, first, pivotIndex - 1);
10      quickSort(list, pivotIndex + 1, last);
11    }
12  }
13
14  /** Partition the array list[first..last] */
15  private static int partition(int[] list, int first, int last) {
16    // Same as in Listing 26.8, so omitted
17  }
18 }
```

FIGURE 26.5 The partition method returns the index of the pivot after it is put in the right place.

26.4.1 Quick Sort Time

To partition an array of n elements, it takes n comparisons and n moves in the worst case. So, the time required for partition is $O(n)$.

In the worst case, the pivot divides the array each time into one big subarray with the other empty. The size of the big subarray is one less than the one before divided. The algorithm requires $(n - 1) + (n - 2) + \ldots + 2 + 1 = O(n^2)$ time.

In the best case, the pivot divides the array each time into two parts of about the same size. Let $T(n)$ denote the time required for sorting an array of n elements using quick sort. So,

$$T(n) = T\left(\frac{n}{2}\right) + T\left(\frac{n}{2}\right) + n.$$

Similar to the merge sort analysis, $T(n) = O(n\log n)$.

On the average, each time the pivot will not divide the array into two parts of the same size nor one empty part. Statistically, the sizes of the two parts are very close. So the average time is $O(n\log n)$. The exact average-case analysis is beyond the scope of this book.

Both merge sort and quick sort employ the divide-and-conquer approach. For merge sort, the bulk of work is to merge two sublists, which takes place *after* the sublists are sorted. For quick sort, the bulk of work is to partition the list into two sublists, which takes place *before* the sublists are sorted. Merge sort is more efficient than quick sort in the worst case, but the two are equally efficient in the average case. Merge sort requires a temporary array for merging two subarrays. Quick sort does not need additional array space. So, quick sort is more space efficient than merge sort.

26.5 Heap Sort

Heap sort uses a binary heap to sort an array. The binary heap was introduced in §25.6, "Heaps." Recall that a heap is a complete binary tree. Each node in the tree is greater than or equal to its descendants. To sort an array using a heap, first create an object using the **Heap** class, add all the elements to the heap using the **add** method, and remove all the elements from the heap using the **remove** method. The elements are removed in descending order. Listing 26.10 gives an algorithm for sorting an array using a heap.

LISTING 26.10 HeapSort.java

```java
 1 public class HeapSort {
 2   public static void main(String[] args) {
 3     Integer[] list = {2, 3, 2, 5, 6, 1, -2, 3, 14, 12};
 4     heapSort(list);
 5     for (int i = 0; i < list.length; i++)
 6       System.out.print(list[i] + " ");
 7   }
 8
 9   public static void heapSort(Object[] list) {
10     Heap heap = new Heap(); // Create a Heap
11
12     // Add elements to the heap
13     for (int i = 0; i < list.length; i++)
14       heap.add(list[i]);
15
16     // Remove elements from the heap
17     for (int i = list.length - 1; i >= 0; i--)
```

remove element

```
18        list[i] = heap.remove();
19    }
20 }
```

```
-2 1 2 2 3 3 5 6 12 14
```

heap sort time

The algorithm first inserts *n* elements into the heap. Since it takes $O(\log n)$ time to insert an element, the total time for constructing an initial heap is $O(n\log n)$. The algorithm removes *n* elements from the heap. Since it takes $O(\log n)$ time to remove an element, the total time for removing all elements from the heap is $O(n\log n)$.

heap sort vs. merge sort

Both merge sort and heap sort requires $O(n\log n)$ time. Merge sort requires a temporary array for merging two subarrays. Heap sort does not need additional array space. So, heap sort is more space efficient than merge sort.

Note

lower bound on sort

The best sort algorithm presented so far takes $O(n\log n)$ time. It is natural to ask whether a sort algorithm exists that would take less than $O(n\log n)$ time. It has been proven that the *lower bound* for any sort algorithm is $O(n\log n)$. So, it is impossible to discover an algorithm better than $O(n\log n)$.

Video Note
Bucket sort and radix sort

26.6 Bucket Sort and Radix Sort

All sort algorithms discussed so far are general sorting algorithms that work for any types of keys (e.g., integers, strings, and any comparable objects). These algorithms sort the elements by comparing their keys. The lower bound for general sorting algorithms is $O(n\log n)$. So, no sorting algorithms based on comparisons can perform better than $O(n\log n)$. However, if the keys are small integers, you can use bucket sort without having to compare the keys.

The bucket sort algorithm works as follows. Assume the keys are in the range from 0 to N-1. We need N buckets labeled 0, 1, ..., and N-1. If an element's key is i, the element is put into the bucket i. Each bucket holds the elements with the same key value. You can use an `ArrayList` to implement a bucket.

The bucket sort algorithm for sorting a list of elements can be described as follows:

```java
void bucketSort(E[] list) {
  E[] buckets = (E[])new java.util.ArrayList[N];

  // Distribute the elements from list to buckets
  for (int i = 0; i < list.length; i++) {
    int key = list[i].getKey();

    if (buckets[key] == null)
      buckets[key] = new java.util.ArrayList();
    buckets[key].add(list[i]);
  }

  // Now move the elements from the buckets back to list
  int k = 0; // k is an index for list
  for (int i = 0; i < buckets.length; i++) {
    if (buckets[i] != null) {
      for (int j = 0; j < buckets[i].size(); j++)
        list[k++] = buckets[i].get(j);
    }
  }
}
```

Clearly, it takes $O(n + N)$ time to sort the list and uses $O(n + N)$ space, where n is the list size.

Note that if N is too large, bucket sort is not desirable. You can use radix sort. Radix sort is based on bucket sort, but it is more efficient than bucket sort.

It is worthwhile to note that bucket sort is *stable*, meaning that if two elements in the original list have the same key value, the order of the two elements is not changed in the sorted list. That is, if element e_1 and element e_2 have the same key and e_1 precedes e_2 in the original list, e_1 still precedes e_2 in the sorted list.   stable

Again assume that the keys are positive integers. The idea for the radix sort is to divide the keys into subgroups based on their radix positions. For example, 934 is divided into {9, 3, 4} and 1344 is divided into {1, 3, 4, 4}. Radix sort is to apply the bucket sort repeatedly for the key values on radix positions, starting from the least-significant position from the left to right. Each time when you apply the bucket sort, you only need ten buckets.

Consider sorting the elements with the keys:

331, 454, 230, 34, 343, 45, 59, 453, 345, 231, 9

Apply the bucket sort on the last radix position. The elements are put into the buckets as follows:

230	331 231		343 453	454 34	45 345				59 9
buckets[0]	buckets[1]	buckets[2]	buckets[3]	buckets[4]	buckets[5]	buckets[6]	buckets[7]	buckets[8]	buckets[9]

After removing the elements from the buckets, the elements are in the following order:

230, 331, 231, 343, 453, 454, 34, 45, 345, 59, 9

Apply the bucket sort on the second last radix position. The elements are put into the buckets as follows:

9			230 331 231 34	343 45 345	453 454 59				
buckets[0]	buckets[1]	buckets[2]	buckets[3]	buckets[4]	buckets[5]	buckets[6]	buckets[7]	buckets[8]	buckets[9]

After removing the elements from the buckets, the elements are in the following order:

9, 230, 331, 231, 34, 343, 45, 345, 453, 454, 59

(Note that 9 is 009).

Apply the bucket sort on the third last radix position. The elements are put into the buckets as follows:

9 34 45 59		230 231	331 343 345	453					
buckets[0]	buckets[1]	buckets[2]	buckets[3]	buckets[4]	buckets[5]	buckets[6]	buckets[7]	buckets[8]	buckets[9]

After removing the elements from the buckets, the elements are in the following order:

9, 34, 45, 59, 230, 231, 331, 343, 345, 453

The elements are now sorted.

In general, radix sort takes $O(dn)$ time to sort n elements with integer keys, where d is the maximum number of the radix positions among all keys.

26.7 External Sort

All the sort algorithms discussed in the preceding sections assume that all data to be sorted are available at one time in internal memory such as an array. To sort data stored in an external file, you may first bring data to the memory, then sort them internally. However, if the file is too large, all data in the file cannot be brought to memory at one time. This section discusses how to sort data in a large external file.

For simplicity, assume that two million **int** values are stored in a binary file named largedata.dat. This file was created using the program in Listing 26.11.

LISTING 26.11 CreateLargeFile.java

```
1  import java.io.*;
2
3  public class CreateLargeFile {
4    public static void main(String[] args) throws Exception {
5      DataOutputStream output = new DataOutputStream(
6        new BufferedOutputStream(
7          new FileOutputStream("largedata.dat")));
8
9      for (int i = 0; i < 2000000; i++)
10         output.writeInt((int)(Math.random() * 1000000));
11
12       output.close();
13   }
14 }
```

a binary output stream (line 5)

output an int value (lines 9–10)

close the file (line 12)

A variation of merge sort can be used to sort this file in two phases:

Phase I: Repeatedly bring data from the file to an array, sort the array using an internal sorting algorithm, and output the data from the array to a temporary file. This process is shown in Figure 26.6. Ideally, you want to create a large array, but the maximum size of the array depends on how much memory is allocated to the JVM by the operating system. Assume that the maximum array size is of 100000 **int** values. In the temporary file, every 100000 **int** values are sorted. They are denoted as $S_1, S_2, \ldots$, and S_k, where the last segment, S_k, may contain less than 100000 values.

FIGURE 26.6 The original file is sorted in segments.

Phase II: Merge a pair of sorted segments (e.g., S_1 with S_2, S_3 with $S_4, \ldots$, and so on) into a larger sorted segment and save the new segment into a new temporary file. Continue the same process until one sorted segment results. Figure 26.7 shows how to merge eight segments.

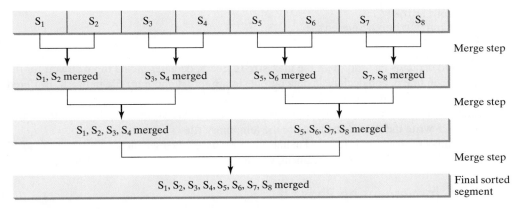

FIGURE 26.7 Sorted segments are merged iteratively.

Note

It is not necessary to merge two successive segments. For example, you may merge S_1 with S_5, S_2 with S_6, S_3 with S_7, and S_4 with S_8, in the first merge step. This observation is useful to implement Phase II efficiently.

26.7.1 Implementing Phase I

Assume `MAX_ARRAY_SIZE` is declared as a constant 100000. Listing 26.12 gives the method that sorts every 100000 in largedata.dat and stores the sorted segments into a new file named f1.dat. The method returns the number of segments.

LISTING 26.12 Creating Initial Sorted Segments

```
1  /** Sort original file into sorted segments */
2  private static int initializeSegments
3      (int segmentSize, String originalFile, String f1)
4      throws Exception {
5    int[] list = new int[segmentSize];                              original file
6    DataInputStream input = new DataInputStream(
7      new BufferedInputStream(new FileInputStream(originalFile)));   file with sorted segments
8    DataOutputStream output = new DataOutputStream(
9      new BufferedOutputStream(new FileOutputStream(f1)));
10
11   int numberOfSegments = 0;
12   while (input.available() > 0) {
13     numberOfSegments++;
14     int i = 0;
15     for ( ; input.available() > 0 && i < segmentSize; i++) {
16       list[i] = input.readInt();
17     }
18
19     // Sort an array list[0..i-1]                                 sort a segment
20     java.util.Arrays.sort(list, 0, i);
21
22     // Write the array to f1.dat
23     for (int j = 0; j < i; j++) {                                 output to file
24       output.writeInt(list[j]);
25     }
26   }
27
28   input.close();                                                 close file
```

return # of segments

```
29    output.close();
30    return numberOfSegments;
31 }
```

The method declares an array with the max size in line 5, declares a data input stream for the original file in line 6, and declares a data output stream for a temporary file in line 8. Buffered streams are used to improve performance.

Lines 14–17 read a segment of data from the file into the array. Line 19 sorts the array. Lines 23–25 write the data in the array to the temporary file.

The number of segments is returned in line 30. Note that every segment has `MAX_ARRAY_SIZE` number of elements except the last segment, which may have a smaller number of elements.

26.7.2   Implementing Phase II

In each merge step, two sorted segments are merged to form a new segment. The size of the new segment is doubled. The number of segments is reduced by half after each merge step. A segment is too large to be brought to an array in memory. To implement a merge step, copy half the number of segments from file f1.dat to a temporary file f2.dat. Then merge the first remaining segment in f1.dat with the first segment in f2.dat into a temporary file named f3.dat, as shown in Figure 26.8.

FIGURE 26.8   Sorted segments are merged iteratively.

Note
f1.dat may have one segment more than f2.dat. If so, move the last segment into f3.dat after the merge.

Listing 26.13 gives a method that copies the first half of the segments in f1.dat to f2.dat. Listing 26.14 gives a method that merges a pair of segments in f1.dat and f2.dat. Listing 26.15 gives a method that merges two segments.

LISTING 26.13   Copying First Half Segments

input stream f1
output stream f2

segments copied

```
1 private static void copyHalfToF2(int numberOfSegments,
2     int segmentSize, DataInputStream f1, DataOutputStream f2)
3     throws Exception {
4   for (int i = 0; i < (numberOfSegments / 2) * segmentSize; i++) {
5     f2.writeInt(f1.readInt());
6   }
7 }
```

LISTING 26.14   Merging All Segments

input stream f1 and f2

```
1 private static void mergeSegments(int numberOfSegments,
2     int segmentSize, DataInputStream f1, DataInputStream f2,
```

```
 3      DataOutputStream f3) throws Exception {          output stream f3
 4    for (int i = 0; i < numberOfSegments; i++) {
 5      mergeTwoSegments(segmentSize, f1, f2, f3);       merge two segments
 6    }
 7
 8    // f1 may have one extra segment, copy it to f3
 9    while (f1.available() > 0) {                        extra segment in f1
10      f3.writeInt(f1.readInt());
11    }
12  }
```

LISTING 26.15 Merging Two Segments

```
 1  private static void mergeTwoSegments(int segmentSize,
 2      DataInputStream f1, DataInputStream f2,           input stream f1 and f2
 3      DataOutputStream f3) throws Exception {           output stream f3
 4    int intFromF1 = f1.readInt();                       read from f1
 5    int intFromF2 = f2.readInt();                       read from f2
 6    int f1Count = 1;
 7    int f2Count = 1;
 8
 9    while (true) {
10      if (intFromF1 < intFromF2) {
11        f3.writeInt(intFromF1);                         write to f3
12        if (f1.available() == 0 || f1Count++ >= segmentSize) {
13          f3.writeInt(intFromF2);
14          break;                                        segment in f1 finished
15        }
16        else {
17          intFromF1 = f1.readInt();
18        }
19      }
20      else {
21        f3.writeInt(intFromF2);                         write to f3
22        if (f2.available() == 0 || f2Count++ >= segmentSize) {
23          f3.writeInt(intFromF1);
24          break;                                        segment in f2 finished
25        }
26        else {
27          intFromF2 = f2.readInt();
28        }
29      }
30    }
31
32    while (f1.available() > 0 && f1Count++ < segmentSize) {   remaining f1 segment
33      f3.writeInt(f1.readInt());
34    }
35
36    while (f2.available() > 0 && f2Count++ < segmentSize) {   remaining f2 segment
37      f3.writeInt(f2.readInt());
38    }
39  }
```

26.7.3 Combining Two Phases

Listing 26.16 gives the complete program for sorting `int` values in largedata.dat and storing the sorted data in sortedlargedata.dat.

LISTING 26.16 SortLargeFile.java

```java
 1  import java.io.*;
 2
 3  public class SortLargeFile {
 4    public static final int MAX_ARRAY_SIZE = 100000;
 5    public static final int BUFFER_SIZE = 100000;
 6
 7    public static void main(String[] args) throws Exception {
 8      // Implement Phase 1: Create initial segments
 9      int numberOfSegments =
10        initializeSegments(MAX_ARRAY_SIZE, "largedata.dat", "f1.dat");
11
12      // Implement Phase 2: Merge segments recursively
13      merge(numberOfSegments, MAX_ARRAY_SIZE,
14        "f1.dat", "f2.dat", "f3.dat");
15    }
16
17    /** Sort original file into sorted segments */
18    private static int initializeSegments
19        (int segmentSize, String originalFile, String f1)
20        throws Exception {
21      // Same as Listing 26.12, so omitted
22    }
23
24    private static void merge(int numberOfSegments,
25        int segmentSize, String f1, String f2, String f3)
26        throws Exception {
27      if (numberOfSegments > 1) {
28        mergeOneStep(numberOfSegments, segmentSize, f1, f2, f3);
29        merge((numberOfSegments + 1) / 2, segmentSize * 2, f3, f1, f2);
30      }
31      else { // Rename f1 as the final sorted file
32        File sortedFile = new File("sortedlargedata.dat");
33        if (sortedFile.exists()) sortedFile.delete();
34        new File(f1).renameTo(sortedFile);
35      }
36    }
37
38    private static void mergeOneStep(int numberOfSegments,
39        int segmentSize, String f1, String f2, String f3)
40        throws Exception {
41      DataInputStream f1Input = new DataInputStream(
42        new BufferedInputStream(new FileInputStream(f1), BUFFER_SIZE));
43      DataOutputStream f2Output = new DataOutputStream(
44        new BufferedOutputStream(new FileOutputStream(f2),
45          BUFFER_SIZE));
46
47      // Copy half number of segments from f1.dat to f2.dat
48      copyHalfToF2(numberOfSegments, segmentSize, f1Input, f2Output);
49      f2Output.close();
50
51      // Merge remaining segments in f1 with segments in f2 into f3
52      DataInputStream f2Input = new DataInputStream(
53        new BufferedInputStream(new FileInputStream(f2), BUFFER_SIZE));
54      DataOutputStream f3Output = new DataOutputStream(
55        new BufferedOutputStream(new FileOutputStream(f3),
56          BUFFER_SIZE));
57
58      mergeSegments(numberOfSegments / 2,
```

Margin annotations:
- max array size (line 4)
- IO stream buffer size (line 5)
- create segments (line 10)
- merge recursively (line 13)
- merge one step (line 28)
- merge recursively (line 29)
- final sorted file (line 31)
- input stream f1Input (line 41)
- output stream f2Output (line 43)
- copy half segments to f2 (line 48)
- close f2Output (line 49)
- input stream f2Input (line 52)
- output stream f3Output (line 54)
- merge two segments (line 58)

```
59        segmentSize, f1Input, f2Input, f3Output);
60
61     f1Input.close();
62     f2Input.close();
63     f3Output.close();
64   }
65
66   /** Copy first half number of segments from f1.dat to f2.dat */
67   private static void copyHalfToF2(int numberOfSegments,
68       int segmentSize, DataInputStream f1, DataOutputStream f2)
69       throws Exception {
70     // Same as Listing 26.13, so omitted
71   }
72
73   /** Merge all segments */
74   private static void mergeSegments(int numberOfSegments,
75       int segmentSize, DataInputStream f1, DataInputStream f2,
76       DataOutputStream f3) throws Exception {
77     // Same as Listing 26.14, so omitted
78   }
79
80   /** Merges two segments */
81   private static void mergeTwoSegments(int segmentSize,
82     DataInputStream f1, DataInputStream f2,
83     DataOutputStream f3) throws Exception {
84     // Same as Listing 26.15, so omitted
85   }
86 }
```

close streams

Line 10 creates initial segments from the original array and stores the sorted segments in a new file f1.dat. Line 13 produces a sorted file in sortedlargedata.dat. The merge method

```
merge(int numberOfSegments,
      int segmentSize, String f1, String f2, String f3)
```

merges the segments in f1 into f3 using f2 to assist the merge. The merge method is invoked recursively with many merge steps. Each merge step reduces the numberOfSegments by half and doubles the sorted segment size. After completion of one merge step, the next merge step merges the new segments in f3 to f2 using f1 to assist the merge. So the statement to invoke the new merge method is

```
merge((numberOfSegments + 1) / 2, segmentSize * 2, f3, f1, f2);
```

The numberOfSegments for the next merge step is (numberOfSegments + 1) / 2. For example, if numberOfSegments is 5, numberOfSegments is 3 for the next merge step, because every two segments are merged but one is left unmerged.

The recursive merge method ends when numberOfSegments is 1. In this case, f1 contains sorted data. Rename it to sortedlargedata.dat in line 34.

26.7.4 External Sort Analysis

In the external sort, the dominating cost is on I/O. Assume n is the number of the elements to be sorted in the file. In Phase I, n number of elements are read from the original file and output to a temporary file. So, the I/O for Phase I is $O(n)$.

In Phase II, before the first merge step, the number of sorted segments is $\dfrac{n}{c}$, where c is MAX_ARRAY_SIZE. Each merge step reduces the number of segments by half. So, after the first merge step, the number of segments is $\dfrac{n}{2c}$. After the second merge step, the number of segments is $\dfrac{n}{2^2c}$. After the third merge step, the number of segments is $\dfrac{n}{2^3c}$. After $\log\left(\dfrac{n}{c}\right)$ merge steps, the number of segments has been reduced to 1. Therefore, the total number of merge steps is $\log\left(\dfrac{n}{c}\right)$.

In each merge step, half the number of segments are read from file f1 and then written into a temporary file f2. The remaining segments in f1 are merged with the segments in f2. The number of I/Os in each merge step is $O(n)$. Since the total number of merge steps is $\log\left(\dfrac{n}{c}\right)$, the total number of I/Os is

$$O(n) \times \log\left(\dfrac{n}{c}\right) = O(n\log n)$$

Therefore, the complexity of the external sort is $O(n\log n)$.

KEY TERMS

bubble sort 836	merge sort 838
bucket sort 846	quick sort 842
external sort 846	radix sort 847
heap sort 845	

CHAPTER SUMMARY

- The worst-time complexity for selection sort, insertion sort, bubble sort, and quick sort is $O(n^2)$.

- The average-time and worst-time complexity for merge sort is $O(n\log n)$. The average time for quick sort is also $O(n\log n)$.

- The time complexity for heap sort is $O(n\log n)$.

- Bucket sort and radix sort are specialized sorting algorithms for integer keys. These algorithms sort keys using buckets rather than comparing keys. They are more efficient than general sorting algorithms.

- A variation of merge sort can be applied to sort large data from external files.

REVIEW QUESTIONS

Sections 21.2–21.6

26.1 Use Figure 26.1 as an example to show how to apply bubble sort on $\{45, 11, 50, 59, 60, 2, 4, 7, 10\}$.

26.2 Use Figure 26.2 as an example to show how to apply merge sort on $\{45, 11, 50, 59, 60, 2, 4, 7, 10\}$.

26.3 Use Figure 26.4 as an example to show how to apply quick sort on $\{45, 11, 50, 59, 60, 2, 4, 7, 10\}$.

26.4 Show the steps of creating a heap using $\{45, 11, 50, 59, 60, 2, 4, 7, 10\}$.

26.5 Given the following heap, show the steps of removing all nodes from the heap.

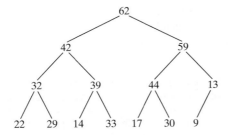

26.6 Ten numbers {2, 3, 4, 0, 5, 6, 7, 9, 8, 1} are stored in the external file largedata.dat. Trace the SortLargeFile program by hand with `MAX_ARRAY_SIZE` 2.

PROGRAMMING EXERCISES

26.1 (*Generic bubble sort*) Write the following two generic methods using bubble sort. The first method sorts the elements using the Comparable interface and the second uses the Comparator interface.

```
public static <E extends Comparable<E>> void bubbleSort
  (E[] list)
public static <E> void bubbleSort(E[] list,
  Comparator<? super E> comparator)
```

26.2 (*Generic merge sort*) Write the following two generic methods using merge sort. The first method sorts the elements using the Comparable interface and the second uses the Comparator interface.

```
public static <E extends Comparable<E>> void mergeSort
  (E[] list)
public static <E> void mergeSort(E[] list,
  Comparator<? super E> comparator)
```

26.3 (*Generic quick sort*) Write the following two generic methods using quick sort. The first method sorts the elements using the Comparable interface and the second uses the Comparator interface.

```
public static <E extends Comparable<E>> void quickSort
  (E[] list)
public static <E> void quickSort(E[] list,
  Comparator<? super E> comparator)
```

26.4 (*Improving quick sort*) The quick sort algorithm presented in the book selects the first element in the list as the pivot. Revise it by selecting the medium among the first, middle, and last elements in the list.

Video Note
Improve quick sort

26.5* (*Generic heap sort*) Write the following two generic methods using heap sort. The first method sorts the elements using the Comparable interface and the second uses the Comparator interface.

```
public static <E extends Comparable<E>> void heapSort(E[] list)
public static <E> void heapSort(E[] list,
  Comparator<? super E> comparator)
```

26.6 (*Checking order*) Write the following overloaded methods that check whether an array is ordered in ascending order or descending order. By default, the method checks ascending order. To check descending order, pass `false` to the ascending argument in the method.

```
public static boolean ordered(int[] list)
public static boolean ordered(int[] list, boolean ascending)
public static boolean ordered(double[] list)
public static boolean ordered(double[] list, boolean descending)
public static <E extends Comparable<E>> boolean ordered
  (E[] list)
public static <E extends Comparable<E>> boolean ordered
  (E[] list, boolean ascending)
public static <E> boolean ordered(E[] list,
  Comparator<? super E> comparator)
public static <E> boolean ordered(E[] list,
  Comparator<? super E> comparator, boolean ascending)
```

26.7* (*Execution time for sorting*) Write a program that obtains the execution time of selection sort, insertion sort, bubble sort, merge sort, nonrecursive quick sort, and heap sort for input size 50,000, 100,000, 150,000, 200,000, 250,000, and 300,000. Your program should create data randomly and print a table like this:

Array size	Selection Sort	Insertion Sort	Bubble Sort	Merge Sort	Quick Sort	Heap Sort
50000						
100000						
150000						
200000						
250000						
300000						

Hint: You can use the following code template to obtain the execution time:

```
long startTime = System.currentTimeMillis();
perform the task;
long endTime = System.currentTimeMillis();
long executionTime = endTime - startTime;
```

26.8* (*Execution time for external sorting*) Write a program that obtains the execution time of external sort for integers of size 5,000,000, 10,000,000, 15,000,000, 20,000,000, 25,000,000, and 30,000,000. Your program should print a table like this:

File size	5000000	10000000	15000000	20000000	25000000	30000000
Time						

26.9* (Radix sort) Write a program that randomly generates 1000000 integers and sorts them using radix sort.

CHAPTER 27

GRAPH APPLICATIONS

Objectives

- To model real-world problems using graphs and explain the Seven Bridges of Königsberg problem (§27.1).

- To describe the graph terminologies: vertices, edges, simple graphs, weighted/unweighted graphs, and directed/undirected graphs (§27.2).

- To represent vertices and edges using lists, adjacent matrices, and adjacent lists (§27.3).

- To model graphs using the `Graph` interface, the `AbstractGraph` class, and the `UnweightedGraph` class (§27.4).

- To represent the traversal of a graph using the `AbstractGraph.Tree` class (§27.5).

- To design and implement depth-first search (§27.6).

- To design and implement breadth-first search (§27.7).

- To solve the nine-tail problem using breadth-first search (§27.8).

- To solve the Knight's Tour problem by reducing it to a Hamiltonian path problem (§27.9)

27.1 Introduction

Shortest distance

Graphs play an important role in modeling real-world problems. For example, the problem to find the shortest distance between two cities can be modeled using a graph, where the vertices represent cities and edges represent the roads and distances between two adjacent cities, as shown in Figure 27.1. The problem of finding the shortest distance between two cities is reduced to finding a shortest path between two vertices in a graph.

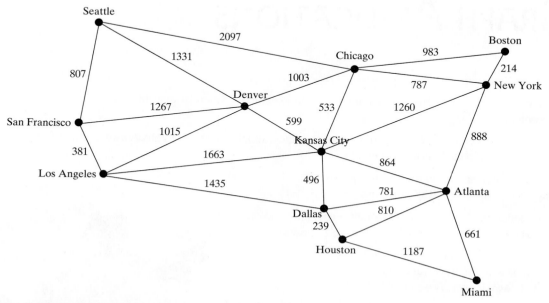

FIGURE 27.1 A graph can be used to model the distance between the cities.

graph theory

Seven Bridges of Königsberg

The study of graph problems is known as *graph theory*. Graph theory was founded by Leonard Euler in 1736, when he introduced graph terminology to solve the famous *Seven Bridges of Königsberg* problem. The city of Königsberg, Prussia (now Kaliningrad, Russia) was divided by the Pregel River. There were two islands on the river. The city and islands were connected by seven bridges, as shown in Figure 27.2(a). The question is, can one take a walk, cross each bridge exactly once, and return to the starting point? Euler proved that it was not possible.

To establish a proof, Euler first abstracted the Königsberg city map into the sketch shown in Figure 27.2(a), by eliminating all streets. Second, he replaced each land mass with a dot, called a vertex or a node, and each bridge with a line, called an edge, as shown in Figure 27.2(b). This structure with vertices and edges is called a graph.

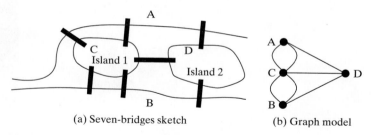

(a) Seven-bridges sketch   (b) Graph model

FIGURE 27.2 Seven bridges connected islands and land.

Looking at the graph, we ask whether there is a path starting from any vertex, traversing all edges exactly once, and returning to the starting vertex. Euler proved that for such path to exist, each vertex must have an even number of edges. Therefore, the *Seven Bridges of Königsberg* problem has no solution.

Graph problems are often solved using algorithms. Graph algorithms have many applications in various areas, such as in computer science, mathematics, biology, engineering, economics, genetics, and social sciences. This chapter presents the algorithms for depth-first search and breadth-first search, and their applications. The next chapter presents the algorithms for finding a minimum spanning tree and shortest paths in weighted graphs, and their applications.

27.2 Basic Graph Terminologies

This chapter does not assume that the reader has prior knowledge of graph theory or discrete mathematics. We use plain and simple terms to define graphs.

What is a graph? A *graph* is a mathematical structure that represents relationships among entities in the real world. For example, the graph is Figure 27.1 represents the roads and their distances among cities, and the graph in Figure 27.2(b) represents the bridges among land masses.

what is a graph?

A graph consists of a nonempty set of vertices, nodes, or points, and a set of edges that connect the vertices. For convenience, we define a graph as G = (V, E), where V represents a set of vertices and E represents a set of edges. For example, V and E for the graph in Figure 27.1 are as follows:

define a graph

```
V = {"Seattle", "San Francisco", "Los Angeles",
    "Denver", "Kansas City", "Chicago", "Boston", "New York",
    "Atlanta", "Miami", "Dallas", "Houston"};

E = {{"Seattle", "San Francisco"},{"Seattle", "Chicago"},
    {"Seattle", "Denver"}, {"San Francisco", "Denver"},
        ...
    };
```

Video Note
Graph terminologies and representation

A graph may be directed or undirected. In a directed graph, each edge has a direction, which indicates that you can move from one vertex to the other through the edge. You may model parent/child relationships using a directed graph, where an edge from vertex A to B indicates that A is a parent of B.

directed vs. undirected

Figure 27.3(a) shows a directed graph. In an undirected graph, you can move in both directions between vertices. The graph in Figure 27.1 is undirected.

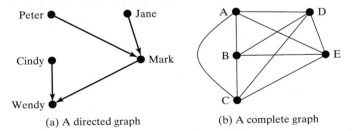

(a) A directed graph   (b) A complete graph

FIGURE 27.3 Graphs may appear in many forms.

Edges may be weighted or unweighted. For example, each edge in the graph in Figure 27.1 has a weight that represents the distance between two cities.

weighted vs. unweighted

Two vertices in a graph are said to be *adjacent* if they are connected by the same edge. Similarly two edges are said to be *adjacent* if they are connected to the same vertex. An edge

adjacent

incident
degree
neighbor

loop
parallel edge
simple graph
complete graph
spanning tree

in a graph that joins two vertices is said to be *incident* to both vertices. The *degree* of a vertex is the number of edges incident to it.

Two vertices are called *neighbors* if they are adjacent. Similarly two edges are called *neighbors* if they are incident.

A *loop* is an edge that links a vertex to itself. If two vertices are connected by two or more edges, these edges are called *parallel edges*. A simple graph is one that has no loops and parallel edges. A complete graph is the one in which every two pairs of vertices are connected, as shown in Figure 27.3(b).

Assume that the graph is connected and undirected. A *spanning tree* of a graph is a subgraph that is a tree and connects all vertices in the graph.

27.3 Representing Graphs

To write a program that processes and manipulates graphs, you have to store or represent graphs in the computer.

27.3.1 Representing Vertices

The vertices can be stored in an array. For example, you can store all the city names in the graph in Figure 27.1 using the following array:

```
String[] vertices = {"Seattle", "San Francisco", "Los Angeles",
   "Denver", "Kansas City", "Chicago", "Boston", "New York",
   "Atlanta", "Miami", "Dallas", "Houston"};
```

Note

vertex type

The vertices can be objects of any type. For example, you may consider cities as objects that contain the information such as name, population, mayor, etc. So, you may define vertices as follows:

```
City city0 = new City("Seattle", 563374, "Greg Nickels");
...
City city11 = new City("Houston", 1000203, "Bill White");
Object[] vertices = {city0, city1, ..., city11};

public class City {
  private String cityName;
  private int population;
  private String mayor;

  public City(String cityName, int population, String mayor) {
    this.cityName = cityName;
    this.population = population;
    this.mayor = mayor;
  }

  public String getCityName() {
    return cityName;
  }

  public int getPopulation() {
    return population;
  }

  public String getCityName() {
    return cityName;
  }
```

```java
    public void setMayor(String mayor) {
      this.mayor = mayor;
    }

    public void setPopulation(int population) {
      this.population = population;
    }
  }
```

The vertices can be conveniently labeled using natural numbers $0, 1, 2, \ldots, n - 1$, for a graph for n vertices. So, `vertices[0]` represents `"Seattle"`, `vertices[1]` represents `"San Francisco"`, and so on, as shown in Figure 27.4.

`vertices[0]`	Seattle
`vertices[1]`	San Francisco
`vertices[2]`	Los Angeles
`vertices[3]`	Denver
`vertices[4]`	Kansas City
`vertices[5]`	Chicago
`vertices[6]`	Boston
`vertices[7]`	New York
`vertices[8]`	Atlanta
`vertices[9]`	Miami
`vertices[10]`	Dallas
`vertices[11]`	Houston

FIGURE 27.4 An array stores the vertex names.

Note

You can reference a vertex by its name or its index, whichever is convenient. Obviously, it is easy to access a vertex via its index in a program.

reference vertex

27.3.2 Representing Edges: Edge Array

The edges can be represented using a two-dimensional array. For example, you can store all the edges in the graph in Figure 27.1 using the following array:

```java
int[][] edges = {
  {0, 1}, {0, 3}, {0, 5},
  {1, 0}, {1, 2}, {1, 3},
  {2, 1}, {2, 3}, {2, 4}, {2, 10},
  {3, 0}, {3, 2}, {3, 4}, {3, 5},
  {4, 2}, {4, 3}, {4, 5}, {4, 7}, {4, 8}, {4, 10},
  {5, 0}, {5, 3}, {5, 4}, {5, 6}, {5, 7},
  {6, 5}, {6, 7},
  {7, 4}, {7, 5}, {7, 6}, {7, 8},
  {8, 4}, {8, 7}, {8, 9}, {8, 10}, {8, 11},
  {9, 8}, {9, 11},
```

```
      {10, 2}, {10, 4}, {10, 8}, {10, 11},
      {11, 8}, {11, 9}, {11, 10}
    };
```

array edge

This is known as the *edge representation using arrays*.

27.3.3 Representing Edges: Edge Objects

Another way to represent the edges is to define edges as objects and store the edges in a `java.util.ArrayList`. The `Edge` class can be defined as follows:

```java
public class Edge {
  int u;
  int v;

  public Edge(int u, int v) {
    this.u = u;
    this.v = v;
  }
}
```

For example, you can store all the edges in the graph in Figure 27.1 using the following list:

```java
java.util.ArrayList<Edge> list = new java.util.ArrayList<Edge>();
list.add(new Edge(0, 1));
list.add(new Edge(0, 3));
list.add(new Edge(0, 5));
...
```

Storing `Edge` objects in an `ArrayList` is useful if you don't know the edges in advance.

Representing edges using an array or array list is intuitive for input, but not efficient for internal processing. The next two sections introduce the representation of graphs using adjacency matrices and adjacency lists. These two data structures are efficient for processing graphs.

27.3.4 Representing Edges: Adjacency Matrices

Assume that the graph has n vertices. You can use a two-dimensional $n \times n$ matrix, say `adjacencyMatrix`, to represent edges. Each element in the array is 0 or 1. `adjacencyMatrix[i][j]` is 1 if there is an edge from vertex i to vertex j; otherwise, `adjacencyMatrix[i][j]` is 0. If the graph is undirected, the matrix is symmetric, because `adjacencyMatrix[i][j]` is the same as `adjacencyMatrix[j][i]`. For example, the edges in the graph in Figure 27.1 can be represented using an adjacency matrix as follows:

```java
int[][] adjacencyMatrix = {
  {0, 1, 0, 1, 0, 1, 0, 0, 0, 0, 0, 0}, // Seattle
  {1, 0, 1, 1, 0, 0, 0, 0, 0, 0, 0, 0}, // San Francisco
  {0, 1, 0, 1, 1, 1, 0, 0, 0, 0, 0, 0}, // Los Angeles
  {1, 1, 1, 0, 1, 1, 0, 0, 0, 0, 0, 0}, // Denver
  {0, 0, 1, 1, 0, 1, 0, 1, 1, 0, 1, 0}, // Kansas City
  {1, 0, 0, 1, 1, 0, 1, 1, 0, 0, 0, 0}, // Chicago
  {0, 0, 0, 0, 0, 1, 0, 1, 0, 0, 0, 0}, // Boston
  {0, 0, 0, 0, 1, 1, 1, 0, 1, 0, 0, 0}, // New York
  {0, 0, 0, 1, 1, 0, 0, 1, 0, 1, 1, 1}, // Atlanta
  {0, 0, 0, 0, 0, 0, 0, 0, 1, 0, 0, 1}, // Miami
  {0, 0, 1, 0, 1, 0, 0, 0, 1, 0, 0, 1}, // Dallas
  {0, 0, 0, 0, 0, 0, 0, 0, 1, 1, 1, 0}  // Houston
};
```

Note

Since the matrix is symmetric for an undirected graph, to save storage, you may use a ragged array.   ragged array

The adjacency matrix for the directed graph in Figure 27.3(a) can be represented as follows:

```
int[][] a = {{0, 0, 1, 0, 0}, // Peter
             {0, 0, 1, 0, 0}, // Jane
             {0, 0, 0, 0, 1}, // Mark
             {0, 0, 0, 0, 1}, // Cindy
             {0, 0, 0, 0, 0}  // Wendy
            };
```

27.3.5 Representing Edges: Adjacency Lists

To represent edges using adjacency lists, define an array of linked lists. The array has n entries. Each entry represents a vertex. The linked list for vertex i contains all the vertices j such that there is an edge from vertex i to vertex j. For example, to represent the edges in the graph in Figure 27.1, you may create an array of linked lists as follows:

```
java.util.LinkedList[] neighbors = new java.util.LinkedList(12);
```

`lists[0]` contains all vertices adjacent to vertex 0 (i.e., Seattle), `lists[1]` contains all vertices adjacent to vertex 1 (i.e., San Francisco), and so on, as shown in Figure 27.5.

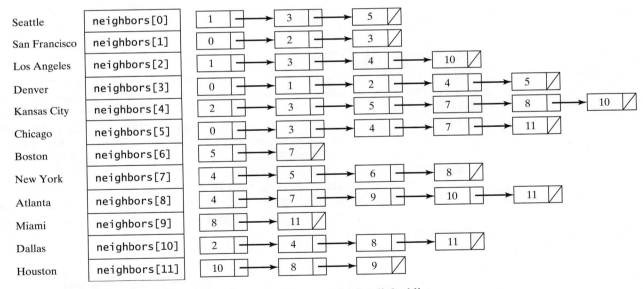

FIGURE 27.5 Edges in the graph in Figure 27.1 are represented using linked lists.

To represent the edges in the graph in Figure 27.3(a), you may create an array of linked list as follows:

```
java.util.LinkedList[] lists = new java.util.LinkedList(5);
```

`lists[0]` contains all vertices pointed from vertex 0 via directed edges, `lists[1]` contains all vertices pointed from vertex 1 via directed edges, and so on, as shown in Figure 27.6.

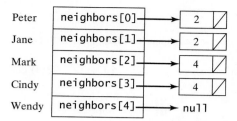

FIGURE 27.6 Edges in the graph in Figure 27.3(a) are represented using linked lists.

Note

You can represent a graph using an adjacency matrix or adjacency lists. Which one is better? If the graph is dense (i.e., there are a lot of edges), using an adjacency matrix is preferred. If the graph is very sparse (i.e., very few edges), using adjacency lists is better, because using an adjacency matrix would waste a lot of space.

Both adjacency matrices and adjacency lists may be used in a program to make algorithms more efficient. For example, it takes $O(1)$ constant time to check whether two vertices are connected using an adjacency matrix and it takes linear time $O(m)$ to print all edges in a graph using adjacency lists, where m is the number of edges.

Note

Adjacency matrices and adjacency lists are two common representations for graphs, but they are not the only ways to represent graphs. For example, you may define a vertex as an object with a method `getNeighbors()` that returns all its neighbors. For simplicity, the text will use adjacency matrices and adjacency lists to represent graphs. Other representations will be explored in the exercises.

27.4 Modeling Graphs

The Java Collections Framework serves as a good example for designing complex data structures. The common features of data structures are defined in the interfaces (e.g., `Collection`, `Set`, `List`), as shown in Figure 22.1. Abstract classes (e.g., `AbstractCollection`, `AbstractSet`, `AbstractList`) partially implement the interfaces. Concrete classes (e.g., `HashSet`, `LinkedHashSet`, `TreeSet`, `ArrayList`, `LinkedList`) provide concrete implementations. This design pattern is useful in the design of graphs. We will define an interface named `Graph` that contains all common operations of graphs and an abstract class named `AbstractGraph` that partially implements the `Graph` interface. Many concrete graphs may be added to the design. For example, we will define such graphs named `UnweightedGraph` and `WeightedGraph`. The relationships of these interfaces and classes are illustrated in Figure 27.7.

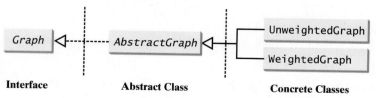

FIGURE 27.7 Graphs can be modeled using interfaces, abstract classes and concrete classes.

What are the common operations for a graph? In general, you need to get the number of vertices in a graph, get all vertices in a graph, get the vertex object with a specified index, get the index of the vertex with a specified name, get the neighbors for a vertex, get the adjacency matrix, get the degree for a vertex, perform a depth-first search, and perform a breadth-first search. Depth-first search and breadth-first search will be introduced in the next section. Figure 27.8 illustrates these methods in the UML diagram.

`AbstractGraph` does not introduce any new methods. An array of vertices and an array of adjacency lists for the vertices are defined in the `AbstractGraph` class. With these data fields, it is sufficient to implement all the methods defined in the `Graph` interface.

`UnweightedGraph` simply extends `AbstractGraph` with four constructors for creating the concrete `Graph` instances. `UnweightedGraph` inherits all methods from `AbstractGraph`, and it does not introduce any new methods.

<<interface>> *Graph*	
+getSize(): int	Returns the number of vertices in the graph.
+getVertices(): Object[]	Returns the vertices in the graph.
+getVertices(index: int): Object	Returns the vertex object for the specified vertex label.
+getIndex(v: Object): int	Returns the index for the specified vertex object.
+getNeighbors(v: int): java.util.LinkedList	Returns the neighbors of vertex v.
+getDegree(v: int): int	Returns the degree for a specified vertex.
+getAdjacencyMatrix(): int[][]	Returns the adjacency matrix.
+printAdjacencyMatrix(): void	Prints the adjacency matrix.
+printEdges(): void	Prints the edges.
+dfs(int v): AbstractGraph.Tree	Obtains a depth-first search tree.
+bfs(int v): AbstractGraph.Tree	Obtains a breadth-first search tree.

AbstractGraph	
#vertices: Object[]	Vertices in the graph.
#neighbors: java.util.LinkedList[]	Neighbors for each vertex in the graph.
#AbstractGraph(edges: int[][], vertices: Object[])	Constructs a graph with the specified edges and vertices in arrays.
#AbstractGraph(edges: List<Edge>, vertices: List)	Constructs a graph with the specified edges and vertices stored in lists.
#AbstractGraph(edges: int[][], numberOfVertices: int)	Constructs a graph with the specified edges in an array and the number of vertices.
#AbstractGraph(edges: List<Edge>, numberOfVertices: int)	Constructs a graph with the specified edges in a list and the number of vertices.
Inner classes Tree and PathIterator are defined here	

UnweightedGraph	
+UnweightedGraph(edges: int[][], vertices: Object[])	Constructs a graph with the specified edges and vertices in arrays.
+UnweightedGraph(edges: List<Edge>, vertices:List)	Constructs a graph with the specified edges and vertices stored in lists.
+UnweightedGraph(edges: List<Edge>, numberOfVertices: int)	Constructs a graph with the specified edges in a list and the number of vertices.
+UnweightedGraph(edges: int[][], numberOfVertices: int)	Constructs a graph with the specified edges in an array and the number of vertices.

FIGURE 27.8 The Graph interface defines the common operations for all types of graphs.

why **AbstractGraph**?

Note

The **AbstractGraph** class implements all the methods in the **Graph** interface. So, why is it defined as abstract? In the future, you may need to add new methods to the **Graph** interface that cannot be implemented in **AbstractGraph**. To make the classes easy to maintain, it is desirable to define the **AbstractGraph** class as abstract.

Assume all these interfaces and classes are available. Listing 27.1 gives a test program that creates a graph for the one in Figure 27.1 and another graph for the one in Figure 27.3(a).

LISTING 27.1 TestGraph.java

vertices

edges

create a graph

print adjacency matrix

print edges

create a graph

print adjacency matrix

print edges

```java
1 public class TestGraph {
2   public static void main(String[] args) {
3     String[] vertices = {"Seattle", "San Francisco", "Los Angeles",
4       "Denver", "Kansas City", "Chicago", "Boston", "New York",
5       "Atlanta", "Miami", "Dallas", "Houston"};
6
7     int[][] edges = {
8       {0, 1}, {0, 3}, {0, 5},
9       {1, 0}, {1, 2}, {1, 3},
10      {2, 1}, {2, 3}, {2, 4}, {2, 10},
11      {3, 0}, {3, 2}, {3, 4}, {3, 5},
12      {4, 2}, {4, 3}, {4, 5}, {4, 7}, {4, 8}, {4, 10},
13      {5, 0}, {5, 3}, {5, 4}, {5, 6}, {5, 7},
14      {6, 5}, {6, 7},
15      {7, 4}, {7, 5}, {7, 6}, {7, 8},
16      {8, 4}, {8, 7}, {8, 9}, {8, 10}, {8, 11},
17      {9, 8}, {9, 11},
18      {10, 2}, {10, 4}, {10, 8}, {10, 11},
19      {11, 8}, {11, 9}, {11, 10}
20    };
21
22    Graph graph1 = new UnweightedGraph(edges, vertices);
23    System.out.println("Adjacency matrix for graph1:");
24    graph1.printAdjacencyMatrix();
25    System.out.println("The edges for graph1:");
26    graph1.printEdges();
27
28    edges = new int[][]{{0, 2}, {1, 2}, {2, 4}, {3, 4}};
29    Graph graph2 = new UnweightedGraph(edges, 5);
30    System.out.println("\nAdjacency matrix for graph2:");
31    graph2.printAdjacencyMatrix();
32    System.out.println("The edges for graph2:");
33    graph2.printEdges();
34  }
35 }
```

```
Adjacency matrix for graph1:
0 1 0 1 0 1 0 0 0 0 0 0
1 0 1 1 0 0 0 0 0 0 0 0
0 1 0 1 1 0 0 0 0 0 1 0
1 0 1 0 1 1 0 0 0 0 0 0
0 0 1 1 0 1 0 1 1 0 1 0
1 0 0 1 1 0 1 1 0 0 0 0
0 0 0 0 0 1 0 1 0 0 0 0
0 0 0 0 1 1 1 0 1 0 0 0
0 0 0 0 1 0 0 1 0 1 0 1 1
```

```
0 0 0 0 0 0 0 0 1 0 0 1
0 0 1 0 1 0 0 0 1 0 0 1
0 0 0 0 0 0 0 0 1 1 1 0

The edges for graph1:
Vertex 0: (0, 1) (0, 3) (0, 5)
Vertex 1: (1, 0) (1, 2) (1, 3)
Vertex 2: (2, 1) (2, 3) (2, 4) (2, 10)
Vertex 3: (3, 0) (3, 2) (3, 4) (3, 5)
Vertex 4: (4, 2) (4, 3) (4, 5) (4, 7) (4, 8) (4, 10)
Vertex 5: (5, 0) (5, 3) (5, 4) (5, 6) (5, 7)
Vertex 6: (6, 5) (6, 7)
Vertex 7: (7, 4) (7, 5) (7, 6) (7, 8)
Vertex 8: (8, 4) (8, 7) (8, 9) (8, 10) (8, 11)
Vertex 9: (9, 8) (9, 11)
Vertex 10: (10, 2) (10, 4) (10, 8) (10, 11)
Vertex 11: (11, 8) (11, 9) (11, 10)

Adjacency matrix for graph2:
0 0 1 0 0
0 0 1 0 0
0 0 0 0 1
0 0 0 0 1
0 0 0 0 0

The edges for graph2:
Vertex 0: (0, 2)
Vertex 1: (1, 2)
Vertex 2: (2, 4)
Vertex 3: (3, 4)
Vertex 4:
```

The program creates **graph1** for the graph in Figure 27.1 in lines 3–22. The vertices for **graph1** are defined in lines 3–5. The edges for **graph1** are defined in 7–20. The edges are represented using a two-dimensional array. For each row **i** in the array, **edges[i][0]** and **edges[i][1]** indicate that there is an edge from vertex **edges[i][0]** to vertex **edges[i][1]**. For example, the first row $\{0, 1\}$ represents the edge from vertex 0 (**edges[0][0]**) to vertex 1 (**edges[0][1]**). The row $\{0, 5\}$ represents the edge from vertex 0 (**edges[2][0]**) to vertex 5 (**edges[2][1]**). Line 24 invokes the **printAdjacencyMatrix()** method on **graph1** to display the adjacency matrix for **graph1**. Line 26 invokes the **printEdges()** method on **graph1** to display all edges in **graph1**.

The program creates **graph2** for the graph in Figure 27.3(a) in lines 28–29. The edges for **graph2** are defined in line 28. Line 31 invokes the **printAdjacencyMatrix()** method on **graph2** to display the adjacency matrix for **graph1**. Line 33 invokes the **printEdges()** method on **graph2** to display all edges in **graph2**.

Now we turn our attention to implementing the interface and classes. Listings 27.2, 27.3, and 27.4 give the **Graph** interface, the **AbstractGraph** class, and the **UnweightedGraph** class, respectively.

LISTING 27.2 Graph.java

```
1 public interface Graph {
2    /** Return the number of vertices in the graph */
3    public int getSize();
4
5    /** Return the vertices in the graph */
6    public Object[] getVertices();
```

getSize

getVertices

```
                    7
getVertex           8     /** Return the object for the specified vertex index */
                    9     public Object getVertex(int index);
                   10
getIndex           11     /** Return the index for the specified vertex object */
                   12     public int getIndex(Object v);
                   13
getNeighbors       14     /** Return the neighbors of vertex v */
                   15     public java.util.List getNeighbors(int v);
                   16
getDegree          17     /** Return the degree for a specified vertex */
                   18     public int getDegree(int v);
                   19
getAdjacencyMatrix 20     /** Return the adjacency matrix */
                   21     public int[][] getAdjacencyMatrix();
                   22
printAdjacencyMatrix 23   /** Print the adjacency matrix */
                   24     public void printAdjacencyMatrix();
                   25
printEdges         26     /** Print the edges */
                   27     public void printEdges();
                   28
dfs                29     /** Obtain a depth-first search tree */
                   30     public AbstractGraph.Tree dfs(int v);
                   31
bfs                32     /** Obtain a breadth-first search tree */
                   33     public AbstractGraph.Tree bfs(int v);
                   34   }
```

LISTING 27.3   AbstractGraph.java

```
                    1  import java.util.*;
                    2
                    3  public abstract class AbstractGraph implements Graph {
                    4    protected Object[] vertices; // Store vertices
                    5    protected List<Integer>[] neighbors; // Adjacency lists
                    6
                    7    /** Construct a graph from edges and vertices stored in arrays */
constructor         8    protected AbstractGraph(int[][] edges, Object[] vertices) {
                    9      this.vertices = vertices;
                   10      createAdjacencyLists(edges, vertices.length);
                   11    }
                   12
                   13    /** Construct a graph from edges and vertices stored in ArrayList */
constructor        14    protected AbstractGraph(List<Edge> edges, List vertices) {
                   15      this.vertices = vertices.toArray();
                   16      createAdjacencyLists(edges, vertices.size());
                   17    }
                   18
                   19    /** Construct a graph from edges and vertices in ArrayList */
constructor        20    protected AbstractGraph(List<Edge> edges, int numberOfVertices) {
                   21      vertices = new Integer[numberOfVertices]; // Create vertices
                   22      for (int i = 0; i < numberOfVertices; i++) {
                   23        vertices[i] = new Integer(i); // vertices is {0, 1, 2, ...}
                   24      }
                   25      createAdjacencyLists(edges, numberOfVertices);
                   26    }
                   27
                   28    /** Construct a graph from edges in array */
constructor        29    protected AbstractGraph(int[][] edges, int numberOfVertices) {
```

```
30      vertices = new Integer[numberOfVertices]; // Create vertices
31      for (int i = 0; i < numberOfVertices; i++) {
32        vertices[i] = new Integer(i); // vertices is {0, 1, 2, ...}
33      }
34      createAdjacencyLists(edges, numberOfVertices);
35    }
36
37    /** Create adjacency lists for each vertex */
38    private void createAdjacencyLists(
39        int[][] edges, int numberOfVertices) {
40      // Create a linked list
41      neighbors = new LinkedList[numberOfVertices];
42      for (int i = 0; i < numberOfVertices; i++) {
43        neighbors[i] = new java.util.LinkedList<Integer>();
44      }
45
46      for (int i = 0; i < edges.length; i++) {
47        int u = edges[i][0];
48        int v = edges[i][1];
49        neighbors[u].add(v);
50      }
51    }
52
53    /** Create adjacency lists for each vertex */
54    private void createAdjacencyLists(
55        List<Edge> edges, int numberOfVertices) {
56      // Create a linked list
57      neighbors = new LinkedList[numberOfVertices];
58      for (int i = 0; i < numberOfVertices; i++) {
59        neighbors[i] = new java.util.LinkedList<Integer>();
60      }
61
62      for (Edge edge: edges) {
63        neighbors[edge.u].add(edge.v);
64      }
65    }
66
67    /** Return the number of vertices in the graph */
68    public int getSize() {                                       getSize
69      return vertices.length;
70    }
71
72    /** Return the vertices in the graph */
73    public Object[] getVertices() {                              getVertices
74      return vertices;
75    }
76
77    /** Return the object for the specifed vertex */
78    public Object getVertex(int v) {                             getVertex
79      return vertices[v];
80    }
81
82    /** Return the index for the specified vertex object */
83    public int getIndex(Object vertex) {                         getIndex
84      for (int i = 0; i < getSize(); i++) {
85        if (vertex.equals(vertices[i])) {
86          return i;
87        }
88      }
89
```

```
90        return -1; // If vertex is not in the graph
91      }
92
93      /** Return the neighbors of vertex v */
```

getNeighbors
```
94      public java.util.List getNeighbors(int v) {
95        return neighbors[v];
96      }
97
98      /** Return the degree for a specified vertex */
```

getDegrees
```
99      public int getDegree(int v) {
100       return neighbors[v].size();
101     }
102
103     /** Return the adjacency matrix */
```

getAdjacencyMatrix
```
104     public int[][] getAdjacencyMatrix() {
105       int[][] adjacencyMatrix = new int[getSize()][getSize()];
106
107       for (int i = 0; i < neighbors.length; i++) {
108         for (int j = 0; j < neighbors[i].size(); j++) {
109           int v = neighbors[i].get(j);
110           adjacencyMatrix[i][v] = 1;
111         }
112       }
113
114       return adjacencyMatrix;
115     }
116
117     /** Print the adjacency matrix */
```

printAdjacencyMatrix
```
118     public void printAdjacencyMatrix() {
119       int[][] adjacencyMatrix = getAdjacencyMatrix();
120       for (int i = 0; i < adjacencyMatrix.length; i++) {
121         for (int j = 0; j < adjacencyMatrix[0].length; j++) {
122           System.out.print(adjacencyMatrix[i][j] + " ");
123         }
124
125         System.out.println();
126       }
127     }
128
129     /** Print the edges */
```

printEdges
```
130     public void printEdges() {
131       for (int u = 0; u < neighbors.length; u++) {
132         System.out.print("Vertex " + u + ": ");
133         for (int j = 0; j < neighbors[u].size(); j++) {
134           System.out.print("(" + u + ", " +
135             neighbors[u].get(j) + ") ");
136         }
137         System.out.println();
138       }
139     }
140
141     /** Edge inner class inside the AbstractGraph class */
```

Edge inner class
```
142     public static class Edge {
143       public int u; // Starting vertex of the edge
144       public int v; // Ending vertex of the edge
145
146       /** Construct an edge for (u, v) */
147       public Edge(int u, int v) {
148         this.u = u;
149         this.v = v;
```

```
150      }
151  }
152
153  /** Obtain a DFS tree starting from vertex v */
154  /** To be discussed in Section 27.6 */
155  public Tree dfs(int v) {                                              dfs method
156    List<Integer> searchOrders = new ArrayList<Integer>();
157    int[] parent = new int[vertices.length];
158    for (int i = 0; i < parent.length; i++)
159      parent[i] = -1; // Initialize parent[i] to -1
160
161    // Mark visited vertices
162    boolean[] isVisited = new boolean[vertices.length];
163
164    // Recursively search
165    dfs(v, parent, searchOrders, isVisited);
166
167    // Return a search tree
168    return new Tree(v, parent, searchOrders);
169  }
170
171  /** Recursive method for DFS search */
172  private void dfs(int v, int[] parent, List<Integer> searchOrders,
173      boolean[] isVisited) {
174    // Store the visited vertex
175    searchOrders.add(v);
176    isVisited[v] = true; // Vertex v visited
177
178    for (int i : neighbors[v]) {
179      if (!isVisited[i]) {
180        parent[i] = v; // The parent of vertex i is v
181        dfs(i, parent, searchOrders, isVisited); // Recursive search
182      }
183    }
184  }
185
186  /** Starting bfs search from vertex v */
187  /** To be discussed in Section 27.7 */
188  public Tree bfs(int v) {                                              bfs method
189    List<Integer> searchOrders = new ArrayList<Integer>();
190    int[] parent = new int[vertices.length];
191    for (int i = 0; i < parent.length; i++)
192      parent[i] = -1; // Initialize parent[i] to -1
193
194    java.util.LinkedList<Integer> queue =
195      new java.util.LinkedList<Integer>(); // list used as a queue
196    boolean[] isVisited = new boolean[vertices.length];
197    queue.offer(v); // Enqueue v
198    isVisited[v] = true; // Mark it visited
199
200    while (!queue.isEmpty()) {
201      int u = queue.poll(); // Dequeue to u
202      searchOrders.add(u); // u searched
203      for (int w : neighbors[u]) {
204        if (!isVisited[w]) {
205          queue.offer(w); // Enqueue w
206          parent[w] = u; // The parent of w is u
207          isVisited[w] = true; // Mark it visited
208        }
209      }
210    }
```

```
211
212      return new Tree(v, parent, searchOrders);
213    }
214
215  /** Tree inner class inside the AbstractGraph class */
216  /** To be discussed in Section 27.5 */
217  public class Tree {
218    private int root; // The root of the tree
219    private int[] parent; // Store the parent of each vertex
220    private List<Integer> searchOrders; // Store the search order
221
222    /** Construct a tree with root, parent, and searchOrder */
223    public Tree(int root, int[] parent, List<Integer> searchOrders) {
224      this.root = root;
225      this.parent = parent;
226      this.searchOrders = searchOrders;
227    }
228
229    /** Construct a tree with root and parent without a
230     *  particular order */
231    public Tree(int root, int[] parent) {
232      this.root = root;
233      this.parent = parent;
234    }
235
236    /** Return the root of the tree */
237    public int getRoot() {
238      return root;
239    }
240
241    /** Return the parent of vertex v */
242    public int getParent(int v) {
243      return parent[v];
244    }
245
246    /** Return an array representing search order */
247    public List<Integer> getSearchOrders() {
248      return searchOrders;
249    }
250
251    /** Return number of vertices found */
252    public int getNumberOfVerticesFound() {
253      return searchOrders.size();
254    }
255
256    /** Return the iterator for a path starting from the root to v */
257    public java.util.Iterator pathIterator(int v) {
258      return new PathIterator(v);
259    }
260
261    /** PathIterator inner class inside the tree */
262    public class PathIterator implements java.util.Iterator {
263      private Stack<Integer> stack;
264
265      /** Construct an iterator for the vertices on the path */
266      public PathIterator(int v) {
267        stack = new Stack<Integer>();
268        do {
269          stack.add(v);
270          v = parent[v];
271        }
```

```
272          while (v != -1);
273        }
274
275        /** Has next element in the iterator? */
276        public boolean hasNext() {
277          return !stack.isEmpty();
278        }
279
280        /* Get the current element in the iterator and move the
281         * iterator to point to the next element */
282        public Object next() {
283          return vertices[stack.pop()];
284        }
285
286        /* This remove method is defined in the Iterator interface
287         * Do not implement it */
288        public void remove() {
289          // Do nothing
290        }
291      }
292
293      /** Print a path from the root to vertex v */
294      public void printPath(int v) {
295        Iterator iterator = pathIterator(v);
296        System.out.print("A path from " + vertices[root] + " to " +
297          vertices[v] + ": ");
298        while (iterator.hasNext()) {
299          System.out.print(iterator.next() + " ");
300        }
301      }
302
303      /** Print the whole tree */
304      public void printTree() {
305        System.out.println("Root is: " + vertices[root]);
306        System.out.print("Edges: ");
307        for (int i = 0; i < parent.length; i++) {
308          if (parent[i] != -1) {
309            // Display an edge
310            System.out.print("(" + vertices[parent[i]] + ", " +
311              vertices[i] + ") ");
312          }
313        }
314        System.out.println();
315      }
316    }
317 }
```

LISTING 27.4 UnweightedGraph.java

```
1 import java.util.*;
2
3 public class UnweightedGraph extends AbstractGraph {
4   /** Construct a graph with the specified edges and vertices in
5    *  arrays
6    */
7   public UnweightedGraph(int[][] edges, Object[] vertices) {          constructor
8     super(edges, vertices);
9   }
10
```

```
11    /** Construct a graph with the specified edges and vertices in
12     *  lists
13     */
```
constructor
```
14    public UnweightedGraph(List<Edge> edges, List vertices) {
15      super(edges, vertices);
16    }
17
18    /** Construct a graph with the specified edges in a list and
19     *  the number of vertices
20     */
```
constructor
```
21    public UnweightedGraph(List<Edge> edges, int numberOfVertices) {
22      super(edges, numberOfVertices);
23    }
24
25    /** Construct a graph with the specified edges in an array and
26     *  the number of vertices
27     */
```
constructor
```
28    public UnweightedGraph(int[][] edges, int numberOfVertices) {
29      super(edges, numberOfVertices);
30    }
31  }
```

The code in the **Graph** interface in Listing 27.2 and the **UnweightedGraph** class are straightforward. Let us digest the code in the **AbstractGraph** class in Listing 27.3.

The **AbstractGraph** class defines the data field **vertices** (line 4) to store vertices and **neighbors** (line 5) to store edges in adjacency lists. **neighbors[i]** stores all vertices adjacent to vertex **i**. Four overloaded constructors are defined in lines 8–35 to create graphs from arrays or lists of edges and vertices. The **createAdjacencyLists(int[][] edges, int numberOfVertice)** method creates adjacency lists from edges in an array (lines 38–51). The **createAdjacencyLists(List<Edge> edges, int numberOfVertice)** method creates adjacency lists from edges in a list (lines 54–65).

The **getAdjacencyMatrix()** method (lines 104–115) returns a two-dimensional array for representing an adjacency matrix of the edges. The **printAdjacencyMatrix()** method (lines 118–127) displays the adjacency matrix. The **printEdges()** method (lines 130–139) displays all vertices and edges adjacent to each vertex.

The code in lines 155–213 gives the methods for finding a depth-first search tree and a breadth-first search tree, which will be introduced in the following sections.

27.5 Graph Traversals

depth-first
breadth-first

Graph traversal is the process of visiting each vertex in the graph exactly once. There are two popular ways to traverse a graph: *depth-first traversal* (or *depth-first search*) and *breadth-first traversal* (or *breadth-first search*). Both traversals result in a spanning tree, which can be modeled using a class, as shown in Figure 27.9. Note that **Tree** is an inner class defined in the **AbstractGraph** class. **AbstractGraph.Tree** is different from the **Tree** interface defined in §25.2.5. **AbstractGraph.Tree** describes a search order of the nodes in the graph, whereas the **Tree** interface defines common features in a tree.

The **Tree** class is defined as an inner class in the **AbstractGraph** class in lines 217–316 in Listing 27.3.

The **Tree** class defines seven methods. The **getRoot()** method returns the root of the tree. You can get the order of the vertices searched by invoking the **getSearchOrders()** method. You can invoke **getParent(v)** to find the parent of vertex **v** in the search. Invoking **getNumberOfVerticesFound()** returns the number of vertices searched. Invoking **printPath(v)** displays a path from the root to **v**. You can display all edges in the tree using the **printTree()** method.

AbstractGraph.Tree	
−root: int −parent: int[] −searchOrders: java.util.List\<Integer>	The root of the tree. The parents of the vertices. The orders for traversing the vertices.

+Tree(root: int, parent: int[],
   searchOrders: List\<Integer>)
+Tree(root: int, parent: int[])
	Constructs a tree with the specified root, parent, and
	  searchOrders.
	Constructs a tree with the specified root and parent with
	  no specified searchOrders.

+getRoot(): int +getSearchOrders(): List +getParent(v: int): int +getNumberOfVerticesFound(): int +pathIterator(v: int): java.util.Iterator +printPath(v: int): void +printTree(): void	Returns the root of the tree. Returns the order of vertices searched. Returns the parent of vertex v. Returns the number of vertices searched. Returns an iterator for the path from the root to vertex v. Displays a path from the root to the specified vertex. Displays tree with the root and all edges.

FIGURE 27.9 The Tree class describes a tree with a search order for the nodes.

The Tree class provides the pathIterator(int v) method that returns an iterator for a path from the root to vertex v. The iterator is an instance of the PathIterator class, which implements java.util.Iterator (line 262). The Iterator interface defines three methods: hasNext(), next(), and remove(). The PathIterator class must implement all these three methods. To avoid actually removing any vertices from the path, the body of the remove() method is empty (line 289). The PathIterator constructor uses a stack to store vertices from v to the root (lines 268–273). hasNext() returns true if the stack is not empty (line 277). Invoking next() removes a vertex from the stack (line 283). The root is on the top of stack, so it is removed first. The iterator traverses the vertices for the path from the root to the specified vertex.

PathIterator class

Sections 27.6 and 27.7 will introduce depth-first search and breadth-first search, respectively. Both searches will result in an instance of the Tree class.

27.6 Depth-First Search

The depth-first search of a graph is like the depth-first search of a tree discussed in §25.2.4, "Tree Traversal." In the case of a tree, the search starts from the root. In a graph, the search can start from any vertex.

A depth-first search of a tree first visits the root, then recursively visits the subtrees of the root. Similarly, the depth-first search of a graph first visits a vertex, then recursively visits all vertices adjacent to that vertex. The difference is that the graph may contain cycles, which may lead to an infinite recursion. To avoid this problem, you need to track the vertices that have already been visited.

The search is called depth-first, because it searches "deeper" in the graph as much as possible. The search starts from some vertex v. After visiting v, the next vertex to be visited is first unvisited neighbor of v. If v has no unvisited neighbor, backtrack to the vertex from which we reached v.

Video Note
Depth-first search

27.6.1 Depth-First Search Algorithm

The algorithm for the depth-first search can be described in Listing 27.5.

LISTING 27.5 Depth-first Search Algorithm

```
1 dfs(vertex v) {
2   visit v;
3   for each neighbor w of v
```

visit v

check a neighbor
recursive search

```
4     if (w has not been visited) {
5         dfs(w);
6     }
7 }
```

You may use an array named **isVisited** to denote whether a vertex has been visited. Initially, **isVisited[i]** is **false** for each vertex *i*. Once a vertex, say *v*, is visited, **isVisited[v]** is set to **true**.

Consider the graph in Figure 27.10(a). Suppose you start the depth-first search from vertex 0. First visit 0, then any of its neighbors, say 1. Now 1 is visited, as shown in Figure 27.10(b). Vertex 1 has three neighbors 0, 2, and 4. Since 0 has already been visited, you will visit either 2 or 4. Let us pick 2. Now 2 is visited, as shown in Figure 27.10(c). 2 has three neighbors 0, 1, and 3. Since 0 and 1 have already been visited, pick 3. 3 is now visited, as shown in Figure 27.10(d). At this point, the vertices have been visited are in this order:

0, 1, 2, 3

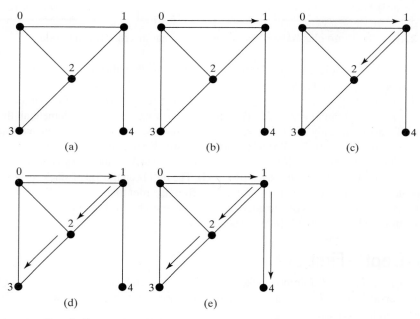

FIGURE 27.10 Depth-first search visits a node and its neighbors recursively.

Since all the neighbors of 3 have been visited, backtrack to 2. Since all the vertices of 2 have been visited, backtrack to 1. 4 is adjacent to 1, but 4 has not been visited. So, visit 4, as shown in Figure 27.9(e). Since all the neighbors of 4 have been visited, backtrack to 1. Since all the neighbors of 1 have been visited, backtrack to 0. Since all the neighbors of 0 have been visited, the search ends.

DFS time complexity

Since each edge and vertex is visited only once, the time complexity of the **dfs** method is $O(|E| + |V|)$, where $|E|$ denotes the number of edges and $|V|$ the number of vertices.

27.6.2 Implementation of Depth-First Search

The algorithm is described in Listing 27.5 using recursion. It is natural to use recursion to implement it. Alternatively, you can use a stack (see Exercise 27.1).

The **dfs(int v)** method is implemented in lines 155–184 in Listing 27.3. It returns an instance of the **Tree** class with vertex **v** as the root. The method stores the vertices searched in a list **searchOrders** (line 156), the parent of each vertex in an array **parent** (line 157), and uses the `isVisited` array to indicate whether a vertex has been visited (line 162). It invokes the helper method `dfs(v, parent, searchOrders, isVisited)` to perform a depth-first search (line 165).

In the recursive helper method, the search starts from vertex `v`. `v` is added to `searchOrders` in line 175 and is marked visited (line 176). For each unvisited neighbor of `v`, the method is recursively invoked to perform a depth-first search. When a vertex `i` is visited, the parent of `i` is stored in `parent[i]` (line 180). The method returns when all vertices are visited for a connected graph, or in a connected component.

Listing 27.6 gives a test program that displays a DFS for the graph in Figure 27.1 starting from Chicago.

LISTING 27.6 TestDFS.java

```
 1 public class TestDFS {
 2   public static void main(String[] args) {
 3     String[] vertices = {"Seattle", "San Francisco", "Los Angeles",      vertices
 4       "Denver", "Kansas City", "Chicago", "Boston", "New York",
 5       "Atlanta", "Miami", "Dallas", "Houston"};
 6
 7     int[][] edges = {                                                     edges
 8       {0, 1}, {0, 3}, {0, 5},
 9       {1, 0}, {1, 2}, {1, 3},
10       {2, 1}, {2, 3}, {2, 4}, {2, 10},
11       {3, 0}, {3, 2}, {3, 4}, {3, 5},
12       {4, 2}, {4, 3}, {4, 5}, {4, 7}, {4, 8}, {4, 10},
13       {5, 0}, {5, 3}, {5, 4}, {5, 6}, {5, 7},
14       {6, 5}, {6, 7},
15       {7, 4}, {7, 5}, {7, 6}, {7, 8},
16       {8, 4}, {8, 7}, {8, 9}, {8, 10}, {8, 11},
17       {9, 8}, {9, 11},
18       {10, 2}, {10, 4}, {10, 8}, {10, 11},
19       {11, 8}, {11, 9}, {11, 10}
20     };
21
22     Graph graph = new UnweightedGraph(edges, vertices);                  create a graph
23     AbstractGraph.Tree dfs = graph.dfs(5); // Vertex 5 is Chicago        get DFS
24
25     java.util.List<Integer> searchOrders = dfs.getSearchOrders();        get search order
26     System.out.println(dfs.getNumberOfVerticesFound() +
27       " vertices are searched in this DFS order:");
28     for (int i = 0; i < searchOrders.size(); i++)
29       System.out.print(graph.getVertex(searchOrders.get(i)) + " ");
30     System.out.println();
31
32     for (int i = 0; i < searchOrders.size(); i++)
33       if (dfs.getParent(i) != -1)
34         System.out.println("parent of " + graph.getVertex(i) +
35           " is " + graph.getVertex(dfs.getParent(i)));
36   }
37 }
```

```
12 vertices are searched in this DFS order:
Chicago Seattle San Francisco Los Angeles Denver Kansas City
New York Boston Atlanta Miami Houston Dallas

parent of Seattle is Chicago
parent of San Francisco is Seattle
parent of Los Angeles is San Francisco
```

```
parent of Denver is Los Angeles
parent of Kansas City is Denver
parent of Chicago is Chicago
parent of Boston is New York
parent of New York is Kansas City
parent of Atlanta is New York
parent of Miami is Atlanta
parent of Dallas is Houston
parent of Houston is Miami
```

The graphical illustration of the DFS starting from Chicago is shown in Figure 27.11.

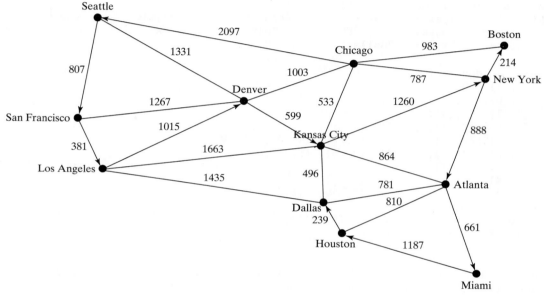

FIGURE 27.11   DFS search starts from Chicago.

27.6.3   Applications of the DFS

The depth-first search can be used to solve many problems such as follows:

- Detecting whether a graph is connected. A graph is connected if there is a path between any two vertices in the graph. (See Exercise 27.2.)

- Detecting whether there is a path between two vertices. (See Exercise 27.3.)

- Finding a path between two vertices. (See Exercise 27.3.)

- Finding all connected components. A connected component is a maximal connected subgraph in which every pair of vertices are connected by a path. (See Exercise 27.2.)

- Detecting whether there is a cycle in the graph. (See Exercise 27.4.)

- Finding a cycle in the graph. (See Exercise 27.5.)

The first four problems can be easily solved using the **dsf** method in Listing 27.3. To detect or find a cycle in the graph, you have to slightly modify the **dfs** method.

27.7 Breadth-First Search

The breadth-first traversal of a graph is like the breadth-first traversal of a tree discussed in §25.2.4, "Tree Traversal." With breadth-first traversal of a tree, the nodes are visited level by level. First the root is visited, then all the children of the root, then the grandchildren of the root from left to right, and so on. Similarly, the breadth-first search of a graph first visits a vertex, then all its adjacent vertices, then all the vertices adjacent to those vertices, and so on. To ensure that each vertex is visited only once, skip a vertex if it has already been visited.

Video Note
Breadth-first search

27.7.1 Breadth-First Search Algorithm

The algorithm for the breadth-first search starting from vertex *v* in a graph can be described in Listing 27.7.

LISTING 27.7 Breadth-first Search Algorithm

```
 1 bfs(vertex v) {
 2    create an empty queue for storing vertices to be visited;
 3    add v into the queue;
 4    mark v visited;
 5
 6    while the queue is not empty {
 7      dequeue a vertex, say u, from the queue
 8      visit u;
 9      for each neighbor w of u
10        if w has not been visited {
11          add w into the queue;
12          mark w visited;
13        }
14    }
15 }
```

create a queue
enqueue v

dequeue into u
visit u
check a neighbor w
is w visited?
enqueue w

Consider the graph in Figure 27.12(a). Suppose you start the breadth-first search from vertex 0. First visit 0, then all its visited neighbors, 1, 2, and 3, as shown in 27.13(b). Vertex 1 has three neighbors, 0, 2, and 4. Since 0 and 2 have already been visited, you will now visit just 4, as shown in Figure 27.12(c). Vertex 2 has three neighbors, 0, 1, and 3, which are all visited. Vertex 3 has three neighbors, 0, 2, and 4, which are all visited. Vertex 4 has two neighbors, 1 and 3, which are all visited. So, the search ends.

Since each edge and vertex is visited only once, the time complexity of the **bfs** method is $O(|E| + |V|)$, where $|E|$ denotes the number of edges and $|V|$ the number of vertices.

BFS time complexity

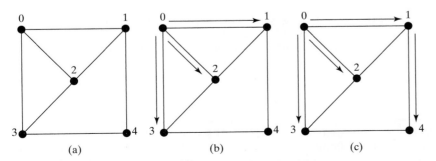

FIGURE 27.12 Breadth-first search visits a node, then its neighbors, and then its neighbors' neighbors, and so on.

27.7.2 Implementation of Breadth-First Search

The `bfs(int v)` method is defined in the `Graph` interface and implemented in the `AbstractGraph` class (lines 188–213). It returns an instance of the `Tree` class with vertex `v` as the root. The method stores the vertices searched in a list `searchOrders` (line 189), the parent of each vertex in an array `parent` (line 190), uses a linked list for a queue (line 194), and uses the `isVisited` array to indicate whether a vertex has been visited (line 196). The search starts from vertex `v`. `v` is added to the queue in line 197 and is marked visited (line 198). The method now examines each vertex `u` in the queue (line 200) and adds it to `searchOrders` (line 202). The method adds each unvisited neighbor `w` of `u` to the queue (line 205), set its parent to `u` (line 206), and mark it visited (line 207).

Listing 27.8 gives a test program that displays a BFS for the graph in Figure 27.1 starting from Chicago.

LISTING 27.8 TestBFS.java

vertices

edges

create a graph
create a bfs tree

get search order

```
1 public class TestBFS {
2   public static void main(String[] args) {
3     String[] vertices = {"Seattle", "San Francisco", "Los Angeles",
4       "Denver", "Kansas City", "Chicago", "Boston", "New York",
5       "Atlanta", "Miami", "Dallas", "Houston"};
6
7     int[][] edges = {
8       {0, 1}, {0, 3}, {0, 5},
9       {1, 0}, {1, 2}, {1, 3},
10      {2, 1}, {2, 3}, {2, 4}, {2, 10},
11      {3, 0}, {3, 2}, {3, 4}, {3, 5},
12      {4, 2}, {4, 3}, {4, 5}, {4, 7}, {4, 8}, {4, 10},
13      {5, 0}, {5, 3}, {5, 4}, {5, 6}, {5, 7},
14      {6, 5}, {6, 7},
15      {7, 4}, {7, 5}, {7, 6}, {7, 8},
16      {8, 4}, {8, 7}, {8, 9}, {8, 10}, {8, 11},
17      {9, 8}, {9, 11},
18      {10, 2}, {10, 4}, {10, 8}, {10, 11},
19      {11, 8}, {11, 9}, {11, 10}
20    };
21
22    Graph graph = new UnweightedGraph(edges, vertices);
23    AbstractGraph.Tree bfs = graph.bfs(5); // Vertex 5 is Chicago
24
25    java.util.List<Integer> searchOrders = bfs.getSearchOrders();
26    System.out.println(bfs.getNumberOfVerticesFound() +
27      " vertices are searched in this order:");
28    for (int i = 0; i < searchOrders.size(); i++)
29      System.out.println(graph.getVertex(searchOrders.get(i)));
30
31    for (int i = 0; i < searchOrders.size(); i++)
32      if (bfs.getParent(i) != -1)
33        System.out.println("parent of " + graph.getVertex(i) +
34          " is " + graph.getVertex(bfs.getParent(i)));
35  }
36 }
```

```
12 vertices are searched in this BFS order:
Chicago Seattle Denver Kansas City Boston New York San Francisco
Los Angeles Atlanta Dallas Miami Houston
```

```
parent of Seattle is Chicago
parent of San Francisco is Seattle
parent of Los Angeles is Denver
parent of Denver is Chicago
parent of Kansas City is Chicago
parent of Chicago is Seattle
parent of Boston is Chicago
parent of New York is Chicago
parent of Atlanta is Kansas City
parent of Miami is Atlanta
parent of Dallas is Kansas City
parent of Houston is Atlanta
```

The graphical illustration of the BFS starting from Chicago is shown in Figure 27.13.

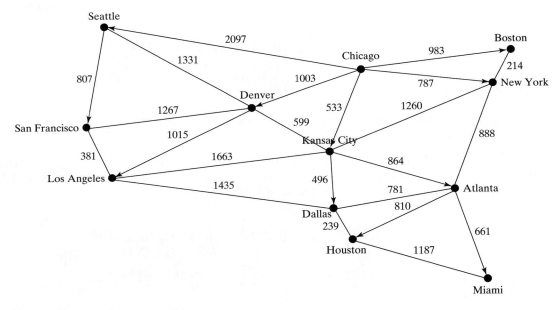

FIGURE 27.13 BFS search starts from Chicago.

27.7.3 Applications of the BFS

Many of the problems solved by the DFS can also be solved using the breadth-first search. Specifically, the BFS can be used to solve the following problems:

■ Detecting whether a graph is connected. A graph is connected if there is a path between any two vertices in the graph.

■ Detecting whether there is a path between two vertices.

■ Finding a shortest path between two vertices. You can prove that the path between the root and any node in the BFS tree is the shortest path between the root and the node (see Review Question 27.10).

■ Finding all connected components. A connected component is a maximal connected subgraph in which every pair of vertices are connected by a path.

■ Detecting whether there is a cycle in the graph. (See Exercise 27.4.)

- Finding a cycle in the graph. (See Exercise 27.5.)

- Testing whether a graph is bipartite. A graph is bipartite if the vertices of the graph can be divided into two disjoint sets such that no edges exist between vertices in the same set. (See Exercise 27.6.)

27.8 Case Study: The Nine Tail Problem

The DFS and BFS algorithms have many applications. This section applies the BFS to solve the nine tail problem.

The problem is stated as follows. Nine coins are placed in a three-by-three matrix with some face up and some face down. A legal move is to take any coin that is face up and reverse it, together with the coins adjacent to it (this does not include coins that are diagonally adjacent). Your task is to find the minimum number of moves that lead to all coins face down. For example, you start with the nine coins as shown in Figure 27.14(a). After flipping the second coin in the last row, the nine coins are now as shown in Figure 27.14(b). After flipping the second coin in the first row, the nine coins are all face down, as shown in Figure 27.14(c).

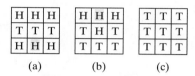

    (a)   (b)   (c)

FIGURE 27.14 The problem is solved when all coins are face down.

We will write a Java applet that lets the user set an initial state of the nine coins (see Figure 27.15(a)) and click the *Solve* button to display the solution, as shown in Figure 27.15(b). Initially, the user can click the mouse button to flip a coin.

    (a)   (b)

FIGURE 27.15 The applet solves the nine tail problem.

We will create two classes: `NineTailApp` and `NineTailModel`. The `NineTailApp` class is responsible for user interaction and for displaying the solution, and the `NineTailModel` class creates a graph for modeling this problem, as shown in Figure 27.16.

Each state of the nine coins represents a node in the graph. For example, the three states in Figure 27.14 correspond to three nodes in the graph. For convenience, we use a 3×3 matrix to represent all nodes and use `0` for head and `1` for tail. Since there are nine cells and each cell is either `0` or `1`, there are a total of 2^9(512) nodes, labeled `0`, `1`, ..., and `511`, as shown in Figure 27.17.

We assign an edge from node `u` to `v` if there is a legal move from `v` to `u`. The last node in Figure 27.17 represents the state of nine face-down coins. For convenience, we call this last node the *target node*. So the target node is labeled `511`. Suppose the initial state of the nine tail problem corresponds to the node `u`. The problem is reduced to finding a shortest path

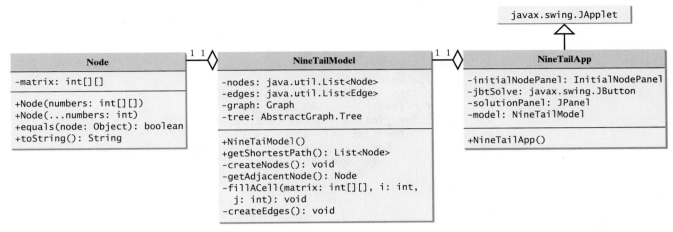

FIGURE 27.16 `NineTailModel` creates a graph for modeling the problem and `NineTailApp` presents the model in a view.

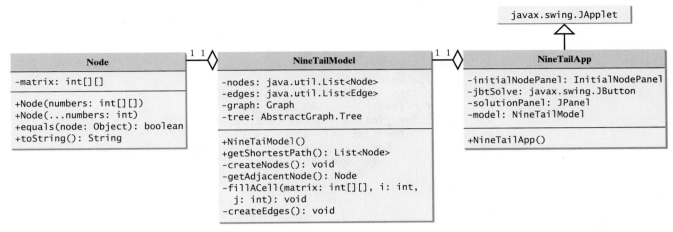

FIGURE 27.17 There are total of 512 nodes, labeled in this order as 0, 1, 2, . . . , and 511.

from node u to the target node, which is equivalent to finding a path from node u to the target node in a BFS tree rooted at the target node.

The `NineTailModel` class is given in Listing 27.9 to create the nodes and the edges, and it obtains a BFS tree rooted from the target node. The `Node` class defines a node (lines 47–92). You can create a node by passing nine numbers as a variable-length argument (line 51) or as a two dimensional array (line 61). The `createNodes()` method (lines 23–44) creates all nodes and adds them to the `nodes` list. The `createEdges()` method (lines 95–111) creates all edges and adds them to the `edges` list. For each node u, you get a new node v (line 104) by flipping a head cell and its neighboring cells in u, and add an edge (v, u) to the edges list (line 106). The `getShortestPath(Node node)` method (lines 144–153) returns a list that contains all vertices on a path from the specified node to the target node in this order.

LISTING 27.9 `NineTailModel.java`

```java
 1 import java.util.*;
 2
 3 public class NineTailModel {
 4   private ArrayList<Node> nodes = new ArrayList<Node>(); // Vertices
 5   private ArrayList<AbstractGraph.Edge> edges =
 6     new ArrayList<AbstractGraph.Edge>(); // Store edges
 7   private UnweightedGraph graph; // Define a graph
 8   private AbstractGraph.Tree tree; // Define a tree
 9
10   /** Construct a model */
11   public NineTailModel() {
12     createNodes(); // Create nodes
13     createEdges(); // Create edges
14
15     // Create a graph
16     graph = new UnweightedGraph(edges, nodes);
17
```

vertices
edges
declare a graph
declare a tree

create nodes
create edges

create graph

```
18        // Obtain a tree rooted at the target node
19        tree = graph.bfs(511);
20      }
21
22      /** Create all nodes for the graph */
23      private void createNodes() {
24        for (int k1 = 0; k1 <= 1; k1++) {
25          for (int k2 = 0; k2 <= 1; k2++) {
26            for (int k3 = 0; k3 <= 1; k3++) {
27              for (int k4 = 0; k4 <= 1; k4++) {
28                for (int k5 = 0; k5 <= 1; k5++) {
29                  for (int k6 = 0; k6 <= 1; k6++) {
30                    for (int k7 = 0; k7 <= 1; k7++) {
31                      for (int k8 = 0; k8 <= 1; k8++) {
32                        for (int k9 = 0; k9 <= 1; k9++) {
33                          nodes.add(new Node(k1, k2, k3, k4,
34                            k5, k6, k7, k8, k9));
35                        }
36                      }
37                    }
38                  }
39                }
40              }
41            }
42          }
43        }
44      }
45
46      /** Node inner class */
47      public static class Node {
48        int[][] matrix = new int[3][3];
49
50        /** Construct a Node from nine numbers */
51        Node(int ...numbers) { // Variable-length argument
52          int k = 0;
53          for (int i = 0; i < 3; i++) {
54            for (int j = 0; j < 3; j++) {
55              matrix[i][j] = numbers[k++];
56            }
57          }
58        }
59
60        /** Construct a Node from nine numbers in a 3-by-3 array */
61        Node(int[][] numbers) {
62          this.matrix = numbers;
63        }
64
65        /** Override the equals method to compare two nodes */
66        public boolean equals(Object o) {
67          int[][] anotherMatrix = ((Node)o).matrix;
68          for (int i = 0; i < 3; i++) {
69            for (int j = 0; j < 3; j++) {
70              if (matrix[i][j] != anotherMatrix[i][j]) {
71                return false;
72              }
73            }
74          }
75
76          return true; // Nodes with the same matrix values
77        }
78
```

Margin notes:

create tree

create 512 nodes

Node inner class

construct a node

construct a node

compare two nodes

string representation

```
79      /** Return a string representation for the node */
80      public String toString() {
81        StringBuilder result = new StringBuilder();
82
83        for (int i = 0; i < 3; i++) {
84          for (int j = 0; j < 3; j++) {
85            result.append(matrix[i][j] + " ");
86          }
87          result.append("\n");
88        }
89
90        return result.toString();
91      }
92    }
93
94    /** Create all edges for the graph */
95    private void createEdges() {
96      for (Node node : nodes) {
97        int u = nodes.indexOf(node); // node index
98        int[][] matrix = node.matrix; // matrix for the node
99
100       for (int i = 0; i < 3; i++) {
101         for (int j = 0; j < 3; j++) {
102           if (matrix[i][j] == 0) {
103             Node adjacentNode = getAdjacentNode(matrix, i, j);
104             int v = nodes.indexOf(adjacentNode);
105             // Add edge (v, u) for a legal move from node u to node v
106             edges.add(new AbstractGraph.Edge(v, u));
107           }
108         }
109       }
110     }
111   }
112
113   /** Get the adjacent node after flipping the cell at i and j */
114   private Node getAdjacentNode(int[][] matrix, int i, int j) {
115     int[][] matrixOfNextNode = new int[3][3];
116     for (int i1 = 0; i1 < 3; i1++) {
117       for (int j1 = 0; j1 < 3; j1++) {
118         matrixOfNextNode[i1][j1] = matrix[i1][j1];
119       }
120     }
121
122     flipACell(matrixOfNextNode, i - 1, j); // Top neighbor
123     flipACell(matrixOfNextNode, i + 1, j); // Bottom neighbor
124     flipACell(matrixOfNextNode, i, j - 1); // Left neighbor
125     flipACell(matrixOfNextNode, i, j + 1); // Right neighbor
126     flipACell(matrixOfNextNode, i, j);     // Flip self
127
128     return new Node(matrixOfNextNode);
129   }
130
131   /** Change a valid cell from 0 to 1 and 1 to 0 */
132   private void flipACell(int[][] matrix, int i, int j) {
133     if (i >= 0 && i <= 2 && j >= 0 && j <= 2) { // Within boundary
134       if (matrix[i][j] == 0) {
135         matrix[i][j] = 1; // Flip from 0 to 1
136       }
137       else {
138         matrix[i][j] = 0; // Flip from 1 to 0
139       }
```

create edges

get adjacent node

flip a cell

```
140      }
141    }
142
143    /** Return the shortest path from the specified node to the root */
144    public LinkedList<Node> getShortestPath(Node node) {
145      Iterator iterator = tree.pathIterator(nodes.indexOf(node));
146      LinkedList list = new LinkedList();
147
148      // Insert the vertices on the path starting from the root to list
149      while (iterator.hasNext())
150        list.addFirst(iterator.next());
151
152      return list;
153    }
154  }
```

shortest path

The `NineTailApp` class is given in Listing 27.10 to create the GUI. A node in the model is displayed in a `NodePanel` (lines 58–72) of nine cells. Each cell is a label, defined in the `Cell` class (lines 75–82). Each cell represents a coin. The `InitialNodePanel` class (lines 85–115) displays the starting node. The cells in `InitialNodePanel` are clickable. You can use the mouse to click on a cell in a starting node to flip a coin. The `ClickableCell` class (lines 118–132) extends `Cell` to enable the user to click on a cell.

LISTING 27.10 NineTailApp.java

```
 1  import java.awt.*;
 2  import java.awt.event.*;
 3  import javax.swing.*;
 4  import javax.swing.border.LineBorder;
 5
 6  public class NineTailApp extends JApplet {
 7    // Create the initial board
 8    private InitialNodePanel initialNodePanel = new InitialNodePanel();
 9    private JButton jbtSolve = new JButton("Solve");
10    private JButton jbtStartOver = new JButton("Start Over");
11    // solutionPanel holds a sequeunce of panels for displaying nodes
12    private JPanel solutionPanel =
13      new JPanel(new FlowLayout(FlowLayout.LEFT, 10, 10));
14    private NineTailModel model = new NineTailModel();
15
16    /** Initialize UI */
17    public NineTailApp() {
18      // Place solutionPanel in a scroll pane
19      solutionPanel.add(initialNodePanel);
20      add(new JScrollPane(solutionPanel), BorderLayout.CENTER);
21
22      // buttonPanel holds two buttons
23      JPanel buttonPanel = new JPanel();
24      buttonPanel.add(jbtSolve);
25      buttonPanel.add(jbtStartOver);
26      add(buttonPanel, BorderLayout.SOUTH);
27
28      // Listener for the Solve button
29      jbtSolve.addActionListener(new ActionListener() {
30        public void actionPerformed(ActionEvent e) {
31          solutionPanel.removeAll();
32
33          // Get a shortest path
34          java.util.List<NineTailModel.Node> list =
```

initial node panel

solution panel

model

add **initialNodePanel**
enable scrolling

button listener

remove all components

get solution

```
35          model.getShortestPath(new NineTailModel.Node(
36            initialNodePanel.getMatrix()));
37
38          // Display nodes in the shortest path
39          for (NineTailModel.Node node: list) {
40            solutionPanel.add(new NodePanel(node.matrix));
41          }
42
43          solutionPanel.revalidate();
44        }
45      });
46
47      // Listener for the Start Over button
48      jbtStartOver.addActionListener(new ActionListener() {
49        public void actionPerformed(ActionEvent e) {
50          solutionPanel.removeAll();
51          solutionPanel.add(initialNodePanel); // Display initial node
52          solutionPanel.repaint();
53        }
54      });
55    }
56
57    /** An inner class for displaying a node on a panel */
58    static class NodePanel extends JPanel {
59      public NodePanel(int[][] matrix) {
60        this.setLayout(new GridLayout(3, 3));
61        for (int i = 0; i < 3; i++) {
62          for (int j = 0; j < 3; j++) {
63            if (matrix[i][j] == 0) {
64              add(new Cell("H")); // Display H for cell 0
65            }
66            else {
67              add(new Cell("T")); // Display T for cell 1
68            }
69          }
70        }
71      }
72    }
73
74    /** An inner class for displaying a cell */
75    static class Cell extends JLabel {
76      public Cell(String s) {
77        this.setBorder(new LineBorder(Color.black, 1)); // Cell border
78        this.setHorizontalAlignment(JLabel.CENTER);
79        this.setFont(new Font("TimesRoman", Font.BOLD, 20));
80        setText(s);
81      }
82    }
83
84    /** An inner class for displaying the initial node */
85    static class InitialNodePanel extends JPanel {
86      // Each cell represents a coin, which can be flipped
87      ClickableCell[][] clickableCells = new ClickableCell[3][3];
88
89      public InitialNodePanel() {
90        this.setLayout(new GridLayout(3, 3));
91
92        for (int i = 0; i < 3; i++) {
93          for (int j = 0; j < 3; j++) {
94            add(clickableCells[i][j] = new ClickableCell("H"));
```

display solution

redisplay **solutionPanel**

button listener
remove all components

add **initialNodePanel**
redisplay **solutionPanel**

inner class **NodePanel**

add cells to panel

inner class **Cell**

set cell properties

inner class
    InitialNodePanel
clickable cells

add clickable cells

get cell values

```
 95          }
 96        }
 97      }
 98
 99      /** Get a 3-by-3 matrix from GUI cells */
100      public int[][] getMatrix() {
101        int[][] matrix = new int[3][3];
102        for (int i = 0; i < 3; i++) {
103          for (int j = 0; j < 3; j++) {
104            if (clickableCells[i][j].getText().equals("H")) {
105              matrix[i][j] = 0; // 0 is for head
106            }
107            else {
108              matrix[i][j] = 1; // 0 is for tail
109            }
110          }
111        }
112
113        return matrix;
114      }
115    }
116
117    /** An inner class for displaying a clickable cell */
118    static class ClickableCell extends Cell {
119      public ClickableCell(String s) {
120        super(s);
121        addMouseListener(new MouseAdapter() {
122          public void mouseClicked(MouseEvent e) {
123            if (getText().equals("H")) {
124              setText("T"); // Flip from H to T
125            }
126            else {
127              setText("H"); // Flip from T to H
128            }
129          }
130        });
131      }
132    }
133 }
```

inner class **ClickableCell**

mouse listener

main method omitted

27.9 Case Study: The Knight's Tour Problem

Graph algorithms are used in every day life. Delivery companies such as UPS and FedEx use graph algorithms to determine the best delivery routes for their drivers. Google uses graph algorithms to map the best travel routes among cities. The key to solve a real-world problem using graph algorithms is to model the problem into a graph problem. In the preceding section, we model the Nine Tail problem into the problem of finding a shortest path between two vertices in a graph. This section introduces how to solve the Knight's Tour problem using graph algorithms.

The Knight's Tour is a well-known classic problem. The objective is to move a knight, starting from any square on a chessboard, to every other square once. Note that the knight makes only L-shape moves (two spaces in one direction and one space in a perpendicular direction). As shown in Figure 27.18(a), the knight can move to eight squares.

Hamiltonian path
Hamiltonian cycle

There are several approaches to solve this problem. One approach is to reduce the problem into a problem for finding a Hamiltonian path in a graph. A *Hamiltonian path* in a graph is a path that visits each vertex in the graph exactly once. A *Hamiltonian cycle* is a cycle that visits each vertex in the graph exactly once and returns to the starting vertex. To solve the Knight's Tour problem, create a graph with 64 vertices representing all the squares in the chessboard. Two vertices are connected if a knight can move between the two vertices.

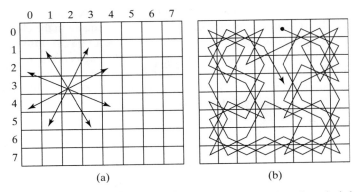

FIGURE 27.18 (a) A knight makes an L-shape move. (b) A solution for a knight to traverse all squares once.

We will write an applet that lets the user specify a starting square and displays a tour, as shown in Figure 27.19.

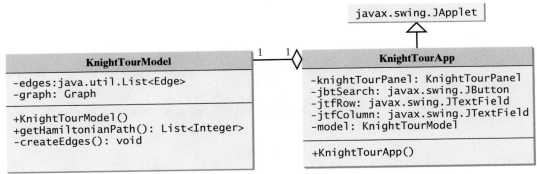

FIGURE 27.19 The applet displays a knight tour.

A graph model was built for the Nine Tail problem in the preceding section. Following the same spirit, we will build a graph model for the Knight's Tour problem. We will create two classes: **KnightTourApp** and **KnightTourModel**. The **KnightTourApp** class is responsible for user interaction and for displaying the solution and the **KnightTourModel** class creates a graph for modeling this problem, as shown in Figure 27.20.

FIGURE 27.20 **KnightTourModel** creates a graph for modeling the problem and **KnightTourApp** presents a view for the solution.

The KnightTourModel class is given in Listing 27.11 to create the vertices and the edges. For convenience, the vertices are labeled 0, 1, 2, ..., 63. A square in the chessboard at row i and column j corresponds to the vertex (i * 8 + j). The createEdges() method (lines 22–68) creates all edges and adds them to the edges list. For each node u at square (i, j), check eight possible edges from u (lines 28–66), as shown in Figure 27.21. The model builds a graph from the edges and nodes (line 13). The method getHamiltonianPath(int v) returns a Hamiltonian path from the specified starting vertex v by applying the getHamiltonianPath method on the graph.

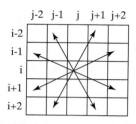

FIGURE 27.21 Each node may be connected with eight other vertices.

LISTING 27.11 KnightTourModel.java

```java
1 import java.util.*;
2
3 public class KnightTourModel {
4   private ArrayList<AbstractGraph.Edge> edges
5     = new ArrayList<AbstractGraph.Edge>(); // Store edges
6   private UnweightedGraph graph; // Define a graph
7
8   public KnightTourModel() {
9     // (u, v) is an edge if a knight can move from u and v
10    createEdges();
11
12    // Create a graph with 64 vertices labeled 0 to 63
13    graph = new UnweightedGraph(edges, 64);
14  }
15
16  /** Get a Hamiltonian path starting from vertex v */
17  public List<Integer> getHamiltonianPath(int v) {
18    return graph.getHamiltonianPath(v);
19  }
20
21  /** Create edges for the graph */
22  public void createEdges() {
23    for (int i = 0; i < 8; i++)
24      for (int j = 0; j < 8; j++) {
25        int u = i * 8 + j; // The vertex label
26
27        // Check eight possible edges from u
28        if (i - 1 >= 0 && j - 2 >= 0) {
29          int v1 = (i - 1) * 8 + (j - 2);
30          edges.add(new AbstractGraph.Edge(u, v1));
31        }
32
33        if (i - 2 >= 0 && j - 1 >= 0) {
34          int v2 = (i - 2) * 8 + (j - 1);
35          edges.add(new AbstractGraph.Edge(u, v2));
36        }
37
```

edges

declare a graph

create edges

Hamiltonian path

create edges

vertex label

find an edge

```
38        if (i - 2 >= 0 && j + 1 <= 7) {
39          int v3 = (i - 2) * 8 + (j + 1);
40          edges.add(new AbstractGraph.Edge(u, v3));
41        }
42
43        if (i - 1 >= 0 && j + 2 <= 7) {
44          int v4 = (i - 1) * 8 + (j + 2);
45          edges.add(new AbstractGraph.Edge(u, v4));
46        }
47
48        if (i + 1 <= 7 && j + 2 <= 7) {
49          int v5 = (i + 1) * 8 + (j + 2);
50          edges.add(new AbstractGraph.Edge(u, v5));
51        }
52
53        if (i + 2 <= 7 && j + 1 <= 7) {
54          int v6 = (i + 2) * 8 + (j + 1);
55          edges.add(new AbstractGraph.Edge(u, v6));
56        }
57
58        if (i + 2 <= 7 && j - 1 >= 0) {
59          int v7 = (i + 2) * 8 + (j - 1);
60          edges.add(new AbstractGraph.Edge(u, v7));
61        }
62
63        if (i + 1 <= 7 && j - 2 >= 0) {
64          int v8 = (i + 1) * 8 + (j - 2);
65          edges.add(new AbstractGraph.Edge(u, v8));
66        }
67      }
68    }
69 }
```

Now the question is how to find a Hamiltonian path in a graph? You can apply the DFS approach to search for a subpath that contains unvisited vertices as deep as you can. In the DFS, after a vertex is visited, it will never be revisited. In the process of finding a Hamiltonian path, you may have to backtrack to revisit the same vertex. The algorithm can be described in Listing 27.12.

LISTING 27.12 Hamiltonian Path Algorithm

```
 1 /** hamiltonianPath(v) is to find a Hamiltonian path for
 2  *  all unvisited vertices. */
 3 boolean hamiltonianPath(vertex v) {
 4   isVisited[v] = true;                                    visit v
 5
 6   if (all vertices are marked visited)                    all visited?
 7     return true;
 8
 9   for each neighbor u of v                                check a neighbor
10     if (u is not visited && hamiltonianPath(u)) {         recursive search
11       next[v] = u; // u is the next vertex in the path from v
12       return true;
13     }
14
15   isVisited[v] = false; // Backtrack
16   return false; // No path starting from v
17 }
```

To find a Hamiltonian path starting from v, the algorithm first visits v and then recursively finds a Hamiltonian path for the remaining unvisited vertices starting from a neighbor of v (line 10). If so, a Hamiltonian path is found; otherwise, a Hamiltonian path from v does not exist (line 16).

time complexity

Let $T(n)$ denote the time for finding a Hamiltonian path in a graph of n vertices and d be the largest degree among all vertices. Clearly,

$$T(n) = O(d \times T(n - 1)) = O(d \times d \times T(n - 2)) = O(d^n)$$

NP-complete

This is an exponential-time algorithm. Can you develop an algorithm in polynomial time? No. It has been proven that the Hamiltonian path problem is *NP-complete*, meaning that no polynomial time algorithm for such problems can be found. However, you can apply some heuristic to speed up the search. Intuitively, you should attempt to search the vertices with small degrees and leave those vertices with large degrees open, so there will be a better chance of success in the end of the search.

Add the following two methods in the **Graph** interface.

```
/** Return a Hamiltonian path from the specified vertex object
 * Return null if the graph does not contain a Hamiltonian path */
public List<Integer> getHamiltonianPath(Object vertex);

/** Return a Hamiltonian path from the specified vertex label
 * Return null if the graph does not contain a Hamiltonian path */
public List<Integer> getHamiltonianPath(int v);
```

Implement these methods in the **AbstractGraph** class as follows:

```
1    /** Return a Hamiltonian path from the specified vertex object
2     * Return null if the graph does not contain a Hamiltonian path */
3    public List<Integer> getHamiltonianPath(Object vertex) {
4      return getHamiltonianPath(getIndex(vertex));
5    }
6
7    /** Return a Hamiltonian path from the specified vertex label
8     * Return null if the graph does not contain a Hamiltonian path */
9    public List<Integer> getHamiltonianPath(int v) {
10     // A path starts from v. (i, next[i]) represents an edge in
11     // the path. isVisited[i] tracks whether i is currently in the
12     // path.
13     int[] next = new int[getSize()];
14     for (int i = 0; i < next.length; i++)
15       next[i] = -1; // Indicate no subpath from i is found yet
16
17     boolean[] isVisited = new boolean[getSize()];
18
19     // The vertices in the Hamiltonian path are stored in result
20     List<Integer> result = null;
21
22     // To speed up search, reorder the adjacency list for each
23     // vertex so that the vertices in the list are in increasing
24     // order of their degrees
25     for (int i = 0; i < getSize(); i++)
26       reorderNeigborsBasedOnDegree(neighbors[i]);
27
28     if (getHamiltonianPath(v, next, isVisited)) {
29       result = new ArrayList<Integer>(); // Create a list for path
30       int vertex = v; // Starting from v
31       while (vertex != -1) {
32         result.add(vertex); // Add vertex to the result list
33         vertex = next[vertex]; // Get the next vertex in the path
```

reorder adjacency list

recursive search

```
34       }
35     }
36
37     return result; // return null if no Hamiltionian path is found
38   }
39
40   /** Reorder the adjacency list in increasing order of degrees */
41   private void reorderNeigborsBasedOnDegree(List<Integer> list) {
42     for (int i = list.size() - 1; i >= 1; i--) {
43       // Find the maximum in the list[0..i]
44       int currentMaxDegree = getDegree(list.get(0));
45       int currentMaxIndex = 0;
46
47       for (int j = 1; j <= i; j++) {
48         if (currentMaxDegree < getDegree(list.get(j))) {
49           currentMaxDegree = getDegree(list.get(j));
50           currentMaxIndex = j;
51         }
52       }
53
54       // Swap list[i] with list[currentMaxIndex] if necessary;
55       if (currentMaxIndex != i) {
56         int temp = list.get(currentMaxIndex);
57         list.set(currentMaxIndex, list.get(i));
58         list.set(i, temp);
59       }
60     }
61   }
62
63   /** Return true if all elements in array isVisited are true */
64   private boolean allVisited(boolean[] isVisited) {
65     boolean result = true;
66
67     for (int i = 0; i < getSize(); i++)
68       result = result && isVisited[i];
69
70     return result;
71   }
72
73   /** Search for a Hamiltonian path from v */
74   private boolean getHamiltonianPath(int v, int[] next,
75       boolean[] isVisited) {
76     isVisited[v] = true; // Mark vertex v visited
77
78     if (allVisited(isVisited))
79       return true; // The path now includes all vertices, thus found
80
81     for (int i = 0; i < neighbors[v].size(); i++) {
82       int u = neighbors[v].get(i);
83       if (!isVisited[u] &&
84           getHamiltonianPath(u, next, isVisited)) {
85         next[v] = u; // Edge (v, u) is in the path
86         return true;
87       }
88     }
89
90     isVisited[v] = false; // Backtrack, v is marked unvisited now
91     return false; // No Hamiltonian path exists from vertex v
92   }
```

The `getHamiltonianPath(Object vertex)` finds a Hamiltonian path for the specified vertex object and the `getHamiltonianPath(int v)` finds a Hamiltonian path for the specified vertex label. `getIndex(vertex)` returns the label for the vertex object (line 4).

To implement the `getHamiltonianPath(int v)` method, first create an array `next`, which keeps track of the `next` vertex in the path (line 13). `next[v]` denotes the next vertex in the path after `v`. Initially, `next[i]` is set to `-1` for all vertices `i` (line 15). The `isVisited` array keeps track the vertices that are currently in the path (line 17). Initially, all elements in `isVisited` are false.

heuristics

To speed up search, the adjacency list for every vertex is reordered in increasing order of their degrees (line 26). So the vertex with small degrees will be visited earlier.

The recursive `getHamiltonianPath(v, next, isVisited)` method is invoked to find a Hamiltonian path starting from `v`. When a vertex `v` is visited, `isVisited[v]` is set to true (line 76). If all the vertices are visited, the search returns true (line 79). For each neighbor of `v`, recursively search a Hamiltonian subpath starting from a neighbor of `v` (line 84). If a subpath is found, set `u` to `next[v]` and return true (line 85). After all neighbors of `v` are searched without success, backtrack by setting `v` unvisited (line 90) and return false to indicate a path or a subpath is not found (line 91).

The `KnightTourApp` class is given in Listing 27.13 to create the GUI. An instance of the `KnightTourModel` class is created in line 7. The path of the knight tour is displayed in an instance of `PaintKnightTour` panel (line 8). The user specifies the row and column of the starting square and clicks the *Search* button to display path (line 27).

LISTING 27.13 KnightTourApp.java

```
 1  import java.util.List;
 2  import javax.swing.*;
 3  import java.awt.*;
 4  import java.awt.event.*;
 5
 6  public class KnightTourApp extends JApplet {
 7    private KnightTourModel model = new KnightTourModel();
 8    private PaintKnightTour paintKnightTour = new PaintKnightTour();
 9    private JTextField jtfRow = new JTextField(2);
10    private JTextField jtfColumn = new JTextField(2);
11    private JButton jbtSearch = new JButton("Search");
12
13    public KnightTourApp() {
14      JPanel panel = new JPanel();
15      panel.add(new JLabel("Specify a starting position, row: "));
16      panel.add(jtfRow);
17      panel.add(new JLabel("column: "));
18      panel.add(jtfColumn);
19      panel.add(jbtSearch);
20      add(paintKnightTour, BorderLayout.CENTER);
21      add(panel, BorderLayout.SOUTH);
22
23      jbtSearch.addActionListener(new ActionListener() {
24        public void actionPerformed(ActionEvent e) {
25          int position = Integer.parseInt(jtfRow.getText()) * 8 +
26            Integer.parseInt(jtfColumn.getText());
27          paintKnightTour.displayPath(
28            model.getHamiltonianPath(position));
29        }
30      });
31    }
32
```

model
paint panel
button listener
display path
find path

```
33   /** A panel to paint the chessboard and the knight tour */
34   private static class PaintKnightTour extends JPanel {
35     private List<Integer> path; // A Knight tour path
36
37     public PaintKnightTour() {
38       setBorder(BorderFactory.createLineBorder(Color.black, 1));
39     }
40
41     public void displayPath(List<Integer> path) {
42       this.path = path;
43       repaint();
44     }
45
46     protected void paintComponent(Graphics g) {
47       super.paintComponent(g);
48
49       // Display horizontal lines
50       for (int i = 0; i < 8; i++)
51         g.drawLine(0, i * getHeight() / 8,
52           getWidth(), i * getHeight() / 8);
53
54       // Display vertical lines
55       for (int i = 0; i < 8; i++)
56         g.drawLine(i * getWidth() / 8, 0,
57           (int)i * getWidth() / 8, getHeight());
58
59       if (path == null) return; // No path to be displayed yet
60
61       for (int i = 0; i < path.size() - 1; i++) {
62         int u = path.get(i);
63         int v = path.get(i + 1);
64
65         // Knight moves from u and v. Draw a line to connect u and v
66         g.drawLine((u % 8) * getWidth() / 8 + getWidth() / 16,
67           (u / 8) * getHeight() / 8 + getHeight() / 16,
68           (v % 8) * getWidth() / 8 + getWidth() / 16,
69           (v / 8) * getHeight() / 8 + getHeight() / 16);
70       }
71     }
72   }
73 }
```

display path

main method omitted

KEY TERMS

adjacency list   863
adjacent vertices   859
adjacency matrix   862
breadth-first search   879
complete graph   860
degree   860
depth-first search   874
directed graph   859
graph   859

incident edges   860
parallel edge   860
Seven Bridges of Königsberg   858
simple graph   860
spanning tree   860
weighted graph   859
undirected graph   859
unweighted graph   859

CHAPTER SUMMARY

■ A graph is a useful mathematical structure that represents relationships among entities in the real world. You learned how to model graphs using classes and interfaces, how to represent vertices and edges using arrays and linked lists, and how to implement operations for vertices and edges.

■ Graph traversal is the process of visiting each vertex in the graph exactly once. You learned two popular ways for traversing a graph: depth-first search and breadth-first search.

REVIEW QUESTIONS

Sections 27.1–27.3

27.1 What is the famous *Seven Bridges of Königsberg* problem?

27.2 What is a graph? Explain terms: undirected graph, directed graph, weighted graph, degree of a vertex, parallel edge, simple graph, and complete graph.

27.3 How do you represent vertices in a graph? How do you represent edges using an edge array? How do you represent an edge using an edge object? How do you represent edges using an adjacency matrix? How do you represent edges using adjacency lists?

27.4 Represent the following graph using an edge array, a list of edge objects, an adjacent list, an adjacent matrix, and an adjacent list, respectively.

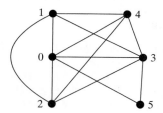

Sections 27.4–27.7

27.5 Describe the relationships among Graph, AbstractGraph, and Unweighted-Graph.

27.6 What is the return type from invoking dfs(v) and bfs(v)?

27.7 What are depth-first search and breadth-first search?

27.8 Show the DFS and BFS for the graph in Figure 27.1 starting from vertex Atlanta.

27.9 The depth-first search algorithm described in Listing 27.5 uses recursion. Alternatively you may use a stack to implement it, as shown below. Point out the error in this algorithm and give a correct algorithm.

```
// Wrong version
dfs(vertex v) {
  push v into the stack;
  mark v visited;

  while (the stack is not empty) {
    pop a vertex, say u, from the stack
    visit u;
    for each neighbor w of u
```

```
        if (w has not been visited)
          push w into the stack;
    }
  }
```

27.10 Prove that the path between the root and any node in the BFS tree is the shortest path between the root and the node.

Section 27.8

27.11 Lines 115–120 in Listing 27.9 copy array `matrix` to `matrixOfNextNode`. Will it work if you replace these lines using the following code?

```
int[][] matrixOfNextNode = (int[][])matrix.clone();
```

PROGRAMMING EXERCISES

Sections 27.6–27.7

27.1* (*Implementing DFS using a stack*) The depth-first search algorithm described in Listing 27.5 uses recursion. Implement it without using recursion.

27.2* (*Finding connected components*) Add a new method in `AbstractGraph` to find all connected components in a graph with the following header:

```
public List getConnectedComponents();
```

The method returns a `List`. Each element in the list is another list that contains all the vertices in a connected component. For example, if the graph has three connected components, the method returns a list with three elements, each of which contains the vertices in a connected component.

27.3* (*Finding paths*) Add a new method in `AbstractGraph` to find a path between two vertices with the following header:

```
public List getPath(int u, int v);
```

The method returns a `List` that contains all the vertices in a path from u to v in this order. Using the BFS approach, you can obtain a shortest path from u to v. If there is no path from u to v, the method returns `null`.

27.4* (*Detecting cycles*) Add a new method in `AbstractGraph` to determine whether there is a cycle in the graph with the following header:

```
public boolean isCyclic();
```

27.5* (*Finding a cycle*) Add a new method in `AbstractGraph` to find a cycle in the graph with the following header:

```
public List getACycle();
```

The method returns a `List` that contains all the vertices in a cycle from u to v in this order. If the graph has no cycles, the method returns `null`.

27.6** (*Testing bipartite*) Recall that a graph is bipartite if its vertices can be divided into two disjoint sets such that no edges exist between vertices in the same set. Add a new method in `AbstractGraph` to detect whether the graph is bipartite:

```
public boolean isBipartite();
```

Video Note
Nine tail problem

27.7** (*Getting bipartite sets*) Add a new method in `AbstractGraph` to return two bipartite sets if the graph is bipartite:

```
public List isBipartite();
```

The method returns a `List` that contains two sublists, each of which contains a set of vertices. If the graph is not bipartite, the method returns `null`.

27.8** (*Revising Listing 27.9, NineTailModel.java*) In Listing 27.9, a 3 × 3 array is used to store the cell values for a node. Revise the model to store cell values using integers 0, 1, 2, …, and 511. Value 0 represents the node with all heads and 511 the node with all tails, as shown below:

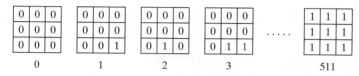

This leads to a simple implementation for the model class. For example, line 48 in Listing 27.9

```
int[][] matrix = new int[3][3];
```

can be replaced by

```
int value;
```

The `createNodes()` (line 23 in Listing 27.9) method can be implemented using just one loop as follows:

```
for (int i = 0; i < 512; i++)
```

27.9** (*Variation of the nine tail problem*) In the nine tail problem, when you flip a head, the horizontal and vertical neighboring cells are also flipped. Rewrite the program, assuming that all neighboring cells including the diagonal neighbors are also flipped.

27.10** (*4 × 4 16 tail model*) The nine tail problem in the text uses a 3 × 3 matrix. Assume that you have 16 coins placed in a 4 × 4 matrix. Create a new model class named `TailModel16`. Create an instance of the model and save the object into a file named Exercise27_10.dat.

27.11** (*4 × 4 16 tail view*) Listing 27.10, NineTailApp.java, presents a view for the nine tail problem. Revise this program for the 4 × 4 16 tail problem. Your program should read the model object created from the preceding exercise.

27.12** (*Dynamic graphs*) Add the following methods in the `Graph` interface to dynamically add and remove vertices and edges:

```
// Add a vertex to the graph and return true if succeeded
public boolean add(Object vertex)

// Remove a vertex from the graph and return true if succeeded
public boolean remove(Object vertex)

// Add an edge to the graph and return true if succeeded
public boolean add(Edge edge)

// Remove an edge from the graph and return true if succeeded
public boolean remove(Edge edge)
```

For simplicity, assume the vertices are labeled with integers 1, 2, …, and so on.

27.13**   (*Induced subgraph*) Given an undirected graph G = (V, E) and an integer k, find an induced subgraph H of G of maximum size such that all vertices of H have degree $>= k$, or conclude that no such induced subgraph exists. Implement the method with the following header:

```
public static Graph maxInducedSubgraph(Graph edge, int k)
```

The method returns `null` if such subgraph does not exist.

(*Hint*: An intuitive approach is to remove vertices whose degree is less than k. As vertices are removed with their adjacent edges, the degrees of other vertices may be reduced. Continue the process until no vertices can be removed, or all the vertices are removed.)

27.14***   (*Hamiltonian cycle*) Add the following methods in the `Graph` interface and implement them in the `AbstractGraph` class:

```
/** Return a Hamiltonian cycle
  * Return null if the graph contain no a Hamiltonian cycle */
public List<Integer> getHamiltonianCycle()
```

27.15***   (*Knight's Tour cycle*) Rewrite Listing 27.13, KnightTourApp.java, to find a knight's tour that visits each square in the chessboard and return to the starting square. Reduce the Knight's Tour cycle problem to the problem of finding a Hamiltonian cycle.

CHAPTER 28

WEIGHTED GRAPHS APPLICATIONS

Objectives

- To represent weighted edges using adjacency matrices and priority queues (§28.2).

- To model weighted graphs using the `WeightedGraph` class that extends the `AbstractGraph` class (§28.3).

- To design and implement the algorithm for finding a minimum spanning tree (§28.4).

- To define the `MST` class that extends the `Tree` class (§28.4).

- To design and implement the algorithm for finding single-source shortest paths (§28.5).

- To define the `ShortestPathTree` class that extends the `Tree` class (§28.5).

- To solve the weighted nine tail problem using the shortest-path algorithm (§28.6).

28.1 Introduction

The preceding chapter introduced the concept of graphs. You learned how to represent edges using edge arrays, edge lists, adjacency matrices, and adjacency lists, and how to model a graph using the `Graph` interface, the `AbstractGraph` class, and the `UnweightedGraph` class. The preceding chapter also introduced two important techniques for traversing graphs: depth-first search and breadth-first search, and applied traversal to solve practical problems. This chapter will introduce weighted graphs. You will learn the algorithm for finding a minimum spanning tree in §28.4 and the algorithm for finding shortest paths in §28.5.

Video Note

Representation of weighted graphs

28.2 Representing Weighted Graphs

There are two types of weighted graphs: vertex weighted and edge weighted. In a vertex-weighted graph, each vertex is assigned a weight. In an edge-weighted graph, each edge is assigned a weight. Of the two types, edge-weighted graphs have more applications. This chapter considers edge-weighted graphs.

Weighted graphs can be represented in the same way as unweighted graphs except that you have to represent the weights on the edges. As with unweighted graphs, the vertices in weighted graphs can be stored in an array. This section introduces three representations for the edges in weighted graphs.

28.2.1 Representing Weighted Edges: Edge Array

Weighted edges can be represented using a two-dimensional array. For example, you can store all the edges in the graph in Figure 28.1 using the following array:

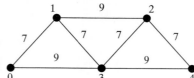

```
int[][] edges = {{0, 1, 7}, {0, 3, 9},
    {1, 0, 7}, {1, 2, 9}, {1, 3, 7},
    {2, 1, 9}, {2, 3, 7}, {2, 4, 7},
    {3, 0, 9}, {3, 1, 7}, {3, 2, 7}, {3, 4, 9},
    {4, 2, 7}, {4, 3, 9}
};
```

FIGURE 28.1 Each edge is assigned a weight on an edge-weighted graph.

Note

integer weights

For simplicity, we assume that the *weights are integers*. Weights can be of any type. In that case, you may use a two-dimensional array of the `Object` type as follows:

```
Object[][] edges = {
  {new Integer(0), new Integer(1), new SomeTypeForWeight(7)},
```

```
      {new Integer(0), new Integer(3), new SomeTypeForWeight(9)},
      ...
   };
```

28.2.2 Weighted Adjacency Matrices

Assume that the graph has n vertices. You can use a two-dimensional $n \times n$ matrix, say `weights`, to represent the weights on edges. `weights[i][j]` represents the weight on edge (i, j). If vertices i and j are not connected, `weights[i][j]` is `null`. For example, the weights in the graph in Figure 28.1 can be represented using an adjacency matrix as follows:

```
Integer[][] adjacencyMatrix = {
   {null, 7, null, 9, null },
   {7, null, 9, 7, null },
   {0, 9, null, 7, 7},
   {9, 7, 7, null, 9},
   {null, null, 7, 9, null}
};
```

28.2.3 Priority Adjacency Lists

Another way to represent the edges is to define edges as objects. The `AbstractGraph.Edge` class was defined to represent edges in unweighted graphs. For weighted edges, we define the `WeightedEdge` class as shown in Listing 28.1.

LISTING 28.1 WeightedEdge.java

```
 1 public class WeightedEdge extends AbstractGraph.Edge
 2     implements Comparable<WeightedEdge> {
 3   public int weight; // The weight on edge (u, v)                    edge weight
 4
 5   /** Create a weighted edge on (u, v) */
 6   public WeightedEdge(int u, int v, int weight) {                    constructor
 7     super(u, v);
 8     this.weight = weight;
 9   }
10
11   /** Compare two edges on weights */
12   public int compareTo(WeightedEdge edge) {                          compare edges
13     if (weight > edge.weight) {
14       return 1;
15     }
16     else if (weight == edge.weight) {
17       return 0;
18     }
19     else {
20       return -1;
21     }
22   }
23 }
```

`AbstractGraph.Edge` is an inner class defined in the `AbstractGraph` class. It represents an edge from vertex `u` to `v`. `WeightedEdge` extends `AbstractGraph.Edge` with a new property `weight`.

To create an `Edge` object, use `new Edge(i, j, w)`, where `w` is the weight on edge (`i`, `j`). Often it is desirable to store a vertex's adjacent edges in a priority queue so that you can remove the edges in increasing order of their weights. For this reason, the `Edge` class implements the `Comparable` interface.

For unweighted graphs, we use adjacency lists to represent edges. For weighted graphs, we still use adjacency lists, but the lists are priority queues. For example, the adjacency lists for the vertices in the graph in Figure 28.1 can be represented as follows:

```
java.util.PriorityQueue<Edge>[5] queues =
    new java.util.PriorityQueue<Edge>();
```

queues[0]	WeightedEdge(0, 1, 7)	WeightedEdge(0, 3, 9)		
queues[1]	WeightedEdge(1, 0, 7)	WeightedEdge(1, 3, 7)	WeightedEdge(1, 2, 9)	
queues[2]	WeightedEdge(2, 3, 7)	WeightedEdge(2, 4, 7)	WeightedEdge(2, 1, 9)	
queues[3]	WeightedEdge(3, 1, 7)	WeightedEdge(3, 2, 7)	WeightedEdge(3, 0, 9)	WeightedEdge(3, 4, 9)
queues[4]	WeightedEdge(4, 2, 7)	WeightedEdge(4, 3, 9)		

`queues[i]` stores all edges adjacent to vertex `i`.

28.3 The **WeightedGraph** Class

The preceding chapter designed the `Graph` interface, the `AbstractGraph` class, and the `UnweightedGraph` class for modeling graphs. Following this pattern, we design `WeightedGraph` as a subclass of `AbstractGraph`, as shown in Figure 28.2.

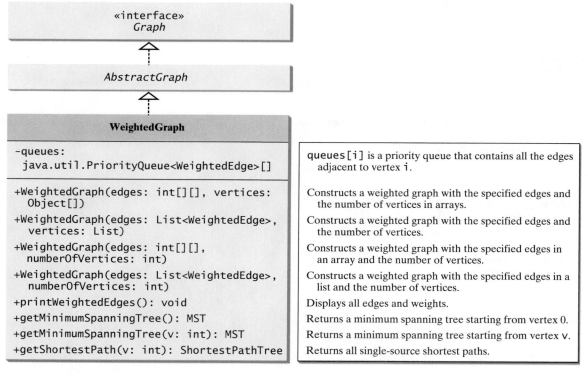

FIGURE 28.2 `WeightedGraph` extends `AbstractGraph`.

`WeightedGraph` simply extends `AbstractGraph` with four constructors for creating concrete weighted `Graph` instances. `WeightedGraph` inherits all methods from `AbstractGraph` and also introduces the new methods for obtaining minimum spanning trees and for finding single-source all shortest paths. Minimum spanning trees and shortest paths will be introduced in §28.4 and §28.5, respectively.

Listing 28.2 implements `WeightedGraph`. Priority adjacency lists (line 5) are used internally to store adjacent edges for a vertex. When a `WeightedGraph` is constructed, its priority adjacency lists are created (lines 11, 18, 25, 33, and 36). The methods `getMinimum-SpanningTree()` (lines 83–131) and `getShortestPaths()` (lines 164–217) will be introduced in the upcoming sections.

LISTING 28.2 WeightedGraph.java

```java
1  import java.util.*;
2
3  public class WeightedGraph extends AbstractGraph {
4    // Priority adjacency lists
5    private PriorityQueue<WeightedEdge>[] queues;          priority queue
6
7    /** Construct a WeightedGraph with specified edges and vertice in
8     *  arrays */
9    public WeightedGraph(int[][] edges, Object[] vertices) {    constructor
10     super(edges, vertices);                                superclass constructor
11     createQueues(edges, vertices.length);                  create priority queues
12   }
13
14   /** Construct a WeightedGraph with specified edges in
15    *  an array and the number of vertices */
16   public WeightedGraph(int[][] edges, int numberOfVertices) {    constructor
17     super(edges, numberOfVertices);
18     createQueues(edges, numberOfVertices);
19   }
20
21   /** Construct a WeightedGraph with specified edges and vertices in
22    *  lists */
23   public WeightedGraph(List<WeightedEdge> edges, List vertices) {    constructor
24     super((List)edges, vertices);
25     createQueues(edges, vertices.size());
26   }
27
28   /** Construct a WeightedGraph with specified edges in
29    *  a list and the number of vertices */
30   public WeightedGraph(List<WeightedEdge> edges,                constructor
31       int numberOfVertices) {
32     super((List)edges, numberOfVertices);
33     createQueues(edges, numberOfVertices);
34   }
35
36   /** Create priority adjacency lists from edge arrays */
37   public void createQueues(int[][] edges, int numberOfVertices) {   create priority queues
38     queues = new java.util.PriorityQueue[numberOfVertices];
39     for (int i = 0; i < queues.length; i++) {
40       queues[i] = new java.util.PriorityQueue(); // Create a queue    create queues
41     }
42
43     for (int i = 0; i < edges.length; i++) {
44       int u = edges[i][0];
45       int v = edges[i][1];
46       int weight = edges[i][2];
47       // Insert an edge into the queue
48       queues[u].offer(new WeightedEdge(u, v, weight));            fill queues
49     }
50   }
51
52   /** Create priority adjacency lists from edge lists */
```

```
53    public void createQueues(List<WeightedEdge> edges,
54        int numberOfVertices) {
55      queues = new PriorityQueue[numberOfVertices];
56      for (int i = 0; i < queues.length; i++) {
57        queues[i] = new java.util.PriorityQueue(); // Create a queue
58      }
59
60      for (WeightedEdge edge: edges) {
61        queues[edge.u].offer(edge); // Insert an edge into the queue
62      }
63    }
64
65    /** Display edges with weights */
66    public void printWeightedEdges() {
67      for (int i = 0; i < queues.length; i++) {
68        System.out.print("Vertex " + i + ": ");
69        for (WeightedEdge edge : queues[i]) {
70          System.out.print("(" + edge.u +
71            ", " + edge.v + ", " + edge.weight + ") ");
72        }
73        System.out.println();
74      }
75    }
76
77    /** Get a minimum spanning tree rooted at vertex 0 */
78    public MST getMinimumSpanningTree() {
79      return getMinimumSpanningTree(0);
80    }
81
82    /** Get a minimum spanning tree rooted at a specified vertex */
83    public MST getMinimumSpanningTree(int startingVertex) {
84      Set<Integer> T = new HashSet<Integer>();
85      // T initially contains the startingVertex;
86      T.add(startingVertex);
87
88      int numberOfVertices = vertices.length; // Number of vertices
89      int[] parent = new int[numberOfVertices]; // Parent of a vertex
90      // Initially set the parent of all vertices to -1
91      for (int i = 0; i < parent.length; i++)
92        parent[i] = -1;
93      int totalWeight = 0; // Total weight of the tree thus far
94
95      // Clone the priority queue, so to keep the original queue intact
96      PriorityQueue<WeightedEdge>[] queues = deepClone(this.queues);
97
98      // All vertices are found?
99      while (T.size() < numberOfVertices) {
100       // Search for the vertex with the smallest edge adjacent to
101       // a vertex in T
102       int v = -1;
103       double smallestWeight = Double.MAX_VALUE;
104       for (int u : T) {
105         while (!queues[u].isEmpty() &&
106           T.contains(queues[u].peek().v)) {
107           // Remove the edge from queues[u] if the adjacent
108           // vertex of u is already in T
109           queues[u].remove();
110         }
111
```

Margin annotations (left column):
- create priority queues (line 53)
- create queues (line 57)
- fill queues (line 61)
- print edges (line 66)
- minimum spanning tree / start from vertex 0 (line 78)
- minimum spanning tree (line 83)
- vertices in tree (line 84)
- add to tree (line 86)
- number of vertices (line 88)
- parent array (line 89)
- initialize parent (line 92)
- total weight (line 93)
- deep clone / a copy of queues (line 96)
- more vertices? (line 99)
- every u in tree (line 104)
- remove visited vertex (line 109)

```
112      if (queues[u].isEmpty()) {                              queues[u] is empty
113        continue; // Consider the next vertex in T
114      }
115
116      // Current smallest weight on an edge adjacent to u
117      WeightedEdge edge = queues[u].peek();                   smallest edge to u
118      if (edge.weight < smallestWeight) {
119        v = edge.v;
120        smallestWeight = edge.weight;                         update smallestWeight
121        // If v is added to the tree, u will be its parent
122        parent[v] = u;
123      }
124    } // End of for
125
126    T.add(v); // Add a new vertex to the tree                 add to tree
127    totalWeight += smallestWeight;                            update totalWeight
128  } // End of while
129
130  return new MST(startingVertex, parent, totalWeight);
131 }
132
133 /** Clone an array of queues */
134 private PriorityQueue<WeightedEdge>[] deepClone(            clone queue
135   PriorityQueue<WeightedEdge>[] queues) {
136   PriorityQueue<WeightedEdge> [] copiedQueues =
137     new PriorityQueue[queues.length];
138
139   for (int i = 0; i < queues.length; i++) {
140     copiedQueues[i] = new PriorityQueue<WeightedEdge>();
141     for (WeightedEdge e : queues[i]) {
142       copiedQueues[i].add(e);                               clone every element
143     }
144   }
145
146   return copiedQueues;
147 }
148
149 /** MST is an inner class in WeightedGraph */
150 public class MST extends Tree {                             MST inner class
151   private int totalWeight; // Total weight of all edges in the tree   total weight in tree
152
153   public MST(int root, int[] parent, int totalWeight) {
154     super(root, parent);
155     this.totalWeight = totalWeight;
156   }
157
158   public int getTotalWeight() {
159     return totalWeight;
160   }
161 }
162
163 /** Find single-source shortest paths */
164 public ShortestPathTree getShortestPath(int sourceVertex) {
165   // T stores the vertices whose path found so far
166   Set<Integer> T = new HashSet<Integer>();                  vertices found
167   // T initially contains the sourceVertex;
168   T.add(sourceVertex);                                      add source
169
170   // vertices is defined in AbstractGraph
171   int numberOfVertices = vertices.length;                   number of vertices
```

```
172
173        // parent[v] stores the previous vertex of v in the path
174        int[] parent = new int[numberOfVertices];
175        parent[sourceVertex] = -1; // The parent of source is set to -1
176
177        // costs[v] stores the cost of the path from v to the source
178        int[] costs = new int[numberOfVertices];
179        for (int i = 0; i < costs.length; i++) {
180          costs[i] = Integer.MAX_VALUE; // Initial cost set to infinity
181        }
182        costs[sourceVertex] = 0; // Cost of source is 0
183
184        // Get a copy of queues
185        PriorityQueue<WeightedEdge> [] queues = deepClone(this.queues);
186
187        // Expand verticesFound
188        while (T.size() < numberOfVertices) {
189          int v = -1; // Vertex to be determined
190          int smallestCost = Integer.MAX_VALUE; // Set to infinity
191          for (int u : T) {
192            while (!queues[u].isEmpty() &&
193              T.contains(queues[u].peek().v)) {
194              queues[u].remove(); // Remove the vertex in verticesFound
195            }
196
197            if (queues[u].isEmpty()) {
198              // All vertices adjacent to u are in verticesFound
199              continue;
200            }
201
202            WeightedEdge e = queues[u].peek();
203            if (costs[u] + e.weight < smallestCost) {
204              v = e.v;
205              smallestCost = costs[u] + e.weight;
206              // If v is added to the tree, u will be its parent
207              parent[v] = u;
208            }
209          } // End of for
210
211          T.add(v); // Add a new vertex to the set
212          costs[v] = smallestCost;
213        } // End of while
214
215        // Create a ShortestPathTree
216        return new ShortestPathTree(sourceVertex, parent, costs);
217      }
218
219      /** ShortestPathTree is an inner class in WeightedGraph */
220      public class ShortestPathTree extends Tree {
221        private int[] costs; // costs[v] is the cost from v to source
222
223        /** Construct a path */
224        public ShortestPathTree(int source, int[] parent, int[] costs) {
225          super(source, parent);
226          this.costs = costs;
227        }
228
229        /** Return the cost for a path from the root to vertex v */
230        public int getCost(int v) {
```

Margin notes:

parent array (174)
parent of root (175)
costs array (178)
source cost (182)
a copy of queues (185)
more vertices left? (188)
determine one (189)
remove visited vertex (194)
queues[u] is empty (199)
smallest edge to u (204)
update **smallestCost** (205)
v now found (207)
add to T (211)
create a path (216)
costs (221)
constructor (224)
get cost (230)

```
231        return costs[v];
232      }
233
234      /** Print paths from all vertices to the source */
235      public void printAllPaths() {                                    print all paths
236        System.out.println("All shortest paths from " +
237          vertices[getRoot()] + " are:");
238        for (int i = 0; i < costs.length; i++) {
239          printPath(i); // Print a path from i to the source
240          System.out.println("(cost: " + costs[i] + ")"); // Path cost
241        }
242      }
243    }
244 }
```

When you construct a WeightedGraph, its superclass's constructor is invoked (lines 10, 17, 24, 32) to initialize the properties **vertices** and **neighbors** in AbstractGraph. Additionally, priority queues are created for instances of WeightedGraph.

Listing 28.3 gives a test program that creates a graph for the one in Figure 27.1 and another graph for the one in Figure 28.1.

LISTING 28.3 TestWeightedGraph.java

```
1 public class TestWeightedGraph {
2   public static void main(String[] args) {
3     String[] vertices = {"Seattle", "San Francisco", "Los Angeles",    vertices
4       "Denver", "Kansas City", "Chicago", "Boston", "New York",
5       "Atlanta", "Miami", "Dallas", "Houston"};
6
7     int[][] edges = {                                                   edges
8       {0, 1, 807}, {0, 3, 1331}, {0, 5, 2097},
9       {1, 0, 807}, {1, 2, 381}, {1, 3, 1267},
10      {2, 1, 381}, {2, 3, 1015}, {2, 4, 1663}, {2, 10, 1435},
11      {3, 0, 1331}, {3, 2, 1015}, {3, 4, 599}, {3, 5, 1003},
12      {4, 2, 1663}, {4, 3, 599}, {4, 5, 533}, {4, 7, 1260},
13        {4, 8, 864}, {4, 10, 496},
14      {5, 0, 2097}, {5, 3, 1003}, {5, 4, 533},
15        {5, 6, 983}, {5, 7, 787},
16      {6, 5, 983}, {6, 7, 214},
17      {7, 4, 1260}, {7, 5, 787},
18      {8, 4, 864}, {8, 7, 888}, {8, 9, 661},
19        {8, 10, 781}, {8, 11, 810},
20      {9, 8, 661}, {9, 11, 1187},
21      {10, 2, 1435}, {10, 4, 496}, {10, 8, 781}, {10, 11, 239},
22      {11, 8, 810}, {11, 9, 1187}, {11, 10, 239}
23    };
24
25    WeightedGraph graph1 = new WeightedGraph(edges, vertices);         create graph
26    System.out.println("The edges for graph1:");
27    graph1.printWeightedEdges();                                       print edges
28
29    edges = new int[][]{                                              edges
30      {0, 1, 7}, {0, 3, 9},
31      {1, 0, 7}, {1, 2, 9}, {1, 3, 7},
32      {2, 1, 9}, {2, 3, 7}, {2, 4, 7},
33      {3, 0, 9}, {3, 1, 7}, {3, 2, 7}, {3, 4, 9},
34      {4, 2, 7}, {4, 3, 9}
35    };
```

create graph

print edges

```
36     WeightedGraph graph2 = new WeightedGraph(edges, 5);
37     System.out.println("The edges for graph2:");
38     graph2.printWeightedEdges();
39 }
40 }
```

```
The edges for graph1:
Vertex 0: (0, 1, 807) (0, 3, 1331) (0, 5, 2097)
Vertex 1: (1, 2, 381) (1, 0, 807) (1, 3, 1267)
Vertex 2: (2, 1, 381) (2, 3, 1015) (2, 4, 1663) (2, 10, 1435)
Vertex 3: (3, 4, 599) (3, 5, 1003) (3, 2, 1015) (3, 0, 1331)
Vertex 4: (4, 10, 496) (4, 8, 864) (4, 5, 533) (4, 2, 1663)
          (4, 7, 1260) (4, 3, 599)
Vertex 5: (5, 4, 533) (5, 7, 787) (5, 3, 1003) (5, 0, 2097)
          (5, 6, 983)
Vertex 6: (6, 7, 214) (6, 5, 983)
Vertex 7: (7, 5, 787) (7, 4, 1260)
Vertex 8: (8, 9, 661) (8, 10, 781) (8, 4, 864) (8, 7, 888)
          (8, 11, 810)
Vertex 9: (9, 8, 661) (9, 11, 1187)
Vertex 10: (10, 11, 239) (10, 4, 496) (10, 8, 781) (10, 2, 1435)
Vertex 11: (11, 10, 239) (11, 9, 1187) (11, 8, 810)

The edges for graph2:
Vertex 0: (0, 1, 7) (0, 3, 9)
Vertex 1: (1, 0, 7) (1, 2, 9) (1, 3, 7)
Vertex 2: (2, 3, 7) (2, 1, 9) (2, 4, 7)
Vertex 3: (3, 1, 7) (3, 0, 9) (3, 2, 7) (3, 4, 9)
Vertex 4: (4, 2, 7) (4, 3, 9)
```

The program creates `graph1` for the graph in Figure 27.1 in lines 3–25. The vertices for `graph1` are defined in lines 3–5. The edges for `graph1` are defined in lines 7–23. The edges are represented using a two-dimensional array. For each row `i` in the array, `edges[i][0]` and `edges[i][1]` indicate that there is an edge from vertex `edges[i][0]` to vertex `edges[i][1]` and the weight for the edge is `edges[i][2]`. For example, the first row {0, 1, 807} represents the edge from vertex 0 (`edges[0][0]`) to vertex 1 (`edges[0][1]`) with weight 807 (`edges[0][2]`). The row {0, 5, 2097} represents the edge from vertex 0 (`edges[2][0]`) to vertex 5 (`edges[2][1]`) with weight 2097 (`edges[2][2]`). Line 27 invokes the `printWeightedEdges()` method on `graph1` to display all edges in `graph1`.

The program creates the edges for `graph2` for the graph in Figure 28.1 in lines 29–36. Line 38 invokes the `printWeightedEdges()` method on `graph2` to display all edges in `graph2`.

Traversing priority queue

Note

The adjacent edges for each vertex are stored in a priority queue. When you remove an edge from the queue, the one with the smallest weight is always removed. However, if you traverse the edges in the queue, the edges are not necessarily in increasing order of weights.

Video Note

Minimum spanning trees

28.4 Minimum Spanning Trees

A graph may have many spanning trees. Suppose that the edges are weighted. A minimum spanning tree is a spanning tree with the minimum total weights. For example, the trees in Figures 28.3(b), 28.3(c), 28.3(d) are spanning trees for the graph in Figure 28.3(a). The trees in Figures 28.3(c) and 28.3(d) are minimum spanning trees.

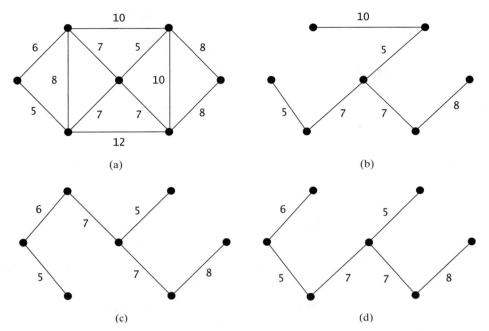

FIGURE 28.3 The trees in (c) and (d) are minimum spanning trees of the graph in (a).

The problem of finding a minimum spanning tree has many applications. Consider a company with branches in many cities. The company wants to lease telephone lines to connect all branches together. The phone company charges different amounts of money to connect different pairs of cities. There are many ways to connect all branches together. The cheapest way is to find a spanning tree with the minimum total rates.

28.4.1 Minimum Spanning Tree Algorithms

How do you find a minimum spanning tree? There are several well-known algorithms for doing so. This section introduces Prim's algorithm. Prim's algorithm starts with a spanning tree T that contains an arbitrary vertex. The algorithm expands the tree by adding a vertex with the smallest edge incident to a vertex already in the tree. The algorithm is described in Listing 28.4.

Prim's algorithm

LISTING 28.4 Prim's Minimum Spanning Tree Algorithm

```
 1 minimumSpanningTree() {
 2   Let V denote the set of vertices in the graph;
 3   Let T be a set for the vertices in the spanning tree;
 4   Initially, add the starting vertex to T;
 5
 6   while (size of T < n) {
 7     find u in T and v in V - T with the smallest weight
 8       on the edge (u, v), as shown in Figure 28.4;
 9     add v to T;
10   }
11 }
```

add initial vertex

more vertices?
find a vertex

add to tree

The algorithm starts by adding the starting vertex into T. It then continuously adds a vertex (say v) from V − T into T. v is the vertex that is adjacent to a vertex in T with the smallest weight on the edge. For example, there are five edges connecting vertices in T and V − T, as shown in Figure 28.4, (u, v) is the one with the smallest weight.

Vertices already in
the spanning tree

V – T

Vertices not currently in
the spanning tree

T

v

u

FIGURE 28.4 Find a vertex *u* in *T* that connects a vertex *v* in *V − T* with the smallest weight.

example

Consider the graph in Figure 28.3(a). The algorithm adds the vertices to T in this order:

1. Add vertex 0 to T.

2. Add vertex 5 to T, since Edge(5, 1, 5) has the smallest weight, as shown in Figure 28.5(a).

3. Add vertex 1 to T, since Edge(1, 0, 6) has the smallest weight among all edges adjacent to the vertices in T, as shown in Figure 28.5(b).

4. Add vertex 6 to T, since Edge(6, 1, 7) has the smallest weight among all edges adjacent to the vertices in T, as shown in Figure 28.5(c).

5. Add vertex 2 to T, since Edge(2, 6, 5) has the smallest weight among all edges adjacent to the vertices in T, as shown in Figure 28.5(d).

6. Add vertex 4 to T, since Edge(4, 6, 7) has the smallest weight among all edges adjacent to the vertices in T, as shown in Figure 28.5(e).

7. Add vertex 3 to T, since Edge(3, 2, 8) has the smallest weight among all edges adjacent to the vertices in T, as shown in Figure 28.5(f).

Note

unique tree?

A minimum spanning tree is not unique. For example, both (c) and (d) in Figure 28.3 are minimum spanning trees for the graph in Figure 28.1(a). However, if the weights are distinct, the graph has a unique minimum spanning tree.

Note

connected and undirected

Assume that the graph is connected and undirected. If a graph is not connected or directed, the program may not work. You may modify the program to find a spanning forest for any undirected graph.

28.4.2 Implementation of the MST Algorithm

getMinimumSpanning-
Tree()

The getMinimumSpanningTree(int v) method is defined in the WeightedGraph class. It returns an instance of the MST class, as shown in Figure 28.2. The MST class is defined as an inner class in the WeightedGraph class, which extends the Tree class, as shown in Figure 28.6. The Tree class was shown in Figure 27.9. The MST class was implemented in lines 152–161 in Listing 28.2.

The getMinimumSpanningTree method was implemented in lines 83–131 in Listing 28.2. The getMinimumSpanningTree(int startingVertex) method first adds starting-Vertex to T (line 86). T is a set that stores the vertices currently in the spanning tree (line

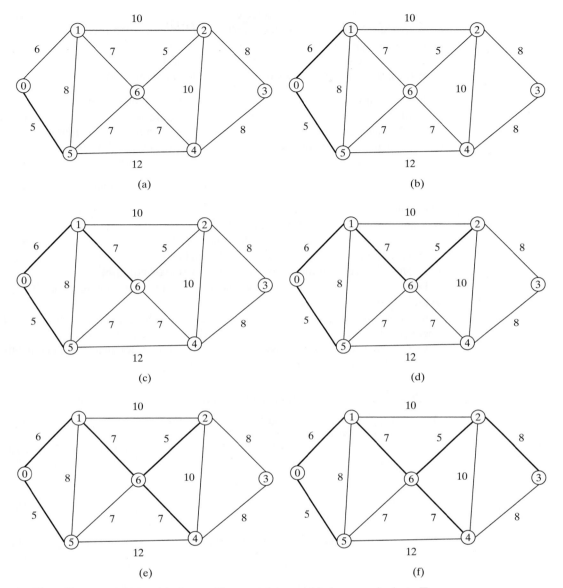

FIGURE 28.5 The adjacent vertices with the smallest weight are added successively to T.

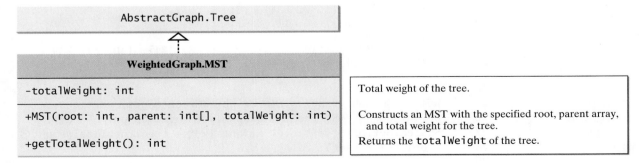

FIGURE 28.6 The MST class extends the Tree class.

84). `vertices` is defined as a protected data field in the `AbstractGraph` class, which is an array that stores all vertices in the graph. `vertices.length` returns the number of the vertices in the graph (line 88).

A vertex is added to T if it is adjacent to one of the vertices in T with the smallest weight (line 126). Such a vertex is found using the following procedure:

1. For each vertex u in T, find its neighbor with the smallest weight to u. All the neighbors of u are stored in `queues[u]`. `queues[u].peek()` (line 106) returns the adjacent edge with the smallest weight. If a neighbor is already in T, remove it (line 109). To keep the original queues intact, a copy is created in line 96. After lines 105–114, `queues[u].peek()` (line 118) returns the vertex with the smallest weight to u.

2. Compare all these neighbors and find the one with the smallest weight (lines 118–123).

After a new vertex is added to T (line 129), `totalWeight` is updated (line 127). Once all vertices are added to T, an instance of `MST` is created (line 130).

The `MST` class extends the `Tree` class (line 151). To create an instance of `MST`, pass `root`, `parent`, and `totalWeight` (lines 131). The data fields `root` and `parent` are defined in the `Tree` class, which is an inner class defined in `AbstractGraph`.

For each vertex, the program constructs a priority queue for its adjacent edges. It takes $O(\log|V|)$ time to insert an edge into a priority queue and the same time to remove an edge from the priority queue. So the overall time complexity for the program is $O(|E|\log|V|)$, where $|E|$ denotes the number of edges and $|V|$ the number of vertices.

Listing 28.5 gives a test program that displays minimum spanning trees for the graph in Figure 27.1 and the graph in Figure 28.1, respectively.

LISTING 28.5 TestMinimumSpanningTree.java

```java
public class TestMinimumSpanningTree {
  public static void main(String[] args) {
    String[] vertices = {"Seattle", "San Francisco", "Los Angeles",
      "Denver", "Kansas City", "Chicago", "Boston", "New York",
      "Atlanta", "Miami", "Dallas", "Houston"};

    int[][] edges = {
      {0, 1, 807}, {0, 3, 1331}, {0, 5, 2097},
      {1, 0, 807}, {1, 2, 381}, {1, 3, 1267},
      {2, 1, 381}, {2, 3, 1015}, {2, 4, 1663}, {2, 10, 1435},
      {3, 0, 1331}, {3, 2, 1015}, {3, 4, 599}, {3, 5, 1003},
      {4, 2, 1663}, {4, 3, 599}, {4, 5, 533}, {4, 7, 1260},
        {4, 8, 864}, {4, 10, 496},
      {5, 0, 2097}, {5, 3, 1003}, {5, 4, 533},
        {5, 6, 983}, {5, 7, 787},
      {6, 5, 983}, {6, 7, 214},
      {7, 4, 1260}, {7, 5, 787}, {7, 6, 214},
      {8, 4, 864}, {8, 7, 888}, {8, 9, 661},
        {8, 10, 781}, {8, 11, 810},
      {9, 8, 661}, {9, 11, 1187},
      {10, 2, 1435}, {10, 4, 496}, {10, 8, 781}, {10, 11, 239},
      {11, 8, 810}, {11, 9, 1187}, {11, 10, 239}
    };

    WeightedGraph graph1 = new WeightedGraph(edges, vertices);
    WeightedGraph.MST tree1 = graph1.getMinimumSpanningTree();
    System.out.println("Total weight is " + tree1.getTotalWeight());
    tree1.printTree();
```

Margin notes:
- time complexity
- create vertices
- create edges
- create graph1
- MST for graph1
- total weight
- print tree

```
30      edges = new int[][]{                                          create edges
31        {0, 1, 7}, {0, 3, 9},
32        {1, 0, 7}, {1, 2, 9}, {1, 3, 7},
33        {2, 1, 9}, {2, 3, 7}, {2, 4, 7},
34        {3, 0, 9}, {3, 1, 7}, {3, 2, 7}, {3, 4, 9},
35        {4, 2, 7}, {4, 3, 9}
36      };
37
38      WeightedGraph graph2 = new WeightedGraph(edges, 5);            create graph2
39      WeightedGraph.MST tree2 = graph2.getMinimumSpanningTree(1);    MST for graph2
40      System.out.println("Total weight is " + tree2.getTotalWeight());  total weight
41      tree2.printTree();                                            print tree
42    }
43 }
```

```
Total weight is 6513
Root is: Seattle
Edges: (Seattle, San Francisco) (San Francisco, Los Angeles)
(Los Angeles, Denver) (Denver, Kansas City) (Kansas City, Chicago)
(New York, Boston) (Chicago, New York) (Dallas, Atlanta)
(Atlanta, Miami) (Kansas City, Dallas) (Dallas, Houston)

Total weight is 28
Root is: 1
Edges: (1, 0) (3, 2) (1, 3) (2, 4)
```

The program creates a weighted graph for Figure 27.1 in line 25. It then invokes `getMinimumSpanningTree()` (line 26) to return a `MST` that represents a minimum spanning tree for the graph. Invoking `printTree()` (line 28) on the `MST` object displays the edges in the tree. Note that `MST` is a subclass of `Tree`. The `printTree()` method is defined in the `Tree` class.

The graphical illustration of the minimum spanning tree is shown in Figure 28.7. The vertices are added to the tree in this order: Seattle, San Francisco, Los Angeles, Denver, Kansas City, Dallas, Houston, Chicago, New York, Boston, Atlanta, and Miami.

graphical illustration

28.5 Finding Shortest Paths

§27.1 introduced the problem of finding the shortest distance between two cities for the graph in Figure 27.1. The answer to this problem is to find a shortest path between two vertices in the graph.

Video Note
Shortest path

28.5.1 Shortest Path Algorithms

Given a graph with nonnegative weights on the edges, a well-known algorithm for finding a single-source shortest path was discovered by Edsger Dijkstra, a Dutch computer scientist. Dijkstra's algorithm uses `costs[v]` to store the cost of the shortest path from vertex `v` to the source vertex `s`. So `costs[s]` is `0`. Initially assign infinity to `costs[v]` to indicate that no path is found from `v` to `s`. Let `V` denote all vertices in the graph and `T` denote the set of the vertices whose costs have been found so far. Initially, the source vertex `s` is in `T`. The algorithm repeatedly finds a vertex `u` in `T` and a vertex `v` in `V − T` such that `costs[u] + w(u, v)` is the smallest, and moves `v` to `T`. Here `w(u, v)` denotes the weight on edge `(u, v)`.

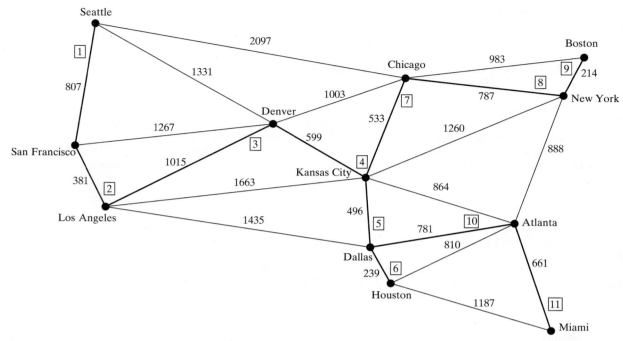

FIGURE 28.7 The edges in the minimum spanning tree for the cities are highlighted.

The algorithm is described in Listing 28.6.

LISTING 28.6 Dijkstra's Single Source Shortest Path Algorithm

```
1 shortestPath(s) {
2   Let V denote the set of vertices in the graph;
3   Let T be a set that contains the vertices whose
4     paths to s have been found;
5   Initially T contains source vertex s with costs[s] = 0;
6
7   while (size of T < n) {
8     find v in V - T with the smallest costs[u] + w(u, v) value
9       among all u in T;
10      add v to T and costs[v] = costs[u] + w(u, v);
11  }
12 }
```

add initial vertex → line 5

more vertex → line 7
find next vertex → lines 8–9

add a vertex → line 10

This algorithm is very similar to Prim's for finding a minimum spanning tree. Both algorithms divide the vertices into two sets T and V – T. In the case of Prim's algorithm, set T contains the vertices that are already added to the tree. In the case of Dijkstra's, set T contains the vertices whose shortest paths to the source have been found. Both algorithms repeatedly find a vertex from V – T and add it to T. In the case of Prim's algorithm, the vertex is adjacent to some vertex in the set with the minimum weight on the edge. In the case of Dijkstra's, the vertex is adjacent to some vertex in the set with the minimum total cost to the source.

The algorithm starts by adding the source vertex s into T and sets costs[s] to 0 (line 5) It then continuously adds a vertex (say v) from V – T into T. v is the vertex that is adjacent to a vertex in T with the smallest costs[u] + w(u, v). For example, there are five edges connecting vertices in T and V – T, as shown in Figure 28.8; (u, v) is the one with the smallest costs[u] + w(u, v). After v is added to T, set costs[v] to costs[u] + w(u, v) (line 10).

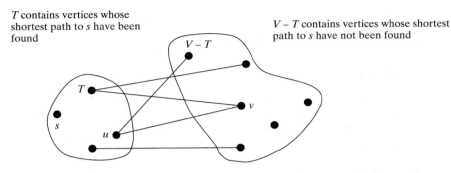

FIGURE 28.8 Find a vertex u in T that connects a vertex v in V – T with the smallest costs[u] + w(u, v).

Let us illustrate Dijkstra's algorithm using the graph in Figure 28.9(a). Suppose the source vertex is 1. So, costs[1] is 0 and the costs for all other vertices are initially ∞, as shown in Figure 28.9(b).

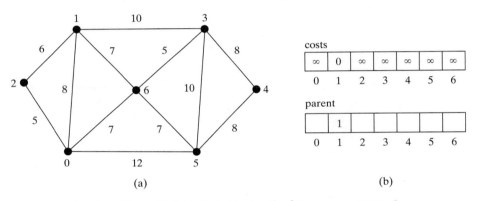

(a)   (b)

FIGURE 28.9 The algorithm will find all shortest paths from source vertex 1.

Initially set T contains the source vertex. Vertices 2, 0, 6, and 3 are adjacent to the vertices in T, and vertex 2 has the path of smallest cost to source vertex 1. So add 2 to T. costs[2] now becomes 6, as shown in Figure 28.10.

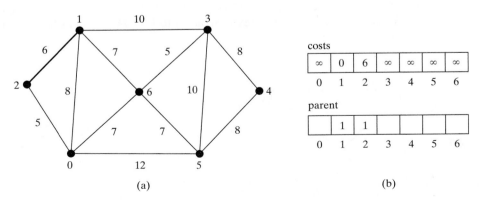

(a)   (b)

FIGURE 28.10 Now vertices 1 and 2 are in the set T.

Now T contains {1, 2}. Vertices 0, 6, and 3 are adjacent to the vertices in T, and vertex 6 has a path of smallest cost to source vertex 1. So add 6 to T. costs[6] now becomes 7, as shown in Figure 28.11.

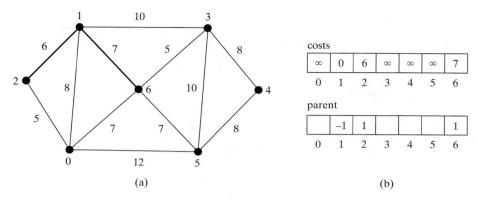

(a)   (b)

FIGURE 28.11   Now vertices $\{1, 2, 6\}$ are in the set T.

Now T contains $\{1, 2, 6\}$. Vertices 0, 5, and 3 are adjacent to the vertices in T, and vertex 0 has the path of smallest cost to source vertex 1. So add 0 to T. costs[0] now becomes 8, as shown in Figure 28.12.

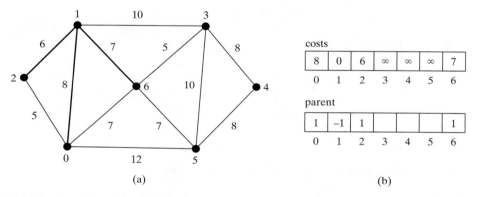

(a)   (b)

FIGURE 28.12   Now vertices $\{1, 2, 6, 0\}$ are in the set T.

Now T contains $\{1, 2, 6, 0\}$. Vertices 5 and 3 are adjacent to the vertices in T, and vertex 3 has the path of smallest cost to source vertex 1. So add 3 to T. costs[3] now becomes 10, as shown in Figure 28.13.

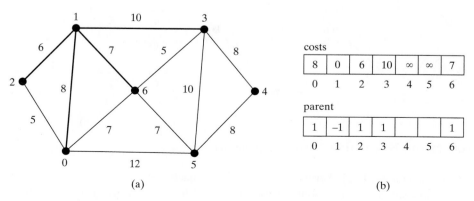

(a)   (b)

FIGURE 28.13   Now vertices $\{1, 2, 6, 0, 3\}$ are in the set T.

Now T contains $\{1, 2, 6, 0, 3\}$. Vertices 4 and 5 are adjacent to the vertices in T, and vertex 5 has the path of smallest cost to source vertex 1. So add 5 to T. costs[5] now becomes 14, as shown in Figure 28.14.

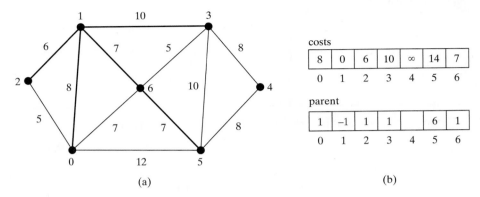

FIGURE 28.14 Now vertices $\{1, 2, 6, 0, 3, 5\}$ are in the set T.

Now T contains $\{1, 2, 6, 0, 3, 5\}$. The smallest cost for a path to connect 4 with 1 is 18, as shown in Figure 28.15.

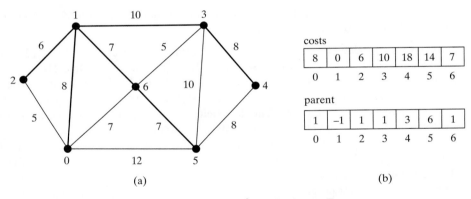

FIGURE 28.15 Now vertices $\{1, 2, 6, 0, 3, 5, 4\}$ are in the set T.

28.5.2 Implementation of the shortest-paths algorithm

As you see, the algorithm essentially finds all shortest paths from a source vertex, which produces a tree rooted at the source vertex. We call this tree a *single-source all-shortest-path tree* (or simply a *shortest-path tree*). To model this tree, define a class named ShortestPathTree   shortest-path tree that extends the Tree class, as shown in Figure 28.16. ShortestPathTree is defined as an inner class in WeightedGraph in lines 220–243 in Listing 28.2.

The getShortestPath(int sourceVertex) method was implemented in lines 164–217 in Listing 28.2. The method first adds sourceVertex to T (line 168). T is a set that stores the vertices whose path has been found (line 166). vertices is defined as a protected data field in the AbstractGraph class, which is an array that stores all vertices in the graph. vertices.length returns the number of the vertices in the graph (line 171).

Each vertex is assigned a cost. The cost of the source vertex is 0 (line 182). The cost of all other vertices is initially assigned infinity (line 180).

The method needs to remove the elements from the queues in order to find the one with the smallest total cost. To keep the original queues intact, queues are cloned in line 185.

FIGURE 28.16 `WeightedGraph.ShortestPathTree` extends `AbstractGraph.Tree`.

A vertex is added to T if it is adjacent to one of the vertices in T with the smallest cost (line 211). Such a vertex is found using the following procedure:

1. For each vertex u in T, find its incident edge e with the smallest weight to u. All the incident edges to u are stored in `queues[u]`. `queues[u].peek()` (line 193) returns the incident edge with the smallest weight. If e.v is already in T, remove e from `queues[u]` (line 194). After lines 192–200, `queues[u].peek()` returns the edge e such that e has the smallest weight to u and e.v is not in T (line 202).

2. Compare all these edges and find the one with the smallest value on `costs[u]` + + `e.getWeight()` (line 206).

After a new vertex is added to T (line 211), the cost of this vertex is updated (line 212). Once all vertices are added to T, an instance of **ShortestPathTree** is created (line 216).

ShortestPathTree class

The **ShortestPathTree** class extends the **Tree** class (line 220). To create an instance of **ShortestPathTree**, pass **sourceVertex**, **parent**, and **costs** (lines 216). **source-Vertex** becomes the root in the tree. The data fields **root** and **parent** are defined in the **Tree** class, which is an inner class defined in **AbstractGraph**.

Dijkstra's algorithm time complexity

Dijkstra's algorithm is implemented essentially in the same way as Prim's. So, the time complexity for Dijkstra's algorithm is $O(|E|\log|V|)$, where $|E|$ denotes the number of edges and $|V|$ the number of vertices.

Listing 28.7 gives a test program that displays all shortest paths from Chicago to all other cities in Figure 27.1 and all shortest paths from vertex 3 to all vertices for the graph in Figure 28.1, respectively.

LISTING 28.7 TestShortestPath.java

```
1 public class TestShortestPath {
2   public static void main(String[] args) {
3     String[] vertices = {"Seattle", "San Francisco", "Los Angeles",
4       "Denver", "Kansas City", "Chicago", "Boston", "New York",
5       "Atlanta", "Miami", "Dallas", "Houston"};
6
7     int[][] edges = {
8       {0, 1, 807}, {0, 3, 1331}, {0, 5, 2097},
9       {1, 0, 807}, {1, 2, 381}, {1, 3, 1267},
10      {2, 1, 381}, {2, 3, 1015}, {2, 4, 1663}, {2, 10, 1435},
11      {3, 0, 1331}, {3, 1, 1267}, {3, 2, 1015}, {3, 4, 599},
12        {3, 5, 1003},
13      {4, 2, 1663}, {4, 3, 599}, {4, 5, 533}, {4, 7, 1260},
14        {4, 8, 864}, {4, 10, 496},
15      {5, 0, 2097}, {5, 3, 1003}, {5, 4, 533},
```

vertices

edges

```
16          {5, 6, 983}, {5, 7, 787},
17         {6, 5, 983}, {6, 7, 214},
18         {7, 4, 1260}, {7, 5, 787},
19         {8, 4, 864}, {8, 7, 888}, {8, 9, 661},
20          {8, 10, 781}, {8, 11, 810},
21         {9, 8, 661}, {9, 11, 1187},
22         {10, 2, 1435}, {10, 4, 496}, {10, 8, 781}, {10, 11, 239},
23         {11, 8, 810}, {11, 9, 1187}, {11, 10, 239}
24       };
25
26       WeightedGraph graph1 = new WeightedGraph(edges, vertices);          create graph1
27       WeightedGraph.ShortestPathTree tree1 = graph1.getShortestPath(5);   shortest path
28       tree1.printAllPaths();
29
30       // Display shortest paths from Chicago to Houston
31       System.out.print("Shortest path from Chicago to Houston: ");
32       java.util.Iterator iterator = tree1.pathIterator(11);
33       while (iterator.hasNext())
34         System.out.print(iterator.next() + " ");
35       System.out.println();
36
37       edges = new int[][]{                                                create edges
38         {0, 1, 7}, {0, 3, 9},
39         {1, 0, 7}, {1, 2, 9}, {1, 3, 7},
40         {2, 1, 9}, {2, 3, 7}, {2, 4, 7},
41         {3, 0, 9}, {3, 1, 7}, {3, 2, 7}, {3, 4, 9},
42         {4, 2, 7}, {4, 3, 9}
43       };
44       WeightedGraph graph2 = new WeightedGraph(edges, 5);                 create graph2
45       WeightedGraph.ShortestPathTree tree2 = graph2.getShortestPath(3);
46       tree2.printAllPaths();                                             print paths
47   }
48 }
```

```
All shortest paths from Chicago are:
A path from Chicago to Seattle: Chicago Seattle (cost: 2097)
A path from Chicago to San Francisco:
  Chicago Denver San Francisco (cost: 2270)
A path from Chicago to Los Angeles:
  Chicago Denver Los Angeles (cost: 2018)
A path from Chicago to Denver: Chicago Denver (cost: 1003)
A path from Chicago to Kansas City:
  Chicago Kansas City (cost: 533)
A path from Chicago to Chicago: Chicago (cost: 0)
A path from Chicago to Boston: Chicago Boston (cost: 983)
A path from Chicago to New York: Chicago New York (cost: 787)
A path from Chicago to Atlanta:
  Chicago Kansas City Atlanta (cost: 1397)
A path from Chicago to Miami:
  Chicago Kansas City Atlanta Miami (cost: 2058)
A path from Chicago to Dallas:
  Chicago Kansas City Dallas (cost: 1029)
A path from Chicago to Houston:
  Chicago Kansas City Dallas Houston (cost: 1268)

Shortest path from Chicago to Houston:
  Chicago Kansas City Dallas Houston

All shortest paths from 3 are:
A path from 3 to 0:3 0 (cost: 9)
```

```
A path from 3 to 1:3 1 (cost: 7)
A path from 3 to 2:3 2 (cost: 7)
A path from 3 to 3:3 (cost: 0)
A path from 3 to 4:3 4 (cost: 9)
```

The program creates a weighted graph for Figure 27.1 in line 26. It then invokes the `getShortestPath(5)` method to return a `Path` object that contains all shortest paths from vertex `5` (i.e., Chicago). Invoking `printPath()` on the `ShortestPathTree` object displays all the paths.

The graphical illustration of all shortest paths from `Chicago` is shown in Figure 28.17. The shortest paths from Chicago to the cities are found in this order: Kansas City, New York, Boston, Denver, Dallas, Houston, Atlanta, Los Angeles, Miami, San Francisco, and Seattle.

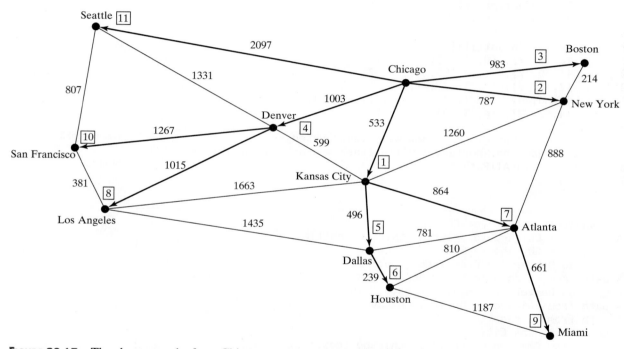

FIGURE 28.17 The shortest paths from Chicago to all other cities are highlighted.

28.6 Case Study: The Weighted Nine Tail Problem

§27.8 presented the nine tail problem and solved it using the BFS algorithm. This section presents a modification of the problem and solves it using the shortest-path algorithm.

The nine tail problem is to find the minimum number of the moves that lead to all coins face down. Each move flips a head coin and its neighbors. The weighted nine tail problem assigns the number of flips as a weight on each move. For example, you can move from the coins in Figure 28.18(a) to Figure 28.18(b) by flipping the three coins. So the weight for this move is `3`.

The weighted nine tail problem is to find the minimum number of flips that lead to all coins face down. The problem can be reduced to finding the shortest path from a starting node to the target node in an edge-weighted graph. The graph has 512 nodes. Create an

H	H	H
T	T	T
H	H	H

(a)

T	T	H
H	T	T
H	H	H

(b)

FIGURE 28.18   The weight for each move is the number of flips for the move.

edge from node v to u if there is a move from node u to node v. Assign the number of flips to the edge.

Recall that we created two classes, `NineTailApp` and `NineTailModel`, for the nine tail problem in §27.8. The `NineTailApp` class is responsible for user interaction and for displaying the solution, and the `NineTailModel` class creates a graph for modeling this problem. We may reuse the same classes to solve the weighted nine tail problem. The only change is to modify the implementation of `NineTailModel`. For convenience, let us name the new classes `WeightedNineTailApp` and `WeightedNineTailModel`.

`WeightedNineTailApp` is exactly the same as `NineTailApp` except that the words `NineTailApp` and `NineTailModel` in the code are replaced by `WeightedNineTailApp` and `WeightedNineTailModel`, respectively. The code listing is omitted. You can download WeightedNineTailApp.java from the companion Web site.

The public method headers in `WeightedNineTailModel` are the same as those in `NineTailModel` except that `UnweightedGraph` is replaced by `WeightedGraph` and `Edge` is replaced by `WeightedEdge`. Listing 28.8 gives the new implementation of the methods.

LISTING 28.8   WeightedNineTailModel.java

```
 1 import java.util.*;
 2
 3 public class WeightedNineTailModel {
 4   private List<Node> nodes = new ArrayList<Node>(); // Vertices
 5   private List<WeightedEdge> edges =
 6     new ArrayList<WeightedEdge>(); // Store edges
 7   private WeightedGraph graph; // Define a graph
 8   private WeightedGraph.Tree tree; // Define a tree
 9
10   /** Construct a model */
11   public WeightedNineTailModel() {
12     createNodes(); // Create nodes
13     createEdges(); // Create edges
14
15     // Create a graph
16     graph = new WeightedGraph(edges, nodes);
17
18     // Obtain a tree rooted at the target node
19     tree = graph.getShortestPath(511);
20   }
21
22   /** Create all nodes for the graph */
23   private void createNodes() {
24     for (int k1 = 0; k1 <= 1; k1++) {
25       for (int k2 = 0; k2 <= 1; k2++) {
26         for (int k3 = 0; k3 <= 1; k3++) {
27           for (int k4 = 0; k4 <= 1; k4++) {
```

vertices
edges

declare a graph
declare a tree

create nodes
weighted edges

weighted graph

shortest-path tree

create 512 nodes

```
28                    for (int k5 = 0; k5 <= 1; k5++) {
29                      for (int k6 = 0; k6 <= 1; k6++) {
30                        for (int k7 = 0; k7 <= 1; k7++) {
31                          for (int k8 = 0; k8 <= 1; k8++) {
32                            for (int k9 = 0; k9 <= 1; k9++) {
33                              nodes.add(new Node(k1, k2, k3, k4,
34                                k5, k6, k7, k8, k9));
35                            }
36                          }
37                        }
38                      }
39                    }
40                  }
41                }
42              }
43            }
44   }
45
46   /** Node inner class */
47   public static class Node {
48     int[][] matrix = new int[3][3];
49
50     /** Construct a Node from nine numbers */
51     Node(int ...numbers) { // Variable-length argument
52       int k = 0;
53       for (int i = 0; i < 3; i++) {
54         for (int j = 0; j < 3; j++) {
55           matrix[i][j] = numbers[k++];
56         }
57       }
58     }
59
60     /** Construct a Node from nine numbers in a 3-by-3 array */
61     Node(int[][] numbers) {
62       this.matrix = numbers;
63     }
64
65     /** Override the equals method to compare two nodes */
66     public boolean equals(Object o) {
67       int[][] anotherMatrix = ((Node)o).matrix;
68       for (int i = 0; i < 3; i++) {
69         for (int j = 0; j < 3; j++) {
70           if (matrix[i][j] != anotherMatrix[i][j]) {
71             return false;
72           }
73         }
74       }
75
76       return true; // Nodes with the same matrix values
77     }
78
79     /** Return a string representation for the node */
80     public String toString() {
81       StringBuilder result = new StringBuilder();
82
83       for (int i = 0; i < 3; i++) {
84         for (int j = 0; j < 3; j++) {
85           result.append(matrix[i][j] + " ");
```

Node inner class

construct a node

construct a node

compare two nodes

string representation

```
86          }
87          result.append("\n");
88       }
89
90       return result.toString();
91    }
92  }
93
94    /** Create all edges for the graph */
95    private void createEdges() {
96      for (Node node : nodes) {
97        int u = nodes.indexOf(node); // node index
98        int[][] matrix = node.matrix; // matrix for the node
99
100       for (int i = 0; i < 3; i++) {
101         for (int j = 0; j < 3; j++) {
102           if (matrix[i][j] == 0) { // For a head cell
103             Node adjacentNode = getAdjacentNode(matrix, i, j);
104             int v = nodes.indexOf(adjacentNode);
105             int numberOfFlips = getNumberOfFlips(adjacentNode,
106               node);
107             // Add edge (v, u) for a legal move from node u to node v
108             edges.add(new WeightedEdge(v, u, numberOfFlips));
109           }
110         }
111       }
112     }
113   }
114
115   /** Get the adjacent node after flipping the cell at i and j */
116   private Node getAdjacentNode(int[][] matrix, int i, int j) {
117     int[][] matrixOfNextNode = new int[3][3];
118     for (int i1 = 0; i1 < 3; i1++) {
119       for (int j1 = 0; j1 < 3; j1++) {
120         matrixOfNextNode[i1][j1] = matrix[i1][j1];
121       }
122     }
123
124     flipACell(matrixOfNextNode, i - 1, j); // Top neighbor
125     flipACell(matrixOfNextNode, i + 1, j); // Bottom neighbor
126     flipACell(matrixOfNextNode, i, j - 1); // Left neighbor
127     flipACell(matrixOfNextNode, i, j + 1); // Right neighbor
128     flipACell(matrixOfNextNode, i, j);     // Flip self
129
130     return new Node(matrixOfNextNode);
131   }
132
133   /** Change a valid cell from 0 to 1 and 1 to 0 */
134   private void flipACell(int[][] matrix, int i, int j) {
135     if (i >= 0 && i <= 2 && j >= 0 && j <= 2) { // Within boundary
136       if (matrix[i][j] == 0) {
137         matrix[i][j] = 1; // Flip from 0 to 1
138       }
139       else {
140         matrix[i][j] = 0; // Flip from 1 to 0
141       }
142     }
143   }
```

create edges

number of flips

add edges

get adjacent node

flip a cell

shortest path

```
144
145    /** Return the shortest path from the specified node to the root */
146    public List<Node> getShortestPath(Node node) {
147      Iterator iterator = tree.pathIterator(nodes.indexOf(node));
148      LinkedList list = new LinkedList();
149
150      // Insert the vertices on the path starting from the root to list
151      while (iterator.hasNext())
152        list.addFirst(iterator.next());
153
154      return list;
155    }
156
157    /** Get the number of the flips */
158    private int getNumberOfFlips(Node node1, Node node2) {
159      int[][] matrix1 = node1.matrix;
160      int[][] matrix2 = node2.matrix;
161
162      int count = 0; // Count the number of different cells
163      for (int i = 0; i < 3; i++) {
164        for (int j = 0; j < 3; j++) {
165          if (matrix1[i][j] != matrix2[i][j]) count++;
166        }
167      }
168
169      return count;
170    }
171  }
```

number of flips

Line 19 obtains a tree that represents the shortest paths rooted at the target node 511. Line 108 adds a weighted edge to the graph. The getNumberOfFlips(node1, node2) compares node1 with node2 to return the number of different cells, which is the number of the flips for the move from node1 to node2.

KEY TERMS

Dijkstra's algorithm   915
edge-weighted graph   902
minimum spanning tree   908
Prim's algorithm   910

shortest path   915
single-source shortest path   915
vertex-weighted graph   902

CHAPTER SUMMARY

■ You can use adjacency matrices or priority queues to represent weighted edges.

■ A spanning tree of a graph is a subgraph that is a tree and connects all vertices in the graph. You learned how to implement Prim's algorithm for finding a minimum spanning tree.

■ You learned how to implement Dijkstra's algorithm for finding shortest paths.

REVIEW QUESTIONS

Section 28.4 Minimum Spanning Trees

28.1   Find a minimum spanning tree for the following graph.

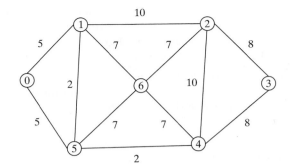

28.2 Is the minimum spanning tree unique if all edges have different weights?

28.3 If you use an adjacency matrix to represent weighted edges, what would be the time complexity for Prim's algorithm?

Section 28.5 The Shortest Paths

28.4 Trace Dijkstra's algorithm for finding shortest paths from Boston to all other cities in Figure 27.1.

28.5 Is the shortest path between two vertices unique if all edges have different weights?

28.6 If you use an adjacency matrix to represent weighted edges, what would be the time complexity for Dijkstra's algorithm?

PROGRAMMING EXERCISES

28.1* (*Kruskal's algorithm*) The text introduced Prim's algorithm for finding a minimum spanning tree. Kruskal's algorithm is another well-known algorithm for finding a minimum spanning tree. The algorithm repeatedly finds a minimum-weight edge and adds it to the tree if it does not cause a cycle. The process ends when all vertices are in the tree. Design and implement an algorithm for finding a MST using Kruskal's algorithm.

28.2* (*Implementing Prim's algorithm using adjacency matrix*) The text implements Prim's algorithm using priority queues on adjacent edges. Implement the algorithm using adjacency matrix for weighted graphs.

28.3* (*Implementing Dijkstra's algorithm using adjacency matrix*) The text implements Dijkstra's algorithm using priority queues on adjacent edges. Implement the algorithm using adjacency matrix for weighted graphs.

28.4* (*Modifying weight in the nine tail problem*) In the text, we assign the number of the flips as the weight for each move. Assuming that the weight is three times of the number of flips, revise the program.

28.5* (*Prove or disprove*) The conjecture is that both `NineTailModel` and `Weighted-NineTailModel` result in the same shortest path. Write a program to prove or disprove it.

(*Hint*: Add a new method named `depth(int v)` in the `AbstractGraph.Tree` class to return the depth of the `v` in the tree. Let `tree1` and `tree2` denote the trees obtained from `NineTailModel` and `WeightedNineTailModel`, respectively. If the depth of a node `u` is the same in `tree1` and in `tree2`, the length of the path from `u` to the target is the same.)

Video Note
4 by 4 16 tail model

28.6** (*Weighted 4 × 4 16 tail model*) The weighted nine tail problem in the text uses a 3 × 3 matrix. Assume that you have 16 coins placed in a 4 × 4 matrix. Create a new model class named `WeightedTailModel16`. Create an instance of the model and save the object into a file named Exercise28_6.dat.

28.7** (*Weighted 4 × 4 16 tail view*) Listing 27.12, NineTailApp.java, presents a view for the nine tail problem. Revise this program for the weighted 4 × 4 16 tail problem. Your program should read the model object created from the preceding exercise.

28.8** (*Traveling salesman problem*) The traveling salesman problem (TSP) is to find a shortest round-trip route that visits each city exactly once and then returns to the starting city. The problem is equivalent to finding a shortest Hamiltonian cycle. Add the following method in the `WeightedGraph` class:

```
// Return a shortest cycle
// Return null if no such cycle exists
public List<Integer> getShortestHamiltonianCycle()
```

CHAPTER 29

MULTITHREADING

Objectives

- To get an overview of multithreading (§29.2).
- To develop task classes by implementing the `Runnable` interface (§29.3).
- To create threads to run tasks using the `Thread` class (§29.3).
- To control threads using the methods in the `Thread` class (§29.4).
- To control animations using threads (§§29.5, 29.7).
- To run code in the event dispatch thread (§29.6).
- To execute tasks in a thread pool (§29.8).
- To use synchronized methods or blocks to synchronize threads to avoid race conditions (§29.9).
- To synchronize threads using locks (§29.10).
- To facilitate thread communications using conditions on locks (§§29.11–29.12).
- To use blocking queues to synchronize access to an array queue, linked queue, and priority queue (§29.13).
- To restrict the number of accesses to a shared resource using semaphores (§29.14).
- To use the resource-ordering technique to avoid deadlocks (§29.15).
- To describe the life cycle of a thread (§29.16).
- To create synchronized collections using the static methods in the `Collections` class (§29.17).
- To run time-consuming tasks in a `SwingWorker` rather than in the event dispatch thread (§29.18).
- To display the completion status of a task using `JProgressBar` (§29.19).

29.1 Introduction

multithreading

One of the powerful feature of Java is its built-in support for multithreading—the concurrent running of multiple tasks within a program. In many programming languages, you have to invoke system-dependent procedures and functions to implement multithreading. This chapter introduces the concepts of threads and how to develop multithreading programs in Java.

29.2 Thread Concepts

thread

task

A *thread* is the flow of execution, from beginning to end, of a task in a program. A *task* is a program unit that is executed independently of other parts of the program. A thread provides the mechanism for running a task. With Java, you can launch multiple threads from a program concurrently. These threads can be executed simultaneously in multiprocessor systems, as shown in Figure 29.1(a).

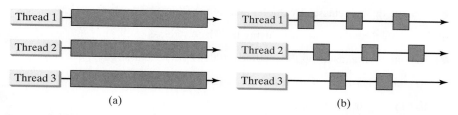

FIGURE 29.1   (a) Here multiple threads are running on multiple CPUs. (b) Here multiple threads share a single CPU.

In single-processor systems, as shown in Figure 29.1(b), the multiple threads share CPU time, and the operating system is responsible for scheduling and allocating resources to them. This arrangement is practical, because most of the time the CPU is idle. It does nothing, for example, while waiting for the user to enter data.

Multithreading can make your program more responsive and interactive, as well as enhance performance. For example, a good word processor lets you print or save a file while you are typing. In some cases, multithreaded programs run faster than single-threaded programs even on single-processor systems. Java provides exceptionally good support for creating and running threads and for locking resources to prevent conflicts.

Java task

When your program executes as an application, the Java interpreter starts a thread for the main method. When your program executes as an applet, the Web browser starts a thread to run the applet. You can create additional threads to run concurrent tasks in the program. In

runnable object

thread

Java, each task is an instance of the **Runnable** interface, also called a *runnable object*. A *thread* is essentially an object that facilitates the execution of a task.

29.3 Creating Tasks and Threads

Thread class

Runnable interface

run() method

Tasks are objects. To create tasks, you have to first declare a class for tasks. A task class must implement the **Runnable** interface. The **Runnable** interface is rather simple. All it contains is the **run** method. You need to implement this method to tell the system how your thread is going to run. A template for developing a task class is shown in Figure 29.2(a).

Once you have declared a **TaskClass**, you can create a task using its constructor. For example,

creating a task

```
TaskClass task = new TaskClass(...);
```

FIGURE 29.2 Define a task class by implementing the Runnable interface.

A task must be executed in a thread. The Thread class contains the constructors for creating threads and many useful methods for controlling threads. To create a thread for a task, use

```
Thread thread = new Thread(task);
```

creating a thread

You can then invoke the start() method to tell the JVM that the thread is ready to run, as follows:

```
thread.start();
```

starting a thread

The JVM will execute the task by invoking the task's run() method. Figure 29.2(b) outlines the major steps for creating a task, a thread, and starting the thread.

Listing 29.1 gives a program that creates three tasks and three threads to run them:

- The first task prints the letter *a* 100 times.

- The second task prints the letter *b* 100 times.

- The third task prints the integers 1 through 100.

If you run this program on a multiple-CPU system, all three threads will execute simultaneously. If you run the program on a single-CPU system, the three threads will share the CPU and take turns printing letters and numbers on the console. This is known as *time sharing*. Figure 29.3 shows a sample run of the program.

time sharing

FIGURE 29.3 Tasks printA, printB, and print100 are executed simultaneously to display the letter a 100 times, the letter b 100 times, and the numbers from 1 to 100.

LISTING 29.1 TaskThreadDemo.java

```java
 1 public class TaskThreadDemo {
 2   public static void main(String[] args) {
 3     // Create tasks
 4     Runnable printA = new PrintChar('a', 100);
 5     Runnable printB = new PrintChar('b', 100);
 6     Runnable print100 = new PrintNum(100);
 7
 8     // Create threads
 9     Thread thread1 = new Thread(printA);
10     Thread thread2 = new Thread(printB);
11     Thread thread3 = new Thread(print100);
12
13     // Start threads
14     thread1.start();
15     thread2.start();
16     thread3.start();
17   }
18 }
19
20 // The task for printing a character a specified number of times
21 class PrintChar implements Runnable {
22   private char charToPrint; // The character to print
23   private int times; // The number of times to repeat
24
25   /** Construct a task with specified character and number of
26    *  times to print the character
27    */
28   public PrintChar(char c, int t) {
29     charToPrint = c;
30     times = t;
31   }
32
33   /** Override the run() method to tell the system
34    *  what task to perform
35    */
36   public void run() {
37     for (int i = 0; i < times; i++) {
38       System.out.print(charToPrint);
39     }
40   }
41 }
42
43 // The task class for printing numbers from 1 to n for a given n
44 class PrintNum implements Runnable {
45   private int lastNum;
46
47   /** Construct a task for printing 1, 2, ... i */
48   public PrintNum(int n) {
49     lastNum = n;
50   }
51
52   /** Tell the thread how to run */
53   public void run() {
54     for (int i = 1; i <= lastNum; i++) {
55       System.out.print(" " + i);
56     }
57   }
58 }
```

create tasks

create threads

start threads

task class

run

task class

run

The program creates three tasks (lines 4–6). To run them concurrently, three threads are created (lines 9–11). The `start()` method (lines 14–16) is invoked to start a thread that causes the `run()` method in the task to be executed. When the `run()` method completes, the thread terminates.

Because the first two tasks, `printA` and `printB`, have similar functionality, they can be defined in one task class `PrintChar` (lines 21–41). The `PrintChar` class implements `Runnable` and overrides the `run()` method (lines 36–40) with the print-character action. This class provides a framework for printing any single character a given number of times. The runnable objects `printA` and `printB` are instances of the `PrintChar` class.

The `PrintNum` class (lines 44–58) implements `Runnable` and overrides the `run()` method (lines 53–57) with the print-number action. This class provides a framework for printing numbers from *1* to *n*, for any integer *n*. The runnable object `print100` is an instance of the class `printNum` class.

Note

If you don't see the effect of these three threads running concurrently, increase the number of characters to be printed. For example, change line 4 to

effect of concurrency

```
Runnable printA = new PrintChar('a', 10000);
```

Important Note

The `run()` method in a task specifies how to perform the task. This method is automatically invoked by the JVM. You should not invoke it. Invoking `run()` directly merely executes this method in the same thread; no new thread is started.

run() *method*

29.4 The **Thread** Class

The `Thread` class contains the constructors for creating threads for tasks, and the methods for controlling threads, as shown in Figure 29.4.

«interface» java.lang.Runnable	

java.lang.Thread	
+Thread()	Creates a default thread.
+Thread(task: Runnable)	Creates a thread for a specified task.
+start(): void	Starts the thread that causes the run() method to be invoked by the JVM.
+isAlive(): boolean	Tests whether the thread is currently running.
+setPriority(p: int): void	Sets priority p (ranging from 1 to 10) for this thread.
+join(): void	Waits for this thread to finish.
+sleep(millis: long): void	Puts the runnable object to sleep for a specified time in milliseconds.
+yield(): void	Causes this thread to pause temporarily and allow other threads to execute.
+interrupt(): void	Interrupts this thread.

FIGURE 29.4 The `Thread` class contains the methods for controlling threads.

Note

Since the `Thread` class implements `Runnable`, you could declare a class that extends `Thread` and implements the `run` method, as shown in Figure 29.5(a), and then create an object from the class and invoke its `start` method in a client program to start the thread, as shown in Figure 29.5(b).

separating task from thread

(a)   (b)

FIGURE 29.5 Define a thread class by extending the Thread class.

This approach is, however, not recommended, because it mixes the task and the mechanism of running the task. Separating the task from the thread is a preferred design.

Note

deprecated method

The Thread class also contains the stop(), suspend(), and resume() methods. As of Java 2, these methods are *deprecated* (or *outdated*) because they are known to be inherently unsafe. Instead of using the stop() method, you should assign null to a Thread variable to indicate that it is stopped.

yield()

You can use the yield() method to temporarily release time for other threads. For example, suppose you modify the code in the run() method (lines 53–57 in PrintNum in TaskThread-Demo.java) in Listing 29.1 as follows:

```java
public void run() {
  for (int i = 1; i <= lastNum; i++) {
    System.out.print(" " + i);
    Thread.yield();
  }
}
```

Every time a number is printed, the thread of the print100 task is yielded. So each number is followed by some characters.

sleep(long)

The sleep(long millis) method puts the thread to sleep for the specified time in milliseconds to allow other threads to execute. For example, suppose you modify the code in lines 53–57 in TaskThreadDemo.java in Listing 29.1 as follows:

```java
public void run() {
  try {
    for (int i = 1; i <= lastNum; i++) {
      System.out.print(" " + i);
      if (i >= 50) Thread.sleep(1);
    }
  }
  catch (InterruptedException ex) {
  }
}
```

Every time a number (`>= 50`) is printed, the thread of the `print100` task is put to sleep for 1 millisecond.

The `sleep` method may throw an `InterruptedException`, which is a checked exception. **InterruptedException** Such an exception may occur when a sleeping thread's `interrupt()` method is called. The `interrupt()` method is very rarely invoked on a thread, so an `InterruptedException` is unlikely to occur. But since Java forces you to catch checked exceptions, you have to put it in a try-catch block. If a `sleep` method is invoked in a loop, you should wrap the loop in a try-catch block, as shown in (a) below. If the loop is outside the try-catch block, as shown in (b), the thread may continue to execute even though it is being interrupted.

```
public void run() {
  try {
    while (...) {
      ...
      Thread.sleep(1000);
    }
  }
  catch (InterruptedException ex) {
    ex.printStackTrace();
  }
}
```

(a) Correct

```
public void run() {
  while (...) {
    try {
      ...
      Thread.sleep(sleepTime);
    }
    catch (InterruptedException ex) {
      ex.printStackTrace();
    }
  }
}
```

(b) Incorrect

You can use the `join()` method to force one thread to wait for another thread to finish. For ex- **join()** ample, suppose you modify the code in lines 53–57 in TaskThreadDemo.java in Listing 29.1 as follows:

```
public void run() {
  Thread thread4 = new Thread(
    new PrintChar('c', 40));
  thread4.start();
  try {
    for (int i = 1; i <= lastNum; i++) {
      System.out.print (" " + i);
      if (i == 50) thread4.join();
    }
  }
  catch (InterruptedException ex) {
  }
}
```

Thread print100   Thread thread4

thread4.join()

Wait for thread4 to finish

thread4 finished

A new `thread4` is created. It prints character c 40 times. The numbers from 50 to 100 are printed after thread `thread4` is finished.

Java assigns every thread a priority. By default, a thread inherits the priority of the thread that spawned it. You can increase or decrease the priority of any thread by using the `setPriority` **setPriority(int)** method, and you can get the thread's priority by using the `getPriority` method. Priorities are numbers ranging from 1 to 10. The `Thread` class has the `int` constants `MIN_PRIORITY`, `NORM_PRIORITY`, and `MAX_PRIORITY`, representing 1, 5, and 10, respectively. The priority of the main thread is `Thread.NORM_PRIORITY`.

The JVM always picks the currently runnable thread with the highest priority. If several runnable threads have equally high priorities, the CPU is allocated to all of them in round-robin fashion. A lower-priority thread can run only when no higher-priority threads are running. For example, suppose you insert the following code in line 16 in TaskThreadDemo.java in Listing 29.1:

```
thread3.setPriority(Thread.MAX_PRIORITY);
```

The thread for the `print100` task will be finished first.

Tip
The priority numbers may be changed in a future version of Java. To minimize the impact of any changes, use the constants in the `Thread` class to specify thread priorities.

Tip
contention or starvation

A thread may never get a chance to run if there is always a higher-priority thread running or a same-priority thread that never yields. This situation is known as *contention* or *starvation*. To avoid contention, the thread with high priority must periodically invoke the sleep or yield method to give a thread with a lower or the same priority a chance to run.

29.5 Example: Flashing Text

The use of a `Timer` object to control animations was introduced in §15.6, "Animation Using the `Timer` Class." You can also use a thread to control animation. Listing 29.2 gives an example that displays a flashing text on a label, as shown in Figure 29.6.

FIGURE 29.6 The text Welcome blinks.

LISTING 29.2 FlashingText.java

implements Runnable
create a label

add a label
start a thread

how to run

sleep

main method omitted

```java
 1 import javax.swing.*;
 2
 3 public class FlashingText extends JApplet implements Runnable {
 4   private JLabel jlblText = new JLabel("Welcome", JLabel.CENTER);
 5
 6   public FlashingText() {
 7     add(jlblText);
 8     new Thread(this).start();
 9   }
10
11   /** Set the text on/off every 200 milliseconds */
12   public void run() {
13     try {
14       while (true) {
15         if (jlblText.getText() == null)
16           jlblText.setText("Welcome");
17         else
18           jlblText.setText(null);
19
20         Thread.sleep(200);
21       }
22     }
23     catch (InterruptedException ex) {
24     }
25   }
26 }
```

`FlashingText` implements `Runnable` (line 3), so it is a task class. Line 8 wraps the task in a thread and starts the thread. The `run` method dictates how to run the thread. It sets a text in the label if the label does not have a text (line 15), and sets its text `null` (line 18) if the label has a text. The text is set and unset to simulate a flashing effect.

You can use a timer or a thread to control animation. Which one is better? A timer is a source component that fires an `ActionEvent` at a "fixed rate." When an action event occurs, the timer invokes the listener's `actionPerformed` method to handle the event. The timer and event handling run on the same event dispatch thread. If it takes a long time to handle the event, the actual delay time between two events will be longer than the requested delay time. In this case, you should run event handling on a separate thread. The next section will give an example to illustrate the problem and fix it by running the event handling on a separate thread. In general, threads are more reliable and responsive than timers. If you need a precise delay time or a quick response, it is better to use a thread. Otherwise, using a timer is simpler and more efficient. Timers consume less system resource because they run on the GUI event dispatch thread, so you don't need to spawn new threads for timers.

thread vs. timer

29.6 GUI Event Dispatch Thread

GUI event handling and painting code executes in a single thread called the *event dispatch thread*. This ensures that each event handler finishes executing before the next one executes and the painting isn't interrupted by events.

In certain situations, you need to run the code in the event dispatch thread to avoid possible deadlock. You can use the static methods, `invokeLater` and `invokeAndWait` in the `javax.swing.SwingUtilities` class to run the code in the event dispatch thread. You must put this code in the `run` method of a `Runnable` object and specify the `Runnable` object as the argument to `invokeLater` and `invokeAndWait`. The `invokeLater` method returns immediately, without waiting for the event dispatch thread to execute the code. The `invokeAndWait` method is just like `invokeLater`, except that `invokeAndWait` doesn't return until the event dispatching thread has executed the specified code.

invokeLater

invokeAndWait

So far, you have launched your GUI application from the main method by creating a frame and making it visible. This works fine for most applications, but in certain situations it could cause problems. To avoid possible thread deadlock, you should launch GUI creation from the event dispatch thread, as follows:

```
public static void main(String[] args) {
  SwingUtilities.invokeLater(new Runnable() {
    public void run() {
      // Place the code for creating a frame and setting it properties
    }
  });
}
```

For example, Listing 29.3 gives a simple program that launches the frame from the event dispatch thread.

LISTING 29.3 EventDispatcherThreadDemo.java

```
1  import javax.swing.*;
2
3  public class EventDispatcherThreadDemo extends JApplet {
4    public EventDispatcherThreadDemo() {
5      add(new JLabel("Hi, it runs from an event dispatch thread"));
6    }
7
8    /** Main method */
9    public static void main(String[] args) {
10     SwingUtilities.invokeLater(new Runnable() {
11       public void run() {
12         JFrame frame = new JFrame("EventDispatcherThreadDemo");
13         frame.add(new EventDispatcherThreadDemo());
```

create frame

```
14              frame.setSize(200, 200);
15              frame.setDefaultCloseOperation(JFrame.EXIT_ON_CLOSE);
16              frame.setLocationRelativeTo(null); // Center the frame
17              frame.setVisible(true);
18          }
19      });
20   }
21 }
```

29.7 Case Study: Clock with Audio

The example creates an applet that displays a running clock and announces the time at one-minute intervals. For example, if the current time is 6:30:00, the applet announces, "six o'-clock thirty minutes A.M." If the current time is 20:20:00, the applet announces, "eight o'clock twenty minutes P.M." Also add a label to display the digital time, as shown in Figure 29.7.

FIGURE 29.7 The applet displays a clock and announces the time every minute.

audio clips
audio files

To announce the time, the applet plays three audio clips. The first clip announces the hour, the second announces the minute, and the third announces A.M. or P.M. All of the audio files are stored in the directory `audio`, a subdirectory of the applet's class directory. The 12 audio files used to announce the hours are stored in the files **hour0.au**, **hour1.au**, and so on, to **hour11.au**. The 60 audio files used to announce the minutes are stored in the files **minute0.au**, **minute1.au**, and so on, to **minute59.au**. The two audio files used to announce A.M. or P.M. are stored in the file **am.au** and **pm.au**.

You need to play three audio clips on a separate thread to avoid animation delays. To illustrate the problem, let us first write a program without playing the audio on a separate thread.

In §14.12, the `StillClock` class was developed to draw a still clock to show the current time. Create an applet named `ClockWithAudio` (Listing 29.4) that contains an instance of `StillClock` to display an analog clock, and an instance of `JLabel` to display the digit time. Override the `init` method to load the audio files. Use a `Timer` object to set and display the current time continuously at a fixed rate. When the second is zero, announce the current time.

LISTING 29.4 ClockWithAudio.java

```
1 import java.applet.*;
2 import javax.swing.*;
3 import java.awt.event.*;
4 import java.awt.*;
5
6 public class ClockWithAudio extends JApplet {
7   protected AudioClip[] hourAudio = new AudioClip[12];
8   protected AudioClip[] minuteAudio = new AudioClip[60];
9
10    // Create audio clips for pronouncing am and pm
```

audio clips

```
11    protected AudioClip amAudio =                                              am clip
12       Applet.newAudioClip(this.getClass().getResource("audio/am.au")) ;
13    protected AudioClip pmAudio =                                              pm clip
14       Applet.newAudioClip(this.getClass().getResource("audio/pm.au "));
15
16    // Create a clock
17    private StillClock clock = new StillClock();                               still clock
18
19    // Create a timer
20    private Timer timer = new Timer(1000, new TimerListener());                timer
21
22    // Create a label to display time
23    private JLabel jlblDigitTime = new JLabel("", JLabel.CENTER);              label
24
25    /** Initialize the applet */
26    public void init() {
27       // Create audio clips for pronouncing hours
28       for (int i = 0; i < 12; i++)
29          hourAudio[i] = Applet.newAudioClip(                                  create audio clips
30             this.getClass().getResource("audio/hour" + i + ".au" ));
31
32       // Create audio clips for pronouncing minutes
33       for (int i = 0; i < 60; i++)
34          minuteAudio[i] = Applet.newAudioClip(
35             this.getClass().getResource("audio/minute" + i + ".au" ));
36
37       // Add clock and time label to the content pane of the applet
38       add(clock, BorderLayout.CENTER);
39       add(jlblDigitTime, BorderLayout.SOUTH);
40    }
41
42    /** Override the applet's start method */
43    public void start() {
44       timer.start(); // Resume clock                                          start timer
45    }
46
47    /** Override the applet's stop method */
48    public void stop() {
49       timer.stop(); // Suspend clock                                          stop timer
50    }
51
52    private class TimerListener implements ActionListener {                    timer listener
53       public void actionPerformed(ActionEvent e) {
54          clock.setCurrentTime();                                             set new time
55          clock.repaint();
56          jlblDigitTime.setText(clock.getHour() + ":" + clock.getMinute()
57             + ":" + clock.getSecond());
58          if (clock.getSecond() == 0)
59             announceTime(clock.getHour(), clock.getMinute());                announce time
60       }
61    }
62
63    /** Announce the current time at every minute */
64    public void announceTime(int hour, int minute) {
65       // Announce hour
66       hourAudio[hour % 12].play();                                            announce hour
67
68       try {
69          // Time delay to allow hourAudio play to finish
```

```
70        Thread.sleep(1500);
71
72        // Announce minute
73        minuteAudio[minute].play();
74
75        // Time delay to allow minuteAudio play to finish
76        Thread.sleep(1500);
77      }
78      catch(InterruptedException ex) {
79      }
80
81      // Announce am or pm
82      if (hour < 12)
83        amAudio.play();
84      else
85        pmAudio.play();
86    }
87  }
```

announce minute *(margin, line 73)*
announce am *(margin, line 83)*
announce pm *(margin, line 85)*
main method omitted *(margin, line 87)*

The `hourAudio` is an array of twelve audio clips that are used to announce the 12 hours of the day (line 7); the `minuteAudio` is an audio clip that is used to announce the minutes in an hour (line 8). The `amAudio` announces A.M. (line 11); the `pmAudio` announces P.M. (line 13).

The `init()` method creates hour audio clips (lines 29–30) and minute audio clips (lines 34–35), and places a clock and a label in the applet (lines 38–39).

An `ActionEvent` is fired by the timer every second. In the listener's `actionPerformed` method (lines 53–60), the clock is repainted with the new current time, and the digital time is displayed in the label.

In the `announceTime` method (lines 64–86), the `sleep()` method (lines 70, 76) is purposely invoked to ensure that one clip finishes before the next clip starts, so that the clips do not interfere with each other.

The applet's `start()` and `stop()` methods (lines 43–50) are overridden to ensure that the timer starts or stops when the applet is restarted or stopped.

abnormal problem *(margin)*

When you run the preceding program, you will notice that the second hand does not display at the first, second, and third seconds of the minute. This is because `sleep(1500)` is invoked twice in the `announceTime()` method, which takes three seconds to announce the time at the beginning of each minute. Thus, the next action event is delayed for three seconds during the first three seconds of each minute. As a result of this delay, the time is not updated and the clock was not repainted for these three seconds. To fix this problem, you should announce the time on a separate thread. This can be accomplished by modifying the `announceTime` method. Listing 29.5 gives the new program.

LISTING 29.5 ClockWithAudioOnSeparateThread.java

omitted *(margin, line 1)*

```
1  // same import statements as in Listing 29.4, so omitted
2
3  public class ClockWithAudioOnSeparateThread extends JApplet {
```

omitted *(margin, line 4)*

```
4    // same as in lines 7-61 in Listing 29.4, so omitted
5
6    /** Announce the current time at every minute */
7    public void announceTime(int h, int m) {
```

create a thread *(margin, line 8)*

```
8      new Thread(new AnnounceTimeOnSeparateThread(h, m)).start();
9    }
10
11   /** Inner class for announcing time */
```

task class *(margin, line 12)*

```
12   class AnnounceTimeOnSeparateThread implements Runnable {
13     private int hour, minute;
14
```

```
15        /** Get Audio clips */
16        public AnnounceTimeOnSeparateThread(int hour, int minute) {
17          this.hour = hour;
18          this.minute = minute;
19        }
20
21        public void run() {                                              run thread
22          // Announce hour
23          hourAudio[hour % 12].play();
24
25          try {
26            // Time delay to allow hourAudio play to finish
27            Thread.sleep(1500);
28
29            // Announce minute
30            minuteAudio[minute].play();
31
32            // Time delay to allow minuteAudio play to finish
33            Thread.sleep(1500);
34          }
35          catch (InterruptedException ex) {
36          }
37
38          // Announce am or pm
39          if (hour < 12)
40            amAudio.play();
41          else
42            pmAudio.play();
43        }
44      }
45 }                                                                main method omitted
```

The new class `ClockWithAudioOnSeparateThread` is the same as `ClockWithAudio` except that the `announceTime` method is new. The new `announceTime` method creates a thread (line 8) for the task of announcing time. The task class is declared an inner class (lines 12–44). The `run` method (line 21) announces the time on a separate thread.

When running this program, you will discover that the audio does not interfere with the clock animation because an instance of `AnnounceTimeOnSeparateThread` starts on a separate thread to announce the current time. This thread is independent of the thread on which the `actionPerformed` method runs.

29.8 Thread Pools

In §29.3, "Creating Tasks and Threads," you learned how to declare a task class by implementing `java.lang.Runnable`, and how to create a thread to run a task like this:

```
Runnable task = new TaskClass(task);
new Thread(task).start();
```

This approach is convenient for a single task execution, but it is not efficient for a large number of tasks, because you have to create a thread for each task. Starting a new thread for each task could limit throughput and cause poor performance. A thread pool is ideal to manage the number of tasks executing concurrently. JDK 1.5 uses the `Executor` interface for executing tasks in a thread pool and the `ExecutorService` interface for managing and controlling tasks. `ExecutorService` is a subinterface of `Executor`, as shown in Figure 29.8.

To create an `Executor` object, use the static methods in the `Executors` class, as shown in Figure 29.9. The `newFixedThreadPool(int)` method creates a fixed number of threads in

FIGURE 29.8 Executor executes threads, and ExecutorService manages threads.

FIGURE 29.9 The Executors class provides static methods for creating Executor objects.

a pool. If a thread completes executing a task, it can be reused to execute another task. If a thread terminates due to a failure prior to shutdown, a new thread will be created to replace it if all the threads in the pool are not idle and there are tasks waiting for execution. The newCachedThreadPool() method creates a new thread if all the threads in the pool are not idle and there are tasks waiting for execution. A thread in a cached pool will be terminated if it has not been used for 60 seconds. A cached pool is efficient for many short tasks.

Listing 29.6 shows how to rewrite Listing 29.1, TaskThreadDemo.java, using a thread pool.

LISTING 29.6 ExecutorDemo.java

```
 1  import java.util.concurrent.*;
 2
 3  public class ExecutorDemo {
 4    public static void main(String[] args) {
 5      // Create a fixed thread pool with maximum three threads
 6      ExecutorService executor = Executors.newFixedThreadPool(3);
 7
 8      // Submit runnable tasks to the executor
 9      executor.execute(new PrintChar('a', 100));
10      executor.execute(new PrintChar('b', 100));
11      executor.execute(new PrintNum(100));
12
13      // Shut down the executor
14      executor.shutdown();
15    }
16  }
```

create executor — (line 6)

submit task — (line 9)

shut down executor — (line 14)

Line 6 creates a thread pool executor with three threads maximum. Classes `PrintChar` and `PrintNum` were declared in TaskThreadDemo.java in Listing 29.1. Line 9 creates a task `new PrintChar('a', 100)` and adds it to the pool. Another two runnable tasks are created and added to the same pool in lines 10–11 similarly. The executor creates three threads to execute three tasks concurrently. Suppose that you replace line 6 by

```
ExecutorService executor = Executors.newFixedThreadPool(1);
```

What will happen? The three runnable tasks will be executed sequentially, because there is only one thread in the pool.

Suppose you replace line 6 by

```
ExecutorService executor = Executors.newCachedThreadPool();
```

What will happen? New threads will be created for each waiting task, so all the tasks will be executed concurrently.

The `shutdown()` method in line 14 tells the executor to shut down. No new tasks can be accepted, but the existing task will continue to finish.

Tip
If you need to create a thread for one task, use the Thread class. If you need to create threads for multiple tasks, it is better to use a thread pool.

29.9 Thread Synchronization

A shared resource may be corrupted if it is accessed simultaneously by multiple threads. The following example demonstrates the problem.

Suppose that you create and launch 100 threads, each of which adds a penny to an account. Create a class named `Account` to model the account, a class named `AddAPennyTask` to add a penny to the account, and a main class that creates and launches threads. The relationships of these classes are shown in Figure 29.10. The program is given in Listing 29.7.

LISTING 29.7 AccountWithoutSync.java

```
 1  import java.util.concurrent.*;
 2
 3  public class AccountWithoutSync {
 4    private static Account account = new Account();
 5
 6    public static void main(String[] args) {
 7      ExecutorService executor = Executors.newCachedThreadPool();      create executor
 8
 9      // Create and launch 100 threads
10      for (int i = 0; i < 100; i++) {
11        executor.execute(new AddAPennyTask());                        submit task
12      }
13
14      executor.shutdown();                                           shut down executor
15
16      // Wait until all tasks are finished
17      while (!executor.isTerminated()) {                             wait for all tasks to terminate
18      }
19
20      System.out.println("What is balance? " + account.getBalance());
21    }
22
```

```
23    // A thread for adding a penny to the account
24    private static class AddAPennyTask implements Runnable {
25      public void run() {
26        account.deposit(1);
27      }
28    }
29
30    // An inner class for account
31    private static class Account {
32      private int balance = 0;
33
34      public int getBalance() {
35        return balance;
36      }
37
38      public void deposit(int amount) {
39        int newBalance = balance + amount;
40
41        // This delay is deliberately added to magnify the
42        // data-corruption problem and make it easy to see.
43        try {
44          Thread.sleep(5);
45        }
46        catch (InterruptedException ex) {
47        }
48
49        balance = newBalance;
50      }
51    }
52  }
```

FIGURE 29.10 `AccountWithoutSync` contains an instance of `Account` and 100 threads of `AddAPennyTask`.

The classes `AddAPennyTask` and `Account` in lines 24–51 are inner classes. Line 4 creates an `Account` with initial balance `0`. Line 11 creates a task to add a penny to the account and submit the task to the executor. Line 11 is repeated 100 times in lines 10–12. The program repeatedly checks whether all tasks are completed in lines 17–18. The account balance is displayed in line 20 after all tasks are completed.

The program creates 100 threads executed in a thread pool `executor` (lines 10–12). The `isTerminated()` method (line 17) is used to test whether the thread is terminated.

The balance of the account is initially `0` (line 32). When all the threads are finished, the balance should be `100`, but the output is unpredictable. As can be seen in Figure 29.11, the answers are wrong in the sample run. This demonstrates the data-corruption problem that occurs when all the threads have access to the same data source simultaneously.

FIGURE 29.11 The `AccountWithoutSync` program causes data inconsistency.

Lines 39–49 could be replaced by one statement:

```
balance = balance + amount;
```

However, it is highly unlikely, although plausible, that the problem can be replicated using this single statement. The statements in lines 39–49 are deliberately designed to magnify the data-corruption problem and make it easy to see. If you run the program several times but still do not see the problem, increase the sleep time in line 44. This will increase the chances for showing the problem of data inconsistency.

What, then, caused the error in this program? Here is a possible scenario, as shown in Figure 29.12.

Step	Balance	Task 1	Task 2
1	0	newBalance = balance + 1;	
2	0		newBalance = balance + 1;
3	1	balance = newBalance;	
4	1		balance = newBalance;

FIGURE 29.12 Task 1 and Task 2 both add 1 to the same balance.

In Step 1, Task 1 gets the balances from the account. In Step 2, Task 2 gets the same balances from the account. In Step 3, Task 1 writes a new balance to the account. In Step 4, Task 2 writes a new balance to the account.

The effect of this scenario is that Task 1 does nothing, because in Step 4 Task 2 overrides Task 1's result. Obviously, the problem is that Task 1 and Task 2 are accessing a common resource in a way that causes conflict. This is a common problem, known as a *race condition*, in multithreaded programs. A class is said to be *thread-safe* if an object of the class does not cause a race condition in the presence of multiple threads. As demonstrated in the preceding example, the `Account` class is not thread-safe.

race condition
thread-safe

29.9.1 The `synchronized` Keyword

To avoid race conditions, it is necessary to prevent more than one thread from simultaneously entering a certain part of the program, known as the *critical region*. The critical region in Listing 29.7 is the entire `deposit` method. You can use the keyword `synchronized` to synchronize the method so that only one thread can access the method at a time. There are several ways to correct the problem in Listing 29.7. One approach is to make `Account` thread-safe by adding the keyword `synchronized` in the `deposit` method in line 38, as follows:

critical region

```
public synchronized void deposit(double amount)
```

A synchronized method acquires a lock before it executes. In the case of an instance method, the lock is on the object for which the method was invoked. In the case of a static method, the lock is on the class. If one thread invokes a synchronized instance method (respectively, static method) on an object, the lock of that object (respectively, class) is acquired first, then the method is executed, and finally the lock is released. Another thread invoking the same method of that object (respectively, class) is blocked until the lock is released.

With the `deposit` method synchronized, the preceding scenario cannot happen. If Task 1 enters the method, Task 2 is blocked until Task 1 finishes the method, as shown in Figure 29.13.

FIGURE 29.13 Task 1 and Task 2 are synchronized.

29.9.2 Synchronizing Statements

Invoking a synchronized instance method of an object acquires a lock on the object, and invoking a synchronized static method of a class acquires a lock on the class. A synchronized statement can be used to acquire a lock on any object, not just *this* object, when executing a block of the code in a method. This block is referred to as a *synchronized block*. The general form of a synchronized statement is as follows:

synchronized block

```
synchronized (expr) {
  statements;
}
```

The expression `expr` must evaluate to an object reference. If the object is already locked by another thread, the thread is blocked until the lock is released. When a lock is obtained on the object, the statements in the synchronized block are executed, and then the lock is released.

Synchronized statements enable you to synchronize part of the code in a method instead of the entire method. This increases concurrency. Synchronized statements enable you to acquire a lock on any object so that you can synchronize the access to an object instead of to a method. You can make Listing 29.7 thread-safe by placing the statement in line 26 inside a synchronized block:

```
synchronized (account) {
  account.deposit(1);
}
```

Note
Any synchronized instance method can be converted into a synchronized statement. For example, the following synchronized instance method in (a) is equivalent to (b):

```
public synchronized void xMethod() {
   // method body
}
```

```
public void xMethod() {
   synchronized (this) {
      // method body
   }
}
```

(a)   (b)

29.10 Synchronization Using Locks

In Listing 29.7, 100 tasks deposit a penny to the same account concurrently, which causes conflict. To avoid it, you can simply use the `synchronized` keyword in the `deposit` method, as follows:

```
public synchronized void deposit(double amount)
```

A synchronized instance method implicitly acquires a lock on the instance before it executes the method.

JDK 1.5 enables you to use locks explicitly. The new locking features are flexible and give you more control for coordinating threads. A lock is an instance of the `Lock` interface, which declares the methods for acquiring and releasing locks, as shown in Figure 29.14. A lock may also use the `newCondition()` method to create any number of `Condition` objects, which can be used for thread communications.

FIGURE 29.14 The `ReentrantLock` class implements the `Lock` interface to represent a lock.

`ReentrantLock` is a concrete implementation of `Lock` for creating mutually exclusive locks. You can create a lock with the specified fairness policy. True fairness policies guarantee that the longest-wait thread will obtain the lock first. False fairness policies grant a lock to a waiting thread without any access order. Programs using fair locks accessed by many threads may have poorer overall performance than those using the default setting, but have smaller variances in times to obtain locks and prevent starvation.

fairness policy

Listing 29.8 revises AccountWithoutSync.java in Listing 29.7 to synchronize the account modification using explicit locks.

LISTING 29.8 AccountWithSyncUsingLock.java

package for locks

create a lock

acquire the lock

```java
 1 import java.util.concurrent.*;
 2 import java.util.concurrent.locks.*;
 3
 4 public class AccountWithSyncUsingLock {
 5   private static Account account = new Account();
 6
 7   public static void main(String[] args) {
 8     ExecutorService executor = Executors.newCachedThreadPool();
 9
10     // Create and launch 100 threads
11     for (int i = 0; i < 100; i++) {
12       executor.execute(new AddAPennyTask());
13     }
14
15     executor.shutdown();
16
17     // Wait until all tasks are finished
18     while (!executor.isTerminated()) {
19     }
20
21     System.out.println("What is balance ? " + account.getBalance());
22   }
23
24   // A thread for adding a penny to the account
25   public static class AddAPennyTask implements Runnable {
26     public void run() {
27       account.deposit(1);
28     }
29   }
30
31   // An inner class for account
32   public static class Account {
33     private static Lock lock = new ReentrantLock(); // Create a lock
34     private int balance = 0;
35
36     public int getBalance() {
37       return balance;
38     }
39
40     public void deposit(int amount) {
41       lock.lock(); // Acquire the lock
42
43       try {
44         int newBalance = balance + amount;
45
46         // This delay is deliberately added to magnify the
47         // data-corruption problem and make it easy to see.
48         Thread.sleep(5);
49
50         balance = newBalance;
51       }
52       catch (InterruptedException ex) {
53       }
54       finally {
```

```
55          lock.unlock(); // Release the lock
56        }
57      }
58    }
59 }
```
release the lock

Line 33 creates a lock, line 41 acquires the lock, and line 55 releases the lock.

> **Tip**
> It is a good practice to always immediately follow a call to `lock()` with a `try-catch` block and
> release the lock in the `finally` clause, as shown in lines 41–57, to ensure that the lock is always
> released.

The example in Listing 29.7 using the synchronized method is simpler than the one in Listing 29.8 using a lock. In general, using `synchronized` methods or statements is simpler than
using explicit locks for mutual exclusion. However, using explicit locks is more intuitive and
flexible to synchronize threads with conditions, as you will see in the next section.

29.11 Cooperation among Threads

Thread synchronization suffices to avoid race conditions by ensuring the mutual exclusion of
multiple threads in the critical region, but sometimes you also need a way for threads to coop-
erate. Conditions can be used to facilitate communications among threads. A thread can specify what to do under a certain condition. Conditions are objects created by invoking the
`newCondition()` method on a `Lock` object. Once a condition is created, you can use its
`await()`, `signal()`, and `signalAll()` methods for thread communications, as shown in
Figure 29.15. The `await()` method causes the current thread to wait until the condition is sig-
naled. The `signal()` method wakes up one waiting thread, and the `signalAll()` method wakes
all waiting threads.

«interface» *java.util.concurrent.Condition*	
+await(): void	Causes the current thread to wait until the condition is signaled.
+signal(): void	Wakes up one waiting thread.
+signalAll(): Condition	Wakes up all waiting threads.

FIGURE 29.15 The `Condition` interface defines the methods for performing synchronization.

Let us use an example to demonstrate thread communications. Suppose that you create and
launch two tasks, one that deposits to an account, and one that withdraws from the same account. The withdraw task has to wait if the amount to be withdrawn is more than the current
balance. Whenever new funds are deposited to the account, the deposit task notifies the withdraw thread to resume. If the amount is still not enough for a withdrawal, the withdraw thread
has to continue to wait for a new deposit.

To synchronize the operations, use a lock with a condition: `newDeposit` (i.e., new deposit
added to the account). If the balance is less than the amount to be withdrawn, the withdraw
task will wait for the `newDeposit` condition. When the deposit task adds money to the account, the task signals the waiting withdraw task to try again. The interaction between the two
tasks is shown in Figure 29.16.

You create a condition from a `Lock` object. To use a condition, you have to first obtain a
lock. The `await()` method causes the thread to wait and automatically releases the lock on the
condition. Once the condition is right, the thread reacquires the lock and continues executing.

condition

thread cooperation example

FIGURE 29.16 The condition `newDeposit` is used for communications between the two threads.

Assume that the initial balance is 0 and the amounts to deposit and withdraw are randomly generated. Listing 29.9 gives the program. A sample run of the program is shown in Figure 29.17.

```
Command Prompt                                          _ | □ | x
C:\book>java ThreadCooperation
Thread 1                        Thread 2              Balance
Deposit 4                                             4
Deposit 6                                             10
                                Withdraw 6            4
                                Withdraw 2            2
Deposit 6                                             8
                                Withdraw 5            3
Deposit 7                                             10
```

FIGURE 29.17 The withdraw task waits if there are not sufficient funds to withdraw.

LISTING 29.9 ThreadCooperation.java

```java
1  import java.util.concurrent.*;
2  import java.util.concurrent.locks.*;
3
4  public class ThreadCooperation {
5    private static Account account = new Account();
6
7    public static void main(String[] args) {
8      // Create a thread pool with two threads
9      ExecutorService executor = Executors.newFixedThreadPool(2);
10     executor.execute(new DepositTask());
11     executor.execute(new WithdrawTask());
12     executor.shutdown();
13
14     System.out.println("Thread 1\t\tThread 2\t\tBalance");
15   }
16
17   // A task for adding an amount to the account
18   public static class DepositTask implements Runnable {
19     public void run() {
20       try { // Purposely delay it to let the withdraw method proceed
21         while (true) {
22           account.deposit((int)(Math.random() * 10) + 1);
23           Thread.sleep(1000);
24         }
25       }
26       catch (InterruptedException ex) {
27         ex.printStackTrace();
```

create two threads

```
28            }
29          }
30    }
31
32    // A task for subtracting an amount from the account
33    public static class WithdrawTask implements Runnable {
34      public void run() {
35        while (true) {
36          account.withdraw((int)(Math.random() * 10) + 1);
37        }
38      }
39    }
40
41    // An inner class for account
42    private static class Account {
43      // Create a new lock
44      private static Lock lock = new ReentrantLock();                create a lock
45
46      // Create a condition
47      private static Condition newDeposit = lock.newCondition();     create a condition
48
49      private int balance = 0;
50
51      public int getBalance() {
52        return balance;
53      }
54
55      public void withdraw(int amount) {
56        lock.lock(); // Acquire the lock                            acquire the lock
57        try {
58          while (balance < amount)
59            newDeposit.await();                                     wait on the condition
60
61          balance -= amount;
62          System.out.println("\t\t\tWithdraw " + amount +
63            "\t\t" + getBalance());
64        }
65        catch (InterruptedException ex) {
66          ex.printStackTrace();
67        }
68        finally {
69          lock.unlock(); // Release the lock                        release the lock
70        }
71      }
72
73      public void deposit(int amount) {
74        lock.lock(); // Acquire the lock                            acquire the lock
75        try {
76          balance += amount;
77          System.out.println("Deposit " + amount +
78            "\t\t\t\t\t" + getBalance());
79
80          // Signal thread waiting on the condition
81          newDeposit.signalAll();                                   signal threads
82        }
83        finally {
84          lock.unlock(); // Release the lock                        release the lock
85        }
86      }
87    }
88  }
```

The example creates a new inner class named `Account` to model the account with two methods, `deposit(int)` and `withdraw(int)`, a class named `DepositTask` to add an amount to the balance, a class named `WithdrawTask` to withdraw an amount from the balance, and a main class that creates and launches two threads.

The program creates and submits the deposit task (line 10) and the withdraw task (line 11). The deposit task is purposely put to sleep (line 23) to let the withdraw task run. When there are not enough funds to withdraw, the withdraw task waits (line 59) for notification of the balance change from the deposit task (line 81).

A lock is created in line 44. A condition named `newDeposit` on the lock is created in line 47. A condition is bound to a lock. Before waiting or signaling the condition, a thread must first acquire the lock for the condition. The withdraw task acquires the lock in line 56, waits for the `newDeposit` condition (line 59) when there is not a sufficient amount to withdraw, and releases the lock in line 69. The deposit task acquires the lock in line 74, and signals all waiting threads (line 81) for the `newDeposit` condition after a new deposit is made.

What will happen if you replace the `while` loop in lines 58–59 with the following `if` statement?

```
if (balance < amount)
  newDeposit.await();
```

The deposit task will notify the withdraw task whenever the balance changes. `(balance < amount)` may still be true when the withdraw task is awakened. Using the `if` statement, the withdraw task may wait forever. Using the loop statement, the withdraw task will have a chance to recheck the condition. Thus you should always test the condition in a loop.

Caution

Once a thread invokes `await()` on a condition, the thread is put to wait for a signal to resume. If you forget to call `signal()` or `signalAll()` on the condition, the thread will wait forever.

Caution

A condition is created from a `Lock` object. To invoke any method (e.g., `await()`, `signal()`, and `signalAll()`), you must first own the lock. If you invoke these methods without acquiring the lock, an `IllegalMonitorStateException` will be thrown.

ever-waiting threads (margin note)

IllegalMonitorState-Exception (margin note)

29.11.1 Java's Built-in Monitor

Locks and conditions are new in Java 5. Prior to Java 5, thread communications were programmed using the object's built-in monitors. Locks and conditions are more powerful and flexible than the built-in monitor, and in consequence, this section can be completely ignored. However, if you are working with legacy Java code, you may encounter Java's built-in monitor.

A *monitor* is an object with mutual exclusion and synchronization capabilities. Only one thread at a time can execute a method in the monitor. A thread enters the monitor by acquiring a lock on it and exits by releasing the lock. *Any object can be a monitor.* An object becomes a monitor once a thread locks it. Locking is implemented using the `synchronized` keyword on a method or a block. A thread must acquire a lock before executing a synchronized method or block. A thread can wait in a monitor if the condition is not right for it to continue executing in the monitor. You can invoke the `wait()` method on the monitor object to release the lock so that some other thread can get in the monitor and perhaps change the monitor's state. When the condition is right, the other thread can invoke the `notify()` or `notifyAll()` method to signal one or all waiting threads to regain the lock and resume execution. The template for invoking these methods is shown in Figure 29.18.

```
          Task 1                                          Task 2
synchronized (anObject) {                     synchronized (anObject) {
  try {                                         // When condition becomes true
    // Wait for the condition to become true    anObject.notify(); or anObject.notifyAll();
    while (!condition)        resume            ...
      anObject.wait();                        }

    // Do something when condition is true
  }
  catch (InterruptedException ex) {
    ex.printStackTrace();
  }
}
```

FIGURE 29.18 The `wait()`, `notify()`, and `notifyAll()` methods coordinate thread communication.

The `wait()`, `notify()`, and `notifyAll()` methods must be called in a synchronized method or a synchronized block on the receiving object of these methods. Otherwise, an `IllegalMonitorStateException` will occur.

When `wait()` is invoked, it pauses the thread and simultaneously releases the lock on the object. When the thread is restarted after being notified, the lock is automatically reacquired.

The `wait()`, `notify()`, and `notifyAll()` methods on an object are analogous to the `await()`, `signal()`, and `signalAll()` methods on a condition.

29.12 Case Study: Producer/Consumer

Consider the classic Consumer/Producer example. Suppose you use a buffer to store integers. The buffer size is limited. The buffer provides the method `write(int)` to add an `int` value to the buffer and the method `read()` to read and delete an `int` value from the buffer. To synchronize the operations, use a lock with two conditions: `notEmpty` (i.e., buffer is not empty) and `notFull` (i.e., buffer is not full). When a task adds an `int` to the buffer, if the buffer is full, the task will wait for the `notFull` condition. When a task deletes an `int` from the buffer, if the buffer is empty, the task will wait for the `notEmpty` condition. The interaction between the two tasks is shown in Figure 29.19.

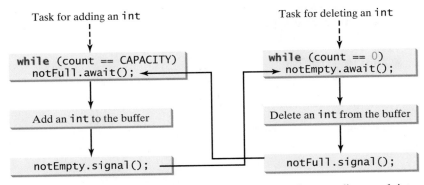

FIGURE 29.19 The conditions `notFull` and `notEmpty` are used to coordinate task interactions.

Listing 29.10 presents the complete program. The program contains the `Buffer` class (lines 48–95) and two tasks for repeatedly producing and consuming numbers to and from the buffer (lines 16–45). The `write(int)` method (line 60) adds an integer to the buffer. The `read()` method (line 77) deletes and returns an integer from the buffer.

For simplicity, the buffer is implemented using a linked list (lines 48–49). The conditions notEmpty and notFull on the lock are created in lines 55–56. The conditions are bound to a lock. A lock must be acquired before a condition can be applied. If you use the wait() and notify() methods to rewrite this example, you have to designate two objects as monitors.

LISTING 29.10 ConsumerProducer.java

```java
import java.util.concurrent.*;
import java.util.concurrent.locks.*;

public class ConsumerProducer {
  private static Buffer buffer = new Buffer();

  public static void main(String[] args) {
    // Create a thread pool with two threads
    ExecutorService executor = Executors.newFixedThreadPool(2);
    executor.execute(new ProducerTask());
    executor.execute(new ConsumerTask());
    executor.shutdown();
  }

  // A task for adding an int to the buffer
  private static class ProducerTask implements Runnable {
    public void run() {
      try {
        int i = 1;
        while (true) {
          System.out.println("Producer writes " + i);
          buffer.write(i++); // Add a value to the buffer
          // Put the thread to sleep
          Thread.sleep((int)(Math.random() * 10000));
        }
      } catch (InterruptedException ex) {
        ex.printStackTrace();
      }
    }
  }

  // A task for reading and deleting an int from the buffer
  private static class ConsumerTask implements Runnable {
    public void run() {
      try {
        while (true) {
          System.out.println("\t\t\tConsumer reads " + buffer.read());
          // Put the thread into sleep
          Thread.sleep((int)(Math.random() * 10000));
        }
      } catch (InterruptedException ex) {
        ex.printStackTrace();
      }
    }
  }

  // An inner class for buffer
  private static class Buffer {
    private static final int CAPACITY = 1; // buffer size
    private java.util.LinkedList<Integer> queue =
      new java.util.LinkedList<Integer>();
```

Margin notes:
- create a buffer (line 5)
- create two threads (line 9)
- producer task (line 16)
- consumer task (line 33)

```java
53     // Create a new lock
54     private static Lock lock = new ReentrantLock();
55
56     // Create two conditions
57     private static Condition notEmpty = lock.newCondition();
58     private static Condition notFull = lock.newCondition();
59
60     public void write(int value) {
61       lock.lock(); // Acquire the lock
62       try {
63         while (queue.size() == CAPACITY) {
64           System.out.println("Wait for notFull condition");
65           notFull.await();
66         }
67
68         queue.offer(value);
69         notEmpty.signal(); // Signal notEmpty condition
70       } catch (InterruptedException ex) {
71         ex.printStackTrace();
72       } finally {
73         lock.unlock(); // Release the lock
74       }
75     }
76
77     public int read() {
78       int value = 0;
79       lock.lock(); // Acquire the lock
80       try {
81         while (queue.isEmpty()) {
82           System.out.println("\t\t\tWait for notEmpty condition");
83           notEmpty.await();
84         }
85
86         value = queue.remove();
87         notFull.signal(); // Signal notFull condition
88       } catch (InterruptedException ex) {
89         ex.printStackTrace();
90       } finally {
91         lock.unlock(); // Release the lock
92         return value;
93       }
94     }
95   }
96 }
```

create a lock

create a condition
create a condition

acquire the lock

wait on notFull

signal notEmpty

release the lock

acquire the lock

wait on notEmpty

signal notFull

release the lock

A sample run of the program is shown in Figure 29.20.

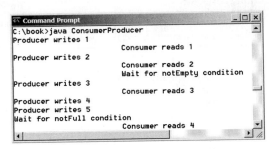

FIGURE 29.20 Locks and conditions are used for communications between the Producer and Consumer threads.

29.13 Blocking Queues

blocking queue

Queues and priority queues were introduced in §22.9. A *blocking queue* causes a thread to block when you try to add an element to a full queue or to remove an element from an empty queue. The `BlockingQueue` interface extends `java.util.Queue` and provides the synchronized `put` and `take` methods for adding an element to the head of the queue and for removing an element from the tail of the queue, as shown in Figure 29.21.

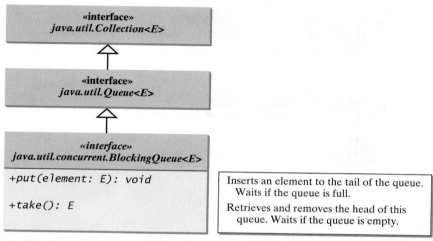

FIGURE 29.21 `BlockingQueue` is a subinterface of `Queue`.

Three concrete blocking queues `ArrayBlockingQueue`, `LinkedBlockingQueue`, and `PriorityBlockingQueue` are supported in JDK 1.5, as shown in Figure 29.22. All are in the `java.util.concurrent` package. `ArrayBlockingQueue` implements a blocking queue using an array. You have to specify a capacity or an optional fairness to construct an `ArrayBlockingQueue`. `LinkedBlockingQueue` implements a blocking queue using a linked list. You may create an unbounded or bounded `LinkedBlockingQueue`. `PriorityBlockingQueue` is a priority queue. You may create an unbounded or bounded priority queue.

FIGURE 29.22 `ArrayBlockingQueue`, `LinkedBlockingQueue`, and `PriorityBlockingQueue` are concrete blocking queues.

Note

You may create an unbounded `LinkedBlockingQueue` or `PriorityBlockingQueue`. For an unbounded queue, the `put` method will never block.

unbounded queue

Listing 29.11 gives an example of using an `ArrayBlockingQueue` to simplify the Consumer/Producer example in Listing 29.10. Line 5 creates an `ArrayBlockingQueue` to store integers. The Producer thread puts an integer to the queue (line 22), and the Consumer thread takes an integer from the queue (line 37).

LISTING 29.11 `ConsumerProducerUsingBlockingQueue.java`

```
1  import java.util.concurrent.*;
2
3  public class ConsumerProducerUsingBlockingQueue {
4    private static ArrayBlockingQueue<Integer> buffer =
5      new ArrayBlockingQueue<Integer>(2);
6
7    public static void main(String[] args) {
8      // Create a thread pool with two threads
9      ExecutorService executor = Executors.newFixedThreadPool(2);
10     executor.execute(new ProducerTask());
11     executor.execute(new ConsumerTask());
12     executor.shutdown();
13   }
14
15   // A task for adding an int to the buffer
16   private static class ProducerTask implements Runnable {
17     public void run() {
18       try {
19         int i = 1;
20         while (true) {
21           System.out.println("Producer writes " + i);
22           buffer.put(i++); // Add any value to the buffer, say, 1
23           // Put the thread to sleep
24           Thread.sleep((int)(Math.random() * 10000));
25         }
26       } catch (InterruptedException ex) {
27         ex.printStackTrace();
28       }
29     }
30   }
31
32   // A task for reading and deleting an int from the buffer
33   private static class ConsumerTask implements Runnable {
34     public void run() {
35       try {
36         while (true) {
37           System.out.println("\t\t\tConsumer reads " + buffer.take());
38           // Put the thread to sleep
39           Thread.sleep((int)(Math.random() * 10000));
40         }
41       } catch (InterruptedException ex) {
42         ex.printStackTrace();
43       }
44     }
45   }
46 }
```

create a buffer

create two threads

producer task

put

consumer task

take

In Listing 29.10, you used locks and conditions to synchronize the Producer and Consumer threads. In this program, hand coding is not necessary, because synchronization is already implemented in `ArrayBlockingQueue`.

29.14 Semaphores

Semaphores can be used to restrict the number of threads that access a shared resource. Before accessing the resource, a thread must acquire a permit from the semaphore. After finishing with the resource, the thread must return the permit back to the semaphore, as shown in Figure 29.23.

FIGURE 29.23 A limited number of threads can access a shared resource controlled by a semaphore.

To create a semaphore, you have to specify the number of permits with an optional fairness policy, as shown in Figure 29.24. A task acquires a permit by invoking the semaphore's `acquire()` method and releases the permit by invoking the semaphore's `release()` method. Once a permit is acquired, the total number of available permits in a semaphore is reduced by 1. Once a permit is released, the total number of available permits in a semaphore is increased by 1.

A semaphore with just one permit can be used to simulate a mutually exclusive lock. Listing 29.12 revises the `Account` inner class in Listing 29.10 using a semaphore to ensure that only one thread at a time can access the `deposit` method.

LISTING 29.12 New Account Inner Class

```
1  // An inner class for account
2  private static class Account {
3    // Create a semaphore
4    private static Semaphore semaphore = new Semaphore(1);
5    private int balance = 0;
6
7    public int getBalance() {
8      return balance;
9    }
10
11   public void deposit(int amount) {
12     try {
13       semaphore.acquire(); // Acquire a permit
14       int newBalance = balance + amount;
15
16       // This delay is deliberately added to magnify the
17       // data-corruption problem and make it easy to see
18       Thread.sleep(5);
19
20       balance = newBalance;
21     }
```

create a semaphore

acquire a permit

```
22      catch (InterruptedException ex) {
23      }
24      finally {
25        semaphore.release(); // Release a permit
26      }
27    }
28 }
```

release a permit

java.util.concurrent.Semaphore	
+Semaphore(numberOfPermits: int)	Creates a semaphore with the specified number of permits. The fairness policy is false.
+Semaphore(numberOfPermits: int, fair: boolean)	Creates a semaphore with the specified number of permits and the fairness policy.
+acquire(): void	Acquires a permit from this semaphore. If no permit is available, the thread is blocked until one is available.
+release(): void	Releases a permit back to the semaphore.

FIGURE 29.24 The Semaphore class contains the methods for accessing a semaphore.

A semaphore with one permit is created in line 4. A thread first acquires a permit when executing the deposit method in line 13. After the balance is updated, the thread releases the permit in line 25. It is a good practice to always place the release() method in the finally clause to ensure that the permit is finally released even in the case of exceptions.

29.15 Avoiding Deadlocks

Sometimes two or more threads need to acquire the locks on several shared objects. This could cause a *deadlock*, in which each thread has the lock on one of the objects and is waiting for the lock on the other object. Consider the scenario with two threads and two objects, as shown in Figure 29.25. Thread 1 has acquired a lock on object1, and Thread 2 has acquired a lock on object2. Now Thread 1 is waiting for the lock on object2, and Thread 2 for the lock on object1. Each thread waits for the other to release the lock it needs, and until that happens, neither can continue to run.

deadlock

FIGURE 29.25 Thread 1 and Thread 2 are deadlocked.

Deadlock is easily avoided by using a simple technique known as *resource ordering*. With this technique, you assign an order to all the objects whose locks must be acquired and ensure that each thread acquires the locks in that order. For the example in Figure 29.25, suppose that

resource ordering

the objects are ordered as `object1` and `object2`. Using the resource ordering technique, Thread 2 must acquire a lock on `object1` first, then on `object2`. Once Thread 1 acquires a lock on `object1`, Thread 2 has to wait for a lock on `object1`. So Thread 1 will be able to acquire a lock on `object2` and no deadlock will occur.

29.16 Thread States

Tasks are executed in threads. Threads can be in one of five states: New, Ready, Running, Blocked, or Finished (see Figure 29.26).

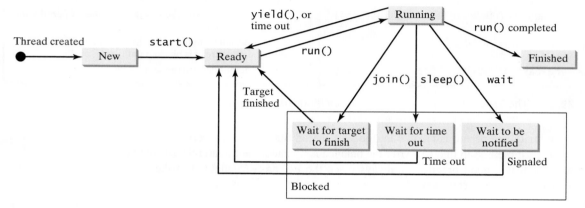

FIGURE 29.26 A thread can be in one of five states: New, Ready, Running, Blocked, or Finished.

When a thread is newly created, it enters the *New state*. After a thread is started by calling its `start()` method, it enters the *Ready state*. A ready thread is runnable but may not be running yet. The operating system has to allocate CPU time to it.

When a ready thread begins executing, it enters the *Running state*. A running thread may enter the *Ready* state if its given CPU time expires or its `yield()` method is called.

A thread can enter the *Blocked state* (i.e., become inactive) for several reasons. It may have invoked the `join()`, `sleep()`, `wait()`, or `lock()` method, or some other thread may have invoked these methods. It may be waiting for an I/O operation to finish. A blocked thread may be reactivated when the action inactivating it is reversed. For example, if a thread has been put to sleep and the sleep time has expired, the thread is reactivated and enters the **Ready** state.

Finally, a thread is *finished* if it completes the execution of its `run()` method.

The `isAlive()` method is used to find out the state of a thread. It returns `true` if a thread is in the **Ready**, **Blocked**, or **Running** state; it returns `false` if a thread is new and has not started or if it is finished.

The `interrupt()` method interrupts a thread in the following way: If a thread is currently in the **Ready** or **Running** state, its interrupted flag is set; if a thread is currently blocked, it is awakened and enters the **Ready** state, and an `java.lang.InterruptedException` is thrown.

29.17 Synchronized Collections

synchronized collection

The classes in the Java Collections Framework are not thread-safe; that is, their contents may be corrupted if they are accessed and updated concurrently by multiple threads. You can protect the data in a collection by locking the collection or by using synchronized collections.

The `Collections` class provides six static methods for wrapping a collection into a synchronized version, as shown in Figure 29.27. The collections created using these methods are called *synchronization wrappers*.

synchronization wrapper

java.util.Collections	
+synchronizedCollection(c: Collection): Collection	Returns a synchronized collection.
+synchronizedList(list: List): List	Returns a synchronized list from the specified list.
+synchronizedMap(m: Map): Map	Returns a synchronized map from the specified map.
+synchronizedSet(s: Set): Set	Returns a synchronized set from the specified set.
+synchronizedSortedMap(s: SortedMap): SortedMap	Returns a synchronized sorted map from the specified sorted map.
+synchronizedSortedSet(s: SortedSet): SortedSet	Returns a synchronized sorted set.

FIGURE 29.27 You can obtain synchronized collections using the methods in the `Collections` class.

Invoking `synchronizedCollection(Collection c)` returns a new `Collection` object, in which all the methods that access and update the original collection `c` are synchronized. These methods are implemented using the `synchronized` keyword. For example, the `add` method is implemented like this:

```
public boolean add(E o) {
  synchronized (this) { return c.add(o); }
}
```

Synchronized collections can be safely accessed and modified by multiple threads concurrently.

Note

The methods in `java.util.Vector`, `java.util.Stack`, and `java.util.Hashtable` are already synchronized. These are old classes introduced in JDK 1.0. In JDK 1.5, you should use `java.util.ArrayList` to replace `Vector`, `java.util.LinkedList` to replace `Stack`, and `java.util.Map` to replace `Hashtable`. If synchronization is needed, use a synchronization wrapper.

The synchronization wrapper classes are thread-safe, but the iterator is *fail-fast*. This means that if you are using an iterator to traverse a collection while the underlying collection is being modified by another thread, then the iterator will immediately fail by throwing `java.util.ConcurrentModificationException`, which is a subclass of `RuntimeException`. To avoid this error, you need to create a synchronized collection object and acquire a lock on the object when traversing it. For example, suppose you want to traverse a set; you have to write the code like this:

fail-fast

```
Set hashSet = Collections.synchronizedSet(new HashSet());

synchronized (hashSet) { // Must synchronize it
  Iterator iterator = hashSet.iterator();

  while (iterator.hasNext()) {
    System.out.println(iterator.next());
  }
}
```

Failure to do so may result in nondeterministic behavior, such as `ConcurrentModificationException`.

29.18 SwingWorker

event dispatch thread

As discussed in §29.6, all Swing GUI events are processed in a single *event dispatch thread*. If an event requires a long time to process, the thread cannot attend to other tasks in the queue. To solve this problem, you should run the time-consuming task for processing the event in a separate thread. Java 6 introduced `SwingWorker`. `SwingWorker` is an abstract class that implements `Runnable`. You can define a task class that extends `SwingWorker`, run the time-consuming task and update the GUI using the results produced from the task. Figure 29.28 defines `SwingWorker`.

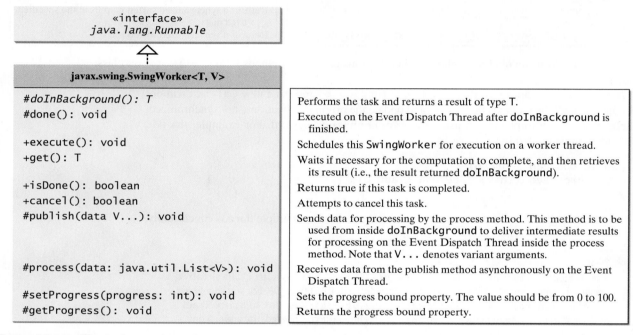

FIGURE 29.28 The `SwingWorker` class can be used to process time-consuming tasks.

This section demonstrates basic use of `SwingWorker`. The next section gives an example involving advanced features of `SwingWorker`.

doInBackground()

done()

To use `SwingWorker`, your task class should override `doInBackground()` to perform a time-consuming task and override the `done()` method to update GUI components if necessary. Listing 29.13 gives an example that lets the user specify a number and displays the number of prime numbers less than or equal to the specified number, as shown in Figure 29.29.

FIGURE 29.29 You can compare the effect of using versus not using `SwingWorker`.

LISTING 29.13 SwingWorkerDemo.java

```java
 1  import javax.swing.*;
 2  import java.awt.*;
 3  import java.awt.event.*;
 4
 5  public class SwingWorkerDemo extends JApplet {
 6    private JButton jbtComputeWithSwingWorker = new JButton("Compute");     GUI components
 7    private JTextField jtfLimit1 = new JTextField(8);
 8    private JTextField jtfResult1 = new JTextField(6);
 9    private JButton jbtCompute = new JButton("Compute");
10    private JTextField jtfLimit2 = new JTextField(8);
11    private JTextField jtfResult2 = new JTextField(6);
12
13    public SwingWorkerDemo() {                                              create UI
14      JPanel panel1 = new JPanel(new GridLayout(2, 1));                     left panel
15      panel1.setBorder(BorderFactory.createTitledBorder(
16        "Using SwingWorker"));
17      JPanel panel11 = new JPanel();
18      panel11.add(new JLabel("The number of prime numbers <= "));
19      panel11.add(jtfLimit1);
20      panel11.add(new JLabel("is"));
21      panel11.add(jtfResult1);
22      JPanel panel12 = new JPanel();
23      panel12.add(jbtComputeWithSwingWorker);
24      panel1.add(panel11);
25      panel1.add(panel12);
26
27      JPanel panel2 = new JPanel(new GridLayout(2, 1));                     right panel
28      panel2.setBorder(BorderFactory.createTitledBorder(
29        "Without Using SwingWorker"));
30      JPanel panel21 = new JPanel();
31      panel21.add(new JLabel("The number of prime numbers <= "));
32      panel21.add(jtfLimit2);
33      panel21.add(new JLabel("is"));
34      panel21.add(jtfResult2);
35      JPanel panel22 = new JPanel();
36      panel22.add(jbtCompute);
37      panel2.add(panel21);
38      panel2.add(panel22);
39
40      setLayout(new GridLayout(1, 2));
41      add(panel1);
42      add(panel2);
43
44      jbtComputeWithSwingWorker.addActionListener(new ActionListener() {    add listener
45        public void actionPerformed(ActionEvent e) {
46          new ComputePrime(Integer.parseInt(jtfLimit1.getText()),          create task
47            jtfResult1).execute(); // Execute SwingWorker                   create task
48        }
49      });
50
51      jbtCompute.addActionListener(new ActionListener() {                   add listener
52        public void actionPerformed(ActionEvent e) {
53          int count = ComputePrime.getNumberOfPrimes(
54            Integer.parseInt(jtfLimit2.getText()));
55          jtfResult2.setText(count + "");
56        }
57      });
```

```
58    }
59
60    /** Task class for SwingWorker */
61    static class ComputePrime extends SwingWorker<Integer, Object> {
62      private int limit;
63      private JTextField result; // Text field in the UI
64
65      /** Construct a runnable Task */
66      public ComputePrime(int limit, JTextField result) {
67        this.limit = limit;
68        this.result = result;
69      }
70
71      /** Code run on a background thread */
72      protected Integer doInBackground() {
73        return getNumberOfPrimes(limit);
74      }
75
76      /** Code executed after the background thread finishes */
77      protected void done() {
78        try {
79          result.setText(get().toString()); // Display in text field
80        }
81        catch (Exception ex) {
82          result.setText(ex.getMessage());
83        }
84      }
85
86      /** Return the number of primes <= limit */
87      public static int getNumberOfPrimes(int limit) {
88        int count = 0; // Count the number of prime numbers
89        int number = 2; // A number to be tested for primeness
90
91        // Repeatedly find prime numbers
92        while (number <= limit) {
93          // Print the prime number and increase the count
94          if (isPrime(number)) {
95            count++; // Increase the count
96          }
97
98          // Check if the next number is prime
99          number++;
100       }
101
102       return count;
103     }
104
105     /** Check whether number is prime */
106     private static boolean isPrime(int number) {
107       for (int divisor = 2; divisor <= number / 2; divisor++) {
108         if (number % divisor == 0) { // If true, number is not prime
109           return false; // number is not a prime
110         }
111       }
112
113       return true; // number is prime
114     }
115   }
116 }
```

Margin annotations:

- (line 66) constructor
- (line 72) override **doInBackground()**
- (line 77) override **done()**
- (line 87) **getNumberOfPrimes**
- (line 116) main method omitted

The UI consists of two panels. The left panel demonstrates how to compute the number of prime numbers using a SwingWorker. The right panel demonstrates how to compute the number of prime numbers without using a SwingWorker. You enter a number (e.g., 100000) in the first text field in the panel and click the *Compute* button to display the number of primes in the second text field. When you click the *Compute* button in the left panel, a SwingWorker task is created and executed (lines 46–47). Since the task is run on a separate thread, you can continue to use the GUI. However, when you click the *Compute* button in the right panel, the GUI is frozen, because the getNumberOfPrimes method is executed on the event dispatch thread (lines 53–54).

using or not using **SwingWorker**

The inner class ComputePrime is a SwingWorker (line 61). It overrides the doInBackground method to run getNumberOfPrimes in a background thread (lines 72–74). It also overrides the done method to display the result in a text field, once the background thread finishes (lines 77–84).

override **doInBackground**

override **done**

The ComputePrime class defines the static getNumberOfPrimes method for computing the number of primes (lines 87–103). When you click the *Compute* button in the left panel, this method is executed on a background thread (lines 46–47). When you click the *Compute* button in the right panel, this method is executed in the event dispatch thread (lines 53–54).

static **getNumberOfPrimes**

Tip
Two things to remember when writing Swing GUI programs:

GUI and **SwingWorker**

- Time-consuming tasks should be run in SwingWorker.
- Swing components should be accessed from the event dispatch thread only.

29.19 Displaying Progress Using **JProgressBar**

In the preceding example, it may take a long time to finish the computation in the background thread. It is better to inform the user the progress of the computation. You can use the JProgressBar to display the progress.

JProgressBar is a component that displays a value graphically within a bounded interval. A progress bar is typically used to show the percentage of completion of a lengthy operation; it comprises a rectangular bar that is "filled in" from left to right horizontally or from bottom to top vertically as the operation is performed. It provides the user with feedback on the progress of the operation. For example, when a file is being read, it alerts the user to the progress of the operation, thereby keeping the user attentive.

JProgressBar is often implemented using a thread to monitor the completion status of other threads. The progress bar can be displayed horizontally or vertically, as determined by its orientation property. The minimum, value, and maximum properties determine the minimum, current, and maximum lengths on the progress bar, as shown in Figure 29.30. Figure 29.31 lists frequently used features of JProgressBar.

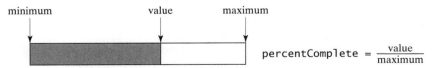

FIGURE 29.30 JProgressBar displays the progress of a task.

Listing 29.14 gives an example that lets the user specify the number of primes, say *n*, and displays the first *n* primes starting from 2, as shown in Figure 29.32. The program displays the primes in the text area and updates the completion status in a progress bar.

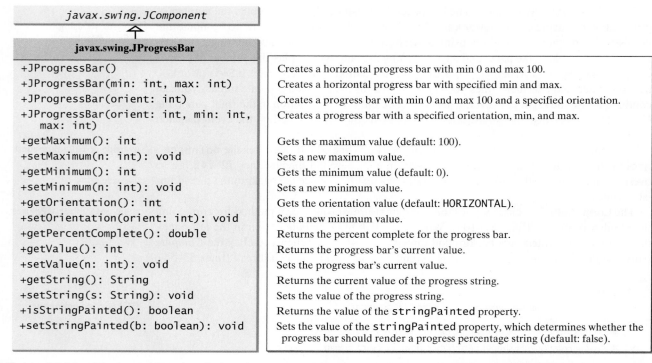

javax.swing.JComponent	

javax.swing.JProgressBar	
+JProgressBar()	Creates a horizontal progress bar with min 0 and max 100.
+JProgressBar(min: int, max: int)	Creates a horizontal progress bar with specified min and max.
+JProgressBar(orient: int)	Creates a progress bar with min 0 and max 100 and a specified orientation.
+JProgressBar(orient: int, min: int, max: int)	Creates a progress bar with a specified orientation, min, and max.
+getMaximum(): int	Gets the maximum value (default: 100).
+setMaximum(n: int): void	Sets a new maximum value.
+getMinimum(): int	Gets the minimum value (default: 0).
+setMinimum(n: int): void	Sets a new minimum value.
+getOrientation(): int	Gets the orientation value (default: HORIZONTAL).
+setOrientation(orient: int): void	Sets a new minimum value.
+getPercentComplete(): double	Returns the percent complete for the progress bar.
+getValue(): int	Returns the progress bar's current value.
+setValue(n: int): void	Sets the progress bar's current value.
+getString(): String	Returns the current value of the progress string.
+setString(s: String): void	Sets the value of the progress string.
+isStringPainted(): boolean	Returns the value of the **stringPainted** property.
+setStringPainted(b: boolean): void	Sets the value of the **stringPainted** property, which determines whether the progress bar should render a progress percentage string (default: false).

FIGURE 29.31 JProgressBar is a Swing component with many properties that enable you to customize a progress bar.

FIGURE 29.32 The user enters the number of prime numbers and clicks the Display Prime button to display the primes starting from 2 to the text area.

LISTING 29.14 ProgressBarDemo.java

```
 1  import javax.swing.*;
 2  import java.awt.*;
 3  import java.awt.event.*;
 4  import java.beans.*;
 5
 6  public class ProgressBarDemo extends JApplet {
 7    private JProgressBar jpb = new JProgressBar();
 8    private JTextArea jtaResult = new JTextArea();
 9    private JTextField jtfPrimeCount = new JTextField(8);
10    private JButton jbtDisplayPrime = new JButton("Display Prime");
11
12    public ProgressBarDemo() {
13      jpb.setStringPainted(true); // Paint the percent in a string
14      jpb.setValue(0);
15      jpb.setMaximum(100);
16
```

progress bar

JProgressBar properties UI

```
17      jtaResult.setWrapStyleWord(true);                                    wrap word
18      jtaResult.setLineWrap(true);                                         wrap line
19
20      JPanel panel = new JPanel();
21      panel.add(new JLabel("Enter the prime number count"));
22      panel.add(jtfPrimeCount);
23      panel.add(jbtDisplayPrime);
24
25      add(jpb, BorderLayout.NORTH);
26      add(new JScrollPane(jtaResult), BorderLayout.CENTER);
27      add(panel, BorderLayout.SOUTH);
28
29      jbtDisplayPrime.addActionListener(new ActionListener() {             add button listener
30        public void actionPerformed(ActionEvent e) {
31          ComputePrime task = new ComputePrime(                            create task
32            Integer.parseInt(jtfPrimeCount.getText()), jtaResult);
33
34          task.addPropertyChangeListener(new PropertyChangeListener() {    add property listener
35            public void propertyChange(PropertyChangeEvent e) {
36              if ("progress".equals(e.getPropertyName())) {
37                jpb.setValue((Integer)e.getNewValue());                    get property value
38              }
39            }
40          });
41
42          task.execute(); // Execute SwingWorker                           execute task
43        }
44      });
45    }
46
47    /** Task class for SwingWorker */
48    static class ComputePrime extends SwingWorker<Integer, Integer> {       task class
49      private int count;
50      private JTextArea result; // Textarea in the UI
51
52      /** Construct a runnable Task */
53      public ComputePrime(int count, JTextArea result) {
54        this.count = count;
55        this.result = result;
56      }
57
58      /** Code run on a background thread */
59      protected Integer doInBackground() {                                 override doInBackground
60        publishPrimeNumbers(count);
61
62        return 0; // doInBackground must return a value
63      }
64
65      /** Override process to display published prime values */
66      protected void process(java.util.List<Integer> list) {               override process
67        for (int i = 0; i < list.size(); i++)
68          result.append(list.get(i) + " ");
69      }
70
71      /** Publish the first n primes number */
72      private void publishPrimeNumbers(int n) {                            compute primes
73        int count = 0; // Count the number of prime numbers
74        int number = 2; // A number to be tested for primeness
75
```

set progress property
publish a prime

```
76        // Repeatedly find prime numbers
77        while (count <= n) {
78          // Print the prime number and increase the count
79          if (isPrime(number)) {
80            count++; // Increase the count
81            setProgress(100 * count / n); // Update progress
82            publish(number); // Publish the prime number
83          }
84
85          // Check if the next number is prime
86          number++;
87        }
88      }
89
90      /** Check whether number is prime */
91      private static boolean isPrime(int number) {
92        for (int divisor = 2; divisor <= number / 2; divisor++) {
93          if (number % divisor == 0) { // If true, number is not prime
94            return false; // number is not a prime
95          }
96        }
97
98        return true; // number is prime
99      }
100   }
101 }
```

main method omitted

The **SwingWorker** class generates a **PropertyChangeEvent** whenever the **setProgress** method is invoked. The **setProgress** method (line 81) sets a new progress value between 0 and 100. This value is wrapped in the **PropertyChangeEvent**. The listener of this event can obtain the progress value using the **getNewValue()** method (line 37). The progress bar is updated using this new progress value (line 37).

The program creates a **JProgressBar** (line 7) and sets its properties (lines 13–15).

override **doInBackground**

The inner class **ComputePrime** is a **SwingWorker** (line 48). It overrides the **do-InBackground** method to run **publishPrimeNumbers** in a background thread (line 60). The **publishPrimeNumbers** method finds the specified number of primes starting from 2. When a prime is found, the **setProgress** method is invoked to set a new progress value (line 81). This causes a **PropertyChangeEvent** to be fired, which is notified to the listener.

override **process**

When a prime is found, the **publish** method is invoked to send the data to the **process** method (line 82). The **process** method is overridden (lines 66–69) to display the primes sent from the **publish** method. The primes are displayed in the text area (line 68).

KEY TERMS

condition 949	multithreading 930
deadlock 959	race condition 945
event dispatch thread 937	synchronization wrapper 961
fail-fast 961	synchronized 945
fairness policy 947	thread 930
lock 947	thread-safe 945
monitor 952	

CHAPTER SUMMARY

■ Each task is an instance of the **Runnable** interface. A *thread* is an object that facilitates the execution of a task. You can declare a task class by implementing the **Runnable** interface and create a thread by wrapping a task using a **Thread** constructor.

- After a thread object is created, use the `start()` method to start a thread, and the `sleep(long)` method to put a thread to sleep so that other threads get a chance to run.

- A thread object never directly invokes the `run` method. The JVM invokes the `run` method when it is time to execute the thread. Your class must override the `run` method to tell the system what the thread will do when it runs.

- To prevent threads from corrupting a shared resource, use synchronized methods or blocks. A synchronized method acquires a lock before it executes. In the case of an instance method, the lock is on the object for which the method was invoked. In the case of a static (class) method, the lock is on the class.

- A synchronized statement can be used to acquire a lock on any object, not just *this* object, when executing a block of the code in a method. This block is referred to as a *synchronized block*.

- You can use explicit locks and conditions to facilitate communications among threads, as well as using the built-in monitor for objects.

- *Deadlock* occurs when two or more threads acquire locks on multiple objects and each has a lock on one object and is waiting for the lock on the other object. The *resource ordering technique* can be used to avoid deadlock.

- You can define a task class that extends `SwingWorker`, run the time-consuming task, and update the GUI using the results produced from the task.

- You can use a `JProgressBar` to track the progress of a thread.

REVIEW QUESTIONS

Sections 29.1–29.4

29.1 Why do you need multithreading? How can multiple threads run simultaneously in a single-processor system?

29.2 How do you declare a task class? How do you create a thread for a task?

29.3 What would happen if you replaced the `start()` method by the `run()` method in lines 14–16 in Listing 29.1?

```
print100.start();        print100.run();
printA.start();   ──Replaced by──▶   printA.run();
printB.start();          printB.run();
```

29.4 What is wrong in the following two programs? Correct the errors.

```java
public class Test implements Runnable {
  public static void main(String[] args) {
    new Test();
  }

  public Test() {
    Test task = new Test();
    new Thread(task).start();
  }

  public void run(){
    System.out.println("test");
  }
}
```

(a)

```java
public class Test implements Runnable {
  public static void main(String[] args) {
    new Test();
  }

  public Test() {
    Thread t = new Thread(this);
    t.start();
    t.start();

  }

  public void run() {
    System.out.println("test");
  }
}
```

(b)

29.5 Which of the following methods are instance methods in `java.lang.Thread`? Which method may throw an `InterruptedException`? Which of them are deprecated in Java 2?

```
run, start, stop, suspend, resume, sleep, interrupt, yield, join,
```

29.6 If a loop contains a method that throws an `InterruptedException`, why should the loop be placed inside a try-catch block?

29.7 How do you set a priority for a thread? What is the default priority?

Sections 29.5–29.7

29.8 When should you use a timer or a thread to control animation? What are the advantages and disadvantages of using a thread and a timer?

29.9 What is the event dispatch thread? How do you let a task run from the event dispatch thread?

Section 29.8 Thread Pools

29.10 What are the benefits of using a thread pool?

29.11 How do you create a thread pool with three fixed threads? How do you submit a task to the thread pool? How do you know that all the tasks are finished?

Sections 29.9–29.12

29.12 Give some examples of possible resource corruption when running multiple threads. How do you synchronize conflicting threads?

29.13 Suppose you place the statement in line 30 of Listing 29.7 AccountWithoutSync.java inside a synchronized block to avoid race conditions, as follows:

```
synchronized (this) {
  account.deposit(1);
}
```

Does it work?

29.14 How do you create a lock object? How do you acquire a lock and release a lock?

29.15 How do you create a condition on a lock? What are the `await()`, `signal()`, and `signalAll()` methods for?

29.16 What would happen if the `while` loop in lines 56–57 of Listing 29.9 ThreadCooperation.java were changed to an `if` statement?

```
while (balance < amount)        Replaced by        if (balance < amount)
  wait();                    ───────────────►        wait();
```

29.17 Why does the following class have a syntax error?

```
 1 import javax.swing.*;
 2
 3 public class Test extends JApplet implements Runnable {
 4    public void init() throws InterruptedException {
 5      Thread thread = new Thread(this);
 6      thread.sleep(1000);
 7    }
 8
 9    public synchronized void run() {
10    }
11 }
```

29.18 What is the possible cause for `IllegalMonitorStateException`?

29.19 Can the `wait()`, `notify()`, and `notifyAll()` be invoked from any object? What is the purpose of these methods?

29.20 What is wrong in the following code?

```
synchronized (object1) {
  try {
    while (!condition) object2.wait();
  }
  catch (InterruptedException ex) {
  }
}
```

Section 29.13 Blocking Queues

29.21 What blocking queues are supported in JDK 1.5?

29.22 What method do you use to add an element to an `ArrayBlockingQueue`? What happens if the queue is full?

29.23 What method do you use to retrieve an element from an `ArrayBlockingQueue`? What happens if the queue is empty?

Section 29.14 Semaphores

29.24 What are the similarities and differences between a lock and a semaphore?

29.25 How do you create a semaphore that allows three concurrent threads? How do you acquire a semaphore? How do you release a semaphore?

Section 29.15 Avoiding Deadlocks

29.26 What is deadlock? How can you avoid deadlock?

Section 29.17 Synchronized Collections

29.27 What is a synchronized collection? Is `ArrayList` synchronized? How do you make it synchronized?

29.28 Explain why an iterator is fail-fast.

Section 29.19 `JProgressBar`

29.29 For a `JProgressBar`, what is the property that displays the percentage of work completed? How do you set its orientation?

PROGRAMMING EXERCISES

Sections 29.1–29.5

29.1* (*Revising Listing 29.1*) Rewrite Listing 29.1 to display the output in a text area, as shown in Figure 29.33.

FIGURE 29.33 The output from three threads is displayed in a text area.

29.2 (*Racing cars*) Rewrite Exercise 17.17 using a thread to control car racing. Compare the program with Exercise 17.17 by setting the delay time to 10 in both programs. Which one runs animation faster?

29.3 (*Raising flags*) Rewrite Exercise 17.23 using a thread to animate flag rising. Compare the program with Exercise 17.23 by setting the delay time to 10 in both programs. Which one runs animation faster?

Sections 29.8–29.12

29.4 (*Synchronizing threads*) Write a program that launches 1000 threads. Each thread adds 1 to a variable sum that initially is 0. You need to pass sum by reference to each thread. In order to pass it by reference, define an Integer wrapper object to hold sum. Run the program with and without synchronization to see its effect.

29.5 (*Running fans*) Rewrite Exercise 17.11 using a thread to control fan animation.

29.6 (*Bouncing balls*) Rewrite Exercise 17.19 using a thread to control car racing.

29.7 (*Controlling a group of clocks*) Rewrite Exercise 17.14 using a thread to control clock animation.

29.8 (*Account synchronization*) Rewrite Listing 29.9, ThreadCoorporation.java, using object's wait() and notifyAll() methods.

29.9 (*Demonstrating ConcurrentModificationException*) The iterator is *fail-fast*. Write a program to demonstrate it by creating two threads that concurrently access and modify a set. The first thread creates a hash set filled with numbers, and adds a new number to the set every second. The second thread obtains an iterator for the set and traverses the set back and forth through the iterator every second. You will receive a Concurrent-ModificationException because the underlying set is being modified in the first thread while the set in the second thread is being traversed.

29.10* (*Using synchronized sets*) Using synchronization, correct the problem in the preceding exercise so that the second thread does not throw ConcurrentM-odificationException.

Section 29.15 Avoiding Deadlocks

29.11* (*Demonstrating deadlock*) Write a program that demonstrates deadlock.

Section 29.18 **JProgressBar**

29.12* (*Using JProgressBar*) Create a program that displays an instance of JProgressBar and sets its value property randomly every 500 milliseconds infinitely.

Comprehensive

29.13* (*Sorting animation*) Write an animation applet for selection sort, insertion sort, and bubble sort, as shown in Figure 29.34. Create an array of integers 1, 2, ..., 50. Shuffle it randomly. Create a panel to display the array. You should invoke each sort method in a separate thread.

(a) Sorting in progress

(b) Sorted

FIGURE 29.34   Three sorting algorithms are illustrated in the animation.

29.14**   (*Copying files*) Write a GUI application that copies files. A progress bar is used
to display the progress of the copying operation, as shown in Figure 29.35(a).

(a)   (b)

FIGURE 29.35   (a) The user enters the files in the text fields and clicks the *Copy* button to
start copying files. (b) The program split a file into several smaller files.

29.15**   (*Splitting a file*) Modify Exercise 19.11 to display the percentage of work
done in a progress bar, as shown in Figure 29.35(b).

CHAPTER 30

NETWORKING

Objectives

- To explain terms: TCP, IP, domain name, domain name server, stream-based communication, and packet-based communications (§30.2).

- To create servers using server sockets (§30.2.1) and create clients using client sockets (§30.2.2).

- To implement Java networking programs using stream sockets (§30.2.3).

- To obtain Internet addresses using the `InetAddress` class (§30.3).

- To develop servers for multiple clients (§30.4).

- To develop applets that communicate with the server (§30.5).

- To send and receive objects on a network (§30.6).

- To create applications or applets to retrieve files from a network (§30.7).

- To render HTML files using the `JEditorPane` class (§30.8).

- To develop an interactive `TicTacToe` game played on the Internet (§30.9).

30.1 Introduction

To browse the Web or send email, your computer must be connected to the Internet. The Internet is the global network of millions of computers. Your computer may connect to the Internet through an Internet Service Provider (ISP) using dialup, DSL, or cable modem, or through a local area network (LAN).

IP address

domain name
domain name server

When a computer needs to communicate with another computer, it needs to know the other computer's address. An *Internet Protocol* (IP) address uniquely identifies the computer on the Internet. An IP address consists of four dotted decimal numbers between 0 and 255, such as 130.254.204.36. Since it is not easy to remember so many numbers, they are often mapped to meaningful names called *domain names*, such as drake.armstrong.edu. Special servers called *Domain Name Servers* (DNS) on the Internet translate host names into IP addresses. When a computer contacts drake.armstrong.edu, it first asks the DNS to translate this domain name into a numeric IP address and then sends the request using the IP address.

TCP

The Internet Protocol is a low-level protocol for delivering data from one computer to another across the Internet in packets. Two higher-level protocols used in conjunction with the IP are the *Transmission Control Protocol* (TCP) and the *User Datagram Protocol* (UDP). TCP enables two hosts to establish a connection and exchange streams of data. TCP guarantees delivery of data and also guarantees that packets will be delivered in the same order in which they were sent. UDP is a standard, low-overhead, connectionless, host-to-host protocol that is used over the IP. UDP allows an application program on one computer to send a datagram to an application program on another computer.

stream-based

packet-based

Java supports both *stream-based* and *packet-based communications*. *Stream-based communications* use TCP (Transmission Control Protocol) for data transmission, whereas *packet-based communications* use UDP (User Datagram Protocol). Since TCP can detect lost transmissions and resubmit them, transmissions are lossless and reliable. UDP, in contrast, cannot guarantee lossless transmission. Stream-based communications are used in most areas of Java programming and are the focus of this chapter. Packet-based communications are introduced in Supplement III.T, "Networking Using Datagram Protocol."

30.2 Client/Server Computing

socket

Networking is tightly integrated in Java. Java API provides the classes for creating sockets to facilitate program communications over the Internet. *Sockets* are the endpoints of logical connections between two hosts and can be used to send and receive data. Java treats socket communications much as it treats I/O operations; thus programs can read from or write to sockets as easily as they can read from or write to files.

Network programming usually involves a server and one or more clients. The client sends requests to the server, and the server responds. The client begins by attempting to establish a connection to the server. The server can accept or deny the connection. Once a connection is established, the client and the server communicate through sockets.

The server must be running when a client attempts to connect to the server. The server waits for a connection request from a client. The statements needed to create sockets on a server and a client are shown in Figure 30.1.

30.2.1 Server Sockets

To establish a server, you need to create a *server socket* and attach it to a port, which is where the server listens for connections. The port identifies the TCP service on the socket. Port numbers range from 0 to 65536, but port numbers 0 to 1024 are reserved for privileged services. For instance, the email server runs on port 25, and the Web server usually runs on port 80.

FIGURE 30.1 The server creates a server socket and, once a connection to a client is established, connects to the client with a client socket.

You can choose any port number that is not currently used by any other process. The following statement creates a server socket `serverSocket`:

```
ServerSocket serverSocket = new ServerSocket(port);
```

server socket

Note

Attempting to create a server socket on a port already in use would cause the `java.net.BindException`.

BindException

30.2.2 Client Sockets

After a server socket is created, the server can use the following statement to listen for connections:

```
Socket socket = serverSocket.accept();
```

This statement waits until a client connects to the server socket. The client issues the following statement to request a connection to a server:

connect to client

```
Socket socket = new Socket(serverName, port);
```

This statement opens a socket so that the client program can communicate with the server. *serverName* is the server's Internet host name or IP address. The following statement creates a socket at port 8000 on the client machine to connect to the host 130.254.204.36:

client socket

```
Socket socket = new Socket("130.254.204.36", 8000)
```

use IP address

Alternatively, you can use the domain name to create a socket, as follows:

```
Socket socket = new Socket("drake.armstrong.edu", 8000);
```

use domain name

When you create a socket with a host name, the JVM asks the DNS to translate the host name into the IP address.

Note

A program can use the host name `localhost` or the IP address `127.0.0.1` to refer to the machine on which a client is running.

localhost

Note

The `Socket` constructor throws a `java.net.UnknownHostException` if the host cannot be found.

UnknownHostException

30.2.3 Data Transmission through Sockets

After the server accepts the connection, communication between server and client is conducted the same as for I/O streams. The statements needed to create the streams and to exchange data between them are shown in Figure 30.2.

```
Server                                          Client

int port = 8000;                                int port = 8000;
DataInputStream in;                             String host = "localhost"
DataOutputStream out;                           DataInputStream in;
ServerSocket server;                            DataOutputStream out;
Socket socket;                                  Socket socket;

                            Connection
server = new ServerSocket(port);  Request
socket = server.accept();                       socket = new Socket(host, port);
in = new DataInputStream                        in = new DataInputStream
  (socket.getInputStream());                      (socket.getInputStream());
out = new DataOutStream            I/O           out = new DataOutputStream
  (socket.getOutputStream());    Streams           (socket.getOutputStream());
System.out.println(in.readDouble());            out.writeDouble(aNumber);
out.writeDouble(aNumber);                       System.out.println(in.readDouble());
```

FIGURE 30.2   The server and client exchange data through I/O streams on top of the socket.

To get an input stream and an output stream, use the `getInputStream()` and `getOutputStream()` methods on a socket object. For example, the following statements create an `InputStream` stream called `input` and an `OutputStream` stream called `output` from a socket:

```
InputStream input = socket.getInputStream();
OutputStream output = socket.getOutputStream();
```

The `InputStream` and `OutputStream` streams are used to read or write bytes. You can use `DataInputStream`, `DataOutputStream`, `BufferedReader`, and `PrintWriter` to wrap on the `InputStream` and `OutputStream` to read or write data, such as `int`, `double`, or `String`. The following statements, for instance, create a `DataInputStream` stream, `input`, and a `DataOutput` stream, `output`, to read and write primitive data values:

```
DataInputStream input = new DataInputStream
  (socket.getInputStream());
DataOutputStream output = new DataOutputStream
  (socket.getOutputStream());
```

The server can use `input.readDouble()` to receive a `double` value from the client, and `output.writeDouble(d)` to send `double` value `d` to the client.

 Tip
Recall that binary I/O is more efficient than text I/O because text I/O requires encoding and decoding. Therefore it is better to use binary I/O for transmitting data between a server and a client to improve performance.

30.2.3   A Client/Server Example

This example presents a client program and a server program. The client sends data to a server. The server receives the data, uses it to produce a result, and then sends the result back to the client. The client displays the result on the console. In this example, the data sent from the client comprise the radius of a circle, and the result produced by the server is the area of the circle (see Figure 30.3).

FIGURE 30.3 The client sends the radius to the server; the server computes the area and sends it to the client.

The client sends the radius through a `DataOutputStream` on the output stream socket, and the server receives the radius through the `DataInputStream` on the input stream socket, as shown in Figure 30.4(a). The server computes the area and sends it to the client through a `DataOutputStream` on the output stream socket, and the client receives the area through a `DataInputStream` on the input stream socket, as shown in Figure 30.4(b). The server and client programs are given in Listings 30.1 and 30.2. Figure 30.5 contains a sample run of the server and the client.

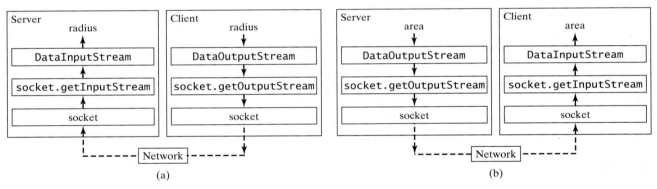

FIGURE 30.4 (a) The client sends the radius to the server. (b) The server sends the area to the client.

FIGURE 30.5 The client sends the radius to the server. The server receives it, computes the area, and sends the area to the client.

LISTING 30.1 Server.java

```java
1 import java.io.*;
2 import java.net.*;
3 import java.util.*;
4 import java.awt.*;
5 import javax.swing.*;
6
```

```
 7 public class Server extends JFrame {
 8   // Text area for displaying contents
 9   private JTextArea jta = new JTextArea();
10
11   public static void main(String[] args) {
12     new Server();
13   }
14
15   public Server() {
16     // Place text area on the frame
17     setLayout(new BorderLayout());
18     add(new JScrollPane(jta), BorderLayout.CENTER);
19
20     setTitle("Server");
21     setSize(500, 300);
22     setDefaultCloseOperation(JFrame.EXIT_ON_CLOSE);
23     setVisible(true); // It is necessary to show the frame here!
24
25     try {
26       // Create a server socket
27       ServerSocket serverSocket = new ServerSocket(8000);
28       jta.append("Server started at " + new Date() + '\n');
29
30       // Listen for a connection request
31       Socket socket = serverSocket.accept();
32
33       // Create data input and output streams
34       DataInputStream inputFromClient = new DataInputStream(
35         socket.getInputStream());
36       DataOutputStream outputToClient = new DataOutputStream(
37         socket.getOutputStream());
38
39       while (true) {
40         // Receive radius from the client
41         double radius = inputFromClient.readDouble();
42
43         // Compute area
44         double area = radius * radius * Math.PI;
45
46         // Send area back to the client
47         outputToClient.writeDouble(area);
48
49         jta.append("Radius received from client: " + radius + '\n');
50         jta.append("Area found: " + area + '\n');
51       }
52     }
53     catch(IOException ex) {
54       System.err.println(ex);
55     }
56   }
57 }
```

Margin notes, top to bottom:
launch server
server socket
connect client
input from client
output to client
read radius
write area

LISTING 30.2   Client.java

```
1 import java.io.*;
2 import java.net.*;
3 import java.awt.*;
4 import java.awt.event.*;
5 import javax.swing.*;
```

```
6
7  public class Client extends JFrame {
8    // Text field for receiving radius
9    private JTextField jtf = new JTextField();
10
11   // Text area to display contents
12   private JTextArea jta = new JTextArea();
13
14   // IO streams
15   private DataOutputStream toServer;
16   private DataInputStream fromServer;
17
18   public static void main(String[] args) {
19     new Client();                                                    launch client
20   }
21
22   public Client() {
23     // Panel p to hold the label and text field
24     JPanel p = new JPanel();
25     p.setLayout(new BorderLayout());
26     p.add(new JLabel("Enter radius"), BorderLayout.WEST);
27     p.add(jtf, BorderLayout.CENTER);
28     jtf.setHorizontalAlignment(JTextField.RIGHT);
29
30     setLayout(new BorderLayout());
31     add(p, BorderLayout.NORTH);
32     add(new JScrollPane(jta), BorderLayout.CENTER);
33
34     jtf.addActionListener(new TextFieldListener());                  register listener
35
36     setTitle("Client");
37     setSize(500, 300);
38     setDefaultCloseOperation(JFrame.EXIT_ON_CLOSE);
39     setVisible(true); // It is necessary to show the frame here!
40
41     try {
42       // Create a socket to connect to the server
43       Socket socket = new Socket("localhost", 8000);                 request connection
44       // Socket socket = new Socket("130.254.204.36", 8000);
45       // Socket socket = new Socket("drake.Armstrong.edu", 8000);
46
47       // Create an input stream to receive data from the server      input from server
48       fromServer = new DataInputStream(
49         socket.getInputStream());
50
51       // Create an output stream to send data to the server
52       toServer =                                                     output to server
53         new DataOutputStream(socket.getOutputStream());
54     }
55     catch (IOException ex) {
56       jta.append(ex.toString() + '\n');
57     }
58   }
59
60   private class TextFieldListener implements ActionListener {
61     public void actionPerformed(ActionEvent e) {
62       try {
63         // Get the radius from the text field
64         double radius = Double.parseDouble(jtf.getText().trim());
```

```
65
66          // Send the radius to the server
67          toServer.writeDouble(radius);
68          toServer.flush();
69
70          // Get area from the server
71          double area = fromServer.readDouble();
72
73          // Display to the text area
74          jta.append("Radius is " + radius + "\n");
75          jta.append("Area received from the server is "
76            + area + '\n');
77        }
78      catch (IOException ex) {
79          System.err.println(ex);
80        }
81      }
82    }
83  }
```

write radius — lines 67, 68

read radius — line 71

You start the server program first, then start the client program. In the client program, enter a radius in the text field and press *Enter* to send the radius to the server. The server computes the area and sends it back to the client. This process is repeated until one of the two programs terminates.

The networking classes are in the package `java.net`. This should be imported when writing Java network programs.

The `Server` class creates a `ServerSocket serverSocket` and attaches it to port 8000, using this statement (line 27 in Server.java):

```
ServerSocket serverSocket = new ServerSocket(8000);
```

The server then starts to listen for connection requests, using the following statement (line 31 in Server.java):

```
Socket socket = serverSocket.accept();
```

The server waits until a client requests a connection. After it is connected, the server reads the radius from the client through an input stream, computes the area, and sends the result to the client through an output stream.

The `Client` class uses the following statement to create a socket that will request a connection to the server on the same machine (localhost) at port 8000 (line 43 in Client.java).

```
Socket socket = new Socket("localhost", 8000);
```

If you run the server and the client on different machines, replace `localhost` with the server machine's host name or IP address. In this example, the server and the client are running on the same machine.

If the server is not running, the client program terminates with a `java.net.ConnectException`. After it is connected, the client gets input and output streams—wrapped by data input and output streams—in order to receive and send data to the server.

If you receive a `java.net.BindException` when you start the server, the server port is currently in use. You need to terminate the process that is using the server port and then restart the server.

What happens if the `setVisible(true)` statement in line 23 in Server.java is moved after the `try-catch` block in line 56 in Server.java? The frame will not be displayed, because the `while` loop in the `try-catch` block will not finish until the program terminates.

Note

When you create a server socket, you have to specify a port (e.g., 8000) for the socket. When a client connects to the server (line 43 in Client.java), a socket is created on the client. This socket has its own local port. This port number (e.g., 2047) is automatically chosen by the JVM, as shown in Figure 30.6.

client socket port

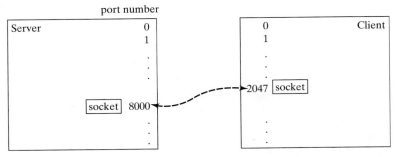

FIGURE 30.6 The JVM automatically chooses an available port to create a socket for the client.

To see the local port on the client, insert the following statement in line 46 in Client.java.

```
System.out.println("local port: " + socket.getLocalPort());
```

30.3 The **InetAddress** Class

Occasionally, you would like to know who is connecting to the server. You can use the InetAddress class to find the client's host name and IP address. The InetAddress class models an IP address. You can use the statement shown below to create an instance of InetAddress for the client on a socket.

```
InetAddress inetAddress = socket.getInetAddress();
```

Next, you can display the client's host name and IP address, as follows:

```
System.out.println("Client's host name is " +
  inetAddress.getHostName());
System.out.println("Client's IP Address is " +
  inetAddress.getHostAddress());
```

You can also create an instance of InetAddress from a host name or IP address using the static getByName method. For example, the following statement creates an InetAddress for the host liang.armstrong.edu.

```
InetAddress address = InetAddress.getByName("liang.armstrong.edu");
```

Listing 30.3 gives a program that identifies the host name and IP address of the arguments you pass in from the command line. Line 7 creates an InetAddress using the getByName method. Lines 8–9 use the getHostName and getHostAddress methods to get the host name and IP address. Figure 30.7 shows a sample run of the program.

LISTING 30.3 IdentifyHostNameIP.java

```
1 import java.net.*;
2
3 public class IdentifyHostNameIP {
4   public static void main(String[] args) {
```

```
 5      for (int i = 0; i < args.length; i++) {
 6        try {
 7          InetAddress address = InetAddress.getByName(args[i]);
 8          System.out.println("Host name: " + address.getHostName());
 9          System.out.println("IP address: " + address.getHostAddress());
10        }
11        catch (UnknownHostException ex) {
12          System.err.println("Unknown host or IP address " + args[i]);
13        }
14      }
15    }
16  }
```

get an InetAddress
get host name
get host IP

```
Command Prompt                                                    _ □ ×
C:\book>java IdentifyHostNameIP www.whitehouse.gov 130.254.204.34
Host name: www.whitehouse.gov
IP address: 72.247.31.27
Host name: panda.Armstrong.EDU
IP address: 130.254.204.34

C:\book>
```

FIGURE 30.7 The program identifies host names and IP addresses.

30.4 Serving Multiple Clients

Multiple clients are quite often connected to a single server at the same time. Typically, a server runs constantly on a server computer, and clients from all over the Internet may want to connect to it. You can use threads to handle the server's multiple clients simultaneously. Simply create a thread for each connection. Here is how the server handles the establishment of a connection:

```
while (true) {
  Socket socket = serverSocket.accept();
  Thread thread = new ThreadClass(socket);
  thread.start();
}
```

The server socket can have many connections. Each iteration of the `while` loop creates a new connection. Whenever a connection is established, a new thread is created to handle communication between the server and the new client; and this allows multiple connections to run at the same time.

Listing 30.4 creates a server class that serves multiple clients simultaneously. For each connection, the server starts a new thread. This thread continuously receives input (the radius of a circle) from clients and sends the results (the area of the circle) back to them (see Figure 30.8). The client program is same as in Listing 30.2. A sample run of the server with two clients is shown in Figure 30.9.

LISTING 30.4 MultiThreadServer.java

```
1 import java.io.*;
2 import java.net.*;
3 import java.util.*;
4 import java.awt.*;
5 import javax.swing.*;
6
7 public class MultiThreadServer extends JFrame {
8   // Text area for displaying contents
```

```
 9    private JTextArea jta = new JTextArea();
10
11    public static void main(String[] args) {
12      new MultiThreadServer();
13    }
14
15    public MultiThreadServer() {
16      // Place text area on the frame
17      setLayout(new BorderLayout());
18      add(new JScrollPane(jta), BorderLayout.CENTER);
19
20      setTitle("MultiThreadServer");
21      setSize(500, 300);
22      setDefaultCloseOperation(JFrame.EXIT_ON_CLOSE);
23      setVisible(true); // It is necessary to show the frame here!
24
25      try {
26        // Create a server socket
27        ServerSocket serverSocket = new ServerSocket(8000);          server socket
28        jta.append("MultiThreadServer started at " + new Date() + '\n');
29
30        // Number a client
31        int clientNo = 1;
32
33        while (true) {
34          // Listen for a new connection request
35          Socket socket = serverSocket.accept();                     connect client
36
37          // Display the client number
38          jta.append("Starting thread for client " + clientNo +
39            " at " + new Date() + '\n');
40
41          // Find the client's host name, and IP address
42          InetAddress inetAddress = socket.getInetAddress();         network information
43          jta.append("Client " + clientNo + "'s host name is "
44            + inetAddress.getHostName() + "\n");
45          jta.append("Client " + clientNo + "'s IP Address is "
46            + inetAddress.getHostAddress() + "\n");
47
48          // Create a new thread for the connection
49          HandleAClient task = new HandleAClient(socket);            create task
50
51          // Start the new thread
52          new Thread(task).start();                                  start thread
53
54          // Increment clientNo
55          clientNo++;
56        }
57      }
58      catch(IOException ex) {
59        System.err.println(ex);
60      }
61    }
62
63    // Inner class
64    // Define the thread class for handling new connection
65    class HandleAClient implements Runnable {                        task class
66      private Socket socket; // A connected socket
67
68      /** Construct a thread */
```

I/O

```
69      public HandleAClient(Socket socket) {
70        this.socket = socket;
71      }
72
73      /** Run a thread */
74      public void run() {
75        try {
76          // Create data input and output streams
77          DataInputStream inputFromClient = new DataInputStream(
78            socket.getInputStream());
79          DataOutputStream outputToClient = new DataOutputStream(
80            socket.getOutputStream());
81
82          // Continuously serve the client
83          while (true) {
84            // Receive radius from the client
85            double radius = inputFromClient.readDouble();
86
87            // Compute area
88            double area = radius * radius * Math.PI;
89
90            // Send area back to the client
91            outputToClient.writeDouble(area);
92
93            jta.append("radius received from client: " +
94              radius + '\n');
95            jta.append("Area found: " + area + '\n');
96          }
97        }
98        catch(IOException e) {
99          System.err.println(e);
100       }
101     }
102   }
103 }
```

The server creates a server socket at port 8000 (line 27) and waits for a connection (line 35). When a connection with a client is established, the server creates a new thread to handle the communication (line 49). It then waits for another connection in an infinite `while` loop (lines 33–56).

The threads, which run independently of one another, communicate with designated clients. Each thread creates data input and output streams that receive and send data to a client.

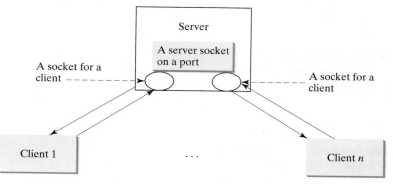

FIGURE 30.8 Multithreading enables a server to handle multiple independent clients.

FIGURE 30.9 The server spawns a thread in order to serve a client.

30.5 Applet Clients

Because of security constraints, applets can connect only to the host from which they were loaded. Therefore, the HTML file must be located on the machine on which the server is running. You can obtain the server's host name by invoking `getCodeBase().getHost()` on an applet, so you can write the applet without the host name fixed. Below is an example of how to use an applet to connect to a server.

The applet shows the number of visits made to a Web page. The count should be stored in a file on the server side. Every time the page is visited or reloaded, the applet sends a request to the server, and the server increases the count and sends it to the applet. The applet then displays the new count in a message, such as **You are visitor number 11**, as shown in Figure 30.10. The server and client programs are given in Listings 30.5 and 30.6.

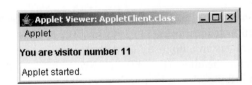

FIGURE 30.10 The applet displays the access count on a Web page.

LISTING 30.5 CountServer.java

```
1 import java.io.*;
2 import java.net.*;
3
4 public class CountServer {
5   private RandomAccessFile raf;
6   private int count; // Count the access to the server
7
8   public static void main(String[] args) {
9     new CountServer();                                    launch server
10  }
11
12  public CountServer() {
13    try {
14      // Create a server socket
15      ServerSocket serverSocket = new ServerSocket(8000);  server socket
16      System.out.println("Server started ");
17
18      // Create or open the count file
19      raf = new RandomAccessFile("count.dat", "rw");       random access file
20
```

```
21        // Get the count
22        if (raf.length() == 0)
23          count = 0;
24        else
25          count = raf.readInt();
26
27        while (true) {
28          // Listen for a new connection request
29          Socket socket = serverSocket.accept();
30
31          // Create a DataOutputStream for the socket
32          DataOutputStream outputToClient =
33            new DataOutputStream(socket.getOutputStream());
34
35          // Increase count and send the count to the client
36          count++;
37          outputToClient.writeInt(count);
38
39          // Write new count back to the file
40          raf.seek(0);
41          raf.writeInt(count);
42        }
43      }
44      catch(IOException ex) {
45        ex.printStackTrace();
46      }
47    }
48 }
```

new file (line 23)
get count (line 25)
connect client (line 29)
send to client (lines 32–33)
update count (line 36)

The server creates a ServerSocket in line 15 and creates or opens a file using RandomAccessFile in line 19. It reads the count from the file in lines 22–31. The server then waits for a connection request from a client (line 29). After a connection with a client is established, the server creates an output stream to the client (lines 32–33), increases the count (line 36), sends the count to the client (line 37), and writes the new count back to the file. This process continues in an infinite while loop to handle all clients.

LISTING 30.6 AppletClient.java

```
 1 import java.io.*;
 2 import java.net.*;
 3 import javax.swing.*;
 4
 5 public class AppletClient extends JApplet {
 6   // Label for displaying the visit count
 7   private JLabel jlblCount = new JLabel();
 8
 9   // Indicate if it runs as application
10   private boolean isStandAlone = false;
11
12   // Host name or ip
13   private String host = "localhost";
14
15   /** Initialize the applet */
16   public void init() {
17     add(jlblCount);
18
19     try {
20       // Create a socket to connect to the server
21       Socket socket;
22       if (isStandAlone)
```

```
23              socket = new Socket(host, 8000);                        for standalone
24          else
25              socket = new Socket(getCodeBase().getHost(), 8000);      for applet
26
27          // Create an input stream to receive data from the server
28          DataInputStream inputFromServer =
29            new DataInputStream(socket.getInputStream());
30
31          // Receive the count from the server and display it on label
32          int count = inputFromServer.readInt();                       receive count
33          jlblCount.setText("You are visitor number " + count);
34
35          // Close the stream
36          inputFromServer.close();
37        }
38        catch (IOException ex) {
39          ex.printStackTrace();
40        }
41    }
42
43    /** Run the applet as an application */
44    public static void main(String[] args) {
45      // Create a frame
46      JFrame frame = new JFrame("Applet Client");
47
48      // Create an instance of the applet
49      AppletClient applet = new AppletClient();
50      applet.isStandAlone = true;
51
52      // Get host
53      if (args.length == 1) applet.host = args[0];
54
55      // Add the applet instance to the frame
56      frame.getContentPane().add(applet, java.awt.BorderLayout.CENTER);
57
58      // Invoke init() and start()
59      applet.init();
60      applet.start();
61
62      // Display the frame
63      frame.pack();
64      frame.setVisible(true);
65    }
66  }
```

The client is an applet. When it runs as an applet, it uses **getCodeBase().getHost()** (line 25) to return the IP address for the server. When it runs as an application, it passes the URL from the command line (line 53). If the URL is not passed from the command line, by default "localhost" is used for the URL (line 13).

The client creates a socket to connect to the server (lines 21–25), creates an input stream from the socket (lines 28–29), receives the count from the server (line 32), and displays it in the text field (line 33).

30.6 Sending and Receiving Objects

In the preceding examples, you learned how to send and receive data of primitive types. You can also send and receive objects using **ObjectOutputStream** and **ObjectInputStream** on socket streams. To enable passing, the objects must be serializable. The following example demonstrates how to send and receive objects.

The example consists of three classes: StudentAddress.java (Listing 30.7), StudentClient.java (Listing 30.8), and StudentServer.java (Listing 30.9). The client program collects student information from a client and sends it to a server, as shown in Figure 30.11.

The StudentAddress class contains the student information: name, street, state, and zip. The StudentAddress class implements the Serializable interface. Therefore, it can be sent and received using the object output and input streams.

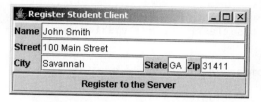

FIGURE 30.11 The client sends the student information in an object to the server.

LISTING 30.7 StudentAddress.java

serialized

```
1 public class StudentAddress implements java.io.Serializable {
2   private String name;
3   private String street;
4   private String city;
5   private String state;
6   private String zip;
7
8   public StudentAddress(String name, String street, String city,
9     String state, String zip) {
10    this.name = name;
11    this.street = street;
12    this.city = city;
13    this.state = state;
14    this.zip = zip;
15  }
16
17  public String getName() {
18    return name;
19  }
20
21  public String getStreet() {
22    return street;
23  }
24
25  public String getCity() {
26    return city;
27  }
28
29  public String getState() {
30    return state;
31  }
32
33  public String getZip() {
34    return zip;
35  }
36 }
```

The client sends a StudentAddress object through an ObjectOutputStream on the output stream socket, and the server receives the Student object through the ObjectInputStream on the input stream socket, as shown in Figure 30.12. The client uses the `writeObject` method in the `ObjectOutputStream` class to send a student to the server, and the server receives the student using the `readObject` method in the `ObjectInputStream` class. The server and client programs are given in Listings 30.8 and 30.9.

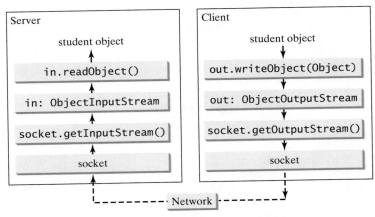

FIGURE 30.12   The client sends a `StudentAddress` object to the server.

LISTING 30.8 `StudentClient.java`

```java
1  import java.io.*;
2  import java.net.*;
3  import java.awt.*;
4  import java.awt.event.*;
5  import javax.swing.*;
6  import javax.swing.border.*;
7
8  public class StudentClient extends JApplet {
9    private JTextField jtfName = new JTextField(32);
10   private JTextField jtfStreet = new JTextField(32);
11   private JTextField jtfCity = new JTextField(20);
12   private JTextField jtfState = new JTextField(2);
13   private JTextField jtfZip = new JTextField(5);
14
15   // Button for sending a student to the server
16   private JButton jbtRegister = new JButton("Register to the Server");
17
18   // Indicate if it runs as application
19   private boolean isStandAlone = false;
20
21   // Host name or ip
22   String host = "localhost";
23
24   public void init() {
25     // Panel p1 for holding labels Name, Street, and City
26     JPanel p1 = new JPanel();
27     p1.setLayout(new GridLayout(3, 1));
28     p1.add(new JLabel("Name"));
29     p1.add(new JLabel("Street"));
30     p1.add(new JLabel("City"));
31
32     // Panel jpState for holding state
33     JPanel jpState = new JPanel();
```

create UI

```
34        jpState.setLayout(new BorderLayout());
35        jpState.add(new JLabel("State"), BorderLayout.WEST);
36        jpState.add(jtfState, BorderLayout.CENTER);
37
38        // Panel jpZip for holding zip
39        JPanel jpZip = new JPanel();
40        jpZip.setLayout(new BorderLayout());
41        jpZip.add(new JLabel("Zip"), BorderLayout.WEST);
42        jpZip.add(jtfZip, BorderLayout.CENTER);
43
44        // Panel p2 for holding jpState and jpZip
45        JPanel p2 = new JPanel();
46        p2.setLayout(new BorderLayout());
47        p2.add(jpState, BorderLayout.WEST);
48        p2.add(jpZip, BorderLayout.CENTER);
49
50        // Panel p3 for holding jtfCity and p2
51        JPanel p3 = new JPanel();
52        p3.setLayout(new BorderLayout());
53        p3.add(jtfCity, BorderLayout.CENTER);
54        p3.add(p2, BorderLayout.EAST);
55
56        // Panel p4 for holding jtfName, jtfStreet, and p3
57        JPanel p4 = new JPanel();
58        p4.setLayout(new GridLayout(3, 1));
59        p4.add(jtfName);
60        p4.add(jtfStreet);
61        p4.add(p3);
62
63        // Place p1 and p4 into StudentPanel
64        JPanel studentPanel = new JPanel(new BorderLayout());
65        studentPanel.setBorder(new BevelBorder(BevelBorder.RAISED));
66        studentPanel.add(p1, BorderLayout.WEST);
67        studentPanel.add(p4, BorderLayout.CENTER);
68
69        // Add the student panel and button to the applet
70        add(studentPanel, BorderLayout.CENTER);
71        add(jbtRegister, BorderLayout.SOUTH);
72
73        // Register listener
74        jbtRegister.addActionListener(new ButtonListener());
75
76        // Find the IP address of the Web server
77        if (!isStandAlone)
78          host = getCodeBase().getHost();
79      }
80
81      /** Handle button action */
82      private class ButtonListener implements ActionListener {
83        public void actionPerformed(ActionEvent e) {
84          try {
85            // Establish connection with the server
86            Socket socket = new Socket(host, 8000);
87
88            // Create an output stream to the server
89            ObjectOutputStream toServer =
90              new ObjectOutputStream(socket.getOutputStream());
91
92            // Get text field
93            String name = jtfName.getText().trim();
```

register listener   74

get server name   78

server socket   86

output stream   89

```
94          String street = jtfStreet.getText().trim();
95          String city = jtfCity.getText().trim();
96          String state = jtfState.getText().trim();
97          String zip = jtfZip.getText().trim();
98
99          // Create a StudentAddress object and send to the server
100         StudentAddress s =
101           new StudentAddress(name, street, city, state, zip);
102         toServer.writeObject(s);                              send to server
103       }
104     catch (IOException ex) {
105         System.err.println(ex);
106       }
107     }
108 }
109
110 /** Run the applet as an application */
111 public static void main(String[] args) {
112   // Create a frame
113   JFrame frame = new JFrame("Register Student Client");
114
115   // Create an instance of the applet
116   StudentClient applet = new StudentClient();
117   applet.isStandAlone = true;
118
119   // Get host
120   if (args.length == 1) applet.host = args[0];
121
122   // Add the applet instance to the frame
123   frame.add(applet, BorderLayout.CENTER);
124
125   // Invoke init() and start()
126   applet.init();
127   applet.start();
128
129   // Display the frame
130   frame.pack();
131   frame.setVisible(true);
132   }
133 }
```

LISTING 30.9   StudentServer.java

```
1 import java.io.*;
2 import java.net.*;
3
4 public class StudentServer {
5   private ObjectOutputStream outputToFile;
6   private ObjectInputStream inputFromClient;
7
8   public static void main(String[] args) {
9     new StudentServer();
10   }
11
12   public StudentServer() {
13     try {
14       // Create a server socket
15       ServerSocket serverSocket = new ServerSocket(8000);        server socket
16       System.out.println("Server started ");
17
```

```
18        // Create an object ouput stream
19        outputToFile = new ObjectOutputStream(
20          new FileOutputStream("student.dat", true));
21
22        while (true) {
23          // Listen for a new connection request
24          Socket socket = serverSocket.accept();
25
26          // Create an input stream from the socket
27          inputFromClient =
28            new ObjectInputStream(socket.getInputStream());
29
30          // Read from input
31          Object object = inputFromClient.readObject();
32
33          // Write to the file
34          outputToFile.writeObject(object);
35          System.out.println("A new student object is stored");
36        }
37      }
38      catch(ClassNotFoundException ex) {
39        ex.printStackTrace();
40      }
41      catch(IOException ex) {
42        ex.printStackTrace();
43      }
44      finally {
45        try {
46          inputFromClient.close();
47          outputToFile.close();
48        }
49        catch (Exception ex) {
50          ex.printStackTrace();
51        }
52      }
53    }
54  }
```

output to file (line 19)

connect to client (line 24)

input stream (line 27)

get from client (line 31)

write to file (line 34)

On the client side, when the user clicks the "Register to the Server" button, the client creates a socket to connect to the host (line 86), creates an ObjectOutputStream on the output stream of the socket (lines 89–90), and invokes the writeObject method to send the StudentAddress object to the server through the object output stream (line 102).

On the server side, when a client connects to the server, the server creates an ObjectInputStream on the input stream of the socket (lines 27–28), invokes the readObject method to receive the StudentAddress object through the object input stream (line 31), and writes the object to a file (line 34).

This program can run either as an applet or as an application. To run it as an application, the host name is passed as a command-line argument.

30.7 Retrieving Files from Web Servers

In previous sections you developed client/server applications. Java allows you to develop clients that retrieve files on a remote host through a Web server. In this case, you don't have to create a custom server program. The Web server can be used to send the files, as shown in Figure 30.13.

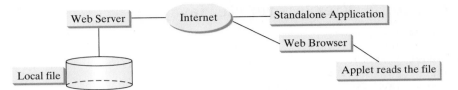

FIGURE 30.13 The applet client or the application client retrieves files from a Web server.

To retrieve a file, first create a URL object for the file. The `java.net.URL` class was introduced in §17.9, "Locating Resource Using the URL Class." You can create a URL object using the following constructor:

public URL(String spec) **throws** MalformedURLException

For example, the statement given below creates a URL object for http://www.cs.armstrong.edu/ liang/index.html.

```
try {
  URL url = new URL("http://www.cs.armstrong.edu/liang/index.html");
}
catch (MalformedURLException ex) {
}
```

A `MalformedURLException` is thrown if the URL string has a syntax error. For example, the URL string "http:/www.cs.armstrong.edu/liang/index.html" would cause a `Malformed-URLException` runtime error because two slashes (`//`)are required after the colon (`:`).

You can then use the `openStream()` method defined in the URL class to open an input stream to the file's URL.

```
InputStream inputStream = url.openStream();
```

Now you can read the data from the input stream. Listing 30.10 gives an example that demonstrates how to retrieve a file from a Web server. The program can run as an application or an applet. The user interface includes a text field in which to enter the URL of the file name, a text area in which to show the file, and a button that can be used to submit an action. A label is added at the bottom of the applet to indicate the status, such as *File loaded successfully* or *Network connection problem*. A sample run of the program is shown in Figure 30.14.

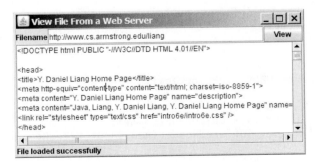

FIGURE 30.14 The program displays the contents of a specified file on the Web server.

LISTING 30.10 ViewRemoteFile.java

```
1  import java.awt.*;
2  import java.awt.event.*;
3  import java.io.*;
4  import java.net.*;
5  import javax.swing.*;
6
7  public class ViewRemoteFile extends JApplet {
8    // Button to view the file
9    private JButton jbtView = new JButton("View");
10
11   // Text field to receive file name
12   private JTextField jtfURL = new JTextField(12);
13
14   // Text area to store file
15   private JTextArea jtaFile = new JTextArea();
16
17   // Label to display status
18   private JLabel jlblStatus = new JLabel();
19
20   /** Initialize the applet */
21   public void init() {
22     // Create a panel to hold a label, a text field, and a button
23     JPanel p1 = new JPanel();
24     p1.setLayout(new BorderLayout());
25     p1.add(new JLabel("Filename"), BorderLayout.WEST);
26     p1.add(jtfURL, BorderLayout.CENTER);
27     p1.add(jbtView, BorderLayout.EAST);
28
29     // Place text area and panel p to the applet
30     setLayout(new BorderLayout());
31     add(new JScrollPane(jtaFile), BorderLayout.CENTER);
32     add(p1, BorderLayout.NORTH);
33     add(jlblStatus, BorderLayout.SOUTH);
34
35     // Register listener to handle the "View" button
36     jbtView.addActionListener(new ActionListener() {
37       public void actionPerformed(ActionEvent e) {
38         showFile();
39       }
40     });
41   }
42
43   private void showFile() {
44     // Declare buffered stream for reading text for the URL
45     BufferedReader infile = null;
46     URL url = null;
47
48     try {
49       // Obtain URL from the text field
50       url = new URL(jtfURL.getText().trim());
51
52       // Create a buffered stream
53       InputStream is = url.openStream();
54       infile = new BufferedReader(new InputStreamReader(is));
55
56       // Get file name from the text field
57       String inLine;
58
```

create UI (line 23)

register listener (line 36)

get URL (line 50)

input stream (line 53)

```
59        // Read a line and append the line to the text area
60        while ((inLine = infile.readLine()) != null) {
61          jtaFile.append(inLine + '\n');
62        }
63
64        jlblStatus.setText("File loaded successfully");
65      }
66      catch (FileNotFoundException e) {
67        jlblStatus.setText("URL " + url + " not found.");
68      }
69      catch (IOException e) {
70        jlblStatus.setText(e.getMessage());
71      }
72      finally {
73        try {
74          if (infile != null) infile.close();
75        }
76        catch (IOException ex) {}
77      }
78    }
79 }
```

main method omitted

Line 50 `new URL(jtfURL.getText().trim())` creates a `URL` for the file name entered from the text field. Line 53 `url.openStream()` creates an `InputStream` from the URL. After the input stream is established, reading data from the remote file is just like reading data locally. A `BufferedReader` object is created from the input stream (line 54). The text from the file is displayed in the text area (line 61).

30.8 JEditorPane

Swing provides a GUI component named `javax.swing.JEditorPane` that can display plain text, HTML, and RTF files automatically. Using it, you don't have to write code to explicitly read data from the files. `JEditorPane` is a subclass of `JTextComponent`. Thus it inherits all the behavior and properties of `JTextComponent`.

To display the content of a file, use the `setPage(URL)` method, as follows:

```
public void setPage(URL url) throws IOException
```

`JEditorPane` generates `javax.swing.event.HyperlinkEvent` when a hyperlink in the editor pane is clicked. Through this event, you can get the URL of the hyperlink and display it using the `setPage(url)` method.

Listing 30.11 gives an example that creates a simple Web browser to render HTML files. The program lets the user enter an HTML file in a text field and press the *Enter* key to display it in an editor pane, as shown in Figure 30.15.

FIGURE 30.15 You can specify a URL in the text field and display the HTML file in an editor pane.

LISTING 30.11   WebBrowser.java

```java
1  import java.awt.*;
2  import java.awt.event.*;
3  import javax.swing.*;
4  import java.net.URL;
5  import javax.swing.event.*;
6  import java.io.*;
7
8  public class WebBrowser extends JApplet {
9    // JEditor pane to view HTML files
10   private JEditorPane jep = new JEditorPane();
11
12   // Label for URL
13   private JLabel jblURL = new JLabel("URL");
14
15   // Text field for entering URL
16   private JTextField jtfURL = new JTextField();
17
18   /** Initialize the applet */
19   public void init() {
20     // Create a panel jpURL to hold the label and text field
21     JPanel jpURL = new JPanel();
22     jpURL.setLayout(new BorderLayout());
23     jpURL.add(jblURL, BorderLayout.WEST);
24     jpURL.add(jtfURL, BorderLayout.CENTER);
25
26     // Create a scroll pane to hold JEditorPane
27     JScrollPane jspViewer = new JScrollPane();
28     jspViewer.getViewport().add(jep, null);
29
30     // Place jpURL and jspViewer in the applet
31     add(jspViewer , BorderLayout.CENTER);
32     add(jpURL, BorderLayout.NORTH);
33
34     // Set jep noneditable
35     jep.setEditable(false);
36
37     // Register listener
38     jep.addHyperlinkListener(new HyperlinkListener() {
39       public void hyperlinkUpdate(HyperlinkEvent e) {
40         try {
41           jep.setPage(e.getURL());
42         }
43         catch (IOException ex) {
44           System.out.println(ex);
45         }
46       }
47     });
48     jtfURL.addActionListener(new ActionListener() {
49       public void actionPerformed(ActionEvent e) {
50         try {
51           // Get the URL from text field
52           URL url = new URL(jtfURL.getText().trim());
53
54           // Display the HTML file
55           jep.setPage(url);
56         }
57         catch (IOException ex) {
```

create UI

register listener

register listener

get URL

display HTML

```
58              System.out.println(ex);
59          }
60      }
61    });
62  }
63 }
```
main method omitted

In this example, a simple Web browser is created using the `JEditorPane` class (line 10). `JEditorPane` is capable of displaying files in HTML format. To enable scrolling, the editor pane is placed inside a scroll pane (lines 27–28).

The user enters the URL of the HTML file in the text field and presses the *Enter* key to fire an action event to display the URL in the editor pane. To display the URL in the editor pane, simply set the URL in the `page` property of the editor pane (line 55).

The editor pane does not have all the functions of a commercial Web browser, but it is convenient for displaying HTML files, including embedded images.

There are two shortcomings in this program: (1) it cannot view a local HTML file, and (2) to view a remote HTML file, you have to enter a URL beginning with http://. In Exercise 30.11, you will modify the program so that it can also view an HTML file from the local host and accept URLs beginning with either http:// or www.

30.9 Case Studies: Distributed TicTacToe Games

In §17.7, "Case Study: TicTacToe," you developed an applet for the TicTacToe game that enables two players to play on the same machine. In this section, you will learn how to develop a distributed TicTacToe game using multithreads and networking with socket streams. A distributed TicTacToe game enables users to play on different machines from anywhere on the Internet.

You need to develop a server for multiple clients. The server creates a server socket and accepts connections from every two players to form a session. Each session is a thread that communicates with the two players and determines the status of the game. The server can establish any number of sessions, as shown in Figure 30.16.

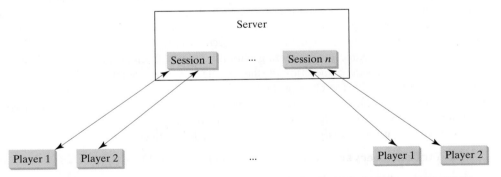

FIGURE 30.16 The server can create many sessions, each of which facilitates a TicTacToe game for two players.

For each session, the first client connecting to the server is identified as player 1 with token `'X'`, and the second client connecting is identified as player 2 with token `'O'`. The server notifies the players of their respective tokens. Once two clients are connected to it, the server starts a thread to facilitate the game between the two players by performing the steps repeatedly, as shown in Figure 30.17.

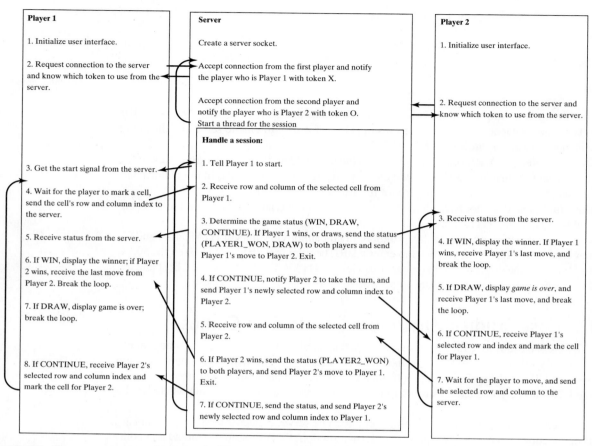

Player 1

1. Initialize user interface.

2. Request connection to the server and know which token to use from the server.

3. Get the start signal from the server.

4. Wait for the player to mark a cell, send the cell's row and column index to the server.

5. Receive status from the server.

6. If WIN, display the winner; if Player 2 wins, receive the last move from Player 2. Break the loop.

7. If DRAW, display game is over; break the loop.

8. If CONTINUE, receive Player 2's selected row and column index and mark the cell for Player 2.

Server

Create a server socket.

Accept connection from the first player and notify the player who is Player 1 with token X.

Accept connection from the second player and notify the player who is Player 2 with token O. Start a thread for the session

Handle a session:

1. Tell Player 1 to start.

2. Receive row and column of the selected cell from Player 1.

3. Determine the game status (WIN, DRAW, CONTINUE). If Player 1 wins, or draws, send the status (PLAYER1_WON, DRAW) to both players and send Player 1's move to Player 2. Exit.

4. If CONTINUE, notify Player 2 to take the turn, and send Player 1's newly selected row and column index to Player 2.

5. Receive row and column of the selected cell from Player 2.

6. If Player 2 wins, send the status (PLAYER2_WON) to both players, and send Player 2's move to Player 1. Exit.

7. If CONTINUE, send the status, and send Player 2's newly selected row and column index to Player 1.

Player 2

1. Initialize user interface.

2. Request connection to the server and know which token to use from the server.

3. Receive status from the server.

4. If WIN, display the winner. If Player 1 wins, receive Player 1's last move, and break the loop.

5. If DRAW, display *game is over*, and receive Player 1's last move, and break the loop.

6. If CONTINUE, receive Player 1's selected row and index and mark the cell for Player 1.

7. Wait for the player to move, and send the selected row and column to the server.

FIGURE 30.17 The server starts a thread to facilitate communications between the two players.

The server does not have to be a graphical component, but creating it as a frame in which game information can be viewed is user friendly. You can create a scroll pane to hold a text area in the frame and display game information in the text area. The server creates a thread to handle a game session when two players are connected to the server.

The client is responsible for interacting with the players. It creates a user interface with nine cells, and displays the game title and status to the players in the labels. The client class is very similar to the TicTacToe class presented in §17.7, "Case Study: TicTacToe." However, the client in this example does not determine the game status (win or draw), it simply passes the moves to the server and receives the game status from the server.

Based on the foregoing analysis, you can create the following classes:

- **TicTacToeServer** serves all the clients in Listing 30.13.

- **HandleASession** facilitates the game for two players in Listing 30.13. It is in the same file with TicTacToeServer.java.

- **TicTacToeClient** models a player in Listing 30.14.

- **Cell** models a cell in the game in Listing 30.14. It is an inner class in TicTacToeClient.

- **TicTacToeConstants** is an interface that defines the constants shared by all the classes in the example in Listing 30.12.

The relationships of these classes are shown in Figure 30.18.

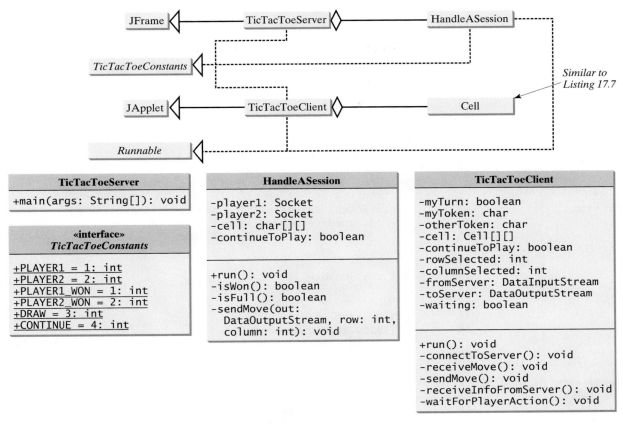

FIGURE 30.18 `TicTacToeServer` creates an instance of `HandleASession` for each session of two players. `TicTacToeClient` creates nine cells in the UI.

LISTING 30.12 `TicTacToeConstants.java`

```
1  public interface TicTacToeConstants {
2    public static int PLAYER1 = 1; // Indicate player 1
3    public static int PLAYER2 = 2; // Indicate player 2
4    public static int PLAYER1_WON = 1; // Indicate player 1 won
5    public static int PLAYER2_WON = 2; // Indicate player 2 won
6    public static int DRAW = 3; // Indicate a draw
7    public static int CONTINUE = 4; // Indicate to continue
8  }
```

LISTING 30.13 `TicTacToeServer.java`

```
1  import java.io.*;
2  import java.net.*;
3  import javax.swing.*;
4  import java.awt.*;
5  import java.util.Date;
6
7  public class TicTacToeServer extends JFrame
8      implements TicTacToeConstants {
9    public static void main(String[] args) {
10     TicTacToeServer frame = new TicTacToeServer();
11   }
12
```
run server

```
13   public TicTacToeServer() {
14     JTextArea jtaLog = new JTextArea();
15
16     // Create a scroll pane to hold text area
17     JScrollPane scrollPane = new JScrollPane(jtaLog);
18
19     // Add the scroll pane to the frame
20     add(scrollPane, BorderLayout.CENTER);
21
22     setDefaultCloseOperation(JFrame.EXIT_ON_CLOSE);
23     setSize(300, 300);
24     setTitle("TicTacToeServer");
25     setVisible(true);
26
27     try {
28       // Create a server socket
29       ServerSocket serverSocket = new ServerSocket(8000);
30       jtaLog.append(new Date() +
31         ": Server started at socket 8000\n");
32
33       // Number a session
34       int sessionNo = 1;
35
36       // Ready to create a session for every two players
37       while (true) {
38         jtaLog.append(new Date() +
39           ": Wait for players to join session " + sessionNo + '\n');
40
41         // Connect to player 1
42         Socket player1 = serverSocket.accept();
43
44         jtaLog.append(new Date() + ": Player 1 joined session " +
45           sessionNo + '\n');
46         jtaLog.append("Player 1's IP address" +
47           player1.getInetAddress().getHostAddress() + '\n');
48
49         // Notify that the player is Player 1
50         new DataOutputStream(
51           player1.getOutputStream()).writeInt(PLAYER1);
52
53         // Connect to player 2
54         Socket player2 = serverSocket.accept();
55
56         jtaLog.append(new Date() +
57           ": Player 2 joined session " + sessionNo + '\n');
58         jtaLog.append("Player 2's IP address" +
59           player2.getInetAddress().getHostAddress() + '\n');
60
61         // Notify that the player is Player 2
62         new DataOutputStream(
63           player2.getOutputStream()).writeInt(PLAYER2);
64
65         // Display this session and increment session number
66         jtaLog.append(new Date() + ": Start a thread for session " +
67           sessionNo++ + '\n');
68
69         // Create a new thread for this session of two players
70         HandleASession task = new HandleASession(player1, player2);
71
72         // Start the new thread
```

Margin notes:
- create UI (line 13–14)
- server socket (line 29)
- connect to client (line 42)
- to player1 (line 50)
- to player2 (line 62)
- a session for two players (line 70)

```
73            new Thread(task).start();
74          }
75        }
76        catch(IOException ex) {
77          System.err.println(ex);
78        }
79      }
80    }
81
82    // Define the thread class for handling a new session for two players
83    class HandleASession implements Runnable, TicTacToeConstants {
84      private Socket player1;
85      private Socket player2;
86
87      // Create and initialize cells
88      private char[][] cell =  new char[3][3];
89
90      private DataInputStream fromPlayer1;
91      private DataOutputStream toPlayer1;
92      private DataInputStream fromPlayer2;
93      private DataOutputStream toPlayer2;
94
95      // Continue to play
96      private boolean continueToPlay = true;
97
98      /** Construct a thread */
99      public HandleASession(Socket player1, Socket player2) {
100       this.player1 = player1;
101       this.player2 = player2;
102
103       // Initialize cells
104       for (int i = 0; i < 3; i++)
105         for (int j = 0; j < 3; j++)
106           cell[i][j] = ' ';
107     }
108
109     /** Implement the run() method for the thread */
110     public void run() {
111       try {
112         // Create data input and output streams
113         DataInputStream fromPlayer1 = new DataInputStream(
114           player1.getInputStream());
115         DataOutputStream toPlayer1 = new DataOutputStream(
116           player1.getOutputStream());
117         DataInputStream fromPlayer2 = new DataInputStream(
118           player2.getInputStream());
119         DataOutputStream toPlayer2 = new DataOutputStream(
120           player2.getOutputStream());
121
122         // Write anything to notify player 1 to start
123         // This is just to let player 1 know to start
124         toPlayer1.writeInt(1);
125
126         // Continuously serve the players and determine and report
127         // the game status to the players
128         while (true) {
129           // Receive a move from player 1
130           int row = fromPlayer1.readInt();
131           int column = fromPlayer1.readInt();
132           cell[row][column] = 'X';
```

```
133
134                     // Check if Player 1 wins
135                     if (isWon('X')) {
136                       toPlayer1.writeInt(PLAYER1_WON);
137                       toPlayer2.writeInt(PLAYER1_WON);
138                       sendMove(toPlayer2, row, column);
139                       break; // Break the loop
140                     }
141                     else if (isFull()) { // Check if all cells are filled
142                       toPlayer1.writeInt(DRAW);
143                       toPlayer2.writeInt(DRAW);
144                       sendMove(toPlayer2, row, column);
145                       break;
146                     }
147                     else {
148                       // Notify player 2 to take the turn
149                       toPlayer2.writeInt(CONTINUE);
150
151                       // Send player 1's selected row and column to player 2
152                       sendMove(toPlayer2, row, column);
153                     }
154
155                     // Receive a move from Player 2
156                     row = fromPlayer2.readInt();
157                     column = fromPlayer2.readInt();
158                     cell[row][column] = 'O';
159
160                     // Check if Player 2 wins
161                     if (isWon('O')) {
162                       toPlayer1.writeInt(PLAYER2_WON);
163                       toPlayer2.writeInt(PLAYER2_WON);
164                       sendMove(toPlayer1, row, column);
165                       break;
166                     }
167                     else {
168                       // Notify player 1 to take the turn
169                       toPlayer1.writeInt(CONTINUE);
170
171                       // Send player 2's selected row and column to player 1
172                       sendMove(toPlayer1, row, column);
173                     }
174                   }
175                 }
176               catch(IOException ex) {
177                 System.err.println(ex);
178               }
179           }
180
181           /** Send the move to other player */
182           private void sendMove(DataOutputStream out, int row, int column)
183               throws IOException {
184             out.writeInt(row); // Send row index
185             out.writeInt(column); // Send column index
186           }
187
188           /** Determine if the cells are all occupied */
189           private boolean isFull() {
190             for (int i = 0; i < 3; i++)
191               for (int j = 0; j < 3; j++)
192                 if (cell[i][j] == ' ')
```

```
193            return false; // At least one cell is not filled
194
195    // All cells are filled
196    return true;
197  }
198
199  /** Determine if the player with the specified token wins */
200  private boolean isWon(char token) {
201    // Check all rows
202    for (int i = 0; i < 3; i++)
203      if ((cell[i][0] == token)
204          && (cell[i][1] == token)
205          && (cell[i][2] == token)) {
206        return true;
207      }
208
209    /** Check all columns */
210    for (int j = 0; j < 3; j++)
211      if ((cell[0][j] == token)
212          && (cell[1][j] == token)
213          && (cell[2][j] == token)) {
214        return true;
215      }
216
217    /** Check major diagonal */
218    if ((cell[0][0] == token)
219        && (cell[1][1] == token)
220        && (cell[2][2] == token)) {
221      return true;
222    }
223
224    /** Check subdiagonal */
225    if ((cell[0][2] == token)
226        && (cell[1][1] == token)
227        && (cell[2][0] == token)) {
228      return true;
229    }
230
231    /** All checked, but no winner */
232    return false;
233  }
234 }
```

LISTING 30.14 TicTacToeClient.java

```
1 import java.awt.*;
2 import java.awt.event.*;
3 import javax.swing.*;
4 import javax.swing.border.LineBorder;
5 import java.io.*;
6 import java.net.*;
7
8 public class TicTacToeClient extends JApplet
9     implements Runnable, TicTacToeConstants {
10   // Indicate whether the player has the turn
11   private boolean myTurn = false;
12
13   // Indicate the token for the player
14   private char myToken = ' ';
15
```

```
16    // Indicate the token for the other player
17    private char otherToken = ' ';
18
19    // Create and initialize cells
20    private Cell [][] cell =  new Cell[3][3];
21
22    // Create and initialize a title label
23    private JLabel jlblTitle = new JLabel();
24
25    // Create and initialize a status label
26    private JLabel jlblStatus = new JLabel();
27
28    // Indicate selected row and column by the current move
29    private int rowSelected;
30    private int columnSelected;
31
32    // Input and output streams from/to server
33    private DataInputStream fromServer;
34    private DataOutputStream toServer;
35
36    // Continue to play?
37    private boolean continueToPlay = true;
38
39    // Wait for the player to mark a cell
40    private boolean waiting = true;
41
42    // Indicate if it runs as application
43    private boolean isStandAlone = false;
44
45    // Host name or ip
46    private String host = "localhost";
47
48    /** Initialize UI */
49    public void init() {
50      // Panel p to hold cells
51      JPanel p = new JPanel();
52      p.setLayout(new GridLayout(3, 3, 0, 0));
53      for (int i = 0; i < 3; i++)
54        for (int j = 0; j < 3; j++)
55          p.add(cell[i][j] = new Cell(i, j));
56
57      // Set properties for labels and borders for labels and panel
58      p.setBorder(new LineBorder(Color.black, 1));
59      jlblTitle.setHorizontalAlignment(JLabel.CENTER);
60      jlblTitle.setFont(new Font("SansSerif", Font.BOLD, 16));
61      jlblTitle.setBorder(new LineBorder(Color.black, 1));
62      jlblStatus.setBorder(new LineBorder(Color.black, 1));
63
64      // Place the panel and the labels to the applet
65      add(jlblTitle, BorderLayout.NORTH);
66      add(p, BorderLayout.CENTER);
67      add(jlblStatus, BorderLayout.SOUTH);
68
69      // Connect to the server
70      connectToServer();
71    }
72
73    private void connectToServer() {
74      try {
75        // Create a socket to connect to the server
```

create UI (line 49)

connect to server (line 70)

```
76        Socket socket;
77        if (isStandAlone)
78          socket = new Socket(host, 8000);              standalone
79        else
80          socket = new Socket(getCodeBase().getHost(), 8000);   applet
81
82        // Create an input stream to receive data from the server
83        fromServer = new DataInputStream(socket.getInputStream());    input from server
84
85        // Create an output stream to send data to the server
86        toServer = new DataOutputStream(socket.getOutputStream());    output to server
87      }
88      catch (Exception ex) {
89        System.err.println(ex);
90      }
91
92      // Control the game on a separate thread
93      Thread thread = new Thread(this);
94      thread.start();
95    }
96
97    public void run() {
98      try {
99        // Get notification from the server
100       int player = fromServer.readInt();
101
102       // Am I player 1 or 2?
103       if (player == PLAYER1) {
104         myToken = 'X';
105         otherToken = 'O';
106         jlblTitle.setText("Player 1 with token 'X'");
107         jlblStatus.setText("Waiting for player 2 to join");
108
109         // Receive startup notification from the server
110         fromServer.readInt(); // Whatever read is ignored
111
112         // The other player has joined
113         jlblStatus.setText("Player 2 has joined. I start first");
114
115         // It is my turn
116         myTurn = true;
117       }
118       else if (player == PLAYER2) {
119         myToken = 'O';
120         otherToken = 'X';
121         jlblTitle.setText("Player 2 with token 'O'");
122         jlblStatus.setText("Waiting for player 1 to move");
123       }
124
125       // Continue to play
126       while (continueToPlay) {
127         if (player == PLAYER1) {
128           waitForPlayerAction(); // Wait for player 1 to move
129           sendMove();  // Send the move to the server
130           receiveInfoFromServer(); // Receive info from the server
131         }
132         else if (player == PLAYER2) {
133           receiveInfoFromServer(); // Receive info from the server
134           waitForPlayerAction(); // Wait for player 2 to move
135           sendMove(); // Send player 2's move to the server
```

```
136            }
137          }
138        }
139      catch (Exception ex) {
140      }
141    }
142
143    /** Wait for the player to mark a cell */
144    private void waitForPlayerAction() throws InterruptedException {
145      while (waiting) {
146        Thread.sleep(100);
147      }
148
149      waiting = true;
150    }
151
152    /** Send this player's move to the server */
153    private void sendMove() throws IOException {
154      toServer.writeInt(rowSelected); // Send the selected row
155      toServer.writeInt(columnSelected); // Send the selected column
156    }
157
158    /** Receive info from the server */
159    private void receiveInfoFromServer() throws IOException {
160      // Receive game status
161      int status = fromServer.readInt();
162
163      if (status == PLAYER1_WON) {
164        // Player 1 won, stop playing
165        continueToPlay = false;
166        if (myToken == 'X') {
167          jlblStatus.setText("I won! (X)");
168        }
169        else if (myToken == '0') {
170          jlblStatus.setText("Player 1 (X) has won!");
171          receiveMove();
172        }
173      }
174      else if (status == PLAYER2_WON) {
175        // Player 2 won, stop playing
176        continueToPlay = false;
177        if (myToken == '0') {
178          jlblStatus.setText("I won! (0)");
179        }
180        else if (myToken == 'X') {
181          jlblStatus.setText("Player 2 (0) has won!");
182          receiveMove();
183        }
184      }
185      else if (status == DRAW) {
186        // No winner, game is over
187        continueToPlay = false;
188        jlblStatus.setText("Game is over, no winner!");
189
190        if (myToken == '0') {
191          receiveMove();
192        }
193      }
194      else {
195        receiveMove();
```

```
196        jlblStatus.setText("My turn");
197        myTurn = true; // It is my turn
198      }
199    }
200
201    private void receiveMove() throws IOException {
202      // Get the other player's move
203      int row = fromServer.readInt();
204      int column = fromServer.readInt();
205      cell[row][column].setToken(otherToken);
206    }
207
208    // An inner class for a cell
209    public class Cell extends JPanel {                                    model a cell
210      // Indicate the row and column of this cell in the board
211      private int row;
212      private int column;
213
214      // Token used for this cell
215      private char token = ' ';
216
217      public Cell(int row, int column) {
218        this.row = row;
219        this.column = column;
220        setBorder(new LineBorder(Color.black, 1)); // Set cell's border
221        addMouseListener(new ClickListener());  // Register listener      register listener
222      }
223
224      /** Return token */
225      public char getToken() {
226        return token;
227      }
228
229      /** Set a new token */
230      public void setToken(char c) {
231        token = c;
232        repaint();
233      }
234
235      /** Paint the cell */
236      protected void paintComponent(Graphics g) {
237        super.paintComponent(g);
238
239        if (token == 'X') {
240          g.drawLine(10, 10, getWidth() - 10, getHeight() - 10);         draw X
241          g.drawLine(getWidth() - 10, 10, 10, getHeight() - 10);
242        }
243        else if (token == 'O') {
244          g.drawOval(10, 10, getWidth() - 20, getHeight() - 20);         draw O
245        }
246      }
247
248      /** Handle mouse click on a cell */
249      private class ClickListener extends MouseAdapter {                  mouse listener
250        public void mouseClicked(MouseEvent e) {
251          // If cell is not occupied and the player has the turn
252          if ((token == ' ') && myTurn) {
253            setToken(myToken);  // Set the player's token in the cell
254            myTurn = false;
255            rowSelected = row;
```

```
256            columnSelected = column;
257            jlblStatus.setText("Waiting for the other player to move");
258            waiting = false; // Just completed a successful move
259          }
260        }
261      }
262    }
263 }
```

main method omitted

The server can serve any number of sessions. Each session takes care of two players. The client can be a Java applet or a Java application. To run a client as a Java applet from a Web browser, the server must run from a Web server. Figures 30.19 and 30.20 show sample runs of the server and the clients.

FIGURE 30.19 `TicTacToeServer` accepts connection requests and creates sessions to serve pairs of players.

FIGURE 30.20 `TicTacToeClient` can run as an applet or an application.

The `TicTacToeConstants` interface defines the constants shared by all the classes in the project. Each class that uses the constants needs to implement the interface. Centrally defining constants in an interface is a common practice in Java. For example, all the constants shared by Swing classes are defined in `java.swing.SwingConstants`.

Once a session is established, the server receives moves from the players in alternation. Upon receiving a move from a player, the server determines the status of the game. If the game is not finished, the server sends the status (`CONTINUE`) and the player's move to the other player. If the game is won or drawn, the server sends the status (`PLAYER1_WON`, `PLAYER2_WON`, or `DRAW`) to both players.

The implementation of Java network programs at the socket level is tightly synchronized. An operation to send data from one machine requires an operation to receive data from the other machine. As shown in this example, the server and the client are tightly synchronized to send or receive data.

CHAPTER SUMMARY

■ Java supports stream sockets and datagram sockets. *Stream sockets* use TCP (Transmission Control Protocol) for data transmission, whereas *datagram sockets* use UDP (User Datagram Protocol). Since TCP can detect lost transmissions and resubmit them, transmissions are lossless and reliable. UDP, in contrast, cannot guarantee lossless transmission.

■ To create a server, you must first obtain a server socket, using `new ServerSocket(port)`. After a server socket is created, the server can start to listen for connections, using the `accept()` method on the server socket. The client requests a connection to a server by using `new socket(serverName, port)` to create a client socket.

■ Stream socket communication is very much like input/output stream communication after the connection between a server and a client is established. You can obtain an input stream using the `getInputStream()` method and an output stream using the `getOutputStream()` method on the socket.

■ A server must often work with multiple clients at the same time. You can use threads to handle the server's multiple clients simultaneously by creating a thread for each connection.

■ Applets are good for deploying multiple clients. They can be run anywhere with a single copy of the program. However, because of security restrictions, an applet client can connect only to the server where the applet is loaded.

■ Java programs can retrieve data from a file on a remote host through a Web server. To do so, first create a URL object using `new URL(urlString)`, then use `openStream()` to get an `InputStream` to read the data from the file.

■ Swing provides a GUI component named `javax.swing.JEditorPane` that can be used to display text, HTML, and RTF files automatically without writing the code to read data from the file explicitly.

REVIEW QUESTIONS

Section 30.2 Client/Server Computing

30.1 How do you create a server socket? What port numbers can be used? What happens if a requested port number is already in use? Can a port connect to multiple clients?

30.2 What are the differences between a server socket and a client socket?

30.3 How does a client program initiate a connection?

30.4 How does a server accept a connection?

30.5 How are data transferred between a client and a server?

Sections 30.3–30.4

30.6 How do you find the IP address of a client that connects to a server?

30.7 How do you make a server serve multiple clients?

Sections 30.5–30.6

30.8 Can an applet connect to a server that is different from the machine where the applet is located?

30.9 How do you find the host name of an applet?

30.10 How do you send and receive an object?

Sections 30.7–30.8

30.11 Can an application retrieve a file from a remote host? Can an application update a file on a remote host?

30.12 How do you retrieve a file from a Web server?

30.13 What types of files can be displayed in a `JEditorPane`? How do you display a file in a `JEditorPane`?

PROGRAMMING EXERCISES

Section 30.2

30.1* (*Loan server*) Write a server for a client. The client sends loan information (annual interest rate, number of years, and loan amount) to the server (see Figure 30.21(b)). The server computes monthly payment and total payment and sends them back to the client (see Figure 30.21(a)). Name the client Exercise30_1Client and the server Exercise30_1Server.

         (a)   (b)

FIGURE 30.21 The client in (a) sends the annual interest rate, number of years, and loan amount to the server and receives the monthly payment and total payment from the server in (b).

30.2 (*Network I/O using `Scanner` and `PrintWriter`*) Rewrite the client and server programs in Listings 30.1 and 30.2 using a `Scanner` for input and a `PrintWriter` for output. Name the client Exercise30_2Client and the server Exercise30_2Server.

Sections 30.3–30.4

30.3* (*Loan server for multiple clients*) Revise Exercise 30.1 to write a server for multiple clients.

Section 30.5

30.4 (*Web visit count*) The example in §30.5, "Applet Clients," created an applet that shows the number of visits made to a Web page. The count is stored in a file on the server side. Every time the page is visited or reloaded, the applet sends a request to the server, and the server increases the count and sends it to the applet. The count is stored using a random-access file. When the applet is loaded, the server reads the count from the file, increases it, and saves it back to the file. Rewrite the program to improve its performance. Read the count from the file when the server starts, and save the count to the file when the server stops, using the Stop button, as shown in Figure 30.22. When the server is alive, use a variable to store the count. Name the client Exercise30_4Client and the server Exercise30_4Server. The client program should be the same as in Listing 30.5. Rewrite the server as a GUI application with a *Stop* button that exits the server.

FIGURE 30.22 The applet displays how many times this Web page has been accessed. The server stores the count.

30.5 (*Creating a stock ticker in an applet*) Write an applet like the one in Exercise 17.16 (*Simulating a stock ticker*). Assume that the applet gets the stock index from a file named Exercise30_5.txt stored on the Web server. Enable the applet to run standalone.

Section 30.6

30.6 (*Displaying and adding addresses*) Develop a client/server application to view and add addresses, as shown in Figure 30.23(a).

- Declare an **Address** class to hold name, street, city, state, and zip in an object.
- The user can use the buttons *First*, *Next*, *Previous*, and *Last* to view an address, and the *Add* button to add a new address.
- Limit the concurrent connections to two clients.

Name the client Exercise30_6Client and the server Exercise30_6Server.

(a) (b)

FIGURE 30.23 (a) You can view and add an address in this applet; (b) The HTML files are displayed in a JEditorPane.

30.7* (*Transferring last 100 numbers in an array*) Exercise 23.7 retrieves the last 100 prime numbers from a file Exercise23_7.dat. Write a client program that requests the server to send the last 100 prime numbers in an array. Name the server program Exercise30_7Server and the client program Exercise30_7Client. Assume that the numbers of the **long** type are stored in Exercise23_7.dat in binary format.

30.8* (*Transferring last 100 numbers in an ArrayList*) Exercise 23.7 retrieves the last 100 prime numbers from a file Exercise23_7.dat. Write a client program that requests the server to send the last 100 prime numbers in an **ArrayList**. Name the server program Exercise30_8Server and the client program Exercise30_8Client. Assume that the numbers of the **long** type are stored in Exercise23_7.dat in binary format.

Section 30.7

30.9*   (*Retrieving remote files*) Revise Listing 30.10, ViewRemoteFile.java, to use `JEditorPane` instead of `JTextArea`.

Section 30.8

30.10*   (*Using `JEditorPane`*) Write a program to get descriptions of the layout manager from an HTML file and display it in a `JEditorPane`, as shown in Figure 30.23(b). The descriptions are stored in three files: FlowLayout.html, GridLayout.html, and BoxLayout.html.

30.11*   (*Web browser*) Modify Listing 30.11, WebBrowser.java, as follows:

- It accepts an HTML file from a local host. Assume that a local HTML file name begins neither with http:// nor with www.
- It accepts a remote HTML file. A remote HTML file name begins with either http:// or www.

Sections 30.9

30.12**   (*Chat*) Write a program that enables two users to chat. Implement one user as the server (Figure 30.24(a)) and the other as the client (Figure 30.24(b)). The server has two text areas: one for entering text and the other (noneditable) for displaying text received from the client. When the user presses the *Enter* key, the current line is sent to the client. The client has two text areas: one for receiving text from the server, and the other for entering text. When the user presses the Enter key, the current line is sent to the server. Name the client Exercise30_12Client and the server Exercise30_12Server.

(a)   (b)

FIGURE 30.24   The server and client send and receive text from each other.

30.13***   (*Multiple client chat*) Write a program that enables any number of clients to chat. Implement one server that serves all the clients, as shown in Figure 30.25. Name the client Exercise30_13Client and the server Exercise30_13Server.

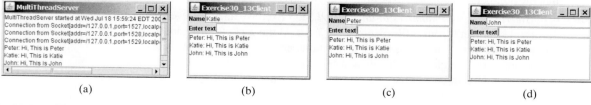

(a)   (b)   (c)   (d)

FIGURE 30.25   The server starts in (a) with three clients in (b), (c), and (d).

CHAPTER 31

INTERNATIONALIZATION

Objectives

- To describe Java's internationalization features (§31.1).

- To construct a locale with language, country, and variant (§31.2).

- To display date and time based on locale (§31.3).

- To display numbers, currencies, and percentages based on locale (§31.4).

- To develop applications for international audiences using resource bundles (§31.5).

- To specify encoding schemes for text I/O (§31.6).

31.1 Introduction

Many Web sites maintain several versions of Web pages so that readers can choose one written in a language they understand. Because there are so many languages in the world, it would be highly problematic to create and maintain enough different versions to meet the needs of all clients everywhere. Java comes to the rescue. Java is the first language designed from the ground up to support internationalization. In consequence, it allows your programs to be customized for any number of countries or languages without requiring cumbersome changes in the code.

Here are the major Java features that support internationalization:

Unicode

- Java characters use *Unicode*, a 16-bit encoding scheme established by the Unicode Consortium to support the interchange, processing, and display of written texts in the world's diverse languages. The use of Unicode encoding makes it easy to write Java programs that can manipulate strings in any international language. (To see all the Unicode characters, visit http://mindprod.com/jgloss/reuters.html.)

`Locale` class

- Java provides the `Locale` class to encapsulate information about a specific locale. A `Locale` object determines how locale-sensitive information, such as date, time, and number, is displayed, and how locale-sensitive operations, such as sorting strings, are performed. The classes for formatting date, time, and numbers, and for sorting strings are grouped in the `java.text` package.

`ResourceBundle`

- Java uses the `ResourceBundle` class to separate locale-specific information, such as status messages and GUI component labels, from the program. The information is stored outside the source code and can be accessed and loaded dynamically at runtime from a `ResourceBundle`, rather than hard-coded into the program.

In this chapter, you will learn how to format dates, numbers, currencies, and percentages for different regions, countries, and languages. You will also learn how to use resource bundles to define which images and strings are used by a component, depending on the user's locale and preferences.

31.2 The **Locale** Class

A `Locale` object represents a geographical, political, or cultural region in which a specific language or custom is used. For example, Americans speak English, and the Chinese speak Chinese. The conventions for formatting dates, numbers, currencies, and percentages may differ from one country to another. The Chinese, for instance, use year/month/day to represent the date, while Americans use month/day/year. It is important to realize that locale is not defined only by country. For example, Canadians speak either Canadian English or Canadian French, depending on which region of Canada they reside in.

Note

`locale` property in **Component**

Every Swing user-interface class has a `locale` property inherited from the **Component** class.

To create a `Locale` object, use one of the three constructors with a specified language and optional country and variant, as shown in Figure 31.1.

language

The `language` should be a valid language code—that is, one of the lowercase two-letter codes defined by ISO-639. For example, zh stands for Chinese, da for Danish, en for English, de for German, and ko for Korean. Table 31.1 lists the language codes.

country

The country should be a valid ISO country code—that is, one of the uppercase, two-letter codes defined by ISO-3166. For example, CA stands for Canada, CN for China, DK for Denmark, DE for Germany, and US for the United States. Table 31.2 lists the country codes.

java.util.Locale	
+Locale(language: String)	Constructs a locale from a language code.
+Locale(language: String, country: String)	Constructs a locale from language and country codes.
+Locale(language: String, country: String, variant: String)	Constructs a locale from language, country, and variant codes.
+getCountry(): String	Returns the country/region code for this locale.
+getLanguage(): String	Returns the language code for this locale.
+getVariant(): String	Returns the variant code for this locale.
+getDefault(): Locale	Gets the default locale on the machine.
+getDisplayCountry(): String	Returns the name of the country as expressed in the current locale.
+getDisplayLanguage(): String	Returns the name of the language as expressed in the current locale.
+getDisplayName(): String	Returns the name for the locale. For example, the name is `Chinese (China)` for the locale `Locale.CHINA`.
+getDisplayVariant(): String	Returns the name for the locale's variant if it exists.
+getAvailableLocales(): Locale[]	Returns the available locales in an array.

FIGURE 31.1 The `Locale` class encapsulates a locale.

TABLE 31.1 Common Language Codes

Code	Language	Code	Language
da	Danish	ja	Japanese
de	German	ko	Korean
el	Greek	nl	Dutch
en	English	no	Norwegian
es	Spanish	pt	Portuguese
fi	Finnish	sv	Swedish
fr	French	tr	Turkish
it	Italian	zh	Chinese

TABLE 31.2 Common Country Codes

Code	Country	Code	Country
AT	Austria	IE	Ireland
BE	Belgium	HK	Hong Kong
CA	Canada	IT	Italy
CH	Switzerland	JP	Japan
CN	China	KR	Korea
DE	Germany	NL	Netherlands
DK	Denmark	NO	Norway
ES	Spain	PT	Portugal
FI	Finland	SE	Sweden
FR	France	TR	Turkey
GB	United Kingdom	TW	Taiwan
GR	Greece	US	United States

variant

The argument variant is rarely used and is needed only for exceptional or system-dependent situations to designate information specific to a browser or vendor. For example, the Norwegian language has two sets of spelling rules, a traditional one called *bokmål* and a new one called *nynorsk*. The locale for traditional spelling would be created as follows:

```
new Locale("no", "NO", "B");
```

For convenience, the `Locale` class contains many predefined locale constants. `Locale.CANADA` is for the country Canada and language English; `Locale.CANADA_FRENCH` is for the country Canada and language French. Several other common constants are:

```
Locale.US, Locale.UK, Locale.FRANCE, Locale.GERMANY, Locale.ITALY,
Locale.CHINA, Locale.KOREA, Locale.JAPAN, and Locale.TAIWAN
```

The `Locale` class also provides the following constants based on language:

```
Locale.CHINESE, Locale.ENGLISH, Locale.FRENCH, Locale.GERMAN,
Locale.ITALIAN, Locale.JAPANESE, Locale.KOREAN,
Locale.SIMPLIFIED_CHINESE, and Locale.TRADITIONAL_CHINESE
```

Tip
You can invoke the static method `getAvailableLocales()` in the `Locale` class to obtain all the available locales supported in the system. For example,

```
Locale[] availableLocales = Calendar.getAvailableLocales();
```

returns all the locales in an array.

Tip
Your machine has a default locale. You may override it by supplying the language and region parameters when you run the program, as follows:

```
java -Duser.language=zh -Duser.region=CN MainClass
```

locale sensitive

An operation that requires a `Locale` to perform its task is called *locale sensitive*. Displaying a number such as a date or time, for example, is a locale-sensitive operation; the number should be formatted according to the customs and conventions of the user's locale. The sections that follow introduce locale-sensitive operations.

31.3 Displaying Date and Time

Applications often need to obtain date and time. Java provides a system-independent encapsulation of date and time in the `java.util.Date` class; it also provides `java.util.TimeZone` for dealing with time zones, and `java.util.Calendar` for extracting detailed

Date

information from `Date`. Different locales have different conventions for displaying date and time. Should the year, month, or day be displayed first? Should slashes, periods, or colons be used to separate fields of the date? What are the names of the months in the language? The `java.text.DateFormat` class can be used to format date and time in a locale-sensitive way for display to the user. The `Date` class was introduced in §7.5.1, "The `Date` Class," and the

Calendar

`Calendar` class and its subclass `GregorianCalendar` were introduced in §11.3, "Example: `Calendar` and `GregorianCalendar`."

31.3.1 The `TimeZone` Class

TimeZone

`TimeZone` represents a time zone offset and also figures out daylight savings. To get a `TimeZone` object for a specified time zone ID, use `TimeZone.getTimeZone(id)`. To set a time zone in a

`Calendar` object, use the `setTimeZone` method with a time zone ID. For example, `cal.setTimeZone(TimeZone.getTimeZone("CST"))` sets the time zone to Central Standard Time. To find all the available time zones supported in Java, use the static method `getAvailableIDs()` in the `TimeZone` class. In general, the international time zone ID is a string in the form of continent/city like Europe/Berlin, Asia/Taipei, and America/Washington. You can also use the static method `getDefault()` in the `TimeZone` class to obtain the default time zone on the host machine.

31.3.2 The `DateFormat` Class

The `DateFormat` class can be used to format date and time in a number of styles. The `DateFormat` class supports several standard formatting styles. To format date and time, simply create an instance of `DateFormat` using one of the three static methods `getDateInstance`, `getTimeInstance`, and `getDateTimeInstance` and apply the `format(Date)` method on the instance, as shown in Figure 31.2.

`DateFormat`

java.text.DateFormat	
+format(date: Date): String	Formats a date into a date/time string.
+getDateInstance(): DateFormat	Gets the date formatter with the default formatting style for the default locale.
+getDateInstance(dateStyle: int): DateFormat	Gets the date formatter with the given formatting style for the default locale.
+getDateInstance(dateStyle: int, aLocale: Locale): DateFormat	Gets the date formatter with the given formatting style for the given locale.
+getDateTimeInstance(): DateFormat	Gets the date and time formatter with the default formatting style for the default locale.
+getDateTimeInstance(dateStyle: int, timeStyle: int): DateFormat	Gets the date and time formatter with the given date and time formatting styles for the default locale.
+getDateTimeInstance(dateStyle: int, timeStyle: int, aLocale: Locale): DateFormat	Gets the date and time formatter with the given formatting styles for the given locale.
+getInstance(): DateFormat	Gets a default date and time formatter that uses the SHORT style for both the date and the time.

FIGURE 31.2 The `DateFormat` class formats date and time.

The `dateStyle` and `timeStyle` are one of the following constants: `DateFormat.SHORT`, `DateFormat.MEDIUM`, `DateFormat.LONG`, `DateFormat.FULL`. The exact result depends on the locale, but generally,

- `SHORT` is completely numeric, such as 7/24/98 (for date) and 4:49 PM (for time).

- `MEDIUM` is longer, such as 24-Jul-98 (for date) and 4:52:09 PM (for time).

- `LONG` is even longer, such as July 24, 1998 (for date) and 4:53:16 PM EST (for time).

- `FULL` is completely specified, such as Friday, July 24, 1998 (for date) and 4:54:13 o'clock PM EST (for time).

The statements given below display current time with a specified time zone (CST), formatting style (full date and full time), and locale (US).

```
GregorianCalendar calendar = new GregorianCalendar();
DateFormat formatter = DateFormat.getDateTimeInstance(
    DateFormat.FULL, DateFormat.FULL, Locale.US);
TimeZone timeZone = TimeZone.getTimeZone("CST");
formatter.setTimeZone(timeZone);
System.out.println("The local time is " +
    formatter.format(calendar.getTime()));
```

31.3.3 The `SimpleDateFormat` Class

The date and time formatting subclass, `SimpleDateFormat`, enables you to choose any user-defined pattern for date and time formatting. The constructor shown below can be used to create a `SimpleDateFormat` object, and the object can be used to convert a `Date` object into a string with the desired format.

```
public SimpleDateFormat(String pattern)
```

The parameter `pattern` is a string consisting of characters with special meanings. For example, `y` means year, `M` means month, `d` means day of the month, `G` is for era designator, `h` means hour, `m` means minute of the hour, `s` means second of the minute, and `z` means time zone. Therefore, the following code will display a string like "Current time is 1997.11.12 AD at 04:10:18 PST" because the pattern is "yyyy.MM.dd G 'at' hh:mm:ss z".

```
SimpleDateFormat formatter
  = new SimpleDateFormat("yyyy.MM.dd G 'at' hh:mm:ss z");
date currentTime = new Date();
String dateString = formatter.format(currentTime);
System.out.println("Current time is " + dateString);
```

31.3.4 The `DateFormatSymbols` Class

The `DateFormatSymbols` class encapsulates localizable date-time formatting data, such as the names of the months and the names of the days of the week, as shown in Figure 31.3.

For example, the following statement displays the month names and weekday names for the default locale.

```
DateFormatSymbols symbols = new DateFormatSymbols();
String[] monthNames = symbols.getMonths();
for (int i = 0; i < monthNames.length; i++) {
  System.out.println(monthNames[i]);
}

String[] weekdayNames = symbols.getWeekdays();
for (int i = 0; i < weekdayNames.length; i++) {
  System.out.println(weekdayNames[i]);
}
```

java.text.DateFormatSymbols	
+DateFormatSymbols()	Constructs a `DateFormatSymbols` object for the default locale.
+DateFormatSymbols(locale: Locale)	Constructs a `DateFormatSymbols` object for the given locale.
+getAmPmStrings(): String[]	Gets AM/PM strings. For example: "AM" and "PM".
+getEras(): String[]	Gets era strings. For example: "AD" and "BC".
+getMonths(): String[]	Gets month strings. For example: "January", "February", etc.
+setMonths(newMonths: String[]): void	Sets month strings for this locale.
+getShortMonths(): String[]	Gets short month strings. For example: "Jan", "Feb", etc.
+setShortMonths(newShortMonths: String[]): void	Sets short month strings for this locale.
+getWeekdays(): String[]	Gets weekday strings. For example: "Sunday", "Monday", etc.
+setWeekdays(newWeekdays: String[]): void	Sets weekday strings.
+getShortWeekdays(): String[]	Gets short weekday strings. For example: "Sun", "Mon", etc.
+setShortWeekdays(newWeekdays: String[]): void	Sets short weekday strings.

FIGURE 31.3 The `DateFormatSymbols` class encapsulates localizable date-time formatting data.

The following two examples demonstrate how to display date, time, and calendar based on locale. The first example creates a clock and displays date and time in locale-sensitive format. The second example displays several different calendars with the names of the days shown in the appropriate local language.

31.3.5 Example: Displaying an International Clock

Write a program that displays a clock to show the current time based on the specified locale and time zone. The locale and time zone are selected from the combo boxes that contain the available locales and time zones in the system, as shown in Figure 31.4.

FIGURE 31.4 The program displays a clock that shows the current time with the specified locale and time zone.

Here are the major steps in the program:

1. Create a subclass of **JPanel** named **WorldClock** (Listing 31.1) to contain an instance of the **StillClock** class (developed in Listing 14.12, StillClock.java), and place it in the center. Create a **JLabel** to display the digit time, and place it in the south. Use the **GreogorianCalendar** class to obtain the current time for a specific locale and time zone.

2. Create a subclass of **JPanel** named **WorldClockControl** (Listing 31.2) to contain an instance of **WorldClock** and two instances of **JComboBox** for selecting locales and time zones.

3. Create an applet named **WorldClockApp** (Listing 31.3) to contain an instance of **WorldClockControl** and enable the applet to run standalone.

The relationship among these classes is shown in Figure 31.5.

FIGURE 31.5 `WorldClockApplet` contains `WorldClockControl`, and `WorldClockControl` contains `WorldClock`.

LISTING 31.1 WorldClock.java

```java
1  import javax.swing.*;
2  import java.awt.*;
3  import java.awt.event.*;
4  import java.util.Calendar;
5  import java.util.TimeZone;
6  import java.util.GregorianCalendar;
7  import java.text.*;
8
9  public class WorldClock extends JPanel {
10   private TimeZone timeZone = TimeZone.getTimeZone("EST");
11   private Timer timer = new Timer(1000, new TimerListener());
12   private StillClock clock = new StillClock();
13   private JLabel jlblDigitTime = new JLabel("", JLabel.CENTER);
14
15   public WorldClock() {
16     setLayout(new BorderLayout());
17     add(clock, BorderLayout.CENTER);
18     add(jlblDigitTime, BorderLayout.SOUTH);
19     timer.start();
20   }
21
22   public void setTimeZone(TimeZone timeZone) {
23     this.timeZone = timeZone;
24   }
25
26   private class TimerListener implements ActionListener {
27     public void actionPerformed(ActionEvent e) {
28       Calendar calendar = new GregorianCalendar(timeZone, getLocale());
29       clock.setHour(calendar.get(Calendar.HOUR));
30       clock.setMinute(calendar.get(Calendar.MINUTE));
31       clock.setSecond(calendar.get(Calendar.SECOND));
32
33       // Display digit time on the label
34       DateFormat formatter = DateFormat.getDateTimeInstance
35         (DateFormat.MEDIUM, DateFormat.LONG, getLocale());
36       formatter.setTimeZone(timeZone);
37       jlblDigitTime.setText(formatter.format(calendar.getTime()));
38     }
39   }
40 }
```

Margin notes for Listing 31.1:
- create timer (line 11)
- create clock (line 12)
- timer listener class (line 26)

LISTING 31.2 WorldClockControl.java

```java
1  import javax.swing.*;
2  import java.awt.*;
3  import java.awt.event.*;
4  import java.util.*;
5
6  public class WorldClockControl extends JPanel {
7    // Obtain all available locales and time zone ids
8    private Locale[] availableLocales = Locale.getAvailableLocales();
9    private String[] availableTimeZones = TimeZone.getAvailableIDs();
10
11   // Combo boxes to display available locales and time zones
12   private JComboBox jcbLocales = new JComboBox();
13   private JComboBox jcbTimeZones = new JComboBox();
14
```

Margin notes for Listing 31.2:
- locales (line 8)
- time zones (line 9)
- combo boxes (line 12)

```
15    // Create a clock                                              create clock
16    private WorldClock clock = new WorldClock();
17
18    public WorldClockControl()  {
19      // Initialize jcbLocales with all available locales
20      setAvailableLocales();
21
22      // Initialize jcbTimeZones with all available time zones
23      setAvailableTimeZones();
24
25      // Initialize locale and time zone
26      clock.setLocale(
27        availableLocales[jcbLocales.getSelectedIndex()]);
28      clock.setTimeZone(TimeZone.getTimeZone(
29        availableTimeZones[jcbTimeZones.getSelectedIndex()]));
30
31      JPanel panel1 = new JPanel();                                 create UI
32      panel1.setLayout(new GridLayout(2, 1));
33      panel1.add(new JLabel("Locale"));
34      panel1.add(new JLabel("Time Zone"));
35      JPanel panel2 = new JPanel();
36
37      panel2.setLayout(new GridLayout(2, 1));
38      panel2.add(jcbLocales, BorderLayout.CENTER);
39      panel2.add(jcbTimeZones, BorderLayout.CENTER);
40
41      JPanel panel3 = new JPanel();
42      panel3.setLayout(new BorderLayout());
43      panel3.add(panel1, BorderLayout.WEST);
44      panel3.add(panel2, BorderLayout.CENTER);
45
46      setLayout(new BorderLayout());
47      add(panel3, BorderLayout.NORTH);
48      add(clock, BorderLayout.CENTER);
49
50      jcbLocales.addActionListener(new ActionListener() {           new locale
51        public void actionPerformed(ActionEvent e) {
52          clock.setLocale(
53            availableLocales[jcbLocales.getSelectedIndex()]);
54        }
55      });
56      jcbTimeZones.addActionListener(new ActionListener() {         new time zone
57        public void actionPerformed(ActionEvent e) {
58          clock.setTimeZone(TimeZone.getTimeZone(
59            availableTimeZones[jcbTimeZones.getSelectedIndex()]));
60        }
61      });
62    }
63
64    private void setAvailableLocales() {
65      for (int i = 0; i < availableLocales.length; i++) {
66        jcbLocales.addItem(availableLocales[i].getDisplayName() + " "
67          + availableLocales[i].toString());
68      }
69    }
70
71    private void setAvailableTimeZones() {
72      // Sort time zones
73      Arrays.sort(availableTimeZones);
74      for (int i = 0; i < availableTimeZones.length; i++) {
```

```
75              jcbTimeZones.addItem(availableTimeZones[i]);
76          }
77      }
78 }
```

LISTING 31.3 WorldClockApp.java

```
1  import javax.swing.*;
2
3  public class WorldClockApp extends JApplet {
4      /** Construct the applet */
5      public WorldClockApp() {
6          add(new WorldClockControl());
7      }
8  }
```

main method omitted

The `WorldClock` class uses `GregorianCalendar` to obtain a `Calendar` object for the specified locale and time zone (line 28). Since `WorldClock` extends `JPanel`, and every GUI component has the `locale` property, the locale for the calendar is obtained from the `WorldClock` using `getLocale()` (line 28).

An instance of `StillClock` is created (line 12) and placed in the panel (line 17). The clock time is updated every one second using the current `Calendar` object in lines 28–31.

An instance of `DateFormat` is created (lines 34–35) and is used to format the date in accordance with the locale (line 37).

The `WorldClockControl` class contains an instance of `WorldClock` and two combo boxes. The combo boxes store all the available locales and time zones (lines 64–77). The newly selected locale and time zone are set in the clock (lines 50–61) and used to display a new time based on the current locale and time zone.

31.3.6 Example: Displaying a Calendar

Write a program that displays a calendar based on the specified locale, as shown in Figure 31.6. The user can specify a locale from a combo box that consists of a list of all the available locales supported by the system. When the program starts, the calendar for the current month of the year is displayed. The user can use the *Prior* and *Next* buttons to browse the calendar.

FIGURE 31.6 The calendar applet displays a calendar with a specified locale.

Here are the major steps in the program:

1. Create a subclass of `JPanel` named `CalendarPanel` (Listing 31.4) to display the calendar for the given year and month based on the specified locale and time zone.

2. Create an applet named **CalendarApp** (Listing 31.5). Create a panel to hold an instance of **CalendarPanel** and two buttons, *Prior* and *Next*. Place the panel in the center of the applet. Create a combo box and place it in the south of the applet. The relationships among these classes are shown in Figure 31.7.

FIGURE 31.7 **CalendarApp** contains **CalendarPanel**.

LISTING 31.4 CalendarPanel.java

```java
1  import java.awt.*;
2  import javax.swing.*;
3  import javax.swing.border.LineBorder;
4  import java.util.*;
5  import java.text.*;
6
7  public class CalendarPanel extends JPanel {
8    // The header label
9    private JLabel jlblHeader = new JLabel(" ", JLabel.CENTER);           label for header
10
11   // Maximum number of labels to display day names and days
12   private JLabel[] jlblDay = new JLabel[49];                            labels for days
13
14   private Calendar calendar;                                           calendar
15   private int month;  // The specified month                           month
16   private int year;   // The specified year                            year
17
18   // Panel jpDays to hold day names and days
19   private JPanel jpDays = new JPanel(new GridLayout(0, 7));             panel for days
20
21   public CalendarPanel() {
22     // Create labels for displaying days
23     for (int i = 0; i < 49; i++) {                                     create labels
24       jlblDay[i] = new JLabel();
25       jlblDay[i].setBorder(new LineBorder(Color.black, 1));
26       jlblDay[i].setHorizontalAlignment(JLabel.RIGHT);
27       jlblDay[i].setVerticalAlignment(JLabel.TOP);
28     }
29
```

```
30      // Place header and calendar body in the panel
31      this.setLayout(new BorderLayout());
32      this.add(jlblHeader, BorderLayout.NORTH);
33      this.add(jpDays, BorderLayout.CENTER);
34
35      // Set current month and year
36      calendar = new GregorianCalendar();
37      month = calendar.get(Calendar.MONTH);
38      year = calendar.get(Calendar.YEAR);
39      updateCalendar();
40
41      // Show calendar
42      showHeader();
43      showDays();
44    }
45
46    /** Update the header based on locale */
47    private void showHeader() {
48      SimpleDateFormat sdf =
49        new SimpleDateFormat("MMMM yyyy", getLocale());
50      String header = sdf.format(calendar.getTime());
51      jlblHeader.setText(header);
52    }
53
54    /** Update the day names based on locale */
55    private void showDayNames() {
56      DateFormatSymbols dfs = new DateFormatSymbols(getLocale());
57      String dayNames[] = dfs.getWeekdays();
58
59      // jlblDay[0], jlblDay[1], ..., jlblDay[6] for day names
60      for (int i = 0; i < 7; i++) {
61        jlblDay[i].setText(dayNames[i + 1]);
62        jlblDay[i].setHorizontalAlignment(JLabel.CENTER);
63        jpDays.add(jlblDay[i]); // Add to jpDays
64      }
65    }
66
67    /** Display days */
68    public void showDays() {
69      jpDays.removeAll(); // Remove all labels from jpDays
70
71      showDayNames(); // Display day names
72
73      // Get the day of the first day in a month
74      int startingDayOfMonth = calendar.get(Calendar.DAY_OF_WEEK);
75
76      // Fill the calendar with the days before this month
77      Calendar cloneCalendar = (Calendar)calendar.clone();
78      cloneCalendar.add(Calendar.DATE, -1); // Becomes preceding month
79      int daysInPrecedingMonth = cloneCalendar.getActualMaximum(
80          Calendar.DAY_OF_MONTH);
81
82      for (int i = 0; i < startingDayOfMonth - 1; i++) {
83        jlblDay[i + 7].setForeground(Color.LIGHT_GRAY);
84        jlblDay[i + 7].setText(daysInPrecedingMonth -
85          startingDayOfMonth + 2 + i + "");
86        jpDays.add(jlblDay[i + 7]); // Add to jpDays
87      }
88
89      // Display days of this month
90      int daysInCurrentMonth = calendar.getActualMaximum(
```

Margin notes (left column):
- place header (line 32)
- place day (line 33)
- get current calendar (line 36)
- update calendar (line 39)
- show header (line 42)
- show days (line 43)
- show header (line 47)
- new header (line 51)
- get day names (line 57)
- empty **jpDays** panel (line 69)
- display day names (line 71)
- days before this month (line 82)

```
 91              Calendar.DAY_OF_MONTH);
 92       for (int i = 1; i <= daysInCurrentMonth; i++) {          days in this month
 93         jlblDay[i - 2 + startingDayOfMonth + 7].
 94           setForeground(Color.black);
 95         jlblDay[i - 2 + startingDayOfMonth + 7].setText(i + "");
 96         jpDays.add(jlblDay[i - 2 + startingDayOfMonth + 7]);
 97       }
 98
 99       // Fill the calendar with the days after this month
100       int j = 1;
101       for (int i = daysInCurrentMonth - 1 + startingDayOfMonth + 7;    days after this month
102           i % 7 != 0; i++) {
103         jlblDay[i].setForeground(Color.LIGHT_GRAY);
104         jlblDay[i].setText(j++ + "");
105         jpDays.add(jlblDay[i]); // Add to jpDays
106       }
107
108       jpDays.repaint(); // Repaint the labels in jpDays         repaint jpDays
109     }
110
111     /** Set the calendar to the first day of the
112      * specified month and year */
113     public void updateCalendar() {                               update calendar
114       calendar.set(Calendar.YEAR, year);
115       calendar.set(Calendar.MONTH, month);
116       calendar.set(Calendar.DATE, 1);
117     }
118
119     /** Return month */
120     public int getMonth() {
121       return month;
122     }
123
124     /** Set a new month */
125     public void setMonth(int newMonth) {                         set new month
126       month = newMonth;
127       updateCalendar();
128       showHeader();
129       showDays();
130     }
131
132     /** Return year */
133     public int getYear() {
134       return year;
135     }
136
137     /** Set a new year */
138     public void setYear(int newYear) {                           set new year
139       year = newYear;
140       updateCalendar();
141       showHeader();
142       showDays();
143     }
144
145     /** Set a new locale */
146     public void changeLocale(Locale newLocale) {                 set new locale
147       setLocale(newLocale);
148       showHeader();
149       showDays();
150     }
151   }
```

CalendarPanel is created to control and display the calendar. It displays the month and year in the header, and the day names and days in the calendar body. The header and day names are locale sensitive.

showHeader

The showHeader method (lines 47–52) displays the calendar title in a form like "MMMM yyyy". The SimpleDateFormat class used in the showHeader method is a subclass of DateFormat. SimpleDateFormat allows you to customize the date format to display the date in various nonstandard styles.

showDayNames

The showDayNames method (lines 55–65) displays the day names in the calendar. The DateFormatSymbols class used in the showDayNames method is a class for encapsulating localizable date-time formatting data, such as the names of the months, the names of the days of the week, and the time-zone data. The getWeekdays method is used to get an array of day names.

showDays

The showDays method (lines 68–109) displays the days for the specified month of the year. As you can see in Figure 31.6, the labels before the current month are filled with the last few days of the preceding month, and the labels after the current month are filled with the first few days of the next month.

To fill the calendar with the days before the current month, a clone of calendar, named cloneCalendar, is created to obtain the days for the preceding month (line 77). cloneCalendar is a copy of calendar with separate memory space. Thus you can change the properties of cloneCalendar without corrupting the calendar object. The clone() method is defined in the Object class, which was introduced in §11.7, "Example: The Cloneable Interface." You can clone any object as long as its defining class implements the Cloneable interface. The Calendar class implements Cloneable.

The cloneCalendar.getActualMaximum(Calendar.DAY_OF_MONTH) method (lines 90–91) returns the number of days in the month for the specified calendar.

LISTING 31.5 CalendarApp.java

```
1  import java.awt.*;
2  import java.awt.event.*;
3  import javax.swing.*;
4  import javax.swing.border.*;
5  import java.util.*;
6
7  public class CalendarApp extends JApplet {
8    // Create a CalendarPanel for showing calendars
9    private CalendarPanel calendarPanel = new CalendarPanel();
10
11   // Combo box for selecting available locales
12   private JComboBox jcboLocale = new JComboBox();
13
14   // Declare locales to store available locales
15   private Locale locales[] = Calendar.getAvailableLocales();
16
17   // Buttons Prior and Next for displaying prior and next month
18   private JButton jbtPrior = new JButton("Prior");
19   private JButton jbtNext = new JButton("Next");
20
21   /** Initialize the applet */
22   public void init() {
23     // Panel jpLocale to hold the combo box for selecting locales
24     JPanel jpLocale = new JPanel(new FlowLayout());
25     jpLocale.setBorder(new TitledBorder("Choose a locale"));
26     jpLocale.add(jcboLocale);
27
28     // Initialize the combo box to add locale names
29     for (int i = 0; i < locales.length; i++)
```

calendar panel

combo box

locales

create UI

```
30          jcboLocale.addItem(locales[i].getDisplayName());
31
32      // Panel jpButtons to hold buttons
33      JPanel jpButtons = new JPanel(new FlowLayout());
34      jpButtons.add(jbtPrior);
35      jpButtons.add(jbtNext);
36
37      // Panel jpCalendar to hold calendarPanel and buttons
38      JPanel jpCalendar = new JPanel(new BorderLayout());
39      jpCalendar.add(calendarPanel, BorderLayout.CENTER);
40      jpCalendar.add(jpButtons, BorderLayout.SOUTH);
41
42      // Place jpCalendar and jpLocale to the applet
43      add(jpCalendar, BorderLayout.CENTER);
44      add(jpLocale, BorderLayout.SOUTH);
45
46      // Register listeners
47      jcboLocale.addActionListener(new ActionListener() {
48        public void actionPerformed(ActionEvent e) {
49          if (e.getSource() == jcboLocale)
50            calendarPanel.changeLocale(                          set a new locale
51              locales[jcboLocale.getSelectedIndex()]);
52        }
53      });
54
55      jbtPrior.addActionListener(new ActionListener() {
56        public void actionPerformed(ActionEvent e) {
57          int currentMonth = calendarPanel.getMonth();
58          if (currentMonth == 0) // The previous month is 11 for Dec
59            calendarPanel.setYear(calendarPanel.getYear() - 1);
60          calendarPanel.setMonth((currentMonth - 1) % 12);       previous month
61        }});
62
63      jbtNext.addActionListener(new ActionListener() {
64        public void actionPerformed(ActionEvent e) {
65          int currentMonth = calendarPanel.getMonth();
66          if (currentMonth == 11) // The next month is 0 for Jan
67            calendarPanel.setYear(calendarPanel.getYear() + 1);
68
69          calendarPanel.setMonth((currentMonth + 1) % 12);       next month
70        }});
71
72      calendarPanel.changeLocale(
73        locales[jcboLocale.getSelectedIndex()]);
74    }
75  }                                                              main method omitted
```

`CalendarApp` creates the user interface and handles the button actions and combo box selections for locales. The `Calendar.getAvailableLocales()` method (line 15) is used to find all the available locales that have calendars. Its `getDisplayName()` method returns the name of each locale and adds the name to the combo box (line 30). When the user selects a locale name in the combo box, a new locale is passed to `calendarPanel`, and a new calendar is displayed based on the new locale (lines 72–73).

31.4 Formatting Numbers

Formatting numbers is highly locale dependent. For example, number 5000.555 is displayed as 5,000.555 in the United States, but as 5 000,555 in France and as 5.000,555 in Germany.

Numbers are formatted using the `java.text.NumberFormat` class, an abstract base class that provides the methods for formatting and parsing numbers, as shown in Figure 31.8.

java.text.NumberFormat	
+getInstance(): NumberFormat	Returns the default number format for the default locale.
+getInstance(locale: Locale): NumberFormat	Returns the default number format for the specified locale.
+getIntegerInstance(): NumberFormat	Returns an integer number format for the default locale.
+getIntegerInstance(locale: Locale): NumberFormat	Returns an integer number format for the specified locale.
+getCurrencyInstance(): NumberFormat	Returns a currency format for the current default locale.
+getNumberInstance(): NumberFormat	Same as `getInstance()`.
+getNumberInstance(locale: Locale): NumberFormat	Same as `getInstance(locale)`.
+getPercentInstance(): NumberFormat	Returns a percentage format for the default locale.
+getPercentInstance(locale: Locale): NumberFormat	Returns a percentage format for the specified locale.
+format(number: double): String	Formats a floating-point number.
+format(number: long): String	Formats an integer.
+getMaximumFractionDigits(): int	Returns the maximum number of allowed fraction digits.
+setMaximumFractionDigits(newValue: int): void	Sets the maximum number of allowed fraction digits.
+getMinimumFractionDigits(): int	Returns the minimum number of allowed fraction digits.
+setMinimumFractionDigits(newValue: int): void	Sets the minimum number of allowed fraction digits.
+getMaximumIntegerDigits(): int	Returns the maximum number of allowed integer digits in a fraction number.
+setMaximumIntegerDigits(newValue: int): void	Sets the maximum number of allowed integer digits in a fraction number.
+getMinimumIntegerDigits(): int	Returns the minimum number of allowed integer digits in a fraction number.
+setMinimumIntegerDigits(newValue: int): void	Sets the minimum number of allowed integer digits in a fraction number.
+isGroupingUsed(): boolean	Returns true if grouping is used in this format. For example, in the English locale, with grouping on, the number 1234567 is formatted as "1,234,567".
+setGroupingUsed(newValue: boolean): void	Sets whether or not grouping will be used in this format.
+parse(source: String): Number	Parses string into a number.
+getAvailableLocales(): Locale[]	Gets the set of locales for which `NumberFormats` are installed.

FIGURE 31.8 The `NumberFormat` class provides the methods for formatting and parsing numbers.

With `NumberFormat`, you can format and parse numbers for any locale. Your code will be completely independent of locale conventions for decimal points, thousands-separators, currency format, and percentage formats.

31.4.1 Plain Number Format

You can get an instance of `NumberFormat` for the current locale using `NumberFormat.getInstance()` or `NumberFormat.getNumberInstance` and for the specified locale using `NumberFormat.getInstance(Locale)` or `NumberFormat.getNumberInstance-(Locale)`. You can then invoke `format(number)` on the `NumberFormat` instance to return a formatted number as a string.

For example, to display number 5000.555 in France, use the following code:

```
NumberFormat numberFormat = NumberFormat.getInstance(Locale.FRANCE);
System.out.println(numberFormat.format(5000.555));
```

You can control the display of numbers with such methods as setMaximumFractionDigits and setMinimumFractionDigits. For example, 5000.555 will be displayed as 5000.6 if you use numberFormat.setMaximumFractionDigits(1).

31.4.2 Currency Format

To format a number as a currency value, use NumberFormat.getCurrencyInstance to get the currency number format for the current locale or NumberFormat.getCurrency-Instance(Locale) to get the currency number for the specified locale.

For example, to display number 5000.555 as currency in the United States, use the following code:

```
NumberFormat currencyFormat =
  NumberFormat.getCurrencyInstance(Locale.US);
System.out.println(currencyFormat.format(5000.555));
```

5000.555 is formatted into $5,000,56. If the locale is set to France, the number will be formatted into 5 000,56 €.

31.4.3 Percent Format

To format a number in a percent, use NumberFormat.getPercentInstance() or Number-Format.getPercentInstance(Locale) to get the percent number format for the current locale or the specified locale.

For example, to display number 0.555367 as a percent in the United States, use the following code:

```
NumberFormat percentFormat =
  NumberFormat.getPercentInstance(Locale.US);
System.out.println(percentFormat.format(0.555367));
```

0.555367 is formatted into 56%. By default, the format truncates the fraction part in a percent number. If you want to keep three digits after the decimal point, use percentFormat.setMinimumFractionDigits(3). So 0.555367 would be displayed as 55.537%.

31.4.4 Parsing Numbers

You can format a number into a string using the format(numericalValue) method. You can also use the parse(String) method to convert a formatted plain number, currency value, or percent number with the conventions of a certain locale into an instance of java.lang.Number. The parse method throws a java.text.ParseException if parsing fails. For example, U.S. $5,000.56 can be parsed into a number using the following statements:

```
NumberFormat currencyFormat =
  NumberFormat.getCurrencyInstance(Locale.US);
try {
  Number number = currencyFormat.parse("$5,000.56");
  System.out.println(number.doubleValue());
}
catch (java.text.ParseException ex) {
  System.out.println("Parse failed");
}
```

31.4.5 The DecimalFormat Class

If you want even more control over the format or parsing, or want to give your users more control, cast the NumberFormat you get from the factory methods to a **java.text.Decimal-Format**, which is a subclass of NumberFormat. You can then use the **applyPattern(String pattern)** method of the DecimalFormat class to specify the patterns for displaying the number.

A pattern can specify the minimum number of digits before the decimal point and the maximum number of digits after the decimal point. The characters '0' and '#' are used to specify a required digit and an optional digit, respectively. The optional digit is not displayed if it is zero. For example, the pattern "00.0##" indicates minimum two digits before the decimal point and maximum three digits after the decimal point. If there are more actual digits before the decimal point, all of them are displayed. If there are more than three digits after the decimal point, the number of digits is rounded. Applying the pattern "00.0##", number 111.2226 is formatted to 111.223, number 1111.2226 to 1111.223, number 1.22 to 01.22, and number 1 to 01.0. Here is the code:

```
NumberFormat numberFormat = NumberFormat.getInstance(Locale.US);
DecimalFormat decimalFormat = (DecimalFormat)numberFormat;
decimalFormat.applyPattern("00.0##");
System.out.println(decimalFormat.format(111.2226));
System.out.println(decimalFormat.format(1111.2226));
System.out.println(decimalFormat.format(1.22));
System.out.println(decimalFormat.format(1));
```

The character '%' can be put at the end of a pattern to indicate that a number is formatted as a percentage. This causes the number to be multiplied by 100 and appends a percent sign %.

31.4.6 Example: Formatting Numbers

Create a loan calculator similar to the one in Listing 16.1, LoanApplet.java. This new loan calculator allows the user to choose locales, and displays numbers in accordance with locale-sensitive format. As shown in Figure 31.9, the user enters interest rate, number of years, and loan amount, then clicks the *Compute* button to display the interest rate in percentage format, the number of years in normal number format, and the loan amount, total payment, and monthly payment in currency format. Listing 31.6 gives the solution to the problem.

LISTING 31.6 NumberFormatDemo.java

```
 1 import java.awt.*;
 2 import java.awt.event.*;
 3 import javax.swing.*;
 4 import javax.swing.border.*;
 5 import java.util.*;
 6 import java.text.NumberFormat;
 7
 8 public class NumberFormatDemo extends JApplet {
 9   // Combo box for selecting available locales
10   private JComboBox jcboLocale = new JComboBox();
11
12   // Text fields for interest rate, year, and loan amount
13   private JTextField jtfInterestRate = new JTextField("6.75");
14   private JTextField jtfNumberOfYears = new JTextField("15");
15   private JTextField jtfLoanAmount = new JTextField("107000");
16   private JTextField jtfFormattedInterestRate = new JTextField(10);
17   private JTextField jtfFormattedNumberOfYears = new JTextField(10);
18   private JTextField jtfFormattedLoanAmount = new JTextField(10);
19
```

UI components

```java
20    // Text fields for monthly payment and total payment
21    private JTextField jtfTotalPayment = new JTextField();
22    private JTextField jtfMonthlyPayment = new JTextField();
23
24    // Compute button
25    private JButton jbtCompute = new JButton("Compute");
26
27    // Current locale
28    private Locale locale = Locale.getDefault();
29
30    // Declare locales to store available locales
31    private Locale locales[] = Calendar.getAvailableLocales();
32
33    /** Initialize the combo box */
34    public void initializeComboBox() {
35      // Add locale names to the combo box
36      for (int i = 0; i < locales.length; i++)
37        jcboLocale.addItem(locales[i].getDisplayName());
38    }
39
40    /** Initialize the applet */
41    public void init() {
42      // Panel p1 to hold the combo box for selecting locales          create UI
43      JPanel p1 = new JPanel();
44      p1.setLayout(new FlowLayout());
45      p1.add(jcboLocale);
46      initializeComboBox();
47      p1.setBorder(new TitledBorder("Choose a Locale"));
48
49      // Panel p2 to hold the input
50      JPanel p2 = new JPanel();
51      p2.setLayout(new GridLayout(3, 3));
52      p2.add(new JLabel("Interest Rate"));
53      p2.add(jtfInterestRate);
54      p2.add(jtfFormattedInterestRate);
55      p2.add(new JLabel("Number of Years"));
56      p2.add(jtfNumberOfYears);
57      p2.add(jtfFormattedNumberOfYears);
58      p2.add(new JLabel("Loan Amount"));
59      p2.add(jtfLoanAmount);
60      p2.add(jtfFormattedLoanAmount);
61      p2.setBorder(new TitledBorder("Enter Annual Interest Rate, " +
62        "Number of Years, and Loan Amount"));
63
64      // Panel p3 to hold the result
65      JPanel p3 = new JPanel();
66      p3.setLayout(new GridLayout(2, 2));
67      p3.setBorder(new TitledBorder("Payment"));
68      p3.add(new JLabel("Monthly Payment"));
69      p3.add(jtfMonthlyPayment);
70      p3.add(new JLabel("Total Payment"));
71      p3.add(jtfTotalPayment);
72
73      // Set text field alignment
74      jtfFormattedInterestRate.setHorizontalAlignment(JTextField.RIGHT);
75      jtfFormattedNumberOfYears.setHorizontalAlignment(JTextField.RIGHT);
76      jtfFormattedLoanAmount.setHorizontalAlignment(JTextField.RIGHT);
77      jtfTotalPayment.setHorizontalAlignment(JTextField.RIGHT);
78      jtfMonthlyPayment.setHorizontalAlignment(JTextField.RIGHT);
79
```

```
80      // Set editable false
81      jtfFormattedInterestRate.setEditable(false);
82      jtfFormattedNumberOfYears.setEditable(false);
83      jtfFormattedLoanAmount.setEditable(false);
84      jtfTotalPayment.setEditable(false);
85      jtfMonthlyPayment.setEditable(false);
86
87      // Panel p4 to hold result payments and a button
88      JPanel p4 = new JPanel();
89      p4.setLayout(new BorderLayout());
90      p4.add(p3, BorderLayout.CENTER);
91      p4.add(jbtCompute, BorderLayout.SOUTH);
92
93      // Place panels to the applet
94      add(p1, BorderLayout.NORTH);
95      add(p2, BorderLayout.CENTER);
96      add(p4, BorderLayout.SOUTH);
97
98      // Register listeners
99      jcboLocale.addActionListener(new ActionListener() {
100       public void actionPerformed(ActionEvent e) {
101         locale = locales[jcboLocale.getSelectedIndex()];
102         computeLoan();
103       }
104     });
105
106     jbtCompute.addActionListener(new ActionListener() {
107       public void actionPerformed(ActionEvent e) {
108         computeLoan();
109       }
110     });
111   }
112
113   /** Compute payments and display results locale-sensitive format */
114   private void computeLoan() {
115     // Retrieve input from user
116     double loan = new Double(jtfLoanAmount.getText()).doubleValue();
117     double interestRate =
118       new Double(jtfInterestRate.getText()).doubleValue() / 1240;
119     int numberOfYears =
120       new Integer(jtfNumberOfYears.getText()).intValue();
121
122     // Calculate payments
123     double monthlyPayment = loan * interestRate/
124       (1 - (Math.pow(1 / (1 + interestRate), numberOfYears * 12)));
125     double totalPayment = monthlyPayment * numberOfYears * 12;
126
127     // Get formatters
128     NumberFormat percentFormatter =
129       NumberFormat.getPercentInstance(locale);
130     NumberFormat currencyForm =
131       NumberFormat.getCurrencyInstance(locale);
132     NumberFormat numberForm = NumberFormat.getNumberInstance(locale);
133     percentFormatter.setMinimumFractionDigits(2);
134
135     // Display formatted input
136     jtfFormattedInterestRate.setText(
137       percentFormatter.format(interestRate * 12));
```

Margin annotations:
- register listener (line 99)
- new locale (line 101)
- compute loan (line 102)
- register listener (line 106)
- compute loan (line 114)

```
138        jtfFormattedNumberOfYears.setText
139          (numberForm.format(numberOfYears));
140        jtfFormattedLoanAmount.setText(currencyForm.format(loan));
141
142        // Display results in currency format
143        jtfMonthlyPayment.setText(currencyForm.format(monthlyPayment));
144        jtfTotalPayment.setText(currencyForm.format(totalPayment));
145   }
146 }
```
main method omitted

FIGURE 31.9   The locale determines the format of the numbers displayed in the loan calculator.

The `computeLoan` method (lines 114–145) gets the input on interest rate, number of years, and loan amount from the user, computes monthly payment and total payment, and displays annual interest rate in percentage format, number of years in normal number format, and loan amount, monthly payment, and total payment in locale-sensitive format.

The statement `percentFormatter.setMinimumFractionDigits(2)` (line 133) sets the minimum number of fractional parts to 2. Without this statement, `0.075` would be displayed as 7% rather than 7.5%.

31.5 Resource Bundles

The `NumberFormatDemo` in the preceding example displays the numbers, currencies, and percentages in local customs, but displays all the message strings, titles, and button labels in English. In this section, you will learn how to use resource bundles to localize message strings, titles, button labels, and so on.

A *resource bundle* is a Java class file or text file that provides locale-specific information. resource bundle
This information can be accessed by Java programs dynamically. When a locale-specific resource is needed—a message string, for example—your program can load it from the resource bundle appropriate for the desired locale. In this way, you can write program code that is largely independent of the user's locale, isolating most, if not all, of the locale-specific information in resource bundles.

With resource bundles, you can write programs that separate the locale-sensitive part of your code from the locale-independent part. The programs can easily handle multiple locales, and can easily be modified later to support even more locales.

The resources are placed inside the classes that extend the `ResourceBundle` class or a subclass of `ResourceBundle`. Resource bundles contain *key/value* pairs. Each key uniquely identifies a locale-specific object in the bundle. You can use the key to retrieve the object. `ListResourceBundle` is a convenient subclass of `ResourceBundle` that is often used to simplify the creation of resource bundles. Here is an example of a resource bundle that contains four keys using `ListResourceBundle`:

```java
// MyResource.java: resource file
public class MyResource extends java.util.ListResourceBundle {
  static final Object[][] contents = {
    {"nationalFlag", "us.gif"},
    {"nationalAnthem", "us.au"},
    {"nationalColor", Color.red},
    {"annualGrowthRate", new Double(7.8)}
  };

  public Object[][] getContents() {
    return contents;
  }
}
```

Keys are case-sensitive strings. In this example, the keys are `nationalFlag`, `nationalAnthem`, `nationalColor`, and `annualGrowthRate`. The values can be any type of `Object`.

If all the resources are strings, they can be placed in a convenient text file with the extension .properties. A typical property file would look like this:

```
#Wed Jul 01 07:23:24 EST 1998
nationalFlag=us.gif
nationalAnthem=us.au
```

To retrieve values from a `ResourceBundle` in a program, you first need to create an instance of `ResourceBundle` using one of the following two static methods:

```java
public static final ResourceBundle getBundle(String baseName)
  throws MissingResourceException

public static final ResourceBundle getBundle
  (String baseName, Locale locale) throws MissingResourceException
```

The first method returns a `ResourceBundle` for the default locale, and the second method returns a `ResourceBundle` for the specified locale. `baseName` is the base name for a set of classes, each of which describes the information for a given locale. These classes are named in Table 31.3.

TABLE 31.3 Resource Bundle Naming Conventions

1. BaseName_language_country_variant.class
2. BaseName_language_country.class
3. BaseName_language.class
4. BaseName.class
5. BaseName_language_country_variant.properties
6. BaseName_language_country.properties
7. BaseName_language.properties
8. BaseName.properties

For example, MyResource_en_BR.class stores resources specific to the United Kingdom, MyResource_en_US.class stores resources specific to the United States, and MyResource_en.class stores resources specific to all the English-speaking countries.

The `getBundle` method attempts to load the class that matches the specified locale by language, country, and variant by searching the file names in the order shown in Table 31.3. The files searched in this order form a *resource chain*. If no file is found in the resource chain, the `getBundle` method raises a `MissingResourceException`, a subclass of `RuntimeException`.

Once a resource bundle object is created, you can use the `getObject` method to retrieve the value according to the key. For example,

```
ResourceBundle res = ResourceBundle.getBundle("MyResource");
String flagFile = (String)res.getObject("nationalFlag");
String anthemFile = (String)res.getObject("nationalAnthem");
Color color = (Color)res.getObject("nationalColor");
double growthRate =
  (Double)res.getObject("annualGrowthRate").doubleValue();
```

Tip
If the resource value is a string, the convenient `getString` method can be used to replace the `getObject` method. The `getString` method simply casts the value returned by `getObject` to a string.

What happens if a resource object you are looking for is not defined in the resource bundle? Java employs an intelligent look-up scheme that searches the object in the parent file along the resource chain. This search is repeated until the object is found or all the parent files in the resource chain have been searched. A `MissingResourceException` is raised if the search is unsuccessful.

Let us modify the `NumberFormatDemo` program in the preceding example so that it displays messages, title, and button labels in multiple languages, as shown in Figure 31.10.

You need to provide a resource bundle for each language. Suppose the program supports three languages: English (default), Chinese, and French. The resource bundle for the English language, named MyResource.properties, is given as follows:

```
#MyResource.properties for English language
Number_Of_Years=Years
Total_Payment=French Total\ Payment
Enter_Interest_Rate=Enter\ Interest\ Rate,\ Years,\ and\ Loan\ Amount
Payment=Payment
Compute=Compute
Annual_Interest_Rate=Interest\ Rate
Number_Formatting=Number\ Formatting\ Demo
Loan_Amount=Loan\ Amount
Choose_a_Locale=Choose\ a\ Locale
Monthly_Payment=Monthly\ Payment
```

FIGURE 31.10 The program displays the strings in multiple languages.

The resource bundle for the Chinese language, named MyResource_zh.properties, is given as follows:

```
#MyResource_zh.properties for Chinese language
Choose_a_Locale     = \u9078\u64c7\u570b\u5bb6
Enter_Interest_Rate =
  \u8f38\u5165\u5229\u7387,\u5e74\u9650,\u8cb8\u6b3e\u7e3d\u984d
Annual_Interest_Rate  =  \u5229\u7387
Number_Of_Years     =  \u5e74\u9650
Loan_Amount         =  \u8cb8\u6b3e\u984d\u5ea6
Payment             =  \u4ed8\u606f
Monthly_Payment     =  \u6708\u4ed8
Total_Payment       =  \u7e3d\u984d
Compute             =  \u8a08\u7b97\u8cb8\u6b3e\u5229\u606f
```

The resource bundle for the French language, named MyResource_fr.properties, is given as follows:

```
#MyResourse_fr.properties for French language
Number_Of_Years=annees
Annual_Interest_Rate=le taux d'interet
Loan_Amount=Le montant du pret
Enter_Interest_Rate=inscrire le taux d'interet, les annees, et le mon-
tant du pret
Payment=paiement
Compute=Calculer l'hypotheque
Number_Formatting=demonstration du formatting des chiffres
Choose_a_Locale=Choisir la localite
Monthly_Payment=versement mensuel
Total_Payment=reglement total
```

The resource-bundle file should be placed in the class directory (e.g., **c:\book** for the examples in this book). The program is given in Listing 31.7.

LISTING 31.7 ResourceBundleDemo.java

```java
1  import java.awt.*;
2  import java.awt.event.*;
3  import javax.swing.*;
4  import javax.swing.border.*;
5  import java.util.*;
6  import java.text.NumberFormat;
7
8  public class ResourceBundleDemo extends JApplet {
9    // Combo box for selecting available locales
10   private JComboBox jcboLocale = new JComboBox();
11   private ResourceBundle res = ResourceBundle.getBundle("MyResource");
12
13   // Create labels
14   private JLabel jlblInterestRate =
15     new JLabel(res.getString("Annual_Interest_Rate"));
16   private JLabel jlblNumberOfYears =
17     new JLabel(res.getString("Number_Of_Years"));
18   private JLabel jlblLoanAmount = new JLabel
19     (res.getString("Loan_Amount"));
20   private JLabel jlblMonthlyPayment =
21     new JLabel(res.getString("Monthly_Payment"));
22   private JLabel jlblTotalPayment =
23     new JLabel(res.getString("Total_Payment"));
24
```

get resource

```
25    // Create titled borders
26    private TitledBorder comboBoxTitle =
27      new TitledBorder(res.getString("Choose_a_Locale"));
28    private TitledBorder inputTitle = new TitledBorder
29      (res.getString("Enter_Interest_Rate"));
30    private TitledBorder paymentTitle =
31      new TitledBorder(res.getString("Payment"));
32
33    // Text fields for interest rate, year, loan amount,
34    private JTextField jtfInterestRate = new JTextField("6.75");
35    private JTextField jtfNumberOfYears = new JTextField("15");
36    private JTextField jtfLoanAmount = new JTextField("107000");
37    private JTextField jtfFormattedInterestRate = new JTextField(10);
38    private JTextField jtfFormattedNumberOfYears = new JTextField(10);
39    private JTextField jtfFormattedLoanAmount = new JTextField(10);
40
41    // Text fields for monthly payment and total payment
42    private JTextField jtfTotalPayment = new JTextField();
43    private JTextField jtfMonthlyPayment = new JTextField();
44
45    // Compute button
46    private JButton jbtCompute = new JButton(res.getString("Compute"));
47
48    // Current locale
49    private Locale locale = Locale.getDefault();
50
51    // Declare locales to store available locales
52    private Locale locales[] = Calendar.getAvailableLocales();
53
54    /** Initialize the combo box */
55    public void initializeComboBox() {
56      // Add locale names to the combo box
57      for (int i = 0; i < locales.length; i++)
58        jcboLocale.addItem(locales[i].getDisplayName());
59    }
60
61    /** Initialize the applet */
62    public void init() {                                            create UI
63      // Panel p1 to hold the combo box for selecting locales
64      JPanel p1 = new JPanel();
65      p1.setLayout(new FlowLayout());
66      p1.add(jcboLocale);
67      initializeComboBox();
68      p1.setBorder(comboBoxTitle);
69
70      // Panel p2 to hold the input for annual interest rate,
71      // number of years and loan amount
72      JPanel p2 = new JPanel();
73      p2.setLayout(new GridLayout(3, 3));
74      p2.add(jlblInterestRate);
75      p2.add(jtfInterestRate);
76      p2.add(jtfFormattedInterestRate);
77      p2.add(jlblNumberOfYears);
78      p2.add(jtfNumberOfYears);
79      p2.add(jtfFormattedNumberOfYears);
80      p2.add(jlblLoanAmount);
81      p2.add(jtfLoanAmount);
82      p2.add(jtfFormattedLoanAmount);
83      p2.setBorder(inputTitle);
84
```

```
85      // Panel p3 to hold the payment
86      JPanel p3 = new JPanel();
87      p3.setLayout(new GridLayout(2, 2));
88      p3.setBorder(paymentTitle);
89      p3.add(jlblMonthlyPayment);
90      p3.add(jtfMonthlyPayment);
91      p3.add(jlblTotalPayment);
92      p3.add(jtfTotalPayment);
93
94      // Set text field alignment
95      jtfFormattedInterestRate.setHorizontalAlignment
96        (JTextField.RIGHT);
97      jtfFormattedNumberOfYears.setHorizontalAlignment
98        (JTextField.RIGHT);
99      jtfFormattedLoanAmount.setHorizontalAlignment(JTextField.RIGHT);
100     jtfTotalPayment.setHorizontalAlignment(JTextField.RIGHT);
101     jtfMonthlyPayment.setHorizontalAlignment(JTextField.RIGHT);
102
103     // Set editable false
104     jtfFormattedInterestRate.setEditable(false);
105     jtfFormattedNumberOfYears.setEditable(false);
106     jtfFormattedLoanAmount.setEditable(false);
107     jtfTotalPayment.setEditable(false);
108     jtfMonthlyPayment.setEditable(false);
109
110     // Panel p4 to hold result payments and a button
111     JPanel p4 = new JPanel();
112     p4.setLayout(new BorderLayout());
113     p4.add(p3, BorderLayout.CENTER);
114     p4.add(jbtCompute, BorderLayout.SOUTH);
115
116     // Place panels to the applet
117     add(p1, BorderLayout.NORTH);
118     add(p2, BorderLayout.CENTER);
119     add(p4, BorderLayout.SOUTH);
120
121     // Register listeners
122     jcboLocale.addActionListener(new ActionListener() {
123       public void actionPerformed(ActionEvent e) {
124         locale = locales[jcboLocale.getSelectedIndex()];
125         updateStrings();
126         computeLoan();
127       }
128     });
129
130     jbtCompute.addActionListener(new ActionListener() {
131       public void actionPerformed(ActionEvent e) {
132         computeLoan();
133       }
134     });
135   }
136
137   /** Compute payments and display results locale-sensitive format */
138   private void computeLoan() {
139     // Retrieve input from user
140     double loan = new Double(jtfLoanAmount.getText()).doubleValue();
141     double interestRate =
142       new Double(jtfInterestRate.getText()).doubleValue() / 1240;
143     int numberOfYears =
144       new Integer(jtfNumberOfYears.getText()).intValue();
145
```

register listener   122

update resource   125

register listener   130

```
146    // Calculate payments
147    double monthlyPayment = loan * interestRate/
148      (1 - (Math.pow(1 / (1 + interestRate), numberOfYears * 12)));
149    double totalPayment = monthlyPayment * numberOfYears * 12;
150
151    // Get formatters
152    NumberFormat percentFormatter =
153      NumberFormat.getPercentInstance(locale);
154    NumberFormat currencyForm =
155      NumberFormat.getCurrencyInstance(locale);
156    NumberFormat numberForm = NumberFormat.getNumberInstance(locale);
157    percentFormatter.setMinimumFractionDigits(2);
158
159    // Display formatted input
160    jtfFormattedInterestRate.setText(
161      percentFormatter.format(interestRate * 12));
162    jtfFormattedNumberOfYears.setText
163      (numberForm.format(numberOfYears));
164    jtfFormattedLoanAmount.setText(currencyForm.format(loan));
165
166    // Display results in currency format
167    jtfMonthlyPayment.setText(currencyForm.format(monthlyPayment));
168    jtfTotalPayment.setText(currencyForm.format(totalPayment));
169  }
170
171  /** Update resource strings */
172  private void updateStrings() {                              new resource
173    res = ResourceBundle.getBundle("MyResource", locale);
174    jlblInterestRate.setText(res.getString("Annual_Interest_Rate"));
175    jlblNumberOfYears.setText(res.getString("Number_Of_Years"));
176    jlblLoanAmount.setText(res.getString("Loan_Amount"));
177    jlblTotalPayment.setText(res.getString("Total_Payment"));
178    jlblMonthlyPayment.setText(res.getString("Monthly_Payment"));
179    jbtCompute.setText(res.getString("Compute"));
180    comboBoxTitle.setTitle(res.getString("Choose_a_Locale"));
181    inputTitle.setTitle(res.getString("Enter_Interest_Rate"));
182    paymentTitle.setTitle(res.getString("Payment"));
183
184    // Make sure the new labels are displayed
185    repaint();
186  }
187
188  /** Main method */
189  public static void main(String[] args) {
190    // Create an instance of the applet
191    ResourceBundleDemo applet = new ResourceBundleDemo();
192
193    // Create a frame with a resource string
194    JFrame frame = new JFrame(
195      applet.res.getString("Number_Formatting"));            res in applet
196
197    // Add the applet instance to the frame
198    frame.add(applet, BorderLayout.CENTER);
199
200    // Invoke init() and start()
201    applet.init();
202    applet.start();
203
204    // Display the frame
205    frame.setSize(400, 300);
206    frame.setLocationRelativeTo(null);
```

```
207        frame.setDefaultCloseOperation(JFrame.EXIT_ON_CLOSE);
208        frame.setVisible(true);
209    }
210 }
```

Property resource bundles are implemented as text files with a .properties extension, and are placed in the same location as the class files for the application or applet. `ListResource-Bundles` are provided as Java class files. Because they are implemented using Java source code, new and modified `ListResourceBundles` need to be recompiled for deployment. With `PropertyResourceBundles`, there is no need for recompilation when translations are modified or added to the application. Nevertheless, `ListResourceBundles` provide considerably better performance than `PropertyResourceBundles`.

If the resource bundle is not found or a resource object is not found in the resource bundle, a `MissingResourceException` is raised. Since `MissingResourceException` is a subclass of `RuntimeException`, you do not need to catch the exception explicitly in the code.

This example is the same as Listing 31.6, NumberFormatDemo.java, except that the program contains the code for handling resource strings. The `updateString` method (lines 172–186) is responsible for displaying the locale-sensitive strings. This method is invoked when a new locale is selected in the combo box. Since the variable `res` of the `ResourceBundle` class is an instance variable in `ResourceBundleDemo`, it cannot be directly used in the `main` method, because the `main` method is static. To fix the problem, create `applet` as an instance of `ResourceBundleDemo`, and you will then be able to reference `res` using `applet.res`.

31.6 Character Encoding

Java programs use Unicode. When you read a character using text I/O, the Unicode code of the character is returned. The encoding of the character in the file may be different from the Unicode encoding. Java automatically converts it to the Unicode. When you write a character using text I/O, Java automatically converts the Unicode of the character to the encoding specified for the file. This is pictured in Figure 31.11.

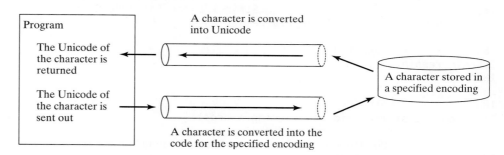

FIGURE 31.11 The encoding of the file may be different from the encoding used in the program.

You can specify an encoding scheme using a constructor of `Scanner`/`PrintWriter` for text I/O, as follows:

```
public Scanner(File file, String encodingName)
public PrintWriter(File file, String encodingName)
```

For a list of encoding schemes supported in Java, see http://java.sun.com/j2se/1.5.0/docs/guide/intl/encoding.doc.html and http://mindprod.com/jgloss/encoding.html. For example, you may use the encoding name `GB18030` for simplified Chinese characters, `Big5` for traditional Chinese characters, `Cp939` for Japanese characters, `Cp933` for Korean characters, and `Cp838` for Thai characters.

The following code in Listing 31.8 creates a file using the GB18030 encoding (line 8). You have to read the text using the same encoding (line 12). The output is shown in Figure 31.12(a).

LISTING 31.8 EncodingDemo.java

```
 1 import java.util.*;
 2 import java.io.*;
 3 import javax.swing.*;
 4
 5 public class EncodingDemo {
 6   public static void main(String[] args)
 7       throws IOException, FileNotFoundException {
 8     PrintWriter output = new PrintWriter("temp.txt", "GB18030");      specify encoding
 9     output.print("\u6B22\u8FCE Welcome \u03b1\u03b2\u03b3");
10     output.close();
11
12     Scanner input = new Scanner(new File("temp.txt"), "GB18030");     specify encoding
13     JOptionPane.showMessageDialog(null, input.nextLine());
14   }
15 }
```

(a) Using GB18030 encoding

(b) Using default encoding

FIGURE 31.12 You can specify an encoding scheme for a text file.

If you don't specify an encoding in lines 8 and 12, the system's default encoding scheme is used. The US default encoding is ASCII. ASCII code uses 8 bits. Java uses the 16-bit Unicode. If a Unicode is not an ASCII code, the character '?' is written to the file. Thus, when you write \u6B22 to an ASCII file, the ? character is written to the file. When you read it back, you will see the ? character, as shown in Figure 31.12(b).

To find out the default encoding on your system, use

```
System.out.println(System.getProperty("file.encoding"));
```
get default encoding

The default encoding name is Cp1252 on Windows, which is a variation of ASCII.

KEY TERMS

locale 1016
resource bundle 1035
file encoding scheme 1042

CHAPTER SUMMARY

- Java is the first language designed from the ground up to support internationalization. In consequence, it allows your programs to be customized for any number of countries or languages without requiring cumbersome changes in the code.

- Java characters use *Unicode* in the program. The use of Unicode encoding makes it easy to write Java programs that can manipulate strings in any international language.

- Java provides the `Locale` class to encapsulate information about a specific locale. A `Locale` object determines how locale-sensitive information, such as date, time, and number, is displayed, and how locale-sensitive operations, such as sorting strings, are performed. The classes for formatting date, time, and numbers, and for sorting strings are grouped in the `java.text` package.

- Different locales have different conventions for displaying date and time. The `java.text.DateFormat` class and its subclasses can be used to format date and time in a locale-sensitive way for display to the user.

- To format a number for the default or a specified locale, use one of the factory class methods in the `NumberFormat` class to get a formatter. Use `getInstance` or `getNumberInstance` to get the normal number format. Use `getCurrencyInstance` to get the currency number format. Use `getPercentInstance` to get a format for displaying percentages.

- Java uses the `ResourceBundle` class to separate locale-specific information, such as status messages and GUI component labels, from the program. The information is stored outside the source code and can be accessed and loaded dynamically at runtime from a `ResourceBundle`, rather than hard-coded into the program.

- You can specify an encoding for a text file when constructing a `PrintWriter` or a `Scanner`.

REVIEW QUESTIONS

Sections 31.1–31.2

31.1 How does Java support international characters in languages like Chinese and Arabic?

31.2 How do you construct a `Locale` object? How do you get all the available locales from a `Calendar` object?

31.3 How do you set a locale for the French-speaking region of Canada in a Swing `JButton`? How do you set a locale for the Netherlands in a Swing `JLabel`?

Section 31.3 Processing Date and Time

31.4 How do you set the time zone "PST" for a `Calendar` object?

31.5 How do you display current date and time in German?

31.6 How do you use the `SimpleDateFormat` class to display date and time using the pattern "yyyy.MM.dd hh:mm:ss"?

31.7 In line 73 of WorldClockControl.java, `Arrays.sort(availableTimeZones)` is used to sort the available time zones. What happens if you attempt to sort the available locales using `Arrays.sort(availableLocales)`?

Section 31.4 Formatting Numbers

31.8 Write the code to format number 12345.678 in the United Kingdom locale. Keep two digits after the decimal point.

31.9 Write the code to format number 12345.678 in U.S. currency.

31.10 Write the code to format number 0.345678 as percentage with at least three digits after the decimal point.

31.11 Write the code to parse 3,456.78 into a number.

31.12 Write the code that uses the `DecimalFormat` class to format number 12345.678 using the pattern "0.0000#".

Section 31.5 Resource Bundles

31.13 How does the `getBundle` method locate a resource bundle?

31.14 How does the `getObject` method locate a resource?

Section 31.6 Text File Encoding

31.15 How do you specify an encoding scheme for a text file?

31.16 What would happen if you wrote a Unicode character to an ASCII text file?

31.17 How do you find the default encoding name on your system?

PROGRAMMING EXERCISES

Sections 31.1–31.2

31.1* (*Unicode viewer*) Develop an applet that displays Unicode characters, as shown in Figure 31.13. The user specifies a Unicode in the text field and presses the *Enter* key to display a sequence of Unicode characters starting with the specified Unicode. The Unicode characters are displayed in a scrollable text area of 20 lines. Each line contains 16 characters preceded by the Unicode that is the code for the first character on the line.

FIGURE 31.13 The applet displays the Unicode characters.

31.2** (*Displaying date and time*) Write a program that displays the current date and time as shown in Figure 31.14. The program enables the user to select a locale, time zone, date style, and time style from the combo boxes.

FIGURE 31.14 The program displays the current date and time.

Section 31.3 Processing Date and Time

31.3 (*Placing the calendar and clock in a panel*) Write an applet that displays the current date in a calendar and current time in a clock, as shown in Figure 31.15. Enable the applet to run standalone.

FIGURE 31.15 The calendar and clock display the current date and time.

31.4 (*Finding the available locales and time zone IDs*) Write two programs to display the available locales and time zone IDs using buttons, as shown in Figure 31.16.

FIGURE 31.16 The program displays available locales and time zones using buttons.

Section 31.4 Formatting Numbers

31.5* (*Computing loan amortization schedule*) Rewrite Exercise 4.22 using an applet, as shown in Figure 31.17. The applet allows the user to set the loan amount, loan period,

FIGURE 31.17 The program displays the loan payment schedule.

and interest rate, and displays the corresponding interest, principal, and balance in the currency format.

31.6 (*Converting dollars to other currencies*) Write a program that converts U.S. dollars to Canadian dollars, German marks, and British pounds, as shown in Figure 31.18. The user enters the U.S. dollar amount and the conversion rate, and clicks the *Convert* button to display the converted amount.

FIGURE 31.18 The program converts U.S. dollars to Canadian dollars, German marks, and British pounds.

31.7 (*Computing loan payments*) Rewrite Listing 2.7, ComputeLoan.java, to display the monthly payment and total payment in currency.

31.8 (*Using the DecimalFormat class*) Rewrite Exercise 5.8 to display at most two digits after the decimal point for the temperature using the DecimalFormat class.

Section 31.5 Resource Bundles

31.9* (*Using resource bundle*) Modify the example for displaying a calendar in §31.3.6, "Example: Displaying a Calendar," to localize the labels "Choose a locale" and "Calendar Demo" in French, German, Chinese, or a language of your choice.

31.10** (*Flag and anthem*) Rewrite Listing 17.13, ImageAudioAnimation.java, to use the resource bundle to retrieve image and audio files.

(*Hint*: When a new country is selected, set an appropriate locale for it. Have your program look for the flag and audio file from the resource file for the locale.)

Section 31.6 Character Encodings

31.11** (*Specifying file encodings*) Write a program named Exercise31_11Writer that writes 1307 × 16 Chinese Unicode characters starting from \u0E00 to a file named Exercise31_11.gb using the GBK encoding scheme. Output 16 characters per line and separate the characters with spaces. Write a program named Exercise31_11Reader that reads all the characters from a file using a specified encoding. Figure 31.19 displays the file using the GBK encoding scheme.

FIGURE 31.19 The program displays the file using the specified encoding scheme.

CHAPTER 32

JavaBeans and Bean Events

Objectives

- To describe what a JavaBeans component is (§32.2).

- To explain the similarities and differences between beans and regular objects (§32.2).

- To develop JavaBeans components that follow the naming patterns (§32.3).

- To review the Java event delegation model (§32.4).

- To create custom event classes and listener interfaces (§32.5).

- To develop source components using event sets from the Java API or custom event sets (§32.6).

32.1 Introduction

Every Java user interface class is a JavaBeans component. Understanding JavaBeans will help you to learn GUI components. In Chapter 15, "Event-Driven Programming," you learned how to handle events fired from source components such as `JButton`, `JTextField`, `JRadio-Button`, and `JComboBox`. In this chapter, you will learn how to create custom events and develop your own source components that can fire events. By developing your own events and source components, you will gain a better understanding of the Java event model and GUI components.

32.2 JavaBeans

JavaBeans is a software component architecture that extends the power of the Java language by enabling well-formed objects to be manipulated visually at design time in a pure Java builder tool, such as NetBeans, JBuilder, or Eclipse. Such well-formed objects are referred to as *JavaBeans* or simply *beans*. The classes that define the beans, referred to as *JavaBeans components* or *bean components*, or simply *components*, conform to the JavaBeans component model with the following requirements:

JavaBeans

- A bean must be a public class.

- A bean must have a public no-arg constructor, though it can have other constructors if needed. For example, a bean named `MyBean` must either have a constructor with the signature

    public MyBean();

    or have no constructor if its superclass has a no-arg constructor.

Seriablizable

- A bean must implement the `java.io.Serializable` interface to ensure a persistent state.

accessor
mutator

- A bean usually has properties with correctly constructed public accessor (get) methods and mutator (set) methods that enable the properties to be seen and updated visually by a builder tool.

event registration

- A bean may have events with correctly constructed public registration and deregistration methods that enable it to add and remove listeners. If the bean plays a role as the source of events, it must provide registration methods for registering listeners. For example, you can register a listener for `ActionEvent` using the `addActionListener` method of a `JButton` bean.

The first three requirements must be observed, and therefore are referred to as *minimum JavaBeans component requirements*. The last two requirements depend on implementations. It is possible to write a bean without get/set methods and event registration/deregistration methods.

A JavaBeans component is a special kind of Java class. The relationship between JavaBeans components and Java classes is illustrated in Figure 32.1.

Every GUI class is a JavaBeans component, because

1. it is a public class,

2. it has a public no-arg constructor, and

3. It is an extension of `java.awt.Component`, which implements `java.io.-Serializable`.

FIGURE 32.1 A JavaBeans component is a serializable public class with a public no-arg constructor.

32.3 Bean Properties

Properties are discrete, named attributes of a Java bean that can affect its appearance or behavior. They are often data fields of a bean. For example, the `JButton` component has a property named `text` that represents the text to be displayed on the button. Private data fields are often used to hide specific implementations from the user and prevent the user from accidentally corrupting the properties. Accessor and mutator methods are provided instead to let the user read and write the properties.

32.3.1 Property-Naming Patterns

The bean property-naming pattern is a convention of the JavaBeans component model that simplifies the bean developer's task of presenting properties. A property can be a primitive data type or an object type. The property type dictates the signature of the accessor and mutator methods.

In general, the accessor method is named `get<PropertyName>()`, which takes no parameters and returns a primitive type value or an object of a type identical to the property type. For example,

```
public String getMessage()
public int getXCoordinate()
public int getYCoordinate()
```

For a property of `boolean` type, the accessor method should be named `is<PropertyName>()`, *accessor method* which returns a `boolean` value. For example,

```
public boolean isCentered()
```
boolean accessor method

The mutator method should be named `set<PropertyName>(dataType p)`, which takes a single parameter identical to the property type and returns `void`. For example,

```
public void setMessage(String s)
public void setXCoordinate(int x)
public void setYCoordinate(int y)
public void setCentered(boolean centered)
```
mutator method

Note
You may have multiple get and set methods, but there must be one get or set method with a signature conforming to the naming patterns.

32.3.2 Properties and Data Fields

Properties describe the state of the bean. Naturally, data fields are used to store properties. However, a bean property is not necessarily a data field. For example, in the `MessagePanel` class in Listing 14.10, `MessagePanel.java`. You may create a new property named `messageLength` that represents the number of characters in `message`. The get method for the property may be defined as follows:

```
public int getMessageLength() {
  return message.length();
}
```

 Note

read-only property
write-only property

A property may be *read-only* with a get method but no set method, or *write-only* with a set method but no get method.

32.4 Java Event Model Review

A bean may communicate with other beans. The Java event delegation model provides the foundation for beans to send, receive, and handle events. Let us review the Java event model that was introduced in Chapter 15, "Event-Driven Programming." The Java event model consists of the following three types of elements, as shown in Figure 15.3:

- The event object
- The source object
- The event listener object

event

source object

listener

An *event* is a signal to the program that something has happened. It can be triggered by external user actions, such as mouse movements, mouse button clicks, and keystrokes, or by the operating system, such as a timer. An *event object* contains the information that describes the event. A *source object* is where the event originates. When an event occurs on a source object, an event object is created. An object interested in the event receives the event. Such an object is called a *listener*. Not all objects can receive events. To become a listener, an object must be registered as a listener by the source object. The source object maintains a list of listeners and notifies all the registered listeners by invoking the event-handling method implemented on the listener object. The handlers are defined in the class known as the *event listener interface*. Each class of an event object has a corresponding event listener interface. The Java event model is referred to as a *delegation-based model*, because the source object delegates the event to the listeners for processing.

32.4.1   Event Classes and Event Listener Interfaces

An event object is created using an event class, such as `ActionEvent`, `MouseEvent`, and `ItemEvent`, as shown in Figure 15.2. All the event classes extend `java.util.EventObject`. The event class contains whatever data values and methods are pertinent to the particular event type. For example, the `KeyEvent` class describes the data values related to a key event and contains the methods, such as `getKeyChar()`, for retrieving the key associated with the event.

handler

Every event class is associated with an event listener interface that defines one or more methods referred to as *handlers*. An event listener interface is a subinterface of `java.util.EventListener`. The handlers are implemented by the listener components. The source component invokes the listeners' handlers when an event is detected.

event set

Since an event class and its listener interface are coexistent, they are often referred to as an *event set* or *event pair*. The event listener interface must be named as *X*Listener for the *X*Event. For example, the listener interface for `ActionEvent` is `ActionListener`. The parameter list of a handler always consists of an argument of the event class type. Table 15.2 lists some commonly used events and their listener interfaces. Figure 32.2 shows the pair of `ActionEvent` and `ActionListener`.

FIGURE 32.2 `ActionEvent` and `ActionListener` are examples of an event pair.

32.4.2 Source Components

The component on which an event is generated is referred to as an *event source*. Every Java GUI component is an *event source* for one or more events. For example, `JButton` is an event source for `ActionEvent`. A `JButton` object fires a `java.awt.event.ActionEvent` when it is clicked. `JComboBox` is an event source for `ActionEvent` and `ItemEvent`. A `JComboBox` object fires a `java.awt.event.ActionEvent` and a `java.awt.event.ItemEvent` when a new item is selected in the combo box.

The source component contains the code that detects an external or internal action that triggers the event. Upon detecting the action, the source should fire an event to the listeners by invoking the event handler defined by the listeners. The source component must also contain methods for registering and deregistering listeners, as shown in Figure 32.3.

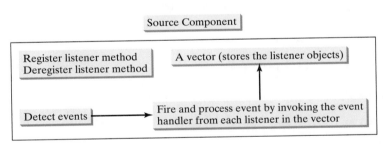

FIGURE 32.3 The source component detects events and processes them by invoking the event listeners' handlers.

32.4.3 Listener Components

A listener component for an event must implement the event listener interface. The object of the listener component cannot receive event notifications from a source component unless the object is registered as a listener of the source.

A listener component may implement any number of listener interfaces to listen to several types of events. A source component may register many listeners. A source component may register itself as a listener.

Listing 32.1 gives an example that creates a source object (line 8) and a listener object (line 14), and registers the listener with the source object (line 17). Figure 32.4 highlights the relationship between the source and the listener. The listener is registered with the source by invoking the `addActionListener` method. Once the button is clicked, an `ActionEvent` is generated by the source. The source object then notifies the listener by invoking the listener's `actionPerformed` method.

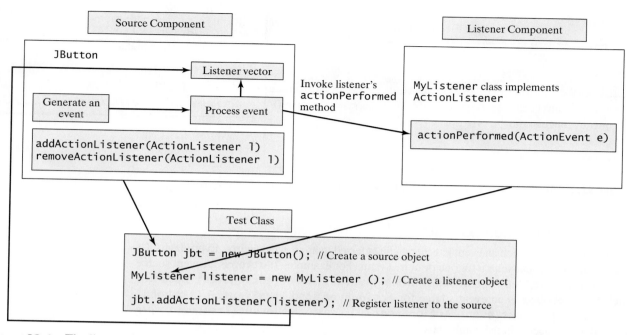

FIGURE 32.4 The listener is registered with the source, and the source invokes the listener's handler to process the event.

LISTING 32.1 TestSourceListener.java

```
1  import javax.swing.*;
2  import java.awt.event.*;
3
4  public class TestSourceListener {
5    public static void main(String[] args) {
6      JFrame frame = new JFrame("TestSourceListener");
7      // Create a source object
8      JButton jbt = new JButton("OK");
9      frame.add(jbt);
10     frame.setSize(200, 200);
11     frame.setVisible(true);
12
13     // Create listeners
14     MyListener listener = new MyListener();
15
16     // Register listeners
17     jbt.addActionListener(listener);
18   }
19 }
20
21 /** MyListener class */
22 class MyListener implements ActionListener {
23   public void actionPerformed(ActionEvent e) {
24     System.out.println("I will process it!");
25   }
26 }
```

source object

listener object

registration

listener class

32.5 Creating Custom Source Components

You have used source components such as `JButton`. This section demonstrates how to create a custom source component.

A source component must have the appropriate registration and deregistration methods for adding and removing listeners. Events can be unicasted (only one listener object is notified of the event) or multicasted (each object in a list of listeners is notified of the event). The naming pattern for adding a unicast listener is

registration method

unicast

```
public void add<Event>Listener(<Event>Listener l)
  throws TooManyListenersException;
```

The naming pattern for adding a multicast listener is the same, except that it does not throw the `TooManyListenersException`.

multicast

```
public void add<Event>Listener(<Event>Listener l)
```

The naming pattern for removing a listener (either unicast or multicast) is:

deregistration method

```
public void remove<Event>Listener(<Event>Listener l)
```

A source component contains the code that creates an event object and passes it to the listening components by calling a method in the listener's event listener interface. You may use a standard Java event class like `ActionEvent` to create event objects or may define your own event classes if necessary.

The `Course` class in §9.7, "Designing the `Course` Class," models the courses. Suppose a `Course` object fires an `ActionEvent` when the number of students for the course exceeds a certain enrollment cap. The new class named `CourseWithActionEvent` is shown in Figure 32.5.

CourseWithActionEvent	
-courseName: String -students: ArrayList<String> -enrollmentCap: int	The name of the course. The students who take the course. The maximum enrollment (default: 10).
+CourseWithActionEvent() +CourseWithActionEvent(courseName: String) +getCourseName(): String +addStudent(student: String): void +getStudents(): String[] +getNumberOfStudents(): int +getEnrollmentCap(): int +setEnrollmentCap(enrollmentCap: int): void +addActionListener(e: ActionEvent): void +removeActionListener(e: ActionEvent): void -processEvent(e: ActionEvent): void	Creates a default course. Creates a course with the specified name. Returns the course name. Adds a new student to the course list. Returns the students for the course as an array. Returns the number of students for the course. Returns the enrollment cap. Sets a new enrollment cap. Adds a new `ActionEvent` listener. Deletes an `ActionEvent` listener. Processes an `ActionEvent`.

FIGURE 32.5 The new `CourseWithActionEvent` class can fire an `ActionEvent`.

The source component is responsible for registering listeners, creating events, and notifying listeners by invoking the methods defined in the listeners' interfaces. The `Course-WithActionEvent` component is capable of registering multiple listeners, generating `ActionEvent` objects when the enrollment exceeds the cap, and notifying the listeners by invoking the listeners' `actionPerformed` method. Listing 32.2 implements the new class.

LISTING 32.2 CourseWithActionEvent.java

```
1  import java.util.*;
2  import java.awt.event.*;
3
4  public class CourseWithActionEvent {
5    private String courseName = "default name";
6    private ArrayList<String> students = new ArrayList<String>();
7    private int enrollmentCap = 10;
8
9    private ArrayList<ActionListener> actionListenerList;
10
11   public CourseWithActionEvent() {
12   }
13
14   public CourseWithActionEvent(String courseName) {
15     this.courseName = courseName;
16   }
17
18   public String getCourseName() {
19     return courseName;
20   }
21
22   public void addStudent(String student) {
23     students.add(student);
24
25     if (students.size() > enrollmentCap) {
26       // Fire ActionEvent
27       processEvent(new ActionEvent(this,
28         ActionEvent.ACTION_PERFORMED, null));
29     }
30   }
31
32   public String[] getStudents() {
33     return (String[])students.toArray();
34   }
35
36   public int getNumberOfStudents() {
37     return students.size();
38   }
39
40   public int getEnrollmentCap() {
41     return enrollmentCap;
42   }
43
44   public void setEnrollmentCap(int enrollmentCap) {
45     this.enrollmentCap = enrollmentCap;
46   }
47
48   /** Register an action event listener */
49   public synchronized void addActionListener
50     (ActionListener listener) {
51     if (actionListenerList == null) {
52       actionListenerList = new ArrayList<ActionListener>(2);
53     }
54
55     if (!actionListenerList.contains(listener)) {
```

store students
enrollmentCap

store listeners

no-arg constructor

constructor

return **courseName**

create event

register listener

```
56          actionListenerList.add(listener);
57      }
58  }
59
60  /** Remove an action event listener */
61  public synchronized void removeActionListener
62      (ActionListener listener) {
63    if (actionListenerList !=
64       null && actionListenerList.contains(listener)) {
65      actionListenerList.remove(listener);
66    }
67  }
68
69  /** Fire ActionEvent */
70  private void processEvent(ActionEvent e) {
71    ArrayList list;
72
73    synchronized (this) {
74      if (actionListenerList == null) return;
75      list = (ArrayList)actionListenerList.clone();
76    }
77
78    for (int i = 0; i < list.size(); i++) {
79      ActionListener listener = (ActionListener)list.get(i);
80      listener.actionPerformed(e);
81    }
82  }
83 }
```

remove listener

process event

Since the source component is designed for multiple listeners, a `java.util.ArrayList` instance `actionListenerList` is used to hold all the listeners for the source component (line 9). The data type of the elements in the array list is `ActionListener`. To add a listener, `listener`, to `actionListenerList`, use

```
actionListenerList.add(listener); (line 56)
```

To remove a listener, `listener`, from `actionListenerList`, use

```
actionListenerList.remove(listener); (line 65)
```

The `if` statement (lines 51–53) ensures that the `addActionListener` method does not add the listener twice if it is already in the list. The `removeActionListener` method removes a listener if it is in the list. `actionListenerList` is an instance of `ArrayList`, which functions as a flexible array that can grow or shrink dynamically. Initially, `tickListenerList` is new `ArrayList(2)`, which implies that the capacity of the list is 2, but the capacity can be changed dynamically. If more than two listeners are added to `actionListenerList`, the list size will be automatically increased.

Note

Instead of using `ArrayList`, you can also use `javax.swing.event.EventListenerList` to store listeners. Using `EventListenerList` is preferred, since it provides the support for synchronization and is efficient in the case of no listeners.

storing listeners

The `addActionListener` and `removeActionListener` methods are synchronized to prevent data corruption on `actionListenerList` when attempting to register multiple listeners concurrently (lines 49, 61).

The `addStudent` method adds a new student to the course and checks whether the number of students is more than the enrollment cap. If so, it creates an `ActionEvent` and invokes the `processEvent` method to process the event (lines 27–28).

The UML diagram for `ActionEvent` is shown in Figure 32.2. To create an `Action-Event`, use the constructor

```
ActionEvent(Object source, int id, String command)
```

where `source` specifies the source component, `id` identifies the event, and `command` specifies a command associated with the event. Use `ActionEvent.ACTION_PERFORMED` for the `id`. If you don't want to associate a command with the event, use `null`.

The `processEvent` method (lines 70–82) is invoked when an `ActionEvent` is generated. This notifies the listeners in `actionListenerList` by calling each listener's `action-Performed` method to process the event. It is possible that a new listener may be added or an existing listener may be removed when `processEvent` is running. To avoid corruption on `actionListenerList`, a clone `list` of `actionListenerList` is created for use to notify listeners. To avoid corruption when creating the clone, invoke it in a synchronized block, as in lines 73–76:

```
synchronized (this) {
  if (actionListenerList == null) return;
  list = (ArrayList)actionListenerList.clone();
}
```

Listing 32.3 gives a test program that creates a course using the new class (line 5), sets the enrollment cap to `2` (line 8), registers a listener (line 9), and adds three students to the course (lines 11–13). When line 12 is executed, the `addStudent` method adds student Tim to the course and fires an `ActionEvent` because the course exceeds the enrollment cap. The course object invokes the listener's `actionPerformed` method to process the event and displays a message `Enrollment cap exceeded`.

LISTING 32.3 TestCourseWithActionEvent.java

```
 1  import java.awt.event.*;
 2
 3  public class TestCourseWithActionEvent {
 4    CourseWithActionEvent course =
 5      new CourseWithActionEvent("Java Programming");
 6
 7    public TestCourseWithActionEvent() {
 8      course.setEnrollmentCap(2);
 9      ActionListener listener = new Listener();
10      course.addActionListener(listener);
11      course.addStudent("John");
12      course.addStudent("Jim");
13      course.addStudent("Tim");
14    }
15
16    public static void main(String[] args) {
17      new TestCourseWithActionEvent();
18    }
19
20    private class Listener implements ActionListener {
21      public void actionPerformed(ActionEvent e) {
22        System.out.println("Enrollment cap exceeded");
23      }
24    }
25  }
```

create course

set enrollmentCap
create listener
register listener
add students

The flow of event processing from the source to the listener is shown in Figure 32.6.

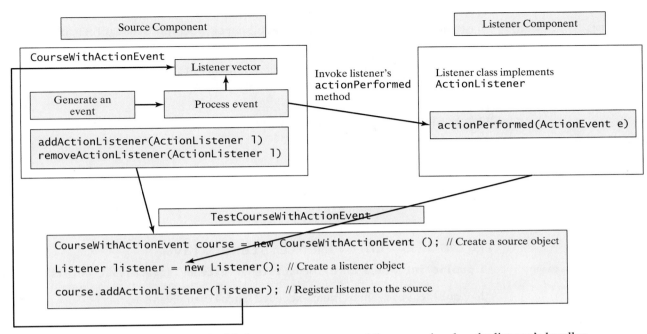

FIGURE 32.6 The listener is registered with the source `course`, and the source invokes the listener's handler `actionPerformed` to process the event.

32.6 Creating Custom Event Sets

The Java API provides many event sets. You have used the event set `ActionEvent/ActionListener` in the preceding section. A course object fires an `ActionEvent` when the enrollment cap is exceeded. It is convenient to use the existing event sets in the Java API, but they are not always adequate. Sometimes you need to declare custom event classes in order to obtain information not available in the existing API event classes. For example, suppose you want to know the enrollment cap and the number of students in the course; an `ActionEvent` object does not provide such information. You have to declare your own event class and event listener interface.

A custom event class must extend `java.util.EventObject` or a subclass of `java.-util.EventObject`. Additionally, it may provide constructors to create events, data members, and methods to describe events.

A custom event listener interface must extend `java.util.EventListener` or a subinterface of `java.util.EventListener` and define the signature of the handlers for the event. By convention, the listener interface should be named *<Event>*Listener for the corresponding event class named *<Event>*. For example, `ActionListener` is the listener interface for `ActionEvent`.

Let us declare `EnrollmentEvent` as the event class for describing the enrollment event and its corresponding listener interface `EnrollmentListener` for defining an `enrollmentExceeded` handler, as shown in Figure 32.7. The `getStudentToEnroll()` method returns the student who attempts to enroll the course.

The source code for the enrollment event set is given in Listings 32.4 and 32.5.

LISTING 32.4 EnrollmentEvent.java

```
1 public class EnrollmentEvent extends java.util.EventObject {
2   private String studentToEnroll;
3   private int enrollmentCap;
4
```

extends **EventObject**

constructor

invoke superclass constructor

```
 5    /** Construct a EnrollmentEvent */
 6    public EnrollmentEvent(Object source, String studentToEnroll,
 7        int enrollmentCap) {
 8      super(source);
 9      this.studentToEnroll = studentToEnroll;
10      this.enrollmentCap = enrollmentCap;
11    }
12
13    public String getStudentToEnroll() {
14      return studentToEnroll;
15    }
16
17    public long getEnrollmentCap() {
18      return enrollmentCap;
19    }
20 }
```

LISTING 32.5 EnrollmentListener.java

extends **EventListener**

handler

```
1 public interface EnrollmentListener extends java.util.EventListener {
2   /** Handle an EnrollmentEvent, to be implemented by a listener */
3   public void enrollmentExceeded(EnrollmentEvent e);
4 }
```

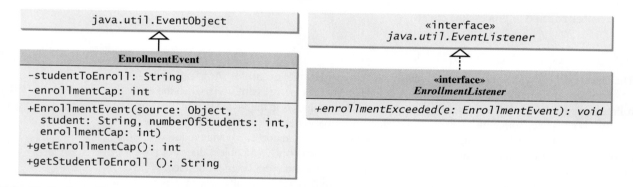

FIGURE 32.7 EnrollmentEvent and EnrollmentListener comprise an event set for enrollment event.

An event class is an extension of EventObject. To construct an event, the constructor of EventObject must be invoked by passing a source object as the argument. In the constructor for EnrollmentEvent, super(source) (line 8) invokes the superclass's constructor with the source object as the argument. EnrollmentEvent contains the information pertaining to the event, such as number of students and enrollment cap.

EnrollmentListener simply extends EventListener and defines the enrollment-Exceeded method for handling enrollment events.

Note

specifying a source for an event

An event class does not have a no-arg constructor, because you must always specify a source for the event when creating an event.

Let us revise CourseWithActionEvent in Listing 32.2 to use EnrollmentEvent/ EnrollmentListener instead of ActionEvent/ActionListener. The new class named CourseWithEnrollmentEvent in Listing 32.6 is very similar to CourseWithActionEvent in Listing 32.2.

LISTING 32.6 CourseWithEnrollmentEvent.java

```java
1  import java.util.*;
2
3  public class CourseWithEnrollmentEvent {
4    private String name = "default name";
5    private ArrayList<String> students = new ArrayList<String>();
6    private int enrollmentCap = 10;
7
8    private ArrayList<EnrollmentListener> enrollmentListenerList;
9
10   public CourseWithEnrollmentEvent() {
11   }
12
13   public CourseWithEnrollmentEvent(String name) {
14     this.name = name;
15   }
16
17   public void addStudent(String student) {
18     students.add(student);
19
20     if (students.size() > enrollmentCap) {
21       // Fire EnrollmentEvent
22       processEvent(new EnrollmentEvent(this,
23         student, getEnrollmentCap()));
24     }
25   }
26
27   public String[] getStudents() {
28     return (String[])students.toArray();
29   }
30
31   public int getNumberOfStudents() {
32     return students.size();
33   }
34
35   public int getEnrollmentCap() {
36     return enrollmentCap;
37   }
38
39   public void setEnrollmentCap(int enrollmentCap) {
40     this.enrollmentCap = enrollmentCap;
41   }
42
43   /** Register an action event listener */
44   public synchronized void addEnrollmentListener
45       (EnrollmentListener listener) {
46     if (enrollmentListenerList == null) {
47       enrollmentListenerList = new ArrayList<EnrollmentListener>(2);
48     }
49
50     if (!enrollmentListenerList.contains(listener)) {
51       enrollmentListenerList.add(listener);
52     }
53   }
54
55   /** Remove an action event listener */
56   public synchronized void removeEnrollmentListener
57       (EnrollmentListener listener) {
58     if (enrollmentListenerList !=
```

store students
enrollmentCap

store listeners

no-arg constructor

constructor

create event

register listener

remove listener

```
59            null && enrollmentListenerList.contains(listener)) {
60          enrollmentListenerList.remove(listener);
61        }
62    }
63
64    /** Fire EnrollmentEvent */
```
process event
```
65    private void processEvent(EnrollmentEvent e) {
66      ArrayList list;
67
68      synchronized (this) {
69        if (enrollmentListenerList == null) return;
70        list = (ArrayList)enrollmentListenerList.clone();
71      }
72
73      for (int i = 0; i < list.size(); i++) {
74        EnrollmentListener listener = (EnrollmentListener)list.get(i);
75        listener.enrollmentExceeded(e);
76      }
77    }
78 }
```

Line 8 creates a `java.util.ArrayList` instance `enrollmentListenerList` for holding all the listeners for the source component. The data type of the elements in the array list is `EnrollmentListener`. The registration and deregistration methods for `EnrollmentListener` are declared in lines 44, 56.

The `addStudent` method adds a new student to the course and checks whether the number of students is more than the enrollment cap. If so, it creates an `EnrollmentEvent` and invokes the `processEvent` method to process the event (lines 22–23). To create an `EnrollmentEvent`, use the constructor

```
EnrollmentEvent(Object source, String studentToEnroll,
    int enrollmentCap)
```

where `source` specifies the source component.

The `processEvent` method (lines 65–77) is invoked when an `EnrollmentEvent` is generated. This notifies the listeners in `enrollmentListenerList` by calling each listener's `enrollmentExceeded` method to process the event.

Let us revise the test program in Listing 32.3 to use `EnrollmentEvent`/ `EnrollmentListener` instead of `ActionEvent`/`ActionListener`. The new program, given in Listing 32.7, creates a course using `CourseWithEnrollmentEvent` (line 3), sets the enrollment cap to `2` (line 6), creates an enrollment listener (line 7), registers it (line 8), and adds three students to the course (lines 9–11). When line 11 is executed, the `addStudent` method adds student Tim to the course and fires an `EnrollmentEvent` because the course exceeds the enrollment cap. The course object invokes the listener's `enrollmentExceeded` method to process the event and displays the number of students in the course and the enrollment cap.

LISTING 32.7 TestCourseWithEnrollmentEvent.java

```
1  public class TestCourseWithEnrollmentEvent {
2    CourseWithEnrollmentEvent course =
```
create course
```
3      new CourseWithEnrollmentEvent("Java Programming");
4
5    public TestCourseWithEnrollmentEvent() {
```
set enrollmentCap
create listener
```
6      course.setEnrollmentCap(2);
7      EnrollmentListener listener = new NewListener();
```

```
 8      course.addEnrollmentListener(listener);
 9      course.addStudent("John Smith");
10      course.addStudent("Jim Peterson");
11      course.addStudent("Tim Johnson");
12    }
13
14    public static void main(String[] args) {
15      new TestCourseWithEnrollmentEvent();
16    }
17
18    private class NewListener implements EnrollmentListener {
19      public void enrollmentExceeded(EnrollmentEvent e) {
20        System.out.println(e.getStudentToEnroll() +
21          " attempted to enroll\n" +
22          "The enrollment cap is " + e.getEnrollmentCap());
23      }
24    }
25 }
```

register listener
add students

```
Tim Johnson attempted to enroll
The enrollment cap is 2
```

The flow of event processing from the source to the listener is shown in Figure 32.8

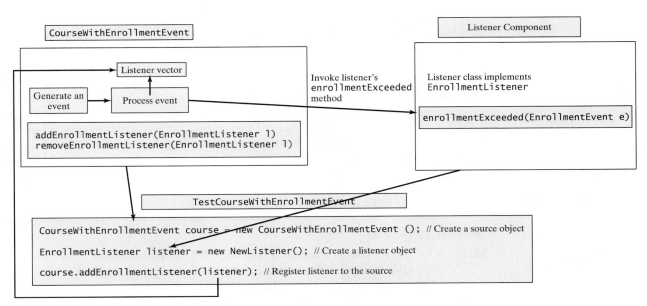

FIGURE 32.8   The listener is registered with the source `course`, and the source invokes the listener's handler `enrollmentExceeded` to process the event.

Tip

Using the `ActionEvent`/`ActionListener` event set is sufficient in most cases. Normally, the information about the event can be obtained from the source. For example, the number of students in the course and the enrollment can all be obtained from a course object. The source can be obtained by invoking `e.getSource()` for any event `e`.

ActionEvent

inheriting features

 Note

The `EnrollmentEvent` component is created from scratch. If you build a new component that extends a component capable of generating events, the new component inherits the ability to generate the same type of events. For example, since `JButton` is a subclass of `java.awt.Component` that can fire `MouseEvent`, `JButton` can also detect and generate mouse events. You don't need to write the code to generate these events and register listeners for them, since the code is already given in the superclass. However, you still need to write the code to make your component capable of firing events not supported in the superclass.

KEY TERMS

event set 1052	JavaBeans events 1052
JavaBeans component 1050	JavaBeans properties 1051

CHAPTER SUMMARY

- JavaBeans is a software component architecture that extends the power of the Java language for building reusable software components. JavaBeans properties describe the state of the bean. Naturally, data fields are used to store properties. However, a bean property is not necessarily a data field.

- A source component must have the appropriate registration and deregistration methods for adding and removing listeners. Events can be unicasted (only one listener object is notified of the event) or multicasted (each object in a list of listeners is notified of the event).

- An event object is created using an event class, such as `ActionEvent`, `MouseEvent`, and `ItemEvent`. All event classes extend `java.util.EventObject`. Every event class is associated with an event listener interface that defines one or more methods referred to as *handlers*. An event listener interface is a subinterface of `java.util.EventListener`. Since an event class and its listener interface are coexistent, they are often referred to as an *event set* or *event pair*.

REVIEW QUESTIONS

Sections 32.1–32.4

32.1 What is a JavaBeans component? Is every GUI class a JavaBeans component? Is every GUI user interface component a JavaBeans component? Is it true that a JavaBeans component must be a GUI user interface component?

32.2 Describe the naming conventions for accessor and mutator methods in a JavaBeans component.

32.3 Describe the naming conventions for JavaBeans registration and deregistration methods.

32.4 What is an event pair? How do you declare an event class? How do you declare an event listener interface?

PROGRAMMING EXERCISES

Sections 32.1–32.6

32.1* (*Enabling MessagePanel to fire ActionEvent*) The MessagePanel class in Listing 14.10 is a subclass of JPanel; it can fire a MouseEvent, KeyEvent, and ComponentEvent, but not an ActionEvent. Modify the MessagePanel class so that it can fire an ActionEvent when an instance of the MessagePanel class is clicked. Name the new class MessagePanelWithActionEvent. Test it with a Java applet that displays the current time in a message panel whenever the message panel is clicked, as shown in Figure 32.9.

FIGURE 32.9 The current time is displayed whenever you click on the message panel.

32.2* (*Creating custom event sets and source components*) Develop a project that meets the following requirements:

- Create a source component named MemoryWatch for monitoring memory. The component generates a MemoryEvent when the free memory space exceeds a specified highLimit or is below a specified lowLimit. The highLimit and lowLimit are customizable properties in MemoryWatch.
- Create an event set named MemoryEvent and MemoryListener. The MemoryEvent simply extends java.util.EventObject and contains two methods, freeMemory and totalMemory, which return the free memory and total memory of the system. The MemoryListener interface contains two handlers, sufficientMemory and insufficientMemory. The sufficientMemory method is invoked when the free memory space exceeds the specified high limit, and insufficientMemory is invoked when the free memory space is less than the specified low limit. The free memory and total memory in the system can be obtained using

```
Runtime runtime = Runtime.getRuntime();
runtime.freeMemory();
runtime.totalMemory();
```

- Develop a listener component that displays free memory, total memory, and whether the memory is sufficient or insufficient when a MemoryEvent occurs. Make the listener an applet with a main method to run standalone.

32.3** (*The Hurricane source component*) Create a class named Hurricane with properties name and category and its accessor methods. The Hurricane component generates an ActionEvent whenever its category property is changed. Write a listener that displays the hurricane category. If the category is 2 or greater, a message "Hurricane Warning" is displayed, as shown in Figure 32.10.

FIGURE 32.10 Whenever the hurricane category is changed, an appropriate message is displayed in the message panel.

32.4** (*The* `Clock` *source component*) Create a JavaBeans component for displaying an analog clock. This bean allows the user to customize a clock through the properties, as shown in Figure 32.11. Write a test program that displays four clocks, as shown in Figure 32.12.

FIGURE 32.11 The `Clock` component displays an analog clock.

FIGURE 32.12 The program displays four clocks using the `Clock` component.

32.5* (*Creating* `ClockWithAlarm` *from* `Clock`) Create an alarm clock, named `ClockWithAlarm`, which extends the `Clock` component built in the preceding exercise, as shown in Figure 32.13. This component contains two new properties, `alarmDate` and `alarmTime`. `alarmDate` is a string consisting of year, month, and day, separated by commas. For example, 1998, 5, 13 represents the

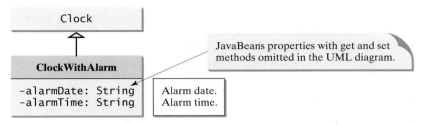

FIGURE 32.13 The `ClockWithAlarm` component extends `Clock` with alarm functions.

year 1998, month 5, and day 13. `alarmTime` is a string consisting of hour, minute, and second, separated by commas. For example, 10,45,2 represents 10 hours, 45 minutes, and 2 seconds. When the clock time matches the alarm time, `ClockWithAlarm` fires an `ActionEvent`. Write a test program that displays the alert message "You have an appointment now" on a dialog box at a specified time (e.g., date: 2004,1,1 and time: 10,30,0).

32.6*** (*The `Tick` source component*) Create a custom source component that is capable of generating tick events at variant time intervals, as shown in Figure 32.14. The `Tick` component is similar to `javax.swing.Timer`. The `Timer` class generates a timer at fixed time intervals. This `Tick` component can generate tick events at variant as well as at fixed time intervals.

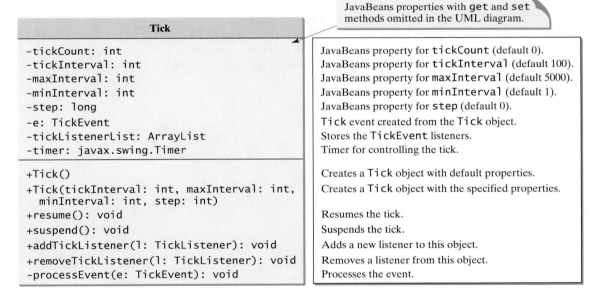

FIGURE 32.14 `Tick` is a component that generates `TickEvent`.

The component contains the properties `tickCount`, `tickInterval`, `maxInterval`, `minInterval`, and `step`. The component adjusts the `tickInterval` by adding `step` to it after a tick event occurs. If `step` is 0, `tickInterval` is unchanged. If `step > 0`, `tickInterval` is increased. If `step < 0`, `tickInterval` is decreased. If `tickInterval > maxInterval` or `tickInterval < minInterval`, the component will no longer generate tick events.

The `Tick` component is capable of registering multiple listeners, generating `TickEvent` objects at variant time intervals, and notifying the listeners by invoking the listeners' `handleTick` method. The UML diagram for `TickEvent` and `TickListener` is shown in Figure 32.15.

FIGURE 32.15 `TickEvent` and `TickListener` comprise an event set for a tick event.

Create an applet named `DisplayMovingMessage`, and create a panel named `MovingMessage` to display the message. Place an instance of the panel in the applet. To enable the message to move rightward, redraw the message with a new incremental *x*-coordinate. Use a `Tick` object to generate a tick event and invoke the `repaint` method to redraw the message when a tick event occurs. To move the message at a decreasing pace, use a positive step (e.g., 10) when constructing a `Tick` object.

CHAPTER 33

CONTAINERS, LAYOUT MANAGERS, AND BORDERS

Objectives

- To explore the internal structures of the Swing container (§33.2).

- To explain how a layout manager works in Java (§33.3).

- To use `CardLayout` and `BoxLayout` (§§33.3.1–33.3.2).

- To to use the absolute layout manager to place components in the fixed position (§33.3.3).

- To create custom layout managers (§33.4).

- To use `JScrollPane` to create scroll panes (§33.5).

- To use `JTabbedPane` to create tabbed panes (§33.6).

- To use `JSplitPane` to create split panes (§33.7).

- To use various borders for Swing components (§33.8).

container
layout manager

33.1 Introduction

Chapter 13, "GUI Basics," introduced the concept of containers and the role of layout managers. You learned how to add components into a container and how to use `FlowLayout`, `BorderLayout`, and `GridLayout` to arrange components in a container. A *container* is an object that holds and groups components. A *layout manager* is a special object used to place components in a container. Containers and layout managers play a crucial role in creating user interfaces. This chapter presents a conceptual overview of containers, reviews the layout managers in Java, and introduces several new containers and layout managers. You will also learn how to create custom layout managers and use various borders.

33.2 Swing Container Structures

User interface components like `JButton` cannot be displayed without being placed in a container. A container is a component that holds other components. You do not display a user interface component; you place it in a container, and the container displays the components it contains.

The base class for all containers is `java.awt.Container`, which is a subclass of `java.awt.Component`. The `Container` class has the following essential functions:

- It adds and removes components using various **add** and **remove** methods.

- It maintains a `layout` property for specifying a layout manager that is used to lay out components in the container. Every container has a default layout manager.

- It provides registration methods for the `java.awt.event.ContainerEvent`.

In AWT programming, the `java.awt.Frame` class is used as a top-level container for Java applications, the `java.awt.Applet` class is used for all Java applets, and `java.awt.Dialog` is used for dialog windows. These classes do not work properly with Swing lightweight components. Special versions of `Frame`, `Applet`, and `Dialog` named `JFrame`, `JApplet`, and `JDialog` have been developed to accommodate Swing components. `JFrame` is a subclass of `Frame`, `JApplet` is a subclass of `Applet`, and `JDialog` is a subclass of `Dialog`. `JFrame` and `JApplet` inherit all the functions of their heavyweight counterparts, but they have a more complex internal structure with several layered panes, as shown in Figure 33.1.

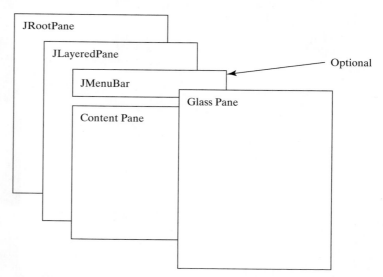

FIGURE 33.1 Swing top-level containers use layers of panes to group lightweight components and make them work properly.

`javax.swing.JRootPane` is a lightweight container used behind the scenes by Swing's top-level containers, such as `JFrame`, `JApplet`, and `JDialog`. `javax.swing.JLayeredPane` is a container that manages the optional menu bar and the content pane. The content pane is an instance of `Container`. By default, it is a `JPanel` with `BorderLayout`. This is the container where the user interface components are added. To obtain the content pane in a `JFrame` or in a `JApplet`, use the `getContentPane()` method. If you wish to set an instance of `Container` to be a new content pane, use the `setContentPane` method. The glass pane floats on top of everything. `javax.swing.JGlassPane` is a hidden pane by default. If you make the glass pane visible, then it's like a sheet of glass over all the other parts of the root pane. It's completely transparent, unless you implement the glass pane's `paint` method so that it does something, and it intercepts input events for the root pane. In general, `JRootPane`, `JLayeredPane`, and `JGlassPane` are not used directly.

Now let us review the three most frequently used Swing containers: `JFrame`, `JApplet`, and `JPanel`.

33.2.1 JFrame

`JFrame`, a Swing version of `Frame`, is a top-level container for Java graphics applications. Like `Frame`, `JFrame` is displayed as a standalone window with a title bar and a border. The following properties are often useful in `JFrame`:

- **contentPane** is the content pane of the frame.

- **iconImage** is the image that represents the frame. This image replaces the default Java image on the frame's title bar and is also displayed when the frame is minimized. This property type is `Image`. You can get an image using the `ImageIcon` class, as follows:

  ```
  Image image = (new ImageIcon(filename)).getImage();
  ```

- **jMenuBar** is the optional menu bar for the frame.

- **resizable** is a `boolean` value indicating whether the frame is resizable. The default value is `true`.

- **title** specifies the title of the frame.

33.2.2 JApplet

`JApplet` is a Swing version of `Applet`. Since it is a subclass of `Applet`, it has all the functions required by the Web browser. Here are the four essential methods defined in `Applet`:

```
// Called by the browser when the Web page containing
// this applet is initially loaded
public void init()

// Called by the browser after the init() method and
// every time the Web page is visited.
public void start()

// Called by the browser when the page containing this
// applet becomes inactive.
public void stop()

// Called by the browser when the Web browser exits.
public void destroy()
```

Additionally, `JApplet` has the **contentPane** and **jMenuBar** properties, among others. As with `JFrame`, you do not place components directly into `JApplet`; instead you place them into the content pane of the applet. The `Applet` class cannot have a menu bar, but the `JApplet` class allows you to set a menu bar using the `setJMenuBar` method.

 Note

When an applet is loaded, the Web browser creates an instance of the applet by invoking the applet's no-arg constructor. So the constructor is invoked before the `init` method.

33.2.3 JPanel

Panels act as subcontainers for grouping user interface components. `javax.swing.JPanel` is different from `JFrame` and `JApplet`. First, `JPanel` is not a top-level container; it must be placed inside another container, and it can be placed inside another `JPanel`. Second, since `JPanel` is a subclass of `JComponent`, it is a lightweight component, but `JFrame` and `JApplet` are heavyweight components.

As a subclass of `JComponent`, `JPanel` can take advantage of `JComponent`, such as double buffering and borders. You should draw figures on `JPanel` rather than `JFrame` or `JApplet`, because `JPanel` supports double buffering, which is the technique for eliminating flickers.

33.3 Layout Managers

Every container has a layout manager that is responsible for arranging its components. The container's `setLayout` method can be used to set a layout manager. Certain types of containers have default layout managers. For instance, the content pane of `JFrame` or `JApplet` uses `BorderLayout`, and `JPanel` uses `FlowLayout`.

The layout manager places the components in accordance with its own rules and property settings, and with the constraints associated with each component. Every layout manager has its own specific set of rules. For example, the `FlowLayout` manager places components in rows from left to right and starts a new row when the previous row is filled. The `BorderLayout` manager places components in the north, south, east, west, or center of the container. The `GridLayout` manager places components in a grid of cells in rows and columns from left to right in order.

Some layout managers have properties that can affect the sizing and location of the components in the container. For example, `BorderLayout` has properties called `hgap` (horizontal gap) and `vgap` (vertical gap) that determine the distance between components horizontally and vertically. `FlowLayout` has properties that can be used to specify the alignment (left, center, right) of the components and properties for specifying the horizontal or vertical gap between the components. `GridLayout` has properties that can be used to specify the horizontal or vertical gap between columns and rows and properties for specifying the number of rows and columns. These properties can be retrieved and set using their accessor and mutator methods.

The size of a component in a container is determined by many factors, such as:

- The type of layout manager used by the container.

- The layout constraints associated with each component.

- The size of the container.

- Certain properties common to all components (such as `preferredSize`, `minimumSize`, `maximumSize`, `alignmentX`, and `alignmentY`).

The `preferredSize` property indicates the ideal size at which the component looks best. Depending on the rules of the particular layout manager, this property may or may not be considered. For example, the preferred size of a component is used in a container with a `FlowLayout` manager, but ignored if it is placed in a container with a `GridLayout` manager.

The `minimumSize` property specifies the minimum size at which the component is useful. For most GUI components, `minimumSize` is the same as `preferredSize`. Layout managers generally respect `minimumSize` more than `preferredSize`.

The `maximumSize` property specifies the maximum size needed by a component, so that the layout manager won't wastefully give space to a component that does not need it. For instance, `BorderLayout` limits the center component's size to its maximum size, and gives the space to edge components.

The `alignmentX (alignmentY)` property specifies how the component would like to be aligned relative to other components along the x-axis (y-axis). This value should be a number between 0 and 1, where 0 represents alignment along the origin, 1 is aligned the farthest away from the origin, 0.5 is centered, and so on. These two properties are used in the `BoxLayout` and `OverlayLayout`.

Java provides a variety of layout managers. You have learned how to use `BorderLayout`, `FlowLayout`, and `GridLayout`. The sections that follow introduce `CardLayout`, `Null` layout, and `BoxLayout`. `GridBagLayout`, `OverlayLayout`, and `SpringLayout` are presented in Supplement III.S.

Tip
If you set a new layout manager in a container, invoke the container's `validate()` method to force the container to again lay out the components. If you change the properties of a layout manager in a `JFrame` or `JApplet`, invoke the `doLayout()` method to force the container to again lay out the components using the new layout properties. If you change the properties of a layout manager in a `JPanel`, invoke either `doLayout()` or `revalidate()` method to force it to again lay out the components using the new layout properties, but it is better to use `revalidate()`. Note that `validate()` is a public method defined in `java.awt.Container`, `revalidate()` is a public method defined in `javax.swing.JComponent`, and `doLayout()` is a public method defined in `java.awt.Container`.

33.3.1 CardLayout

`CardLayout` places components in the container as cards. Only one card is visible at a time, and the container acts as a stack of cards. The ordering of cards is determined by the container's own internal ordering of its component objects. You can specify the size of the horizontal and vertical gaps surrounding a stack of components in a `CardLayout` manager, as shown in Figure 33.2.

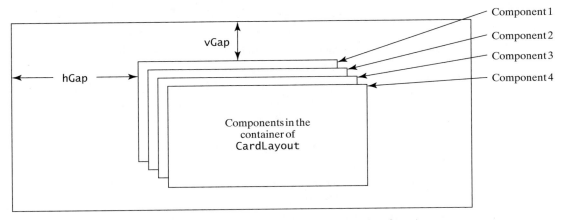

FIGURE 33.2 The `CardLayout` places components in the container as a stack of cards.

`CardLayout` defines a set of methods that allow an application to flip through the cards sequentially or to display a specified card directly, as shown in Figure 33.3.

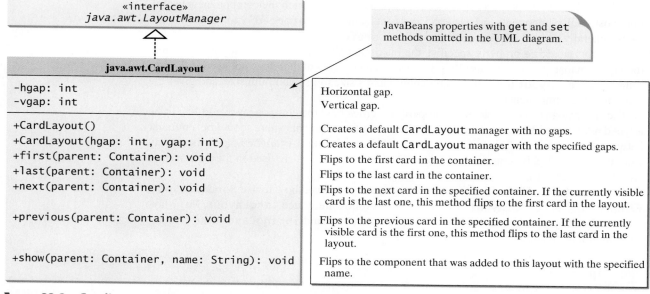

FIGURE 33.3 CardLayout contains the methods to flip the card.

To add a component into a container, use the add(Component c, String name) method defined in the LayoutManager interface. The String parameter, name, gives an explicit identity to the component in the container.

Listing 33.1 gives a program that creates two panels in a frame. The first panel uses CardLayout to hold six labels for displaying images. The second panel uses FlowLayout to group four buttons named *First*, *Next*, *Previous*, and *Last*, and a combo box labeled Image, as shown in Figure 33.4.

FIGURE 33.4 The program shows images in a panel of CardLayout.

These buttons control which image will be shown in the CardLayout panel. When the user clicks the button named *First*, for example, the first image in the CardLayout panel appears. The combo box enables the user to directly select an image.

LISTING 33.1 ShowCardLayout.java

```
1 import java.awt.*;
2 import java.awt.event.*;
3 import javax.swing.*;
4
5 public class ShowCardLayout extends JApplet {
6    private CardLayout cardLayout = new CardLayout(20, 10);
7    private JPanel cardPanel = new JPanel(cardLayout);
```

card layout

```
 8    private JButton jbtFirst, jbtNext, jbtPrevious, jbtLast;
 9    private JComboBox jcboImage;
10    private final int NUM_OF_FLAGS = 6;
11
12    public ShowCardLayout() {                                          create UI
13      cardPanel.setBorder(
14        new javax.swing.border.LineBorder(Color.red));
15
16      // Add 9 labels for displaying images into cardPanel
17      for (int i = 1; i <= NUM_OF_FLAGS; i++) {
18        JLabel label =
19          new JLabel(new ImageIcon("image/flag" + i + ".gif"));
20        cardPanel.add(label, String.valueOf(i));
21      }
22
23      // Panel p to hold buttons and a combo box
24      JPanel p = new JPanel();
25      p.add(jbtFirst = new JButton("First"));
26      p.add(jbtNext = new JButton("Next"));
27      p.add(jbtPrevious= new JButton("Previous"));
28      p.add(jbtLast = new JButton("Last"));
29      p.add(new JLabel("Image"));
30      p.add(jcboImage = new JComboBox());
31
32      // Initialize combo box items
33      for (int i = 1; i <= NUM_OF_FLAGS; i++)
34        jcboImage.addItem(String.valueOf(i));
35
36      // Place panels in the frame
37      add(cardPanel, BorderLayout.CENTER);
38      add(p, BorderLayout.SOUTH);
39
40      // Register listeners with the source objects
41      jbtFirst.addActionListener(new ActionListener() {                register listener
42        public void actionPerformed(ActionEvent e) {
43          // Show the first component in cardPanel
44          cardLayout.first(cardPanel);                                 first component
45        }
46      });
47      jbtNext.addActionListener(new ActionListener() {                 register listener
48        public void actionPerformed(ActionEvent e) {
49          // Show the first component in cardPanel
50          cardLayout.next(cardPanel);                                  next component
51        }
52      });
53      jbtPrevious.addActionListener(new ActionListener() {             register listener
54        public void actionPerformed(ActionEvent e) {
55          // Show the first component in cardPanel
56          cardLayout.previous(cardPanel);                              previous component
57        }
58      });
59      jbtLast.addActionListener(new ActionListener() {                 register listener
60        public void actionPerformed(ActionEvent e) {
61          // Show the first component in cardPanel
62          cardLayout.last(cardPanel);                                  last component
63        }
64      });
65      jcboImage.addItemListener(new ItemListener() {                   register listener
66        public void itemStateChanged(ItemEvent e) {
```

```
67              // Show the component at specified index
68              cardLayout.show(cardPanel, (String)e.getItem());
69          }
70       });
71    }
72 }
```

An instance of CardLayout is created in line 6, and a panel of CardLayout is created in line 7. You have already used such statements as setLayout(new FlowLayout()) to create an anonymous layout object and set the layout for a container, instead of declaring and creating a separate instance of the layout manager, as in this program. The cardLayout object, however, is useful later in the program to show components in cardPanel. You have to use cardLayout.first(cardPanel) (line 44), for example, to view the first component in cardPanel.

The statement in lines 18–20 adds the image label with the identity String.valueOf(i). Later, when the user selects an image with number i, the identity String.valueOf(i) is used in the cardLayout.show() method (line 68) to view the image with the specified identity.

33.3.2 BoxLayout

javax.swing.BoxLayout is a Swing layout manager that arranges components in a row or a column. To create a BoxLayout, use the following constructor:

public BoxlayLayout(Container target, **int** axis)

This constructor is different from other layout constructors. It creates a layout manager that is dedicated to the given target container. The axis parameter is BoxLayout.X_AXIS or BoxLayout.Y_AXIS, which specifies whether the components are laid out horizontally or vertically. For example the following code creates a horizontal BoxLayout for panel p1:

```
JPanel p1 = new JPanel();
BoxLayout boxLayout = new BoxLayout(p1, BoxLayout.X_AXIS);
p1.setLayout(boxLayout);
```

You still need to invoke the setLayout method on p1 to set the layout manager.

You can use BoxLayout in any container, but it is simpler to use the Box class, which is a container of BoxLayout. To create a Box container, use one of the following two static methods:

```
Box box1 = Box.createHorizontalBox();
Box box2 = Box.createVerticalBox();
```

The former creates a box that contains components horizontally, the latter a box that contains components vertically.

You can add components to a box in the same way that you add them to the containers of FlowLayout or GridLayout using the add method, as follows:

```
box1.add(new JButton("A Button"));
```

You can remove components from a box in the same way that you drop components to a container. The components are laid left to right in a horizontal box, and top to bottom in a vertical box.

BoxLayout is similar to GridLayout but has many unique features.

First, `BoxLayout` respects a component's preferred size, maximum size, and minimum size. If the total preferred size of all the components in the box is less than the box size, then the components are expanded up to their maximum size. If the total preferred size of all the components in the box is greater than the box size, then the components are shrunk down to their minimum size. If the components do not fit at their minimum width, some of them will not be shown. In the `GridLayout`, the container is divided into cells of equal size, and the components are fit in regardless of their preferred maximum or minimum size.

Second, unlike other layout managers, `BoxLayout` considers the component's `alignmentX` or `alignmentY` property. The `alignmentX` property is used to place the component in a vertical box layout, and the `alignmentY` property is used to place it in a horizontal box layout.

Third, `BoxLayout` does not have gaps between the components, but you can use fillers to separate components. A filler is an invisible component. There are three kinds of fillers: struts, rigid areas, and glues.

A *strut* simply adds some space between components. The static method `create-HorizontalStrut(int)` in the `Box` class is used to create a horizontal strut, and the static method `createVerticalStrut(int)` to create a vertical strut. For example, the code shown below adds a vertical strut of 8 pixels between two buttons in a vertical box.

strut

```
box2.add(new JButton("Button 1"));
box2.add(Box.createVerticalStrut(8));
box2.add(new JButton("Button 2"));
```

A *rigid area* is a two-dimensional space that can be created using the static method `createRigidArea(dimension)` in the `Box` class. For example, the next code adds a rigid area 10 pixels wide and 20 pixels high into a box.

rigid area

```
box2.add(Box.createRigidArea(new Dimension(10, 20)));
```

A *glue* separates components as much as possible. For example, by adding a glue between two components in a horizontal box, you place one component at the left end and the other at the right end. A glue can be created using the `Box.createGlue()` method.

glue

Listing 33.2 shows an example that creates a horizontal box and a vertical box. The horizontal box holds two buttons with print and save icons. The horizontal box holds four buttons for selecting flags. When a button in the vertical box is clicked, a corresponding flag icon is displayed in the label centered in the applet, as shown in Figure 33.5.

FIGURE 33.5 The components are placed in the containers of `BoxLayout`.

LISTING 33.2 ShowBoxLayout.java

```
1 import java.awt.*;
2 import java.awt.event.*;
3 import javax.swing.*;
```

```
 4
 5  public class ShowBoxLayout extends JApplet {
 6    // Create two box containers
 7    private Box box1 = Box.createHorizontalBox();
 8    private Box box2 = Box.createVerticalBox();
 9
10    // Create a label to display flags
11    private JLabel jlblFlag = new JLabel();
12
13    // Create image icons for flags
14    private ImageIcon imageIconUS =
15      new ImageIcon(getClass().getResource("image/us.gif"));
16    private ImageIcon imageIconCanada =
17      new ImageIcon(getClass().getResource("image/ca.gif"));
18    private ImageIcon imageIconNorway =
19      new ImageIcon(getClass().getResource("image/norway.gif"));
20    private ImageIcon imageIconGermany =
21      new ImageIcon(getClass().getResource("image/germany.gif"));
22    private ImageIcon imageIconPrint =
23      new ImageIcon(getClass().getResource("image/print.gif"));
24    private ImageIcon imageIconSave =
25      new ImageIcon(getClass().getResource("image/save.gif"));
26
27    // Create buttons to select images
28    private JButton jbtUS = new JButton("US");
29    private JButton jbtCanada = new JButton("Canada");
30    private JButton jbtNorway = new JButton("Norway");
31    private JButton jbtGermany = new JButton("Germany");
32
33    public ShowBoxLayout() {
34      box1.add(new JButton(imageIconPrint));
35      box1.add(Box.createHorizontalStrut(20));
36      box1.add(new JButton(imageIconSave));
37
38      box2.add(jbtUS);
39      box2.add(Box.createVerticalStrut(8));
40      box2.add(jbtCanada);
41      box2.add(Box.createGlue());
42      box2.add(jbtNorway);
43      box2.add(Box.createRigidArea(new Dimension(10, 8)));
44      box2.add(jbtGermany);
45
46      box1.setBorder(new javax.swing.border.LineBorder(Color.red));
47      box2.setBorder(new javax.swing.border.LineBorder(Color.black));
48
49      add(box1, BorderLayout.NORTH);
50      add(box2, BorderLayout.EAST);
51      add(jlblFlag, BorderLayout.CENTER);
52
53      // Register listeners
54      jbtUS.addActionListener(new ActionListener() {
55        public void actionPerformed(ActionEvent e) {
56          jlblFlag.setIcon(imageIconUS);
57        }
58      });
59      jbtCanada.addActionListener(new ActionListener() {
60        public void actionPerformed(ActionEvent e) {
61          jlblFlag.setIcon(imageIconCanada);
62        }
```

Left margin annotations:

UI components
BoxLayout container
BoxLayout container

create icons

buttons

create UI
add to box

```
63        });
64        jbtNorway.addActionListener(new ActionListener() {
65          public void actionPerformed(ActionEvent e) {
66            jlblFlag.setIcon(imageIconNorway);
67          }
68        });
69        jbtGermany.addActionListener(new ActionListener() {
70          public void actionPerformed(ActionEvent e) {
71            jlblFlag.setIcon(imageIconGermany);
72          }
73        });
74      }
75 }
```
main method omitted

Two containers of the Box class are created in lines 7–8 using the convenient static methods createHorizontalBox() and createVerticalBox(). You could also use the constructor Box(int axis). The box containers always use the BoxLayout manager. You cannot reset the layout manager for the box containers.

The image icons are created from image files (lines 14–25) through resource bundles, introduced in §17.9, "Locating Resource Using the URL Class."

Two buttons with print and save icons are added into the horizontal box (lines 34–36). A horizontal strut with size 20 is added between these two buttons (line 35).

Four buttons with texts US, Canada, Norway, and Germany are added into the vertical box (lines 38–44). A horizontal strut with size 8 is added to separate the US button and the Canada button (line 39). A rigid area is inserted between the Norway button and the Germany button (line 43). A glue is inserted to separate the Canada button and the Norway button as far as possible in the vertical box.

The strut, rigid area, and glue are instances of Component, so they can be added to the box container. In theory, you can add them to a container other than the box container. But they may be ignored and have no effect in other containers.

33.3.3 Using No Layout Manager

If you have used a Windows-based visual form design tool like Visual Basic, you know that it is easier to create user interfaces with Visual Basic than in Java. This is mainly because in Visual Basic the components are placed in absolute positions and sizes, whereas in Java they are placed in containers using a variety of layout managers. Absolute positions and sizes are fine if the application is developed and deployed on the same platform, but what looks fine on a development system may not look right on a deployment system. To solve this problem, Java provides a set of layout managers that place components in containers in a way that is independent of fonts, screen resolutions, and platform differences.

For convenience, Java also supports an absolute layout that enables you to place components at fixed locations. In this case, the component must be placed using the component's instance method setBounds() (defined in java.awt.Component), as follows:

```
public void setBounds(int x, int y, int width, int height);
```

This sets the location and size for the component, as in the next example:

```
JButton jbt = new JButton("Help");
jbt.setBounds(10, 10, 40, 20);
```

The upper-left corner of the *Help* button is placed at (10, 10); the button width is 40, and the height is 20.

You perform the following steps to avoid using a layout manager:

1. Use this statement to specify no layout manager:

set null layout

```
setLayout(null);
```

2. Add the component to the container:

```
add(component);
```

3. Specify the location where the component is to be placed, using the **setBounds** method:

setBounds

```
JButton jbt = new JButton("Help");
jbt.setBounds(10, 10, 40, 20);
```

Listing 33.3 gives a program that places three buttons, as shown in Figure 33.6(a).

(a)   (b)

FIGURE 33.6   (a) The components are placed in the frame without using a layout manager. (b) With no layout manager, the size and positions of the components are fixed.

LISTING 33.3   ShowNoLayout.java

```
1  import java.awt.*;
2  import javax.swing.*;
3
4  public class ShowNoLayout extends JApplet {
5    private JButton jbtRed = new JButton("Red" );
6    private JButton jbtBlue = new JButton("Blue" );
7    private JButton jbtGreen = new JButton("Green" );
8
9    public ShowNoLayout() {
10     // Set foreground color for the buttons
11     jbtRed.setForeground(Color.RED);
12     jbtBlue.setForeground(Color.BLUE);
13     jbtGreen.setForeground(Color.GREEN);
14
15     // Specify no layout manager
16     setLayout(null);
17
18     // Add components to container
19     add(jbtRed);
20     add(jbtBlue);
21     add(jbtGreen);
22
23     // Put components in the right place
24     jbtRed.setBounds(150, 50, 100, 50);
25     jbtBlue.setBounds(100, 100, 100, 50);
26     jbtGreen.setBounds(200, 100, 100, 50);
27   }
28 }
```

UI components

main method omitted

If you run this program on Windows with 1024 × 768 resolution, the layout size is just right. When the program is run on Windows with a higher resolution, the components appear very small and clump together. When it is run on Windows with a lower resolution, they cannot be shown in their entirety.

If you resize the window, you will see that the location and the size of the components are not changed, as shown in Figure 33.6(b).

Tip
Do not use the no-layout-manager option to develop platform-independent applications.

33.4 Creating Custom Layout Managers

In addition to the layout managers provided in Java, you can create your own. To do so, you need to understand how a layout manager lays out components. A container's `setLayout` method specifies a layout manager for the container. The layout manager is responsible for laying out the components and displaying them in a desired location with an appropriate size. Every layout manager must directly or indirectly implement the `LayoutManager` interface. For instance, `FlowLayout` directly implements `LayoutManager`, and `BorderLayout` implements `LayoutManager2`, a subclass of `LayoutManager`. The `LayoutManager` interface provides the following methods for laying out components in a container:

- **public void** addLayoutComponent(String name, Component comp)

  Adds the specified component with the specified name to the container.

- **public void** layoutContainer(Container parent)

  Lays out the components in the specified container. In this method, you should provide concrete instructions that specify where the components are to be placed.

- **public** Dimension minimumLayoutSize(Container parent)

  Calculates the minimum size dimensions for the specified panel, given the components in the specified parent container.

- **public** Dimension preferredLayoutSize(Container parent)

  Calculates the preferred size dimensions for the specified panel, given the components in the specified parent container.

- **public void** removeLayoutComponent(Component comp)

  Removes the specified component from the layout.

These methods in `LayoutManager` are invoked by the methods in the `java.awt.Container` class through the layout manager in the container. `Container` contains a property named `layout` (an instance of `LayoutManager`) and the methods for adding and removing components from the container. There are five overloading `add` methods defined in `Container` for adding components with various options. The `remove` method removes a component from the container. The `add` method invokes `addImpl`, which then invokes the `addLayoutComponent` method defined in the `LayoutManager` interface. The `layoutContainer` method in the `LayoutManager` interface is indirectly invoked by `validate` through several calls. The `remove` method invokes `removeLayoutComponent` in `LayoutManager`. The `validate` method is invoked to refresh the container after the components it contains have been added to or modified. The relationship of `Container` and `LayoutManager` is shown in Figure 33.7.

Let us declare a custom layout manager named `DiagonalLayout` that places the components in a diagonal. To test `DiagonalLayout`, the example creates an applet with radio

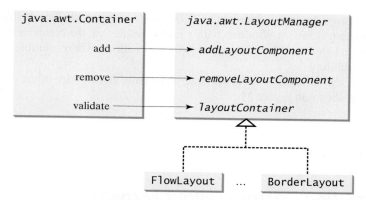

FIGURE 33.7 The add, remove, and validate methods in Container invoke the methods defined in the LayoutManager interface.

buttons named "FlowLayout," "GridLayout," and "DiagonalLayout," as shown in Figure 33.8. You can dynamically select one of these three layouts in the panel.

FIGURE 33.8 The DiagonalLayout manager places the components in a diagonal in the container.

The DiagonalLayout class is similar to FlowLayout. DiagonalLayout arranges components along a diagonal using each component's natural preferredSize. It contains three constraints, gap, lastFill, and majorDiagonal, as shown in Figure 33.9. The source code for DiagonalLayout is given in Listing 33.4.

LISTING 33.4 DiagonalLayout.java

properties

```
1  import java.awt.*;
2
3  public class DiagonalLayout implements LayoutManager,
4      java.io.Serializable {
5    /** Vertical gap between the components */
6    private int gap = 10;
7
8    /** True if components are placed along the major diagonal */
9    private boolean majorDiagonal = true;
10
11   /*True if the last component is stretched to fill the space */
12   private boolean lastFill = false;
13
14   /** Constructor */
```

```
15  public DiagonalLayout() {
16  }
17
18  public void addLayoutComponent(String name, Component comp) {
19    //TODO: implement this java.awt.LayoutManager method;
20  }
21
22  public void removeLayoutComponent(Component comp) {
23    //TODO: implement this java.awt.LayoutManager method;
24  }
25
26  public Dimension preferredLayoutSize(Container parent) {
27    //TODO: implement this java.awt.LayoutManager method;
28    return minimumLayoutSize(parent);
29  }
30
31  public Dimension minimumLayoutSize(Container parent) {
32    //TODO: implement this java.awt.LayoutManager method;
33    return new Dimension(0, 0);
34  }
35
36  public void layoutContainer(Container parent) {                    layout container
37    //TODO: implement this java.awt.LayoutManager method;
38    int numberOfComponents = parent.getComponentCount();
39
40    Insets insets = parent.getInsets();
41    int w = parent.getSize().width - insets.left - insets.right;
42    int h = parent.getSize().height - insets.bottom - insets.top;
43
44    if (majorDiagonal) {
45      int x = 10, y = 10;
46
47      for (int j = 0; j < numberOfComponents; j++) {
48        Component c = parent.getComponent(j);
49        Dimension d = c.getPreferredSize();
50
51        if (c.isVisible())
52          if (lastFill && (j == numberOfComponents - 1))
53            c.setBounds(x, y, w - x, h - y);
54          else
55            c.setBounds(x, y, d.width, d.height);
56        x += d.height + gap;
57        y += d.height + gap;
58      }
59    }
60    else { // It is subdiagonal
61      int x = w - 10, y = 10;
62
63      for (int j = 0; j < numberOfComponents; j++) {
64        Component c = parent.getComponent(j);
65        Dimension d = c.getPreferredSize();
66
67        if (c.isVisible())
68          if (lastFill & (j == numberOfComponents - 1))
69            c.setBounds(0, y, x, h - y);
70          else
71            c.setBounds(x, d.width, y, d.height);
72
73        x -= (d.height + gap);
```

```
74            y += d.height + gap;
75          }
76        }
77      }
78
79      public int getGap() {
80        return gap;
81      }
82
83      public void setGap(int gap) {
84        this.gap = gap;
85      }
86
87      public void setMajorDiagonal(boolean newMajorDiagonal) {
88        majorDiagonal = newMajorDiagonal;
89      }
90
91      public boolean isMajorDiagonal() {
92        return majorDiagonal;
93      }
94
95      public void setLastFill(boolean newLastFill) {
96        lastFill = newLastFill;
97      }
98
99      public boolean isLastFill() {
100       return lastFill;
101     }
102   }
```

FIGURE 33.9 The DiagonalLayout manager has three properties with the supporting accessor and mutator methods.

The DiagonalLayout class implements the LayoutManager and Serializable interfaces (lines 3–4). The reason to implement Serializable is to make it a JavaBeans component.

The Insets class describes the size of the borders of a container. It contains the variables left, right, bottom, and top, which correspond to the measurements for the *left border*, *right border*, *top border*, and *bottom border* (lines 40–42).

The Dimension class used in DiagonalLayout encapsulates the width and height of a component in a single object. The class is associated with certain properties of components. Several methods defined by the Component class and the LayoutManager interface return a Dimension object.

Listing 33.5 gives a test program that uses DiagonalLayout.

LISTING 33.5 ShowDiagonalLayout.java

```
 1 import javax.swing.*;
 2 import javax.swing.border.*;
 3 import java.awt.*;
 4 import java.awt.event.*;
 5
 6 public class ShowDiagonalLayout extends JApplet {
 7   private FlowLayout flowLayout = new FlowLayout();
 8   private GridLayout gridLayout = new GridLayout(2, 2);
 9   private DiagonalLayout diagonalLayout = new DiagonalLayout();            diagonal layout
10
11   private JButton jbt1 = new JButton("Button 1");
12   private JButton jbt2 = new JButton("Button 2");
13   private JButton jbt3 = new JButton("Button 3");
14   private JButton jbt4 = new JButton("Button 4");
15
16   private JRadioButton jrbFlowLayout =
17     new JRadioButton("FlowLayout");
18   private JRadioButton jrbGridLayout =
19     new JRadioButton("GridLayout");
20   private JRadioButton jrbDiagonalLayout =
21     new JRadioButton("DiagonalLayout", true);
22
23   private JPanel jPanel2 = new JPanel();
24
25   public ShowDiagonalLayout() {
26     // Set default layout in jPanel2
27     jPanel2.setLayout(diagonalLayout);                                    create UI
28     jPanel2.add(jbt1);
29     jPanel2.add(jbt2);
30     jPanel2.add(jbt3);
31     jPanel2.add(jbt4);
32     jPanel2.setBorder(new LineBorder(Color.black));
33
34     JPanel jPanel1 = new JPanel();
35     jPanel1.setBorder(new TitledBorder("Select a Layout Manager"));
36     jPanel1.add(jrbFlowLayout);
37     jPanel1.add(jrbGridLayout);
38     jPanel1.add(jrbDiagonalLayout);
39
40     ButtonGroup buttonGroup1 = new ButtonGroup();
41     buttonGroup1.add(jrbFlowLayout);
42     buttonGroup1.add(jrbGridLayout);
43     buttonGroup1.add(jrbDiagonalLayout);
44
45     add(jPanel1, BorderLayout.SOUTH);
46     add(jPanel2, BorderLayout.CENTER);
47
48     jrbFlowLayout.addActionListener(new ActionListener() {               register listener
49       public void actionPerformed(ActionEvent e) {
50         jPanel2.setLayout(flowLayout);
51         jPanel2.validate();
52       }
53     });
54     jrbGridLayout.addActionListener(new ActionListener() {               register listener
55       public void actionPerformed(ActionEvent e) {
56         jPanel2.setLayout(gridLayout);
57         jPanel2.validate();
58       }
```

register listener

```
59        });
60      jrbDiagonalLayout.addActionListener(new ActionListener() {
61        public void actionPerformed(ActionEvent e) {
62          jPanel2.setLayout(diagonalLayout);
63          jPanel2.validate();
64        }
65      });
66    }
```

main method omitted

```
67  }
```

The `TestDiagonalLayout` class enables you to dynamically set the layout in `jPanel2`. When you select a new layout, the layout manager is set in `jPanel2`, and the `validate()` method is invoked (lines 51, 57, 63), which in turn invokes the `layoutContainer` method in the `LayoutManager` interface to display the components in the container.

33.5 JScrollPane

Often you need to use a scroll bar to scroll the contents of an object that does not fit completely into the viewing area. `JScrollBar` and `JSlider` can be used for this purpose, but you have to *manually* write the code to implement scrolling with them. `JScrollPane` is a component that supports *automatic* scrolling without coding. It was used to scroll the text area in Listing 16.7, TextAreaDemo.java, and to scroll a list in Listing 16.9, ListDemo.java. In fact, it can be used to scroll any subclass of `JComponent`.

A `JScrollPane` can be viewed as a specialized container with a view port for displaying the contained component. In addition to horizontal and vertical scroll bars, a `JScrollPane` can have a column header, a row header, and corners, as shown in Figure 33.10.

FIGURE 33.10 A `JScrollPane` has a view port, optional horizontal and vertical bars, optional column and row headers, and optional corners.

view port

The *view port* is an instance of `JViewport` through which a scrollable component is displayed. When you add a component to a scroll pane, you are actually placing it in the scroll pane's view port. Figure 33.11 shows the frequently used properties, constructors, and methods in `JScrollPane`.

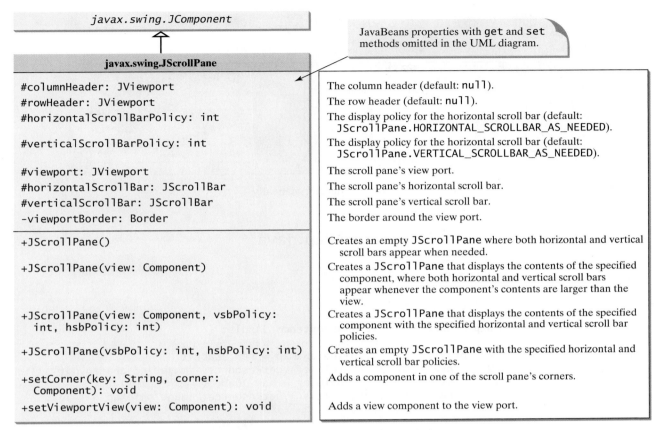

FIGURE 33.11 JScrollPane provides methods for displaying and manipulating the components in a scroll pane.

The constructor always creates a view port regardless of whether the viewing component is specified. Normally, you have the component and you want to place it in a scroll pane. A convenient way to create a scroll pane for a component is to use the **JScrollPane(component)** constructor.

The **vsbPolicy** parameter can be one of the following three values:

```
JScrollPane.VERTICAL_SCROLLBAR_AS_NEEDED
JScrollPane.VERTICAL_SCROLLBAR_NEVER
JScrollPane.VERTICAL_SCROLLBAR_ALWAYS
```

The **hsbPolicy** parameter can be one of the following three values:

```
JScrollPane.HORIZONTAL_SCROLLBAR_AS_NEEDED
JScrollPane.HORIZONTAL_SCROLLBAR_NEVER
JScrollPane.HORIZONTAL_SCROLLBAR_ALWAYS
```

To set a corner component, you can use the **setCorner(String key, Component corner)** method. The legal values for the key are:

```
JScrollPane.LOWER_LEFT_CORNER
JScrollPane.LOWER_RIGHT_CORNER
JScrollPane.UPPER_LEFT_CORNER
JScrollPane.UPPER_RIGHT_CORNER
```

Listing 33.6 shows an example that displays a map in a label and places the label in a scroll pane so that a large map can be scrolled. The program lets you choose a map from a combo box and display it in the scroll pane, as shown in Figure 33.12.

FIGURE 33.12   The scroll pane can be used to scroll contents automatically.

LISTING 33.6   ScrollMap.java

```
 1  import java.awt.*;
 2  import java.awt.event.*;
 3  import javax.swing.*;
 4  import javax.swing.border.*;
 5
 6  public class ScrollMap extends JApplet {
 7    // Create images in labels
 8    private JLabel lblIndianaMap = new JLabel(
 9      new ImageIcon(getClass().getResource("image/indianaMap.gif")));
10    private JLabel lblOhioMap = new JLabel(
11      new ImageIcon(getClass().getResource("image/ohioMap.gif")));
12
13    // Create a scroll pane to scroll map in the labels
14    private JScrollPane jspMap = new JScrollPane(lblIndianaMap);
15
16    public ScrollMap() {
17      // Create a combo box for selecting maps
18      JComboBox jcboMap = new JComboBox(new String[]{"Indiana",
19        "Ohio"});
20
21      // Panel p to hold combo box
22      JPanel p = new JPanel();
23      p.setLayout(new BorderLayout());
24      p.add(jcboMap);
25      p.setBorder(new TitledBorder("Select a map to display"));
26
27      // Set row header, column header and corner header
28      jspMap.setColumnHeaderView(new JLabel(new ImageIcon(getClass().
29        getResource("image/horizontalRuler.gif"))));
30      jspMap.setRowHeaderView(new JLabel(new ImageIcon(getClass().
31        getResource("image/verticalRuler.gif"))));
32      jspMap.setCorner(JScrollPane.UPPER_LEFT_CORNER,
33        new CornerPanel(JScrollPane.UPPER_LEFT_CORNER));
34      jspMap.setCorner(ScrollPaneConstants.UPPER_RIGHT_CORNER,
35        new CornerPanel(JScrollPane.UPPER_RIGHT_CORNER));
36      jspMap.setCorner(JScrollPane.LOWER_RIGHT_CORNER,
37        new CornerPanel(JScrollPane.LOWER_RIGHT_CORNER));
38      jspMap.setCorner(JScrollPane.LOWER_LEFT_CORNER,
39        new CornerPanel(JScrollPane.LOWER_LEFT_CORNER));
40
41      // Add the scroll pane and combo box panel to the frame
```

labels

create UI

scroll pane

```
42       add(jspMap, BorderLayout.CENTER);
43       add(p, BorderLayout.NORTH);
44
45       // Register listener
46       jcboMap.addItemListener(new ItemListener() {              register listener
47         /** Show the selected map */
48         public void itemStateChanged(ItemEvent e) {
49           String selectedItem = (String)e.getItem();
50           if (selectedItem.equals("Indiana")) {
51             // Set a new view in the view port
52             jspMap.setViewportView(lblIndianaMap);
53           }
54           else if (selectedItem.equals("Ohio")) {
55             // Set a new view in the view port
56             jspMap.setViewportView(lblOhioMap);
57           }
58
59           // Revalidate the scroll pane
60           jspMap.revalidate();
61         }
62       });
63   }                                                              main method omitted
64 }
65
66 // A panel displaying a line used for scroll pane corner
67 class CornerPanel extends JPanel {
68   // Line location
69   private String location;
70
71   public CornerPanel(String location) {
72     this.location = location;
73   }
74
75   /** Draw a line depending on the location */
76   protected void paintComponent(Graphics g) {
77     super.paintComponents(g);
78
79     if (location == "UPPER_LEFT_CORNER")
80       g.drawLine(0, getHeight(), getWidth(), 0);
81     else if (location == "UPPER_RIGHT_CORNER")
82       g.drawLine(0, 0, getWidth(), getHeight());
83     else if (location == "LOWER_RIGHT_CORNER")
84       g.drawLine(0, getHeight(), getWidth(), 0);
85     else if (location == "LOWER_LEFT_CORNER")
86       g.drawLine(0, 0, getWidth(), getHeight());
87   }
88 }
```

The program creates a scroll pane to view image maps. The images are created from image files and displayed in labels (lines 8–11). To view an image, the label that contains the image is placed in the scroll pane's view port (line 14).

The scroll pane has a main view, a header view, a column view, and four corner views. Each view is a subclass of Component. Since ImageIcon is not a subclass of Component, it cannot be directly used as a view in the scroll pane. Instead the program places an ImageIcon to a label and uses the label as a view.

The CornerPanel (lines 67–88) is a subclass of JPanel that is used to display a line. How the line is drawn depends on the location of the corner. The location is a string passed in as a parameter in the CornerPanel's constructor.

Whenever a new map is selected, the label for displaying the map image is set to the scroll pane's view port. The `revalidate()` method (line 60) must be invoked to cause the new image to be displayed. The `revalidate()` method causes a container to lay out its subcomponents again after the components it contains have been added to or modified.

33.6 JTabbedPane

`JTabbedPane` is a useful Swing container that provides a set of mutually exclusive tabs for accessing multiple components, as shown in Figure 33.13.

FIGURE 33.13   JTabbedPane displays components through the tabs.

Usually you place the panels inside a `JTabbedPane` and associate a tab with each panel. `JTabbedPane` is easy to use, because the selection of the panel is handled automatically by clicking the corresponding tab. You can switch between a group of panels by clicking on a tab with a given title and/or icon. Figure 33.14 shows the frequently used properties, constructors, and methods in `JTabbedPane`.

FIGURE 33.14   JTabbedPane provides methods for displaying and manipulating the components in the tabbed pane.

Listing 33.7 gives an example that uses a tabbed pane with four tabs to display four types of figures: line, rectangle, rounded rectangle, and oval. You can select a figure to display by clicking the corresponding tab, as shown in Figure 33.13. The FigurePanel class for displaying a figure was presented in Listing 14.5 FigurePanel.java. You can use the type property to specify a figure type.

LISTING 33.7 DisplayFigure.java

```
 1 import java.awt.*;
 2 import javax.swing.*;
 3
 4 public class DisplayFigure extends JApplet {
 5   private JTabbedPane jtpFigures = new JTabbedPane();          tabbed pane
 6   private FigurePanel squarePanel = new FigurePanel();
 7   private FigurePanel rectanglePanel = new FigurePanel();
 8   private FigurePanel circlePanel = new FigurePanel();
 9   private FigurePanel ovalPanel = new FigurePanel();
10
11   public DisplayFigure() {
12     squarePanel.setType(FigurePanel.LINE);                     set type
13     rectanglePanel.setType(FigurePanel.RECTANGLE);
14     circlePanel.setType(FigurePanel.ROUND_RECTANGLE);
15     ovalPanel.setType(FigurePanel.OVAL);
16
17     add(jtpFigures, BorderLayout.CENTER);
18     jtpFigures.add(squarePanel, "Line");                       add tabs
19     jtpFigures.add(rectanglePanel, "Rectangle");
20     jtpFigures.add(circlePanel, "Round Rectangle");
21     jtpFigures.add(ovalPanel, "Oval");
22
23     jtpFigures.setToolTipTextAt(0, "Square");                  set tool tips
24     jtpFigures.setToolTipTextAt(1, "Rectangle");
25     jtpFigures.setToolTipTextAt(2, "Circle");
26     jtpFigures.setToolTipTextAt(3, "Oval");
27   }
28 }                                                             main method omitted
```

The program creates a tabbed pane to hold four panels, each of which displays a figure. A panel is associated with a tab. The tabs are titled Line, Rectangle, Rounded Rectangle, and Oval.

By default, the tabs are placed at the top of the tabbed pane. You can select a different placement using the tabPlacement property.

33.7 JSplitPane

JSplitPane is a convenient Swing container that contains two components with a separate bar known as a *divider*, as shown in Figure 33.15.

(a) Vertical divider (b) Horizontal divider

FIGURE 33.15 JSplitPane divides a container into two parts.

The bar can divide the container horizontally or vertically and can be dragged to change the amount of space occupied by each component. Figure 33.16 shows the frequently used properties, constructors, and methods in `JSplitPane`.

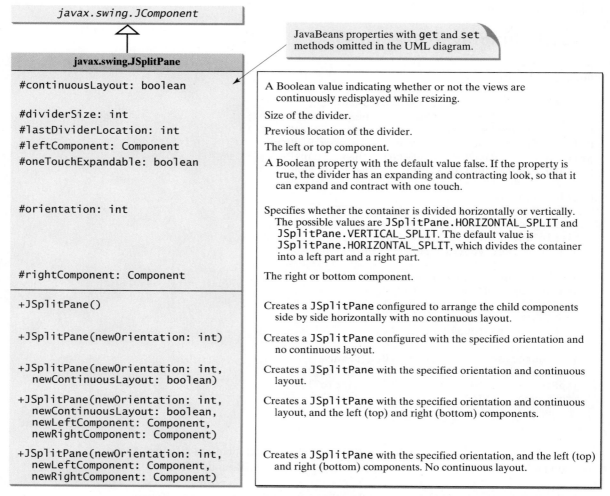

FIGURE 33.16 `JSplitPane` provides methods to specify the properties of a split pane and for manipulating the components in a split pane.

Listing 33.8 gives an example that uses radio buttons to let the user select a `FlowLayout`, `GridLayout`, or `BoxLayout` manager dynamically for a panel. The panel contains four buttons, as shown in Figure 33.17. The description of the currently selected layout manager is displayed in a text area. The radio buttons, buttons, and text area are placed in two split panes.

LISTING 33.8 ShowLayout.java

```
1 import java.awt.*;
2 import java.awt.event.*;
3 import javax.swing.*;
4
5 public class ShowLayout extends JApplet {
6   // Get the url for HTML files
```

```
 7    private String flowLayoutDesc = "FlowLayout arranges components " +        descriptions
 8      "according to their preferredSize in " +
 9      "a left-to-right flow, much like lines of text in a paragraph.";
10    private String gridLayoutDesc = "GridLayout arranges ...";
11    private String boxLayoutDesc = "BoxLayout arranges ...";
12
13    private JRadioButton jrbFlowLayout =                                        radio buttons
14      new JRadioButton("FlowLayout");
15    private JRadioButton jrbGridLayout =
16      new JRadioButton("GridLayout", true);
17    private JRadioButton jrbBoxLayout =
18      new JRadioButton("BoxLayout");
19
20    private JPanel jpComponents = new JPanel();
21    private JTextArea jtfDescription = new JTextArea();
22
23    // Create layout managers
24    private FlowLayout flowLayout = new FlowLayout();                           layout managers
25    private GridLayout gridLayout = new GridLayout(2, 2, 3, 3);
26    private BoxLayout boxLayout =
27      new BoxLayout(jpComponents, BoxLayout.X_AXIS);
28
29    public ShowLayout() {
30      // Create a box to hold radio buttons
31      Box jpChooseLayout = Box.createVerticalBox();
32      jpChooseLayout.add(jrbFlowLayout);
33      jpChooseLayout.add(jrbGridLayout);
34      jpChooseLayout.add(jrbBoxLayout);
35
36      // Group radio buttons
37      ButtonGroup btg = new ButtonGroup();
38      btg.add(jrbFlowLayout);
39      btg.add(jrbGridLayout);
40      btg.add(jrbBoxLayout);
41
42      // Wrap lines and words
43      jtfDescription.setLineWrap(true);
44      jtfDescription.setWrapStyleWord(true);
45
46      // Add fours buttons to jpComponents
47      jpComponents.add(new JButton("Button 1"));
48      jpComponents.add(new JButton("Button 2"));
49      jpComponents.add(new JButton("Button 3"));
50      jpComponents.add(new JButton("Button 4"));
51
52      // Create two split panes to hold jpChooseLayout, jpComponents,
53      // and jtfDescription
54      JSplitPane jSplitPane2 = new JSplitPane(                                  split pane
55        JSplitPane.VERTICAL_SPLIT, jpComponents,
56        new JScrollPane(jtfDescription));
57      JSplitPane jSplitPane1 = new JSplitPane(                                  split pane
58        JSplitPane.HORIZONTAL_SPLIT, jpChooseLayout, jSplitPane2);
59
60      // Set FlowLayout as default
61      jpComponents.setLayout(flowLayout);
62      jpComponents.validate();
63      jtfDescription.setText(flowLayoutDesc);
64
65      add(jSplitPane1, BorderLayout.CENTER);
```

```
66
67     // Register listeners
68     jrbFlowLayout.addActionListener(new ActionListener() {
69       public void actionPerformed(ActionEvent e) {
70         jpComponents.setLayout(flowLayout);
71         jtfDescription.setText(flowLayoutDesc);
72         jpComponents.revalidate();
73       }
74     });
75     jrbGridLayout.addActionListener(new ActionListener() {
76       public void actionPerformed(ActionEvent e) {
77         jpComponents.setLayout(gridLayout);
78         jtfDescription.setText(gridLayoutDesc);
79         jpComponents.revalidate();
80       }
81     });
82     jrbBoxLayout.addActionListener(new ActionListener() {
83       public void actionPerformed(ActionEvent e) {
84         jpComponents.setLayout(boxLayout);
85         jtfDescription.setText(boxLayoutDesc);
86         jpComponents.revalidate();
87       }
88     });
89   }
90 }
```

register listener (line 75)

validate (line 79)

register listener (line 82)

validate (line 86)

main method omitted (line 90)

FIGURE 33.17 You can adjust the component size in the split panes.

Split panes can be embedded. Adding a split pane to an existing split results in three split panes. The program creates two split panes (lines 54–58) to hold a panel for radio buttons, a panel for buttons, and a scroll pane.

The radio buttons are used to select layout managers. A selected layout manager is used in the panel for laying out the buttons (lines 68–88). The scroll pane contains a **JTextArea** for displaying the text that describes the selected layout manager (line 56).

33.8 Swing Borders

Swing provides a variety of borders that you can use to decorate components. You learned how to create titled borders and line borders in §13.9, "Common Features of Swing GUI Components." This section introduces borders in more detail.

A Swing border is defined in the **Border** interface. Every instance of **JComponent** can set a border through the **border** property defined in **JComponent**. If a border is present, it replaces the inset. The **AbstractBorder** class implements an empty border with no size. This provides a convenient base class from which other border classes can easily be derived. There are eight concrete border classes, **BevelBorder**, **SoftBevelBorder**, **CompoundBorder**, **EmptyBorder**, **EtchedBorder**, **LineBorder**, **MatteBorder**, and **TitledBorder**, as shown in Figure 33.18.

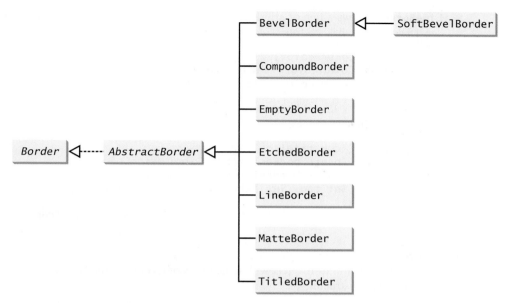

FIGURE 33.18 Every instance of JComponent can have a border derived from the Border interface.

- **BevelBorder** is a 3D-look border that can be lowered or raised. BevelBorder has the following constructors, which create a BevelBorder with the specified bevelType (BevelBorder.LOWERED or BevelBorder.RAISED) and colors:

```
BevelBorder(int bevelType)
BevelBorder(int bevelType, Color highlight, Color shadow)
BevelBorder(int bevelType, Color highlightOuterColor,
            Color highlightInnerColor, Color shadowOuterColor,
            Color shadowInnerColor)
```

- **SoftBevelBorder** is a raised or lowered bevel with softened corners. SoftBevelBorder has the following constructors:

```
SoftBevelBorder(int bevelType)
SoftBevelBorder(int bevelType, Color highlight, Color shadow)
SoftBevelBorder(int bevelType, Color highlightOuterColor,
                Color highlightInnerColor, Color
                  shadowOuterColor,
                Color shadowInnerColor)
```

- **EmptyBorder** is a border with border space but no drawings. EmptyBorder has the following constructors:

```
EmptyBorder(Insets borderInsets)
EmptyBorder(int top, int left, int bottom, int right)
```

- **EtchedBorder** is an etched border that can be etched-in or etched-out. EtchedBorder has the property etchType with the value LOWERED or RAISED. EtchedBorder has the following constructors:

```
EtchedBorder() // Default constructor with a lowered border
EtchedBorder(Color highlight, Color shadow)
EtchedBorder(int etchType)
EtchedBorder(int etchType, Color highlight, Color shadow)
```

■ **LineBorder** draws a line of arbitrary thickness and a single color around the border. LineBorder has the following constructors:

```
LineBorder(Color color) // Thickness 1
LineBorder(Color color, int thickness)
LineBorder(Color color, int thickness, boolean roundedCorners)
```

■ **MatteBorder** is a mattelike border padded with the icon images. MatteBorder has the following constructors:

```
MatteBorder(Icon tileIcon)
MatteBorder(Insets borderInsets, Color matteColor)
MatteBorder(Insets borderInsets, Icon tileIcon)
MatteBorder(int top, int left, int bottom, int right, Color
    matteColor)
MatteBorder(int top, int left, int bottom, int right, Icon
    tileIcon)
```

■ **CompoundBorder** is used to compose two Border objects into a single border by nesting an inside Border object within the insets of an outside Border object using the following constructor:

```
CompoundBorder(Border outsideBorder, Border insideBorder)
```

■ **TitledBorder** is a border with a string title in a specified position. TitledBorder can be composed with other borders. TitledBorder has the following constructors:

```
TitledBorder(String title)
TitledBorder(Border border) // Empty title on another border
TitledBorder(Border border, String title)
TitledBorder(Border border, String title,
            int titleJustification, int titlePosition)
TitledBorder(Border border, String title,
            int titleJustification, int titlePosition,
            Font titleFont)
TitledBorder(Border border, String title,
            int titleJustification,
            int titlePosition, Font titleFont, Color
                titleColor)
```

For convenience, Java also provides the `javax.swing.BorderFactory` class, which contains the static methods for creating borders shown in Figure 33.19.

For example, to create an etched border, use the following statement:

```
Border border = BorderFactory.createEtchedBorder();
```

Note

All the border classes and interfaces are grouped in the package `javax.swing.border` except `javax.swing.BorderFactory`.

Note

Borders and icons can be shared. Thus you can create a border or icon and use it to set the `border` or `icon` property for any GUI component. For example, the following statements set a border `b` for two panels `p1` and `p2`:

```
p1.setBorder(b);
p2.setBorder(b);
```

javax.swing.BorderFactory
+createBevelBorder(type: int): Border
+createBevelBorder(type: int, highlight: Color, shadow: Color): Border
+createBevelBorder(type: int, highlightOuter: Color, highlightInner: Color, shadowOuter: Color, shadowInner: Color): Border
+createCompoundBorder(): CompoundBorder
+createCompoundBorder(outsideBorder: Border, insideBorder: Border): CompoundBorder
+createEmptyBorder(): Border
+createEmptyBorder(top: int, left: int, bottom: int, right: int): Border
+createEtchedBorder(): Border
+createEtchedBorder(highlight: Color, shadow: Color): Border
+createEtchedBorder(type: int): Border
+createEtchedBorder(type: int, highlight: Color, shadow: Color): Border
+createLineBorder(color: Color): Border
+createLineBorder(color: Color, thickness: int): Border
+createLoweredBevelBorder(): Border
+createMatteBorder(top: int, left: int, bottom: int, right: int, color: Color): MatteBorder
+createMatteBorder(top: int, left: int, bottom: int, right: int, tileIcon: Icon): MatteBorder
+createRaisedBevelBorder(): Border
+createTitledBorder(border: Border): TitledBorder
+createTitledBorder(border: Border, title: String): TitledBorder
+createTitledBorder(border: Border, title: String, titleJustification: int, titlePosition: int): TitledBorder
+createTitledBorder(border: Border, title: String, titleJustification: int, titlePosition: int, titleFont: Font): TitledBorder
+createTitledBorder(border: Border, title: String, titleJustification: int, titlePosition: int, titleFont: Font, titleColor: Color): TitledBorder
+createTitledBorder(title: String): TitledBorder

FIGURE 33.19 BorderFactory contains the static methods for creating various types of borders.

Listing 33.9 gives an example that creates and displays various types of borders. You can select a border with or without a title. For a border without a title, you can choose a border style from Lowered Bevel, Raised Bevel, Etched, Line, Matte, or Empty. For a border with a title, you can specify the title position and justification. You can also embed another border into a titled border. Figure 33.20 displays a sample run of the program.

Here are the major steps in the program:

1. Create the user interface.

   a. Create a JLabel object and place it in the center of the frame.

   b. Create a panel named jpPositon to group the radio buttons for selecting the border title position. Set the border of this panel in the titled border with the title "Position".

   c. Create a panel named jpJustification to group the radio buttons for selecting the border title justification. Set the border of this panel in the titled border with the title "Justification".

   d. Create a panel named jpTitleOptions to hold the jpPosition panel and the jpJustification panel.

   e. Create a panel named jpTitle to hold a check box named "Titled" and the jpTitleOptions panel.

f. Create a panel named `jpBorderStyle` to group the radio buttons for selecting border styles.

g. Create a panel named `jpAllChoices` to hold the panels `jpTitle` and `jpBorderStyle`. Place `jpAllChoices` in the south of the frame.

2. Process the event.

   Create and register listeners to implement the `actionPerformed` handler to set the border for the label according to the events from the check box, and from all the radio buttons.

(a)   (b)

FIGURE 33.20 The program demonstrates various types of borders.

LISTING 33.9 BorderDemo.java

```java
 1 import java.awt.*;
 2 import java.awt.event.ActionListener;
 3 import java.awt.event.ActionEvent;
 4 import javax.swing.*;
 5 import javax.swing.border.*;
 6
 7 public class BorderDemo extends JApplet {
 8   // Declare a label for displaying message
 9   private JLabel jLabel1 = new JLabel("Display the border type",
10     JLabel.CENTER);
11
12   // A check box for selecting a border with or without a title
13   private JCheckBox jchkTitled;
14
15   // Radio buttons for border styles
16   private JRadioButton jrbLoweredBevel, jrbRaisedBevel,
17     jrbEtched, jrbLine, jrbMatte, jrbEmpty;
18
19   // Radio buttons for titled border options
20   private JRadioButton jrbAboveBottom, jrbBottom,
21     jrbBelowBottom, jrbAboveTop, jrbTop, jrbBelowTop,
22     jrbLeft, jrbCenter, jrbRight;
23
24   // TitledBorder for the label
25   private TitledBorder jLabel1Border;
26
27   /** Constructor */
28   public BorderDemo() {
29     // Create a JLabel instance and set colors
30     jLabel1.setBackground(Color.yellow);
```

create UI

```
31      jLabel1.setBorder(jLabel1Border);
32
33      // Place title position radio buttons
34      JPanel jpPosition = new JPanel();
35      jpPosition.setLayout(new GridLayout(3, 2));
36      jpPosition.add(
37        jrbAboveBottom = new JRadioButton("ABOVE_BOTTOM"));
38      jpPosition.add(jrbAboveTop = new JRadioButton("ABOVE_TOP"));
39      jpPosition.add(jrbBottom = new JRadioButton("BOTTOM"));
40      jpPosition.add(jrbTop = new JRadioButton("TOP"));
41      jpPosition.add(
42        jrbBelowBottom = new JRadioButton("BELOW_BOTTOM"));
43      jpPosition.add(jrbBelowTop = new JRadioButton("BELOW_TOP"));
44      jpPosition.setBorder(new TitledBorder("Position"));
45
46      // Place title justification radio buttons
47      JPanel jpJustification = new JPanel();
48      jpJustification.setLayout(new GridLayout(3,1));
49      jpJustification.add(jrbLeft = new JRadioButton("LEFT"));
50      jpJustification.add(jrbCenter = new JRadioButton("CENTER"));
51      jpJustification.add(jrbRight = new JRadioButton("RIGHT"));
52      jpJustification.setBorder(new TitledBorder("Justification"));
53
54      // Create panel jpTitleOptions to hold jpPosition and
55      // jpJustification
56      JPanel jpTitleOptions = new JPanel();
57      jpTitleOptions.setLayout(new BorderLayout());
58      jpTitleOptions.add(jpPosition, BorderLayout.CENTER);
59      jpTitleOptions.add(jpJustification, BorderLayout.EAST);
60
61      // Create Panel jpTitle to hold a check box and title position
62      // radio buttons, and title justification radio buttons
63      JPanel jpTitle = new JPanel();
64      jpTitle.setBorder(new TitledBorder("Border Title"));
65      jpTitle.setLayout(new BorderLayout());
66      jpTitle.add(jchkTitled = new JCheckBox("Titled"),
67        BorderLayout.NORTH);
68      jpTitle.add(jpTitleOptions, BorderLayout.CENTER);
69
70      // Group radio buttons for title position
71      ButtonGroup btgTitlePosition = new ButtonGroup();
72      btgTitlePosition.add(jrbAboveBottom);
73      btgTitlePosition.add(jrbBottom);
74      btgTitlePosition.add(jrbBelowBottom);
75      btgTitlePosition.add(jrbAboveTop);
76      btgTitlePosition.add(jrbTop);
77      btgTitlePosition.add(jrbBelowTop);
78
79      // Group radio buttons for title justification
80      ButtonGroup btgTitleJustification = new ButtonGroup();
81      btgTitleJustification.add(jrbLeft);
82      btgTitleJustification.add(jrbCenter);
83      btgTitleJustification.add(jrbRight);
84
85      // Create Panel jpBorderStyle to hold border style radio buttons
86      JPanel jpBorderStyle = new JPanel();
87      jpBorderStyle.setBorder(new TitledBorder("Border Style"));
88      jpBorderStyle.setLayout(new GridLayout(6, 1));
89      jpBorderStyle.add(jrbLoweredBevel =
90        new JRadioButton("Lowered Bevel"));
```

```
91       jpBorderStyle.add(jrbRaisedBevel =
92         new JRadioButton("Raised Bevel"));
93       jpBorderStyle.add(jrbEtched = new JRadioButton("Etched"));
94       jpBorderStyle.add(jrbLine = new JRadioButton("Line"));
95       jpBorderStyle.add(jrbMatte = new JRadioButton("Matte"));
96       jpBorderStyle.add(jrbEmpty = new JRadioButton("Empty"));
97
98       // Group radio buttons for border styles
99       ButtonGroup btgBorderStyle = new ButtonGroup();
100      btgBorderStyle.add(jrbLoweredBevel);
101      btgBorderStyle.add(jrbRaisedBevel);
102      btgBorderStyle.add(jrbEtched);
103      btgBorderStyle.add(jrbLine);
104      btgBorderStyle.add(jrbMatte);
105      btgBorderStyle.add(jrbEmpty);
106
107      // Create Panel jpAllChoices to place jpTitle and jpBorderStyle
108      JPanel jpAllChoices = new JPanel();
109      jpAllChoices.setLayout(new BorderLayout());
110      jpAllChoices.add(jpTitle, BorderLayout.CENTER);
111      jpAllChoices.add(jpBorderStyle, BorderLayout.EAST);
112
113      // Place panels in the frame
114      setLayout(new BorderLayout());
115      add(jLabel1, BorderLayout.CENTER);
116      add(jpAllChoices, BorderLayout.SOUTH);
117
118      // Register listeners
119      ActionListener listener = new EventListener();
120      jchkTitled.addActionListener(listener);
121      jrbAboveBottom.addActionListener(listener);
122      jrbBottom.addActionListener(listener);
123      jrbBelowBottom.addActionListener(listener);
124      jrbAboveTop.addActionListener(listener);
125      jrbTop.addActionListener(listener);
126      jrbBelowTop.addActionListener(listener);
127      jrbLeft.addActionListener(listener);
128      jrbCenter.addActionListener(listener);
129      jrbRight.addActionListener(listener);
130      jrbLoweredBevel.addActionListener(listener);
131      jrbRaisedBevel.addActionListener(listener);
132      jrbLine.addActionListener(listener);
133      jrbEtched.addActionListener(listener);
134      jrbMatte.addActionListener(listener);
135      jrbEmpty.addActionListener(listener);
136    }
137
138    private class EventListener implements ActionListener {
139      /** Handle ActionEvents on check box and radio buttons */
140      public void actionPerformed(ActionEvent e) {
141        // Get border style
142        Border border = new EmptyBorder(2, 2, 2, 2);
143
144        if (jrbLoweredBevel.isSelected()) {
145          border = new BevelBorder(BevelBorder.LOWERED);
146          jLabel1.setText("Lowered Bevel Style");
147        }
148        else if (jrbRaisedBevel.isSelected()) {
149          border = new BevelBorder(BevelBorder.RAISED);
150          jLabel1.setText("Raised Bevel Style");
```

empty border

bevel border

bevel border

```
151          }
152        else if (jrbEtched.isSelected()) {
153          border = new EtchedBorder();                              etched border
154          jLabel1.setText("Etched Style");
155        }
156        else if (jrbLine.isSelected()) {
157          border = new LineBorder(Color.black, 5);                  line border
158          jLabel1.setText("Line Style");
159        }
160        else if (jrbMatte.isSelected()) {
161          border = new MatteBorder(15, 15, 15, 15,                  matte border
162            new ImageIcon(getClass().getResource
163              ("image/caIcon.gif")));
164          jLabel1.setText("Matte Style");
165        }
166        else if (jrbEmpty.isSelected()) {
167          border = new EmptyBorder(2, 2, 2, 2);                     empty border
168          jLabel1.setText("Empty Style");
169        }
170
171        if (jchkTitled.isSelected()) {
172          // Get the title position and justification
173          int titlePosition = TitledBorder.DEFAULT_POSITION;
174          int titleJustification = TitledBorder.DEFAULT_JUSTIFICATION;
175
176          if (jrbAboveBottom.isSelected())
177            titlePosition = TitledBorder.ABOVE_BOTTOM;
178          else if (jrbBottom.isSelected())
179            titlePosition = TitledBorder.BOTTOM;
180          else if (jrbBelowBottom.isSelected())
181            titlePosition = TitledBorder.BELOW_BOTTOM;
182          else if (jrbAboveTop.isSelected())
183            titlePosition = TitledBorder.ABOVE_TOP;
184          else if (jrbTop.isSelected())
185            titlePosition = TitledBorder.TOP;
186          else if (jrbBelowTop.isSelected())
187            titlePosition = TitledBorder.BELOW_TOP;
188
189          if (jrbLeft.isSelected())
190            titleJustification = TitledBorder.LEFT;
191          else if (jrbCenter.isSelected())
192            titleJustification = TitledBorder.CENTER;
193          else if (jrbRight.isSelected())
194            titleJustification = TitledBorder.RIGHT;
195
196          jLabel1Border = new TitledBorder("A Title");
197          jLabel1Border.setBorder(border);                          border on border
198          jLabel1Border.setTitlePosition(titlePosition);
199          jLabel1Border.setTitleJustification(titleJustification);
200          jLabel1.setBorder(jLabel1Border);
201        }
202        else {
203          jLabel1.setBorder(border);
204        }
205      }
206    }
207 }                                                                  main method omitted
```

This example uses many panels to group UI components to achieve the desired look. Figure 33.20
illustrates the relationship of the panels. The Border Title panel groups all the options for setting

title properties. The position options are grouped in the Position panel. The justification options are grouped in the Justification panel. The Border Style panel groups the radio buttons for choosing Lowered Bevel, Raised Bevel, Etched, Line, Matte, and Empty borders.

The label displays the selected border with or without a title, depending on the selection of the title check box. The label also displays a text indicating which type of border is being used, depending on the selection of the radio button in the Border Style panel.

The `TitledBorder` can be mixed with other borders. To do so, simply create an instance of `TitledBorder`, and use the `setBorder` method to embed a new border in `TitledBorder`.

The `MatteBorder` can be used to display icons on the border, as shown in Figure 33.20(b).

CHAPTER SUMMARY

■ `javax.swing.JRootPane` is a lightweight container used behind the scenes by Swing's top-level containers, such as `JFrame`, `JApplet`, and `JDialog`. `javax.swing.JLayeredPane` is a container that manages the optional menu bar and the content pane. The content pane is an instance of `Container`. By default, it is a `JPanel` with `BorderLayout`. This is the container where the user interface components are added. To obtain the content pane in a `JFrame` or in a `JApplet`, use the `getContentPane()` method. You can set any instance of `Container` to be a new content pane using the `setContentPane` method.

■ Every container has a layout manager that is responsible for arranging its components. The container's `setLayout` method can be used to set a layout manager. Certain types of containers have default layout managers.

■ The layout manager places the components in accordance with its own rules and property settings, and with the constraints associated with each component. Every layout manager has its own specific set of rules. Some layout managers have properties that can affect the sizing and location of the components in the container.

■ Java also supports absolute layout, which enables you to place components at fixed locations. In this case, the component must be placed using the component's instance method `setBounds()` (defined in `java.awt.Component`). Absolute positions and sizes are fine if the application is developed and deployed on the same platform, but what looks fine on a development system may not look right on a deployment system on a different platform. To solve this problem, Java provides a set of layout managers that place components in containers in a way that is independent of fonts, screen resolutions, and operating systems.

■ In addition to the layout managers provided in Java, you can create custom layout managers by implementing the `LayoutManager` interface.

■ Java provides specialized containers `Box`, `JScrollPane`, `JTabbedPane`, and `JSplitPane` with fixed layout managers.

■ A Swing border is defined in the `Border` interface. Every instance of `JComponent` can set a border through the `border` property defined in `JComponent`. If a border is present, it replaces the inset. There are eight concrete border classes: `BevelBorder`, `SoftBevelBorder`, `CompoundBorder`, `EmptyBorder`, `EtchedBorder`,

`LineBorder`, `MatteBorder`, and `TitledBorder`. You can use the constructors of these classes or the static methods in `javax.swing.BorderFactory` to create borders.

Review Questions

Section 33.2 Swing Container Structures

33.1 Since `JButton` is a subclass of `Container`, can you add a button inside a button?

33.2 How do you set an image icon in a `JFrame`'s title bar? Can you set an image icon in a `JApplet`'s title bar?

33.3 Which of the following are the properties in `JFrame`, `JApplet`, and `JPanel`?

```
contentPane, iconImage, jMenuBar, resizable, title
```

Section 33.3 Layout Managers

33.4 How does the layout in Java differ from those in Visual Basic?

33.5 Discuss the factors that determine the size of the components in a container.

33.6 Discuss the properties `preferredSize`, `minimumSize`, and `maximumSize`.

33.7 Discuss the properties `alignmentX` and `alignmentY`.

33.8 What is a `CardLayout` manager? How do you create a `CardLayout` manager?

33.9 Can you use absolute positioning in Java? How do you use absolute positioning? Why should you avoid using it?

33.10 What is `BoxLayout`? How do you use `BoxLayout`? How do you use fillers to separate the components?

Sections 33.4–33.7

33.11 How do you create a custom layout manager?

33.12 What is `JScrollPane`? How do you use `JScrollPane`?

33.13 What is `JTabbedPane`? How do you use `JTabbedPane`?

33.14 What is `JSplitPane`? How do you use `JSplitPane`?

33.15 Can you specify a layout manager in `Box`, `JScrollPane`, `JTabbedPane`, and `JSplitPane`?

Section 33.8 Swing Borders

33.16 How do you create a titled border, a line border, a bevel border, and an etched border?

33.17 Can you set a border for every Swing GUI component? Can a border object be shared by different GUI components?

33.18 What package contains `Border`, `BevelBorder`, `CompoundBorder`, `EmptyBorder`, `EtchedBorder`, `LineBorder`, `MatteBorder`, `TitledBorder`, and `BorderFactory`?

Programming Exercises

Section 33.3 Layout Managers

33.1* (*Demonstrating FlowLayout properties*) Create a program that enables the user to set the properties of a `FlowLayout` manager dynamically, as shown in Figure 33.21. The `FlowLayout` manager is used to place 15 components in a panel. You can set the `alignment`, `hgap`, and `vgap` properties of the `FlowLayout` dynamically.

FIGURE 33.21   The program enables you to set the properties of a `FlowLayout` manager dynamically.

33.2* (*Demonstrating* `GridLayout` *properties*) Create a program that enables the user to set the properties of a `GridLayout` manager dynamically, as shown in Figure 33.22(a). The `GridLayout` manager is used to place 15 components in a panel. You can set the `rows`, `columns`, `hgap`, and `vgap` properties of the `GridLayout` dynamically.

FIGURE 33.22   (a) The program enables you to set the properties of a `GridLayout` manager dynamically. (b) The program enables you to set the properties of a `BorderLayout` manager dynamically.

33.3* (*Demonstrating* `BorderLayout` *properties*) Create a program that enables the user to set the properties of a `BorderLayout` manager dynamically, as shown in Figure 33.22(b). The `BorderLayout` manager is used to place five components in a panel. You can set the `hgap` and `vgap` properties of the `BorderLayout` dynamically.

33.4* (*Using* `CardLayout`) Write an applet that does arithmetic on integers and rationals. The program uses two panels in a `CardLayout` manager, one for integer arithmetic and the other for rational arithmetic. The program provides a combo box with two items Integer and Rational. When the user chooses the Integer item, the integer panel is activated. When the user chooses the Rational item, the rational panel is activated (see Figure 33.23).

FIGURE 33.23 `CardLayout` is used to select panels that perform integer operations and rational number operations.

33.5* (*Using absolute layout*) Use absolute layout to lay out a calculator, as shown in Figure 17.18(a).

Sections 33.4–33.8

33.6* (*Using tabbed panes*) Modify Listing 33.7, DisplayFigure.java, to add a panel of radio buttons for specifying the tab placement of the tabbed pane, as shown in Figure 33.24.

FIGURE 33.24 The radio buttons let you choose the tab placement of the tabbed pane.

33.7* (*Using tabbed pane*) Rewrite Exercise 33.4 using tabbed panes instead of `CardLayout` (see Figure 33.25).

FIGURE 33.25 A tabbed pane is used to select panels that perform integer operations and rational number operations.

33.8* (*Using `JSplitPane`*) Create a program that displays four figures in split panes, as shown in Figure 33.26. Use the `FigurePanel` class defined in Listing 14.5, FigurePanel.java.

FIGURE 33.26   Four figures are displayed in split panes.

33.9*   (*Demonstrating JSplitPane properties*) Create a program that enables the user to set the properties of a split pane dynamically, as shown in Figure 33.27.

FIGURE 33.27   The program enables you to set the properties of a split pane dynamically.

CHAPTER 34

MENUS, TOOLBARS, AND DIALOGS

Objectives

- To create menus using components `JMenuBar`, `JMenu`, `JMenuItem`, `JCheckBoxMenuItem`, and `JRadioButtonMenuItem` (§34.2).

- To create popup menus using components `JPopupMenu`, `JMenuItem`, `JCheckBoxMenuItem`, and `JRadioButtonMenuItem` (§34.3).

- To use `JToolBar` to create toolbars (§34.4).

- To use `Action` objects to generalize the code for processing actions (§34.5).

- To create standard dialogs using the `JOptionPane` class (§34.6).

- To extend the `JDialog` class to create custom dialogs (§34.7).

- To select colors using `JColorChooser` (§34.8).

- To use `JFileChooser` to display Open and Save File dialogs (§34.9).

34.1 Introduction

Java provides a comprehensive solution for building graphical user interfaces. This chapter introduces menus, popup menus, toolbars, and dialogs. You will also learn how to use `Action` objects to generalize the code for processing actions.

34.2 Menus

menu

Menus make selection easier and are widely used in window applications. Java provides five classes that implement menus: `JMenuBar`, `JMenu`, `JMenuItem`, `JCheckBoxMenuItem`, and `JRadioButtonMenuItem`.

menu item

`JMenuBar` is a top-level menu component used to hold the menus. A menu consists of *menu items* that the user can select (or toggle on or off). A menu item can be an instance of `JMenuItem`, `JCheckBoxMenuItem`, or `JRadioButtonMenuItem`. Menu items can be associated with icons, keyboard mnemonics, and keyboard accelerators. Menu items can be separated using separators.

34.2.1 Creating Menus

The sequence of implementing menus in Java is as follows:

1. Create a menu bar and associate it with a frame or an applet by using the `setJMenuBar` method. For example, the following code creates a frame and a menu bar, and sets the menu bar in the frame:

```
JFrame frame = new JFrame();
frame.setSize(300, 200);
frame.setVisible(true);
JMenuBar jmb = new JMenuBar();
frame.setJMenuBar(jmb); // Attach a menu bar to a frame
```

2. Create menus and associate them with the menu bar. You can use the following constructor to create a menu:

public JMenu(String label)

Here is an example of creating menus:

```
JMenu fileMenu = new JMenu("File");
JMenu helpMenu = new JMenu("Help");
```

This creates two menus labeled `File` and `Help`, as shown in Figure 34.1(a). The menus will not be seen until they are added to an instance of `JMenuBar`, as follows:

```
jmb.add(fileMenu);
jmb.add(helpMenu);
```

(a)

(b)

(c)

FIGURE 34.1 (a) The menu bar appears below the title bar on the frame. (b) Clicking a menu on the menu bar reveals the items under the menu. (c) Clicking a menu item reveals the submenu items under the menu item.

3. Create menu items and add them to the menus.

```
fileMenu.add(new JMenuItem("New"));
fileMenu.add(new JMenuItem("Open"));
fileMenu.addSeparator();
fileMenu.add(new JMenuItem("Print"));
fileMenu.addSeparator();
fileMenu.add(new JMenuItem("Exit"));
```

This code adds the menu items New, Open, a separator bar, Print, another separator bar, and Exit, in this order, to the File menu, as shown in Figure 34.1(b). The `addSeparator()` method adds a separator bar in the menu.

3.1 Creating submenu items. You can also embed menus inside menus so that the embedded menus become submenus. Here is an example:

```
JMenu softwareHelpSubMenu = new JMenu("Software");
JMenu hardwareHelpSubMenu = new JMenu("Hardware");
helpMenu.add(softwareHelpSubMenu);
helpMenu.add(hardwareHelpSubMenu);
softwareHelpSubMenu.add(new JMenuItem("Unix"));
softwareHelpSubMenu.add(new JMenuItem("NT"));
softwareHelpSubMenu.add(new JMenuItem("Win95"));
```

This code adds two submenus, `softwareHelpSubMenu` and `hardwareHelp-SubMenu`, in `helpMenu`. The menu items `Unix`, `NT`, and `Win95` are added to `softwareHelpSubMenu` (see Figure 34.1(c)).

3.2 Creating check-box menu items. You can also add a `JCheckBoxMenuItem` to a `JMenu`. `JCheckBoxMenuItem` is a subclass of `JMenuItem` that adds a Boolean state to the `JMenuItem`, and displays a check when its state is true. You can click a menu item to turn it on or off. For example, the following statement adds the check-box menu item `Check it` (see Figure 34.2(a)).

```
helpMenu.add(new JCheckBoxMenuItem("Check it"));
```

3.3 Creating radio-button menu items. You can also add radio buttons to a menu, using the `JRadioButtonMenuItem` class. This is often useful when you have a group of mutually exclusive choices in the menu. For example, the following statements add a submenu named Color and a set of radio buttons for choosing a color (see Figure 34.2(b)):

```
JMenu colorHelpSubMenu = new JMenu("Color");
helpMenu.add(colorHelpSubMenu);

JRadioButtonMenuItem jrbmiBlue, jrbmiYellow, jrbmiRed;
colorHelpSubMenu.add(jrbmiBlue =
  new JRadioButtonMenuItem("Blue"));
colorHelpSubMenu.add(jrbmiYellow =
  new JRadioButtonMenuItem("Yellow"));
colorHelpSubMenu.add(jrbmiRed =
  new JRadioButtonMenuItem("Red"));

ButtonGroup btg = new ButtonGroup();
btg.add(jrbmiBlue);
btg.add(jrbmiYellow);
btg.add(jrbmiRed);
```

4. The menu items generate `ActionEvent`. Your listener class must implement the `ActionListener` and the `actionPerformed` handler to respond to the menu selection.

(a)

(b)

(c)

FIGURE 34.2 (a) A check box menu item lets you check or uncheck a menu item just like a check box. (b) You can use `JRadioButtonMenuItem` to choose among mutually exclusive menu choices. (c) You can set image icons, keyboard mnemonics, and keyboard accelerators in menus.

34.2.2 Image Icons, Keyboard Mnemonics, and Keyboard Accelerators

The menu components `JMenu`, `JMenuItem`, `JCheckBoxMenuItem`, and `JRadioButton-MenuItem` have the `icon` and `mnemonic` properties. For example, using the following code, you can set icons for the New and Open menu items, and set keyboard mnemonics for File, Help, New, and Open:

```
JMenuItem jmiNew, jmiOpen;
fileMenu.add(jmiNew = new JMenuItem("New"));
fileMenu.add(jmiOpen = new JMenuItem("Open"));
jmiNew.setIcon(new ImageIcon("image/new.gif"));
jmiOpen.setIcon(new ImageIcon("image/open.gif"));
helpMenu.setMnemonic('H');
fileMenu.setMnemonic('F');
jmiNew.setMnemonic('N');
jmiOpen.setMnemonic('O');
```

The new icons and mnemonics are shown in Figure 34.2(c). You can also use `JMenuItem` constructors like the ones that follow to construct and set an icon or mnemonic in one statement.

```
public JMenuItem(String label, Icon icon);
public JMenuItem(String label, int mnemonic);
```

By default, the text is at the right of the icon. Use `setHorizontalTextPosition-(SwingConstants.LEFT)` to set the text to the left of the icon.

To select a menu, press the ALT key and the mnemonic key. For example, press ALT+F to select the File menu, and then press ALT+O to select the Open menu item. Keyboard mnemonics are useful, but they only let you select menu items from the currently open menu. Key accelerators, however, let you select a menu item directly by pressing the CTRL and accelerator keys. For example, by using the following code, you can attach the accelerator key CTRL+O to the Open menu item:

accelerator

```
jmiOpen.setAccelerator(KeyStroke.getKeyStroke
  (KeyEvent.VK_O, ActionEvent.CTRL_MASK));
```

The `setAccelerator` method takes a `KeyStroke` object. The static method `getKeyStroke` in the `KeyStroke` class creates an instance of the keystroke. `VK_O` is a constant representing the O key, and `CTRL_MASK` is a constant indicating that the `CTRL` key is associated with the keystroke.

Note
As shown in Figure 16.1, `AbstractButton` is the superclass for `JButton` and `JMenuItem`, and `JMenuItem` is a superclass for `JCheckBoxMenuItem`, `JMenu`, and `JRadioButtonMenuItem`. The menu components are very similar to buttons.

34.2.3 Example: Using Menus

This section gives an example that creates a user interface to perform arithmetic. The interface contains labels and text fields for Number 1, Number 2, and Result. The Result text field displays the result of the arithmetic operation between Number 1 and Number 2. Figure 34.3 contains a sample run of the program.

FIGURE 34.3 Arithmetic operations can be performed by clicking buttons or by choosing menu items from the Operation menu.

Here are the major steps in the program (Listing 34.1):

1. Create a menu bar and set it in the applet. Create the menus Operation and Exit, and add them to the menu bar. Add the menu items Add, Subtract, Multiply, and Divide under the Operation menu, and add the menu item Close under the Exit menu.

2. Create a panel to hold labels and text fields, and place the panel in the center of the applet.

3. Create a panel to hold the four buttons labeled Add, Subtract, Multiply, and Divide. Place the panel in the south of the applet.

4. Implement the `actionPerformed` handler to process the events from the menu items and the buttons.

LISTING 34.1 MenuDemo.java

```java
1  import java.awt.*;
2  import java.awt.event.*;
3  import javax.swing.*;
4
5  public class MenuDemo extends JApplet {
6    // Text fields for Number 1, Number 2, and Result
7    private JTextField jtfNum1, jtfNum2, jtfResult;
8
9    // Buttons "Add", "Subtract", "Multiply" and "Divide"
10   private JButton jbtAdd, jbtSub, jbtMul, jbtDiv;
11
12   // Menu items "Add", "Subtract", "Multiply","Divide" and "Close"
13   private JMenuItem jmiAdd, jmiSub, jmiMul, jmiDiv, jmiClose;
14
15   public MenuDemo() {
16     // Create menu bar
17     JMenuBar jmb = new JMenuBar();                        menu bar
18
```

<table>
<tr><td>set menu bar</td><td>

```
19       // Set menu bar to the applet
20       setJMenuBar(jmb);
21
22       // Add menu "Operation" to menu bar
23       JMenu operationMenu = new JMenu("Operation");
24       operationMenu.setMnemonic('O');
25       jmb.add(operationMenu);
26
```
</td></tr>
</table>

```
27       // Add menu "Exit" to menu bar
```
exit menus
```
28       JMenu exitMenu = new JMenu("Exit");
29       exitMenu.setMnemonic('E');
30       jmb.add(exitMenu);
31
32       // Add menu items with mnemonics to menu "Operation"
```
add menu items
```
33       operationMenu.add(jmiAdd= new JMenuItem("Add", 'A'));
34       operationMenu.add(jmiSub = new JMenuItem("Subtract", 'S'));
35       operationMenu.add(jmiMul = new JMenuItem("Multiply", 'M'));
36       operationMenu.add(jmiDiv = new JMenuItem("Divide", 'D'));
37       exitMenu.add(jmiClose = new JMenuItem("Close", 'C'));
38
39       // Set keyboard accelerators
```
accelerator
```
40       jmiAdd.setAccelerator(
41         KeyStroke.getKeyStroke(KeyEvent.VK_A, ActionEvent.CTRL_MASK));
42       jmiSub.setAccelerator(
43         KeyStroke.getKeyStroke(KeyEvent.VK_S, ActionEvent.CTRL_MASK));
44       jmiMul.setAccelerator(
45         KeyStroke.getKeyStroke(KeyEvent.VK_M, ActionEvent.CTRL_MASK));
46       jmiDiv.setAccelerator(
47         KeyStroke.getKeyStroke(KeyEvent.VK_D, ActionEvent.CTRL_MASK));
48
49       // Panel p1 to hold text fields and labels
50       JPanel p1 = new JPanel(new FlowLayout());
51       p1.add(new JLabel("Number 1"));
52       p1.add(jtfNum1 = new JTextField(3));
53       p1.add(new JLabel("Number 2"));
54       p1.add(jtfNum2 = new JTextField(3));
55       p1.add(new JLabel("Result"));
56       p1.add(jtfResult = new JTextField(4));
57       jtfResult.setEditable(false);
58
59       // Panel p2 to hold buttons
60       JPanel p2 = new JPanel(new FlowLayout());
```
buttons
```
61       p2.add(jbtAdd = new JButton("Add"));
62       p2.add(jbtSub = new JButton("Subtract"));
63       p2.add(jbtMul = new JButton("Multiply"));
64       p2.add(jbtDiv = new JButton("Divide"));
65
66       // Add panels to the frame
67       setLayout(new BorderLayout());
68       add(p1, BorderLayout.CENTER);
69       add(p2, BorderLayout.SOUTH);
70
71       // Register listeners
```
register listener
```
72       jbtAdd.addActionListener(new ActionListener() {
73         public void actionPerformed(ActionEvent e) {
74           calculate('+');
75         }
76       });
```
register listener
```
77       jbtSub.addActionListener(new ActionListener() {
```

```
78        public void actionPerformed(ActionEvent e) {
79          calculate('-');
80        }
81      });
82      jbtMul.addActionListener(new ActionListener() {                    register listener
83        public void actionPerformed(ActionEvent e) {
84          calculate('*');
85        }
86      });
87      jbtDiv.addActionListener(new ActionListener() {                    register listener
88        public void actionPerformed(ActionEvent e) {
89          calculate('/');
90        }
91      });
92      jmiAdd.addActionListener(new ActionListener() {                    register listener
93        public void actionPerformed(ActionEvent e) {
94          calculate('+');
95        }
96      });
97      jmiSub.addActionListener(new ActionListener() {                    register listener
98        public void actionPerformed(ActionEvent e) {
99          calculate('-');
100       }
101     });
102     jmiMul.addActionListener(new ActionListener() {                    register listener
103       public void actionPerformed(ActionEvent e) {
104         calculate('*');
105       }
106     });
107     jmiDiv.addActionListener(new ActionListener() {                    register listener
108       public void actionPerformed(ActionEvent e) {
109         calculate('/');
110       }
111     });
112     jmiClose.addActionListener(new ActionListener() {                  register listener
113       public void actionPerformed(ActionEvent e) {
114         System.exit(0);
115       }
116     });
117   }
118
119   /** Calculate and show the result in jtfResult */
120   private void calculate(char operator) {                             calculator
121     // Obtain Number 1 and Number 2
122     int num1 = (Integer.parseInt(jtfNum1.getText().trim()));
123     int num2 = (Integer.parseInt(jtfNum2.getText().trim()));
124     int result = 0;
125
126     // Perform selected operation
127     switch (operator) {
128       case '+': result = num1 + num2;
129                 break;
130       case '-': result = num1 - num2;
131                 break;
132       case '*': result = num1 * num2;
133                 break;
134       case '/': result = num1 / num2;
135     }
136
```

```
137        // Set result in jtfResult
138        jtfResult.setText(String.valueOf(result));
139    }
140 }
```

The program creates a menu bar, `jmb`, which holds two menus: `operationMenu` and `exitMenu` (lines 17–30). The `operationMenu` contains four menu items for doing arithmetic: Add, Subtract, Multiply, and Divide. The `exitMenu` contains the menu item Close for exiting the program. The menu items in the Operation menu are created with keyboard mnemonics and accelerators.

The user enters two numbers in the number fields. When an operation is chosen from the menu, its result, involving two numbers, is displayed in the Result field. The user can also click the buttons to perform the same operation.

The private method `calculate(char operator)` (lines 120–139) retrieves operands from the text fields in Number 1 and Number 2, applies the binary operator on the operands, and sets the result in the Result text field.

Note

placing menus

The menu bar is usually attached to the window using the `setJMenuBar` method. However, like any other component, it can be placed in a container. For instance, you can place a menu bar in the south of the container with `BorderLayout`.

34.3 Popup Menus

popup menu

A *popup menu*, also known as *a context menu*, is like a regular menu, but does not have a menu bar and can float anywhere on the screen. Creating a popup menu is similar to creating a regular menu. First, you create an instance of `JPopupMenu`, then you can add `JMenuItem`, `JCheckBoxMenuItem`, `JRadioButtonMenuItem`, and separators to the popup menu. For example, the following code creates a `JPopupMenu` and adds `JMenuItems` into it:

```
JPopupMenu jPopupMenu = new JPopupMenu();
jPopupMenu.add(new JMenuItem("New"));
jPopupMenu.add(new JMenuItem("Open"));
```

A regular menu is always attached to a menu bar using the `setJMenuBar` method, but a popup menu is associated with a parent component and is displayed using the `show` method in the `JPopupMenu` class. You specify the parent component and the location of the popup menu, using the coordinate system of the parent like this:

```
jPopupMenu.show(component, x, y);
```

popup trigger

The popup menu usually contains the commands for an object. Customarily, you display a popup menu by pointing to the object and clicking a certain mouse button, the so-called *popup trigger*. Popup triggers are system dependent. In Windows, the popup menu is displayed when the right mouse button is released. In Motif, the popup menu is displayed when the third mouse button is pressed and held down.

Listing 34.2 gives an example that creates a text area in a scroll pane. When the mouse points to the text area, it triggers the popup menu display, as shown in Figure 34.4.

Here are the major steps in the program (Listing 34.2):

1. Create a popup menu using `JPopupMenu`. Create menu items for New, Open, Print, and Exit using `JMenuItem`. For the menu items with both labels and icons, it is convenient to use the `JMenuItem(label, icon)` constructor.

2. Add the menu items into the popup menu.

Figure 34.4 A popup menu is displayed when the popup trigger is issued on the text area.

3. Create a scroll pane and add a text area into it. Place the scroll pane in the center of the applet.

4. Implement the `actionPerformed` handler to process the events from the menu items.

5. Implement the `mousePressed` and `mouseReleased` methods to process the events for handling popup triggers.

LISTING 34.2 PopupMenuDemo.java

```java
1  import javax.swing.*;
2  import java.awt.*;
3  import java.awt.event.*;
4
5  public class PopupMenuDemo extends JApplet {
6    private JPopupMenu jPopupMenu1 = new JPopupMenu();
7    private JMenuItem jmiNew = new JMenuItem("New",
8      new ImageIcon(getClass().getResource("image/new.gif")));
9    private JMenuItem jmiOpen = new JMenuItem("Open",
10     new ImageIcon(getClass().getResource("image/open.gif")));
11   private JMenuItem jmiPrint = new JMenuItem("Print",
12     new ImageIcon(getClass().getResource("image/print.gif")));
13   private JMenuItem jmiExit = new JMenuItem("Exit");
14   private JTextArea jTextArea1 = new JTextArea();
15
16   public PopupMenuDemo() {
17     jPopupMenu1.add(jmiNew);
18     jPopupMenu1.add(jmiOpen);
19     jPopupMenu1.addSeparator();
20     jPopupMenu1.add(jmiPrint);
21     jPopupMenu1.addSeparator();
22     jPopupMenu1.add(jmiExit);
23     jPopupMenu1.add(jmiExit);
24
25     add(new JScrollPane(jTextArea1), BorderLayout.CENTER);
26
27     jmiNew.addActionListener(new ActionListener() {
28       public void actionPerformed(ActionEvent e) {
29         System.out.println("Process New");
30       }
31     });
32     jmiOpen.addActionListener(new ActionListener() {
33       public void actionPerformed(ActionEvent e) {
34         System.out.println("Process Open");
35       }
36     });
37     jmiPrint.addActionListener(new ActionListener() {
38       public void actionPerformed(ActionEvent e) {
```

popup menu

add menu items

register listener

register listener

register listener

register listener

register listener

show popup menu

show popup menu

main method omitted

```
39              System.out.println("Process Print");
40          }
41      });
42      jmiExit.addActionListener(new ActionListener() {
43          public void actionPerformed(ActionEvent e) {
44              System.exit(0);
45          }
46      });
47      jTextArea1.addMouseListener(new MouseAdapter() {
48          public void mousePressed(MouseEvent e) { // For Motif
49              showPopup(e);
50          }
51
52          public void mouseReleased(MouseEvent e) { // For Windows
53              showPopup(e);
54          }
55      });
56  }
57
58  /** Display popup menu when triggered */
59  private void showPopup(java.awt.event.MouseEvent evt) {
60      if (evt.isPopupTrigger())
61          jPopupMenu1.show(evt.getComponent(), evt.getX(), evt.getY());
62  }
63 }
```

The process of creating popup menus is similar to the process for creating regular menus. To create a popup menu, create a JPopupMenu as the basis (line 6) and add JMenuItems to it (lines 17–23).

To show a popup menu, use the **show** method by specifying the parent component and the location for the popup menu (line 47). The **show** method is invoked when the popup menu is triggered by a particular mouse click on the text area. Popup triggers are system dependent. The listener implements the **mouseReleased** handler for displaying the popup menu in Windows (lines 52–54) and the **mousePressed** handler for displaying the popup menu in Motif (lines 48–50).

Tip

simplifying popup menu

JDK 1.5 provides a new setComponentPopupMenu(JPopupMenu) method in the JComponent class, which can be used to add a popup menu on a component. This method automatically handles mouse listener registration and popup display. Using this method, you may delete the showPopup method in lines 59–62 and replace the code in lines 47–55 with the following statement:

```
jTextArea1.setComponentPopupMenu(jPopupMenu1);
```

Owing to a bug, this method does not work with JPanel.

34.4 JToolBar

In user interfaces, a *toolbar* is often used to hold commands that also appear in the menus. Frequently used commands are placed in a toolbar for quick access. Clicking a command in the toolbar is faster than choosing it from the menu.

toolbar

Swing provides the JToolBar class as the container to hold toolbar components. JToolBar uses BoxLayout to manage components by default. You can set a different layout manager if desired. The components usually appear as icons. Since icons are not components, they cannot be placed into a toolbar directly. Instead you place buttons into the toolbar and set the icons on the buttons. An instance of JToolBar is like a regular container. Often it is placed in the north, west, or east of a container of BorderLayout.

The following properties in the JToolBar class are often useful:

- **orientation** specifies whether the items in the toolbar appear horizontally or vertically. The possible values are JToolBar.HORIZONTAL and JToolBar.VERTICAL. The default value is JToolBar.HORIZONTAL.

- **floatable** is a boolean value that specifies whether the toolbar can be floated. By default, a toolbar is floatable.

Listing 34.3 gives an example that creates a JToolBar to hold three buttons with the icons representing the commands New, Open, and Print, as shown in Figure 34.5.

FIGURE 34.5 The toolbar contains the icons representing the commands New, Open, and Print.

LISTING 34.3 ToolBarDemo.java

```java
1  import javax.swing.*;
2  import java.awt.*;
3
4  public class ToolBarDemo extends JApplet {
5    private JButton jbtNew = new JButton(
6      new ImageIcon(getClass().getResource("image/new.gif")));
7    private JButton jbtOpen = new JButton(
8      new ImageIcon(getClass().getResource("image/open.gif")));
9    private JButton jbPrint = new JButton(
10     new ImageIcon(getClass().getResource("image/print.gif")));
11
12   public ToolBarDemo() {
13     JToolBar jToolBar1 = new JToolBar("My Toolbar");
14     jToolBar1.setFloatable(true);
15     jToolBar1.add(jbtNew);
16     jToolBar1.add(jbtOpen);
17     jToolBar1.add(jbPrint);
18
19     jbtNew.setToolTipText("New");
20     jbtOpen.setToolTipText("Open");
21     jbPrint.setToolTipText("Print");
22
23     jbtNew.setBorderPainted(false);
24     jbtOpen.setBorderPainted(false);
25     jbPrint.setBorderPainted(false);
26
27     add(jToolBar1, BorderLayout.NORTH);
28   }
29 }
```

buttons

toolbar

add toolbar

main method omitted

A `JToolBar` is created in line 13. The toolbar is a container with `BoxLayout` by default. Using the `orientation` property, you can specify whether components in the toolbar are organized horizontally or vertically. By default, it is horizontal.

By default, the toolbar is floatable, and a floatable controller is displayed in front of its components. You can drag the floatable controller to move the toolbar to different locations of the window or can show the toolbar in a separate window, as shown in Figure 34.6.

FIGURE 34.6 The toolbar buttons are floatable.

You can also set a title for the floatable toolbar, as shown in Figure 34.7(a). To do so, create a toolbar using the `JToolBar(String title)` constructor. If you set `floatable` false, the floatable controller is not displayed, as shown in Figure 34.7(b). If you set a border (e.g., a line border), as shown in Figure 34.7(c), the line border is displayed and the floatable controller is not displayed.

    (a)   (b)   (c)

FIGURE 34.7 The toolbar buttons can be customized in many forms.

 Tip
For the floatable feature to work properly, do the following: (1) place a toolbar to one side of the container of `BorderLayout` and add no components to the other sides; (2) don't set border on a toolbar. Setting a border would make it non-floatable.

34.5 Processing Actions Using the `Action` Interface

Often menus and toolbars contain some common actions. For example, you can save a file by choosing *File*, *Save*, or by clicking the save button in the toolbar. Swing provides the `Action` interface, which can be used to create action objects for processing actions. Using `Action` objects, common action processing can be centralized and separated from the other application code.

The `Action` interface is a subinterface of `ActionListener`, as shown in Figure 34.8. Additionally, it defines several methods for checking whether the action is enabled, for enabling

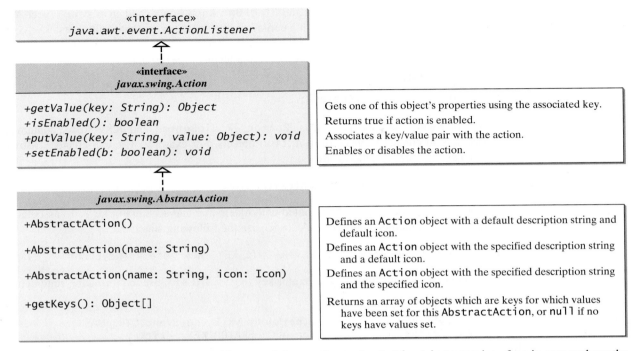

FIGURE 34.8   The `Action` interface provides a useful extension to the `ActionListener` interface in cases where the same functionality may be accessed by several controls. The `AbstractAction` class provides a default implementation for `Action`.

and disabling the action, and for retrieving and setting the associated action value using a key. The key can be any string, but four keys have predefined meanings:

Key	Description
Action.NAME	A name for the action
Action.SMALL_ICON	A small icon for the action
Action.SHORT_DESCRIPTION	A tool tip for the action
Action.LONG_DESCRIPTION	A description for online help

`AbstractAction` is a default implementation of the `Action` interface, as shown in Figure 34.8. It implements all the methods in the `Action` interface except the `actionPerformed` method. Additionally, it defines the `getKeys()` method.

Since `AbstractAction` is an abstract class, you cannot create an instance using its constructor. However, you can create a concrete subclass of `AbstractAction` and implement the `actionPerformed` method. This subclass can be conveniently defined as an anonymous inner class. For example, the following code creates an `Action` object for terminating a program.

```java
Action exitAction = new AbstractAction("Exit") {
  public void actionPerformed(ActionEvent e) {
    System.exit(0);
  }
};
```

Certain containers, such as `JMenu` and `JToolBar`, know how to ad[...]tion object. When an `Action` object is added to such a container, the container auto[...]y creates an appropriate component for the `Action` object and registers a listener with [...]ction object. Here is an example of adding an `Action` object to a menu and a toolbar:

```
jMenu.add(exitAction);
jToolBar.add(exitAction);
```

Several Swing components, such as `JButton`, `JRadioButton`, and `JCheckBox`, contain constructors to create instances from `Action` objects. For example, you can create a `JButton` from an `Action` object, as follows:

```
JButton jbt = new JButton(exitAction);
```

`Action` objects can also be associated with mnemonic and accelerator keys. To associate actions with a mnemonic key (e.g., ALT+E), use the following statement:

```
exitAction.putValue(Action.MNEMONIC_KEY, new Integer(KeyEvent.VK_E));
```

To associate actions with an accelerator key (e.g., CTRL+E), use the following statement:

```
KeyStroke exitKey =
  KeyStroke.getKeyStroke(KeyEvent.VK_E, KeyEvent.CTRL_MASK);
exitAction.putValue(Action.ACCELERATOR_KEY, exitKey);
```

Listing 34.4 gives an example that creates three menu items, Left, Center, and Right, three toolbar buttons, Left, Center, and Right, and three regular buttons, Left, Center, and Right, in a panel, as shown in Figure 34.9. The panel that holds the buttons uses the `FlowLayout`. The actions of the left, center, and right buttons set the alignment of the `FlowLayout` to left, right, and center, respectively. The actions of the menu items, the toolbar buttons, and the buttons in the panel can be processed through common action handlers using the `Action` interface.

FIGURE 34.9 Left, Center, and Right appear in the menu, in the toolbar, and in regular buttons.

LISTING 34.4 ActionInterfaceDemo.java

```
1 import java.awt.*;
2 import java.awt.event.*;
3 import javax.swing.*;
4
5 public class ActionInterfaceDemo extends JApplet {
6   private JPanel buttonPanel = new JPanel();
7   private FlowLayout flowLayout = new FlowLayout();
8
9   public ActionInterfaceDemo() {
10    // Create image icons
11    ImageIcon leftImageIcon = new ImageIcon(getClass().getResource(
```

image icon

```
12        "image/leftAlignment.png"));
13      ImageIcon centerImageIcon = new ImageIcon(getClass().getResource(
14        "image/centerAlignment.png"));
15      ImageIcon rightImageIcon = new ImageIcon(getClass().getResource(
16        "image/rightAlignment.png"));
17
18      // Create actions
19      Action leftAction = new MyAction("Left", leftImageIcon,                 create action
20        "Left alignment for the buttons in the panel",
21        new Integer(KeyEvent.VK_L),
22        KeyStroke.getKeyStroke(KeyEvent.VK_L, ActionEvent.CTRL_MASK));
23      Action centerAction = new MyAction("Center", centerImageIcon,
24        "Center alignment for the buttons in the panel",
25        new Integer(KeyEvent.VK_C),
26        KeyStroke.getKeyStroke(KeyEvent.VK_C, ActionEvent.CTRL_MASK));
27      Action rightAction = new MyAction("Right", rightImageIcon,
28        "Right alignment for the buttons in the panel",
29        new Integer(KeyEvent.VK_R),
30        KeyStroke.getKeyStroke(KeyEvent.VK_R, ActionEvent.CTRL_MASK));
31
32      // Create menus
33      JMenuBar jMenuBar1 = new JMenuBar();                                   menu
34      JMenu jmenuAlignment = new JMenu("Alignment");
35      setJMenuBar(jMenuBar1);
36      jMenuBar1.add(jmenuAlignment);
37
38      // Add actions to the menu
39      jmenuAlignment.add(leftAction);
40      jmenuAlignment.add(centerAction);
41      jmenuAlignment.add(rightAction);
42
43      // Add actions to the toolbar
44      JToolBar jToolBar1 = new JToolBar(JToolBar.VERTICAL);                  toolbar
45      jToolBar1.setBorder(BorderFactory.createLineBorder(Color.red));
46      jToolBar1.add(leftAction);
47      jToolBar1.add(centerAction);
48      jToolBar1.add(rightAction);
49
50      // Add buttons to the button panel
51      buttonPanel.setLayout(flowLayout);
52      JButton jbtLeft = new JButton(leftAction);                            button
53      JButton jbtCenter = new JButton(centerAction);
54      JButton jbtRight = new JButton(rightAction);
55      buttonPanel.add(jbtLeft);
56      buttonPanel.add(jbtCenter);
57      buttonPanel.add(jbtRight);
58
59      // Add toolbar to the east and panel to the center
60      add(jToolBar1, BorderLayout.EAST);
61      add(buttonPanel, BorderLayout.CENTER);
62    }
63
64    private class MyAction extends AbstractAction {                         custom action
65      String name;
66
67      MyAction(String name, Icon icon) {                                    constructor
68        super(name, icon);
69        this.name = name;
70      }
71
```

constructor

```
72    MyAction(String name, Icon icon, String desc, Integer mnemonic,
73        KeyStroke accelerator) {
74      super(name, icon);
75      putValue(Action.SHORT_DESCRIPTION, desc);
76      putValue(Action.MNEMONIC_KEY, mnemonic);
77      putValue(Action.ACCELERATOR_KEY, accelerator);
78      this.name = name;
79    }
80
```

handler

```
81    public void actionPerformed(ActionEvent e) {
82      if (name.equals("Left"))
83        flowLayout.setAlignment(FlowLayout.LEFT);
84      else if (name.equals("Center"))
85        flowLayout.setAlignment(FlowLayout.CENTER);
86      else if (name.equals("Right"))
87        flowLayout.setAlignment(FlowLayout.RIGHT);
88
89      buttonPanel.revalidate();
90    }
91  }
```

main method omitted

```
92 }
```

The inner class `MyAction` extends `AbstractAction` with a constructor to construct an action with a name and an icon (lines 67–70) and another constructor to construct an action with a name, icon, description, mnemonic, and accelerator (lines 72–79). The constructors invoke the `putValue` method to associate the name, icon, decription, mnemonic, and accelerator. It implements the `actionPerformed` method to set a new alignment in the panel of the `FlowLayout` (line 81–90). The `revalidate()` method validates the new alignment (line 89).

Three actions, `leftAction`, `centerAction`, and `rightAction`, were created from the `MyAction` class (lines 19–30). Each action has a name, icon, decription, mnemonic, and accelerator. The actions are for the menu items and the buttons in the toolbar and in the panel. The menu and toolbar know how to add these objects automatically (lines 39–41, 46–48). Three regular buttons are created with the properties taken from the actions (lines 51–54).

34.6 JOptionPane Dialogs

You have used `JOptionPane` to create input and output dialog boxes. This section provides a comprehensive introduction to `JOptionPane` and other dialog boxes. A *dialog box* is normally used as a temporary window to receive additional information from the user or to provide notification that some event has occurred. Java provides the `JOptionPane` class, which can be used to create standard dialogs. You can also build custom dialogs by extending the `JDialog` class.

The `JOptionPane` class can be used to create four kinds of standard dialogs:

- **Message dialog** shows a message and waits for the user to click OK.

- **Confirmation dialog** shows a question and asks for confirmation, such as OK or Cancel.

- **Input dialog** shows a question and gets the user's input from a text field, combo box, or list.

- **Option dialog** shows a question and gets the user's answer from a set of options.

These dialogs are created using the static methods *showXxxDialog* and generally appear as shown in Figure 34.10(a).

FIGURE 34.10   (a) A JOptionPane dialog can display an icon, a message, an input, and option buttons. (b) The message dialog displays a message and waits for the user to click OK.

For example, you can use the following method to create a message dialog box, as shown in Figure 34.10(b):

```
JOptionPane.showMessageDialog(null, "SSN not found",
   "For Your Information", JOptionPane.INFORMATION_MESSAGE);
```

34.6.1 Message Dialogs

A *message dialog* box displays a message that alerts the user and waits for the user to click the *OK* button to close the dialog. The methods for creating message dialogs are:

```
public static void showMessageDialog(Component parentComponent,
                                   Object message)
public static void showMessageDialog(Component parentComponent,
                                   Object message,
                                   String title,
                                   int messageType)
public static void showMessageDialog(Component parentComponent,
                                   Object message,
                                   String title,
                                   int messageType,
                                   Icon icon)
```

The **parentComponent** can be any component or **null**. The **message** is an object, but often a string is used. These two parameters must always be specified. The **title** is a string displayed in the title bar of the dialog with the default value "Message".

The **messageType** is one of the following constants:

```
JOptionPane.ERROR_MESSAGE
JOptionPane.INFORMATION_MESSAGE
JOptionPane.PLAIN_MESSAGE
JOptionPane.WARNING_MESSAGE
JOptionPane.QUESTION_MESSAGE
```

By default, **messageType** is **JOptionPane.INFORMATION_MESSAGE**. Each type has an associated icon except the **PLAIN_MESSAGE** type, as shown in Figure 34.11. You can also supply your own icon in the **icon** parameter.

The **message** parameter is an object. If it is a GUI component, the component is displayed. If it is a non-GUI component, the string representation of the object is displayed. For example, the following statement displays a clock in a message dialog, as shown in Figure 34.12.

```
JOptionPane.showMessageDialog(null, new StillClock(),
   "Current Time", JOptionPane.PLAIN_MESSAGE);
```

FIGURE 34.11   There are five types of message dialog boxes.

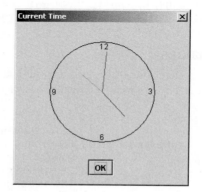

FIGURE 34.12   A clock is displayed in a message dialog.

34.6.2   Confirmation Dialogs

A message dialog box displays a message and waits for the user to click the *OK* button to dismiss the dialog. The message dialog does not return any value. A *confirmation dialog* asks a question and requires the user to respond with an appropriate button. The confirmation dialog returns a value that corresponds to a selected button.

The methods for creating confirmation dialogs are:

```
public static int showConfirmDialog(Component parentComponent,
                                    Object message)
public static int showConfirmDialog(Component parentComponent,
                                    Object message,
                                    String title,
                                    int optionType)
public static int showConfirmDialog(Component parentComponent,
                                    Object message,
                                    String title,
                                    int optionType,
                                    int messageType)
public static int showConfirmDialog(Component parentComponent,
                                    Object message,
                                    String title,
                                    int optionType,
                                    int messageType,
                                    Icon icon)
```

The parameters **parentComponent**, **message**, **title**, **icon**, and **messageType** are the same as in the **showMessageDialog** method. The default value for **title** is "Select an Option" and for **messageType** is QUESTION_MESSAGE. The **optionType** determines which buttons are displayed in the dialog. The possible values are:

```
JOptionPane.YES_NO_OPTION
JOptionPane.YES_NO_CANCEL_OPTION
JOptionPane.OK_CANCEL_OPTION
```

Figure 34.13 shows the confirmation dialogs with these options.

FIGURE 34.13   The confirmation dialog displays a question and three types of option buttons, and requires responses from the user.

The **showConfirmDialog** method returns one of the following **int** values corresponding to the selected option:

```
JOptionPane.YES_OPTION
JOptionPane.NO_OPTION
JOptionPane.CANCEL_OPTION
JOptionPane.OK_OPTION
JOptionPane.CLOSED_OPTION
```

These options correspond to the button that was activated, except for the CLOSED_OPTION, which implies that the dialog box is closed without buttons activated.

34.6.3   Input Dialogs

An *input dialog* box is used to receive input from the user. The input can be entered from a text field or selected from a combo box or a list. Selectable values can be specified in an array, and one of them can be designated as the initial selected value. If no selectable value is specified when an input dialog is created, a text field is used for entering input. If fewer than twenty selection values are specified, a combo box is displayed in the input dialog. If twenty or more selection values are specified, a list is used in the input dialog.

The methods for creating input dialogs are shown below:

```
public static String showInputDialog(Object message)
public static String showInputDialog(Component parentComponent,
                                     Object message)
public static String showInputDialog(Component parentComponent,
                                     Object message,
                                     String title,
                                     int messageType)
public static Object showInputDialog(Component parentComponent,
                                     Object message,
                                     int messageType,
                                     Icon icon,
                                     Object[] selectionValues,
                                     Object initialSelectionValue)
```

The first three methods listed above use a text field for input, as shown in Figure 34.14(a) . The last method listed above specifies an array of `Object` type as selection values in addition to an object specified as an initial selection. The first three methods return a `String` that is entered from the text field in the input dialog. The last method returns an `Object` selected from a combo box or a list. The input dialog displays a combo box if there are fewer than twenty selection values, as shown in Figure 34.14(b); it displays a list if there are twenty or more selection values, as shown in Figure 34.14(c).

(a) Text field   (b) Combo box   (c) List

FIGURE 34.14   (a) When creating an input dialog without specifying selection values, the input dialog displays a text field for data entry. (b) When creating an input dialog with selection values, the input dialog displays a combo box if there are fewer than twenty selection values. (c) When creating an input dialog with selection values, the input dialog displays a list if there are twenty or more selection values.

Note

The `showInputDialog` method does not have the `optionType` parameter. The buttons for input dialog are not configurable. The *OK* and *Cancel* buttons are always used.

34.6.4 Option Dialogs

An *option dialog* allows you to create custom buttons. You can create an option dialog using the following method:

```
public static int showOptionDialog(Component parentComponent,
                                    Object message,
                                    String title,
                                    int optionType,
                                    int messageType,
                                    Icon icon,
                                    Object[] options,
                                    Object initialValue)
```

The buttons are specified using the `options` parameter. The `initialValue` parameter allows you to specify a button to receive initial focus. The `showOptionDialog` method returns an `int` value indicating the button that was activated. For example, here is the code that creates an option dialog, as shown in Figure 34.15:

```
int value =
  JOptionPane.showOptionDialog(null, "Select a button",
    "Option Dialog", JOptionPane.DEFAULT_OPTION,
    JOptionPane.PLAIN_MESSAGE, null,
    new Object[]{"Button 0", "Button 1", "Button 2"}, "Button 1");
```

FIGURE 34.15 The option dialog displays the custom buttons.

34.6.5 Example: Creating JOptionPane Dialogs

This section gives an example that demonstrates the use of JOptionPane dialogs. The program prompts the user to select the annual interest rate from a list in an input dialog, the number of years from a combo box in an input dialog, and the loan amount from an input dialog, and it displays the loan payment schedule in a text area inside a JScrollPane in a message dialog, as shown in Figure 34.16.

FIGURE 34.16 The input dialogs can contain a list or a combo box for selecting input, and the message dialogs can contain GUI objects like JScrollPane.

Here are the major steps in the program (Listing 34.5):

1. Display an input dialog box to let the user select an annual interest rate from a list.

2. Display an input dialog box to let the user select the number of years from a combo box.

3. Display an input dialog box to let the user enter the loan amount.

4. Compute the monthly payment, total payment, and loan payment schedule, and display the result in a text area in a message dialog box.

LISTING 34.5 JOptionPaneDemo.java

```
 1 import javax.swing.*;
 2
 3 public class JOptionPaneDemo {
 4   public static void main(String args[]) {
 5     // Create an array for annual interest rates
 6     Object[] rateList = new Object[25];
 7     int i = 0;
 8     for (double rate = 5; rate <= 8; rate += 1.0 / 8)
 9       rateList[i++] = new Double(rate);
10
11     // Prompt the user to select an annual interest rate
12     Object annualInterstRateObject = JOptionPane.showInputDialog(
13       null, "Select annual interest rate:", "JOptionPaneDemo",
14       JOptionPane.QUESTION_MESSAGE, null, rateList, null);
15     double annualInterestRate =
16       ((Double)annualInterstRateObject).doubleValue();
17
18     // Create an array for number of years
19     Object[] yearList = {new Integer(7), new Integer(15),
20       new Integer(30)};
21
22     // Prompt the user to enter number of years
23     Object numberOfYearsObject = JOptionPane.showInputDialog(null,
24       "Select number of years:", "JOptionPaneDemo",
25       JOptionPane.QUESTION_MESSAGE, null, yearList, null);
26     int numberOfYears = ((Integer)numberOfYearsObject).intValue();
27
28     // Prompt the user to enter loan amount
29     String loanAmountString = JOptionPane.showInputDialog(null,
30       "Enter loan amount,\nfor example, 150000 for $150000",
31       "JOptionPaneDemo", JOptionPane.QUESTION_MESSAGE);
32     double loanAmount = Double.parseDouble(loanAmountString);
33
34     // Obtain monthly payment and total payment
35     Loan loan = new Loan(
36       annualInterestRate, numberOfYears, loanAmount);
37     double monthlyPayment = loan.getMonthlyPayment();
38     double totalPayment = loan.getTotalPayment();
39
40     // Prepare output string
41     String output = "Interest Rate: " + annualInterestRate + "%" +
42       " Number of Years: " + numberOfYears + " Loan Amount: $"
43       + loanAmount;
44     output += "\nMonthly Payment: " + "$" +
45       (int)(monthlyPayment * 100) / 100.0;
46     output += "\nTotal Payment: $" +
47       (int)(monthlyPayment * 12 * numberOfYears * 100) / 100.0 + "\n";
48
49     // Obtain monthly interest rate
50     double monthlyInterestRate = annualInterestRate / 1200;
51
```

input dialog

input dialog

input dialog

```
52        double balance = loanAmount;
53        double interest;
54        double principal;
55
56        // Display the header
57        output += "\nPayment#\tInterest\tPrincipal\tBalance\n";
58
59        for (i = 1; i <= numberOfYears * 12; i++) {
60          interest = (int)(monthlyInterestRate * balance * 100) / 100.0;
61          principal = (int)((monthlyPayment - interest) * 100) / 100.0;
62          balance = (int)((balance - principal) * 100) / 100.0;
63          output += i + "\t" + interest + "\t" + principal + "\t" +
64            balance + "\n";
65        }
66
67        // Display monthly payment and total payment
68        JScrollPane jsp = new JScrollPane(new JTextArea(output));
69        jsp.setPreferredSize(new java.awt.Dimension(400, 200));
70        JOptionPane.showMessageDialog(null, jsp,                          message dialog
71          "JOptionPaneDemo", JOptionPane.INFORMATION_MESSAGE, null);
72      }
73 }
```

The `JOptionPane` dialog boxes are *modal*, which means that no other window can be accessed until a dialog box is dismissed.

You have used the input dialog box to enter input from a text field. This example shows that input dialog boxes can also contain a list (lines 12–14) or a combo box (lines 23–25) to list input options. The elements of the list are objects. The return value from these input dialog boxes is of the `Object` type. To obtain a `double` value or an `int` value, you have to cast the return object into `Double` or `Integer`, then use the `doubleValue` or `intValue` method to get the `double` or `int` value (lines 15–16 and 26).

You have already used the message dialog box to display a string. This example shows that the message dialog box can also contain GUI objects. The output string is contained in a text area, the text area is inside a scroll pane, and the scroll pane is placed in the message dialog box (lines 68–71).

34.7 Creating Custom Dialogs

Standard `JOptionPane` dialogs are sufficient in most cases. Occasionally, you need to create custom dialogs. In Swing, the `JDialog` class can be extended to create custom dialogs.

As with `JFrame`, components are added to the `contentPane` of `JDialog`. Creating a custom dialog usually involves laying out user interface components in the dialog, adding buttons for dismissing the dialog, and installing listeners that respond to button actions.

The standard dialog is *modal*, which means that no other window can be accessed before the dialog is dismissed. However, the custom dialogs derived from `JDialog` are not modal by default. To make a dialog modal, set its `modal` property to `true`. To display an instance of `JDialog`, set its `visible` property to `true`.

Let us create a custom dialog box for choosing colors, as shown in Figure 34.17(a). Use this dialog to choose the color for the foreground of the button, as shown in Figure 34.17(b). When the user clicks the *Change Button Text Color* button, the Choose Color dialog box is displayed.

Create a custom dialog component named `ColorDialog` by extending `JDialog`. Use three sliders to specify red, green, and blue components of a color. The program is given in Listing 34.6.

FIGURE 34.17   The custom dialog allows you to choose a color for the label's foreground.

LISTING 34.6   ColorDialog.java

```
 1  import java.awt.*;
 2  import java.awt.event.*;
 3  import javax.swing.*;
 4  import javax.swing.event.*;
 5
 6  public class ColorDialog extends JDialog {
 7    // Declare color component values and selected color
 8    private int redValue, greenValue, blueValue;
 9    private Color color = null;
10
11    // Create sliders
12    private JSlider jslRed = new JSlider(0, 128);
13    private JSlider jslGreen = new JSlider(0, 128);
14    private JSlider jslBlue = new JSlider(0, 128);
15
16    // Create two buttons
17    private JButton jbtOK = new JButton("OK");
18    private JButton jbtCancel = new JButton("Cancel");
19
20    // Create a panel to display the selected color
21    private JPanel jpSelectedColor = new JPanel();
22
23    public ColorDialog() {
24      this(null, true);
25    }
26
27    public ColorDialog(java.awt.Frame parent, boolean modal) {
28      super(parent, modal);
29      setTitle("Choose Color");
30
31      // Group two buttons OK and Cancel
32      JPanel jpButtons = new JPanel();
33      jpButtons.add(jbtOK);
34      jpButtons.add(jbtCancel);
35
36      // Group labels
37      JPanel jpLabels = new JPanel();
38      jpLabels.setLayout(new GridLayout(3, 0));
39      jpLabels.add(new JLabel("Red"));
40      jpLabels.add(new JLabel("Green"));
41      jpLabels.add(new JLabel("Blue"));
42
43      // Group sliders for selecting red, green, and blue colors
44      JPanel jpSliders = new JPanel();
45      jpSliders.setLayout(new GridLayout(3, 0));
46      jpSliders.add(jslRed);
```

color value

sliders

buttons

constructor

constructor

create UI

```
47        jpSliders.add(jslGreen);
48        jpSliders.add(jslBlue);
49
50        // Group jpLabels and jpSliders
51        JPanel jpSelectColor = new JPanel();
52        jpSelectColor.setLayout(new BorderLayout());
53        jpSelectColor.setBorder(
54          BorderFactory.createTitledBorder("Select Color"));
55        jpSelectColor.add(jpLabels, BorderLayout.WEST);
56        jpSelectColor.add(jpSliders, BorderLayout.CENTER);
57
58        // Group jpSelectColor and jpSelectedColor
59        JPanel jpColor = new JPanel();
60        jpColor.setLayout(new BorderLayout());
61        jpColor.add(jpSelectColor, BorderLayout.SOUTH);
62        jpColor.add(jpSelectedColor, BorderLayout.CENTER);
63
64        // Place jpButtons and jpColor into the dialog box
65        add(jpButtons, BorderLayout.SOUTH);
66        add(jpColor, BorderLayout.CENTER);
67        pack();
68
69        jbtOK.addActionListener(new ActionListener() {              listeners
70          public void actionPerformed(ActionEvent e) {
71            setVisible(false);
72          }
73        });
74
75        jbtCancel.addActionListener(new ActionListener() {
76          public void actionPerformed(ActionEvent e) {
77            color = null;
78            setVisible(false);
79          }
80        });
81
82        jslRed.addChangeListener(new ChangeListener() {
83          public void stateChanged(ChangeEvent e) {
84            redValue = jslRed.getValue();
85            color = new Color(redValue, greenValue, blueValue);
86            jpSelectedColor.setBackground(color);
87          }
88        });
89
90        jslGreen.addChangeListener(new ChangeListener() {
91          public void stateChanged(ChangeEvent e) {
92            greenValue = jslGreen.getValue();
93            color = new Color(redValue, greenValue, blueValue);
94            jpSelectedColor.setBackground(color);
95          }
96        });
97
98        jslBlue.addChangeListener(new ChangeListener() {
99          public void stateChanged(ChangeEvent e) {
100            blueValue = jslBlue.getValue();
101            color = new Color(redValue, greenValue, blueValue);
102            jpSelectedColor.setBackground(color);
103          }
104        });
105      }
106
```

```
107    public Dimension getPreferredSize() {
108      return new java.awt.Dimension(200, 200);
109    }
110
111    /** Return color */
112    public Color getColor() {
113      return color;
114    }
115 }
```

Create a test class to use the color dialog to select the color for the foreground color of the button in Listing 34.7.

LISTING 34.7 TestColorDialog.java

```
1 import javax.swing.*;
2 import java.awt.*;
3 import java.awt.event.*;
4
5 public class TestColorDialog extends JApplet {
6   private ColorDialog colorDialog1 = new ColorDialog();
7   private JButton jbtChangeColor = new JButton("Choose color");
8
9   public TestColorDialog() {
10     setLayout(new java.awt.FlowLayout());
11     jbtChangeColor.setText("Change Button Text Color");
12     jbtChangeColor.addActionListener(new ActionListener() {
13       public void actionPerformed(ActionEvent e) {
14         colorDialog1.setVisible(true);
15
16         if (colorDialog1.getColor() != null)
17           jbtChangeColor.setForeground(colorDialog1.getColor());
18       }
19     });
20     add(jbtChangeColor);
21   }
22 }
```

listener (margin note at line 12)

main method omitted (margin note at line 22)

The custom dialog box allows the user to use the sliders to select colors. The selected color is stored in the **color** variable. When the user clicks the *Cancel* button, color becomes **null**, which implies that no selection has been made.

The dialog box is displayed when the user clicks the *Change Button Text Color* button and is closed when the *OK* button or the *Cancel* button is clicked.

Tip
Not setting the dialog modal when needed is a common mistake. In this example, the dialog is set modal in line 24 in ColorDialog.java (Listing 34.6). If the dialog is not modal, all the statements in the *Change Button Text Color* button handler are executed before the color is selected from the dialog box.

34.8 JColorChooser

You created a color dialog in the preceding example as a subclass of **JDialog**, which is a subclass of **java.awt.Dialog** (a top-level heavy-weight component). Therefore, it cannot be added to a container as a component. Color dialogs are commonly used in GUI programming. Swing provides a convenient and versatile color dialog named **javax.swing.JColorChooser**. **JColorChooser** is a lightweight component inherited from **JComponent**. It can be added to any container. For example, the following code places a **JColorChooser** in an applet, as shown in Figure 34.18.

FIGURE 34.18 An instance of JColorChooser is displayed in an applet.

```
public class JColorChooserDemo extends javax.swing.JApplet {
  public JColorChooserDemo() {
    this.add(new javax.swing.JColorChooser());
  }
}
```

create **JColorChooser**

Often an instance of JColorChooser is displayed in a dialog box using JColorChooser's static showDialog method:

```
public static Color showDialog(Component parentComponent,
                               String title,
                               Color initialColor)
```

For example, the following code creates a JColorChooser in an applet, as shown in Figure 34.19.

```
import javax.swing.*;
import java.awt.Color;

public class JColorChooserDemo extends javax.swing.JApplet {
  public void init() {
    Color color = JColorChooser.showDialog(this, "Choose a color",
      Color.YELLOW);
  }
}
```

JColorChooser

The showDialog method creates an instance of JDialog with three buttons, *OK*, *Cancel*, and *Reset*, to hold a JColorChooser object, as shown in Figure 34.19(a). The method displays a

(a)   (b)

FIGURE 34.19 An instance of JColorChooser is displayed in a dialog box with the *OK*, *Cancel*, and *Reset* buttons.

modal dialog. If the user clicks the *OK* button, the method dismisses the dialog and returns the selected color. If the user clicks the *Cancel* button or closes the dialog, the method dismisses the dialog and returns `null`.

JColorChooser consists of a tabbed pane and a color preview panel. The tabbed pane has three tabs for choosing colors using Swatches, HSB, and RGB, as shown in Figure 34.19(b). The preview panel shows the effect of the selected color.

Note

JColorChooser is very flexible. It allows you to replace the tabbed pane or the color preview panel with custom components. The default tabbed pane and the color preview panel are sufficient. You rarely need to use custom components.

34.9 JFileChooser

The `javax.swing.JFileChooser` class displays a dialog box from which the user can navigate through the file system and select files for loading or saving, as shown in Figure 34.20.

FIGURE 34.20 The Swing JFileChooser shows files and directories, and enables the user to navigate through the file system visually.

Like JColorChooser, JFileChooser is a lightweight component inherited from JComponent. It can be added to any container if desired, but often you create an instance of JFileChooser and display it standalone.

JFileChooser is a subclass of JComponent. There are several ways to construct a file dialog box. The simplest is to use JFileChooser's no-arg constructor.

The file dialog box can appear in two types: open and save. The *open type* is for opening a file, and the *save type* is for storing a file. To create an open file dialog, use the following method:

```
public int showOpenDialog(Component parent)
```

This method creates a dialog box that contains an instance of JFileChooser for opening a file. The method returns an `int` value, either APPROVE_OPTION or CANCEL_OPTION, which indicates whether the *Open* button or the *Cancel* button was clicked.

Similarly, you can use the following method to create a dialog for saving files:

```
public int showSaveDialog(Component parent)
```

The file dialog box created with showOpenDialog or showSaveDialog is modal. The JFileChooser class has the properties inherited from JComponent. It also has the following useful properties:

- **dialogType** specifies the type of this dialog. Use OPEN_DIALOG when you want to bring up a file chooser that the user can use to open a file. Likewise, use SAVE_DIALOG to let the user choose a file for saving.

- **dialogTitle** is the string that is displayed in the title bar of the dialog box.

- **currentDirectory** is the current directory of the file. The type of this property is java.io.File. If you want the current directory to be used, use setCurrent-Directory(new File(".")).

- **selectedFile** is the file you have selected. You can use getSelectedFile() to return the selected file from the dialog box. The type of this property is java.io.File. If you have a default file name that you expect to use, use setSelected-File(new File(filename)).

- **selectedFiles** is a list of the files selected if the file chooser is set to allow multiselection. The type of this property is File[].

- **multiSelectionEnabled** is a boolean value indicating whether multiple files can be selected. By default, it is false.

Let us create an example of a simple text editor that uses Swing menus, toolbar, file chooser, and color chooser, as shown in Figure 34.21, which allows the user to open and save text files, clear text, and change the color and font of the text. Listing 34.8 shows the program.

FIGURE 34.21 The editor enables you to open and save text files from the File menu or from the toolbar, and to change the color and font of the text from the Edit menu.

LISTING 34.8 TextEditor.java

```
1  import java.io.*;
2  import java.awt.*;
3  import java.awt.event.*;
4  import javax.swing.*;
5
6  public class TextEditor extends JApplet {
7    // Declare and create image icons
8    private ImageIcon openImageIcon =
9      new ImageIcon(getClass().getResource("image/open.gif"));
10   private ImageIcon saveImageIcon =
11     new ImageIcon(getClass().getResource("image/save.gif"));
12
```

create UI

```
13    // Create menu items
14    private JMenuItem jmiOpen = new JMenuItem("Open", openImageIcon);
15    private JMenuItem jmiSave = new JMenuItem("Save", saveImageIcon);
16    private JMenuItem jmiClear = new JMenuItem("Clear");
17    private JMenuItem jmiExit = new JMenuItem("Exit");
18    private JMenuItem jmiForeground = new JMenuItem("Foreground");
19    private JMenuItem jmiBackground = new JMenuItem("Background");
20
21    // Create buttons to be placed in a toolbar
22    private JButton jbtOpen = new JButton(openImageIcon);
23    private JButton jbtSave = new JButton(saveImageIcon);
24    private JLabel jlblStatus = new JLabel();
25
26    // Create a JFileChooser with the current directory
27    private JFileChooser jFileChooser1
28      = new JFileChooser(new File("."));
29
30    // Create a text area
31    private JTextArea jta = new JTextArea();
32
33    public TextEditor() {
34      // Add menu items to the menu
35      JMenu jMenu1 = new JMenu("File");
36      jMenu1.add(jmiOpen);
37      jMenu1.add(jmiSave);
38      jMenu1.add(jmiClear);
39      jMenu1.addSeparator();
40      jMenu1.add(jmiExit);
41
42      // Add menu items to the menu
43      JMenu jMenu2 = new JMenu("Edit");
44      jMenu2.add(jmiForeground);
45      jMenu2.add(jmiBackground);
46
47      // Add menus to the menu bar
48      JMenuBar jMenuBar1 = new JMenuBar();
49      jMenuBar1.add(jMenu1);
50      jMenuBar1.add(jMenu2);
51
52      // Set the menu bar
53      setJMenuBar(jMenuBar1);
54
55      // Create toolbar
56      JToolBar jToolBar1 = new JToolBar();
57      jToolBar1.add(jbtOpen);
58      jToolBar1.add(jbtSave);
59
60      jmiOpen.addActionListener(new ActionListener() {
61        public void actionPerformed(ActionEvent e) {
62          open();
63        }
64      });
65
66      jmiSave.addActionListener(new ActionListener() {
67        public void actionPerformed(ActionEvent evt) {
68          save();
69        }
70      });
71
72      jmiClear.addActionListener(new ActionListener() {
```

```
 73      public void actionPerformed(ActionEvent evt) {
 74        jta.setText(null);
 75      }
 76    });
 77
 78    jmiExit.addActionListener(new ActionListener() {
 79      public void actionPerformed(ActionEvent evt) {
 80        System.exit(0);
 81      }
 82    });
 83
 84    jmiForeground.addActionListener(new ActionListener() {
 85      public void actionPerformed(ActionEvent evt) {
 86        Color selectedColor =
 87          JColorChooser.showDialog(null, "Choose Foreground Color",      color chooser
 88            jta.getForeground());
 89
 90        if (selectedColor != null)
 91          jta.setForeground(selectedColor);
 92      }
 93    });
 94
 95    jmiBackground.addActionListener(new ActionListener() {
 96      public void actionPerformed(ActionEvent evt) {
 97        Color selectedColor =
 98          JColorChooser.showDialog(null, "Choose Background Color",      color chooser
 99            jta.getForeground());
100
101        if (selectedColor != null)
102          jta.setBackground(selectedColor);
103      }
104    });
105
106    jbtOpen.addActionListener(new ActionListener() {
107      public void actionPerformed(ActionEvent evt) {
108        open();
109      }
110    });
111
112    jbtSave.addActionListener(new ActionListener() {
113      public void actionPerformed(ActionEvent evt) {
114        save();
115      }
116    });
117
118    add(jToolBar1, BorderLayout.NORTH);
119    add(jlblStatus, BorderLayout.SOUTH);
120    add(new JScrollPane(jta), BorderLayout.CENTER);
121  }
122
123  /** Open file */
124  private void open() {
125    if (jFileChooser1.showOpenDialog(this) ==                           file chooser
126      JFileChooser.APPROVE_OPTION)
127      open(jFileChooser1.getSelectedFile());
128  }
129
130  /** Open file with the specified File instance */
131  private void open(File file) {
132    try {
```

```
133          // Read from the specified file and store it in jta
134          BufferedInputStream in = new BufferedInputStream(
135            new FileInputStream(file));
136          byte[] b = new byte[in.available()];
137          in.read(b, 0, b.length);
138          jta.append(new String(b, 0, b.length));
139          in.close();
140
141          // Display the status of the Open file operation in jlblStatus
142          jlblStatus.setText(file.getName() + " Opened");
143        }
144        catch (IOException ex) {
145          jlblStatus.setText("Error opening " + file.getName());
146        }
147      }
148
149      /** Save file */
150      private void save() {
151        if (jFileChooser1.showSaveDialog(this) ==
152          JFileChooser.APPROVE_OPTION) {
153            save(jFileChooser1.getSelectedFile());
154        }
155      }
156
157      /** Save file with specified File instance */
158      private void save(File file) {
159        try {
160          // Write the text in jta to the specified file
161          BufferedOutputStream out = new BufferedOutputStream(
162            new FileOutputStream(file));
163          byte[] b = (jta.getText()).getBytes();
164          out.write(b, 0, b.length);
165          out.close();
166
167          // Display the status of the save file operation in jlblStatus
168          jlblStatus.setText(file.getName()  + " Saved ");
169        }
170        catch (IOException ex) {
171          jlblStatus.setText("Error saving " + file.getName());
172        }
173      }
174    }
```

main method omitted

The program creates the File and Edit menus (lines 34–45). The File menu contains the menu commands Open for loading a file, Save for saving a file, Clear for clearing the text editor, and Exit for terminating the program. The Edit menu contains the menu commands Foreground Color and Background Color for setting foreground color and background color in the text. The Open and Save menu commands can also be accessed from the toolbar, which is created in lines 56–58. The status of executing Open and Save is displayed in the status label, which is created in line 35.

jFileChooser1, an instance of JFileChooser, is created for displaying the file dialog box to open and save files (lines 27–28). new File(".") is used to set the current directory to the directory where the class is stored.

The open method is invoked when the user clicks the Open menu command or the Open toolbar button (lines 62, 108). The showOpenDialog method (line 125) displays an Open dialog box, as shown in Figure 34.20. Upon receiving the selected file, the method open(file) (line 127) is invoked to load the file to the text area using a BufferedInputStream wrapped on a FileInputStream.

The `save` method is invoked when the user clicks the Save menu command or the Save toolbar button (lines 68, 114). The `showSaveDialog` method (line 151) displays a Save dialog box. Upon receiving the selected file, the method `save(file)` (line 153) is invoked to save the contents from the text area to the file, using a `BufferedOutputStream` wrapped on a `FileOutputStream`.

The color dialog is displayed using the static method `showDialog` (lines 87, 98) of `JColorChooser`. Thus you don't need to create an instance of `JFileChooser`. The `showDialog` method returns the selected color if the *OK* button is clicked after a color is selected.

CHAPTER SUMMARY

- *Menus* make selection easier and are widely used in window applications. Java provides five classes that implement menus: `JMenuBar`, `JMenu`, `JMenuItem`, `JCheckBoxMenuItem`, and `JRadioButtonMenuItem`. These classes are subclasses of `AbstractButton`. They are very similar to buttons.

- `JMenuBar` is a top-level menu component used to hold menus. A menu consists of *menu items* that the user can select (or toggle on or off). A menu item can be an instance of `JMenuItem`, `JCheckBoxMenuItem`, or `JRadioButtonMenuItem`. Menu items can be associated with icons, keyboard mnemonics, and keyboard accelerators. Menu items can be separated using separators.

- A *popup menu*, also known as a *context menu*, is like a regular menu, but does not have a menu bar and can float anywhere on the screen. Creating a popup menu is similar to creating a regular menu. First, you create an instance of `JPopupMenu`, then you can add `JMenuItem`, `JCheckBoxMenuItem`, `JRadioButtonMenuItem`, and separators to the popup menu.

- A popup menu usually contains the commands for an object. Customarily, you display a popup menu by pointing to the object and clicking a certain mouse button, the so-called *popup trigger*. Popup triggers are system dependent. In Windows, the popup menu is displayed when the right mouse button is released. In Motif, the popup menu is displayed when the third mouse button is pressed and held down.

- Swing provides the `JToolBar` class as the container to hold toolbar components. `JToolBar` uses `BoxLayout` to manage components. The components usually appear as icons. Since icons are not components, they cannot be placed into a toolbar directly. Instead you place buttons into the toolbar and set the icons on the buttons. An instance of `JToolBar` is like a regular container. Often it is placed in the north, west, or east of a container of `BorderLayout`.

- Swing provides the `Action` interface, which can be used to create action objects for processing actions. Using `Action` objects, common action processing for menu items and toolbar buttons can be centralized and separated from the other application code.

- The `JOptionPane` class contains the static methods for creating message dialogs, confirmation dialogs, input dialogs, and option dialogs. You can also create custom dialogs by extending the `JDialog` class.

■ Swing provides a convenient and versatile color dialog named `javax.swing.-JColorChooser`. Like `JOptionPane`, `JColorChooser` is a lightweight component inherited from `JComponent`. It can be added to any container.

■ Swing provides the `javax.swing.JFileChooser` class that displays a dialog box from which the user can navigate through the file system and select files for loading or saving.

REVIEW QUESTIONS

Section 34.2 Menus

34.1 How do you create a menu bar?

34.2 How do you create a submenu? How do you create a check-box menu item? How do you create a radio-button menu item?

34.3 How do you add a separator in a menu?

34.4 How do you set an icon and a text in a menu item? How do you associate keyboard mnemonics and accelerators in a menu item?

Section 34.3 Popup Menus

34.5 How do you create a popup menu? How do you show a popup menu?

34.6 Describe a popup trigger.

Section 34.4 `JToolBar`

34.7 What is the layout manager used in `JToolBar`? Can you change the layout manager?

34.8 How do you add buttons into a `JToolBar`? How do you add a `JToolBar` into a frame or an applet?

Section 34.5 Processing Actions Using the `Action` Interface

34.9 What is the `Action` interface for?

34.10 How do you add an `Action` object to a `JToolBar`, `JMenu`, `JButton`, `JRadioButton`, and `JCheckBox`?

Section 34.6 `JOptionPane` Dialogs

34.11 Describe the standard dialog boxes created using the `JOptionPane` class.

34.12 How do you create a message dialog? What are the message types? What is the button in the message dialog?

34.13 How do you create a confirmation dialog? What are the button option types?

34.14 How do you create an input dialog with a text field for entering input? How do you create a combo box dialog for selecting values as input? How do you create a list dialog for selecting values as input?

Sections 34.7–34.10

34.15 How do you show an instance of `JDialog`? Is a standard dialog box created using the static methods in `JOptionPane` modal? Is an instance of `JDialog` modal?

34.16 How do you display an instance of `JColorChooser`? Is an instance of `JColorChooser` modal? How do you obtain the selected color?

34.17 How do you display an instance of `JFileChooser`? Is an instance of `JFileChooser` modal? How do you obtain the selected file? What is the return type for `getSelectedFile()` and `getSelectedDirectory()`? How do you set the current directory as the default directory for a `JFileChooser` dialog?

PROGRAMMING EXERCISES

Sections 34.2–34.3

34.1* (*Creating an investment value calculator*) Write a program that calculates the future value of an investment at a given interest rate for a specified number of years. The formula for the calculation is as follows:

$$futureValue = investmentAmount \times (1 + monthlyInterestRate)^{years \times 12}$$

Use text fields for interest rate, investment amount, and years. Display the future amount in a text field when the user clicks the *Calculate* button or chooses Calculate from the Operation menu (see Figure 34.22). Show a message dialog box when the user clicks the **About** menu item from the Help menu.

FIGURE 34.22 The user enters the investment amount, years, and interest rate to compute future value.

34.2* (*Using popup menus*) Modify Listing 34.1, MenuDemo.java, to create a popup menu that contains the menus Operations and Exit, as shown in Figure 34.23. The popup is displayed when you click the right mouse button on the panel that contains the labels and the text fields.

FIGURE 34.23 The popup menu contains the commands to perform arithmetic operations.

Sections 34.4–34.5

34.3**(*A paint utility*) Write a program that emulates a paint utility. Your program should enable the user to choose options and draw shapes or get characters from the keyboard based on the selected options (see Figure 34.24). The options are

FIGURE 34.24 This exercise produces a prototype drawing utility that enables you to draw lines, rectangles, ovals, and characters.

displayed in a toolbar. To draw a line, the user first clicks the line icon in the toolbar and then uses the mouse to draw a line in the same way you would draw using Microsoft Paint.

34.4* (*Using actions*) Write a program that contains the menu items and toolbar buttons that can be used to select flags to be displayed in an `ImageViewer`, as shown in Figure 34.25. Use the `Action` interface to centralize the processing for the actions.

FIGURE 34.25   The menu items and tool buttons are used to display selected images in the `ImageViewer`.

Sections 34.6–34.10

34.5* (*Demonstrating* `JOptionPane`) Write a program that creates option panes of all types, as shown in Figure 34.26. Each menu item invokes a static `showXxxDialog` method to display a dialog box.

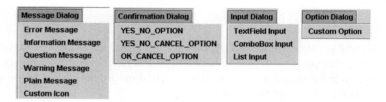

FIGURE 34.26   You can display a dialog box by clicking a menu item.

34.6* (*Creating custom dialog*) Write a program that creates a custom dialog box to gather user information, as shown in Figure 34.27(a).

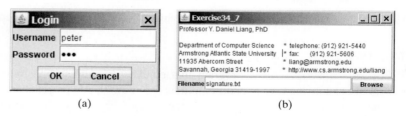

(a)   (b)

FIGURE 34.27   (a) The custom dialog box prompts the user to enter username and password. (b) The program enables the user to view a file by selecting it from a file open dialog box.

34.7* (*Using* `JFileChooser`) Write a program that enables the user to select a file from a file open dialog box. A file open dialog box is displayed when the *Browse* button is clicked, as shown in Figure 34.27(b). The file is displayed in the text area, and the file name is displayed in the text field when the *OK* button is clicked in the file open dialog box. You can also enter the file name in the text field and press the *Enter* key to display the file in the text area.

34.8* (*Selecting an audio file*) Write a program that selects an audio file using the file dialog box, and use three buttons, *Play*, *Loop*, and *Stop*, to control the audio, as shown in Figure 34.28. If you click the *Play* button, the audio file is played once. If you click the *Loop* button, the audio file keeps playing repeatedly. If you click the *Stop* button, the playing stops. The selected audio files are stored in the folder named **anthems** under the exercise directory. The exercise directory contains the class file for this exercise.

FIGURE 34.28   The program allows you to choose an audio file from a dialog box and use the buttons to play, repeatedly play, or stop the audio.

34.9** (*Playing TicTacToe with a computer*) The game in §17.7, "Case Study: TicTac-Toe," facilitates two players. Write a new game that enables a player to play against the computer. Add a File menu with two items, New Game and Exit, as shown in Figure 34.29. When you click New Game, it displays a dialog box. From this dialog box, you can decide whether to let the computer go first.

FIGURE 34.29   The new TicTacToe game enables you to play against the computer.

CHAPTER 35

MVC and Swing Models

Objectives

- To use the model-view-controller approach to separate data and logic from the presentation of data (§35.2).

- To implement the model-view-controller components using the JavaBeans event model (§35.2).

- To explain the Swing model-view-controller architecture (§35.4).

- To use `JSpinner` to scroll the next and previous values (§35.5).

- To create custom spinner models and editors (§35.6).

- To use `JList` to select single or multiple items in a list (§35.7).

- To add and remove items using `ListModel` and `DefaultListModel` (§35.8).

- To render list cells using a default or custom cell renderer (§35.9).

- To create custom combo box models and renderers (§35.10).

35.1 Introduction

The Swing user interface components are implemented using variations of the MVC architecture. You have used simple Swing components without concern for their supporting models, but in order to use advanced Swing components, you have to use their models to store, access, and modify data. This chapter introduces the MVC architecture and Swing models. Specifically, you will learn how to use the models in `JSpinner`, `JList`, and `JComboBox`. The next chapter will introduce `JTable` and `JTree`.

35.2 MVC

The model-view-controller (MVC) approach is a way of developing components by separating data storage and handling from the visual representation of the data. The component for storing and handling data, known as a *model*, contains the actual contents of the component. The component for presenting the data, known as a *view*, handles all essential component behaviors. It is the view that comes to mind when you think of the component. It does all the displaying of the components. The *controller* is a component that is usually responsible for obtaining data, as shown in Figure 35.1.

model
view

controller

FIGURE 35.1 The controller obtains data and stores it in a model. The view displays the data stored in the model.

MVC benefits

Separating a component into a model and a view has two major benefits:

- It makes multiple views possible so that data can be shared through the same model. For example, a model storing student names can be displayed simultaneously in a combo box and a list box.

- It simplifies the task of writing complex applications and makes the components scalable and easy to maintain. Changes can be made to the view without affecting the model, and vice versa.

A model contains data, whereas a view makes the data visible. Once a view is associated with a model, it is synchronized with the model. This ensures that all of the model's views display the same data consistently. To achieve consistency and synchronization with its dependent views, the model should notify the views when there is a change in any of its properties that are used in the view. In response to a change notification, the view is responsible for redisplaying the viewing area affected by the property change.

Prior to JDK 1.1, you would create a model by extending the `java.util.Observable` class and create a view by implementing the `java.util.Observer` interface. `Observable` and `Observer` were introduced in JDK 1.0, and their use is not consistent with the JDK 1.1 event model. With the arrival of the new Java event delegation model, using `Observable` and `Observer` became obsolete. The JDK event delegation model provides a superior architecture for supporting MVC component development. The model can be implemented as a source with appropriate event and event listener registration methods. The view can be implemented as a listener. Thus, if data are changed in the model, the view will be notified. To enable the selection of the model from the view, simply add the model as a property in the view with a set method.

Let us use an example to demonstrate the development of components using the MVC approach. The example creates a model named `CircleModel`, a view named `CircleView`, and a controller named `CircleControl`. `CircleModel` stores the properties (`radius`, `filled`, and `color`) that describe a circle. `filled` is a boolean value that indicates whether a circle is filled.

`CircleView` draws a circle according to the properties of the circle. `CircleControl` enables the user to enter circle properties from a graphical user interface. Create an applet with two buttons named *Show Controller* and *Show View,* as shown in Figure 35.2(a). When you click the *Show Controller* button, the controller is displayed in a frame, as shown in Figure 35.2(b). When you click the *Show View* button, the view is displayed in a separate frame, as shown in Figure 35.2(c).

(a)   (b)   (c)

FIGURE 35.2 The controller obtains circle properties and stores them in a circle model. The view displays the circle specified by the circle model.

The circle model contains the properties `radius`, `filled`, and `color`, as well as the registration/deregistration methods for action event, as shown in Figure 35.3.

When a property value is changed, the listeners are notified. The complete source code for `CircleModel` is given in Listing 35.1.

date model

LISTING 35.1 CircleModel.java

```java
 1 import java.awt.event.*;
 2 import java.util.*;
 3
 4 public class CircleModel {
 5   /** Property radius. */
 6   private double radius = 20;
 7
 8   /** Property filled. */
 9   private boolean filled;
10
11   /** Property color. */
12   private java.awt.Color color;
13
14   /** Utility field used by event firing mechanism. */
15   private ArrayList<ActionListener> actionListenerList;
16
17   public double getRadius() {
18     return radius;
19   }
20
21   public void setRadius(double radius) {
22     this.radius = radius;
23
24     // Notify the listener for the change on radius
25     processEvent(
26       new ActionEvent(this, ActionEvent.ACTION_PERFORMED, "radius"));
27   }
28
29   public boolean isFilled() {
30     return filled;
31   }
32
33   public void setFilled(boolean filled) {
34     this.filled = filled;
35
36     // Notify the listener for the change on filled
```

properties

fire event

```
fire event              37        processEvent(
                        38          new ActionEvent(this, ActionEvent.ACTION_PERFORMED, "filled"));
                        39      }
                        40
                        41      public java.awt.Color getColor() {
                        42        return color;
                        43      }
                        44
                        45      public void setColor(java.awt.Color color) {
                        46        this.color = color;
                        47
                        48        // Notify the listener for the change on color
fire event              49        processEvent(
                        50          new ActionEvent(this, ActionEvent.ACTION_PERFORMED, "color"));
                        51      }
                        52
                        53      /** Register an action event listener */
standard code           54      public synchronized void addActionListener(ActionListener l) {
                        55        if (actionListenerList == null)
                        56          actionListenerList = new ArrayList<ActionListener>();
                        57
                        58        actionListenerList.add(l);
                        59      }
                        60
                        61      /** Remove an action event listener */
standard code           62      public synchronized void removeActionListener(ActionListener l) {
                        63        if (actionListenerList != null && actionListenerList.contains(l))
                        64          actionListenerList.remove(l);
                        65      }
                        66
                        67      /** Fire TickEvent */
standard code           68      private void processEvent(ActionEvent e) {
                        69        ArrayList list;
                        70
                        71        synchronized (this) {
                        72          if (actionListenerList == null) return;
                        73          list = (ArrayList)actionListenerList.clone();
                        74        }
                        75
                        76        for (int i = 0; i < list.size(); i++) {
                        77          ActionListener listener = (ActionListener)list.get(i);
                        78          listener.actionPerformed(e);
                        79        }
                        80      }
                        81 }
```

FIGURE 35.3 The circle model stores the data and notifies the listeners if the data change.

Note
The registration/deregistration/processEvent methods (lines 54–80) are the same as in Listing 32.2, CourseWithActionEvent.java. If you use a GUI builder tool such as NetBeans, Eclipse, or JBuilder, the code can be generated automatically.

The view implements `ActionListener` to listen for notifications from the model. It contains the model as its property. When a model is set in the view, the view is registered with the model. The view extends `JPanel` and overrides the `paintComponent` method to draw the circle according to the property values specified in the model. The UML diagram for `CircleView` is shown in Figure 35.4 and its source code is given in Listing 35.2.

view

FIGURE 35.4 The view displays the circle according to the model.

LISTING 35.2 CircleView.java

```java
1  import java.awt.*;
2  import java.awt.event.*;
3
4  public class CircleView extends javax.swing.JPanel
5      implements ActionListener {
6    private CircleModel model;
7
8    public void actionPerformed(ActionEvent actionEvent) {
9      repaint();
10   }
11
12   /** Set a model */
13   public void setModel(CircleModel newModel) {
14     model = newModel;
15
16     if (model != null)
17       // Register the view as listener for the model
18       model.addActionListener(this);
19
20     repaint();
21   }
22
23   public CircleModel getModel() {
24     return model;
25   }
26
27   public void paintComponent(Graphics g) {
28     super.paintComponent(g);
29
30     if (model == null) return;
31
32     g.setColor(model.getColor());
33
```

model

set model

paint view

```
34       int xCenter = getWidth() / 2;
35       int yCenter = getHeight() / 2;
36       int radius = (int)model.getRadius();
37
38       if (model.isFilled()) {
39         g.fillOval(xCenter - radius, yCenter - radius,
40           2 * radius, 2 * radius);
41       }
42       else {
43         g.drawOval(xCenter - radius, yCenter - radius,
44           2 * radius, 2 * radius);
45       }
46   }
47 }
```

The controller presents a GUI interface that enables the user to enter circle properties **radius**, **filled**, and **color**. It contains the model as its property. You can use the **setModel** method to associate a circle model with the controller. It uses a text field to obtain a new radius and a combo box to obtain a **boolean** value to specify whether the circle is filled. The source code for **CircleController** is given in Listing 35.3.

LISTING 35.3 CircleController.java

model

create UI

```
1 import java.awt.event.*;
2 import java.awt.*;
3 import javax.swing.*;
4
5 public class CircleController extends JPanel {
6   private CircleModel model;
7   private JTextField jtfRadius = new JTextField();
8   private JComboBox jcboFilled = new JComboBox(new Boolean[]{
9     new Boolean(false), new Boolean(true)});
10
11   /** Creates new form CircleController */
12   public CircleController() {
13     // Panel to group labels
14     JPanel panel1 = new JPanel();
15     panel1.setLayout(new GridLayout(2, 1));
16     panel1.add(new JLabel("Radius"));
17     panel1.add(new JLabel("Filled"));
18
19     // Panel to group text field, combo box, and another panel
20     JPanel panel2 = new JPanel();
21     panel2.setLayout(new GridLayout(2, 1));
22     panel2.add(jtfRadius);
23     panel2.add(jcboFilled);
24
25     setLayout(new BorderLayout());
26     add(panel1, BorderLayout.WEST);
27     add(panel2, BorderLayout.CENTER);
28
29     // Register listeners
30     jtfRadius.addActionListener(new ActionListener() {
31       public void actionPerformed(ActionEvent e) {
32         if (model == null) return; // No model associated yet.
33         model.setRadius(new
34           Double(jtfRadius.getText()).doubleValue());
35       }
36     });
```

```
37        jcboFilled.addActionListener(new ActionListener() {
38          public void actionPerformed(ActionEvent e) {
39            if (model == null) return;
40            model.setFilled(
41              ((Boolean)jcboFilled.getSelectedItem()).booleanValue());
42          }
43        });
44      }
45
46      public void setModel(CircleModel newModel) {          set model
47        model = newModel;
48      }
49
50      public CircleModel getModel() {
51        return model;
52      }
53    }
```

Finally, let us create an applet named MVCDemo with two buttons, *Show Controller* and *Show View*. The *Show Controller* button displays a controller in a frame, and the *Show View* button displays a view in a separate frame. The program is shown in Listing 35.4.

LISTING 35.4   MVCDemo.java

```
1  import java.awt.*;
2  import java.awt.event.*;
3  import javax.swing.*;
4
5  public class MVCDemo extends JApplet  {
6    private JButton jbtController = new JButton("Show Controller");
7    private JButton jbtView = new JButton("Show View");
8    private CircleModel model = new CircleModel();              create model
9
10   public MVCDemo() {
11     setLayout(new FlowLayout());                              create UI
12     add(jbtController);
13     add(jbtView);
14
15     jbtController.addActionListener(new ActionListener() {
16       public void actionPerformed(ActionEvent e) {
17         JFrame frame = new JFrame("Controller");
18         CircleController controller = new CircleController();
19         controller.setModel(model);                           set model
20         frame.add(controller);
21         frame.setSize(200, 200);
22         frame.setLocation(200, 200);
23         frame.setVisible(true);
24       }
25     });
26
27     jbtView.addActionListener(new ActionListener() {
28       public void actionPerformed(ActionEvent e) {
29         JFrame frame = new JFrame("View");
30         CircleView view = new CircleView();
31         view.setModel(model);                                 set model
32         frame.add(view);
33         frame.setSize(500, 200);
34         frame.setLocation(200, 200);
35         frame.setVisible(true);
```

```
36       }
37     });
38   }
39 }
```

main method omitted

The model stores and handles data, and the views are responsible for presenting data. The fundamental issue in the model-view approach is to ensure consistency between the views and the model. Any change in the model should be notified to the dependent views, and all the views should display the same data consistently. The data in the model is changed through the controller.

The methods `setRadius` and `setFilled`, and `setColor` (lines 21, 33, 45) in `CircleModel` invoke the `processEvent` method to notify the listeners of any change in the properties.

The `setModel` method in `CircleView` sets a new model and registers the view with the model by invoking the model's `addActionListener` method (line 18). When the data in the model are changed, the view's `actionPerformed` method is invoked to repaint the circle (line 9).

The controller `CircleController` presents a GUI. You can enter the radius from the radius text field. You can specify whether the circle is filled from the combo box that contains two `Boolean` objects, `new Boolean(false)` and `new Boolean(true)` (lines 8–9). Several controllers or views can share a model.

In `MVCDemo`, every time you click the *Show Controller* button, a new controller is created (line 18). Every time you click the *Show View* button, a new view is created (line 30). All the controllers and views share the same model.

35.3 MVC Variations

A variation of the model-view-controller architecture combines the controller with the view. In this case, a view not only presents the data, but is also used as an interface to interact with the user and accept user input, as shown in Figure 35.5.

FIGURE 35.5 The view can interact with the user as well as displaying data.

For example, you can modify the view in the preceding example to enable the user to change the circle's radius using the mouse. When the left mouse button is clicked, the radius is increased by 5 pixels. When the right mouse button is clicked, the radius is decreased by 5 pixels. The new view, named `ViewController`, can be implemented by extending `CircleView`, as follows:

mouse listener

right button?

```
1 public class ViewController extends CircleView {
2   public ViewController() {
3     // Register mouse listener
4     addMouseListener(new java.awt.event.MouseAdapter() {
5       public void mousePressed(java.awt.event.MouseEvent e) {
6         CircleModel model = getModel(); // Get model
7
8         if (model == null) return;
9
10        if (e.isMetaDown())
11          model.setRadius(model.getRadius() - 5); // Right button
```

```
12              else
13                  model.setRadius(model.getRadius() + 5); // Left button
14          }
15      });
16   }
17 }
```

Another variation of the model-view-controller architecture adds some of the data from the model to the view so that frequently used data can be accessed directly from the view. Swing components are designed using the MVC architecture. Each Swing GUI component is a view that uses a model to store data. A Swing GUI component contains some data in the model, so that it can be accessed directly from the component.

35.4 Swing Model-View-Controller Architecture

Every Swing user interface component (except some containers and dialog boxes, such as JPanel, JSplitPane, JFileChooser, and JColorChooser) has a property named *model* that refers to its data model. The data model is defined in an interface whose name ends with Model. For example, the model for button component is ButtonModel. Most model interfaces have a default implementation class, commonly named DefaultX, where X is its model interface name. For example, the default implementation class for ButtonModel is DefaultButtonModel. The relationship of a Swing component, its model interface, and its default model implementation class is illustrated in Figure 35.6.

(a) Generic Swing model-view architecture   (b) JButton model-view implementation

FIGURE 35.6 Swing components are implemented using the MVC architecture.

For convenience, most Swing components contain some properties of their models, and these properties can be accessed and modified directly from the component without the existence of the model being known. For example, the properties actionCommand and mnemonic are defined in both ButtonModel and JButton. Actually, these properties are in the AbstractButton class. Since JButton is a subclass of AbstractButton, it inherits all the properties from AbstractButton.

When you create a Swing component without specifying a model, a default data model is assigned to the model property. For example, lines 9–10 in the following code set the actionCommand and mnemonic properties of a button through its model.

```
1 public class TestSwingModel1 {
2   public static void main(String[] args) {
3     javax.swing.JButton jbt = new javax.swing.JButton();
4
5     // Obtain the default model from the component
6     javax.swing.ButtonModel model = jbt.getModel();          get model
7
8     // Set properties in the model
9     model.setActionCommand("OK");                            set model properties
10    model.setMnemonic('O');
11
```

```
12      // Display the property values from the component
13      System.out.println("actionCommand is " + jbt.getActionCommand());
14      System.out.println("mnemonic is " + (char)(jbt.getMnemonic()));
15    }
16  }
```

```
actionCommand is OK
mnemonic is O
```

You can also create a new model and assign it to a Swing component. For example, the following code creates an instance of `ButtonModel` (line 7) and assigns it to an instance of `JButton` (line 14).

```
 1  public class TestSwingModel2 {
 2    public static void main(String[] args) {
 3      javax.swing.JButton jbt = new javax.swing.JButton();
 4
 5      // Create a new button model
 6      javax.swing.ButtonModel model =
 7        new javax.swing.DefaultButtonModel();
 8
 9      // Set properties in the model
10      model.setActionCommand("OK");
11      model.setMnemonic('O');
12
13      // Assign the model to the button
14      jbt.setModel(model);
15
16      // Display the property values from the component
17      System.out.println("actionCommand is " + jbt.getActionCommand());
18      System.out.println("mnemonic is " + jbt.getMnemonic());
19    }
20  }
```

create model

set model properties

set a new model

```
actionCommand is OK
mnemonic is 79
```

It is unnecessary to use the models for simple Swing components, such as `JButton`, `JToggleButton`, `JCheckBox`, `JRadioButton`, `JTextField`, and `JTextArea`, because the frequently used properties in the models of these Swing components are also the properties in these components. You can access and modify these properties directly through the components. For advanced components, such as `JSpinner`, `JList`, `JComboBox`, `JTable`, and `JTree`, you have to work with their models to store, access, and modify data.

35.5 JSpinner

A spinner is a text field with a pair of tiny arrow buttons on its right side that enable the user to select numbers, dates, or values from an ordered sequence, as shown in Figure 35.7. The keyboard up/down arrow keys also cycle through the elements. The user may also be allowed to type a (legal) value directly into the spinner. A spinner is similar to a combo box but is sometimes preferred because it doesn't require a drop-down list that can obscure important data.

Spinner   Spinner

FIGURE 35.7 Two JSpinner components enable the user to select a month and a year for the calendar.

Figure 35.8 shows the constructors and commonly used methods in JSpinner. A JSpinner's sequence value is defined by the SpinnerModel interface, which manages a potentially unbounded sequence of elements. The model doesn't support indexed random access to sequence elements. Only three sequence elements are accessible at a time—current, next, and previous—using the methods getValue(), getNextValue(), and getPreviousValue(), respectively. The current sequence element can be modified using the setValue method. When the current value in a spinner is changed, the model invokes the stateChanged(javax.swing.event.ChangeEvent e) method of the registered listeners. The listeners must implement javax.swing.event.ChangeListener. All these methods in SpinnerModel are also defined in JSpinner for convenience, so you can access the data in the model from JSpinner directly.

JavaBeans properties with get and set methods omitted in the UML diagram.

javax.swing.JSpinner	javax.swing.SpinnerModel
-model: SpinnerModel	Specifies a model with get/set methods.
-editor:JComponent	Specifies an editor with get/set methods.
+JSpinner()	Constructs a JSpinner with a SpinnerNumberModel with initial value 0 and no minimum or maximum limits.
+JSpinner(model: SpinnerModel)	Constructs a JSpinner with a specified SpinnerModel.
+getNextValue(): Object	Gets the next element value in this JSpinner.
+getPreviousValue(): Object	Gets the previous element value in this JSpinner.
+getValue(): Object	Gets the current element value in this JSpinner.
+setValue(value: Object): void	Sets the current element value.
+addChangeListener(l: ChangeListener): void	Adds a listener for value change.
+removeChangeListener(l: ChangeListener): void	Removes a listener.

FIGURE 35.8 JSpinner uses a spinner model to store data.

Note

If you create a JSpinner object without specifying a model, the spinner displays a sequence of integers.

Listing 35.5 gives an example that creates a JSpinner object for a sequence of numbers and displays the previous, current, and next numbers from the spinner on a label, as shown in Figure 35.9.

LISTING 35.5 SimpleSpinner.java

```
 1 import javax.swing.*;
 2 import javax.swing.event.*;
 3 import java.awt.BorderLayout;
 4
 5 public class SimpleSpinner extends JApplet {
 6   // Create a JSpinner
 7   private JSpinner spinner = new JSpinner();
 8
 9   // Create a JLabel
10   private JLabel label = new JLabel("", JLabel.CENTER);
11
12   public SimpleSpinner() {
13     // Add spinner and label to the UI
14     add(spinner, BorderLayout.NORTH);
15     add(label, BorderLayout.CENTER);
16
17     // Register and create a listener
18     spinner.addChangeListener(new ChangeListener() {
19       public void stateChanged(javax.swing.event.ChangeEvent e) {
20         label.setText("Previous value: " + spinner.getPreviousValue()
21           + " Current value: " + spinner.getValue()
22           + " Next value: " + spinner.getNextValue());
23       }
24     });
25   }
26 }
```

spinner (line 7)

spinner listener (line 18)

main method omitted (line 26)

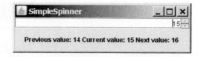

FIGURE 35.9 The previous, current, and next values in the spinner are displayed on the label.

A `JSpinner` object is created using its no-arg constructor (line 7). By default, a spinner displays a sequence of integers.

An anonymous inner class event adapter is created to process the value change event on the spinner (lines 18–24). The previous, current, and next values in a spinner can be obtained using the `JSpinner`'s instance methods `getPreviousValue()`, `getValue()`, and `getNextValue()`.

To display a sequence of values other than integers, you have to use spinner models.

35.6 Spinner Models and Editors

`SpinnerModel` is an interface for all spinner models. `AbstractSpinnerModel` is a convenient abstract class that implements `SpinnerModel` and provides the implementation for its registration/deregistration methods. `SpinnerListModel`, `SpinnerNumberModel`, and `SpinnerDateModel` are concrete implementations of `SpinnerModel`. The relationship among them is illustrated in Figure 35.10. Besides these models, you can create a custom spinner model that extends `AbstractSpinnerModel` or directly implements `SpinnerModel`.

FIGURE 35.10 SpinnerListModel, SpinnerNumberModel, and SpinnerDateModel are concrete implementations for SpinnerModel.

35.6.1 SpinnerListModel

SpinnerListModel (see Figure 35.11) is a simple implementation of SpinnerModel whose values are stored in a java.util.List.

FIGURE 35.11 SpinnerListModel uses a java.util.List to store a sequence of data in the model.

You can create a SpinnerListModel using an array or a list. For example, the following code creates a model that consists of values Freshman, Sophomore, Junior, Senior, and Graduate in an array.

```
// Create an array
String[] grades = {"Freshman", "Sophomore", "Junior",
  "Senior", "Graduate"};

// Create a model from an array
model = new SpinnerListModel(grades);
```

Alternatively, the following code creates a model using a list:

```
// Create an array
String[] grades = {"Freshman", "Sophomore", "Junior",
  "Senior", "Graduate"};

// Create an ArrayList from the array
list = new ArrayList(Arrays.asList(grades));

// Create a model from the list
model = new SpinnerListModel(list);
```

The alternative code seems unnecessary. However, it is useful if you need to add or remove elements from the model. The size of the array is fixed once the array is created. The list is a flexible data structure that enables you to add or remove elements dynamically.

35.6.2 SpinnerNumberModel

SpinnerNumberModel (see Figure 35.12) is a concrete implementation of SpinnerModel that represents a sequence of numbers. It contains the properties maximum, minimum, and stepSize. The maximum and minimum properties specify the upper and lower bounds of the sequence. The stepSize specifies the size of the increase or decrease computed by the nextValue and previousValue methods defined in SpinnerModel. The minimum and maximum properties can be null to indicate that the sequence has no lower or upper limit. All of the properties in this class are defined as Number or Comparable, so that all Java numeric types may be accommodated.

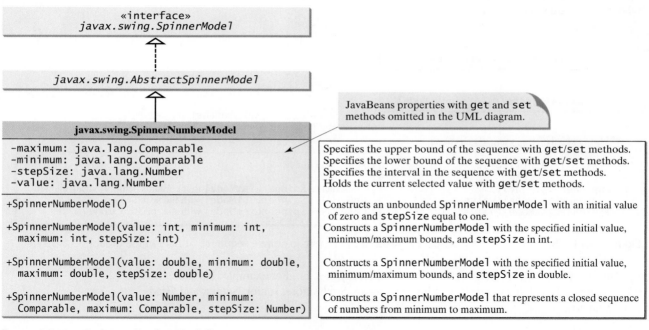

FIGURE 35.12 SpinnerNumberModel represents a sequence of numbers.

You can create a SpinnerNumberModel with integers or double. For example, the following code creates a model that represents a sequence of numbers from 0 to 3000 with initial value 2004 and interval 1.

```
// Create a spinner number model
SpinnerNumberModel model = new SpinnerNumberModel(2004, 0, 3000, 1);
```

The following code creates a model that represents a sequence of numbers from 0 to 120 with initial value 50 and interval 0.1.

```
// Create a spinner number model
SpinnerNumberModel model = new SpinnerNumberModel(50, 0, 120, 0.1);
```

35.6.3 `SpinnerDateModel`

`SpinnerDateModel` (see Figure 35.13) is a concrete implementation of `SpinnerModel` that represents a sequence of dates. The upper and lower bounds of the sequence are defined by properties called `start` and `end`, and the size of the increase or decrease computed by the `nextValue` and `previousValue` methods is defined by a property called `calendarField`. The `start` and `end` properties can be `null` to indicate that the sequence has no lower or upper limit. The value of the `calendarField` property must be one of the `java.util.Calendar` constants that specify a field within a `Calendar`. The `getNextValue` and `getPreviousValue` methods change the date forward or backward by this amount. For example, if `calendarField` is `Calendar.DAY_OF_WEEK`, then `nextValue` produces a date that is 24 hours after the current value, and `previousValue` produces a date that is 24 hours earlier.

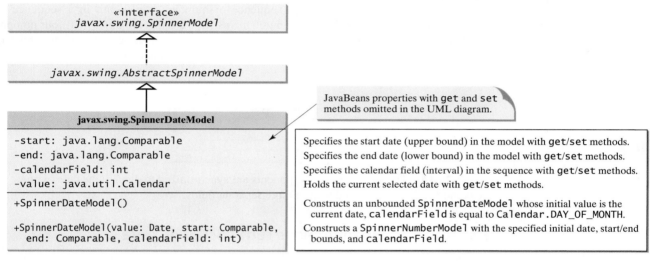

FIGURE 35.13 `SpinnerDateModel` represents a sequence of dates.

For example, the following code creates a spinner model that represents a sequence of dates, starting from the current date without an upper limit and with calendar field on month.

```
SpinnerDateModel model = new SpinnerDateModel(new Date(), null, null,
  Calendar.MONTH);
```

35.6.4 Spinner Editors

A `JSpinner` has a single child component, called the *editor*, which is responsible for displaying the current element or value of the model. Four editors are defined as static inner classes inside `JSpinner`.

- **`JSpinner.DefaultEditor`** is a simple base class for all other specialized editors to display a read-only view of the model's current value with a `JFormattedTextField`. `JFormattedTextField` extends `JTextField`, adding support for formatting arbitrary values, as well as retrieving a particular object once the user has edited the text.

- **`JSpinner.NumberEditor`** is a specialized editor for a `JSpinner` whose model is a `SpinnerNumberModel`. The value of the editor is displayed with a `JFormattedTextField` whose format is defined by a `NumberFormatter` instance.

- **`JSpinner.DateEditor`** is a specialized editor for a `JSpinner` whose model is a `SpinnerDateModel`. The value of the editor is displayed with a `JFormattedTextField` whose format is defined by a `DateFormatter` instance.

■ **JSpinner.ListEditor** is a specialized editor for a JSpinner whose model is a SpinnerListModel. The value of the editor is displayed with a JFormatted-TextField.

The JSpinner's constructor creates a NumberEditor for SpinnerNumberModel, a DateEditor for SpinnerDateModel, a ListEditor for SpinnerListModel, and a DefaultEditor for all other models. The editor can also be changed using the setEditor method. The JSpinner's editor stays in sync with the model by listening for ChangeEvents. The commitEdit() method should be used to commit the currently edited value to the model.

35.6.5 Example: Using Spinner Models and Editors

This example uses a JSpinner component to display the date and three other JSpinner components to display the day in a sequence of numbers, the month in a sequence of strings, and the year in a sequence of numbers, as shown in Figure 35.14. All four components are synchronized. For example, if you change the year in the spinner for year, the date value in the date spinner is updated accordingly. The source code of the example is given in Listing 35.6.

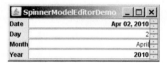

FIGURE 35.14   The four spinner components are synchronized to display the date in one field and the day, month, and year in three separate fields.

LISTING 35.6   SpinnerModelEditorDemo.java

```
1  import javax.swing.*;
2  import javax.swing.event.*;
3  import java.util.*;
4  import java.text.*;
5  import java.awt.*;
6
7  public class SpinnerModelEditorDemo extends JApplet {
8    // Create four spinners for date, day, month, and year
9    private JSpinner jspDate =
10     new JSpinner(new SpinnerDateModel());
11   private JSpinner jspDay =
12     new JSpinner(new SpinnerNumberModel(1, 1, 31, 1));
13   private String[] monthNames = new DateFormatSymbols().getMonths();
14   private JSpinner jspMonth = new JSpinner
15     (new SpinnerListModel(Arrays.asList(monthNames).subList(0, 12)));
16   private JSpinner spinnerYear =
17     new JSpinner(new SpinnerNumberModel(2004, 1, 3000, 1));
18
19   public SpinnerModelEditorDemo() {
20     // Group labels
21     JPanel panel1 = new JPanel();
22     panel1.setLayout(new GridLayout(4, 1));
23     panel1.add(new JLabel("Date"));
24     panel1.add(new JLabel("Day"));
25     panel1.add(new JLabel("Month"));
26     panel1.add(new JLabel("Year"));
27
```

spinners

create UI

```
28        // Group spinners
29        JPanel panel2 = new JPanel();
30        panel2.setLayout(new GridLayout(4, 1));
31        panel2.add(jspDate);
32        panel2.add(jspDay);
33        panel2.add(jspMonth);
34        panel2.add(spinnerYear);
35
36        // Add spinner and label to the UI
37        add(panel1, BorderLayout.WEST);
38        add(panel2, BorderLayout.CENTER);
39
40        // Set editor for date
41        JSpinner.DateEditor dateEditor =                          date editor
42          new JSpinner.DateEditor(jspDate, "MMM dd, yyyy");
43        jspDate.setEditor(dateEditor);
44
45        // Set editor for year
46        JSpinner.NumberEditor yearEditor =                        number editor
47          new JSpinner.NumberEditor(spinnerYear, "####");
48        spinnerYear.setEditor(yearEditor);
49
50        // Update date to synchronize with the day, month, and year
51        updateDate();
52
53        // Register and create a listener for jspDay
54        jspDay.addChangeListener(new ChangeListener() {           spinner listener
55          public void stateChanged(javax.swing.event.ChangeEvent e) {
56            updateDate();
57          }
58        });
59
60        // Register and create a listener for jspMonth
61        jspMonth.addChangeListener(new ChangeListener() {         spinner listener
62          public void stateChanged(javax.swing.event.ChangeEvent e) {
63            updateDate();
64          }
65        });
66
67        // Register and create a listener for spinnerYear
68        spinnerYear.addChangeListener(new ChangeListener() {      spinner listener
69          public void stateChanged(javax.swing.event.ChangeEvent e) {
70            updateDate();
71          }
72        });
73      }
74
75      /** Update date spinner to synchronize with the other spinners */
76      private void updateDate() {
77        // Get current month and year in int
78        int month = ((SpinnerListModel)jspMonth.getModel()).
79            getList().indexOf(jspMonth.getValue());
80        int year = ((Integer)spinnerYear.getValue()).intValue();
81
82        // Set a new maximum number of days for the new month and year
83        SpinnerNumberModel numberModel =
84          (SpinnerNumberModel)jspDay.getModel();
85        numberModel.setMaximum(new Integer(maxDaysInMonth(year, month)));
86
```

```
87       // Set a new current day if it exceeds the maximum
88       if (((Integer)(numberModel.getValue())).intValue() >
89           maxDaysInMonth(year, month))
90         numberModel.setValue(new Integer(maxDaysInMonth(year, month)));
91
92       // Get the current day
93       int day = ((Integer)jspDay.getValue()).intValue();
94
95       // Set a new date in the date spinner
96       jspDate.setValue(
97         new GregorianCalendar(year, month, day).getTime());
98     }
99
100    /** Return the maximum number of days in a month. For example,
101      Feb 2004 has 29 days. */
102    private int maxDaysInMonth(int year, int month) {
103      Calendar calendar = new GregorianCalendar(year, month, 1);
104      return calendar.getActualMaximum(Calendar.DAY_OF_MONTH);
105    }
106  }
```

main method omitted

A `JSpinner` object for dates, `jspDate`, is created with a default `SpinnerDateModel` (lines 9–10). The format of the date displayed in the spinner is MMM dd, yyyy (e.g., Feb 01, 2006). This format is created using the `JSpinner`'s inner class constructor `DateEditor` (lines 41–42) and is set as `jspDate`'s editor (line 43).

A `JSpinner` object for days, `jspDay`, is created with a `SpinnerNumberModel` with a sequence of integers between 1 and 31 in which the initial value is 1 and the interval is 1 (lines 11–12). The maximum number is reset in the `updateDate()` method based on the current month and year (lines 88–90). For example, February 2004 has 29 days, so the maximum in `jspDay` is set to 29 for February 2004.

A `JSpinner` object for months, `jspMonth`, is created with a `SpinnerListModel` with a list of month names (lines 14–15). Month names are locale specific and can be obtained using the `new DateFormatSymbols().getMonths()` (line 13). Some calendars can have 13 months. `Arrays.asList(monthNames)` creates a list from an array of strings, and `subList(0, 12)` returns the first 12 elements in the list.

A `JSpinner` object for years, `spinnerYear`, is created with a `SpinnerNumberModel` with a sequence of integers between 1 and 3000 in which the initial value is 2004 and the interval is 1 (lines 16–17). By default, locale-specific number separators are used. For example, 2004 would be displayed as 2,004 in the spinner. To display the number without separators, the number pattern `####` is specified to construct a new `NumberEditor` for `spinnerYear` (lines 46–47). The editor is set as `spinnerYear`'s editor (line 48).

The `updateDate()` method synchronizes the date spinner with the day, month, and year spinners. Whenever a new value is selected in the day, month, or year spinner, a new date is set in the date spinner. The `maxDaysInMonth` method (lines 102–105) returns the maximum number of days in a month. For example, February 2004 has 29 days.

A `JSpinner` object can fire `javax.swing.event.ChangeEvent` to notify the listeners of the state change in the spinner. The anonymous event adapters are created to process spinner state changes for the day, month, and year spinners (lines 54–73). Whenever a new value is selected in one of these three spinners, the date spinner value is updated accordingly. In Exercise 35.3, you will improve the example to synchronize the day, month, and year spinners with the date spinner. Then, when a new value is selected in the date spinner, the values in the day, month, and year spinners will be updated accordingly.

This example uses `SpinnerNumberModel`, `SpinnerDateModel`, and `SpinnerList-Model`. They are predefined concrete spinner models in the API. You can also create custom spinner models (see Exercise 35.4).

35.7 **JList** and its Models

The basic features of **JList** were introduced in §16.9, "Lists," without using list models. You learned how to create a list and how to respond to list selections. However, you cannot add or remove elements from a list without using list models. This section introduces list models and gives a detailed discussion on how to use **JList**.

JList has two supporting models: a list model and a list-selection model. The *list model* is for storing and processing data. The *list-selection model* is for selecting items. By default, items are rendered as strings or icons. You can also create a custom renderer implementing the **ListCellRenderer** interface. The relationship of these interfaces and classes is shown in Figure 35.15.

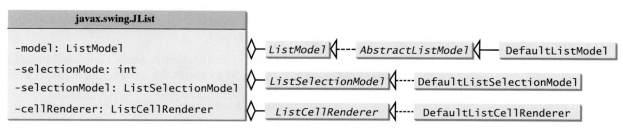

FIGURE 35.15 **JList** contains several supporting interfaces and classes.

35.7.1 **JList** Constructors, Properties, and Methods

Figure 35.16 shows the properties and constructors of **JList**. You can create a list from a list model, an array of objects, or a vector.

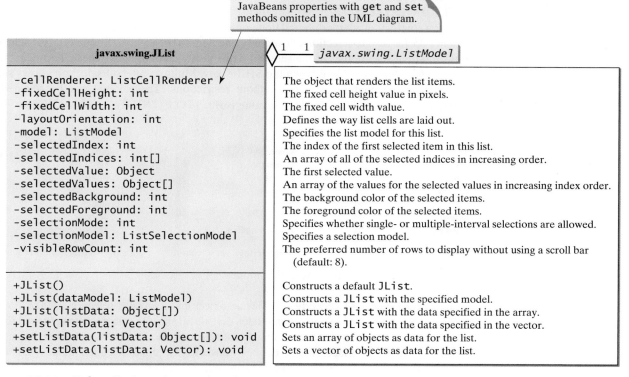

FIGURE 35.16 **JList** displays elements in a list.

35.7.2 List Layout Orientations

The `layoutOrientation` property, introduced in JDK 1.4, specifies the layout of the items using one of the following three values:

- `JList.VERTICAL` specifies that the cells should be laid out vertically in one column. This is the default value.

- `JList.HORIZONTAL_WRAP` specifies that the cells should be laid out horizontally, wrapping to a new row as necessary. The number of rows to use is determined by the `visibleRowCount` property if its value is greater than `0`; otherwise the number of rows is determined by the width of the `JList`.

- `JList.VERTICAL_WRAP` specifies that the cells should be laid out vertically, wrapping to a new column as necessary. The number of rows to use is determined by the `visibleRowCount` property if its value is greater than `0`; otherwise the number of rows is determined by the height of the `JList`.

For example, suppose there are five elements (item1, item2, item3, item4, and item5) in the list and the `visibleRowCount` is 2. Figure 35.17 shows the layout in these three cases.

| (a) Vertical | (b) Vertical wrap | (c) Horizontal wrap |

Figure 35.17 Layout orientation specifies how elements are laid out in a list.

35.7.3 List-Selection Modes and List-Selection Models

The **selectionMode** property is one of the three values (`SINGLE_SELECTION`, `SINGLE_INTERVAL_SELECTION`, `MULTIPLE_INTERVAL_SELECTION`) that indicate whether a single item, single-interval item, or multiple-interval item can be selected, as shown in Figure 35.18. Single selection allows only one item to be selected. Single-interval selection allows multiple selections, but the selected items must be contiguous. These items can be selected all together by holding down the SHIFT key. Multiple-interval selection allows selections of multiple contiguous items without restrictions. These items can be selected by holding down the *Ctrl* key. The default value is `MULTIPLE_INTERVAL_SELECTION`.

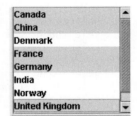

| (a) Single selection | (b) Single-interval selection | (c) Multiple-interval selection |

Figure 35.18 A list has three selection modes.

The **selectionModel** property specifies an object that tracks list selection. `JList` has two models: a list model and a list-selection model. *List models* handle data management, and *list-selection models* deal with data selection. A list-selection model must implement the `ListSelectionModel` interface, which defines constants for three selection modes (`SINGLE_SELECTION`, `SINGLE_INTERVAL_SELECTION`, and `MULTIPLE_INTERVAL_SELECTION`), and registration methods for `ListSectionListener`. It also defines the methods for adding and removing selection intervals, and the access methods for the properties, such as selectionMode, anchorSelectionIndex, leadSelectionIndex, and valueIsAdjusting.

By default, an instance of JList uses DefaultListSelectionModel, which is a concrete implementation of ListSelectionModel. Usually, you do not need to provide a custom list-selection model, because the DefaultListSelectionModel class is sufficient in most cases. List-selection models are rarely used explicitly, because you can set the selection mode directly in JList.

35.7.4   Example: List Properties Demo

This example creates a list of a fixed number of items displayed as strings. The example enables you to dynamically set visibleRowCount from a spinner, layoutOrientation from a combo box, and selectionMode from a combo box, as shown in Figure 35.19. When you select one or more items, their values are displayed in a status label below the list. The source code of the example is given in Listing 35.7.

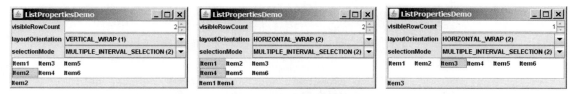

FIGURE 35.19   You can dynamically set the properties for visibleRowCount, layoutOrientation, and selectionMode in a list.

LISTING 35.7 **ListPropertiesDemo.java**

```
 1  import java.awt.*;
 2  import java.awt.event.*;
 3  import javax.swing.*;
 4  import javax.swing.event.*;
 5
 6  public class ListPropertiesDemo extends JApplet {
 7    private JList jlst = new JList(new String[]); {"Item1",          list
 8      "Item2", "Item3", "Item4", "Item5", "Item6"});
 9    private JSpinner jspVisibleRowCount =                             spinner
10      new JSpinner(new SpinnerNumberModel(8, -1, 20, 1));
11    private JComboBox jcboLayoutOrientation =                        combo box
12      new JComboBox(new String[]{"VERTICAL (0)",
13        "VERTICAL_WRAP (1)", "HORIZONTAL_WRAP (2)"});
14    private JComboBox jcboSelectionMode =                            combo box
15      new JComboBox(new String[]{"SINGLE_SELECTION (0)",
16        "SINGLE_INTERVAL_SELECTION (1)",
17        "MULTIPLE_INTERVAL_SELECTION (2)"});
18    private JLabel jlblStatus = new JLabel();
19
20    /** Construct the applet */
21    public ListPropertiesDemo() {
22      // Place labels in a panel                                    create UI
23      JPanel panel1 = new JPanel();
24      panel1.setLayout(new GridLayout(3, 1));
25      panel1.add(new JLabel("visibleRowCount"));
26      panel1.add(new JLabel("layoutOrientation"));
27      panel1.add(new JLabel("selectionMode"));
28
```

```
29        // Place text fields in a panel
30        JPanel panel2 = new JPanel();
31        panel2.setLayout(new GridLayout(3, 1));
32        panel2.add(jspVisibleRowCount);
33        panel2.add(jcboLayoutOrientation);
34        panel2.add(jcboSelectionMode);
35
36        // Place panel1 and panel2
37        JPanel panel3 = new JPanel();
38        panel3.setLayout(new BorderLayout(5, 5));
39        panel3.add(panel1, BorderLayout.WEST);
40        panel3.add(panel2, BorderLayout.CENTER);
41
42        // Place elements in the applet
43        add(panel3, BorderLayout.NORTH);
44        add(new JScrollPane(jlst), BorderLayout.CENTER);
45        add(jlblStatus, BorderLayout.SOUTH);
46
47        // Set initial property values
48        jlst.setFixedCellWidth(50);
49        jlst.setFixedCellHeight(20);
50        jlst.setSelectionMode(ListSelectionModel.SINGLE_SELECTION);
51
52        // Register listeners
53        jspVisibleRowCount.addChangeListener(new ChangeListener() {
54          public void stateChanged(ChangeEvent e) {
55            jlst.setVisibleRowCount(
56              ((Integer)jspVisibleRowCount.getValue()).intValue());
57          }
58        });
59
60        jcboLayoutOrientation.addActionListener(new ActionListener() {
61          public void actionPerformed(ActionEvent e) {
62            jlst.setLayoutOrientation(
63              jcboLayoutOrientation.getSelectedIndex());
64          }
65        });
66
67        jcboSelectionMode.addActionListener(new ActionListener() {
68          public void actionPerformed(ActionEvent e) {
69            jlst.setSelectionMode(
70              jcboSelectionMode.getSelectedIndex());
71          }
72        });
73
74        jlst.addListSelectionListener(new ListSelectionListener() {
75          public void valueChanged(ListSelectionEvent e) {
76            Object[] values = jlst.getSelectedValues();
77            String display = "";
78
79            for (int i = 0; i < values.length; i++) {
80              display += (String)values[i] + " ";
81            }
82
83            jlblStatus.setText(display);
84          }
85        });
86      }
87  }
```

Margin notes:

spinner listener (line 53)

combo box listener (line 60)

combo box listener (line 67)

list listener (line 74)

main method omitted (line 87)

A `JList` is created with six string values (lines 7–8). A `JSpinner` is created using a `SpinnerNumberModel` with initial value `8`, minimum value `–1`, maximum value `20`, and step `1` (lines 9–10). A `JComboBox` is created with string values `VERTICAL` (`0`), `VERTICAL_WRAP` (`1`), and `HORIZONTAL_WRAP` (`2`) for choosing layout orientation (lines 11–13). A `JComboBox` is created with string values `SINGLE_SELECTION` (`0`), `INTERVAL_SELECTION` (`1`), and `MULTIPLE_INTERVAL_SELECTION` (`2`) for choosing a selection mode (lines 14–17). A `JLabel` is created to display the selected elements in the list (lines 18).

A `JList` does not support scrolling. To create a scrollable list, create a `JScrollPane` and add an instance of `JList` to it (line 44).

The fixed list cell width and height are specified in lines 48–49. The default selection mode is multiple-interval selection. Line 50 sets the selection mode to single selection.

When a new visible row count is selected from the spinner, the `setVisibleRowCount` method is used to set the count (lines 53–58). When a new layout orientation is selected from the `jcboLayoutOrientation` combo box, the `setLayoutOrientation` method is used to set the layout orientation (lines 60–65). Note that the constant values for `VERTICAL`, `VERTICAL_WRAP`, and `HORIZONTAL_WRAP` are `0`, `1`, and `2`, which correspond to the index values of these items in the combo box. When a new selection mode is selected from the `jcboSelectionMode` combo box, the `setSelectionMode` method is used to set the selection mode (lines 67–72). Note that the constant values for `SINGLE_SELECTION`, `SINGLE_INTERVAL_SELECTION`, and `MULTIPLE_INTERVAL_SELECTION` are `0`, `1`, and `2`, which correspond to the index value of these items in the combo box.

`JList` generates `javax.swing.event.ListSelectionEvent` to notify the listeners of the selections. The listener must implement the `valueChanged` handler to process the event. When the user selects an item in the list, the `valueChanged` handler is executed, which gets the selected items and displays all the items in the label (lines 74–85).

35.8 List Models

The preceding example constructs a list with a fixed set of strings. If you want to add new items to the list or delete existing items, you have to use a list model. This section introduces list models.

The `JList` class delegates the responsibilities of storing and maintaining data to its data model. The `JList` class itself does not have methods for adding or removing items from the list. These methods are supported in `ListModel`, as shown in Figure 35.20.

All list models implement the `ListModel` interface, which defines the registration methods for `ListDataEvent`. The instances of `ListDataListener` are notified when the items in the list are modified. `ListModel` also defines the methods `getSize` and `getElementAt`. The `getSize` method returns the length of the list, and the `getElementAt` method returns the element at the specified index.

`AbstractListModel` implements the `ListModel` and `Serializable` interfaces. `AbstractListModel` implements the registration methods in the `ListModel`, but does not implement the `getSize` and `getElementAt` methods.

`DefaultListModel` extends `AbstractListModel` and implements the two methods `getSize` and `getElementAt`, which are not implemented by `AbstractListModel`.

The methods in `DefaultListModel` are similar to those in the `java.util.Vector` class. You use the `add` method to insert an element to the list, the `remove` method to remove an element from the list, the `clear` method to clear the list, the `getSize` method to return the number of elements in the list, and the `getElementAt` method to retrieve an element. In fact, the `DefaultListModel` stores data in an instance of `Vector`, which is essentially a resizable array. Swing components were developed before the Java Collections Framework. In future implementations, `Vector` may be replaced by `java.util.ArrayList`.

FIGURE 35.20 `ListModel` stores and manages data in a list.

 Note

In most cases, if you create a Swing GUI object without specifying a model, an instance of the default model class is created. But this is not true for `JList`. By default, the `model` property in `JList` is not an instance of `DefaultListModel`. To use a list model, you should explicitly create one using `DefaultListModel`.

default list model

Listing 35.8 gives an example that creates a list using a list model and allows the user to add and delete items in the list, as shown in Figure 35.21. When the user clicks the *Add new item* button, an input dialog box is displayed to receive a new item.

LISTING 35.8 `ListModelDemo.java`

```
1 import java.awt.*;
2 import java.awt.event.*;
3 import javax.swing.*;
4
```

```
 5 public class ListModelDemo extends JApplet {                              list model
 6   private DefaultListModel listModel = new DefaultListModel();
 7   private JList jlst = new JList(listModel);                              list
 8   private JButton jbtAdd = new JButton("Add new item");
 9   private JButton jbtRemove = new JButton("Remove selected item");
10
11   /** Construct the applet */
12   public ListModelDemo() {
13     // Add items to the list model
14     listModel.addElement("Item1");                                       add items
15     listModel.addElement("Item2");
16     listModel.addElement("Item3");
17     listModel.addElement("Item4");
18     listModel.addElement("Item5");
19     listModel.addElement("Item6");
20
21     JPanel panel = new JPanel();
22     panel.add(jbtAdd);
23     panel.add(jbtRemove);
24
25     add(panel, BorderLayout.NORTH);
26     add(new JScrollPane(jlst), BorderLayout.CENTER);
27
28     // Register listeners
29     jbtAdd.addActionListener(new ActionListener() {                      button listener
30       public void actionPerformed(ActionEvent e) {
31         String newItem =
32           JOptionPane.showInputDialog("Enter a new item");
33
34         if (newItem != null)
35           if (jlst.getSelectedIndex() == -1)
36             listModel.addElement(newItem);
37           else
38             listModel.add(jlst.getSelectedIndex(), newItem);
39       }
40     });
41
42     jbtRemove.addActionListener(new ActionListener() {                   button listener
43       public void actionPerformed(ActionEvent e) {
44         listModel.remove(jlst.getSelectedIndex());
45       }
46     });
47   }
48 }                                                                        main method omitted
```

FIGURE 35.21 You can add elements and remove elements in a list using list models.

The program creates `listModel` (line 6), which is an instance of `DefaultListModel`, and uses it to manipulate data in the list. The model enables you to add and remove items in the list.

A list is created from the list model (line 7). The initial elements are added into the model using the `addElement` method (lines 13–19).

To add an element, the user clicks the *Add new item* button to display an input dialog box. Type a new item in the dialog box. The new item is inserted before the currently selected element in the list (line 38). If no element is selected, the new element is appended to the list (line 36).

To remove an element, the user has to select the element and then click the *Remove selected item* button. Note that only the first selected item is removed. You can modify the program to remove all the selected items (see Exercise 35.6).

What would happen if you clicked the *Remove selected item* button but no items were currently selected? This would cause an error. To fix it, see Exercise 35.6.

35.9 List Cell Renderer

The preceding example displays items as strings in a list. JList is very flexible and versatile, and it can be used to display images and GUI components in addition to simple text. This section introduces list cell renderers for displaying graphics.

In addition to delegating data storage and processing to list models, JList delegates the rendering of list cells to list cell renderers. All list cell renderers implement the ListCellRenderer interface, which defines a single method, getListCellRendererComponent, as follows:

```
public Component getListCellRendererComponent
  (JList list, Object value, int index, boolean isSelected,
  boolean cellHasFocus)
```

This method is passed with a list, the value associated with the cell, the index of the value, and information regarding whether the value is selected and whether the cell has the focus. The component returned from the method is painted on the cell in the list. By default, JList uses DefaultListCellRenderer to render its cells. The DefaultListCellRenderer class implements ListCellRenderer, extends JLabel, and can display either a string or an icon, but not both in the same cell.

For example, you can use JList's default cell renderer to display strings, as shown in Figure 35.22(a), using the following code:

```
JList list = new JList(new String[]{"Denmark", "Germany",
  "China", "India", "Norway", "UK", "US"});
```

(a) Strings   (b) Icons   (c) Icons and strings

FIGURE 35.22 The cell renderer displays list items in a list.

You can use JList's default cell renderer to display icons, as shown in Figure 35.22(b), using the following code:

```
ImageIcon denmarkIcon = new ImageIcon(getClass().getResource(
  "image/denmarkIcon.gif"));
...
JList list = new JList(new ImageIcon[]{denmarkIcon, germanyIcon,
  chinaIcon, indiaIcon, norwayIcon, ukIcon, usIcon});
```

How do you display a string along with an icon in one cell, as shown in Figure 35.22(c)? You need to create a custom renderer by implementing `ListCellRenderer`, as shown in Figure 35.23.

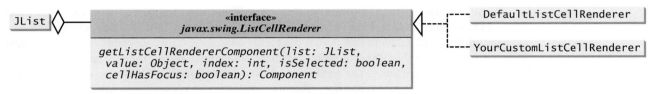

FIGURE 35.23 `ListCellRenderer` defines how cells are rendered in a list.

Suppose a list is created as follows:

```
JList list = new JList(new Object[][]{{denmarkIcon, "Denmark"},
  {germanyIcon, "Germany"}, {chinaIcon, "China"},
  {indiaIcon, "India"}, {norwayIcon, "Norway"}, {ukIcon, "UK"},
  {usIcon, "US"}});
```

Each item in the list is an array that consists of an icon and a string. You can create a custom cell renderer that retrieves an icon and a string from the list data model and display them in a label. The custom cell renderer class is given in Listing 35.9.

LISTING 35.9 MyListCellRenderer.java

```
 1 import java.awt.*;
 2 import javax.swing.*;
 3 import javax.swing.border.*;
 4
 5 public class MyListCellRenderer implements ListCellRenderer {
 6   private JLabel jlblCell = new JLabel(" ", JLabel.LEFT);         cell component
 7   private Border lineBorder =
 8     BorderFactory.createLineBorder(Color.black, 1);
 9   private Border emptyBorder =
10     BorderFactory.createEmptyBorder(2, 2, 2, 2);
11
12   /** Implement this method in ListCellRenderer */
13   public Component getListCellRendererComponent
14      (JList list, Object value, int index, boolean isSelected,
15       boolean cellHasFocus) {
16     Object[] pair = (Object[])value; // Cast value into an array
17     jlblCell.setOpaque(true);
18     jlblCell.setIcon((ImageIcon)pair[0]);                         set icon
19     jlblCell.setText(pair[1].toString());                        set text
20
21     if (isSelected) {
22       jlblCell.setForeground(list.getSelectionForeground());     cell selected
23       jlblCell.setBackground(list.getSelectionBackground());
24     }
25     else {
26       jlblCell.setForeground(list.getForeground());
27       jlblCell.setBackground(list.getBackground());
28     }
29
30     jlblCell.setBorder(cellHasFocus ? lineBorder : emptyBorder);
31
```

return rendering cell

```
32        return jlblCell;
33    }
34 }
```

The **MyListCellRenderer** class implements the **getListCellRendererComponent** method in the **ListCellRenderer** interface. This method is passed with the parameters **list**, **value**, **index**, **isSelected**, and **isFocused** (lines 13–15). The **value** represents the current item value. In this case, it is an array consisting of two elements. The first element is an image icon (line 18). The second element is a string (line 19). Both image icon and string are displayed on a label. The **getListCellRendererComponent** method returns the label (line 32), which is painted on the cell in the list.

If the cell is selected, the background and foreground of the cell are set to the list's selection background and foreground (lines 22–23). If the cell is focused, the cell's border is set to the line border (line 30); otherwise, it is set to the empty border (line 30). The empty border serves as a divider between the cells.

 Note

any GUI renderer

The example in Listing 35.9 uses a **JLabel** as a renderer. You may use any GUI component as a renderer, returned from the **getListCellRendererComponent** method.

Let us develop an example (Listing 35.10) that creates a list of countries and displays the flag image and name for each country as one item in the list, as shown in Figure 35.24. When a country is selected in the list, its flag is displayed in a label next to the list.

Small icon ———→ ←——— Large icon

FIGURE 35.24 The image and the text are displayed in the list cell.

LISTING 35.10 ListCellRendererDemo.java

```
1  import javax.swing.*;
2  import javax.swing.event.*;
3  import java.awt.*;
4
5  public class ListCellRendererDemo extends JApplet {
6    private final static int NUMBER_OF_NATIONS = 7;
7    private String[] nations = new String[]
8      {"Denmark", "Germany", "China", "India", "Norway", "UK", "US"};
9    private ImageIcon[] icons = new ImageIcon[NUMBER_OF_NATIONS];
10   private ImageIcon[] bigIcons = new ImageIcon[NUMBER_OF_NATIONS];
11
12   // Create a list model
13   private DefaultListModel listModel = new DefaultListModel();
```

nation strings

small icons
big icons

list model

```
14
15      // Create a list using the list model
16      private JList jlstNations = new JList(listModel);                          list
17
18      // Create a list cell renderer
19      private ListCellRenderer renderer = new MyListCellRenderer();              list cell renderer
20
21      // Create a split pane
22      private JSplitPane jSplitPane1 = new JSplitPane();                         split pane
23
24      // Create a label for displaying iamge
25      private JLabel jlblImage = new JLabel("", JLabel.CENTER);                   image label
26
27      /** Construct ListCellRenderer */
28      public ListCellRendererDemo() {
29        // Load small and large image icons
30        for (int i = 0; i < NUMBER_OF_NATIONS; i++) {
31          icons[i] = new ImageIcon(getClass().getResource(                       load image icons
32            "image/flagIcon" + i + ".gif"));
33          listModel.addElement(new Object[]{icons[i], nations[i]});              add elements
34
35          bigIcons[i] = new ImageIcon(getClass().getResource(                    load image icons
36            "image/flag" + i + ".gif"));
37        }
38
39        // Set list cell renderer
40        jlstNations.setCellRenderer(renderer);                                   set renderer
41        jlstNations.setPreferredSize(new Dimension(200, 200));
42        jSplitPane1.setLeftComponent(new JScrollPane(jlstNations));
43        jSplitPane1.setRightComponent(jlblImage);
44        jlstNations.setSelectedIndex(0);
45        jlblImage.setIcon(bigIcons[0]);
46        add(jSplitPane1, BorderLayout.CENTER);
47
48        // Register listener
49        jlstNations.addListSelectionListener(new ListSelectionListener() {       list listener
50          public void valueChanged(ListSelectionEvent e) {
51            jlblImage.setIcon(bigIcons[jlstNations.getSelectedIndex()]);
52          }
53        });
54      }
55    }                                                                            main method omitted
```

Two types of icons are used in this program. The small icons are created from files
flagIcon0.gif, ..., **flagIcon6.gif** (lines 31–32). These image files are the flags for Denmark, Germany, China, India, Norway, UK, and US. The small icons are rendered inside the list.
The large icons for the same countries are created from files **flag0.gif**, ..., **flag6.gif**
(lines 35–36). The large icons are displayed on a label on the right side of the split pane.

The **ListCellRendererDemo** class creates a list model (line 13) and adds the items to
the model (line 33). Each item is an array of two elements (image icon and string). The list is
created using the list model (line 16). The list cell renderer is created (line 19) and associated
with the list (line 40).

The **ListCellRendererDemo** class creates a split pane (line 22) and places the list on the
left (line 42) and a label on the right (line 43).

When you choose a country in the list, the list-selection event handler is invoked (lines
49–53) to set a new image to the label in the right side of the split pane (line 51).

35.10 **JComboBox** and its Models

The basic features of JComboBox were introduced in §16.8, "Combo Boxes," without using combo box models. This section introduces combo models and discusses the use of JComboBox in some detail.

A combo box is similar to a list. Combo boxes and lists are both used for selecting items from a list. A combo box allows the user to select one item at a time, whereas a list permits multiple selections. When a combo box is selected, it displays a drop-down list contained in a popup menu. The selected item can be edited in the cell as if it were a text field. Figure 35.25 shows the properties and constructors of JComboBox. The data for a combo box are stored in ComboBoxModel. You can create a combo box from a combo box model, an array of objects, or a vector.

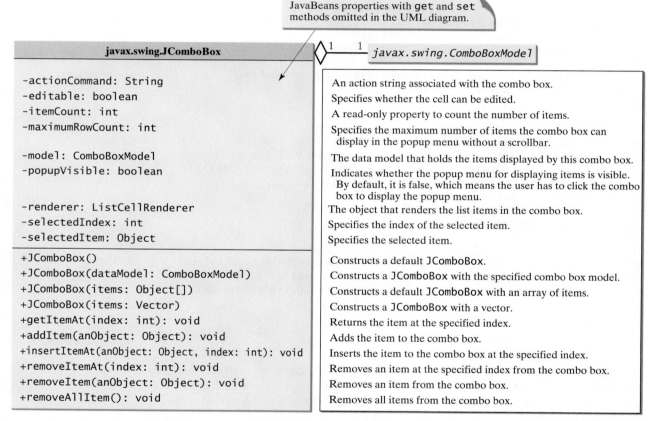

FIGURE 35.25 JComboBox displays elements in a list.

JComboBox delegates the responsibilities of storing and maintaining data to its data model. All combo box models implement the ComboBoxModel interface, which extends the ListModel interface and defines the getSelectedItem and setSelectedItem methods for retrieving and setting a selected item. The methods for adding and removing items are defined in the MutableComboBoxModel interface, which extends ComboBoxModel. When an instance of JComboBox is created without explicitly specifying a model, an instance of DefaultComboBoxModel is used. The DefaultComboBoxModel class extends AbstractListModel and implements MutableComboBoxModel, as shown in Figure 35.26.

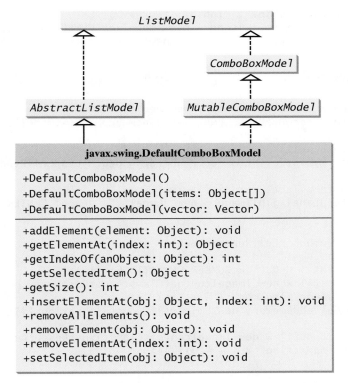

FIGURE 35.26 ComboBoxModel stores and manages data in a combo box.

Usually you don't need to use combo box models explicitly, because JComboBox contains the methods for retrieving (getItemAt, getSelectedItem, and getSelectedIndex), adding (addItem and insertItemAt), and removing (removeItem, removeItemAt, and removeAllItems) items from the list.

JComboBox can generate ActionEvent and ItemEvent, among many other events. Whenever a new item is selected, JComboBox generates ItemEvent twice, once for deselecting the previously selected item, and the other for selecting the currently selected item. JComboBox generates an ActionEvent after generating an ItemEvent.

Combo boxes render cells exactly like lists, because the combo box items are displayed in a list contained in a popup menu. Therefore, a combo box cell renderer can be created exactly like a list cell renderer by implementing the ListCellRenderer interface. Like JList, JComboBox has a default cell renderer that displays a string or an icon, but not both at the same time. To display a combination of a string and an icon, you need to create a custom renderer. The custom list cell renderer MyListCellRenderer in Listing 35.9 can be used as a combo box cell renderer without any modification.

Listing 35.11 gives an example that creates a combo box to display the flag image and name for each country as one item in the list, as shown in Figure 35.27. When a country is selected in the list, its flag is displayed in a panel below the combo box.

LISTING 35.11 ComboBoxCellRendererDemo.java

```
1 import java.awt.*;
2 import java.awt.event.*;
3 import javax.swing.*;
4
5 public class ComboBoxCellRendererDemo extends JApplet {
6   private final static int NUMBER_OF_NATIONS = 7;
7   private String[] nations = new String[] {"Denmark",
```

nation strings

```
  8      "Germany", "China", "India", "Norway", "UK", "US"};
  9    private ImageIcon[] icons = new ImageIcon[NUMBER_OF_NATIONS];
 10    private ImageIcon[] bigIcons = new ImageIcon[NUMBER_OF_NATIONS];
 11
 12    // Create a combo box model
 13    private DefaultComboBoxModel model = new DefaultComboBoxModel();
 14
 15    // Create a combo box with the specified model
 16    private JComboBox jcboCountries = new JComboBox(model);
 17
 18    // Create a list cell renderer
 19    private MyListCellRenderer renderer = new MyListCellRenderer();
 20
 21    // Create a label for displaying iamge
 22    private JLabel jlblImage = new JLabel("", JLabel.CENTER);
 23
 24    /** Construct the applet */
 25    public ComboBoxCellRendererDemo() {
 26      // Load small and large image icons
 27      for (int i = 0; i < NUMBER_OF_NATIONS; i++) {
 28        icons[i] = new ImageIcon(getClass().getResource(
 29          "image/flagIcon" + i + ".gif"));
 30        model.addElement(new Object[]{icons[i], nations[i]});
 31
 32        bigIcons[i] = new ImageIcon(getClass().getResource(
 33          "image/flag" + i + ".gif"));
 34      }
 35
 36      // Set list cell renderer for the combo box
 37      jcboCountries.setRenderer(renderer);
 38      jlblImage.setIcon(bigIcons[0]);
 39      add(jcboCountries, java.awt.BorderLayout.NORTH);
 40      add(jlblImage, java.awt.BorderLayout.CENTER);
 41
 42      // Register listener
 43      jcboCountries.addActionListener(new ActionListener() {
 44        public void actionPerformed(java.awt.event.ActionEvent e) {
 45          jlblImage.setIcon
 45            (bigIcons[jcboCountries.getSelectedIndex()]);
 46        }
 47      });
 48    }
 49  }
```

Side labels:
- small icons (line 9)
- big icons (line 10)
- combo box model (line 13)
- combo box (line 16)
- list cell renderer (line 19)
- image label (line 22)
- load image icons (line 28)
- add elements (line 30)
- load image icons (line 32)
- set renderer (line 37)
- action listener (line 43)
- main method omitted (line 49)

FIGURE 35.27 The image and the text are displayed in the list cell of a combo box.

The program is very similar to the preceding example in Listing 35.10. Two types of image icons are loaded for each country and stored in the arrays **icons** and **bigIcons** (lines 27–34). Each item in the combo box is an array that consists of an icon and a string (line 30).

`MyListCellRenderer`, defined in the preceding example, is used to create a cell renderer in line 19. The cell renderer is plugged into the combo box in line 37.

When you choose a country from the combo box, the action event handler is invoked (lines 44–46). This handler sets a new image on the label (line 45).

KEY TERMS

controller 1146	MVC architecture 1146
model 1146	view 1146

CHAPTER SUMMARY

- The fundamental issue in the model-view approach is to ensure consistency between the views and the model. Any change in the model should be notified to the dependent views, and all the views should display the same data consistently. The model can be implemented as a source with appropriate event and event listener registration methods. The view can be implemented as a listener. Thus, if data are changed in the model, the view will be notified.

- Every Swing user interface component (e.g., `JButton`, `JTextField`, `JList`, and `JComboBox`) has a property named *model* that refers to its data model. The data model is defined in an interface whose name ends with `Model` (e.g., `SpinnerModel`, `ListModel`, `ListSelectionModel`, and `ComboBoxModel`).

- Most simple Swing components (e.g., `JButton`, `JTextField`, `JTextArea`) contain some properties of their models, and these properties can be accessed and modified directly from the component without the existence of the model being known.

- A `JSpinner` is displayed as a text field with a pair of tiny arrow buttons on its right side that enable the user to select numbers, dates, or values from an ordered sequence. A `JSpinner`'s sequence value is defined by the `SpinnerModel` interface. `AbstractSpinnerModel` is a convenient abstract class that implements `SpinnerModel` and provides the implementation for its registration/deregistration methods. `SpinnerListModel`, `SpinnerNumberModel`, and `SpinnerDateModel` are concrete implementations of `SpinnerModel`. `SpinnerNumberModel` represents a sequence of numbers with properties `maximum`, `minimum`, and `stepSize`. `SpinnerDateModel` represents a sequence of dates. `SpinnerListModel` can store a list of any object values.

- A `JSpinner` has a single child component, called the *editor*, which is responsible for displaying the current element or value of the model. Four editors are defined as static inner classes inside `JSpinner`: `JSpinner.DefaultEditor`, `JSpinner.NumberEditor`, `JSpinner.DateEditor`, and `JSpinner.ListEditor`.

- `JList` has two supporting models: a list model and a list-selection model. The *list model* is for storing and processing data. The *list-selection model* is for selecting items. By default, items are rendered as strings or icons. You can also create a custom renderer implementing the `ListCellRenderer` interface.

- `JComboBox` delegates the responsibilities of storing and maintaining data to its data model. All combo box models implement the `ComboBoxModel` interface, which extends the `ListModel` interface and defines the `getSelectedItem` and `setSelectedItem` methods for retrieving and setting a selected item. The methods for adding and removing items are defined in the `MutableComboBoxModel` interface, which extends `ComboBoxModel`. When an instance of `JComboBox` is created without explicitly specifying a model, an instance of `DefaultComboBoxModel` is used. The `DefaultComboBoxModel` class extends `AbstractListModel` and implements `MutableComboBoxModel`.

■ Combo boxes render cells exactly like lists, because the combo box items are displayed in a list contained in a popup menu. Therefore, a combo box cell renderer can be created exactly like a list cell renderer by implementing the `ListCellRenderer` interface.

REVIEW QUESTIONS

Sections 35.2–35.3

35.1 What is model-view-controller architecture?

35.2 How do you do implement models, views, and controllers?

35.3 What are the variations of MVC architecture?

Section 35.4 Swing Model-View-Controller Architecture

35.4 Does each Swing GUI component (except containers such as `JPanel`) have a property named `model`? Is the type of `model` the same for all the components?

35.5 Does each model interface have a default implementation class? If so, does a Swing component use the default model class if no model is specified?

Sections 35.5–35.6

35.6 If you create a `JSpinner` without specifying a data model, what is the default model?

35.7 What is the internal data structure for storing data in `SpinnerListModel`? How do you convert an array to a list?

Sections 35.7–35.9

35.8 Does `JList` have a method, such as `addItem`, for adding an item to a list? How do you add items to a list? Can `JList` display icons and custom GUI objects in a list? Can a list item be edited? How do you initialize data in a list? How do you specify the maximum number of visible rows in a list without scrolling? How do you specify the height of a list cell? How do you specify the horizontal margin of list cells?

35.9 How do you create a list model? How do you add items to a list model? How do you remove items from a list model?

35.10 What are the three list-selection modes? Can you set the selection modes directly in an instance of `JList`? How do you obtain the selected item(s)?

35.11 How do you create a custom list cell renderer?

35.12 What is the handler for handling the `ListSelectionEvent`?

Section 35.10 JComboBox

35.13 Can multiple items be selected from a combo box? Can a combo box item be edited? How do you specify the maximum number of visible rows in a combo box without scrolling? Can you specify the height of a combo box cell using a method in `JComboBox`? How do you obtain the selected item in a combo box?

35.14 How do you add or remove items from a combo box?

35.15 Why is the cell renderer for a combo box the same as the renderer for a list?

PROGRAMMING EXERCISES

Section 35.2 MVC

35.1* (*Creating MVC components*) Create a model, named `ChartModel`, which holds data in an array of double elements named `data`, and the names for the data in an array of strings named `dataName`. For example, the enrollment data {200, 40, 50, 100, 40} stored in the array `data` are for {"CS", "Math", "Chem", "Biol", "Phys"} in the array `dataName`. These two properties have their respective get methods, but not individual set methods. Both properties are set together in the `setChartData(String[] newDataName, double[] newData)` method so that they can be displayed properly. Create a view named `PieChart` to present the data in a pie chart, and create a view named `BarChart` to present the data in a bar chart, as shown in Figure 35.28(a).

(a)   (b)

FIGURE 35.28 (a) The two views, `PieChart` and `BarChart`, receive data from the `ChartModel`; (b) Clicking the eclipse button displays the color chooser dialog box for specifying a color.

(*Hint*: Each pie represents a percentage of the total data. Color the pie using the colors from an array named colors, which is {`Color.red`, `Color.yellow`, `Color.green`, `Color.blue`, `Color.cyan`, `Color.magenta`, `Color.orange`, `Color.pink`, `Color.darkGray`}. Use `colors[i % colors.length]` for the *i*th pie. Use black color to display the data names.)

35.2* (*Revising Listing 35.3 CircleController.java*) `CircleController` uses a text field to obtain a new radius and a combo box to obtain a Boolean value to specify whether the circle is filled. Add a new row in `CircleController` to let the user choose color using the `JColorChooser` component, as shown in Figure 35.28(b). The new row consists of a label with text Color, a label to display color, and an eclipse button. The user can click the eclipse button to display a `JColorChooser` dialog box. Once the user selects a color, the color is displayed as the background for the label on the left of the eclipse button.

Sections 35.5–35.6

35.3** (*Synchronizing spinners*) The date spinner is synchronized with the day, month, and year spinners in Listing 35.6, SpinnerModelEditorDemo.java. Improve it to synchronize the day, month, and year spinners with the date spinner. In other words, when a new value is selected in the date spinner, the values in the day, month, and year spinners are updated accordingly.

35.4* (*Custom spinner model*) Develop a custom spinner model that represents a sequence of numbers of power 2—that is, 1, 2, 4, 8, 16, 32, and so on. Your model should implement `AbstractSpinnerModel`. The registration/dereg-istration methods for `ChangeListener` have already been implemented in `AbstractSpinnerModel`. You need to implement `getNextValue()`, `getPreviousValue()`, `getValue()`, and `setValue(Object)` methods.

35.5* (*Reversing the numbers displayed in a spinner*) The numbers displayed in a spinner increase when the up-arrow button is clicked and decrease when the down-arrow button is clicked. You can reverse the sequence by creating a new model that extends `SpinnerNumberModel` and overrides the `getNextValue` and `getPreviousValue` methods.

Sections 35.7–35.9

35.6* (*Removing selected items in a list*) Modify Listing 35.8, ListModelDemo.java, to meet the following requirements:

- Remove all the selected items from the list when the *Remove selected item* button is clicked.
- Enable the items to be deleted using the DELETE key.

35.7* (*Custom list cell renderer*) Listing 35.10, ListCellRendererDemo.java, has two types of images for each country. The small images are used for display in the list, and the large ones are used for display outside the list. Assume that only the large images are available. Rewrite the custom cell renderer to use a `JPanel` instead of a `JLabel` for rendering a cell. Each cell consists of an image and a string. Display the image in an `ImageViewer` and the string in a label. The `ImageViewer` component was introduced in Listing 13.15, ImageViewer.java. The image can be stretched in an `ImageViewer`. Set the dimension of an image viewer to 32 by 32, as shown in Figure 35.29. Revise Listing 35.10 to test the new custom cell renderer.

FIGURE 35.29 `ImageViewer` is used to render the image in the list.

35.8* (*Deleting selected items in a list using the DELETE key*) Modify Listing 35.10, ListCellRendererDemo.java, to delete selected items from the list using the DELETE key. After some items are deleted from the list, the index of a select-ed item in the list does not match the index of the item in the `bigIcons` array. As a result, you cannot use the image icon in the `bigIcons` array to display the image to the right side of the split pane. Revise the program to retrieve the icon from the selected item in the list and display it, as shown in Figure 35.30.

FIGURE 35.30 Images in the list are also used for display in the label placed in the right side of a split pane.

35.9**   (*Rendering figures*) Create a program that shows a list of geometrical shapes along with a label in an instance of `JList`, as shown in Figure 35.31(a). Display the selected figure in a panel when selecting a figure from the list. The figures can be drawn using the `FigurePanel` class in Listing 14.5, FigurePanel.java.

35.10**   (*List of clocks*) Write a program that displays a list of cities and their local times in a clock, as shown in Figure 35.31(b). When a city is selected in the list, its clock is displayed in a large picture on the right.

(a)   (b)

FIGURE 35.31   (a) The list displays geometrical shapes and their names; (b) The list displays cities and clocks.

Section 35.10 JComboBox

35.11**   (*Creating custom cell renderer in a combo box*) Create a program that shows a list of geometrical shapes along with a label in a combo box, as shown in Figure 35.32(a). This exercise may share the list cell renderer with Exercise 35.9.

(a)   (b)

FIGURE 35.32   (a) The combo box contains a list of geometrical shapes and the shape names. (b) The combo box contains a list of color names, each using its own color for its foreground.

35.12**   (*Rendering colored text*) Write a program that enables the user to choose the foreground colors for a label, as shown in Figure 35.32(b). The combo box contains 13 standard colors (BLACK, BLUE, CYAN, DARK_GRAY, GRAY, GREEN, LIGHT_GRAY, MAGENTA, ORANGE, PINK, RED, WHITE, YELLOW). Each color name in the combo box uses its own color for its foreground.

35.13*   (*Deleting a selected item in a combo box using the DELETE key*) Modify Listing 35.11, ComboBoxCellRendererDemo.java, to delete the selected item from the combo box using the DELETE key.

Comprehensive

35.14* (*Calendar*) Write a program that controls a calendar using a spinner, as shown in Figure 35.7. Use the `CalendarPanel` class (see Listing 31.4) to display the calendar.

CHAPTER 36

JTABLE AND JTREE

Objectives

- To display tables using `JTable` (§36.2).

- To process rows and columns using `TableModel`, `DefaultTableModel`, `TableColumnModel`, `DefaultTableColumnModel`, and `ListSelectionModel` (§§36.3–36.5).

- To enable auto sort and filtering on table model (§36.4).

- To add rows and columns, delete rows and columns (§36.5).

- To render and edit table cells using the default renderers and editors (§36.6).

- To render and edit table cells using the custom renderers and editors (§36.7).

- To handle table model events (§36.8).

- To display data in a tree hierarchy using `JTree` (§36.9).

- To model the structure of a tree using using `TreeModel` and `DefaultTreeModel` (§36.10).

- To add, remove, and process tree nodes using `TreeNode`, `DefaultMutableTreeNode`, and `TreePath` (§36.11).

- To select tree nodes and paths using `TreeSelectionModel` and `DefaultTreeSe-lectionModel` (§36.12).

- To render and edit tree nodes using the default and custom renderers and editors (§36.14).

36.1 Introduction

The preceding chapter introduced the model-view architecture, Swing MVC, and the models in **JSpinner**, **JList**, and **JComboBox**. This chapter introduces **JTable** and **JTree**, and how to use the models to process data in **JTable** and **JTree**.

36.2 **JTable**

JTable is a Swing component that displays data in rows and columns in a two-dimensional grid, as shown in Figure 36.1.

Country	Capital	Population in Millions	Democracy
USA	Washington DC	280	true
Canada	Ottawa	32	true
United Kingdom	London	60	true
Germany	Berlin	83	true
France	Paris	60	true
Norway	Oslo	4.5	true
India	New Delhi	1046	true

FIGURE 36.1 **JTable** displays data in a table.

JTable doesn't directly support scrolling. To create a scrollable table, you need to create a **JScrollPane** and add an instance of **JTable** to the scroll pane. If a table is not placed in a scroll pane, its column header will not be visible, because the column header is placed in the header of the view port of a scroll pane.

JTable has three supporting models: a table model, a column model, and a list-selection model. The *table model* is for storing and processing data. The *column model* represents all the columns in the table. The *list-selection model* is the same as the one used by **JList** for selecting rows, columns, and cells in a table. **JTable** also has two useful supporting classes, **TableColumn** and **JTableHeader**. **TableColumn** contains the information on a particular column. **JTableHeader** can be used to display the header of a **JTable**. Each column has a default editor and renderer. You can also create a custom editor by implementing the **TableCellEditor** interface, and create a custom renderer by implementing the **TableCellRenderer** interface. The relationship of these interfaces and classes is shown in Figure 36.2.

FIGURE 36.2 **JTable** contains many supporting interfaces and classes.

Note

All the supporting interfaces and classes for **JTable** are grouped in the `javax.swing.table` package.

Figure 36.3 shows the constructors, properties, and methods of **JTable**.

> JavaBeans properties with `get` and `set` methods omitted in the UML diagram.

javax.swing.JTable	
-autoCreateColumnsFromModel: boolean	Indicates whether the columns are created in the table (default: true).
-autoResizeMode: int	Specifies how columns are resized (default: SUBSEQUENT_COLUMNS).
-cellEditor: TableCellEditor	Specifies a cell editor.
-columnModel: TableColumnModel	Maintains the table column data.
-columnSelectionAllowed: boolean	Specifies whether the column can be selected (default: false).
-editingColumn: int	Specifies the column of the cell that is currently being edited.
-editingRow: int	Specifies the row of the cell that is currently being edited.
-gridColor: java.awt.Color	The color used to draw grid lines (default: GRAY).
-intercellSpacing: Dimension	Specifies horizontal and vertical margins between cells (default: 1, 1).
-model: TableModel	Maintains the table model.
-rowCount: int	Read-only property that counts the number of rows in the table.
-rowHeight: int	Specifies the row height of the table (default: 16 pixels).
-rowMargin: int	Specifies the vertical margin between rows (default: 1 pixel).
-rowSelectionAllowed: boolean	Specifies whether the rows can be selected (default: true).
-selectionBackground: java.awt.Color	The background color of selected cells.
-selectionForeground: java.awt.Color	The foreground color of selected cells.
-showGrid: boolean	Specify whether the grid lines are displayed (write-only, default: true).
-selectionMode: int	Specifies a selection mode (write-only).
-selectionModel: ListSelectionModel	Specifies a selection model.
-showHorizontalLines: boolean	Specifies whether the horizontal grid lines are displayed (default: true).
-showVerticalLines: boolean	Specifies whether the vertical grid lines are displayed (default: true).
-tableHeader: JTableHeader	Specifies a table header.
+JTable()	Creates a default JTable with all the default models.
+JTable(numRows: int, numColumns: int)	Creates a JTable with the specified number of empty rows and columns.
+JTable(rowData: Object[][], columnData: Object[])	Creates a JTable with the specified row data and column header names.
+JTable(dm: TableModel)	Creates a JTable with the specified table model.
+JTable(dm: TableModel, cm: TableColumnModel)	Creates a JTable with the specified table model and table column model.
+JTable(dm: TableModel, cm: TableColumnModel, sm: ListSelectionModel)	Creates a JTable with the specified table model, table column model, and selection model.
+JTable(rowData: Vector, columnNames: Vector)	Creates a JTable with the specified row data and column data in vectors.
+addColumn(aColumn: TableColumn): void	Adds a new column to the table.
+clearSelection(): void	Deselects all selected columns and rows.
+editCellAt(row: int, column: int): void	Edits the cell if it is editable.
+getDefaultEditor(column: Class): TableCellEditor	Returns the default editor for the column.
+getDefaultRenderer(col: Class): TableCellRenderer	Returns the default renderer for the column.
+setDefaultEditor(column: Class, editor: TableCellEditor): void	Sets the default editor for the column.
+setDefaultRenderer(column: Class, editor: TableCellRenderer): void	Sets the default renderer for the column.

FIGURE 36.3 The `JTable` class is for creating, customizing, and manipulating tables.

The `JTable` class contains seven constructors for creating tables. You can create a table using its no-arg constructor, its models, row data in a two-dimensional array, and column header names in an array, or row data and column header names in vectors. Listing 36.1 creates a table with the row data and column names (line 20) and places it in a scroll pane (line 23). The table is displayed in Figure 36.1.

LISTING 36.1 TestTable.java

```java
1  import javax.swing.*;
2
3  public class TestTable extends JApplet {
4    // Create table column names
5    private String[] columnNames =
6      {"Country", "Capital", "Population in Millions", "Democracy"};
7
8    // Create table data
9    private Object[][] data = {
10     {"USA", "Washington DC", 280, true},
11     {"Canada", "Ottawa", 32, true},
12     {"United Kingdom", "London", 60, true},
13     {"Germany", "Berlin", 83, true},
14     {"France", "Paris", 60, true},
15     {"Norway", "Oslo", 4.5, true},
16     {"India", "New Delhi", 1046, true}
17   };
18
19   // Create a table
20   private JTable jTable1 = new JTable(data, columnNames);
21
22   public TestTable() {
23     add(new JScrollPane(jTable1));
24   }
25 }
```

column names — lines 4–6

row data — lines 8–17

create table — line 20

scroll pane — line 23

main method omitted — line 25

 Note

autoboxing

Primitive type values such as **280** and **true** in line 10 are autoboxed into **new Integer(280)** and **new Boolean(true)**.

JTable is a powerful control with a variety of properties that provide many ways to customize tables. All the frequently used properties are documented in Figure 36.3. The **autoResizeMode** property specifies how columns are resized (you can resize table columns but not rows). Possible values are:

```
JTable.AUTO_RESIZE_OFF
JTable.AUTO_RESIZE_LAST_COLUMN
JTable.AUTO_RESIZE_SUBSEQUENT_COLUMNS
JTable.AUTO_RESIZE_NEXT_COLUMN
JTable.AUTO_RESIZE_ALL_COLUMNS
```

The default mode is **JTable.AUTO_RESIZE_SUBSEQUENT_COLUMNS**. Initially, each column in the table occupies the same width (75 pixels). With **AUTO_RESIZE_OFF**, resizing a column does not affect the widths of the other columns. With **AUTO_RESIZE_LAST_COLUMN**, resizing a column affects the width of the last column. With **AUTO_RESIZE_SUBSEQUENT_COLUMNS**, resizing a column affects the widths of all the subsequent columns. With **AUTO_RESIZE_NEXT_COLUMN**, resizing a column affects the widths of the next columns. With **AUTO_RESIZE_ALL_COLUMNS**, resizing a column affects the widths of all the columns.

Listing 36.2 gives an example that demonstrates the use of several **JTable** properties. The example creates a table and allows the user to choose an Auto Resize Mode, specify the row height and margin, and indicate whether the grid is shown. A sample run of the program is shown in Figure 36.4.

FIGURE 36.4 You can specify an autoresizing mode, the table's row height and row margin, and whether to show the grid in the table.

LISTING 36.2 TablePropertiesDemo.java

```java
1  import java.awt.*;
2  import java.awt.event.*;
3  import javax.swing.*;
4  import javax.swing.event.*;
5
6  public class TablePropertiesDemo extends JApplet {
7    // Create table column names
8    private String[] columnNames =
9      {"Country", "Capital", "Population in Millions", "Democracy"};
10
11   // Create table data
12   private Object[][] rowData = {
13     {"USA", "Washington DC", 280, true},
14     {"Canada", "Ottawa", 32, true},
15     {"United Kingdom", "London", 60, true},
16     {"Germany", "Berlin", 83, true},
17     {"France", "Paris", 60, true},
18     {"Norway", "Oslo", 4.5, true},
19     {"India", "New Delhi", 1046, true}
20   };
21
22   // Create a table
23   private JTable jTable1 = new JTable(rowData, columnNames);
24
25   // Create two spinners
26   private JSpinner jspiRowHeight =
27     new JSpinner(new SpinnerNumberModel(16, 1, 50, 1));
28   private JSpinner jspiRowMargin =
29     new JSpinner(new SpinnerNumberModel(1, 1, 50, 1));
30
31   // Create a check box
32   private JCheckBox jchkShowGrid = new JCheckBox("showGrid", true);
33
34   // Create a combo box
35   private JComboBox jcboAutoResizeMode = new JComboBox(new String[]{
36     "AUTO_RESIZE_OFF", "AUTO_RESIZE_LAST_COLUMN",
37     "AUTO_RESIZE_SUBSEQUENT_COLUMNS", "AUTO_RESIZE_NEXT_COLUMN",
38     "AUTO_RESIZE_ALL_COLUMNS"});
39
40   public TablePropertiesDemo() {
41     JPanel panel1 = new JPanel();
42     panel1.add(new JLabel("rowHeight"));
43     panel1.add(jspiRowHeight);
```

column names

table data

table

spinners

combo box

create UI

```
44      panel1.add(new JLabel("rowMargin"));
45      panel1.add(jspiRowMargin);
46      panel1.add(jchkShowGrid);
47
48      JPanel panel2 = new JPanel();
49      panel2.add(new JLabel("autoResizeMode"));
50      panel2.add(jcboAutoResizeMode);
51
52      add(panel1, BorderLayout.SOUTH);
53      add(panel2, BorderLayout.NORTH);
54      add(new JScrollPane(jTable1));
55
56      // Initialize jTable1
57      jTable1.setAutoResizeMode(JTable.AUTO_RESIZE_OFF);
58      jTable1.setGridColor(Color.BLUE);
59      jTable1.setSelectionMode(ListSelectionModel.SINGLE_SELECTION);
60      jTable1.setSelectionBackground(Color.RED);
61      jTable1.setSelectionForeground(Color.WHITE);
62
63      // Register and create a listener for jspiRowHeight
64      jspiRowHeight.addChangeListener(new ChangeListener() {
65        public void stateChanged(ChangeEvent e) {
66          jTable1.setRowHeight (
67            ((Integer)(jspiRowHeight.getValue())).intValue());
68        }
69      });
70
71      // Register and create a listener for jspiRowMargin
72      jspiRowMargin.addChangeListener(new ChangeListener() {
73        public void stateChanged(ChangeEvent e) {
74          jTable1.setRowMargin (
75            ((Integer)(jspiRowMargin.getValue())).intValue());
76        }
77      });
78
79      // Register and create a listener for jchkShowGrid
80      jchkShowGrid.addActionListener(new ActionListener() {
81        public void actionPerformed(ActionEvent e) {
82          jTable1.setShowGrid (jchkShowGrid.isSelected());
83        }
84      });
85
86      // Register and create a listener for jcboAutoResizeMode
87      jcboAutoResizeMode.addActionListener(new ActionListener() {
88        public void actionPerformed(ActionEvent e) {
89          String selectedItem =
90            (String)jcboAutoResizeMode.getSelectedItem();
91
92          if (selectedItem.equals("AUTO_RESIZE_OFF"))
93            jTable1.setAutoResizeMode(JTable.AUTO_RESIZE_OFF);
94          else if (selectedItem.equals("AUTO_RESIZE_LAST_COLUMN"))
95            jTable1.setAutoResizeMode(JTable.AUTO_RESIZE_LAST_COLUMN);
96          else if (selectedItem.equals
97              ("AUTO_RESIZE_SUBSEQUENT_COLUMNS"))
98            jTable1.setAutoResizeMode(
99              JTable.AUTO_RESIZE_SUBSEQUENT_COLUMNS);
100         else if (selectedItem.equals("AUTO_RESIZE_NEXT_COLUMN"))
101           jTable1.setAutoResizeMode(JTable.AUTO_RESIZE_NEXT_COLUMN);
102         else if (selectedItem.equals("AUTO_RESIZE_ALL_COLUMNS"))
103           jTable1.setAutoResizeMode(JTable.AUTO_RESIZE_ALL_COLUMNS);
```

table properties

spinner listener

spinner listener

check-box listener

combo box listener

```
104        }
105      });
106    }
107 }
```
main method omitted

If you know the row data in advance, creating a table using the constructor `JTable-(Object[][] rowData, Object[] columnNames)` is convenient. As shown in line 23, a `JTable` is created using this constructor.

Two `JSpinner` objects (`jspiRowHeight`, `jspiRowMargin`) for selecting row height and row margin are created in lines 26–29. The initial value for `jspiRowHeight` is set to `16`, which is the default property value for `rowHeight`. The initial value for `jspiRowMargin` is set to `1`, which is the default property value for `rowMargin`. A check box (`jchkShowGrid`) is created with label showGrid and initially selected in line 32. A combo box for selecting `autoResizeMode` is created in lines 35–38.

The values of the `JTable` properties (`autoResizeMode`, `gridColor`, `selectionMode`, `selectionBackground`, and `selectionForeground`) are set in lines 57–61.

The code for processing spinners, check boxes, and combo boxes is given in lines 64–105.

36.3 Table Models and Table Column Models

`JTable` delegates data storing and processing to its table data model. A table data model must implement the `TableModel` interface, which defines the methods for registering table model listeners, manipulating cells, and obtaining row count, column count, column class, and column name.

TableModel

The `AbstractTableModel` class provides partial implementations for most of the methods in `TableModel`. It takes care of the management of listeners and provides some conveniences for generating `TableModelEvent`s and dispatching them to the listeners. To create a concrete `TableModel`, you simply extend `AbstractTableModel` and implement at least the following three methods:

AbstractTableModel

- **public int** getRowCount()

- **public int** getColumnCount()

- **public** Object getValueAt(**int** row, **int** column)

The `DefaultTableModel` class extends `AbstractTableModel` and implements these three methods. Additionally, `DefaultTableModel` provides concrete storage for data. The data are stored in a vector. The elements in the vector are arrays of objects, each of which represents an individual cell value. The methods in `DefaultTableModel` for accessing and modifying data are shown in Figure 36.5.

DefaultTableModel

Listing 36.3 gives an example that demonstrates table models. The example creates a table model (line 16), plugs the model to the table (line 20), appends a row to the table (line 25), inserts a row before the first row (line 26), removes a row with index 1 (line 28), adds a new column (line 29), and sets new values at specified cells (lines 30–32). Figure 36.6 shows the output of the program.

LISTING 36.3 TestTableModel.java

```
1 import javax.swing.*;
2 import javax.swing.table.*;
3
4 public class TestTableModel extends JApplet {
5   // Create table column names
6   private String[] columnNames =
7     {"Country", "Capital", "Population in Millions", "Democracy"};
8
9   // Create table data
10   private Object[][] data = {
```

column names

row data

```
11     {"USA", "Washington DC", 280, true},
12     {"Canada", "Ottawa", 32, true}
13   };
14
15   // Create a model
```

create table model
```
16   private DefaultTableModel tableModel =
17     new DefaultTableModel(data, columnNames);
18
19   // Create a table
```

create table
```
20   private JTable jTable1 = new JTable(tableModel);
21
22   public TestTableModel() {
```

scroll pane
```
23     add(new JScrollPane(jTable1));
24
```

add row
insert row
```
25     tableModel.addRow(new Object[]{"France", "Paris", 60, true});
26     tableModel.insertRow(0, new Object[]
27       {"India", "New Delhi", 1046, true});
```

remove row
add column
set value
```
28     tableModel.removeRow(1);
29     tableModel.addColumn("Area");
30     tableModel.setValueAt(10, 0, 4);
31     tableModel.setValueAt(20, 1, 4);
32     tableModel.setValueAt(30, 2, 4);
33   }
```

main method omitted
```
34 }
```

«interface» *javax.swing.table.TableModel*
+getColumnClass(columnIndex: int): Class
+getColumnName(columnIndex: int): String
+getColumnCount(): int
+getRowCount(): int
+getValueAt(rowIndex: int, columnIndex: int): Object
+setValueAt(aValue: Object, rowIndex: int, columnIndex: int): void
+isCellEditable(rowIndex: int, columnIndex: int): boolean
+addTableModelListener(l: TableModelListener): void
+removeTableModelListener(l: TableModelListener): void

javax.swing.table.AbstractTableModel

javax.swing.table.DefaultTableModel
+DefaultTableModel()
+DefaultTableModel(rowCount: int, columnCount: int)
+DefaultTableModel(columnNames: Object[], rowCount: int)
+DefaultTableModel(data: Object[][], columnNames: Object[])
+DefaultTableModel(columnNames: Vector, rowCount: int)
+DefaultTableModel(data: Vector, columnNames: Vector)
+DefaultTableModel(rowData: Vector, columnNames: Vector)
+addColumn(columnName: Object): void
+addColumn(columnName: Object, columnData: Vector)
+addRow(rowData: Object[]): void
+addRow(rowData: Vector): void
+getColumnCount(): int
+getDataVector(): Vector
+getRowCount(): int
+insertRow(row: int, rowData: Object[]): void
+insertRow(row: int, rowData: Vector): void
+removeRow(row: int): void
+setColumnCount(columnCount: int): void
+setColumnIdentifiers(newIdentifiers: Object[]): void
+setColumnIdentifiers(columnIdentifiers: Vector): void
+setDataVector(dataVector: Object[][], columnIdentifiers: Object[]): void
+setDataVector(dataVector: Vector, columnIdentifiers: Vector): void
+setRowCount(rowCount: int): void

FIGURE 36.5   `TableModel` stores and manages data in a table and `DefaultTableModel` provides a default implentation for `TableMobel`.

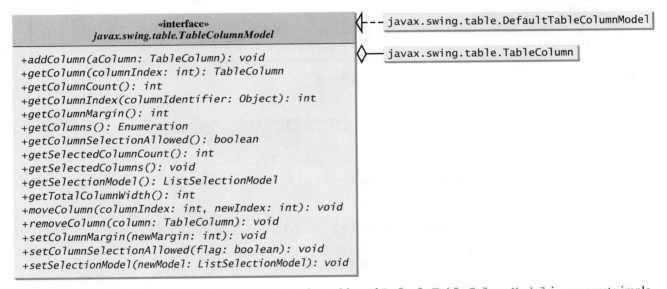

FIGURE 36.6 `TableModel` and `DefaultTableModel` contain the methods for adding, updating, and removing table data.

`TableModel` manages table data. You can add and remove rows through a `TableModel`. You can also add a column through a `TableModel`. However, you cannot remove a column through a `TableModel`. To remove a column from a `JTable`, you have to use a table column model.

Table column models manage columns in a table. They can be used to select, add, move, and remove table columns. A table column model must implement the `TableColumnModel` interface, which defines the methods for registering table column model listeners, and for accessing and manipulating columns, as shown in Figure 36.7.

`TableColumnModel`

```
              «interface»
    javax.swing.table.TableColumnModel
─────────────────────────────────────────
+addColumn(aColumn: TableColumn): void
+getColumn(columnIndex: int): TableColumn
+getColumnCount(): int
+getColumnIndex(columnIdentifier: Object): int
+getColumnMargin(): int
+getColumns(): Enumeration
+getColumnSelectionAllowed(): boolean
+getSelectedColumnCount(): int
+getSelectedColumns(): void
+getSelectionModel(): ListSelectionModel
+getTotalColumnWidth(): int
+moveColumn(columnIndex: int, newIndex: int): void
+removeColumn(column: TableColumn): void
+setColumnMargin(newMargin: int): void
+setColumnSelectionAllowed(flag: boolean): void
+setSelectionModel(newModel: ListSelectionModel): void
```

`javax.swing.table.DefaultTableColumnModel`

`javax.swing.table.TableColumn`

FIGURE 36.7 `TableColumnModel` manages columns in a table and `DefaultTableColumnModel` is a concrete implemention of it.

`DefaultTableColumnModel` is a concrete class that implements `TableColumnModel` and `PropertyChangeListener`. The `DefaultTableColumnModel` class stores its columns in a vector and contains an instance of `ListSelectionModel` for selecting columns.

`DefaultTableColumnModel`

The column model deals with all the columns in a table. The `TableColumn` class is used to model an individual column in the table. An instance of `TableColumn` for a specified column can be obtained using the `getColumn(index)` method in `TableColumnModel` or the `getColumn(columnIdentifier)` method in `JTable`.

`TableColumn`

Figure 36.8 shows the properties, constructors, and methods in `TableColumn` for manipulating column width and specifying the cell renderer, cell editor, and header renderer.

Listing 36.4 gives an example that demonstrates table column models. The example obtains the table column model from the table (line 21), moves the first column to the second (line 22), and removes the last column (lines 23). Figure 36.9 shows the output of the program.

```
        javax.swing.table.TableColumn
```

JavaBeans properties with `get` and `set` methods omitted in the UML diagram.

#cellEditor: TableCellEditor	The editor for editing a cell in this column.
#cellRenderer: TableCellRenderer	The renderer for displaying a cell in this column.
#headerRenderer: TableCellRenderer	The renderer for displaying the header of this column.
#headerValue: Object	The header value of this column.
#identifier: Object	The identifier for this column.
#maxWidth: int	The maximum width of this column.
#minWidth: int	The minimum width of this column (default: 15 pixels).
#modelIndex: int	The index of the column in the table model (default: 0).
#preferredWidth: int	The preferred width of this column (default: 75 pixels).
#resizable: boolean	Indicates whether this column can be resized (default: true).
#width: int	Specifies the width of this column (default: 75 pixels).
+TableColumn()	Constructs a default table column.
+TableColumn(modelIndex: int)	Constructs a table column for the specified column.
+TableColumn(modelIndex: int, width: int)	Constructs a table column with the specified column and width.
+TableColumn(modelIndex: int, width: int, cellRenderer: TableCellRenderer)	Constructs a table column with the specified column, width, and cell renderer.
+sizeWidthToFit(): void	Resizes the column to fit the width of its header cell.

FIGURE 36.8 The `TableColumn` class models a single column.

FIGURE 36.9 `TableColumnModel` contains the methods for moving and removing columns.

LISTING 36.4 TestTableColumnModel.java

```java
 1  import javax.swing.*;
 2  import javax.swing.table.*;
 3
 4  public class TestTableColumnModel extends JApplet {
 5    // Create table column names
 6    private String[] columnNames =
 7      {"Country", "Capital", "Population in Millions", "Democracy"};
 8
 9    // Create table data
10    private Object[][] data = {
11      {"USA", "Washington DC", 280, true},
12      {"Canada", "Ottawa", 32, true}
13    };
14
15    // Create a table
16    private JTable jTable1 = new JTable(data, columnNames);
17
18    public TestTableColumnModel() {
19      add(new JScrollPane(jTable1));
20
21      TableColumnModel columnModel = jTable1.getColumnModel();
22      columnModel.moveColumn(0, 1);
```

column names

row data

create table

scroll pane

column model
move a column

```
23        columnModel.removeColumn(columnModel.getColumn(3));
24   }
25 }
```

remove a column

main method omitted

 Note

Some of the methods defined in the table model and the table column model are also defined in the `JTable` class for convenience. For instance, the `getColumnCount()` method is defined in `JTable`, `TableModel`, and `TableColumnModel`, the `addColumn` method defined in the column model is also defined in the table model, and the `getColumn()` method defined in the column model is also defined in the `JTable` class.

`JTableHeader` is a GUI component that displays the header of the `JTable` (see Figure 36.10). When you create a `JTable`, an instance of `JTableHeader` is automatically created and stored in the `tableHeader` property. By default, you can reorder the columns by dragging the header of the column. To disable it, set the `reorderingAllowed` property to `false`.

TableHeader

FIGURE 36.10 The `JTableHeader` class displays the header of the `JTable`.

36.4 Auto Sort and Filtering

Auto sort and filtering are two useful new features in JDK 1.6. To enable auto sort on any column in a `JTable`, create an instance of `TableRowSet` with a table model and set `JTable`'s `rowSorter` as follows:

```
TableRowSorter<TableModel> sorter =
   new TableRowSorter<TableModel>(tableModel);
jTable.setRowSorter(sorter);
```

create a **TableRowSorter**

setRowSorter

When the table is displayed, you can sort the table by clicking a column head, as shown in Figure 36.11.

You can specify a filter to select rows in the table. The filter can be applied on one column or all columns. The `javax.swing.RowFilter` class contains several static methods for creating filters. You can use the `regexFilter` method to create a `RowFilter` with the specified regular expression. For example, the following statement creates a filter for the rows whose first column or second column begin with letter U.

```
RowFilter rowFilter = RowFilter.regexFilter("U.*", int[]{0, 1});
```

create a filter

(a)

(b)

FIGURE 36.11 (a) The table is sorted on Country. (b) The table is sorted on Capital.

The second argument in the `regexFilter` method specifies a set of column indices. If no indices are specified, all columns are searched in the filter.

set filter in **JTable**

To enable filtering, you have to associate a filter with a `TableRowSorter`, which is set to the `JTable`'s `rowSorter` property.

Listing 36.5 gives an example that demonstrates auto sort and filtering in `JTable`.

LISTING 36.5 TestTableSortFilter.java

```
 1 import javax.swing.*;
 2 import javax.swing.table.*;
 3 import java.awt.BorderLayout;
 4
 5 public class TestTableSortFilter extends JApplet {
 6   // Create table column names
 7   private String[] columnNames =
 8     {"Country", "Capital", "Population in Millions", "Democracy"};
 9
10   // Create table data
11   private Object[][] data = {
12     {"USA", "Washington DC", 280, true},
13     {"Canada", "Ottawa", 32, true},
14     {"United Kingdom", "London", 60, true},
15     {"Germany", "Berlin", 83, true},
16     {"France", "Paris", 60, true},
17     {"Norway", "Oslo", 4.5, true},
18     {"India", "New Delhi", 1046, true}
19   };
20
21   // Create a table
22   private JTable jTable1 = new JTable(data, columnNames);
23
24   // Create a TableRowSorter
25   private TableRowSorter<TableModel> sorter =
26     new TableRowSorter<TableModel>(jTable1.getModel());
27
28   private JTextField jtfFilter = new JTextField();
29   private JButton btFilter = new JButton("Filter");
30
31   public TestTableSortFilter() {
32     // Enable auto sorter
33     jTable1.setRowSorter(sorter);
34
35     JPanel panel = new JPanel(new java.awt.BorderLayout());
36     panel.add(new JLabel("Sepecify a word to match:"),
37       BorderLayout.WEST);
38     panel.add(jtfFilter, BorderLayout.CENTER);
39     panel.add(btFilter, BorderLayout.EAST);
```

column names

row data

create table

create **TableRowSorter**

set sorter

```
40
41        add(panel, BorderLayout.SOUTH);
42        add(new JScrollPane(jTable1), BorderLayout.CENTER);
43
44        btFilter.addActionListener(new java.awt.event.ActionListener() {
45          public void actionPerformed(java.awt.event.ActionEvent e) {
46            String text = jtfFilter.getText();
47            if (text.trim().length() == 0)
48              sorter.setRowFilter(null);                                    remove filter
49            else
50              sorter.setRowFilter(RowFilter.regexFilter(text));            set a filter
51          }
52        });
53      }
54 }                                                                          main method omitted
```

The example creates a `TableRowSorter` (line 25) and sets the sorter in `jTable1` (line 33). The program lets the user enter a filter pattern from a text field, as shown in Figure 36.12. If nothing is entered, no filter is set (line 48). If a regex is entered, clicking the *Filter* button sets the filter to `jTable1` (line 50).

FIGURE 36.12   (a) Filter the table with regex `U.*`. (b) Filter the table with regex `w`.

36.5 Case Study: Modifying Rows and Columns

This case study demonstrates the use of table models, table column models, list-selection models, and the `TableColumn` class. The program allows the user to choose selection mode and selection type, add or remove rows and columns, and save, clear, or restore the table, as shown in Figure 36.13(a).

The *Add New Row* button adds a new empty row before the currently selected row, as shown in Figure 36.13(b). If no row is currently selected, a new empty row is appended to the end of the table.

FIGURE 36.13   You can add, remove, and modify rows and columns in a table interactively.

When you click the *Add New Column* button, an input dialog box is displayed to receive the title of the column, as shown in Figure 36.14(a). The new column is appended in the table, as shown in Figure 36.14(b).

(a)　　　　　　　　　　　　　　(b)

FIGURE 36.14 You can add a new column in a table.

The *Delete Selected Row* button deletes the first selected row. The *Delete Selected Column* button deletes the first selected column.

The *Save* button saves the current table data and column names. The *Clear* button clears the row data in the table. The *Restore* button restores the saved table.

Listing 36.6 gives the program.

LISTING 36.6 ModifyTable.java

```java
1  import java.awt.*;
2  import java.awt.event.*;
3  import javax.swing.*;
4  import javax.swing.table.*;
5  import java.io.*;
6  import java.util.Vector;
7
8  public class ModifyTable extends JApplet {
9    // Create table column names
10   private String[] columnNames =
11     {"Country", "Capital", "Population in Millions", "Democracy"};
12
13   // Create table data
14   private Object[][] rowData = {
15     {"USA", "Washington DC", 280, true},
16     {"Canada", "Ottawa", 32, true},
17     {"United Kingdom", "London", 60, true},
18     {"Germany", "Berlin", 83, true},
19     {"France", "Paris", 60, true},
20     {"Norway", "Oslo", 4.5, true},
21     {"India", "New Delhi", 1046, true}
22   };
23
24   // Create a table model
25   private DefaultTableModel tableModel = new DefaultTableModel(
26     rowData, columnNames);
27
28   // Create a table
29   private JTable jTable1 = new JTable(tableModel);
```

column names — line 10
table data — line 14
table model — line 25
table — line 29

```
30
31    // Create buttons
32    private JButton jbtAddRow = new JButton("Add New Row");                buttons
33    private JButton jbtAddColumn = new JButton("Add New Column");
34    private JButton jbtDeleteRow = new JButton("Delete Selected Row");
35    private JButton jbtDeleteColumn = new JButton(
36      "Delete Selected Column");
37    private JButton jbtSave = new JButton("Save");
38    private JButton jbtClear = new JButton("Clear");
39    private JButton jbtRestore = new JButton("Restore");
40
41    // Create a combo box for selection modes
42    private JComboBox jcboSelectionMode =                                  combo box
43      new JComboBox(new String[] {"SINGLE_SELECTION",
44        "SINGLE_INTERVAL_SELECTION", "MULTIPLE_INTERVAL_SELECTION"});
45
46    // Create check boxes
47    private JCheckBox jchkRowSelectionAllowed =                            check boxes
48      new JCheckBox("RowSelectionAllowed", true);
49    private JCheckBox jchkColumnSelectionAllowed =
50      new JCheckBox("ColumnSelectionAllowed", false);
51
52    public ModifyTable() {
53      JPanel panel1 = new JPanel();                                       create UI
54      panel1.setLayout(new GridLayout(2, 2));
55      panel1.add(jbtAddRow);
56      panel1.add(jbtAddColumn);
57      panel1.add(jbtDeleteRow);
58      panel1.add(jbtDeleteColumn);
59
60      JPanel panel2 = new JPanel();
61      panel2.add(jbtSave);
62      panel2.add(jbtClear);
63      panel2.add(jbtRestore);
64
65      JPanel panel3 = new JPanel();
66      panel3.setLayout(new BorderLayout(5, 0));
67      panel3.add(new JLabel("Selection Mode"), BorderLayout.WEST);
68      panel3.add(jcboSelectionMode, BorderLayout.CENTER);
69
70      JPanel panel4 = new JPanel();
71      panel4.setLayout(new FlowLayout(FlowLayout.LEFT));
72      panel4.add(jchkRowSelectionAllowed);
73      panel4.add(jchkColumnSelectionAllowed);
74
75      JPanel panel5 = new JPanel();
76      panel5.setLayout(new GridLayout(2, 1));
77      panel5.add(panel3);
78      panel5.add(panel4);
79
80      JPanel panel6 = new JPanel();
81      panel6.setLayout(new BorderLayout());
82      panel6.add(panel1, BorderLayout.SOUTH);
83      panel6.add(panel2, BorderLayout.CENTER);
84
85      add(panel5, BorderLayout.NORTH);
86      add(new JScrollPane(jTable1),
87        BorderLayout.CENTER);
88      add(panel6, BorderLayout.SOUTH);
89
```

```
 90      // Initialize table selection mode
 91      jTable1.setSelectionMode(ListSelectionModel.SINGLE_SELECTION);
 92
 93      jbtAddRow.addActionListener(new ActionListener() {
 94        public void actionPerformed(ActionEvent e) {
 95          if (jTable1.getSelectedRow() >= 0)
 96            tableModel.insertRow(jTable1.getSelectedRow(),
 97              new java.util.Vector());
 98          else
 99            tableModel.addRow(new java.util.Vector());
100        }
101      });
102
103      jbtAddColumn.addActionListener(new ActionListener() {
104        public void actionPerformed(ActionEvent e) {
105          String name = JOptionPane.showInputDialog("New Column Name");
106          tableModel.addColumn(name, new java.util.Vector());
107        }
108      });
109
110      jbtDeleteRow.addActionListener(new ActionListener() {
111        public void actionPerformed(ActionEvent e) {
112          if (jTable1.getSelectedRow() >= 0)
113            tableModel.removeRow(jTable1.getSelectedRow());
114        }
115      });
116
117      jbtDeleteColumn.addActionListener(new ActionListener() {
118        public void actionPerformed(ActionEvent e) {
119          if (jTable1.getSelectedColumn() >= 0) {
120            TableColumnModel columnModel = jTable1.getColumnModel();
121            TableColumn tableColumn =
122                columnModel.getColumn(jTable1.getSelectedColumn());
123            columnModel.removeColumn(tableColumn);
124          }
125        }
126      });
127
128      jbtSave.addActionListener(new ActionListener() {
129        public void actionPerformed(ActionEvent e) {
130          try {
131            ObjectOutputStream out = new ObjectOutputStream(
132              new FileOutputStream("tablemodel.dat"));
133            out.writeObject(tableModel.getDataVector());
134            out.writeObject(getColumnNames());
135            out.close();
136          }
137          catch (Exception ex) {
138            ex.printStackTrace();
139          }
140        }
141      });
142
143      jbtClear.addActionListener(new ActionListener() {
144        public void actionPerformed(ActionEvent e) {
145          tableModel.setRowCount(0);
146        }
147      });
148
149      jbtRestore.addActionListener(new ActionListener() {
```

Marginal labels (left column):
- add row — line 93
- add column — line 103
- delete row — line 110
- delete column — line 117
- save table — line 128
- clear table — line 143
- restore table — line 149

```
150        public void actionPerformed(ActionEvent e) {
151          try {
152            ObjectInputStream in = new ObjectInputStream(
153              new FileInputStream("tablemodel.dat"));
154            Vector rowData = (Vector)in.readObject();
155            Vector columnNames = (Vector)in.readObject();
156            tableModel.setDataVector(rowData, columnNames);
157            in.close();
158          }
159          catch (Exception ex) {
160            ex.printStackTrace();
161          }
162        }
163      });
164
165      jchkRowSelectionAllowed.addActionListener(new ActionListener() {    row selection allowed
166        public void actionPerformed(ActionEvent e) {
167          jTable1.setRowSelectionAllowed(
168            jchkRowSelectionAllowed.isSelected());
169        }
170      });
171
172      jchkColumnSelectionAllowed.addActionListener(              column selection allowed
173        new ActionListener() {
174        public void actionPerformed(ActionEvent e) {
175          jTable1.setColumnSelectionAllowed(
176            jchkColumnSelectionAllowed.isSelected());
177        }
178      });
179
180      jcboSelectionMode.addActionListener(new ActionListener() {     choose selection mode
181        public void actionPerformed(ActionEvent e) {
182          String selectedItem =
183            (String) jcboSelectionMode.getSelectedItem();
184
185          if (selectedItem.equals("SINGLE_SELECTION"))
186            jTable1.setSelectionMode(
187              ListSelectionModel.SINGLE_SELECTION);
188          else if (selectedItem.equals("SINGLE_INTERVAL_SELECTION"))
189            jTable1.setSelectionMode(
190              ListSelectionModel.SINGLE_INTERVAL_SELECTION);
191          else if (selectedItem.equals("MULTIPLE_INTERVAL_SELECTION"))
192            jTable1.setSelectionMode(
193              ListSelectionModel.MULTIPLE_INTERVAL_SELECTION);
194        }
195      });
196    }
197
198    private Vector getColumnNames() {                    get column names
199      Vector<String> columnNames = new Vector<String>();
200
201      for (int i = 0; i < jTable1.getColumnCount(); i++)
202        columnNames.add(jTable1.getColumnName(i));
203
204      return columnNames;
205    }
206 }                                                    main method omitted
```

A table model is created using `DefaultTableModel` with row data and column names (lines 25–26). This model is used to create a `JTable` (line 29).

The GUI objects (buttons, combo box, check boxes) are created in lines 32–50 and are placed in the UI in lines 53–88.

The table-selection mode is the same as the list-selection mode. By default, the selection mode is MULTIPLE_INTERVAL_SELECTION. To match the initial value in the selection combo box (jcboSelectionMode), the table's selection mode is set to SINGLE_SELECTION.

The *Add New Row* button action is processed in lines 93–101. The insertRow method inserts a new row before the selected row (lines 96–97). If no row is currently selected, the addRow method appends a new row into the table model (line 99).

The *Add New Column* button action is processed in lines 103–108. The addColumn method appends a new column into the table model (line 106).

The *Delete Selected Row* button action is processed in lines 110–115. The removeRow(rowIndex) method removes the selected row from the table model (line 113).

The *Delete Selected Column* button action is processed in lines 117–126. To remove a column, you have to use the removeColumn method in TableColumnModel (line 123).

The *Save* button action is processed in lines 128–141. It writes row data and column names to an output file using object stream (lines 133–134). The column names are obtained using the getColumnNames() method (lines 198–205). You may attempt to save tableModel, because tableModel is an instance of DefaultTableModel (lines 25–26) and DefaultTableModel is serializable. However, tableModel may contain nonserializable listeners for TableModel event.

The *Clear* button action is processed in lines 143–147. It clears the table by setting the row count to 0 (line 145).

The *Restore* button action is processed in lines 149–163. It reads row data and column names from the file using object stream (lines 154–155) and sets the new data and column names to the table model (line 156).

36.6 Table Renderers and Editors

Table cells are painted by cell renderers. By default, a cell object's string representation (toString()) is displayed and the string can be edited as it was in a text field. JTable maintains a set of predefined renderers and editors, listed in Table 36.1, which can be specified to replace default string renderers and editors.

The predefined renderers and editors are automatically located and loaded to match the class returned from the getColumnClass() method in the table model. To use a predefined renderer or editor for a class other than String, you need to create your own table model by extending a subclass of TableModel. In your table model class, you need to override the getColumnClass() method to return the class of the column, as follows:

```
public Class getColumnClass(int column) {
  return getValueAt(0, column).getClass();
}
```

TABLE 36.1 Predefined renderers and editors for tables

Class	Renderer	Editor
Object	JLabel (left aligned)	JTextField
Date	JLabel (right aligned)	JTextField
Number	JLabel (right aligned)	JTextField
ImageIcon	JLabel (center aligned)	
Boolean	JCheckBox (center aligned)	JCheckBox (center aligned)

By default, all cells are editable. To prohibit a cell from being edited, override the `isCellEditable(int rowIndex, int columnIndx)` method in `TableModel` to return `false`. By default, this method returns `true` in `AbstractTableModel`.

To demonstrate predefined table renderers and editors, let us write a program that displays a table for books. The table consists of three rows with the column names Title, Copies Needed, Publisher, Date Published, In-Stock, and Book Photo, as shown in Figure 36.15. Assume that dates and icons are not editable; prohibit users from editing these two columns.

FIGURE 36.15 You need to use a custom table model to enable predefined renderers for Boolean and image cells.

Listing 36.7 gives a custom table model named `MyTableModel` that overrides the `getColumnClass` method (lines 15–17) to enable predefined renderers for Boolean and image cells. `MyTableModel` also overrides the `isCellEditable()` method (lines 20–24). By default, `isCellEditable()` returns `true`. The example does not allow the user to edit image icons and dates, so this method is overridden to return `false` to disable editing of date and image columns. For a cell to be editable, both `isCellEditable()` in the table model and `isEditing` in `JTable` class must be `true`.

LISTING 36.7 MyTableModel.java

```
1 import javax.swing.*;
2 import javax.swing.table.*;
3 import java.util.*;
4
5 public class MyTableModel extends DefaultTableModel {
6   public MyTableModel() {
7   }
8
9   /** Construct a table model with specified data and columnNames */
10  public MyTableModel(Object[][] data, Object[] columnNames) {
11    super(data, columnNames);
12  }
13
14  /** Override this method to return a class for the column */
15  public class getColumnClass(int column) {                          column class
16    return getValueAt(0, column).getClass();
17  }
18
19  /** Override this method to return true if cell is editable */
20  public boolean isCellEditable(int row, int column) {               cell editable?
21    Class columnClass = getColumnClass(column);
22    return columnClass != ImageIcon.class &&
23      columnClass != Date.class;
24  }
25 }
```

If you create a `JTable` using a table model created from `MyTableModel`, the default renderers and editors for numbers, Boolean values, dates, and icons are used to display and edit these columns. Listing 36.8 gives a test program. The program creates a table model using **MyTableModel** (line 36). **JTable** assigns a predefined cell renderer and a predefined editor to the cell, whose class is specified in the **getColumnClass()** method in **MyTableModel**.

LISTING 36.8   TableCellRendererEditorDemo.java

```
1  import java.awt.*;
2  import javax.swing.*;
3  import java.util.*;
4
5  public class TableCellRendererEditorDemo extends JApplet {
6    // Create table column names
7    private String[] columnNames =
8      {"Title", "Copies Needed", "Publisher", "Date Published",
9       "In-stock", "Book Photo"};
10
11   // Create image icons
12   private ImageIcon intro1eImageIcon = new ImageIcon(
13     getClass().getResource("image/intro1e.gif"));
14   private ImageIcon intro2eImageIcon = new ImageIcon(
15     getClass().getResource("image/intro2e.gif"));
16   private ImageIcon intro3eImageIcon = new ImageIcon(
17     getClass().getResource("image/intro3e.jpg"));
18
19   // Create table data
20   private Object[][] rowData = {
21     {"Introduction to Java Programming", 120,
22      "Que Education & Training",
23      new GregorianCalendar(1998, 1-1, 6).getTime(),
24      false, intro1eImageIcon},
25     {"Introduction to Java Programming, 2E", 220,
26      "Que Education & Training",
27      new GregorianCalendar(1999, 1-1, 6).getTime(),
28      false, intro2eImageIcon},
29     {"Introduction to Java Programming, 3E", 220,
30      "Prentice Hall",
31      new GregorianCalendar(2000, 12-1, 0).getTime(),
32      true, intro3eImageIcon},
33   };
34
35   // Create a table model
36   private MyTableModel tableModel = new MyTableModel(
37     rowData, columnNames);
38
39   // Create a table
40   private JTable jTable1 = new JTable(tableModel);
41
42   public TableCellRendererEditorDemo() {
43     jTable1.setRowHeight(60);
44     add(new JScrollPane(jTable1),
45       BorderLayout.CENTER);
46   }
47 }
```

Marginal notes, top to bottom:
- column names
- image icons
- row data
- table model
- table
- main method omitted

The example creates two classes: **MyTableModel** and **TableCellRendererEditorDemo**. **MyTableModel** is an extension of **DefaultTableModel**. The purpose of **MyTableModel** is to override the default implementation of the **getColumnClass()** method to return the class of the column, so that an appropriate predefined **JTable** can be used for the column. By default, **getColumnClass()** returns **Object.class**.

36.7 Custom Table Renderers and Editors

Predefined renderers and editors are convenient and easy to use, but their functions are limited. The predefined image icon renderer displays the image icon in a label. The image icon cannot be scaled. If you want the whole image to fit in a cell, you need to create a custom renderer.

A custom renderer can be created by extending the `DefaultTableCellRenderer`, which is a default implementation for the `TableCellRenderer` interface. The custom renderer must override the `getTableCellRendererComponent()` to return a component for rendering the table cell. The `getTableCellRendererComponent()` is defined as follows:

```
public Component getTableCellRendererComponent
  (JTable table, Object value, boolean isSelected,
   boolean isFocused, int row, int column)
```

This method signature is very similar to the `getListCellRendererComponent()` method used to create custom list cell renderers.

This method is passed with a `JTable`, the value associated with the cell, information regarding whether the value is selected and the cell has the focus, and the row and column indices of the value. The component returned from the method is painted on the cell in the table. The class in Listing 36.9, `MyImageCellRenderer`, creates a renderer for displaying image icons in a panel.

LISTING 36.9 `MyImageCellRenderer.java`

```
 1  import javax.swing.*;
 2  import javax.swing.table.*;
 3  import java.awt.*;
 4
 5  public class MyImageCellRenderer extends DefaultTableCellRenderer {
 6    /** Override this method in DefaultTableCellRenderer */
 7    public Component getTableCellRendererComponent             override method
 8      (JTable table, Object value, boolean isSelected,
 9       boolean isFocused, int row, int column) {
10      Image image = ((ImageIcon)value).getImage();            getImage()
11      ImageViewer imageViewer = new ImageViewer(image);       create image viewer
12                                                              return image viewer
13      return imageViewer;
14    }
15  }
```

You can also create a custom editor. `JTable` provides the `DefaultCellEditor` class, which can be used to edit a cell in a text field, a check box, or a combo box. To use it, simply create a text field, a check box, or a combo box, and pass it to `DefaultCellEditor`'s constructor to create an editor.

Using a custom renderer and editor, the preceding example can be revised to display scaled images and to use a custom combo editor to edit the cells in the Publisher column, as shown in Figure 36.16. The program is given in Listing 36.10.

FIGURE 36.16 A custom renderer displays a scaled image, and a custom editor edits the Publisher column using a combo box.

LISTING 36.10 CustomTableCellRendererEditorDemo.java

```java
import java.awt.*;
import javax.swing.*;
import javax.swing.table.*;
import java.util.*;

public class CustomTableCellRendererEditorDemo extends JApplet {
  // Create table column names
  private String[] columnNames =
    {"Title", "Copies Needed", "Publisher", "Date Published",
      "In-stock", "Book Photo"};

  // Create image icons
  private ImageIcon intro1eImageIcon =
    new ImageIcon(getClass().getResource("image/intro1e.gif"));
  private ImageIcon intro2eImageIcon =
    new ImageIcon(getClass().getResource("image/intro2e.gif"));
  private ImageIcon intro3eImageIcon =
    new ImageIcon(getClass().getResource("image/intro3e.jpg"));

  // Create table data
  private Object[][] rowData = {
    {"Introduction to Java Programming", 120,
      "Que Education & Training",
      new GregorianCalendar(1998, 1-1, 6).getTime(),
      false, intro1eImageIcon},
    {"Introduction to Java Programming, 2E", 220,
      "Que Education & Training",
      new GregorianCalendar(1999, 1-1, 6).getTime(),
      false, intro2eImageIcon},
    {"Introduction to Java Programming, 3E", 220,
      "Prentice Hall",
      new GregorianCalendar(2000, 12-1, 0).getTime(),
      true, intro3eImageIcon},
  };

  // Create a table model
  private MyTableModel tableModel = new MyTableModel(
    rowData, columnNames);

  // Create a table
  private JTable jTable1 = new JTable(tableModel);

  public CustomTableCellRendererEditorDemo() {
    // Set custom renderer for displaying images
    TableColumn bookCover = jTable1.getColumn("Book Photo");
    bookCover.setCellRenderer(new MyImageCellRenderer());

    // Create a combo box for publishers
    JComboBox jcboPublishers = new JComboBox();
    jcboPublishers.addItem("Prentice Hall");
    jcboPublishers.addItem("Que Education & Training");
    jcboPublishers.addItem("McGraw-Hill");

    // Set combo box as the editor for the publisher column
    TableColumn publisherColumn = jTable1.getColumn("Publisher");
    publisherColumn.setCellEditor(
      new DefaultCellEditor(jcboPublishers));
```

column names

image icons

row data

table model

table

set renderer

combo box

set editor

```
59        jTable1.setRowHeight(60);
60        add(new JScrollPane(jTable1),
61          BorderLayout.CENTER);
62     }
63  }
```

main method omitted

This example uses the same table model (`MyTableModel`) that was created in the preceding example (lines 37–38). By default, image icons are displayed using the predefined image icon renderer. To use `MyImageCellRenderer` to display the image, you have to explicitly specify the `MyImageCellRenderer` renderer for the Book Photo column (line 46). Likewise, you have to explicitly specify the combo box editor for the Publisher column (lines 56–57); otherwise the default editor would be used.

When you edit a cell in the Publisher column, a combo box of three items is displayed. When you select an item from the box, it is displayed in the cell. You did not write the code for handling selections. The selections are handled by the `DefaultCellEditor` class.

When you resize the Book Photo column, the image is resized to fit into the whole cell. With the predefined image renderer, you can see only part of the image if the cell is smaller than the image.

36.8 Table Model Events

`JTable` does not fire table events. It fires events like `MouseEvent`, `KeyEvent`, and `ComponentEvent` that are inherited from its superclass, `JComponent`. Table events are fired by table models, table column models, and table-selection models whenever changes are made to these models. Table models fire `TableModelEvent` when table data are changed. Table column models fire `TableColumnModelEvent` when columns are added, removed, or moved, or when the column selection changes. Table-selection models fire `ListSelectionEvent` when the selection changes.

To listen for these events, a listener must be registered with an appropriate model and implement the correct listener interface. Listing 36.11 gives an example that demonstrates how to use these events. The program displays messages on a text area when a row or a column is selected, when a cell is edited, or when a column is removed. Figure 36.17 is a sample run of the program.

FIGURE 36.17 Table event handlers display table events on a text area.

LISTING 36.11 TableEventsDemo.java

```
1  import java.awt.*;
2  import java.awt.event.*;
3  import javax.swing.*;
4  import javax.swing.event.*;
5  import javax.swing.table.*;
```

```
 6  import java.util.*;
 7
 8  public class TableEventsDemo extends JApplet {
 9    // Create table column names
10    private String[] columnNames =
11      {"Title", "Copies Needed", "Publisher", "Date Published",
12       "In-stock", "Book Photo"};
13
14    // Create image icons
15    private ImageIcon intro1eImageIcon =
16      new ImageIcon(getClass().getResource("image/intro1e.gif"));
17    private ImageIcon intro2eImageIcon =
18      new ImageIcon(getClass().getResource("image/intro2e.gif"));
19    private ImageIcon intro3eImageIcon =
20      new ImageIcon(getClass().getResource("image/intro3e.jpg"));
21
22    // Create table data
23    private Object[][] rowData = {
24      {"Introduction to Java Programming", 120,
25       "Que Education & Training",
26       new GregorianCalendar(1998, 1-1, 6).getTime(),
27       false, intro1eImageIcon},
28      {"Introduction to Java Programming, 2E", 220,
29       "Que Education & Training",
30       new GregorianCalendar(1999, 1-1, 6).getTime(),
31       false, intro2eImageIcon},
32      {"Introduction to Java Programming, 3E", 220,
33       "Prentice Hall",
34       new GregorianCalendar(2000, 12-1, 0).getTime(),
35       true, intro3eImageIcon},
36    };
37
38    // Create a table model
39    private MyTableModel tableModel = new MyTableModel(
40      rowData, columnNames);
41
42    // Create a table
43    private JTable jTable1 = new JTable(tableModel);
44
45    // Get table column model
46    private TableColumnModel tableColumnModel =
47      jTable1.getColumnModel();
48
49    // Get table selection model
50    private ListSelectionModel selectionModel =
51      jTable1.getSelectionModel();
52
53    // Create a text area
54    private JTextArea jtaMessage = new JTextArea();
55
56    // Create a button
57    private JButton jbtDeleteColumn =
58      new JButton("Delete Selected Column");
59
60    public TableEventsDemo() {
61      // Set custom renderer for displaying images
62      TableColumn bookCover = jTable1.getColumn("Book Photo");
63      bookCover.setCellRenderer(new MyImageCellRenderer());
64
```

column names

image icons

table data

table model

table

column model

selection model

```
65        // Create a combo box for publishers
66        JComboBox jcboPublishers = new JComboBox();
67        jcboPublishers.addItem("Prentice Hall");
68        jcboPublishers.addItem("Que Education & Training");
69        jcboPublishers.addItem("McGraw-Hill");
70
71        // Set combo box as the editor for the publisher column
72        TableColumn publisherColumn = jTable1.getColumn("Publisher");
73        publisherColumn.setCellEditor(
74          new DefaultCellEditor(jcboPublishers));
75
76        jTable1.setRowHeight(60);
77        jTable1.setColumnSelectionAllowed(true);
78
79        JSplitPane jSplitPane1 = new JSplitPane(
80          JSplitPane.VERTICAL_SPLIT);
81        jSplitPane1.add(new JScrollPane(jTable1), JSplitPane.LEFT);
82        jSplitPane1.add(new JScrollPane(jtaMessage), JSplitPane.RIGHT);
83        add(jbtDeleteColumn, BorderLayout.NORTH);
84        add(jSplitPane1, BorderLayout.CENTER);
85
86        tableModel.addTableModelListener(new TableModelListener() {       table model listener
87          public void tableChanged(TableModelEvent e) {
88            jtaMessage.append("Table changed at row " +
89              e.getFirstRow() + " and column " + e.getColumn() + "\n");
90          }
91        });
92
93        tableColumnModel.addColumnModelListener(                           column model listener
94          new TableColumnModelListener() {
95          public void columnRemoved(TableColumnModelEvent e) {
96            jtaMessage.append("Column indexed at " + e.getFromIndex() +
97              " is deleted \n");
98          }
99          public void columnAdded(TableColumnModelEvent e) {
100         }
101         public void columnMoved(TableColumnModelEvent e) {
102         }
103         public void columnMarginChanged(ChangeEvent e) {
104         }
105         public void columnSelectionChanged(ListSelectionEvent e) {
106         }
107       });
108
109       jbtDeleteColumn.addActionListener(new ActionListener() {
110         public void actionPerformed(ActionEvent e) {
111           if (jTable1.getSelectedColumn() >= 0) {
112             TableColumnModel columnModel = jTable1.getColumnModel();
113             TableColumn tableColumn =
114               columnModel.getColumn(jTable1.getSelectedColumn());
115             columnModel.removeColumn(tableColumn);
116           }
117         }
118       });
119
120       selectionModel.addListSelectionListener(                           selection model listener
121         new ListSelectionListener() {
122         public void valueChanged(ListSelectionEvent e) {
123           jtaMessage.append("Row " + jTable1.getSelectedRow() +
```

```
124                  " and column " + jTable1.getSelectedColumn() +
125                  " selected\n");
126            }
127       });
128   }
129 }
```

main method omitted

To respond to the row and column selection events, you need to implement the `valueChanged` method in `ListSelectionListener`. To respond to the cell-editing event, you need to implement the `tableChanged` method in `TableModelListener`. To respond to the column-deletion event, you need to implement the `columnRemoved` method in `TableColumnModelListener`. Let's use the same table from the preceding example, but with a button added for deleting the selected column and a text area for displaying the messages.

A table model is created using `MyTableModel` (lines 39–40), which was given in Listing 36.7. When a table is created (line 43), its default column model and selection model are also created. Therefore, you can obtain the table column model and selection model from the table (lines 46–51).

When a row or a column is selected, a `ListSelectionEvent` is fired by `selectionModel`, which invokes the handler to display the selected row and column in the text area (lines 120–127). When the content or structure of the table is changed, a `TableModelEvent` is fired by `tableModel`, which invokes the handler to display the last row and last column of the changed data in the text area (lines 86–91). When a column is deleted by clicking the *Delete Selected Column* button, a `ColumnModelEvent` is fired by `tableColumnModel`, which invokes the handler to display the index of the deleted column (lines 93–107).

36.9 JTree

`JTree` is a Swing component that displays data in a treelike hierarchy, as shown in Figure 36.18.

FIGURE 36.18 `JTree` displays data in a treelike hierarchy.

All the nodes displayed in the tree are in the form of a hierarchical indexed list. The tree can be used to navigate structured data with hierarchical relationships. A node can have child nodes. A node is called a *leaf* if it has no children; a node with no parent is called the *root* of its tree. A tree may consist of many subtrees, each node acting as the root for its own subtree.

A nonleaf node can be expanded or collapsed by double-clicking on the node or on the node's handle in front of the node. The handle usually has a visible sign to indicate whether the node is expanded or collapsed. For example, on Windows, the + symbol indicates that the node can be expanded, and the − symbol, that it can be collapsed.

Like `JTable`, `JTree` is a very complex component with many supporting interfaces and classes. `JTree` is in the `javax.swing` package, but its supporting interfaces and classes are all included in the `javax.swing.tree` package. The supporting interfaces are `TreeModel`, `TreeSelectionModel`, `TreeNode`, and `MutableTreeNode`, and the supported classes are `DefaultTreeModel`, `DefaultMutableTreeNode`, `DefaultTreeCellEditor`, `DefaultTreeCellRenderer`, and `TreePath`.

While `JTree` displays the tree, the data representation of the tree is handled by `TreeModel`, `TreeNode`, and `TreePath`. `TreeModel` represents the entire tree, `TreeNode` represents a node, and `TreePath` represents a path to a node. Unlike the `ListModel` or `TableModel`, `TreeModel` does not directly store or manage tree data. Tree data are stored and managed in `TreeNode` and `TreePath`. `DefaultTreeModel` is a concrete implementation of `TreeModel`. `MutableTreeNode` is a subinterface of `TreeNode`, which represents a tree node that can be mutated by adding or removing child nodes, or by changing the contents of a user object stored in the node.

The `TreeSelectionModel` interface handles tree node selection. The `DefaultTreeCellRenderer` class provides a default tree node renderer that can display a label and/or an icon in a node. The `DefaultTreeCellEditor` can be used to edit the cells in a text field.

A `TreePath` is an array of `Object`s that are vended from a `TreeModel`. The elements of the array are ordered such that the root is always the first element (index 0) of the array. Figure 36.19 shows how these interfaces and classes are interrelated.

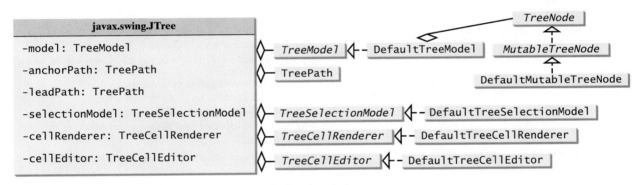

FIGURE 36.19 `JTree` contains many supporting interfaces and classes.

Figure 36.20 shows the constructors, frequently used properties, and methods of `JTree`.

The `JTree` class contains seven constructors for creating trees. You can create a tree using its no-arg constructor, a tree model, a tree node, a `Hashtable`, an array, or a vector. Using the no-arg constructor, a sample tree is created as shown in Figure 36.18. Using a `Hashtable`, an array, or a vector, a root is created but not displayed. All the keys in a `Hashtable`, all the objects in an array, and all the elements in a vector are added into the tree as children of the root. If you wish the root to be displayed, set the `rootVisible` property to true.

All the methods related to path selection are also defined in the `TreeSelectionModel` interface, which will be covered in §36.9, "`TreePath` and `TreeSelectionModel`."

Listing 36.12 gives an example that creates four trees: a default tree using the no-arg constructor, a tree created from an array of objects, a tree created from a vector, and a tree created from a hash table, as shown in Figure 36.21. Enable the user to dynamically set the properties for `rootVisible`, `rowHeight`, and `showsRootHandles`.

> JavaBeans properties with `get` and `set` methods omitted in the UML diagram.

javax.swing.JTree	
#cellEditor: TreeCellEditor	Specifies a cell editor used to edit entries in the tree.
#cellRenderer: TreeCellRenderer	Specifies a cell renderer.
#editable: boolean	Specifies whether the cells are editable (default: false).
#model: TreeModel	Maintains the tree model.
#rootVisible: boolean	Specifies whether the root is displayed (depending on the constructor).
#rowHeight: int	Specifies the height of the row for the node displayed in the tree (default: 16 pixels).
#scrollsOnExpand: boolean	If true, when a node is expanded, as many of the descendants as possible are scrolled to be visible (default: 16 pixels).
#selectionModel: TreeSelectionModel	Models the set of selected nodes in this tree.
#showsRootHandles: boolean	Specifies whether the root handles are displayed (default: true).
#toggleClickCount: int	Number of mouse clicks before a node is expanded (default: 2).
-anchorSelectionPath: TreePath	The path identified as the anchor.
-expandsSelectedPaths: boolean	True if paths in the selection should be expanded (default: true).
-leadSelectionPaths: TreePath	The path identified as the lead.
+JTree()	Creates a JTree with a sample tree model, as shown in Figure 31.16.
+JTree(value: java.util.Hashtable)	Creates a JTree with an invisible root and the keys in the Hashtable key/value pairs as its children.
+JTree(value: Object[])	Creates a JTree with an invisible root and the elements in the array as its children.
+JTree(newModel: TreeModel)	Creates a JTree with the specified tree model.
+JTree(root: TreeNode)	Creates a JTree with the specified tree node as its root.
+JTree(root: TreeNode, asksAllowsChildren: boolean)	Creates a JTree with the specified tree node as its root and decides whether a node is a leaf node in the specified manner.
+JTree(value: Vector)	Creates a JTree with an invisible root and the elements in the vector as its children.
+addSelectionPath(path: TreePath): void	Adds the specified TreePath to the current selection.
+addSelectionPaths(paths: TreePath[]): void	Adds the specified TreePaths to the current selection.
+addSelectionRow(row: int): void	Adds the path at the specified row to the current selection.
+addSelectionRows(rows: int[]): void	Adds the path at the specified rows to the current selection.
+clearSelection(): void	Clears the selection.
+collapsePath(path: TreePath): void	Ensures that the node identified by the specified path is collapsed and viewable.
+getSelectionPath(): TreePath	Returns the path from the root to the first selected node.
+getSelectionPaths(): TreePath[]	Returns the paths from the root to all the selected nodes.
+getLastSelectedPathComponent()	Returns the last node in the first selected TreePath.
+getRowCount(): int	Returns the number of rows currently being displayed.
+removeSelectionPath(path: TreePath): void	Removes the node in the specified path.
+removeSelectionPaths(paths: TreePath[]): void	Removes the node in the specified paths.

FIGURE 36.20   The JTree class is for creating, customizing, and manipulating trees.

FIGURE 36.21   You can dynamically set the properties for rootVisible, rowHeight, and showRootHandles in a tree.

LISTING 36.12 SimpleTreeDemo.java

```java
 1 import java.awt.*;
 2 import java.awt.event.*;
 3 import javax.swing.*;
 4 import javax.swing.event.*;
 5 import java.util.*;
 6
 7 public class SimpleTreeDemo extends JApplet {
 8   // Create a default tree
 9   private JTree jTree1 = new JTree();                          tree 1
10
11   // Create a tree with an array of Objects.
12   private JTree jTree2 = new JTree(new String[]              tree 2
13     {"dog", "cow", "cat", "pig", "rabbit"});
14
15   // Create a tree with a Hashtable
16   private Vector vector = new Vector(Arrays.asList(          tree 3
17     new Object[]{"red", "green", "black", "white", "purple"}));
18   private JTree jTree3 = new JTree(vector);
19
20   private Hashtable<Integer, String> hashtable =
21     new Hashtable<Integer, String>();
22   private JTree jTree4;                                       tree 4
23
24   // Create a combo box for selecting rootVisible
25   private JComboBox jcboRootVisible = new JComboBox(
26     new String[]{"false", "true"});
27
28   // Create a combo box for selecting showRootHandles
29   private JComboBox jcboShowsRootHandles = new JComboBox(
30     new String[] {"false", "true"});
31
32   // Create a spinner for selecting row height
33   private JSpinner jSpinnerRowHeight = new JSpinner(
34     new SpinnerNumberModel(16, 1, 50, 1));
35
36   public SimpleTreeDemo() {
37     jTree1.setRootVisible(false);
38
39     hashtable.put(1, "red");
40     hashtable.put(2, "green");
41     hashtable.put(3, "blue");
42     hashtable.put(4, "yellow");
43     jTree4 = new JTree(hashtable);                           tree
44
45     JPanel panel1 = new JPanel(new GridLayout(1, 4));
46     panel1.add(new JScrollPane(jTree1));
47     panel1.add(new JScrollPane(jTree2));
48     panel1.add(new JScrollPane(jTree3));
49     panel1.add(new JScrollPane(jTree4));
50
51     JPanel panel2 = new JPanel();
52     panel2.add(new JLabel("rootVisible"));
53     panel2.add(jcboRootVisible);
54     panel2.add(new JLabel("rowHeight"));
55     panel2.add(jSpinnerRowHeight);
56     panel2.add(new JLabel("showsRootHandles"));
57     panel2.add(jcboShowsRootHandles);
58
```

combo box listener

```
59        add(panel1, BorderLayout.CENTER);
60        add(panel2, BorderLayout.SOUTH);
61
62        // Register listeners
63        jcboRootVisible.addActionListener(new ActionListener() {
64          public void actionPerformed(ActionEvent e) {
65            boolean rootVisible =
66              jcboRootVisible.getSelectedItem().equals("true");
67            jTree1.setRootVisible(rootVisible);
68            jTree2.setRootVisible(rootVisible);
69            jTree3.setRootVisible(rootVisible);
70            jTree4.setRootVisible(rootVisible);
71          }
72        });
73
74        jcboShowsRootHandles.addActionListener(new ActionListener() {
75          public void actionPerformed(ActionEvent e) {
76            boolean showsRootHandles =
77              jcboShowsRootHandles.getSelectedItem().equals("true");
78            jTree1.setShowsRootHandles(showsRootHandles);
79            jTree2.setShowsRootHandles(showsRootHandles);
80            jTree3.setShowsRootHandles(showsRootHandles);
81            jTree4.setShowsRootHandles(showsRootHandles);
82          }
83        });
84
85        jSpinnerRowHeight.addChangeListener(new ChangeListener() {
86          public void stateChanged(ChangeEvent e) {
87            int height =
88              ((Integer)(jSpinnerRowHeight.getValue())).intValue();
89            jTree1.setRowHeight(height);
90            jTree2.setRowHeight(height);
91            jTree3.setRowHeight(height);
92            jTree4.setRowHeight(height);
93          }
94        });
95      }
96 }
```

spinner listener

main method omitted

Four trees are created in this example. The first is created using the no-arg constructor (line 9) with a sample tree. The second is created using an array of objects (lines 12–13). All the objects in the array become the children of the root. The third is created using a vector (lines 16–18). All the elements in the vector become the children of the root. The fourth is created using a hash table (lines 39–43). A Hashtable is like a Map. Hashtable was introduced earlier than Java 2 and has since been replaced by Map. It is used in the Java API (e.g., JTree), which was developed before Java 2. The keys of the hash table become the children of the root.

JTree doesn't directly support scrolling. To create a scrollable tree, create a JScrollPane and add an instance of JTree to the scroll pane (lines 46–49).

The example enables you to specify whether the root is visible and whether the root handles are visible from two combo boxes (lines 63–83). It also lets you specify the row height of the node in a spinner (lines 85–94).

36.10 TreeModel and DefaultTreeModel

The TreeModel interface represents the entire tree. Unlike ListModel or TableModel, TreeModel does not directly store or manage tree data. TreeModel contains the structural information about the tree, and tree data are stored and managed by TreeNode.

«interface» *javax.swing.tree.TreeModel*	
+getChild(parent: Object, index: int): Object	Returns the child of the parent at the index in the parent's child array.
+getChildCount(parent: Object): int	Returns the number of children of the specified parent in the tree model.
+getIndexOfChild(parent: Object, child: Object): int	Returns the index of the child in the parent. If the parent or child is null, returns –1.
+getRoot(): Object	Returns the root of the tree. Returns null if the tree is empty.
+isLeaf(node: Object): boolean	Returns true if the specified node is a leaf.
+addTreeModelListener(listener: TreeModelListener): void	Adds a listener for the TreeModelEvent posted after the tree changes.
+removeTreeModelListener(listener: TreeModelListener): void	Removes a listener previously added with addTreeModelListener.

+valueForPathChanged(path: TreePath, newValue:
  Object): void
	Messaged when the user has altered the value for the item identified by
	  path to newValue.

javax.swing.tree.DefaultTreeModel	
#asksAllowsChildren: boolean	Tells how leaf nodes are determined. True if only nodes that do not allow children are leaf nodes, false if nodes that have no children are leaf nodes.
#root: TreeNode	The root of the tree.
+DefaultTreeModel(root: TreeNode)	Creates a DefaultTreeModel with the specified root.

+DefaultTreeModel(root: TreeNode,
  asksAllowsChildren: boolean)
	Creates a DefaultTreeModel with the specified root and decides whether a
	  node is a leaf node in the specified manner.

+asksAllowsChildren(): boolean	Returns asksAllowsChildren.
+getPathToRoot(aNode: TreeNode): TreeNode[]	Returns the nodes in an array from root to the specified node.
+insertNodeInto(newChild: MutableTreeNode, parent: MutableTreeNode, index: int): void	Inserts newChild at location index in parent's children.
+reload(): void	Reloads the model (invoke this method if the tree has been modified).
+removeNodeFromParent(node: MutableTreeNode): void	Removes the node from its parent.

FIGURE 36.22 TreeModel represents an entire tree and DefaultTreeModel is a concrete implementation of it.

DefaultTreeModel is a concrete implementation for TreeModel that uses TreeNodes. Figure 36.22 shows TreeModel and DefaultTreeModel.

Once a tree is created, you can obtain its tree model using the getModel method. Listing 36.13 gives an example that traverses all the nodes in a tree using the tree model. Line 1 creates a tree using JTree's no-arg constructor with the default sample nodes, as shown in Figure 36.18. The tree model for the tree is obtained in line 4. Line 5 invokes the traversal method to traverse the nodes in the tree.

LISTING 36.13 TestTreeModel.java

```
 1 public class TestTreeModel {
 2   public static void main(String[] args) {
 3     javax.swing.JTree jTree1 = new javax.swing.JTree();          default tree
 4     javax.swing.tree.TreeModel model = jTree1.getModel();        tree model
 5     traversal(model, model.getRoot());                           getRoot
 6   }
 7
 8   private static void traversal
 9       (javax.swing.tree.TreeModel model, Object root) {
10     System.out.print(root + " ");
11     if (model.isLeaf(root)) return;                              is leaf?
12     for (int i = 0; i < model.getChildCount(model.getRoot()); i++) {   getChildCount
13       traversal(model, model.getChild(root, i));                getChild
```

```
14      }
15    }
16 }
```

```
JTree colors blue violet red sports basketball soccer football
food hot dogs pizza ravioli
```

The `traversal` method starts from the root of the tree. The root is obtained by invoking the `getRoot` method (line 5). If the root is a leaf, the method returns (line 11). Otherwise, it recursively invokes the `traversal` method to start from the children of the root (line 13).

36.11 TreeNode, MutableTreeNode, and DefaultMutableTreeNode

While `TreeModel` represents the entire tree, `TreeNode` stores a single node of the tree. `MutableTreeNode` defines a subinterface of `TreeNode` with additional methods for changing the content of the node, for inserting and removing a child node, for setting a new parent, and for removing the node itself.

    `DefaultMutableTreeNode` is a concrete implementation of `MutableTreeNode` that maintains a list of children in a vector and provides the operations for creating nodes, for examining and modifying a node's parent and children, and also for examining the tree to which the node belongs. Normally, you should use `DefaultMutableTreeNode` to create a tree node. Figure 36.23 shows `TreeNode`, `MutableTreeNode`, and `DefaultMutableTreeNode`.

depth-first traversal

Note
In graph theory, depth-first traversal is defined the same as preorder traversal, but in the `depthFirstEnumeration()` method in `DefaultMutableTreeNode`, it is the same as postorder traversal.

creating trees

Note
You can create a `JTree` from a root using `new JTree(TreeNode)` or from a model using `new JTree(TreeModel)`. To create a tree model, you first create an instance of `TreeNode` to represent the root of the tree, and then create an instance of `DefaultTreeModel` fitted with the root.

Listing 36.14 gives an example that creates two trees to display world, continents, countries, and states. The two trees share the same nodes and thus display identical contents. The program also displays the properties of the tree in a text area, as shown in Figure 36.24.

LISTING 36.14 TreeNodeDemo.java

```java
1  import java.awt.*;
2  import javax.swing.*;
3  import javax.swing.tree.*;
4  import java.util.*;
5
6  public class TreeNodeDemo extends JApplet {
7    public TreeNodeDemo() {
8      // Create the first tree
9      DefaultMutableTreeNode root, europe, northAmerica, us;
10
11     europe = new DefaultMutableTreeNode("Europe");
12     europe.add(new DefaultMutableTreeNode("UK"));
```

tree nodes

add children

```
13    europe.add(new DefaultMutableTreeNode("Germany"));
14    europe.add(new DefaultMutableTreeNode("France"));
15    europe.add(new DefaultMutableTreeNode("Norway"));
16
17    northAmerica = new DefaultMutableTreeNode("North America");
18    us = new DefaultMutableTreeNode("US");
19    us.add(new DefaultMutableTreeNode("California"));                add children
20    us.add(new DefaultMutableTreeNode("Texas"));
21    us.add(new DefaultMutableTreeNode("New York"));
22    us.add(new DefaultMutableTreeNode("Florida"));
23    us.add(new DefaultMutableTreeNode("Illinois"));
24    northAmerica.add(us);
25    northAmerica.add(new DefaultMutableTreeNode("Canada"));
26
27    root = new DefaultMutableTreeNode("World");
28    root.add(europe);
29    root.add(northAmerica);
30
31    JPanel panel = new JPanel();
32    panel.setLayout(new GridLayout(1, 2));
33    panel.add(new JScrollPane(new JTree(root)));
34    panel.add(new JScrollPane(new JTree(new DefaultTreeModel(root))));
35
36    JTextArea jtaMessage = new JTextArea();
37    jtaMessage.setWrapStyleWord(true);
38    jtaMessage.setLineWrap(true);
39    add(new JSplitPane(JSplitPane.VERTICAL_SPLIT,
40      panel, new JScrollPane(jtaMessage)), BorderLayout.CENTER);
41
42    // Get tree information
43    jtaMessage.append("Depth of the node US is " + us.getDepth());
44    jtaMessage.append("\nLevel of the node US is " + us.getLevel());
45    jtaMessage.append("\nFirst child of the root is " +
46      root.getFirstChild());
47    jtaMessage.append("\nFirst leaf of the root is " +
48      root.getFirstLeaf());
49    jtaMessage.append("\nNumber of the children of the root is " +
50      root.getChildCount());
51    jtaMessage.append("\nNumber of leaves in the tree is " +
52      root.getLeafCount());
53    String breadthFirstSearchResult = "";
54
55    // Breadth-first traversal
56    Enumeration bf = root.breadthFirstEnumeration();
57    while (bf.hasMoreElements())
58      breadthFirstSearchResult += bf.nextElement().toString() + " ";
59    jtaMessage.append("\nBreath-first traversal from the root is "
60      + breadthFirstSearchResult);
61  }
62 }
```
main method omitted

You can create a **JTree** using a **TreeNode** root (line 33) or a **TreeModel** (line 34), whichever is convenient. A **TreeModel** is actually created using a **TreeNode** root (line 34). The two trees have the same contents because the root is the same. However, it is important to note that the two **JTree** objects are different, and so are their **TreeModel** objects, although both trees have the same root.

A tree is created by adding the nodes to the tree (lines 9–29). Each node is created using the **DefaultMutableTreeNode** class. This class provides many methods to manipulate the tree (e.g., adding a child, removing a child) and obtaining information about the tree

<table>
<tr><td>

«interface»
javax.swing.tree.TreeNode

</td><td></td></tr>
<tr><td>

+*children(): java.util.Enumeration*
+*getAllowsChildren(): boolean*
+*getChildAt(childIndex: int): TreeNode*
+*getChildCount(): int*
+*getIndex(node: TreeNode): int*
+*getParent(): TreeNode*
+*isLeaf(): boolean*

</td><td>

Returns the children of this node.
Returns true if this node can have children.
Returns the child TreeNode at index childIndex.
Returns the number of children under this node.
Returns the index of the specified node in the current node's children.
Returns the parent of this node.
Returns true if this node is a leaf.

</td></tr>
</table>

<table>
<tr><td>

«interface»
javax.swing.tree.MutableTreeNode

</td><td></td></tr>
<tr><td>

+*insert(child: MutableTreeNode, index: int): void*
+*remove(index: int): void*
+*remove(node: MutableTreeNode): void*
+*removeFromParent(): void*
+*setParent(newParent: MutableTreeNode): void*
+*setUserObject(object: Object): void*

</td><td>

Adds the specified child under this node at the specified index.
Removes the child at the specified index from this node's child list.
Removes the specified node from this node's child list.
Removes this node from its parent.
Sets the parent of this node to the specified newParent.
Resets the user object of this node to the specified object.

</td></tr>
</table>

<table>
<tr><td>

javax.swing.tree.DefaultMutableTreeNode

</td><td></td></tr>
<tr><td>

#allowsChildren: Boolean
#parent: MutableTreeNode
#userObject: Object

</td><td>

True if the node is able to have children.
Stores the parent of this node.
Stores the content of this node.

</td></tr>
<tr><td>

+DefaultMutableTreeNode()
+DefaultMutableTreeNode(userObject: Object)
+DefaultMutableTreeNode(userObject: Object,
 allowsChildren: boolean)
+add(newChild: MutableTreeNode)
+getChildAfter(aChild: TreeNode): TreeNode
+getChildBefore(aChild: TreeNode): TreeNode
+getFirstChild(): TreeNode
+getLastChild(): TreeNode
+getFirstLeaf(): DefaultMutableTreeNode
+getLastLeaf(): DefaultMutableTreeNode
+getNextLeaf(): DefaultMutableTreeNode
+getPreviousLeaf(): DefaultMutableTreeNode
+getLeafCount(): int
+getDepth(): int
+getLevel(): int
+getNextNode(): DefaultMutableTreeNode
+getPreviousNode(): DefaultMutableTreeNode
+getSiblingCount(): int
+getNextSibling(): DefaultMutableTreeNode
+getPath(): TreeNode[]
+getRoot(): TreeNode
+isRoot(): boolean
+breadthFirstEnumeration(): Enumeration
+depthFirstEnumeration(): Enumeration
+postorderEnumeration(): Enumeration
+preorderEnumeration(): Enumeration

</td><td>

Creates a tree node without user object, and allows children.
Creates a tree node with the specified user object, and allows children.
Creates a tree node with the specified user object and the specified mode to indicate whether children are allowed.
Adds the specified node to the end of this node's child vector.
These two methods return the next (previous) sibling of the specified child in this node's child vector.
These two methods return this node's first (last) child in the child's vector of this node.
These four methods return the first (last, next, and previous) leaf that is a descendant of this node. The first (last, next, and previous) leaf is recursively defined as the first (last, next, and previous) child's first (last, next, and previous) leaf.
Returns the total number of leaves that are descendants of this node.
Returns the depth of the tree rooted at this node.
Returns the distance from the root to this node.
Returns the node that follows (precedes) this node in a preorder traversal of this node.
Returns the number of siblings of this node.
Returns the next sibling of this node in the parent's child vector.
Returns the path from the root to this node.
Returns the root of the tree that contains this node.
Returns true if this node is the root of the tree.
These four methods create and return an enumeration that traverses the subtree rooted at this node in breadth-first order (depth-first order, postorder, preorder). These traversals were discussed in §25.2.4, "Tree Traversal."

</td></tr>
</table>

FIGURE 36.23 TreeNode represents a node.

FIGURE 36.24 The two trees have the same data because their roots are the same.

(e.g., level, depth, number of children, number of leaves, traversals). Some examples of using these methods are given in lines 43–60.

As shown in this example, often you don't have to directly use `TreeModel`. Using `DefaultMutableTreeNode` is sufficient, since the tree data are stored in `Default-MutableTreeNode`, and `DefaultMutableTreeNode` contains all the methods for modifying the tree and obtaining tree information.

36.12 `TreePath` and `TreeSelectionModel`

The `JTree` class contains the methods for selecting tree paths. The `TreePath` class represents a path from an ancestor to a descendant in a tree. Figure 36.25 shows `TreePath`.

javax.swing.tree.TreePath	
+TreePath(singlePath: Object)	Constructs a `TreePath` containing only a single element.
+TreePath(path: Object[])	Constructs a path from an array of objects.
+getLastPathComponent(): Object	Returns the last component of this path.
+getParentPath(): TreePath	Returns a path containing all but the last path component.
+getPath(): Object[]	Returns an ordered array of objects containing the components of this `TreePath`.
+getPathComponent(element: int): Object	Returns the path component at the specified index.
+getPathCount(): int	Returns the number of elements in the path.
+isDescendant(aTreePath: TreePath): boolean	Returns true if aTreePath contains all the components in this `TreePath`.
+pathByAddingChild(child: Object): TreePath	Returns a new path containing all the elements of this `TreePath` plus child.

FIGURE 36.25 `TreePath` represents a path from an ancestor to a descendant in a tree.

You can construct a `TreePath` from a single object or an array of objects, but often instances of `TreePath` are returned from the methods in `JTree` and `TreeSelectionModel`. For instance, the `getLeadSelectionPath()` method in `JTree` returns the path from the root to the selected node. There are many ways to extract the nodes from a tree path. Often you use the `getLastPathComponent()` method to obtain the last node in the path, and then the `getParent()` method to get all the nodes in the path upward through the link.

The selection of tree nodes is defined in the `TreeSelectionModel` interface, as shown in Figure 36.26. The `DefaultTreeSelectionModel` class is a concrete implementation of the `TreeSelectionModel` that maintains an array of `TreePath` objects representing the current selection. The last `TreePath` selected, called the *lead path*, can be obtained using the `getLeadSelectionPath()` method. To obtain all the selection paths, use the `getSelectionPaths()` method, which returns an array of tree paths.

obtain tree paths

«interface» *javax.swing.tree.TreeSelectionModel*	
+addSelectionPath(path: TreePath): void	Adds the specified TreePath to the current selection.
+addSelectionPaths(paths: TreePath[]): void	Adds the specified TreePaths to the current selection.
+clearSelection(): void	Clears the selection.
+getLeadSelectionPath(): TreePath	Returns the last path in the selection.
+getSelectionCount(): int	Returns the number of paths in the selection.
+getSelectionPath(): TreePath	Returns the first path in the selection.
+getSelectionPaths(): TreePath[]	Returns all the paths in the selection.
+getSelectionMode(): int	Returns the current selection mode.
+removeSelectionPath(path: TreePath): void	Removes path from the selection.
+removeSelectionPaths(paths: TreePath[]): void	Removes paths from the selection.
+setSelectionMode(mode: int): void	Sets the selection mode.
+setSelectionPath(path: TreePath): void	Sets the selection to path.
+setSelectionPaths(paths: TreePath[]): void	Sets the selection to paths.
+addTreeSelectionListener(x: TreeSelectionListener): void	Registers a TreeSelectionListener.
+removeTreeSelectionListener(x: TreeSelectionListener): void	Removes a TreeSelectionListener.

```
javax.swing.tree.DefaultTreeSelectionModel
```

FIGURE 36.26 The `TreeSelectionModel` handles selection in a tree and `DefaultTreeSelectionModel` is a concretate implementation of it.

tree selection modes

`TreeSelectionModel` supports three selection modes: contiguous selection, discontiguous selection, and single selection. *Single selection* allows only one item to be selected. *Contiguous selection* allows multiple selections, but the selected items must be contiguous. *Discontiguous selection* is the most flexible; it allows any item to be selected at a given time. The default tree selection mode is discontiguous. To set a selection mode, use the `setSelectionMode(int mode)` method in `TreeSelectionModel`. The constants for the three modes are:

- CONTIGUOUS_TREE_SELECTION

- DISCONTIGUOUS_TREE_SELECTION

- SINGLE_TREE_SELECTION

Note

When you create a `JTree`, a `DefaultTreeSelectionModel` is automatically created, and thus you rarely need to create an instance of `TreeSelectionModel` explicitly. Since most of the methods in `TreeSelectionModel` are also in `JTree`, you can get selection paths and process the selection without directly dealing with `TreeSelectionModel`.

bypass
TreeSelectionModel

Listing 36.15 gives an example that displays a selected path or selected paths in a tree. The user may select a node or multiple nodes and click the *Show Path* button to display the properties of the first selected path or the *Show Paths* button to display all the selected paths in a text area, as shown in Figure 36.27. The *Show Path* button displays a path from the last node up to the root.

LISTING 36.15 `TestTreePath.java`

```
1 import java.awt.*;
2 import java.awt.event.*;
3 import javax.swing.*;
4 import javax.swing.tree.*;
```

```
5
6  public class TestTreePath extends JApplet {                           default tree
7    private JTree jTree = new JTree();                                  text area
8    private JTextArea jtaOutput = new JTextArea();                      Show Path button
9    private JButton jbtShowPath = new JButton("Show Path");             Show Paths button
10   private JButton jbtShowPaths = new JButton("Show Paths");
11
12   public TestTreePath() {
13     JSplitPane splitPane = new JSplitPane(JSplitPane.HORIZONTAL_SPLIT,  split pane
14       new JScrollPane(jTree), new JScrollPane(jtaOutput));
15
16     JPanel panel = new JPanel();
17     panel.add(jbtShowPath);
18     panel.add(jbtShowPaths);
19
20     add(splitPane, BorderLayout.CENTER);
21     add(panel, BorderLayout.NORTH);
22
23     jbtShowPath.addActionListener(new ActionListener() {              Show Path button
24       public void actionPerformed(ActionEvent e) {
25         TreePath path = jTree.getSelectionPath();                     selected path
26         jtaOutput.append("\nProcessing a single path\n");
27         jtaOutput.append("# of elements: " + path.getPathCount());    path count
28         jtaOutput.append("\nlast element: "
29           + path.getLastPathComponent());
30         jtaOutput.append("\nfrom last node in the path to the root: ");
31         TreeNode node = (TreeNode)path.getLastPathComponent();        last node
32         while (node != null) {
33           jtaOutput.append(node.toString() + " ");
34           node = node.getParent();                                    get parent
35         }
36     }});
37
38     jbtShowPaths.addActionListener(new ActionListener() {             Show Paths button
39       public void actionPerformed(ActionEvent e) {
40         jtaOutput.append("\nProcessing multiple paths\n");
41         javax.swing.tree.TreePath[] paths = jTree.getSelectionPaths();  selected paths
42         for (int i = 0; i < paths.length; i++)
43           jtaOutput.append(paths[i].toString() + "\n");              display a path
44     }});
45   }                                                                   main method omitted
46 }
```

FIGURE 36.27 The selected path(s) are processed.

The `getSelectionPath()` method invoked from a **JTree** returns a **TreePath** in line 25. The first node in the path is always the root of the tree. The `getPathCount()` invoked from a **TreePath** returns the number of the nodes in the path (line 27). The `getLast-PathComponent()` invoked from a **TreePath** returns the last node in the path (line 29). The return node type is **Object**. You need to cast it to a **TreeNode** (line 31) in order to invoke the `getParent()` method from a **TreeNode** (line 34).

While the `getSelectionPath()` method (line 25) returns the first selected path, the `getSelectionPaths()` method (line 41) returns all the selected paths in an array of paths.

36.13 Case Study: Modifying Trees

Write a program to create two trees that display the same contents: world, continents, countries, and states, as shown in Figure 36.28. For the tree on the left, enable the user to choose a selection mode, specify whether it can be edited, add a new child under the first selected node, and remove all the selected nodes.

(a)   (b)

FIGURE 36.28   You can rename a node, add a child, and remove nodes in a tree dynamically.

You can choose a selection mode from the selectionMode combo box. You can specify whether the left tree nodes can be edited from the editable check box.

When you click a button, if no nodes are currently selected in the left tree, a message dialog box is displayed, as shown in Figure 36.29(a). When you click the *Add a Child for Selected Node* button, an input dialog box is displayed to prompt the user to enter a child name for the selected node, as shown in Figure 36.29(b). The new node becomes a child of the first selected node. When you click the *Remove Selected Nodes* button, all the selected nodes in the left tree are removed.

(a)   (b)

FIGURE 36.29   You can add a new node to the tree.

Listing 36.16 gives the program.

LISTING 36.16   ModifyTree.java

```
1 import java.awt.*;
2 import java.awt.event.*;
3 import javax.swing.*;
4 import javax.swing.tree.*;
```

```
 5
 6  public class ModifyTree extends JApplet {
 7    // Create a combo box for choosing selection modes
 8    private JComboBox jcboSelectionMode = new JComboBox(new String[]{          combo box
 9      "CONTIGUOUS_TREE_SELECTION", "DISCONTIGUOUS_TREE_SELECTION",
10      "SINGLE_TREE_SELECTION"});
11
12    // Create a check box for specifying editable
13    private JCheckBox jchkEditable = new JCheckBox();                          check box
14
15    // Create two buttons
16    private JButton jbtAdd =                                                   buttons
17      new JButton("Add a Child for Selected Node");
18    private JButton jbtRemove = new JButton("Remove Selected Nodes");
19
20    // Declare two trees
21    private JTree jTree1, jTree2;                                              trees
22
23    public ModifyTree() {
24      // Create the first tree
25      DefaultMutableTreeNode root, europe, northAmerica, us;                  tree nodes
26
27      europe = new DefaultMutableTreeNode("Europe");                          fill nodes
28      europe.add(new DefaultMutableTreeNode("UK"));
29      europe.add(new DefaultMutableTreeNode("Germany"));
30      europe.add(new DefaultMutableTreeNode("France"));
31      europe.add(new DefaultMutableTreeNode("Norway"));
32
33      northAmerica = new DefaultMutableTreeNode("North America");
34      us = new DefaultMutableTreeNode("US");
35      us.add(new DefaultMutableTreeNode("California"));
36      us.add(new DefaultMutableTreeNode("Texas"));
37      us.add(new DefaultMutableTreeNode("New York"));
38      us.add(new DefaultMutableTreeNode("Florida"));
39      us.add(new DefaultMutableTreeNode("Illinois"));
40      northAmerica.add(us);
41      northAmerica.add(new DefaultMutableTreeNode("Canada"));
42
43      root = new DefaultMutableTreeNode("World");
44      root.add(europe);
45      root.add(northAmerica);
46
47      jcboSelectionMode.setSelectedIndex(1);
48
49      JPanel p1 = new JPanel();
50      p1.add(new JLabel("selectionMode"));
51      p1.add(jcboSelectionMode);
52      p1.add(new JLabel("editable"));
53      p1.add(jchkEditable);
54
55      JPanel p2 = new JPanel(new GridLayout(1, 2));
56      p2.add(new JScrollPane(jTree1 = new JTree(root)));                       create jTree1
57      p2.add(new JScrollPane(jTree2 =                                         create jTree2
58        new JTree(new DefaultTreeModel(root)))); // Same root as jTree1
59
60      JPanel p3 = new JPanel();
61      p3.add(jbtAdd);
62      p3.add(jbtRemove);
63
64      add(p1, BorderLayout.NORTH);
```

```
65        add(p2, BorderLayout.CENTER);
66        add(p3, BorderLayout.SOUTH);
67
68        // Register listeners
69        jcboSelectionMode.addActionListener(new ActionListener() {
70          public void actionPerformed(ActionEvent e) {
71            if (jcboSelectionMode.getSelectedItem().
72              equals("CONTIGUOUS_TREE_SELECTION"))
73              jTree1.getSelectionModel().setSelectionMode(
74                TreeSelectionModel.CONTIGUOUS_TREE_SELECTION);
75            else if (jcboSelectionMode.getSelectedItem().
76              equals("DISCONTIGUOUS_TREE_SELECTION"))
77              jTree1.getSelectionModel().setSelectionMode(
78                TreeSelectionModel.DISCONTIGUOUS_TREE_SELECTION);
79            else
80              jTree1.getSelectionModel().setSelectionMode(
81                TreeSelectionModel.SINGLE_TREE_SELECTION);
82          }
83        });
84
85        jchkEditable.addActionListener(new ActionListener() {
86          public void actionPerformed(ActionEvent e) {
87            jTree1.setEditable(jchkEditable.isSelected());
88          }
89        });
90
91        jbtAdd.addActionListener(new ActionListener() {
92          public void actionPerformed(ActionEvent e) {
93            DefaultMutableTreeNode parent = (DefaultMutableTreeNode)
94              jTree1.getLastSelectedPathComponent();
95
96            if (parent == null) {
97              JOptionPane.showMessageDialog(null,
98                "No node in the left tree is selected");
99              return;
100           }
101
102           // Enter a new node
103           String nodeName = JOptionPane.showInputDialog(
104             null, "Enter a child node for "+ parent, "Add a Child",
105             JOptionPane.QUESTION_MESSAGE);
106
107           // Insert the new node as a child of treeNode
108           parent.add(new DefaultMutableTreeNode(nodeName));
109
110           // Reload the model since a new tree node is added
111           ((DefaultTreeModel)(jTree1.getModel())).reload();
112           ((DefaultTreeModel)(jTree2.getModel())).reload();
113         }
114       });
115
116       jbtRemove.addActionListener(new ActionListener() {
117         public void actionPerformed(ActionEvent e) {
118           // Get all selected paths
119           TreePath[] paths = jTree1.getSelectionPaths();
120
121           if (paths == null) {
122             JOptionPane.showMessageDialog(null,
123               "No node in the left tree is selected");
124             return;
125           }
```

```
126
127          // Remove all selected nodes
128          for (int i = 0; i < paths.length; i++) {
129            DefaultMutableTreeNode node = (DefaultMutableTreeNode)
130              (paths[i].getLastPathComponent());
131
132            if (node.isRoot()) {
133              JOptionPane.showMessageDialog(null,
134                "Cannot remove the root");
135            }
136            else
137              node.removeFromParent();                               remove node
138          }
139
140          // Reload the model since a new tree node is added
141          ((DefaultTreeModel)(jTree1.getModel())).reload();          reload tree model
142          ((DefaultTreeModel)(jTree2.getModel())).reload();
143        }
144      });
145    }
146 }                                                                   main method omitted
```

Two JTree objects (jTree1 and jTree2) are created with the same root (lines 56–58), but each has its own TreeSelectionModel. When you choose a selection mode in the combo box, the new selection mode is set in jTree1's selection model (line 69–83). The selection mode for jTree2 is not affected.

When the editable check box is checked or unchecked, the editable property in jTree1 is set accordingly. If editable is true, you can edit a node in the left tree.

When you click the *Add a Child for Selected Node* button, the first selected node is returned as parent (lines 93–94). Suppose you selected Europe, UK, and US in this order; parent is Europe. If parent is null, no node is selected in the left tree (lines 96–100). Otherwise, prompt the user to enter a new node from an input dialog box (lines 103–105) and add this node as a child of parent (line 108). Since the tree has been modified, you need to invoke the reload() method to notify that the models for both trees have been changed (lines 111–112). Otherwise, the new node may not be displayed in jTree1 and jTree2.

When you click the *Remove Selected Nodes* button, all the tree paths for each selected node are obtained in paths (line 119). Suppose you selected Europe, UK, and US in this order; three tree paths are obtained. Each path starts from the root to a selected node. If no node is selected, paths is null. To delete a selected node is to delete the last node in each selected tree path (128–138). The last node in a path is obtained using getLastPathComponent(). If the node is the root, it cannot be removed (lines 132–135). The removeFromParent() method removes a node (line 137).

36.14 Tree Node Rendering and Editing

JTree delegates node rendering to a renderer. All renderers are instances of the TreeCellRenderer interface, which defines a single method, getTreeCellRenderer-Component, as follows:

```
public Component getTreeCellRendererComponent
  (JTree tree, Object value, boolean selected, boolean expanded,
  boolean leaf, int row, boolean hasFocus);
```

You can create a custom tree cell renderer by implementing the TreeCellRenderer interface, or use the DefaultTreeCellRenderer class, which provides a default implementation for TreeCellRenderer. When a new JTree is created, an instance of Default-TreeCellRenderer is assigned to the tree renderer. The DefaultTreeCellRenderer class maintains three icon properties named `leafIcon`, `openIcon`, and `closedIcon` for leaf nodes, expanded nodes, and collapsed nodes. It also provides colors for text and background. The following code sets new leaf, open and closed icons, and new background selection color in the tree:

```
DefaultTreeCellRenderer renderer =
  (DefaultTreeCellRenderer)jTree1.getCellRenderer();
renderer.setLeafIcon(yourCustomLeafImageIcon);
renderer.setOpenIcon(yourCustomOpenImageIcon);
renderer.setClosedIcon(yourCustomClosedImageIcon);
renderer.setBackgroundSelectionColor(Color.red);
```

Note

The default leaf, open icon, and closed icon are dependent on the look-and-feel. For instance, on Windows look-and-feel, the open icon is − and the closed icon is +.

JTree comes with a default cell editor. If **JTree**'s `editable` property is `true`, the default editor activates a text field for editing when the node is clicked three times. By default, this property is set to `false`. To create a custom editor, you need to extend the **DefaultCellEditor** class, which is the same class you used in table cell editing. You can use a text field, a check box, or a combo box, and pass it to **DefaultCellEditor**'s constructor to create an editor. The following code uses a combo box for editing colors. The combo box editor is shown in Figure 36.30(a).

```
// Customize editor
JComboBox jcboColor = new JComboBox();
jcboColor.addItem("red");
jcboColor.addItem("green");
jcboColor.addItem("blue");
jcboColor.addItem("yellow");
jcboColor.addItem("orange");

jTree1.setCellEditor(new javax.swing.DefaultCellEditor(jcboColor));
jTree1.setEditable(true);
```

(a)   (b)

FIGURE 36.30 You can supply a custom editor for editing tree nodes.

There are two annoying problems with the editor created in the preceding code. First, it is activated with just one mouse click. Second, it overlaps the node's icon, as shown in Figure 36.30(a). These two problems can be fixed by using the **DefaultTreeCellEditor**, as shown in the following code:

```
jTree1.setCellEditor
  (new javax.swing.tree.DefaultTreeCellEditor(jTree1,
   new javax.swing.tree.DefaultTreeCellRenderer(),
   new javax.swing.DefaultCellEditor(jcboColor)));
```

The new editor is shown in Figure 36.30(b). Editing using `DefaultTreeCellEditor` starts on a triple mouse click. The combo box does not overlap the node's icon.

36.15 Tree Events

`JTree` can fire `TreeSelectionEvent` and `TreeExpansionEvent`, among many other events. Whenever a new node is selected, `JTree` fires a `TreeSelectionEvent`. Whenever a node is expanded or collapsed, `JTree` fires a `TreeExpansionEvent`. To handle the tree-selection event, a listener must implement the `TreeSelectionListener` interface, which contains a single handler named `valueChanged` method. `TreeExpansionListener` contains two handlers named `treeCollapsed` and `treeExpanded` for handling node expansion or node closing.

The following code displays a selected node in a listener class for `TreeSelectionEvent`:

```java
public void valueChanged(TreeSelectionEvent e) {
  TreePath path = e.getNewLeadSelectionPath();
  TreeNode treeNode = (TreeNode)path.getLastPathComponent();
  System.out.println("The selected node is " + treeNode.toString());
}
```

CHAPTER SUMMARY

■ `JTable` has three supporting models: a table model, a column model, and a list-selection model. The *table model* is for storing and processing data. The *column model* represents all the columns in the table. The *list-selection model* is the same as the one used by `JList` for selecting rows, columns, and cells in a table. `JTable` also has two useful supporting classes, `TableColumn` and `JTableHeader`. `TableColumn` contains the information on a particular column. `JTableHeader` contains the information on the header of a `JTable`. Each column has a default editor and renderer. You can also create a custom editor by implementing the `TableCellEditor` interface, and you can create a custom renderer by implementing the `TableCellRenderer` interface.

■ Like `JTable`, `JTree` is a very complex component with many supporting interfaces and classes. While `JTree` displays the tree, the data representation of the tree is handled by `TreeModel`, `TreeNode`, and `TreePath`. `TreeModel` represents the entire tree, `TreeNode` represents a node, and `TreePath` represents a path to a node. Unlike the `ListModel` or `TableModel`, the tree model does not directly store or manage tree data. Tree data are stored and managed in `TreeNode` and `TreePath`. A `TreePath` is an array of `Object`s that are vended from a `TreeModel`. The elements of the array are ordered such that the root is always the first element (index 0) of the array. The `TreeSelectionModel` interface handles tree node selection. The `DefaultTreeCellRenderer` class provides a default tree node renderer that can display a label and/or an icon in a node. The `DefaultTreeCellEditor` can be used to edit the cells in a text field. The `TreePath` class is a support class that represents a set of nodes in a path.

■ `JTable` and `JTree` are in the `javax.swing` package, but their supporting interfaces and classes are all included in the `javax.swing.tree` and `javax.swing.table` packages, respectively.

REVIEW QUESTIONS

Sections 36.2–36.7

36.1   How do you initialize a table? Can you specify the maximum number of visible rows in a table without scrolling? How do you specify the height of a table cell? How do you specify the horizontal margin of table cells?

36.2   How do you modify table contents? How do you add or remove a row? How do you add or remove a column?

36.3   What is autoresizing of a table column? How many types of autoresizing are available?

36.4   What are the properties that show grids, horizontal grids, and vertical grids? What are the properties that specify the table row height, vertical margin, and horizontal margin?

36.5   What are the default table renderers and editors? How do you create a custom table cell renderer and editor?

36.6   What are the default tree renderers and editors? How do you create a custom tree cell renderer and editor?

36.7   How do you disable table cell editing?

Sections 36.8–36.14

36.8   How do you create a tree? How do you specify the row height of a tree node? How do you obtain the default tree model and tree-selection model from an instance of `JTree`?

36.9   How do you initialize data in a tree using `TreeModel`? How do you add a child to an instance of `DefaultMutableTreeNode`?

36.10   How do you enable tree node editing?

36.11   How do you add or remove a node from a tree?

36.12   How do you obtain a selected tree node?

PROGRAMMING EXERCISES

Sections 36.2–36.7

36.1*   (*Creating a table for a loan schedule*) Exercise 31.5 displays an amortization schedule in a text area. Write a program that enables the user to enter or choose the loan amount, number of years, and interest rate from spinners and displays the schedule in a table, as shown in Figure 36.31. The step for loan amount is $500, for number of years is 1, and for annual interest rate is 0.125%.

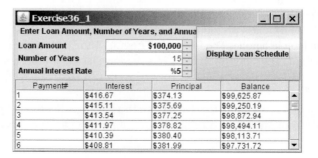

FIGURE 36.31   The table shows the loan schedule.

36.2* (*Deleting rows and columns*) Listing 36.6, ModifyTable.java, allows you to delete only the first selected row or column. Enable the program to delete all the selected rows or columns. Also enable the program to delete a row or a column by pressing the DELETE key.

36.3** (*Creating a student table*) Create a table for student records. Each record consists of name, birthday, class status, in-state, and a photo, as shown in Figure 36.32(a). The name is of the **String** type; birthday is of the **Date** type; class status is one of the following five values: Freshman, Sophomore, Junior, Senior, or Graduate; in-state is a **boolean** value indicating whether the student is a resident of the state; and photo is an image icon. Use the default editors for name, birthday, and in-state. Supply a combo box as custom editor for class status.

Exercise36_3

Name	Birthday	Class Stat...	In-State	Photo
Jeff F. Smith	Sep 29, 1998	Fresh... ▼	☐	
John F. Kay	Sep 29, 1997	Freshman Sophomore Junior Senior Graduate	☐	

Exercise36_4

Country	Capital	Population	Democracy
USA	Washington DC	280	true
Canada	Ottawa	32	true
United Kingdom	London	60	true
Germany	Berlin	83	true
France	Paris	60	true

(a)   (b)

FIGURE 36.32 (a) The table displays student records. (b) The data in the file are displayed in a **JTable**.

36.4* (*Displaying a table for data from a text file*) Suppose that a table named Exercise36_4Table.txt is stored in a text file. The first line in the file is the header, and the remaining lines correspond to rows in the table. The elements are separated by commas. Write a program to display the table using the **JTable** component. For example, the following text file is displayed in a table, as shown in Figure 36.32(b).

```
Country, Capital, Population, Democracy
USA, Washington DC, 280, true
Canada, Ottawa, 32, true
United Kingdom, London, 60, true
Germany, Berlin, 83, true
France, Paris, 60, true
Norway, Oslo, 4.5, true
India, New Delhi, 1046, true
```

36.5*** (*Creating a controller using* **JTable**) In Exercise 35.1, you created a chart model (**ChartModel**) and two views (**PieChart** and **BarChart**). Create a controller that enables the user to modify the data, as shown in Figure 36.33.

FIGURE 36.33 You can modify the data in the controller. The views are synchronized with the controller.

You will see the changes take effect in the pie-chart view and the bar-chart view. Your exercise consists of the following classes:

- The controller named **ChartController**. This class uses a table to display data. You can modify the data in the table. Click the *Insert* button to insert a new row above the selected row in the table, click the *Delete* button to delete the selected row in the table, and click the *Update* button to update the changes you made in the table.
- The class **MyTableModel**. This class extends **DefaultTableModel** to override the **getColumnClass** method so that you can use the **JTable**'s default editor for numerical values. This class is the same as in Listing 36.7.
- The classes **ChartModel**, **PieChart**, and **BarChart** from Exercise 35.1.
- The main class **Exercise36_5**. This class creates a user interface with a controller and two buttons, *View Pie Chart* and *View Bar Chart*. Click the *View Pie Chart* button to pop up a frame to display a pie chart, and click the *View Bar Chart* button to pop up a frame to display a bar chart.

Sections 36.8–36.14

36.6* (*Creating a tree for book chapters*) Create a tree to display the table of contents for a book. When a node is selected in the tree, display a paragraph to describe the selected node, as shown in Figure 36.34(a).

(a)   (b)

FIGURE 36.34 (a) The content of the node is displayed in a text area when the node is clicked. (b) You can store tree data to a file and restore them later.

36.7* (*Storing and restoring trees*) Modify Listing 36.16, ModifyTree.java, to add two buttons, as shown in Figure 36.34(b) to store and restore trees. Use the object I/O to store the tree model.

36.8* (*Traversing trees*) Create a tree using the default **JTree** constructor and traverse the nodes in breadth-first, depth-first, preorder, and postorder.

36.9*** (*File explorer*) Use JTree to develop a file explorer. The program lets the user enter a directory and displays all files under the directory, as shown in Figure 36.35.

FIGURE 36.35   The file explorer explores the files in a directory.

36.10**   (*Adding and deleting tree nodes using the INSERT and DELETE keys*) Modify
Listing 36.16, ModifyTree.java, to add a new child node by pressing the IN-
SERT key, and delete a node by pressing the DELETE key.

CHAPTER 37

JAVA DATABASE PROGRAMMING

Objectives

- To understand the concept of database and database management systems (§37.2).

- To understand the relational data model: relational data structures, constraints, and languages (§37.2).

- To use SQL to create and drop tables and to retrieve and modify data (§37.3).

- To learn how to load a driver, connect to a database, execute statements, and process result sets using JDBC (§37.4).

- To use prepared statements to execute precompiled SQL statements (§37.5).

- To use callable statements to execute stored SQL procedures and functions (§37.6).

- To explore database metadata using the `DatabaseMetaData` and `ResultSetMetaData` interfaces (§37.7).

37.1 Introduction

You may have heard a lot about database systems. Database systems are everywhere. Your social security information is stored in a database by the government. If you shop online, your purchase information is stored in a database by the company. If you attend a university, your academic information is stored in a database by the university. Database systems not only store data, they also provide means of accessing, updating, manipulating, and analyzing data. Your social security information is updated periodically, and you can register in courses online. Database systems play an important role in society and in commerce.

This chapter introduces database systems, SQL, and how to develop database applications using Java. If you already know SQL, you may skip §§37.2–37.3.

37.2 Relational Database Systems

database system

A *database system* consists of a database, the software that stores and manages data in the database, and the application programs that present data and enable the user to interact with the database system, as shown in Figure 37.1.

FIGURE 37.1 A database system consists of data, database management software, and application programs.

DBMS

A database is a repository of data that form information. When you purchase a database system, such as MySQL, Oracle, IBM, Microsoft, or Sybase, from a software vendor, you actually purchase the software comprising a *database management system* (DBMS). Database management systems are designed for use by professional programmers and are not suitable for ordinary customers. Application programs are built on top of the DBMS for customers to access and update the database. Thus application programs can be viewed as the interfaces between the database system and its users. Application programs may be standalone GUI applications or Web applications, and may access several different database systems in the network, as shown in Figure 37.2.

Most of today's database systems are *relational database systems*. They are based on the relational data model, which has three key components: structure, integrity, and language. *Structure* defines the representation of the data. *Integrity* imposes constraints on the data. *Language* provides the means for accessing and manipulating data.

FIGURE 37.2 An application program may access multiple database systems.

37.2.1 Relational Structures

The relational model is built around a simple and natural structure. A relation is actually a table that consists of nonduplicate rows. Tables are easy to understand and easy to use. The relational model provides a simple yet powerful way to represent data.

A row of a table represents a record, and a column of a table represents the value of a single attribute of the record. In relational database theory, a row is called a *tuple* and a column is called an *attribute*. Figure 37.3 shows a sample table that stores information about the courses offered by a university. The table has eight tuples, and each tuple has five attributes.

relational model

tuple

attribute

FIGURE 37.3 A table has a table name, column names, and rows.

Tables describe the relationship among data. Each row in a table represents a record of related data. For example, "11111", "CSCI", "1301", "Introduction to Java I", and "4" are related to form a record (the first row in Figure 37.3) in the **Course** table. Just as data in the same row are related, so too data in different tables may be related through common attributes. Suppose the database has two other tables, **Student** and **Enrollment**, as shown in Figures 37.4 and 37.5. The **Course** table and the **Enrollment** table are related through their common attribute **courseId**, and the **Enrollment** table and the **Student** table are related through **ssn**.

Student Table

ssn	firstName	mi	lastName	phone	birthDate		street	zipCode	deptID
444111110	Jacob	R	Smith	9129219434	1985-04-09	99	Kingston Street	31435	BIOL
444111111	John	K	Stevenson	9129219434	null	100	Main Street	31411	BIOL
444111112	George	K	Smith	9129213454	1974-10-10	1200	Abercorn St.	31419	CS
444111113	Frank	E	Jones	9125919434	1970-09-09	100	Main Street	31411	BIOL
444111114	Jean	K	Smith	9129219434	1970-02-09	100	Main Street	31411	CHEM
444111115	Josh	R	Woo	7075989434	1970-02-09	555	Franklin St.	31411	CHEM
444111116	Josh	R	Smith	9129219434	1973-02-09	100	Main Street	31411	BIOL
444111117	Joy	P	Kennedy	9129229434	1974-03-19	103	Bay Street	31412	CS
444111118	Toni	R	Peterson	9129229434	1964-04-29	103	Bay Street	31412	MATH
444111119	Patrick	R	Stoneman	9129229434	1969-04-29	101	Washington St.	31435	MATH
444111120	Rick	R	Carter	9125919434	1986-04-09	19	West Ford St.	31411	BIOL

FIGURE 37.4 A Student table stores student information.

Enrollment Table

ssn	courseId	dateRegistered	grade
444111110	11111	2004-03-19	A
444111110	11112	2004-03-19	B
444111110	11113	2004-03-19	C
444111111	11111	2004-03-19	D
444111111	11112	2004-03-19	F
444111111	11113	2004-03-19	A
444111112	11114	2004-03-19	B
444111112	11115	2004-03-19	C
444111112	11116	2004-03-19	D
444111113	11111	2004-03-19	A
444111113	11113	2004-03-19	A
444111114	11115	2004-03-19	B
444111115	11115	2004-03-19	F
444111115	11116	2004-03-19	F
444111116	11111	2004-03-19	D
444111117	11111	2004-03-19	D
444111118	11111	2004-03-19	A
444111118	11112	2004-03-19	D
444111118	11113	2004-03-19	B

FIGURE 37.5 An Enrollment table stores student enrollment information.

37.2.2 Integrity Constraints

integrity constraint

An *integrity constraint* imposes a condition that all the legal values in a table must satisfy. Figure 37.6 shows an example of some integrity constraints in the Subject and Course tables.

In general, there are three types of constraints: domain constraints, primary key constraints, and foreign key constraints. *Domain constraints* and *primary key constraints* are known as *intrarelational constraints*, meaning that a constraint involves only one relation. The *foreign key constraint* is *interrelational*, meaning that a constraint involves more than one relation.

Domain Constraints

domain constraint

Domain constraints specify the permissible values for an attribute. Domains can be specified using standard data types, such as integers, floating-point numbers, fixed-length strings, and variant-length strings. The standard data type specifies a broad range of values. Additional constraints can be specified to narrow the ranges. For example, you can specify that the numOfCredits attribute (in the Course table) must be greater than 0 and less than 5. You can

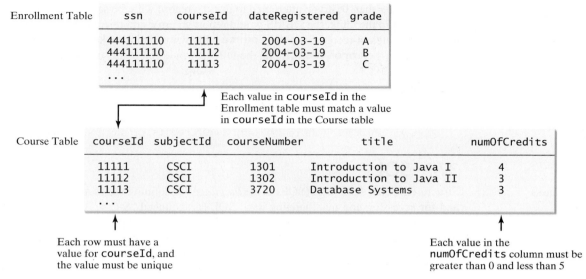

FIGURE 37.6 The Enrollment table and the Course table have integrity constraints.

also specify whether an attribute can be null, which is a special value in a database meaning unknown or not applicable. As shown in the Student table, birthDate may be null.

Primary Key Constraints

To understand primary keys, it is helpful to know superkeys, keys, and candidate keys. A *superkey* is an attribute or a set of attributes that uniquely identifies the relation. That is, no two tuples have the same values on a superkey. By definition, a relation consists of a set of distinct tuples. The set of all attributes in the relation forms a superkey.

primary key
superkey

A *key* K is a minimal superkey, meaning that any proper subset of K is not a superkey. A relation can have several keys. In this case, each of the keys is called a *candidate key*. The *primary* key is one of the candidate keys designated by the database designer. The primary key is often used to identify tuples in a relation. As shown in Figure 37.6, courseId is the primary key in the Course table.

Foreign Key Constraints

In a relational database, data are related. Tuples in a relation are related, and tuples in different relations are related through their common attributes. Informally speaking, the common attributes are foreign keys. The *foreign key constraints* define the relationships among relations.

foreign key

Formally, a set of attributes *FK* is a *foreign key* in a relation *R* that references relation *T* if it satisfies the following two rules:

- The attributes in *FK* have the same domain as the primary key in *T*.

- A nonnull value on *FK* in *R* must match a primary key value in *T*.

As shown in Figure 37.6, courseId is the foreign key in Enrollment that references the primary key courseId in Course. Every courseId value must match a courseId value in Course.

Enforcing Integrity Constraints

The database management system enforces integrity constraints and rejects operations that would violate them. For example, if you attempted to insert a new record ('11115', 'CSCI', '2490', 'C++ Programming', 0) into the Course table, it would fail because the credit hours

auto enforcement

must be greater than 0; if you attempted to insert a record with the same primary key as an existing record in the table, the DBMS would report an error and reject the operation; if you attempted to delete a record from the **Course** table whose primary key value is referenced by the records in the **Enrollment** table, the DBMS would reject this operation.

Note

All relational database systems support primary key constraints and foreign key constraints. Not all database systems support domain constraints. On the Microsoft Access database, for example, you cannot specify the constraint that **numOfCredits** is greater than 0 and less than 5.

37.3 SQL

database language

Structured Query Language (SQL) is the *language* for defining tables and integrity constraints and for accessing and manipulating data. SQL (pronounced "S-Q-L" or "sequel") is the universal language for accessing relational database systems. Application programs may allow users to access a database without directly using SQL, but these applications themselves must use SQL to access the database. This section introduces some basic SQL commands.

Note

standard SQL

There are hundreds of relational database management systems. They share the common SQL language but do not all support every feature of SQL. Some systems have their own extensions to SQL. This section introduces standard SQL supported by all systems.

SQL can be used on MySQL, Oracle, Sybase, IBM DB2, IBM Informix, Borland Interbase, MS Access, or any other relational database system. This chapter uses MySQL to demonstrate SQL and uses MySQL, Access, and Oracle to demonstrate JDBC programming. The book's Web site contains the following supplements on how to install and use three popular databases: MySQL, Oracle, and Access:

MySQL Tutorial

Oracle Tutorial

Access Tutorial

- Supplement IV.B: Tutorial for MySQL
- Supplement IV.C: Tutorial for Oracle
- Supplement IV.D: Tutorial for Microsoft Access

37.3.1 Creating a User Account on MySQL

Assume that you have installed MySQL 5 with the default configuration. To match all the examples in this book, you should create a user named *scott* with password *tiger*. You can perform the administrative tasks using the MySQL GUI Administrator tool or using the command line. Here are the steps to create a user from the command line:

1. From the DOS command prompt, type

   mysql –uroot -p

   You will be prompted to enter the root password, as shown in Figure 37.7.

2. At the mysql prompt, enter

   use mysql;

3. To create user **scott** with password **tiger**, enter

   create user 'scott'@'localhost' identified by 'tiger';

   grant select, insert, update, delete, create, drop,
   **   execute, references on *.* to 'scott'@'localhost';**

FIGURE 37.7 You can access a MySQL database server from the command window.

4. Enter

exit;

to exit the MySQL console.

Note

On Windows, your MySQL database server starts every time your computer starts. You can stop it by typing the command `net stop mysql` and restart it by typing the command `net start mysql`.

start mysql
stop mysql

By default, the server contains two databases named **mysql** and **test**. The **mysql** database contains the tables that store information about the server and its users. This database is intended for the server administrator to use. For example, the administrator can use it to create users and grant or revoke user privileges. Since you are the owner of the server installed on your system, you have full access to the mysql database. However, you should not create user tables in the mysql database. You can use the test database to store data or create new databases. You can also create a new database using the command `create database` *databasename* or drop an existing database using the command `drop database` *databasename*.

37.3.2 Creating a Database

To match the examples in the book, you should create a database named **javabook**. Here are the steps to create it:

1. From the DOS command prompt, type

mysql –uscott -ptiger

to login to mysql, as shown in Figure 37.8.

```
Command Prompt - mysql -uscott -ptiger                    _|□|×|
C:\>mysql -uscott -ptiger
Welcome to the MySQL monitor.  Commands end with ; or \g.
Your MySQL connection id is 33
Server version: 5.0.37-community-nt MySQL Community Edition (GPL)

Type 'help;' or '\h' for help. Type '\c' to clear the buffer.

mysql> create database javabook;
Query OK, 1 row affected (0.02 sec)

mysql> show databases;
```

FIGURE 37.8 You can create databases in MySQL.

2. At the mysql prompt, enter

create database javabook;

For your convenience, the SQL statements for creating and initializing tables used in the book is provided in Supplement IV.A. You can download the script for MySQL and save it to script.sql. To execute the script, first switch to the **javabook** database and then type

run script file

source script.sql;

as shown in Figure 37.9.

FIGURE 37.9 You can run SQL commands in a script file.

37.3.3 Creating and Dropping Tables

Tables are the essential objects in a database. To create a table, use the `create table` statement to specify a table name, attributes, and types, as in the following example:

create table

```
create table Course (
  courseId char(5),
  subjectId char(4) not null,
  courseNumber integer,
  title varchar(50) not null,
  numOfCredits integer,
  primary key (courseId)
);
```

This statement creates the Course table with attributes courseId, subjectId, course-Number, title, and numOfCredits. Each attribute has a data type that specifies the type of data stored in the attribute. char(5) specifies that courseId consists of five characters. varchar(50) specifies that title is a variant-length string with a maximum of 50 characters. integer specifies that courseNumber is an integer. The primary key is courseId.

The tables Student and Enrollment can be created as follows:

```
create table Student (
  ssn char(9),
  firstName varchar(25),
  mi char(1),
  lastName varchar(25),
  birthDate date,
  street varchar(25),
  phone char(11),
  zipCode char(5),
  deptId char(4),
  primary key (ssn)
);
```

```
create table Enrollment (
  ssn char(9),
  courseId char(5),
  dateRegistered date,
  grade char(1),
  primary key (ssn, courseId),
  foreign key (ssn) references Student,
  foreign key (courseId) references Course
);
```

Note

SQL keywords are not case sensitive. This book adopts the following naming conventions: Tables are named in the same way as Java classes, and attributes are named in the same way as Java variables. SQL keywords are named in the same way as Java keywords.

naming convention

If a table is no longer needed, it can be dropped permanently using the drop table command. For example, the following statement drops the Course table:

```
drop table Course;
```

create table

If a table to be dropped is referenced by other tables, you have to drop the other tables first. For example, if you have created the tables Course, Student, and Enrollment and want to drop Course, you have to first drop Enrollment, because Course is referenced by Enrollment.

Figure 37.10 shows how to enter the create table statement from the mysql console.

FIGURE 37.10 The execution result of the SQL statements is displayed in the MySQL console.

If you make typing errors, you have to retype the whole command. To avoid retyping, you can save the command in a file, and then run the command from the file. To do so, create a text file to contain commands, named, for example, test.sql. You can create the text file using any text editor, such as NotePad, as shown in Figure 37.11(a). To comment a line, precede it with two dashes. You can now run the script file by typing source test.sql from the SQL command prompt, as shown in Figure 37.11(b).

(a)   (b)

FIGURE 37.11 (a) You can use Notepad to create a text file for SQL commands. (b) You can run the SQL commands in a script file from MySQL.

37.3.4 Simple Insert, Update, and Delete

Once a table is created, you can insert data into it. You can also update and delete records. This section introduces simple insert, update, and delete statements.

The general syntax to insert a record into a table is:

```
insert into tableName [(column1, column2, ..., column)]
values (value1, value2, ..., valuen);
```

For example, the following statement inserts a record into the Course table. The new record has the courseId '11113', subjectId 'CSCI', courseNumber 3720, title 'Database Systems', and creditHours 3.

```
insert into Course (courseId, subjectId, courseNumber, title, numOfCredits)
values ('11113', 'CSCI', '3720', 'Database Systems', 3);
```

The column names are optional. If they are omitted, all the column values for the record must be entered, even though the columns have default values. String values are case sensitive and enclosed inside single quotation marks in SQL.

The general syntax to update a table is:

```
update tableName
set column1 = newValue1 [, column2 = newValue2, ...]
[where condition];
```

For example, the following statement changes the numOfCredits for the course whose title is Database Systems to 4.

```
update Course
set numOfCredits = 4
where title = 'Database Systems';
```

The general syntax to delete records from a table is:

```
delete [from] tableName
[where condition];
```

For example, the following statement deletes the Database Systems course from the Course table:

```
delete Course
where title = 'Database System';
```

The following statement deletes all the records from the Course table:

```
delete Course;
```

37.3.5 Simple Queries

To retrieve information from tables, use a select statement with the following syntax:

```
select column-list
from table-list
[where condition];
```

The select clause lists the columns to be selected. The from clause refers to the tables involved in the query. The optional where clause specifies the conditions for the selected rows.

Query 1: Select all the students in the CS department, as shown in Figure 37.12.

```
select firstName, mi, lastName
from Student
where deptId = 'CS';
```

37.3.6 Comparison and Boolean Operators

SQL has six comparison operators, as shown in Table 37.1, and three Boolean operators, as shown in Table 37.2.

FIGURE 37.12 The result of the select statement is displayed in a window.

TABLE 37.1 Comparison Operators

Operator	Description
=	Equal to
<> or !=	Not equal to
<	Less than
<=	Less or equal to
>	Greater than
>=	Greater than or equal to

TABLE 37.2 Boolean Operators

Operator	Description
not	logical negation
and	logical conjunction
or	logical disjunction

Note
The comparison and Boolean operators in SQL have the same meaning as in Java. In SQL the equal to operator is =, but in Java it is ==. In SQL the not equal to operator is <> or !=, but in Java it is !=. The not, and, and or operators are !, && (&), and in Java || (|).

Query 2: Get the names of the students who are in the CS dept and live in the zip code 31411.

```
select firstName, mi, lastName
from Student
where deptId = 'CS' and zipCode = '31411';
```

Note
To select all the attributes from a table, you don't have to list all the attribute names in the select clause. Instead you can just specify an *asterisk* (*), which stands for all the attributes. For example, the following query displays all the attributes of the students who are in the CS dept and live in zip code 31411:

```
select *
from Student
where deptId = 'CS' and zipCode = '31411';
```

37.3.7 The `like`, `between-and`, and `is null` Operators

SQL has a `like` operator that can be used for pattern matching. The syntax to check whether a string `s` has a pattern `p` is

`s like p` or `s not like p`

You can use the wild-card characters % (percent symbol) and _ (underline symbol) in the pattern `p`. % matches zero or more characters, and _ matches any single character in `s`. For example, `lastName like '_mi%'` matches any string whose second and third letters are `m` and `i`. `lastName not like '_mi%'` excludes any string whose second and third letters are `m` and `i`.

Note

On the earlier version of MS Access, the wild-card character is *, and the character ? matches any single character.

The **between-and** operator checks whether a value v is between two other values, v1 and v2, using the following syntax:

> v between v1 and v2 or v not between v1 and v2

> v between v1 and v2 is equivalent to v >= v1 and v <= v2, and v not between v1 and v2 is equivalent to v < v1 or v > v2.

The **is null** operator checks whether a value v is **null** using the following syntax:

> v is null or v is not null

Query 3: Get the social security numbers of the students whose grades are between 'C' and 'A'.

```
select ssn
from Enrollment
where grade between 'C' and 'A';
```

37.3.8   Column Alias

When a query result is displayed, SQL uses the column names as column headings. Usually the user gives abbreviated names for the columns, and the columns cannot have spaces when the table is created. Sometimes it is desirable to give more descriptive names in the result heading. You can use the column aliases with the following syntax:

```
select columnName [as] alias
```

Query 4: Get the last name and zip code of the students in the CS department. Display the column headings as Last Name for lastName and Zip Code for zipCode. The query result is shown in Figure 37.13.

```
select lastName as "Last Name", zipCode as "Zip Code"
from Student
where deptId = 'CS';
```

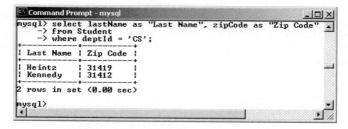

FIGURE 37.13   You can use a column alias in the display.

Note

The **as** keyword is optional in MySQL and Oracle but is required in MS Access.

37.3.9   The Arithmetic Operators

You can use the arithmetic operators * (multiplication), / (division), + (addition), and – (subtraction) in SQL.

Query 5: Assume that a credit hour is 50 minutes of lectures; get the total minutes for each course with the subject CSCI. The query result is shown in Figure 37.14.

```
select title, 50 * numOfCredits as "Lecture Minutes Per Week"
from Course
where subjectId = 'CSCI';
```

FIGURE 37.14 You can use arithmetic operators in SQL.

37.3.10 Displaying Distinct Tuples

SQL provides the `distinct` keyword, which can be used to suppress duplicate tuples in the output. For example, the following statement displays all the subject IDs used by the courses:

```
select subjectId as "Subject ID"
from Course;
```

This statement displays all the subject IDs. To display distinct tuples, add the `distinct` keyword in the `select` clause, as follows:

```
select distinct subjectId as "Subject ID"
from Course;
```

When there is more than one item in the `select` clause, the `distinct` keyword applies to all the items that find distinct tuples.

37.3.11 Displaying Sorted Tuples

SQL provides the `order by` clause to sort the output using the following general syntax:

```
select column-list
from table-list
[where condition]
[order by columns-to-be-sorted];
```

In the syntax, `columns-to-be-sorted` specifies a column or a list of columns to be sorted. By default, the order is ascending. To sort in descending order, append the `desc` keyword after `columns-to-be-sorted`. You could also append the `asc` keyword, but it is not necessary. When multiple columns are specified, the rows are sorted based on the first column, then the rows with the same values on the first column are sorted based on the second column, and so on.

Query 6: List the full names of the students in the CS department, ordered primarily on their last names in descending order and secondarily on their first names in ascending order. The query result is shown in Figure 37.15.

```
select lastName, firstName, deptId
from Student
where deptId = 'CS'
order by lastName desc, firstName asc;
```

FIGURE 37.15 You can sort results using the order by clause.

37.3.12 Joining Tables

Often you need to get information from multiple tables, as demonstrated in the next query.

Query 7: List the courses taken by student Jacob Smith. To solve this query, you need to join tables Student and Enrollment, as shown in Figure 37.16.

FIGURE 37.16 Student and Enrollment are joined on ssn.

You can write the query in SQL:

```
select distinct lastName, firstName, courseId
from Student, Enrollment
where Student.ssn = Enrollment.ssn and
    lastName = 'Smith' and firstName = 'Jacob';
```

The tables Student and Enrollment are listed in the from clause. The query examines every pair of rows, each made of one item from Student and another from Enrollment, and selects the pairs that satisfy the condition in the where clause. The rows in Student have the last name, Smith, and the first name, Jacob, and both rows from Student and Enrollment have the same ssn values. For each pair selected, lastName and firstName from Student and courseId from Enrollment are used to produce the result, as shown in Figure 37.17. Student and Enrollment have the same attribute ssn. To distinguish them in a query, use Student.ssn and Enrollment.ssn.

For more features of SQL, see Supplement IV.H and Supplement IV.I.

37.4 JDBC

The Java API for developing Java database applications is called *JDBC*. JDBC is the trade-marked name of a Java API that supports Java programs that access relational databases. JDBC is not an acronym, but it is often thought to stand for Java Database Connectivity.

JDBC provides Java programmers with a uniform interface for accessing and manipulating a wide range of relational databases. Using the JDBC API, applications written in the

```
Command Prompt - mysql                                    _ | □ | x |
mysql> select distinct lastName, firstName, courseId
    -> from Student, Enrollment
    -> where Student.ssn = Enrollment.ssn and
    ->    lastName = 'Smith' and firstName = 'Jacob';
+----------+-----------+----------+
| lastName | firstName | courseId |
+----------+-----------+----------+
| Smith    | Jacob     | 11111    |
| Smith    | Jacob     | 11112    |
| Smith    | Jacob     | 11113    |
+----------+-----------+----------+
3 rows in set (0.06 sec)

mysql>
```

FIGURE 37.17   Query 7 demonstrates queries involving multiple tables.

Java programming language can execute SQL statements, retrieve results, present data in a user-friendly interface, and propagate changes back to the database. The JDBC API can also be used to interact with multiple data sources in a distributed, heterogeneous environment.

The relationships between Java programs, JDBC API, JDBC drivers, and relational databases are shown in Figure 37.18. The JDBC API is a set of Java interfaces and classes used to write Java programs for accessing and manipulating relational databases. Since a JDBC driver serves as the interface to facilitate communications between JDBC and a proprietary database, JDBC drivers are database specific and are normally provided by the database vendors. You need MySQL JDBC drivers to access the MySQL database, and Oracle JDBC drivers to access the Oracle database. For the Access database, use the JDBC-ODBC bridge driver included in JDK. ODBC is a technology developed by Microsoft for accessing databases on the Windows platform. An ODBC driver is preinstalled on Windows. The JDBC-ODBC bridge driver allows a Java program to access any ODBC data source.

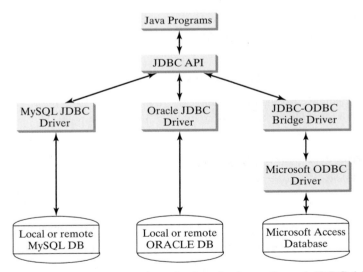

FIGURE 37.18   Java programs access and manipulate databases through JDBC drivers.

37.4.1 Developing Database Applications Using JDBC

The JDBC API is a Java application program interface to generic SQL databases that enables Java developers to develop DBMS-independent Java applications using a uniform interface.

The JDBC API consists of classes and interfaces for establishing connections with databases, sending SQL statements to databases, processing the results of the SQL statements, and obtaining database metadata. Four key interfaces are needed to develop any database application using Java: `Driver`, `Connection`, `Statement`, and `ResultSet`. These interfaces define a framework for generic SQL database access. The JDBC API defines these interfaces. The JDBC driver vendors provide implementation for them. Programmers use the interfaces.

The relationship of these interfaces is shown in Figure 37.19. A JDBC application loads an appropriate driver using the `Driver` interface, connects to the database using the `Connection` interface, creates and executes SQL statements using the `Statement` interface, and processes the result using the `ResultSet` interface if the statements return results. Note that some statements, such as SQL data definition statements and SQL data modification statements, do not return results.

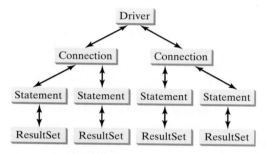

FIGURE 37.19 JDBC classes enable Java programs to connect to the database, send SQL statements, and process results.

The JDBC interfaces and classes are the building blocks in the development of Java database programs. A typical Java program takes the steps outlined below to access the database.

1. Loading drivers.

An appropriate driver must be loaded using the statement shown below before connecting to a database.

```
Class.forName("JDBCDriverClass");
```

A driver is a concrete class that implements the `java.sql.Driver` interface. The drivers for Access, MySQL, and Oracle are listed in Table 37.3.

TABLE 37.3 JDBC Drivers

Database	Driver Class	Source
Access	`sun.jdbc.odbc.JdbcOdbcDriver`	Already in JDK
MySQL	`com.mysql.jdbc.Driver`	Companion Web site
Oracle	`oracle.jdbc.driver.OracleDriver`	Companion Web site

mysqljdbc.jar
ojdbc14.jar

The JDBC-ODBC driver for Access is bundled in JDK. The MySQL JDBC driver is contained in `mysqljdbc.jar` (downloadable from www.cs.armstrong.edu/liang/intro7e/book/lib/mysqljdbc.jar). The Oracle JDBC driver is contained in `ojdbc14.jar` (downloadable from www.cs.armstrong.edu/liang/intro7e/book/lib/ojdbc14.jar). To use the MySQL and Oracle drivers, you have to add mysqljdbc.jar and ojdbc14.jar in the classpath using the following DOS command on Windows:

```
set classpath=%classpath%;c:\book\mysqljdbc.jar;c:\book\ojdbc14.jar
```

If your program accesses several different databases, all their respective drivers must be loaded.

Note

com.mysql.jdbc.Driver is a class in mysqljdbc.jar, and oracle.jdbc.driver.
OracleDriver is a class in ojdbc14.jar. mysqljdbc.jar and ojdbc14.jar contain
many classes to support the driver. These classes are used by JDBC, but not directly by JDBC programmers. When you use a class explicitly in the program, it is automatically loaded by the JVM.
The driver classes, however, are not used explicitly in the program, so you have to write the code
to tell the JVM to load them.

why load a driver?

Note

Java 6 supports automatic driver discovery, so you don't have to load the driver explicitly. At the
time of this writing, however, this feature is not supported for Oracle and MySQL drivers.

automatic driver discovery

2. Establishing connections.

To connect to a database, use the static method getConnection(databaseURL) in the
DriverManager class, as follows:

```
Connection connection = DriverManager.getConnection(databaseURL);
```

where databaseURL is the unique identifier of the database on the Internet. Table 37.4 lists
the URLs for the MySQL, Oracle, and Access databases.

TABLE 37.4 JDBC URLs

Database	URL Pattern
Access	jdbc:odbc:dataSource
MySQL	jdbc:mysql://hostname/dbname
Oracle	jdbc:oracle:thin:@hostname:port#:oracleDBSID

For an ODBC data source, the databaseURL is jdbc:odbc:dataSource. An ODBC
data source can be created using the ODBC Data Source Administrator on Windows. See
Supplement IV.D, "Tutorial for Microsoft Access," on how to create an ODBC data source for
an Access database.

Suppose a data source named ExampleMDBDataSource has been created for an Access
database. The following statement creates a Connection object:

```
Connection connection = DriverManager.getConnection
    ("jdbc:odbc:ExampleMDBDataSource");
```

connect Access DB

The databaseURL for a MySQL database specifies the host name and database name to locate a database. For example, the following statement creates a Connection object for the
local MySQL database javabook with username *scott* and password *tiger*:

```
Connection connection = DriverManager.getConnection
    ("jdbc:mysql://localhost/javabook", "scott", "tiger");
```

connect MySQL DB

Recall that by default MySQL contains two databases named *mysql* and *test*. §37.3.2, "Creating a Database," created a custom database named javabook. We will use javabook in the
examples.

The databaseURL for an Oracle database specifies the *hostname*, the *port#* where the database listens for incoming connection requests, and the *oracleDBSID* database name to locate a

database. For example, the following statement creates a `Connection` object for the Oracle database on liang.armstrong.edu with username *scott* and password *tiger*:

connect Oracle DB

```
Connection connection = DriverManager.getConnection
    ("jdbc:oracle:thin:@liang.armstrong.edu:1521:orcl",
     "scott", "tiger");
```

3. Creating statements.

If a `Connection` object can be envisioned as a cable linking your program to a database, an object of `Statement` can be viewed as a cart that delivers SQL statements for execution by the database and brings the result back to the program. Once a `Connection` object is created, you can create statements for executing SQL statements as follows:

```
Statement statement = connection.createStatement();
```

4. Executing statements.

An SQL DDL or update statement can be executed using `executeUpdate(String sql)`, and an SQL query statement can be executed using `executeQuery(String sql)`. The result of the query is returned in `ResultSet`. For example, the following code executes the SQL statement *create table Temp (col1 char(5), col2 char(5))*:

```
statement.executeUpdate
    ("create table Temp (col1 char(5), col2 char(5))");
```

The next code executes the SQL query `select firstName, mi, lastName from Student where lastName = 'Smith'`:

```
// Select the columns from the Student table
ResultSet resultSet = statement.executeQuery
    ("select firstName, mi, lastName from Student where lastName "
     + " = 'Smith'");
```

5. Processing `ResultSet`.

The `ResultSet` maintains a table whose current row can be retrieved. The initial row position is `null`. You can use the `next` method to move to the next row and the various get methods to retrieve values from a current row. For example, the code given below displays all the results from the preceding SQL query.

```
// Iterate through the result and print the student names
while (resultSet.next())
    System.out.println(resultSet.getString(1) + " " +
        resultSet.getString(2) + ". " + resultSet.getString(3));
```

The `getString(1)`, `getString(2)`, and `getString(3)` methods retrieve the column values for `firstName`, `mi`, and `lastName`, respectively. Alternatively, you can use `getString("firstName")`, `getString("mi")`, and `getString("lastName")` to retrieve the same three column values. The first execution of the `next()` method sets the current row to the first row in the result set, and subsequent invocations of the `next()` method set the current row to the second row, third row, and so on, to the last row.

Listing 37.1 is a complete example that demonstrates connecting to a database, executing a simple query, and processing the query result with JDBC. The program connects to a local MySQL database and displays the students whose last name is Smith.

LISTING 37.1 SimpleJDBC.java

```
1 import java.sql.*;
2
3 public class SimpleJdbc {
4   public static void main(String[] args)
5       throws SQLException, ClassNotFoundException {
6     // Load the JDBC driver
7     Class.forName("com.mysql.jdbc.Driver");                                    load driver
8     System.out.println("Driver loaded");
9
10    // Establish a connection
11    Connection connection = DriverManager.getConnection               connect database
12      ("jdbc:mysql://localhost/javabook" , "scott", "tiger");
13    System.out.println("Database connected");
14
15    // Create a statement
16    Statement statement = connection.createStatement();                create statement
17
18    // Execute a statement
19    ResultSet resultSet = statement.executeQuery                       execute statement
20      ("select firstName, mi, lastName from Student where lastName "
21       + " = 'Smith'");
22
23    // Iterate through the result and print the student names
24    while (resultSet.next())                                           get result
25      System.out.println(resultSet.getString(1) + "\t" +
26        resultSet.getString(2) + "\t" + resultSet.getString(3));
27
28    // Close the connection
29    connection.close();                                                close connection
30  }
31 }
```

The statement in line 7 loads a JDBC driver for MySQL, and the statement in lines 11–13 connects to a local MySQL database. You may change them to connect to an Access or Oracle database. The last statement (line 29) closes the connection and releases resource related to the connection.

Note

If you run this program from the DOS prompt, specify the appropriate driver in the classpath, as shown in Figure 37.20.

run from DOS prompt

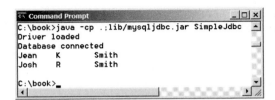

FIGURE 37.20 You must include the driver file to run Java database programs.

The classpath directory and jar files are separated by commas. The period (.) represents the current directory. For convenience, the driver files are placed under the **lib** directory.

Caution

Do not use a semicolon (;) to end the Oracle SQL command in a Java program. The semicolon may not work with the Oracle JDBC drivers. It does work, however, with the other drivers used in the book.

the semicolon issue

auto commit

Note

The `Connection` interface handles transactions and specifies how they are processed. By default, a new connection is in autocommit mode, and all its SQL statements are executed and committed as individual transactions. The commit occurs when the statement completes or the next execute occurs, whichever comes first. In the case of statements returning a result set, the statement completes when the last row of the result set has been retrieved or the result set has been closed. If a single statement returns multiple results, the commit occurs when all the results have been retrieved. You can use the `setAutoCommit(false)` method to disable autocommit, so that all SQL statements are grouped into one transaction that is terminated by a call to either the `commit()` or the `rollback()` method. The `rollback()` method undoes all the changes made by the transaction.

37.4.2 Accessing a Database from a Java Applet

Using the JDBC-ODBC bridge driver, your program cannot run as an applet from a Web browser because the ODBC driver contains non-Java native code. The JDBC drivers for MySQL and Oracle are written in Java and can run from the JVM in a Web browser. This section gives an example that demonstrates connecting to a database from a Java applet. The applet lets the user enter the SSN and the course ID to find a student's grade, as shown in Figure 37.21. The code in Listing 37.2 uses the MySQL database on the host liang.armstrong.edu.

FIGURE 37.21 A Java applet can access the database on the server.

LISTING 37.2 FindGrade.java

```
1  import javax.swing.*;
2  import java.sql.*;
3  import java.awt.*;
4  import java.awt.event.*;
5
6  public class FindGrade extends JApplet {
7    private JTextField jtfSSN = new JTextField(9);
8    private JTextField jtfCourseId = new JTextField(5);
9    private JButton jbtShowGrade = new JButton("Show Grade");
10
11   // Statement for executing queries
12   private Statement stmt;
13
14   /** Initialize the applet */
15   public void init() {
16     // Initialize database connection and create a Statement object
17     initializeDB();
18
```

```
19      jbtShowGrade.addActionListener(                                    button listener
20        new java.awt.event.ActionListener() {
21        public void actionPerformed(ActionEvent e) {
22          jbtShowGrade_actionPerformed(e);
23        }
24      });
25
26      JPanel jPanel1 = new JPanel();
27      jPanel1.add(new JLabel("SSN"));
28      jPanel1.add(jtfSSN);
29      jPanel1.add(new JLabel("Course ID"));
30      jPanel1.add(jtfCourseId);
31      jPanel1.add(jbtShowGrade);
32
33      add(jPanel1, BorderLayout.NORTH);
34    }
35
36    private void initializeDB() {
37      try {
38        // Load the JDBC driver
39        Class.forName("com.mysql.jdbc.Driver");                          load driver
40 //       Class.forName("oracle.jdbc.driver.OracleDriver");             Oracle drive commented
41        System.out.println("Driver loaded");
42
43        // Establish a connection
44        Connection connection = DriverManager.getConnection             connect database
45          ("jdbc:mysql://localhost/javabook", "scott", "tiger");
46 //       ("jdbc:oracle:thin:@liang.armstrong.edu:1521:orcl",           connect to Oracle commented
47 //        "scott", "tiger");
48        System.out.println("Database connected");
49
50        // Create a statement
51        stmt = connection.createStatement();                            create statement
52      }
53      catch (Exception ex) {
54        ex.printStackTrace();
55      }
56    }
57
58    private void jbtShowGrade_actionPerformed(ActionEvent e) {
59      String ssn = jtfSSN.getText();
60      String courseId = jtfCourseId.getText();
61      try {
62        String queryString = "select firstName, mi, " +
63          "lastName, title, grade from Student, Enrollment, Course " +
64          "where Student.ssn = '" + ssn + "' and Enrollment.courseId "
65          + "= '" + courseId +
66          "' and Enrollment.courseId = Course.courseId " +
67          " and Enrollment.ssn = Student.ssn";
68
69        ResultSet rset = stmt.executeQuery(queryString);                execute statement
70
71        if (rset.next()) {                                              show result
72          String lastName = rset.getString(1);
73          String mi = rset.getString(2);
74          String firstName = rset.getString(3);
75          String title = rset.getString(4);
76          String grade = rset.getString(5);
77
```

```
78              // Display result in a dialog box
79              JOptionPane.showMessageDialog(null, firstName + " " + mi +
80                " " + lastName + "'s grade on course " + title + " is " +
81                grade);
82            } else {
83              // Display result in a dialog box
84              JOptionPane.showMessageDialog(null, "Not found");
85            }
86          }
87          catch (SQLException ex) {
88            ex.printStackTrace();
89          }
90        }
91      }
```

main method omitted

The `initializeDB()` method (lines 36–56) loads the MySQL driver (line 39), connects to the MySQL database on host liang.armstrong.edu (lines 44–45), and creates a statement (line 51).

You can run the applet standalone from the `main` method (note that the listing for the `main` method is omitted for all the applets in the book for brevity) or test the applet using the appletviewer utility, as shown in Figure 37.21. If this applet is deployed on the server where the database is located, any client on the Internet can run it from a Web browser. Since the client may not have a MySQL driver, you should specify the driver in the archive attribute in the applet tag, as follows:

```
<applet
  code = "FindGrade"
  archive = "FindGrade.jar, lib/mysqljdbc.jar"
  width = 380
  height = 80
>
</applet>
```

Note

create archive file

For information on how to *create an archive file*, see Supplement I I I.Q, "Packaging and Deploying Java Projects." The FindGrade.jar file can be created using the following command:

```
c:\book>jar -cf FindGrade.jar FindGrade.class FindGrade$1.class
```

Note

applet security restriction

To access the database from an applet, *security restrictions* make it necessary for the applet to be downloaded from the server where the database is located. Therefore, you have to deploy the applet on the server.

Note

security hole

There is a *security hole* in this program. If you enter `1' or true or '1` in the SSN field, you will get the first student's score, because the query string now becomes

```
select firstName, mi, lastName, title, grade
from Student, Enrollment, Course
where Student.ssn = 1' or true or '1 and
      Enrollment.courseId = ' ' and
      Enrollment.courseId = Course.courseId and
      Enrollment.ssn = Student.ssn;
```

You can avoid this problem by using the `PreparedStatement`.

37.5 **PreparedStatement**

Once a connection to a particular database is established, it can be used to send SQL statements from your program to the database. The Statement interface is used to execute static SQL statements that contain no parameters. The PreparedStatement interface, extending Statement, is used to execute a precompiled SQL statement with or without parameters. Since the SQL statements are precompiled, they are efficient for repeated executions.

A PreparedStatement object is created using the preparedStatement method in the Connection interface. For example, the following code creates a PreparedStatement preparedStatement on a particular Connection connection for an SQL insert statement:

```
Statement preparedStatement = connection.prepareStatement
    ("insert into Student (firstName, mi, lastName) " +
    "values (?, ?, ?)");
```

This insert statement has three question marks as placeholders for parameters representing values for firstName, mi, and lastName in a record of the Student table.

As a subinterface of Statement, the PreparedStatement interface inherits all the methods defined in Statement. It also provides the methods for setting parameters in the object of PreparedStatement. These methods are used to set the values for the parameters before executing statements or procedures. In general, the set methods have the following name and signature:

```
setX(int parameterIndex, X value);
```

where X is the type of the parameter, and parameterIndex is the index of the parameter in the statement. The index starts from 1. For example, the method setString(int paramterIndex, String value) sets a String value to the specified parameter.

The following statements pass the parameters "Jack", "A", and "Ryan" to the placeholders for firstName, mi, and lastName in PreparedStatement preparedStatement:

```
preparedStatement.setString(1, "Jack");
preparedStatement.setString(2, "A");
preparedStatement.setString(3, "Ryan");
```

After setting the parameters, you can execute the prepared statement by invoking executeQuery() for a SELECT statement and executeUpdate() for a DDL or update statement.

The executeQuery() and executeUpdate() methods are similar to the ones defined in the Statement interface except that they have no parameters, because the SQL statements are already specified in the preparedStatement method when the object of PreparedStatement is created.

Using a prepared SQL statement, Listing 37.2 can be improved as in Listing 37.3.

LISTING 37.3 FindGradeUsingPreparedStatement.java

```
1 import javax.swing.*;
2 import java.sql.*;
3 import java.awt.*;
4 import java.awt.event.*;
5
6 public class FindGradeUsingPreparedStatement extends JApplet {
7     private JTextField jtfSSN = new JTextField(9);
8     private JTextField jtfCourseId = new JTextField(5);
9     private JButton jbtShowGrade = new JButton("Show Grade");
10
```

```
11    // PreparedStatement for executing queries
12    private PreparedStatement preparedStatement;
13
14    /** Initialize the applet */
15    public void init() {
16      // Initialize database connection and create a Statement object
17      initializeDB();
18
19      jbtShowGrade.addActionListener(
20        new java.awt.event.ActionListener() {
21        public void actionPerformed(ActionEvent e) {
22          jbtShowGrade_actionPerformed(e);
23        }
24      });
25
26      JPanel jPanel1 = new JPanel();
27      jPanel1.add(new JLabel("SSN"));
28      jPanel1.add(jtfSSN);
29      jPanel1.add(new JLabel("Course ID"));
30      jPanel1.add(jtfCourseId);
31      jPanel1.add(jbtShowGrade);
32
33      add(jPanel1, BorderLayout.NORTH);
34    }
35
36    private void initializeDB() {
37      try {
38        // Load the JDBC driver
39        Class.forName("com.mysql.jdbc.Driver");
40  //      Class.forName("oracle.jdbc.driver.OracleDriver");
41        System.out.println("Driver loaded");
42
43        // Establish a connection
44        Connection connection = DriverManager.getConnection
45          ("jdbc:mysql://localhost/javabook", "scott", "tiger");
46  //      ("jdbc:oracle:thin:@liang.armstrong.edu:1521:orcl",
47  //       "scott", "tiger");
48        System.out.println("Database connected");
49
50        String queryString = "select firstName, mi, " +
51          "lastName, title, grade from Student, Enrollment, Course " +
52          "where Student.ssn = ? and Enrollment.courseId = ? " +
53          "and Enrollment.courseId = Course.courseId";
54
55        // Create a statement
56        preparedStatement = connection.prepareStatement(queryString);
57      }
58      catch (Exception ex) {
59        ex.printStackTrace();
60      }
61    }
62
63    private void jbtShowGrade_actionPerformed(ActionEvent e) {
64      String ssn = jtfSSN.getText();
65      String courseId = jtfCourseId.getText();
66      try {
67        preparedStatement.setString(1, ssn);
68        preparedStatement.setString(2, courseId);
69        ResultSet rset = preparedStatement.executeQuery();
70
```

Margin notes:
load driver (line 39)
connect database (line 44)
placeholder (line 52)
prepare statement (line 56)
execute statement (line 69)

```
71      if (rset.next()) {                                            show result
72        String lastName = rset.getString(1);
73        String mi = rset.getString(2);
74        String firstName = rset.getString(3);
75        String title = rset.getString(4);
76        String grade = rset.getString(5);
77
78        // Display result in a dialog box
79        JOptionPane.showMessageDialog(null, firstName + " " + mi +
80          " " + lastName + "'s grade on course " + title + " is " +
81          grade);
82      }
83      else {
84        // Display result in a dialog box
85        JOptionPane.showMessageDialog(null, "Not found");
86      }
87    }
88    catch (SQLException ex) {
89      ex.printStackTrace();
90    }
91  }
92 }                                                                   main method omitted
```

This example does exactly the same thing as Listing 37.2 except that it uses the prepared statement to dynamically set the parameters. The code in this example is almost the same as in the preceding example. The new code is highlighted.

A prepared query string is defined in lines 50–53 with `ssn` and course ID as parameters. An SQL prepared statement is obtained in line 56. Before executing the query, the actual values of `ssn` and `courseId` are set to the parameters in lines 67–68. Line 69 executes the prepared statement.

37.6 **CallableStatement**

The `CallableStatement` interface is designed to execute SQL-stored procedures. The procedures may have `IN`, `OUT` or `IN OUT` parameters. An `IN` parameter receives a value passed to the procedure when it is called. An `OUT` parameter returns a value after the procedure is completed, but it contains no value when the procedure is called. An `IN OUT` parameter contains a value passed to the procedure when it is called, and returns a value after it is completed. For example, the following procedure in Oracle PL/SQL has `IN` parameter `p1`, `OUT` parameter `p2`, and `IN OUT` parameter `p3`.

IN parameter
OUT parameter
IN OUT parameter

```
create or replace procedure sampleProcedure
  (p1 in varchar, p2 out number, p3 in out integer) is
begin
  -- do something
end sampleProcedure;
/
```

 Note
The syntax of stored procedures is vendor specific. Oracle PL/SQL is used for demonstrations of stored procedures in this book. PL/SQL is a procedural language extension of SQL. It is a fully functional programming language whose syntax is very similar to Ada's.

A `CallableStatement` object can be created using the `prepareCall(String call)` method in the `Connection` interface. For example, the following code creates a `Callable-Statement cstmt` on `Connection connection` for procedure `sampleProcedure`.

```
CallableStatement callableStatement = connection.prepareCall(
  "{call sampleProcedure(?, ?, ?)}");
```

`{call sampleProcedure(?, ?, ...)}` is referred to as the *SQL escape syntax*, which signals the driver that the code within it should be handled differently. The driver parses the escape syntax and translates it into code that the database understands. For this case, `sampleProcedure` is an Oracle PL/SQL procedure. The call is translated to a string `"begin sampleProcedure(?, ?, ?); end"` and passed to an Oracle database for execution.

You can call procedures as well as functions. The syntax to create a SQL callable statement for a function is:

```
{? = call functionName(?, ?, ...)}
```

`CallableStatement` inherits `PreparedStatement`. Additionally, the `CallableStatement` interface provides methods for registering `OUT` parameters and for getting values from `OUT` parameters.

Before calling a SQL procedure, you need to use appropriate set methods to pass values to `IN` and `IN OUT` parameters, and use `registerOutParameter` to register `OUT` and `IN OUT` parameters. For example, before calling procedure `sampleProcedure`, the following statements pass values to parameters `p1` (`IN`) and `p3` (`IN OUT`) and register parameters `p2` (`OUT`) and `p3` (`IN OUT`):

```
callableStatement.setString(1, "Dallas"); // Set Dallas to p1
callableStatement.setLong(3, 1); // Set 1 to p3
// Register OUT parameters
callableStatement.registerOutParameter(2, java.sql.Types.DOUBLE);
callableStatement.registerOutParameter(3, java.sql.Types.INTEGER);
```

You may use `execute()` or `executeUpdate()` to execute the procedure depending on the type of SQL statement, then use get methods to retrieve values from the OUT parameters. For example, the next statements retrieve the values from parameters `p2` and `p3`.

```
double d = callableStatement.getDouble(2);
int i = callableStatement.getInt(3);
```

Let us define an Oracle function that returns the number of the records in the table that match the specified `firstName` and `lastName` in the `Student` table.

```
create or replace function studentFound
  (first varchar2, last varchar2)
  -- Do not name firstName and lastName. 6/4/00 YDL
  return number is
  numberOfSelectedRows number := 0;
begin
  select count(*) into numberOfSelectedRows
  from Student
  where Student.firstName = first and
    Student.lastName = last;

  return numberOfSelectedRows;
end studentFound;
/
```

Suppose the function `studentFound` is already created in the database. Listing 37.4 gives an example that tests this function using callable statements.

LISTING 37.4 TestCallableStatement.java

```
 1 import java.sql.*;
 2
 3 public class TestCallableStatement {
 4   /** Creates new form TestTableEditor */
 5   public static void main(String[] args) throws Exception {
 6     Class.forName("oracle.jdbc.driver.OracleDriver");          load driver
 7     Connection connection = DriverManager.getConnection(        connect database
 8       "jdbc:oracle:thin:@liang.armstrong.edu:1521:orcl",
 9       "scott", "tiger");
10
11     // Create a callable statement
12     CallableStatement callableStatement = connection.prepareCall(   create callable statement
13       "{? = call studentFound(?, ?)}");
14
15     java.util.Scanner input = new java.util.Scanner(System.in);
16     System.out.print("Enter student's first name: ");
17     String firstName = input.nextLine();                        enter firstName
18     System.out.print("Enter student's last name: ");
19     String lastName = input.nextLine();                         enter lastName
20
21     callableStatement.setString(2, firstName);                  set IN parameter
22     callableStatement.setString(3, lastName);                   set IN parameter
23     callableStatement.registerOutParameter(1, Types.INTEGER);   register OUT parameter
24     callableStatement.execute();                                execute statement
25
26     if (callableStatement.getInt(1) >= 1)                       get OUT parameter
27       System.out.println(firstName + " " + lastName +
28         " is in the database");
29     else
30       System.out.println(firstName + " " + lastName +
31         " is not in the database");
32   }
33 }
```

```
Enter student's first name: Jacob  ↵Enter
Enter student's last name: Smith  ↵Enter
Jacob Smith is in the database
```

```
Enter student's first name: John  ↵Enter
Enter student's last name: Smith  ↵Enter
John Smith is not in the database
```

The program loads an Oracle driver (line 6), connects to an Oracle database (lines 7–9), and creates a callable statement for executing the function **studentFound** (lines 12–13).

The function's first parameter is the return value; its second and third parameters correspond to the first and last names. Before executing the callable statement, the program sets the first name and last name (lines 21–22) and registers the **OUT** parameter (line 23). The statement is executed in line 26).

The function's return value is obtained in line 26. If the value is greater or equal to 1, the student with the specified first and last name is found in the table.

You can define procedures and functions in MySQL 5. The equivalent function for `studentFound` in MySQL can be defined as follows:

MySQL function

```
drop function if exists studentFound;

delimiter //

create function studentFound(first varchar(20), last varchar(20))
  returns int
begin
  declare result int;

  select count(*) into result
  from Student
  where Student.firstName = first and
    Student.lastName = last;

  return result;
end;
//

delimiter ;
```

37.7 Retrieving Metadata

database metadata

JDBC provides the `DatabaseMetaData` interface for obtaining databasewide information and the `ResultSetMetaData` interface for obtaining information on the specific `ResultSet`, such as column count and column names.

37.7.1 Database Metadata

The `Connection` interface establishes a connection to a database. It is within the context of a connection that SQL statements are executed and results are returned. A connection also provides access to database metadata information that describes the capabilities of the database, supported SQL grammar, stored procedures, and so on. To obtain an instance of `Database-MetaData` for a database, use the `getMetaData` method on a `connection` object like this:

```
DatabaseMetaData dbMetaData = connection.getMetaData();
```

If your program connects to a local MySQL database, Listing 37.5 displays the database information, as shown in Figure 37.22.

```
C:\book>java -cp .;lib/mysqljdbc.jar TestDatabaseMetaData
Driver loaded
Database connected
database URL: jdbc:mysql://localhost/javabook
database username: scott@localhost
database product name: MySQL
database product version: 5.0.37-community-nt
JDBC driver name: MySQL-AB JDBC Driver
JDBC driver version: mysql-connector-java-5.0.4 ( $Date: 2006-10-19 17:47:48
00 (Thu, 19 Oct 2006) $, $Revision: 5908 $ )
JDBC driver major version: 5
JDBC driver minor version: 0
Max number of connections: 0
MaxTableNameLength: 64
MaxColumnsInTable: 512

C:\book>_
```

FIGURE 37.22 The `DatabaseMetaData` interface enables you to obtain database information.

LISTING 37.5 TestDatabaseMetaData.java

```
1 import java.sql.*;
2
3 public class TestDatabaseMetaData {
4   public static void main(String[] args)
5       throws SQLException, ClassNotFoundException {
6     // Load the JDBC driver
7     Class.forName("com.mysql.jdbc.Driver");
8     System.out.println("Driver loaded");
9
10    // Establish a connection
11    Connection connection = DriverManager.getConnection
12      ("jdbc:mysql://localhost/javabook", "scott", "tiger");
13    System.out.println("Database connected");
14
15    DatabaseMetaData dbMetaData = connection.getMetaData();
16    System.out.println("database URL: " + dbMetaData.getURL() );
17    System.out.println("database username: " +
18      dbMetaData.getUserName());
19    System.out.println("database product name: " +
20      dbMetaData.getDatabaseProductName());
21    System.out.println("database product version: " +
22      dbMetaData.getDatabaseProductVersion());
23    System.out.println("JDBC driver name: " +
24      dbMetaData.getDriverName());
25    System.out.println("JDBC driver version: " +
26      dbMetaData.getDriverVersion());
27    System.out.println("JDBC driver major version: " +
28      dbMetaData.getDriverMajorVersion());
29    System.out.println("JDBC driver minor version: " +
30      dbMetaData.getDriverMinorVersion());
31    System.out.println("Max number of connections: " +
32      dbMetaData.getMaxConnections());
33    System.out.println("MaxTableNameLength: " +
34      dbMetaData.getMaxTableNameLength());
35    System.out.println("MaxColumnsInTable: " +
36      dbMetaData.getMaxColumnsInTable());
37
38    // Close the connection
39    connection.close();
40  }
41 }
```

load driver

connect database

database metadata
get metadata

37.7.2 Obtaining Database Tables

You can find out the tables in the database through database metadata using the `getTables` method. Listing 37.6 displays all the user tables in the test database on a local MySQL. Figure 37.23 shows a sample output of the program.

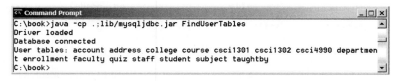

FIGURE 37.23 You can find all the tables in the database.

LISTING 37.6 FindUserTables.java

```
1  import java.sql.*;
2
3  public class FindUserTables {
4    public static void main(String[] args)
5      throws SQLException, ClassNotFoundException {
6      // Load the JDBC driver
7      Class.forName("com.mysql.jdbc.Driver");
8      System.out.println("Driver loaded");
9
10     // Establish a connection
11     Connection connection = DriverManager.getConnection
12       ("jdbc:mysql://localhost/javabook", "scott", "tiger");
13     System.out.println("Database connected");
14
15     DatabaseMetaData dbMetaData = connection.getMetaData();
16
17     ResultSet rsTables = dbMetaData.getTables(null, null, null,
18       new String[] {"TABLE"});
19     System.out.print("User tables: ");
20     while (rsTables.next())
21       System.out.print(rsTables.getString("TABLE_NAME") + " ");
22
23     // Close the connection
24     connection.close();
25   }
26 }
```

Margin notes:
- load driver (line 7)
- connect database (line 11)
- database metadata (line 15)
- obtain tables (line 17)
- get table names (line 21)

Line 17 obtains table information in a result set using the `getTables` method. One of the columns in the result set is TABLE_NAME. Line 21 retrieves the table name from this result set column.

37.7.3 Result Set Metadata

The `ResultSetMetaData` interface describes information pertaining to the result set. A `ResultSetMetaData` object can be used to find the types and properties of the columns in a `ResultSet`. To obtain an instance of `ResultSetMetaData`, use the `getMetaData` method on a result set like this:

```
ResultSetMetaData rsMetaData = resultSet.getMetaData();
```

You can use the `getColumnCount()` method to find the number of columns in the result and the `getColumnName(int)` method to get the column names. For example, Listing 37.7 displays all the column names and contents resulting from the SQL SELECT statement *select * from Enrollment*. The output is shown in Figure 37.24.

```
C:\book>java -cp .;lib/mysqljdbc.jar TestResultSetMetaData
Driver loaded
Database connected
ssn          courseId       dateRegistered   grade
444111110    11111          2007-04-13       A
444111110    11113          2007-04-13       C
444111111    11111          2007-04-13       D
```

FIGURE 37.24 The `ResultSetMetaData` interface enables you to obtain resultset information.

LISTING 37.7 TestResultSetMetaData.java

```java
 1 import java.sql.*;
 2
 3 public class TestResultSetMetaData {
 4   public static void main(String[] args)
 5       throws SQLException, ClassNotFoundException {
 6     // Load the JDBC driver
 7     Class.forName("com.mysql.jdbc.Driver");
 8     System.out.println("Driver loaded");
 9
10     // Establish a connection
11     Connection connection = DriverManager.getConnection
12       ("jdbc:mysql://localhost/javabook", "scott", "tiger");
13     System.out.println("Database connected");
14
15     // Create a statement
16     Statement statement = connection.createStatement();
17
18     // Execute a statement
19     ResultSet resultSet = statement.executeQuery
20       ("select * from Enrollment");
21
22     ResultSetMetaData rsMetaData = resultSet.getMetaData();
23     for (int i = 1; i <= rsMetaData.getColumnCount(); i++)
24       System.out.printf("%-12s\t", rsMetaData.getColumnName(i));
25     System.out.println();
26
27     // Iterate through the result and print the student names
28     while (resultSet.next()) {
29       for (int i = 1; i <= rsMetaData.getColumnCount(); i++)
30         System.out.printf("%-12s\t", resultSet.getObject(i));
31       System.out.println();
32     }
33
34     // Close the connection
35     connection.close();
36   }
37 }
```

(margin annotations: load driver · connect database · create statement · create resultset · resultset metadata · column count · column name)

KEY TERMS

database system   1232
domain constraint   1234
foreign key constraint   1235
integrity constraint   1234

primary key constraint   1235
relational database   1232
Structured Query Language
  (SQL)   1236

CHAPTER SUMMARY

- This chapter introduced the concepts of database systems, relational databases, relational data models, data integrity, and SQL. You learned how to develop database applications using Java.

- The Java API for developing Java database applications is called *JDBC*. JDBC provides Java programmers with a uniform interface for accessing and manipulating a wide range of relational databases.

■ The JDBC API consists of classes and interfaces for establishing connections with databases, sending SQL statements to databases, processing the results of SQL statements, and obtaining database metadata.

■ Since a JDBC driver serves as the interface to facilitate communications between JDBC and a proprietary database, JDBC drivers are database specific. A JDBC-ODBC bridge driver is included in JDK to support Java programs that access databases through ODBC drivers. If you use a driver other than the JDBC-ODBC bridge driver, make sure it is on the classpath before running the program.

■ Four key interfaces are needed to develop any database application using Java: `Driver`, `Connection`, `Statement`, and `ResultSet`. These interfaces define a framework for generic SQL database access. The JDBC driver vendors provide implementation for them.

■ A JDBC application loads an appropriate driver using the `Driver` interface, connects to the database using the `Connection` interface, creates and executes SQL statements using the `Statement` interface, and processes the result using the `ResultSet` interface if the statements return results.

■ The `PreparedStatement` interface is designed to execute dynamic SQL statements with parameters. These SQL statements are precompiled for efficient use when repeatedly executed.

■ Database *metadata* is information that describes the database itself. JDBC provides the `DatabaseMetaData` interface for obtaining databasewide information and the `ResultSetMetaData` interface for obtaining information on the specific `ResultSet`.

REVIEW QUESTIONS

Section 37.2 Relational Database Systems

37.1 What are superkeys, candidate keys, and primary keys? How do you create a table with a primary key?

37.2 What is a foreign key? How do you create a table with a foreign key?

37.3 Can a relation have more than one primary key or foreign key?

37.4 Does a foreign key need to be a primary key in the same relation?

37.5 Does a foreign key need to have the same name as its referenced primary key?

37.6 Can a foreign key value be null?

Section 37.3 SQL

37.7 Create the tables `Course`, `Student`, and `Enrollment` using the `create table` statements in Section 37.3.1, "Creating and Dropping Tables." Insert rows into `Course`, `Student`, and `Enrollment` using the data in Figures 37.3, 37.4, and 37.5.

37.8 List all CSCI courses with at least four credit hours.

37.9 List all students whose last names contain the letter *e* two times.

37.10 List all students whose birthdays are null.

37.11 List all students who take Math courses.

37.12 List the number of courses in each subject.

37.13 Assume that each credit hour is 50 minutes of lectures. Get the total minutes for the courses that each student takes.

Section 37.4 JDBC

37.14 What are the advantages of developing database applications using Java?

37.15 Describe the following JDBC interfaces: `Driver`, `Connection`, `Statement`, and `ResultSet`.

37.16 How do you load a JDBC driver? What are the driver classes for MySQL, Access, and Oracle?

37.17 How do you create a database connection? What are the URLs for MySQL, Access, and Oracle?

37.18 How do you create a `Statement` and execute an SQL statement?

37.19 How do you retrieve values in a `ResultSet`?

37.20 Does JDBC automatically commit a transaction? How do you set autocommit to false?

Section 37.5 `PreparedStatement`

37.21 Describe prepared statements. How do you create instances of `Prepared-Statement`? How do you execute a `PreparedStatement`? How do you set parameter values in a `PreparedStatement`?

37.22 What are the benefits of using prepared statements?

Section 37.6 `CallableStatement`

37.23 Describe callable statements. How do you create instances of `CallableStatement`? How do you execute a `CallableStatement`? How do you register `OUT` parameters in a `CallableStatement`?

Section 37.7 Retrieving Metadata

37.24 What is `DatabaseMetaData` for? Describe the methods in `DatabaseMetaData`. How do you get an instance of `DatabaseMetaData`?

37.25 What is `ResultSetMetaData` for? Describe the methods in `ResultSetMeta-Data`. How do you get an instance of `ResultSetMetaData`?

37.26 How do you find the number of columns in a result set? How do you find the column names in a result set?

PROGRAMMING EXERCISES

37.1* (*Accessing and updating a* `Staff` *table*) Write a Java applet that views, inserts, and updates staff information stored in a database, as shown in Figure 37.25(a). The *View* button displays a record with a specified ID. The `Staff` table is created as follows:

```
create table Staff (
  id char(9) not null,
  lastName varchar(15),
  firstName varchar(15),
  mi char(1),
  address varchar(20),
  city varchar(20),
  state char(2),
```

```
                    telephone char(10),
                    email varchar(40),
                    primary key (id)
                );
```

(a)   (b)

FIGURE 37.25 (a) The applet lets you view, insert, and update staff information. (b) The `PieChart` and `BarChart` components display the query data obtained from the data module.

37.2**(*Displaying data*) Write a program that displays the number of students in each department in a pie chart and a bar chart, as shown in Figure 37.25(b). The number of students for each department can be obtained from the `Student` table (see Figure 37.4) using the following SQL statement:

```
select deptId, count(*)
from Student
where deptId is not null
group by deptId;
```

Use the `PieChart` component and the `BarChart` component created in Exercise 35.1 to display the data.

37.3*(*Connection dialog*) Develop a JavaBeans component named `DBConnectionPanel` that enables the user to select or enter a JDBC driver and a URL and to enter a username and password, as shown in Figure 37.26. When the *OK* button is clicked, a `Connection` object for the database is stored in the `connection` property. You can then use the `getConnection()` method to return the connection.

FIGURE 37.26 The `DBConnectionPanel` component enables the user to enter database information.

37.4* (*Finding grades*) Listing 37.2, FindGrade.java, presented an applet that finds a student's grade for a specified course. Rewrite the program to find all the grades for a specified student, as shown in Figure 37.27.

FIGURE 37.27 The applet displays the grades for the courses for a specified student.

37.5* (*Displaying table contents*) Write a program that displays the content for a given table. As shown in Figure 37.28(a), you enter a table and click the *Show Contents* button to display the table contents in the text area.

        (a)   (b)

FIGURE 37.28 (a) Enter a table name to display the table contents. (b) Select a table name from the combo box to display its contents.

37.6* (*Finding tables and showing their contents*) Write a program that fills in table names in a combo box, as shown in Figure 37.28(b). You can select a table from the combo box to display its contents in the text area.

37.7**(*Populating database*) Create a table named `Quiz` as follows:

```
create table Quiz(
  questionId int,
  question varchar(4000),
  choicea varchar(1000),
  choiceb varchar(1000),
  choicec varchar(1000),
  choiced varchar(1000),
  answer varchar(5));
```

The `Quiz` table stores multiple-choice questions. Suppose the multiple-choice questions are stored in a text file named Exercise37_7.txt in the following format:

```
1. question1
a. choice a
b. choice b
c. choice c
d. choice d
Answer:cd
```

```
2. question2
a. choice a
b. choice b
c. choice c
d. choice d
Answer:a
...
```

Write a program that reads the data from the file and stores it in the Quiz table. (Exercise37_7.txt is contained in **c:\book**).

APPENDIXES

Appendix A
Java Keywords

Appendix B
The ASCII Character Set

Appendix C
Operator Precedence Chart

Appendix D
Java Modifiers

Appendix E
Special Floating-Point Values

Java Keywords

The following fifty keywords are reserved for use by the Java language:

abstract	double	int	super
assert	else	interface	switch
boolean	enum	long	synchronized
break	extends	native	this
byte	for	new	throw
case	final	package	throws
catch	finally	private	transient
char	float	protected	try
class	goto	public	void
const	if	return	volatile
continue	implements	short	while
default	import	static	
do	instanceof	strictfp*	

The keywords **goto** and **const** are C++ keywords reserved, but not currently used, in Java. This enables Java compilers to identify them and to produce better error messages if they appear in Java programs.

The literal values `true`, `false`, and `null` are not keywords, just like literal value `100`. However, you cannot use them as identifiers, just as you cannot use `100` as an identifier.

assert is a keyword added in JDK 1.4 and **enum** is a keyword added in JDK 1.5.

---

*The `strictfp` keyword is a modifier for method or class to use strict floating-point calculations. Floating-point arithmetic can be executed in one of two modes: *strict* or *nonstrict*. The strict mode guarantees that the evaluation result is the same on all Java Virtual Machine implementations. The nonstrict mode allows intermediate results from calculations to be stored in an extended format different from the standard IEEE floating-point number format. The extended format is machine-dependent and enables code to be executed faster. However, when you execute the code using the nonstrict mode on different JVMs, you may not always get precisely the same results. By default, the nonstrict mode is used for floating-point calculations. To use the strict mode in a method or a class, add the `strictfp` keyword in the method or the class declaration. Strict floating-point may give you slightly better precision than nonstrict floating-point, but the distinction will only affect some applications. Strictness is not inherited; that is, the presence of `strictfp` on a class or interface declaration does not cause extended classes or interfaces to be strict.

APPENDIX B

The ASCII Character Set

Tables B.1 and B.2 show ASCII characters and their respective decimal and hexadecimal codes. The decimal or hexadecimal code of a character is a combination of its row index and column index. For example, in Table B.1, the letter A is at row 6 and column 5, so its decimal equivalent is 65; in Table B.2, letter A is at row 4 and column 1, so its hexadecimal equivalent is 41.

TABLE B.1   ASCII Character Set in the Decimal Index

	0	1	2	3	4	5	6	7	8	9
0	nul	soh	stx	etx	eot	enq	ack	bel	bs	ht
1	nl	vt	ff	cr	so	si	dle	dcl	dc2	dc3
2	dc4	nak	syn	etb	can	em	sub	esc	fs	gs
3	rs	us	sp	!	"	#	$	%	&	'
4	(	)	*	+	,	−	.	/	0	1
5	2	3	4	5	6	7	8	9	:	;
6	<	=	>	?	@	A	B	C	D	E
7	F	G	H	I	J	K	L	M	N	O
8	P	Q	R	S	T	U	V	W	X	Y
9	Z	[	\	]	^	_	`	a	b	c
10	d	e	f	g	h	i	j	k	l	m
11	n	o	p	q	r	s	t	u	v	w
12	x	y	z	{	|	}	~	del		

TABLE B.2   ASCII Character Set in the Hexadecimal Index

	0	1	2	3	4	5	6	7	8	9	A	B	C	D	E	F
0	nul	soh	stx	etx	eot	enq	ack	bel	bs	ht	nl	vt	ff	cr	so	si
1	dle	dcl	dc2	dc3	dc4	nak	syn	etb	can	em	sub	esc	fs	gs	rs	us
2	sp	!	"	#	$	%	&	'	(	)	*	+	,	−	.	/
3	0	1	2	3	4	5	6	7	8	9	:	;	<	=	>	?
4	@	A	B	C	D	E	F	G	H	I	J	K	L	M	N	O
5	P	Q	R	S	T	U	V	W	X	Y	Z	[	\	]	^	_
6	`	a	b	c	d	e	f	g	h	i	j	k	l	m	n	o
7	p	q	r	s	t	u	v	w	x	y	z	{	|	}	~	del

APPENDIX C

Operator Precedence Chart

The operators are shown in decreasing order of precedence from top to bottom. Operators in the same group have the same precedence, and their associativity is shown in the table.

Operator	Name	Associativity
()	Parentheses	Left to right
()	Function call	Left to right
[]	Array subscript	Left to right
.	Object member access	Left to right
++	Postincrement	Right to left
--	Postdecrement	Right to left
++	Preincrement	Right to left
--	Predecrement	Right to left
+	Unary plus	Right to left
-	Unary minus	Right to left
!	Unary logical negation	Right to left
(type)	Unary casting	Right to left
new	Creating object	Right to left
*	Multiplication	Left to right
/	Division	Left to right
%	Remainder	Left to right
+	Addition	Left to right
-	Subtraction	Left to right
<<	Left shift	Left to right
>>	Right shift with sign extension	Left to right
>>>	Right shift with zero extension	Left to right
<	Less than	Left to right
<=	Less than or equal to	Left to right
>	Greater than	Left to right
>=	Greater than or equal to	Left to right
instanceof	Checking object type	Left to right

Operator	Name	Associativity
==	Equal comparison	Left to right
!=	Not equal	Left to right
&	(Unconditional AND)	Left to right
^	(Exclusive OR)	Left to right
|	(Unconditional OR)	Left to right
&&	Conditional AND	Left to right
||	Conditional OR	Left to right
?:	Ternary condition	Right to left
=	Assignment	Right to left
+=	Addition assignment	Right to left
-=	Subtraction assignment	Right to left
*=	Multiplication assignment	Right to left
/=	Division assignment	Right to left
%=	Remainder assignment	Right to left

Appendix D

Java Modifiers

Modifiers are used on classes and class members (constructors, methods, data, and class-level blocks), but the final modifier can also be used on local variables in a method. A modifier that can be applied to a class is called a *class modifier*. A modifier that can be applied to a method is called a *method modifier*. A modifier that can be applied to a data field is called a *data modifier*. A modifier that can be applied to a class-level block is called a block modifier. The following table gives a summary of the Java modifiers.

Modifier	class	constructor	method	data	block	Explanation
`(default)`*	√	√	√	√	√	A class, constructor, method, or data field is visible in this package.
`public`	√	√	√	√		A class, constructor, method, or data field is visible to all the programs in any package.
`private`		√	√	√		A constructor, method or data field is only visible in this class.
`protected`		√	√	√		A constructor, method or data field is visible in this package and in subclasses of this class in any package.
`static`			√	√	√	Define a class method, or a class data field or a static initialization block.
`final`	√		√	√		A final class cannot be extended. A final method cannot be modified in a subclass. A final data field is a constant.
`abstract`	√		√			An abstract class must be extended. An abstract method must be implemented in a concrete subclass.
`native`			√			A native method indicates that the method is implemented using a language other than Java.

*Default access has no modifier associated with it. For example: `class Test {}`

Modifier	class	constructor	method	data	block	Explanation
synchronized			√		√	Only one thread at a time can execute this method.
strictfp	√	√				Use strict floating-point calculations to guarantee that the evaluation result is the same on all JVMs.
transient				√		Mark a nonserializable instance data field.

APPENDIX E

Special Floating-Point Values

Dividing an integer by zero is invalid and throws `ArithmeticException`, but dividing a floating-point value by zero does not cause an exception. Floating-point arithmetic can overflow to infinity if the result of the operation is too large for a `double` or a `float`, or underflow to zero if the result is too small for a double or a `float`. Java provides the special floating-point values `POSITIVE_INFINITY`, `NEGATIVE_INFINITY`, and `NaN` (Not a Number) to denote these results. These values are defined as special constants in the `Float` class and the Double class.

If a positive floating-point number is divided by zero, the result is `POSITIVE_INFINITY`. If a negative floating-point number is divided by zero, the result is `NEGATIVE_INFINITY`. If a floating-point zero is divided by zero, the result is NaN, which means that the result is undefined mathematically. The string representation of these three values are Infinity, -Infinity, and NaN. For example,

```
System.out.print(1.0 / 0); // Print Infinity
System.out.print(-1.0 / 0); // Print -Infinity
System.out.print(0.0 / 0); // Print NaN
```

These special values can also be used as operands in computations. For example, a number divided by `POSITIVE_INFINITY` yields a positive zero. Table E.1 summarizes various combinations of the /, *, %, +, and – operators.

TABLE E.1 Special Floating-Point Values

x	y	x/y	x*y	x%y	x + y	x − y
Finite	± 0.0	± ∞	± 0.0	NaN	Finite	Finite
Finite	± ∞	± 0.0	± 0.0	x	± ∞	∞
± 0.0	± 0.0	NaN	± 0.0	NaN	± 0.0	± 0.0
± ∞	Finite	± ∞	± 0.0	NaN	± ∞	± ∞
± ∞	± ∞	NaN	± 0.0	NaN	± ∞	∞
± 0.0	± ∞	± 0.0	NaN	± 0.0	± ∞	± 0.0
NaN	Any	NaN	NaN	NaN	NaN	NaN
Any	NaN	NaN	NaN	NaN	NaN	NaN

Note
If one of the operands is NaN, the result is NaN.

INDEX

Symbols

- (subtraction), 33–34
-= (subtraction assignment operator), 37
--var (predecrement), 37–38
!= (not equal to), 68, 1241
! operator, truth table for, 69
&& operator, truth table for, 69
$ character, 29
% (remainder), 33–34
%= (remainder assignment operator), 37
* character (all), 282–283
* (multiplication), 33–34
*= (multiplication assignment operator), 37
/ (division), 33–34
/= (division assignment operator), 37
\ (backslash), 42, 283
^ operator, truth table for, 69
|| operator, truth table for, 69
+ (addition), 33–34
+= (addition assignment operator), 37
++var (preincrement), 37–38
var++ (postincrement), 37–38
< (less than), 68, 1241
<= (less than or equal to), 68, 1241
<> (not equal to) comparison operator, 1241
<applet> tag, syntax of, 562
<param> tag, 562
== (equal to), 68
= (equal to) comparison operator, 1241
> (greater than), 68, 1241
>= (greater than or equal to), 68, 1241
var-- (postdecrement), 37–38

A

abs method, Math class, 156
Absolute file name, 283
Abstract classes, 362–366, 864
  Calendar class, 366–367
    field constants in, 367
    TestCalendar.java, 367–368
  Circle.java, 363
  defined, 362
  GeometricObject.java, 362–364
  GregorianCalendar class, 366–367
  interesting points on, 365–366
  for interfaces, 768
  interfaces vs., 377–380
  Rectangle.java, 363–364
Abstract methods, 362, 364–365
abstract modifier, 362, 1274
Abstract Windows Toolkit (AWT),
    Swing vs., 420
AbstractAction class, 1119, 1122
AbstractBorder class, 1094
  BevelBorder class, 1094–1095
  CompoundBorder class, 1094–1096
  EmptyBorder class, 1094–1095
  EtchedBorder class, 1094–1095
  LineBorder class, 1094–1096
  MatteBorder class, 1094–1096
  SoftBevelBorder class, 1094–1095
  TitledBorder class, 1094–1096
AbstractButton class, 514–515, 637
AbstractCollection interface,
    413, 707–708
AbstractGraph class, 864–866, 904

AbstractGraph.java, 868–869
  class diagram, 865
  createAdjacencyList methods, 874
  getAdjacencyMatrix() method, 874
  printAdjacencyMatrix() method, 874
  printEdges() method, 874
  vertices data field, 874
AbstractGraph.java, 868–869
Abstraction:
  class, 307
  in system design, 395
AbstractList class, 717
AbstractListModel class, 1167, 1174
AbstractMap class, 729
AbstractSet class, 413, 708
AbstractSpinnerModel class, 1156
AbstractTableModel class, 1189
AbstractTree class, 804
  AbstractTree.java, 805–806
Accessibility modifiers, 350–351
Accessible method, overriding, 339
AccountWithSyncUsingLock.java, 948–949
acquire() method, Semaphore
    class, 958–959
action-after-each-iteration, 112
Action interface, 1118–1122
  ActionInterfaceDemo.java, 1120–1122
ActionEvent, 486–487, 1052–1053,
    1057–1058, 1063
ActionListener interface, 373–374,
    484, 486–487, 1052–1053,
    1057, 1119, 1149
actionListenerList, 1057
actionPerformed method,
    1053, 1058, 1119, 1122
Actual parameter, 143
Adapter classes, 6
AdapterDemo.java, 498
add method, 724
addActionListener method,
    486, 1053, 1056–1057
addColumn method, 1200
addElement method, 724
addFirst(e) method, MyLinkedList
    class, 779
add(index, e) method, MyLinkedList
    class, 780–781
Addition (+), 33–34
Addition assignment operator (+=), 37
AdditionQuiz.java, 71
addLast(e) method, MyLinkedList
    class, 779–780
addMatrix method, 697–699
Address book, creating (problem), 642–643
  AddressBook.java, 644–648
    readAddress() method, 648
    writeAddress() method, 648
  FixedLengthStringIO.java, 643–644
Address.java, 402–403
addRow method, 1200
addSeparator() method, 1109
addStudent method, 1057–1058, 1062
Adjacent edges, 859
Adjacent vertices, 859
AdjustmentEvent, 487
AdjustmentListener interface, 487
Aggregated class, 397

Aggregated objects (subject object), 397
Aggregating class, 397
Aggregating object (owner object), 397
Aggregation, 397–398, 415
Aggregation relationship, representation
    of, 397–398
Algorithm efficiency, 741–766
  algorithm for finding a closest pair in
    step 3 (listing), 759–760
  algorithm for finding a closest pair
    (listing), 758–759
  big O notation, 742–745
    examples of determining, 743–745
  binary search algorithm, 745
  closest pair of points (case studies),
    758–760
  common growth functions,
    comparing, 747
  exponential algorithm, 746
  Fibonacci numbers, finding
    (case studies), 747–748
  greatest common divisors, finding
    (case studies), 749–752
  insertion sort algorithm, 746
  prime numbers, finding (case studies),
    752–758
  quadratic algorithms, 743
  recurrence functions, 760
  selection sort algorithm, 745–746
  Towers of Hanoi problem,
    analyzing, 746
Algorithms, 26
  graphs, 859
alignment property, FlowLayout
    manager, 431
Alignments, 516–517
alt attribute, 562
anchorSelectionIndex method, 1165
and operator, 1241
Animal class, 378–379
Animation, binary tree, 822–823
AnimationDemo.java, 504–505
Anonymous arrays, 189
Anonymous class listeners, 492–494
Anonymous objects, 233
AnonymousListenerDemo.java, 492–493
  enlarging or shrinking a circle
    (example), 494–495
Applet class, 558–560, 1070
  destroy method, 560
  getParameter method, 570
  init method, 559
  start method, 559
  stop method, 560
  subclasses of, 558
Applet clients, 987–989
  AppletClient.java, 988–989
  CountServer.java, 987–988
Applets, 12–13, 15
  audio, playing in Java programs, 581–582
  bouncing ball (case study), 577–580
  demos, 566
  enabling to run as applications, 567–568
  HTML file and the <applet> tag, 561–566
  JApplet class, 420, 435
  loan applet, creating, 564–566
  LoanApplet.html, 566

Applets (*continued*)
  LoanApplet.java, 564–565
    with main method, 568
  and multimedia, 557–596
  multimedia animations, 582–585
  passing strings to, 568–572
  TicTacToe game (case study), 572–577
  viewing from a Web browser, 563
  viewing using the applet viewer
    utility, 562–563
appletviewer command, 563
Application program interface (API), 14
Applications, 15
applyPattern(String pattern)
    method, DecimalFormat
    class, 1032
arcAngle, 456
archive attribute, 562
Arcs, drawing, 456–458
  DrawArcs.java, 456–457
Arguments, 143
Arithmetic/logic unit (ALU), 2–3
Arithmetic operators, in SQL, 1242–1243
ArithmeticException, 385, 600
Array elements, analyzing (problem), 185–186
  grade assignment (problem), 186–187
  TestArray.java, 185
Array initializers, 182–183
Array length, 182
Array lists, 349, 350
Array objects, 233
Array variables:
  arrays vs., 182
  declaring, 180
Array variables, declaring, 180
ArrayBlockingQueue, 956–957
arraycopy method, 188–189, 377
ArrayIndexOutOfBoundsException, 186
ArrayList class, 345–349, 717–720, 823
  add(Object) method, 346
  class diagram, 687
  defined, 717
  differences and similarities between
    arrays and, 348
  remove(index) method, 346
  remove(Object) method, 346
  size() method, 346
  TestArrayAndLinkedList.java, 719
  TestArrayList.java, 347–348
  toString() method, 347
  trimToSize() method, 718
Arrays, 179–228, 768
  anonymous, 189
  Arrays class, 202–203
  basics of, 180–188
  binary search approach, 196–199
  conversion between strings and, 271
  copying, 188–189
  creating, 180–182
  defined, 179
  elements, analyzing (problem), 185–186
  initializers, 182–183
  insertion sort, 200–202
  length, 182
  linear search approach, 196
  multidimensional, 215–218
  of objects, 251–253
  passing to methods, 189–192
  printing, 183
  processing, 183–184
  returning from a method, 192–195
  searching, 196–199
  selection sort, 199–200
  serializing, 638–639

sorting, 199–202, 382–384
  GenericSort.java, 382–383
  two-dimensional, 203–215
  variable-length argument lists, 195
  variables, declaring, 180
Arrays class, 202–203
  binarySearch method, 202–203
  sort method, 202
Arrow keys, 5
Ascent, 460
ASCII (American Standard Code for
    Information Interchange), 40–41
  character set, 1270–1271
Assembler, 6
Assembly language, 5–6, 21
assert keyword, 1269
AssignGrade.java, 186–188
Assignment expression, 30
Assignment operator, 30
Assignment statement, 30
Association, 396–397, 415
Associativity, 91–92
Attributes, 1233
Audio:
  ImageAudioAnimation.java, 583–584
  playing in Java programs, 581–582
Autoboxing, 687
Autocommit mode, 1250
Automatic driver discovery, 1247
autoResizeMode property, 1186
Autounboxing, 688
Average-case analysis, 742
await() method, 949–950, 953
AWTError class, 602
AWTException, 603

B

Backslash (\), 42, 283
Backward compatibility, 691
Backward pointer, 788
BallCanvas class, 495
BallControl.java, 578–579
Ball.java, 577–578
Base case, 656
  testing, 666
Base, decimal number system, 9
BASIC, 6
Beans, *See* JavaBeans
Behavior, of objects, 230
Best-case input, 742
between-and operator, 1242
BevelBorder class, 1094–1095
Big *O* notation, 742–745
  examples of determining, 743–745
BigDecimal class, 385
BigInteger class, 385
Binary files, 624
Binary I/O, 624, 626–633
  address book, creating
    (problem), 642–643
  characters/strings in, 630–631
  copying files (problem), 633–635
  DataInputStream class, 629–632
  DataOutputStream class, 629–632
  efficiency of, 626
  object I/O, 635–637
  random access files, 639–642
  Serializable interface, 637–638
  TestFileStream.java, 628
  text I/O vs., 625
Binary numbers, 3, 9
  conversions between decimal
    numbers and, 9–10

conversions between hexadecimal
    numbers and, 11–12
Binary operator, 34
Binary search, 196–199, 664–665
  benefits of, 199
  binarySearch method, 665
  BinarySearch.java, 197–198
  recursive binary search method, 664
Binary search algorithm, 745
Binary search trees (BST), 800–812
  deleting elements in, 812–816
  depth of a node, 800
  element:
    inserting, 802–803
    searching for, 801–802
  height of, 800
  leaf, 800
  left subtree, 800
  length of a path, 800
  level of, 800
  representing, 800–801
  right subtree, 800
  root, 800
  siblings, 800
  tree traversal, 803–804
Binary tree:
  animation, 822–823
  complete, 822
  deleting an element from (listing), 812–813
  time complexity, 815–816
binarySearch method, Collections class, 721
BinaryTree class, 804–812
  BinaryTree.java, 806–811
  class diagram, 804
  TestBinaryTree.java, 811–812
  Tree.java, 805
Birth dates, guessing (problem),
    83–86, 217–218
  GuessBirthDateUsingArray.java,
    217–218
Bits, 3, 9
Block, 16
Block comment, 15
Block styles, 52–53
Blocking queues, 956–957
  ArrayBlockingQueue, 956–957
  concrete, 956
  ConsumerProducerUsingBlockingQueue.java,
    957
  defined, 956
  LinkedBlockingQueue, 956
  PriorityBlockingQueue, 956
BlockingQueue interface, 956
BMI class, 311–313
  BMI.java, 312–313
  getBMI() instance method, 313
  getStatus() instance method, 313
  UseBMIClass.java, 312
Body Mass Index (BMI), computing
    (problem), 80–81
Body, method, 143
Boolean literal, 69
Boolean operators, 69
boolean value:
  casting, 70
  testing, 77
Boolean variables, 68
Boolean wrapper class, 380
BorderDemo.java, 1098–1102
BorderLayout manager, 429–431, 1072, 1081
  hgap property, 431, 1072
  setHgap method, 431
  ShowBorderLayout.java, 430–431
  vgap property, 431, 1072

Borders:
  sharing, 438
  Swing, 1094–1102
Borland Interbase, 1236
Borrower.java, 404–405
BorrowLoan.java, 405
Bottom-up design, 163
BounceBallApp.java, 579–580
Bouncing ball (case study), 577–580
  BallControl.java, 578–579
  Ball.java, 577–578
  BounceBallApp.java, 579–580
Bounded wildcard, 693
Box class:
  createHorizontalBox() method, 1079
  createlHorizontalStrut(int)
      method, 1077
  createVerticalBox() method, 1079
Boxing, 384–385
BoxLayout manager, 1076–1079
  and component's alignmentX or
     alignmentY property, 1077
  glue, 1077
  rigid area, 1077
  ShowBoxLayout.java, 1077–1079
  strut, 1077
  unique features of, 1076–1077
Braces, 16
Breadth-first search, 879–882
  algorithm (listing), 879
  applications of, 881–882
  defined, 879
  implementation of, 880–881
  nine tail problem, 882–888
    NineTailApp class, 882–883, 886, 923
    NineTailApp.java, 886–888
    NineTailModel class, 882–883, 923
    NineTailModel.java, 883–886
  TestBFS.java, 880–881
Breadth-first traversal:
  graphs, 874
  trees, 803–804
break keyword, 122–127
  GuessNumberUsingBreak.java, 124
  TestBreak.java, 122–123
break statement, 87–88
Breakpoints, 55
Bubble sort, 836–838
  algorithm (listing), 836–837
  bubble sort time, 838
  BubbleSort.java, 837–838
  defined, 836
  improved algorithm (listing), 836
Bucket sort, 846–847
  algorithm (listing), 846
  stability of, 847
BufferedInputStream, 632–633
BufferedOutputStream, 632–633
Bugs, 55
Bus, 2
ButtonModel, 1153–1154
Buttons, 514–520
  AbstractButton class, 514–515
  alignments, 516–517
  defined, 514
  icons, 515–516
  pressed icons, 515–516
  rollover icons, 515–516
  TestButtonIcons.java, 516
  text positions, 517
  using, 518–520
byte type, 32–33
Byte wrapper class, 380
Bytecode, 7

Bytecode verifier, 19
Bytes, 3

C

C, 6
C#, 6
Cable modem, 5, 976
calculate method, 1114
Calculator (problem), 281–283
  Calculator.java, 282–283
Calendar class, 366–367, 1018
  field constants in, 367
  get(int field) method, 367
  getActualMaximum(Calendar.
     DAY_OF_MONTH) method, 1028
  TestCalendar.java, 367–368
Calendar, displaying, 1024–1029
  CalendarApp class, 1025
  CalendarApp.java, 1028–1029
  CalendarPanel class, 1024–1025
  CalendarPanel.java, 1025–1028
Call stacks, 145
CallableStatement interface, 1255–1258
  TestCallableStatement.java, 1257–1258
Calling methods, 143–145
Calling object, 233
Candidate key, 1235
capacity() method, StringBuilder, 278
CardLayout manager, 1073–1076
  add method, 1073
  methods, 1073
  ShowCardLayout.java, 1074–1076
Case sensitivity:
  of Java source programs, 18
  of name identifiers, 29
case statement, 87
Casting, 687, See Type casting
Casting objects, 343–345
  TestPolymorphismCasting.java, 344–345
catch block, 600, 601
CD-R/CD-RW, 4
CDs/DVDs, 4
Cell class, 1000
centerAction, MyAction class, 1122
Central processing unit (CPU), 2–3
  sharing, 8
  speed, 3
Chained exceptions, 613
ChangeEvent, 1160, 1162
char (data type), 40–41
  casting between numeric types and, 42–43
  increment/decrement, 41
Character class, 273–276
  charValue() method, 274
  CountEachLetter.java, 275
  counting each letter in a string
    (problem), 274–276
  methods for manipulating a character, 274
  static methods, 274
Character encoding, 40
Character literal, 40
Character wrapper class, 380
Characters:
  converting to strings, 272
  finding in strings, 270–271
charAt(index) method, String
    class, 268
charAt(index) method,
    StringBuilder, 278
Check-box menu items, 1109–1110
Check boxes, 520–523
  CheckBoxDemo.java, 521–522
  toggle button, 520

Checked exceptions, 603–604, 607
CheckPalindrome.java, 272–273
Child classes, See Subclasses
Choice lists, See Combo boxes
Circle class, 230–231, 233, 330–331
  Circle1.java, 235–236
  Circle2.java, 242–243
  Circle3.java, 247–248
  Circle4.java, 332–333
  Circle.java, 363
CircleControl class, 1146–1147
CircleController.java, 1150–1151
CircleModel class, 1146–1147
CircleModel.java, 1147–1149
CircleView class, 1146–1147
CircleView.java, 1149–1150
Circular doubly l lists, 787–788
Circular singly linked lists, 787
Clarity, 415
  in class design, 411
Class abstraction, 307
Class block, 16
Class design guidelines, 410–413
  clarity, 411
  cohesion, 410
  completeness, 412
  consistency, 410–411
  encapsulation, 411
  inheritance vs. aggregation, 412
  instance vs. static, 412
  interfaces vs. abstract classes, 413
Class diagrams, 231
Class encapsulation, 307
class keyword, 22
Class loaders, 19
Class variables, See Static variables
ClassCastException, 372, 696
.class file, 18, 20
Classes, 230
  Date class, 238
  Java, 231
  from Java library, 238–241
  naming, 52
  naming convention, 378
  Random class, 239
  reusing, 467
ClassNotFoundException, 603
Class's contract, 307
clear method, Map interface, 728
Client class, 982
Client.java, 980–982
Clock with audio (case study), 938–941
  ClockWithAudio.java, 938–940
    announceTime method, 940
    hourAudio array, 940
    start() method, 940
    stop() method, 940
  ClockWithAudioOnSeparateThread.java,
    940–941
    announceTime method, 941
    run method, 941
ClockAnimation.java, 505–506
clone method, Object class, 376–377
Cloneable interface, 374–375
  House.java, 375–376
cloneCalendar method, 1028
CloneNotSupportedException, 376, 603
close() method, 286
Close stream, 629
closedIcon property, 1224
Closest pair, finding (problem), 209–210
  FindNearestPoints.java, 209–210
Closest pair of points (case studies), 758–760
COBOL, 6

Code, modularizing, 149–151
Code incrementally, use of term, 106
Code sharing, and methods, 145
codebase attribute, 562
Cohesion, 415
  in class design, 410
Collaborator, 395
Collection interface, 413, 707–708, 726, 728
  add method, 708
  basic operations for adding/removing
      elements in a collection, 708
  class diagram, 707
  clear() method, 708
  iterator method, 708
  query methods, 708
  removeAll method, 708
  retainAll method, 708
  toArray() method, 708
Collection objects, 705
Collections:
  defined, 705–706
  static methods for, 720–722
  types of, 705
Collections class, 733–734, 961
  binarySearch method, 721
  copy method, 722
  disjoint method, 722
  fill method, 722
  frequency method, 722
  max and min methods, 722
  methods, 720, 733
  nCopies method, 722
  reverse method, 721
  shuffle method, 721
  singleton method, 734
  singletonList method, 734
  singletonMap method, 734
  unmodifiableCollection class, 734
  unmodifiableList class, 734
  unmodifiableMap class, 734
  unmodifiableSet class, 734
  unmodifiableSortedMap class, 734
  unmodifiableSortedSet class, 734
Color class, 420, 422, 432
color property, 1147, 1150
ColorDialog.java, 1130–1132
Column alias, 1242
columnRemoved method,
    TableColumnModelListener, 1208
columns property, GridLayout
    manager, 431
columns-to-be-sorted, 1243
Combining strings, 267–268
Combo boxes, 531–534
  ComboBoxDemo.java, 533–534
  defined, 531, 1174
  JComboBox class, 532
ComboBoxCellRendererDemo.java, 1175–1176
ComboBoxModel interface, 1174
Command-line arguments, 280–283
Comment styles, 51
Comments, 15, 51
commit() method, 1250
commitEdit() method, 1160
Common design error, 245
Communication devices, 2, 5
com.mysql.jdbc.Driver class, 1247
Comparable interface, 370–371, 385,
    413, 690, 691, 713
  ComparableRectangle.java, 372–373
  compareTo method, 720
  reverseOrder() method, 720–721
Comparator interface, 714–716
  Comparable interface vs., 716

GeometricObjectComparator.java, 715
  TestTreeSetWithComparator.java, 715–716
Comparator, order by, 713
compareTo method, 371, 373, 713
  String class, 266
compareToIgnoreCase method, String
    class, 266
Comparing characters, 68
Comparison operators, 68
Compile warning, unavoidable, 696
Compiler, 6–7, 17, 21
Compiling vs. interpreting, 7
Complete binary tree, 822
Complete graphs, 860
Completeness, 415
  in class design, 412
Component class, 421, 435, 471, 485, 1070
  setFont method, 432
Component classes, 420
ComponentAdapter class, 498
ComponentEvent, 485, 1205
ComponentListener interface, 498
Components:
  JavaBeans, 1050
  naming convention for, 514
Composition, 350, 397–398, 415
Compound expression, 790–791
CompoundBorder class, 1094–1096
ComputeArea.java, 27–28
ComputeBMI.java, 80–81, 311
ComputeChange.java, 48–49
ComputeFactorial.java, 657
ComputeFibonacci.java, 659–660
ComputeLoan.java, 47–48, 307–308
ComputeLoanUsingInputDialog.java, 57–58
ComputePrime.java, 968
  as SwingWorker, 965
ComputeTax.java, 82–83
Concatenating strings, 28, 43–44
Concrete blocking queues, 956
Concrete classes, 864
  in the Java Collections Framework, 707
ConcurrentModificationException, 961
Condition interface, 949
Conditional expressions, 72–73, 88
Conditional operator, 71
Conditions, 949
  and Java's built-in monitor, 182
Confirmation dialogs, 92–94, 1124–1125
  controlling a loop with, 127–128
  defined, 1122
  showConfirmDialog method, 1125
Connected and undirected graph, 912
Connection interface, 1250, 1253, 1258
connectLeftChild, 820
connectRightChild, 820
Console input, using Scanner class, 44–46
Console output, formatting, 89–90
const keyword, 1269
Constant base, omission of, 743
Constant time, 742–743, 746, 747
Constants, 31–32, 120, 241–245
  benefits of, 32
  naming, 32, 52
Constructor chaining, 337

Constructors, 231
  compared to methods, 232
  constructing objects using, 232
  default, 232
  no-arg, 232
  overloaded, 232
ConsumerProducer.java, 954–955
ConsumerProducerUsingBlockingQueue.java, 957
Container class, 422, 436, 1070, 1081
Container class:
  add methods, 1081–1082
  layoutContainer method, 1081
  remove method, 1081–1082
  validate method, 1081–1082
Container classes, 420, 422
Container objects, 705
ContainerAdapter class, 498
ContainerEvent, 487
ContainerListener interface, 487, 498
containsKey method, Map interface, 729
containsValue method, Map interface, 729
Content pane delegation, 425, 561
Contention, 936
Context menus, See Popup menus
Contiguous selection mode, 1218
continue keyword, 122–124
  TestContinue.java, 123–124
Contract, class, 307
Control unit, 2–3
Control variable, 112–113
ControlBall.java, 494–495
Controller, 1146
Convenience adapters, 497–498
Convenience classes, 413
Convenience listener adapter, 497
Converting strings, 269
copy method, Collections class, 722
Copy reference, 188
Copying files (problem), 633–635
  Copy.java, 634–635
CornerPanel class, 1089
CountLettersInArray.java, 193–194
CountOccurrenceOfWords.java, 732–733
Country codes, 1016–1017
Course class, 313–315, 1055
  Course.java, 315
  modeling the courses, 314
  TestCourse.java, 314–315
Course table, 1234–1235
CourseWithActionEvent class, 1055–1056
CourseWithActionEvent.java, 1056–1057
  addActionListener method, 1056–1057
CourseWithEnrollmentEvent.java, 1060
CPU, See Central processing unit (CPU)
CRC (classes/responsibilities/collaborators)
    cards, 395
createAdjacencyList methods,
    AbstractGraph class, 874
createGlue() method, 1077
createHorizontalBox() method, 1079
  Box class, 1079
CreateLargeFile.java, 848
createlHorizontalStrut(int) method,
    Box class, 1077
createVerticalBox() method, Box
    class, 1079
Critical region, 945
Cubic time, 747
Currency format, 1031
Current time, displaying
    (case study), 50–55
currentDirectory property,
    JFileChooser class, 1135
currentTimeMillis method, 50

Custom dialogs, creating, 1129–1132
   ColorDialog.java, 1130–1132
   TestColorDialog.java, 1132
Custom event sets, creating, 1059–1064
   CourseWithEnrollmentEvent.java,
      1060, 1061–1062
   EnrollmentEvent class, 1059–1160, 1064
   EnrollmentEvent.java, 1059–1060
   enrollmentExceeded method, 1062–1063
   EnrollmentListener class, 1060
   EnrollmentListener.java, 1060–1061
   TestCourseWithEnrollmentEvent.java,
      1062–1063
Custom exception classes, 614–615
Custom layout managers, creating, 1081–1086
Custom source components, creating, 1055–1059
   CourseWithActionEvent class, 1055–1056
   CourseWithActionEvent.java, 1056–1057
   deregistration method, 1055
   multicast listener, 1055
   registration method, 1055
   TestCourseWithActionEvent.java, 1058–1059
Custom stack class, 349–350
Custom table renderers and editors, 1203–1205
   CustomTableCellRendererEditorDemo.java,
      1204–1205
   MyImageCellRenderer.java, 1203
CustomFrame class, 336

D

Data encapsulation, benefit of, 321
Data field encapsulation, 247–249
   Circle3.java, 247–248
   TestCircle3.java, 248–249
Data fields, 230, 231, 305
   hidden, 306
Data structures, 26, 705, 864
Data types, 29
Database, defined, 1232
Database management system (DBMS), 1232
Database systems, *See also* Java database
      programming
   connecting to, 1247
   database language, 1236
   defined, 1231
DatabaseMetaData interface, 1258
databaseURL:
   for a MySQL database, 1247
   for an ODBC data source, 1247
   for an Oracle database, 1247–1248
Datagram sockets, 976
DataInput interface, 639
DataInputStream class, 629–630, 635
   TestDataStream.java, 631–632
   using, 631
DataOutput interface, 639
DataOutputStream class, 629–630, 635
   TestDataStream.java, 631–632
   using, 631
Date class, 238, 285, 1018
Date constructor, 238
Date/time, displaying, 1018–1029, 1019
   calendar, displaying, 1024–1029
      CalendarApp class, 1025
      CalendarApp.java, 1028–1029
      CalendarPanel class, 1024–1025
      CalendarPanel.java, 1025–1028
   DateFormat class, 1019
   DateFormatSymbols class, 1020–1021
   international clock display, 1021–1024
      WorldClockApp.java, 1024
      WorldClockControl.java, 1022–1024
      WorldClock.java, 1022

   SimpleDateFormat class, 1020, 1028
   TimeZone class, 1018–1019
   DateFormat class, 1018, 1019
   DateFormatSymbols class, 1020–1021
De Morgan's law, 71
Deadlocks, 959–960
Debuggers, 55
Debugging, 54–55
   defined, 55
Decimal numbers, 9
   conversions between binary numbers and, 9–10
   conversions between hexadecimal
      numbers and, 10–11
DecimalFormat class, 1032
   applyPattern(String pattern)
      method, 1032
Declarations, 28, 29–30
Declared type, 341, 343
Declaring exceptions, 604
Decrement operator, 37–38
Deep copy, 376
Default constructor, 232
Default field values, 236
Default modifiers, 245
Default values, 182
DefaultCellEditor class, 1224
DefaultComboBoxModel class, 1174–1175
DefaultListCellRenderer, 1170
DefaultListModel class, 1167
DefaultMutableTreeNode, 1217
   depthFirstEnumeration() method, 1214
DefaultTableColumnModel class, 1191
DefaultTableModel class, 1189, 1200
   methods in, 1189–1190
DefaultTreeCellEditor, 1224–1225
DefaultTreeCellRenderer
      class, 1223–1224
DefaultTreeModel class, 1212–1214
DefaultTreeSelectionModel class, 1217
Degree of a vertex, 860
Delete key, 5
Delimiters, changing, 288
Delphi, 6
Dependency, 398, 399, 415
deposit method, 945–947
Deprecated methods, 934
Depth-first search (DFS), 875–878
   algorithm (listing), 875–876
   applications of, 878
   defined, 875
   implementation of, 876–878
   isVisited array, 876–878
   TestDFS.java, 877
   time complexity, 876
Depth-first traversal:
   graphs, 874
   trees, 803
depthFirstEnumeration() method,
      DefaultMutableTreeNode, 1214
Deque interface, 726–727
   TestQueue.java, 726–727
Derived classes, *See* Subclasses
Descent, 461
Descriptive names, 27
   full, 52
   identifiers, 29
Deserialization, 638
Design Patterns, 414
destroy method, Applet class, 560
DiagonalLayout class, 1081–1082
   DiagonalLayout.java, 1082–1085
   gap property, 1082, 1084
   lastfill property, 1082, 1084
   majorDiagonal property, 1082, 1084

   ShowDiagonalLayout.java, 1085–1086
   TestDiagonalLayout class, 1086
Dialog boxes, defined, 1122
dialogTitle property, JFileChooser
      class, 1135
dialogType property, JFileChooser
      class, 1135
Dialup modem, 5, 976
Dijkstra, Edsger, 915
Dijkstra's algorithm, 915
Dimension class, 420, 422, 1084
Directed graphs, 859
Directory path, 283
Directory size, finding (problem), 665–666
   directory size, defined, 665
   DirectorySize.java, 665–666
Discontiguous selection mode, 1218
disjoint method, Collections class, 722
Disks, 4
DisplayFigure.java, 1091
DisplayImagePlayAudio.java, 582
DisplayImageWithURL.java, 580–581
DisplayMessage applet, parameter
      names/values for, 569
DisplayMessageApp.java, 570–572
DisplayMessage.html, 569
DisplayMessage.java, 569–570
displayObject method,
      TestPolymorphismCasting.java, 344–345
DisplayTime.java, 34
DisplayUnicode.java, 41
distinct SQL keyword, 1243
Distinct tuples, displaying, 1243–1244
Distributed TicTacToe game, 999–1010
   Cell class, 1000
   HandleASession class, 1000–1001
   TicTacToeClient class, 1000–1001
   TicTacToeClient.java, 1005–1010
   TicTacToeConstants interface, 1000
   TicTacToeConstants.java, 1001
   TicTacToeServer class, 1000–1001
   TicTacToeServer.java, 1001–1005
Divide-and-conquer strategy, 159
Division (/), 33–34
Division by zero, and runtime errors, 54
do-while loop, 110–111
Documentation, 51–53
   defined, 51
doInBackground() method, 962
doLayout method, 431
Domain constraints, 1234–1235
Domain Name Servers (DNS), 976
Domain names, 976
done() method, 962
Dot operator (.), 233
Dot pitch, 5
Double precision, 33, 116
double type, 32, 36
double type values vs. float type
      values, 35
Double wrapper class, 380
Double.parseDouble method, 56
Doubly linked lists, 787–788
draw3DRect method, 452
drawArc method, 456
drawImage method, 471
drawLine method, 451
drawOval method, 452, 456
drawPolygon method, 459
drawPolyline method, 459
drawRect method, 451
drawRoundRect method, 452
drawString method, 451
Drives, 4

Drop-down lists, *See* Combo boxes
DSL (digital subscriber line), 5, 976
Duplicate-free elements, storing using
    `HashSet` class, 709
Duplicate objects, and object stream, 638
DVDs, 4
Dynamic binding, 342–343

E

Eclipse, 55, 1050
Edge-weighted graphs, 902
`Edible` interface, 380
EfficientPrimeNumbers.java, 755–756
Eight Queens puzzle, 656, 673–675
    defined, 673
    EightQueens.java, 673–675
    `isValid(row, column)` method, 675
    `search(row)` method, 675
`element()` method, `Queue` interface, 726
Elementary programming, 25–66
`empty()` method, `Stack` class, 725
`EmptyBorder` class, 1094–1095
Encapsulating string, 267
Encapsulation, 159, 415
    benefit of, 321
    class, 307
    in class design, 411
    data field, 247–249
encoding, 40
Encoding scheme, 40–41
EncodingDemo.java, 1043
End-of-line style, 52–53
End tag, 562
Enrollment table, 1234–1235
`EnrollmentEvent` class, 1059–1160, 1064
EnrollmentEvent.java, 1059–1060
`enrollmentExceeded` method, 1062–1063
EnrollmentListener.java, 1060–1061
`entrySet()` method, `Map` interface, 729
`enum` keyword, 687
`Enumeration` interface, 724
`equalArea` method, 690
`equals` method:
    `AbstractSet` class, 708
    `Object` class, 340–341, 373
`equalsIgnoreCase` method, `String` class, 266
Erroneous solutions, 118
`Error` class, 602
    subclasses of, 602–603
Escape sequences for special characters, 41–42
`EtchedBorder` class, 1094–1095
Euclidean algorithm, 118
Euler, Leonard, 858
EvaluateExpression.java, 792–795
Event, defined, 484
Event dispatch thread, 937–938, 962
Event-driven programming, 483–512
    defined, 484
Event pair, 1052
Event set, 1052
EventDispatcherThreadDemo.java, 937–938
`EventListener`, 1060
`EventListenerList`, 1057
`EventObject` class, 484
Events:
    key, 501–503
    mouse, 498–501
    SimpleEventDemo.java, 489–490
Ever-waiting threads, 952
`Exception` class, 602
Exception classes, types of, 602–603
Exception handling, 597–622
    advantages of, 600–601

custom exception classes, 614–615
exception types, 601–604
`finally` clause, 611–612
overview, 598–600
Quotient.java, 598
QuotientWithException.java, 599
QuotientWithIF.java, 598–599
QuotientWithMethod.cpp, 600–601
rethrowing exceptions, 612–613
understanding, 604–610
when to use exceptions, 612
Exception propagation, 605, 612
Exception types, 601–604
Exceptions, 602
    chained, 613
    chained exceptions, 613
    checked, 603–604, 607
    declaring, 604
    defined, 600
    propagation, 605, 612
    throwing, 600
    unchecked, 603–604, 615
`executeQuery()` method, `Statement`
    interface, 1253
`executeUpdate()` method, `Statement`
    interface, 1253
Execution time, 741
`Executor` interface, 941–942
ExecutorDemo.java, 942–943
`Executors` class, 942
`ExecutorService` interface, 941
exitMenu menu, 1114
Exponent methods, `Math` class, 155
Exponential algorithm, 746
Exponential time, 746, 747
Expression statement, 38
Expressions, 30
    compound, 790–791
    conditional, 72–73, 88
    EvaluateExpression.java, 792–795
    evaluating, 36–37
        case study, 790–795
Extended classes, *See* Subclasses
Extending, prevention of, 351
External sort, 848–854
    analysis, 852–854
    copying first half segments
        (listing), 850
    CreateLargeFile.java, 848
    creating initial sorted segments
        (listing), 849–850
    defined, 848
    merging all segments (listing),
        850–851
    merging two segments (listing), 851
    phase I, implementation of, 849–850
    phase II, implementation of, 850–851
    sort phases, defined, 848
    SortLargeFile.java, 852–853
    two phases, combining, 851–852

F

`factorial` method, 657–659
Factorials, computing:
    base case, 656
    ComputeFactorial.java, 657
    problem, 656–659
    stopping condition, 656
FahrenheitToCelsius.java, 36–37
Fail-fast, use of term, 961
Fairness policy, and locks, 947
Fall-through behavior, 87
Fibonacci, Leonardo, 659

Fibonacci numbers, computing
    (problem), 659–661
    ComputeFibonacci.java, 659–660
    `fib` method, 659–661
Fibonacci numbers, finding
    (case studies), 747–748
    ImprovedFibonacci.java, 748
`FigurePanel` class (case study):
    FigurePanel.java, 454–455
    TestFigurePanel.java, 453–454
    UML diagram, 452–453
`File` class, 283–285, 288
    `lastModified()` method, 285
    obtaining file and directory properties
        using, 284
    TestFileClass.java, 284–285
File dialogs, 290–291
    ReadFileUsingJFileChooser.java, 290–291
File encoding scheme, 1042
File input and output, 285–290
    `PrintWriter` class, writing data
        using, 285–286
    `Scanner` class, reading data using,
        286–290
    WriteData.java, 285–286
File names:
    absolute, 283
    relative, 283
File pointer, 640
`FileInputStream` class, 627–629
    constructors, 627
`FileOutputStream` class, 627–629
    constructors, 627
Files, naming consistently, 438
`fill` method, `Collections` class, 722
`fill3DRect` method, 452
`filled` property, 1147, 1150
`fillOval` method, 452
`fillRect` method, 451
`fillRoundRect` method, 452
Filter streams, 629
`FilterInputStream` class, 629
`FilterOutputStream` class, 629
`final` modifier, 31, 351–353, 1274
`finally` clause, 611–612
FindGrade.java, 1250–1252
FindGradeUsingPreparedStatement.java,
    1253–1255
FindNearestPoints.java, 209–210
FindSalesAmount.java, 119–120
Fired event, 484
FixedLengthStringIO.java, 643–644
Flash drives, 4
`float` type, 32, 36
`Float` wrapper class, 380
Floating-point approximation, 34
Floating-point literals, 35
Floating-point numbers, 26, 33
    defined, 36
Floppy disks, 4
`FlowLayout` manager, 425–428, 456,
        1072, 1081
    `hgap` property, 431
    order of components added to a
        container, 429
    placing components in a frame
        using, 427
    properties, 431
    ShowFlowLayout.java, 426–427
    `vgap` property, 431
`flush()` method, 632
`focusable` property, 503
`FocusAdapter` class, 498
`FocusEvent`, 485, 487

FocusListener interface, 487, 498
Font class, 420, 422, 432–433
  finding available fonts, 433
FontMetrics class, 420, 422, 460–462
  TestCenterMessage.java, 461–462
for-each loops, 184
for loop, 111–113
Foreign key, 1235
Foreign key constraints, 1235
Formal parameters, 143
Format specifier, 89–90
FORTRAN, 6
Forward pointer, 788
Fractals:
  defined, 670
  problem, 670–673
  Sierpinski triangle, 670–673
    defined, 670
    SierpinskiTriangle.java, 671–673
Frame class, 1070
Frames, 423–425
  adding components to, 424–425
  creating, 423, *See also* JFrame class
  MyFrame.java, 423–424
  MyFrameWithComponents.java, 424–425
Framework-based programming using, 413–414
frequency method, Collections class, 722
Full descriptive names, 52
Function keys, 4–5
Functions, 143

G

Gang-of-four book, 414
Garbage collection, 188, 238
Garbage, defined, 238
GCD1.java, 749–750
GCD2.java, 751–752
Generated event, 484
Generic matrix class (case study), 697–701
  GenericMatrix class:
    addMatrix method, 697–699
    class diagram, 697
    GenericMatrix.java, 698–699
    IntegerMatrix class, 697, 699–700
    IntegerMatrix.java, 699–700
    multiplyMatrix method, 697–699
    RationalMatrix class, 697, 700
    RationalMatrix.java, 700
    TestIntegerMatrix.java, 700–701
    TestRationalMatrix.java, 701
Generic programming, 343, 384
  and interfaces, 373
Generic types, 687
GenericMatrix.java, 698–699
Generics, 685–704
  actual concrete type, 686
  benefit of, 686
  bounded generic type, 690
  BoundedTypeDemo.java, 690–691
  defined, 686
  erasing of, 694–695
  erasure and restrictions on, 694–697
  formal generic type, 686
  generic class constructor, 689
  generic class parameter, 691
  generic classes and interfaces:
    declaring, 688–690
    multiple generic parameters, 689
  generic instantiation, 686
  generic matrix class (case study), 697–701
  generic method parameter, 691
  generic methods, 690–691
    invoking, 690

generic types, benefits of using, 689
GenericMethodDemo.java, 690
GenericStack class, 688, 690
GenericStack.java, 688, 691
  inheritance with, 690
  motivations and benefits, 686–688
  raw type and backward compatibility, 691–692
  unbounded generic type, 691
  wildcard generic types, 692–694
GenericSort.java, 382–383
Geometric objects, 330
GeometricObject class, 330–331
  Circle4.java, 332–333
  GeometricObject1.java, 331–332
  Rectangle1.java, 333
GeometricObjectComparator.java, 715
GeometricObject.java, 362–364
GeometricObject.java:
  abstract methods, 362
    benefits of defining, 364–365
  TestGeometricObject.java, 364–365
getAdjacencyMatrix() method, AbstractGraph class, 874
getArea() method, 230, 235, 241
  Circle class, 330
getArea() method, Rectangle class, 330
getAvailableFontFamilyNames() method, 433
getAvailableLocales() method, 1018, 1029
getBMI() instance method, 313
getBundle method, 1037
getByName method, 983–984
getClass() method, 580–581
getCodeBase().getHost() method, 987, 989
getColumnClass() method, 1200
getColumn(columnIdentifier) method, JTable class, 1191
getColumn(index) method, TableColumnModel interface, 1191
getColumnNames() method, 1200
getCurrencyInstance method, NumberFormat class, 1031
getDateInstance method, 1019
getDateTimeInstance method, 1019
getDiammeter() method, Circle class, 330
getDisplayName() method, 1029
getElementAt method, ListModel, 1167
getFontMetrics methods, Graphics class, 461
getHamiltonianPath(int v) method, 894
getHamiltonianPath(Object vertex) method, 894
getHamiltonianPath(v, next, isVisited) method, 894
getHeight() method, 462
getHostAddress method, 983–984
getHostName method, 983–984
getInputStream() method, 978
getInstance method, NumberFormat class, 1030
get(int field) method, Calendar class, 367
getKeyChar() method, 1052
getKeyCode() method, 502
getKeys() method, 1119
getKeyStroke method, 1110
getLeadSelectionPath() method, 1217
getListCellRendererComponent() method, 1203
getLocalGraphicsEnvironment() method, 433
getMinimumSpanningTree method, 912–913
getNumberInstance method, NumberFormat class, 1030
getNumberOfObjects, 241–243

getNumberOfPrimes method, 965
getOutputStream() method, 978
getParameter method, Applet class, 570
getParent(v) method, Tree class, 874
getPercentInstance method, NumberFormat class, 1031
getPerimeter() method:
  Circle class, 330
  Rectangle class, 330
getPreferredSize() method, 456
getPriority method, 935
getRadius method, 241
getRoot() method, Tree class, 874
getSearchOrders() method, Tree class, 874
getSelectionPaths() method, 1217
getShortestPath method, 919
getSize method, ListModel, 1167
getSize() method, MyStack class, 350
getSource() method, 484
getStatus() instance method, 313
getString method, 1037
getTableCellRendererComponent() method, 1203
getTestTime method, 724
getTime() method, Date class, 238
getTimeInstance method, 1019
getTreeCellRendererComponent method, 1223
getWeekdays method, 1028
getWidth() method, 462
GIF (Graphics Interchange Format), 437
Gigahertz (GHz), 3
Glue, 1077
Gosling, James, 12, 22
goto keyword, 1269
goto statement, 124
Grade assignment (problem), 186–187
  AssignGrade.java, 186–188
GradeExam.java, 208
Graph applications, 857–899
Graph interface, 864–866, 892, 902, 904
  class diagram, 865
Graph traversals, 874–875
  breadth-first traversal, 874
  defined, 874
  depth-first traversal, 874
Graphical user interface (GUI), 514,
    See also GUI programming
  displaying components, 239–240
  GUIComponents.java, 240–241
  TestFrame.java, 240
Graphics, 445–482
  drawing on panels, 450–451
  graphical coordinate systems, 446
  Graphics class, 446–449
  images, displaying, 471–472
  ImageViewer class, 473–475
  MessagePanel class (case study), 462–467
  paintComponent method, 449–450
  StillClock class, 467–471
Graphics class, 420, 422, 446–449
  getGraphics() method, 447–448
  methods, 447
  TestGetGraphics.java, 448
GraphicsEnvironment class, 433
Graphs:
  AbstractGraph class, 868–873
  AbstractGraph.java, 864–866
  adjacency lists, 863–864
  adjacency matrices, 863–864
    adjacency lists vs, 864
  algorithms, 859
  basic terminologies, 859–860

Graphs:(*continued*)
　breadth-first search, 879–882
　　algorithm (listing), 879
　　applications of, 881–882
　　defined, 879
　　implementation of, 880–881
　　Nine Tail Problem, 882–888
　　TestBFS.java, 880–881
　common operations for, 864–865
　complete, 860
　components of, 859
　defined, 859
　depth-first search (DFS), 875–878
　　algorithm (listing), 875–876
　　defined, 875
　　implementation of, 876–878
　　TestDFS.java, 877
　　time complexity, 876
　directed, 859
　edge array, 861–862
　edge objects, 861–862
　edges, 859
　edges, representing, 861–863
　Graph.java, 867–868
　Knight's Tour problem, 888–895
　　defined, 888
　　Hamiltonian cycle, 888
　　Hamiltonian path, 888
　　Hamiltonian path algorithm
　　　(listing), 891–892
　　KnightTourApp class, 889
　　KnightTourApp.java, 894–895
　　KnightTourModel class, 889
　　KnightTourModel.java, 890–891
　　NP-complete, use of term, 892
　　time complexity, 892
　modeling, 864–874
　and modeling of real-world problems, 858
　problems, 859
　representing, 860–864
　simple, 860
　TestGraph.java, 866–867
　theory, 858
　undirected, 859
　UnweightedGraph class, 864–865, 873–874
　UnweightedGraph.java, 873–874
　vertices, representing, 860–861
　WeightedGraph class, 904
　WeightedGraph.java, 905–909
Greatest common divisor, finding:
　case studies, 749–752
　GCD1.java, 749–750
　GCD2.java, 751–752
　problem, 117–118
GreatestCommonDivisor.java, 118
GreatestCommonDivisorMethod.java, 149–150
GregorianCalendar class, 366–367, 1018
GridLayout manager, 428–429, 456, 1072
　properties, 431
　ShowGridLayout.java, 429
　specifying the number of rows/columns
　　in a grid, 428
Growth functions, comparing, 747
Growth rate, 741
GuessBirthDate.java, 84–86, 318
GuessBirthDateUsingArray.java, 217–218, 318
GuessBirthDateUsingConfirmationDialog.java,
　92–94
GuessDate class:
　designing, 318–320
　GuessDate.java, 320–322
　UseGuessDateClass.java, 319–320
Guessing numbers (problem), 105–106
GuessNumber.java, 106–107

GuessNumberOneTime.java, 106
GuessNumberUsingBreak.java, 124
GUI event dispatch thread, 937–938
　EventDispatcherThreadDemo.java, 937–938
GUI programming, 419–444
　arcs, drawing, 456–458
　classes, 421
　Color class, 420, 422, 432
　component classes, 420
　container classes, 420, 422
　Font class, 420, 422, 432–433
　frames, 423–425
　GUI classes, classification of, 420
　helper classes, 420, 422–423
　image icons, 437–439
　Java GUI API, 420–423
　layout managers, 425–431
　　BorderLayout manager, 429–431
　　doLayout method, 431
　　FlowLayout manager, 425–428
　　GridLayout manager, 428–429
　　properties of, 431
　　setLayout method, 425, 435
　　validate method, 431
　panels, using as subcontainers, 433–435
　polygons/polylines, drawing, 458–460
　Swing GUI components, 421–422
　　common features of, 435–437
　Swing vs. AWT, 420

H

Hand-traces, 55
HandleASession class, 1000–1001
HandleEvent.java, 373–374
Handlers, 486, 1052
Handling the exception, use of term, 600
Hard disks, 4
Hardware, 2, 21
Hash map, 709, 731
Hash sets, 709–710
hashCode method, 708–709
HashMap class, 730, 732
HashSet class, 708, 709–712
Hashtable class, 730–731
hasNext() method, Iterator
　　interface, 821, 875
Heap class, 825–827
　class diagram, 826
　heap time complexity, 828
　Heap.java, 826–827
　TestHeap.java, 827
Heap sort, 845–846
　HeapSort.java, 845–846
　merge sort vs., 846
　sort time, 846
Heaps, 822–828
　defined, 822
　Heap class, 825–827
　height of, 828
　new node, adding, 823–824
　representing, 823
　root, removing, 824–825
Heavyweight Swing components, 420
Height, 461
Helper classes, 420, 422–423
Hertz (Hz), 3
Heuristics, 894–895
Hexadecimal literals, 35
Hexadecimal numbers, 9
　conversions between binary numbers
　　and, 11–12
　conversions between decimal numbers
　　and, 10–11

hgap property:
　BorderLayout manager, 431, 1072
　FlowLayout manager, 431
　GridLayout manager, 431
Hidden data fields, 306
Hidden static methods, 339
High-level languages, 6, 21
Histogram.java, 545–546
Hoare, C. A. R., 841
Horizontal alignment, 516
Horizontal text position, 517
House.java, 375–376
howToEat method, 378–380
hspace attribute, 562
HTML tag, 562
Hypertext Markup Language (HTML), 12

I

I/O, in Java, 624
IBM DB2, 1236
IBM Informix, 1236
Icons:
　alignments, 516–517
　sharing, 438
　text positions, 517
Identifiers, 28–29
　using abbreviations for, 52
IdentifyHostNameIP.java, 983–984
IEEE 754, 32
if...else statements, 72, 74–75
if statements, 72–73
　nested, 72–73, 75–76
　simple, 73–74
IllegalArgumentException, 432
Image icons, 437–439, 1110–1111
　TestImageIcon.java, 438–439
ImageIcon, 1089
ImageObserver interface, 471
Images, displaying, 471–472
　DisplayImage.java, 472
ImageViewer class, 473–475
　ImageViewer.java, 474–475
　SixFlags.java, 473–474
Immutable classes, 304–305, 385
Immutable objects, 304–305
Immutable strings, 264–265
Implicit import, 20
ImprovedFibonacci.java, 748
Incident, sue of term, 860
Incompatible operands, 70
Increment and decrement operators, 37–38
Incremental development and testing, 166
Increment.java, 147–148
Indent code, 52
Indentation style, 52
Indexed variables, 182
indexOf method, String class, 270–271
InetAddress class, 983–984
Infinite loop, 105
Infinite recursion, 657
Information hiding, 159
Inheritance, 415
　aggregation vs., in class design, 412
　casting objects, 343–345
　defined, 330–341
　and modeling of the *is-a* relationship, 334
　multiple, 334–335
　Object class, 340–341
　and object-oriented programming, 399–400
　overriding methods, 338–339
　overriding vs. overloading
　　methods, 339–340
　single, 335, 377

subclasses, 330–335
super keyword, 336–338
superclass, 330–335
using to design stack and queue
classes, 788
init method, Applet class, 559
initial-action, 112
Inner class, 490–492
SimpleEventDemoInnerClass.java, 491–492
Inner class listeners, 490–492
InnerClass class, 490
Inorder traversal, 803, 821
InorderIterator class, 821
inorderIterator() method, 821
Input dialogs, 55–58, 1125–1126
defined, 1122, 1125
using, 56–57
Input errors, 54
Input/output devices, 2, 4–5
keyboard, 4–5
monitor, 5
mouse, 5
Input stream, defined, 624
InputMismatchException, 288
InputStream class, 626
Insert key, 5
insert(element) method, 812
Insertion sort, 200–202
InsertionSort.java, 202
Insertion sort algorithm, 746
insertRow method, 1200
Insets class, 1084
Inside access, 246
Instance, 230
static vs., in class design, 412
Instance method, 233
Instance variables, 241, 305
Instantiation, 230
generic, 686
int, 32
Integer literals, 35
Integer vs. decimal division, 37
Integer weights, 902
Integer wrapper class, 380
IntegerMatrix class, 697, 699–700
IntegerMatrix.java, 699–700
Integer.parseInt method, 56
Integrated Development Environment (IDE), 14
debugging in, 55
Integrity component, relational database
systems, 1232
Integrity constraints, 1234–1236
domain constraints, 1234–1235
enforcing, 1235–1236
foreign key constraints, 1234, 1235
primary key constraints, 1235
Intelligent guesses, 105
Interface inheritance, 369
Interfaces, 362, 369–370, 415, 864
abstract classes vs., 377–380, 413
in class design, 413
ActionListener interface, 373–374
Cloneable interface, 374–375
defined, 369
distinguishing from a class, 369
flexibility of, 413
and generic programming, 373
in the Java Collections Framework, 707
marker, 374–375
naming convention, 378
TestEdible.java, 369–370
International clock display, 1021–1024
WorldClockApp.java, 1021, 1024
WorldClockControl.java, 1021, 1022–1024

WorldClock.java, 1021, 1022
Internationalization, 1015–1047
character encoding, 1042–1043
EncodingDemo.java, 1043
date/time, displaying, 1018–1029
Locale class, 1016–1018
constants based on language, 1016
country codes, 1016–1017
getAvailableLocales() method, 1018
language codes, 1016–1017
local sensitive operations, 1018
locale property, 1016
numbers, formatting, 1029–1035
currency format, 1031
DecimalFormat class, 1032
example of, 1032–1035
locale dependence of, 1029
NumberFormat class, 1030–1032
NumberFormatDemo.java, 1032–1035
parsing numbers, 1031
percent format, 1031
plain number format, 1030–1031
resource bundles, 1035–1042
for the Chinese language (example), 1038
defined, 1035
for the English language
(example), 1037
for the French language
(example), 1038
getBundle method, 1037
ListResourceBundle class, 1035–1036
MissingResourceException, 1037, 1042
naming conventions, 1036
property resource bundles, 1042
ResourceBundle class, 1035–1036, 1042
ResourceBundleDemo.java, 1038–1042
updateString method, 1042
ResourceBundle class, 1016
Unicode, 1016
Interned strings, 265
Internet, defined, 976
Internet Protocol (IP), 976
Internet Protocol (IP) address, 976
Internet Service Provider (ISP), 976
Interrelational constraints, 1234
interrupt() method, 960
InterruptedException, 935
Intrarelational constraints, 1234
invokeAndWait method, 937
invokeLater method, 937
Invoking a second constructor, 306
IOException class, 603
IP address, 976
is-a relationships, 378
is-kind-of relationship, 378, 413
is null operator, 1242
isAlive() method, 960
isCellEditable method,
TableModel, 1201
isDigit method, Character class, 274
isEmpty method, Map interface, 729
isEmpty() method, MyStack class, 350
isFocusable property, 503
isLetter method, Character class, 274
isLetterOrDigit method, Character
class, 274
isLowerCase method, Character class, 274
isPalindrome method, 662
isVisited array, 876–878
ItemEvent, 487, 1052
ItemListener interface, 487
Iteration of a loop, 104
Iteration, recursion vs., 675
Iterator interface, 708, 821, 875

Iterators, 820–822
advantages of, 822
defined, 820
Iterator interface, 821
Iterator pattern, 822
TestBinaryTreeWithIterator.java, 821–822
variations of, 822

J

JApplet class, 420, 435, 560–561,
1070, 1071–1072
Java, 6
anatomy of characteristics of, 12
defined, 2, 12
versatility of, 14
Java API (Application Program Interface):
defined, 413
framework-based programming using, 413–414
Java API packages, 413–414
Java applet, accessing a database from, 1250–1252
FindGrade.java, 1250–1252
Java bytecode, running, 18
Java class, 231
java ClassName, 18
Java Collections Framework, 705–740, 864, 960
AbstractCollection interface, 707–708
Collection interface, 707–708
Comparator interface, 714–716
GeometricObjectComparator.java, 715–716
constructors, for concrete classes in, 714
defined, 705
design of, 707
interfaces and classes defined in, 707
maps, 728–733
priority queues, 726–728
queues, 726–728
sets, 706, 708–717
Set interface, 708
Stack class, 724–725
types of collections supported by, 706
Vector class, 724–725
java command, 18, 22
Java compiler, 21
Java database programming, 1231–1268,
1250–1252, *See also* Database systems
database systems, defined, 1231
JDBC, 1244–1252, *See also* JDBC
URLs, 1247
PreparedStatement interface, 1253
preparedStatement method, 1253
relational database systems, 1231–1236
attributes, 1233
integrity, 1232
integrity constraints, 1234–1236
language, 1232
relational data model, 1232
structure, 1232
tables, 1233–1234
tuples, 1233
relational structures, 1233–1234
Structured Query Language
(SQL), 1236–1244
arithmetic operators, 1242–1243
between-and operator, 1242
Boolean operators, 1240–1241
from clause, 1240
column alias, 1242
comparison operators, 1240–1241
creating a database, 1237–1238
creating a user account on, 1236–1237
creating and dropping tables, 1238–1239
defined, 1236
delete records, 1240

Java database programming (*continued*)
  distinct tuples, displaying, 1243–1244
  inserting records, 1239–1240
  `is null` operator, 1242
  `like` operator, 1241
  `select` clause, 1240
  simple queries, 1240
  standard SQL, 1236
  tables, joining, 1244
  updating records, 1240
Java Development Toolkit (JDK), 14
Java Enterprise Edition (Java EE), 14
Java expressions, evaluating, 36–37
.java extension, 22
.java file, 20
Java GUI API, 420–423
Java keywords, *See* Keywords
Java language specification, 14
Java Micro Edition (Java ME), 14
Java modifiers, *See* Modifiers
Java program-development process, 17
Java program, simple, 15–16
Java servlets, 14
Java source-code file, creating, 17
Java source programs, case sensitivity of, 18
Java Standard Edition (Java SE), 14
Java Virtual Machine (JVM), 7, 188, 935
`java.applet`, 413
`java.awt`, 413
`java.awt` package, 420, 423
`java.awt.Applet` class, 1070
`java.awt.Color` class, 432
`java.awt.Component`, 1070
`java.awt.Container`, 422, 1070, 1081
`java.awt.Dialog`, 1132
`java.awt.Dimension`, 422
`java.awt.Font`, 420, 422, 432–433
`java.awt.FontMetrics`, 420, 422
`java.awt.Frame` class, 1070
`java.awt.Graphics`, 420, 422
`java.awt.GraphicsEnvironment`, 433
`java.awt.LayoutManager`, 422
JavaBeans, 1049–1068
  components, 1050
    relationship between Java classes
      and, 1050–1051
  custom event sets, creating, 1059–1064
    CourseWithEnrollmentEvent.java,
      1061–1062
    `EnrollmentEvent` class, 1059–1160, 1064
    EnrollmentEvent.java, 1059–1060
    `enrollmentExceeded` method, 1062–1063
    `EnrollmentListener` class, 1060
    EnrollmentListener.java, 1060–1061
    TestCourseWithEnrollmentEvent.java,
      1062–1063
  custom source components, creating,
    1055–1059
    `CourseWithActionEvent` class,
      1055–1056
    CourseWithActionEvent.java, 1056–1057
    deregistration method, 1055
    multicast listener, 1055
    registration method, 1055
    TestCourseWithActionEvent.java,
      1058–1059
  defined, 1050
  delegation-based model, 1052
  event, 1052
  event classes, 1052–1053
  event listener interface, 1052–1053
  event object, 1052
  event set, 1052
Java event model, 1052–1054

listener, 1052
listener components, 1053–1054
minimum component requirements, 1050
properties, 1051–1052
  and data fields, 1051
property-naming patterns, 1051
source components, 1053
source object, 1052
javac command, 17, 22
javadoc comments, 51
`java.io`, 413–414
`java.io.FileNotFoundException`, 627
`java.io.IOException`, 627, 628
`java.lang`, 413–414
`java.lang` package, 20, 46–48
`java.lang.Class` class, 580–581
`java.lang.ClassNotFoundException`, 637
`java.lang.Comparable`, 371
`java.lang.InterruptedException`, 960
`java.lang.Number`, 1031
`java.lang.UnsupportedOperationException`,
  708
`java.math`, 413
`java.net`, 413
`java.net.BindException`, 982
`java.net.ConnectException`, 982
`java.net.URL` class, 995
Java's built-in monitor, 952–953
JavaServer Pages, 14
`java.sun.com`, 12, 14
`java.swing.SwingConstants`, 1010
`java.text.DateFormat`, 1018
`java.text.DecimalFormat`, 1032
`java.text.ParseException`, 1031
`java.util` package, 45
`java.util.ArrayList`, 961, 1167
`java.util.Calendar`, 1018
`java.util.Collection`, 726
`java.util.concurrent` package, 956
`java.util.Date`, 1018
`java.util.EventListener`, 1052, 1059
`java.util.EventObject`, 1052, 1059
`java.util.Hashtable`, 730–731, 961
`java.util.Map`, 961
`java.util.Observer` interface, 1146
`java.util.Queue`, 956
`java.util.TimeZone`, 1018
`java.util.Vector`, `java.util.Stack`, 961
`javax.swing` package, 413–414, 420, 1209
`javax.swing.Border` package, 1096
`javax.swing.BorderFactory`, 1096–1097
`javax.swing.BoxLayout`, 1076
`javax.swing.event` package, 485
`javax.swing.event.ChangeEvent`, 1162
`javax.swing.event.EventListenerList`,
  1057
`javax.swing.event.HyperlinkEvent`, 997
`javax.swing.JApplet`, 422
`javax.swing.JDialog`, 1070
`javax.swing.JEditorPane`, 997
`javax.swing.JFileChooser`, 1132–1134
`javax.swing.JFrame`, 422
`javax.swing.JPanel`, 422, 1072
`javax.swing.ListSelectionModel`, 534
`javax.swing.RowFilter`, 1193
`javax.swing.SwingUtilities`, 937
`javax.swing.Timer`, 503–504
`javax.swing.tree` package, 1209
JBuilder, 55, 1050
`JButton` class, 239, 414, 420, 435, 486, 637,
  1064, 1070, 1153–1154
  GUIComponents.java, 241
`JCheckBox` class, 520, 523
  GUIComponents.java, 241

`JCheckBoxMenuItem` class, 1108, 1109
`JColorChooser` class, 1132–1134, 1153
  color preview panel, 1134
  defined, 1132
  showDialog method, 1133–1134, 1139
  tabbed pane, 1134
`JComboBox` class, 239, 420, 532, 1174–1177
  ComboBoxCellRendererDemo.java, 1175–1176
  GUIComponents.java, 241
  properties/constructors, 1174
`JComponent` class, 420, 421–422,
  435–436, 451, 1095
JDBC, 1244–1252
  `CallableStatement` interface, 1255–1258
  classes, 1246
  connections, establishing, 1247–1248
  defined, 1244
  developing database applications using,
    1245–1250
  drivers, 1245, 1246
    loading, 1246–1247
  FindGradeUsingPreparedStatement.java,
    1253–1255
  interfaces, 1246
  Java applet, accessing a database from,
    1250–1252
  metadata retrieval, 1258–1259
    database tables, obtaining, 1259–1260
    `DatabaseMetaData` interface, 1258
    `ResultSetMetaData` interface, 1260–1261
    TestDatabaseMetaData.java, 1259
    TestResultSetMetaData.java, 1261
  `PreparedStatement` interface, 1253
  relationships between Java programs, JDBC
    API, JDBC drivers, and relational
    databases, 1245
  `ResultSet`, processing, 1248
  SimpleJDBC.java, 1248
  statements, executing, 1248
JDBC-ODBC bridge driver, 1245, 1250
jdbc:odbc:dataSource, 1247
`JDialog` class, 435, 1070, 1129
JDK 1.6, 14, 55
`JEditorPane` class, 997–999
  WebBrowser.java, 998–999
`JFileChooser` class, 290, 1134–1139, 1153
  `currentDirectory` property, 1135
  `dialogTitle` property, 1135
  `dialogType` property, 1135
  `multiSelectionEnabled` property, 1135
  no-arg constructor, 1134
  ReadFileUsingJFileChooser.java, 290–291
  `selectedFile` property, 1135
  `selectedFiles` property, 1135
  showOpenDialog method, 1135
  showSaveDialog method, 1135
  TextEditor.java, 1135–1138
`JFrame` class, 239–240, 335–336, 420, 423, 435,
  529, 543, 1070, 1071
  compared to `JApplet` class, 567
  `CustomFrame` class, 336
  `setDefaultCloseOpeartion` method, 240
  `setLocation` method, 240
  `setSize` method, 240
  `setTitle` method, 240
  `setVisible` method, 240
  UseCustomFrame.java, 335–336
`JLabel` class, 435, 526
`JList` class, 239, 420, 535, 1163–1167
  constructors, 1163
  `DefaultListCellRenderer`, 1170
  `DefaultListModel`, 1167
  HORIZONTAL_WRAP, 1164
  list layout orientations, 1164

list-selection models, 1164–1165
list-selection modes, 1164–1165
methods, 1163
properties, 1163
scrollable list, creating, 1167
string values, 1167
VERTICAL, 1164
VERTICAL_WRAP, 1164
JMenu class, 420, 1108, 1110
JMenuBar class, 1108
JMenuItem class, 1108–1109, 1110
JOptionPane class, 55–58, 1122–1129
  confirmation dialog, 1124–1125
    defined, 1122
  creating, 1127–1129
  dialogs created using, 1122
  input dialog, 1125–1126
    defined, 1122, 1125
  message dialogs, 1123–1124
    defined, 1122
  option dialog, 1126–1127
    defined, 1122, 1126
  showMessageDialog method, 19–20
JOptionPaneDemo.java, 1128–1129
JPanel class, 241, 420, 433, 435, 529, 1072, 1153
  as a canvas for drawing, 450
JPasswordField class, 528
JPEG (Joint Photographic Experts Group), 437
JProgressBar, 965–968
  class diagram, 966
  ProgressBarDemo.java, 966–968
  PropertyChangeEvent, 968
JRadioButton class, 239, 420, 520, 523
  GUIComponents.java, 241
JRadioButtonMenuItem class, 1108–1110
JScrollBar class, 538
JScrollPane class, 1086–1090
  hsbPolicy parameter, 1087
  methods, 1087
  ScrollMap.java, 1088–1089
  setCorner method, 1087
  viewport, 1086
  vsbPolicy parameter, 1087
JScrollPane class, 529
JSlider class, 541
jspDate, 1162
jspDay, 1162
JSpinner class, 1154–1157
  getNextValue() method, 1155
  getPreviousValue() method, 1155
  getValue() method, 1155
  methods, 1155
  sequence value, 1155
  SimpleSpinner.java, 1156–1157
JSpinner.DateEditortor, 1159
JSpinner.DefaultEditor, 1159
JSpinner.ListEditor, 1160
JSpinner.NumberEditor, 1159
JSplitPane class, 1091–1094, 1153
  defined, 1091
  properties/constructors/methods, 1092
  ShowLayout.java, 1092–1094
jspMonth, 1162
JTabbedPane class, 1090–1091
  defined, 1090
  DisplayFigure.java, 1091
JTable class, 1184, 1184–1208
  auto sort and filtering, 1193–1195
  classes, 1184
  column model, 1184
  constructors, 1184–1185
    for creating tables, 1185
  defined, 1184
  and events, 1205

interfaces, 1184
JTableHeader, as supporting class, 1184
list-selection model, 1184
methods, 1184–1185
properties, 1184–1185, 1189
rows/columns, modifying (case study),
    1195–1200
rowSorter method, 1193–1194
scrollable table, creating, 1184
table column models, 1189, 1191, 1195, 1205
  AbstractTableModel class, 1189
  DefaultTableModel class, 1189
  TableModel interface, 1189
  TableModelEvents, 1189
  TestTableModel.java, 1189–1190
table model events, 1205–1208
table models, 1184, 1189–1193
table renderers and editors, 1200–1202
  custom, 1203–1205
TableColumn, as supporting class, 1184
TablePropertiesDemo.java, 1187–1189
TestTable.java, 1186
TestTableSortFilter.java, 1194–1195
JTableHeader class, 1184, 1193
JTextArea class, 420, 528
  constructors/methods, 528
JTextComponent class, 997
JTextField class, 420, 435, 527–528
  GUIComponents.java, 241
JToggleButton class, 520
JToolBar class, 1116–1118
  floatable toolbar, 1118
  ToolBarDemo.java, 1117–1118
JTree class, 1208–1225
  classes, 1209
  complexity of, 1209
  constructors for creating tables, 1209
  data representation of the tree, 1209
  defined, 1208
  editable property, 1224
  interfaces, 1209
  modifying trees (case study), 1220–1223
    ModifyTree.java, 1220–1223
  SimpleTreeDemo.java, 1211–1212
  supporting interfaces and classes, 1209
  TestTreeModel.java, 1213–1214
  TestTreePath.java, 1218–1220
  tree events, 12225
  tree node rendering and editing, 1223–1225
JViewport class, 1086

K

Key codes, 501–502
Key constants, 502
Key events, 501–503
  defined, 501
  KeyEventDemo.java, 502–503
KeyAdapter class, 498
Keyboard, 4–5
  accelerators, 1110–1111
  mnemonics, 1110–1111
KeyEvent class, 485, 487, 501, 1052, 1205
KeyEventDemo.java, 502–503
KeyListener interface, 487, 498, 501
keyPressed handler, 501
keyReleased handler, 501
keySet() method, Map interface, 729
KeyStroke class, 1110
keyTyped handler, 501
Keywords, 15, 1269
Knight's Tour problem:
  defined, 888
  Hamiltonian cycle, 888

Hamiltonian path, 888
Hamiltonian path algorithm (listing), 891–892
KnightTourApp class, 889
KnightTourModel class, 889
  class diagram, 889
KnightTourModel.java, 890–891
NP-complete, use of term, 892
time complexity, 892

L

Labeled continue statement, 128
Labels, 525–526
  defined, 525
LAN (local area network), 5
Language codes, 1016–1017
Language component, relational database
    systems, 1232
Large input size, 742
LargeFactorial.java, 385–386
lastIndexOf method, String class, 270–271
lastModified() method, File class, 285
Layout managers, 425–431, 1072–1081
  alignmentX (alignmentY) property, 1073
  BorderLayout manager, 429–431, 1072, 1081
    hgap property, 431, 1072
    setHgap method, 431
    ShowBorderLayout.java, 430–431
    vgap property, 431, 1072
  BoxLayout manager, 1076–1079
    and component's alignmentX or
        alignmentY property, 1077
    glue, 1077
    rigid area, 1077
    ShowBoxLayout.java, 1077–1079
    strut, 1077
    unique features of, 1076–1077
  CardLayout manager, 1073–1076
    add method, 1073
    methods, 1073
    ShowCardLayout.java, 1074–1076
  custom, creating, 1081–1086
  defined, 1072
  doLayout method, 431
  FlowLayout manager, 425–428, 456,
      1072, 1081
    hgap property, 431
    order of components added to a
        container, 431
    placing components in a frame using, 427
    properties, 431
    setHgap method, 431
    setVgap method, FlowLayout
        manager, 431
    ShowFlowLayout.java, 426–427
    vgap property, 431
  GridLayout manager, 428–429, 456, 1072
    properties, 431
    ShowGridLayout.java, 429
    specifying the number of rows/columns
        in a grid, 428
  maximumSize property, 1073
  minimumSize property, 1073
  no layout manager, using, 1079–1081
    ShowNoLayout.java, 1080–1081
  preferredSize property, 1072–1073, 1082
  properties affecting sizing/location of
      components in container, 1072
  setLayout method, 425, 435
  validate method, 431
LayoutManager interface, 1081, 1084
  layoutContainer method, 1086
Lead path, 1217
Leading, 460

leadSelectionIndex method, 1165
leafIcon property, 1224
Leap year, determining (problem), 71
LeapYear.java, 71
Left-associative operators, 91
Left child of a node, 800
Left justification, 90
Left subtree, 800
leftAction, MyAction class, 1122
length() method, StringBuilder, 278
Level of a tree, 800
Lightweight Swing components, 420
like operator, 1241
Line comment, 15
Line numbers, 15
Line separator sting, 288
Linear search algorithm, 742
Linear time, 747
LinearSearch.java, 196
LineBorder class, 1094–1096
Lines, drawing, 451–452
LinkageError class, 602–603
Linked hash map, 709
Linked hash set, 709, 723
Linked lists, 709, 717, 776–787
    LinkedList class, 777–778
    MyLinkedList class, 777–778
        addFirst(e) method, 779
        add(index, e) method, 780–781
        addLast(e) method, 779–780
        implementing, 779–786
        MyArrayList class vs., 786–787
        removeFirst() method, 781–782
        remove(index) method, 783–784
        removeLast() method, 782–783
    MyLinkedList.java, 784–786
    nodes, 776–777
    TestLinkedList.java, 777–778
    variations of, 787–788
LinkedBlockingQueue, 956
LinkedHashMap class, 730, 732
LinkedHashSet class, 708–709, 712–713
LinkedList class, 717–720, 726–727
    defined, 717–718
    methods, 718
    TestArrayAndLinkedList.java, 719
Linux, 7
List cell renderer, 1170–1173
List interface, 182, 716–717, 769
    add method, 716
    addAll method, 716–717
    indexof method, 717
    methods in, 716
    remove method, 717
    set method, 717
List layout orientations, 1164
List models, 1164, 1167–1170
    and ListModel interface, 1167
    ListModelDemo.java, 1168–1170
List properties demo (example), 1165
List-selection models/list-selection modes, 1164–1165
ListCellRenderer class, 1170
    getListCellRendererComponent method, 1170
    ListCellRendererDemo.java, 1172–1173
    MyListCellRenderer.java, 1171–1172
ListCellRenderer interface, 1175
ListDataEvent, 1167
ListDataListener, 1167
Listener components, 1053–1054
    TestSourceListener.java, 1054
ListenerClass class, 492
Listeners, 485–496

anonymous class listeners, 492–494
    defined, 485–486
    inner class listeners, 490–492
    listener interface adapters, 497–498
        AdapterDemo.java, 498
    SimpleEventDemo.java, 489–490
ListIterator interface, 717–718
    add method, 717
    hasNext() method, 717
    next() method, 717
    previous() method, 717
    set method, 717
ListModel interface, 1167, 1174
ListPropertiesDemo.java, 1165–1167
ListResourceBundle class, 1035–1036
Lists, 534–537, 706, 716–720
    array lists, 771–776
        MyArrayList.java, 772–775
        TestList.java, 775–776
    ArrayList class, 717–720
        defined, 717
        TestArrayAndLinkedList.java, 719
        trimToSize() method, 718
    circular doubly l, 787–788
    circular, singly linked, 787
    common features for, 768–771
    compared to sets, 724
    defined, 534
    doubly linked, 787–788
    expressions, evaluating (case study), 790–795
    JList class, 535
    linked lists, 776–787
        variations of, 787–788
    linked structure, 768
    LinkedList class, 717–720
        defined, 717–718
        LinkedList(Collection), 718
        methods, 718
        TestArrayAndLinkedList.java, 719
    List interface, 716–717
    ListDemo.java, 536–537
    performance of, 723–724
    queues, 788–790
    SetListPerformanceTest.java, 723–724
    stacks, 788–790
    static methods for, 720–722
ListSectionListener, 1164
ListSelectionEvent, 485
Literals, defined, 35
LiveLab, 13
Load factor, 709
Loan applet, creating, 564–566
Loan class, 307–308, 467
    class diagram, 308
    Loan.java, 309–310
    test program, writing, 311
    TestLoanClass.java, 308–309
Loan payments, computing (case study), 46–48
LoanApplet.html, 566
LoanApplet.java, 564–565
    with main method, 568
Local area network (LAN), 976
Local variables, 153, 305
Locale class, 1016–1018
    constants based on language, 1016
    country codes, 1016–1017
    getAvailableLocales() method, 1018
    language codes, 1016–1017
    local sensitive operations, 1018
    locale property, 1016
Lock interface, 947–949
Locks
    and Java's built-in monitor, 182
    synchronization using, 947–949

AccountWithSyncUsingLock.java, 948–949
    ReentrantLock class, 947–948
Log-linear time, 747
Logarithmic time, 745, 747
Logic errors, 54–55
Logical operators, 69
long, 32
long literal, 35
Long string, breaking, 28
Long wrapper class, 380
Loop body, 104
loop-continuation-condition, 112–113
Loop statement, 38
Loops, 103–139, 860
    body, 104
    case studies, 117–122
    controlling, with a confirmation dialog, 127–128
    controlling with a sentinel value, 108–109
    defined, 103
    do-while loop, 110–111
    infinite, 105
    iteration of, 104
    for loop, 111–113
    nested, 115–116
    pre-test, 113
    while loop, 103–110
Loss of precision, 49
Lottery (problem), 79–80
Lottery.java, 79–80
Lower-bound wildcard, 693

M

Mac OS, 7
Machine language, 5, 21
Main class, 231
main method, 15–16, 22, 144, 558, 572
    passing strings to, 281
Main window, 543
MalformedURLException, 995
Map, 706
Map interface, 182
Maps, 728–733
    AbstractMap class, 729
    HashMap class, 730, 732
    LinkedHashMap class, 730, 732
    Map interface, 728
        concrete implementations of, 730
        methods, 728–729
        query methods, 729
        update methods, 728
    SortedMap interface, 730
    TestMap.java, 731
    TreeMap class, 730;, 732
Marker interface, 374–375
matches method, String class, 270
Matching braces, 16
Math class, 154–157, 246, 351
    abs method, 156
    exponent methods, 155
    max method, 156
    min method, 156
    random method, 156–157
    rounding methods, 155–156
    trigonometric methods, 154–155
Math learning tool, 71
    advanced, 107–108
    improved, 77–78
MatteBorder class, 1094–1096, 1102
max and min methods, Collections class, 722
max method, 144–145, 371–372
    Math class, 156
Max1.java, 692

maxDaysInMonth method, 1162
Max.java, 691
Mbps (million bits per second), 5
Megabyte (MB), 3
Megahertz (mHz), 3
Memory chips, 3
Memory (main memory), 2, 3
Menu bar, creating, 1108
Menus, 1108–1114
    check-box menu items, 1109–1110
    classes, 1108
    creating, 1110
    menu bar, 1108
    menu items, 1109–1110
    MenuDemo.java, 1111–1114
    popup, 1114–1116
    radio-button menu items, 1109
    submenu items, 1109
    using, 1111–1114
Merge sort, 838–841
    algorithm (listing), 838
    illustration, 838–839
    merge sort time, 840–841
    method for merging two arrays (listing), 839
    quick sort vs., 845
    time analysis, 840–841
Message dialog box, displaying text in, 19–20
Message dialogs, 1123–1124
    defined, 1122
MessagePanel class (case study), 462–467
    implementation of, 464
    MessagePanel.java, 464–466
    TestMessagePanel.java, 463–464
    xCoordinate property, 466
    yCoordinate property, 466
MessagePanel.java, 1052
Meta object, 580–581
Metadata retrieval, 1258–1259
    database tables, obtaining, 1259–1260
    DatabaseMetaData interface, 1258
    ResultSetMetaData interface, 1260–1261
    TestDatabaseMetaData.java, 1259
    TestResultSetMetaData.java, 1261
Method abstraction, 159–161
    bottom-up design, 163
    PrintCalendar.java, 163–166
    top-down design, 160–161, 162–163
Method block, 16
Method header, 142
Method name, 142
Method overloading, 151–153
Method signature, 143
Methods, 22, 141–178, 231, 241–245
    body, 143
    call stacks, 145
    calling, 143–145
    defined, 142
    modularizing code, 149–150
    naming, 52
    overloading, 151–153
    parameters, 142–143
    passing arrays to, 189–192
    passing objects to, 249–251
    passing parameters by values, 147–149
    syntax for defining, 142
    value-returning, 143
    void, 143
Microsoft Windows, 6, 7
min method, Math class, 156
Minimum spanning trees (MSTs), 910–915
    getMinimumSpanningTree method, 912–913
    implementation of, 912–913
    MST class, 912–914
    Prim's algorithm, 911–912

TestMinimumSpanningTree.java, 914–915
    time complexity, 914
    uniqueness of, 912
MissingResourceException, 1037, 1042
Modal dialogs, 1132
Model-view-controller (MVC), See MVC
Models, 1146
Modem, 5
Modifier key, 5
Modifiers, 350–353, 1274–1275
    methods, 142
ModifyTree.java, 1220–1223
Modularizing code, 149–151
    GreatestCommonDivisorMethod.java, 149–150
    PrimeNumberMethod.java, 150–151
Monetary units, counting (case study), 48–50
Monitor, 5
    defined, 952
Mouse, 5
Mouse events, 498–501
    MoveMessageDemo.java, 500–501
    moving a message on a panel using a mouse
        (example), 499–501
MouseAdapter class, 498
mouseDragged method, 501
MouseEvent, 485, 487, 499, 1052, 1064, 1205
MouseListener interface, 487, 498–499
MouseMotionAdapter class, 498
MouseMotionListener interface, 485–486, 487,
    498–499
mousePressed handler, 1116
mouseReleased handler, 1116
MovableMessagePanel class, 501
MoveMessageDemo.java, 500–501
MS Access, 1236
    JDBC-ODBC driver, 1246
    URL, 1247
MST class, 912–914
Multidimensional arrays, 215–218
    birth dates, guessing (problem), 217–218
    student scores, computing (problem), 216–217
Multimedia, 557–596
    animations, 582–585
Multiple-choice test, grading (problem), 207–208
    GradeExam.java, 208
Multiple clients, serving, 984–987
Multiple inheritance, 334–335
Multiple solutions, 118
Multiple windows:
    creating, 543–547
    Histogram.java, 545–546
    MultipleWindowsDemo.java, 544–545
Multiplication (*), 33–34
MultiplicationTable.java, 115–116
Multiplicative constants, ignoring, 742
Multiplicity, 396
multiplyMatrix method, 697–699
Multiprocessing, 8
Multiprogramming, 8
multiSelectionEnabled property,
    JFileChooser class, 1135
Multithreading, 8, 929–973, 958–959
    blocking queues, 956–957
        ArrayBlockingQueue, 956–957
        concrete, 956
        ConsumerProducerUsing-
            BlockingQueue.java, 957
        defined, 956
        LinkedBlockingQueue, 956
        PriorityBlockingQueue, 956
    cooperation among threads, 949–953
    deadlocks, 959–960
        avoiding, 959–960
    defined, 930

FlashingText.java, 936–937
GUI event dispatch thread, 937–938
JProgressBar, 965–968
    class diagram, 966
    ProgressBarDemo.java, 966–968
Producer/Consumer (case study), 953–955
and program responsiveness/interactivity, 930
Semaphore class:
    acquire() method, 958–959
    class diagram, 959
    release() method, 958–959
semaphores, 958–959
SwingWorker class, 962–965
synchronized collections, 960–961
synchronized keyword, 945–947
tasks, 930
thread concepts, 930
thread pools, 941–943
thread states, 960
thread synchronization, 943–947
MultiThreadServer.java, 984–986
MutableComboBoxModel interface, 1174
MutableTreeNode, 1209, 1214
Mutator method, 247
MVC, 1146–1154
    MVCDemo.java, 1151–1152
    Swing architecture, 1153–1154
    variations, 1152–1153
MyAbstractList interface, 768–769
    MyAbstractList.java, 770–771
MyAction class, 1122
MyArrayList class, time complexities for
    methods in, 787
MyArrayList.java, 772–775
    add method, 774
    clear method, 774
    contains method, 774
    ensureCapacity method, 774
    get method, 774
    indexOf method, 774
    lastIndexOf method, 774
    remove method, 775
    set method, 775
    toString method, 775
MyFrame.java, 423–424
MyFrameWithComponents.java,
    424–425
MyImageCellRenderer.java,
    1203, 1205
MyLinkedList class, 777–778
    addFirst(e) method, 779
    add(index, e) method, 780–781
    addLast(e) method, 779–780
    implementing, 779–786
    MyArrayList class vs., 786–787
    removeFirst() method, 781–782
    remove(index) method, 783–784
    removeLast() method, 782–783
MyLinkedList.java, 784–786
    time complexities for methods
        in, 787
MyList interface, 768–769
    MyList.java, 769–770
MyListCellRenderer.java, 1171–1172,
    1175, 1177
MyPriorityQueue class, 828
MyPriorityQueue.java, 828–829
MyQueue class, 788
MySQL, 1236–1237
    JDBC driver, 1246
    URL, 1247
MyStack class, 788
MyStack.java, 349–350, 788, 789
MyTableModel.java, 1201–1202

N

Name.java, 402
Naming conflicts, avoiding, 331
Naming conventions, 52
Narrowing a type, 39
native keyword, 376
native modifier, 1274
Natural order, 713
nCopies method, Collections class, 722
Neighbors, 860
Nested blocks, 16
Nested class, 490–492
Nested if statements, 72–73, 75–76
Nested loops, 115–116
NetBeans, 55, 1050
NetBeans console input, 46
Network interface card (NIC), 5
Networking:
    applet clients, 987–989
    client/server computing, 976–983
        client sockets, 977
        Client.java, 980–982
        data transmission through sockets, 978
        example of, 978–983
        server sockets, 976–977
        Server.java, 979–980
    distributed TicTacToe game, 999–1010
        Cell class, 1000
        HandleASession class, 1000–1001
        TicTacToeClient class, 1000–1001
        TicTacToeClient.java, 1005–1010
        TicTacToeConstants class, 1000
        TicTacToeConstants.java, 1001
        TicTacToeServer class, 1000–1001
        TicTacToeServer.java, 1001–1005
    Domain Name Servers (DNS), 976
    domain names, 976
    IdentifyHostNameIP.java, 983–984
    InetAddress class, 983–984
    Internet Protocol (IP) address, 976
    JEditorPane class, 997–999
    multiple clients, serving, 984–987
    packet-based communications, 976
    sending and receiving objects, 989–994
        ObjectInputStream, 989
        ObjectOutputStream, 989
        StudentAddress class, 990
        StudentAddress.java, 990–991
        StudentClient.java, 991–993
        StudentServer.java, 993–994
    stream-based communications, 976
    Transmission Control Protocol (TCP), 976
    User Datagram Protocol (UDP), 976
    Web servers, retrieving files from, 994–997
        java.net.URL class, 995
        MalformedURLException, 995
        openStream() method, 995
        ViewRemoteFile.java, 996–997
New account inner class (listing), 958–959
new operator, 232
newCondition() method, 947–949
    Condition interface, 949
newDeposit condition, 949–952
newFixedThreadPool(int)
        method, 941–942
NewInterface, 377
next(), 44
Next-line style, 52–53
next() method, Iterator interface, 875
nextByte() method, 44, 288
nextDouble() method, 44, 288
nextFloat() method, 44, 288
nextInt() method, 44, 288

nextLine() method, 44, 288–289
nextLong() method, 44, 288
nextShort() method, 44, 288
NIC, 5
Nine tail problem, 882–888
    InitialNodePanel class, 886
    NineTailApp class, 882–883, 886
    NineTailApp.java, 886–888
    NineTailModel class, 882–883, 923
    NineTailModel.java, 883–886
    NodePanel class, 886
No-arg constructor, 232
NoClassDefFoundError, 18
Nondominating terms, ignoring, 742
Nonextensible is-a relationship, 334
Nonserializable fields, 638
Nonstrict mode, floating-point arithmetic, 1269fn
NoSuchMethodError, 18
not operator, 1241
notify() method, 952–953
notifyAll() method, 952–953
NotSerializableException, 638
null keyword, 20
null value, 236
NullPointerException, 237, 466
Number class, 380, 385
Number systems, 8–12
NumberFormat class, 1030–1032
    getCurrencyInstance method, 1031
    getInstance method, 1030
    getNumberInstance method, 1030
    getPercentInstance method, 1031
    setMaximumFractionDigits method, 1031
    setMinimumFractionDigits method, 1031
NumberFormatDemo.java, 1032–1035,
        1036–1037
numberOfObjects, 241–243
Numbers, formatting, 48, 1029–1035
    converting to strings, 56
    currency format, 1031
    DecimalFormat class, 1032
    example of, 1032–1035
    locale dependence of, 1029
    NumberFormat class, 1030
    NumberFormatDemo.java, 1032–1035
    parsing numbers, 1031
    percent format, 1031
    plain number format, 1030–1031
Numeric data types, 32–38
Numeric errors:
    avoiding, 117
    minimizing, 116–117
Numeric keypad, 5
Numeric literals, 35–36
Numeric operators, 33–34
    on characters, 43
Numeric types:
    conversions, 39–40
    range of, 39
Numeric values, converting to strings, 272
Numeric wrapper classes, 380–381
    abstract methods implemented by, 381
numOfCredits attribute, 1234

O

Oak language, 12
Object class, 340–341, 378
    clone method, 376–377
    equals method, 340–341, 373
    toString method, 340
Object I/O, 635–637
    TestObjectInputStream.java, 637
    TestObjectOutputStream.java, 636–637

Object member access operator (.), and casting
        operator, 345
Object-oriented design:
    case study, 400–405
        Address.java, 402–403
        Borrower.java, 404–405
        BorrowLoan.java, 405
        describing attributes, 401
        establishing relationships, 400
        identifying classes, 400
        Name.java, 402
        Person1.java, 403–404
        writing code for classes, 401–402
    class design guidelines, 410–413
        clarity, 411
        cohesion, 410
        completeness, 412
        consistency, 410–411
        encapsulation, 411
        inheritance vs. aggregation, 412
        instance vs. static, 412
        interfaces vs. abstract classes, 413
    design patterns, 414–415
        learning, 414
    and patterns, 393–418
    Rational class, 405–410
        limitations of, 410
        overflow, 410
        properties/constructors/methods, 406
        Rational.java, 407–410
        TestRationalClass.java, 406–407
    Singleton pattern, 414
    software life cycle, 394–395
Object-oriented programming (OOP), 311–313
    class relationships, 396–400
        aggregation, 397–398
        association, 396–397, 399
        comparing dependency, association,
            aggregation, and composition, 399
        composition, 397–398
        dependency, 398
    classes, discovering, 395–396
    ComputeBMI.java, 311
    defined, 230
    inheritance, 399–400
    key to, 395
Object serialization, 638
ObjectInputStream class, 635–637, 989, 991,
        994
    readObject method, 991
ObjectOutputStream class, 989, 991, 994
    writeObject method, 991
Objects:
    anonymous, 233
    array of, 251–253
    behavior of, 230
    calling, 233
    defined, 230
    object reference variables vs., 233
    passing to methods, 249–251
    processing primitive data type values as,
        380–382
    state of, 230
Observable class, 1146
Observer interface, 1146
Occurrences of letters, counting (case study),
        192–195
    CountLettersInArray.java, 193–194
Occurrences of words (case study), 732–733
Octal literals, 35
Octal numbers, 12
ODBC, 1245
Off-by-one error, 120, 186
offer method, Queue interface, 726

openIcon property, 1224
openStream() method, 995
Operands, converting, 39–40
operandStack, 790–791
Operating system (OS), 7–8, 22
    defined, 8
    scheduling operations, 8
    system activities, controlling/monitoring, 8
    system resources, allocating/assigning, 8
operationMenu menu, 1114
Operator associativity, 91–92
Operator precedence, 91–92
Operator precedence chart, 1272–1273
operatorStack, 790–791
Option buttons, See Radio buttons
Option dialog, 1126–1127
    defined, 1122, 1126
or operator, 1241
Oracle, 1236
    JDBC driver, 1246
    URL, 1247
Order by comparator, 713
orientation property, 1118
OuterClass class, 490
Output stream, defined, 624
OutputStream class, 626–627
Ovals, drawing, 451–452
Overflow, 33
Overloaded constructors, 232
Overloading methods, 151–153
    TestMethodOverloading.java, 151–152
Overriding:
    methods, 338–339
    prevention of, 351

P

pack() method, 493, 528
Package-access, 245–246
Package-private, 245
Packages, using, 19, 245
Packet-based communications, 976
Page Up/Page Dn keys, 5
paintComponent method, 449–450, 455–456,
        466, 1149
    invoking, 456
    TestPaintComponent.java, 449–450
Palindromes, checking (problem), 272–273
Panels:
    drawing graphics on, 450–451
    TestPanelDrawing.java, 450
Panels, using as subcontainers, 433–435
    TestPanels.java, 434
Parallel edges, 860
Parameter list, 143
Parameter order association, 147–149
Parameters, methods, 142–143
Parent classes, See Superclasses
parse method, 1031
parseDouble method, Double class, 381
parseInt method, Integer class, 381
Parsing numbers, 1031
Partition:
    illustration, 843
    method, 843
Pascal, 6
Pass-by-sharing, 189, 251
Pass-by-value, use of term, 147
Passing arrays to methods, 189–192
    TestPassArray.java, 190–192
Passing parameters by values, 147–149
    Increment.java, 147–148
    TestPassByValue.java, 148
PathIterator class, 875

pathIterator(int v) method, Tree
        class, 875
peek method:
    Queue interface, 726
    Stack class, 725
Peers, 420
Percent format, 1031
Person1.java, 403–404
Pixels, 5, 424
Plain number format, 1030–1031
Plus sign (+), 28
PNG (Portable Network Graphics), 437
Point class, 498, 672
poll method, Queue interface, 726
Polygons/polylines, drawing, 458–460
    DrawPolygon.java, 459–460
polyLine method, 459
Polymorphism, 341–352
    defined, 342
    dynamic binding, 342–343
    generic programming, 343, 384
    matching vs. binding, 343
    PolymorphismDemo.java, 341–342
pop() method, MyStack.java, 350
pop() method, Stack class, 725
Popup menus, 1114–1116
    popup triggers, 1114
    PopupMenuDemo.java, 1115–1116
Post-test loop, 113
Postdecrement operator, 37–38
Postincrement operator, 37–38
Postorder traversal, 803–804, 821
PostorderIterator class, 821
postorderIterator() method, 821
pow(a, b) method, 46
Pre-test loop, 113
Precedence, 91–92
Predecrement operator, 37–38
Predefined renderers and editors, 1200, 1203
preferredSize property, 1072–1073, 1082
Preincrement operator, 37–38
Preorder traversal, 803–804, 821
PreorderIterator class, 821
preorderIterator() method, 821
presentNation(index) method, 585
Pressed icons, 515–516
Primary key, 1235
Primary key constraints, 1234, 1235
Prime number algorithms, comparisons of, 758
Prime numbers:
    displaying (problem), 125–127
    finding (case studies), 752–758
        EfficientPrimeNumbers.java, 755–756
        PrimeNumbers.java, 753–754
        SieveOfEratosthenes.java, 757–758
PrimeNumber.java, 125–126
PrimeNumberMethod.java, 150–151
Primitive data types, 26
Prim's minimum spanning tree algorithm,
        911–912
print method, 286
    println method compared to, 45
printAdjacencyMatrix() method,
        AbstractGraph class, 874
PrintCalendar.java, 163–166
PrintChar class, 933
printEdges() method, AbstractGraph
        class, 874
PrintNum class, 933
printPath(v) method, Tree class, 874
PrintPyramid.java, 121–122
printTree() method, Tree class, 874
PrintWriter class, writing data using,
        285–286

Priority queues, 727–728, 828–829
    MyPriorityQueue class, 828
    MyPriorityQueue.java, 828–829
    TestPriorityQueue.java, 829
PriorityBlockingQueue, 956
PriorityQueue class, 727
PriorityQueueDemo.java, 728
private constructor, 246
Private constructor, 321
Private data fields, 339
private modifier, 245–246, 350–351, 1274
Problem, 68
Procedures, 143
process method, 968
processEvent method, 1057–1058, 1062
Processing arrays, 183–184
Producer/Consumer (case study), 953–955
    ConsumerProducer.java, 954–955
Programming errors, 53–54
    debugging, 54–55
    logic errors, 54–55
    runtime errors, 54
    syntax errors, 53–54
Programming style, 51–53
    defined, 51
Programs, 5–7, 21
    creating/compiling/executing, 16–19
    problem, 26–27
ProgressBarDemo.java, 966–968
Properties, 230
Property default values, 437
Protected data fields, 771
protected modifier, 350–351, 1274
Pseudocode, 68
public modifier, 245–246, 350–351, 1274
publish method, 968
publishPrimeNumbers, 968
push() method, Stack class, 725
push(Object element) method,
        MyStack.java, 350
put method, Map interface, 728
putAll method, Map interface, 728
Pyramid of numbers, displaying
        (problem), 121–122

Q

Quadratic algorithm, 743
Quadratic time, 743, 747
Queue classes, designing, 788
Queue interface, 726
Queues, defined, 788
Quick sort:
    algorithm (listing), 841–842
    defined, 841
    illustration, 842
    merge sort vs., 845
    partition method, 843
    partitioning, 842–844
    quick sort time, 845–846
    QuickSort.java, 844–845
quickSort methods, 843
Quotient.java, 598
QuotientWithException.java, 599
QuotientWithIF.java, 598–599
QuotientWithMethod.cpp, 600–601

R

Race condition, 945
Radio-button menu items, 1109
Radio buttons, 523–525
    defined, 523
    RadioButtonDemo.java, 524–525

radius data field, 233, 235
radius property, 1147, 1150
Radix, decimal number system, 9
Radix sort, 847
Ragged array, 205–206
RAM (random-access memory), 3
Random access files, 639–642
  defined, 639
  and processing of files of record, 642
  TestRandomAccessFile.java, 641–642
Random class, 239
random() method, Math class, 77–78
random method, Math class, 156
Random numbers, generating (case study),
    157–159
  RandomCharacter.java, 157–158
  TestRandomCharacter.java, 158–159
RandomAccessFile class:
  defined, 639
  UML diagram, 640
Rational class, 405–410
  limitations of, 410
  overflow, 410
  properties/constructors/methods, 406
  Rational.java, 407–410
  TestRationalClass.java, 406–407
RationalMatrix class, 697, 700
RationalMatrix.java, 700
Raw type, 691–692
  and backward compatibility, 691
    Max1.java, 692
    Max.java, 691
Read-only property, 1052
Read-only streams, 639
ReadFileUsingJFileChooser.java, 290–291
readObject() method, 637, ObjectInputStream
    class, 991
Rectangle class, 330–331
  Rectangle1.java, 333
Rectangle class, TestCircleRectangle.java, 334
Rectangle.java, 363–364
Rectangles, drawing, 451–452
Recurrence functions, 760
Recursion, 655–684, 673–675
  advantages of, 675
  defined, 656
  directory size, finding (problem), 665–666
  Eight Queens puzzle, 673–675
    defined, 673–675
    EightQueens.java, 673–675
  factorials, computing, 656–659
    base case, 656
    ComputeFactorial.java, 657
    stopping condition, 656
  Fibonacci numbers, computing
      (problem), 659–661
  fractals (problem), 670–673
    Sierpinski triangle, 670–673
    SierpinskiTriangle.java, 671–673
  infinite, 657
  iteration vs., 675
  overhead, 675
  and performance concern, 675
  problem solving using, 661–662
    RecursivePalindromeUsingSubstring.java, 662
  recursive helper methods, 662–665
    binary search, 664–665
    RecursivePalindrome.java, 662
    selection sort, 663–664
  Tower of Hanoi (problem), 666–670
Recursive call, 656
Recursive methods, 656
Recursive thinking, 661
RecursivePalindrome.java, 662

RecursivePalindromeUsingSubstring.java, 662
RecursiveSelectionSort.java, 663–664
ReentrantLock class, 947
Reference type, defined, 232
Reference variables:
  accessing an object's data and methods, 233
  accessing objects via, 232–238
  Circle1.java, 235–236
  declaring classes and creating objects
      (example), 233–234
  defined, 232
  reference data fields and the null value, 236–237
  and reference types, 232–233
  TestCircle1.java, 234–235
  variables of primitive types and reference types,
      differences between, 237–238
regionMatches method, String class, 266–267
Register listener, 486
Regular expression, 270
Relational database systems, 1231–1236
  attributes, 1233
  integrity, 1232
  integrity constraints, 1234–1236
  language, 1232
  relational data model, 1232
  structure, 1232
  tables, 1233–1234
  tuples, 1233
Relational operators, 68
Relational structures, 1233–1234
Relative file name, 283
release() method, Semaphore class, 958–959
Remainder (%), 33–34
remove method:
  Map interface, 728
  Queue interface, 726
remove() method, Iterator interface, 821, 875
removeActionListener method, 1057
removeColumn method,
    TableColumnModel, 1200
removeFirst() method, MyLinkedList
    class, 781–782
remove(index) method, MyLinkedList
    class, 783–784
removeLast() method, MyLinkedList
    class, 782–783
removeRow(rowIndex) method, 1200
reorderingAllowed property, 1193
repaint method, Component class, 455–456
replaceAll method, String class, 270
replaceFirst method, String class, 270
ReplaceText.java, 289–290
Replacing strings, 269
requestFocusInWindow() method, 528
Reserved words, 15
Resolution, 5, 424
Resource bundles, 1035–1042
  for the Chinese language (example), 1038
  defined, 1035
  for the English language (example), 1037
  for the French language (example), 1038
  getBundle method, 1037
  ListResourceBundle class, 1035–1036
  MissingResourceException, 1037, 1042
  naming conventions, 1036
  property resource bundles, 1042
  ResourceBundle class, 1035–1036, 1042
  ResourceBundleDemo.java, 1038–1042
  updateString method, 1042
Resource ordering, 959–960
ResourceBundle class, 1042
ResultSetMetaData interface, 1260–1261
Rethrowing exceptions, 612–613
return statement, 145

Return value type, methods, 142
Reusing classes, 467
Reusing experience, 414, 416
Reusing methods, 145
revalidate() method, 1090
reverse method, Collections class, 721
RGB model, 432, 439
Right-associative operators, 91
Right child of a node, 800
rightAction, MyAction class, 1122
Rigid area, 1077
rollback() method, 1250
Rollover icons, 515–516
Rounding methods, Math class, 155–156
RowFilter class, 1193
Rows/columns, modifying (case study),
    1195–1200
  Add New Column button, 1196, 1200
  Add New Row button, 1195, 1200
  Clear button, 1196, 1200
  Delete Selected Row button, 1196, 1200
  ModifyTable.java, 1196–1200
  Restore button, 1196, 1200
  Save button, 1196, 1200
rows property, GridLayout manager, 431
rowSorter method, JTable class, 1193–1194
Runnable interface, 930–931
Runnable object, 930
Runtime errors, 54
RuntimeException, 708, 961

S

Sales amount, finding (problem), 119–120
SalesTax.java, 40
Scanner class:
  console input using, 44–46
  how it works, 288–289
  input errors, avoiding, 46
  InputMismatchException, 288
  methods, 44–45, 287
  next() method/nextLine() method, 288
  nextByte() method, 288
  nextDouble() method, 288
  nextFloat() method, 288
  nextInt() method, 288
  nextLine() method, 288–289
  nextLong() method, 288
  nextShort() method, 288
  ReadData.java, 287–288
  reading data using, 286–290
  ReplaceText.java, 289–290
  replacing text (problem), 289–290
Scientific notation, 35–36
Scope of variables, 153–154
Screen resolution, 5
Scroll bars, 538–540
  JScrollBar class, 538
  ScrollBarDemo.java, 539–540
ScrollMap.java, 1088–1089
search() method, Stack class, 725
Search word problem, 656
search(Object element) method,
    MyStack.java, 350
selectedFile property, JFileChooser
    class, 1135
selectedFiles property, JFileChooser
    class, 1135
Selection sort, 199–200, 663–664
  defined, 199, 663
  RecursiveSelectionSort.java, 663–664
  SelectionSort.java, 200
Selection sort algorithm, 745–746.

Selection statements, 72
selectionMode method, 534, 1165
selectionMode property, 1164
selectionModel property, 1164
Selections, 67–101
Semaphore class:
  acquire() method, 958–959
  class diagram, 959
  release() method, 958–959
Semaphores, 958–959
Semicolon (statement terminator), 15
Sentinel value, 108–109
SentinelValue.java, 109
SentinelValueUsingConfirmationDialog.java,
  127–128
Sequential access file, 639
Serializable interface, 637–638, 990,
  1050, 1084
  serializing arrays, 638–639
  TestObjectStreamForArray.java, 638–639
Serializable objects, defined, 637
Serialization, 638
Server class, 982
Server.java, 979–980
Set interface, 182
setAccelerator method, 1110
setAlignment method, FlowLayout
  manager, 431
setAutoCommit(false) method, 1250
setBackground method, Component class,
  432, 451, 467
setBorder method, 1102
setColor method, 1152
  Graphics class., 467
setColumns method, GridLayout manager, 431
setComponentPopupMenu(JPopupMenu)
  method, 1116
setDefaultCloseOpeartion method, JFrame
  class, 240
setEditor method, 1160
setFilled method, 1152
setFont method:
  Component class, 432, 467
  Graphics class, 467
setForeground method, Component
  class, 432, 467
setHgap method:
  BorderLayout manager, 431
  FlowLayout manager, 431
  GridLayout manager, 431
setHorizontalTextPosition method, 1110
setJMenuBar method, 1108
setLayout method, 425, 435
setlength() method, StringBuilder, 278
setLocation method, JFrame class, 240
setLocationRelativeTo(null), 424
setMaximumFractionDigits method,
  NumberFormat class, 1031
setMinimumFractionDigits method,
  NumberFormat class, 1031
setModel method, CircleView class, 1152
setPage(url) method, 997
setPriority method, 935
setRadius method, 241, 1152
setRows method, GridLayout manager, 431
Sets, 706, 708–709, 708–717
  compared to lists, 724
  HashSet class, 708, 709–712
  LinkedHashSet class, 712–713
  and nonduplicate elements, 716
  performance of, 723–724
  SetListPerformanceTest.java, 723–724
  TestHashSet.java, 710
  TestLinkedHashSet.java, 712–713

TestMethodsInCollection.java, 710–712
TestTreeSet.java, 713–714
  TreeSet class, 713–714
setSize method, JFrame class, 240, 493
setSize(w, h) method, 424
Setter method, 247
setTitle method, 427
  JFrame class, 240
setVgap method:
  BorderLayout manager, 431
  FlowLayout manager, 431
  GridLayout manager, 431
setVisible method, JFrame class, 240
setVisibleRowCount method, 1167
Seven Bridges of Königsberg problem, 858–859
Shallow copy, 376
Short-circuit operator, 71
short type, 32
Short wrapper class, 380
Shortest-path tree, 919–920
Shortest paths, 915–922
  algorithms, 915–919
    implementation of, 919–922
  ShortestPathTree class, 919–20
  TestShortestPath.java, 920–922
Shorthand operators, 37–38
ShowBoxLayout.java, 1077–1079
ShowCardLayout.java, 1074–1076
showConfirmDialog method, 1125
ShowCurrentTime.java, 50–51, 238
showDayNames method, 1028
showDays method, 1028
ShowDiagonalLayout.java, 1085–1086
ShowGridLayout.java, 429
showHeader method, 1028
showInputDialog method, 56, 58, 1126
ShowLayout.java, 1092–1094
showMessageDialog method, JOptionPane
  class, 19–20
ShowNoLayout.java, 1080–1081
showOpenDialog method, JFileChooser
  class, 1135, 1138
showPopup method, 1116
showSaveDialog method, JFileChooser
  class, 1135
shuffle method, Collections
  class, 721
Sierpinski triangle, 670–673
  creation of, 670–671
  defined, 670
  SierpinskiTriangle.java, 671–673
    Point class, 672
Sieve of Eratosthenes algorithm, 756–758
SieveOfEratosthenes.java, 757–758
signal() method, 949, 953
signalAll() method, 949, 953
Simple graphs, 860
SimpleDateFormat class, 1020, 1028
SimpleEventDemoInnerClass.java, 491–492
SimpleEventDemo.java, 489–490
SimpleSpinner.java, 1156–1157
SimpleTreeDemo.java, 1211–1212
Single inheritance, 335, 377
Single precision, 33
Single selection mode, 1218
Single space, 52
Single-source all-shortest-path tree, 919
Single space, 52
Singleton pattern, 414
Singleton.java, 414–415
size method, Map interface, 729
Sliders, 541–543
  JSlider class, 541
  SliderDemo.java, 542–543
SoftBevelBorder class, 1094–1095

Software, 2, 5–7, 21
  defined, 5
Software life cycle, 394–395
  deployment, 395
  implementation, 394
  maintenance, 395
  requirements specification, 394
  system analysis, 394
  system design, 394
  testing, 394
Sorted tuples, displaying, 1243–1244
SortedMap interface, 730
SortedSet interface, 713
Sorting, 835–856
  bubble sort, 836–838
    algorithm (listing), 836–837
    bubble sort time, 838
    BubbleSort.java, 837–838
    defined, 836
    improved algortihm (listing), 836
  bucket sort, 846–847
    algorithm (listing), 846
    stability of, 847
  defined, 835
  external sort, 848–854
    analysis, 852–854
    copying first half segments (listing), 850
    CreateLargeFile.java, 848
    creating initial sorted segments (listing),
      849–850
    defined, 848
    merging all segments (listing), 850–851
    merging two segments (listing), 851
    phase I, implementation of, 849–850
    phase II, implementation of, 850–851
    sort phases, defined, 848
    SortLargeFile.java, 852–853
    two phases, combining, 851–852
  heap sort, 845–846
    HeapSort.java, 845–846
    merge sort vs., 846
    sort time, 846
  lower bound on sort, 846
  merge sort, 838–841
    algorithm (listing), 838
    illustration, 838–839
    merge sort time, 840–841
    method for merging two arrays
      (listing), 839
    time analysis, 840–841
  quick sort, 841–845
    algorithm (listing), 841–842
    defined, 841
    illustration, 842
    merge sort vs., 845
    partition method, 843
    partitioning, 842–844
    quick sort time, 845–846
    QuickSort.java, 844–845
  radix sort, 847
  reasons for studying, 836
SortLargeFile.java, 852–853
Source components, 1053
Source file, 6, 15
Source object (source component), 484
Source program (source code), 6–7, 21
Spacing, 52
Spanning tree, 860
Special characters, escape sequences for, 41–42
Special floating-point values, 1276
Specific import, 20
Specifier, 89–90
Speed, CPU, 3
Spinner, defined, 1154

Spinner editors, 1159–1162
    JSpinner.DateEditortor, 1159
    JSpinner.DefaultEditor, 1159
    JSpinner.ListEditor, 1160
    JSpinner.NumberEditor, 1159
    SpinnerModelEditorDemo.java, 1160–1162
    using, 1160–1162
Spinner models, 1156–1159
    SpinnerModelEditorDemo.java, 1160–1162
    using, 1160–1162
SpinnerDateModel, 1156–1157, 1159, 1162
SpinnerListModel, 1156–1158, 1162
SpinnerModel interface, 1156
SpinnerNumberModel, 1156, 1158, 1162
spinnerYear, 1162
Splash screen, 439
split method, String class, 270
Splitting strings, 269
SQL, See Structured Query Language (SQL)
sqrt method, 110
Stack class, 724–725
    empty() method, 725
    peek() method, 725
    pop() method, 725
    push() method, 725
    search() method, 725
Stack classes, designing, 788
StackOfIntegers class, 316, 316–318
    StackOfIntegers.java, 317–318
    TestStackOfIntegers.java, 316–317
    UML diagram, 316
Stacks, 145, 307
    defined, 788
    TestStackQueue.java, 789–790
start method, Applet class, 559
Start tag, 562
startAngle, 456
Starvation, 936
State, of objects, 230
Statement, 15
Statement interface, 1253
Statement terminator, 15
static inner class, 490
Static methods, 241
    hidden, 339
static modifier, 1274
Static variables, 241–245, 305
    Circle2.java, 242–243
    TestCircle2.java, 243–244
Stepwise refinement, 159
StillClock class, 467–471, 505, 938
    DisplayClock.java, 467–469
    StillClock.java, 469–471
    UML diagram, 467
stop method, Applet class, 560
Stopping condition, 656
Storage devices, 2, 4
Stream-based communications, 976
Stream, defined, 624
Stream sockets, 978
Strict mode, floating-point arithmetic, 1269fn
strictfp keyword, 1269fn
strictfp modifier, 1275
String class, 264–273
    characters, 267
    combining strings, 267–268
    compareTo method, 266
    as immutable class, 304
    methods for comparing strings, 266
    string length, 267
String concatenation operator, 28
String literal, 40
String type, 43–44
StringBuffer class, 276–280, 351

StringBuilder class, 276–280, 351
    capacity() method, 278
    charAt(index) method, 278
    constructors, 276
    initial capacity, 278–279
    length() method, 278
    methods for modifying string builders, 277
    setlength() method, 278
Strings:
    calculator (problem), 281–283
    characters, finding in, 270–271
    CheckPalindrome.java, 272–273
    command-line arguments, 280–283
    comparisons, 265–266
    constructing, 264
    conversion between arrays and, 271
    converting, 269
    converting characters and numeric
        values to, 272
    drawing, 451–452
    immutable, 264–265
    index range, 268
    interned, 265
    matching, by patterns, 270
    PalindromeIgnoreNonAlphanumeric.java,
        279–280
    palindromes, checking (problem), 272–273
    palindromes, ignoring nonalphanumeric
        characters when checking
        (problem), 279
    passing to the main method, 281
    replacing, 269
        by patterns, 270
    splitting, 269
        by patterns, 270
    stack of, creating, 689
    string literal, 267
    string literal object, 264
    string object, 264
    string value, 264, 267
    string variable, 264
    substrings:
        finding in, 270–271
        obtaining, 268–269
Strings, converting to numbers, 56
Strong is-a relationship, 378, 399, 413, 415
Structure component, relational database
    systems, 1232
Structured Query Language (SQL), 1236–1244
    arithmetic operators, 1242–1243
    between-and operator, 1242
    Boolean operators, 1240–1241
    from clause, 1240
    column alias, 1242
    comparison operators, 1240–1241
    creating a database, 1237–1238
    creating a user account on, 1236–1237
    creating and dropping tables, 1238–1239
    defined, 1236
    delete records, 1240
    distinct tuples, displaying, 1243–1244
    inserting records, 1239–1240
    is null operator, 1242
    like operator, 1241
    select clause, 1240
    simple queries, 1240
    standard SQL, 1236
    tables, joining, 1244
    updating records, 1240
Strut, 1077
Stubs, 162–163
Student class, 304
Student scores, computing (problem), 216–217
    TotalScore.java, 216–217

Student table, joining Enrollment table and, 1244
StudentAddress.java, 990–991
StudentClient.java, 991–993
StudentServer.java, 993–994
Subclasses, overriding of a protected
        method with, 351
Subinterface, 377
Subproblem, 126
substring method, String class, 268
Substrings:
    finding in a string, 270–271
    obtaining, 268–269
Subtraction (-), 33–34
SubtractionQuiz.java, 78
SubtractionQuizLoop.java, 107–108
Subtype, 341
Subwindows, 543
Sudoku game, developing an applet for, 558
Sudoku (problem), 210–215
    Sudoku.java, 212–215
Sun Java Website, 12, 14
super keyword, 336–338
    constructor chaining, 337
    superclass constructors, 336–337
    superclass methods, calling, 338
Superkey, 1235
Supertype, 341
Supplementary Unicode, 41, 625
Supplier, 398
Swing:
    AWT vs., 420
    components, 420
Swing borders, 1094–1102
    and Border interface, 1094
    BorderDemo.java, 1098–1102
    defined, 1094
Swing container structures, 1070–1072
    JApplet class, 1071–1072
    JFrame class, 1071
    JPanel class, 1072
Swing GUI components, 421–422, 514
    common features of, 435–437
    TestSwingCommonFeatures.java, 436–437
Swing MVC architecture, 1153–1154
SwingUtilities class, 937
SwingWorker class, 962–965
    class diagram, 962
    defined, 962
    and GUI, 965
    SwingWorkerDemo.java, 963–965
switch statements, 72–73, 86–88
    and break statement, 87
Sybase, 1236
Synchronization using locks, 947–949
Synchronization wrapper, 961
Synchronized block, 946
Synchronized collections, 960–961
    defined, 960
synchronized keyword, 945–947, 952, 961
    synchronizing statements, 946–947
synchronized methods, 949
synchronized modifier, 1275
Syntax errors, 53–54
Syntax rules, 16
System errors, 602
System.currentTimeMillis(), 50–51, 77
System.out.println, 15

T

Table model events, 1205–1208
Table renderers and editors, 1200–1202
    custom, 1203–1205
    MyTableModel.java, 1201–1202

predefined, 1200
TableCellRendererEditorDemo.java, 1202
TableCellEditor interface, 1184
TableCellRenderer interface, 1184, 1203
TableCellRendererEditorDemo.java, 1202
tableChanged method,
    TableModelListener, 1208
TableColumn, as supporting class, 1184
TableColumn class, 1184, 1191–1192
    properties/constructors/methods, 1191–1192
TableColumnModel interface, 1191
    TestTableColumnModel.java, 1192–1193
TableEventsDemo.java, 1205–1208
tableHeader property, 1193
TableModel interface, 1189, 1190–1191
    and table data management, 1191
TableModelEvents, 1189
TablePropertiesDemo.java, 1187–1189
TableRowSet, 1193
Tables, joining, 1244
Tables, relational database systems, 1233–1234
Tag, defined, 561
Tag name, defined, 561
Tapes, 4
Target mode, 882–883
Tasks:
    creating, 930–931
    defined, 930
    TaskThreadDemo.java, 932–933, 935
        run() method, 933
        start() method, 933
TaskThreadDemo.java, 932–933, 935
    run() method, 933
    start() method, 933
Taxes, computing (problem), 81–83
TCP (Transmission Control Protocol), 976
Ternary operator, 88
TestArrayAndLinkedList.java, 719
TestArrayList.java, 347–348
TestBFS.java, 880–881
TestBinaryTreeDelete.java, 815–816
TestBinaryTree.java, 811–812
TestBinaryTreeWithIterator.java, 821–822
TestBoolean.java, 70
TestBreak.java, 122–123
TestButtonIcons.java, 516
TestCalendar.java, 367–368
TestCallableStatement.java, 1257–1258
TestCenterMessage.java, 461–462
TestCircle1.java, 234–235
TestCircle2.java, 243–244
TestCircle3.java, 248–249
TestColorDialog.java, 1132
TestContinue.java, 123–124
TestCourse.java, 314–315
TestCourseWithActionEvent.java, 1058–1059
TestCourseWithEnrollmentEvent.java,
    1062–1063
TestDatabaseMetaData.java, 1259
TestDFS.java, 877
TestDiagonalLayout class, 1086
TestDoWhile.java, 110–111
TestEdible.java, 369–370
TestFileClass.java, 284–285
TestFrame.java, 240
TestGeometricObject.java, 364–365, 690
TestHashSet.java, 710
TestHeap.java, 827
TestImageIcon.java, 438–439
TestIntegerMatrix.java, 700–701
TestLinkedHashSet.java, 712–713
TestList.java, 775–776
TestLoanClass.java, 308–309
TestMap.java, 731

TestMax.java, 144
TestMethodOverloading.java, 151–152
TestMethodsInCollection.java, 710–712
TestMinimumSpanningTree.java, 914–915
TestObjectInputStream.java, 637
TestObjectOutputStream.java, 636–637
TestObjectStreamForArray.java, 638–639
TestPaintComponent.java, 449–450
TestPanelDrawing.java, 450
TestPanels.java, 434
TestPassArray.java, 190–192
TestPassByValue.java, 148
TestPassObject.java, 249–250
TestPolymorphismCasting.java, 344–345
TestPriorityQueue.java, 829
TestQueue.java, 727
TestRandomAccessFile.java, 641–642
TestRandomCharacter.java, 158–159
TestRationalMatrix.java, 701
TestResultSetMetaData.java, 1261
TestScanner.java, 45
TestShortestPath.java, 920–922
TestStackOfIntegers.java, 316–317
TestStackQueue.java, 789–790
TestSum.java, 116
TestSwingCommonFeatures.java, 436–437
TestTableColumnModel.java, 1192–1193
TestTable.java, 1186
TestTableModel.java, 1189–1190
TestTableSortFilter.java, 1194–1195
TestTreeModel.java, 1213–1214
TestTreeSet.java, 713–714
TestTreeSetWithComparator.java, 715–716
TestVoidMethod.java, 146
TestWeightedGraph.java, 909–910
TestWindowEvent.jav, 495–497
Text areas, 528–531
    DescriptionPanel.java, 530
    TextAreaDemo.java, 531
Text fields, 526–528
    defined, 526
    TextFieldDemo.java, 527–528
Text files, 624
    appending, 629
Text I/O, binary I/O vs., 624–626
Text I/O classes, 624
TextAreaDemo class, 529
TextEditor.java, 1135–1138
    open method, 1138
    save method, 1139
Think before coding, use of term, 106
Thinking before you type, use of term, 118
this keyword, 306
this(arg-list) statement, 307
Thread class, 933–936
    class diagram, 933
    extending, 934
    join method, 935
    methods, 933
    resume() method, 934
    sleep method, 934–935
    stop() method, 934
    suspend() method, 934
    yield() method, 934
Thread cooperation, 949–953
    ever-waiting, 952
    Java's built-in monitor, 952–953
    ThreadCooperation.java, 950–952
Thread-safe class, 945
Thread states, 960
Thread synchronization, 943–947
    AccountWithoutSync.java, 943–945
        Account class, 944
        AddAPennyTaskAddAPennyTask class, 944

and data inconsistency, 944–945
    isTerminated() method, 944
Threads:
    Blocked state, 960
    concurrent, 933
    cooperation among, 949–953
    creating, 931
    defined, 930
    interrupt() method, 960
    isAlive() method, 960
    and monitors, 182
    New state, 960
    Ready state, 960
    Running state, 960
    separating tasks from, 933
    starting, 931
    Thread class, 933–936
        class diagram, 933
        extending, 934
        join method, 935
        methods, 933
        resume() method, 934
        sleep method, 934–935
        stop() method, 934
        suspend() method, 934
        yield() method, 934
    time sharing, 931
    timers vs., 937
Throwable class, 601–602
Throwing exceptions, 600
throws Exception, 286, 288
tickListenerList, 1057
TicTacToe game (case study), 572–577
    TicTacToe.java, 574–576
TicTacToeClient class, 1000–1001
TicTacToeClient.java, 1005–1010
TicTacToeConstants class, 1000
TicTacToeConstants interface, 1010
TicTacToeConstants.java, 1001
TicTacToeServer class, 1000–1001
TicTacToeServer.java, 1001–1005
Time sharing, 931
Timer class, animation using, 503–504
    AnimationDemo.java, 504–505
    ClockAnimation.java, 505–506
Timers, threads vs., 937
TimeZone class, 1018–1019
TitledBorder class, 1094–1096, 1102
toCharArray method, 271
Toggle button, 520
Token-reading methods, 288
toLowerCase method, Character class, 274
Tool tip, 436
Toolbars, 1116
Top-down design, 160–161, 162–163
toString method:
    Date class, 238
    GeometricObject class, 338–339
    MyStack.java, 350
TotalArea.java, 251–253
TotalScore.java, 216–217
toUpperCase method, Character class, 274
Tower of Hanoi (problem), 666–670
    analyzing, 746
    defined, 666
    TowersOfHanoi.java, 668–669
transient keyword, 638
Transient modifier, 1275
Transmission Control Protocol (TCP), 976
Traversals:
    graphs, 874–875
    trees, 803–804, 821
Tree class, 874, 875, 912
    class diagram, 875

Tree events, 1225
Tree interface, 804
TreeMap, 730, 731–733
Tree node rendering and editing, 1223–1225
Tree sets, 713–716, 715
Tree traversal, 803–804
   breadth-first traversal, 803–804
   depth-first traversal, 803
   inorder traversal, 803, 821
   postorder traversal, 803–804, 821
   preorder traversal, 803–804, 821
Tree visualization, 816–820
   BinaryTreeView.java, 818–820
   DisplayBinaryTree.java, 818
TreeCellRenderer interface, 1223
treeCollapsed, 1225
TreeExpansionEvent, 1225
TreeExpansionListener, 1225
treeExtended, 1225
Tree.java, 805
TreeMap class, 730;, 732
TreeModel class, 1209
TreeModel interface, 1212–1214
TreeNode class, 1209, 1214, 1216
TreeNodeDemo.java, 1214–1215
TreePath class, 1209, 1217–1220
Trees:
   binary search trees, 800–812
      deleting elements in, 812–816
   defined, 800
   iterators, 820–822
TreeSelectionEvent, 1225
TreeSelectionListener interface, 1225
TreeSelectionModel interface, 1209,
   1217–1218
TreeSet class, 708–709, 713–714, 720
Trigonometric methods, Math class, 154–155
Truncation, 39
try-throw-catch block, template for, 600
Tuples, 1233
   distinct, displaying, 1243–1244
   sorted, displaying, 1243–1244
Two-dimensional arrays, 203–215
   closest pair, finding (problem), 209–210
   creating, 203–205
   declaring variables of, 203–205
   multiple-choice test, grading (problem),
      207–208
   obtaining the lengths of, 205
   processing, 206–207
   ragged array, 205–206
   Sudoku (problem), 210–215
Type casting, 31, 39–40
   defined, 39
   explicit casting, 42–43
   implicit casting, 42
   and loss of precision, 39
   syntax for, 39
Type erasure, 694

U

UDP (User Datagram Protocol), 976
UML (Unified Modeling Language):
   class diagram, 231
   notation, 231
Unary operator, 34
Unbounded wildcard, 693
Unboxing, 384–385
Unchecked exceptions, 603–604, 615
Underflow, 33
Unicode, 40–41, 1016
   supplementary, 41, 625
Unix epoch, 50

UnmodifiableCollection class, 734
UnmodifiableList class, 734
UnmodifiableMap class, 734
UnmodifiableSet class, 734
UnmodifiableSortedMap class, 734
UnmodifiableSortedSet class, 734
UnsupportedOperationException, 708
Unweighted edges, 859
UnweightedGraph class, 864–865, 904
updateDate() method, 1162
updateString method, 1042
URL class, 580–581
   DisplayImagePlayAudio.java, 582
   DisplayImageWithURL.java, 580–581
USB flash drives, 4
UseCustomFrame.java, 335–336
UseGuessDateClass.java, 319–320
User actions, source object and event type, 485
User Datagram Protocol (UDP), 976
User interfaces:
   buttons, 514–520
      AbstractButton class, 514–515
      alignments, 516–517
      ButtonDemo.java, 516–517
      defined, 514
      icons, 515–516
      pressed icons, 515–516
      rollover icons, 515–516
      TestButtonIcons.java, 516
      text positions, 517
      using, 518–520
   check boxes, 520–523
      CheckBoxDemo.java, 521–522
      toggle button, 520
   combo boxes, 531–534
      ComboBoxDemo.java, 533–534
      defined, 531, 1174
      JComboBox class, 532
   creating, 513–555
   labels, 525–526
   lists, 534–537
   multiple windows, creating, 543–547
   radio buttons, 523–525
      defined, 523
      RadioButtonDemo.java, 524–525
   scroll bars, 538–540
      JScrollBar class, 538
      ScrollBarDemo.java, 539–540
   sliders, 541–543
      JSlider class, 541
      SliderDemo.java, 542–543
   text areas, 528–531
      DescriptionPanel.java, 530
      TextAreaDemo class, 529
      TextAreaDemo.java, 531
   text fields, 526–528
      defined, 526
      TextFieldDemo.java, 527–528
UTF-8 format, 630–631

V

validate method, 431
Value-returning method, 143
valueChanged method:
   ListSelectionListener, 1208
   TreeSelectionListener interface, 1225
valueIsAdjusting method, 1165
valueOf method, String class, 272
values() method, Map interface, 729
VarArgsDemo.java, 195
Variable-length argument lists, 195
Variables, 27
   class's, 305

control, 112–113
declarations, 28, 29–30
delaring/initializing in one step, 31
indexed, 182
instance, 241, 244, 305
local, 153, 305
naming, 30, 52
scope of, 153–154, 305–306
static, 241–245, 305
used as expressions, 30
Vector class, 724–725
   methods, 724
Vertex-weighted graph, 902
Vertical alignment, 516–517
Vertical text position, 517
vertices data field, 874
vgap property:
   BorderLayout manager, 431, 1072
   FlowLayout manager, 431
   GridLayout manager, 431
ViewRemoteFile.java, 996–997
Views, 1146
VirtualMachineError class, 602
Visibility, changing of, 351
Visibility modifiers, 245–246, 350–351
visible property, JFrame, 437
visibleRowCount method, 1164–1165
Visual Basic, 6
Visualization, trees, 816–820
void keyword, 232
Void method, 143
void method, 145–147
   invoking, 146
   return in, 146–147
   TestVoidMethod.java, 146
vspace attribute, 562

W

wait() method, 952–953
Weak is-a relationship, 378, 399, 413, 415
Web servers, retrieving files from, 994–997
   java.net.URL class, 995
   MalformedURLException, 995
   openStream() method, 995
   ViewRemoteFile.java, 996–997
WebBrowser.java, 998–999
Weighted edges, 859
   representing, 902–903
      edge array, 902–903
      priority adjacency lists, 903–904
      weighted adjacency matrices, 903
      WeightedEdge.java, 903–904
Weighted graphs:
   applications, 901–928
   representing, 902–904
Weighted nine tail problem (case study), 922–926
   WeightedNineTailApp class, 923
   WeightedNineTailMode class, 923
   WeightedNineTailModel.java, 923–926
WeightedEdge.java, 903–904
WeightedGraph class, 864, 904–910
   TestWeightedGraph.java, 909–910
WeightedGraph.java, 905–909
WelcomeInMessageDialogBox.java, 19–20
Welcome.java, 15, 17
while loop, 103–110
Whitespace, 45
Whitespace character, 45
Widening a type, 39
Wildcard generic types, 692–694
   <? extends E> type, 693
   <? super T> wildcard, 693, 694–695
   <?> type, 693

bounded wildcard, 693
lower-bound wildcard, 693
unbounded wildcard, 693
WildCardDemo1.java, 692–693
WildCardDemo2.java, 693–694
WildCardDemo3.java, 694
Wildcard import, 20
WildCardDemo3.java, 694
Window events, handling, 495–497
windowActivated method, 497
WindowAdapter class, 497
windowClosed method, 497
windowClosing method, 497
windowDeactivated method, 497
windowDeiconified method, 497
WindowEvent, 487, 497
windowIconified method, 497
WindowListener interface, 487, 497, 498

windowOpened method, 497
Windows Calculator, 10
World Wide Web (WWW), defined, 12
WorldClockApp.java, 1021, 1024
WorldClockControl.java, 1021, 1022–1024
WorldClock.java, 1021, 1022
Worst-case input, 742
Wrapper class, 380–382
naming convention, 380
and no-arg constructors, 380
Wrapper class types, automatic conversion
between primitive types and, 384–386
Wrapper objects, constructing, 380
Write-only property, 1052
Write-only streams, 639
writeBytes(String s) method, 630
writeChar(char c) method, 630
writeChars(String s) method, 630

WriteData.java, 285–286
writeObject method, ObjectOutputStream
class, 991
writeUTF(String s) method, 630–631

X

xCoordinate, Component class, 462

Y

yCoordinate, Component class, 462

Z

Zero, division by, and runtime errors, 54
0 based array indices, 182